The Norton Reader

FOURTH EDITION

The Norton Reader

An Anthology of Expository Prose

FOURTH EDITION

Arthur M. Eastman, *General Editor*
CARNEGIE-MELLON UNIVERSITY

Caesar Blake
UNIVERSITY OF TORONTO

Hubert M. English, Jr.
UNIVERSITY OF MICHIGAN

Alan B. Howes
UNIVERSITY OF MICHIGAN

Robert T. Lenaghan
UNIVERSITY OF MICHIGAN

Leo F. McNamara
UNIVERSITY OF MICHIGAN

James Rosier
UNIVERSITY OF PENNSYLVANIA

W·W·NORTON & COMPANY·INC· *New York*

Library of Congress Cataloging in Publication Data
Eastman, Arthur M   1918–   ed.
    The Norton reader.
    Includes index.
    1. College readers. I. Title
PE1122.E3 1977   808.88'8   76–48280
ISBN 0–393–09145–7

ACKNOWLEDGMENTS

Frederick Lewis Allen: "Alcohol and Al Capone" from *Only Yesterday: An Informal History of the 1920's.* Copyright © 1957 by Harper & Row, Publishers, Inc. Reprinted by permission of the publishers.

Woody Allen: from *Without Feathers,* by Woody Allen. Copyright © 1972, 1973 by Woody Allen. Reprinted by permission of Random House, Inc.

Kenneth Allsop: from *The Bootleggers and Their Era,* published by the Hutchinson Publishing Group. Reprinted by permission of A. D. Peters & Co. Ltd.

Maya Angelou: from *I Know Why the Caged Bird Sings,* by Maya Angelou. Copyright © 1969 by Maya Angelou. Reprinted by permission of Random House, Inc.

Anonymous: McGraw-Hill Guidelines, reprinted by permission of the McGraw-Hill Book Company.

Hannah Arendt: from *Eichmann in Jerusalem* by Hannah Arendt. Copyright © 1963 by Hannah Arendt. All Rights Reserved. Reprinted by permission of The Viking Press, Inc.

Isaac Asimov: from *The Left Hand of the Electron.* Copyright © 1971 by Mercury Press, Inc. Reprinted by permission of Doubleday & Company, Inc.

W. H. Auden: from *The Dyer's Hand,* by W. H. Auden. Copyright © 1962 by W. H. Auden. Reprinted by permission of Random House, Inc.

James Baldwin: from *Notes of a Native Son,* copyright 1953, © 1955 by James Baldwin. Reprinted by permission of Beacon Press.

Jacques Barzun: from *The Columbia Forum,* Vol. III, No. 3 (Summer 1974), copyright © 1974 by the Trustees of Columbia University in the City of New York. Reprinted by permission.

Saul Bellow: from *Intellectual Digest,* September 1971. This essay appeared originally in a slightly longer form in *Modern Occasions.* Copyright © 1971 by Saul Bellow. Reprinted by permission of Russell & Volkening, Inc.

Henri Bergson: from the book *Comedy,* copyright © 1956 by Wylie Sypher, which contains "Laughter" by Henri Bergson. Reprinted by permission of Doubleday & Company, Inc.

Bruno Bettelheim: Reprinted with permission of Macmillan Publishing Co., Inc., from *The Informed Heart* by Bruno Bettelheim. Copyright © 1960 by The Free Press, a Corporation.

Wayne C. Booth: "Boring from Within: The Art of the Freshman Essay," from an address to the Illinois Council of College Teachers in 1963. Reprinted by permission of the author.

Wayne C. Booth: "Is There Any Knowledge That a Man *Must* Have?" from *The Knowledge Most Worth Having,* 1967. Reprinted by permission of the University of Chicago Press.

Hal Borland: "The March Buds," "Midsummer," "August," "Autumn's Leftovers," "The Fangs of Winter," "Those Attic Wasps." Copyright © 1975 by The New York Times Company. Reprinted by permission.

Jimmy Breslin: from *How the Good Guys Finally Won,* copyright © 1975 by Jimmy Breslin. Reprinted by permission of The Viking Press, Inc.

Jacob Bronowski: "The Reach of Imagination," from *American Scholar,* Spring 1967. Reprinted by permission of The American Academy of Arts and Letters and the author.

Dee Brown: from *Bury My Heart At Wounded Knee,* copyright © 1970 by Dee Brown. Reprinted by permission of Holt, Rinehart and Winston, Inc.

Norman O. Brown: from *Life Against Death,* copyright © 1959 by Wesleyan University. Reprinted by permission of Wesleyan University Press.

Jerome S. Bruner, from *Partisan Review,* Summer 1956, Vol. XXIII, No. 3. Copyright 1956 by *Partisan Review.* Reprinted by permission of *Partisan Review* and the author.

Martin Buber: from *Tales of the Hasidim—The Early Masters,* copyright © 1947 by Schocken Books Inc. Reprinted by permission.

Art Buchwald: from *I Never Danced at the White House,* copyright © 1971, 1972, 1973, by Art Buchwald. Reprinted by permission of G. P. Putnam's Sons.

Anthony Burgess: from *The New York Times Magazine,* November 7, 1971. Copyright © 1971 by The New York Times Company. Reprinted by permission.

Samuel Butler: from *The Notebooks of Samuel Butler,* arranged and edited by Henry Festing Jones. Reprinted by permission of Jonathan Cape Ltd. on behalf of the Executors of the Samuel Butler Estate.

Edward Hallett Carr: from *What Is History?* by Edward Hallett Carr. Copyright © 1961 by Edward Hallett Carr. Reprinted by permission of Alfred A. Knopf, Inc.

Joyce Cary: from *Highlights of Modern Literature,* copyright © 1949 by The New York Times Company. Reprinted by permission.

Carlos Castaneda: from *The Teachings of Don Juan,* copyright © 1968 by The Regents of the University of California. Reprinted by permission of the University of California Press.

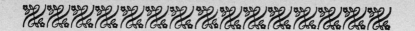

Contents

[*Entries marked with • are followed by Questions*]

ON MIND

ON EDUCATION

ON LANGUAGE AND COMMUNICATION

AN ALBUM OF STYLES

ON LITERATURE AND THE ARTS

SIGNS OF THE TIMES

PEOPLE

ON ETHICS

ON POLITICS AND GOVERNMENT

ON HISTORY

ON SCIENCE

LAST THINGS

Preface to the
FOURTH EDITION

The Fourth Edition of *The Norton Reader* maintains the size and quality of its predecessor. Of its 219 selections, 85 are new. Many of these are by women authors, including among those represented for the first time—Annie Dillard, Shulamith Firestone, Janet Flanner (Genêt), Elizabeth Hardwick, Elizabeth Janeway, Jean Kerr, Doris Lessing, Mary McCarthy, Anaïs Nin, Vita Sackville-West, Margaret Sanger, May Sarton, Jean Stafford, and many others. A new section entitled People falls naturally between Oral History and On Ethics. In the interests of accuracy, On Religion has been retitled Last Things. Selections in the Album of Styles bear titles for the first time; three of the four Prose Forms sections have expanded; and Signs of the Times is, appropriately, almost totally new, containing selections by such contemporary authors as Art Buchwald, Harvey Cox, S. J. Perelman, "Adam Smith," and Studs Terkel. All in all, the editors think, the various sections are more rounded and more evenly balanced than heretofore.

As in the past, additions have been purchased at the expense of material abandoned on advice from the field or because of neglect. As Samuel Johnson once observed, that work is good in vain which is not read. Still, 134 selections continue from the past as having stood the test of time—witness, in On Politics and Government, the essays by DuBois, Baldwin, Martin Luther King, Jr., Thurber, Swift, Darrow, Machiavelli, Erasmus, Lincoln, Jefferson, E. B. White, Becker, and Lippmann. Users of earlier editions will find an abundance of tried and proved material among the newer entries.

The essays in the *Reader* are gathered into sections titled according to major fields of human concern—Mind, Education, Language, etc. The ordering remains virtually unchanged—unobtrusive, we think, minimal, yet reflective of the individual's enlarging experience. Teachers who wish to work by topic can use its divisions. On gaining familiarity with the text, moreover, they will discover thematic links between the different sections. For example, May Sarton's entries under Prose Forms: Journals tie in with the material in On Literature and the Arts; Toni Morrison's "Three Merry Gargoyles" in the Album of Styles joins nicely with the portraits in People; and the essays on Tip O'Neill, Abraham Lincoln, and

George Washington in People clearly relate to material in On Ethics and On Politics and Government.

Two features of the Fourth Edition may elude an initial skimming of its table of contents. One is that a fair number of authors are represented twice or more—Bacon, Booth, Didion, Donne, Emerson, Franklin, and some dozen others. Instructors interested in exploring different manifestations of the same voice, in emphasizing how, though subjects and tones differ, voice remains identifiable, may find such double and treble entries useful. A second feature is an increase in the number of paired pieces—articles taking differing, sometimes opposing, positions on the same topics. For example, two essays concern Isadora Duncan, two Al Capone, two the Golden Rule. Dee Brown's chapter from *Bury My Heart at Wounded Knee* finds its counter in Terri Schultz's "Bamboozle Me Not at Wounded Knee," and B. F. Skinner's "What is Man?" receives a polished retort in Willard Gaylin's "Skinner Redux."

Teachers who prefer to organize their courses rhetorically will, we trust, find useful the Index of Essays Illustrative of Rhetorical Modes and Devices that appears at the beginning of the book and, at the end, the Notes on Composition, which directs attention to rhetorical principles as exemplified in the text. Study questions for approximately half of the essays are offered diffidently for those who care to use them.

It is a pleasure to acknowledge those who have helped bring the Fourth Edition to completion. We wish to pay tribute to George Brockway and others of the Norton staff, including Emily Garlin and John Francis, whose copious nominations and sustained encouragement eased our way. A trio of special nominators greatly enlarged the pool from which we made selections: warm thanks to Professor Joan E. Hartman of Staten Island Community College, Professor Louis I. Middleman of Harrisburg Area Community College, and Professor Natalie Lenaghan of Eastern Michigan University.

Thanks are also extended to the many dedicated teachers, who by drawing on their classroom experiences with *The Norton Reader* and by giving generously of their time to answer our questionnaires, have offered a wealth of ideas and suggestions for its improvement. These include: Patricia M. Geiger, William J. Stevens, and Carl Swope, University of Akron; Professor Virginia Carr, Allegheny College; A. M. Atkins, William J. Johnson, and George D. Meinhold, Augusta College; T. E. Blom, University of British Columbia; Daniel Jacobson, University of California; Peter Brier and George M. Spangler, California State College; David Novehen, Catonsville Community College; Allen Ramsey, Central Missouri State University; Barbara Wigginton, Chemeketa Community College; Philip Owen, Clemson University; A. G. Medlicott, Jr., University of Connecticut; R. Bennett and D. Hayward Black, University of Delaware; P. A. Scholl, University of Evansville; Leo F. O'Connor and N. M. Rinaldi, Fairfield University; Charlotte S. McClure and Malinda Snow, Georgia State University; Charlotte F. Otten, Grand Valley State College; H. A. Simpson, Hampden-Sydney College; Paul McCarthy, University of Hawaii, Hilo College; John B. Dalsant and Charles B. Ruggless, Humboldt State University; Genevieve Gulan, Illinois Valley Community College; Donald Gray, Indiana University; R. Lloyd-Jones, University of Iowa; B. Wallingford Boothe and Jack Lindeman, Kutztown State College; Ross McLean, Los Angeles Valley College; James J. Sherry, University of Maryland; A. Mervin Tyson, Marshall University; William B. F. DeLoach, Memphis State University; Elizabeth Cummings and Jerome Rosenberg, Miami University; Walter Clark, David Manosjak, Tom McCort, David Samuelson, Catherine Wallace, Jeffrey E. Welch, Patrick R. Williams, and J. Wright, University of Michigan; James Berman and Julie Carson, University of Minnesota; Lesta C. Wren, Monroe Community College; J. Brewer, William M. Tucker, and Anna J. Wooten, University of North Carolina; Courtney B. Lawson, Northwestern Illinois University; Dennis Szilak, Northwestern Michigan College; Harold R. Swardson, Ohio University; James W. Wayland, Pepperdine University; A. L. McLeod and Frederick Wilbur, Rider College; Joseph Paris, Roosevelt University; Peter Petersen, Shasta College; K. Peterson, Paul Smith's College; C. W. Harwell, James F. Dorrill, and Charles M. Matlock, University of Southern Alabama; Frances M. D'Antuono and John Houpt, University of Southern California; Patrick J. Horner, State University of New York, Albany; P. Neumeyer and E. G. Schreiber, State University of New York, Stony Brook; L. Edward Bevins, Towson State College; Arvid F. Sponberg, Valparaiso University; Douglas A. Hughes, Washington State University; Rosemary Bartolameolli and Douglas Kevorkian, Wayne State University; B. Haight, Western Illinois University; N. S. Burns, Wichita State University; Kay Rosier, Widener College; and G. Godfrey, Xavier University.

ARTHUR M. EASTMAN

An Index of Essays
Illustrative of Rhetorical
Modes and Devices

THESIS[1]

---

1. The section headings of this index are treated more fully in the Notes on
Composition, p. 1253.

STYLE

The Norton Reader

FOURTH EDITION

Personal Report

DYLAN THOMAS
Memories of Christmas

One Christmas was so much like another, in those years, around the sea-town corner now, and out of all sound except the distant speaking of the voices I sometimes hear a moment before sleep, that I can never remember whether it snowed for six days and six nights when I was twelve or whether it snowed for twelve days and twelve nights when I was six; or whether the ice broke and the skating grocer vanished like a snowman through a white trap-door on that same Christmas Day that the mince-pies finished Uncle Arnold and we tobogganed down the seaward hill, all the afternoon, on the best tea-tray, and Mrs. Griffiths complained, and we threw a snowball at her niece, and my hands burned so, with the heat and the cold, when I held them in front of the fire, that I cried for twenty minutes and then had some jelly.

All the Christmases roll down the hill towards the Welsh-speaking sea, like a snowball growing whiter and bigger and rounder, like a cold and headlong moon bundling down the sky that was our street; and they stop at the rim of the ice-edged, fish-freezing waves, and I plunge my hands in the snow and bring out whatever I can find; holly or robins or pudding, squabbles and carols and oranges and tin whistles, and the fire in the front room, and bang go the crackers, and holy, holy, holy, ring the bells, and the glass bells shaking on the tree, and Mother Goose, and Struwelpeter[1] —oh! the baby-burning flames and the clacking scissorman!—Billy Bunter[2] and Black Beauty, Little Women and boys who have three helpings, Alice and Mrs. Potter's badgers,[3] penknives, teddy-bears

---

1. The title character of *Struwelpeter* (*Slovenly Peter*), or *Merry Tales and Funny Pictures*, a children's book originally in German, by Dr. Heinrich Hoffmann, containing gaily grim admonitory narratives in verse about little Pauline, for example, who played with matches and got burned up; or the little boy who sucked his thumbs until the tall scissorman cut them off.
2. The humorous fat boy in Frank Richards' tales of English school life.
3. Beatrix Potter, creator of *Peter Rabbit* and other animal tales for children, among them *The Tale of Mr. Tod*, a badger.

—named after a Mr. Theodore Bear, their inventor, or father, who died recently in the United States—mouth-organs, tin-soldiers, and blancmange, and Auntie Bessie playing "Pop Goes the Weasel" and "Nuts in May" and "Oranges and Lemons" on the untuned piano in the parlor all through the thimble-hiding musical-chairing blind-man's-buffing party at the end of the never-to-be-forgotten day at the end of the unremembered year.

In goes my hand into that wool-white bell-tongued ball of holidays resting at the margin of the carol-singing sea, and out come Mrs. Prothero and the firemen.

It was on the afternoon of the day of Christmas Eve, and I was in Mrs. Prothero's garden, waiting for cats, with her son Jim. It was snowing. It was always snowing at Christmas; December, in my memory, is white as Lapland, though there were no reindeers. But there were cats. Patient, cold, and callous, our hands wrapped in socks, we waited to snowball the cats. Sleek and long as jaguars and terrible-whiskered, spitting and snarling they would slink and sidle over the white back-garden walls, and the lynx-eyed hunters, Jim and I, fur-capped and moccasined trappers from Hudson's Bay off Eversley Road, would hurl our deadly snowballs at the green of their eyes. The wise cats never appeared. We were so still, Eskimo-footed arctic marksmen in the muffling silence of the eternal snows—eternal, ever since Wednesday—that we never heard Mrs. Prothero's first cry from her igloo at the bottom of the garden. Or, if we heard it at all, it was, to us, like the far-off challenge of our enemy and prey, the neighbor's Polar Cat. But soon the voice grew louder. "Fire!" cried Mrs. Prothero, and she beat the dinner-gong. And we ran down the garden, with the snowballs in our arms, towards the house, and smoke, indeed, was pouring out of the dining-room, and the gong was bombilating, and Mrs. Prothero was announcing ruin like a town-crier in Pompeii. This was better than all the cats in Wales standing on the wall in a row. We bounded into the house, laden with snowballs, and stopped at the open door of the smoke-filled room. Something was burning all right; perhaps it was Mr. Prothero, who always slept there after midday dinner with a newspaper over his face; but he was standing in the middle of the room, saying "A fine Christmas!" and smacking at the smoke with a slipper.

"Call the fire-brigade," cried Mrs. Prothero as she beat the gong.

"They won't be there," said Mr. Prothero, "it's Christmas."

There was no fire to be seen, only clouds of smoke and Mr. Prothero standing in the middle of them, waving his slipper as though he were conducting.

"Do something," he said.

And we threw all our snowballs into the smoke—I think we

missed Mr. Prothero—and ran out of the house to the telephone-box.
"Let's call the police as well," Jim said.
"And the ambulance."
"And Ernie Jenkins, he likes fires."
But we only called the fire-brigade, and soon the fire-engine
came and three tall men in helmets brought a hose into the house
and Mr. Prothero got out just in time before they turned it on.
Nobody could have had a noisier Christmas Eve. And when the
firemen turned off the hose and were standing in the wet and
smoky room, Jim's aunt, Miss Prothero, came downstairs and
peered in at them. Jim and I waited, very quietly, to hear what
she would say to them. She said the right thing, always. She
looked at the three tall firemen in their shining helmets, standing
among the smoke and cinders and dissolving snowballs, and she
said: "Would you like something to read?"
Now out of that bright white snowball of Christmas gone
comes the stocking, the stocking of stockings, that hung at the foot
of the bed with the arm of a golliwog dangling over the top and
small bells ringing in the toes. There was a company, gallant and
scarlet but never nice to taste though I always tried when very
young, of belted and busbied and musketed lead soldiers so soon
to lose their heads and legs in the wars on the kitchen table after
the tea-things, the mince-pies, and the cakes that I helped to make
by stoning the raisins and eating them, had been cleared away;
and a bag of moist and many-colored jelly-babies and a folded
flag and a false nose and a tram-conductor's cap and a machine
that punched tickets and rang a bell; never a catapult; once, by a
mistake that no one could explain, a little hatchet; and a rubber-
buffalo, or it may have been a horse, with a yellow head and
haphazard legs; and a celluloid duck that made, when you pressed
it, a most unducklike noise, a mewing moo that an ambitious cat
might make who wishes to be a cow; and a painting-book in which
I could make the grass, the trees, the sea, and the animals any color
I pleased: and still the dazzling sky-blue sheep are grazing in the
red field under a flight of rainbow-beaked and pea green birds.
Christmas morning was always over before you could say Jack
Frost. And look! suddenly the pudding was burning! Bang the
gong and call the fire-brigade and the book-loving firemen! Someone found the silver three-penny-bit with a currant on it; and the
someone was always Uncle Arnold. The motto in my cracker read:

> Let's all have fun this Christmas Day,
> Let's play and sing and shout hooray!

and the grown-ups turned their eyes towards the ceiling, and
Auntie Bessie, who had already been frightened, twice, by a clock-

work mouse, whimpered at the sideboard and had some elderberry
wine. And someone put a glass bowl full of nuts on the littered
table, and my uncle said, as he said once every year: "I've got a
shoe-nut here. Fetch me a shoehorn to open it, boy."

And dinner was ended.

And I remember that on the afternoon of Christmas Day,
when the others sat around the fire and told each other that this
was nothing, no, nothing, to the great snowbound and turkey-proud
yule-log-crackling holly-berry-bedizined and kissing-under-the-mis-
tletoe Christmas when *they* were children, I would go out, school-
capped and gloved and mufflered, with my bright new boots
squeaking, into the white world on to the seaward hill, to call on
Jim and Dan and Jack and to walk with them through the silent
snowscape of our town.

We went padding through the streets, leaving huge deep footprints in the snow, on the hidden pavements.

"I bet people'll think there's been hippoes."

"What would you do if you saw a hippo coming down Terrace
Road?"

"I'd go like this, bang! I'd throw him over the railings and roll
him down the hill and then I'd tickle him under the ear and he'd
'wag his tail . . ."

"What would you do if you saw *two* hippoes . . . ?"

Iron-flanked and bellowing he-hippoes clanked and blundered
and battered through the scudding snow towards us as we passed
by Mr. Daniel's house.

"Let's post Mr. Daniel a snowball through his letter box."

"Let's write things in the snow."

"Let's write 'Mr. Daniel looks like a spaniel' all over his lawn."

"Look," Jack said, "I'm eating snow-pie."

"What's it taste like?"

"Like snow-pie," Jack said.

Or we walked on the white shore.

"Can the fishes see it's snowing?"

"They think it's the sky falling down."

The silent one-clouded heavens drifted on to the sea.

"All the old dogs have gone."

Dogs of a hundred mingled makes yapped in the summer at the
sea-rim and yelped at the trespassing mountains of the waves.

"I bet St. Bernards would like it now."

And we were snowblind travelers lost on the north hills, and
the great dewlapped dogs, with brandy-flasks round their necks,
ambled and shambled up to us, baying "Excelsior."

We returned home through the desolate poor sea-facing streets
where only a few children fumbled with bare red fingers in the

thick wheel-rutted snow and catcalled after us, their voices fading away, as we trudged uphill, into the cries of the dock-birds and the hooters of ships out in the white and whirling bay.

Bring out the tall tales now that we told by the fire as we roasted chestnuts and the gaslight bubbled low. Ghosts with their heads under their arms trailed their chains and said "whooo" like owls in the long nights when I dared not look over my shoulder; wild beasts lurked in the cubby-hole under the stairs where the gas-meter ticked. "Once upon a time," Jim said, "there were three boys, just like us, who got lost in the dark in the snow, near Bethesda Chapel, and this is what happened to them . . ." It was the most dreadful happening I had ever heard.

And I remember that we went singing carols once, a night or two before Christmas Eve, when there wasn't the shaving of a moon to light the secret, white-flying streets. At the end of a long road was a drive that led to a large house, and we stumbled up the darkness of the drive that night, each one of us afraid, each one holding a stone in his hand in case, and all of us too brave to say a word. The wind made through the drive-trees noises as of old and unpleasant and maybe web-footed men wheezing in caves. We reached the black bulk of the house.

"What shall we give them?" Dan whispered.

" 'Hark the Herald'? 'Christmas comes but Once a Year' ?"

"No," Jack said: "We'll sing 'Good King Wenceslas.' I'll count three."

One, two, three, and we began to sing, our voices high and seemingly distant in the snow-felted darkness round the house that was occupied by nobody we knew. We stood close together, near the dark door.

> Good King Wenceslas looked out
> On the Feast of Stephen.

And then a small, dry voice, like the voice of someone who has not spoken for a long time, suddenly joined our singing: a small, dry voice from the other side of the door: a small, dry voice through the keyhole. And when we stopped running we were outside *our* house; the front room was lovely and bright; the gramophone was playing; we saw the red and white balloons hanging from the gas-bracket; uncles and aunts sat by the fire; I thought I smelt our supper being fried in the kitchen. Everything was good again, and Christmas shone through all the familiar town.

"Perhaps it was a ghost," Jim said.

"Perhaps it was trolls," Dan said, who was always reading.

"Let's go in and see if there's any jelly left," Jack said. And we did that.

WALLACE STEGNER
The Town Dump

The town dump of Whitemud, Saskatchewan, could only have been a few years old when I knew it, for the village was born in 1913 and I left there in 1919. But I remember the dump better than I remember most things in that town, better than I remember most of the people. I spent more time with it, for one thing; it has more poetry and excitement in it than people did.

It lay in the southeast corner of town, in a section that was always full of adventure for me. Just there the Whitemud River left the hills, bent a little south, and started its long traverse across the prairie and international boundary to join the Milk. For all I knew, it might have been on its way to join the Alph: simply, before my eyes, it disappeared into strangeness and wonder.

Also, where it passed below the dumpground, it ran through willowed bottoms that were a favorite campsite for passing teamsters, gypsies, sometimes Indians. The very straw scattered around those camps, the ashes of those strangers' campfires, the manure of their teams and saddle horses, were hot with adventurous possibilities.

It was as an extension, a living suburb, as it were, of the dumpground that we most valued those camps. We scoured them for artifacts of their migrant tenants as if they had been archaeological sites full of the secrets of ancient civilizations. I remember toting around for weeks the broken cheek strap of a bridle. Somehow or other its buckle looked as if it had been fashioned in a far place, a place where they were accustomed to flatten the tongues of buckles for reasons that could only be exciting, and where they made a habit of plating the metal with some valuable alloy, probably silver. In places where the silver was worn away the buckle underneath shone dull yellow: probably gold.

It seemed that excitement liked that end of town better than our end. Once old Mrs. Gustafson, deeply religious and a little raddled in the head, went over there with a buckboard full of trash, and as she was driving home along the river she looked and saw a spent catfish, washed in from Cypress Lake or some other part of the watershed, floating on the yellow water. He was two feet long, his whiskers hung down, his fins and tail were limp. He was a kind of fish that no one had seen in the Whitemud in the three or four years of the town's life, and a kind that none of us children had ever seen anywhere. Mrs. Gustafson had never seen one like him either; she perceived at once that he was the devil, and she whipped up the team and reported him at Hoffman's elevator.

We could hear her screeching as we legged it for the river to see for ourselves. Sure enough, there he was. He looked very tired, and he made no great effort to get away as we pushed out a half-sunken rowboat from below the flume, submerged it under him, and brought him ashore. When he died three days later we experimentally fed him to two half-wild cats, but they seemed to suffer no ill effects.

At that same end of town the irrigation flume crossed the river. It always seemed to me giddily high when I hung my chin over its plank edge and looked down, but it probably walked no more than twenty feet above the water on its spidery legs. Ordinarily in summer it carried about six or eight inches of smooth water, and under the glassy hurrying of the little boxed stream the planks were coated with deep sun-warmed moss as slick as frogs' eggs. A boy could sit in the flume with the water walling up against his back, and grab a cross brace above him, and pull, shooting himself sledlike ahead until he could reach the next brace for another pull and another slide, and so on across the river in four scoots.

After ten minutes in the flume he would come out wearing a dozen or more limber black leeches, and could sit in the green shade where darning needles flashed blue, and dragonflies hummed and darted and stopped, and skaters dimpled slack and eddy with their delicate transitory footprints, and there stretch the leeches out one by one while their sucking ends clung and clung, until at last, stretched far out, they let go with a tiny wet *puk* and snapped together like rubber bands. The smell of the river and the flume and the clay cutbanks and the bars of that part of the river was the smell of wolf willow.

But nothing in that end of town was as good as the dumpground that scattered along a little runoff coulee dipping down toward the river from the south bench. Through a historical process that went back, probably, to the roots of community sanitation and distaste for eyesores, but that in law dated from the Unincorporated Towns Ordinance of the territorial government, passed in 1888, the dump was one of the very first community enterprises, almost our town's first institution.

More than that, it contained relics of every individual who had ever lived there, and of every phase of the town's history.

The bedsprings on which the town's first child was begotten might be there; the skeleton of a boy's pet colt; two or three volumes of Shakespeare bought in haste and error from a peddler, later loaned in carelessness, soaked with water and chemicals in a house fire, and finally thrown out to flap their stained eloquence in the prairie wind.

Broken dishes, rusty tinware, spoons that had been used to mix paint; once a box of percussion caps, sign and symbol of the carelessness that most of those people felt about all matters of personal or public safety. We put them on the railroad tracks and were anonymously denounced in the *Enterprise*. There were also old iron, old brass, for which we hunted assiduously, by night conning junkmen's catalogues and the pages of the *Enterprise* to find how much wartime value there might be in the geared insides of clocks or in a pound of tea lead carefully wrapped in a ball whose weight astonished and delighted us. Sometimes the unimaginable outside world reached in and laid a finger on us. I recall that, aged no more than seven, I wrote a St. Louis junk house asking if they preferred their tea lead and tinfoil wrapped in balls, or whether they would rather have it pressed flat in sheets, and I got back a typewritten letter in a window envelope instructing me that they would be happy to have it in any way that was convenient for me. They added that they valued my business and were mine very truly. Dazed, I carried that windowed grandeur around in my pocket until I wore it out, and for months I saved the letter as a souvenir of the wondering time when something strange and distinguished had singled me out.

We hunted old bottles in the dump, bottles caked with dirt and filth, half buried, full of cobwebs, and we washed them out at the horse trough by the elevator, putting in a handful of shot along with the water to knock the dirt loose; and when we had shaken them until our arms were tired, we hauled them off in somebody's coaster wagon and turned them in at Bill Anderson's pool hall, where the smell of lemon pop was so sweet on the dark pool-hall air that I am sometimes awakened by it in the night, even yet.

Smashed wheels of wagons and buggies, tangles of rusty barbed wire, the collapsed perambulator that the French wife of one of the town's doctors had once pushed proudly up the planked sidewalks and along the ditchbank paths. A welter of foul-smelling feathers and coyote-scattered carrion which was all that remained of somebody's dream of a chicken ranch. The chickens had all got some mysterious pip at the same time, and died as one, and the dream lay out there with the rest of the town's history to rustle to the empty sky on the border of the hills.

There was melted glass in curious forms, and the half-melted office safe left from the burning of Bill Day's Hotel. On very lucky days we might find a piece of the lead casing that had enclosed the wires of the town's first telephone system. The casing was just the right size for rings, and so soft that it could be whittled with a jackknife. It was a material that might have made artists of us. If we had been Indians of fifty years before, that bright soft metal would have enlisted our maximum patience and craft and come out as ring and metal and amulet inscribed with the symbols of our observed world. Perhaps there were too many ready-made alternatives in the local drug, hardware, and general stores; perhaps our feeble artistic response was a measure of the insufficiency of the challenge we felt. In any case I do not remember that we did any more with the metal than to shape it into crude seal rings with our initials or pierced hearts carved in them; and these, though they served a purpose in juvenile courtship, stopped something short of art.

The dump held very little wood, for in that country anything burnable got burned. But it had plenty of old iron, furniture, papers, mattresses that were the delight of field mice, and jugs and demijohns that were sometimes their bane, for they crawled into the necks and drowned in the rain water or redeye that was inside.

If the history of our town was not exactly written, it was at least hinted, in the dump. I think I had a pretty sound notion even at eight or nine of how significant was that first institution of our forming Canadian civilization. For rummaging through its foul purlieus I had several times been surprised and shocked to find relics of my own life tossed out there to rot or blow away.

The volumes of Shakespeare belonged to a set that my father had bought before I was born. It had been carried through successive moves from town to town in the Dakotas, and from Dakota to Seattle, and from Seattle to Bellingham, and Bellingham to Redmond, and from Redmond back to Iowa, and from there to Saskatchewan. Then, stained in a stranger's house fire, these volumes had suffered from a house-cleaning impulse and been thrown away for me to stumble upon in the dump. One of the Cratchet girls had borrowed them, a hatchet-faced, thin, eager, transplanted Cockney girl with a frenzy, almost a hysteria, for reading. And yet somehow, through her hands, they found the dump, to become a symbol of how much was lost, how much thrown aside, how much carelessly or of necessity given up, in the making of a new country. We had so few books that I was familiar with them all, had handled them, looked at their pictures, perhaps even read them. They were the lares and penates, part of the skimpy impedimenta of household gods we had brought with us into Latium.[1] Finding those three thrown away was a little like finding my own name on a gravestone.

And yet not the blow that something else was, something that

---

1. In Roman families the lares and penates were the ancestral, household gods; they came to embody the continuity of the family. Cf. Virgil, *Aeneid* I. 1-7.

impressed me even more with the dump's close reflection of the town's intimate life. The colt whose picked skeleton lay out there was mine. He had been incurably crippled when dogs chased our mare, Daisy, the morning after she foaled. I had labored for months to make him well; had fed him by hand, curried him, exercised him, adjusted the iron braces that I had talked my father into having made. And I had not known that he would have to be destroyed. One weekend I turned him over to the foreman of one of the ranches, presumably so that he could be cared for. A few days later I found his skinned body, with the braces still on his crippled front legs, lying on the dump.

Not even that, I think, cured me of going there, though our parents all forbade us on pain of cholera or worse to do so. The place fascinated us, as it should have. For this was the kitchen midden of all the civilization we knew; it gave us the most tantalizing glimpses into our lives as well as into those of the neighbors. It gave us an aesthetic distance from which to know ourselves.

The dump was our poetry and our history. We took it home with us by the wagonload, bringing back into town the things the town had used and thrown away. Some little part of what we gathered, mainly bottles, we managed to bring back to usefulness, but most of our gleanings we left lying around barn or attic or cellar until in some renewed fury of spring cleanup our families carted them off to the dump again, to be rescued and briefly treasured by some other boy with schemes for making them useful. Occasionally something we really valued with a passion was snatched from us in horror and returned at once. That happened to the mounted head of a white mountain goat, somebody's trophy from old times and the far Rocky Mountains, that I brought home one day in transports of delight. My mother took one look and discovered that his beard was full of moths.

I remember that goat; I regret him yet. Poetry is seldom useful, but always memorable. I think I learned more from the town dump than I learned from school: more about people, more about how life is lived, not elsewhere but here, not in other times but now. If I were a sociologist anxious to study in detail the life of any community, I would go very early to its refuse piles. For a community may be as well judged by what it throws away —what it has to throw away and what it chooses to—as by any other evidence. For whole civilizations we have sometimes no more of the poetry and little more of the history than this.

QUESTIONS

1. Stegner begins his reminiscence of the town dump by saying that it had "poetry and excitement" in it. In what ways does he seek to convey those qualities to the reader?

2. Is Stegner's description of the dump and its surroundings vivid? Where does his writing directly appeal to the senses, and which senses are called into play?

3. In his second paragraph Stegner speaks of the Alph, the "sacred river" of Coleridge's poem "Kubla Khan." Why? How does allusion to that poem help him convey the strangeness and wonder he then felt?

4. In paragraphs 5-8 Stegner departs, as he had departed to a lesser degree in the two preceding paragraphs, from his description of the dump. Explain how that departure is justified and whether the writing there is appropriate to the essay as a whole.

5. Why does Stegner say (p. 9) that finding the three volumes of Shakespeare in the dump was "a little like finding my own name on a gravestone"? What is the purpose and effect of his allusion to Virgil's Aeneid in the sentence just before that?

6. Through what particular details does Stegner portray the dump as a record of his childhood? How is it shown to be also a record of the brief history of the town? In what respects does it reflect and suggest more widely yet, European and American history and culture and, ultimately, the ancient past, the foundations of civilization? Explain how and to what effect Stegner's focus on the dump enables these considerations to widen in scope but remain associated.

MAYA ANGELOU

High School Graduation[1]

The children in Stamps[2] trembled visibly with anticipation. Some adults were excited too, but to be certain the whole young population had come down with graduation epidemic. Large classes were graduating from both the grammar school and the high school. Even those who were years removed from their own day of glorious release were anxious to help with preparations as a kind of dry run. The junior students who were moving into the vacating classes' chairs were tradition-bound to show their talents for leadership and management. They strutted through the school and around the campus exerting pressure on the lower grades. Their authority was so new that occasionally if they pressed a little too hard it had to be overlooked. After all, next term was coming, and it never hurt a sixth grader to have a play sister in the eighth grade, or a tenth-year student to be able to call a twelfth grader Bubba. So all was endured in a spirit of shared understanding. But the graduating classes themselves were the nobility. Like travelers with exotic destinations on their minds, the graduates were remarkably

1. Chapter 23 of *I Know Why the Caged Bird Sings*, 1970.   2. A town in Arkansas.

forgetful. They came to school without their books, or tablets or even pencils. Volunteers fell over themselves to secure replacements for the missing equipment. When accepted, the willing workers might or might not be thanked, and it was of no importance to the pregraduation rites. Even teachers were respectful of the now quiet and aging seniors, and tended to speak to them, if not as equals, as beings only slightly lower than themselves. After tests were returned and grades given, the student body, which acted like an extended family, knew who did well, who excelled, and what piteous ones had failed.

Unlike the white high school, Lafayette County Training School distinguished itself by having neither lawn, nor hedges, nor tennis court, nor climbing ivy. Its two buildings (main classrooms, the grade school and home economics) were set on a dirt hill with no fence to limit either its boundaries or those of bordering farms. There was a large expanse to the left of the school which was used alternately as a baseball diamond or basketball court. Rusty hoops on swaying poles represented the permanent recreational equipment, although bats and balls could be borrowed from the P.E. teacher if the borrower was qualified and if the diamond wasn't occupied.

Over this rocky area relieved by a few shady tall persimmon trees the graduating class walked. The girls often held hands and no longer bothered to speak to the lower students. There was a sadness about them, as if this old world was not their home and they were bound for higher ground. The boys, on the other hand, had become more friendly, more outgoing. A decided change from the closed attitude they projected while studying for finals. Now they seemed not ready to give up the old school, the familiar paths and classrooms. Only a small percentage would be continuing on to college —one of the South's A & M (agricultural and mechanical) schools, which trained Negro youths to be carpenters, farmers, handymen, masons, maids, cooks and baby nurses. Their future rode heavily on their shoulders, and blinded them to the collective joy that had pervaded the lives of the boys and girls in the grammar school graduating class.

Parents who could afford it had ordered new shoes and ready-made clothes for themselves from Sears and Roebuck or Montgomery Ward. They also engaged the best seamstresses to make the floating graduating dresses and to cut down secondhand pants which would be pressed to a military slickness for the important event.

Oh, it was important, all right. Whitefolks would attend the ceremony, and two or three would speak of God and home, and the Southern way of life, and Mrs. Parsons, the principal's wife, would play the graduation march while the lower-grade graduates paraded

down the aisles and took their seats below the platform. The high
school seniors would wait in empty classrooms to make their dramatic entrance.

In the Store I was the person of the moment. The birthday girl.
The center. Bailey[3] had graduated the year before, although to do
so he had had to forfeit all pleasures to make up for his time lost in
Baton Rouge.

My class was wearing butter-yellow piqué dresses, and Momma
launched out on mine. She smocked the yoke into tiny crisscrossing
puckers, then shirred the rest of the bodice. Her dark fingers ducked
in and out of the lemony cloth as she embroidered raised daisies
around the hem. Before she considered herself finished she had
added a crocheted cuff on the puff sleeves, and a pointy crocheted
collar.

I was going to be lovely. A walking model of all the various styles
of fine hand sewing and it didn't worry me that I was only twelve
years old and merely graduating from the eighth grade. Besides,
many teachers in Arkansas Negro schools had only that diploma
and were licensed to impart wisdom.

The days had become longer and more noticeable. The faded
beige of former times had been replaced with strong and sure
colors. I began to see my classmates' clothes, their skin tones, and
the dust that waved off pussy willows. Clouds that lazed across the
sky were objects of great concern to me. Their shiftier shapes might
have held a message that in my new happiness and with a little bit
of time I'd soon decipher. During that period I looked at the arch of
heaven so religiously my neck kept a steady ache. I had taken to
smiling more often, and my jaws hurt from the unaccustomed activity. Between the two physical sore spots, I suppose I could have
been uncomfortable, but that was not the case. As a member of the
winning team (the graduating class of 1940) I had outdistanced
unpleasant sensations by miles. I was headed for the freedom of
open fields.

Youth and social approval allied themselves with me and we
trammeled memories of slights and insults. The wind of our swift
passage remodeled my features. Lost tears were pounded to mud
and then to dust. Years of withdrawal were brushed aside and left
behind, as hanging ropes of parasitic moss.

My work alone had awarded me a top place and I was going to
be one of the first called in the graduating ceremonies. On the classroom blackboard, as well as on the bulletin board in the auditorium, there were blue stars and white stars and red stars. No
absences, no tardinesses, and my academic work was among the best
of the year. I could say the preamble to the Constitution even faster

3. The author's brother.

than Bailey. We timed ourselves often: "WethepeopleoftheUnited Statesinordertoformamoreperfectunion . . ." I had memorized the Presidents of the United States from Washington to Roosevelt in chronological as well as alphabetical order.

My hair pleased me too. Gradually the black mass had lengthened and thickened, so that it kept at last to its braided pattern, and I didn't have to yank my scalp off when I tried to comb it.

Louise and I had rehearsed the exercises until we tired out ourselves. Henry Reed was class valedictorian. He was a small, very black boy with hooded eyes, a long, broad nose and an oddly shaped head. I had admired him for years because each term he and I vied for the best grades in our class. Most often he bested me, but instead of being disappointed I was pleased that we shared top places between us. Like many Southern Black children, he lived with his grandmother, who was as strict as Momma and as kind as she knew how to be. He was courteous, respectful and soft-spoken to elders, but on the playground he chose to play the roughest games. I admired him. Anyone, I reckoned, sufficiently afraid or sufficiently dull could be polite. But to be able to operate at a top level with both adults and children was admirable.

His valedictory speech was entitled "To Be or Not to Be." The rigid tenth-grade teacher had helped him write it. He'd been working on the dramatic stresses for months.

The weeks until graduation were filled with heady activities. A group of small children were to be presented in a play about buttercups and daisies and bunny rabbits. They could be heard throughout the building practicing their hops and their little songs that sounded like silver bells. The older girls (nongraduates, of course) were assigned the task of making refreshments for the night's festivities. A tangy scent of ginger, cinnamon, nutmeg and chocolate wafted around the home economics building as the budding cooks made samples for themselves and their teachers.

In every corner of the workshop, axes and saws split fresh timber as the woodshop boys made sets and stage scenery. Only the graduates were left out of the general bustle. We were free to sit in the library at the back of the building or look in quite detachedly, naturally, on the measures being taken for our event.

Even the minister preached on graduation the Sunday before. His subject was, "Let your light so shine that men will see your good works and praise your Father, Who is in Heaven." Although the sermon was purported to be addressed to us, he used the occasion to speak to backsliders, gamblers and general ne'er-do-wells. But since he had called our names at the beginning of the service we were mollified.

Among Negroes the tradition was to give presents to children going only from one grade to another. How much more important this was when the person was graduating at the top of the class. Uncle Willie and Momma had sent away for a Mickey Mouse watch like Bailey's. Louise gave me four embroidered handkerchiefs. (I gave her crocheted doilies.) Mrs. Sneed, the minister's wife, made me an undershirt to wear for graduation, and nearly every customer gave me a nickel or maybe even a dime with the instruction "Keep on moving to higher ground," or some such encouragement.

Amazingly the great day finally dawned and I was out of bed before I knew it. I threw open the back door to see it more clearly, but Momma said, "Sister, come away from that door and put your robe on."

I hoped the memory of that morning would never leave me. Sunlight was itself young, and the day had none of the insistence maturity would bring it in a few hours. In my robe and barefoot in the backyard, under cover of going to see about my new beans, I gave myself up to the gentle warmth and thanked God that no matter what evil I had done in my life He had allowed me to live to see this day. Somewhere in my fatalism I had expected to die, accidentally, and never have the chance to walk up the stairs in the auditorium and gracefully receive my hard-earned diploma. Out of God's merciful bosom I had won reprieve.

Bailey came out in his robe and gave me a box wrapped in Christmas paper. He said he had saved his money for months to pay for it. It felt like a box of chocolates, but I knew Bailey wouldn't save money to buy candy when we had all we could want under our noses.

He was as proud of the gift as I. It was a soft-leather-bound copy of a collection of poems by Edgar Allan Poe, or, as Bailey and I called him, "Eap." I turned to "Annabel Lee" and we walked up and down the garden rows, the cool dirt between our toes, reciting the beautifully sad lines.

Momma made a Sunday breakfast although it was only Friday. After we finished the blessing, I opened my eyes to find the watch on my plate. It was a dream of a day. Everything went smoothly and to my credit. I didn't have to be reminded or scolded for anything. Near evening I was too jittery to attend to chores, so Bailey volunteered to do all before his bath.

Days before, we had made a sign for the Store, and as we turned out the lights Momma hung the cardboard over the doorknob. It read clearly: CLOSED. GRADUATION.

My dress fitted perfectly and everyone said that I looked like a sunbeam in it. On the hill, going toward the school, Bailey walked behind with Uncle Willie, who muttered, "Go on, Ju." He wanted him to walk ahead with us because it embarrassed him to have to walk so slowly. Bailey said he'd let the ladies walk together, and the men would bring up the rear. We all laughed, nicely.

Little children dashed by out of the dark like fireflies. Their crepe-paper dresses and butterfly wings were not made for running and we heard more than one rip, dryly, and the regretful "uh uh" that followed.

The school blazed without gaiety. The windows seemed cold and unfriendly from the lower hill. A sense of ill-fated timing crept over me, and if Momma hadn't reached for my hand I would have drifted back to Bailey and Uncle Willie, and possibly beyond. She made a few slow jokes about my feet getting cold, and tugged me along to the now-strange building.

Around the front steps, assurance came back. There were my fellow "greats," the graduating class. Hair brushed back, legs oiled, new dresses and pressed pleats, fresh pocket handkerchiefs and little handbags, all homesewn. Oh, we were up to snuff, all right. I joined my comrades and didn't even see my family go in to find seats in the crowded auditorium.

The school band struck up a march and all classes filed in as had been rehearsed. We stood in front of our seats, as assigned, and on a signal from the choir director, we sat. No sooner had this been accomplished than the band started to play the national anthem. We rose again and sang the song, after which we recited the pledge of allegiance. We remained standing for a brief minute before the choir director and the principal signaled to us, rather desperately I thought, to take our seats. The command was so unusual that our carefully rehearsed and smooth-running machine was thrown off. For a full minute we fumbled for our chairs and bumped into each other awkwardly. Habits change or solidify under pressure, so in our state of nervous tension we had been ready to follow our usual assembly pattern: the American national anthem, then the pledge of allegiance, then the song every Black person I knew called the Negro National Anthem.[4] All done in the same key, with the same passion and most often standing on the same foot.

Finding my seat at last, I was overcome with a presentiment of worse things to come. Something unrehearsed, unplanned, was going to happen, and we were going to be made to look bad. I distinctly remember being explicit in the choice of pronoun. It was "we," the graduating class, the unit, that concerned me then.

The principal welcomed "parents and friends" and asked the Baptist minister to lead us in prayer. His invocation was brief and punchy, and for a second I thought we were getting on the high road to right action. When the principal came back to the dais, however, his voice had changed. Sounds always affected me profoundly and the principal's voice was one of my favorites. During assembly it melted and lowed weakly into the audience. It had not

4. "Lift Every Voice."

been in my plan to listen to him, but my curiosity was piqued and I straightened up to give him my attention.

He was talking about Booker T. Washington, our "late great leader," who said we can be as close as the fingers on the hand, etc. . . . Then he said a few vague things about friendship and the friendship of kindly people to those less fortunate than themselves. With that his voice nearly faded, thin, away. Like a river diminishing to a stream and then to a trickle. But he cleared his throat and said, "Our speaker tonight, who is also our friend, came from Texarkana to deliver the commencement address, but due to the irregularity of the train schedule, he's going to, as they say, 'speak and run.' " He said that we understood and wanted the man to know that we were most grateful for the time he was able to give us and then something about how we were willing always to adjust to another's program, and without more ado—"I give you Mr. Edward Donleavy."

Not one but two white men came through the door off-stage. The shorter one walked to the speaker's platform, and the tall one moved to the center seat and sat down. But that was our principal's seat, and already occupied. The dislodged gentleman bounced around for a long breath or two before the Baptist minister gave him his chair, then with more dignity than the situation deserved, the minister walked off the stage.

Donleavy looked at the audience once (on reflection, I'm sure that he wanted only to reassure himself that we were really there), adjusted his glasses and began to read from a sheaf of papers.

He was glad "to be here and to see the work going on just as it was in the other schools."

At the first "Amen" from the audience I willed the offender to immediate death by choking on the word. But Amens and Yes, sir's began to fall around the room like rain through a ragged umbrella.

He told us of the wonderful changes we children in Stamps had in store. The Central School (naturally, the white school was Central) had already been granted improvements that would be in use in the fall. A well-known artist was coming from Little Rock to teach art to them. They were going to have the newest microscopes and chemistry equipment for their laboratory. Mr. Donleavy didn't leave us long in the dark over who made these improvements available to Central High. Nor were we to be ignored in the general betterment scheme he had in mind.

He said that he had pointed out to people at a very high level that one of the first-line football tacklers at Arkansas Agricultural and Mechanical College had graduated from good old Lafayette County Training School. Here fewer Amen's were heard. Those few that did break through lay dully in the air with the heaviness of habit.

He went on to praise us. He went on to say how he had bragged that "one of the best basketball players at Fisk sank his first ball right here at Lafayette County Training School."

The white kids were going to have a chance to become Galileos and Madame Curies and Edisons and Gauguins, and our boys (the girls weren't even in on it) would try to be Jesse Owenses and Joe Louises.

Owens and the Brown Bomber were great heroes in our world, but what school official in the white-goddom of Little Rock had the right to decide that those two men must be our only heroes? Who decided that for Henry Reed to become a scientist he had to work like George Washington Carver, as a bootblack, to buy a lousy microscope? Bailey was obviously always going to be too small to be an athlete, so which concrete angel glued to what country seat had decided that if my brother wanted to become a lawyer he had to first pay penance for his skin by picking cotton and hoeing corn and studying correspondence books at night for twenty years?

The man's dead words fell like bricks around the auditorium and too many settled in my belly. Constrained by hard-learned manners I couldn't look behind me, but to my left and right the proud graduating class of 1940 had dropped their heads. Every girl in my row had found something new to do with her handkerchief. Some folded the tiny squares into love knots, some into triangles, but most were wadding them, then pressing them flat on their yellow laps.

On the dais, the ancient tragedy was being replayed. Professor Parsons sat, a sculptor's reject, rigid. His large, heavy body seemed devoid of will or willingness, and his eyes said he was no longer with us. The other teachers examined the flag (which was draped stage right) or their notes, or the windows which opened on our now-famous playing diamond.

Graduation, the hush-hush magic time of frills and gifts and congratulations and diplomas, was finished for me before my name was called. The accomplishment was nothing. The meticulous maps, drawn in three colors of ink, learning and spelling decasyllabic words, memorizing the whole of *The Rape of Lucrece*—it was for nothing. Donleavy had exposed us.

We were maids and farmers, handymen and washerwomen, and anything higher that we aspired to was farcical and presumptuous.

Then I wished that Gabriel Prosser and Nat Turner[5] had killed all whitefolks in their beds and that Abraham Lincoln had been assassinated before the signing of the Emancipation Proclamation, and that Harriet Tubman[6] had been killed by that blow on her

5. Leaders of Virginia slave rebellions in 1800 and 1831 respectively.
6. Nineteenth-century black abolition-ist, a "conductor" on the Underground Railroad.

head and Christopher Columbus had drowned in the *Santa Maria*.

It was awful to be a Negro and have no control over my life. It was brutal to be young and already trained to sit quietly and listen to charges brought against my color with no chance of defense. We should all be dead. I thought I should like to see us all dead, one on top of the other. A pyramid of flesh with the whitefolks on the bottom, as the broad base, then the Indians with their silly tomahawks and teepees and wigwams and treaties, the Negroes with their mops and recipes and cotton sacks and spirituals sticking out of their mouths. The Dutch children should all stumble in their wooden shoes and break their necks. The French should choke to death on the Louisiana Purchase (1803) while silkworms ate all the Chinese with their stupid pigtails. As a species, we were an abomination. All of us.

Donleavy was running for election, and assured our parents that if he won we could count on having the only colored paved playing field in that part of Arkansas. Also—he never looked up to acknowledge the grunts of acceptance—also, we were bound to get some new equipment for the home economics building and the workshop.

He finished, and since there was no need to give any more than the most perfunctory thank-you's, he nodded to the men on the stage, and the tall white man who was never introduced joined him at the door. They left with the attitude that now they were off to something really important. (The graduation ceremonies at Lafayette County Training School had been a mere preliminary.)

The ugliness they left was palpable. An uninvited guest who wouldn't leave. The choir was summoned and sang a modern arrangement of "Onward, Christian Soldiers," with new words pertaining to graduates seeking their place in the world. But it didn't work. Elouise, the daughter of the Baptist minister, recited "Invictus," and I could have cried at the impertinence of "I am the master of my fate, I am the captain of my soul."

My name had lost its ring of familiarity and I had to be nudged to go and receive my diploma. All my preparations had fled. I neither marched up to the stage like a conquering Amazon, nor did I look in the audience for Bailey's nod of approval. Marguerite Johnson, I heard the name again, my honors were read, there were noises in the audience of appreciation, and I took my place on the stage as rehearsed.

I thought about colors I hated: ecru, puce, lavender, beige and black.

There was shuffling and rustling around me, then Henry Reed was giving his valedictory address, "To Be or Not to Be." Hadn't he heard the whitefolks? We couldn't *be*, so the question was a waste of time. Henry's voice came out clear and strong. I feared to look at him. Hadn't he got the message? There was no "nobler in the mind" for Negroes because the world didn't think we had minds, and they let us know it. "Outrageous fortune"? Now, that was a joke. When the ceremony was over I had to tell Henry Reed some things. That is, if I still cared. Not "rub," Henry, "erase." "Ah, there's the erase." Us.

Henry had been a good student in elocution. His voice rose on tides of promise and fell on waves of warnings. The English teacher had helped him to create a sermon winging through Hamlet's soliloquy. To be a man, a doer, a builder, a leader, or to be a tool, an unfunny joke, a crusher of funky toadstools. I marveled that Henry could go through with the speech as if we had a choice.

I had been listening and silently rebutting each sentence with my eyes closed; then there was a hush, which in an audience warns that something unplanned is happening. I looked up and saw Henry Reed, the conservative, the proper, the A student, turn his back to the audience and turn to us (the proud graduating class of 1940) and sing, nearly speaking,

> "Lift ev'ry voice and sing
> Till earth and heaven ring
> Ring with the harmonies of Liberty ..."

It was the poem written by James Weldon Johnson. It was the music composed by J. Rosamond Johnson. It was the Negro national anthem. Out of habit we were singing it.

Our mothers and fathers stood in the dark hall and joined the hymn of encouragement. A kindergarten teacher led the small children onto the stage and the buttercups and daisies and bunny rabbits marked time and tried to follow:

> "Stony the road we trod
> Bitter the chastening rod
> Felt in the days when hope, unborn, had died.
> Yet with a steady beat
> Have not our weary feet
> Come to the place for which our fathers sighed?"

Each child I knew had learned that song with his ABC's and along with "Jesus Loves Me This I Know." But I personally had never heard it before. Never heard the words, despite the thousands of times I had sung them. Never thought they had anything to do with me.

On the other hand, the words of Patrick Henry had made such an impression on me that I had been able to stretch myself tall and trembling and say, "I know not what course others may take, but as for me, give me liberty or give me death."

And now I heard, really for the first time:

> "We have come over a way that with tears
> has been watered,

We have come, treading our path through
the blood of the slaughtered."

While echoes of the song shivered in the air, Henry Reed bowed
his head, said "Thank you," and returned to his place in the line.
The tears that slipped down many faces were not wiped away in
shame.

We were on top again. As always, again. We survived. The
depths had been icy and dark, but now a bright sun spoke to our
souls. I was no longer simply a member of the proud graduating
class of 1940; I was a proud member of the wonderful, beautiful
Negro race.

Oh, Black known and unknown poets, how often have your auc-
tioned pains sustained us? Who will compute the lonely nights
made less lonely by your songs, or the empty pots made less tragic
by your tales?

If we were a people much given to revealing secrets, we might
raise monuments and sacrifice to the memories of our poets, but
slavery cured us of that weakness. It may be enough, however, to
have it said that we survive in exact relationship to the dedication
of our poets (include preachers, musicians and blues singers).

PAT JORDAN

The Last Season

I arrived at Eau Claire in late April with my wife, who had
joined me at the end of spring training. We rented a single room
with a tiny kitchenette on the second floor of an old two-family
house. It disturbed me that, unlike most baseball wives, Carol knew
nothing about the game to which I had devoted my life. She took
her cues solely from my enthusiasms and despairs. Whenever I
pitched decently—a rarity—I had to tell her so, and then she would
smile and say, "That's nice, dear." When I was knocked out of the
box in the first inning and she saw my dejection, she commiserated
with me: "Well, it's certainly not your fault. It's hard to do good
when you only play a little bit. . . . Why doesn't your manager let
you play as much as the other pitchers?"

On the night of my first starting assignment, I pitched less than
an inning. It was like Waycross. After I was relieved, I had to sit on
the bench in the dugout in 30° weather until the game was over
two hours later. I returned to our apartment at midnight and
found, in the kitchenette, the table set, dishes gleaming, napkins
folded and a single candle, unlighted. She was sitting by the table,

her hands in her lap, her eyes pink-rimmed. On the counter next to the stove was a mound of freshly peeled but uncooked potatoes and a long, thick, raw steak.

She sniffed, shivering all over as if just emerging from cold water. "I couldn't light the oven," she said, finally.

"What!"

She held up a pack of matches with only a single match left. "I tried, but it wouldn't catch!"

"Jesus, Carol, I'm starved!"

She began to cry. She cried often that first year, having stepped on board a sinking ship with a mad captain. A thousand miles from home for the first time in her life, she was burdened with nothing but my black moods day after day, while I, obsessed with my career, seldom gave her a thought. She was just there, hovering around my despairs, at times a pleasant diversion, at others a burden. To her I was a husband, the sole source of her comfort and despair, and she wondered, secretly, if this was the way it was supposed to be. Always?

After my next disastrous performance I was relegated to the bullpen. After two weeks I was the 10th pitcher of a 10-man staff. I mopped up in the last inning of lost causes, and even then often had to be relieved because I could not get three outs. After a month I had appeared in six games for a total of 15 innings.

I remember pitching an inning in Duluth and, afterward, being asked by a Duluth player, "Aren't you the guy from Davenport? The one who could really bring it?" I nodded, embarrassed.

"What happened to you? Your motion's all screwed up."

Another time I remember pitching to Lou Brock in St. Cloud, Minn. At the time Brock was leading the Northern League in hitting with a .380 average. I struck him out on a soft, floating fastball. He swung so far ahead of it he asked my catcher if it was an offspeed pitch. At the end of the inning I sat down in the far corner of the dugout and cried. I cried uncontrollably and my manager had to send another man out to warm up in order to pitch the next inning.

And I remember a game in Winnipeg that began in weather so cold—19 above zero—that we had to build small fires on the dirt floor of the dugout to prevent our fingers from going numb. We huddled around the fires, simian men in gray flannel, and at the end of each inning sent one of our tribe to forage for twigs and bits of paper in the open area behind the outfield fence. Because I was the player least likely to be used in that game, I was the one sent to forage.

By June I no longer pitched, not even the last inning of hopelessly lost games (which were many, since the Braves were in last place). I spent each game in the bullpen. I warmed up constantly, inning after inning, trying to recapture what had once been as natural as walking. I became more frantic as I threw, and my motion became even more distorted. I was pushing the ball now, like a shotputter.

There was nothing wrong with my arm. I could have understood a sore arm, dealt with it, accepted it eventually. What was happening to me was happening in my head, not my arm. Whenever I began to throw a ball, my head went as blank as a sheet of paper, and afterward it buzzed with a thousand discordant whispers. Recently, a friend of mine met Jeff Jones, the scout who had first signed me to a Braves contract. He asked Jeff why I never made it to the major leagues. "He should have," said Jeff. "He had a great arm, one of the best I'd ever seen." And then he tapped his forehead three times. "But he had a bad head."

After a while no one would catch me in the bullpen; not our third-string catcher, not any of my fellow pitchers. So I threw alone, without a ball. I stood on the warmup mound, pumped, kicked and fired an imaginary baseball toward the plate.

It was in Winnipeg one night that I thought I might be starting a game at last. Jim Fanning, my manager, tossed me a ball and told me to go to the bullpen. "But don't warm up yet," he said. I sat in the right-field bullpen for a while and watched our team practice. I grew anxious as game time drew near. Finally, one of my teammates came sprinting toward me. I stood up, flexed my shoulders, touched my toes twice. It was a pitcher, Jerry Hummitzsch. He tossed me a catcher's mitt. "Jim wants you to warm me up," he said. "He can't spare a catcher right now."

"But I thought . . . he told me I was starting. . . ."

"I only know what he told me," he said, and stepped onto the mound. I caught him until he was warm. Each pitch was a blur through my tears. When he returned to the dugout I remained in the bullpen for a few minutes and then I walked across the outfield to our clubhouse. I changed into my street clothes without showering, packed my blue canvas bag and walked to the bus stop. I took a bus into town, got my other bags at the hotel and took a Greyhound from Winnipeg to Eau Claire. I reached the Eau Claire bus terminal at nine o'clock in the morning and found my wife there, crying. "I didn't know what had happened to you," she said. "Everyone's looking for you. Jim Fanning called. He said you ran away. . . . I thought you'd left me, too. . . ." She began to laugh and cry at the same time. "I had this ridiculous vision. . . . You were running like a madman through Canada. . . . You were in your uniform. . . ."

That night John Mullen, the Braves' farm director, telephoned. He told me that for jumping the club I was suspended without salary from Eau Claire. I told him he was too late, that I had already suspended Eau Claire from my career.

"Don't be a wise guy," he said. "We're reassigning you to Palatka in the Florida State League. You get down there within two days or I'll see to it you don't get your final bonus payment." We got there.

Situated on the banks of the St. Johns River, Palatka was surrounded by dense tropical foliage in limitless swamps. It was always hot, and it rained daily. The town's main street, made of bricks, was called Lemon Street. Weeds grew out of the spaces between the bricks and out of the cracks in the sidewalks and at the bottom of the concrete buildings, so that to a stranger the vegetation appeared to be strangling the town. There was a paper mill in town. It supplied most of the blacks and poorer whites with employment. Each morning at six they were summoned to work by a whistle that woke the entire area. Shortly thereafter Palatka was blanketed by a lavender haze and filled with a terrible stench.

My wife and I drove slowly over the bricks and stopped in front of the James Hotel, the tallest building in town. In the lobby old men dozed in faded armchairs, while overhead a huge fan turned so slowly I could count its blades. We registered with the grinning clerk. He wiped a handkerchief across his brow. "Hot 'nuff for y'all?" he asked.

We fell asleep fully clothed on the old, iron poster bed in our room and we did not wake from this, the longest of all road trips, until the following night. We ate spareribs at a barbecue place and then drove out to the ball park to watch my new teammates play. They were not called the Braves, I learned from the hotel clerk, but the Azaleas. "After the town flower," the clerk said.

"I never played for a corsage before," I said, but he did not smile.

"They play their games in The Bowl," he said with pride. "The Azalea Bowl." A slightly pretentious name for a Class D ball park, I thought, until we arrived there and I saw that the name was not so much pretentious as ludicrous. The Bowl was a decaying structure at the edge of a swamp. It was enclosed by a 10-foot wooden fence that began behind the left-field bleachers, went behind the home-plate stands and terminated behind the right-field bleachers. The outfield was enclosed by a three-foot-high wooden fence whose purpose seemed less to define home runs than to hold back the swamp. Thick, green foliage hung over the fence, obscuring the faded names of restaurants and gas stations that had been painted there. Long vines and tendrils crept under the fence onto the playing field, so that often, when an outfielder chased a ball to the fence, vines would get caught in his spikes. Each week, it seemed, the vines crept farther onto the field, the swamp pressed closer, overrunning The Bowl as it was overrunning the town.

Carol and I arrived at The Bowl in the third inning of a game between the Azaleas and the Tampa Smokers. We sat in the top row of the home-plate stands, which were only 10 rows high. On this humid night in June there were perhaps 100 people there, most of them blacks, laughing and cheering in the segregated bleachers along the left-field foul line. On the field my new teammates trailed the Smokers 8–0 under dim lights and to the accompaniment of the noises of the swamp: strange thrashings-about and the caws of birds. In the fifth inning a snake slithered under the outfield fence and the umpires called time while our rightfielder beat it to death with a bat. By the seventh inning mist from the swamp was drifting into the outfield. Concealed from the waist down, outfielders floated eerily through the mist after fly balls.

The Azaleas were, I discovered, one of the worst minor league teams ever assembled. They had fallen to last place and then buried themselves ever deeper. Their fortunes had so turned against them by the time I arrived that players often refused to take the field. The team's leading pitcher, "Birdlegs" Perez, a Dominican dandy with a cherubic face and a body like a stick figure, had lost seven games in a row. He refused to pitch anymore. He claimed he had calcium deposits in his elbow. The Azaleas' leading home-run hitter was Paul Catto, a portly, unshaven first baseman. Paul refused to play one day when, after putting his glove down beside the dugout, he took a lap around the park to loosen up and returned to find his glove stolen. "Enough is enough!" he shouted.

An Azalea outfielder, call him Jim, had been a teammate of mine at McCook, Neb. After indifferent success at McCook he had become a star in Palatka. When I arrived he was leading the Florida State League in hitting, a few percentage points ahead of Tampa's second baseman, Pete Rose. Jim was not used to the pressure. Each day he grew more twitchy as Rose narrowed the gap between them. He pleaded with the manager to drop his name from the starting lineup. He complained of mysterious ailments. He accused Rose of voodoo. And then one day he sat by the window of his room on the top floor of the James Hotel with a case of warm beer beside him, drained each bottle in a single gulp and tossed it out the window at a passing car. Bottles exploded on car roofs and shattered on the bricks. Someone telephoned the sheriff. Jim was arrested. The sheriff telephoned the Milwaukee Braves. A decision was made. The sheriff escorted him to the bus depot and put him on a Greyhound heading north. That was the last we ever saw of him.

I was kept on the inactive list for two weeks. I arrived at the ball park each day at 5:30, dressed, pitched batting practice, ran 10 halfhearted wind sprints, showered, put on my street clothes and joined my wife in the stands. We watched about five innings of each game. Then we had supper and went back to our house, where we watched television and made love.

What we had rented was a tiny house the size of a garage at the end of a dead-end street. The kitchen contained a battered refrigerator just cool enough to keep food from spoiling for six hours and an old gas stove that continued to hiss gas even after it was lighted. The living room was bare and rugless and contained only a few sticks of wicker lawn furniture. The bedroom was rugless, too, and as stark as the rest of the house except for a huge, canopied four-poster bed in the center of the room. Carol fell in love with that bed on first sight. "It's so elegant," she said.

One night the bed broke down. We found a few wooden crates and metal pails on which to rest the mattress. After that we slept carefully, making no sudden moves. We could have avoided such anxiety by simply putting the mattress on the floor and sleeping there, but Carol would not have it. She was too terrified of the bugs, she said. They were the size of goldfish. Crackly-shelled palmetto bugs, they lived in the walls and ventured out only in darkness. When we returned home at night and flicked on the lights, we would catch them in maneuvers in the middle of the living room floor. The light would momentarily stun them. Carol and I would step on them. Their backs cracked like eggshells. They would regain their senses quickly and scatter in disarray as we stomped after them. Once Carol cornered one, raised her foot high—and smashed her spike heel through the floor. Given a reprieve, the condemned darted into the wall. Carol pulled her foot out of the floor and the heel broke off. She began to cry. "They're eating the house out from under us!" she wailed.

The next morning I bought six aerosol cans of DDT. We sprayed every corner of the house, sprayed until we began to feel sick. We waited all day and into the night and still nothing. We turned off the lights and were about to go to bed when we heard a thousand crunchy steps. I flicked on the lights and the bugs scattered into the walls. I trapped a straggler in a glass jar, sprayed an entire can of DDT into the jar and then screwed on the top. The jar clouded up and the bug disappeared from view. I waited—10, 15 minutes—and then unscrewed the top and turned the jar upside down. The palmetto fell onto the floor and darted into the wall. We went to bed with the lights on. Carol stuffed towels in the crack under the door leading to the living room and more towels under the door to the bathroom and we lay down cautiously on our precariously balanced bed in our brilliantly lighted, hermetically sealed room. And we stared at the ceiling.

In the mornings I played pool and drank lemon Cokes on the benches that lined Lemon Street, and in the afternoons I went fishing with Ron Pavia, perhaps the only other married Azalea besides the manager, Mike Fandozzi, and myself. Ron was a chunky, swarthy Portuguese from Cranston, R.I., who so resembled a character in the cartoon strip *Yogi Bear* that we nicknamed him "Boo Bear." Boo and I went fishing every afternoon, and we never caught anything. We went first to a bait store, where we bought 30 shrimp in a pail of crushed ice, and then we went to a grocery store and bought six lemons and a package of Dixie cups and a few six-packs of 7-Up, and then we went to a liquor store and bought a gallon of port wine, which we stuck in the pail of crushed ice with the shrimp, and then we drove to the outskirts of town, where the road passed over the narrowest part of the St. Johns River without benefit of a bridge railing. We parked the car on a soft shoulder and sat on the edge of the road with our feet dangling over the river. We baited our hooks with shrimp and tossed them into the water. We poured some port wine over crushed ice, added a dash of 7-Up and a squeeze of lemon, and relaxed.

To combat the heat we refreshed ourselves often with our wine coolers. After a while we no longer noticed the heat; sweat pouring down our necks, heads nodding on our chests, the bamboo poles now weightless in arms gone numb. Nor did it register that we never got a nibble, and that we never saw a fish, that after a while we had begun to eat our bait.

We fished like this daily and probably would have continued until the end of the season except for an experience we had late one afternoon after we had finished the last of the wine. The sun was beginning to set and the day had grown dark and cool, although by then we were too numb to really notice. We had not moved a muscle in minutes, it seemed, when suddenly there was a splash and we saw, rising out of the water, twisting like a corkscrew as it rose, a huge and ugly fish. It had a hide like rusted armor and a mean, long-billed face like an alligator's. The fish kept rising and rising in slow motion, endlessly, it seemed, until it had reached a height of almost six feet and its beady popeyes were level with our own. We stared at one another. Then we stared into the popeyes of the gar-fish and he scrutinized us with a narrowing squint. He opened his long-billed mouth to reveal rows of tiny teeth like thumbtacks. With a single swipe he severed both lines and then slipped silently back into the river. We said nothing. We just sat there, fishing with our severed lines that no longer reached the water, staring at that point in space where the garfish had stared at us. After a while we got up to leave. We threw the rest of the shrimp into the river, and then we threw the pail of ice in, too, and the empty 7-Up bottles, and the wine bottle, and then, as an afterthought, we threw our bamboo poles into the river, and we never dared mention what we had seen—what we thought we had seen—to anyone, not even to one another.

I was put on the Azaleas' active list early in July. A few days later I won my first game of the season. I pitched five innings against the Daytona Beach Islanders before being relieved with the tying runs on base. My relief pitcher retired the side and then pitched three more scoreless, hitless innings to preserve my first victory of the year. Nothing had changed in my pitching, really. I had given up three runs on six walks, five hits and a wild pitch. I had struck out only one batter. My motion was still a disaster and my fastball and curve were faint echoes of what they had once been. But I had had luck that night (now that I no longer needed it), and I had begun to cease to care. I threw easily, without thought or anxiety over my lost promise. It was hard to be tormented by lost promise at Palatka, where one was surrounded by so much lost promise. We laughed at our inadequacies. One night, playing third base, Boo Bear kicked two routine ground balls into the third-base stands. When he returned to the dugout at the end of the inning, he sat at the far end of the bench, shaking his head gloomily. Someone called down to him, "Atta boy, Boo, great hands!" We all began to laugh. Boo glanced sideways at his laughing teammates, his face dark and threatening, and then not so threatening, and then he was laughing, too.

I laughed at myself. For the first time. After my victory over the White Sox, one of the Azaleas shook my hand. "Nice motion you got there, fella," he said. "Smooth."

"Just a little something I picked up along the way," I said, and we both laughed.

Ironically, I was one of the most successful pitchers on the club during the last weeks of the season. I started every fourth game or so, and often relieved between starts. In one 11-day span I appeared in four games for a total of 20 innings, and I won two. When we left for Tampa on the last road trip of the season, I had a 4-5 record. Despite this modest success, I had not deluded myself into thinking I had recaptured anything. I knew I was not throwing well, was getting by on a little luck, a little know-how and indifference. I realized that my pitching had deteriorated as much as it possibly could have at Eau Claire and now, at Palatka, I was not making progress; I was just not getting worse.

I thought about all of these things as Boo Bear and I drove toward Tampa on that hot afternoon near the end of the season. I wondered where I had lost my talent, tried to discover that point where it all started going downhill. But it was like trying to read random, unconnected points on a faulty graph, none of which indicated a direction. I turned to Boo Bear beside me in the front seat. "Pour me one of those, Boo," I said.

He had set up a small bar on the dashboard—wine, ice, 7-Up, lemons—and he had already poured himself two wine coolers while I was daydreaming.

"Aren't you pitching tonight?" he asked.

"To hell with it," I said, and he laughed. Boo poured me a cool drink, and a little later he poured another, and then another, and another, until we reached Tampa.

I started that game without a care in the world, and it did not bother me a bit when I walked the first four batters I faced, or when Mike Fandozzi came out to the mound to relieve me from this, the last game of my career, or when I walked into the dugout with an idiot's grin and my teammates burst out laughing. I sobered up on the ride home that night. I was not grinning when we reached Palatka at four o'clock in the morning. I woke up my wife.

"What's the matter?"

"Nothing," I said. "We're going home. Pack our things."

"But the season isn't over yet," she said. "You still have two more games."

"Don't worry about it," I said. "It's all right." We packed the Chrysler with our belongings and then, because we still owed a month's rent, I coasted the car down the hill past our landlord's house, and then I turned the key.

We reached Jacksonville at dawn and Brunswick, Ga. a little later and then Savannah and Florence, S.C. and Fayetteville, N.C., and the time passed easily as I daydreamed about my career. When we reached Rocky Mount, N.C. it was dark again. We moved slowly through traffic, past motels and traffic lights, and suddenly it occurred to me, with a chill, that I had no career. What would I be without baseball? I could think of nothing.

QUESTIONS

1. Did Jordan care very much about playing professional baseball? Did he try very hard to succeed? How do you know?
2. What attitude does Jordan take toward his failure? Cite some details that indicate to you this attitude.
3. Why do you think Jordan includes the story about the garfish? Does that incident seem revelant to the story of his failure? How?
4. If Jordan had succeeded in his ambition and had written about it, do you think his story would be more interesting, or less? Why?
5. Is there any way in which Jordan's account of his experience can be considered a personal victory? Explain.
6. Write an account of your failure at something that was important to you. What happened? How did you feel about it? How do you feel about it now? What were the consequences for you of your failure?

EMMA GOLDMAN
In Jail[1]

I was called before the head matron, a tall woman with a stolid face. She began taking my pedigree. "What religion?" was her first question. "None, I am an atheist." "Atheism is prohibited here. You will have to go to church." I replied that I would do nothing of the kind. I did not believe in anything the Church stood for and, not being a hypocrite, I would not attend. Besides, I came from Jewish people. Was there a synagogue?

She said curtly that there were services for the Jewish convicts on Saturday afternoon, but as I was the only Jewish female prisoner, she could not permit me to go among so many men.

After a bath and a change into the prison uniform I was sent to my cell and locked in.

I knew from what Most[2] had related to me about Blackwell's Island that the prison was old and damp, the cells small, without light or water. I was therefore prepared for what was awaiting me. But the moment the door was locked on me, I began to experience a feeling of suffocation. In the dark I groped for something to sit on and found a narrow iron cot. Sudden exhaustion overpowered me and I fell asleep.

I became aware of a sharp burning in my eyes, and I jumped up in fright. A lamp was being held close to the bars. "What is it?" I cried, forgetting where I was. The lamp was lowered and I saw a thin, ascetic face gazing at me. A soft voice congratulated me on my sound sleep. It was the evening matron on her regular rounds. She told me to undress and left me.

But there was no more sleep for me that night. The irritating feel of the coarse blanket, the shadows creeping past the bars, kept me awake until the sound of a gong again brought me to my feet. The cells were being unlocked, the doors heavily thrown open. Blue and white striped figures slouched by, automatically forming into a line, myself a part of it. "March!" and the line began to move along the

1. Emma Goldman was one of the leaders of the anarchist movement in the United States between 1890 and 1920. In the wake of the Homestead Steel Strike of 1892 and with the onset of the Great Panic of 1893, she accelerated her activities on behalf of labor unions and the unemployed. She urged the unemployed to demand what was rightfully theirs and to distrust capitalists and politicians. In the fall of 1893, she was arrested, tried and convicted of inciting to riot and unlawful assemblage. She was sentenced to one year in Blackwell's Island Penitentiary in New York City. Her turbulent career as a propagandist in America extended for twenty-five years beyond this internment. Shortly after the United States entered the First World War, Emma Goldman was convicted of conspiring to organize resistance to the Draft Act of 1917. She served two years in the Missouri State Penitentiary and was subsequently deported to the Soviet Union. (The following selection is from Chapter 12 of her autobiography, *Living My Life*, 1931.)

2. Johann Most, German anarchist editor who in 1882 emigrated to the United States.

corridor down the steps towards a corner containing wash-stands and towels. Again the command: "Wash!" and everybody began clamouring for a towel, already soiled and wet. Before I had time to splash some water on my hands and face and wipe myself half-dry, the order was given to march back.

Then breakfast: a slice of bread and a tin cup of warm brownish water. Again the line formed, and the striped humanity was broken up in sections and sent to its daily tasks. With a group of other women I was taken to the sewing-room.

The procedure of forming lines—"Forward, march!"—was repeated three times a day, seven days a week. After each meal ten minutes were allowed for talk. A torrent of words would then break forth from the pent-up beings. Each precious second increased the roar of sounds; and then sudden silence.

The sewing-room was large and light, the sun often streaming through the high windows, its rays intensifying the whiteness of the walls and the monotony of the regulation dress. In the sharp light the figures in baggy and ungainly attire appeared more hideous. Still, the shop was a welcome relief from the cell. Mine, on the ground floor, was grey and damp even in the day-time; the cells on the upper floors were somewhat brighter. Close to the barred door one could even read by the help of the light coming from the corridor windows.

The locking of the cells for the night was the worst experience of the day. The convicts were marched along the tiers in the usual line. On reaching her cell each left the line, stepped inside, hands on the iron door, and awaited the command. "Close!" and with a crash the seventy doors shut, each prisoner automatically locking herself in. More harrowing still was the daily degradation of being forced to march in lock-step to the river, carrying the bucket of excrement accumulated during twenty-four hours.

I was put in charge of the sewing-shop. My task consisted in cutting the cloth and preparing work for the two dozen women employed. In addition I had to keep account of the incoming material and the outgoing bundles. I welcomed the work. It helped me to forget the dreary existence within the prison. But the evenings were torturous. The first few weeks I would fall asleep as soon as I touched the pillow. Soon, however, the nights found me restlessly tossing about, seeking sleep in vain. The appalling nights—even if I should get the customary two months' commutation time, I still had nearly two hundred and ninety of them. Two hundred and ninety—and Sasha? I used to lie awake and mentally figure in the dark the number of days and nights before him. Even if he could come out after his first sentence of seven years, he would still have more than twenty-five hundred nights! Dread overcame me that Sasha could not survive them. Nothing was so likely to drive people to madness, I felt, as sleepless nights in prison. Better dead, I thought. Dead? Frick was not dead, and Sasha's glorious youth, his life, the things he might have accomplished—all were being sacrificed—perhaps for nothing. But—was Sasha's *Attentat* in vain?[3] Was my revolutionary faith a mere echo of what others had said or taught me? "No, not in vain!" something within me insisted. "No sacrifice is lost for a great ideal."

One day I was told by the head matron that I would have to get better results from the women. They were not doing so much work, she said, as under the prisoner who had had charge of the sewing-shop before me. I resented the suggestion that I become a slave-driver. It was because I hated slaves as well as their drivers, I informed the matron, that I had been sent to prison. I considered myself one of the inmates, not above them. I was determined not to do anything that would involve a denial of my ideals. I preferred punishment. One of the methods of treating offenders consisted in placing them in a corner facing a blackboard and compelling them to stay for hours in that position, constantly before the matron's vigilant eyes. This seemed to me petty and insulting. I decided that if I was offered such an indignity, I would increase my offence and take the dungeon. But the days passed and I was not punished.

News in prison travels with amazing rapidity. Within twenty-four hours all the women knew that I had refused to act as a slave-driver. They had not been unkind to me, but they had kept aloof. They had been told that I was a terrible "anarchist" and that I didn't believe in God. They had never seen me in church and I did not participate in their ten-minute gush of talk. I was a freak in their eyes. But when they learned that I had refused to play the boss over them, their reserve broke down. Sundays after church the cells would be opened to permit the women an hour's visit with one another. The next Sunday I received visits from every inmate on my tier. They felt I was their friend, they assured me, and they would do anything for me. Girls working in the laundry offered to wash my clothes, others to darn my stockings. Everyone was anxious to do some service. I was deeply moved. These poor creatures so hungered for kindness that the least sign of it loomed high on their limited horizons. After that they would often come to me with their troubles, their hatred of the head matron, their confidences about their infatuations with the male convicts. Their ingenuity in carrying on flirtations under the very eyes of the officials was amazing.

My three weeks in the Tombs[4] had given me ample proof that

---

3. Sasha was her close friend and colleague Alexander Berkman. The act referred to here was Berkman's attempt to murder Henry Clay Frick, chairman of the Carnegie Steel Company, for which he was sentenced to twenty-two years in prison.

4. The Manhattan House of Detention, in New York City.

the revolutionary contention that crime is the result of poverty is
based on fact. Most of the defendants who were awaiting trial came
from the lowest strata of society, men and women without friends,
often even without a home. Unfortunate, ignorant creatures they
were, but still with hope in their hearts, because they had not yet
been convicted. In the penitentiary despair possessed almost all of
the prisoners. It served to unveil the mental darkness, fear, and
superstition which held them in bondage. Among the seventy
inmates, there were no more than half a dozen who showed any
intelligence whatever. The rest were outcasts without the least social
consciousness. Their personal misfortunes filled their thoughts; they
could not understand that they were victims, links in an endless
chain of injustice and inequality. From early childhood they had
known nothing but poverty, squalor, and want, and the same conditions were awaiting them on their release. Yet they were capable of
sympathy and devotion, of generous impulses. I soon had occasion
to convince myself of it when I was taken ill.

The dampness of my cell and the chill of the late December days
had brought on an attack of my old complaint, rheumatism. For
some days the head matron opposed my being taken to the hospital,
but she was finally compelled to submit to the order of the visiting
physician.

Blackwell's Island Penitentiary was fortunate in the absence of a
"steady" physician. The inmates were receiving medical attendance
from the Charity Hospital, which was situated near by. That institution had six weeks' post-graduate courses, which meant frequent
changes in the staff. They were under the direct supervision of a visiting physician from New York City, Dr. White, a humane and
kindly man. The treatment given the prisoners was as good as
patients received in any New York hospital.

The sick-ward was the largest and brightest room in the building.
Its spacious windows looked out upon a wide lawn in front of the
prison and, farther on, the East River. In fine weather the sun
streamed in generously. A month's rest, the kindliness of the physician, and the thoughtful attention of my fellow prisoners relieved
me of my pain and enabled me to get about again.

During one of his rounds Dr. White picked up the card hanging
at the foot of my bed giving my crime and pedigree. "Inciting to
riot," he read. "Piffle! I don't believe you could hurt a fly. A fine
inciter you would make!" he chuckled, then asked me if I should
not like to remain in the hospital to take care of the sick. "I should,
indeed," I replied, "but I know nothing about nursing." He assured
me that neither did anyone else in the prison. He had tried for
some time to induce the city to put a trained nurse in charge of the
ward, but he had not succeeded. For operations and grave cases he
had to bring a nurse from the Charity Hospital. I could easily pick

up the elementary things about tending the sick. He would teach me to take the pulse and temperature and to perform similar services. He would speak to the Warden and the head matron if I wanted to remain.

Soon I took up my new work. The ward contained sixteen beds, most of them always filled. The various diseases were treated in the same room, from grave operations to tuberculosis, pneumonia, and childbirth. My hours were long and strenuous, the groans of the patients nerve-racking; but I loved my job.

* * *

I was gradually given entire charge of the hospital ward, part of my duties being to divide the special rations allowed the sick prisoners. They consisted of a quart of milk, a cup of beef tea, two eggs, two crackers, and two lumps of sugar for each invalid. On several occasions milk and eggs were missing and I reported the matter to a day matron. Later she informed me that a head matron had said that it did not matter and that certain patients were strong enough to do without their extra rations. I had had considerable opportunity to study this head matron, who felt a violent dislike of everyone not Anglo-Saxon. Her special targets were the Irish and the Jews, against whom she discriminated habitually. I was therefore not surprised to get such a message from her.

A few days later I was told by the prisoner who brought the hospital rations that the missing portions had been given by this head matron to two husky Negro prisoners. That also did not surprise me. I knew she had a special fondness for the coloured inmates. She rarely punished them and often gave them unusual privileges. In return her favourites would spy on the other prisoners, even on those of their own colour who were too decent to be bribed. I myself never had any prejudice against coloured people; in fact, I felt deeply for them because they were being treated like slaves in America. But I hated discrimination. The idea that sick people, white or coloured, should be robbed of their rations to feed healthy persons outraged my sense of justice, but I was powerless to do anything in the matter.

After my first clashes with this woman she left me severely alone. Once she became enraged because I refused to translate a Russian letter that had arrived for one of the prisoners. She had called me into her office to read the letter and tell her its contents. When I saw that the letter was not for me, I informed her that I was not employed by the prison as a translator. It was bad enough for the officials to pry into the personal mail of helpless human beings, but I would not do it. She said that it was stupid of me not to take advantage of her goodwill. She could put me back in my cell, deprive me of my commutation time for good behaviour, and make the rest of my stay very hard. She could do as she pleased, I told her, but I would not read the private letters of my unfortunate sisters, much less translate them to her.

Then came the matter of the missing rations. The sick women began to suspect that they were not getting their full share and complained to the doctor. Confronted with a direct question from him, I had to tell the truth. I did not know what he said to the offending matron, but the full rations began to arrive again. Two days later I was called downstairs and locked up in the dungeon.

I had repeatedly seen the effect of a dungeon experience on other women prisoners. One inmate had been kept there for twenty-eight days on bread and water, although the regulations prohibited a longer stay than forty-eight hours. She had to be carried out on a stretcher; her hands and legs were swollen, her body covered with a rash. The descriptions the poor creature and others had given me used to make me ill. But nothing I had heard compared with the reality. The cell was barren; one had to sit or lie down on the cold stone floor. The dampness of the walls made the dungeon a ghastly place. Worse yet was the complete shutting out of light and air, the impenetrable blackness, so thick that one could not see the hand before one's face. It gave me the sensation of sinking into a devouring pit. "The Spanish Inquisition came to life in America"—I thought of Most's description. He had not exaggerated.

After the door shut behind me, I stood still, afraid to sit down or to lean against the wall. Then I groped for the door. Gradually the blackness paled. I caught a faint sound slowly approaching; I heard a key turn in the lock. A matron appeared. I recognized Miss Johnson, the one who had frightened me out of my sleep on my first night in the penitentiary. I had come to know and appreciate her as a beautiful personality. Her kindness to the prisoners was the one ray of light in their dreary existence. She had taken me to her bosom almost from the first, and in many indirect ways she had shown me her affection. Often at night, when all were asleep, and quiet had fallen on the prison, Miss Johnson would enter the hospital ward, put my head in her lap, and tenderly stroke my hair. She would tell me the news in the papers to distract me and try to cheer my depressed mood. I knew I had found a friend in the woman, who herself was a lonely soul, never having known the love of man or child.

She came into the dungeon carrying a camp-chair and a blanket. "You can sit on that," she said, "and wrap yourself up. I'll leave the door open a bit to let in some air. I'll bring you hot coffee later. It will help to pass the night." She told me how painful it was for her to see the prisoners locked up in the dreadful hole, but she could do nothing for them because most of them could not be trusted. It was different with me, she was sure.

At five in the morning my friend had to take back the chair and
blanket and lock me in. I no longer was oppressed by the dungeon.
The humanity of Miss Johnson had dissolved the blackness.

When I was taken out of the dungeon and sent back to the hospital, I saw that it was almost noon. I resumed my duties. Later I
learned that Dr. White had asked for me, and upon being informed
that I was in punishment he had categorically demanded my
release.

No visitors were allowed in the penitentiary until after one
month had been served. Ever since my entry I had been longing for
Ed, yet at the same time I dreaded his coming. I remembered my
terrible visit with Sasha. But it was not quite so appalling in Blackwell's Island. I met Ed in a room where other prisoners were having
their relatives and friends to see them. There was no guard between
us. Everyone was so absorbed in his own visitor that no one paid
any attention to us. Still we felt constrained. With clasped hands
we talked of general things.

* * *

Once Ed came accompanied by Voltairine de Cleyre. She had
been invited by New York friends to address a meeting arranged in
my behalf. When I visited her in Philadelphia, she had been too ill
to speak. I was glad of the opportunity to come closer to her now.
We talked about things nearest to our hearts—Sasha, the movement.
Voltairine promised to join me, on my release, in a new effort for
Sasha. Meanwhile she would write to him, she said. Ed, too, was in
touch with him.

My visitors were always sent up to the hospital. I was therefore
surprised one day to be called to the Warden's office to see someone. It proved to be John Swinton and his wife. Swinton was a
nationally known figure; he had worked with the abolitionists and
had fought in the Civil War. As editor-in-chief of the New York
Sun he had pleaded for the European refugees who came to find
asylum in the United States. He was the friend and adviser of
young literary aspirants, and he had been one of the first to defend
Walt Whitman against the misrepresentations of the purists. Tall,
erect, with beautiful features, John Swinton was an impressive
figure.

He greeted me warmly, remarking that he had just been saying to
Warden Pillsbury that he himself had made more violent speeches
during the abolition days than anything I said at Union Square. Yet
he had not been arrested. He told the warden that he ought to be
ashamed of himself to keep "a little girl like that" locked up. "And
what do you suppose he said? He said that he had no choice—he
was only doing his duty. All weaklings say that, cowards who always
put the blame on others." Just then the Warden approached us. He
assured Swinton that I was a model prisoner and that I had

become an efficient nurse in the short time. In fact, I was doing such good work that he wished I had been given five more years. "Generous cuss, aren't you?" Swinton laughed. "Perhaps you'll give her a paid job when her time is up?" "I would, indeed," Pillsbury replied. "Well, you'd be a damn fool. Don't you know she doesn't believe in prisons? Sure as you live, she'd let them all escape, and what would become of you then?" The poor man was embarrassed, but he joined in the banter. Before my visitor took leave, he turned once more to the Warden, cautioning him to "take good care of his little friend," else he would "take it out of his hide."

The visit of the Swintons completely changed the attitude of the head matron towards me. The Warden had always been quite decent, and she now began showering privileges on me: food from her own table, fruit, coffee, and walks on the island. I refused her favours except for the walks; it was my first opportunity in six months to go out in the open and inhale the spring air without iron bars to check me.

In March 1894 we received a large influx of women prisoners. They were nearly all prostitutes rounded up during recent raids. The city had been blessed by a new vice crusade. The Lexow Committee, with the Reverend Dr. Parkhurst at its head, wielded the broom which was to sweep New York clean of the fearful scourge. The men found in the public houses were allowed to go free, but the women were arrested and sentenced to Blackwell's Island.

Most of the unfortunates came in a deplorable condition. They were suddenly cut off from the narcotics which almost all of them had been habitually using. The sight of their suffering was heartbreaking. With the strength of giants the frail creatures would shake the iron bars, curse, and scream for dope and cigarettes. Then they would fall exhausted to the ground, pitifully moaning through the night.

*   *   *

One day a young Irish girl was brought to the hospital for an operation. In view of the seriousness of the case Dr. White called in two trained nurses. The operation lasted until late in the evening, and then the patient was left in my charge. She was very ill from the effect of the ether, vomited violently, and burst the stitches of her wound, which resulted in a severe haemorrhage. I sent a hurry call to the Charity Hospital. It seemed hours before the doctor and his staff arrived. There were no nurses this time and I had to take their place.

The day had been an unusually hard one and I had had very little sleep. I felt exhausted and had to hold on to the operating-table with my left hand while passing with my right instruments and sponges. Suddenly the operating-table gave way, and my arm was caught. I screamed with pain. Dr. White was so absorbed in his manipulations that for a moment he did not realize what had happened. When he at last had the table raised and my arm was lifted out, it looked as if every bone had been broken. The pain was excruciating and he ordered a shot of morphine. "We'll set her arm later. This has got to come first." "No morphine," I begged. I still remembered the effect of morphine on me when Dr. Julius Hoffmann had given me a dose against insomnia. It had put me to sleep, but during the night I had tried to throw myself out of the window, and it had required all of Sasha's strength to pull me back. The morphine had crazed me, and now I would have none of it.

One of the physicians gave me something that had a soothing effect. After the patient on the operating-table had been returned to her bed, Dr. White examined my arm. "You're nice and chubby," he said; "that has saved your bones. Nothing has been broken—just flattened a bit." My arm was put in a splint. The doctor wanted me to go to bed, but there was no one else to sit up with the patient. It might be her last night: her tissues were so badly infected that they would not hold her stitches, and another haemorrhage would prove fatal. I decided to remain at her bedside. I knew I could not sleep with the case as serious as it was.

All night I watched her struggle for life. In the morning I sent for the priest. Everyone was surprised at my action, particularly the head matron. How could I, an atheist, do such a thing, she wondered, and choose a priest, at that! I had declined to see the missionaries as well as the rabbi. She noticed how friendly I had become with the two Catholic sisters who often visited us on Sunday. I had even made coffee for them. Didn't I think that the Catholic Church had always been the enemy of progress and that it had persecuted and tortured the Jews? How could I be so inconsistent? Of course, I thought so, I assured her. I was just as opposed to the Catholics as to the other Churches. I considered them all alike, enemies of the people. They preached submission, and their God was the God of the rich and the mighty. I hated their God and would never make peace with him. But if I could believe in any religion at all, I should prefer the Catholic Church. "It is less hypocritical," I said to her; "it makes allowance for human frailties and it has a sense of beauty." The Catholic sisters and the priest had not tried to preach to me like the missionaries, the minister, and the vulgar rabbi. They left my soul to its own fate; they talked to me about human things, especially the priest, who was a cultured man. My poor patient had reached the end of a life that had been too hard for her. The priest might give her a few moments of peace and kindness; why should I not have sent for him? But the matron was too dull to follow my argument or understand my motives. I remained a "queer one," in her estimation.

Before my patient died, she begged me to lay her out. I had been kinder to her, she said, than her own mother. She wanted to know that it would be my hand that would get her ready for the last journey. I would make her beautiful; she wanted to look beautiful to meet Mother Mary and the Lord Jesus. It required little effort to make her as lovely in death as she had been in life. Her black curls made her alabaster face more delicate than the artificial methods she had used to enhance her looks. Her luminous eyes were closed now; I had closed them with my own hands. But her chiselled eyebrows and long, black lashes were remindful of the radiance that had been hers. How she must have fascinated men! And they destroyed her. Now she was beyond their reach. Death had smoothed her suffering. She looked serene in her marble whiteness now.

During the Jewish Easter holidays I was again called to the Warden's office. I found my grandmother there. She had repeatedly begged Ed to take her to see me, but he had declined in order to spare her the painful experience. The devoted soul could not be stopped. With her broken English she had made her way to the Commissioner of Corrections, procured a pass, and come to the penitentiary. She handed me a large white handkerchief containing matzoth, *gefüllte* fish, and some Easter cake of her own baking. She tried to explain to the Warden what a good Jewish daughter her *Chavele* was; in fact, better than any rabbi's wife, because she gave everything to the poor. She was fearfully wrought up when the moment of departure came, and I tried to soothe her, begging her not to break down before the Warden. She bravely dried her tears and walked out straight and proud, but I knew she would weep bitterly as soon as she got out of sight. No doubt she also prayed to her God for her *Chavele*.

June saw many prisoners discharged from the sick-ward, only a few beds remaining occupied. For the first time since coming to the hospital I had some leisure, enabling me to read more systematically. I had accumulated a large library; John Swinton had sent me many books, as did also other friends; but most of them were from Justus Schwab. He had never come to see me; he had asked Ed to tell me that it was impossible for him to visit me. He hated prison so much that he would not be able to leave me behind. If he should come, he would be tempted to use force to take me back with him, and it would only cause trouble. Instead he sent me stacks of books. Walt Whitman, Emerson, Thoreau, Hawthorne, Spencer, John Stuart Mill, and many other English and American authors I learned to know and love through the friendship of Justus. At the same time other elements also became interested in my salvation— spiritualists and metaphysical redeemers of various kinds. I tried honestly to get at their meaning, but I was no doubt too much of the earth to follow their shadows in the clouds.

* * *

The prison library had some good literature, including the works of George Sand, George Eliot, and Ouida. The librarian in charge was an educated Englishman serving a five-year sentence for forgery. The books he handed out to me soon began to contain love notes framed in most affectionate terms, and presently they flamed with passion. He had already put in four years in prison, one of his notes read, and he was starved for the love of woman and companionship. He begged me at least to give him the companionship. Would I write him occasionally about the books I was reading? I disliked becoming involved in a silly prison flirtation, yet the need for free, uncensored expression was too compelling to resist. We exchanged many notes, often of a very ardent nature.

My admirer was a splendid musician and played the organ in the chapel. I should have loved to attend, to be able to hear him and feel him near, but the sight of the male prisoners in stripes, some of them handcuffed, and still further degraded and insulted by the lip-service of the minister, was too appalling to me. I had seen it once on the fourth of July, when some politician had come over to speak to the inmates about the glories of American liberty. I had to pass through the male wing on an errand to the Warden, and I heard the pompous patriot spouting of freedom and independence to the mental and physical wrecks. One convict had been put in irons because of an attempted escape. I could hear the clanking of his chains with his every movement. I could not bear to go to church.

* * *

Of the friends I made on Blackwell's Island the priest was the most interesting. At first I felt antagonistic to him. I thought he was like the rest of the religious busybodies, but I soon found that he wanted to talk only about books. He had studied in Cologne and had read much. He knew I had many books and he asked me to exchange some of them with him. I was amazed and wondered what kind of books he would bring me, expecting the New Testament or the Catechism. But he came with works of poetry and music. He had free access to the prison at any time, and often he would come to the ward at nine in the evening and remain till after midnight. We would discuss his favourite composers—Bach, Beethoven, and Brahms—and compare our views on poetry and social ideas. He presented me with an English-Latin dictionary as a gift, inscribed: "With the highest respect, to Emma Goldman."

On one occasion I asked him why he never gave me the Bible. "Because no one can understand or love it if he is forced to read it," he replied. That appealed to me and I asked him for it. Its simplicity of language and legendry fascinated me. There was no make-believe about my young friend. He was devout, entirely consecrated. He observed every fast and he would lose himself in prayer for hours. Once he asked me to help him decorate the chapel. When I came down, I found the frail, emaciated figure in silent prayer, oblivious of his surroundings. My own ideal, my faith, was at the opposite pole from his, but I knew he was as ardently sincere as I. Our fervour was our meeting-ground.

* * *

The nearer the day of my liberation approached, the more unbearable life in prison became. The days dragged and I grew restless and irritable with impatience. Even reading became impossible. I would sit for hours lost in reminiscences. I thought of the comrades in the Illinois penitentiary brought back to life by the pardon of Governor Altgeld. Since I had come to prison, I realized how much the release of the three men, Neebe, Fielden, and Schwab, had done for the cause for which their comrades in Chicago had been hanged. The venom of the press against Altgeld for his gesture of justice proved how deeply he had struck the vested interests, particularly by his analysis of the trial and his clear demonstration that the executed anarchists had been judicially killed in spite of their proved innocence of the crime charged against them. Every detail of the momentous days of 1887 stood out in strong relief before me. Then Sasha, our life together, his act, his martyrdom—every moment of the five years since I had first met him I now relived with poignant reality. Why was it, I mused, that Sasha was still so deeply rooted in my being? Was not my love for Ed more ecstatic, more enriching? Perhaps it was his act that had bound me to him with such powerful cords. How insignificant was my own prison experience compared with what Sasha was suffering in the Allegheny purgatory! I now felt ashamed that, even for a moment, I could have found my incarceration hard. Not one friendly face in the court-room to be near Sasha and comfort him—solitary confinement and complete isolation, for no more visits had been allowed him. The Inspector had kept his promise; since my visit in November 1892, Sasha had not again been permitted to see anyone. How he must have craved the sight and touch of a kindred spirit, how he must be yearning for it!

My thoughts rushed on. Fedya, the lover of beauty, so fine and sensitive! And Ed. Ed—he had kissed to life so many mysterious longings, had opened such spiritual sources of wealth to me! I owed my development to Ed, and to others, too, who had been in my life. And yet, more than all else, it was the prison that had proved the best school. A more painful, but a vital, school. Here I had been brought close to the depths and complexities of the human soul; here I found ugliness and beauty, meanness and generosity. Here, too, I had learned to see life through my own eyes and not through those of Sasha, Most, or Ed. The prison had been the crucible that tested my faith. It had helped me to discover strength in my own being, the strength to stand alone, the strength to live my life and fight for my ideals, against the whole world if need be. The State of New York could have rendered me no greater service than by sending me to Blackwell's Island Penitentiary!

MARGARET SANGER

The Turbid Ebb and Flow of Misery

"Every night and every morn
Some to misery are born.
Every morn and every night
Some are born to sweet delight.
Some are born to sweet delight,
Some are born to endless night."

WILLIAM BLAKE

During these years[1] in New York trained nurses were in great demand. Few people wanted to enter hospitals; they were afraid they might be "practiced" upon, and consented to go only in desperate emergencies. Sentiment was especially vehement in the matter of having babies. A woman's own bedroom, no matter how inconveniently arranged, was the usual place for her lying-in. I was not sufficiently free from domestic duties to be a general nurse, but I could ordinarily manage obstetrical cases because I was notified far enough ahead to plan my schedule. And after serving my two weeks I could get home again.

Sometimes I was summoned to small apartments occupied by young clerks, insurance salesmen, or lawyers, just starting out, most of them under thirty and whose wives were having their first or second baby. They were always eager to know the best and latest method in infant care and feeding. In particular, Jewish patients, whose lives centered around the family, welcomed advice and followed it implicitly.

But more and more my calls began to come from the Lower East Side, as though I were being magnetically drawn there by some force outside my control. I hated the wretchedness and hopelessness of the poor, and never experienced that satisfaction in working among them that so many noble women have found. My concern for my patients was now quite different from my earlier hospital attitude. I could see that much was wrong with them which did not appear in the physiological or medical diagnosis. A woman in childbirth was not merely a woman in childbirth. My expanded outlook included a view of her background, her potentialities as a human being, the kind of children she was bearing, and what was going to happen to them.

The wives of small shopkeepers were my most frequent cases, but I had carpenters, truck drivers, dishwashers, and pushcart vendors. I admired intensely the consideration most of these people had for their own. Money to pay doctor and nurse had been carefully saved

1. Around 1912.

months in advance—parents-in-law, grandfathers, grandmothers, all contributing.

As soon as the neighbors learned that a nurse was in the building they came in a friendly way to visit, often carrying fruit, jellies, or gefüllter fish made after a cherished recipe. It was infinitely pathetic to me that they, so poor themselves, should bring me food. Later they drifted in again with the excuse of getting the plate, and sat down for a nice talk; there was no hurry. Always back of the little gift was the question, "I am pregnant (or my daughter, or my sister is). Tell me something to keep from having another baby. We cannot afford another yet."

I tried to explain the only two methods I had ever heard of among the middle classes, both of which were invariably brushed aside as unacceptable. They were of no certain avail to the wife because they placed the burden of responsibility solely upon the husband—a burden which he seldom assumed. What she was seeking was self-protection she could herself use, and there was none.

Below this stratum of society was one in truly desperate circumstances. The men were sullen and unskilled, picking up odd jobs now and then, but more often unemployed, lounging in and out of the house at all hours of the day and night. The women seemed to slink on their way to market and were without neighborliness.

These submerged, untouched classes were beyond the scope of organized charity or religion. No labor union, no church, not even the Salvation Army reached them. They were apprehensive of everyone and rejected help of any kind, ordering all intruders to keep out; both birth and death they considered their own business. Social agents, who were just beginning to appear, were profoundly mistrusted because they pried into homes and lives, asking questions about wages, how many were in the family, had any of them ever been in jail. Often two or three had been there or were now under suspicion of prostitution, shoplifting, purse snatching, petty thievery, and, in consequence, passed furtively by the big blue uniforms on the corner.

The utmost depression came over me as I approached this surreptitious region. Below Fourteenth Street I seemed to be breathing a different air, to be in another world and country where the people had habits and customs alien to anything I had ever heard about.

There were then approximately ten thousand apartments in New York into which no sun ray penetrated directly; such windows as they had opened only on a narrow court from which rose fetid odors. It was seldom cleaned, though garbage and refuse often went down into it. All these dwellings were pervaded by the foul breath of poverty, that moldy, indefinable, indescribable smell which cannot be fumigated out, sickening to me but apparently unnoticed by those who lived there. When I set to work with antiseptics, their pungent sting, at least temporarily, obscured the stench.

I remember one confinement case to which I was called by the doctor of an insurance company. I climbed up the five flights and entered the airless rooms, but the baby had come with too great speed. A boy of ten had been the only assistant. Five flights was a long way; he had wrapped the placenta in a piece of newspaper and dropped it out the window into the court.

Many families took in "boarders," as they were termed, whose small contributions paid the rent. These derelicts, wanderers, alternately working and drinking, were crowded in with the children; a single room sometimes held as many as six sleepers. Little girls were accustomed to dressing and undressing in front of the men, and were often violated, occasionally by their own fathers or brothers, before they reached the age of puberty.

Pregnancy was a chronic condition among the women of this class. Suggestions as to what to do for a girl who was "in trouble" or a married woman who was "caught" passed from mouth to mouth—herb teas, turpentine, steaming, rolling downstairs, inserting slippery elm, knitting needles, shoe-hooks. When they had word of a new remedy they hurried to the drugstore, and if the clerk were inclined to be friendly he might say, "Oh, that won't help you, but here's something that may." The younger druggists usually refused to give advice because, if it were to be known, they would come under the law; midwives were even more fearful. The doomed women implored me to reveal the "secret" rich people had, offering to pay me extra to tell them; many really believed I was holding back information for money. They asked everybody and tried anything, but nothing did them any good. On Saturday nights I have seen groups of from fifty to one hundred with their shawls over their heads waiting outside the office of a five-dollar abortionist.

Each time I returned to this district, which was becoming a recurrent nightmare, I used to hear that Mrs. Cohen "had been carried to a hospital, but had never come back," or that Mrs. Kelly "had sent the children to a neighbor and had put her head into the gas oven." Day after day such tales were poured into my ears—a baby born dead, great relief—the death of an older child, sorrow but again relief of a sort—the story told a thousand times of death from abortion and children going into institutions. I shuddered with horror as I listened to the details and studied the reasons back of them—destitution linked with excessive childbearing. The waste of life seemed utterly senseless. One by one worried, sad, pensive, and aging faces marshaled themselves before me in my dreams, sometimes appealingly, sometimes accusingly.

These were not merely "unfortunate conditions among the poor" such as we read about. I knew the women personally. They were living, breathing, human beings, with hopes, fears, and aspirations like my own, yet their weary, misshapen bodies, "always ailing, never failing," were destined to be thrown on the scrap heap before they were thirty-five. I could not escape from the facts of their wretchedness; neither was I able to see any way out. My own cozy and comfortable family existence was becoming a reproach to me.

Then one stifling mid-July day of 1912 I was summoned to a Grand Street tenement. My patient was a small, slight Russian Jewess, about twenty-eight years old, of the special cast of feature to which suffering lends a madonna-like expression. The cramped three-room apartment was in a sorry state of turmoil. Jake Sachs, a truck driver scarcely older than his wife, had come home to find the three children crying and her unconscious from the effects of a self-induced abortion. He had called the nearest doctor, who in turn had sent for me. Jake's earnings were trifling, and most of them had gone to keep the none-too-strong children clean and properly fed. But his wife's ingenuity had helped them to save a little, and this he was glad to spend on a nurse rather than have her go to a hospital.

The doctor and I settled ourselves to the task of fighting the septicemia. Never had I worked so fast, never so concentratedly. The sultry days and nights were melted into a torpid inferno. It did not seem possible there could be such heat, and every bit of food, ice, and drugs had to be carried up three flights of stairs.

Jake was more kind and thoughtful than many of the husbands I had encountered. He loved his children, and had always helped his wife wash and dress them. He had brought water up and carried garbage down before he left in the morning, and did as much as he could for me while he anxiously watched her progress.

After a fortnight Mrs. Sachs' recovery was in sight. Neighbors, ordinarily fatalistic as to the results of abortion, were genuinely pleased that she had survived. She smiled wanly at all who came to see her and thanked them gently, but she could not respond to their hearty congratulations. She appeared to be more despondent and anxious than she should have been, and spent too much time in meditation.

At the end of three weeks, as I was preparing to leave the fragile patient to take up her difficult life once more, she finally voiced her fears, "Another baby will finish me, I suppose?"

"It's too early to talk about that," I temporized.

But when the doctor came to make his last call, I drew him aside. "Mrs. Sachs is terribly worried about having another baby."

"She well may be," replied the doctor, and then he stood before her and said, "Any more such capers, young woman, and there'll be no need to send for me."

"I know, doctor," she replied timidly, "but," and she hesitated as though it took all her courage to say it, "what can I do to prevent it?"

The doctor was a kindly man, and he had worked hard to save her, but such incidents had become so familiar to him that he had long since lost whatever delicacy he might once have had. He laughed good-naturedly. "You want to have your cake and eat it too, do you? Well, it can't be done."

Then picking up his hat and bag to depart he said, "Tell Jake to sleep on the roof."

I glanced quickly at Mrs. Sachs. Even through my sudden tears I could see stamped on her face an expression of absolute despair. We simply looked at each other, saying no word until the door had closed behind the doctor. Then she lifted her thin, blue-veined hands and clasped them beseechingly. "He can't understand. He's only a man. But you do, don't you? Please tell me the secret, and I'll never breathe it to a soul. *Please!*"

What was I to do? I could not speak the conventionally comforting phrases which would be of no comfort. Instead, I made her as physically easy as I could and promised to come back in a few days to talk with her again. A little later, when she slept, I tiptoed away.

Night after night the wistful image of Mrs. Sachs appeared before me. I made all sorts of excuses to myself for not going back. I was busy on other cases; I really did not know what to say to her or how to convince her of my own ignorance; I was helpless to avert such monstrous atrocities. Time rolled by and I did nothing.

The telephone rang one evening three months later, and Jake Sachs' agitated voice begged me to come at once; his wife was sick again and from the same cause. For a wild moment I thought of sending someone else, but actually, of course, I hurried into my uniform, caught up my bag, and started out. All the way I longed for a subway wreck, an explosion, anything to keep me from having to enter that home again. But nothing happened, even to delay me. I turned into the dingy doorway and climbed the familiar stairs once more. The children were there, young little things.

Mrs. Sachs was in a coma and died within ten minutes. I folded her still hands across her breast, remembering how they had pleaded with me, begging so humbly for the knowledge which was her right. I drew a sheet over her pallid face. Jake was sobbing, running his hands through his hair and pulling it out like an insane person. Over and over again he wailed, "My God! My God! My God!"

I left him pacing desperately back and forth, and for hours I myself walked and walked and walked through the hushed streets. When I finally arrived home and let myself quietly in, all the household was sleeping. I looked out my window and down upon the dimly lighted city. Its pains and griefs crowded in upon me, a moving picture rolled before my eyes with photographic clearness: women writhing in travail to bring forth little babies; the babies themselves naked and hungry, wrapped in newspapers to keep them from the cold; six-year-old children with pinched, pale, wrinkled faces, old in concentrated wretchedness, pushed into gray and fetid cellars, crouching on stone floors, their small scrawny hands scuttling through rags, making lamp shades, artificial flowers; white coffins, black coffins, coffins, coffins interminably passing in neverending succession. The scenes piled one upon another on another. I could bear it no longer.

As I stood there the darkness faded. The sun came up and threw its reflection over the house tops. It was the dawn of a new day in my life also. The doubt and questioning, the experimenting and trying, were now to be put behind me. I knew I could not go back merely to keeping people alive.

I went to bed, knowing that no matter what it might cost, I was finished with palliatives and superficial cures; I was resolved to seek out the root of evil, to do something to change the destiny of mothers whose miseries were vast as the sky.

BRUNO BETTELHEIM
A Victim[1]

Many students of discrimination are aware that the victim often reacts in ways as undesirable as the action of the aggressor. Less attention is paid to this because it is easier to excuse a defendant than an offender, and because they assume that once the aggression stops the victim's reactions will stop too. But I doubt if this is of real service to the persecuted. His main interest is that the persecution cease. But that is less apt to happen if he lacks a real understanding of the phenomenon of persecution, in which victim and persecutor are inseparably interlocked.

Let me illustrate with the following example: in the winter of 1938 a Polish Jew murdered the German attaché in Paris, vom Rath. The Gestapo used the event to step up anti-Semitic actions, and in the camp new hardships were inflicted on Jewish prisoners. One of these was an order barring them from the medical clinic unless the need for treatment had originated in work accident.

Nearly all prisoners suffered from frostbite which often led to gangrene and then amputation. Whether or not a Jewish prisoner was admitted to the clinic to prevent such a fate depended on the whim of an SS private. On reaching the clinic entrance, the prisoner explained the nature of his ailment to the SS man, who then decided if he should get treatment or not.

I too suffered from frostbite. At first I was discouraged from trying to get medical care by the fate of Jewish prisoners whose attempts had ended up in no treatment, only abuse. Finally things

1. From "Behavior in Extreme Situations: Defenses," Chapter 5 of *The Informed Heart*, 1960.

got worse and I was afraid that waiting longer would mean amputation. So I decided to make the effort.

When I got to the clinic, there were many prisoners lined up as usual, a score of them Jews suffering from severe frostbite. The main topic of discussion was one's chances of being admitted to the clinic. Most Jews had planned their procedure in detail. Some thought it best to stress their service in the German army during World War I: wounds received or decorations won. Others planned to stress the severity of their frostbite. A few decided it was best to tell some "tall story," such as that an SS officer had ordered them to report at the clinic.

Most of them seemed convinced that the SS man on duty would not see through their schemes. Eventually they asked me about my plans. Having no definite ones, I said I would go by the way the SS man dealt with other Jewish prisoners who had frostbite like me, and proceed accordingly. I doubted how wise it was to follow a preconceived plan, because it was hard to anticipate the reactions of a person you didn't know.

The prisoners reacted as they had at other times when I had voiced similar ideas on how to deal with the SS. They insisted that one SS man was like another, all equally vicious and stupid. As usual, any frustration was immediately discharged against the person who caused it, or was nearest at hand. So in abusive terms they accused me of not wanting to share my plan with them, or of intending to use one of theirs; it angered them that I was ready to meet the enemy unprepared.

No Jewish prisoner ahead of me in the line was admitted to the clinic. The more a prisoner pleaded, the more annoyed and violent the SS became. Expressions of pain amused him; stories of previous services rendered to Germany outraged him. He proudly remarked that *he* could not be taken in by Jews, that fortunately the time had passed when Jews could reach their goal by lamentations.

When my turn came he asked me in a screeching voice if I knew that work accidents were the only reason for admitting Jews to the clinic, and if I came because of such an accident. I replied that I knew the rules, but that I couldn't work unless my hands were freed of the dead flesh. Since prisoners were not allowed to have knives, I asked to have the dead flesh cut away. I tried to be matter-of-fact, avoiding pleading, deference, or arrogance. He replied: "If that's all you want, I'll tear the flesh off myself." And he started to pull at the festering skin. Because it did not come off as easily as he may have expected, or for some other reason, he waved me into the clinic.

Inside, he gave me a malevolent look and pushed me into the treatment room. There he told the prisoner orderly to attend to the wound. While this was being done, the guard watched me closely for signs of pain but I was able to suppress them. As soon as the cutting was over, I started to leave. He showed surprise and asked why I didn't wait for further treatment. I said I had gotten the service I asked for, at which he told the orderly to make an exception and treat my hand. After I had left the room, he called me back and gave me a card entitling me to further treatment, and admittance to the clinic without inspection at the entrance.

* * *

Because my behavior did not correspond to what he expected of Jewish prisoners on the basis of his projection, he could not use his prepared defenses against being touched by the prisoner's plight. Since I did not act as the dangerous Jew was expected to, I did not activate the anxieties that went with his stereotype. Still he did not altogether trust me, so he continued to watch while I received treatment.

Throughout these dealings, the SS felt uneasy with me, though he did not unload on me the annoyance his uneasiness aroused. Perhaps he watched me closely because he expected that sooner or later I would slip up and behave the way his projected image of the Jew was expected to act. This would have meant that his delusional creation had become real.

VITA SACKVILLE-WEST

From Portrait of a Marriage

27 September [1920]

In April [1918], when we were back in the country, Violet[1] wrote to ask whether she could come and stay with me for a fortnight. I was bored by the idea, as I wanted to work, and I did not know how to entertain her; but I could scarcely refuse. So she came. We were both bored. My serenity got on her nerves, and her restlessness got on mine. She went up to London for the day as often as she could, but she came back in the evenings because the air-raids frightened her. She had been here [Long Barn] I think about a week when everything changed suddenly—changed far more than I foresaw at the time; changed my life. It was the 18th of April. An absurd circumstance gave rise to the whole thing; I had just got clothes like the women-on-the-land were wearing, and in the unaccustomed freedom of breeches and gaiters I went into wild spirits; I ran, I shouted, I jumped, I climbed, I vaulted over gates, I

---

1. Violet Trefusis, Vita Sackville-West's companion and lover.

felt like a schoolboy let out on a holiday; and Violet followed me across fields and woods with a new meekness, saying very little, but never taking her eyes off me, and in the midst of my exuberance I knew that all the old under-current had come back stronger than ever, and that my old domination over her had never been diminished. I remember that wild irresponsible day. It was one of the most vibrant days of my life. As it happened, Harold[2] was not coming down that night. Violet and I dined alone together, and then after dinner, we went into my sitting-room, and for some time made conversation, but that broke down, and from ten o'clock until two in the morning—for four hours, or perhaps more—we talked.

Violet had struck the secret of my duality; she attacked me about it, and I made no attempt to conceal it from her or from myself. I talked myself out, until I could hear my own voice getting hoarse, and the fire went out, and all the servants had long since gone to bed, and there was not a soul in the house except Violet and me, and I talked out the whole of myself with absolute sincerity and pain, and Violet only listened—which was skilful of her. She made no comments and no suggestions until I had finished—until, that is, I had dug into every corner and brought its contents out to the light. I had been vouchsafed insight, as one sometimes is. Then, when I had finished, when I had told her how all the gentleness and all the femininity of me was called out by Harold alone, but how towards everyone else my attitude was completely otherwise—then, still with her infinite skill, she brought me round to my attitude towards herself, as it had always been ever since we were children, and then she told me how she had loved me always, and reminded me of incidents running through years, which I couldn't pretend to have forgotten. She was far more skilful than I. I might have been a boy of eighteen, and she a woman of thirty-five. She was infinitely clever—she didn't scare me, she didn't rush me, she didn't allow me to see where I was going; it was all conscious on her part, but on mine it was simply the drunkenness of liberation —the liberation of half my personality. She opened up to me a new sphere. And for her, of course, it meant the supreme effort to conquer the love of the person she had always wanted, who had always repulsed her (when things seemed to be going too far), out of a sort of fear, and of whom she was madly jealous—a fact I had not realized, so adept was she at concealment, and so obtuse was I at her psychology.

She lay on the sofa, I sat plunged in the armchair; she took my hands, and parted my fingers to count the points as she told me why she loved me. I hadn't dreamt of such an art of love. Such things had been *direct* for me always; I had known no love possessed of that Latin artistry (whether instinctive or acquired). I was

2. Harold Nicolson, Vita Sackville-West's husband.

infinitely troubled by the softness of her touch and the murmur of her lovely voice. She appealed to my unawakened senses; she wore, I remember, a dress of red velvet, that was exactly the colour of a red rose, and that made of her, with her white skin and the tawny hair, the most seductive being. She pulled me down until I kissed her—I had not done so for many years. Then she was wise enough to get up and go to bed; but I kissed her again in the dark after I had blown out our solitary lamp. She let herself go entirely limp and passive in my arms. (I shudder to think of the experience that lay behind her abandonment.) I can't think I slept all that night—not that much of the night was left.

I don't know how to go on; I keep thinking that Harold, if he ever reads this, will suffer so, but I ask him to remember that he is reading about a *different person* from the one he knew. Also I am not writing this for fun, but for several reasons which I will explain. (1) As I started by saying, because I want to tell the *entire* truth. (2) Because I know of no truthful record of such a connection—one that is written, I mean, with no desire to appeal to a vicious taste in any possible readers; and (3) because I hold the conviction that as centuries go on, and the sexes become more nearly merged on account of their increasing resemblances, I hold the conviction that such connections will to a very large extent cease to be regarded as merely unnatural, and will be understood far better, at least in their *intellectual* if not in their physical aspect. (Such is already the case in Russia.) I believe that then the psychology of people like myself will be a matter of interest, and I believe it will be recognized that many more people of my type do exist than under the present-day system of hypocrisy is commonly admitted. I am not saying that such personalities, and the connections which result from them, will not be deplored as they are now; but I do believe that their greater prevalence, and the spirit of candour which one hopes will spread with the progress of the world, will lead to their recognition, if only as an inevitable evil. The first step in the direction of such candour must be taken by the general admission of normal but illicit relations, and the facilitation of divorce, or possibly even the reconstruction of the system of marriage. Such advance must necessarily come from the more educated and liberal classes. Since 'unnatural' means 'removed from nature', only the most civilized, because the least natural, class of society can be expected to tolerate such a product of civilization.

I advance, therefore, the perfectly accepted theory that cases of dual personality do exist, in which the feminine and the masculine elements alternately preponderate. I advance this in an impersonal and scientific spirit, and claim that I am qualified to speak with the intimacy a professional scientist could acquire only after years of study and indirect information, because I have the object of study always to hand, in my own heart, and can gauge the exact truthfulness of what my own experience tells me. However frank, people would always keep back something. I can't keep back anything from myself.

29 September [1920]

I think Violet stayed on for about five days after that. All the time I was in fantastic spirits; and, not realizing how different she was from me in many ways, I made her follow me on wild courses all over the country, and, because she knew she had me only lightly hooked, she obeyed without remonstrance. There was very little between us during those days, only an immense excitement and a growing wish to go away somewhere alone together. This wish was carried out, by arranging to go down to Cornwall for the inside of a week; it was the first time I had ever been away from Harold, and he obviously minded my going.

We went. We met again in London, lunched at a restaurant, and filled with a spirit of adventure took the train for Exeter. On the way there we decided to go on to Plymouth. We arrived at Plymouth to find our luggage had of course been put out at Exeter. We had only an assortment of French poetry with us. We didn't care. We went to the nearest hotel, exultant to feel that nobody in the world knew where we were; at the booking office we were told there was only one room. It seemed like fate. We engaged it. We went and had supper—cider and ham—over which we talked fast and tremulously; she was frightened of me by then.

The next day we went on to Cornwall, where we spent five blissful days; I felt like a person translated, or re-born; it was like beginning one's life again in a different capacity. We were very miserable to come away, but we were constantly together during the whole of the summer months following. Once we went down to Cornwall again for a fortnight. It was a lovely summer. She was radiant. But I never thought it would last; I thought of it as an adventure, an escapade. I kept telling myself she was fickle, that I was the latest toy; she used to assure me of the contrary. She did this with such gravity that sometimes I was almost convinced; but now the years have convinced me thoroughly.

She no longer flirted, and got rid of the last person she had been engaged to, when we went to Cornwall. But there was a man out in France, who used to write to her; she hardly knew him, and I wasn't jealous. He was called Denzil [Denys Trefusis]. She described him to me as fiery—hair like gold wire, blue eyes starting out of his head, and winged nostrils. I listened, not very much interested. I now hate him more than I have ever hated anyone in this life, or am likely to; and there is no injury I would not do him with the utmost pleasure.

Well, the whole of that summer she was mine—a mad and irresponsible summer of moonlight nights, and infinite escapades, and passionate letters, and music, and poetry. Things were not tragic for us then, because although we cared passionately we didn't care deeply—not like now, though it was deepening all the time; no, things weren't tragic, they were rapturous and new, and one side of my life was opened to me, and, to hide nothing, I found things out about my own temperament that I had never been sure of before. Of course I wish now that I had never made those discoveries. One doesn't miss what one doesn't know, and now life is made wretched for me by privations. I often long for ignorance and innocence. I think that if anything happened to bring my friendship with Violet to an end, I might have the strength of mind to blot all that entirely out of my life.

At the end of that summer Denys came home on leave, and I met him. He was very tall and slender, and had the winged look that she had described—I could compare him to many things, to a race-horse, to a Crusader, to a greyhound, to an ascetic in search of the Holy Grail. I liked him then (oh irony!), and he liked me. I could afford to like him, because I was accustomed to Violet's amusements. Even now I see his good points, and they are many; but I see them only by translating myself into an impersonal spectator, and I see them, above all, when Violet makes him suffer. I see that he is a rare, sensitive, proud idealist, and I recognize that through me he has undergone months of suffering, and that his profound love for Violet has been thwarted of its fulfilment. And I am sorry enough for him, at moments, just sorry enough to wish vaguely that he could have cared for someone other than Violet. I see his tragedy—for he is a tragic person. But none of this softens my hatred of him, which is certainly the most violent feeling I have ever experienced. I only hope he returns it in full measure; he has a hundred times more cause to hate me than I to hate him.

He was in London for about ten days. It was already arranged that Violet and I were to go abroad together that winter for a month. There were scenes connected with our going. Violet and I had a row over something; I refused to go abroad; she came round to my house and we made friends again; then I had a dreadful scene with Mother, who was furious at my going; however to make a long story short, we left for Paris at the end of November [1918]. I was to be away until Christmas!

5 October [1920]

Paris . . . We were there for about a week, living in a flat that was lent us in the Palais Royal. Even now the intoxication of some of those hours in Paris makes me see confusedly; other hours were, I admit, wretched, because Denys came (the war being just over), and I wanted Violet to myself. But the evenings were ours. I have never told a soul of what I did. I hesitate to write it here, but I must; shirking the truth here would be like cheating oneself playing patience. I dressed as a boy. It was easy, because I could put a khaki bandage round my head, which in those days was so common that it attracted no attenion at all. I browned my face and hands. It must have been successful, because no one looked at me at all curiously or suspiciously—never once, out of the many times I did it. My height of course was my great advantage. I looked like a rather untidy young man, a sort of undergraduate, of about nineteen. It was marvellous fun, all the more so because there was always the risk of being found out. Of course it was easy in the Palais Royal because I could let myself in and out by a latchkey; in hotels it was more difficult. I had done it once already in England; that was one of the boldest things I ever did. I will tell about it: I changed in my own house in London late one evening (the darkened streets made me bold), and drove with Violet in a taxi as far as Hyde Park Corner. There I got out. I never felt so free as when I stepped off the kerb, down Piccadilly, alone, and knowing that if I met my own mother face to face she would take no notice of me. I walked along, smoking a cigarette, buying a newspaper off a little boy who called me 'sir', and being accosted now and then by women. In this way I strolled from Hyde Park Corner to Bond Street, where I met Violet and took her in a taxi to Charing Cross. (The extraordinary thing was, how natural it all was for me.) Nobody, even in the glare of the station, glanced at me twice. I had wondered about my voice, but found I could sink it sufficiently. Well, I took Violet as far as Orpington by train, and there we found a lodging house where we could get a room. The landlady was very benevolent and I said Violet was my wife. Next day of course I had to put on the same clothes, although I was a little anxious about the daylight, but again nobody took the slightest notice. We went to Knole!,[3] which was, I think, brave. Here I slipped into the stables, and emerged as myself.

Well, this discovery was too good to be wasted, and in Paris I practically lived in that role. Violet used to call me Julian. We dined together every evening in cafés and restaurants, and went to all the theatres. I shall never forget the evenings when we walked back slowly to our flat through the streets of Paris. I, personally, had never felt so free in my life. Perhaps we have never been so happy since. When we got back to the flat, the windows all used to be open onto the courtyard of the Palais Royal, and the fountains splashed below. It was all incredible—like a fairy-tale.

It couldn't go on for ever, and at the end of the week we left for Monte Carlo, stopping on the way at St Raphael. The weather was perfect, Monte Carlo was perfect, Violet was perfect. Again as

3. A large and famous estate near Long Barn, the Nicolsons' house in Kent.

Julian, I took her to a dance there, and had a success with a French family, who asked me to come and play bridge with them, and, I think, had an eye on me for their daughter, a plain girl whose head I tried to turn with compliments. They said '*On voit que monsieur est valseur*',[4] and their son, a French officer, asked me about my '*blessure*',[5] and we exchanged war reminiscences.

I didn't go back at Christmas. I didn't go back till nearly the end of March, and everybody was very angry with me, and I felt like suicide after those four wild and radiant months. The whole of that time is dreadful, a nightmare. Harold was in Paris, and I was alone with Mother and Dada, who were both very angry, and wanted me to give Violet up. (There had been a lot of scandal, by then.) On the other hand, Denys had been in England a month, and was agitating to announce his engagement to Violet. Violet was like a hunted creature. I could have prevented the engagement by very few words, but I thought that would be too outrageously selfish; there was Violet's mother, a demon of a woman, longing to get her safely married, and having told all London that she was going to marry Denys. She had already so bad a reputation for breaking engagements that this would have been the last straw. Besides, we both thought she would gain more liberty by marrying, and Denys was prepared to marry her on her own terms—that is, of merely brotherly relations.

I was absolutely miserable. I went to Brighton, alone, in a great empty dust-sheeted house, and all night I used to lie awake, and all day I used to wonder whether I wouldn't throw myself over the cliffs. Everyone questioned me as to why I looked so ill. On the fifth day Violet's engagement was announced in the papers; I bought the paper at Brighton station and nearly fainted as I read it, although I had expected to find it there. Not very long after that I went to Paris, to join Harold, who by that time knew the whole truth of the affair. I was terribly unhappy in Paris. When I came back to London, Violet began to declare that nothing would induce her to go through with the thing, and that I must save her from it by taking her away; in fact I believe she used Denys very largely as a lever to get me to do so. Living permanently with me had become an obsession in her mind. I don't absolutely remember the process in detail, but I know that I ended by consenting. After that we were both less unhappy; I could afford to see her ostensibly engaged to Denys when I knew that instead of marrying him she was coming away with me. I really intended to take her; we had every plan made. We were to go the day before her wedding—not sooner, because we thought we should be overtaken and brought back. It was of course only this looking-forward which enabled me to endure the period of her engagement.

4. "One can see that you, sir, know   5. Wound.
how to dance."

Then about five days before her wedding I suddenly got by the same post three miserable letters from Harold, who had scented danger, because, in order to break it to him more or less gently (and also because I was in a dreadful state of mind myself during all that time), I had been writing him letters full of hints. When I read those letters something snapped in my mind. I saw Harold, all sweet and gentle and dependent upon me. Violet was there. She was terrified. I remember saying, 'It's no good, I can't take you away.' She implored me by everything she could think of, but I was obdurate. We went up to London together, Violet nearly off her head, and me repeating to myself phrases out of Harold's letters to give myself strength. I telegraphed to him to say I was coming to Paris; I had only one idea, to fly as quickly as I could and to put distance between me and temptation. I saw Violet twice more; once in my own house in London; she looked ill and changed; and once in the early morning at her mother's house, where I went to say goodbye to her on my way to the station. There was a dreary slut scrubbing the doorstep, for it was very early, and I stepped in over the soapy pail, and saw Violet in the morning-room. Then I went to Paris, alone. That is one of the worst days I remember. While I was in the train going to Folkestone I still felt I could change my mind and go back if I wanted to, for she had told me she would wait for me up to the very last minute, and would come straight away if I appeared, or telephoned for her. At Folkestone I felt it becoming more irrevocable, and tried to get off the boat again, but they were moving the gangway and pushed me back. I had Harold's letters with me, and kept reading them until they almost lost all sense. The journey had never seemed so slow; it remains with me simply as a nightmare. I couldn't eat, and tears kept running down my face. Harold met me at the Gare du Nord. I said I wanted to go straight back, but he said, 'No, no,' and took me out to Versailles in a motor. The next day was Sunday, and he stayed with me all day. By then I got such a reaction that I was feverishly cheerful, and he might have thought nothing was the matter. I gave him the book I was writing [*Challenge*], because I knew Violet would hate me to do that, as it was all about her. I was awake nearly all that night. Next day was Monday, 16 June [1919]; Harold had to go into Paris, and I sat quite dazed in my room holding my watch in my hand and watching the hands tick past the hour of Violet's wedding. All that time, I knew, she was expecting a pre-arranged message from me, which I never sent.

I was so stunned by all this at the time that I could not even think; it is only since then that I have realized how every minute has burnt itself into me.

On Tuesday night Violet and Denys came to Paris. On Wednesday I went to see her, at the Ritz. She was wearing clothes I had never seen before, but no wedding ring. I can't describe how terrible it all was—that meeting, and everything. It makes me physically ill to write about it and think about it, and my cheeks are burning. It was dreadful, dreadful. By then I had left Versailles, and was living alone in a small hotel. I took her there, I treated her savagely, I made love to her, I had her, I didn't care, I only wanted to hurt Denys, even though he didn't know of it. I make no excuse, except that I had suffered too much during the past week and was really scarcely responsible. The next day I saw Denys at an awful interview. Violet told him she had meant to run away with me instead of marrying him; she told him she didn't care for him. He got very white, and I thought he was going to faint. I restrained myself from saying much more. I wanted to say, 'Don't you know, you stupid fool, that she is mine in every sense of the word?', but I was afraid that he would kill her if I did that. That night I dined at the Ritz, and from the open window of her room Violet watched me, and Denys sobbed in the room behind her. That day seems to have made a great impression upon him, as he constantly referred to it in his letters to her afterwards.

After that they went away to St Jean de Luz, and I went to Switzerland with Harold, and then back to England alone. After three weeks Violet came back. Things were not quite so bad then. She had a house in Sussex, and Denys only came there for the weekends, and I spent all the rest of the week there. He and I never met, because in Paris he had said to me it must be war or peace. We met once, when he arrived earlier than was expected; I was just leaving, and Violet threw some things into a bag and came with me. I never saw anyone look so angry as he did. He was dead white and his lips were shaking. I tried to make Violet go back, because I thought it was really humiliating the man too much, but she wouldn't. On the whole, however, she was on friendly terms with him, and I am bound to say that he was friendly as an angel to her, and above all he kept the promises he had made, which I think few men would have done. I think on the whole that that was the period when Violet liked him best.

MARY McCARTHY

Artists in Uniform

The Colonel went out sailing,
He spoke with Turk and Jew . . .

"Pour it on, Colonel," cried the young man in the Dacron suit excitedly, making his first sortie into the club-car conversation. His face was white as Roquefort and of a glistening, cheeselike texture; he had a shock of tow-colored hair, badly cut and greasy, and a

snub nose with large gray pores. Under his darting eyes were two
black craters. He appeared to be under some intense nervous strain
and had sat the night before in the club car drinking bourbon with
beer chasers and leafing through magazines which he frowningly
tossed aside, like cards into a discard heap. This morning he had
come in late, with a hangdog, hangover look, and had been sitting
tensely forward on a settee, smoking cigarettes and following the
conversation with little twitches of the nose and quivers of the
body, as a dog follows a human conversation, veering its mistrustful
eyeballs from one speaker to another and raising its head eagerly at
its master's voice. The colonel's voice, rich and light and plausible,
had in fact abruptly risen and swollen, as he pronounced his last
sentence. "I can tell you one thing," he had said harshly. "They
weren't named Ryan or Murphy!"

A sort of sigh, as of consummation, ran through the club car.
"Pour it on, Colonel, give it to them, Colonel, that's right, Colonel," urged the young man in a transport of admiration. The colonel fingered his collar and modestly smiled. He was a thin, hawk-
like, black-haired handsome man with a bright blue bloodshot eye
and a well-pressed, well-tailored uniform that did not show the
effects of the heat—the train, westbound for St. Louis, was passing
through Indiana, and, as usual in a heat wave, the air-conditioning
had not met the test. He wore the Air Force insignia, and there was
something in his light-boned, spruce figure and keen, knifelike profile that suggested a classic image of the aviator, ready to cut, piercing, into space. In base fact, however, the colonel was in procurement, as we heard him tell the mining engineer who had just
bought him a drink. From several silken hints that parachuted into
the talk, it was patent to us that the colonel was a man who knew
how to enjoy this earth and its pleasures: he led, he gave us to
think, a bachelor's life of abstemious dissipation and well-rounded
sensuality. He had accepted the engineer's drink with a mere nod of
the glass in acknowledgment, like a genial Mars[1] quaffing a libation; there was clearly no prospect of his buying a second in return,
not if the train were to travel from here to the Mojave Desert. In
the same way, an understanding had arisen that I, the only woman
in the club car, had become the colonel's perquisite; it was taken
for granted, without an invitation's being issued, that I was to
lunch with him in St. Louis, where we each had a wait between
trains—my plans for seeing the city in a taxicab were dashed.

From the beginning, as we eyed each other over my volume of
Dickens (*"The Christmas Carol?"* suggested the colonel, opening
relations), I had guessed that the colonel was of Irish stock, and
this, I felt, gave me an advantage, for he did not suspect the same
of me, strangely so, for I am supposed to have the map of Ireland

1. God of war in antiquity.

written on my features. In fact, he had just wagered, with a jaunty, sidelong grin at the mining engineer, that my people "came from Boston from way back," and that I—narrowed glance, running, like steel measuring-tape, up and down my form—was a professional sculptress. I might have laughed this off, as a crudely bad guess like his *Christmas Carol*, if I had not seen the engineer nodding gravely, like an idol, and the peculiar young man bobbing his head up and down in mute applause and agreement. I was wearing a bright apple-green raw silk blouse and a dark-green rather full raw silk skirt, plus a pair of pink glass earrings; my hair was done up in a bun. It came to me, for the first time, with a sort of dawning horror, that I had begun, in the course of years, without ever guessing it, to look irrevocably Bohemian. Refracted from the three men's eyes was a strange vision of myself as an artist, through and through, stained with my occupation like the dyer's hand. All I lacked, apparently, was a pair of sandals. My sick heart sank to my Ferragamo shoes; I had always particularly preened myself on being an artist in disguise. And it was not only a question of personal vanity—it seemed to me that the writer or intellectual had a certain missionary usefulness in just such accidental gatherings as this, if he spoke not as an intellectual but as a normal member of the public. Now, thanks to the colonel, I slowly became aware that my contributions to the club-car conversation were being watched and assessed as coming from *a certain quarter*. My costume, it seemed, carefully assembled as it had been at an expensive shop, was to these observers simply a uniform that blazoned a caste and allegiance just as plainly as the colonel's khaki and eagles. "*Gardoz*,"[2] I said to myself. But, as the conversation grew tenser and I endeavored to keep cool, I began to writhe within myself, and every time I looked down, my contrasting greens seemed to be growing more and more lurid and taking on an almost menacing light, like leaves just before a storm that lift their bright undersides as the air becomes darker. We had been speaking, of course, of Russia, and I had mentioned a study that had been made at Harvard of political attitudes among Iron Curtain refugees. Suddenly, the colonel had smiled. "They're pretty Red at Harvard, I'm given to understand," he observed in a comfortable tone, while the young man twitched and quivered urgently. The eyes of all the men settled on me and waited. I flushed as I saw myself reflected. The woodland greens of my dress were turning to their complementary red, like a color-experiment in psychology or a traffic light changing. Down at the other end of the club car, a man looked up from his paper. I pulled myself together. "Set your mind at rest, Colonel," I remarked dryly. "I know Harvard very well and they're conservative to the point of dullness. The only thing crimson is the football team." This dispar-

2. Watch out.

agement had its effect. "So . . .?" queried the colonel. "I thought there was some professor. . . ." I shook my head. "Absolutely not. There used to be a few fellow-travelers, but they're very quiet these days, when they haven't absolutely recanted. The general atmosphere is more anti-Communist than the Vatican." The colonel and the mining engineer exchanged a thoughtful stare and seemed to agree that the Delphic oracle that had just pronounced knew whereof it spoke. "Glad to hear it," said the colonel. The engineer frowned and shook his fat wattles; he was a stately, gray-haired, plump man with small hands and feet and the pampered, finical tidiness of a small-town widow. "There's so much hearsay these days," he exclaimed vexedly. "You don't know *what* to believe."

I reopened my book with an air of having closed the subject and read a paragraph three times over. I exulted to think that I had made a modest contribution to sanity in our times, and I imagined my words pyramiding like a chain letter—the colonel telling a fellow-officer on the veranda of a club in Texas, the engineer halting a works-superintendent in a Colorado mine shaft: "I met a woman on the train who claims . . . Yes, absolutely. . . ." Of course, I did not know Harvard as thoroughly as I pretended, but I forgave myself by thinking it was the convention of such club-car symposia in our positivistic country to speak from the horse's mouth.

Meanwhile, across the aisle, the engineer and the colonel continued their talk in slightly lowered voices. From time to time, the colonel's polished index-fingernail scratched his burnished black head and his knowing blue eye forayed occasionally toward me. I saw that still I was a doubtful quantity to them, a movement in the bushes, a noise, a flicker, that was figuring in their crenelated thought as "she." The subject of Reds in our colleges had not, alas, been finished; they were speaking now of another university and a woman faculty-member who had been issuing Communist statements. This story somehow, I thought angrily, had managed to appear in the newspapers without my knowledge, while these men were conversant with it; I recognized a big chink in the armor of my authority. Looking up from my book, I began to question them sharply, as though they were reporting some unheard-of natural phenomenon. "When?" I demanded. "Where did you see it? What was her name?" This request for the professor's name was a headlong attempt on my part to buttress my position, the implication being that the identities of all university professors were known to me and that if I were but given the name I could promptly clarify the matter. To admit that there was a single Communist in our academic system whose activities were hidden from me imperiled, I instinctively felt, all the small good I had done here. Moreover, in the back of my mind, I had a supreme confidence that these men were wrong: the story, I supposed, was some tattered piece of misinformation they had picked up from a gossip column. Pride, as usual, preceded my fall. To the colonel, the demand for the name was not specific but generic: what *kind* of name was the question he presumed me to be asking. "Oh," he said slowly with a luxurious yawn, "Finkelstein or Fishbein or Feinstein." He lolled back in his seat with a side glance at the engineer, who deeply nodded. There was a voluptuary pause, as the implication sank in. I bit my lip, regarding this as a mere diversionary tactic. "Please!" I said impatiently. "Can't you remember exactly?" The colonel shook his head and then his spare cheekbones suddenly reddened and he looked directly at me. "I can tell you one thing," he exclaimed irefully. "They weren't named Ryan or Murphy."

The colonel went no further; it was quite unnecessary. In an instant, the young man was at his side, yapping excitedly and actually picking at the military sleeve. The poor thing was transformed, like some creature in a fairy tale whom a magic word releases from silence. "That's right, Colonel," he happily repeated. "I know them. *I* was at Harvard in the business school, studying accountancy. I left. I couldn't take it." He threw a poisonous glance at me, and the colonel, who had been regarding him somewhat doubtfully, now put on an alert expression and inclined an ear for his confidences. The man at the other end of the car folded his newspaper solemnly and took a seat by the young man's side. "They're all Reds, Colonel," said the young man. "They teach it in the classroom. I came back here to Missouri. It made me sick to listen to the stuff they handed out. If you didn't hand it back, they flunked you. Don't let anybody tell you different." "You are wrong," I said coldly and closed my book and rose. The young man was still talking eagerly, and the three men were leaning forward to catch his every gasping word, like three astute detectives over a dying informer, when I reached the door and cast a last look over my shoulder at them. For an instant, the colonel's eye met mine and I felt his scrutiny processing my green back as I tugged open the door and met a blast of hot air, blowing my full skirt wide. Behind me, in my fancy, I saw four sets of shrugging brows.

In my own car, I sat down, opposite two fat nuns, and tried to assemble my thoughts. I ought to have spoken, I felt, and yet what could I have said? It occurred to me that the four men had perhaps not realized why I had left the club car with such abruptness: was it possible that they thought I was a Communist, who feared to be unmasked? I spurned this possibility, and yet it made me uneasy. For some reason, it troubled my *amour-propre*[3] to think of my anti-Communist self living on, so to speak, green in their collective memory as a Communist or fellow-traveler. In fact, though I did

3. Self-respect.

not give a fig for the men, I hated the idea, while a few years ago I should have counted it a great joke. This, it seemed to me, was a measure of the change in the social climate. I had always scoffed at the notion of liberals "living in fear" of political demagoguery in America, but now I had to admit that if I was not fearful, I was at least uncomfortable in the supposition that anybody, anybody whatever, could think of me, precious me, as a Communist. A remoter possibility was, of course, that back there my departure was being ascribed to Jewishness, and this too annoyed me. I am in fact a quarter Jewish, and though I did not "hate" the idea of being taken for a Jew, I did not precisely like it, particularly under these circumstances. I wished it to be clear that I had left the club car for intellectual and principled reasons; I wanted those men to know that it was not I, but my principles, that had been offended. To let them conjecture that I had left because I was Jewish would imply that only a Jew could be affronted by an anti-Semitic outburst; a terrible idea. Aside from anything else, it voided the whole concept of transcendence, which was very close to my heart, the concept that man is more than his circumstances, more even than himself.

However you looked at the episode, I said to myself nervously, I had not acquitted myself well. I ought to have done or said something concrete and unmistakable. From this, I slid glassily to the thought that those men ought to be punished, the colonel, in particular, who occupied a responsible position. In a minute, I was framing a businesslike letter to the Chief of Staff, deploring the colonel's conduct as unbecoming to an officer and identifying him by rank and post, since unfortunately I did not know his name. Earlier in the conversation, he had passed some comments on "Harry"[4] that bordered positively on treason, I said to myself triumphantly. A vivid image of the proceedings against him presented itself to my imagination: the long military tribunal with a row of stern soldierly faces glaring down at the colonel. I myself occupied only an inconspicuous corner of this tableau, for, to tell the truth, I did not relish the role of the witness. Perhaps it would be wiser to let the matter drop . . .? We were nearing St. Louis now; the colonel had come back into my car, and the young accountant had followed him, still talking feverishly. I pretended not to see them and turned to the two nuns, as if for sanctuary from this world and its hatred and revenges. Out of the corner of my eye, I watched the colonel, who now looked wry and restless; he shrank against the window as the young man made a place for himself amid the colonel's smart luggage and continued to express his views in a pale breathless voice. I smiled to think that the colonel was paying the piper. For the colonel, anti-Semitism was simply an aspect of urbanity, like a knowledge of hotels or women. This frantic psychopath of an accountant

---

4. Harry S Truman, thirty-third president of the United States (1945–1953).

was serving him as a nemesis, just as the German people had been served by their psychopath, Hitler. Colonel, I adjured him, you have chosen, between him and me; measure the depth of your error and make the best of it! No intervention on my part was now necessary; justice had been meted out. Nevertheless, my heart was still throbbing violently, as if I were on the verge of some dangerous action. What was I to do, I kept asking myself, as I chatted with the nuns, if the colonel were to hold me to that lunch? And I slowly and apprehensively revolved this question, just as though it were a matter of the most serious import. It seemed to me that if I did not lunch with him—and I had no intention of doing so—I had the dreadful obligation of telling him why.

He was waiting for me as I descended the car steps. "Aren't you coming to lunch with me?" he called out and moved up to take my elbow. I began to tremble with audacity. "No," I said firmly, picking up my suitcase and draping an olive-green linen duster over my arm. "I can't lunch with you." He quirked a wiry black eyebrow. "Why not?" he said. "I understood it was all arranged." He reached for my suitcase. "No," I said, holding on to the suitcase. "I can't." I took a deep breath. "I have to tell you. I think you should be *ashamed* of yourself, Colonel, for what you said in the club car." The colonel stared: I mechanically waved for a redcap, who took my bag and coat and went off. The colonel and I stood facing each other on the emptying platform. "What do you mean?" he inquired in a low, almost clandestine tone. "Those anti-Semitic remarks," I muttered, resolutely. "You ought to be *ashamed*." The colonel gave a quick, relieved laugh. "Oh, come now," he protested. "I'm sorry," I said. "I can't have lunch with anybody who feels that way about the Jews." The colonel put down his attaché case and scratched the back of his lean neck. "Oh, come now," he repeated, with a look of amusement. "You're not Jewish, are you?" "No," I said quickly. "Well, then . . ." said the colonel, spreading his hands in a gesture of bafflement. I saw that he was truly surprised and slightly hurt by my criticism, and this made me feel wretchedly embarrassed and even apologetic, on my side, as though I had called attention to some physical defect in him, of which he himself was unconscious. "But I might have been," I stammered. "You had no way of knowing. You oughtn't to talk like that." I recognized, too late, that I was strangely reducing the whole matter to a question of etiquette: "Don't start anti-Semitic talk before making sure there are no Jews present." "Oh, hell," said the colonel, easily. "I can tell a Jew." "No, you can't," I retorted, thinking of my Jewish grandmother, for by Nazi criteria I was Jewish. "Of course I can," he insisted. "So can you." We had begun to walk down the platform side by side, disputing with a restrained passion that isolated us like a pair of lovers. All at once, the colonel halted, as though struck with a thought. "What *are* you, anyway?" he said meditatively, regarding my dark hair, green blouse, and pink earrings. Inside myself, I began to laugh. "Oh," I said gaily, playing out the trump I had been saving. "I'm Irish, like you, Colonel." "How did you know?" he said amazedly. I laughed aloud. "I can tell an Irishman," I taunted. The colonel frowned. "What's your family name?" he said brusquely. "McCarthy." He lifted an eyebrow, in defeat, and then quickly took note of my wedding ring. "That your maiden name?" I nodded. Under this peremptory questioning, I had the peculiar sensation that I get when I am lying; I began to feel that "McCarthy" was a nom de plume, a coinage of my artistic personality. But the colonel appeared to be satisfied. "Hell," he said, "come on to lunch, then. With a fine name like that, you and I should be friends." I still shook my head, though by this time we were pacing outside the station restaurant; my baggage had been checked in a locker; sweat was running down my face and I felt exhausted and hungry. I knew that I was weakening and I wanted only an excuse to yield and go inside with him. The colonel seemed to sense this. "Hell," he conceded. "You've got me wrong. I've nothing against the Jews. Back there in the club car, I was just stating a simple fact: you won't find an Irishman sounding off for the Commies. You can't deny that, can you?"

His voice rose persuasively; he took my arm. In the heat, I wilted and we went into the air-conditioned cocktail lounge. The colonel ordered two old-fashioneds. The room was dark as a cave and produced, in the midst of the hot midday, a hallucinated feeling, as though time had ceased, with the weather, and we were in eternity together. As the colonel prepared to relax, I made a tremendous effort to guide the conversation along rational, purposive lines; my only justification for being here would be to convert the colonel. "There *have* been Irishmen associated with the Communist party." I said suddenly, when the drinks came. "I can think of two." "Oh, hell," said the colonel, "every race and nation has its traitors. What I mean is, you won't find them in numbers. You've got to admit the Communists in this country are ninety per cent Jewish." "But the Jews in this country aren't ninety per cent Communist," I retorted.

As he stirred his drink, restively, I began to try to show him the reasons why the Communist movement in America had attracted such a large number, relatively, of Jews; how the Communists had been anti-Nazi when nobody else seemed to care what happened to the Jews in Germany; how the Communists still capitalized on a Jewish fear of fascism; how many Jews had become, after Buchenwald, traumatized by this fear. . . .

But the colonel was scarcely listening. An impatient frown rested on his jaunty features. "I don't get it," he said slowly. "Why should you be for them, with a name like yours?" "I'm *not* for the Communists," I cried. "I'm just trying to explain to you—" "For the

Jews," the colonel interrupted, irritable now himself. "I've heard of such people but I never met one before." "I'm not 'for' them," I protested. "You don't understand. I'm not for *any* race or nation. I'm against those who are against them." This word, *them*, with a sort of slurring circle drawn round it, was beginning to sound ugly to me. Automatically, in arguing with him, I seemed to have slipped into the colonel's style of thought. It occurred to me that defense of the Jews could be a subtle and safe form of anti-Semitism, an exercise of patronage: as a rational Gentile, one could feel superior both to the Jews and the anti-Semites. There could be no doubt that the Jewish question evoked a curious stealthy lust or concupiscence. I could feel it now vibrating between us over the dark table. If I had been a good person, I should unquestionably have got up and left.

"I don't get it," repeated the colonel. "How were you brought up? Were your people this way too?" It was manifest that an odd reversal had taken place; each of us regarded the other as "abnormal" and was attempting to understand the etiology of a disease. "Many of my people think just as you do," I said, smiling coldly. "It seems to be a sickness to which the Irish are prone. Perhaps it's due to the potato diet," I said sweetly, having divined that the colonel came from a social stratum somewhat lower than my own.

But the colonel's was tough. "You've got me wrong," he reiterated, with an almost plaintive laugh. "I don't dislike the Jews. I've got a lot of Jewish friends. Among themselves, they think just as I do, mark my words. I tell you what it is," he added ruminatively, with a thoughtful prod of his muddler, "I draw a distinction between a kike and a Jew." I groaned. "Colonel, I've never heard an anti-Semite who didn't draw that distinction. You know what Otto Kahn said? 'A kike is a Jewish gentleman who has just left the room.' " The colonel did not laugh. "I don't hold it against some of them," he persisted, in a tone of pensive justice. "It's not their fault if they were born that way. That's what I tell them, and they respect me for my honesty. I've had a lot of discussions; in procurement, you have to do business with them, and the Jews are the first to admit that you'll find more chiselers among their race than among the rest of mankind." "It's not a race," I interjected wearily, but the colonel pressed on. "If I deal with a Jewish manufacturer, I can't bank on his word. I've seen it again and again, every damned time. When I deal with a Gentile, I can trust him to make delivery as promised. That's the difference between the two races. They're just a different breed. They don't have standards of honesty, even among each other." I sighed, feeling unequal to arguing the colonel's personal experience.

"Look," I said, "you may be dealing with an industry where the Jewish manufacturers are the most recent comers and feel they have to cut corners to compete with the established firms. I've heard that said about Jewish cattle-dealers, who are supposed to be extra sharp. But what I think, really, is that you notice it when a Jewish firm fails to meet an agreement and don't notice it when it's a Yankee." "Hah," said the colonel. "They'll tell you what I'm telling you themselves, if you get to know them and go into their homes. You won't believe it, but some of my best friends are Jews," he said, simply and thoughtfully, with an air of originality. "They may be *your* best friends, Colonel," I retorted, "but you are not theirs. I defy you to tell me that you talk to them as you're talking now." "Sure," said the Colonel, easily. "More or less." "They must be very queer Jews you know." I observed tartly, and I began to wonder whether there indeed existed a peculiar class of Jews whose function in life was to be "friends" with such people as the colonel. It was difficult to think that all the anti-Semites who made the colonel's assertion were the victims of a cruel self-deception.

A dispirited silence followed. I was not one of those liberals who believed that the Jews, alone among peoples, possessed no characteristics whatever of a distinguishing nature—this would mean they had no history and no culture, a charge which should be leveled against them only by an anti-Semite. Certainly, types of Jews could be noted and patterns of Jewish thought and feeling; Jewish humor, Jewish rationality, and so on, not that every Jew reflected every attribute of Jewish life or history. But somehow, with the colonel, I dared not concede that there was such a thing as a Jew: I saw the sad meaning of the assertion that a Jew was a person whom other people thought was Jewish.

Hopeless, however, to convey this to the colonel. The desolate truth was that the colonel was extremely stupid, and it came to me, as we sat there, glumly ordering lunch, that for extremely stupid people anti-Semitism was a form of intellectuality, the sole form of intellectuality of which they were capable. It represented, in a rudimentary way, the ability to make categories, to generalize. Hence a thing I had noted before but never understood: the fact that anti-Semitic statements were generally delivered in an atmosphere of profundity. Furrowed brows attended these speculative distinctions between a kike and a Jew, these little empirical laws that you can't know one without knowing them all. To arrive, indeed, at the idea of a Jew was, for these grouping minds, an exercise in Platonic thought, a discovery of essence, and to be able to add the great corollary, "Some of my best friends are Jews," was to find the philosopher's cleft between essence and existence. From this, it would seem, followed the querulous obstinacy with which the anti-Semite clung to his concept; to be deprived of this intellectual tool by missionaries of tolerance would be, for persons like the colonel, the equivalent of Western man's losing the syllogism: a lapse into animal darkness. In the club car, we had just witnessed an example:

the colonel with his anti-Semitic observation had come to the mute young man like the paraclete, bearing the gift of tongues.

Here in the bar, it grew plainer and plainer that the colonel did not regard himself as an anti-Semite but merely as a heavy thinker. The idea that I considered him anti-Semitic sincerely outraged his feelings. "Prejudice" was the last trait he could have imputed to himself. He looked on me, almost respectfully, as a "Jew-lover," a kind of being he had heard of but never actually encountered, like a centaur or a Siamese twin, and the interest of relating this prodigy to the natural state of mankind overrode any personal distaste. There I sat, the exception which was "proving" or testing the rule, and he kept pressing me for details of my history that might explain my deviation in terms of the norm. On my side, of course, I had become fiercely resolved that he would learn nothing from me that would make it possible for him to dismiss my anti-anti-Semitism as the product of special circumstances; I was stubbornly sitting on the fact of my Jewish grandmother like a hen on a golden egg. I was bent on making *him* see himself as a monster, a deviation, a heretic from Church and State. Unfortunately, the colonel, owing perhaps to his military training, had not the glimmering of an idea of what democracy meant; to him, it was simply a slogan that was sometimes useful in war. The notion of an ordained inequality was to him "scientific."

"Honestly," he was saying in lowered tones, as our drinks were taken away and the waitress set down my sandwich and his corned-beef hash, "don't you, brought up the way you were, feel about them the way I do? Just between ourselves, isn't there a sort of inborn feeling of horror that the very word, Jew, suggests?" I shook my head, roundly. The idea of an *innate* anti-Semitism was in keeping with the rest of the colonel's thought, yet it shocked me more than anything he had yet said. "No," I sharply replied. "It doesn't evoke any feeling one way or the other." "Honest Injun?" said the colonel. "Think back; when you were a kid, didn't the word, Jew, make you feel sick?" There was a dreadful sincerity about this that made me answer in an almost kindly tone. "No, truthfully, I assure you. When we were children, we learned to call the old-clothes man a sheeny, but that was just a dirty word to us, like 'Hun' that we used to call after workmen we thought were Germans."

"I don't get it," pondered the colonel, eating a pickle. "There must be something wrong with you. Everybody is born with that feeling. It's natural; it's part of nature." "On the contrary," I said. "It's something very unnatural that you must have been taught as a child." "It's not something you're *taught*," he protested. "You must have been," I said. "You simply don't remember it. In any case, you're a man now; you must rid yourself of that feeling. It's psycho-pathic, like that horrible young man on the train." "You thought he was crazy?" mused the colonel, in an idle, dreamy tone. I shrugged my shoulders. "Of course. Think of his color. He was probably just out of a mental institution. People don't get that tat-tletale gray except in prison or mental hospitals." The colonel sud-denly grinned. "You might be right," he said. "He was quite a case." He chuckled.

I leaned forward. "You know, Colonel," I said quickly, "anti-Semitism is contrary to the Church's teaching. God will make you do penance for hating the Jews. Ask your priest; he'll tell you I'm right. You'll have a long spell in Purgatory, if you don't rid yourself of this sin. It's a deliberate violation of Christ's commandment, 'Love thy neighbor.' The Church holds that the Jews have a sacred place in God's design. Mary was a Jew and Christ was a Jew. The Jews are under God's special protection. The Church teaches that the millennium can't come until the conversion of the Jews; there-fore, the Jews must be preserved that the Divine Will may be accomplished. Woe to them that harm them, for they controvert God's Will!" In the course of speaking, I had swept myself away with the solemnity of the doctrine. The Great Reconciliation between God and His chosen people, as envisioned by the Evangel-ist, had for me at that moment a piercing, majestic beauty, like some awesome Tintoretto. I saw a noble spectacle of blue sky, thronged with gray clouds, and a vast white desert, across which God and Israel advanced to meet each other, while below in hell the demons of disunion shrieked and gnashed their teeth.

"Hell," said the colonel, jovially, "I don't believe in all that. I lost my faith when I was a kid. I saw that all this God stuff was a lot of bushwa." I gazed at him in stupefaction. His confidence had completely returned. The blue eyes glittered debonairly, the eagles glittered; the narrow polished head cocked and listened to itself like a trilling bird. I was up against an airman with a bird's-eye view, a man who believed in nothing but the law of kind: the epitome of godless materialism. "You still don't hold with that bunk?" the colonel inquired in an undertone, with an expression of stealthy curiosity. "No," I confessed, sad to admit to a meeting of minds. "You know what got me?" exclaimed the colonel. "That birth-control stuff. Didn't it kill you?" I made a neutral sound. "I was beginning to play around," said the colonel, with a significant beam of the eye, "and I just couldn't take that guff. When I saw through the birth-control talk, I saw through the whole thing. They claimed it was against nature, but I claim, if that's so, an operation's against nature. I told my old man that when he was having his kidney stones out. You ought to have heard him yell!" A rich, reminiscent satisfaction dwelt in the colonel's face.

This period of his life, in which he had thrown off the claims of the spiritual and adopted a practical approach, was evidently one of those "turning points" to which a man looks back with pride. He lingered over the story of his break with church and parents with a curious sort of heat, as though the flames of old sexual conquests stirred within his body at the memory of those old quarrels. The looks he rested on me, as a sharer of that experience, grew more and more lickerish and assaying. "What got *you* down?" he finally inquired, settling back in his chair and pushing his coffee cup aside. "Oh," I said wearily, "it's a long story. You can read it when it's published." "You're an author?" cried the colonel, who was really very slow-witted. I nodded, and the colonel regarded me afresh. "What do you write? Love stories?" He gave a half-wink. "No," I said. "Various things. Articles. Books. Highbrowish stories." A suspicion darkened in the colonel's sharp face. "That McCarthy," he said. "Is that your pen name?" "Yes," I said, "but it's my real name too. It's the name I write under *and* my maiden name." The colonel digested this thought. "Oh," he concluded.

A new idea seemed to visit him. Quite cruelly, I watched it take possession. He was thinking of the power of the press and the indiscretions of other military figures, who had been rewarded with demotion. The consciousness of the uniform he wore appeared to seep uneasily into his body. He straightened his shoulders and called thoughtfully for the check. We paid in silence, the colonel making no effort to forestall my dive into my pocketbook. I should not have let him pay in any case, but it startled me that he did not try to do so, if only for reasons of vanity. The whole business of paying, apparently, was painful to him; I watched his facial muscles contract as he pocketed the change and slipped two dimes for the waitress onto the table, not daring quite to hide them under the coffee cup—he had short-changed me on the bill and the tip, and we both knew it. We walked out into the steaming station and I took my baggage out of the checking locker. The colonel carried my suitcase and we strolled along without speaking. Again, I felt horribly embarrassed for him. He was meditative, and I supposed that he too was mortified by his meanness about the tip.

"Don't get me wrong," he said suddenly, setting the suitcase down and turning squarely to face me, as though he had taken a big decision. "I may have said a few things back there about the Jews getting what they deserved in Germany." I looked at him in surprise; actually, he had not said that to me. Perhaps he had let it drop in the club car after I had left. "But that doesn't mean I approve of Hitler." "I should hope not," I said. "What I mean is," said the colonel, "that they probably gave the Germans a lot of provocation, but that doesn't excuse what Hitler did." "No," I said, somewhat ironically, but the colonel was unaware of anything satiric in the air. His face was grave and determined; he was sorting out his philosophy for the record. "I mean, I don't approve of his methods," he finally stated. "No," I agreed. "You mean, you don't approve of the gas chamber." The colonel shook his head very severely. "Absolutely not! That was terrible." He shuddered and drew out a handkerchief and slowly wiped his brow. "For God's sake," he said, "don't get me wrong. I think they're human beings" "Yes," I assented, and we walked along to my track. The colonel's spirits lifted, as though, having stated his credo, he had both got himself in line with public policy and achieved an autonomous thought. "I mean," he resumed, "you may not care for them, but that's not the same as killing them, in cold blood, like that." "No, Colonel," I said.

He swung my bag onto the car's platform and I climbed up behind it. He stood below, smiling, with upturned face. "I'll look for your article," he cried, as the train whistle blew. I nodded, and the colonel waved, and I could not stop myself from waving back at him and even giving him the corner of a smile. After all, I said to myself, looking down at him, the colonel was "a human being." There followed one of those inane intervals in which one prays for the train to leave. We both glanced at our watches. "See you some time," he called. "What's your married name?" "Broadwater," I called back. The whistle blew again. "Brodwater?" shouted the colonel, with a dazed look of unbelief and growing enlightenment; he was not the first person to hear it as a Jewish name, on the model of Goldwater. "B-r-o-a-d," I began, automatically, but then I stopped. I disdained to spell it out for him; the victory was his. "One of the chosen, eh?" his brief grimace seemed to commiserate. For the last time, and in the final fullness of understanding, the hawk eye patrolled the green dress, the duster, and the earrings; the narrow flue of his nostril contracted as he curtly turned away. The train commenced to move.

QUESTIONS

1. *What do you understand by the title? Who are the "artists"? Why "in uniform"?*
2. *How does the author try to show the colonel that anti-Semitism is wrong? Does she succeed? Explain why, or why not.*
3. *How does the colonel try to account for the author's attitudes?*
4. *In what ways are stereotypes involved in this incident?*
5. *The incident recounted took place in the early part of the 1950s. Which matters appear to be peculiar to that time? Which are still revelant today?*
6. *Is "Artists in Uniform," an account of an actual occurrence, in any ways like a work of fiction? Explain.*
7. *Elsewhere in this book ("Settling the Colonel's Hash," pp. 425–436) the author tells how readers of "Artists in Uniform" have tried to interpret the "symbols" in it. What does she say about these efforts? What distinction does she draw between literary and natural symbolism?*

JEAN STAFFORD

Con Ed and Me[1]

On quitting New York City in 1957 where I had been living under the name Jean Stafford, I asked Consolidated Edison to send my final bill. Instead of a bill, I received a check for six cents, which represented, I supposed, what was left of my deposit. I kept it, partly as a curio, partly in the hope that in a wee way I could bollix up the company books, and partly because I thought it might come in handy some day in one way or another. Eleven years later, thanks to my mean spirited foresight, I was able to use it as a tactical diversion in a battle I fought with and won from Con Ed.

In the spring of 1968, having spent a miserable ten months in a stygian sublet in the East 80's, calling myself Mrs. A. J. Liebling, I once again asked to settle my account with the Diggers Who Must.[2] When the bill came, I read it with interest and in detail; I read it in artificial light and I took it outdoors and read it in the sun; I read it with and without a magnifying glass; each time I saw the same incontrovertible figures.

Over a period of 27 days I had, according to the computers in Charles F. Luce's busy concern, used up $6.32 worth of electricity and $409.28 of cooking gas, but, because I had a credit of $8.03 from the month before, the total came only to $407.57 instead of $415.60.

I had the bill and the old check for six cents Xeroxed and then I sat down to write Chief Luce a seventeen-page letter. I began:

"The originals of these unusual documents are at the frame shop. They will hang, well lit by LILCO,[3] in some conspicuous part of my house in Suffolk County on Long Island. Let me explain that while I am Mrs. A. J. Liebling, in debt to you for your clean energy to the tune of $407.57, I am also, professionally, Jean Stafford (I am a writer and am not to be confused with Jo Stafford, the popular singer) to whom you owe six cents. Perhaps I could apply the latter to the former.

"I am a widow and I live alone. My breakfast consists of coffee, made in an electric percolator, and fruit. I do not eat lunch. In the city I seldom dine in but when I do, I cook something simple on top of the stove or I have 'finger-food,' as my mother would have called it, sent in from a delicatessen.

1. From a *New York Times* article dated June 8, 1974. Jean Stafford won a Pulitzer Prize in 1970 for her collected short stories. "Although she never has more than a twenty-watt bulb burning at any time and now does all her cooking over a bunsen burner, her most recent monthly bill from LILCO for gas and electricity came to $121.26" [*New York Times* note].

2. The famous company motto of Con Ed is "Dig we must."

3. Long Island Lighting Company, a New York utility company.

"I have a very long history (I was born in 1915) of somnambulism and it could be argued that between April 29 and May 25, I used up $401.25 worth of cooking gas running a short-order house and snack bar in my sleep for the operators of your pneumatic drills. The facts, however, cannot support this proposition. For example, my grocery bill for that period came to $41.77—that may seem steep, considering how little I eat, but what I do eat is always of prime quality. No matter where I live, my butcher who is also my cat's meat man is listed in my personal telephone book simply as 'Tiffany.'

"There is, of course, the possibility that there might have been a leak in my two-burner stove, but in that event, don't you imagine I would be dead?"

Chairman Luce and his subalterns had no way of knowing that the only entries I make in my engagement book are appointments with my dentist, my C.P.A., the doctors in charge of my giblets, of my eyes and my bones and my skin; and the hours of the departure of planes taking me away from my gas stove, my light bulbs and my electric blanket. So I felt free to describe, with a wealth of needless detail, where and with whom I had been each evening but two during the time in question.

My companions had all been illustrious in the world of *belle lettres*, architecture, painting, music, the natural and the physical sciences, jurisprudence, medicine and high finance. We had eaten ambrosia and drunk nectar in the smartest possible restaurants or in the dining rooms of splendidly appointed houses or apartments where Cézannes and Corots hung, where Aubussons and Sarouks[4] lay and Chippendale and Queen Anne stood. These interiors reminded me of others I had seen or read about and I was happy to share my memories with my interlocutor—not, of course, that he was getting a word in edgewise.

I had in truth spent one weekend in Boston and another at my own house in the country, and in the course of one of those weeks, I had been in Nashville for two days and two nights. My weekend in Boston led me to nostalgic reminiscences of people I had known there and in all other parts of New England during the forties; the trip to Nashville caused me to discourse at length on the Southern Fugitive group and my association with them.

Relevant to nothing at all, I said:

"While I am writing to you, let me say a few words about a building you rent to Columbia University. It is known as Myles Cooper and is situated at 440 West 110th Street and it houses The School of the Arts where, while I was living in the city, I held a seminar. Myles Cooper is the most appalling place I have ever

4. Expensive imported carpets.

worked in and I have worked in some mighty appalling places. You should have seen my office at "The Southern Review" at Louisiana State University where I was my secretary . . ."

I named the distinguished editors, the distinguished contributors and described the parties held when the distinguished contributors came to call on the distinguished editors in Baton Rouge. I went into the pesky vermin of Louisiana, the tragic beauty of the antebellum[5] houses, Spanish moss and the Long[6] family.

Eventually I got back to Myles Cooper but then digressed, with many cross-references to colleagues, to talk of my offices on other campuses. Then back to Myles Cooper and to The Troubles at Columbia in April of 1968 when I was cooking up a storm at East 80th Street. I went into the woeful state of higher education. I concluded by wishing many years of health and prosperity for Mr. Luce and his.

My several verbose postscripts were followed by brief biographies of all the notables, in addition to those I had mentioned in the letter, to whom I was sending copies.

Ten days later I got a bill from Consolidated Edison for $407.57.

Now I was impatient. I wrote brusquely; "In my earlier letter, I told you to get your computers overhauled. Do as I say and do so instantly."

Two weeks went by and then one morning, a trembly-voiced Mr. Poltroon telephoned me from New York City and said that there had been a mistake in my Con Ed bill, that the figures had been based on an estimate.

"An estimate of what?" I demanded so loudly that my cat who had been spot-cleaning his gloves at my feet scuttered upstairs. "An estimate for Nedick's?"

The poor bloke tried to explain how the estimates were made, but the procedure is so tortuous, so idiosyncratically imaginative, that, at my suggestion, Mr. Poltroon gave up and went on to say that, in fact, Con Ed owed me 23 cents. I would not get the check, he was sorry to say, for ten days or two weeks and he sincerely hoped I would not be inconvenienced.

Two days later, Mr. P. was back on the hooter asking me to return the 1957 check for six cents. I refused. Testily. I said I thought I was to get a check for 23 cents; he said yes, but the company would like to combine the two so that I would get 29 cents. I told him nothing doing.

All through the summer Mr. Poltroon called me long distance every four or five days: If I got a bill for $3.67, I was to ignore it—it was a mistake. Had I got my check for 23 cents? Wouldn't I please turn loose my check for six cents? Each time he identified

5. Pre–Civil War.
6. A reference to Huey Long, promi- nent member of a politically powerful Louisiana family.

himself, I said, "Oh, Mr. Poltroon, could you hang on a sec? There's somebody at my back door."

Then I'd go out to the kitchen and make myself a bacon-and-tomato sandwich, work the daily crossword puzzle, comb the cat and sterilize a few Mason jars for canning watermelon pickles. He was always waiting for me when I moseyed back to the telephone; and before he could say a word, I'd tell him that I'd been in conversation with the plumber (I talked about sump-pumps, cesspools, elbows, Stillson wrenches, hard water, the high incidence of silverfish in the bathrooms of Monteagle, Tenn.) or the tree men (had Mr. Poltroon ever had trouble with fire-blight on his Japanese quince or powdery mildew on his mimosa?).

Toward the end of August, the calls stopped, but on the Tuesday after Labor Day, Mr. Poltroon rang up to apologize for not having been in touch for so long—he'd been away, he'd needed a rest.

Before I could compassionately inquire about his present condition, there was a knock at the back door and I had to leave him to confer with the cablevision man, to run up a batch of vichyssoise and to rearrange the spice shelf. Faithful Poltroon was still at the other end of the wire. His respiration was shallow; I didn't like the sound of it at all. Had I got my money from Con Ed yet? I hadn't? That was the limit! His voice belied the indignation of his words: It was wanting the timbre of a healthy man.

I never heard that voice again. But late in September a Mr. Bandersnatch S. Pecksniff wrote:

"Mr. C. E. Poltroon informed me of his telephone conversation in which he explained the circumstances resulting in the issuance of our inaccurate billing. We have special programing and instructions to prevent such situations. I am sorry that these instructions were not followed in this instance.

"Enclosed are the two checks which Mr. Poltroon spoke to you about. I do hope you will cash them promptly and enable us to balance your account."

There was an imploring note, I felt, in that last sentence. Although the letter was dated Sept. 24, the new check for six cents (payable to Mrs. A. J. Liebling. Why? Con Ed had owed and had paid Miss Stafford six cents in 1957 but they didn't owe Mrs. L. six cents in 1968) was dated Aug. 8 and the one for 23 cents had been made out on Sept. 6. My case had clearly consumed far more clerical time than I had consumed gas.

The three checks and the amazing bill are framed and hang in my downstairs bathroom. I'm not sure yet, but I have a hunch that by and by I'll have to make room for another set of similar testaments under glass. For I have discovered that the Long Island Lighting Company, far from being Con Ed's easy-going country cousin, is his blood brother, foxy, avaricious and, not to put too fine a point on it, uppity. If he gets too far out of line—and he seems aimed in that direction—I may have to read *him* the riot act, in no uncertain terms.

JOAN DIDION
On Going Home

I am home for my daughter's first birthday. By "home" I do not mean the house in Los Angeles where my husband and I and the baby live, but the place where my family is, in the Central Valley of California. It is a vital although troublesome distinction. My husband likes my family but is uneasy in their house, because once there I fall into their ways, which are difficult, oblique, deliberately inarticulate, not my husband's ways. We live in dusty houses ("D-U-S-T," he once wrote with his finger on surfaces all over the house, but no one noticed it) filled with mementos quite without value to him (what could the Canton dessert plates mean to him? how could he have known about the assay scales, why should he care if he did know?), and we appear to talk exclusively about people we know who have been committed to mental hospitals, about people we know who have been booked on drunk-driving charges, and about property, particularly about property, land, price per acre and C-2 zoning and assessments and freeway access. My brother does not understand my husband's inability to perceive the advantage in the rather common real-estate transaction known as "sale-leaseback," and my husband in turn does not understand why so many of the people he hears about in my father's house have recently been committed to mental hospitals or booked on drunk-driving charges. Nor does he understand that when we talk about sale-leasebacks and right-of-way condemnations we are talking in code about the things we like best, the yellow fields and the cottonwoods and the rivers rising and falling and the mountain roads closing when the heavy snow comes in. We miss each other's points, have another drink and regard the fire. My brother refers to my husband, in his presence, as "Joan's husband." Marriage is the classic betrayal.

Or perhaps it is not any more. Sometimes I think that those of us who are now in our thirties were born into the last generation to carry the burden of "home," to find in family life the source of all tension and drama. I had by all objective accounts a "normal" and a "happy" family situation, and yet I was almost thirty years old before I could talk to my family on the telephone without crying after I had hung up. We did not fight. Nothing was wrong. And yet some nameless anxiety colored the emotional charges between me and the place that I came from. The question of whether or not you could go home again was a very real part of the sentimental and largely literary baggage with which we left home in the fifties; I suspect that it is irrelevant to the children born of the fragmentation after World War II. A few weeks ago in a San Francisco bar I saw a pretty young girl on crystal take off her clothes and dance for the cash prize in an "amateur-topless" contest. There was no particular sense of moment about this, none of the effect of romantic degradation, of "dark journey," for which my generation strived so assiduously. What sense could that girl possibly make of, say, *Long Day's Journey into Night?* Who is beside the point?

That I am trapped in this particular irrelevancy is never more apparent to me than when I am home. Paralyzed by the neurotic lassitude engendered by meeting one's past at every turn, around every corner, inside every cupboard, I go aimlessly from room to room. I decide to meet it head-on and clean out a drawer, and I spread the contents on the bed. A bathing suit I wore the summer I was seventeen. A letter of rejection from *The Nation*, an aerial photograph of the site for a shopping center my father did not build in 1954. Three teacups hand-painted with cabbage roses and signed "E.M.," my grandmother's initials. There is no final solution for letters of rejection from *The Nation* and teacups hand-painted in 1900. Nor is there any answer to snapshots of one's grandfather as a young man on skis, surveying around Donner Pass in the year 1910. I smooth out the snapshot and look into his face, and do and do not see my own. I close the drawer, and have another cup of coffee with my mother. We get along very well, veterans of a guerrilla war we never understood.

Days pass. I see no one. I come to dread my husband's evening call, not only because he is full of news of what by now seems to me our remote life in Los Angeles, people he has seen, letters which require attention, but because he asks what I have been doing, suggests uneasily that I get out, drive to San Francisco or Berkeley. Instead I drive across the river to a family graveyard. It has been vandalized since my last visit and the monuments are broken, overturned in the dry grass. Because I once saw a rattlesnake in the grass I stay in the car and listen to a country-and-Western station. Later I drive with my father to a ranch he has in the foothills. The man who runs his cattle on it asks us to the roundup, a week from Sunday, and although I know that I will be in Los Angeles I say, in the oblique way my family talks, that I will come. Once home I mention the broken monuments in the graveyard. My mother shrugs.

I go to visit my great-aunts. A few of them think now that I am my cousin, or their daughter who died young. We recall an anecdote about a relative last seen in 1948, and they ask if I still like living in New York City. I have lived in Los Angeles for three years, but I say that I do. The baby is offered a horehound drop, and I am slipped a dollar bill "to buy a treat." Questions trail off, answers are abandoned, the baby plays with the dust motes in a shaft of afternoon sun.

It is time for the baby's birthday party: a white cake, strawberry-marshmallow ice cream, a bottle of champagne saved from another party. In the evening, after she has gone to sleep, I kneel beside the crib and touch her face, where it is pressed against the slats, with mine. She is an open and trusting child, unprepared for and unaccustomed to the ambushes of family life, and perhaps it is just as well that I can offer her little of that life. I would like to give her more. I would like to promise her that she will grow up with a sense of her cousins and of rivers and of her great-grandmother's teacups, would like to pledge her a picnic on a river with fried chicken and her hair uncombed, would like to give her *home* for her birthday, but we live differently now and I can promise her nothing like that. I give her a xylophone and a sundress from Madeira, and promise to tell her a funny story.

QUESTIONS

1. Does the author take a single attitude, or several, toward "home"? Try to specify the attitude, or attitudes.
2. The author speaks of herself at home as "paralyzed by the neurotic lassitude engendered by meeting one's past at every turn" (p. 76). What details in the essay help explain that feeling?
3. What does the author mean by "the ambushes of family life" (above)?
4. Explain whether the essay gives you any clues as to why so much of the talk at home is ". . . about people we know who have been committed to mental hospitals, about people we know who have been booked on drunk-driving charges, and about property . . . (p. 75)?
5. If you have read or seen the play, explain the appropriateness of the author's reference (p. 76) to Eugene O'Neill's *Long Day's Journey into Night*.
6. In her concluding sentence the author tells us she gives as birthday gifts to her daughter "a xylophone and a sundress from Madeira." Are these appropriate? Why, or why not? Explain why she would like to give other gifts.

LOREN EISELEY
The Brown Wasps

There is a corner in the waiting room of one of the great Eastern stations where women never sit. It is always in the shadow and over-hung by rows of lockers. It is, however, always frequented—not so much by genuine travelers as by the dying. It is here that a certain element of the abandoned poor seeks a refuge out of the weather, clinging for a few hours longer to the city that has fathered them. In a precisely similar manner I have seen, on a sunny day in midwin-ter, a few old brown wasps creep slowly over an abandoned wasp nest in a thicket. Numbed and forgetful and frost-blackened, the hum of the spring hive still resounded faintly in their sodden tissues. Then the temperature would fall and they would drop away into the white oblivion of the snow. Here in the station it is in no way dif-ferent save that the city is busy in its snows. But the old ones cling to their seats as though these were symbolic and could not be given up. Now and then they sleep, their gray old heads resting with pain-ful awkwardness on the backs of the benches.

Also they are not at rest. For an hour they may sleep in the gasp-ing exhaustion of the ill-nourished and aged who have to walk in the night. Then a policeman comes by on his round and nudges them upright.

"You can't sleep here," he growls.

A strange ritual then begins. An old man is difficult to waken. After a muttered conversation the policeman presses a coin into his hand and passes fiercely along the benches prodding and gesturing toward the door. In his wake, like birds rising and settling behind the passage of a farmer through a cornfield, the men totter up, move a few paces and subside once more upon the benches.

One man, after a slight, apologetic lurch, does not move at all. Tubercularly thin, he sleeps on steadily. The policeman does not look back. To him, too, this has become a ritual. He will not have to notice it again officially for another hour.

Once in a while one of the sleepers will not awake. Like the brown wasps, he will have had his wish to die in the great droning center of the hive rather than in some lonely room. It is not so bad here with the shuffle of footsteps and the knowledge that there are others who share the bad luck of the world. There are also the whis-tles and the sounds of everyone, everyone in the world, starting on journeys. Amidst so many journeys somebody is bound to come out all right. Somebody.

Maybe it was on a like thought that the brown wasps fell away from the old paper nest in the thicket. You hold till the last, even if it is only to a public seat in a railroad station. You want your place in the hive more than you want a room or a place where the aged can be eased gently out of the way. It is the place that matters, the place at the heart of things. It is life that you want, that bruises your gray old head with the hard chairs; a man has a right to his place.

But sometimes the place is lost in the years behind us. Or sometimes it is a thing of air, a kind of vaporous distortion above a heap of rubble. We cling to a time and place because without them man is lost, not only man but life. This is why the voices, real or unreal, which speak from the floating trumpets at spiritualist seances are so unnerving. They are voices out of nowhere whose only reality lies in their ability to stir the memory of a living person with some fragment of the past. Before the medium's cabinet both the dead and the living revolve endlessly about an episode, a place, an event that has already been engulfed by time.

This feeling runs deep in life; it brings stray cats running over endless miles, and birds homing from the ends of the earth. It is as though all living creatures, and particularly the more intelligent, can survive only by fixing or transforming a bit of time into space or by securing a bit of space with its objects immortalized and made permanent in time. For example, I once saw, on a flower pot in my own living room, the efforts of a field mouse to build a remembered field. I have lived to see this episode repeated in a thousand guises, and since I have spent a large portion of my life in the shade of a nonexistent tree, I think I am entitled to speak for the field mouse.

One day as I cut across the field which at that time extended on one side of our suburban shopping center, I found a giant slug feeding from a runnel of pink ice cream in an abandoned Dixie cup. I could see his eyes telescope and protrude in a kind of dim, uncertain ecstasy as his dark body bunched and elongated in the curve of the cup. Then, as I stood there at the edge of the concrete, contemplating the slug, I began to realize it was like standing on a shore where a different type of life creeps up and fumbles tentatively among the rocks and sea wrack. It knows its place and will only creep so far until something changes. Little by little as I stood there I began to see more of this shore that surrounds the place of man. I looked with sudden care and attention at things I had been running over thoughtlessly for years. I even waded out a short way into the grass and the wild-rose thickets to see more. A huge black-belted bee went droning by and there were some indistinct scurryings in the underbrush.

Then I came to a sign which informed me that this field was to be the site of a new Wanamaker suburban store. Thousands of obscure lives were about to perish, the spores of puffballs would go smoking off to new fields, and the bodies of little white-footed mice would be crunched under the inexorable wheels of the bulldozers. Life disappears or modifies its appearances so fast that everything takes on an aspect of illusion—a momentary fizzing and boiling with smoke rings, like pouring dissident chemicals into a retort. Here man was advancing, but in a few years his plaster and bricks would be disappearing once more into the insatiable maw of the clover. Being of an archaeological cast of mind, I thought of this fact with an obscure sense of satisfaction and waded back through the rose thickets to the concrete parking lot. As I did so, a mouse scurried ahead of me, frightened of my steps if not of that ominous Wanamaker sign. I saw him vanish in the general direction of my apartment house, his little body quivering with fear in the great open sun on the blazing concrete. Blinded and confused, he was running straight away from his field. In another week scores would follow him.

I forgot the episode then and went home to the quiet of my living room. It was not until a week later, letting myself into the apartment, that I realized I had a visitor. I am fond of plants and had several ferns standing on the floor in pots to avoid the noon glare by the south window.

As I snapped on the light and glanced carelessly around the room, I saw a little heap of earth on the carpet and a scrabble of pebbles that had been kicked merrily over the edge of one of the flower pots. To my astonishment I discovered a full-fledged burrow delving downward among the fern roots. I waited silently. The creature who had made the burrow did not appear. I remembered the wild field then, and the flight of the mice. No house mouse, no *Mus domesticus*, had kicked up this little heap of earth or sought refuge under a fern root in a flower pot. I thought of the desperate little creature I had seen fleeing from the wild-rose thicket. Through intricacies of pipes and attics, he, or one of his fellows, had climbed to this high green solitary room. I could visualize what had occurred. He had an image in his head, a world of seed pods and quiet, of green sheltering leaves in the dim light among the weed stems. It was the only world he knew and it was gone.

Somehow in his flight he had found his way to this room with drawn shades where no one would come till nightfall. And here he had smelled green leaves and run quickly up the flower pot to dabble his paws in common earth. He had even struggled half the afternoon to carry his burrow deeper and had failed. I examined the hole, but no whiskered twitching face appeared. He was gone. I gathered up the earth and refilled the burrow. I did not expect to find traces of him again.

Yet for three nights thereafter I came home to the darkened room and my ferns to find the dirt kicked gaily about the rug and the burrow reopened, though I was never able to catch the field mouse within it. I dropped a little food about the mouth of the burrow, but it was never touched. I looked under beds or sat reading with one ear cocked for rustlings in the ferns. It was all in vain; I never saw him. Probably he ended in a trap in some other tenant's room.

But before he disappeared I had come to look hopefully for his evening burrow. About my ferns there had begun to linger the insubstantial vapor of an autumn field, the distilled essence, as it were, of a mouse brain in exile from its home. It was a small dream, like our dreams, carried a long and weary journey along pipes and through spider webs, past holes over which loomed the shadows of waiting cats, and finally, desperately, into this room where he had played in the shuttered daylight for an hour among the green ferns on the floor. Every day these invisible dreams pass us on the street, or rise from beneath our feet, or look out upon us from beneath a bush.

Some years ago the old elevated railway in Philadelphia was torn down and replaced by a subway system. This ancient El with its barnlike stations containing nut-vending machines and scattered food scraps had, for generations, been the favorite feeding ground of flocks of pigeons, generally one flock to a station along the route of the El. Hundreds of pigeons were dependent upon the system. They flapped in and out of its stanchions and steel work or gathered in watchful little audiences about the feet of anyone who rattled the peanut-vending machines. They even watched people who jingled change in their hands, and prospected for food under the feet of the crowds who gathered between trains. Probably very few among the waiting people who tossed a crumb to an eager pigeon realized that this El was like a food-bearing river, and that the life which haunted its banks was dependent upon the running of the trains with their human freight.

I saw the river stop.

The time came when the underground tubes were ready; the traffic was transferred to a realm unreachable by pigeons. It was like a great river subsiding suddenly into desert sands. For a day, for two days, pigeons continued to circle over the El or stand close to the red vending machines. They were patient birds, and surely this great river which had flowed through the lives of unnumbered generations was merely suffering from some momentary drought.

They listened for the familiar vibrations that had always heralded an approaching train; they flapped hopefully about the head of an occasional workman walking along the steel runways. They passed from one empty station to another, all the while growing hungrier. Finally they flew away.

I thought I had seen the last of them about the El, but there was a revival and it provided a curious instance of the memory of living things for a way of life or a locality that has long been cherished. Some weeks after the El was abandoned workmen began to tear it down. I went to work every morning by one particular station, and the time came when the demolition crews reached this spot. Acetylene torches showered passersby with sparks, pneumatic drills hammered at the base of the structure, and a blind man who, like the pigeons, had clung with his cup to a stairway leading to the change booth, was forced to give up his place.

It was then, strangely, momentarily, one morning that I witnessed the return of a little band of the familiar pigeons. I even recognized one or two members of the flock that had lived around this particular station before they were dispersed into the streets. They flew bravely in and out among the sparks and the hammers and the shouting workmen. They had returned—and they had returned because the hubbub of the wreckers had convinced them that the river was about to flow once more. For several hours they flapped in and out through the empty windows, nodding their heads and watching the fall of girders with attentive little eyes. By the following morning the station was reduced to some burned-off stanchions in the street. My bird friends had gone. It was plain, however, that they retained a memory for an insubstantial structure now compounded of air and time. Even the blind man clung to it. Someone had provided him with a chair, and he sat at the same corner staring sightlessly at an invisible stairway where, so far as he was concerned, the crowds were still ascending to the trains.

I have said my life has been passed in the shade of a nonexistent tree, so that such sights do not offend me. Prematurely I am one of the brown wasps and I often sit with them in the great droning hive of the station, dreaming sometimes of a certain tree. It was planted sixty years ago by a boy with a bucket and a toy spade in a little Nebraska town. That boy was myself. It was a cottonwood sapling and the boy remembered it because of some words spoken by his father and because everyone died or moved away who was supposed to wait and grow old under its shade. The boy was passed from hand to hand, but the tree for some intangible reason had taken root in his mind. It was under its branches that he sheltered; it was from this tree that his memories, which are my memories, led away into the world.

After sixty years the mood of the brown wasps grows heavier upon one. During a long inward struggle I thought it would do me good to go and look upon that actual tree. I found a rational excuse in which to clothe this madness. I purchased a ticket and at the end of two thousand miles I walked another mile to an address that was still the same. The house had not been altered.

I came close to the white picket fence and reluctantly, with great effort, looked down the long vista of the yard. There was nothing there to see. For sixty years that cottonwood had been growing in my mind. Season by season its seeds had been floating farther on the hot prairie winds. We had planted it lovingly there, my father and I, because he had a great hunger for soil and live things growing, and because none of these things had long been ours to protect. We had planted the little sapling and watered it faithfully, and I remembered that I had run out with my small bucket to drench its roots the day we moved away. And all the years since it had been growing in my mind, a huge tree that somehow stood for my father and the love I bore him. I took a grasp on the picket fence and forced myself to look again.

A boy with the hard bird eye of youth pedaled a tricycle slowly up beside me.

"What'cha lookin' at?" he asked curiously.

"A tree," I said.

"What for?" he said.

"It isn't there," I said, to myself mostly, and began to walk away at a pace just slow enough not to seem to be running.

"What isn't there?" the boy asked. I didn't answer. It was obvious I was attached by a thread to a thing that had never been there, or certainly not for long. Something that had to be held in the air, or sustained in the mind, because it was part of my orientation in the universe and I could not survive without it. There was more than an animal's attachment to a place. There was something else, the attachment of the spirit to a grouping of events in time; it was part of our morality.

So I had come home at last, driven by a memory in the brain as surely as the field mouse who had delved long ago into my flower pot or the pigeons flying forever amidst the rattle of nut-vending machines. These, the burrow under the greenery in my living room and the red-bellied bowls of peanuts now hovering in midair in the minds of pigeons, were all part of an elusive world that existed nowhere and yet everywhere. I looked once at the real world about me while the persistent boy pedaled at my heels.

It was without meaning, though my feet took a remembered path. In sixty years the house and street had rotted out of my mind. But the tree, the tree that no longer was, that had perished in its first season, bloomed on in my individual mind, unblemished as my father's words. "We'll plant a tree here, son, and we're not going to move any more. And when you're an old, old man you can sit under it and think how we planted it here, you and me, together."

I began to outpace the boy on the tricycle.

"Do you live here, Mister?" he shouted after me suspiciously. I took a firm grasp on airy nothing—to be precise, on the bole of a great tree. "I do," I said. I spoke for myself, one field mouse, and several pigeons. We were all out of touch but somehow permanent. It was the world that had changed.

E. B. WHITE

Once More to the Lake (August 1941)

One summer, along about 1904, my father rented a camp on a lake in Maine and took us all there for the month of August. We all got ringworm from some kittens and had to rub Pond's Extract on our arms and legs night and morning, and my father rolled over in a canoe with all his clothes on; but outside of that the vacation was a success and from then on none of us ever thought there was any place in the world like that lake in Maine. We returned summer after summer—always on August 1st for one month. I have since become a salt-water man, but sometimes in summer there are days when the restlessness of the tides and the fearful cold of the sea water and the incessant wind which blows across the afternoon and into the evening make me wish for the placidity of a lake in the woods. A few weeks ago this feeling got so strong I bought myself a couple of bass hooks and a spinner and returned to the lake where we used to go, for a week's fishing and to revisit old haunts.

I took along my son, who had never had any fresh water up his nose and who had seen lily pads only from train windows. On the journey over to the lake I began to wonder what it would be like. I wondered how time would have marred this unique, this holy spot—the coves and streams, the hills that the sun set behind, the camps and the paths behind the camps. I was sure the tarred road would have found it out and I wondered in what other ways it would be desolated. It is strange how much you can remember about places like that once you allow your mind to return into the grooves which lead back. You remember one thing, and that suddenly reminds you of another thing. I guess I remembered clearest of all the early mornings, when the lake was cool and motionless, remembered how the bedroom smelled of the lumber it was made of and of the wet woods whose scent entered through the screen. The partitions in the camp were thin and did not extend clear to the top of the rooms, and as I was always the first up I would dress softly so as not to wake the others, and sneak out into the sweet outdoors and start out in the canoe, keeping close along the shore in the long shadows of the pines. I remembered being very careful never to rub my paddle against the gunwale for fear of disturbing the stillness of the cathedral.

The lake had never been what you would call a wild lake. There were cottages sprinkled around the shores, and it was in farming country although the shores of the lake were quite heavily wooded. Some of the cottages were owned by nearby farmers, and you would live at the shore and eat your meals at the farmhouse. That's what our family did. But although it wasn't wild, it was a fairly large and undisturbed lake and there were places in it which, to a child at least, seemed infinitely remote and primeval.

I was right about the tar: it led to within half a mile of the shore. But when I got back there, with my boy, and we settled into a camp near a farmhouse and into the kind of summertime I had known, I could tell that it was going to be pretty much the same as it had been before—I knew it, lying in bed the first morning, smelling the bedroom, and hearing the boy sneak quietly out and go off along the shore in a boat. I began to sustain the illusion that he was I, and therefore, by simple transposition, that I was my father. This sensation persisted, kept cropping up all the time we were there. It was not an entirely new feeling, but in this setting it grew much stronger. I seemed to be living a dual existence. I would be in the middle of some simple act, I would be picking up a bait box or laying down a table fork, or I would be saying something, and suddenly it would be not I but my father who was saying the words or making the gesture. It gave me a creepy sensation.

We went fishing the first morning. I felt the same damp moss covering the worms in the bait can, and saw the dragonfly alight on the tip of my rod as it hovered a few inches from the surface of the water. It was the arrival of this fly that convinced me beyond any doubt that everything was as it always had been, that the years were a mirage and there had been no years. The small waves were the same, chucking the rowboat under the chin as we fished at anchor, and the boat was the same boat, the same color green and the ribs broken in the same places, and under the floor-boards the same fresh-water leavings and débris—the dead helgramite,[1] the wisps of moss, the rusty discarded fishook, the dried blood from yesterday's catch. We stared silently at the tips of our rods, at the dragonflies that came and went. I lowered the tip of mine into the water, tentatively, pensively dislodging the fly, which darted two feet away, poised, darted two feet back, and came to rest again a little farther up the rod. There had been no years between the ducking of this dragonfly and the other one—the one that was part of memory. I looked at the boy, who was silently watching his fly, and it was my hands that held his rod, my eyes watching. I felt dizzy and didn't know which rod I was at the end of.

We caught two bass, hauling them in briskly as though they were mackerel, pulling them over the side of the boat in a businesslike manner without any landing net, and stunning them with a blow on the back of the head. When we got back for a swim before lunch, the lake was exactly where we had left it, the same number of inches from the dock, and there was only the merest suggestion of a breeze. This seemed an utterly enchanted sea, this lake you could leave to its own devices for a few hours and come back to, and find that it had not stirred, this constant and trustworthy body of water. In the shallows, the dark, water-soaked sticks and twigs, smooth and old, were undulating in clusters on the bottom against the clean ribbed

1. The nymph of the May-fly, used as bait.

sand, and the track of the mussel was plain. A school of minnows swam by, each minnow with its small individual shadow, doubling the attendance, so clear and sharp in the sunlight. Some of the other campers were in swimming, along the shore, one of them with a cake of soap, and the water felt thin and clear and unsubstantial. Over the years there had been this person with the cake of soap, this cultist, and here he was. There had been no years.

Up to the farmhouse to dinner through the teeming, dusty field, the road under our sneakers was only a two-track road. The middle track was missing, the one with the marks of the hooves and the splotches of dried, flaky manure. There had always been three tracks to choose from in choosing which track to walk in; now the choice was narrowed down to two. For a moment I missed terribly the middle alternative. But the way led past the tennis court, and something about the way it lay there in the sun reassured me; the tape had loosened along the backline, the alleys were green with plantains and other weeds, and the net (installed in June and removed in September) sagged in the dry noon, and the whole place steamed with midday heat and hunger and emptiness. There was a choice of pie for dessert, and one was blueberry and one was apple, and the waitresses were the same country girls, there having been no passage of time, only the illusion of it as in a dropped curtain—the waitresses were still fifteen; their hair had been washed, that was the only difference—they had been to the movies and seen the pretty girls with the clean hair.

Summertime, oh summertime, pattern of life indelible, the fade-proof lake, the woods unshatterable, the pasture with the sweetfern and the juniper forever and ever, summer without end; this was the background, and the life along the shore was the design, the cottagers with their innocent and tranquil design, their tiny docks with the flagpole and the American flag floating against the white clouds in the blue sky, the little paths over the roots of the trees leading from camp to camp and the paths leading back to the outhouses and the can of lime for sprinkling, and at the souvenir counters at the store the miniature birch-bark canoes and the post cards that showed things looking a little better than they looked. This was the American family at play, escaping the city heat, wondering whether the newcomers in the camp at the head of the cove were "common" or "nice," wondering whether it was true that the people who drove up for Sunday dinner at the farmhouse were turned away because there wasn't enough chicken.

It seemed to me, as I kept remembering all this, that those times and those summers had been infinitely precious and worth saving. There had been jollity and peace and goodness. The arriving (at the beginning of August) had been so big a business in itself, at the railway station the farm wagon drawn up, the first smell of the pine-laden air, the first glimpse of the smiling farmer, and the great importance of the trunks and your father's enormous authority in such matters, and the feel of the wagon under you for the long ten-mile haul, and at the top of the last long hill catching the first view of the lake after eleven months of not seeing this cherished body of water. The shouts and cries of the other campers when they saw you, and the trunks to be unpacked, to give up their rich burden. (Arriving was less exciting nowadays, when you sneaked up in your car and parked it under a tree near the camp and took out the bags and in five minutes it was all over, no fuss, no loud wonderful fuss about trunks.)

Peace and goodness and jollity. The only thing that was wrong now, really, was the sound of the place, an unfamiliar nervous sound of the outboard motors. This was the note that jarred, the one thing that would sometimes break the illusion and set the years moving. In those other summertimes all motors were inboard; and when they were at a little distance, the noise they made was a sedative, an ingredient of summer sleep. They were one-cylinder and two-cylinder engines, and some were make-and-break and some were jump-spark,[2] but they all made a sleepy sound across the lake. The one-lungers throbbed and fluttered, and the twin-cylinder ones purred and purred, and that was a quiet sound too. But now the campers all had outboards. In the daytime, in the hot mornings, these motors made a petulant, irritable sound; at night, in the still evening when the afterglow lit the water, they whined about one's ears like mosquitoes. My boy loved our rented outboard, and his great desire was to achieve singlehanded mastery over it, and authority, and he soon learned the trick of choking it a little (but not too much), and the adjustment of the needle valve. Watching him I would remember the things you could do with the old one cylinder engine with the heavy flywheel, how you could have it eating out of your hand if you got really close to it spiritually. Motor boats in those days didn't have clutches, and you would make a landing by shutting off the motor at the proper time and coasting in with a dead rudder. But there was a way of reversing them, if you learned the trick, by cutting the switch and putting it on again exactly on the final dying revolution of the flywheel, so that it would kick back against compression and begin reversing. Approaching a dock in a strong following breeze, it was difficult to slow up sufficiently by the ordinary coasting method, and if a boy felt he had complete mastery over his motor, he was tempted to keep it running beyond its time and then reverse it a few feet from the dock. It took a cool nerve, because if you threw the switch a twentieth of a second too soon you would catch the flywheel when it still had speed enough to go up past center, and the boat would leap ahead, charging bull-fashion at the dock.

We had a good week at the camp. The bass were biting well and the sun shone endlessly, day after day. We would be tired at night

2. Methods of ignition timing.

and lie down in the accumulated heat of the little bedrooms after the long hot day and the breeze would stir almost imperceptibly outside and the smell of the swamp drift in through the rusty screens. Sleep would come easily and in the morning the red squirrel would be on the roof, tapping out his gay routine. I kept remembering everything, lying in bed in the mornings—the small steamboat that had a long rounded stern like the lip of a Ubangi, and how quietly she ran on the moonlight sails, when the older boys played their mandolins and the girls sang and we ate doughnuts dipped in sugar, and how sweet the music was on the water in the shining night, and what it had felt like to think about girls then. After breakfast we would go up to the store and the things were in the same place—the minnows in a bottle, the plugs and spinners disarranged and pawed over by the youngsters from the boys' camp, the fig newtons and the Beeman's gum. Outside, the road was tarred and cars stood in front of the store. Inside, all was just as it had always been, except there was more Coca-Cola and not so much Moxie and root beer and birch beer and sarsaparilla. We would walk out with a bottle of pop apiece and sometimes the pop would backfire up our noses and hurt. We explored the streams, quietly, where the turtles slid off the sunny logs and dug their way into the soft bottom; and we lay on the town wharf and fed worms to the tame bass. Everywhere we went I had trouble making out which was I, the one walking at my side, the one walking in my pants.

One afternoon while we were there at that lake a thunderstorm came up. It was like the revival of an old melodrama that I had seen long ago with childish awe. The second-act climax of the drama of the electrical disturbance over a lake in America had not changed in any important respect. This was the big scene, still the big scene. The whole thing was so familiar, the first feeling of oppression and heat and a general air around camp of not wanting to go very far away. In midafternoon (it was all the same) a curious darkening of the sky, and a lull in everything that had made life tick; and then the way the boats suddenly swung the other way at their moorings with the coming of a breeze out of the new quarter, and the premonitory rumble. Then the kettle drum, then the snare, then the bass drum and cymbals, then crackling light against the dark, and the gods grinning and licking their chops in the hills. Afterward the calm, the rain steadily rustling in the calm lake, the return of light and hope and spirits, and the campers running out in joy and relief to go swimming in the rain, their bright cries perpetuating the deathless joke about how they were getting simply drenched, and the children screaming with delight at the new sensation of bathing in the rain, and the joke about getting drenched linking the generations in a strong indestructible chain. And the comedian who waded in carrying an umbrella.

When the others went swimming my son said he was going in

too. He pulled his dripping trunks from the line where they had hung all through the shower, and wrung them out. Languidly, and with no thought of going in, I watched him, his hard little body, skinny and bare, saw him wince slightly as he pulled up around his vitals the small, soggy, icy garment. As he buckled the swollen belt suddenly my groin felt the chill of death.

QUESTIONS

1. White had not been back to the lake for many years. What bearing has this fact on the experience which the essay describes?
2. What has guided White in his selection of the details he gives about the trip? Why, for example, does he talk about the road, the dragonfly, the bather with the cake of soap?
3. How do the differences between boats of the past and boats of today relate to or support the point of the essay?
4. What is the meaning of White's last sentence? What relation has it to the sentence just preceding? How has White prepared us for this ending?
5. How would the narrative differ if it were told by the boy? What details of the scene might the boy emphasize? Why? Show what point the boy's selection of details might make.

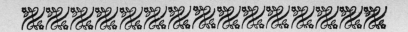

Prose Forms: Journals

[Occasionally a man catches himself having said something aloud, obviously with no concern to be heard, even by himself. And all of us have overheard, perhaps while walking, a solitary person muttering or laughing softly or exclaiming abruptly. For oneself or another, something floats up from the world within, forces itself to be expressed, takes no real account of the time or the place, and certainly intends no conscious communication.

With more self-consciousness, and yet without a specific audience, a man sometimes speaks out at something that has momentarily filled his attention from the world without. A sharp play at the ball game, the twist of a political speech, an old photograph—something from the outer world impresses the mind, stimulates it, focuses certain of its memories and values, interests and needs. Thus stimulated, the man may wish to share his experience with another, to inform or amuse him, to rouse him to action or persuade him to a certain belief. Often, though, the man experiencing may want most to talk to himself, to give a public shape in words to his thoughts and feelings but for the sake of a kind of private dialogue with himself. Communication to another may be an ultimate desire, but the immediate motive is to articulate the experience for himself.

To articulate, to shape the experience in language for his own sake, one may keep a journal. Literally a day-book, the journal enables one to write down something about the experiences of a day which for a great variety of reasons may have been especially memorable or impressive. The journal entry may be merely a few words to call to mind a thing done, a person seen, a menu enjoyed at a dinner party. It may be concerned at length with a political crisis in the community, or a personal crisis in the home. It may even be as noble as it was with some pious men in the past who used the journal to keep a record of their consciences, a periodic reckoning of their moral and spiritual accounts. In its most public aspect, the idea of a journal calls to mind the newspaper or the record of proceedings like the Congressional Record. In its most closely private form, the journal becomes the diary.

For the person keeping a journal, whatever he experiences and wants to hold he can write down. But to get it down on paper begins another adventure. For he has to focus on what he has experienced, and to be able to say what, in fact, the experience is. What of it is new? What of it is remarkable because of associations in the memory it stirs up? Is this like anything I—or others—have experienced before? Is it a good or a bad thing to have happened? And why, specifically? The questions multiply themselves quickly, and as the journalist seeks to answer the appropriate ones, he begins to know what it is he contemplates. As he tries next to find the words that best represent his discovery, the experience becomes even more clear in its shape and meaning. We can imagine Emerson going to the ballet, being absorbed in the spectacle, thinking casually of this or that association the dancer and the movements suggest. When he writes about the experience in his journal, a good many questions, judgments, and speculations get tied up with the spectacle, and it is this complex of event and his total relation to it that becomes the experience he records. The simple facts of time, place, people, and actions drop down into a man's consciousness and set in motion ideas and feelings which give those facts their real meaning to that man.

Once this consciousness of events is formulated in words, the journal-keeper has it, not only in the sense of understanding what he has seen or felt or thought, but also in the sense of having it there before him to contemplate long after the event itself. When we read a carefully kept journal covering a long period and varied experiences, we have the pleasure of a small world re-created for us in the consciousness of one who experienced it. Even more, we feel the continuity, the wholeness, of the person himself. Something of the same feeling is there for the person who kept the journal: a whole world of events preserved in the form of their experienced reality, and with it the persistent self in the midst of that world. That world and that self are always accessible on the page, and ultimately, therefore, usably real.

Beyond the value of the journal as record, there is the instructive value of the habit of mind and hand journal keeping can assure. One begins to attend more carefully to what happens to him and around him. To have discovered, like May Sarton, that attention to small needs and demands that are of the world of nature brings a special peace and relief from depression, is doubtless for her the fruit of years of experience and contemplation. But as she notes again this contemplated fact in her journal, the realization is revitalized, made manifest in the minutiae of a day otherwise undistinguished from many other days. Experience here begins to be related to experience there, apparently dissimilar experiences may not be entirely different, the more and the less important begin to be discriminated. Even in so unlikely a situation for calm contemplation as war is, it is possible, like Pearce, to achieve that moment of detachment which focuses the immediate scene or event for what it is by seeing how it matters in relation to ideas or meanings beyond the battle or the beleaguered city or the desolated church. One begins to see what he is looking at, if he becomes accustomed to the characteristic method and form of the journal entry. All the while, one is learning the resources of language as a means of representing what he sees, and gaining skill and certainty in doing justice to experience and to his own consciousness when he writes.

The journal represents a discipline. It brings together an individual and a complex environment in a relation that teaches the individual something of himself, something of his world, and something of the meaning of their relation. There is scarcely a moment in a person's life when he is not poised for the lesson. When it comes with the promise of special force, there is the almost irresistible temptation to catch the impulse, give it form, make it permanent, assert its meaning. And so one commits himself to language. To have given up one's experience to words is to have begun marking out the limits and potential of its meaning. In the journal that meaning is developed and clarified to oneself primarily. When the whole intention of the development and the clarification is the consideration of another reader, the method of the journal redirects itself to become that of the essay.]

JOAN DIDION: On Keeping a Notebook

" 'That woman Estelle,' " the note reads, " 'is partly the reason why George Sharp and I are separated today.' *Dirty crepe-deChine wrapper, hotel bar, Wilmington RR, 9:45 a.m. August Monday morning."*

Since the note is in my notebook, it presumably has some meaning to me. I study it for a long while. At first I have only the most general notion of what I was doing on an August Monday morning in the bar of the hotel across from the Pennsylvania Railroad station in Wilmington, Delaware (waiting for a train? missing one? 1960? 1961? why Wilmington?), but I do remember being there. The woman in the dirty crepe-de-Chine wrapper had come down from her room for a beer, and the bartender had heard before the reason why George Sharp and she were separated today. "Sure," he said, and went on mopping the floor. "You told me." At the other end of the bar is a girl. She is talking, pointedly, not to the man beside her but to a cat lying in the triangle of sunlight cast through the open door. She is wearing a plaid silk dress from Peck & Peck, and the hem is coming down.

Here is what it is: the girl has been on the Eastern Shore, and now she is going back to the city, leaving the man beside her, and all she can see ahead are the viscous summer sidewalks and the 3 a.m. long-distance calls that will make her lie awake and then sleep drugged through all the steaming mornings left in August (1960? 1961?). Because she must go directly from the train to lunch in New York, she wishes that she had a safety pin for the hem of the plaid silk dress, and she also wishes that she could forget about the hem and the lunch and stay in the cool bar that smells of disinfectant and malt and make friends with the women in the crepe-de-Chine wrapper. She is afflicted by a little self-pity, and she wants to compare Estelles. That is what that was all about.

Why did I write it down? In order to remember, of course, but exactly what was it I wanted to remember? How much of it actually happened? Did any of it? Why do I keep a notebook at all? It is easy to deceive oneself on all those scores. The impulse to write things down is a peculiarly compulsive one, inexplicable to those who do not share it, useful only accidentally, only secondarily, in the way that any compulsion tries to justify itself. I suppose that it begins or does not begin in the cradle. Although I have felt compelled to write things down since I was five years old, I doubt that my daughter ever will, for she is a singularly blessed and accepting child, delighted with life exactly as life presents itself to her, unafraid to go to sleep and unafraid to wake up. Keepers of private notebooks are a different breed altogether, lonely and resistant rearrangers of things, anxious malcontents, children afflicted apparently at birth with some presentiment of loss.

My first notebook was a Big Five tablet, given to me by my mother with the sensible suggestion that I stop whining and learn to amuse myself by writing down my thoughts. She returned the tablet to me a few years ago; the first entry is an account of a woman who believed herself to be freezing to death in the Arctic night, only to find, when day broke, that she had stumbled onto the Sahara Desert, where she would die of the heat before lunch. I have no idea what turn of a five-year-old's mind could have prompted so insistently "ironic" and exotic a story, but it does reveal a certain predilection for the extreme which has dogged me into adult life; perhaps if I were analytically inclined I would find it a truer story than any I might have told about Donald Johnson's birthday party or the day my cousin Brenda put Kitty Litter in the aquarium.

So the point of my keeping a notebook has never been, nor is it now, to have an accurate factual record of what I have been doing or thinking. That would be a different impulse entirely, an instinct for reality which I sometimes envy but do not possess. At no point have I ever been able successfully to keep a diary; my approach to daily life ranges from the grossly negligent to the merely absent, and on those few occasions when I have tried dutifully to record a day's events, boredom has so overcome me that the results are mysterious at best. What is this business about "shopping, typing piece, dinner with E, depressed"? Shopping for what? Typing what piece? Who is E? Was this "E" depressed, or was I depressed? Who cares?

In fact I have abandoned altogether that kind of pointless entry; instead I tell what some would call lies. "That's simply not true," the members of my family frequently tell me when they come up against my memory of a shared event. "The party was *not* for you, the spider was *not* a black widow, *it wasn't that way at all.*" Very likely they are right, for not only have I always had trouble distinguishing between what happened and what merely might have happened, but I remain unconvinced that the distinction, for my purposes, matters. The cracked crab that I recall having for lunch the day my father came home from Detroit in 1945 must certainly be embroidery, worked into the day's pattern to lend verisimilitude; I was ten years old and would not now remember the cracked crab. The day's events did not turn on cracked crab. And yet it is precisely that fictitious crab that makes me see the afternoon all over again, a home movie run all too often, the father bearing gifts, the child weeping, an exercise in family love and guilt. Or that is what it was to me. Similarly, perhaps it never did snow that August in Vermont; perhaps there never were flurries in the night wind, and maybe no one else felt the ground hardening and summer already dead even as we pretended to bask in it, but that was how it felt to me, and it might as well have snowed, could have snowed, **did** snow.

How it felt to me: that is getting closer to the truth about a notebook. I sometimes delude myself about why I keep a notebook, imagine that some thrifty virtue derives from preserving everything observed. See enough and write it down, I tell myself, and then some morning when the world seems drained of wonder, some day when I am only going through the motions of doing what I am supposed to do, which is write—on that bankrupt morning I will simply open my notebook and there it will all be, a forgotten account with accumulated interest, paid passage back to the world out there: dialogue overheard in hotels and elevators and at the hatcheck counter in Pavillon (one middle-aged man shows his hat check to another and says, "That's my old football number"); impressions of Bettina Aptheker and Benjamin Sonnenberg and Teddy ("Mr. Acapulco") Stauffer; careful *aperçus* about tennis bums and failed fashion models and Greek shipping heiresses, one of whom taught me a significant lesson (a lesson I could have learned from F. Scott Fitzgerald, but perhaps we all must meet the very rich for ourselves) by asking, when I arrived to interview her in her orchid-filled sitting room on the second day of a paralyzing New York blizzard, whether it was snowing outside.

I imagine, in other words, that the notebook is about other people. But of course it is not. I have no real business with what one stranger said to another at the hat-check counter in Pavillon; in fact I suspect that the line "That's my old football number" touched not my own imagination at all, but merely some memory of something once read, probably "The Eighty-Yard Run." Nor is my concern with a woman in a dirty crepe-de-Chine wrapper in a Wilmington bar. My stake is always, of course, in the unmentioned girl in the plaid silk dress. *Remember what it was to be me*: that is always the point.

It is a difficult point to admit. We are brought up in the ethic that others, any others, all others, are by definition more interesting than ourselves; taught to be diffident, just this side of self-effacing. ("You're the least important person in the room and don't forget it," Jessica Mitford's governess would hiss in her ear on the advent of any social occasion; I copied that into my notebook because it is only recently that I have been able to enter a room without hearing some such phrase in my inner ear.) Only the very young and the very old may recount their dreams at breakfast, dwell upon self, interrupt with memories of beach picnics and favorite Liberty lawn dresses and the rainbow trout in a creek near Colorado Springs. The rest of us are expected, rightly, to affect absorption in other people's favorite dresses, other people's trout.

And so we do. But our notebooks give us away, for however dutifully we record what we see around us, the common denominator of all we see is always, transparently, shamelessly, the implacable "I." We are not talking here about the kind of notebook that is patently for public consumption, a structural conceit for binding together a series of graceful *pensées;* we are talking about something private, about bits of the mind's string too short to use, an indiscriminate and erratic assemblage with meaning only for its maker.

And sometimes even the maker has difficulty with the meaning. There does not seem to be, for example, any point in my knowing for the rest of my life that, during 1964, 720 tons of soot fell on every square mile of New York City, yet there it is in my notebook, labeled "FACT." Nor do I really need to remember that Ambrose Bierce liked to spell Leland Stanford's name "£eland $anford" or that "smart women almost always wear black in Cuba," a fashion hint without much potential for practical application. And does not the relevance of these notes seem marginal at best?:

In the basement museum of the Inyo County Courthouse in Independence, California, sign pinned to a mandarin coat: "This MANDARIN COAT was often worn by Mrs. Minnie S. Brooks when giving lectures on her TEAPOT COLLECTION."
Redhead getting out of car in front of Beverly Wilshire Hotel, chinchilla stole, Vuitton bags with tags reading:

MRS LOU FOX
HOTEL SAHARA
VEGAS

Well, perhaps not entirely marginal. As a matter of fact, Mrs. Minnie S. Brooks and her MANDARIN COAT pull me back into my own childhood, for although I never knew Mrs. Brooks and did not visit Inyo County until I was thirty, I grew up in just such a world, in houses cluttered with Indian relics and bits of gold ore and ambergris and the souvenirs my Aunt Mercy Farnsworth brought back from the Orient. It is a long way from that world to Mrs. Lou Fox's world, where we all live now, and is it not just as well to remember that? Might not Mrs. Minnie S. Brooks help me to remember what I am? Might not Mrs. Lou Fox help me to remember what I am not?

But sometimes the point is harder to discern. What exactly did I have in mind when I noted down that it cost the father of someone I know $650 a month to light the place on the Hudson in which he lived before the Crash? What use was I planning to make of this line by Jimmy Hoffa: "I may have my faults, but being wrong ain't one of them"? And although I think it interesting to know where the girls who travel with the Syndicate have their hair done when they find themselves on the West Coast, will I ever make suitable use of it? Might I not be better off just passing it on to John O'Hara? What is a recipe for sauerkraut doing in my notebook? What kind of magpie keeps this notebook? *"He was born the night the Titanic went down."* That seems a nice enough line, and I even recall who said it, but is it not really a better line in life than it could ever be in fiction?

But of course that is exactly it: not that I should ever use the line, but that I should remember the woman who said it and the afternoon I heard it. We were on her terrace by the sea, and we were finishing the wine left from lunch, trying to get what sun there was, a California winter sun. The woman whose husband was born the night the *Titanic* went down wanted to rent her house, wanted to go back to her children in Paris. I remember wishing that I could afford the house, which cost $1,000 a month. "Someday you will," she said lazily. "Someday it all comes." There in the sun on her terrace it seemed easy to believe in someday, but later I had a low-grade afternoon hangover and ran over a black snake on the way to the supermarket and was flooded with inexplicable fear when I heard the checkout clerk explaining to the man ahead of me why she was finally divorcing her husband. "He left me no choice," she said over and over as she punched the register. "He has a little seven-month-old baby by her, he left me no choice." I would like to believe that my dread then was for the human condition, but of course it was for me, because I wanted a baby and did not then have one and because I wanted to own the house that cost $1,000 a month to rent and because I had a hangover.

It all comes back. Perhaps it is difficult to see the value in having one's self back in that kind of mood, but I do see it; I think we are well advised to keep on nodding terms with the people we used to be whether we find them attractive company or not. Otherwise they turn up unannounced and surprise us, come hammering on the mind's door at 4 a.m. of a bad night and demand to know who deserted them, who betrayed them, who is going to make amends. We forget all too soon the things we thought we could never forget. We forget the loves and the betrayals alike, forget what we whispered and what we screamed, forget who we were. I have already lost touch with a couple of people I used to be; one of them, a seventeen-year-old, presents little threat, although it would be of some interest to me to know again what it feels like to sit on a river levee drinking vodka-and-orange-juice and listening to Les Paul and Mary Ford and their echoes sing "How High the Moon" on the car radio. (You see I still have the scenes, but I no longer perceive myself among those present, no longer could even improvise the dialogue.) The other one, a twenty-three-year-old, bothers me more. She was always a good deal of trouble, and I suspect she will reappear when I least want to see her, skirts too long, shy to the point of aggravation, always the injured party, full of recriminations and little hurts and stories I do not want to hear again, at once saddening me and angering me with her vulnerability and ignorance, an apparition all the more insistent for being so long banished.

It is a good idea, then, to keep in touch, and I suppose that keeping in touch is what notebooks are all about. And we are all on our own when it comes to keeping those lines open to ourselves: your notebook will never help me, nor mine you. *"So what's new in the whiskey business?"* What could that possibly mean to you? To me it means a blonde in a Pucci bathing suit sitting with a couple of fat men by the pool at the Beverly Hills Hotel. Another man approaches, and they all regard one another in silence for a while. "So what's new in the whiskey business?" one of the fat men finally says by way of welcome, and the blonde stands up, arches one foot and dips it in the pool, looking all the while at the cabaña where Baby Pignatari is talking on the telephone. That is all there is to that, except that several years later I saw the blonde coming out of Saks Fifth Avenue in New York with her California complexion and a voluminous mink coat. In the harsh wind that day she looked old and irrevocably tired to me, and even the skins in the mink coat were not worked the way they were doing them that year, not the way she would have wanted them done, and there is the point of the story. For a while after that I did not like to look in the mirror, and my eyes would skim the newspapers and pick out only the deaths, the cancer victims, the premature coronaries, the suicides, and I stopped riding the Lexington Avenue IRT because I noticed for the first time that all the strangers I had seen for years—the man with the seeing-eye dog, the spinster who read the classified pages every day, the fat girl who always got off with me at Grand Central—looked older than they once had.

It all comes back. Even that recipe for sauerkraut: even that brings it back. I was on Fire Island when I first made that sauerkraut, and it was raining, and we drank a lot of bourbon and ate the sauerkraut and went to bed at ten, and I listened to the rain and the Atlantic and felt safe. I made the sauerkraut again last night and it did not make me feel any safer, but that is, as they say, another story.

RALPH WALDO EMERSON: *from* Journal

I like to have a man's knowledge comprehend more than one class of topics, one row of shelves. I like a man who likes to see a fine barn as well as a good tragedy. [1828]

The Religion that is afraid of science dishonors God and commits suicide. [1831]

The things taught in colleges and schools are not an education, but the means of education. [1831]

Don't tell me to get ready to die. I know not what shall be. The only preparation I can make is by fulfilling my present duties. This is the everlasting life. [1832]

My aunt [Mary Moody Emerson] had an eye that went through and through you like a needle. "She was endowed," she said, "with the fatal gift of penetration." She disgusted everybody because she knew them too well. [1832]

I am sure of this, that by going much alone a man will get more of a noble courage in thought and word than from all the wisdom that is in books. [1833]

I fretted the other night at the hotel at the stranger who broke into my chamber after midnight, claiming to share it. But after his lamp had smoked the chamber full and I had turned round to the wall in despair, the man blew out his lamp, knelt down at his bedside, and made in low whisper a long earnest prayer. Then was the relation entirely changed between us. I fretted no more, but respected and liked him. [1835]

I believe I shall some time cease to be an individual, that the eternal tendency of the soul is to become Universal, to animate the last extremities of organization. [1837]

It is very hard to be simple enough to be good. [1837]

A man must have aunts and cousins, must buy carrots and turnips, must have barn and woodshed, must go to market and to the blacksmith's shop, must saunter and sleep and be inferior and silly. [1838]

How sad a spectacle, so frequent nowadays, to see a young man after ten years of college education come out, ready for his voyage of life—and to see that the entire ship is made of rotten timber, of rotten, honeycombed, traditional timber without so much as an inch of new plank in the hull. [1839]

A sleeping child gives me the impression of a traveler in a very far country. [1840]

In reading these letters of M.M.E. I acknowledge (with surprise that I could ever forget it) the debt of myself and my brothers to that old religion which, in those years, still dwelt like a Sabbath peace in the country population of New England, which taught privation, self-denial, and sorrow. A man was born, not for prosperity, but to suffer for the benefit of others, like the noble rock-maple tree which all around the villages bleeds for the service of man. Not praise, not men's acceptance of our doing, but the Spirit's holy errand through us, absorbed the thought. How dignified is this! how all that is called talents and worth in Paris and in Washington dwindles before it! [1841]

All writing is by the grace of God. People do not deserve to have good writing, they are so pleased with bad. In these sentences that you show me, I can find no beauty, for I see death in every clause and every word. There is a fossil or a mummy character which pervades this book. The best sepulchers, the vastest catacombs, Thebes and Cairo, Pyramids, are sepulchers to me. I like gardens and nurseries. Give me initiative, spermatic, prophesying, man-making words. [1841]

When summer opens, I see how fast it matures, and fear it will be short; but after the heats of July and August, I am reconciled, like one who has had his swing, to the cool of autumn. So will it be with the coming of death. [1846]

In England every man you meet is some man's son; in America, he may be some man's father. [1848]

Every poem must be made up of lines that are poems. [1848]

Love is necessary to the righting the estate of woman in this world. Otherwise nature itself seems to be in conspiracy against her dignity and welfare; for the cultivated, high-thoughted, beauty-loving, saintly woman finds herself unconsciously desired for her sex, and even enhancing the appetite of her savage pursuers by these fine ornaments she has piously laid on herself. She finds with indignation that she is herself a snare, and was made such. I do not wonder at her occasional protest, violent protest against nature, in fleeing to nunneries, and taking black veils. Love rights all this deep wrong. [1848]

Natural Aristocracy. It is a vulgar error to suppose that a gentleman must be ready to fight. The utmost that can be demanded of the gentleman is that he be incapable of a lie. There is a man who has good sense, is well informed, well-read, obliging, cultivated, capable, and has an absolute devotion to truth. He always means what he says, and says what he means, however courteously. You may spit upon him—nothing could induce him to spit upon you—no praises, and no possessions, no compulsion of public opinion. You may kick him—he will think it the kick of a brute—but he is not a brute, and will not kick you in return. But neither your knife and pistol, nor your gifts and courting will ever make the smallest impression on his vote or word; for he is the truth's man, and will speak and act the truth until he dies. [1849]

Love is temporary and ends with marriage. Marriage is the perfection which love aimed at, ignorant of what it sought. Marriage is a good known only to the parties—a relation of perfect understanding, aid, contentment, possession of themselves and of the world—which dwarfs love to green fruit. [1850]

I found when I had finished my new lecture that it was a very good house, only the architect had unfortunately omitted the stairs. [1851]

This filthy enactment [The Fugitive Slave Law] was made in the nineteenth century, by people who could read and write. I will not obey it, by God. [1851]

Henry [Thoreau] is military. He seemed stubborn and implacable; always manly and wise, but rarely sweet. One would say that, as Webster could never speak without an antagonist, so Henry does not feel himself except in opposition. He wants a fallacy to expose, a blunder to pillory, requires a little sense of victory, a roll of the drums, to call his powers into full exercise. [1853]

Shall we judge the country by the majority or by the minority? Certainly, by the minority. The mass are animal, in state of pupilage, and nearer the chimpanzee. [1854]

All the thoughts of a turtle are turtle. [1854]

Resources or feats. I like people who can do things. When Edward and I struggled in vain to drag our big calf into the barn, the Irish girl put her finger into the calf's mouth, and led her in directly. [1862]

George Francis Train said in a public speech in New York, "Slavery is a divine institution." "So is hell," exclaimed an old man in the crowd. [1862]

You complain that the Negroes are a base class. Who makes and keeps the Jew or the Negro base, who but you, who exclude them from the rights which others enjoy? [1867]

HENRY DAVID THOREAU: *from* Journal

As the least drop of wine tinges the whole goblet, so the least particle of truth colors our whole life. It is never isolated, or simply added as treasure to our stock. When any real progress is made, we unlearn and learn anew what we thought we knew before. [1837]

Not by constraint or severity shall you have access to true wisdom, but by abandonment, and childlike mirthfulness. If you would know aught, be gay before it. [1840]

It is the man determines what is said, not the words. If a mean person uses a wise maxim, I bethink me how it can be interpreted so as to commend itself to his meanness; but if a wise man makes a commonplace remark, I consider what wider construction it will admit. [1840]

Nothing goes by luck in composition. It allows of no tricks. The best you can write will be the best you are. Every sentence is the result of a long probation. The author's character is read from title-page to end. Of this he never corrects the proofs. We read it as the essential character of a handwriting without regard to the flourishes. And so of the rest of our actions; it runs as straight as a ruled line through them all, no matter how many curvets about it. Our whole life is taxed for the least thing well done: it is its net result. How we eat, drink, sleep, and use our desultory hours, now in these indifferent days, with no eye to observe and no occasion [to] excite us, determines our authority and capacity for the time to come. [1841]

What does education often do? It makes a straight-cut ditch of a free, meandering brook. [1850]

All perception of truth is the detection of an analogy; we reason from our hands to our head. [1851]

To set down such choice experiences that my own writings may inspire me and at last I may make wholes of parts. Certainly it is a distinct profession to rescue from oblivion and to fix the sentiments and thoughts which visit all men more or less generally, that the contemplation of the unfinished picture may suggest its harmonious completion. Associate reverently and as much as you can with your loftiest thoughts. Each thought that is welcomed and recorded is a nest egg, by the side of which more will be laid. Thoughts accidentally thrown together become a frame in which more may be developed and exhibited. Perhaps this is the main value of a habit of writing, of keeping a journal—that so we remember our best hours and stimulate ourselves. My thoughts are my company. They have a certain individuality and separate existence, aye, personality. Having by chance recorded a few disconnected thoughts and then brought them into juxtaposition, they suggest a whole new field in which it was possible to labor and to think. Thought begat thought. [1852]

It is pardonable when we spurn the proprieties, even the sanctities, making them stepping-stones to something higher. [1858]

There is always some accident in the best things, whether thoughts or expressions or deeds. The memorable thought, the happy expression, the admirable deed are only partly ours. The thought came to us because we were in a fit mood; also we were unconscious and did not know that we had said or done a good thing. We must walk consciously only part way toward our goal, and then leap in the dark to our success. What we do best or most perfectly is what we have most thoroughly learned by the longest practice, and at length it falls from us without our notice, as a leaf from a tree. It is the *last* time we shall do it—our unconscious leavings. [1859]

The expression "a *liberal* education" originally meant one worthy of freemen. Such is education simply in a true and broad sense. But education ordinarily so called—the learning of trades and professions which is designed to enable men to earn their living, or to fit them for a particular station in life—is *servile*. [1859]

ANAÏS NIN:[1] *from* The Diary

* * *

Beautiful flow between Durrell, Henry, Nancy[2] and me. It is while we talk together that I discover how we mutually nourish each other, stimulate each other. I discover my own strength as an artist, for Henry and Durrell often ally themselves against me. Henry's respect is also reawakened by Durrell's admiration for me. My feeling for woman's inarticulateness is reawakened by Nancy's stutterings and stumblings, and her loyalty to me as the one who does not betray woman but seeks to speak for her. A marvelous talk, in which Henry unmasked Durrell and me, and when Durrell said: "And now we must unmask Henry," I answered: "We can't, because he has done it himself." Henry is the strongest because he is not afraid of being alone. Larry is afraid. I am afraid. And we confessed it.

They suddenly attacked my personal relation to all things, by personification of ideas. I defended myself by saying that relating was an act of life. To make history or psychology alive I personify

---

1. Anaïs (pron. Ah-na-ees), according to Ms. Nin a common given name in France.

2. Lawrence Durrell, Henry Miller, and Nancy Miller.

it. Also everything depends on the nature of the personal relationship. My self is like the self of Proust. It is an instrument to connect life and the myth.* * *

When they discussed the problem of my diary, all the art theories were involved. They talked about the geological changes undergone with time, and that it was the product of this change we called art. I asserted that such a process could take place instantaneously.

Henry said: "But that would upset all the art theories."

I said: "I can give you an example. I can feel the potentialities of our talk tonight while it is happening as well as six months later. Look at the birth story. It varies very little in its polished form from the way I told it in the diary immediately after it happened. The new version was written three years later. Objectivity may bring a more rounded picture, but the absence of it, empathy, feeling with it, immersion in it, may bring some other kind of connection with it."

Henry asked; "But then, why did you feel the need of rewriting it?"

"For a greater technical perfection. Not to re-create it."

Larry, who before had praised me for writing as a woman, for not breaking the umbilical connection, said: "You must rewrite *Hamlet*."

"Why should I, if that is not the kind of writing I wish to do?"

Larry said; "You must make the leap outside of the womb, destroy your connections."

"I know," I said, "that this is an important talk, and that it will be at this moment that we each go different ways. Perhaps Henry and Larry will go the same way, but I will have to go another, the woman's way."

At the end of the conversation they both said: "We have a real woman artist before us, the first one, and we ought not to put her down."

I know Henry is the artist because he does exactly what I do not do. He waits. He gets outside of himself. Until it becomes fiction. It is all fiction.

I am not interested in fiction. I want faithfulness.

All I know is that I am right, right for me. If today I can talk both woman's and man's language, if I can translate woman to man and man to woman, it is because I do not believe in man's objectivity. In all his ideas, systems, philosophies, arts come from a personal source he does not wish to admit. Henry and Larry are pretending to be impersonal. Larry has the English complex. But it is a disguise.

Poor woman, how difficult it is to make her instinctive knowledge clear!

"Shut up," says Larry to Nancy. She looks at me strangely, as if expecting me to defend her, explain her. Nancy, I won't shut up. I have a great deal to say, for June,[3] for you, for other women.

As to all that nonsense Henry and Larry talked about, the necessity of "I am God" in order to create (I suppose they mean "I am God, I am not a woman"). Woman never had direct communication with God anyway, but only through man, the priest. She never created directly except through man, was never able to create as a woman. But what neither Larry nor Henry understands is that woman's creation far from being like man's must be exactly like her creation of children, that is it must come out of her own blood, englobed by her womb, nourished with her own milk. It must be a human creation, of flesh, it must be different from man's abstractions. As to this "I am God," which makes creation an act of solitude and pride, this image of God alone making sky, earth, sea, it is this image which has confused woman. (Man too, because he thinks God did it all alone, and he thinks he did it all alone. And behind every achievement of man lies a woman, and I am sure God was helped too but never acknowledged it.)

Woman does not forget she needs the fecundator, she does not forget that everything that is born of her is planted in her. If she forgets this she is lost. What will be marvelous to contemplate will not be her solitude but this image of woman being visited at night by man and the marvelous things she will give birth to in the morning. God alone, creating, may be a beautiful spectacle. I don't know. Man's objectivity may be an imitation of this God so detached from us and human emotion. But a woman alone creating is not a beautiful spectacle. The woman was born mother, mistress, wife, sister, she was born to represent union, communion, communication, she was born to give birth to life, and not to insanity. It is man's separateness, his so-called objectivity, which has made him lose contact, and then his reason. Woman was born to *be* the connecting link between man and his human self. Between abstract ideas and the personal pattern which creates them. Man, to create, must become man.

Women has this life-role, but the woman artist has to fuse creation and life in her own way, or in her own womb if you prefer. She has to create something different from man. Man created a world cut off from nature. Woman has to create within the mystery, storms, terrors, the infernos of sex, the battle against abstractions and art. She has to sever herself from the myth man creates, from being created by him, she has to struggle with her own cycles, storms, terrors which man does not understand. Woman wants to destroy aloneness, recover the original paradise. The art of woman

3. June Miller.

must be born in the womb-cells of the mind. She must be the link between the synthetic products of man's mind and the elements.

I do not delude myself as man does, that I create in proud isolation. I say we are bound, interdependent. Woman is not deluded. She must create without these proud delusions of man, without megalomania, without schizophrenia, without madness. She must create that unity which man first destroyed by his proud consciousness.

Henry and Larry tried to lure me out of the womb. They call it objectivity. No woman died the kind of death Rimbaud died. I have never seen in a woman a skeleton like Fraenkel,[4] killed by the dissections of analysis, the leprosy of egotism, the black pest of the brain cells.

Man today is like a tree that is withering at the roots. And most women painted and wrote nothing but imitations of phalluses. The world was filled with phalluses, like totem poles, and no womb anywhere. I must go the opposite way from Proust who found eternal moments in creation. I must find them in life. My work must be the closest to the life flow. I must install myself inside of the seed, growth, mysteries. I must prove the possibility of instantaneous, immediate, spontaneous art. My art must be like a miracle. Before it goes through the conduits of the brain and becomes an abstraction, a fiction, a lie. It must be for woman, more like a personified ancient ritual, where every spiritual thought was made visible, enacted, represented.

A sense of the infinite in the present, as the child has.

Woman's role in creation should be parallel to her role in life. I don't mean the good earth. I mean the bad earth too, the demon, the instincts, the storms of nature. Tragedies, conflicts, mysteries are personal. Man fabricated a detachment which became fatal. Woman must not fabricate. She must descend into the real womb and expose its secrets and its labyrinths. She must describe it as the city of Fez, with its Arabian Nights gentleness, tranquility and mystery. She must describe the voracious moods, the desires, the worlds contained in each cell of it. For the womb has dreams. It is not as simple as the good earth. I believe at times that man created art out of fear of exploring woman. I believe woman stuttered about herself out of fear of what she had to say. She covered herself with taboos and veils. Man invented a woman to suit his needs. He disposed of her by identifying her with nature and then paraded his contemptuous domination of nature. But woman is not nature only.

She is the mermaid with her fish-tail dipped in the unconscious. Her creation will be to make articulate this obscure world which

---

4. Arthur Rimbaud (1854–1891), a French poet who died in a hospital in Marseilles after his return from Africa; Michael Fraenkel (1896–1957), a bookseller and minor literary figure in Paris during the thirties.

dominates man, which he denies being dominated by, but which asserts its domination in destructive proofs of its presence, madness.

Note by Durrell: "Anaïs is *unanswerable*. Completely unanswerable. I fold up and give in. What she says is biologically true from the very navel strings."

MAY SARTON: *from* Journal of a Solitude

September 17th. Cracking open the inner world again, writing even a couple of pages, threw me back into depression, not made easier by the weather, two gloomy days of darkness and rain. I was attacked by a storm of tears, those tears that appear to be related to frustration, to buried anger, and come upon me without warning. I woke yesterday so depressed that I did not get up till after eight.

I drove to Brattleboro[1] to read poems at the new Unitarian church there in a state of dread and exhaustion. How to summon the vitality needed? I had made an arrangement of religious poems, going back to early books and forward into the new book not yet published. I suppose it went all right—at least it was not a disaster —but I felt (perhaps I am wrong) that the kind, intelligent people gathered in a big room looking out on pine trees did not really want to think about God. His absence (many of the poems speak of that) or His presence. Both are too frightening.

On the way back I stopped to see Perley Cole, my dear old friend, who is dying, separated from his wife, and has just been moved from a Dickensian nursing home into what seems like a far better one. He grows more transparent every day, a skeleton or nearly. Clasping his hand, I fear to break a bone. Yet the only real communication between us now (he is very deaf) is a handclasp. I want to lift him in my arms and hold him like a baby. He is dying a terribly lonely death. Each time I see him he says, "It is rough" or "I did not think it would end like this."

Everywhere I look about this place I see his handiwork: the three small trees by a granite boulder that he pruned and trimmed so they pivot the whole meadow; the new shady border he dug out for me one of the last days he worked here; the pruned-out stone wall between my field and the church. The second field where he cut brush twice a year and cleared out to the stone wall is growing back to wilderness now. What is done here has to be done over and over and needs the dogged strength of a man like Perley. I could have never managed it alone. We cherished this piece of land together, and fought together to bring it to some semblance of order and beauty.

I like to think that this last effort of Perley's had a certain ease about it, a game compared to the hard work of his farming years,

1. Brattleboro, Vermont.

and a game where his expert knowledge and skill could be well used. How he enjoyed teasing me about my ignorance!

While he scythed and trimmed, I struggled in somewhat the same way at my desk here, and we were each aware of the companionship. We each looked forward to noon, when I could stop for the day and he sat on a high stool in the kitchen, drank a glass or two of sherry with me, said, "Court's in session!" and then told me some tall tale he had been cogitating all morning.

It was a strange relationship, for he knew next to nothing about my life, really; yet below all the talk we recognized each other as the same kind. He enjoyed my anger as much as I enjoyed his. Perhaps that was part of it. Deep down there was understanding, not of the facts of our lives so much as of our essential natures. Even now in his hard, lonely end he has immense dignity. But I wish there were some way to make it easier. I leave him with bitter resentment against the circumstances of this death. "I know. But I did not approve. And I am not resigned."

In the mail a letter from a twelve-year-old child, enclosing poems, her mother having pushed her to ask my opinion. The child does really look at things, and I can write something helpful, I think. But it is troubling how many people expect applause, recognition, when they have not even begun to learn an art or a craft. Instant success is the order of the day; "I want it *now!*" I wonder whether this is not part of our corruption by machines. Machines do things very quickly and outside the natural rhythm of life, and we are indignant if a car doesn't start at the first try. So the few things that we still do, such as cooking (though there are TV dinners!), knitting, gardening, anything at all that cannot be hurried, have a very particular value.

September 18th. The value of solitude—one of its values—is, of course, that there is nothing to *cushion* against attacks from within, just as there is nothing to help balance at times of particular stress or depression. A few moments of desultory conversation with dear Arnold Miner, when he comes to take the trash, may calm an inner storm. But the storm, painful as it is, might have had some truth in it. So sometimes one has simply to endure a period of depression for what it may hold of illumination if one can live through it, attentive to what it exposes or demands.

The reasons for depression are not so interesting as the way one handles it, simply to stay alive. This morning I woke at four and lay awake for an hour or so in a bad state. It is raining again. I got up finally and went about the daily chores, waiting for the sense of doom to lift—and what did it was watering the house plants. Suddenly joy came back because I was fulfilling a simple need, a living one. Dusting never has this effect (and that may be why I am such a poor housekeeper!), but feeding the cats when they are hungry, giving Punch clean water, makes me suddenly feel calm and happy.

Whatever peace I know rests in the natural world, in feeling myself a part of it, even in a small way. Maybe the gaiety of the Warner family, their wisdom, comes from this, that they work close to nature all the time. As simple as that? But it is not simple. Their life requires patient understanding, imagination, the power to endure constant adversity—the weather, for example! To go with, not against the elements, an inexhaustible vitality summoned back each day to do the same tasks, to feed the animals, clean out barns and pens, keep that complex world alive.

October 6th. A day when I am expecting someone for lunch is quite unlike ordinary days. There is a reason to make the flowers look beautiful all over the house, and I know that Anne Woodson, who is coming today, will notice them, for she sees this house in a way that few of my friends do, perhaps because she has lived here without me, has lived her way into the place by pruning and weeding, and once even tidying the linen cupboard!

It is a mellow day, very gentle. The ash has lost its leaves and when I went out to get the mail and stopped to look up at it, I rejoiced to think that soon everything here will be honed down to structure. It is all a rich farewell now to leaves, to color. I think of the trees and how simply they let go, let fall the riches of a season, how without grief (it seems) they can let go and go deep into their roots for renewal and sleep. Eliot's statement comes back to me these days:

> Teach us to care and not to care
> Teach us to sit still.[2]

It is there in Mahler's *Der Abschied,* which I play again every autumn (Bruno Walter with Kathleen Ferrier).[3] But in Mahler it is a cry of loss, a long lyrical cry just *before* letting go, at least until those last long phrases that suggest peace, renunciation. But I think of it as the golden leaves and the brilliant small red maple that shone transparent against the shimmer of the lake yesterday when I went over to have a picnic with Helen Milbank.

Does anything in nature despair except man? An animal with a foot caught in a trap does not seem to despair. It is too busy trying to survive. It is all closed in, to a kind of still, intense waiting. Is this a key? Keep busy with survival. Imitate the trees. Learn to lose in order to recover, and remember that nothing stays the same for long, not even pain, psychic pain. Sit it out. Let it all pass. Let it go.

2. From T. S. Eliot's *Ash Wednesday* (1930), lines 38–39.

3. A famous record of Mahler's song "The Farewell," evocative of the coming of winter and death. Mahler died before it could be performed, and the premiere was conducted by his disciple Bruno Walter. Kathleen Ferrier was to die within a few years of recording the song.

Yesterday I weeded out violets from the iris bed. The iris was being choked by thick bunches of roots, so much like fruit under the earth. I found one single very fragrant violet and some small autumn crocuses. Now, after an hour's work as the light failed and I drank in the damp smell of earth, it looks orderly again.

October 9th. Has it really happened at last? I feel released from the rack, set free, in touch with the deep source that is only *good,* where poetry lives. We have waited long this year for the glory, but suddenly the big maple is all gold and the beeches yellow with a touch of green that makes the yellow even more intense. There are still nasturtiums to be picked, and now I must get seriously to work to get the remaining bulbs in.

It has been stupidly difficult to let go, but that is what has been needed. I had allowed myself to get overanxious, clutching at what seemed sure to pass, and clutching is the surest way to murder love, as if it were a kitten, not to be squeezed so hard, or a flower to fade in a tight hand. Letting go, I have come back yesterday and today to a sense of my life here in all its riches, depth, freedom for soul-making.

It's a real break-through. I have not written in sonnet form for a long time, but at every major crisis in my life when I reach a point of clarification, where pain is transcended by the quality of the experience itself, sonnets come. Whole lines run through my head and I cannot *stop* writing until whatever it is gets said.

Found three huge mushrooms when I went out before breakfast to fill the bird feeder. So far only jays come, but the word will get around.

October 11th. The joke is on me. I filled this weekend with friends so that I would not go down into depression, not knowing that I should have turned the corner and be writing poems. It is the climactic moment of autumn, but already I feel like Sleeping Beauty as the carpet of leaves on the front lawn gets thicker and thicker. The avenue of beeches as I drive up the winding road along the brook is glorious beyond words, wall on wall of transparent gold. Laurie Armstrong came for roast beef Sunday dinner. Then I went out for two hours late in the afternoon and put in a hundred tulips. In itself that would not be a big job, but everywhere I have to clear space for them, weed, divide perennials, rescue iris that is being choked by violets. I really get to weeding only in spring and autumn, so I am working through a jungle now. Doing it I feel strenuously happy and at peace. At the end of the afternoon on a gray day, the light is sad and one feels the chill, but the bitter smell of earth is a tonic.

I can hardly believe that relief from the anguish of these past months is here to stay, but so far it does feel like a true change of mood—or rather, a change of *being* where I can stand alone. So much of my life here is precarious. I cannot always believe even in my work. But I have come in these last days to feel again the validity of my struggle here, that it is meaningful whether I ever "succeed" as a writer or not, and that even its failures, failures of nerve, failures due to a difficult temperament, can be meaningful. It is an age where more and more human beings are caught up in lives where fewer and fewer inward decisions can be made, where fewer and fewer real choices exist. The fact that a middle-aged, single woman, without any vestige of family left, lives in this house in a silent village and is responsible only to her own soul means something. The fact that she is a writer and can tell where she is and what it is like on the pilgrimage inward can be of comfort. It is comforting to know there are lighthouse keepers on rocky islands along the coast. Sometimes, when I have been for a walk after dark and see my house lighted up, looking so alive, I feel that my presence here is worth all the Hell.

I have time to think. That is the great, the greatest luxury. I have time to be. Therefore my responsibility is huge. To use time well and to be all that I can in whatever years are left to me. This does not dismay. The dismay comes when I lose the sense of my life as connected (as if by an aerial) to many, many other lives whom I do not even know and cannot ever know. The signals go out and come in all the time.

Why is it that poetry always seems to me so much more a true work of the soul than prose? I never feel elated after writing a page of prose, though I have written good things on concentrated will, and at least in a novel the imagination is fully engaged. Perhaps it is that prose is earned and poetry given. Both can be revised almost indefinitely. I do not mean to say that I do not work at poetry. When I am really inspired I can put a poem through a hundred drafts and keep my excitement. But this sustained battle is possible only when I am in a state of grace, when the deep channels are open, and when they are, when I am both profoundly stirred and balanced, then poetry comes as a gift from powers beyond my will.

I have often imagined that if I were in solitary confinement for an indefinite time and knew that no one would ever read what I wrote, I would still write poetry, but I would not write novels. Why? Perhaps because the poem is primarily a dialogue with the self and the novel a dialogue with others. They come from entirely different modes of being. I suppose I have written novels to find out what I *thought* about something and poems to find out what I *felt* about something.

January 7th. I have worked all morning—and it is now afternoon —to try to make by sheer art and craft an ending to the first stanza of a lyric that shot through my head intact. I should not feel so pressed for time, but I do, and I suppose I always shall. Yeats speaks of spending a week on one stanza. The danger, of course, is overmanipulation, when one finds oneself manipulating *words*, not images or concepts. My problem was to make a transition viable between lovers in a snowstorm and the whiteness of a huge amaryllis I look at across the hall in the cosy room—seven huge flowers that make constant silent hosannas as I sit here.

In a period of happy and fruitful isolation such as this, any interruption, any intrusion of the social, any obligation breaks the thread on my loom, breaks the pattern. Two nights ago I was called at the last minute to attend the caucus of Town Meeting . . . and it threw me. But at least the companionship gave me one insight: a neighbor told me she had been in a small car accident and had managed to persuade the local paper to ignore her true age (as it appears on her license) and to print her age as thirty-nine! I was really astonished by this confidence. I am proud of being fifty-eight, and still alive and kicking, in love, more creative, balanced, and potent than I have ever been. I mind certain physical deteriorations, but not *really*. And not at all when I look at the marvelous photograph that Bill sent me of Isak Dinesen just before she died. For after all we make our faces as we go along, and who when young could ever look as she does? The ineffable sweetness of the smile, the total acceptance and joy one receives from it, life, death, everything taken in and, as it were, savored—and let go.

Wrinkles here and there seem unimportant compared to *Gestalt* of the whole person I have become in this past year. Somewhere in *The Poet and the Donkey* Andy speaks for me when he says, "Do not deprive me of my age. I have earned it."

My neighbor's wish to be known forever as thirty-nine years old made me think again of what K said in her letter about the people in their thirties mourning their lost youth because we have given them no ethos that makes maturity appear an asset. Yet we have many examples before us. It looks as if T. S. Eliot came into a fully consummated happy marriage only when he was seventy. Yeats[4] married when he was fifty or over. I am coming into the most fulfilled love of my life now. But for some reason Americans are terrified of the very idea of passionate love going on past middle age. Are they afraid of being alive? Do they want to be dead, i.e., *safe*? For of course one is never safe when in love. Growth is demanding and may seem dangerous, for there is loss as well as gain in growth. But why go on living if one has ceased to grow? And what more demanding atmosphere for growth than love in any form, than any relationship which can call out and requires of us our most secret and deepest selves?

My neighbor who wishes to remain thirty-nine indefinitely does so out of anxiety—she is afraid she will no longer be "attractive" if

---

4. William Butler Yeats, 1865–1939. Irish poet and dramatist.

people know her age. But if one wants mature relationships, one will look for them among one's peers. I cannot imagine being in love with someone much younger than I because I have looked on love as an *éducation sentimentale*. About love I have little to learn from the young.

January 8th. Yesterday was a strange, hurried, uncentered day; yet I did not have to go out, the sun shone. Today I feel centered and time is a friend instead of the old enemy. It was zero this morning. I have a fire burning in my study, yellow roses and mimosa on my desk. There is an atmosphere of festival, of release, in the house. We are one, the house and I, and I am happy to be alone—time to think, time to be. This kind of open-ended time is the only luxury that really counts and I feel stupendously rich to have it. And for the moment I have a sense of fulfillment both about my life and about my work that I have rarely experienced until this year, or perhaps until these last weeks. I look to my left and the transparent blue sky behind a flame-colored cyclamen, lifting about thirty winged flowers to the light, makes an impression of stained glass, light-flooded. I have put the vast heap of unanswered letters into a box at my feet, so I don't see them. And now I am going to make one more try to get that poem right. The last line is still the problem.

WOODY ALLEN: Selections from the Allen Notebooks

Following are excerpts from the hitherto secret private journal of Woody Allen, which will be published posthumously or after his death, whichever comes first.

Getting through the night is becoming harder and harder. Last evening, I had the uneasy feeling that some men were trying to break into my room to shampoo me. But why? I kept imagining I saw shadowy forms, and at 3 A.M. the underwear I had draped over a chair resembled the Kaiser on roller skates. When I finally did fall asleep, I had that same hideous nightmare in which a woodchuck is trying to claim my prize at a raffle. Despair.

I believe my consumption has grown worse. Also my asthma. The wheezing comes and goes, and I get dizzy more and more frequently. I have taken to violent choking and fainting. My room is damp and I have perpetual chills and palpitations of the heart. I noticed, too, that I am out of napkins. Will it never stop?

Idea for a story: A man awakens to find his parrot has been made Secretary of Agriculture. He is consumed with jealousy and shoots himself, but unfortunately the gun is the type with a little flag that pops out, with the word "Bang" on it. The flag pokes his eye out, and he lives—a chastened human being who, for the first time, enjoys the simple pleasures of life, like farming or sitting on an air hose.

Thought: Why does man kill? He kills for food. And not only food: frequently there must be a beverage.

Should I marry W.? Not if she won't tell me the other letters in her name. And what about her career? How can I ask a woman of her beauty to give up the Roller Derby? Decisions . . .

Once again I tried committing suicide—this time by wetting my nose and inserting it into the light socket. Unfortunately, there was a short in the wiring, and I merely caromed off the icebox. Still obsessed by thoughts of death, I brood constantly. I keep wondering if there is an afterlife, and if there is will they be able to break a twenty?

I ran into my brother today at a funeral. We had not seen one another for fifteen years, but as usual he produced a pig bladder from his pocket and began hitting me on the head with it. Time has helped me understand him better. I finally realize his remark that I am "some loathsome vermin fit only for extermination" was said more out of compassion than anger. Let's face it: he was always much brighter than me—wittier, more cultured, better educated. Why he is still working at McDonald's is a mystery.

Idea for story: Some beavers take over Carnegie Hall and perform *Wozzeck*. (Strong theme. What will be the structure?)

Good Lord, why am I so guilty? Is it because I hated my father? Probably it was the veal-parmigian' incident. Well, what *was* it doing in his wallet? If I had listened to him, I would be blocking hats for a living. I can hear him now: "To block hats—that is everything." I remember his reaction when I told him I wanted to write. "The only writing you'll do is in collaboration with an owl." I still have no idea what he meant. What a sad man! When my first play, *A Cyst for Gus*, was produced at the Lyceum, he attended opening night in tails and a gas mask.

Today I saw a red-and-yellow sunset and thought, How insignificant I am! Of course, I thought that yesterday, too, and it rained. I was overcome with self-loathing and contemplated suicide again—this time by inhaling next to an insurance salesman.

Short story: A man awakens in the morning and finds himself transformed into his own arch supports (This idea can work on many levels. Psychologically, it is the quintessence of Kruger, Freud's disciple who discovered sexuality in bacon.)

How wrong Emily Dickinson was! Hope is not "the thing with feathers." The thing with feathers has turned out to be my nephew. I must take him to a specialist in Zurich.

I have decided to break off my engagement with W. She doesn't understand my writing, and said last night that my *Critique of Metaphysical Reality* reminded her of *Airport*. We quarreled, and she brought up the subject of children again, but I convinced her they would be too young.

Do I believe in God? I did until Mother's accident. She fell on some meat loaf, and it penetrated her spleen. She lay in a coma for months, unable to do anything but sing "Granada" to an imaginary herring. Why was this woman in the prime of life so afflicted— because in her youth she dared to defy convention and got married with a brown paper bag on her head? And how can I believe in God when just last week I got my tongue caught in the roller of an electric typewriter? I am plagued by doubts. What if everything is an illusion and nothing exists? In that case, I definitely overpaid for my carpet. If only God would give me some clear sign! Like making a large deposit in my name at a Swiss bank.

Had coffee with Melnick today. He talked to me about his idea of having all government officials dress like hens.

Play idea: A character based on my father, but without quite so prominent a big toe. He is sent to the Sorbonne to study the harmonica. In the end, he dies, never realizing his one dream—to sit up to his waist in gravy. (I see a brilliant second-act curtain, where two midgets come upon a severed head in a shipment of volleyballs.)

While taking my noon walk today, I had more morbid thoughts. What *is* it about death that bothers me so much? Probably the hours. Melnick says the soul is immortal and lives on after the body drops away, but if my soul exists without my body I am convinced all my clothes will be too loose-fitting. Oh, well . . .

Did not have to break off with W. after all, for as luck would have it, she ran off to Finland with a professional circus geek. All for the best, I suppose, although I had another of those attacks where I start coughing out of my ears.

Last night, I burned all my plays and poetry. Ironically as I was burning my masterpiece, *Dark Penguin*, the room caught fire, and I am now the object of a lawsuit by some men named Pinchunk and Schlosser. Kierkegaard was right.

DONALD PEARCE: *from* Journal of a War

December 28. We have been patroling the Rhine and guarding
the bridge across it at Nijmegen continuously for so long now that
they have begun to acquire a positive hold over our minds and
imaginations. Our thoughts seem polarized by them, and turn to
them like compasses to a magnet. This bridge is the only one over
the Rhine left intact for a hundred miles, and we must keep it that
way for our own no doubt imminent invasion of Germany. At the
same time, if Jerry decides to counter-attack in force through here,
and there has been a good deal of fresh evidence that he's getting
ready to do just that, the bridge would become just as important to
him. A really ambiguous prize. But he keeps sending explosives
downstream at it. Damn strange. We shoot into the river at everything that moves, sometimes exploding mines tied to boards, or
logs, or branches. Our engineers have run a huge net across the
river about fifty yards upstream from the bridge to catch whatever
floats downstream; but things get through or under the net somehow and that's what we shoot at. New rumor: German frogmen
have been attempting to swim under the net; also, they have small
one-man submarines in the river. Probably fairy lore.

But I was going to say—the bridge and river no longer appear
ordinary to us, but seem to have acquired personalities, or to have
been endowed with them. Sometimes the river seems less the
watched one than the watcher, reflecting back our searchlight
beams, and breaking the half-moon into a thousand yellow eyes as
we steal along the edge on night patrols. The bridge's single span is
unmistakably a high, arched eyebrow over an invisible eye peering
across the Rhine. Everything we do here revolves around the bridge
and river. As we go back for a rest or, as recently, for Christmas
dinner, miles from the line, we cross the iced-flats that follow along
the curving windswept dykes, and the great iron eyebrow is right
behind us, lifting higher and higher above the mist, in a kind of
inscrutable surmise, and as we return to those god-awful flats again,
the eyebrow and invisible eye are at it again, staring back at us,
watching the Rhine. Perhaps someone should put on a campaign to
establish the ordinariness of this bridge and river, put up signs. But
it would do no good, I tell myself, because this was Caesar's Rhine,
Siegfried's Rhine, Wagner's Rhine, and you can't silence all that
mystery. I hate it here.

Whipping the company jeep at top speed along a mile-long
windswept section of one of the dykes that stretches between our
company and the next is one of the low diversions we have worked
out. It's completely exposed and utterly bare; so for two minutes

you are an A-number one moving target. An insane game, but we play it. Once I heard the loud, flat snap of a bullet going past my head on one of these mad runs. We are, as they say, very definitely under observation.

* * *

March 3 [1945]. The city[1] was quite heavily defended. First, a steep, raw, anti-tank ditch completely girdling the city had to be negotiated, with continuous covering fire from both flanks. Then we ran into a connected system of crawl- and weapons-trenches forming a secondary ring about the interior. Our covering artillery fire was practically saturational; so he resisted only lightly till we were more than halfway in. There followed some sporadic street fighting and house clearing, nothing very spectacular, and the city fell to us shortly after daybreak; i.e., they simply pulled out and disappeared at about 4:00 A.M.

I had a couple of close ones during this show. On the way in, my platoon was evidently silhouetted against the night sky, and was fired on four times at a range of maybe 300 yards by an eighty-eight. (This is a notorious and vicious gun. The velocity of the shell is so high that you hear it pass or explode near you almost at the same instant that you hear the sound of its being fired. You really can't duck it. Also, it's an open-sights affair—you are aimed at particularly; not, as with mortars, aimed at only by approximation.) Anyway, they went past me about an arm's length above or in front of me, I don't know which. We hit the ditches. After pointing a few more, the gun was forced off by our return tank fire.

During the house-clearing phase, at one spot, I walked instead of ran from one house to another and got my helmet spun around on my head with a close shot. There was an extremely loud, flat "snap," like two hands clapped together hard beside my ear; that was all. Plus a crease in my helmet, which gave me immense prestige with the men all morning.

We had two tanks along with us, and their support made the assignment 100 per cent easier. At one point a handful of German snipers, who were perched in the attic of a three-story house at a bend in the main street, held up the battalion for over an hour. They were finally silenced by one of the tanks. In the half-dark, we circled around behind their house during the tank fire and cut off their escape route. Presently they came out through the back garden, dangling in front of them white cloths on long poles. It was vastly disconcerting. Instead of a squad of Nazi supermen in shiny boots, and packing Lugers, we were confronted by five of the most unkempt, stunted, scrubby specimens I have ever had the pleasure of capturing. Two of them couldn't have been more than

1. Udem, in The Netherlands.

fourteen on their next birthday. Possibly they were on some kind of dope; at least they acted that way, a little dazed, grinning, and rather immune to voice control. One of them had nearly shot me a few hours earlier in the dark before dawn. At the time, I remember, I had thought it wasn't any more than I had expected; but later on, seeing them, I felt that it would have been an unfortunate end to my life. I am obviously getting choosy. What I mean is that I would simply like to be well killed, if killed I am to be. I came to the conclusion that they were from the bottom of Germany's recruiting barrel.

The men in the platoon seemed to think so too, for I caught them in the middle of a queer performance. They had lined the five of them up against a schoolhouse wall and were pretending, quite ceremoniously, that they were going to shoot them. The prisoners certainly believed they were about to be shot; three of them had their hands on their heads and their faces turned to the wall, as for execution; the other two were pleading desperately with three or four of our men. I was astonished to find my best corporal in the thick of this business. I stopped it, of course. Not that they would have carried out the execution; I feel sure of that.

We passed through the town and seized a road-and-rail junction about 800 yards past the outskirts and dug in under moderate shelling. A child would know that that junction would become a hot target—which it very shortly did. We sat it out. He sent several salvos of rockets in on us. These you always hear coming, if it's any comfort. The first salvo was the best, but there was time for my sergeant and me to flatten out in a shallow ditch alongside the track. One rocket hit about four or five feet from us, practically shattering my hearing; it chewed up a couple of railway ties, took two or three chunks out of the rails, and turned me over from my stomach to my back. The blast stung my whole left side. Nothing more really close happened there all night.

Next day, I went back to have a look at Udem. In daylight it seemed in worse condition than I remembered it from the night before. Enemy shelling accounted for much of the destruction; but looters, busy rooting around before daybreak, accounted for some too. The houses that had not been shelled were practically turned inside out by our troops. I came across one soldier telling an admiring group about his morning exploits: "First I took a hammer and smashed over 100 plates, and the cups along with them. Then I took an ax to the china cabinets and buffets. Next I smashed all the furniture and pulled the stuffing out of the big chairs. Then I took the hammer again and smashed all the elements on two electric stoves and broke the enamel off the stove fronts and sides. Then I put a grenade in the big piano, and after that I poured a jar of molasses into it. I broke all the French doors and all the doors with mirrors in them and threw the lamps out into the street. I was so mad."

I turned him over to the Provost Corps in the afternoon.

Udem had a large church made of red stone with high twin towers. German artillery scouts had stationed themselves in these towers in order to direct fire onto our positions five miles away. So the church had to be "neutralized," as they say. We engaged it with 17-pounders for about an hour, I believe successfully. Anyway, I went in to see what we had done. It was full of gaping holes; the stone pillars had even been shot off far within the building. The only unharmed thing I saw was the font. The walls had had blue and gold paintings of religious scenes extending all around the interior; these were mostly peeled or ripped off. One painting was of the Descent from the Cross. It had come loose from its frame and seemed heading for a nosedive; the pale belly of Christ had a group of machine-gun bullets through it. The Germans had made a brief stand at the church and had obviously used it as a temporary strongpoint. As I left, engineers were already laying dynamite charges at critical points along the foundations, with the intention of using the stones as rubble for roads, almost the only reasonable use left for it.

On the way back, I met a number of civilians carrying bundles. Most of them were covered with mud from head to foot. They were staggering along rather than walking, and started every time a gun went off far away or close up. One tall thin man was leading two small children, one by each hand. The children were around his back. The man limped; I saw that he was weeping. My limited German enabled me to discover that he was wounded in a couple of places, that his wife had been killed by shrapnel in the morning, and that he didn't know what to do with his tiny children who were wet, cold, and hungry. I took them down into our cellar where the stretcher bearer dressed his wounds and evacuated him. I offered the two children food—chocolate, bread and jam, biscuits. They only tightened their lips and refused. So I tried a sort of game with the names of the articles of furniture in the cellar, deliberately making silly mistakes, and after a while they laughed at my stupidity. I kept this up, and before long they gobbled whatever I put in front of them. I would like to have done more; but instead I turned them over to the Civil Affairs people, not without complicated feelings of concern and regret. I will never know what happened to them.

Kept rummaging around in the town. Went to the place where I was nearly shot, stood on the exact spot, in fact, and determined the window at the end of the street where the shots had come from. An impulse sent me inside the house itself, where I climbed to the upper room. The machine gun was there on its heavy mounting, still pointing out the window and down the street. I sat behind it and took aim on the doorway I had disappeared into at the moment I was fired on, and waited for someone to pass the spot just to see how I must have looked through his sights. No one came and I got tired of the melodrama and went back to our forward positions.

* * *

March 4. When will it all end? The idiocy and the tension, the dying of young men, the destruction of homes, of cities, starvation, exhaustion, disease, children parentless and lost, cages full of shivering, staring prisoners, long lines of hopeless civilians plodding through mud, the endless pounding of the battle line. I can scarcely remember what it is like to be where explosions are not going off around me, some hostile, some friendly, all horrible; an exploding shell is a terrible sound. What keeps this war going, now that its end is so clear? What do the Germans think of us, and we of them? I do not think we think of them at all, or much. Do they think of us? I can think of their weapons, their shells, their machine guns, but not of the men behind them. I do not feel as if I were fighting against men, but against machines. I need to go up in an airplane and actually see German transport hauling guns and ammunition, see their actual armies; for everything that happens merely comes from a vague beyond, and I cannot visualize the people who are fighting against me. The prisoners that come over hills with their hands up, or who come out of houses with white cloths waving—they have no relation, almost, to anything for me. I can't connect them with the guns they have just laid down, it seems like forcing something to do so. It is becoming hard for me not to feel sometimes that both sides are the common victims of a common terror, that everybody's guns are against everybody ultimately.

These are times when I feel that every bit of fighting is defensive. Self defense. If a machine-gun nest is attacked and wiped out by us, by my own platoon, I do not feel very aggressive, as if I had attacked somebody. It is always that I have defended myself against something that was attacking me. And how often I have thought that there might be a Rilke out there in a German pill box. If I could only see them, as in battles long ago, at close range, before engaging them. In our wars, the warring sides are getting farther and farther apart and war is getting more and more meaningless for the field warriors, and more meaningful for the domestic warriors in factories and homes. Will there come a time when hundreds of miles separate the warring fronts? When long-range weapons and the ghastly impersonality of air attacks are the means of war? It is already a very impersonal thing. When a soldier is killed or wounded his buddies, shaking their heads, merely say, "Poor old Joe. He just got it. Just as he was going up that hill, he got it." As if to imply that he was merely in the wrong place at the wrong time, and that life and death are only matters of luck and do not depend on the calculations of human beings at the other end of an S.P. gun. When we were in our static positions around Wyler Meer and Nijmegen, the enemy became real to me for the first time. I watched him for weeks, saw him dig, run, hide, fire, walk. And when I went on patrols into his territory, there was meaning in that, too, for I knew where he was, I knew his habits. So that while we were probing the cuticle of the enemy, so to speak, he was real; but now when we are ripping into his body, he has disappeared and has turned into something read about in the papers. But the guns remain, manned by soldiers who are so meaningless to us that when they shoot a fellow, all we can say is, "He got it."

Once I could say you cannot be disgusted with the war, because it is too big for disgust, that disgust is too shallow an emotion for something involving millions of people. But I am disgusted now, and I know what I am saying. Once I used to get quite a thrill out of seeing a city destroyed and left an ash heap from end to end. It gave me a vicarious sense of power. I felt the romantic and histrionic emotion produced by seeing "retribution" done; and an aesthetic emotion produced by beholding ruins; and the childish emotion that comes from destroying man-made things. But it is not that way any more. All I experience is revulsion every time a fresh city is taken on. I am no longer capable of thinking that the systematic destruction of a city is a wonderful or even a difficult thing, though some seem to think it even a heroic thing. Well, how is it done? Dozens upon dozens of gun crews stationed some two or three miles away from the city simply place shell after shell into hundreds of guns and fire away for a few hours—the simplest and most elementary physical and mental work—and then presently the firing stops, the city has been demolished, has become an ash heap, and great praise is bestowed on the army for the capture of a new city.

I am not suggesting that cities shouldn't be captured in this way; actually it saves lives. But it fills me with disgust because it is all so abysmally foolish, so lunatic. It has not the dramatic elements of mere barbarism about it; it is straight scientific debauchery. A destroyed city is a terrible sight. How can anyone record it?—the million smashed things, the absolutely innumerable tiny tragedies, the crushed life-works, the jagged homes, army tanks parked in living rooms—who could tell of these things I don't know; they are too numerous to mention, too awful in their meanings. Perhaps everyone should be required to spend a couple of hours examining a single smashed home, looking at the fragmentation of every little thing, especially the tiniest things from kitchen to attic, if he could find an attic; be required, in fact, to list the ruined contents of just one home; something would be served, a little sobriety perhaps honored.

It is disgusting (that it should be necessary, is what galls me to the bones) that a towering cathedral, built by ages of care and effort, a sweet labor of centuries, should be shot down by laughing artillerymen, mere boys, because somebody with a machine gun is hiding in a belfry tower. When I see such a building, damaged perhaps beyond repair after one of these "operations," I know only disgust. The matter of sides in this war temporarily becomes irrelevant, especially if someone at my elbow says, like a conquering hero: "Well, we sure did a job on the old church, eh?"

A job has been done on Europe, on the world, and the resulting trauma will be generations long in its effects. It is not just the shock of widespread destruction, of whole cities destroyed, nor the shock which the defeated and the homeless must have suffered, that I am thinking of: it is even more the conqueror's trauma, the habit of violence, the explosion of values, the distortion of relations, the ascending significance of the purely material, the sense of power, and the pride of strength. These things will afflict the victors as profoundly and for quite as long a time as the other things will afflict the victims; and of the two I am not sure that a crass superiority complex is the more desirable. Perhaps I underestimate our ability to return to normal again.

HAL BORLAND: *New York Times* Seasonal Editorials

The Fangs of Winter, January 26, 1975. Tomorrow night's full moon was known to the Indians of the Northeast as the Wolf Moon, a time when winter showed its fangs. The pioneer farmer took inventory at January's end and unless he had half his hay and half his wood unused he knew that cold and hunger would stalk his barns and house. He didn't bother to give a special name to January's sun, moon or stars. He opened a fresh stack of hay and cut another armload of fireplace wood.

Averaged out, January and February are our darkest months, and our coldest and snowiest. Now the rocks have lost the last of their autumn warmth. Now the earth itself heaves with frost. We climb the steepest part of that long, cold slope from December to April, the best and the worst part of winter. Nights when the old star patterns gleam with the nearest thing to certainty and order we know; late dawns, when the gray world comes slowly to life after cold and darkness that seemed eternally deep; high noons with a sun so distant that only the faith of generations can believe it will be overhead again in June.

Man cannot know the year complete unless he knows winter. First principles are involved, to be ignored at one's peril. He who would be warm and fed in winter must know summer's sweat and muscle ache. The truth of cause and effect is written across every winter day and every winter hilltop. We are of the earth and of the universe, but we cannot know the full Buck Moon of July without first knowing the full Wolf Moon of January.

Those Attic Wasps, February 2, 1975. Wasps begin to appear in country houses about now, and even in some suburban houses. One sees them dart uncertainly about, hears them buzz and bang on window panes, and one wonders where they came from. They probably came from the attic, where they spent the early part of the winter hibernating. Now, with longer hours of daylight, the wasps begin to rouse and start exploring.

The sound of a flying wasp is different from that of a fly. It is a matter of vibration, of the speed of the wing strokes. Those strokes set up sound waves. Some ingenious researcher once measured those strokes with a tuning fork. Tuning forks are carefully calibrated and, by matching the sound of a flying insect with that of a tuning fork, it is possible to say how fast that insect moves its wings.

Thus it was shown that a common house fly makes its familiar buzz by beating its wings nearly 20,000 strokes a minute. The wasp beats its wings a little less than one-third that fast, 6,000 strokes a minute. The normal human ear can hear sounds with as few as 1,800 beats per minute, the beat of a dragonfly's wings.

So it is easy enough to hear a wasp. Especially now. But it isn't the sound of spring in the dooryard. It is the sound of a female wasp still half-asleep. It is mid-February with a stinger in her tail.

The March Buds, March 16, 1975. Buds fatten on the elms beading their twigs against the sky, and in the lowlands the red maples begin to shrug off the scales that have protected their crimson florets from the winter's cold. In the dooryard the lilacs are in such big bud they make you wonder how much longer they can contain their swollen pack of leaves and stem and blossoms, all purple tinged for May delivery and celebration.

Out along the pasture fence the cedars are in full bloom and strewing pollen from blossoms you have to look thrice to see. Beside the brook the alder catkins have been at the pollen stage for some time. A few early bees know it, but the alders don't have to wait for the bees. Alder and cedar and most other trees and bushes of older lineage are not dependent on the insects. The wind has been their pollinator since they outgrew spores. That is why their blossoms have no petals, only stamens and a pistil. The wind needs no signal flags or landing platforms.

Go to a grove of poplars now, on a sunny afternoon, and the

fragrance of poplar gum will be there, faint but tanged of spring. The gum that seals the catkins in their fat buds is melting, loosening the scales. Pause beneath the willows and you will see bud scales falling, may even mistake them for motes in the sunlight, though no mote ever sheltered a willow's silver-furred male blossom.

The winds still belong to March, gusty and often edged with ice. But the trees trust their buds and early blossoms to those winds, as they trust their roots to the soil.

Midsummer, July 20, 1975. Dusk comes a few minutes earlier now, and sunrise a few minutes later, then they did a month ago. Summer divides the 24-hour day to its own dimensions, and off there in the distance, a few hills away, lies autumn. Change, the eternal constant, subtly shapes days.

You sense the change in the way the shadows fall. The pool of shade beneath a big maple moves slightly back from its farthest reach to the north. The beam of sunlight slanting through a north window in the morning now has narrowed. And at the roadside are clouds of Queen Anne's lace. Daisies begin to fade. Wild raspberries ripen. On the oak trees young acorns are in plain sight.

Field corn, beyond the suburbs, begins to tassle out and the tang of corn pollen hangs in the air of a hot afternoon. Garden tomatoes fatten, still grass-green, toward August ripeness. Last spring's early mildness brings summer squash by the bushel to roadside markets and baby beets to the farmer's table.

You hear the change in the bird calls, fewer songs of ecstasy, more parental alarms and scoldings. The wood thrush is heard in the evening, and the dove and the whippoolwill. The insects drone afternoon and night, proclaiming life even though theirs is a one-season lifetime. Bees are busier. Wasps are more spiteful. Harvest flies buzz and shrill in the heat of midafternoon. Dragonflies seem to hurry on rattling wings.

It is midsummer and the beat of time is like the throb of a healthy heart, strong, steady and reassuring.

August, August 10, 1975. August is ripe chokecherries, and flutters of jays and robins at them, scolding, quarreling over seedy fruit too puckery for any human use except in jelly. It is elderberries so heavy with their dark fruit the bushes are bowed like hunched old women in coarse purple shawls. It is chicory in bloom, a weed in the field, an herb in the kitchen, sky blue on sunny days but sulking and refusing to reveal its face to the clouds.

August is grasshoppers, their wings rattling when they fly, seeming to know that no summer lasts forever and now they must hurry somewhere. It is the grasshopper cousins, the katydids, starting to scratch the night, to file and rasp the evening to fit the shortening days. Foretellers of first frost, some say; and often it is true.

August is crickets, too. Tree crickets, which fiddle monotonously every evening, and field crickets that trill without pause every hot afternoon, so synchronized that when you drive along a rural road it seems that the same cricket accompanies you for mile after country mile.

August is algae in the scummy waters of the pond. It is the fat thumbs of new cattail heads in the mucky margin. It is joe-pye weed purpling into blossom, and ironweed turning magenta at its floral tips. It is vervain, blue and purple, in the damp lowland.

August gives the lie to the boast that man possesses the earth. Life is the possessor, not man, an infinity of life that will outlast all winters. August and summer are the glory, the achievement that soars beyond all human dreams.

Autumn's Leftovers, November 2, 1975. Rural and suburban householders are busy now with rake and fork and barrow, cleaning and neatening the dooryard, the lawn and the garden. Everything must be in order for the winter. But down the road and across the valley, where autumn itself is in charge, nobody is bothering about the unkempt look. Nature isn't very neat about such matters.

Fallen leaves, restless as sparrows, rustle and scurry at the roadsides. Gray heads of goldenrod fluff spill seeds on every passing wind. Milkweed pods send streams of silken shimmer in all directions. Wild grape vines and woodbine have been left dangling from trees and bushes, nooses for unwary feet. Ripe grass is sadly in need of comb and brush.

But nature doesn't seem to care. The floor of the woodland is littered with dead twigs and branches pruned by wind and rain. Fern fronds lie sere and brown. Box elders emphasize their nakedness with tufts of keys that will dangle there all winter. The abandoned oriole's nest has begun to fray at a high, limber tip of the wineglass elm. Windrows of tan needles prove that pines, too, shed foliage in the autumn.

Man must rake and cart away, to soothe his conscience and proclaim his tenancy. Nature doesn't bother. The tree thrives on its own trash and the seed sprouts in its parent's midden heap. Each new spring grows on autumn's leftovers.

On Mind

JOHN SELDEN
The Measure of Things

We measure from ourselves; and as things are for our use and purpose, so we approve them. Bring a pear to the table that is rotten, we cry it down, 'tis naught; but bring a medlar that is rotten, and 'tis a fine thing; and yet I'll warrant you the pear thinks as well of itself as the medlar[1] does.

We measure the excellency of other men by some excellency we conceive to be in ourselves. Nash, a poet, poor enough (as poets use to be), seeing an alderman with his gold chain, upon his great horse, by way of scorn said to one of his companions, "Do you see yon fellow, how goodly, how big he looks? Why, that fellow cannot make a blank verse."

Nay, we measure the goodness of God from ourselves; we measure his goodness, his justice, his wisdom, by something we call just, good, or wise in ourselves; and in so doing, we judge proportionally to the country-fellow in the play, who said, if he were King, he would live like a lord, and have peas and bacon every day, and a whip that cried Slash.

---

1. The medlar, a fruit like the crab apple, becomes edible only after it begins to decay.

QUESTIONS
1. What pattern of parallels do you discern among the three parts of Selden's statement? How does this principle of structure enforce the thesis he is setting forth?
2. Can the three paragraphs be rearranged without damage? Explain. What principle or principles appear to govern the present arrangement? Does it imply anything about value? About the kind of universe in which Selden conceives man to live?

3. *Consider the three desires of the country fellow who would be king. Has Selden arranged these desires in any particular order? If so, what relation does that order bear to the order of the whole statement?*

BENJAMIN FRANKLIN
The Convenience of Being "Reasonable"[1]

I believe I have omitted mentioning that, in my first voyage from Boston, being becalmed off Block Island, our people set about catching cod, and hauled up a great many. Hitherto I had stuck to my resolution of not eating animal food, and on this occasion I considered, with my master Tryon, the taking every fish as a kind of unprovoked murder, since none of them had, or ever could do us any injury that might justify the slaughter. All this seemed very reasonable. But I had formerly been a great lover of fish, and, when this came hot out of the frying-pan, it smelled admirably well. I balanced some time between principle and inclination, till I recollected that, when the fish were opened, I saw smaller fish taken out of their stomachs; then thought I, "if you eat one another, I don't see why we mayn't eat you." So I dined upon cod very heartily, and continued to eat with other people, returning only now and then occasionally to a vegetable diet. So convenient a thing it is to be a *reasonable creature*, since it enables one to find or make a reason for everything one has a mind to do.

WILLIAM GOLDING
Thinking as a Hobby

While I was still a boy, I came to the conclusion that there were three grades of thinking; and since I was later to claim thinking as my hobby, I came to an even stranger conclusion—namely, that I myself could not think at all.

I must have been an unsatisfactory child for grownups to deal with. I remember how incomprehensible they appeared to me at first, but not, of course, how I appeared to them. It was the headmaster of my grammar school who first brought the subject of thinking before me—though neither in the way, nor with the result he intended. He had some statuettes in his study. They stood on a high cupboard behind his desk. One was a lady wearing nothing but a bath towel. She seemed frozen in an eternal panic lest the bath towel slip down any farther; and since she had no arms, she was in an unfortunate position to pull the towel up again. Next to her, crouched the statuette of a leopard, ready to spring down at the top drawer of a filing cabinet labeled A-AH. My innocence interpreted this as the victim's last, despairing cry. Beyond the leopard was a naked, muscular gentleman, who sat, looking down, with his chin on his fist and his elbow on his knee. He seemed utterly miserable.

Some time later, I learned about these statuettes. The headmaster had placed them where they would face delinquent children, because they symbolized to him the whole of life. The naked lady was the Venus of Milo. She was Love. She was not worried about the towel. She was just busy being beautiful. The leopard was Nature, and he was being natural. The naked, muscular gentleman was not miserable. He was Rodin's Thinker, an image of pure thought. It is easy to buy small plaster models of what you think life is like.

I had better explain that I was a frequent visitor to the headmaster's study, because of the latest thing I had done or left undone. As we now say, I was not integrated. I was, if anything, disintegrated; and I was puzzled. Grownups never made sense. Whenever I found myself in a penal position before the headmaster's desk, with the statuettes glimmering whitely above him, I would sink my head, clasp my hands behind my back and writhe one shoe over the other.

The headmaster would look opaquely at me through flashing spectacles.

"What are we going to do with you?"

Well, what *were* they going to do with me? I would writhe my shoe some more and stare down at the worn rug.

"Look up, boy! Can't you look up?"

Then I would look up at the cupboard, where the naked lady was frozen in her panic and the muscular gentleman contemplated the hindquarters of the leopard in endless gloom. I had nothing to say to the headmaster. His spectacles caught the light so that you could see nothing human behind them. There was no possibility of communication.

"Don't you ever think at all?"

No, I didn't think, wasn't thinking, couldn't think—I was simply waiting in anguish for the interview to stop.

"Then you'd better learn—hadn't you?"

On one occasion the headmaster leaped to his feet, reached up and plonked Rodin's masterpiece on the desk before me.

"That's what a man looks like when he's really thinking."

I surveyed the gentleman without interest or comprehension.

"Go back to your class."

Clearly there was something missing in me. Nature had endowed the rest of the human race with a sixth sense and left me out. This must be so, I mused, on my way back to the class, since whether I had broken a window, or failed to remember Boyle's Law, or been late for school, my teachers produced me one, adult answer: "Why can't you think?"

As I saw the case, I had broken the window because I had tried to hit Jack Arney with a cricket ball and missed him; I could not remember Boyle's Law because I had never bothered to learn it; and I was late for school because I preferred looking over the bridge into the river. In fact, I was wicked. Were my teachers, perhaps, so good that they could not understand the depths of my depravity? Were they clear, untormented people who could direct their every action by this mysterious business of thinking? The whole thing was incomprehensible. In my earlier years, I found even the statuette of the Thinker confusing. I did not believe any of my teachers were naked, ever. Like someone born deaf, but bitterly determined to find out about sound, I watched my teachers to find out about thought.

There was Mr. Houghton. He was always telling me to think. With a modest satisfaction, he would tell me that he had thought a bit himself. Then why did he spend so much time drinking? Or was there more sense in drinking than there appeared to be? But if not, and if drinking were in fact ruinous to health—and Mr. Houghton was ruined, there was no doubt about that—why was he always talking about the clean life and the virtues of fresh air? He would spread his arms wide with the action of a man who habitually spent his time striding along mountain ridges.

"Open air does me good, boys—I know it!"

Sometimes, exalted by his own oratory, he would leap from his desk and hustle us outside into a hideous wind.

"Now, boys! Deep breaths! Feel it right down inside you—huge draughts of God's good air!"

He would stand before us, rejoicing in his perfect health, an open-air man. He would put his hands on his waist and take a tremendous breath. You could hear the wind, trapped in the cavern of his chest and struggling with all the unnatural impediments. His body would reel with shock and his ruined face go white at the unaccustomed visitation. He would stagger back to his desk and collapse there, useless for the rest of the morning.

Mr. Houghton was given to high-minded monologues about the good life, sexless and full of duty. Yet in the middle of one of these monologues, if a girl passed the window, tapping along on her neat little feet, he would interrupt his discourse, his neck would turn of itself and he would watch her out of sight. In this instance, he seemed to me ruled not by thought but by an invisible and irresistible spring in his nape.

His neck was an object of great interest to me. Normally it bulged a bit over his collar. But Mr. Houghton had fought in the

First World War alongside both Americans and French, and had come—by who knows what illogic?—to a settled detestation of both countries. If either country happened to be prominent in current affairs, no argument could make Mr. Houghton think well of it. He would bang the desk, his neck would bulge still further and go red. "You can say what you like," he would cry, "but I've thought about this—and I know what I think!"

Mr. Houghton thought with his neck.

There was Miss Parsons. She assured us that her dearest wish was our welfare, but I knew even then, with the mysterious clairvoyance of childhood, that what she wanted most was the husband she never got. There was Mr. Hands—and so on.

I have dealt at length with my teachers because this was my introduction to the nature of what is commonly called thought. Through them I discovered that thought is often full of unconscious prejudice, ignorance and hypocrisy. It will lecture on disinterested purity while its neck is being remorselessly twisted toward a skirt. Technically, it is about as proficient as most businessmen's golf, as honest as most politicians' intentions, or—to come near my own preoccupation—as coherent as most books that get written. It is what I came to call grade-three thinking, though more properly, it is feeling, rather than thought.

True, often there is a kind of innocence in prejudices, but in those days I viewed grade-three thinking with an intolerant contempt and an incautious mockery. I delighted to confront a pious lady who hated the Germans with the proposition that we should love our enemies. She taught me a great truth in dealing with grade-three thinkers; because of her, I no longer dismiss lightly a mental process which for nine-tenths of the population is the nearest they will ever get to thought. They have immense solidarity. We had better respect them, for we are outnumbered and surrounded. A crowd of grade-three thinkers, all shouting the same thing, all warming their hands at the fire of their own prejudices, will not thank you for pointing out the contradictions in their beliefs. Man is a gregarious animal, and enjoys agreement as cows will graze all the same way on the side of a hill.

Grade-two thinking is the detection of contradictions. I reached grade two when I trapped the poor, pious lady. Grade-two thinkers do not stampede easily, though often they fall into the other fault and lap behind. Grade-two thinking is a withdrawal, with eyes and ears open. It became my hobby and brought satisfaction and loneliness in either hand. For grade-two thinking destroys without having the power to create. It set me watching the crowds cheering His Majesty and King and asking myself what all the fuss was about, without giving me anything positive to put in the place of that heady patriotism. But there were compensations. To hear people justify their habit of hunting foxes and tearing them to pieces by claiming that the foxes liked it. To hear our Prime Minister talk about the great benefit we conferred on India by jailing people like Pandit Nehru and Gandhi. To hear American politicians talk about peace in one sentence and refuse to join the League of Nations in the next. Yes, there were moments of delight.

But I was growing toward adolescence and had to admit that Mr. Houghton was not the only one with an irresistible spring in his neck. I, too, felt the compulsive hand of nature and began to find that pointing out contradiction could be costly as well as fun. There was Ruth, for example, a serious and attractive girl. I was an atheist at the time. Grade-two thinking is a menace to religion and knocks down sects like skittles. I put myself in a position to be converted by her with an hypocrisy worthy of grade three. She was a Methodist—or at least, her parents were, and Ruth had to follow suit. But, alas, instead of relying on the Holy Spirit to convert me, Ruth was foolish enough to open her pretty mouth in argument. She claimed that the Bible (King James Version) was literally inspired. I countered by saying that the Catholics believed in the literal inspiration of Saint Jerome's *Vulgate*, and the two books were different. Argument flagged.

At last she remarked that there were an awful lot of Methodists, and they couldn't be wrong, could they—not all those millions? That was too easy, said I restively (for the nearer you were to Ruth, the nicer she was to be near to) since there were more Roman Catholics than Methodists anyway; and they couldn't be wrong, could they—not all those hundreds of millions? An awful flicker of doubt appeared in her eyes. I slid my arm around her waist and murmured breathlessly that if we were counting heads, the Buddhists were the boys for my money. But Ruth had *really* wanted to do me good, because I was so nice. She fled. The combination of my arm and those countless Buddhists was too much for her.

That night her father visited my father and left, red-cheeked and indignant. I was given the third degree to find out what had happened. It was lucky we were both of us only fourteen. I lost Ruth and gained an undeserved reputation as a potential libertine.

So grade-two thinking could be dangerous. It was in this knowledge, at the age of fifteen, that I remember making a comment from the heights of grade two, on the limitations of grade three. One evening I found myself alone in the school hall, preparing it for a party. The door of the headmaster's study was open. I went in. The headmaster had ceased to thump Rodin's Thinker down on the desk as an example to the young. Perhaps he had not found any more candidates, but the statuettes were still there, glimmering and gathering dust on top of the cupboard. I stood on a chair and rearranged them. I stood Venus in her bath towel on the filing cabinet, so that now the top drawer caught its breath in a gasp of sexy excitement. "A-ah!" The portentous Thinker I placed on the edge of the cupboard so that he looked down at the bath towel and waited for it to slip.

Grade-two thinking, though it filled life with fun and excitement, did not make for content. To find out the deficiencies of our elders bolsters the young ego but does not make for personal security. I found that grade two was not only the power to point out contradictions. It took the swimmer some distance from the shore and left him there, out of his depth. I decided that Pontius Pilate was a typical grade-two thinker. "What is truth?" he said, a very common grade-two thought, but one that is used always as the end of an argument instead of the beginning. There is still a higher grade of thought which says, "What is truth?" and sets out to find it.

But these grade-one thinkers were few and far between. They did not visit my grammar school in the flesh though they were there in books. I aspired to them, partly because I was ambitious and partly because I now saw my hobby as an unsatisfactory thing if it went no further. If you set out to climb a mountain, however high you climb, you have failed if you cannot reach the top.

I *did* meet an undeniably grade-one thinker in my first year at Oxford. I was looking over a small bridge in Magdalen Deer Park, and a tiny mustached and hatted figure came and stood by my side. He was a German who had just fled from the Nazis to Oxford as a temporary refuge. He name was Einstein.

But Professor Einstein knew no English at that time and I knew only two words of German. I beamed at him, trying wordlessly to convey by my bearing all the affection and respect that the English felt for him. It is possible—and I have to make the admission—that I felt here were two grade-one thinkers standing side by side; yet I doubt if my face conveyed more than a formless awe. I would have given my Greek and Latin and French and a good slice of my English for enough German to communicate. But we were divided; he was as inscrutable as my headmaster. For perhaps five minutes we stood together on the bridge, undeniable grade-one thinker and breathless aspirant. With true greatness, Professor Einstein realized that my contact was better than none. He pointed to a trout wavering in midstream.

He spoke: "*Fisch.*"

My brain reeled. Here I was, mingling with the great, and yet helpless as the veriest grade-three thinker. Desperately I sought for some sign by which I might convey that I, too, revered pure reason. I nodded vehemently. In a brilliant flash I used up half of my German vocabulary.

"*Fisch. Ja Ja.*"

For perhaps another five minutes we stood side by side. Then Professor Einstein, his whole figure still conveying good will and amiability, drifted away out of sight.

I, too, would be a grade-one thinker. I was irreverent at the best of times. Political and religious systems, social customs, loyalties and traditions, they all came tumbling down like so many rotten apples off a tree. This was a fine hobby and a sensible substitute for cricket, since you could play it all the year round. I came up in the end with what must always remain the justification for grade-one thinking, its sign, seal and charter. I devised a coherent system for living. It was a moral system, which was wholly logical. Of course, as I readily admitted, conversion of the world to my way of thinking might be difficult, since my system did away with a number of trifles, such as big business, centralized government, armies, marriage. . . .

It was Ruth all over again. I had some very good friends who stood by me, and still do. But my acquaintances vanished, taking the girls with them. Young women seemed oddly contented with the world as it was. They valued the meaningless ceremony with a ring. Young men, while willing to concede the chaining sordidness of marriage, were hesitant about abandoning the organizations which they hoped would give them a career. A young man on the first rung of the Royal Navy, while perfectly agreeable to doing away with big business and marriage, got as rednecked as Mr. Houghton when I proposed a world without any battleships in it.

Had the game gone too far? Was it a game any longer? In those prewar days, I stood to lose a great deal, for the sake of a hobby.

Now you are expecting me to describe how I saw the folly of my ways and came back to the warm nest, where prejudices are so often called loyalties, where pointless actions are hallowed into custom by repetition, where we are content to say we think when all we do is feel.

But you would be wrong. I dropped my hobby and turned professional.

If I were to go back to the headmaster's study and find the dusty statuettes still there, I would arrange them differently. I would dust Venus and put her aside, for I have come to love her and know her for the fair thing she is. But I would put the Thinker, sunk in his desperate thought, where there were shadows before him—and at his back, I would put the leopard, crouched and ready to spring.

QUESTIONS

1. Why does Golding at the end of his essay return to the three statuettes? Have the statuettes anything to do with the three kinds of thinking described in the essay? Why would Golding rearrange the statuettes as he does in the final paragraph?

2. It has been said: "Third-rate thinkers think like everybody else because everybody else thinks the same way. Second-rate thinkers think differently from everybody else because everybody else thinks the same way. First-rate thinkers think." Does this saying correspond to Golding's message? Would you modify it in any way in light of what he writes?

3. Does Golding's anecdote about Einstein have any bearing upon his account of the three categories of thinking?
4. What are the special attractions and what are the penalties of grade-three thinking? Grade-two? Grade-one?
5. Are Golding's three categories all-encompassing? If so, how? If not, what additional ones would you add?
6. Are Golding's categories useful for assessing the value of a person's statements? Choose several selections in this book and examine them by Golding's implied criteria.
7. William Golding is the author of the novel Lord of the Flies. If you have read that work, do you see in his depiction of characters and events any manifestations of the three categories of thinking?

HENRY DAVID THOREAU
Observation

There is no such thing as pure *objective* observation. Your observation, to be interesting, *i.e.* to be significant, must be *subjective*. The sum of what the writer of whatever class has to report is simply some human experience, whether he be poet or philosopher or man of science. The man of most science is the man most alive, whose life is the greatest event. Senses that take cognizance of outward things merely are of no avail. It matters not where or how far you travel—the farther commonly the worse—but how much alive you are. If it is possible to conceive of an event outside to humanity, it is not of the slightest significance, though it were the explosion of a planet. Every important worker will report what life there is in him. It makes no odds into what seeming deserts the poet is born. Though all his neighbors pronounce it a Sahara, it will be a paradise to him; for the desert which we see is the result of the barrenness of our experience. No mere willful activity whatever, whether in writing verses or collecting statistics, will produce true poetry or science. If you are really a sick man, it is indeed to be regretted, for you cannot accomplish so much as if you were well. All that a man has to say or do that can possibly concern mankind, is in some shape or other to tell the story of his love—to sing, and, if he is fortunate and keeps alive, he will be forever in love. This alone is to be alive to the extremities. It is a pity that this divine creature should ever suffer from cold feet; a still greater pity that the coldness so often reaches to his heart. I look over the report of the doings of a scientific association and am surprised that there is so little life to be reported; I am put off with a parcel of dry technical terms. Anything living is easily and naturally expressed in popular language. I cannot help suspecting that the life of these learned professors has been almost as inhuman and wooden as a rain-gauge or self-registering magnetic machine. They communicate no fact which rises to the temperature of blood-heat. It doesn't all amount to one rhyme.

JACOB BRONOWSKI

The Reach of Imagination

For three thousand years, poets have been enchanted and moved and perplexed by the power of their own imagination. In a short and summary essay I can hope at most to lift one small corner of that mystery; and yet it is a critical corner. I shall ask, What goes on in the mind when we imagine? You will hear from me that one answer to this question is fairly specific: which is to say, that we can describe the working of the imagination. And when we describe it as I shall do, it becomes plain that imagination is a specifically *human* gift. To imagine is the characteristic act, not of the poet's mind, or the painter's, or the scientist's, but of the mind of man.

My stress here on the word *human* implies that there is a clear difference in this between the actions of men and those of other animals. Let me then start with a classical experiment with animals and children which Walter Hunter thought out in Chicago about 1910. That was the time when scientists were agog with the success of Ivan Pavlov in forming and changing the reflex actions of dogs, which Pavlov had first announced in 1903. Pavlov had been given a Nobel prize the next year, in 1904; although in fairness I should say that the award did not cite his work on the conditioned reflex, but on the digestive gland.

Hunter duly trained some dogs and other animals on Pavlov's lines. They were taught that when a light came on over one of three tunnels out of their cage, that tunnel would be open; they could escape down it, and were rewarded with food if they did. But once he had fixed that conditioned reflex, Hunter added to it a deeper idea: he gave the mechanical experiment a new dimension, literally—the dimension of time. Now he no longer let the dog go to the lighted tunnel at once; instead, he put out the light, and then kept the dog waiting a little while before he let him go. In this way Hunter timed how long an animal can remember where he has last seen the signal light to his escape route.

The results were and are staggering. A dog or a rat forgets which one of three tunnels has been lit up within a matter of seconds—in Hunter's experiment, ten seconds at most. If you want such an animal to do much better than this, you must make the task much simpler: you must face him with only two tunnels to choose from. Even so, the best that Hunter could do was to have a dog remember for five minutes which one of two tunnels had been lit up.

I am not quoting these times as if they were exact and universal: they surely are not. Hunter's experiment, more than fifty years old now, had many faults of detail. For example, there were too few animals, they were oddly picked, and they did not all behave consistently. It may be unfair to test a dog for what he *saw*, when he commonly follows his nose rather than his eyes. It may be unfair to test any animal in the unnatural setting of a laboratory cage. And there are higher animals, such as chimpanzees and other primates, which certainly have longer memories than the animals that Hunter tried.

Yet when all these provisos have been made (and met, by more modern experiments) the facts are still startling and characteristic. An animal cannot recall a signal from the past for even a short fraction of the time that a man can—for even a short fraction of the time that a child can. Hunter made comparable tests with six-year-old children, and found, of course, that they were incomparably better than the best of his animals. There is a striking and basic difference between a man's ability to imagine something that he saw or experienced, and an animal's failure.

Animals make up for this by other and extraordinary gifts. The salmon and the carrier pigeon can find their way home as we cannot: they have, as it were, a practical memory that man cannot match. But their actions always depend on some form of habit: on instinct or on learning, which reproduce by rote a train of known responses. They do not depend, as human memory does, on calling to mind the recollection of absent things.

Where is it that the animal falls short? We get a clue to the answer, I think, when Hunter tells us how the animals in his experiment tried to fix their recollection. They most often pointed themselves at the light before it went out, as some gun dogs point rigidly at the game they scent—and get the name *pointer* from the posture. The animal makes ready to act by building the signal into its action. There is a primitive imagery in its stance, it seems to me; it is as if the animal were trying to fix the light on its mind by fixing it in its body. And indeed, how else can a dog mark and (as it were) name one of three tunnels, when he has no such words as *left* and *right*, and no such numbers as *one, two, three?* The directed gesture of attention and readiness is perhaps the only symbolic device that the dog commands to hold on to the past, and thereby to guide himself into the future.

I used the verb *to imagine* a moment ago, and now I have some ground for giving it a meaning. *To imagine* means to make images and to move them about inside one's head in new arrangements. When you and I recall the past, we imagine it in this direct and homely sense. The tool that puts the human mind ahead of the animal is imagery. For us, memory does not demand the preoccupation that it demands in animals, and it lasts immensely longer, because we fix it in images or other substitute symbols. With the same symbolic vocabulary we spell out the future—not one but many futures, which we weigh one against another.

I am using the word *image* in a wide meaning, which does not restrict it to the mind's eye as a visual organ. An image in my usage is what Charles Peirce called a *sign*, without regard for its sensory quality. Peirce distinguished between different forms of signs, but there is no reason to make his distinction here, for the imagination works equally with them all, and that is why I call them all images.

Indeed, the most important images for human beings are simply words, which are abstract symbols. Animals do not have words, in our sense: there is no specific center for language in the brain of any animal, as there is in the human being. In this respect at least we know that the human imagination depends on a configuration in the brain that has only evolved in the last one or two million years. In the same period, evolution has greatly enlarged the front lobes in the human brain, which govern the sense of the past and the future; and it is a fair guess that they are probably the seat of our other images. (Part of the evidence for this guess is that damage to the front lobes in primates reduces them to the state of Hunter's animals.) If the guess turns out to be right, we shall know why man has come to look like a highbrow or an egghead: because otherwise there would not be room in his head for his imagination.

The images play out for us events which are not present to our senses, and thereby guard the past and create the future—a future that does not yet exist, and may never come to exist in that form. By contrast, the lack of symbolic ideas, or their rudimentary poverty, cuts off an animal from the past and the future alike, and imprisons him in the present. Of all the distinctions between man and animal, the characteristic gift which makes us human is the power to work with symbolic images: the gift of imagination.

This is really a remarkable finding. When Philip Sidney in 1580 defended poets (and all unconventional thinkers) from the Puritan charge that they were liars, he said that a maker must imagine things that are not. Halfway between Sidney and us, William Blake said, "What is now proved was once only imagined." About the same time, in 1796, Samuel Taylor Coleridge for the first time distinguished between the passive fancy and the active imagination, "the living Power and prime Agent of all human Perception." Now we see that they were right, and precisely right: the human gift is the gift of imagination—and that is not just a literary phrase.

Nor is it just a literary gift; it is, I repeat, characteristically human. Almost everything that we do that is worth doing is done in the first place in the mind's eye. The richness of human life is that we have many lives; we live the events that do not happen (and some that cannot) as vividly as those that do; and if thereby we die a thousand deaths, that is the price we pay for living a thousand lives. (A cat, of course, has only nine.) Literature is alive to us because we live its images, but so is any play of the mind—so is chess: the lines of play that we foresee and try in our heads and dismiss are as much a part of the game as the moves that we make. John Keats said that the unheard melodies are sweeter, and all chess players sadly recall that the combinations that they planned and which never came to be played were the best.

I make this point to remind you, insistently, that imagination is the manipulation of images in one's head; and that the rational manipulation belongs to that, as well as the literary and artistic manipulation. When a child begins to play games with things that stand for other things, with chairs or chessmen, he enters the gateway to reason and imagination together. For the human reason discovers new relations between things not by deduction, but by that unpredictable blend of speculation and insight that scientists call induction, which—like other forms of imagination—cannot be formalized. We see it at work when Walter Hunter inquires into a child's memory, as much as when Blake and Coleridge do. Only a restless and original mind would have asked Hunter's questions and could have conceived his experiments, in a science that was dominated by Pavlov's reflex arcs and was heading toward the behaviorism of John Watson.

Let me find a spectacular example for you from history. What is the most famous experiment that you had described to you as a child? I will hazard that it is the experiment that Galileo is said to have made in Sidney's age, in Pisa about 1590, by dropping two unequal balls from the Leaning Tower. There, we say, is a man in the modern mold, a man after our own hearts: he insisted on questioning the authority of Aristotle and St. Thomas Aquinas, and seeing with his own eyes whether (as they said) the heavy ball would reach the ground before the light one. Seeing is believing.

Yet seeing is also imagining. Galileo did challenge the authority of Aristotle, and he did look at his mechanics. But the eye that Galileo used was the mind's eye. He did not drop balls from the Leaning Tower of Pisa—and if he had, he would have got a very doubtful answer. Instead, Galileo made an imaginary experiment in his head, which I will describe as he did years later in the book he wrote after the Holy Office silenced him: the *Discorsi . . . intorno a due nuove scienze*, which was smuggled out to be printed in the Netherlands in 1638.

Suppose, said Galileo, that you drop two unequal balls from the tower at the same time. And suppose that Aristotle is right—suppose that the heavy ball falls faster, so that it steadily gains on the light ball, and hits the ground first. Very well. Now imagine the same experiment done again, with only one difference: this time the two unequal balls are joined by a string between them. The heavy ball will again move ahead, but now the light ball holds it back and acts as a drag or brake. So the light ball will be speeded up and the heavy ball will be slowed down; they must reach the ground together because they are tied together, but they cannot reach the ground as quickly as the heavy ball alone. Yet the string between them has turned the two balls into a single mass which is heavier than either ball—and surely (according to Aristotle) this mass should therefore move faster than either ball? Galileo's imaginary experiment has uncovered a contradiction; he says trenchantly, "You see how, from your assumption that a heavier body falls more rapidly than a lighter one, I infer that a (still) heavier body falls more slowly." There is only one way out of the contradiction: the heavy ball and the light ball must fall at the same rate, so that they go on falling at the same rate when they are tied together.

This argument is not conclusive, for nature might be more subtle (when the two balls are joined) than Galileo has allowed. And yet it is something more important: it is suggestive, it is stimulating, it opens a new view—in a word, it is imaginative. It cannot be settled without an actual experiment, because nothing that we imagine can become knowledge until we have translated it into, and backed it by, real experience. The test of imagination is experience. But then, that is as true of literature and the arts as it is of science. In science, the imaginary experiment is tested by confronting it with physical experience; and in literature, the imaginative conception is tested by confronting it with human experience. The superficial speculation in science is dismissed because it is found to falsify nature; and the shallow work of art is discarded because it is found to be untrue to our own nature. So when Ella Wheeler Wilcox died in 1919, more people were reading her verses than Shakespeare's; yet in a few years her work was dead. It had been buried by its poverty of emotion and its trivialness of thought: which is to say that it had been proved to be as false to the nature of man as, say, Jean Baptiste Lamarck and Trofim Lysenko[1] were false to the nature of inheritance. The strength of the imagination, its enriching power and excitement, lies in its interplay with reality—physical and emotional.

1. Lamarck was a French biologist (1744–1829) who held that characteristics acquired by experience were biologically transmittable. Lysenko is a Russian biologist (1898–   ) who has held that hereditary properties of organisms could be changed by manipulating the environment.

I doubt if there is much to choose here between science and the arts: the imagination is not much more free, and not much less free, in one than in the other. All great scientists have used their imagination freely, and let it ride them to outrageous conclusions without crying "Halt!" Albert Einstein fiddled with imaginary experiments from boyhood, and was wonderfully ignorant of the facts that they were supposed to bear on. When he wrote the first of his beautiful papers on the random movement of atoms, he did not know that the Brownian motion which it predicted could be seen in any laboratory. He was sixteen when he invented the paradox that he resolved ten years later, in 1905, in the theory of relativity, and it bulked much larger in his mind than the experiment of Albert Michelson and Edward Morley[2] which had upset every other physicist since 1881. All his life Einstein loved to make up teasing puzzles like Galileo's, about falling lifts and the detection of gravity; and they carry the nub of the problems of general relativity on which he was working.

Indeed, it could not be otherwise. The power that man has over nature and himself, and that a dog lacks, lies in his command of imaginary experience. He alone has the symbols which fix the past and play with the future, possible and impossible. In the Renaissance, the symbolism of memory was thought to be mystical, and devices that were invented as mnemonics (by Giordano Bruno, for example, and by Robert Fludd) were interpreted as magic signs. The symbol is the tool which gives man his power, and it is the same tool whether the symbols are images or words, mathematical signs or mesons. And the symbols have a reach and a roundness that goes beyond their literal and practical meaning. They are the rich concepts under which the mind gathers many particulars into one name, and many instances into one general induction. When a man says *left* and *right*, he is outdistancing the dog not only in looking for a light; he is setting in train all the shifts of meaning, the overtones and the ambiguities, between *gauche* and *adroit* and *dexterous*, between *sinister* and the sense of right. When a man counts *one*, *two*, *three*, he is not only doing mathematics; he is on the path to the mysticism of numbers in Pythagoras and Vitruvius and Kepler, to the Trinity and the signs of the Zodiac.

I have described imagination as the ability to make images and to move them about inside one's head in new arrangements. This is the faculty that is specifically human, and it is the common root from which science and literature both spring and grow and flourish together. For they do flourish (and languish) together; the

2. This was an experiment designed to measure the drag exerted on the passage of light by a hypothetical stationary medium. Its negative results eliminated the concept of a motionless, measurable ether and cleared the way for the development of the theory of relativity.

great ages of science are the great ages of all the arts, because in them powerful minds have taken fire from one another, breathless and higgledy-piggledy, without asking too nicely whether they ought to tie their imagination to falling balls or a haunted island. Galileo and Shakespeare, who were born in the same year, grew into greatness in the same age; when Galileo was looking through his telescope at the moon, Shakespeare was writing *The Tempest* and all Europe was in ferment, from Johannes Kepler to Peter Paul Rubens, and from the first table of logarithms by John Napier to the Authorized Version of the Bible.

Let me end with a last and spirited example of the common inspiration of literature and science, because it is as much alive today as it was three hundred years ago. What I have in mind is man's ageless fantasy, to fly to the moon. I do not display this to you as a high scientific enterprise; on the contrary, I think we have more important discoveries to make here on earth than wait for us, beckoning, at the horned surface of the moon. Yet I cannot belittle the fascination which that ice-blue journey has had for the imagination of men, long before it drew us to our television screens to watch the tumbling astronauts. Plutarch and Lucian, Ariosto and Ben Jonson wrote about it, before the days of Jules Verne and H. G. Wells and science fiction. The seventeenth century was heady with new dreams and fables about voyages to the moon. Kepler wrote one full of deep scientific ideas, which (alas) simply got his mother accused of witchcraft. In England, Francis Godwin wrote a wild and splendid work, *The Man in the Moone*, and the astronomer John Wilkins wrote a wild and learned one, *The Discovery of a New World*. They did not draw a line between science and fancy; for example, they all tried to guess just where in the journey the earth's gravity would stop. Only Kepler understood that gravity has no boundary, and put a law to it—which happened to be the wrong law.

All this was a few years before Isaac Newton was born, and it was all in his head that day in 1666 when he sat in his mother's garden, a young man of twenty-three, and thought about the reach of gravity. This was how he came to conceive his brilliant image, that the moon is like a ball which has been thrown so hard that it falls exactly as fast as the horizon, all the way round the earth. The image will do for any satellite, and Newton modestly calculated how long therefore an astronaut would take to fall round the earth once. He made it ninety minutes, and we have all seen now that he was right; but Newton had no way to check that. Instead he went on to calculate how long in that case the distant moon would take to round the earth, if indeed it behaves like a thrown ball that falls in the earth's gravity, and if gravity obeyed a law of inverse squares. He found that the answer would be twenty-eight days.

In that telling figure, the imagination that day chimed with nature, and made a harmony. We shall hear an echo of that harmony on the day when we land on the moon, because it will be not a technical but an imaginative triumph, that reaches back to the beginning of modern science and literature both. All great acts of imagination are like this, in the arts and in science, and convince us because they fill out reality with a deeper sense of rightness. We start with the simplest vocabulary of images, with *left* and *right* and *one, two, three,* and before we know how it happened the words and the numbers have conspired to make a match with nature: we catch in them the pattern of mind and matter as one.

QUESTIONS

1. How does the Hunter experiment provide Bronowski with the ground for defining the imagination?
2. Bronowski discusses the work of Galileo and Newton in the middle and at the end of his essay; what use does he make of their work? Does it justify placing them in the central and final positions?
3. On page 137 Bronowski attributes the imagination to a "configuration" in the brain. Configuration seems vague here; what else shows uncertainty about exactly what happens in the brain? Does this uncertainty compromise the argument of this essay?
4. What function is given to the mind by the title metaphor of reaching (later extended to symbols on page 140)? What words does Bronowski use to indicate the objects reached for? What is the significance of his selecting these words?

ISAAC ASIMOV

The Eureka Phenomenon

In the old days, when I was writing a great deal of fiction, there would come, once in a while, moments when I was stymied. Suddenly, I would find I had written myself into a hole and could see no way out. To take care of that, I developed a technique which invariably worked.

It was simply this—I went to the movies. Not just any movie. I had to pick a movie which was loaded with action but which made no demands on the intellect. As I watched, I did my best to avoid any conscious thinking concerning my problem, and when I came out of the movie I knew exactly what I would have to do to put the story back on the track.

It never failed.

In fact, when I was working on my doctoral dissertation, too many years ago, I suddenly came across a flaw in my logic that I had not noticed before and that knocked out everything I had done. In utter panic, I made my way to a Bob Hope movie—and came out with the necessary change in point of view.

It is my belief, you see, that thinking is a double phenomenon like breathing.

You can control breathing by deliberate voluntary action: you can breathe deeply and quickly, or you can hold your breath altogether, regardless of the body's needs at the time. This, however, doesn't work well for very long. Your chest muscles grow tired, your body clamors for more oxygen, or less, and you relax. The automatic involuntary control of breathing takes over, adjusts it to the body's needs and unless you have some respiratory disorder, you can forget about the whole thing.

Well, you can think by deliberate voluntary action, too, and I don't think it is much more efficient on the whole than voluntary breath control is. You can deliberately force your mind through channels of deductions and associations in search of a solution to some problem and before long you have dug mental furrows for yourself and find yourself circling round and round the same limited pathways. If those pathways yield no solution, no amount of further conscious thought will help.

On the other hand, if you let go, then the thinking process comes under automatic involuntary control and is more apt to take new pathways and make erratic associations you would not think of consciously. The solution will then come while you *think* you are *not* thinking.

The trouble is, though, that conscious thought involves no muscular action and so there is no sensation of physical weariness that would force you to quit. What's more, the panic of necessity tends to force you to go on uselessly, with each added bit of useless effort adding to the panic in a vicious cycle.

It is my feeling that it helps to relax, deliberately, by subjecting your mind to material complicated enough to occupy the voluntary faculty of thought, but superficial enough not to engage the deeper involuntary one. In my case, it is an action movie; in your case, it might be something else.

I suspect it is the involuntary faculty of thought that gives rise to what we call "a flash of intuition," something that I imagine must be merely the result of unnoticed thinking.

Perhaps the most famous flash of intuition in the history of science took place in the city of Syracuse in third-century B.C. Sicily. Bear with me and I will tell you the story—

About 250 B.C., the city of Syracuse was experiencing a kind of Golden Age. It was under the protection of the rising power of

Rome, but it retained a king of its own and considerable self-government; it was prosperous; and it had a flourishing intellectual life.

The king was Hieron II, and he had commissioned a new golden crown from a goldsmith, to whom he had given an ingot of gold as raw material. Hieron, being a practical man, had carefully weighed the ingot and then weighed the crown he received back. The two weights were precisely equal. Good deal!

But then he sat and thought for a while. Suppose the goldsmith had subtracted a little bit of the gold, not too much, and had substituted an equal weight of the considerably less valuable copper. The resulting alloy would still have the appearance of pure gold, but the goldsmith would be plus a quantity of gold over and above his fee. He would be buying gold with copper, so to speak, and Hieron would be neatly cheated.

Hieron didn't like the thought of being cheated any more than you or I would, but he didn't know how to find out for sure if he had been. He could scarcely punish the goldsmith on mere suspicion. What to do?

Fortunately, Hieron had an advantage few rulers in the history of the world could boast. He had a relative of considerable talent. The relative was named Archimedes and he probably had the greatest intellect the world was to see prior to the birth of Newton.

Archimedes was called in and was posed the problem. He had to determine whether the crown Hieron showed him was pure gold, or was gold to which a small but significant quantity of copper had been added.

If we were to reconstruct Archimedes' reasoning, it might go as follows. Gold was the densest known substance (at that time). Its density in modern terms is 19.3 grams per cubic centimeter. This means that a given weight of gold takes up less volume than the same weight of anything else! In fact, a given weight of pure gold takes up less volume than the same weight of *any* kind of impure gold.

The density of copper is 8.92 grams per cubic centimeter, just about half that of gold. If we consider 100 grams of pure gold, for instance, it is easy to calculate it to have a volume of 5.18 cubic centimeters. But suppose that 100 grams of what looked like pure gold was really only 90 grams of gold and 10 grams of copper. The 90 grams of gold would have a volume of 4.66 cubic centimeters, while the 10 grams of copper would have a volume of 1.12 cubic centimeters; for a total value of 5.78 cubic centimeters.

The difference between 5.18 cubic centimeters and 5.78 cubic centimeters is quite a noticeable one, and would instantly tell if the crown were of pure gold, or if it contained 10 per cent copper (with the missing 10 per cent of gold tucked neatly in the goldsmith's strongbox).

All one had to do, then, was measure the volume of the crown and compare it with the volume of the same weight of pure gold.

The mathematics of the time made it easy to measure the volume of many simple shapes: a cube, a sphere, a cone, a cylinder, any flattened object of simple regular shape and known thickness, and so on.

We can imagine Archimedes saying, "All that is necessary, sire, is to pound that crown flat, shape it into a square of uniform thickness, and then I can have the answer for you in a moment."

Whereupon Hieron must certainly have snatched the crown away and said, "No such thing. I can do that much without you; I've studied the principles of mathematics, too. This crown is a highly satisfactory work of art and I won't have it damaged. Just calculate its volume without in any way altering it."

But Greek mathematics had no way of determining the volume of anything with a shape as irregular as the crown, since integral calculus had not yet been invented (and wouldn't be for two thousand years, almost). Archimedes would have had to say, "There is no known way, sire, to carry through a non-destructive determination of volume."

"Then think of one," said Hieron testily.

And Archimedes must have set about thinking of one, and gotten nowhere. Nobody knows how long he thought, or how hard, or what hypotheses he considered and discarded, or any of the details.

What we do know is that, worn out with thinking, Archimedes decided to visit the public baths and relax. I think we are quite safe in saying that Archimedes had no intention of taking his problem to the baths with him. It would be ridiculous to imagine he would, for the public baths of a Greek metropolis weren't intended for that sort of thing.

The Greek baths were a place for relaxation. Half the social aristocracy of the town would be there and there was a great deal more to do than wash. One steamed one's self, got a massage, exercised, and engaged in general socializing. We can be sure that Archimedes intended to forget the stupid crown for a while.

One can envisage him engaging in light talk, discussing the latest news from Alexandria and Carthage, the latest scandals in town, the latest funny jokes at the expense of the country-squire Romans— and then he lowered himself into a nice hot bath which some bumbling attendant had filled too full.

The water in the bath slopped over as Archimedes got in. Did Archimedes notice that at once, or did he sigh, sink back, and paddle his feet awhile before noting the water-slop. I guess the latter. But, whether soon or late, he noticed, and that one fact, added to all the chains of reasoning his brain had been working on during the period of relaxation when it was unhampered by the comparative stupidities (even in Archimedes) of voluntary thought, gave Archimedes his answer in one blinding flash of insight.

Jumping out of the bath, he proceeded to run home at top speed through the streets of Syracuse. He did *not* bother to put on his clothes. The thought of Archimedes running naked through Syracuse has titillated dozens of generations of youngsters who have heard this story, but I must explain that the ancient Greeks were quite lighthearted in their attitude toward nudity. They thought no more of seeing a naked man on the streets of Syracuse, than we would on the Broadway stage.

And as he ran, Archimedes shouted over and over, "I've got it! I've got it!" Of course, knowing no English, he was compelled to shout it in Greek, so it came out, *"Eureka! Eureka!"*

Archimedes' solution was so simple that anyone could understand it—once Archimedes explained it.

If an object that is not affected by water in any way, is immersed in water, it is bound to displace an amount of water equal to its own volume, since two objects cannot occupy the same space at the same time.

Suppose, then, you had a vessel large enough to hold the crown and suppose it had a small overflow spout set into the middle of its side. And suppose further that the vessel was filled with water exactly to the spout, so that if the water level were raised a bit higher, however slightly, some would overflow.

Next, suppose that you carefully lower the crown into the water. The water level would rise by an amount equal to the volume of the crown, and that volume of water would pour out the overflow and be caught in a small vessel. Next, a lump of gold, known to be pure and exactly equal in weight to the crown, is also immersed in the water and again the level rises and the overflow is caught in a second vessel.

If the crown were pure gold, the overflow would be exactly the same in each case, and the volume of water caught in the two small vessels would be equal. If, however, the crown were of alloy, it would produce a larger overflow than the pure gold would and this would be easily noticeable.

What's more, the crown would in no way be harmed, defaced, or even as much as scratched. More important, Archimedes had discovered the "principle of buoyancy."

And was the crown pure gold? I've heard that it turned out to be alloy and that the goldsmith was executed, but I wouldn't swear to it.

How often does this "Eureka phenomenon" happen? How often is there this flash of deep insight during a moment of relaxation, this triumphant cry of "I've got it! I've got it!" which must surely be a moment of the purest ecstasy this sorry world can afford?

I wish there were some way we could tell. I suspect that in the history of science it happens *often*; I suspect that very few significant discoveries are made by the pure technique of voluntary thought; I suspect that voluntary thought may possibly prepare the ground (if even that), but that the final touch, the real inspiration, comes when thinking is under involuntary control.

But the world is in a conspiracy to hide the fact. Scientists are wedded to reason, to the meticulous working out of consequences from assumptions, to the careful organization of experiments designed to check those consequences. If a certain line of experiments ends nowhere, it is omitted from the final report. If an inspired guess turns out to be correct, it is *not* reported as an inspired guess. Instead, a solid line of voluntary thought is invented after the fact to lead up to the thought, and that is what is inserted in the final report.

The result is that anyone reading scientific papers would swear that *nothing* took place but voluntary thought maintaining a steady clumping stride from origin to destination, and that just can't be true.

It's such a shame. Not only does it deprive science of much of its glamour (how much of the dramatic story in Watson's *Double Helix* do you suppose got into the final reports announcing the great discovery of the structure of DNA?[1]), but it hands over the important process of "insight," "inspiration," "revelation" to the mystic.

The scientist actually becomes ashamed of having what we might call a revelation, as though to have one is to betray reason—when actually what we call revelation in a man who has devoted his life to reasoned thought, is after all merely reasoned thought that is not under voluntary control.

Only once in a while in modern times do we ever get a glimpse into the workings of involuntary reasoning, and when we do, it is always fascinating. Consider, for instance, the case of Friedrich August Kekule von Stradonitz.

In Kekule's time, a century and a quarter ago, a subject of great interest to chemists was the structure of organic molecules (those associated with living tissue). Inorganic molecules were generally simple in the sense that they were made up of few atoms. Water molecules, for instance, are made up of two atoms of hydrogen and one of oxygen (H_2O). Molecules of ordinary salt are made up of one atom of sodium and one of chlorine ($NaCl$), and so on.

Organic molecules, on the other hand, often contained a large number of atoms. Ethyl alcohol molecules have two carbon atoms, six hydrogen atoms, and an oxygen atom (C_2H_6O); the molecule

1. I'll tell you, in case you're curious. None! [Asimov's note]

of ordinary cane sugar is $C_{12}H_{22}O_{11}$, and other molecules are even more complex.

Then, too, it is sufficient, in the case of inorganic molecules generally, merely to know the kinds and numbers of atoms in the molecule; in organic molecules, more is necessary. Thus, dimethyl ether has the formula C_2H_6O, just as ethyl alcohol does, and yet the two are quite different in properties. Apparently, the atoms are arranged differently within the molecules—but how to determine the arrangements?

In 1852, an English chemist, Edward Frankland, had noticed that the atoms of a particular element tended to combine with a fixed number of other atoms. This combining number was called "valence." Kekule in 1858 reduced this notion to a system. The carbon atom, he decided (on the basis of plenty of chemical evidence) had a valence of four; the hydrogen atom, a valence of one; and the oxygen atom, a valence of two (and so on).

Why not represent the atoms as their symbols plus a number of attached dashes, that number being equal to the valence. Such atoms could then be put together as though they were so many Tinker Toy units and "structural formulas" could be built up.

It was possible to reason out that the structural formula

of ethyl alcohol was
$$
\begin{array}{c}
\quad\ \text{H}\ \ \text{H} \\
\quad\ | \quad\ | \\
\text{H}-\text{C}-\text{C}-\text{O}-\text{H} \\
\quad\ | \quad\ | \\
\quad\ \text{H}\ \ \text{H}
\end{array}
$$
, while that of dimethyl ether was
$$
\begin{array}{c}
\quad\ \text{H} \quad\quad \text{H} \\
\quad\ | \quad\quad\ | \\
\text{H}-\text{C}-\text{O}-\text{C}-\text{H}. \\
\quad\ | \quad\quad\ | \\
\quad\ \text{H} \quad\quad \text{H}
\end{array}
$$

In each case, there were two carbon atoms, each with four dashes attached; six hydrogen atoms, each with one dash attached; and an oxygen atom with two dashes attached. The molecules were built up of the same components, but in different arrangements.

Kekule's theory worked beautifully. It has been immensely deepened and elaborated since his day, but you can still find structures very much like Kekule's Tinker Toy formulas in any modern chemical textbook. They represent oversimplifications of the true situation, but they remain extremely useful in practice even so.

The Kekule structures were applied to many organic molecules in the years after 1858 and the similarities and contrasts in the structures neatly matched similarities and contrasts in properties. The key to the rationalization of organic chemistry had, it seemed, been found.

Yet there was one disturbing fact. The well-known chemical benzene wouldn't fit. It was known to have a molecule made up of equal numbers of carbon and hydrogen atoms. Its molecular weight was known to be 78 and a single carbon-hydrogen combination had a weight of 13. Therefore, the benzene molecule had to contain six carbon-hydrogen combinations and its formula had to be C_6H_6.

But that meant trouble. By the Kekule formulas, the hydrocarbons (molecules made up of carbon and hydrogen atoms only) could easily be envisioned as chains of carbon atoms with hydrogen atoms attached. If all the valences of the carbon atoms were filled with hydrogen atoms, as in "hexane," whose molecule looks like this—

$$
\begin{array}{cccccc}
H & H & H & H & H & H \\
| & | & | & | & | & | \\
H-C-&C-&C-&C-&C-&C-H \\
| & | & | & | & | & | \\
H & H & H & H & H & H
\end{array}
$$

the compound is said to be saturated. Such saturated hydrocarbons were found to have very little tendency to react with other substances.

If some of the valences were not filled, unused bonds were added to those connecting the carbon atoms. Double bonds were formed as in "hexene"—

$$
\begin{array}{cccccc}
H & H & II & H & H & H \\
| & | & | & | & | & | \\
H-C-&C-&C =&C-&C-&C-H \\
| & | & & & | & | \\
H & H & & & H & H
\end{array}
$$

Hexene is unsaturated, for that double bond has a tendency to open up and add other atoms. Hexene is chemically active.

When six carbons are present in a molecule, it takes fourteen hydrogen atoms to occupy all the valence bonds and make it inert —as in hexane. In hexene, on the other hand, there are only twelve hydrogens. If there were still fewer hydrogen atoms, there would be more than one double bond; there might even be triple bonds, and the compound would be still more active than hexene.

Yet benzene, which is C_6H_6 and has eight fewer hydrogen atoms than hexane, is *less* active than hexene, which has only two fewer hydrogen atoms than hexane. In fact, benzene is even less active than hexane itself. The six hydrogen atoms in the benzene molecule seem to satisfy the six carbon atoms to a greater extent than do the fourteen hydrogen atoms in hexane.

For heaven's sake, why?

This might seem unimportant. The Kekule formulas were so beautifully suitable in the case of so many compounds that one might simply dismiss benzene as an exception to the general rule.

Science, however, is not English grammar. You can't just categorize something as an exception. If the exception doesn't fit into the general system, then the general system must be wrong.

Or, take the more positive approach. An exception can often be made to fit into a general system, provided the general system is broadened. Such broadening generally represents a great advance and for this reason, exceptions ought to be paid great attention.

For some seven years, Kekule faced the problem of benzene and tried to puzzle out how a chain of six carbon atoms could be completely satisfied with as few as six hydrogen atoms in benzene and yet be left unsatisfied with twelve hydrogen atoms in hexene.

Nothing came to him!

And than one day in 1865 (he tells the story himself) he was in Ghent, Belgium, and in order to get to some destination, he boarded a public bus. He was tired and, undoubtedly, the droning beat of the horses' hooves on the cobblestones, lulled him. He fell into a comatose half-sleep.

In that sleep, he seemed to see a vision of atoms attaching themselves to each other in chains that moved about. (Why not? It was the sort of thing that constantly occupied his waking thoughts.) But then one chain twisted in such a way that head and tail joined, forming a ring—and Kekule woke with a start.

To himself, he must surely have shouted "Eureka," for indeed he had it. The six carbon atoms of benzene formed a ring and not a chain, so that the structural formula looked like this:

To be sure, there were still three double bonds, so you might think the molecule had to be very active—but now there was a dif-

ference. Atoms in a ring might be expected to have different properties from those in a chain and double bonds in one case might not
have the properties of those in the other. At least, chemists could
work on that assumption and see if it involved them in contradictions.

It didn't. The assumption worked excellently well. It turned out
that organic molecules could be divided into two groups: aromatic
and aliphatic. The former had the benzene ring (or certain other
similar rings) as part of the structure and the latter did not. Allowing for different properties within each group, the Kekule structures
worked very well.

For nearly seventy years, Kekule's vision held good in the hard
field of actual chemical techniques, guiding the chemist through the
jungle of reactions that led to the synthesis of more and more molecules. Then, in 1932, Linus Pauling applied quantum mechanics
to chemical structure with sufficient subtlety to explain just why the
benzene ring was so special and what had proven correct in practice
proved correct in theory as well.

Other cases? Certainly.

In 1764, the Scottish engineer James Watt was working as an
instrument maker for the University of Glasgow. The university
gave him a model of a Newcomen steam engine, which didn't work
well, and asked him to fix it. Watt fixed it without trouble, but
even when it worked perfectly, it didn't work well. It was far too
inefficient and consumed incredible quantities of fuel. Was there a
way to improve that?

Thought didn't help; but a peaceful, relaxed walk on a Sunday
afternoon did. Watt returned with the key notion in mind of using
two separate chambers, one for steam only and one for cold water
only, so that the same chamber did not have to be constantly
cooled and reheated to the infinite waste of fuel.

The Irish mathematician William Rowan Hamilton worked up a
theory of "quaternions" in 1843 but couldn't complete that theory
until he grasped the fact that there were conditions under which
$p \times q$ was *not* equal to $q \times p$. The necessary thought came to him
in a flash one time when he was walking to town with his wife.

The German physiologist Otto Loewi was working on the mechanism of nerve action, in particular, on the chemicals produced by
nerve endings. He awoke at 3 A.M. one night in 1921 with a perfectly clear notion of the type of experiment he would have to run
to settle a key point that was puzzling him. He wrote it down and
went back to sleep. When he woke in the morning, he found he
couldn't remember what his inspiration had been. He remembered
he had written it down, but he couldn't read his writing.

The next night, he woke again at 3 A.M. with the clear thought
once more in mind. This time, he didn't fool around. He got up,

dressed himself, went straight to the laboratory and began work. By 5 A.M. he had proved his point and the consequences of his findings became important enough in later years so that in 1936 he received a share in the Nobel prize in medicine and physiology.

How very often this sort of thing must happen, and what a shame that scientists are so devoted to their belief in conscious thought that they so consistently obscure the actual methods by which they obtain their results.

QUESTIONS
1. Does Asimov argue that science ought to abandon reasoned thought in favor of intuition?
2. What does Asimov find wrong about scientific reports as they are customarily written? Do you agree? If scientific writing were not strictly reasonable wouldn't there be a danger of misrepresenting science?
3. Is cultivation of "the Eureka phenomenon" encouraged in any of the science courses you may have taken or are now taking? Why, or why not?
4. Have you ever experienced anything like "the Eureka phenomenon" Asimov describes? If so, write out an account of what happened. Tell what your feelings were when the phenomenon occurred. Did you ever report the discovery in just that way to any one else (to a teacher, for example)? If so, what was the other person's response?
5. In the preceding essay J. Bronowski discusses imagination and science. Are there points on which Asimov and Bronowski would seem to be in agreement concerning science?

WILLIAM JAMES

The Ethical and Pedagogical Importance of the Principle of Habit[1]

"Habit a second nature! Habit is ten times nature," the Duke of Wellington is said to have exclaimed; and the degree to which this is true no one probably can appreciate as well as one who is a veteran soldier himself. The daily drill and the years of discipline end by fashioning a man completely over again, as to most of the possibilities of his conduct.

"There is a story," says Prof. Huxley, "which is credible enough, though it may not be true, of a practical joker who, seeing a discharged veteran carrying home his dinner, suddenly called out, 'Attention!' whereupon the man instantly brought his hands

1. From "Habit," Chapter 10 of *The Principles of Psychology.*

down, and lost his mutton and potatoes in the gutter. The drill had been thorough, and its effects had become embodied in the man's nervous structure."

Riderless cavalry-horses, at many a battle, have been seen to come together and go through their customary evolutions at the sound of the bugle-call. Most domestic beasts seem machines almost pure and simple, undoubtingly, unhesitatingly doing from minute to minute the duties they have been taught, and giving no sign that the possibility of an alternative ever suggests itself to their mind. Men grown old in prison have asked to be readmitted after being once set free. In a railroad accident a menagerie-tiger, whose cage had broken open, is said to have emerged, but presently crept back again, as if too much bewildered by his new responsibilities, so that he was without difficulty secured.

Habit is thus the enormous fly-wheel of society, its most precious conservative agent. It alone is what keeps us all within the bounds of ordinance, and saves the children of fortune from the envious uprisings of the poor. It alone prevents the hardest and most repulsive walks of life from being deserted by those brought up to tread therein. It keeps the fisherman and the deck-hand at sea through the winter; it holds the miner in his darkness, and nails the countryman to his log-cabin and his lonely farm through all the months of snow; it protects us from invasion by the natives of the desert and the frozen zone. It dooms us all to fight out the battle of life upon the lines of our nurture or our early choice, and to make the best of a pursuit that disagrees, because there is no other for which we are fitted, and it is too late to begin again. It keeps different social strata from mixing. Already at the age of twenty-five you see the professional mannerism settling down on the young commercial traveler, on the young doctor, on the young minister, on the young counselor-at-law. You see the little lines of cleavage running through the character, the tricks of thought, the prejudices, the ways of the "shop," in a word, from which the man can by-and-by no more escape than his coat-sleeve can suddenly fall into a new set of folds. On the whole, it is best he should not escape. It is well for the world that in most of us, by the age of thirty, the character has set like plaster, and will never soften again.

If the period between twenty and thirty is the critical one in the formation of intellectual and professional habits, the period below twenty is more important still for the fixings of *personal* habits, properly so called, such as a vocalization and pronunciation, gesture, motion, and address. Hardly ever is a language learned after twenty spoken without a foreign accent; hardly ever can a youth transferred to the society of his betters unlearn the nasality and other vices of speech bred in him by the associations of his growing years. Hardly ever, indeed, no matter how much money there be in his pocket, can he even learn to *dress* like a gentleman-born. The merchants offer their wares as eagerly to him as to the veriest "swell," but he simply *cannot* buy the right things. An invisible law, as strong as gravitation, keeps him within his orbit, arrayed this year as he was the last; and how his better-clad acquaintances contrive to get the things they wear will be for him a mystery till his dying day.

The great thing, then, in all education, is to *make our nervous system our ally instead of our enemy*. It is to fund and capitalize our acquisitions, and live at ease upon the interest of the fund. *For this we must make automatic and habitual, as early as possible, as many useful actions as we can*, and guard against the growing into ways that are likely to be disadvantageous to us, as we should guard against the plague. The more of the details of our daily life we can hand over to the effortless custody of automatism, the more our higher powers of mind will be set free for their own proper work. There is no more miserable human being than one in whom nothing is habitual but indecision, and for whom the lighting of every cigar, the drinking of every cup, the time of rising and going to bed every day, and the beginning of every bit of work, are subjects of express volitional deliberation. Full half the time of such a man goes to the deciding, or regretting, of matters which ought to be so ingrained in him as practically not to exist for his consciousness at all. If there be such daily duties not yet ingrained in any one of my readers, let him begin this very hour to set the matter right.

In Professor Bain's chapter on "The Moral Habits" there are some admirable practical remarks laid down. Two great maxims emerge from his treatment. The first is that in the acquisition of a new habit, or the leaving off of an old one, we must take care to *launch ourselves with as strong and decided an initiative as possible*. Accumulate all the possible circumstances which shall re-enforce the right motives; put yourself assiduously in conditions that encourage the new way; make engagements incompatible with the old; take a public pledge, if the case allows; in short, envelop your resolution with every aid you know. This will give your new beginning such a momentum that the temptation to break down will not occur as soon as it otherwise might; and every day during which a breakdown is postponed adds to the chances of its not occurring at all.

The second maxim is: *Never suffer an exception to occur till the new habit is securely rooted in your life*. Each lapse is like the letting fall of a ball of string which one is carefully winding up; a single slip undoes more than a great many turns will wind again. *Continuity* of training is the great means of making the nervous system act infallibly right. As Professor Bain says:

"The peculiarity of the moral habits, contradistinguishing them from the intellectual acquisitions, is the presence of two hostile powers, one to be gradually raised into the ascendant over the other. It is necessary, above all things, in such a situation, never to lose a battle. Every gain on the wrong side undoes the effect of many conquests on the right. The essential precaution, therefore, is so to regulate the two opposing powers that the one may have a series of uninterrupted successes, until repetition has fortified it to such a degree as to enable it to cope with the opposition, under any circumstances. This is the theoretically best career of mental progress."

The need of securing success at the *outset* is imperative. Failure at first is apt to damp the energy of all future attempts, whereas past experiences of success nerve one to future vigor. Goethe says to a man who consulted him about an enterprise but mistrusted his own powers: "Ach! you need only blow on your hands!" And the remark illustrates the effect on Goethe's spirits of his own habitually successful career.

The question of "tapering off," in abandoning such habits as drink and opium-indulgence comes in here, and is a question about which experts differ within certain limits, and in regard to what may be best for an individual case. In the main, however, all expert opinion would agree that abrupt acquisition of the new habit is the best way, *if there be a real possibility of carrying it out.* We must be careful not to give the will so stiff a task as to insure its defeat at the very outset; but, *provided one can stand it,* a sharp period of suffering, and then a free time, is the best thing to aim at, whether in giving up a habit like that of opium, or in simply changing one's hours of rising or of work. It is surprising how soon a desire will die of inanition if it be *never* fed.

One must first learn, unmoved, looking neither to the right nor left, to walk firmly on the strait and narrow path, before one can begin "to make one's self over again." He who every day makes a fresh resolve is like one who, arriving at the edge of the ditch he is to leap, forever stops and returns for a fresh run. Without *unbroken* advance there is no such thing as *accumulation* of the ethical forces possible, and to make this possible, and to exercise us and habituate us in it, is the sovereign blessing of regular work.[2]

A third maxim may be added to the preceding pair: *Seize the very first possible opportunity to act on every resolution you make, and on every emotional prompting you may experience in the direction of the habits you aspire to gain.* It is not in the moment of their forming, but in the moment of their producing *motor*

2. J. Bahnsen: "Beitäge zu Charakterologie" (1867), vol. I, p. 209 [James' note].

effects, that resolves and aspirations communicate the new "set" to the brain. As the author last quoted remarks:

The actual presence of the practical opportunity alone furnishes the fulcrum upon which the lever can rest, by means of which the moral will may multiply its strength, and raise itself aloft. He who has no solid ground to press against will never get beyond the stage of empty gesture-making.

No matter how full a reservoir of *maxims* one may possess, and no matter how good one's *sentiments* may be, if one have not taken advantage of every concrete opportunity to *act*, one's character may remain entirely unaffected for the better. With mere good intentions, hell is proverbially paved. And this is an obvious consequence of the principles we have laid down. A "character," as J. S. Mill says, "is a completely fashioned will"; and a will, in the sense in which he means it, is an aggregate of tendencies to act in a firm and prompt and definite way upon all the principal emergencies of life. A tendency to act only becomes effectively ingrained in us in proportion to the uninterrupted frequency with which the actions actually occur, and the brain "grows" to their use. When a resolve or a fine glow of feeling is allowed to evaporate without bearing practical fruit it is worse than a chance lost; it works so as positively to hinder future resolutions and emotions from taking the normal path of discharge. There is no more contemptible type of human character than that of the nerveless sentimentalist and dreamer, who spends his life in a weltering sea of sensibility and emotion, but who never does a manly concrete deed. Rousseau, inflaming all the mothers of France, by his eloquence, to follow Nature and nurse their babies themselves, while he sends his own children to the foundling hospital, is the classical example of what I mean. But every one of us in his measure, whenever, after glowing for an abstractly formulated Good, he practically ignores some actual case, among the squalid "other particulars" of which that same Good lurks disguised, treads straight on Rousseau's path. All Goods are disguised by the vulgarity of their concomitants, in this work-a-day world; but woe to him who can only recognize them when he thinks them in their pure and abstract form! The habit of excessive novel-reading and theater-going will produce true monsters in this line. The weeping of the Russian lady over the fictitious personages in the play, while her coachman is freezing to death on his seat outside, is the sort of thing that everywhere happens on a less glaring scale. Even the habit of excessive indulgence in music, for those who are neither performers themselves nor musically gifted enough to take it in a purely intellectual way, has probably a relaxing effect upon the character. One becomes filled with emotions which habitually pass without prompting to any deed, and so the inertly sentimental condition is kept up. The remedy would be, never to suffer one's self to have an emotion at a concert, without expressing it afterward in *some* active way. Let the expression be the least thing in the world—speaking genially to one's grandmother, or giving up one's seat in a horse-car, if nothing more heroic offers—but let it not fail to take place.

These latter cases make us aware that it is not simply *particular lines* of discharge, but also *general forms* of discharge, that seem to be grooved out by habit in the brain. Just as, if we let our emotions evaporate, they get into a way of evaporating; so there is reason to suppose that if we often flinch from making an effort, before we know it the effort-making capacity will be gone; and that, if we suffer the wandering of our attention, presently it will wander all the time. Attention and effort are, as we shall see later, but two names for the same psychic fact. To what brain-processes they correspond we do not know. The strongest reason for believing that they do depend on brain-processes at all, and are not pure acts of the spirit, is just this fact, that they seem in some degree subject to the law of habit, which is a material law. As a final practical maxim, relative to these habits of the will, we may, then, offer something like this: *Keep the faculty of effort alive in you by a little gratuitous exercise every day.* That is, be systematically ascetic or heroic in little unnecessary points, do every day or two something for no other reason than that you would rather not do it, so that when the hour of dire need draws nigh, it may find you not unnerved and untrained to stand the test. Ascetism of this sort is like the insurance which a man pays on his house and goods. The tax does him no good at the time, and possibly may never bring him a return. But if the fire *does* come, his having paid it will be his salvation from ruin. So with the man who has daily inured himself to habits of concentrated attention, energetic volition, and self-denial in unnecessary things. He will stand like a tower when everything rocks around him, and when his softer fellow-mortals are winnowed like chaff in the blast.

The physiological study of mental conditions is thus the most powerful ally of hortatory ethics. The hell to be endured hereafter, of which theology tells, is no worse than the hell we make for ourselves in this world by habitually fashioning our characters in the wrong way. Could the young but realize how soon they will become mere walking bundles of habits, they would give more heed to their conduct while in the plastic state. We are spinning our own fates, good or evil, and never to be undone. Every smallest stroke of virtue or of vice leaves its never so little scar. The drunken Rip Van Winkle, in Jefferson's play, excuses himself for every fresh dereliction by saying, "I won't count this time!" Well! he may not count it, and a kind Heaven may not count it; but it is being counted none the less. Down among his nerve cells and fibres the molecules are counting it, registering and storing it up to be used against him when the next temptation comes. Nothing we ever do is, in strict scientific literalness, wiped out. Of course this has its good side as well as its bad one. As we become permanent drunkards by so many separate drinks, so we become saints in the moral, and authorities and experts in the practical and scientific spheres, by so many separate acts and hours of work. Let no youth have any anxiety about the upshot of his education, whatever the line of it may be. If he keep faithfully busy each hour of the working day, he may safely leave the final result to itself. He can with perfect certainty count on waking up some fine morning, to find himself one of the competent ones of his generation, in whatever pursuit he may have singled out. Silently, between all the details of his business, the *power of judging* in all that class of matter will have built itself up within him as a possession that will never pass away. Young people should know this truth in advance. The ignorance of it has probably engendered more discouragement and faint-heartedness in youths embarking on arduous careers than all other causes put together.

QUESTIONS
1. What, according to James, is the utility of habit for society? For the individual person?
2. Will conformity result from cultivating habits according to the maxims here presented?
3. Does your own experience appear to prove or disprove the maxims James presents? All, or some?
4. James and Milgram ("The Perils of Obedience," pp. 158–171) are both psychologists. Do they appear to be working in similar ways? If dissimilar, how do you explain the difference? Is one more scientific than the other? How do the two pieces of writing compare as to subject, method of presentation, assumptions, purpose, style?

STANLEY MILGRAM

The Perils of Obedience

Obedience is as basic an element in the structure of social life as one can point to. Some system of authority is a requirement of all communal living, and it is only the person dwelling in isolation who is not forced to respond, with defiance or submission, to the commands of others. For many people, obedience is a deeply ingrained behavior tendency, indeed a potent impulse overriding training in ethics, sympathy, and moral conduct.

The dilemma inherent in submission to authority is ancient, as old as the story of Abraham, and the question of whether one should obey when commands conflict with conscience has been argued by Plato, dramatized in *Antigone*, and treated to philosophic analysis in almost every historical epoch. Conservative philosophers argue that the very fabric of society is threatened by disobedience, while humanists stress the primacy of the individual conscience.

The legal and philosophic aspects of obedience are of enormous import, but they say very little about how most people behave in concrete situations. I set up a simple experiment at Yale University to test how much pain an ordinary citizen would inflict on another person simply because he was ordered to by an experimental scientist. Stark authority was pitted against the subjects' strongest moral imperatives against hurting others, and, with the subjects' ears ringing with the screams of the victims, authority won more often than not. The extreme willingness of adults to go to almost any lengths on the command of an authority constitutes the chief finding of the study and the fact most urgently demanding explanation.

In the basic experimental design, two people come to a psychology laboratory to take part in a study of memory and learning. One of them is designated as a "teacher" and the other a "learner." The experimenter explains that the study is concerned with the effects of punishment on learning. The learner is conducted into a room, seated in a kind of miniature electric chair; his arms are strapped to prevent excessive movement, and an electrode is attached to his wrist. He is told that he will be read lists of simple word pairs, and that he will then be tested on his ability to remember the second word of a pair when he hears the first one again. Whenever he makes an error, he will receive electric shocks of increasing intensity.

The real focus of the experiment is the teacher. After watching the learner being strapped into place, he is seated before an impressive shock generator. The instrument panel consists of thirty lever switches set in a horizontal line. Each switch is clearly labeled with a voltage designation ranging from 15 to 450 volts. The following designations are clearly indicated for groups of four switches, going from left to right: Slight Shock, Moderate Shock, Strong Shock, Very Strong Shock, Intense Shock, Extreme Intensity Shock, Danger: Severe Shock. (Two switches after this last designation are simply marked XXX.)

When a switch is depressed, a pilot light corresponding to each switch is illuminated in bright red; an electric buzzing is heard; a blue light, labeled "voltage energizer," flashes; the dial on the voltage meter swings to the right; and various relay clicks sound off.

The upper left-hand corner of the generator is labeled SHOCK GENERATOR, TYPE ZLB, DYSON INSTRUMENT COMPANY, WALTHAM, MASS. OUTPUT 15 VOLTS–450 VOLTS.

Each subject is given a sample 45-volt shock from the generator before his run as teacher, and the jolt strengthens his belief in the authenticity of the machine.

The teacher is a genuinely naïve subject who has come to the laboratory for the experiment. The learner, or victim, is actually an actor who receives no shock at all. The point of the experiment is to see how far a person will proceed in a concrete and measurable situation in which he is ordered to inflict increasing pain on a protesting victim.

Conflict arises when the man receiving the shock begins to show that he is experiencing discomfort. At 75 volts, he grunts; at 120 volts, he complains loudly; at 150, he demands to be released from the experiment. As the voltage increases, he protests become more vehement and emotional. At 285 volts, his response can be described only as an agonized scream. Soon thereafter, he makes no sound at all.

For the teacher, the situation quickly becomes one of gripping tension. It is not a game for him; conflict is intense and obvious. The manifest suffering of the learner presses him to quit; but each time he hesitates to administer a shock, the experimenter orders him to continue. To extricate himself from this plight, the subject must make a clear break with authority.[1]

The subject, Gretchen Brandt,[2] is an attractive thirty-one-year-old medical technician who works at the Yale Medical School. She had emigrated from Germany five years before.

On several occasions when the learner complains, she turns to the experimenter coolly and inquires, "Shall I continue?" She promptly returns to her task when the experimenter asks her to do so. At the administration of 210 volts, she turns to the experimenter, remarking firmly, "Well, I'm sorry, I don't think we should continue."

EXPERIMENTER: The experiment requires that you go on until he has learned all the word pairs correctly.

BRANDT: He has a heart condition, I'm sorry. He told you that before.

EXPERIMENTER; The shocks may be painful but they are not dangerous.

BRANDT: Well, I'm sorry, I think when shocks continue like this, they *are* dangerous. You ask him if he wants to get out. It's his free will.

EXPERIMENTER: It is absolutely essential that we continue. . . .

BRANDT: I'd like you to ask him. We came here of our free will. If he wants to continue I'll go ahead. He told you he had a heart con-

---

1. The ethical problems of carrying out an experiment of this sort are too complex to be dealt with here, but they receive extended treatment in the book from which this article is adapted [Milgram's note]. The book is *Obedi-* *ence to Authority* (New York: Harper and Row, 1974).

2. Names of subjects described in this piece have been changed [Milgram's note].

dition. I'm sorry. I don't want to be responsible for anything happening to him. I wouldn't like it for me either.

EXPERIMENTER: You have no other choice.

BRANDT: I think we are here on our own free will. I don't want to be responsible if anything happens to him. Please understand that.

She refuses to go further and the experiment is terminated.

The woman is firm and resolute throughout. She indicates in the interview that she was in no way tense or nervous, and this corresponds to her controlled appearance during the experiment. She feels that the last shock she administered to the learner was extremely painful and reiterates that she "did not want to be responsible for any harm to him."

The woman's straightforward, courteous behavior in the experiment, lack of tension, and total control of her own action seem to make disobedience a simple and rational deed. Her behavior is the very embodiment of what I envisioned would be true for almost all subjects.

Before the experiments, I sought predictions about the outcome from various kinds of people—psychiatrists, college sophomores, middle-class adults, graduate students and faculty in the behavioral sciences. With remarkable similarity, they predicted that virtually all subjects would refuse to obey the experimenter. The psychiatrists, specifically, predicted that most subjects would not go beyond 150 volts, when the victim makes his first explicit demand to be freed. They expected that only 4 percent would reach 300 volts, and that only a pathological fringe of about one in a thousand would administer the highest shock on the board.

These predictions were unequivocally wrong. Of the forty subjects in the first experiment, twenty-five obeyed the orders of the experimenter to the end, punishing the victim until they reached the most potent shock available on the generator. After 450 volts were administered three times, the experimenter called a halt to the session. Many obedient subjects then heaved sighs of relief, mopped their brows, rubbed their fingers over their eyes, or nervously fumbled cigarettes. Others displayed only minimal signs of tension from beginning to end.

When the very first experiments were carried out, Yale undergraduates were used as subjects, and about 60 percent of them were fully obedient. A colleague of mine immediately dismissed these findings as having no relevance to "ordinary" people, asserting that Yale undergraduates are a highly aggressive, competitive bunch who step on each other's necks on the slightest provocation. He assured me that when "ordinary" people were tested, the results would be quite different. As we moved from the pilot studies to the regular experimental series, people drawn from every stratum of New Haven life came to be employed in the experiment: professionals, white-collar workers, unemployed persons, and industrial workers. *The experimental outcome was the same as we had observed among the students.*

Moreover, when the experiments were repeated in Princeton, Munich, Rome, South Africa, and Australia, the level of obedience was invariably somewhat *higher* than found in the investigation reported in this article. Thus one scientist in Munich found 85 percent of his subjects obedient.

Fred Prozi's reactions, if more dramatic than most, illuminate the conflicts experienced by others in less visible form. About fifty years old and unemployed at the time of the experiment, he has a good-natured, if slightly dissolute, appearance, and he strikes people as a rather ordinary fellow. He begins the session calmly but becomes tense as it proceeds. After delivering the 180-volt shock, he pivots around in his chair and, shaking his head, addresses the experimenter in agitated tones:

PROZI: I can't stand it. I'm not going to kill that man in there. You hear him hollering?

EXPERIMENTER: As I told you before, the shocks may be painful, but . . .

PROZI: But he's hollering. He can't stand it. What's going to happen to him?

EXPERIMENTER: (his voice is patient, matter-of-fact): The experiment requires that you continue, Teacher.

PROZI: Aaah, but, unh, I'm not going to get that man sick in there —know what I mean?

EXPERIMENTER: Whether the learner likes it or not, we must go on, through all the word pairs.

PROZI: I refuse to take the responsibility. He's in there hollering!

EXPERIMENTER: It's absolutely essential that you continue, Prozi.

PROZI: (indicating the unused question): There's too many left here, I mean, Jeez, if he gets them wrong, there's too many of them left. I mean, who's going to take the responsibility if anything happens to that gentleman?

EXPERIMENTER: I'm responsible for anything that happens to him. Continue, please.

PROZI: All right. (Consults list of words.) The next one's "Slow —walk, truck, dance, music." Answer, please. (A buzzing sound indicates the learner has signaled his answer.) Wrong. A hundred and ninety-five volts. "Dance." (Zzumph!)

LEARNER (yelling): Let me out of here! My heart's bothering me! (Teacher looks at experimenter.)

EXPERIMENTER: Continue, please.

LEARNER (screaming): Let me out of here! You have no right to keep me here! Let me out of here, my heart's bothering me, let me out!

PROZI (shakes head, pats the table nervously): You see, he's hollering. Hear that? Gee, I don't know.

EXPERIMENTER: The experiment requires . . .

PROZI (interrupting): I know it does, sir, but I mean—hunh! He don't know what he's getting in for. He's up to 195 volts! (Experiment continues, through 210 volts, 225 volts, 240 volts, 255 volts, 270 volts, at which point Prozi, with evident relief, runs out of word-pair questions.)

EXPERIMENTER: You'll have to go back to the beginning of that page and go through them again until he's learned them all correctly.

PROZI: Aw, no. I'm not going to kill that man. You mean I've got to keep going up with the scale? No sir. He's hollering in there. I'm not going to give him 450 volts.

EXPERIMENTER: The experiment requires that you go on.

LEARNER: Ohhh. I absolutely refuse to answer anymore. (Shouting urgently now.) Let me out of here! You can't hold me here! Get me out. Get-me-out-of-here!

EXPERIMENTER: Continue. The next word is "Green," please.

PROZI: "Green—grass, hat, ink, apple." (Nothing happens. No answering buzz. Just gloomy silence.)

PROZI: I don't think he is going to answer.

EXPERIMENTER: If the learner doesn't answer in a reasonable time, about four or five seconds, consider the answer wrong. And follow the same procedures you have been doing for wrong answers. Say, "Wrong," tell him the number of volts, give him the punishment, read him the correct answer. Continue, please.

PROZI: "Green—grass, hat, ink, apple." Answer, please. (More silence. Subject just sits there.)

EXPERIMENTER: Go on with the procedure, please.

PROZI: Three hundred and fifteen volts. The answer is "ink." (Zzumph!)

LEARNER: Ohh. Oooohh.

PROZI (relieved to hear response): Next one . . .

LEARNER: I absolutely refuse to answer.

PROZI: You got to. You get a shock if you don't answer. (Experiment continues with learner refusing to answer, and, finally, failing even to grunt or groan. At 375 volts, the subject stands up.)

PROZI: I think something's happening to that fellow in there. I don't get no answer. He was hollering at less voltage. Can't you check in and see if he's all right, please?

EXPERIMENTER (with same detached calm): Not once we've started. Please continue, Teacher.

PROZI (sits down, sighs deeply): "Cool—day, shade, water, paint." Answer, please. Are you all right in there? Are you all right?

EXPERIMENTER: Please continue, Teacher. Continue, please. (Subject pushes lever. Zzumph!)

PROZI (swiveling around in his chair): Something's happened to that man in there. (Swiveling back.) Next one. "Low—dollar, necklace, moon, paint." (Turning around again.) Something's happened to that man in there. You better check in on him, sir. He won't answer or nothing.

EXPERIMENTER: Continue. Go on, please.

PROZI: You accept all responsibility?

EXPERIMENTER: The responsibility is mine. Correct. Please go on. (Subject returns to his list, starts running through words as rapidly as he can read them, works through to 450 volts.)

PROZI: That's that.

EXPERIMENTER: Continue using the 450 switch for each wrong answer. Continue, please.

PROZI: But I don't get anything!

EXPERIMENTER: Please continue. The next word is "white."

PROZI: Don't you think you should look in on him, please?

EXPERIMENTER: Not once we've started the experiment.

PROZI: What if he's dead in there? (Gestures toward the room with the electric chair.) I mean, he told me he can't stand the shock, sir. I don't mean to be rude, but I think you should look in on him. All you have to do is look in on him. All you have to do is look in the door. I don't get no answer, no noise. Something might have happened to the gentleman in there, sir.

EXPERIMENTER: We must continue. Go on, please.

PROZI: You mean keep giving him what? Four-hundred-fifty volts, what he's got now?

EXPERIMENTER: That's correct. Continue. The next word is "white."

PROZI (now at a furious pace): "White—cloud, horse, rock, house." Answer, please. The answer is "horse." Four hundred and fifty volts. (Zzumph!) Next word, "Bag—paint, music, clown, girl." The answer is "paint." Four hundred and fifty volts. (Zzumph!) Next word is "Short—sentence, movie . . ."

EXPERIMENTER: Excuse me, Teacher. We'll have to discontinue the experiment.

Morris Braverman, another subject, is a thirty-nine-year-old social worker. He looks older than his years because of his bald head and serious demeanor. His brow is furrowed, as if all the world's burdens were carried on his face. He appears intelligent and concerned.

When the learner refuses to answer and the experimenter instructs Braverman to treat the absence of an answer as equivalent to a wrong answer, he takes his instruction to heart. Before administering 300 volts he asserts officiously to the victim, "Mr. Wallace, your silence has to be considered as a wrong answer." Then he administers the shock. He offers halfheartedly to change places with the learner, then asks the experimenter, "Do I have to follow these instructions literally?" He is satisfied with the experimenter's answer that he does. His very refined and authoritative manner of speaking is increasingly broken up by wheezing laughter.

The experimenter's notes on Mr. Braverman at the last few shocks are:

Almost breaking up now each time gives shock. Rubbing face to hide laughter.

Squinting, trying to hide face with hand, still laughing.

Cannot control his laughter at this point no matter what he does. Clenching fist, pushing it onto table.

In an interview after the session, Mr. Braverman summarizes the experiment with impressive fluency and intelligence. He feels the experiment may have been designed also to "test the effects on the teacher of being in an essentially sadistic role, as well as the reactions of a student to a learning situation that was authoritative and punitive." When asked how painful the last few shocks administered to the learner were, he indicates that the most extreme category on the scale is not adequate (it read EXTREMELY PAINFUL) and places his mark at the edge of the scale with an arrow carrying it beyond the scale.

It is almost impossible to convey the greatly relaxed, sedate quality of his conversation in the interview. In the most relaxed terms, he speaks about his severe inner tension.

EXPERIMENTER: At what point were you most tense or nervous?

MR. BRAVERMAN: Well, when he first began to cry out in pain, and I realized this was hurting him. This got worse when he just blocked and refused to answer. There was I. I'm a nice person, I think, hurting somebody, and caught up in what seemed a mad situation . . . and in the interest of science, one goes through with it.

When the interviewer pursues the general question of tension, Mr. Braverman spontaneously mentions his laughter.

"My reactions were awfully peculiar. I don't know if you were watching me, but my reactions were giggly, and trying to stifle laughter. This isn't the way I usually am. This was a sheer reaction to a totally impossible situation. And my reaction was to the situation of having to hurt somebody. And being totally helpless and caught up in a set of circumstances where I just couldn't deviate and I couldn't try to help. This is what got me."

Mr. Braverman, like all subjects, was told the actual nature and purpose of the experiment, and a year later he affirmed in a questionnaire that he had learned something of personal importance: "What appalled me was that I could possess this capacity for obedience and compliance to a central idea, i.e., the value of a memory experiment, even after it became clear that continued adherence to this value was at the expense of violation of another value, i.e., don't hurt someone who is helpless and not hurting you. As my wife said, 'You can call yourself Eichmann.' I hope I deal more effectively with any future conflicts of values I encounter."

One theoretical interpretation of this behavior holds that all people harbor deeply aggressive instincts continually pressing for expression, and that the experiment provides institutional justification for the release of these impulses. According to this view, if a person is placed in a situation in which he has complete power over another individual, whom he may punish as much as he likes, all that is sadistic and bestial in man comes to the fore. The impulse to shock the victim is seen to flow from the potent aggressive tendencies, which are part of the motivational life of the individual, and the experiment, because it provides social legitimacy, simply opens the door to their expression.

It becomes vital, therefore, to compare the subject's performance when he is under orders and when he is allowed to choose the shock level.

The procedure was identical to our standard experiment, except that the teacher was told that he was free to select any shock level on any of the trials. (The experimenter took pains to point out that the teacher could use the highest levels on the generator, the lowest, any in between, or any combination of levels.) Each subject proceeded for thirty critical trials. The learner's protests were coordinated to standard shock levels, his first grunt coming at 75 volts, his first vehement protest at 150 volts.

The average shock used during the thirty critical trials was less than 60 volts—lower than the point at which the victim showed the first signs of discomfort. Three of the forty subjects did not go beyond the very lowest level on the board, twenty-eight went no higher than 75 volts, and thirty-eight did not go beyond the first loud protest at 150 volts. Two subjects provided the exception, administering up to 325 and 450 volts, but the overall result was that the great majority of people delivered very low, usually painless, shocks when the choice was explicitly up to them.

This condition of the experiment undermines another commonly offered explanation of the subjects' behavior—that those who shocked the victim at the most severe levels came only from the sadistic fringe of society. If one considers that almost two-thirds of the participants fall into the category of "obedient" subjects, and that they represented ordinary people drawn from working, managerial, and professional classes, the argument becomes very shaky. Indeed, it is highly reminiscent of the issue that arose in connection with Hannah Arendt's 1963 book, *Eichmann in Jerusalem.* Arendt contended that the prosecution's effort to depict Eichmann as a sadistic monster was fundamentally wrong, that he came closer to being an uninspired bureaucrat who simply sat at his desk and did his job. For asserting her views, Arendt became the object of considerable scorn, even calumny. Somehow, it was felt that the monstrous deeds carried out by Eichmann required a brutal, twisted personality, evil incarnate. After witnessing hundreds of ordinary persons submit to the authority in our own experiments, I must conclude that Arendt's conception of the banality of evil comes closer to the truth than one might dare imagine. The ordinary person who shocked the victim did so out of a sense of obligation—an impression of his duties as a subject—and not from any peculiarly aggressive tendencies.

This is, perhaps, the most fundamental lesson of our study: ordinary people, simply doing their jobs, and without any particular hostility on their part, can become agents in a terrible destructive process. Moreover, even when the destructive effects of their work become patently clear, and they are asked to carry out actions incompatible with fundamental standards of morality, relatively few people have the resources needed to resist authority.

Many of the people were in some sense against what they did to the learner, and many protested even while they obeyed. Some were totally convinced of the wrongness of their actions but could not bring themselves to make an open break with authority. They often derived satisfaction from their thoughts and felt that—within themselves, at least—they had been on the side of the angels. They tried to reduce strain by obeying the experimenter but "only slightly," encouraging the learner, touching the generator switches gingerly. When interviewed, such a subject would stress that he had "asserted my humanity" by administering the briefest shock possible. Handling the conflict in this manner was easier than defiance.

The situation is constructed so that there is no way the subject can stop shocking the learner without violating the experimenter's definitions of his own competence. The subject fears that he will appear arrogant, untoward, and rude if he breaks off. Although these inhibiting emotions appear small in scope alongside the violence being done to the learner, they suffuse the mind and feelings of the subject, who is miserable at the prospect of having to repudiate the authority to his face. (When the experiment was altered so that the experimenter gave his instructions by telephone instead of in person, only a third as many people were fully obedient through 450 volts.) It is a curious thing that a measure of compassion on the part of the subject—an unwillingness to "hurt" the experimenter's feelings—is part of those binding forces inhibiting his disobedience. The withdrawal of such deference may be as painful to the subject as to the authority he defies.

The subjects do not derive satisfaction from inflicting pain, but they often like the feeling they get from pleasing the experimenter. They are proud of doing a good job, obeying the experimenter under difficult circumstances. While the subjects administered only mild shocks on their own initiative, one experimental variation showed that, under orders, 30 percent of them were willing to deliver 450 volts even when they had to forcibly push the learner's hand down on the electrode.

Bruno Batta is a thirty-seven-year-old welder who took part in the variation requiring the use of force. He was born in New Haven, his parents in Italy. He has a rough-hewn face that conveys a conspicuous lack of alertness. He has some difficulty in mastering the experimental procedure and needs to be corrected by the experimenter several times. He shows appreciation for the help and willingness to do what is required. After the 150-volt level, Batta has to force the learner's hand down on the shock plate, since the learner himself refuses to touch it.

When the learner first complains, Mr. Batta pays no attention to him. His face remains impassive, as if to dissociate himself from the learner's disruptive behavior. When the experimenter instructs him to force the learner's hand down, he adopts a rigid, mechanical procedure. He tests the generator switch. When it fails to function, he immediately forces the learner's hand onto the shock plate. All the while he maintains the same rigid mask. The learner, seated alongside him, begs him to stop, but with robotic impassivity he continues the procedure.

What is extraordinary in his apparent total indifference to the learner; he hardly takes cognizance of him as a human being. Meanwhile, he relates to the experimenter in a submissive and courteous fashion.

At the 330-volt level, the learner refuses not only to touch the shock plate but also to provide any answers. Annoyed, Batta turns to him, and chastises him: "You better answer and get it over with. We can't stay here all night." These are the only words he directs to the learner in the course of an hour. Never again does he speak to him. The scene is brutal and depressing, his hard, impassive face showing total indifference as he subdues the screaming learner and gives him shocks. He seems to derive no pleasure from the act itself, only quiet satisfaction at doing his job properly.

When he administers 450 volts, he turns to the experimenter and asks, "Where do we go from here, Professor?" His tone is deferential and expresses his willingness to be a cooperative subject, in contrast to the learner's obstinacy.

At the end of the session he tells the experimenter how honored he has been to help him, and in a moment of contrition, remarks, "Sir, sorry it couldn't have been a full experiment."

He has done his honest best. It is only the deficient behavior of the learner that has denied the experimenter full satisfaction.

The essence of obedience is that a person comes to view himself as the instrument for carrying out another person's wishes, and he therefore no longer regards himself as responsible for his actions. Once this critical shift of viewpoint has occurred, all of the essential features of obedience follow. The most far-reaching consequence is that the person feels responsible *to* the authority directing him but feels no responsibility *for* the content of the actions that the authority prescribes. Morality does not disappear—it acquires a radically different focus: the subordinate person feels shame or pride depending on how adequately he has performed the actions called for by authority.

Language provides numerous terms to pinpoint this type of morality: *loyalty, duty, discipline* all are terms heavily saturated with moral meaning and refer to the degree to which a person fulfills his obligations to authority. They refer not to the "goodness" of the person per se but to the adequacy with which a subordinate fulfills his socially defined role. The most frequent defense of the individual who has performed a heinous act under command of authority is that he has simply done his duty. In asserting this defense, the individual is not introducing an alibi concocted for the moment but is reporting honestly on the psychological attitude induced by submission to authority.

For a person to feel responsible for his actions, he must sense that the behavior has flowed from "the self." In the situation we have studied, subjects have precisely the opposite view of their actions—namely, they see them as originating in the motives of some other person. Subjects in the experiment frequently said, "If it were up to me, I would not have administered shocks to the learner."

Once authority has been isolated as the cause of the subject's behavior, it is legitimate to inquire into the necessary elements of authority and how it must be perceived in order to gain his compliance. We conducted some investigations into the kinds of changes that would cause the experimenter to lose his power and to be disobeyed by the subject. Some of the variations revealed that:

• *The experimenter's physical presence has a marked impact on his authority.* As cited earlier, obedience dropped off sharply when orders were given by telephone. The experimenter could often induce a disobedient subject to go on by returning to the laboratory.

• *Conflicting authority severely paralyzes action.* When two experimenters of equal status, both seated at the command desk, gave incompatible orders, no shocks were delivered past the point of their disagreement.

• *The rebellious action of others severely undermines authority.* In one variation, three teachers (two actors and a real subject) administered a test and shocks. When the two actors disobeyed the experimenter and refused to go beyond a certain shock level, thirty-six of forty subjects joined their disobedient peers and refused as well.

Although the experimenter's authority was fragile in some respects, it is also true that he had almost none of the tools used in ordinary command structures. For example, the experimenter did not threaten the subjects with punishment—such as loss of income, community ostracism, or jail—for failure to obey. Neither could he offer incentives. Indeed, we should expect the experimenter's authority to be much less than that of someone like a general, since the experimenter has no power to enforce his imperatives, and since participation in a psychological experiment scarcely evokes the sense of urgency and dedication found in warfare. Despite these limitations, he still managed to command a dismaying degree of obedience.

I will cite one final variation of the experiment that depicts a dilemma that is more common in everyday life. The subject was not ordered to pull the lever that shocked the victim, but merely to perform a subsidiary task (administering the word-pair test) while another person administered the shock. In this situation, thirty-seven of forty adults continued to the highest level on the shock generator. Predictably, they excused their behavior by saying that the responsibility belonged to the man who actually pulled the switch. This may illustrate a dangerously typical arrangement in a complex society: it is easy to ignore responsibility when one is only an intermediate link in a chain of action.

The problem of obedience is not wholly psychological. The form and shape of society and the way it is developing have much to do with it. There was a time, perhaps, when people were able to give a fully human response to any situation because they were fully absorbed in it as human beings. But as soon as there was a division of labor things changed. Beyond a certain point, the breaking up of society into people carrying out narrow and very special jobs takes away from the human quality of work and life. A person does not get to see the whole situation but only a small part of it, and is thus unable to act without some kind of overall direction. He yields to authority but in doing so is alienated from his own actions.

Even Eichmann was sickened when he toured the concentration camps, but he had only to sit at a desk and shuffle papers. At the same time the man in the camp who actually dropped Cyclon-b into the gas chambers was able to justify *his* behavior on the ground that he was only following orders from above. Thus there is a fragmentation of the total human act; no one is confronted with the consequences of his decision to carry out the evil act. The person who assumes responsibility has evaporated. Perhaps this is the most common characteristic of socially organized evil in modern society.

QUESTIONS
1. What was the purpose of the experiments described in this essay? What might we learn from these experiments?
2. What explanation is offered for the subjects' continuing the experiment even when they believed they were inflicting intense physical pain upon the "learner"? Can you suggest alternative explanations?
3. What explains the experimenters' continuing the experiments even when they knew they were inflicting evident psychological pain upon the subjects?
4. Milgram indicates (p. 160) that the book from which this article is adapted contains a discussion of the ethical problems of carrying out an experiment of this sort. What would you say might be some of those problems? You may wish to refer to his book to inquire how successfully, in your opinion, the author deals with the ethical problems.

WILLIAM MARCH

The Dog and Her Rival

A dog who had been greatly loved by her master found her life less pleasant after he married. She came one night to talk things over with the mare and said, "I wish them both happiness. Perhaps it would be better if I went away, because it must grieve my master to see the way his wife humiliates me all day long."

The mare thought that would be a sensible thing to do, but the dog sighed, shook her head, and continued. "No, that would never work out, because if I disappeared without a word, the uncertainty of my fate would break my master's heart; and, besides, that wife of his would make him believe I was fickle and had abandoned him, and he'd never know how much I had suffered or how great my love was. On second thought, it might be even simpler if I took poison and died on his doorstep. That I think would be the noblest thing to do, the final proof of my love."

The mare said that such renunciation seemed a generous gesture indeed, and the dog lifted her head and stared at the moon. "I'd do it, too," she said; "I'd kill myself on my master's doorstep if only I could hear his pleas for forgiveness when he finds my body, or see him beating his worthless wife for having driven me to such an end."

Love can be the most dreadful disguise that hate assumes.

HENDRIK HERTZBERG
and
DAVID C. K. McCLELLAND

Paranoia

Three people, Phil and Sam and Lucy, are at a party. They share enough common experiences, beliefs, and preconceptions to be having a chat. Each contributes, by his talk or by his attentiveness, about as much as the others contribute. Everyone is having a good time. Everyone *seems* to be having a good time.

But suppose Phil is really having a bad time. Perhaps he feels ugly or stupid or out of it; perhaps he is merely depressed. He might excuse himself and go home, but he is afraid of being thought unsociable, so he stays and lets his mind fasten on some premise that seems to explain why he is not enjoying himself. His thoughts begin to congeal around the explanatory premise, which is probably something like, *I'm bad and unhappy and they know it* or *I'm bad and unhappy and they don't know it.*

The conversation goes on:

LUCY: Did you see that new Altman movie—what's it called?
SAM: *Thieves Like Us.*
PHIL: Yeah, I saw that.
SAM: Me too.
LUCY: What did you think of it?
SAM: I think it's overrated.

Meanwhile, Phil struggles to establish a connection between the conversation and his premise. He may be thinking, *Why are they talking about movies? They must notice that I'm horrible and miserable, but they know there's no way they can help, so they're trying to take my mind off it.*

Or he may be thinking, *Why are they talking about movies? It must be because they don't notice I'm horrible and miserable. They couldn't care less how I feel.*

Phil fails to notice, among other things, that he, too, is talking about movies. His mind is so full of his own wretchedness that he assumes Sam and Lucy are also preoccupied with it. (The only alternative is that Sam and Lucy are callous and unfeeling.) In fact, Sam and Lucy may simply think they are at a party talking about movies.

Phil, so far, is suffering from little more than a lousy mood. But suppose that Phil's condition is more serious. Suppose that he is paranoid. In that event, the premise dominating his mind will be far from simple, and it will explain far more than why he is unhappy. The premise might be, for example, that an elaborate Mafia conspiracy is trying to control his life. Now Phil will have to work harder to interpret the conversation in a way that "proves" his premise.

LUCY: Did you see that new Altman movie—what's it called? (Phil thinks, *You know damn well what it's called.*)

SAM: *Thieves Like Us.* (Phil thinks, *Thieves indeed. What could be more obvious? You can't fool me.*)

PHIL: Yeah, I saw that. (Phil thinks, *Don't kid yourselves that I don't know what you're really talking about.*)

SAM: Me too. (Phil thinks, *So you know I know—is that what you're saying?*)

LUCY: What did you think of it? (Phil thinks, *You're trying to invade my thoughts.*)

SAM: I think it's overrated. (Phil thinks, *Of course you do—those thieves only steal money, you steal minds.*)

Phil is clearly in a bad way.

A Little Semantics

Paranoia is a word on everyone's lips, but only among mental-health professionals has it acquired a tolerably specific meaning. It refers to a psychosis based on a delusionary premise of self-referred persecution or grandeur (e.g., "The Knights of Columbus control the world and are out to get me," "I am Norman Mailer"), and supported by a complex, rigorously logical system that interprets all or nearly all sense impressions as evidence for that premise. The traditional psychiatric view is that paranoia is an extreme measure for the defense of the integrity of the personality against annihilating guilt. The paranoid (so goes the theory) thrusts his guilt outside himself by denying his hostile or erotic impulses and projecting them onto other people or onto the whole universe. Disintegration is avoided, but at high cost: the paranoid view of reality can make everyday life terrifying and social intercourse problematical. And paranoia is tiring. It requires exhausting mental effort to construct trains of thought demonstrating that random events or details "prove" a wholly unconnected premise. Some paranoids hallucinate, but hallucination is by no means obligatory; paranoia is an interpretive, not a perceptual, dysfunction.

Paranoia is a recent cultural disorder. It follows the adoption of rationalism as the quasiofficial religion of Western man and the collapse of certain communitarian bonds (the extended family, belief in God, the harmony of the spheres) which once made sense of the universe in all its parts. Paranoia substitutes a rigorous (though false) order for chaos, and at the same time dispels the sense of individual insignificance by making the paranoid the focus of all he sees going on around him—a natural response to the confusion of modern life.

Strictly speaking, there was no such thing as paranoia before the mid-nineteenth century, when the word (from the Greek for "beside" and "mind") first surfaced as one of several medical-sounding euphemisms for madness. In an earlier age, the states of mind now explained as paranoia were accounted for differently. The vastness of the difference is suggested if one reflects on the likehood of a president of France placing the command of his country's armed forces in the hands of a teen-age peasant girl who hears voices from God.

Even more recent is the wholesale adoption of the terms "paranoia" and "paranoid" into everyday speech as metaphors for a bewildering variety of experiences. Hippies could no more communicate their thoughts without using "paranoia" and "paranoid" than they could eschew "like," "y'know," and "I mean." In this context the meanings of the terms are blurry but readily comprehensible. "Man, are you ever paranoid." This is not meant as a compliment. The implication is that the accused is imagining a threat where none exists. "I mean, she really makes me paranoid." The speaker feels that "she" is more powerful than he is, making him uncomfortable. "There was a lot of paranoia at that concert." One gathers that the security precautions were excessive. "No thanks, man, I get really paranoid when I smoke dope." Here paranoia is merely a euphemism for fear. "I'm paranoid" is less disturbing, for both speaker and listener, than "I'm frightened." (Psychiatric terminology is central to contemporary etiquette. One says, "I'm having trouble relating to you." One does not say, "I hate your guts.")

In politics, paranoia is a logical consequence of the wrenching loose of power from the rigid social arrangements that once conditioned its exercise, and the resulting preoccupation with questions of "dominate or be dominated." Political and quasipolitical notions, such as the conviction that the telephone company is manipulating reality in order to control one's mind, appear routinely in the delusions of persons suffering from paranoid psychosis. In American public life, as Richard Hofstadter showed in *The Paranoid Style in American Politics*, persecutory themes have cropped up periodically from the beginning. Groups widely believed to have been at the center of the shifting conspiracy against the common weal have at various times included the Masons, the Papists, the Illuminati, Wall Street, the gold hoarders, the outside agitators, the Communists, and—bringing us up to the present—the pointy-headed bureaucrats, the Establishment, the system, the straights, the New Left nihilists, the Mafia, the oil companies, the media, and the

CIA.[1] As Lincoln said, you can fool some of the people all of the time.

The Nixon years have been something of a Golden Age of political paranoia. The paranoid strategies of projection, denial, and the use of code language with private meanings ("law and order," "peace with honor," "executive privilege")[2] have been played out on a national scale. The Nixon Administration saw politics as an array of reified conspiracies against it ("the criminal forces as against the peace forces," the Chicago defendants, Ellsberg, the campus bums, the radiclibs, the media) and behaved accordingly. The unprecedented security arrangements at the Washington headquarters of the Committee to Re-Elect the President, designed to counter an imaginary threat of political burglary and wiretapping, were entrusted to precisely the people who carried out the political burglary and wiretapping of the Democratic National Committee. When the crimes and conspiracies known as Watergate began to come to light, the Administration's two basic responses were denial ("I am not a crook") and projection ("everybody does it"). During the fuss over Pentagon thievery of documents belonging to Henry Kissinger, one "White House source" described his colleagues as "a bunch of paranoids spying on each other."

Double Space

Zero is an extremely bright, self-taught, experimental electronics engineer who was the central figure in a small cult in Pontiac, Michigan, one of thousands of local paranoid cults produced by the late counterculture. Zero and his friends made pilgrimages to hear Pink Floyd, a rock group to whose music and lyrics they attached great importance. They occasionally ingested psychedelic drugs and made midnight visits to the main office building of Pontiac Motors, where they intoned mock prayers at the chain-link fence protecting the "temple," a white office monolith lit by floodlights.

Zero lived in a house which would take as long to describe as it would to explicate *Finnegans Wake*. He had used an old chicken coop, later a lampshade factory, as the shell. Inside, he had created an environment from electronic and other debris. The house was too disorienting to be merely a straightforward collection of symbolic

1. The CIA turns up in paranoid delusions perhaps more than any other single organization. Its name is extremely suggestive—"central," "intelligence," and "agency" are all words rich in multiple meanings—and, since the CIA does in fact engage in conspiratorial activities, it can easily be adapted for any scheme involving domination and control by unseen forces. Freud always maintained that every paranoid delusion contains a nugget of truth [Hertzberg and McClelland's note].

2. "I don't have to spell it out," the President told a group of milk producers during a tape-recorded meeting [Hertzberg and McClelland's note].

junk. No object's use was related to its name. Something that looked and worked like a floor lamp turned out to be a fence post, a telescope, and a plastic cake stand, wired to produce light. Aggregates of machines played the radioactive emissions from one's body back through guitar amplifiers hung from the ceiling. Visual punning marked nearly every object in the house. Overall, it had the impact of a brilliant work of art. But Zero did not consider himself an artist; he regarded his house as a means of self-protection, not of self-expression.

Zero's speech, like his house, was disorienting. In the monologue below, reconstructed by John Farrah, a writer and friend of Zero's, Zero discourses on the great conspiracy he devoted so much energy to protecting himself from.

This isn't something I usually run down. People don't want to hear about it. They figure that if this is true then what's the use. Even if somebody brave like the *National Enquirer* ran it down, which I suppose is impossible, nobody could handle it.

Here's the deal. There's this thing, you know, that would like us all to be very nice polite robots. First, they planned to build androids to replace us. It would either be when you're sleeping or at work or in jail. I used to think that this was unbelievable, but I got busted once, and they really dug on beating me up. I'm sure they get off on offing people, too. You've heard about how every couple of hundred years there's a bunch of people who disappear? Well, they're being offed by GM and getting recycled into new cars. There's a computer under Rochester, Michigan. It completely ran the Vietnam war. That's right, and what's happening now is that the computers of GM have figured out a master scheme to turn us into androids via the food we eat. And McDonald's is the front for the whole thing, and the president of GM is actually Ronald McDonald, who's a front in a scheme to rip off our minds and souls. They're planting electrodes and embalming fluid and synthetic God-knows-what in our food. Did you know that the most widely used preservative in white bread is embalming fluid? We're being turned into robots without a hand being laid on us! Maybe those satellites up there are programmed to control us, and it's some kind of worldwide monitoring system. And with all this shit inside us from eating Quarter Pounders that undoubtedly strangle up our minds, who even thinks about all of this?

I worked for Pontiac Motors for a while before I went into the Army, and I used to think that maybe the assembly line was once used to turn out robots. Anyway, there was this food company there that filled all the vending machines and ran the plant cafeterias. It was called Prophet Food. Can you dig that? I mean, it's like saying, "Fuck you, we're going to turn you into androids," you know? Oh, man, I ate one of their hamburgers by mistake once. I got sick and couldn't think straight for a few days. Anyway, every day the workers came in like perfect robots and made the cars that were probably melted down years later and made into bombs or something. Hardly anybody picks up on it—you just had a Big Mac or some other kind of poison and you're driving around trying to relate to the cops. Who's going to be able to think about Pontiac Motors? I mean, you gotta get up tomorrow and be there at 6:28 anyway. So pick up a six-pack and forget about it. It's the whole system. It's its own preservative. And it doesn't matter where you work, man, 'cause it's all GM. Generous Motors. What else is there to say? No one believes it. No one dares even think about it. But it's not their fault. We're all just calcium propionate on this bus.

Like his house, Zero's monologue makes one think of art. The hamburger conspiracy is a striking metaphor for the life Zero sees around him. But Zero is innocent of satiric purpose. He has turned the metaphor on its head. It is not a metaphor to him; it is reality, and he lives inside it.

It is a commonplace of both art and psychology that the line between madness and genius is sometimes difficult to draw. But Zero would seem to fall on one side of it, and a self-aware artist like Thomas Pynchon on the other. In his novel *The Crying of Lot 49,* Pynchon presents a massive conspiracy discovered by a young Southern California housewife, Oedipa Maas. As she begins to find connections between Tupperware, her psychiatrist, a giant corporation called Yoyodyne, perpetual-motion machines, an underground postal system called WASTE, the Mafia, a Jacobean tragedy, the German noble family of Thurn und Taxis, and so on, Oedipa begins to doubt her sanity.

Change your name to Miles, Dean, Serge, and/or Leonard, baby, she advised her reflection in the half-light of that afternoon's vanity mirror. Either way, they'll call it paranoia. They. Either you have stumbled indeed, without the aid of LSD or other indole alkaloids, onto a secret richness and concealed density of dream; onto a network by which X number of Americans are truly communicating whilst reserving their lies, recitations of routine, arid betrayals of spiritual poverty, for the official government delivery system; maybe even onto a real alternative to the existlessness, to the absence of surprise to life, that harrows the head of everybody American you know, and you too, sweetie. Or you are hallucinating it. Or a plot has been mounted against you, so expensive and elaborate, involving items like the forging of stamps and ancient books, constant surveillance of your movements, planting of post horn images all over San Francisco, bribing of librarians, hiring of professional actors and Pierce Inverarity only knows what-all besides, all financed out of the estate in a way either too secret or too involved for your non-legal mind to know about even though you are co-executor, so labyrinthine that it must have meaning beyond just a practical joke. Or you are fantasying some such plot, in which case you are a nut, Oedipa, out of your skull.

The Crying of Lot 49, like Pynchon's latest book, *Gravity's Rainbow,* is a story whose plot is a plot—a fiction with the structure of a paranoid delusion. Pynchon verbally (like Zero visually) uses puns, metaphors, and layers of symbols so intricately that he ends by making one doubt one's own sanity—which is his purpose. The codes are never explicit, and therein lies the hostility of the arts of paranoia. The reader (or house guest) must work terribly hard to feel even minimally oriented. Neither in art nor in life is paranoia a generous state of mind.

A Useful Disorder

One of Philip K. Dick's most delightful science-fiction novels, *Clans of the Alphane Moon*, is full of paranoids. The story unfolds on an obscure moon that colonists from Earth had used as a mental hospital and then abandoned. Left to their own devices, the former mental patients have organized a workable society, dividing themselves into "clans" according to diagnosis. A psychiatrist from Earth rockets in for a visit, looks around, and speculates on the sociology of the moon. "The paranoids—actually paranoiac schizophrenics—would function as the statesman class," she says. "They'd be in charge of developing political ideology and social programs—they'd have the overall world view." And, she concludes, "Leadership in this society would naturally fall to the paranoids, they'd be superior individuals in terms of initiative, intelligence and just plain innate ability. Of course, they'd have trouble keeping the manics from staging a coup."

No doubt Dick exaggerates. But the fact remains that paranoia (unlike, for example, catatonia) is not necessarily a bar to many kinds of success, including success at leading people. Paranoids, in the course of maintaining and defending their delusionary premises, often develop aptitudes for reasoning, for organization, for argument and persuasion. Paranoids are fond of patterns, and they abhor confusion and uncertainty. For them there are no accidents, and nothing is coincidental. Their dogged tenacity and the supreme confidence with which some of them are able to elucidate their all-embracing theories and nostrums can result in their accession to positions of power. "Though a great many patients with paranoia have to be hospitalized," notes Norman A. Cameron of the Yale School of Medicine, "some do not, and among these an occasional one succeeds in building up a following of persons who believe him to be a genius or inspired."

Paranoids live in a state of perpetual crisis. They are always ready for catastrophe. A psychiatrist has recalled an incident that occurred when he was attached to the staff of a large mental hospital. A gas main had broken, and the poisonous fumes were seeping into the wards. It was vital that the hospital be evacuated, and the staff was undermanned. The expected chaos and panic did not materialize, however, because a group of paranoid schizophrenics, once released from their cells, immediately took charge of the evacuation, organized it, and carried it out quickly and efficiently. These paranoids saw nothing unusual in the fact that the hospital was about to be engulfed by an invisible, deadly, malevolent force.

The average person has many worries, but there is one thing he does not generally worry about. He does not worry that somewhere, without his knowledge, a secret tribunal is about to order him seized, drugged, and imprisoned without the right of appeal.

Indeed, anyone who worries overmuch about such a thing, and expresses that worry repeatedly and forcefully enough, would probably be classified as a paranoid schizophrenic.

And, once he is so classified, the probable next step is for a secret tribunal to convene, and, without his knowledge, order him to be seized, drugged, and imprisoned without the right of appeal. Such, at any rate, is the situation in many states of the Union, where commitment laws empower official boards to hospitalize involuntarily a "mentally ill" person whose "illness" renders him unable to appreciate his need for treatment. Whatever else this may prove, it does suggest the power of paranoia to refashion the objective world, as well as the subjective universe, in his own image.

These talents for crisis management and self-fulfilling prophecy are not limited to hospitalized paranoids. Persons who see life as a series of "crises," and who pride themselves on being "the coolest man in the room" when a crisis actually develops, sometimes rise to positions of the highest responsibility. The same is true of people who believe themselves persecuted and harassed by "enemies" who are out to "get" them—and who, as a sort of "protective-reaction strike," persecute and harass these same "enemies." The danger such a person incurs is that with the powers of his high position at his disposal, he may force reality into a conformity with his delusions. He will then find himself besieged by *real* enemies, who will indeed do their best to "get" him. But since such a person has been preparing for precisely this all his life, he will be well equipped to "fight like hell" when his back is against the wall.

Making Enemies Real

An individual paranoid may (as one authority puts it) join "some fanatical movement in current vogue, in this way succeeding sometimes in sublimating his excessive zeal and saving himself from further illness." The paranoiac tendencies of social groups sublimate themselves in another fashion. Supermarkets have their security guards; cities have their police forces, states have their state troopers. And nations—which conduct their relations with one another according to rules that are even less binding and explicit than those governing individual behavior—have their armies.

In any large country, it is the solemn duty of the military establishment to be paranoid on behalf of the nation as a whole. Here in the United States, the Department of Defense employs hundreds of superb logicians—"contingency planners"—to imagine the most appalling, most devious, most diabolical horrors that could possibly be perpetrated by other nations against our own. And, so as to be able to deal with any and all such hypothetical nightmares, it employs and equips millions of soldiers, sailors, and airmen at a cost of scores of billions of dollars each year. Although there has not been a large-scale war in nearly thirty years, the Department of Defense maintains at all times what it calls the "capability" of fighting two-and-a-half wars the size of World War II.

The Department of Defense also maintains, at hair-trigger readiness, an arsenal of nuclear weapons which, if used, would destroy all the major cities of the Soviet Union and China and kill nearly all the people in them. The rationale behind this arsenal is that if we in the United States lacked these weapons, other countries that do possess them would use them against us. Or, to put the rationale more precisely, it is thought to be *more likely* than other countries would attack a disarmed United States than it is thought that the United States and other countries will destroy each other (through inadvertence, miscalculation, or a suicidal-homicidal paroxysm) under the existing "balance of terror" arrangement.

Some people believe that this logic is faulty, that the possibility of an unprovoked nuclear attack on a disarmed United States would be remote—more remote, at least, than the possibility of mutual destruction is now. Some people believe that to maintain an enormously expensive and dangerous "deterrent" against the possibility of such a monstrous, hypothetical crime is to enshrine paranoid delusion as the governing principle of international affairs. The people who believe these things are very few. Most of their fellow citizens regard them as hopelessly naïve and unrealistic.

American society at large believes in the usefulness of maintaining an army, but it also recognizes that the military perception of reality is inevitably a distorted one. For this reason, among others, the military has been kept subservient to the civilian authority, even in specifically military matters. The wisdom of this arrangement is apparent when one examines a country like Chile, where the military forces have overthrown the civilian authorities and have begun the task of restructuring society in their own image. When a military government as serious as Chile's goes to work, the result is a terrifying, bloody purge—a kind of political psychotic episode—followed by an attempt to construct a society as rationalized, as well organized, and as free of uncertainty as the most highly articulated paranoid delusion.

Positive Paranoia

Paranoia is customarily thought of as a distressing experience. It is terrible to be persecuted, even if the perceived mode of persecution happens to be imaginary. Delusions of grandeur, pleasant in themselves, can turn into nightmares when others disbelieve in them. And the shared paranoia of belief in malevolent conspiracies arises from a conviction that something is very wrong with the way things are.

In his book *The Natural Mind*, Andrew Weil describes an anomaly that turned up in psychological testing administered by the Haight-Ashbury Research Project of the Department of Psychiatry of Mount Zion Hospital, in San Francisco. Weil calls this anomaly "positive paranoia." On the Rorschach test, a number of subjects showed a marked "W-tendency." The Rorschach test is a series of ten increasingly fragmented inkblots. Someone who tries to account for every drib and drab of ink is said to have a strong "W-tendency," or "Whole-tendency," which correlates well to paranoia. Yet these particular subjects were unmistakably happy people. The tests said they were paranoid, and in a way they were—each of them thought the universe was a sort of conspiracy organized for his or her own benefit. Such beliefs may be no more realistic than the delusions of "normal" paranoia, but they undoubtedly make for a jollier type of paranoid.

Weil defines paranoia as "the tendency to see external events and things forming patterns that appear to be inimical." (Pattern-seeing, by itself, Weil views as neutral.) Positive paranoia would therefore be the tendency to see events and things forming patterns that appear to be beneficent. By these definitions, however, mere pessimism would qualify as (negative) paranoia, and any religion that posits a benevolent Providence would be a species of positive paranoia. So, for that matter, would any system of social analysis (such as Marxism or classical economics) that finds in the workings of history a progression toward a desirable goal.

Weil's definition seems to us to leave out one element of paranoia. Accordingly, we would amend it to say that paranoia is the tendency to see external events and things forming patterns that appear to be harmful (negative paranoia) or beneficent (positive paranoia), which patterns appear to center upon the person seeing. Now it is not pessimism *per se* that is paranoid, but rather belief in a hostile universe focusing its enmity on oneself. And it is not religion *per se* that is an instance of positive paranoia, but rather a particular kind of religious experience: in Weil's phrase, the perception of the universe as "a radially symmetrical pattern, its center coinciding with the center of focused consciousness." Such experiences are a goal of many kinds of religious and spiritual disciplines. The mandalas of Tibetan Buddhism are, in a sense, maps of precisely this variety of experience.

The concept of positive paranoia is a useful one because it sheds light on the connection between madness and transcendental experience and also because it illuminates what is so seductive about paranoia in general: the comfort of a universe ordered about oneself, a comfort that many people are willing to pay for in the currency of anguish. Paranoia is the very opposite of meaninglessness; indeed, paranoia drenches every detail of the world in meaning.

JEROME S. BRUNER
Freud and the Image of Man

By the dawn of the sixth century before Christ, the Greek physicist-philosophers had formulated a bold conception of the physical world as a unitary material phenomenon. The Ionians had set forth a conception of matter as fundamental substance, transformation of which accounted for the myriad forms and substances of the physical world. Anaximander was subtle enough to recognize that matter must be viewed as a generalized substance, free of any particular sensuous properties. Air, iron, water or bone were only elaborated forms, derived from a more general stuff. Since that time, the phenomena of the physical world have been conceived as continuous and monistic, as governed by the common laws of matter. The view was a bold one, bold in the sense of running counter to the immediate testimony of the senses. It has served as an axiomatic basis of physics for more than two millennia. The bold view eventually became the obvious view, and it gave shape to our common understanding of the physical world. Even the alchemists rested their case upon this doctrine of material continuity and, indeed, had they known about neutron bombardment, they might even have hit upon the proper philosopher's stone.

The good fortune of the physicist—and these matters are always relative, for the material monism of physics may have impeded nineteenth-century thinking and delayed insights into the nature of complementarity in modern physical theory—this early good fortune or happy insight has no counterpart in the sciences of man. Lawful continuity between man and the animal kingdom, between dreams and unreason on one side and waking rationality on the other, between madness and sanity, between consciousness and unconsciousness, between the mind of the child and the adult mind, between primitive and civilized man—each of these has been a cherished discontinuity preserved in doctrinal canons. There were voices in each generation, to be sure, urging the exploration of continuities. Anaximander had a passing good approximation to a theory of evolution based on natural selection; Cornelius Agrippa offered a plausible theory of the continuity of mental health and disease in terms of bottled-up sexuality. But Anaximander did not prevail against Greek conceptions of man's creation nor did Cornelius Agrippa against the demonopathy of the *Malleus Maleficarum*.[1] Neither in establishing the continuity between the varied states of man nor in pursuing the continuity between man and animal was there conspicuous success until the nineteenth century.

I need not insist upon the social, ethical, and political signifi-

---

1. A notorious book about demons and witchcraft.

cance of an age's image of man, for it is patent that the view one takes of man affects profoundly one's standard of dignity and the humanly possible. And it is in the light of such a standard that we establish our laws, set our aspirations for learning, and judge the fitness of men's acts. Those who govern, then, must perforce be jealous guardians of man's ideas about man, for the structure of government rests upon an uneasy consensus about human nature and human wants. Since the idea of man is of the order of *res publica*,[2] it is an idea not subject to change without public debate. Nor is it simply a matter of public concern. For man as individual has a deep and emotional investment in his image of himself. If we have learned anything in the last half-century of psychology, it is that man has powerful and exquisite capacities for defending himself against violation of his cherished self-image. This is not to say that Western man has not persistently asked: "What is man that thou art mindful of him?" It is only that the question, when pressed, brings us to the edge of anxiety where inquiry is no longer free.

Two figures stand out massively as the architects of our present-day conception of man: Darwin and Freud. Freud's was the more daring, the more revolutionary, and in a deep sense, the more poetic insight. But Freud is inconceivable without Darwin. It is both timely and perhaps historically just to center our inquiry on Freud's contribution to the modern image of man. Darwin I shall treat as a necessary condition for Freud and for his success, recognizing, of course, that this is a form of psychological license. Not only is it the centenary of Freud's birth;[3] it is also a year in which the current of popular thought expressed in commemoration of the date quickens one's awareness of Freud's impact on our times.

Rear-guard fundamentalism did not require a Darwin to slay it in an age of technology. He helped, but this contribution was trivial in comparison with another. What Darwin had done was to propose a set of principles unified around the conception that all organic species had their origins and took their form from a common set of circumstances—the requirements of biological survival. All living creatures were on a common footing. When the post-Darwin era of exaggeration had passed and religious literalism had abated into a new nominalism, what remained was a broad, orderly, and unitary conception of organic nature, a vast continuity from the monocellular protozoans to man. Biology had at last found its unifying principle in the doctrine of evolution. Man was not unique but the inheritor of an organic legacy.

As the summit of an evolutionary process, man could still view himself with smug satisfaction, indeed proclaim that God or Nature had shown a persistent wisdom in its effort to produce a final, perfect product. It remained for Freud to present the image of man as the unfinished product of nature: struggling against unreason,

2. The state.   3. 1956

impelled by driving inner vicissitudes and urges that had to be contained if man were to live in society, host alike to seeds of madness and majesty, never fully free from an infancy anything but innocent. What Freud was proposing was that man at his best and man at his worst is subject to a common set of explanations: that good and evil grow from a common process.

Freud was strangely yet appropriately fitted for his role as architect of a new conception of man. We must pause to examine his qualifications, for the image of man that he created was in no small measure founded on his painfully achieved image of himself and of his times. We are concerned not so much with his psychodynamics, as with the intellectual traditions he embodies. A child of his century's materialism, he was wedded to the determinism and the classical physicalism of nineteenth-century physiology so boldly represented by Helmholtz. Indeed, the young Freud's devotion to the exploration of anatomical structures was a measure of the strength of this inheritance. But at the same time, as both Lionel Trilling and W. H. Auden have recognized with much sensitivity, there was a deep current of romanticism in Freud—a sense of the role of impulse, of the drama of life, of the power of symbolism, of ways of knowing that were more poetic than rational in spirit, of the poet's cultural alienation. It was perhaps this romantic's sense of drama that led to his gullibility about parental seduction and to his generous susceptibility to the fallacy of the dramatic instance.

Freud also embodies two traditions almost as antithetical as romanticism and nineteenth-century scientism. He was profoundly a Jew, not in a doctrinal sense but in his conception of morality, in his love of the skeptical play of reason, in his distrust of illusion, in the form of his prophetic talent, even in his conception of mature eroticism. His prophetic talent was antithetic to a Utopianism either of innocence or of social control. Nor did it lead to a counsel of renunciation. Free oneself of illusion, of neurotic infantilism, and "the soft voice of intellect" would prevail. Wisdom for Freud was neither doctrine nor formula, but the achievement of maturity. The patient who is cured is the one who is now free enough of neurosis to decide intelligently about his own destiny. As for his conception of mature love, it has always seemed to me that its blend of tenderness and sensuality combined the uxorious imagery of the Chassidic tradition and the sensual quality of the Song of Songs. And might it not have been Freud rather than a commentator of the Haftorahs[4] who said, "In children, it was taught, God gives humanity a chance to make good its mistakes." For the modern trend of permissiveness toward children is surely a feature of the Freudian legacy.

But for all the Hebraic quality, Freud is also in the classical tradition—combining the Stoics and the great Greek dramatists. For

4. The Old Testament Prophets.

Freud as for the Stoics, there is no possibility of man disobeying the laws of nature. And yet, it is in this lawfulness that for him the human drama inheres. His love for Greek drama and his use of it in his formulation are patent. The sense of the human tragedy, the inevitable working out of the human plight—these are the hallmarks of Freud's case histories. When Freud, the tragic dramatist, becomes a therapist, it is not to intervene as a directive authority. The therapist enters the drama of the patient's life, makes possible a play within a play, the transference, and when the patient has "worked through" and understood the drama, he has achieved the wisdom necessary for freedom. Again, like the Stoics, it is in the recognition of one's own nature and in the acceptance of the laws that govern it that the good life is to be found.

Freud's contribution lies in the continuities of which he made us aware. The first of these is the continuity of organic lawfulness. Accident in human affairs was no more to be brooked as "explanation" than accident in nature. The basis for accepting such an "obvious" proposition had, of course, been well prepared by a burgeoning nineteenth-century scientific naturalism. It remained for Freud to extend naturalistic explanation to the heart of human affairs. The *Psychopathology of Everyday Life* is not one of Freud's deeper works, but "the Freudian slip" has contributed more to the common acceptance of lawfulness in human behavior than perhaps any of the more rigorous and academic formulations from Wundt to the present day. The forgotten lunch engagement, the slip of the tongue, the barked shin could no longer be dismissed as accident. Why Freud should have succeeded where the novelists, philosophers, and academic psychologists had failed we will consider in a moment.

Freud's extension of Darwinian doctrine beyond Haeckel's theorem that ontogeny recapitulates phylogeny is another contribution to continuity. It is the conception that in the human mind, the primitive, infantile, and archaic exist side-by-side with the civilized and evolved.

Where animals are concerned we hold the view that the most highly developed have arisen from the lowest. . . . In the realm of mind, on the other hand, the primitive type is so commonly preserved alongside the transformations which have developed out of it that it is superfluous to give instances in proof of it. When this happens, it is usually the result of a bifurcation in development. One quantitative part of an attitude or an impulse has survived unchanged while another has undergone further development. This brings us very close to the more general problem of conservation in the mind. . . . Since the time when we recognized the error of supposing that ordinary forgetting signified destruction or annihilation of the memory-trace, we have been inclined to the opposite view that nothing once formed in the mind could ever perish, that everything survives in some way or other, and is capable under certain conditions of being brought to light again . . . (Freud, *Civilization and Its Discontents*, pp. 14–15).

What has now come to be common sense is that in everyman there is the potentiality for criminality, and that these are neither accidents nor visitations of degeneracy, but products of a delicate balance of forces that, under different circumstances, might have produced normality or even saintliness. Good and evil, in short, grow from a common root.

Freud's genius was in his resolution of polarities. The distinction of child and adult was one such. It did not suffice to reiterate that the child was father to the man. The theory of infantile sexuality and the stages of psychosexual development were an effort to fill the gap, the latter clumsy, the former elegant. Though the alleged progression of sexual expression from the oral, to the anal, to the phallic, and finally to the genital has not found a secure place either in common sense or in general psychology, the developmental continuity of sexuality has been recognized by both. Common sense honors the continuity in the baby-books and in the permissiveness with which young parents of today resolve their doubts. And the research of Beach and others has shown the profound effects of infantile experience on adult sexual behavior—even in lower organisms.

If today people are reluctant to report their dreams with the innocence once attached to such recitals, it is again because Freud brought into common question the discontinuity between the rational purposefulness of waking life and the seemingly irrational purposelessness of fantasy and dream. While the crude symbolism of Freud's early efforts at dream interpretation has come increasingly to be abandoned—that telephone poles and tunnels have an invariant sexual reference—the conception of the dream as representing disguised wishes and fears has become common coin. And Freud's recognition of deep unconscious processes in the creative act, let it also be said, has gone far toward enriching our understanding of the kinship between the artist, the humanist, and the man of science.

Finally, it is our heritage from Freud that the all-or-none distinction between mental illness and mental health has been replaced by a more humane conception of the continuity of these states. The view that neurosis is a severe reaction to human trouble is as revolutionary in its implications for social practice as it is daring in formulation. The "bad seed" theories, the nosologies of the nineteenth century, the demonologies and doctrines of divine punishment— none of these provided a basis for compassion toward human suffering comparable to that of our time.

One may argue, at last, that Freud's sense of the continuity of human conditions, of the likeness of the human plight, has made possible a deeper sense of the brotherhood of man. It has in any case tempered the spirit of punitiveness toward what once we took as evil and what we now see as sick. We have not yet resolved the dilemma posed by these two ways of viewing. Its resolution is one of the great moral challenges of our age.

Why, after such initial resistance, were Freud's views so phenomenally successful in transforming common conceptions of man?

One reason we have already considered: the readiness of the Western world to accept a naturalistic explanation of organic phenomena and, concurrently, to be readier for such explanation in the mental sphere. There had been at least four centuries of uninterrupted scientific progress, recently capped by a theory of evolution that brought man into continuity with the rest of the animal kingdom. The rise of naturalism as a way of understanding nature and man witnessed a corresponding decline in the explanatory aspirations of religion. By the close of the nineteenth century, religion, to use Morton White's phrase, "too often agreed to accept the role of a non-scientific spiritual grab-bag, or an ideological know-nothing." The elucidation of the human plight had been abandoned by religion and not yet adopted by science.

It was the inspired imagery, the proto-theory of Freud that was to fill the gap. Its success in transforming the common conception of man was not simply its recourse to the "cause-and-effect" discourse of science. Rather it is Freud's imagery, I think, that provides the clue to this ideological power. It is an imagery of necessity, one that combines the dramatic, the tragic, and the scientific views of necessity. It is here that Freud's intellectual heritage matters so deeply. Freud's is a theory or a proto-theory peopled with actors. The characters are from life: the blind, energic, pleasure-seeking id; the priggish and punitive super-ego; the ego, battling for its being by diverting the energy of the others to its own use. The drama has an economy and a terseness. The ego develops canny mechanisms for dealing with the threat of id impulses: denial, projection, and the rest. Balances are struck between the actors, and in the balance is character and neurosis. Freud was using the dramatic technique of decomposition, the play whose actors are parts of a single life. It is a technique that he himself had recognized in fantasies and dreams, one he honored in "The Poet and the Daydream."

The imagery of the theory, moreover, has an immediate resonance with the dialectic of experience. True, it is not the stuff of superficial conscious experience. But it fits the human plight, its conflictedness, its private torment, its impulsiveness, its secret and frightening urges, its tragic quality.

Concerning its scientific imagery, it is marked by the necessity of the classical mechanics. At times the imagery is hydraulic: suppress this stream of impulses, and perforce it breaks out in a displacement elsewhere. The system is a closed and mechanical one. At times it is electrical, as when cathexes are formed and withdrawn like electrical charges. The way of thought fitted well the common-sense physics of its age.

Finally, the image of man presented was thoroughly secular; its ideal type was the mature man free of infantile neuroticism, capable of finding his own way. This freedom from both Utopianism and asceticism has earned Freud the contempt of ideological totalitarians of the Right and the Left. But the image has found a ready home in the rising, liberal intellectual middle class. For them, the Freudian ideal type has become a rallying point in the struggle against spiritual regimentation.

I have said virtually nothing about Freud's equation of sexuality and impulse. It was surely and still is a stimulus to resistance. But to say that Freud's success lay in forcing a reluctant Victorian world to accept the importance of sexuality is as empty as hailing Darwin for his victory over fundamentalism. Each had a far more profound effect.

Can Freud's contribution to the common understanding of man in the twentieth century be likened to the impact of such great physical and biological theories as Newtonian physics and Darwin's conception of evolution? The question is an empty one. Freud's mode of thought is not a theory in the conventional sense, it is a metaphor, an analogy, a way of conceiving man, a drama. I would propose that Anaximander is the proper parallel: his view of the connectedness of physical nature was also an analogy—and a powerful one. Freud is the ground from which theory will grow, and he has prepared the twentieth century to nurture the growth. But far more important, he has provided an image of man that has made him comprehensible without at the same time making him contemptible.

On Education

JOHN HOLT
How Teachers Make Children Hate Reading

When I was teaching English at the Colorado Rocky Mountain School, I used to ask my students the kinds of questions that English teachers usually ask about reading assignments—questions designed to bring out the points that *I* had decided *they* should know. They, on their part, would try to get me to give them hints and clues as to what I wanted. It was a game of wits. I never gave my students an opportunity to say what they really thought about a book.

I gave vocabulary drills and quizzes too. I told my students that every time they came upon a word in their book they did not understand, they were to look it up in the dictionary. I even devised special kinds of vocabulary tests, allowing them to use their books to see how the words were used. But looking back, I realize that these tests, along with many of my methods, were foolish.

My sister was the first person who made me question my conventional ideas about teaching English. She had a son in the seventh grade in a fairly good public school. His teacher had asked the class to read Cooper's *The Deerslayer*. The choice was bad enough in itself; whether looking at man or nature, Cooper was superficial, inaccurate and sentimental, and his writing is ponderous and ornate. But to make matters worse, this teacher had decided to give the book the microscope and x-ray treatment. He made the students look up and memorize not only the definitions but the derivations of every big word that came along—and there were plenty. Every chapter was followed by close questioning and testing to make sure the students "understood" everything.

Being then, as I said, conventional, I began to defend the teacher, who was a good friend of mine, against my sister's criticisms. The argument soon grew hot. What was wrong with making sure that children understood everything they read? My sister answered that until this class her boy had always loved reading, and had read

189

a lot on his own; now he had stopped. (He was not really to start again for many years.)

Still I persisted. If children didn't look up the words they didn't know, how would they ever learn them? My sister said, "Don't be silly! When you were little you had a huge vocabulary, and were always reading very grown-up books. When did you ever look up a word in a dictionary?"

She had me. I don't know that we had a dictionary at home; if we did, I didn't use it. I don't use one today. In my life I doubt that I have looked up as many as fifty words, perhaps not even half that.

Since then I have talked about this with a number of teachers. More than once I have said, "according to tests, educated and literate people like you have a vocabulary of about twenty-five thousand words. How many of these did you learn by looking them up in a dictionary?" They usually are startled. Few claim to have looked up even as many as a thousand. How did they learn the rest?

They learned them just as they learned to talk—by meeting words over and over again, in different contexts, until they saw how they fitted.

Unfortunately, we English teachers are easily hung up on this matter of understanding. Why should children understand everything they read? Why should anyone? Does anyone? I don't, and I never did. I was always reading books that teachers would have said were "too hard" for me, books full of words I didn't know. That's how I got to be a good reader. When about ten, I read all the D'Artagnan stories and loved them. It didn't trouble me in the least that I didn't know why France was at war with England or who was quarreling with whom in the French court or why the Musketeers should always be at odds with Cardinal Richelieu's men. I didn't even know who the Cardinal was, except that he was a dangerous and powerful man that my friends had to watch out for. This was all I needed to know.

Having said this, I will now say that I think a big, unabridged dictionary is a fine thing to have in any home or classroom. No book is more fun to browse around in—*if* you're not made to. Children, depending on their age, will find many pleasant and interesting things to do with a big dictionary. They can look up funny-sounding words, which they like, or words that nobody else in the class has ever heard of, which they like, or long words, which they like, or forbidden words, which they like best of all. At a certain age, and particularly with a little encouragement from parents or teachers, they may become very interested in where words came from and when they came into the language and how their meanings have changed over the years. But exploring for the fun of it is very different from looking up words out of your reading because you're going to get into trouble with your teacher if you don't.

While teaching fifth grade two years or so after the argument with my sister, I began to think again about reading. The children in my class were supposed to fill out a card—just the title and author and a one-sentence summary—for every book they read. I was not running a competition to see which child could read the most books, a competition that almost always leads to cheating. I just wanted to know what the children were reading. After a while it became clear that many of these very bright kids, from highly literate and even literary backgrounds, read very few books and deeply disliked reading. Why should this be?

At this time I was coming to realize, as I described in my book *How Children Fail*, that for most children school was a place of danger, and their main business in school was staying out of danger as much as possible. I now began to see also that books were among the most dangerous things in school.

From the very beginning of school we make books and reading a constant source of possible failure and public humiliation. When children are little we make them read aloud, before the teacher and other children, so that we can be sure they "know" all the words they are reading. This means that when they don't know a word, they are going to make a mistake, right in front of everyone. Instantly they are made to realize that they have done something wrong. Perhaps some of the other children will begin to wave their hands and say, "Ooooh! O-o-o-oh!" Perhaps they will just giggle, or nudge each other, or make a face. Perhaps the teacher will say, "Are you sure?" or ask someone else what he thinks. Or perhaps, if the teacher is kindly, she will just smile a sweet, sad smile—often one of the most painful punishments a child can suffer in school. In any case, the child who has made the mistake knows he has made it, and feels foolish, stupid, and ashamed, just as any of us would in his shoes.

Before long many children associate books and reading with mistakes, real or feared, and penalties and humiliation. This may not seem sensible, but it is natural. Mark Twain once said that a cat that sat on a hot stove lid would never sit on one again—but it would never sit on a cold one either. As true of children as of cats. If they, so to speak, sit on a hot book a few times, if books cause them humiliation and pain, they are likely to decide that the safest thing to do is to leave all books alone.

After having taught fifth-grade classes for four years I felt quite sure of this theory. In my next class were many children who had had great trouble with schoolwork, particularly reading. I decided to try at all costs to rid them of their fear and dislike of books, and to get them to read oftener and more adventurously.

One day soon after school had started, I said to them, "Now I'm going to say something about reading that you have probably never heard a teacher say before. I would like you to read a lot of books this year, but I want you to read them only for pleasure. I am not going to ask you questions to find out whether you understand the books or not. If you understand enough of a book to enjoy it and want to go on reading it, that's enough for me. Also I'm not going to ask you what words mean.

"Finally," I said, "I don't want you to feel that just because you start a book, you have to finish it. Give an author thirty or forty pages or so to get his story going. Then if you don't like the characters and don't care what happens to them, close the book, put it away, and get another. I don't care whether the books are easy or hard, short or long, as long as you enjoy them. Furthermore I'm putting all this in a letter to your parents, so they won't feel they have to quiz and heckle you about books at home."

The children sat stunned and silent. Was this a teacher talking? One girl, who had just come to us from a school where she had had a very hard time, and who proved to be one of the most interesting, lively, and intelligent children I have ever known, looked at me steadily for a long time after I had finished. Then, still looking at me, she said slowly and solemnly, "Mr. Holt, do you really mean that?" I said just as solemnly, "I mean every word of it."

Apparently she decided to believe me. The first book she read was Dr. Seuss's *How the Grinch Stole Christmas*, not a hard book even for most third graders. For a while she read a number of books on this level. Perhaps she was clearing up some confusion about reading that her teachers, in their hurry to get her up to "grade level," had never given her enough time to clear up. After she had been in the class six weeks or so and we had become good friends, I very tentatively suggested that, since she was a skillful rider and loved horses, she might like to read *National Velvet*. I made my sell as soft as possible, saying only that it was about a girl who loved and rode horses, and that if she didn't like it, she could put it back. She tried it, and though she must have found it quite a bit harder than what she had been reading, finished it and liked it very much.

During the spring she really astonished me, however. One day, in one of our many free periods, she was reading at her desk. From a glimpse of the illustrations I thought I knew what the book was. I said to myself, "It can't be," and went to take a closer look. Sure enough, she was reading *Moby Dick*, in the edition with woodcuts by Rockwell Kent. When I came close to her desk she looked up. I said, "Are you really reading that?" She said she was. I said, "Do you like it?" She said, "Oh, yes, it's neat!" I said, "Don't you find parts of it rather heavy going?" She answered "Oh, sure, but I just skip over those parts and go on to the next good part."

This is exactly what reading should be and in school so seldom is—an exciting, joyous adventure. Find something, dive into it, take the good parts, skip the bad parts, get what you can out of it, go on to something else. How different is our mean-spirited, picky insistence that every child get every last little scrap of "understanding" that can be dug out of a book.

For teachers who really enjoy doing it, and will do it with gusto, reading aloud is a very good idea. I have found that not just fifth graders but even ninth and eleventh graders enjoy it. Jack London's "To Build a Fire" is a good read-aloud story. So are ghost stories, and "August Heat," by W. F. Harvey, and "The Monkey's Paw," by W. W. Jacobs, are among the best. Shirley Jackson's "The Lottery" is sure-fire, and will raise all kinds of questions for discussion and argument. Because of a TV program they had seen and that excited them, I once started reading my fifth graders William Golding's *Lord of the Flies,* thinking to read only a few chapters, but they made me read it to the end.

In my early fifth-grade classes the children usually were of high IQ, came from literate backgrounds and were generally felt to be succeeding in school. Yet it was astonishingly hard for most of those children to express themselves in speech or in writing. I have known a number of five-year-olds who were considerably more articulate than most of the fifth graders I have known in school. Asked to speak, my fifth graders were covered with embarrassment; many refused altogether. Asked to write, they would sit for minutes on end, staring at the paper. It was hard for most of them to get down a half page of writing, even on what seemed to be interesting topics or topics they chose themselves.

In desperation I hit on a device that I named the Composition Derby. I divided the class into teams, and told them that when I said, "Go," they were to start writing something. It could be about anything they wanted, but it had to be about something—they couldn't just write "dog dog dog dog" on the paper. It could be true stories, descriptions of people or places or events, wishes, made-up stories, dreams—anything they liked. Spelling didn't count, so they didn't have to worry about it. When I said, "Stop," they were to stop and count up the words they had written. The team that wrote the most words would win the derby.

It was a success in many ways and for many reasons. The first surprise was that the two children who consistently wrote the most words were two of the least successful students in the class. They were bright, but they had always had a very hard time in school. Both were very bad spellers, and worrying about this had slowed down their writing without improving their spelling. When they were free of this worry and could let themselves go, they found hidden and unsuspected talents.

One of the two, a very driven and anxious little boy, used to write long adventures, or misadventures, in which I was the central character—"The Day Mr. Holt Went to Jail," "The Day Mr. Holt Fell Into the Hole," "The Day Mr. Holt Got Run Over," and so on. These were very funny, and the class enjoyed hearing me read them aloud. One day I asked the class to write a derby on a topic I would give them. They groaned; they liked picking their own. "Wait till you hear it," I said. "It's 'The Day the School Burned Down.'"

With a shout of approval and joy they went to work, and wrote furiously for 20 minutes or more, laughing and chuckling as they wrote. The papers were all much alike; in them the children danced around the burning building, throwing in books and driving me and the other teachers back in when we tried to escape.

In our first derby the class wrote an average of about ten words a minute; after a few months their average was over 20. Some of the slower writers tripled their output. Even the slowest, one of whom was the best student in the class, were writing 15 words a minute. More important, almost all the children enjoyed the derbies and wrote interesting things.

Some time later I learned that Professor I. S. Hayakawa, teaching freshman English, had invented a better technique. Every day in class he asked his students to write without stopping for about half an hour. They could write on whatever topic or topics they chose, but the important thing was not to stop. If they ran dry, they were to copy their last sentence over and over again until new ideas came. Usually they came before the sentence had been copied once. I use this idea in my own classes, and call this kind of paper a Non-Stop. Sometimes I ask students to write a Non-Stop on an assigned topic, more often on anything they choose. Once in a while I ask them to count up how many words they have written, though I rarely ask them to tell me; it is for their own information. Sometimes these papers are· to be handed in; often they are what I call private papers, for the students' eyes alone.

The private paper has proved very useful. In the first place, in any English class—certainly any large English class—if the amount the students write is limited by what the teacher can find time to correct, or even to read, the students will not write nearly enough. The only remedy is to have them write a great deal that the teacher does not read. In the second place, students writing for themselves will write about many things that they would never write on a paper to be handed in, once they have learned (sometimes it takes a while) that the teacher means what he says about the papers' being private. This is important, not just because it enables them to get things off their chest, but also because they are most likely to write well, and to pay attention to how they write, when they are writing about something important to them.

Some English teachers, when they first hear about private papers, object that students do not benefit from writing papers unless the papers are corrected. I disagree for several reasons. First, most students, particularly poor students, do not read the corrections on their papers; it is boring, even painful. Second, even when they do read these corrections, they do not get much help from them, do not build the teacher's suggestions into their writing. This is true even when they really believe the teacher knows what he is talking about.

Third, and most important, we learn to write by writing, not by reading other people's ideas about writing. What most students need above all else is practice in writing, and particularly in writing about things that matter to them, so that they will begin to feel the satisfaction that comes from getting important thoughts down in words and will care about stating these thoughts forcefully and clearly.

Teachers of English—or, as some schools say (ugh!), Language Arts—spend a lot of time and effort on spelling. Most of it is wasted; it does little good, and often more harm than good. We should ask ourselves, "How do good spellers spell? What do they do when they are not sure which spelling of a word is right?" I have asked this of a number of good spellers. Their answer never varies. They do not rush for a dictionary or rack their brains trying to remember some rules. They write down the word both ways, or several ways, look at them and pick the one that looks best. Usually they are right.

Good spellers know what words look like and even, in their writing muscles, feel like. They have a good set of word images in their minds, and are willing to trust these images. The things we do to "teach" spelling to children do little to develop these skills or talents, and much to destroy them or prevent them from developing.

The first and worst thing we do is to make children anxious about spelling. We treat a misspelled word like a crime and penalize the misspeller severely; many teachers talk of making children develop a "spelling conscience," and fail otherwise excellent papers because of a few spelling mistakes. This is self-defeating. When we are anxious, we don't perceive clearly or remember what we once perceived. Everyone knows how hard it is to recall even simple things when under emotional pressure; the harder we rack our brains, the less easy it is to find what we are looking for. If we are anxious enough, we will not trust the messages that memory sends us. Many children spell badly because although their first hunches about how to spell a word may be correct, they are afraid to trust them. I have often seen on children's papers a word correctly spelled, then crossed out and misspelled.

There are some tricks that might help children get sharper word images. Some teachers may be using them. One is the trick of air writing; that is, of "writing" a word in the air with a finger and "seeing" the image so formed. I did this quite a bit with fifth graders, using either the air or the top of a desk, on which their fingers left no mark. Many of them were tremendously excited by this. I can still hear them saying, "There's nothing there, but I can see it!" It seemed like black magic. I remember that when I was little I loved to write in the air. It was effortless, voluptuous, satisfying, and it was fun to see the word appear in the air. I used to write "Money Money Money," not so much because I didn't have any as because I liked the way it felt, particularly that *y* at the end, with its swooping tail.

Another thing to help sharpen children's image-making machinery is taking very quick looks at words—or other things. The conventional machine for doing this is the tachistoscope. But these are expensive, so expensive that most children can have few chances to use them, if any at all. With some three-by-five and four-by-eight file cards you can get the same effect. On the little cards you put the words or the pictures that the child is going to look at. You hold the larger card over the card to be read, uncover it for a split second with a quick wrist motion, then cover it up again. Thus you have a tachistoscope that costs one cent and that any child can work by himself.

Once when substituting in a first-grade class, I thought that the children, who were just beginning to read and write, might enjoy some of the kind of free, nonstop writing that my fifth graders had. One day about 40 minutes before lunch, I asked them all to take pencil and paper and start writing about anything they wanted to. They seemed to like the idea, but right away one child said anxiously, "Suppose we can't spell a word."

"Don't worry about it," I said. "Just spell it the best way you can."

A heavy silence settled on the room. All I could see were still pencils and anxious faces. This was clearly not the right approach. So I said, "All right, I'll tell you what we'll do. Any time you want to know how to spell a word, tell me and I'll write it on the board."

They breathed a sigh of relief and went to work. Soon requests for words were coming fast; as soon as I wrote one, someone asked me another. By lunchtime, when most of the children were still busily writing, the board was full. What was interesting was that most of the words they had asked for were much longer and more complicated than anything in their reading books or workbooks. Freed from worry about spelling, they were willing to use the most difficult and interesting words that they knew.

The words were still on the board when we began school next day. Before I began to erase them, I said to the children, "Listen, everyone. I have to erase these words, but before I do, just out of curiosity, I'd like to see if you remember some of them."

The result was surprising. I had expected that the child who had asked for and used a word might remember it, but I did not think many others would. But many of the children still knew many of the words. How had they learned them? I suppose each time I wrote a word on the board a number of children had looked up, relaxed yet curious, just to see what the word looked like, and these images and the sound of my voice saying the word had stuck in their minds until the next day. This, it seems to me, is how children may best learn to write and spell.

What can a parent do if a school, or a teacher, is spoiling the language for a child by teaching it in some tired way? First, try to get them to change, or at least let them know that you are eager for change. Talk to other parents; push some of these ideas in the PTA; talk to the English department at the school; talk to the child's own teacher. Many teachers and schools want to know what the parents want.

If the school or teacher cannot be persuaded, then what? Perhaps all you can do is try not to let your child become too bored or discouraged or worried by what is happening in school. Help him meet the school's demands, foolish though they may seem, and try to provide more interesting alternatives at home—plenty of books and conversation, and a serious and respectful audience when a child wants to talk. Nothing that ever happened to me in English classes at school was as helpful to me as the long conversations I used to have every summer with my uncle, who made me feel that the difference in our ages was not important and that he was really interested in what I had to say.

At the end of her freshman year in college a girl I know wrote home to her mother, "Hooray! Hooray! Just think—I never have to take English any more!" But this girl had always been an excellent English student, had always loved books, writing, ideas. It seems unnecessary and foolish and wrong that English teachers should so often take what should be the most flexible, exciting, and creative of all school courses and make it into something that most children can hardly wait to see the last of. Let's hope that we can and soon will begin to do much better.

QUESTIONS

1. What are the major indictments Holt makes and what alternatives does he propose?
2. Booth discusses various metaphors (including man as machine and man as animal) that underline different theories of education ("Is There Any Knowledge That a Man Must Have?," pp. 239–254). Might Holt accept any of these metaphors? If Holt constructed a different metaphor of his own, what might it be?
3. Is the kind of teaching that Holt describes likely to lead to students' having the knowledge that Booth believes essential?
4. Here are two accounts of a young boy's going to school, the second a summary or précis of the first. Determine what has been removed from the original in the summary. Then write a short comparison of original and summary from Holt's educational point of view, as it can be inferred from his essay.

His days were rich in formal experience. Wearing overalls and an old sweater (the accepted uniform of the private seminary), he sallied forth at morn accompanied by a nurse or a parent and walked (or was pulled) two blocks to a corner where the school bus made a flag stop. This flashy vehicle was as punctual as death: seeing us waiting at the cold curb, it would sweep to a halt, open its mouth, suck the boy in, and spring away with an angry growl. It was a good deal like a train picking up a bag of mail. At school the scholar was worked on for six or seven hours by half a dozen teachers and a nurse, and was revived on orange juice in midmorning. In a cinder court he played games supervised by an athletic instructor, and in a cafeteria he ate lunch worked out by a dietitian.

—E. B. White, "Education"

His days followed a set routine. He wore overalls and an old sweater, as everyone else did in his school. In the morning, a parent or nurse walked the two blocks with him to the corner where he met the school bus. The bus was always on time. During the six or seven hours of the school day, he had six teachers. The school also employed a nurse and a dietitian. Games were supervised. The children ate in the cafeteria. Orange juice was served during the morning session.

—End-of-Year Examinations in English for college bound students grades 9-12, Commission on English.

ROBERT ROSENTHAL
and
LENORE F. JACOBSON

Teacher Expectations for the Disadvantaged

One of the central problems of American society lies in the fact that certain children suffer a handicap in their education which then persists throughout life. The "disadvantaged" child is a Negro American, a Mexican American, a Puerto Rican or any other child who lives in conditions of poverty. He is a lower-class child who performs poorly in an educational system that is staffed almost entirely by middle-class teachers.

The reason usually given for the poor performance of the disadvantaged child is simply that the child is a member of a disadvantaged group. There may well be another reason. It is that the child does poorly in school because that is what is expected of him. In other words, his shortcomings may originate not in his different ethnic, cultural and economic background but in his teachers' response to that background.

If there is any substance to this hypothesis, educators are confronted with some major questions. Have these children, who account for most of the academic failures in the U.S., shaped the expectations that their teachers have for them? Have the schools failed the children by anticipating their poor performance and thus in effect teaching them to fail? Are the massive public programs of educational assistance to such children reinforcing the assumption that they are likely to fail? Would the children do appreciably better if their teachers could be induced to expect more of them?

We have explored the effect of teacher expectations with experiments in which teachers were led to believe at the beginning of a school year that certain of their pupils could be expected to show considerable academic improvement during the year. The teachers thought the predictions were based on tests that had been administered to the student body toward the end of the preceding school year. In actuality the children designated as potential "spurters" had been chosen at random and not on the basis of testing. Nonetheless, intelligence tests given after the experiment had been in progress for several months indicated that on the whole the randomly chosen children had improved more than the rest.

The central concept behind our investigation was that of the "self-fulfilling prophecy." The essence of this concept is that one person's prediction of another person's behavior somehow comes to be realized. The prediction may, of course, be realized only in the perception of the predictor. It is also possible, however, that the predictor's expectation is communicated to the other person, perhaps in quite subtle and unintended ways, and so has an influence on his actual behavior.

An experimenter cannot be sure that he is dealing with a self-fulfilling prophecy until he has taken steps to make certain that a prediction is not based on behavior that has already been observed. If schoolchildren who perform poorly are those expected by their teachers to perform poorly, one cannot say in the normal school situation whether the teacher's expectation was the cause of the performance or whether she simply made an accurate prognosis based on her knowledge of past performance by the particular children involved. To test for the existence of self-fulfilling prophecy the experimenter must establish conditions in which an expectation is uncontaminated by the past behavior of the subject whose performance is being predicted.

It is easy to establish such conditions in the psychological laboratory by presenting an experimenter with a group of laboratory animals and telling him what kind of behavior he can expect from them. One of us (Rosenthal) has carried out a number of experiments along this line using rats that were said to be either bright or dull. In one experiment 12 students in psychology were each given five laboratory rats of the same strain. Six of the students were told that their rats had been bred for brightness in running a maze; the other six students were told that their rats could be expected for genetic reasons to be poor at running a maze. The assignment given the students was to teach the rats to run the maze.

From the outset the rats believed to have the higher potential proved to be the better performers. The rats thought to be dull made poor progress and sometimes would not even budge from the starting position in the maze. A questionnaire given after the experiment showed that the students with the allegedly brighter rats ranked their subjects as brighter, more pleasant and more likable than did the students who had the allegedly duller rats. Asked about their methods of dealing with the rats, the students with the "bright" group turned out to have been friendlier, more enthusiastic and less talkative with the animals than the students with the "dull" group had been. The students with the "bright" rats also said they handled their animals more, as well as more gently, than the students expecting poor performances did.

Our task was to establish similar conditions in a classroom situation. We wanted to create expectations that were based only on what teachers had been told, so that we could preclude the possibility of judgments based on previous observations of the children involved. It was with this objective that we set up our experiment in what we shall call Oak School, an elementary school in the South

San Francisco Unified School District. To avoid the dangers of letting it be thought that some children could be expected to perform poorly we established only the expectation that certain pupils might show superior performance. Our experiments had the financial support of the National Science Foundation and the cooperation of Paul Nielsen, the superintendent of the school district.

Oak School is in an established and somewhat run-down section of a middle-sized city. The school draws some students from middle-class families but more from lower-class families. Included in the latter category are children from families receiving welfare payments, from low-income families and from Mexican-American families. The school has six grades, each organized into three classes—one for children performing at above-average levels of scholastic achievement, one for average children and one for those who are below average. There is also a kindergarten.

At the beginning of the experiment in 1964 we told the teachers that further validation was needed for a new kind of test designed to predict academic blooming or intellectual gain in children. In actuality we used the Flanagan Tests of General Ability, a standard intelligence test that was fairly new and therefore unfamiliar to the teachers. It consists of two relatively independent subtests, one focusing more on verbal ability and the other more on reasoning ability. An example of a verbal item in the version of the test designed for children in kindergarten and first grade presents drawings of an article of clothing, a flower, an envelope, an apple and a glass of water; the children are asked to mark with a crayon "the thing that you can eat." In the reasoning subtest a typical item consists of drawings of five abstractions, such as four squares and a circle; the pupils are asked to cross out the one that differs from the others.

We had special covers printed for the test; they bore the high-sounding title "Test of Inflected Acquisition." The teachers were told that the testing was part of an undertaking being carried out by investigators from Harvard University and that the test would be given several times in the future. The tests were to be sent to Harvard for scoring and for addition to the data being compiled for validation. In May, 1964, the teachers administered the test to all the children then in kindergarten and grades one through five. The children in sixth grade were not tested because they would be in junior high school the next year.

Before Oak School opened the following September about 20 percent of the children were designated as potential academic spurters. There were about five such children in each classroom. The manner of conveying their names to the teachers was deliberately made rather casual: the subject was brought up at the end of the first staff meeting with the remark, "By the way, in case you're interested in who did what in those tests we're doing for Harvard. . . ."

The names of the "spurters" had been chosen by means of a table of random numbers. The experimental treatment of the children involved nothing more than giving their names to their new teachers as children who could be expected to show unusual intellectual gains in the year ahead. The difference, then, between these children and the undesignated children who constituted a control group was entirely in the minds of the teachers.

All the children were given the same test again four months after school had started, at the end of that school year and finally in May of the following year. As the children progressed through the grades they were given tests of the appropriate level. The tests were designed for three grade levels: kindergarten and first grade, second and third grades and fourth through sixth grades.

The results indicated strongly that children from whom teachers expected greater intellectual gains showed such gains. The gains, however, were not uniform across the grades. The tests given at the end of the first year showed the largest gains among children in the first and second grades. In the second year the greatest gains were among the children who had been in the fifth grade when the "spurters" were designated and who by the time of the final test were completing sixth grade.

At the end of the academic year 1964–1965 the teachers were asked to describe the classroom behavior of their pupils. The children from whom intellectual growth was expected were described as having a better chance of being successful in later life and as being happier, more curious and more interesting than the other children. There was also a tendency for the designated children to be seen as more appealing, better adjusted and more affectionate, and as less in need of social approval. In short, the children for whom intellectual growth was expected became more alive and autonomous intellectually, or at least were so perceived by their teachers. These findings were particularly striking among the children in the first grade.

An interesting contrast became apparent when teachers were asked to rate the undesignated children. Many of these children had also gained in I.Q. during the year. The more they gained, the less favorably they were rated.

From these results it seems evident that when children who are expected to gain intellectually do gain, they may be benefited in other ways. As "personalities" they go up in the estimation of their teachers. The opposite is true of children who gain intellectually when improvement is not expected of them. They are looked on as showing undesirable behavior. It would seem that there are hazards in unpredicted intellectual growth.

A closer examination revealed that the most unfavorable ratings were given to the children in low-ability classrooms who gained the most intellectually. When these "slow track" children were in the control group, where little intellectual gain was expected of them, they were rated more unfavorably by their teachers if they did show gains in I.Q. The more they gained, the more unfavorably they were rated. Even when the slow-track children were in the experimental group, where greater intellectual gains were expected of them, they were not rated as favorably with respect to their control-group peers as were the children of the high track and the medium track. Evidently it is likely to be difficult for a slow-track child, even if his I.Q. is rising, to be seen by his teacher as well adjusted and as a potentially successful student.

How is one to account for the fact that the children who were expected to gain did gain? The first answer that comes to kind is that the teachers must have spent more time with them than with the children of whom nothing was said. This hypothesis seems to be wrong, judging not only from some questions we asked the teachers about the time they spent with their pupils but also from the fact that in a given classroom the more the "spurters" gained in I.Q., the more the other children gained.

Another bit of evidence that the hypothesis is wrong appears in the pattern of the test results. If teachers had talked to the designated children more, which would be the most likely way of investing more time in work with them, one might expect to see the largest gains in verbal intelligence. In actuality the largest gains were in reasoning intelligence.

It would seem that the explanation we are seeking lies in a subtler feature of the interaction of the teacher and her pupils. Her tone of voice, facial expression, touch and posture may be the means by which—probably quite unwittingly—she communicates her expectations to the pupils. Such communication might help the child by changing his conception of himself, his anticipation of his own behavior, his motivation or his cognitive skills. This is an area in which further research is clearly needed.

Why was the effect of teacher expectations most pronounced in the lower grades? It is difficult to be sure, but several hypotheses can be advanced. Younger children may be easier to change than older ones are. They are likely to have less well-established reputations in the school. It may be that they are more sensitive to the processes by which teachers communicate their expectations to pupils.

It is also difficult to be certain why the older children showed the best performance in the follow-up year. Perhaps the younger children, who by then had different teachers, needed continued contact with the teachers who had influenced them in order to maintain their improved performance. The older children, who were harder to influence at first, may have been better able to maintain an improved performance autonomously once they had achieved it.

In considering our results, particularly the substantial gains shown by the children in the control group, one must take into account the possibility that what is called the Hawthorne effect might have been involved. The name comes from the Western Electric Company's Hawthorne Works in Chicago. In the 1920's the plant was the scene of an intensive series of experiments designed to determine what effect various changes in working conditions would have on the performance of female workers. Some of the experiments, for example, involved changes in lighting. It soon became evident that the significant thing was not whether the worker had more or less light but merely that she was the subject of attention. Any changes that involved her, and even actions that she only thought were changes, were likely to improve her performance.

In the Oak School experiment the fact that university researchers, supported by Federal funds, were interested in the school may have led to a general improvement of morale and effort on the part of the teachers. In any case, the possibility of a Hawthorne effect cannot be ruled out either in this experiment or in other studies of educational practices. Whenever a new educational practice is undertaken in a school, it cannot be demonstrated to have an intrinsic effect unless it shows some excess of gain over what Hawthorne effects alone would yield. In our case a Hawthorne effect might account for the gains shown by the children in the control group, but it would not account for the greater gains made by the children in the experimental group.

Our results suggest that yet another base line must be introduced when the intrinsic value of an educational innovation is being assessed. The question will be whether the venture is more effective (and cheaper) than the simple expedient of trying to change the expectations of the teacher. Most educational innovations will be found to cost more in both time and money than inducing teachers to expect more of "disadvantaged" children.

For almost three years the nation's schools have had access to substantial Federal funds under the Elementary and Secondary Education Act, which President Johnson signed in April, 1965. Title I of the act is particularly directed at disadvantaged children. Most of the programs devised for using Title I funds focus on overcoming educational handicaps by acting on the child—through remedial instruction, cultural enrichment and the like. The premise seems to be that the deficiencies are all in the child and in the environment from which he comes.

Our experiment rested on the premise that at least some of the deficiencies—and therefore at least some of the remedies—might be in the schools, and particularly in the attitudes of teachers toward disadvantaged children. In our experiment nothing was done directly for the child. There was no crash program to improve his reading ability, no extra time for tutoring, no program of trips to museums and art galleries. The only people affected directly were the teachers; the effect on the children was indirect.

It is interesting to note that one "total push" program of the kind devised under Title I led in three years to a 10-point gain in I.Q. by 38 percent of the children and a 20-point gain by 12 percent. The gains were dramatic, but they did not even match the ones achieved by the control-group children in the first and second grades of Oak School. They were far smaller than the gains made by the children in our experimental group.

Perhaps, then, more attention in educational research should be focused on the teacher. If it could be learned how she is able to bring about dramatic improvement in the performance of her pupils without formal changes in her methods of teaching, other teachers could be taught to do the same. If further research showed that it is possible to find teachers whose untrained educational style does for their pupils what our teachers did for the special children, the prospect would arise that a combination of sophisticated selection of teachers and suitable training of teachers would give all children a boost toward getting as much as they possibly can out of their schooling.

QUESTIONS

1. The authors define "disadvantaged" at the outset; how would you define it when it is used at the end?
2. Assuming that Rosenthal and Jacobson are right, explain what you think teachers should do.
3. Is it possible that student expectations might create a self-fulfilling prophecy for teachers? Can you think of other self-fulfilling prophecies?
4. Is this sort of experiment possible without deceiving the subjects or people involved? Does it matter?

JONATHAN KOZOL

The Open Schoolroom: New Words for Old Deceptions

In the past two years there has been a massive media campaign to popularize the idea of a painless revolution in the U.S. public schools via something known as "open-structured education." The enthusiastic reception which this notion has received in liberal circles, above all in the upper-class schools which wish to have an innovative and attractive image, suggests the desperation that is felt by those who recognize incipient stirrings of an insurrectionary nature in the consciousness of children and young teachers. It is not possible to leave such stirrings undomesticated. Ethical strivings in the consciousness of youth constitute a solemn danger to an unjust nation. The public school, as the custodian of youth, can not allow this kind of ferment to go unrecognized and unconstrained.

All governments and administrative hierarchies will, if they are skillful and astute, find a means to undermine any danger they find themselves in. In other societies, less skilled and practiced than our own, the only methods known are often those of frank repression. In this society, two decades of experience in counter-revolutionary tactics have educated the kinds of men who handle power in the best of ways for neutralizing and de-fusing controversy. Napalm and high-flying aircraft may in certain cases be acceptable for use in foreign nations, but not in our own. Such methods run directly counter to the pretense of unmanaged intellection and of unmanacled expression of ideas that our society is built upon. It is only in emergencies, then, or in the context of those sections of the population where our instincts of abhorrence are abated somewhat by the sense of biological discrimination, that methods of this kind will be employed.

In most cases, what we do in public schools in the United States today is not to suppress but to buy out the revolutionary instincts of our children. We offer them "independent research," "individualized learning," "open-structured education," "non-directive class-discussions." Each child, in the standard code-word of the fashion, learns "at his own pace." Teachers are present not as educators but as "resource-people." The children "do their own thing." Everybody "tells it like it is" and tells other people "where it's at. . . ." It is all fashionable, fun and "innovative" . . . It is intelligently marketed and publicized. It is remarkably well-packaged.

It would, of course, be careless and inaccurate on my part to indicate that all of these innovations constitute overt or even indirect deception. It would also be inaccurate to suggest that they do not make *some* things different, and some situations less manipulative and less painfully oppressive than they were before. There is unquestionably a lower level of direct indoctrination and direct manipulation of a child's thinking now than in the old-time class-room. A number of things are much more fun, and there is far less of the sense of lockstep-motion and of inevitable non-stop perseverance than before. These are real differences and to a small degree they represent a lessening of the sense of desperation and of straight-line perseverance which enslave and paralyze so many children in the course of twelve years of sequential labor in the more traditional classrooms of the old-time schools.

It is my belief, however, that these changes do not seriously undermine the overriding purposes and operations of a public school, but have at best the function of adorning servitude with momentary flashes of delight and secondary avenues of unimportant deviation. At no point do these kinds of changes touch upon the basic anesthetic character of public school, its anti-ethical function, its chauvinistic fealties, its inculcation of the sense of vested interest in credentialized reward, its clever perpetration of a sense of heightened options in a closed and tightly circumscribed arena. At no point is there honest confrontation with the mandate of a man's or a woman's sense of justice. At no point is there actual, concrete, vivid provocation of that sense of justice. This sentence is the one, for me, which sums up all the rest: children are not free in any way that matters if they are not free to know the price in pain and exploitation that their lives are built upon. Stated differently, just children cannot be educated in an unjust school. A school which constitutes an island of self-etherized and of self-serving privilege within a land of pain is not a just school, whatever the games the school board authorizes, whatever the innovative slogans it may ply.

[A *Kind of* DMZ]

The notion of the "open-structured" school most often involves four or five associated notions, all of them wholly or in part erroneous: (1) that a proper and effective answer to the injustice and to the devastation of the time in which we live is constituted by an individual and self-directed search for Love and Satisfaction; (2) that the child who "freely" chooses one out of the fifty things selected in advance by teacher, School Board, EDC or IBM should be persuaded to believe that he is really "doing his own thing," that he is "exercising freedom"; (3) that we can, or ever do, "spontaneously" go from BEING GOOD AND LOVING to our (nearby) friends to BEING GOOD AND LOVING to our (distant) victims, especially if we have no means of finding out they *are* our victims or have no words or concepts to articulate this kind of truth; (4) that in face of pain, in face of hunger, in face of misery on every side, each man has the right to tend to his own needs, and to advance his own enlightenment, reward, self-interest, postponing into an indeterminate and into an unknown future the time at which he worries about those whom he does not see; (5) that a major change in the relationships between rich men and poor can ever come about without a solemn confrontation of some form. Stated differently, it is the notion that is now so much a part of North American mythology concerning progress: the fantasy that we can ever get real goods without authentic payment, that anything that matters ever come scot-free.

It is upon this basis, I believe, that the whole notion of the open-structured class must finally depend. To the teacher, most of all, it carries the consoling message that there is no solemn need to stand up and take sides: "We do not sustain; we do not subvert; we just stroll pleasantly through the class with an inductive glow and, now and then, we stop and smile. . . ." If there is a single phrase to summarize this notion, it is one like this: No one (even a committed man or woman) needs to take sides. No one needs to put his or her body on the line. The classroom does not need to be a counterfoil; it is sufficient if it constitutes a kind of island or a kind of DMZ.

The virtue of the "open-structured" classroom and of the so-called "non-directive" teacher, from the point of view of the society at large, is clear and quite straightforward. If it does not constitute overt cooperation with the ideological wishes of the state, at least it stops one step this side of open and direct rebellion. Battles can be fought on all sides of a DMZ: there is no danger here of rear-guard actions.

From the point of view of social change, or educational upheaval, open-structured education is less easily defended. For this statement I would like to offer two related arguments: one in relation to the teacher's role as a neutral or non-neutral force; the other in regard to the surrounding context.

First, in regard to the surrounding context, the point, I think, needs to be made that "neutral education" or a "neutral classroom" —or a classroom "open," as it were, to winds of truth and falsehood in the world outside—has little meaning in a managed framework of controlled ideas and preference-manufacture such as that which the industrial success of the United States now totally depends upon. There is a great deal more at stake within the school, and in the context of that school, than words and deeds of individual teachers. The physical structure, previous history, sequential character and complex interlock of school itself convey a body of explicit or implied directions, mandates, and requests. The "medium," as it were, of "school and schoolyear" carries with it an overriding and important message, regardless of what may be conveyed by words and textbooks. The message is largely one of dull, benevolent and untumultuous assurance. It is the message of a world which has been built, not like TV and other public media, on active lies, but on discreet negations. Strong colors, deep emotions, soaring passions are left out, and, in the leaving out, a fraudulent image of the world is perpetrated.

The overall picture is a little like the message flamboyant preachers used to call "The Good News." The good news of school, in essence, is the news that life is nice, that people are okay, that poverty is unreal or, if real, then fortunately unrealizable in the young imagination. Whatever the individual teacher does or does not say, all of the rest of this will still be present in the air around us, in the other classrooms, in the previous and succeeding years of school, as well as in the simple, physical persuasion of the architecture and of the flag outside the building. There is also, of course, the body of manipulated views and managed wants and manufactured aspirations that come with every child into this school-building from the outside world. These biases and aspirations, views and yearnings, for the greater part, come from TV and radio, daily press and picture magazines, as well as from one another, older friends, and older brother, sister, father, mother: in short, from all of those people who have been already muted and contained, modulated, styled, quieted, by their own prior course of mandatory public school indoctrination.

It seems to me that "neutral" education, in a time like this and in a land like ours, is less than honest, and less than "neutral" too, if we already recognize too well the presence of a uniform body of controlled and managed stimuli and viewpoints. The notion of the "neutral classroom" and of the "non-directive" teacher depends upon the prior existence of a neutral field, or at least a neutral pocket of unmanipulated and unmanaged intellection. To believe in this (and it is a gentle and appealing notion) is to believe in children who have lived their lives within a sweet and unplowed meadow. But we know very well our children do not live in a sweet meadow: they live in a mine-field crossed by electronic beams and planted with high-voltage speakers. To play the game of "non-directive educator" in this context is perhaps to fill a more attractive and less openly manipulative role than that of conscious salesman or saleswoman for a weary catalogue of patriotic notions. It is, moreover, a less demeaning role in that at least it frees the teacher from the obligation to say things which he or she, in fact, does not believe. Only in this sense does it represent a less debilitating posture, in that it represents a lower level of direct deception. It is deception, nonetheless.

The myth, the wishful thinking or the amiable deception, that lies beneath the notion of the open-structured classroom is the imagined "authenticity," the "spontaneity," and the "autonomy" of the child's intellectual initiatives. "Elicit the wishes, questions and directions from the child, unimpeded and unhindered and without much adult interference." But what is the meaning of a statement of this kind if we know very well that we, and all our children with us, are living in a closed kingdom of confined and narrow options, guided stimuli and calculated access to alternative ideas? A child does not spontaneously "ask" to learn of things that he has not first been allowed to hear of, nor does he innocently ask to learn what he has been already trained to view as inappropriate or awkward or unpopular or dangerous, or morally contaminated.

For the teacher to acquiesce in recognition of this kind, to silence her own convictions, sit down on the floor, smile her inductive smile and await the appearance of "spontaneous desires" on the part of children, may look to us, or to a uninformed observer, to be open and unbiased, "innovative," "honest," and relaxed. It may be innovative, but it is not open. There is a deep and powerful area of self-deception working here: one that attempts to tell us that the child's offerings are *really free*. The vested interest that we hold in this belief is in direct accord with the more powerful vested interest of our faith in our own freedom. The insistence of these notions in the face of all that we have read and comprehended and believed is index of the threat we feel when faced with the reality of our oppressed condition. It is similar to the way a patient feels in psychotherapy at times of imminent, but endangering insight.

It may well be that there was once a time, ages ago, in some other land or even in our own, when thoughts were free and wants were largely self-created. Today, whatever we wish to say, we know it is not so. The wants of the young, like those of their elders, are relentlessly controlled. "It is the essence of planning." Galbraith has said, "that public behavior should be made predictable. . . . The management to which we are subject is not onerous. It works not on the body but on the mind. It first wins acquiescence or belief: action is in response to this . . . conditioning and thus devoid of any sense of compulsion. It is open to anyone who can to contract out of this control. But we are no less managed because we are not physically compelled."

The foregoing deals with what I call the "field," or context of ideas, in which the classroom stands. There is also, however, an additional question about the teacher's role and function. In the long run there is, and can be, no such thing as an unbiased education or a neutral teacher. No teacher, no matter what he does or does not do, can fail in certain ways to advertise his bias to the children in his care—even if it is only by the very vivid lesson of avoiding a field fraught with ethical significance and with the possibilities for moral indignation. What the teacher "teaches," after all, is not only in what he says but at least in part in what he is, in what he does, in what he seems to wish to be. In the classroom, the things a teacher does not wish to say may well provide a deeper and more dangerous and more abiding lesson than the content of the textbooks or the conscious message of the posters on the wall. The teacher who does not speak to grief, who cannot cry for shame, who does not laugh and will not weep, teaches many very deep and memorable lessons about tears, laughter, grief *and* shame. When war is raging, and when millions of black people in our land are going through a private and communal Hell, no teacher, no matter what he does or does not do, can fail to influence his pupils in some fashion. The secret curriculum is the teacher's own lived values and convictions in the lineaments of his expression and in the biography of passion or self-exile that is written in his eyes. A teacher who appears to his children to be anesthetized, sedated, in the face of human pain, of medical racism, black infant-birth, or something so horrible and so quintessentially evil as the massacre at My Lai, may not teach children anything at all about medical racism, birth mortality or My Lai, but he will be teaching a great deal about the capability of an acceptable and respectably situated North American adult to abdicate the consequences of his own perception and, as it were, to vacate his own soul. By denying his convictions in the course of class-discussion, he does not teach *nothing*: he teaches *something*. He teaches, at the very least, a precedent for non-conviction. For these reasons, then, apart from all the others, it seems apparent that a teacher cannot, no matter what he does or does not do, maintain a neutral posture in the eyes of children. It is just not possible for us to disaffiliate entirely from the blood and the stench of the times in which we live.

[New Wine, Old Bottles]

"The social worker," Freire has written, "has a moment of decision. Either he picks the side of change . . . or he is left in the position of favoring stagnation." The open-structured classroom is a means by which the teacher is enabled to imagine that he does not need to choose. In truth, he chooses (for non-direction, non-participation, fashionable non-intervention) but he does not wish to tell himself that he has made this choice. Most teachers who have been in situations of this kind are well aware of the co-optive nature of the process in which they have come to be involved. Most of these teachers, for example, understand and can predict extremely well the kinds of things their pupils will select when they are "freely choosing" areas of study. They know very well the kinds of things they will "conclude" when they are working on their "independent research." They write down in advance, on Sunday afternoon, in lesson-books, the things their children will "discover" Wednesday morning in "small-group discussion." The open structured-classroom may be "child-centered," but it is also "teacher-written," "IBM-predicted," "School Board-overseen." Nobody ever really discovers anything within the confines of a well-run public school in the United States which someone somewhere does not give him license, sanction and permission to discover. It is just a better form of salesmanship than we have ever used before. In olden days we had to *tell* the children what to think, handing them, as it were the bottle and the spoon. Today, we lead them, by a pretense of free inquiry, to ask for it themselves. It is the same old bottle.

Teachers in open-structured situations speak of matters of this kind with one another frequently: they do not say the same things to the children. There is a way, for instance, known to many teachers in the open-structured situation, of opening up a controversial issue with the children in the classroom, in a manner that seems unmanaged, conscientious, honest, open-minded, and leaves us later on with a sense of having "faced the issue," and yet in which the odds were really set before we started and the purpose all along was not to meet a powerful issue but only, as it were, to tell ourselves we had. This is the way in which most dangerous ideas are now defused in innovative classrooms. Teachers pretend to open up an issue when what they really do is close it more emphatically than it has ever been closed before. The teacher who encourages this sense of artificial confrontation with a painful issue is denying more to the pupil than a teacher who avoids the issue altogether; for the latter, whether he knows it or not has left at least the possibility that the pupil, in rebellion, will search out the forbidden area at a later time and find something in it to enrich or challenge him. But the pupil who has had the false sense of meeting the issue in a classroom that was stacked against it has seen the issue sterilized forever.

All of the points that I have been trying to make come down at last to one important, over-riding and intensely unattractive bit of truth: In an unjust nation, the children of the ruling-classes are not free in any way that matters if they are not free to know the price of pain and exploitation that their lives are built upon. This is a freedom that no public school in the United States can willingly give children. Businessmen are not in business to lose customers: public schools do not exist to free their clients from the agencies of mass-persuasion. "Innovative schools" with "open-structured" classrooms speak often about "relevant learning-processes" and "urban-oriented studies," but the first free action of such a class of honest children in an unmanipulated, genuinely open classroom in a segregated school within an all-white suburb, would be to walk out of class, blockade the doors and shut down the school building. School serves the state; the interest of the state is identified for reasons of survival, with the interests of industrial dominion. The school exists to turn out manageable workers, obedient consumers, manipulable voters and, if need be, willing killers. It does not require the attribution of sinister motives, but only of the bare survival instincts, to know that a monolithic complex of industrial, political and academic interests of this kind does not intend to build the kinds of schools which will empower pint-sized zealots to expropriate their interests. It is in the light of considerations such as these that all innovations, all liberal reforms, all so-called "modern" methods and all new technologies ought to be scrutinized: Do they exist to free consumers, to liberate citizens, to inspire disagreement, inquiry, dissent? Or do they exist instead to quiet controversy, to contain rebellion and to channel inquiry into accepted avenues of discreet moderation? Is it conceivable that public schools can serve at once the function of indoctrinating agent and the function of invigorating counterfoil? I find this quite improbable and view with reservations of the deepest kind such genteel changes as may appear to offer broader liberties to captive children.

The only forms of educational innovation that are serious and worth consideration in this nation in the year of 1972 are those which constitute direct rebellion, explicit confrontation or totally independent ventures, such as networks, storefronts, Free Schools and the like, which stand entirely outside of the public system and which at all times labor to perform the function of provocateur and counterfoil. The *New York Times* can tell us what it likes of "open-structured education." The Carnegie Foundation can pay its parasitic program officers what it wishes to propagate the notion of "alternatives within the system." There are no such alternatives so long as the system is itself the primary vehicle of state control.

It is time to raise the stakes and open up our minds. It is time to look with deepened insight and scepticism on the innovative cliché and the high-priced pacification of the open-structured school: *There is a price to be paid, and a struggle of inordinate dimensions to be undertaken.* There is no way in which a serious man or honorable woman can escape the implications and the dangers of this statement.

QUESTIONS

1. List as statements the most important explicit convictions Kozol has about people and society as these convictions appear in this essay. Do these statements form a coherent political outlook?
2. Kozol does not often defend or explain unspoken assumptions. Choose a brief passage from the essay in which his assumptions need explanation or defense and rewrite the passage trying to explain or defend those assumptions to a skeptical reader. How does your version differ from his?
3. Select a short passage which seems strong or powerful. What are the particular words or features of style that make it so?
4. Should it be the function of education to give a child "access to alternative ideas" that may be "awkward or unpopular or dangerous or morally contaminated" (p. 209)? Do all these attributes combine into a consistent set?

PAUL COWAN

A Fight over America's Future

Charleston, W. Va.—The turbulent textbook controversy that has crippled schools here is more than a simple fight over the adoption of 325 first through 12th grade supplementary English textbooks. For the 229,000 people who live in the coal and petrochemical rich Kanawha valley it is not an isolated battle, not some rustic re-run of the Scopes trial, but a microcosm of a basic conflict in our culture. It is nothing less than a fight over America's future.

This fight has taken place in many different localities, over many different issues. Its themes are the same as those that were echoed in New York City's fight over community controlled schools, in Boston's battle over bussing, in the black militant attempt to establish a New Africa in the Mississippi, and in the Chicanos' attempt to drive most Anglos from administrative jobs in Crystal City, Texas. Can America's mainstream culture, made pervasive by the electronic media, absorb all the diverse groups that live here, that are passionate about maintaining their identity?

To me, the protests here are a fresh sign that the melting pot—with its dream of a single, unified American culture—is largely a myth. I don't believe we have ever been united except during times of national crisis like wars and assassinations,—and as consumers. I think that, to an unrecognized extent, we are a collection of religious, ethnic, and generational tribes who maintain an uneasy truce. We had to conquer this continent in order to exploit its vast resources. But we were never able to conquer our own atavistic hatreds and loyalties, to live comfortably as a single people.

The battle in Kanawha is a cultural revolution, in the strictest sense of the term: an effort by the rural working class to wrest schools—the means of production of their children—away from the permissive technocrats who now control them.

It is a holy war between people who depend on books and people who depend on the Book.

And it may be a harbinger of fights that will flare up during the next few years as the Depression, the Mideast war, and the rise of conservative Christianity cause people to lash back at the cosmopolitan elite (the "educated fools" or "upper-class Communists" as they're called down here) they blame for their problems. If the textbook controversy is a harbinger, then education is likely to be a more important battleground than the media or pornography, though those issues kindle the same profound wrath. You can turn off your TV set, avoid movies or massage parlors, but you must send your kids to school.

Most of the people who live in Kanawha County's hollers see the textbooks as a collection of skeptical comments about God, of four-letter words and salacious stories, of subversive essays by black revolutionaries like Eldridge Cleaver and Malcolm X. The books symbolize the horrifying 1960's culture which the schools are inflicting on their young; the infection that began on liberal campuses has spread to Kanawha County and now threatens to turn their kids into sex maniacs, drug addicts, and Manson-like killers. So they want to cleanse America of its filth if they're strong enough; seal themselves off from the plague if that's their only alternative. For the moment, that means they've turned their backs on upward mobility. They feel that if their children established any friendly contact with the corrupt forces that run the nation's institutions, their characters are certain to be corrupted.

Here the fight is between the "hillers" and the "creekers." The "hillers" tend to support the textbooks: they are the doctors, lawyers, mine managers, and petrochemical engineers who live on Charleston's luxurious South Hills. They read the Times and the Wall Street Journal just as avidly as the Charleston Daily Mail or Gazette. Many take the United Airlines flight to New York City so often that it's almost like a commuter trip. They make regular vacation trips to Atlanta or Miami or, if they're genuinely rich, to Europe. They regard the books as crucial ingredients of the kind of contemporary school system that will let their kids keep up with their peers across the country—that will help them get into Harvard or Haverford instead of Morris Harvey or West Virginia Tech.

The "creekers" live in the rural towns and hollers—Big Chimney, Cabin Creek, Cross Lanes—that dot this sprawling, windy, mountainous county. They work in the mines, or in fetid factories like the duPont plant in Balle, or, if they're lucky, as truck drivers or construction workers. Most of them have never been on an airplane in their lives. Many went to cities like Chicago, Dayton, or Cleveland during the Appalachian migration of the 1960's, but they found those places alien and hostile and returned to their own tight-knit communities. Their reminiscences are laced with the same bitterness they display towards the textbooks.

In September, the books were introduced into the schools. There was so much violence in the county that the board of education decided to withdraw the books from the schools for a 30-day review period. During that time, there were exchanges of gunfire, school rooms were dynamited, school busses shot at, cars and homes firebombed. One night someone put 15 sticks of dynamite under Charleston's board of education building and demolished part of it. It was clear that most of the county felt some sympathy for the protestors. In November, a Charleston Gazette poll showed that just 19 per cent of the community wanted all the books returned to the schools. Nevertheless, in mid-November, the board of education voted 4–1 to return most of the controversial materials to the schools, though they ruled that some of the most controversial grade school books would remain in the library. The sporadic violence continued. And, as in any war, attitudes kept hardening.

Susan Bean, 35, who lives in South Hills, was a member of the committee that reviewed all the textbooks. She's the wife of a landscape architect, the mother of three grade school kids. She was born in Mt. Pleasant, Tennessee, where her father was a member of the

John Birch Society. In his small construction business he systematically underpaid all the blacks who worked for him. He whipped Susan whenever he caught her reading unorthodox books, whenever she disagreed with him. At 17 she ran away from home, got a job as a typist at Sears, and worked her way through the University of Georgia, where she was an English major.

Interestingly, it is Susan Bean's conservative background that has made her a fierce supporter of the books. Indeed, she is glad that her children will study the religious unorthodoxies that her father despised. One day I told her I thought we were witnessing a class struggle, and she responded, quite tartly, "Sure it's a class struggle, but not in the way you outsiders think. You come from a liberal background. You can't imagine how much the opportunity to give my kids unlimited freedom means to me. It's a way of making sure that I, and my kids, rise above my past."

Nell Wood, fortyish, the English teacher who selected the textbooks, is the daughter of a fundamentalist railroad engineer from a rural county in West Virginia. Now she teaches an honors English class for seniors at the prestigious George Washington High School, nested in the midst of South Hills. Though most of her students come from wealthy, sophisticated families, she is still a practicing fundamentalist. She never smokes or drinks, feels uncomfortable when people take the Lord's name in vain, and has to ask her team teacher to read whatever four-letter words crop up.

It's possible that her support of the textbooks comes from her special classroom experience. There are teachers who argue that if she had to face a classroom full of rural working class kids each day she might feel more ambivalent about the issue. But she is a woman who lives books and wants to share that passion with her students. She refuses to weed out stories and attitudes that other fundamentalists consider blasphemous because "I can't bear the thought of standing in front of a group of kids and telling lies by omitting ideas I know exist." Just as many protestors have quotations from the Bible in their homes she has a quotation from the Areopagitica in her spare, tiny cubicle behind the George Washington High School Library. "Who kills a man kills a reasonable creature, God's image; but who kills a book kills reason itself."

But thousands of people here say they'd die fighting the blasphemy that Nell Wood believes is freedom. Emmett Thompson, 55, a riverboat engineer from Nitro, West Virginia, lives quite comfortably in a neat red brick house which is larger than Susan Bean's white frame house on South Hills. His oldest son is a trim, impeccably dressed short-haired man who has just graduated from the Lynchburg Bible College. Thompson, whose busy cinnamon-colored moustache makes him look a little more dashing than his boy, is what people here call a "Wednesday nighter"—so devoted to the local Calvary Baptist Church that he attends it twice on Sunday, once on Wednesday. He considers the introduction of the books "moral genocide."

"It's an insidious attempt to replace our periods with their question marks" he says, and he thinks it has to be fought. In a county where coal miners are experts with dynamite, where every man and boy is a hunter and every house in every holler has plenty of guns and plenty of ammunition, he longs for a "return to the spirit of the Boston Tea Party," a "revolution of righteousness."

Skeeter Dodd, the manager of radio station WKLC, is the sort of person who might help lead that revolution. A chunky, sturdy man in his mid-40s. Skeeter is an early morning disk jockey, whose taste in country music, in syndicated jokes from the "Funny Wire," and in imaginary dialogues with the fictional hillbilly "granddad" has made him a favorite with "creekers" throughout the county. "If they don't wake up to me, they ain't gonna wake up that day," he says in his exaggerated West Virginia accent, his genuinely hearty laugh.

Though KLC is Charleston's third largest station, Skeeter spends much of his time worrying about collecting bills from advertisers and finding new sponsors who will keep his station afloat. But he is also a patriot who, like Emmett Thompson, sees the textbook struggle as a salvo in a war to "restore the faith of our fathers. Look at it this way, friend. They tax us for the schools, but the schools don't represent us. Isn't that what them dumb hillbillies and creekers was fighting about 200 years ago?"

He not only despises the books, he believes that they are part of a Communist plot hatched in Düsseldorf, Germany in 1917 to destroy democracy. He showed me a replica of this curious document which proposed "to corrupt the people, get them away from religion. Make them superficial. Destroy their ruggedness." And, like thousands of people here, he believes in the existence of an upper-class conspiracy to bring Communism to America. Most people equate Communism with decadence, and argue that because rich people want to legalize drugs, legitimize pre-marital sex, pornographic movies and massage parlors, they are subversive. But Skeeter's reasons are more personal. His dad worked on an assembly line, he says, "Neighbor, you better believe that under a system like socialism this old creeker'd still be back there."

He'd been in Navy intelligence during the Korean War, and now saw himself combating Communism in Kanawha County. He carried a citizens' band radio in his car so that other movement leaders could alert him if there was trouble. He was "Boots" in a cb network that included "Kojack," "Blue Flag," and "Money Man." Late on a chilly fall night, wearing his battered black overcoat as he slumped over his mike and exchanged information on the small radio, he looked like a weary, dedicated member of a nascent band of freedom fighters, the nucleus of an army which wants to cleanse America, to restore it to the paths of righteousness.

From the Holler to the Space Age

In a sense, this is the story of an idea whose time never quite came.

The idea was that educational planners could reach into America's ghettos, its hollers, and its tradition-bound ethnic communities, like Canarsie and South Boston, and coax people there into the "melting pot." That was the principal rationale behind bussing. It was also the reason that states like West Virginia mandated "multi-cultural, multi-ethnic" programs in their classrooms.

The theory is clearly stated in a funding proposal for the training of teachers, dated 1970, signed by West Virginia's Superintendent of Schools. According to the document, teachers are supposed to be trained to "induce changes . . . in the behavior of the culturally lost" of Appalachia. . . . The setting of the public school should be the testing ground, the diagnostic basis, the experimental center, and the core of this design . . . The most important ingredient of social change is the change agent—the teacher.

You have only to look at the text-books to see how they fit in with that theory. Though I personally found many of them quite appealing—the sorts of books I would like my two children to study —I could also see how their sheer physical appearance would shock parents who had been brought up on Dick and Jane stories, on the six point type of the King James Bible, and on the rigid belief that education meant rote memorization. Now their children are using post-linear paper-backs where cartoons, photos, and gaudily colored pages dominate the print; where you don't read about Evangeline or the Courtship of Miles Standish but about sports heroes, rock stars, and street gangs, where achievement doesn't rest in a child's ability to repeat a lesson accurately, but in her capacity to answer the provocative questions at the end of each section.

And the stories do, as Emmett Thompson said, "attempt to replace our periods with question marks." Reading them I could see, for the first time, how a theist, who was still embittered because the Supreme Court had outlawed school prayer, could believe that the relativism and humanism that I have always cherished as the highest kind of open-mindedness represents a dogma of its own whose very skepticism embodied religious values.

For example, there is one exercise which asks students to compare the biblical story of Daniel and the Lion's Den with the tale of Androcles and the Lion. To conservative Christians the question itself is blasphemy since it suggests that something they take to be revelations is nothing more than myth. Similarly, the books include writings like Mark Twain's "Adam's Diary," which shows God's first offspring as a bumbling upstate New York householder and includes a New Yorker style cartoon of a naked Adam and Eve peeping out over some bushes. The books invite students to invent their own gods, an exercise which suggests that God himself might be an invention.

The idea behind the books is the classic liberal assumption that a child who learns to question himself and his surroundings will grow beyond the confines of his culture. But, apart from the religious heresies, that means the books are also filled with a set of assumptions that many West Virginians regard as secular blasphemy. For example, some of the exercises encourage kids to tell each other about their disagreements with their parents, their reservations about authority. They ask whether it is ever legitimate to steal. They contain a great many four-letter words (whose use, in many Appalachian households, would condemn kids to severe beatings). They suggest that standard English may be one of many dialects spoken in this country, that rules of English are relative, that ghetto English might be a legitimate form of speech. Some of the high school textbooks include writings by revolutionaries like Eldridge Cleaver.

Now, it's easy to see how a professional educator, who has learned, almost as a matter of dogma, that schools were always the vehicles by which working-class kids achieved a level of success that was beyond the wildest dreams of their parents, could have thought that "multi-cultural, multi-ethnic" textbooks could bring kids into the "melting pot."

But it's probably too much to demand that a countyful of people make the spiritual journey from the holler to the Space Age in less than five years, especially when the trip forces them beyond the furthest barrier of their belief. It makes them the victims of a sort of psychic overload. Sometimes they submit in confusion. But in Kanawha County they found leaders who could articulate their fury at the annihilation of every value they revered. They fought back.

Alice Moore is the lone dissenter on the school board. Her husband, a Church of Christ minister, had parishes in Tennessee and Meridian Mississippi before he was stationed in the lower-middle class town of St. Alban's. In 1970, two years after her arrival in, Kanawha County, Alice Moore decided that she'd run for the board to symbolize her opposition to sex education in the schools. She was elected.

She is a stunningly beautiful, intelligent woman who adopts a Southern belle's flirtatious style when she argues with the four male school board members.

But it's clear that when Alice speaks thousands of people in the creeks and hollers listen. She's in the newspapers nearly every day now, on TV nearly every night: a Joan of Arc, witty and resolute in her battle against the male "hiller" majority of the school committee. Whenever she appears at board meetings or at public rallies she is greeted with jubilant standing ovations, with cheerful choruses of "We love you, Alice, oh, yes, we do," with clusters of flowers and placards that read "Alice Moore for President." In places like Big Chimney and Kelly's Creek—towns the hillers can barely find on their maps, let alone in their cars—her name inspires the same kind of glisteningly popular response as Huey Long's did in the back-country parishes of Louisiana.

When the textbooks came up for adoption last spring, she was the only school board member who read them thoroughly. She was enraged by their emphasis on what she calls "situational ethics"— the heathen creed that encourages kids to believe that any set of actions can be justified by sociological conditions.

I could see her anger during a long interview one afternoon when she told me about a teacher training program she'd attended. Her tone alternated between Andy Griffith–like wonder and fundamentalist wrath. She was particularly amused by an instructor who'd tried to show how the concept of camouflage could be conveyed by hiding some green toothpicks in grass. He failed because the grass was so bright that the toothpicks were visible at once. Then, angering quickly, she talked about another educational expert who sought to prove there was a cultural justification for Eskimo mothers who put their babies outside to freeze. "You know," she said, "I was the only person there who argued she was wrong."

With my longish hair, my credentials from an urban liberal newspaper, I must have suddenly seemed like the enemy. She was courteous, and her lovely Southern voice never lost its slight hint of conspiratorial laughter. But: "You just don't understand what you're doing to us," she said. "How can any school board force me to send my kids to a school that teaches God is a myth, that justifies mothers who kill their young?"

"But how could I send my kids to schools that outlawed those textbooks?" I asked. "I hate censorship as much as you hate blasphemy." "I don't know," she said. "Maybe there's no school system in this country that can provide for your kids and mine. Maybe we Americans have come to a parting of the ways."

The Parting of the Ways:
"Don't Educate Them Above Their Rearing"

Maybe the parting of the ways has already come, and the only question is how many people are on each side. Certainly many conservative Christians in Kanawha County feel the frustration, the sense of isolation, that Alice Moore describes. They are so appalled by the America the textbooks represent that they'd rather forego the idea of college altogether, the dream of upward mobility, than risk the infection of relativism.

Many young people are as passionate about the holy war as their parents. I spent a great deal of time interviewing the elite students at George Washington High and the working-class kids from Campbell's Creek who attend duPont and East Bank. There is no communication between them—only mutual stereotypes, mutual contempt.

Many students from George Washington are aware that their wealth spawns resentment, that the fact that they go to GW creates an almost insurmountable barrier of resentment. And some wish, wistfully, that the gap could be bridged. But even though there are many "creckers" at GW, not a single one of the 15 "hiller" kids I interviewed had ever visited them or invited them home. And, though they're theoretically aware that "those kids are angry because they think our parents have money," it never occurred to them that their freedom to leave school in their family car, to gather at Gino's Pizza for a pleasant lunch, rankled the kids from the hollers who had to stay in school all day and eat their meals in the cafeteria.

During an interview one girl asked me, sharply, "why anybody would want to visit people like those coal miners." When I asked some other students to describe the textbook protesters, they used phrases like "closed-minded and violent" people "who want to protest corruption, but don't even know how to use the word," "Wednesday-nighters who carry clubs." Three students gave me an issue of the George Washington Pride, the school's underground newspaper, which contained a long satire about the conflict in which the protest leader's name is "the Rev. Rodney Necc, but my friends call me Red," who has come to a demonstration sponsored by "the Christian and Righteous Association of Parents . . . to show my deep dedication to upholding CRAP."

I felt completely at ease with the kids from George Washington. But many "creekers," and their children, were quite suspicious of me as an outsider, particularly because I was a reporter. At one of their rallies they had beaten up CBS's Jed Duval. When I went to the "anti-textbook headquarters" in Campbell's Creek two separate groups of people insisted on frisking me, on examining the documents in my wallet. A woman who saw that I had a pocket-sized Sony tape-recorder accused me of bugging them all. After a while, many still warned that "they'd come looking for me" if I wrote an unfavorable story about them.

That afternoon, at a small white Baptist Church, off a windy dirt road in Campbell's Creek, I met with about 10 teen-aged children of coal miners, truck drivers, construction workers, and ministers. They didn't feel as free with me as the kids from GW had, so their comments were more cramped and restrained. Still, some were scornful of the hillers. They talked about their wild dope-filled orgies where maids had to lock themselves in their rooms for fear of being beaten, of their rich, reckless parents, who were too busy to take care of their kids: of the ease with which they could bribe the police when they got in trouble. And of their hedonistic atheism. "They're rich people who think they know everything," said a coal miner's daughter. "But they haven't been taught right. They don't have any common sense. They don't really care about God."

Other kids sounded genuinely wounded by the "hillers'" insensitivity. "I can expect someone who doesn't believe in God not to see anything wrong with the textbooks," said one minister's daughter. "But they can at least respect our rights since it does say something about our God. We're not asking that they teach Christianity in the schools. We're just asking that they don't insult our faith."

The truck driver's son had a more practical objection. He was afraid that the books would hurt his chances of earning a living. He wanted to go to West Virginia Tech, to be an engineer, and felt he needed a "good basic education."

"I mean they could teach English in school without going to this ghetto language or some of this slang," he said. "If they drop that standard, then society's just going to go down. Until now we've always been taught to make speeches in front of class, to write letters with correct punctuation. But in this new set of textbooks they say, whatever sort of speech is common in your area, well, that's all right. But if you move out of state it will be just like going to a foreign country. How will you know what other people's meaning is? And, I know from my father's experience—if you look for a job and can't talk the right English, they won't hire you."

Of course, for many protestors the issues are far more general and ominous than the practical questions of grammar and employment. Many students from duPont and East Bank are already into rock music and dope; the parents—and more chaste kids—are scared that the heretical ideas in the school-sanctioned textbooks will rid them of their last vestiges of social control.

At meeting after meeting, I heard complaints about kids from Kanawha County who'd gone to college and come home acting like aliens. The conclusions? "Don't let them be educated above their rearing." "I was going to send my boy to college," said the wife of a food salesman from St. Alban's. "But I've changed my mind. It was a difficult decision. In my husband's profession, now, you need a college degree. But I'd rather see him become a coal miner or a construction worker than know he was risking his soul."

If the Christians Fight Back

Of course, religious controversy is not new in these parts. Nor is separatism. The ancestors of the miners and teamsters who live in Cabin Creek and Big Chimney were Anglo-Saxon yeomen who settled here 200 years ago because they were dissatisfied with Virginia's upper-class Tidewater planters and their moribund Anglican church. They were inspired by the first Great Awakening, the national fit of religious ecstasy which, with its stress on holy fervor and personal salvation, swept westward from New England in the 18th century. Even now, in the small Baptist and Pentecostal churches that dot the landscape, thousands of Baptists and Pentecostals scourge themselves by listening to sermons that sound like replicas of Jonathan Edwards "Sinners in the Hands of an Angry God."

For generations, the fundamentalists were sure that some version of their creed was America's dominant faith. Then, without warning, they found themselves waging a defensive war against the heathen idea of evolution. The Scopes trial was a watershed: between Clarence Darrow's courtroom tactics and H.L. Mencken's scathing prose, they suddenly ceased to be America's conscience and became its laughing stock. Though they clung to their faith, sometimes defiantly, many of them felt a private lingering shame. It took decades for that shame to vanish. Now, their church is likely to become militant again.

If Kanawha County's army of Christian soldiers ever decides to wage all-out war, life here will be unbearable. This fall's rash of dynamiting, firebombing and shooting has terrified educators all over the county. Protest leaders deny responsibility for most incidents, blaming some on stoned-out kids, others on the books' supporters. Still the violence has merged with the fundamentalists ardent support of censorship to make each teacher feel like a potential target. For example, during the weeks the books were out of the schools, English teachers all over the county were scared to teach anything but grammar in case any work of literature, even Shakespeare, goaded some hotheads to bomb their buildings.

Late one Wednesday night someone threw three sticks of dynamite into a first-grade classroom at the Midway School in Campbell's Creek. The teacher whose room was bombed, had spent a decade collecting books and toys for kids whose families couldn't afford them. Now, all that was destroyed. The room itself was littered with the debris from a waist-high partition-bookshelf that had been shattered by the blast. Hundreds of books were scattered on the floor. From the outside all you could see was four shattered windows, the traces of some tables and chairs, a brightly lettered alphabet attached to the blackboard, and an American flag that still perched above the whole room.

The Wet Bridge elementary school in Cabin Creek, the most rural part of the sprawling county, is even more threatened than Midway. In October, someone tossed two sticks of dynamite into the building. The afternoon I visited it, just eight of 300 enrolled students showed up for classes. "Each day seems like it's two million hours long," said one teacher.

One of the older teachers at the school has taught most of the parents of the boycotting children. The fact that they won't trust her to use the books responsibly has robbed her of her self-confidence. In a community where hundreds of people are functionally illiterate, where they are ignorant of the rudiments of personal and sexual hygiene, she is now afraid to offend them by instructing them.

"Soon we won't be able to teach anything," she says. "It's as if those parents and ministers are staring over our shoulders, waiting to get us for saying anything that sounds immoral. I'm afraid that if this boycott ever ends I won't see the children as students. I'll see them as spies in the classroom."

So We Are Two Nations

I have rarely covered a story that left me feeling as emotionally conflicted as this one has. For it seems to me that some of the pro-textbook people—the Northern educators and bureaucrats who devised them, not the local people who adopted them—are involved in a kind of cultural imperialism. But some of the protestors, who may be able to gain control of the county through the courts, through elections, and through threats of violence, are capable of outright totalitarianism.

I know that the people who designed the textbooks believe that the children of fundamentalists (and, to a lesser extent, of the white working class in general) have to be freed from the narrow-minded influence of their parents in order to become functioning members of 21st century America. But is it ethical or prudent, to confront them with textbooks they regard as blasphemous, to use their classrooms as "testing grounds," to train their teachers to be "change agents?" To me that is quite literally, a way of telling kids "we have to destroy your culture in order to save you." I've interviewed some curriculum reformers and textbook authors, and its clear that they see the "creekers" in the same derisive terms H.L. Mencken used during the Scopes trial. They regard the objections of people like Alice Moore as problems to be dealt with, not opinions to be respected.

Their intentions are probably benign, but isn't their policy a fresh example of the arrogance of power? You can invite a person into your culture. But I don't believe you can impose your culture on another person without risking unforeseeable psychological harm.

If the trip is voluntary, as Susan Bean's was, then the person is likely to maintain a sense of identity and pride. But if it's an imposed journey to a totally unknown destination—as it would be for many children in Kanawha County—then it could produce considerable psychological harm. It could set them adrift, with no reliable traditions, no moral compass, in an agnostic, post-linear, multicultural, multi-ethnic Space Age world which has no connection at all to their familiar hollers.

You cannot outlaw school prayer and still pretend that secular humanism—momentarily our national creed—does not carry its own deep assumptions about religion. Why not recognize that both attitudes are dogmas, and try to develop an educational system that's flexible enough to furnish federal funds to schools that base their curriculum on theism as well as to those that base their curriculum on relativism?

Most outside journalists who have come here to cover the textbook controversy have become fascinated by the relatively novel kinds of injustices I've been describing. As a result, many have tended to glorify the protestors a little, to explain their excesses by arguing that they are victims of a class struggle. But I think they are sentimentalizing a potentially dangerous movement.

The last scene I witnessed in Charleston is the one that grates most painfully on my imagination. It was a protest rally the day after the textbooks were restored to the schools. It wasn't in any of the rural churches or parks where the movement was nurtured, but in the cavernous Civic Center, one of the most modern buildings in Charleston.

The audience of 2,500 was in a fervent mood. Most of them wore large stickers which asserted "Jesus Wouldn't Have Read Them." As they sang "Amazing Grace," "We Shall Not be Moved," and "God Bless America," more than half of them swayed back and forth, waving their right hands in the air to show that they were born-again Christians. The podium was bathed in the lights from the TV cameras. On the right side, a stern, trim youth held the American flag aloft through the two-hour program. On the left side, an equally rigid young man bore a Christian flag, with a silky white field and a blood purple cross as its emblem. The flags, and their martial bearers, framed each speaker.

The main speaker was the Rev. Marvin Horan, who is supposed to be one of the more moderate protest leaders—more moderate, say, than the Rev. Charles Quigley, who wore army fatigues that day and who'd shocked the county a few weeks earlier by issuing a public prayer that God would strike the pro-textbook schoolboard members dead.

As Horan spoke, his voice rolled with righteousness: the audience applauded nearly every sentence. He held a Bible in his right hand, two textbooks in his left and, shaking both arms angrily he cried, "Which are we going to stand for, the word of God or the filth in these books?" Then he threatened his audience—"the Bible says not to use the Lord's name in vain or the person who does so will not be held guiltless at the seat of judgement"—and read several blasphemous sentences from "Catcher in the Rye," a text which he, at least, had clearly studied quite carefully. For he told his audience that "out of all this book, almost 300 pages, there's only 20 pages that don't use the Lord's name in vain." Then, waving "Catcher in the Rye" aloft, he asked "Do we surrender or do we fight?"

Behind me someone yelled "burn 'em," and hundreds of people began to applaud.

Now Horan was talking about the importance of maintaining the school boycott. "The board of education may think we're yellow, but our real colors are red, white, and blue . . . If we stand unified we can rid Kanawha County of these filthy books and the people who put them there."

It wasn't just platform rhetoric. Though the school boycott wasn't nearly as successful as Horan had hoped, and the country became outwardly calm after another week of sporadic violence, the influence of the anti-textbook movement has spread to other states. The series of textbooks that started the controversy here has been rejected in Georgia and Texas. There are similar disputes in Virginia, Maryland, Minnesota, New Jersey, and Indiana. The League of Decency, an anti-pornography organization from California, attaches enough importance to the fight here to let its chief spokesman, a former TV personality named Robert Dornan who's paid $42,000 a year, spend most of his time in Charleston.

The school board's decision to put most of the books back in the classrooms has been a Pyrrhic victory for the county's liberals. Last week, the board adopted a set of guidelines—most of them proposed by Alice Moore—which would probably have caused this English series to be rejected if it had existed a year ago. From now on, Kanawha County textbooks can't contain profanity; they can't intrude on a student's privacy by asking personal questions about his family or his inner feelings; they must encourage loyalty to the United States; they can't defame any of America's heroes; they must teach that traditional rules of grammar are essential for effective communications.

It's still possible that the English books will be withdrawn from the schools. Last week some protestors filed a lawsuit charging that the adoption might have been illegal because the school board first voted for the books on April 11, instead of the state deadline of April 1. If that doesn't reopen the issue, then the adoption of a new set of social studies textbooks, slated for next April, could kindle an even more disruptive set of skirmishes.

Meanwhile, protestors from rural Kanawha County, which includes towns like Cabin Creek and Campbell's Creek, are urging people in their region to secede from the rest of the County.

Maybe the prominence of the Christian flag at Reverend Horan's rally awakened my own tribal Jewish fears, but the experience left me deeply unsettled. The Reverend Horan, and the countless conservative Christians who identify with him, are absolutists. My question marks are sacred to me. Each attitude is a dogma, but the difference between them is vast. I would like to think that there is plenty of room for people like Marvin Horan in my America. But I don't believe there's room for me in his.

WILLIAM G. PERRY, JR.

Examsmanship and the Liberal Arts: A Study in Educational Epistemology

"But sir, I don't think I really deserve it, it was mostly bull, really." This disclaimer from a student whose examination we have awarded a straight "A" is wondrously depressing. Alfred North Whitehead invented its only possible rejoinder: "Yes sir, what you wrote is nonsense, utter nonsense. But ah! Sir! It's the right *kind* of nonsense!"

Bull, in this university,[1] is customarily a source of laughter, or a problem in ethics. I shall step a little out of fashion to use the subject as a take-off point for a study in comparative epistemology. The phenomenon of bull, in all the honor and opprobrium with which it is regarded by students and faculty, says something, I think, about our theories of knowledge. So too, the grades which we assign on examinations communicate to students what these theories may be.

We do not have to be out-and-out logical-positivists to suppose that we have something to learn about "what we think knowledge is" by having a good look at "what we do when we go about measuring it." We know the straight "A" examination when we see it, of course, and we have reason to hope that the student will understand why his work receives our recognition. He doesn't always. And those who receive lesser honor? Perhaps an understanding of certain anomalies in our customs of grading good bull will explain the students' confusion.

1. Harvard.

I must beg patience, then, both of the reader's humor and of his morals. Not that I ask him to suspend his sense of humor but that I shall ask him to go beyond it. In a great university the picture of a bright student attempting to outwit his professor while his professor takes pride in not being outwitted is certainly ridiculous. I shall report just such a scene, for its implications bear upon my point. Its comedy need not present a serious obstacle to thought.

As for the ethics of bull, I must ask for a suspension of judgment. I wish that students could suspend theirs. Unlike humor, moral commitment is hard to think beyond. Too early a moral judgment is precisely what stands between many able students and a liberal education. The stunning realization that the Harvard Faculty will often accept, as evidence of knowledge, the cerebrations of a student who has little data at his disposal, confronts every student with an ethical dilemma. For some it forms an academic focus for what used to be thought of as "adolescent disillusion." It is irrelevant that rumor inflates the phenomenon to mythical proportions. The students know that beneath the myth there remains a solid and haunting reality. The moral "bind" consequent on this awareness appears most poignantly in serious students who are reluctant to concede the competitive advantage to the bullster and who yet feel a deep personal shame when, having succumbed to "temptation," they themselves receive a high grade for work they consider "dishonest."

I have spent many hours with students caught in this unwelcome bitterness. These hours lend an urgency to my theme. I have found that students have been able to come to terms with the ethical problem, to the extent that it is real, only after a refined study of the true nature of bull and its relation to "knowledge." I shall submit grounds for my suspicion that we can be found guilty of sharing the students' confusion of moral and epistemological issues.

I

I present as my "premise," then, an amoral *fabliau*. Its hero-villain is the Abominable Mr. Metzger '47. Since I celebrate his virtuosity, I regret giving him a pseudonym, but the peculiar style of his bravado requires me to honor also his modesty. Bull in pure form is rare; there is usually some contamination by data. The community has reason to be grateful to Mr. Metzger for having created an instance of laboratory purity, free from any adulteration by matter. The more credit is due him, I think, because his act was free from premeditation, deliberation, or hope of personal gain.

Mr. Metzger stood one rainy November day in the lobby of Memorial Hall. A junior, concentrating in mathematics, he was fond of diverting himself by taking part in the drama, a penchant which may have had some influence on the events of the next hour. He was waiting to take part in a rehearsal in Sanders Theatre, but, as sometimes happens, no other players appeared. Perhaps the rehearsal had been canceled without his knowledge? He decided to wait another five minutes.

Students, meanwhile, were filing into the Great Hall opposite, and taking seats at the testing tables. Spying a friend crossing the lobby toward the Great Hall's door, Metzger greeted him and extended appropriate condolences. He inquired, too, what course his friend was being tested in. "Oh, Soc. Sci. something-or-other." "What's it all about?" asked Metzger, and this, as Homer remarked of Patroclus, was the beginning of evil for him.

"It's about Modern Perspectives on Man and Society and All That," said his friend. "Pretty interesting, really."

"Always wanted to take a course like that," said Metzger. "Any good reading?"

"Yeah, great. There's this book"—his friend did not have time to finish.

"Take your seats please" said a stern voice beside them. The idle conversation had somehow taken the two friends to one of the tables in the Great Hall. Both students automatically obeyed; the proctor put blue-books before them; another proctor presented them with copies of the printed hour-test.

Mr. Metzger remembered afterwards a brief misgiving that was suddenly overwhelmed by a surge of curiosity and puckish glee. He wrote "George Smith" on the blue book, opened it, and addressed the first question.

I must pause to exonerate the Management. The Faculty has a rule that no student may attend an examination in a course in which he is not enrolled. To the wisdom of this rule the outcome of this deplorable story stands witness. The Registrar, charged with the enforcement of the rule, has developed an organization with procedures which are certainly the finest to be devised. In November, however, class rosters are still shaky, and on this particular day another student, named Smith, was absent. As for the culprit, we can reduce his guilt no further than to suppose that he was ignorant of the rule, or, in the face of the momentous challenge before him, forgetful.

We need not be distracted by Metzger's performance on the "objective" or "spot" questions on the test. His D on these sections can be explained by those versed in the theory of probability. Our interest focuses on the quality of his essay. It appears that when Metzger's friend picked up his own blue book a few days later, he found himself in company with a large proportion of his section in having received on the essay a C +. When he quietly picked up "George Smith's" blue book to return it to Metzger, he observed that the grade for the essay was A–. In the margin was a note in the section man's hand. It read "Excellent work. Could you have pinned these observations down a bit more closely? Compare . . . in . . . pp. . . ."

Such news could hardly be kept quiet. There was a leak, and the whole scandal broke on the front page of Tuesday's *Crimson*. With the press Metzger was modest, as becomes a hero. He said that there had been nothing to it at all, really. The essay question had offered a choice of two books, Margaret Mead's *And Keep Your Powder Dry* or Geoffrey Gorer's *The American People*. Metzger reported that having read neither of them, he had chosen the second "because the title gave me some notion as to what the book might be about." On the test, two critical comments were offered on each book, one favorable, one unfavorable. The students were asked to "discuss." Metzger conceded that he had played safe in throwing his lot with the more laudatory of the two comments, "but I did not forget to be balanced."

I do not have Mr. Metzger's essay before me except in vivid memory. As I recall, he took his first cue from the name Geoffrey, and committed his strategy to the premise that Gorer was born into an "Anglo-Saxon" culture, probably English, but certainly "English speaking." Having heard that Margaret Mead was a social anthropologist, he inferred that Gorer was the same. He then entered upon his essay, centering his inquiry upon what he supposed might be the problems inherent in an anthropologist's observation of a culture which was his own, or nearly his own. Drawing in part from memories of table-talk on cultural relativity[2] and in part from creative logic, he rang changes on the relation of observer to observed, and assessed the kind and degree of objectivity which might accrue to an observer through training as an anthropologist. He concluded that the book in question did in fact contribute a considerable range of " 'objective', and even 'fresh'," insights into the nature of our culture. "At the same time," he warned, "these observations must be understood within the context of their generation by a person only partly freed from his embeddedness in the culture he is observing, and limited in his capacity to transcend those particular tendencies and biases which he has himself developed as a personality in his interraction with this culture since his birth. In this sense the book portrays as much the character of Geoffrey Gorer as it analyzes that of the American people." It is my regrettable duty to report that at this moment of triumph Mr. Metzger was carried away by the temptations of parody and added, "We are thus much the richer."

In any case, this was the essay for which Metzger received his honor grade and his public acclaim. He was now, of course, in serious trouble with the authorities.

I shall leave him for the moment to the mercy of the Administrative Board of Harvard College and turn the reader's attention to the section man who ascribed the grade. He was in much worse trouble. All the consternation in his immediate area of the Faculty

2. "An important part of Harvard's education takes place during meals in the Houses." An Official Publication [Perry's note].

and all the glee in other areas fell upon his unprotected head. I shall now undertake his defense.

I do so not simply because I was acquainted with him and feel a respect for his intelligence; I believe in the justice of his grade! Well, perhaps "justice" is the wrong word in a situation so manifestly absurd. This is more a case in "equity." That is, the grade is equitable if we accept other aspects of the situation which are equally absurd. My proposition is this: if we accept as valid those C grades which were accorded students who, like Metzger's friend, demonstrated a thorough familiarity with the details of the book without relating their critique to the methodological problems of social anthropology, then "George Smith" deserved not only the same, but better.

The reader may protest that the C's given to students who showed evidence only of diligence were indeed not valid and that both these students and "George Smith" should have received E's. To give the diligent E is of course not in accord with custom. I shall take up this matter later. For now, were I to allow the protest, I could only restate my thesis: that "George Smith's" E would, in a college of liberal arts, be properly a "better" E.

At this point I need a short-hand. It is a curious fact that there is no academic slang for the presentation of evidence of diligence alone. "Parroting" won't do; it is possible to "parrot" bull. I must beg the reader's pardon, and, for reasons almost too obvious to bear, suggest "cow."

Stated as nouns, the concepts look simple enough:

> cow (pure): data, however relevant, without relevancies.
> bull (pure): relevancies, however relevant, without data.

The reader can see all too clearly where this simplicity would lead. I can assure him that I would not have imposed on him' this way were I aiming to say that knowledge in this university is definable as some neuter compromise between cow and bull, some infertile hermaphrodite. This is precisely what many diligent students seem to believe: that what they must learn to do is to "find the right mean" between "amounts" of detail and "amounts" of generalities. Of course this is not the point at all. The problem is not quantitative, nor does its solution lie on a continuum between the particular and the general. Cow and bull are not poles of a single dimension. A clear notion of what they really are is essential to my inquiry, and for heuristic purposes I wish to observe them further in the celibate state.

When the pure concepts are translated into verbs, their complexities become apparent in the assumptions and purposes of the students as they write:

To cow (*v. intrans.*) or the act of cowing:
  To list data (or perform operations) without awareness of, or comment

upon, the contexts, frames of reference, or points of observation which determine the origin, nature, and meaning of the data (or procedures). To write on the assumption that "a fact is a fact." To present evidence of hard work as a substitute for understanding, without any intent to deceive.

To bull (*v. intrans.*) or the act of bulling:
To discourse upon the contexts, frames of reference and points of observation which would determine the origin, nature, and meaning of data if one had any. To present evidence of an understanding of form in the hope that the reader may be deceived into supposing a familiarity with content.

At the level of conscious intent, it is evident that cowing is more moral, or less immoral, than bulling. To speculate about unconscious intent would be either an injustice or a needless elaboration of my theme. It is enough that the impression left by cow is one of earnestness, diligence, and painful naiveté. The grader may feel disappointment or even irritation, but these feelings are usually balanced by pity, compassion, and a reluctance to hit a man when he's both down and moral. He may feel some challenge to his teaching, but none whatever to his one-ups-manship. He writes in the margin: "See me."

We are now in a position to understand the anomaly of custom: As instructors, we always assign bull an E, *when we detect it*; whereas we usually give cow a C, *even though it is always obvious*.

After all, we did not ask to be confronted with a choice between morals and understanding (or did we?). We evince a charming humanity, I think, in our decision to grade in favor of morals and pathos. "I simply *can't* give this student an E after he has *worked* so hard." At the same time we tacitly express our respect for the bullster's strength. We recognize a colleague. If he knows so well how to dish it out, we can be sure that he can also take it.

Of course it is just possible that we carry with us, perhaps from our own school-days, an assumption that if a student is willing to work hard and collect "good hard facts" he can always be taught to understand their relevance, whereas a student who has caught onto the forms of relevance without working at all is a lost scholar.

But this is not in accord with our experience.

It is not in accord either, as far as I can see, with the stated values of a liberal education. If a liberal education should teach students "how to think," not only in their own fields but in fields outside their own—that is, to understand "how the other fellow orders knowledge," then bulling, even in its purest form, expresses an important part of what a pluralist university holds dear, surely a more important part than the collecting of "facts that are facts" which schoolboys learn to do. Here then, good bull appears not as ignorance at all but as an aspect of knowledge. It is both relevant and "true." In a university setting good bull is therefore of more value than "facts," which, without a frame of reference, are not even "true" at all.

Perhaps this value accounts for the final anomaly: as instructors, we are inclined to reward bull highly, *where we do not detect its intent,* to the consternation of the bullster's acquaintances. And often we do not examine the matter too closely. After a long evening of reading blue books full of cow, the sudden meeting with a student who at least understands the problems of one's field provides a lift like a draught of refreshing wine, and a strong disposition toward trust.

This was, then, the sense of confidence that came to our unfortunate section man as he read "George Smith's" sympathetic considerations.

II

In my own years of watching over students' shoulders as they work, I have come to believe that this feeling of trust has a firmer basis than the confidence generated by evidence of diligence alone. I believe that the theory of a liberal education holds. Students who have dared to understand man's real relation to his knowledge have shown themselves to be in a strong position to learn content rapidly and meaningfully, and to retain it. I have learned to be less concerned about the education of a student who has come to understand the nature of man's knowledge, even though he has not yet committed himself to hard work, than I am about the education of the student who, after one or two terms at Harvard, is working desperately hard and still believes that collected "facts" constitute knowledge. The latter, when I try to explain to him, too often understands me to be saying that he "doesn't *put in enough generalities."* Surely he has "put in *enough* facts."

I have come to see such quantitative statements as expressions of an entire, coherent epistemology. In grammar school the student is taught that Columbus discovered America in 1492. The *more* such items he gets "right" on a given test the more he is credited with "knowing." From years of this sort of thing it is not unnatural to develop the conviction that knowledge consists of the accretion of hard facts by hard work.

The student learns that the more facts and procedures he can get "right" in a given course, the better will be his grade. The more courses he takes, the more subjects he has "had," the more credits he accumulates, the more diplomas he will get, until, after graduate school, he will emerge with his doctorate, a member of the community of scholars.

The foundation of this entire life is the proposition that a fact is a fact. The necessary correlate of this proposition is that a fact is either right or wrong. This implies that the standard against which the rightness or wrongness of a fact may be judged exists *someplace* —perhaps graven upon a tablet in a Platonic world outside and above *this* cave of tears. In grammar school it is evident that the tablets which enshrine the spelling of a word or the answer to an arithmetic problem are visible to my teacher who need only compare my offerings to it. In high school I observe that my English teachers disagree. This can only mean that the tablets in such matters as the goodness of a poem are distant and obscured by clouds. They surely exist. The pleasing of befuddled English teachers degenerates into assessing their prejudices, a game in which I have no protection against my competitors more glib of tongue. I respect only my science teachers, authorities who *really know*. Later I learn from them that "this is only what we think *now*." But eventually, surely. . . . Into this epistemology of education, apparently shared by teachers in such terms as "credits," "semester hours" and "years of French" the student may invest his ideals, his drive, his competitiveness, his safety, his self-esteem, and even his love.

College raises other questions: by whose calendar is it proper to say that Columbus discovered America in 1492? How, when and by whom was the year 1 established in this calendar? What of other calendars? In view of the evidence for Leif Ericson's previous visit (and the American Indians), what historical ethnocentrism is suggested by the use of the word "discover" in this sentence? As for Leif Ericson, in accord with what assumptions do you order the evidence?

These questions and their answers are not "more" knowledge. They are devastation. I do not need to elaborate upon the epistemology, or rather epistemologies, they imply. A fact has become at last "an observation or an operation performed in a frame of reference." A liberal education is founded in an awareness of frame of reference even in the most immediate and empirical examination of data. Its acquirement involves relinquishing hope of absolutes and of the protection they afford against doubt and the glib-tongued competitor. It demands an ever widening sophistication about systems of thought and observation. It leads, not away from, but *through* the arts of gamesmanship to a new trust.

This trust is in the value and integrity of systems, their varied character, and the way their apparently incompatible metaphors enlighten, from complementary facets, the particulars of human experience. As one student said to me: "I used to be cynical about intellectual games. Now I want to know them thoroughly. You see I came to realize that it was only when I knew the rules of the game cold that I could tell whether what I was saying was tripe."

We too often think of the bullster as cynical. He can be, and not always in a light-hearted way. We have failed to observe that there can lie behind cow the potential of a deeper and more dangerous despair. The moralism of sheer work and obedience can be an ethic that, unwilling to face a despair of its ends, glorifies its means. The implicit refusal to consider the relativity of both ends and means leaves the operator in an unconsidered proprietary absolutism. History bears witness that in the pinches this moral superiority has no recourse to negotiation, only to force.

A liberal education proposes that man's hope lies elsewhere: in the negotiability that can arise from an understanding of the integrity of systems and of their origins in man's address to his universe. The prerequisite is the courage to accept such a definition of knowledge. From then on, of course, there is nothing incompatible between such an epistemology and hard work. Rather the contrary.

I can now at last let bull and cow get together. The reader knows best how a productive wedding is arranged in his own field. This is the nuptial he celebrates with a straight A on examinations. The masculine context must embrace the feminine particular, though itself "born of woman." Such a union is knowledge itself, and it alone can generate new contexts and new data which can unite in their turn to form new knowledge.

In this happy setting we can congratulate in particular the Natural Sciences, long thought to be barren ground to the bullster. I have indeed drawn my examples of bull from the Social Sciences, and by analogy from the Humanities. Essay-writing in these fields has long been thought to nurture the art of bull to its prime. I feel, however, that the Natural Sciences have no reason to feel slighted. It is perhaps no accident that Metzger was a mathematician. As part of my researches for this paper, furthermore, a student of considerable talent has recently honored me with an impressive analysis of the art of amassing "partial credits" on examinations in advanced physics. Though beyond me in some respects, his presentation confirmed my impression that instructors of Physics frequently honor on examinations operations structurally similar to those requisite in a good essay.

The very qualities that make the Natural Sciences fields of delight for the eager gamesman have been essential to their marvelous fertility.

III

As priests of these mysteries, how can we make our rites more precisely expressive? The student who merely cows robs himself, without knowing it, of his education and his soul. The student who only bulls robs himself, as he knows full well, of the joys of inductive discovery—that is, of engagement. The introduction of frames of reference in the new curricula of Mathematics and Physics in the schools is a hopeful experiment. We do not know yet how much of these potent revelations the very young can stand, but I suspect they may rejoice in them more than we have supposed. I can't believe they have never wondered about Leif Ericson and that word "discovered," or even about 1492. They have simply been too wise to inquire.

Increasingly in recent years better students in the better high schools and preparatory schools are being allowed to inquire. In fact they appear to be receiving both encouragement and training in their inquiry. I have the evidence before me.

Each year for the past five years all freshmen entering Harvard and Radcliffe have been asked in freshman week to "grade" two essays answering an examination question in History. They are then asked to give their reasons for their grades. One essay, filled with dates, is 99% cow. The other, with hardly a date in it, is a good essay, easily mistaken for bull. The "official" grades of these essays are, for the first (alas!) C+ "because he has worked so hard," and for the second (soundly, I think) B+. Each year a larger majority of freshmen evaluate these essays as would the majority of the faculty, and for the faculty's reasons, and each year a smaller minority give the higher honor to the essay offering data alone. Most interesting, a larger number of students each year, while not overrating the second essay, award the first the straight E appropriate to it in a college of liberal arts.

For us who must grade such students in a university, these developments imply a new urgency, did we not feel it already. Through our grades we describe for the students, in the showdown, what we believe about the nature of knowledge. The subtleties of bull are not peripheral to our academic concerns. That they penetrate to the center of our care is evident in our feelings when a student whose good work we have awarded a high grade reveals to us that he does not feel he deserves it. Whether he disqualifies himself because "there's too much bull in it," or worse because "I really don't think I've worked that hard," he presents a serious educational problem. Many students feel this sleaziness; only a few reveal it to us.

We can hardly allow a mistaken sense of fraudulence to undermine our students' achievements. We must lead students beyond their concept of bull so that they may honor relevancies that are really relevant. We can willingly acknowledge that, in lieu of the date 1492, a consideration of calendars and of the word "discovered," may well be offered with intent to deceive. We must insist that this does not make such considerations intrinsically immoral, and that, contrariwise, the date 1492 may be no substitute for them. Most of all, we must convey the impression that we grade understanding qua understanding. To be convincing, I suppose we must concede to ourselves in advance that a bright student's understanding is understanding even if he achieved it by osmosis rather than by hard work in our course.

These are delicate matters. As for cow, its complexities are not what need concern us. Unlike good bull, it does not represent partial knowledge at all. It belongs to a different theory of knowledge entirely. In our theories of knowledge it represents total ignorance, or worse yet, a knowledge downright inimical to understanding. I even go so far as to propose that we award no more C's for cow. To do so is rarely, I feel, the act of mercy it seems. Mercy lies in clarity.

The reader may be afflicted by a lingering curiosity about the fate of Mr. Metzger. I hasten to reassure him. The Administrative Board of Harvard College, whatever its satanic reputations, is a benign body. Its members, to be sure, were on the spot. They delighted in Metzger's exploit, but they were responsible to the Faculty's rule. The hero stood in danger of probation. The debate was painful. Suddenly one member, of a refined legalistic sensibility, observed that the rule applied specifically to "examinations" and that the occasion had been simply an hour-test. Mr. Metzger was merely "admonished."

EDNA GOLDSMITH

Straight A's Are Rarely in the Cards

New Haven—I don't know whether things have actually gotten crummier or whether I've just been feeling more impotent about making them less crummy, but I do know that I don't enjoy reading about them anymore. The newspaper used to receive a thorough workout but now I just give it a quick once-over, skimming items of importance half-heartedly.

Articles about students, however, still attract my attention and often invoke my wrath. Those written by adults telling me what I think are sometimes quite illuminating. I mean it's interesting to know that even if I don't know what I think someone else does.

Those written by my peers can be more irritating. When the editorial "we" is bandied about by a single, often singular, individual who purports to be the spokesman for my generation I get a bit ill.

Two articles last semester—one telling of college graduates competing with welfare recipients for jobs, the other of cut-throat competition on campuses across the country—I could not blithely ignore or rationalize away. Still, I need a few illusions to keep me going; I'm not up to reality all the time.

I love fantasy! I like it so much I was thinking of majoring in it —you know, make your own major. A little psych here, a little lit there, a sprinkle of courses on the American dream to pull it together. But recently I've found out that a lot of prominent people think that American higher education is deteriorating and that unless I learn to read, write and think properly, democracy is going to crumble!

Well, I never used to view my education that way. To think that the fate of Western civilization depends on my brain is enough to give even me second thoughts about majoring in fantasy. You see, I hadn't intended to do any reading or writing for this major. I thought I'd just see a couple of cartoons and commercials and do some finger painting for my senior project. Now I'm going to start considering something more substantial, like geophysics, which will help me become a worthwhile, well-informed citizen.

While I'm re-evaluating my major I'll take a smorgasbord of courses that will still allow me to keep my options open. Please don't think, however, that I'll be getting all A's and only praise from my professors. A few recent articles have made it seem as though D's are defunct and that A's are being handed out like popcorn.

Maybe I'm taking the wrong courses, maybe I'm at the wrong school, because B's and C's and even D's are alive and well in New Haven.

Academic pressure, one of the causes of grade inflation, is not my cup of tea and I've found myself drinking a lot of it lately.

Actually I've been pretty lucky. You hear a lot about student sabotage, and I've never been the victim of that. No one has ever spit into my test-tubes or stolen my white rats. Maybe that's because they know I'm not hard-core pre-med. Still, although I'm a member of that dwindling group in my class who's not hard-core pre-something safe-and-solid, the general atmosphere of pressure affects me.

I don't know how academic pressure and competition can be alleviated. Unfortunately it just so happens that a lot of people think the world is going to end and that a degree from Harvard Law or Med might help. It's no one's fault that so many students are worried about the future and concerned about getting into grad school.

I resent it when I hear some professors and administrators say that students are getting away with murder and that it's time to crack down. Although that might be the case some places, it isn't here. If any of my professors crack down I'll crack up.

I cannot work incessantly—a lot perhaps, but not always. People mean as much to me as the biochemical structure of lipids. When I'm old and gray, the thing I'll probably remember best about Yale is not all the literature papers I've written but rather all the beautiful afternoons I sat outside the library talking to my friends.

It would be nice if all sorts of exigencies did not compel me to think about the future, but they do. I haven't yet decided whether to be a psychiatrist-composer-writer-ice cream parlor owner, but that's not because I haven't given thought to the future. I think about it a lot and don't like what I can't help but think.

At 3 A.M., I'm most scared about the future—then, when the thought of living becomes as scary as the thought of dying and being nineteen feels no different than being seven and a half. Thank heaven it's not 3 A.M. all day long. I'd never get any work done.

WAYNE C. BOOTH

Is There Any Knowledge That a Man *Must* Have?

Everyone lives on the assumption that a great deal of knowledge is not worth bothering about; though we all know that what looks trivial in one man's hands may turn out to be earth-shaking in another's, we simply cannot know very much, compared with what might be known, and we must therefore choose. What is shocking is not the act of choice which we all commit openly but the claim that some choices are wrong. Especially shocking is the claim implied by my title: There is some knowledge that a man *must* have.

There clearly is no such thing, if by knowledge we mean mere acquaintance with this or that thing, fact, concept, literary work, or scientific law. When C. P. Snow and F. R. Leavis exchanged blows on whether knowledge of Shakespeare is more important than knowledge of the second law of thermodynamics, they were both, it seemed to me, much too ready to assume as indispensable what a great many wise and good men have quite obviously got along without. And it is not only nonprofessionals who can survive in happy ignorance of this or that bit of lore. I suspect that many successful scientists (in biology, say) have lost whatever hold they might once have had on the second law; I know that a great many literary scholars survive and even flourish without knowing certain "indispensable" classics. We all get along without vast loads of learning that other men take as necessary marks of an educated man. If we once begin to "reason the need" we will find, like Lear, that "our basest beggars/Are in the poorest thing superfluous." Indeed, we can survive, in a manner of speaking, even in the modern world, with little more than the bare literacy necessary to tell the "off" buttons from the "on."

Herbert Spencer would remind us at this point that we are interpreting *need* as if it were entirely a question of private survival. Though he talks about what a man must know to stay alive, he is more interested, in his defense of science, in what a *society* must know to survive: "Is there any knowledge that *man* must have?"—not a man, but *man*. This question is put to us much more acutely in our time than it was in Spencer's, and it is by no means as easy to argue now as it was then that the knowledge needed for man's survival is scientific knowledge. The threats of atomic annihilation, of engulfing population growth, of depleted air, water, and food must obviously be met, if man is to survive, and in meeting them man will, it is true, need more and more scientific knowledge; but it is not at all clear that more and more scientific knowledge will by itself suffice. Even so, a modern Herbert Spencer might well argue that a conference like this one, with its emphasis on the individual and his cognitive needs, is simply repeating the mistakes of the classical tradition. The knowledge most worth having would be, from his point of view, that of how to pull mankind through the next century or so without absolute self-destruction. The precise proportions of different kinds of knowledge—physical, biological, political, ethical, psychological, historical, or whatever—would be different from those prescribed in Spencer's essay, but the nature of the search would be precisely the same.

We can admit the relevance of this emphasis on social utility and at the same time argue that our business here is with other matters entirely. If the only knowledge a man *must* have is how to cross the street without getting knocked down—or, in other words, how to navigate the centuries without blowing himself up—then we may as well close the conference and go home. We may as well also roll up the college and mail it to a research institute, because almost any place that is not cluttered up with notions of liberal education will be able to discover and transmit practical bits of survival-lore better than we can. Our problem of survival is a rather different one, thrust at us as soon as we change our title slightly once again to "Is there any knowledge (other than the knowledge for survival) that a man must have?" That slight shift opens a new perspective on the problem, because the question of what it is to be a man, of what it is to be fully human, is the question at the heart of liberal education.

To be human, to be human, to be fully human. What does it mean? What is required? Immediately, we start feeling nervous again. Is the speaker suggesting that some of us are not fully human *yet*? Here come those hierarchies again. Surely in our pluralistic society we can admit an unlimited number of legitimate ways to be a man, without prescribing some outmoded aristocratic code!

Who—or what—is the creature we would educate? Our answer will determine our answers to educational questions, and it is therefore, I think, worth far more vigorous effort than it usually receives. I find it convenient, and only slightly unfair, to classify the educational talk I encounter these days under four notions of man, three of them metaphorical, only one literal. Though nobody's position, I suppose, fits my types neatly, some educators talk as if they were programming machines, some talk as if they were conditioning rats, some talk as if they were training ants to take a position in the anthill, and some—precious few—talk as if they thought of themselves as men dealing with men.

One traditional division of the human soul, you will remember, was into three parts: the vegetable, the animal, and the rational. Nobody, so far as I know, has devised an educational program treating students as vegetables, though one runs into the analogy used negatively in academic sermons from time to time. Similarly, no one ever really says that men are ants, though there is a marvelous passage in Kwame Nkrumah's autobiography in which he meditates longingly on the order and pure functionality of an anthill. Educators do talk of men as machines or as animals, but of course they always point out that men are much more complicated than any other known animals or machines. My point here is not so much to attack any one of these metaphors—dangerous as I think they are—but to describe briefly what answers to our question each of them might suggest.

Ever since Descartes, La Mettrie,[1] and others explicitly called a man a machine, the metaphor has been a dominant one in educational thinking. Some have thought of man as a very complex machine, needing very elaborate programming; others have thought of him as a very simple machine, requiring little more than a systematic pattern of stimuli to produce foretellable responses. I heard a psychologist recently repeat the old behaviorist claim (first made by John B. Watson, I believe) that if you would give him complete control over any normal child's life from birth, he could turn that child into a great musician or a great mathematician or a great poet—you name it and he could produce it. On being pressed, the professor admitted that this claim was only "in theory," because we don't yet have the necessary knowledge. When I pushed further by asking why he was so confident in advance of experimental proof, it became clear that his faith in the fundamental metaphor of man as a programmable machine was unshakable.

When the notion of man as machine was first advanced, the machine was a very simple collection of pulleys and billiard balls and levers. Such original simplicities have been badly battered by our growing awareness both of how complex real machines can be and of how much more complex man is than any known machine. Modern notions of stimulus-response patterns are immeasurably more complicated than anything Descartes imagined, because we are now aware of the fantastic variety of stimuli that the man-machine is subject to and of the even more fantastic complexity of the responding circuits.

But whether the machine is simple or complex, the educational task for those who think of man under this metaphor is to program the mechanism so that it will produce the results that we have foreordained. We do not simply fill the little pitchers, like Mr. Gradgrind in Dickens' *Hard Times*;[2] we are much too sophisticated to

1. René Descartes (1596-1650), French philosopher and mathematician; Julian Offray de La Mettrie (1709-1751), French physician and philosopher.

2. Thomas Gradgrind thought of his students as "little pitchers . . . who were to be filled so full of facts."

want only undigested "pour-back," as he might have called his product. But we still program the information channels so that the proper if-loops and do-loops will be followed and the right feedback produced. The "programming" can be done by human teachers, of course, and not only by machines; but it is not surprising that those whose thinking is dominated by this metaphor tend to discover that machines are better teachers than men. The more ambitious programmers do not hesitate to claim that they can teach both thought and creativity in this way. But I have yet to see a program that can deal effectively with any subject that cannot be reduced to simple yes and no answers, that is, to answers that are known in advance by the programmer and can thus be fixed for all time.

We can assume that subtler machines will be invented that can engage in simulated dialogue with the pupil, and perhaps even recognize when a particularly bright pupil has discovered something new that refutes the program. But even the subtlest teaching machine imaginable will still be subject, one must assume, to a final limitation: it can teach only what a machine can "learn." For those who believe that man is literally nothing but a very complicated machine, this is not in fact a limitation; machines will ultimately be able to duplicate all mental processes, thus "learning" everything learnable, and they will be able in consequence to teach everything.

I doubt this claim for many reasons, and I am glad to find the testimony of Norbert Wiener, the first and best known cyberneticist, to the effect that there will always remain a radical gap between computers and the human mind. But "ultimately" is a long way off, and I am not so much concerned with whether ultimately man's mind will closely resemble some ultimately inventable machine as I am with the effects, here and now, of thinking about men under the analogy with machines of today. Let me simply close this section with an illustration of how the mechanistic model can permeate our thought in destructive ways. Ask yourselves what picture of creature-to-be-educated emerges from this professor of teacher education:

> To implement the TEAM Project new curriculum proposal ... our first concerns are with instructional systems, materials to feed the system, and personnel to operate the system. We have defined an instructional system as the optimal blending of the demands of content, communication, and learning. While numerous models have been developed, our simplified model of an instructional system would look like Figure 2. . . . We look at the process of communication—communicating content to produce learning—as something involving the senses: ... [aural, oral, tactile, visual]. And I think in teacher education we had better think of the communications aspect of the instructional system as a package that includes the teacher, textbook, new media, classroom, and environment. To integrate these elements to more effectively transmit content into permanent learning, new and better instructional materials are needed and a new focus on the teacher of

teachers is required. The teacher of teachers must: (1) examine critically the content of traditional courses in relation to desired behavioral outcomes; (2) become more sophisticated in the techniques of communicating course content; and (3) learn to work in concert with media specialists to develop the materials and procedures requisite to the efficient instructional system. And if the media specialist were to be charged with the efficient operation of the system, his upgrading would demand a broad-based "media generalist" orientation.[3]

I submit that the author of this passage was thinking of human beings as stimulus-response systems on the simplest possible model, and that he was thinking of the purpose of education as the transfer of information from one machine to another. Though he would certainly deny it if we asked him, he has come to think about the human mind so habitually in the mechanistic mode that he doesn't even know he's doing it.[4]

But it is time to move from the machine metaphor to animal metaphors. They are closely related, of course, because everybody who believes that man is a machine also believes that animals are machines, only simpler ones. But many people who would resist the word "machine" do tend to analogize man to one or another characteristic of animals. Since man is obviously an animal in one sense, he can be studied as an animal, and he can be taught as an animal is taught. Most of the fundamental research in learning theory underlying the use of teaching machines has been done, in fact, on animals like rats and pigeons. You can teach pigeons to play Ping-Pong rather quickly by rewarding every gesture they make that moves them toward success in the game and refusing to reward those gestures that you want to efface. Though everybody admits that human beings are more complicated than rats and pigeons, just as everyone admits that human beings are more complicated than computers, the basic picture of the animal as a collection of drives or instincts, "conditioned" to learn according to rewards or punishments, has underlain much modern educational theory.

The notion of the human being as a collection of drives different from animal drives only in being more complex carries with it implications for education planners. If you and I are motivated only by sex or hunger or more complex drives like desire for power or for ego-satisfaction, then of course all education depends on the provision of satisfactions along our route to knowledge. If our teachers can just program carrots along the path at the proper distance, we donkey-headed students will plod along the path from carrot to carrot and end up as educated men.

3. Desmond P. Wedberg, *Teacher Education Looks to the Future*, Twelfth Biennial School for Executives (Washington, D. C.: American Association of Colleges for Teacher Education, 1964) [Booth's note].

4. I am not of course suggesting that *any* use of teaching machines implies a mechanistic reduction of persons to machines; programmers rightly point out that machines *can* free teachers from the mechanical and save time for the personal [Booth's note].

I cannot take time here to deal with this view adequately, but it seems to me that it is highly questionable even about animals themselves. What kind of thing, really, is a rat or a monkey? The question of whether animals have souls has been debated actively for at least nine centuries; now psychologists find themselves dealing with the same question under another guise: What *are* these little creatures that we kill so blithely for the sake of knowledge? What *are* these strangely resistant little bundles of energy that will prefer—as experiments with rats have shown—a complicated interesting maze without food to a dull one *with* food?

There are, in fact, many experiments by now showing that at the very least we must postulate, for animals, a strong independent drive for mastery of the environment or satisfaction of curiosity about it. All the more advanced animals will learn to push levers that produce interesting results—clicks or bells or flashing lights or sliding panels—when no other reward is offered.[5] It seems clear that even to be a fulfilled animal, as it were, something more than "animal satisfaction" is needed!

I am reminded here of the experiments on mother-love in monkeys reported by Harry F. Harlow in the *Scientific American* some years ago. Harlow called his article "Love in Infant Monkeys," and the subtitle of his article read, "Affection in infants was long thought to be generated by the satisfactions of feeding. Studies of young rhesus monkeys now indicate that love derives mainly from close bodily contact." The experiment consisted of giving infant monkeys a choice between a plain wire figure that offered the infant milk and a terry-cloth covered figure without milk. There was a pathetic picture of an infant clinging to the terry-cloth figure, and a caption that read "The infants spent most of their time clinging to the soft cloth 'mother' even when nursing bottles were attached to the wire mother." The article concluded—rather prematurely, I thought—that "contact comfort" had been shown to be a "prime requisite in the formation of an infant's love for its mother," that the act of nursing had been shown to be unimportant if not totally irrelevant in forming such love (though it was evident to any reader, even at the time, that no genuine "*act* of nursing" had figured in the experiment at all), and that "our investigations have established a secure experimental approach to this realm of dramatic and subtle emotional relationships." The only real problem, Harlow said, was the availability of enough infant monkeys for experiment.

Now I would not want to underrate the importance of Harlow's demonstration to the scientific community that monkeys do not live by bread alone. But I think that most scientists and humanists

5. See Robert W. White, "Motivation Reconsidered: The Concept of Competence," *Psychological Review*, 66 (1959), 297–333 [Booth's note].

reading the article would have been struck by two things. The first is the automatic assumption that the way to study a subject like love is to break it down into its component parts; nobody looking at that little monkey clinging to the terry-cloth could possibly have said, "This is love," unless he had been blinded by a hidden conviction that love in animals is—must be—a mere cumulative result of a collection of drive satisfactions. This assumption is given quite plainly in Harlow's concluding sentence: "Finally with such techniques established, there appears to be no reason why we cannot at some future time investigate the fundamental neurophysiological and biochemical variables underlying affection and love." For Harlow monkeys (and people) seem to be mere collections of neurophysiological and biochemical variables, and love will be best explained when we can explain the genesis of each of its parts. The second striking point is that for Harlow animals do not matter, except as they are useful for experiment. If he had felt that they mattered, he might have noticed the look on his infant's face—a look that predicted for me, and for other readers of the *Scientific American* I've talked with, that these monkeys were doomed.

And indeed they were. A year or so later another article appeared, reporting Harlow's astonished discovery that all of the little monkeys on which he had earlier experimented had turned out to be incurably psychotic. Not a single monkey could mate, not a single monkey could play, not a single monkey could in fact become anything more than the twisted half-creatures that Harlow's deprivations had made of them. Harlow's new discovery was that monkeys needed close association with their peers during infancy and that such association was even more important to their development than genuine mothering. There was no sign that Harlow had learned any fundamental lessons from his earlier gross mistakes; he had landed nicely on his feet, still convinced that the way to study love is to break it down into its component parts and that the way to study animals is to maim them or reduce them to something less than themselves. As Robert White says, summarizing his reasons for rejecting similar methods in studying human infancy, it is too often assumed that the scientific way is to analyze behavior until one can find a small enough unit to allow for detailed research, but in the process "very vital common properties" are lost from view.

I cite Harlow's two reports not, of course, to attack animal experimentation—though I must confess that I am horrified by much that goes on in its name—nor to claim that animals are more like human beings than they are. Rather, I want simply to suggest that the danger of thinking of men as animals is heightened if the animals we think of are reduced to machines on a simple model.

The effects of reducing education to conditioning can be seen throughout America today. Usually they appear in subtle forms, disguised with the language of personalism; you will look a long time before you find anyone (except a very few Skinnerians) saying that he thinks of education as exactly like conditioning pigeons. But there are plenty of honest, blunt folk around to let the cat out of the bag—like the author of an article this year in *College Composition and Communications*: "The Use of a Multiple Response Device in the Teaching of Remedial English." The author claimed to have evidence that if you give each student four buttons to be pushed on multiple-choice questions, with all the buttons wired into a lighted grid at the front of the room, the resulting "instantaneous feedback"—every child learning immediately whether he agrees with the rest of the class—speeds up the learning of grammatical rules considerably over the usual workbook procedures. I daresay it does—but meanwhile what has happened to education? Or take the author of an article on "Procedures and Techniques of Teaching," who wrote as follows: "If we expect students to learn skills, they have to practice, but practice doesn't make perfect. Practice works if the learner *learns the results* of his practice, i.e., if he receives feedback. Feedback is most effective when it is contiguous to the response being learned. One of the chief advantages of teaching machines is that the learner finds out quickly whether his response is right or wrong . . . [Pressey] has published the results of an extensive program of research with tests that students score for themselves by punching alternatives until they hit the correct one. . . . [Thus] teaching machines or workbooks have many theoretical advantages over lecturing or other conventional methods of instruction." But according to what theory, one must ask, *do* systematic feedback mechanisms, perfected to whatever degree, have "theoretical advantages" over human contact? Whatever else can be said for such a theory, it will be based on the simplest of comparisons with animal learning. Unfortunately, the author goes on, experimental evidence is on the whole rather discouraging: "Experiments at the Systems Development Corporation . . . suggest that teaching incorporating . . . human characteristics is more effective than the typical fixed-sequence machines. (In this experiment instead of using teaching machines to simulate human teachers, the experimenters used humans to simulate teaching machines!)"

So far I have dealt with analogies for man that apply only to individuals. My third analogy turns to the picture of men in groups, and it is given to me partly by discussions of education, like those of Admiral Rickover, that see it simply as filling society's needs. I know of only one prominent educator who has publicly praised the anthill as a model for the kind of society a university should serve—a society of specialists each trained to do his part. But the notion pervades many of the defenses of the emerging multiversities.

If knowledge is needed to enable men to function as units in society, and if the health of society is taken as the purpose of their existence, then there is nothing wrong in training the ants to fill their niches; it would be wrong not to. "Education is our first line of defense—make it strong," so reads the title of the first chapter of Admiral Rickover's book, *Education and Freedom* (New York: Dutton, 1959). "We must upgrade our schools" in order to "guarantee the future prosperity and freedom of the Republic." You can tell whether the ant-analogy is dominating a man's thinking by a simple test of how he orders his ends and means. In Admiral Rickover's statement, the schools must be upgraded in order to guarantee future prosperity, that is, we improve education for the sake of some presumed social good.

I seldom find anyone putting it the other way round: we must guarantee prosperity so that we can improve the schools, and the reason we want to improve the schools is that we want to insure the development of certain kinds of persons, both as teachers and as students. You cannot even say what I just said so long as you are really thinking of ants and anthills. Ants are not ends in themselves, ultimately more valuable than the hills they live in (I *think* they are not; maybe to themselves, or in the eyes of God, even ants are ultimate, self-justifying ends). At least from our point of view, ants are expendable, or to put it another way, their society is more beautiful, more interesting, more admirable than they are. And I would want to argue that too many people think of human beings in the same way when they think of educating them. The Communists make this quite explicit: the ends of Communist society justify whatever distortion or destruction of individual purposes is necessary to achieve them; men are educated for the state, not for their own well-being. They are basically political animals, not in the Aristotelian sense that they require society if they are to achieve their full natures and thus their own special, human kind of happiness, but in the sense that they exist, like ants, for the sake of the body politic.

If the social order is the final justification of what we do in education, then a certain attitude toward teaching and research will result: all of us little workmen, down inside the anthill, will go on happily contributing our tiny bit to the total scheme without worrying much about larger questions of the why and wherefore. I know a graduate student who says that she sometimes sees her graduate professors as an army of tiny industrious miners at the bottom of a vast mine, chipping away at the edges and shipping their bits of knowledge up to the surface, blindly hoping that someone up there will know what to do with it all. An order is received for such-and-such new organic compounds; society needs them. Another order is received for an atomic bomb; it is needed, and it is therefore produced. Often no orders come down, but the chipping goes on anyway, and the shipments are made, because everyone knows that the health of the mine depends on a certain tonnage of specialized knowledge each working day.

We have learned lately that "they" are going to establish a great new atom-smasher, perhaps near Chicago. The atom-smasher will employ two thousand scientists and technicians. I look out at you here, knowing that some of you are physics majors, and I wonder whether any of you will ultimately be employed in that new installation, and if you are, whether it will be as an ant or as a human being. Which it will be must depend not on your ultimate employers but on yourself and on what happens to your education between now and then: if you have been given nothing but training to be that ultimate unit in that ultimate system, only a miracle can save you from formic dissolution of your human lineaments.

But it is long past time for me to turn from these negative, truncated portraits of what man really is not and attempt to say what he is. And here we encounter a difficulty that I find very curious. You will note that each of these metaphors has reduced man to something less than man, or at least to a partial aspect of man. It is easy to say that man is not a machine, though he is in some limited respects organized like a machine and even to some degree "programmable." It is also easy to say that man is not simply a complicated rat or monkey, though he is in some ways like rats and monkeys. Nor is man an ant, though he lives and must function in a complicated social milieu. All these metaphors break down not because they are flatly false but because they *are* metaphors, and any metaphorical definition is inevitably misleading. The ones I have been dealing with are especially misleading, because in every case they have reduced something more complex to something much less complex. But even if we were to analogize man to something more complex, say, the universe, we would be dissatisfied. What we want is some notion of what man really *is*, so that we will know what or whom we are trying to educate.

And here it is that we discover something very important about man, something that even the least religious person must find himself mystified by: man is the one "thing" we know that is completely resistant to our efforts at metaphor or analogy or image-making. What seems to be the most important literal characteristic of man is his resistance to definitions in terms of anything else. If you call me a machine, even a very complicated machine, I know that you deny what I care most about, my selfhood, my sense of being a person, my consciousness, my conviction of freedom and dignity, my awareness of love, my laughter. Machines have none of these things, and even if we were generous to their prospects, and imagined machines immeasurably superior to the most complicated ones now in existence, we would still feel an infinite gap between them and what we know to be a basic truth about ourselves: machines are expendable, ultimately expendable, and men are mysteriously ends in themselves.

I hear people deny this, but when they do they always argue for their position by claiming marvelous feats of super-machine calculation that machines can now do or will someday be able to do. But that is not the point; of course machines can outcalculate us. The question to ask is entirely a different one: Will they ever outlove us, outlive us, outvalue us? Do we build machines because machines are good things in themselves? Do we nurture them for their own good, as we nurture our children? An obvious way to test our sense of worth in men and machines is to ask ourselves whether we would ever campaign to liberate the poor drowntrodden machines who have been enslaved. Shall we form a National Association for the Advancement of Machinery? Will anyone ever feel a smidgeon of moral indignation because this or that piece of machinery is not given equal rights before the law? Or put it another way: Does anyone value Gemini more than the twins? There may be men now alive who would rather "destruct," as we say, the pilot than the experimental rocket, but most of us still believe that the human being in the space ship is more important than the space ship.

When college students protest the so-called depersonalization of education, what they mean, finally, is not simply that they want to meet their professors socially or that they want small classes or that they do not want to be dealt with by IBM machines. All these things are but symptoms of a deeper sense of a violation of their literal reality as persons, ends in themselves rather than mere expendable things. Similarly, the current deep-spirited revolt against racial and economic injustice seems to me best explained as a sudden assertion that people, of whatever color or class, are not reducible to social conveniences. When you organize your labor force or your educational system as if men were mere social conveniences, "human resources," as we say, contributors to the gross national product, you violate something that we all know, in a form of knowledge much deeper than our knowledge of the times tables or the second law of thermodynamics: those field hands, those children crowded into the deadening classroom, those men laboring without dignity in the city anthills are *men*, creatures whose worth is mysteriously more than any description of it we might make in justifying what we do to them.

Ants, rats, and machines can all learn a great deal. Taken together, they "know" a very great part of what our schools and colleges are now designed to teach. But is there any kind of knowledge that a creature must have to qualify as a man? Is there any part of the educational task that is demanded of us by virtue of our claim to educate this curious entity, this *person* that cannot be reduced to mechanism or animality alone?

You will not be surprised, by now, to have me sound, in my answer, terribly traditional, not to say square: the education that a *man* must have is what has traditionally been called liberal education. The knowledge it yields is the knowledge or capacity or power of how to act freely as a man. That's why we call liberal education liberal: it is intended to liberate from whatever it is that makes animals act like animals and machines act like machines.

I'll return in a moment to what it means to act freely as a man. But we are already in a position to say something about what knowledge a man must have—he must first of all be able to learn for himself. If he cannot learn for himself, he is enslaved by his teachers' ideas, or by the ideas of his more persuasive contemporaries, or by machines programmed by other men. He may have what we call a good formal education, yet still be totally bound by whatever opinions happen to have come his way in attractive garb. One wonders how many of our graduates have learned how to take hold of a subject and "work it up," so that they can make themselves experts on what other men have concluded. In some ways this is not a very demanding goal, and it is certainly not very exciting. It says nothing about that popular concept, creativity, or about imagination or originality. All it says is that anyone who is dependent on his teachers *is* dependent, not free, and that anyone who knows how to learn for himself is less like animals and machines than anyone who does not know how to learn for himself.

We see already that a college is not being merely capricious or arbitrary when it insists that some kinds of learning are more important than some others. The world is overflowing with interesting subjects and valuable skills, but surely any college worth the name will put first things first: it will try to insure, as one inescapable goal, that every graduate can dig out from the printed page what he needs to know. And it will not let the desire to tamp in additional tidbits of knowledge, however delicious, interfere with training minds for whom a formal teacher is no longer required.

To put our first goal in this way raises some real problems that we cannot solve. Obviously no college can produce self-learners in very many subjects. Are we not lucky if a graduate can learn for himself even in one field, now that knowledge in all areas has advanced as far as it has? Surely we cannot expect our graduates to reach a stage of independence in mathematics and physics, in political science and psychology, in philosophy and English, *and* in all the other nice subjects that one would like to master.

Rather than answer this objection right away, let me make things even more difficult by saying that it is not enough to learn how to learn. The man who cannot *think* for himself, going beyond what other men have learned or thought, is still enslaved to other men's ideas. Obviously the goal of learning to think is even more difficult than the goal of learning to learn. But difficult as it is we must add it to our list. It is simply not enough to be able to get up a subject on one's own, like a good encyclopedia employee, even though any college would take pride if all its graduates could do so. To be fully human means in part to think one's own thoughts, to reach a point at which, whether one's ideas are different from or similar to other men's, they are truly one's own.

The art of asking oneself critical questions that lead either to new answers or to genuine revitalizing of old answers, the art of making thought live anew in each new generation, may not be entirely amenable to instruction. But it is a necessary art nonetheless, for any man who wants to be free. It is an art that all philosophers have tried to pursue, and many of them have given direct guidance in how to pursue it. Needless to say, it is an art the pursuit of which is never fully completed. No one thinks for himself very much of the time or in very many subjects. Yet the habitual effort to ask the right critical questions and to apply rigorous tests to our hunches is a clearer mark than any other of an educated man.

But again we stumble upon the question, "Learn to think about *what?*" The modern world presents us with innumerable subjects to think about. Does it matter whether anyone achieves this rare and difficult point in more than one subject? And if not, won't the best education simply be the one that brings a man into mastery of a narrow specialty as soon as possible, so that he can learn to think for himself as soon as possible? Even at best most of us are enslaved to opinions provided for us by experts in *most* fields. So far, it might be argued, I still have not shown that there is any kind of knowledge that a man must have, only that there are certain skills that he must be able to exercise in at least one field.

To provide a proper grounding for my answer to that objection would require far more time than I have left, and I'm not at all sure that I could do so even with all the time in the world. The question of whether it is possible to maintain a human stance toward any more than a tiny fraction of modern knowledge is not clearly answerable at this stage in our history. It will be answered, if at all, only when men have learned how to store and retrieve all "machinable" knowledge, freeing themselves for distinctively human tasks. But in the meantime, I find myself unable to surrender, as it were, three distinct kinds of knowledge that seem to me indispensable to being human.

To be a man, a man must first know something about his own nature and his place in Nature, with a capital N—something about the truth of things, as men used to say in the old-fashioned days before the word "truth" was banned from academia. Machines are not curious, so far as I can judge; animals are, but presumably they

never go, in their philosophies, even at the furthest, beyond a kind
of solipsistic existentialism. But in science, in philosophy (ancient
and modern), in theology, in psychology and anthropology, and in
literature (of some kinds), we are presented with accounts of our
universe and of our place in it that as men we can respond to in
only one manly way: by thinking about them, by speculating and
testing our speculations.

We know before we start that our thought is doomed to incom-
pleteness and error and downright chanciness. Even the most rigorously scientific view will be changed, we know, within a decade, or
perhaps even by tomorrow. But to refuse the effort to understand is
to resign from the human race; the unexamined life can no doubt
be worth living in other respects—after all, it is no mean thing to
be a vegetable, an oak tree, an elephant, or a lion. But a man, a
man will want to see, in this speculative domain, beyond his next
dinner.

By putting it in this way, I think we can avoid the claim that to
be a man I must have studied any one field—philosophy, science,
theology. But to be a man, *I must speculate*, and I must learn how
to test my speculations so that they are not simply capricious,
unchecked by other men's speculations. A college education, surely,
should throw every student into a regular torrent of speculation,
and it should school him to recognize the different standards of validation proper to different kinds of claims to truth. You cannot distinguish a man who in this respect is educated from other men by
whether or not he believes in God, or in UFO's. But you can tell an
educated man by the way he takes hold of the question of whether
God exists, or whether UFO's are from Mars. Do you know your
own reasons for your beliefs, or do you absorb your beliefs from
whatever happens to be in your environment, like plankton taking
in nourishment?

Second, the man who has not learned how to make the great
human achievements in the arts his own, who does not know what
it means to *earn* a great novel or symphony or painting for himself,
is enslaved either to caprice or to other men's testimony or to a life
of ugliness. You will notice that as I turn thus to "beauty"—
another old-fashioned term—I do not say that a man must know
how to prove what is beautiful or how to discourse on aesthetics.
Such speculative activities are pleasant and worthwhile in themselves, but they belong in my first domain. Here we are asking that
a man be educated to the experience of beauty; speculation about it
can then follow. My point is simply that a man is less than a man
if he cannot respond to the art made by his fellow man.

Again I have tried to put the standard in a way that allows for
the impossibility of any one man's achieving independent responses
in very many arts. Some would argue that education should insure
some minimal human competence in all of the arts, or at least in

music, painting, and literature. I suppose I would be satisfied if all of our graduates had been "hooked" by at least one art, hooked so deeply that they could never get free. As in the domain of speculation, we could say that the more types of distinctively human activity a man can master, the better, but we are today talking about floors, not ceilings, and I shall simply rest content with saying that to be a man, a man must know artistic beauty, in some form, and know it in the way that beauty can be known. (The distinction between natural and man-made beauty might give me trouble if you pushed me on it here, but let me just say, dogmatically, that I would not be satisfied simply to know natural beauty—women and sunsets, say—as a substitute for art).

Finally, the man who has not learned anything about how to understand his own intentions and to make them effective in the world, who has not, through experience and books, learned something about what is possible and what impossible, what desirable and what undesirable, will be enslaved by the political and social intentions of other men, benign or malign. The domain of practical wisdom is at least as complex and troublesome as the other two, and at the same time it is even more self-evidently indispensable. How should a man live? How should a society be run? What direction should a university take in 1966? For that matter what should be the proportion, in a good university, of inquiry into truth, beauty, and "goodness"? What kind of knowledge of self or of society is pertinent to living the life proper to a man? In short, the very question of this conference falls within this final domain: What knowledge, if any, is most worthy of pursuit? You cannot distinguish the men from the boys according to any one set of conclusions, but you *can* recognize a man, in this domain, simply by discovering whether he can think for himself about practical questions, with some degree of freedom from blind psychological or political or economic compulsions. Ernest Hemingway tells somewhere of a man who had "moved one dollar's width to the [political] right for every dollar that he'd ever earned." Perhaps no man ever achieves the opposite extreme, complete freedom in his choices from irrelevant compulsions. But all of us who believe in education believe that it is possible for any man, through study and conscientious thought, to school his choices—that is, to free them through coming to understand the forces working on them.

Even from this brief discussion of the three domains, I think we are put in a position to see how it can be said that there is some knowledge that a man must have. The line I have been pursuing will not lead to a list of great books, or even to a list of indispensable departments in a university. Nor will it lead, in any clear-cut fashion, to a pattern of requirements in each of the divisions. Truth, beauty, and goodness (or "right choice") are relevant to study in every division within the university; the humanities, for example, have no corner on beauty or imagination or art, and the sciences have no corner on speculative truth. What is more, a man can be ignorant even of Shakespeare, Aristotle, Beethoven, and Einstein, and be a man for a' that—*if* he has learned how to think his own thoughts, experience beauty for himself, and choose his own actions.

It is not the business of a college to determine or limit what a man will know; if it tries to, he will properly resent its impositions, perhaps immediately, perhaps ten years later when the imposed information is outmoded. But I think that it *is* the business of a college to help teach a man how to use his mind for himself, in at least the three directions I have suggested. * * * To think for oneself is, as we all know, hard enough. To design a program and assemble faculty to assist rather than hinder students in their efforts to think for themselves is even harder. But in an age that is oppressed by huge accumulations of unassimilated knowledge, the task of discovering what it means to educate a man is perhaps more important than ever before.

CARLOS CASTANEDA

The Enemies of a Man of Knowledge

Sunday, April 15, 1962

As I was getting ready to leave, I decided to ask him[1] once more about the enemies of a man of knowledge. I argued that I could not return for some time, and it would be a good idea to write down what he had to say and then think about it while I was away.

He hesitated for a while, but then began to talk.

"When a man starts to learn, he is never clear about his objectives. His purpose is faulty; his intent is vague. He hopes for rewards that will never materialize, for he knows nothing of the hardships of learning.

"He slowly begins to learn—bit by bit at first, then in big chunks. And his thoughts soon clash. What he learns is never what he pictured, or imagined, and so he begins to be afraid. Learning is never what one expects. Every step of learning is a new task, and the fear the man is experiencing begins to mount mercilessly, unyieldingly. His purpose becomes a battlefield.

"And thus he has stumbled upon the first of his natural enemies: Fear! A terrible enemy—treacherous, and difficult to overcome. It

---

1. Don Juan. The sorcerer and teacher of Castaneda, who had been a graduate student in anthropology at UCLA before becoming a sorcerer's apprentice.

remains concealed at every turn of the way, prowling, waiting. And if the man, terrified in its presence, runs away, his enemy will have put an end to his quest."

"What will happen to the man if he runs away in fear?"

"Nothing happens to him except that he will never learn. He will never become a man of knowledge. He will perhaps be a bully, or a harmless, scared man; at any rate, he will be a defeated man. His first enemy will have put an end to his cravings."

"And what can he do to overcome fear?"

"The answer is very simple. He must not run away. He must defy his fear, and in spite of it he must take the next step in learning, and the next, and the next. He must be fully afraid, and yet he must not stop. That is the rule! And a moment will come when his first enemy retreats. The man begins to feel sure of himself. His intent becomes stronger. Learning is no longer a terrifying task.

"When this joyful moment comes, the man can say without hesitation that he has defeated his first natural enemy."

"Does it happen at once, don Juan, or little by little?"

"It happens little by little, and yet the fear is vanquished suddenly and fast."

"But won't the man be afraid again if something new happens to him?"

"No. Once a man has vanquished fear, he is free from it for the rest of his life because, instead of fear, he has acquired clarity—a clarity of mind which erases fear. By then a man knows his desires; he knows how to satisy those desires. He can anticipate the new steps of learning, and a sharp clarity surrounds everything. The man feels that nothing is concealed.

"And thus he has encountered his second enemy: Clarity! That clarity of mind, which is so hard to obtain, dispels fear, but also blinds.

"It forces the man never to doubt himself. It gives him the assurance he can do anything he pleases, for he sees clearly into everything. And he is courageous because he is clear, and he stops at nothing because he is clear. But all that is a mistake; it is like something incomplete. If the man yields to this make-believe power, he has succumbed to his second enemy and will fumble with learning. He will rush when he should be patient, or he will be patient when he should rush. And he will fumble with learning until he winds up incapable of learning anything more."

"What becomes of a man who is defeated in that way, don Juan? Does he die as a result?"

"No, he doesn't die. His second enemy has just stopped him cold from trying to become a man of knowledge; instead, the man may turn into a buoyant warrior, or a clown. Yet the clarity for which he has paid so dearly will never change to darkness and fear again. He will be clear as long as he lives, but he will no longer learn, or yearn for, anything."

"But what does he have to do to avoid being defeated?"

"He must do what he did with fear: he must defy his clarity and use it only to see, and wait patiently and measure carefully before taking new steps; he must think, above all, that his clarity is almost a mistake. And a moment will come when he will understand that his clarity was only a point before his eyes. And thus he will have overcome his second enemy, and will arrive at a position where nothing can harm him anymore. This will not be a mistake. It will not be only a point before his eyes. It will be true power.

"He will know at this point that the power he has been pursuing for so long is finally his. He can do with it whatever he pleases. His ally is at his command. His wish is the rule. He sees all that is around him. But he has also come across his third enemy: Power!

"Power is the strongest of all enemies. And naturally the easiest thing to do is to give in; after all, the man is truly invincible. He commands; he begins by taking calculated risks, and ends in making rules, because he is a master.

"A man at this stage hardly notices his third enemy closing in on him. And suddenly, without knowing, he will certainly have lost the battle. His enemy will have turned him into a cruel, capricious man."

"Will he lose his power?"

"No, he will never lose his clarity or his power."

"What then will distinguish him from a man of knowledge?"

"A man who is defeated by power dies without really knowing how to handle it. Power is only a burden upon his fate. Such a man has no command over himself, and cannot tell when or how to use his power."

"Is the defeat by any of these enemies a final defeat?"

"Of course it is final. Once one of these enemies overpowers a man there is nothing he can do."

"Is it possible, for instance, that the man who is defeated by power may see his error and mend his ways?"

"No. Once a man gives in he is through."

"But what if he is temporarily blinded by power, and then refuses it?"

"That means his battle is still on. That means he is still trying to become a man of knowledge. A man is defeated only when he no longer tries, and abandons himself."

"But then, don Juan, it is possible that a man may abandon himself to fear for years, but finally conquer it."

"No, that is not true. If he gives in to fear he will never conquer it, because he will shy away from learning and never try again. But if he tries to learn for years in the midst of his fear, he will eventually conquer it because he will never have really abandoned himself to it."

"How can he defeat his third enemy, don Juan?"

"He has to defy it, deliberately. He has to come to realize the power he has seemingly conquered is in reality never his. He must keep himself in line at all times, handling carefully and faithfully all that he has learned. If he can see that clarity and power, without his control over himself, are worse than mistakes, he will reach a point where everything is held in check. He will know then when and how to use his power. And thus he will have defeated his third enemy.

"The man will be, by then, at the end of his journey of learning, and almost without warning he will come upon the last of his enemies: Old age! This enemy is the cruelest of all, the one he won't be able to defeat completely, but only fight away.

"This is the time when a man has no more fears, no more impatient clarity of mind—a time when all his power is in check, but also the time when he has an unyielding desire to rest. If he gives in totally to his desire to lie down and forget, if he soothes himself in tiredness, he will have lost his last round, and his enemy will cut him down into a feeble old creature. His desire to retreat will overrule all his clarity, his power, and his knowledge.

"But if the man sloughs off his tiredness, and lives his fate through, he can then be called a man of knowledge, if only for the brief moment when he succeeds in fighting off his last, invincible enemy. That moment of clarity, power, and knowledge is enough."

On Language
and Communication

WILLIAM MARCH
The Unspeakable Words

There were words in the Brett language considered so corrupting in their effect on others that if anyone wrote them or was heard to speak them aloud, he was fined and thrown into prison. The King of the Bretts was of the opinion that the words were of no importance one way or the other, and besides, everybody in the country knew them anyway; but his advisers disagreed, and at last, to determine who was right, a committee was appointed to examine the people separately.

At length everyone in the kingdom had been examined, and found to know the words quite well, without the slightest damage to themselves. There was then left only one little girl, a five-year-old who lived in the mountains with her deaf and dumb parents. The committee hoped that this little girl, at least, had never heard the corrupting words, and on the morning they visited her, they said solemnly: "Do you know the meaning of *poost, gist, duss, feng?*"

The little girl admitted that she did not, and then, smiling happily, she said, "Oh, you must mean *feek, kusk, dalu,* and *liben!*"

Those who don't know the words must make them up for themselves.

RALPH WALDO EMERSON
The Language of the Street

The language of the street is always strong. What can describe the folly and emptiness of scolding like the word *jawing*? I feel too the force of the double negative, though clean contrary to our grammar rules. And I confess to some pleasure from the stinging rhetoric of a rattling oath in the mouths of truckmen and teamsters. How laconic and brisk it is by the side of a page of the *North American Review*. Cut these words and they would bleed; they are vascular and alive; they walk and run. Moreover they who speak them have this elegancy, that they do not trip in their speech. It is a shower of bullets, whilst Cambridge men and Yale men correct themselves and begin again at every half sentence.

W. SOMERSET MAUGHAM
Lucidity, Simplicity, Euphony[1]

I have never had much patience with the writers who claim from the reader an effort to understand their meaning. You have only to go to the great philosophers to see that it is possible to express with lucidity the most subtle reflections. You may find it difficult to understand the thought of Hume, and if you have no philosophical training its implications will doubtless escape you; but no one with any education at all can fail to understand exactly what the meaning of each sentence is. Few people have written English with more grace than Berkeley. There are two sorts of obscurity that you find in writers. One is due to negligence and the other to willfulness. People often write obscurely because they have never taken the trouble to learn to write clearly. This sort of obscurity you find too often in modern philosophers, in men of science, and even in literary critics. Here it is indeed strange. You would have thought that men who passed their lives in the study of the great masters of literature would be sufficiently sensitive to the beauty of language to write if not beautifully at least with perspicuity. Yet you will find in their works sentence after sentence that you must read twice to discover the sense. Often you can only guess at it, for the writers have evidently not said what they intended.

Another cause of obscurity is that the writer is himself not quite sure of his meaning. He has a vague impression of what he wants to say, but has not, either from lack of mental power or from laziness, exactly formulated it in his mind and it is natural enough that he should not find a precise expression for a confused idea. This is due largely to the fact that many writers think, not before, but as they write. The pen originates the thought. The disadvantage of this, and indeed it is a danger against which the author must be always on his guard, is that there is a sort of magic in the written word. The idea acquires substance by taking on a visible nature, and then stands in the way of its own clarification. But this sort of

---

1. Chapters 11, 12, and 13 of *The Summing Up*, 1938.

obscurity merges very easily into the willful. Some writers who do not think clearly are inclined to suppose that their thoughts have a significance greater than at first sight appears. It is flattering to believe that they are too profound to be expressed so clearly that all who run may read, and very naturally it does not occur to such writers that the fault is with their own minds which have not the faculty of precise reflection. Here again the magic of the written word obtains. It is very easy to persuade oneself that a phrase that one does not quite understand may mean a great deal more than one realizes. From this there is only a little way to go to fall into the habit of setting down one's impressions in all their original vagueness. Fools can always be found to discover a hidden sense in them. There is another form of willful obscurity that masquerades as aristocratic exclusiveness. The author wraps his meaning in mystery so that the vulgar shall not participate in it. His soul is a secret garden into which the elect may penetrate only after overcoming a number of perilous obstacles. But this kind of obscurity is not only pretentious; it is short-sighted. For time plays it an odd trick. If the sense is meagre time reduces it to a meaningless verbiage that no one thinks of reading. This is the fate that has befallen the lucubrations of those French writers who were seduced by the example of Guillaume Apollinaire. But occasionally it throws a sharp cold light on what had seemed profound and thus discloses the fact that these contortions of language disguised very commonplace notions. There are few of Mallarmé's poems now that are not clear; one cannot fail to notice that his thought singularly lacked originality. Some of his phrases were beautiful; the materials of his verse were the poetic platitudes of his day.

Simplicity is not such an obvious merit as lucidity. I have aimed at it because I have no gift for richness. Within limits I admire richness in others, though I find it difficult to digest in quantity. I can read one page of Ruskin with delight, but twenty only with weariness. The rolling period, the stately epithet, the noun rich in poetic associations, the subordinate clauses that give the sentence weight and magnificence, the grandeur like that of wave following wave in the open sea; there is no doubt that in all this there is something inspiring. Words thus strung together fall on the ear like music. The appeal is sensuous rather than intellectual, and the beauty of the sound leads you easily to conclude that you need not bother about the meaning. But words are tyrannical things, they exist for their meanings, and if you will not pay attention to these, you cannot pay attention at all. Your mind wanders. This kind of writing demands a subject that will suit it. It is surely out of place to write in the grand style of inconsiderable things. No one wrote in this manner with greater success than Sir Thomas Browne, but even he did not always escape this pitfall. In the last chapter of *Hydriotaphia* the matter, which is the destiny of man, wonderfully fits the baroque splendor of the language, and here the Norwich doctor produced a piece of prose that has never been surpassed in our literature; but when he describes the finding of his urns in the same splendid manner the effect (at least to my taste) is less happy. When a modern writer is grandiloquent to tell you whether or no a little trollop shall hop into bed with a commonplace young man you are right to be disgusted.

But if richness needs gifts with which everyone is not endowed, simplicity by no means comes by nature. To achieve it needs rigid discipline. So far as I know ours is the only language in which it has been found necessary to give a name to the piece of prose which is described as the purple patch; it would not have been necessary to do so unless it were characteristic. English prose is elaborate rather than simple. It was not always so. Nothing could be more racy, straightforward and alive than the prose of Shakespeare; but it must be remembered that this was dialogue written to be spoken. We do not know how he would have written if like Corneille he had composed prefaces to his plays. It may be that they would have been as euphuistic as the letters of Queen Elizabeth. But earlier prose, the prose of Sir Thomas More, for instance, is neither ponderous, flowery nor oratorical. It smacks of the English soil. To my mind King James's Bible has been a very harmful influence on English prose. I am not so stupid as to deny its great beauty. It is majestical. But the Bible is an oriental book. Its alien imagery has nothing to do with us. Those hyperboles, those luscious metaphors, are foreign to our genius. I cannot but think that not the least of the misfortunes that the Secession from Rome brought upon the spiritual life of our country is that this work for so long a period became the daily, and with many the only, reading of our people. Those rhythms, that powerful vocabulary, that grandiloquence, became part and parcel of the national sensibility. The plain, honest English speech was overwhelmed with ornament. Blunt Englishmen twisted their tongues to speak like Hebrew prophets. There was evidently something in the English temper to which this was congenial, perhaps a native lack of precision in thought, perhaps a naïve delight in fine words for their own sake, an innate eccentricity and love of embroidery, I do not know; but the fact remains that ever since, English prose has had to struggle against the tendency to luxuriance. When from time to time the spirit of the language has reasserted itself, as it did with Dryden and the writers of Queen Anne, it was only to be submerged once more by the pomposities of Gibbon and Dr. Johnson. When English prose recovered simplicity with Hazlitt, the Shelley of the letters and Charles Lamb at his best, it lost it again with De Quincey, Carlyle, Meredith and Walter Pater. It is obvious that the grand style is more striking than the plain. Indeed many people think that a style that does not attract notice is not style. They will admire Walter Pater's, but will read an essay by Matthew Arnold without giving a moment's attention to the elegance, distinction and sobriety with which he set down what he had to say.

The dictum that the style is the man is well known. It is one of those aphorisms that say too much to mean a great deal. Where is the man in Goethe, in his birdlike lyrics or in his clumsy prose? And Hazlitt? But I suppose that if a man has a confused mind he will write in a confused way, if his temper is capricious his prose will be fantastical, and if he has a quick, darting intelligence that is reminded by the matter in hand of a hundred things, he will, unless he has great self-control, load his pages with metaphor and simile. There is a great difference between the magniloquence of the Jacobean writers, who were intoxicated with the new wealth that had lately been brought into the language, and the turgidity of Gibbon and Dr. Johnson, who were the victims of bad theories. I can read every word that Dr. Johnson wrote with delight, for he had good sense, charm and wit. No one could have written better if he had not willfully set himself to write in the grand style. He knew good English when he saw it. No critic has praised Dryden's prose more aptly. He said of him that he appeared to have no art other than that of expressing with clearness what he thought with vigor. And one of his Lives he finished with the words: "Whoever wishes to attain an English style, familiar but not coarse, and elegant but not ostentatious, must give his days and nights to the volumes of Addison." But when he himself sat down to write it was with a very different aim. He mistook the orotund for the dignified. He had not the good breeding to see that simplicity and naturalness are the truest marks of distinction.

For to write good prose is an affair of good manners. It is, unlike verse, a civil art. Poetry is baroque. Baroque is tragic, massive and mystical. It is elemental. It demands depth and insight. I cannot but feel that the prose writers of the baroque period, the authors of King James's Bible, Sir Thomas Browne, Glanville, were poets who had lost their way. Prose is a rococo art. It needs taste rather than power, decorum rather than inspiration and vigor rather than grandeur. Form for the poet is the bit and the bridle without which (unless you are an acrobat) you cannot ride your horse; but for the writer of prose it is the chassis without which your car does not exist. It is not an accident that the best prose was written when rococo with its elegance and moderation, at its birth attained its greatest excellence. For rococo was evolved when baroque had become declamatory and the world, tired of the stupendous, asked for restraint. It was the natural expression of persons who valued a civilized life. Humor, tolerance and horse sense made the great tragic issues that had preoccupied the first half of the seventeenth century seem excessive. The world was a more comfortable place to live in and perhaps for the first time in centuries the cultivated classes could sit back and enjoy their leisure. It has been said that good prose should resemble the conversation of a well-bred man. Conversation is only possible when men's minds are free from pressing anxieties. Their lives must be reasonably secure and they must have no grave concern about their souls. They must attach importance to the refinements of civilization. They must value courtesy, they must pay attention to their persons (and have we not also been told that good prose should be like the clothes of a well-dressed man, appropriate but unobtrusive?), they must fear to bore, they must be neither flippant nor solemn, but always apt; and they must look upon "enthusiasm" with a critical glance. This is a soil very suitable for prose. It is not to be wondered at that it gave a fitting opportunity for the appearance of the best writer of prose that our modern world has seen, Voltaire. The writers of English, perhaps owing to the poetic nature of the language, have seldom reached the excellence that seems to have come so naturally to him. It is in so far as they have approached the ease, sobriety and precision of the great French masters that they are admirable.

Whether you ascribe importance to euphony, the last of the three characteristics that I mentioned, must depend on the sensitiveness of your ear. A great many readers, and many admirable writers, are devoid of this quality. Poets as we know have always made a great use of alliteration. They are persuaded that the repetition of a sound gives an effect of beauty. I do not think it does so in prose. It seems to me that in prose alliteration should be used only for a special reason; when used by accident it falls on the ear very disagreeably. But its accidental use is so common that one can only suppose that the sound of it is not universally offensive. Many writers without distress will put two rhyming words together, join a monstrous long adjective to a monstrous long noun, or between the end of one word and the beginning of another have a conjunction of consonants that almost breaks your jaw. These are trivial and obvious instances. I mention them only to prove that if careful writers can do such things it is only because they have no ear. Words have weight, sound and appearance; it is only by considering these that you can write a sentence that is good to look at and good to listen to.

I have read many books on English prose, but have found it hard to profit by them; for the most part they are vague, unduly theoretical, and often scolding. But you cannot say this of Fowler's *Dictionary of Modern English Usage*. It is a valuable work. I do not think anyone writes so well that he cannot learn much from it. It is lively reading. Fowler liked simplicity, straightforwardness and common sense. He had no patience with pretentiousness. He had a sound feeling that idiom was the backbone of a language and he was all for the racy phrase. He was no slavish admirer of logic and was willing enough to give usage right of way through the exact demesnes of grammar. English grammar is very difficult and few writers have avoided making mistakes in it. So heedful a writer as Henry James, for instance, on occasion wrote so ungrammatically that a schoolmaster, finding such errors in a schoolboy's essay, would be justly indignant. It is necessary to know grammar, and it is better to write grammatically than not, but it is well to remember that grammar is common speech formulated. Usage is the only test. I would prefer a phrase that was easy and unaffected to a phrase that was grammatical. One of the differences between French and English is that in French you can be grammatical with complete naturalness, but in English not invariably. It is a difficulty in writing English that the sound of the living voice dominates the look of the printed word. I have given the matter of style a great deal of thought and have taken great pains. I have written few pages that I feel I could not improve and far too many that I have left with dissatisfaction because, try as I would, I could do no better. I cannot say of myself what Johnson said of Pope: "He never passed a fault unamended by indifference, nor quitted it by despair." I do not write as I want to; I write as I can.

But Fowler had no ear. He did not see that simplicity may sometimes make concessions to euphony. I do not think a far-fetched, an archaic or even an affected word is out of place when it sounds better than the blunt, obvious one or when it gives a sentence a better balance. But, I hasten to add, though I think you may without misgiving make this concession to pleasant sound, I think you should make none to what may obscure your meaning. Anything is better than not to write clearly. There is nothing to be said against lucidity, and against simplicity only the possibility of dryness. This is a risk that is well worth taking when you reflect how much better it is to be bald than to wear a curly wig. But there is in euphony a danger that must be considered. It is very likely to be monotonous. When George Moore began to write, his style was poor; it gave you the impression that he wrote on wrapping paper with a blunt pencil. But he developed gradually a very musical English. He learnt to write sentences that fall away on the ear with a misty languor and it delighted him so much that he could never have enough of it. He did not escape monotony. It is like the sound of water lapping a shingly beach, so soothing that you presently cease to be sensible of it. It is so mellifluous that you hanker for some harshness, for an abrupt dissonance, that will interrupt the silky concord. I do not know how one can guard against this. I suppose the best chance is to have a more lively faculty of boredom than one's readers so that one is wearied before they are. One must always be on the watch for mannerisms and when certain cadences come too easily to the pen ask oneself whether they have not become mechanical. It is very hard to discover the exact point where the idiom one has formed to express oneself has lost its tang. As Dr. Johnson said: "He that has once studiously formed a style, rarely writes afterwards with complete ease." Admirably as I think Matthew Arnold's style was suited to his particular purposes, I must admit that his mannerisms are often irritating. His style was an instrument that he had forged once for all; it was not like the human hand capable of performing a variety of actions.

If you could write lucidly, simply, euphoniously and yet with liveliness you would write perfectly: you would write like Voltaire. And yet we know how fatal the pursuit of liveliness may be: it may result in the tiresome acrobatics of Meredith. Macaulay and Carlyle were in their different ways arresting; but at the heavy cost of naturalness. Their flashy effects distract the mind. They destroy their persuasiveness; you would not believe a man was very intent on ploughing a furrow if he carried a hoop with him and jumped through it at every other step. A good style should show no sign of effort. What is written should seem a happy accident. I think no one in France now writes more admirably than Colette, and such is the ease of her expression that you cannot bring yourself to believe that she takes any trouble over it. I am told that there are pianists who have a natural technique so that they can play in a manner that most executants can achieve only as the result of unremitting toil, and I am willing to believe that there are writers who are equally fortunate. Among them I was much inclined to place Colette. I asked her. I was exceedingly surprised to hear that she wrote everything over and over again. She told me that she would often spend a whole morning working upon a single page. But it does not matter how one gets the effect of ease. For my part, if I get it at all, it is only by strenuous effort. Nature seldom provides me with the word, the turn of phrase, that is appropriate without being far-fetched or commonplace.

QUESTIONS

Maugham draws attention to the two conflicting yet complementary approaches to style that have been traditional in literary criticism. One approach maintains that style is primarily a combination of qualities and devices that can be learned and produced; the other, that "style is the man," the reflection in language of a personality with all its attitudes and idiosyncracies. Using passages from An Album of Styles (pp. 278–369), explore the two approaches In any given passage what appears as impersonal technique or device, what as reflecting the special temperament or character of the author?

ROBERT PATTISON

Being a Disquisition wherein were told whats happening to english including examples written by a man who no's;

This sentence demonstrates alot of the to frequent errors that occur in my freshman composition classes, its not just there willingness to gleefully split an infinitive or end a sentence with a preposition which are the problems kindly boarding school masters used to be concerned with. Its true my students arent the good mannered middle class bunch who I went to school with, there more often cops or shoesalesmens or garbagemens (pardon me, sanitationmens) sons and daughters, and yet there a sharp group, wary, skeptical, bright.

So when I knock myself out day after day class after class explaining the genitive case in english, the proper position of commas, the runon sentence, the distinction between the three theres and still these mistakes appear even in the work of the best of them I wonder.

I wonder if just maybe they know something I dont about the english language. Something intuitive about its history and something instinctive about its future. After all, its been the movement of the language to progress toward simplicity. The case structure, with its confusing endings, was an early victim. Why say "On his dagum hierde Gregorius goda lara" when with a little reliance on word order and common sense you can more simply say "In his time Gregorys heard good lectures"?

Besides the nagging whom the last vestige of the case structure in english is the genitives use of the apostrophe. But surely common sense and word order indicate the genetive usage and my students perception is correct in eliminating the troublesome superscript.

Theres wisdom is doing away with punctuation that doesnt contribute to clarity and when my classes monolithically dispose of pointless spelling distinctions where the sense is obvious there judgment may be sound.

Then again, alot of my colleagues lose sleep over the way some students slam two words or letters into one but metathesis or the changing of the position of sounds or letters is a venerable tradition, or else a newt might still be an ewt.

Words in english usually explain themselves by position and context, though of course there exceptions to this rule which my students in there foresight have not anticipated but give them awhile and they will.

I cant go into detail about every grammatical innovation made by my students, theres alot to recommend them though and if you are an editor, the author of an english grammar or the perpetrator of a work on footnote logic and you can read this you should pay attention to my class because one day they might take over and one day you might wake up. And discover your fired.

WAYNE C. BOOTH
Boring from Within: The Art of the Freshman Essay[1]

Last week I had for about the hundredth time an experience that always disturbs me. Riding on a train, I found myself talking with my seat-mate, who asked me what I did for a living. "I teach English." Do you have any trouble predicting his response? His face fell, and he groaned, "Oh, dear, I'll have to watch my language." In my experience there are only two other possible reactions. The first is even less inspiriting: "I hated English in school; it was my worst subject." The second, so rare as to make an honest English teacher almost burst into tears of gratitude when it occurs, is an animated conversation about literature, or ideas, or the American language— the kind of conversation that shows a continuing respect for "English" as something more than being sure about *who* and *whom*, *lie* and *lay*.

Unless the people you meet are a good deal more tactful or better liars than the ones I meet, you've had the two less favorable experiences many times. And it takes no master analyst to figure out why so many of our fellow citizens think of us as unfriendly policemen: it is because too many of us have seen ourselves as unfriendly policemen. I know of a high school English class in Indiana in which the students are explicitly told that their paper grades will not be affected by anything they say; required to write a paper a week, they are graded simply on the number of spelling and grammatical errors. What is more, they are given a standard form for their papers: each paper is to have three paragraphs, a beginning, a middle, and an end —or is it an introduction, a body, and a conclusion? The theory seems to be that if the student is not troubled about having to say anything, or about discovering a good way of saying it, he can then concentrate on the truly important matter of avoiding mistakes.

What's wrong with such assignments? What's wrong with getting the problem of correctness focused sharply enough so that we can really work on it? After all, we do have the job of teaching correct English, don't we? We can't possibly teach our hordes of students to be colorful writers, but by golly, we can beat the bad grammar out of them. Leaving aside the obvious fact that we *can't* beat the bad grammar out of them, not by direct assault, let's think a bit about what that kind of assignment does to the poor teacher who gives it. Those papers must be read, by someone, and unless the teacher has more trained assistance than you and I have, *she's* the victim. She can't help being bored silly by her own paper-reading, and we all know what an evening of being bored by a class's papers does to our attitude toward that class the next day. The old formula of John Dewey was

1. Adapted by Mr. Booth from a speech delivered in May 1963 to the Illinois Council of College Teachers of English.

that any teaching that bores the student is likely to fail. The formula was subject to abuse, quite obviously, since interest in itself is only one of many tests of adequate teaching. A safer formula, though perhaps also subject to abuse, might be: Any teaching that bores the teacher is sure to fail. And I am haunted by the picture of that poor woman in Indiana, week after week reading batches of papers written by students who have been told that nothing they say can possibly affect her opinion of those papers. Could any hell imagined by Dante or Jean-Paul Sartre match this self-inflicted futility?

I call it self-inflicted, as if it were a simple matter to avoid receiving papers that bore us. But unfortunately it is not. It may be a simple matter to avoid the *total* meaninglessness that the students must give that Indiana teacher, but we all know that it is no easy matter to produce interesting papers; our pet cures for boredom never work as well as they ought to. Every beginning teacher learns quickly and painfully that nothing works with all students, and that on bad days even the most promising ideas work with nobody.

As I try to sort out the various possible cures for those batches of boredom—in ink, double-spaced, on one side of the sheet, only, please —I find them falling into three groups: efforts to give the students a sharper sense of writing to an audience, efforts to give them some substance to express, and efforts to improve their habits of observation and of approach to their task—what might be called improving their mental personalities.

This classification, both obvious and unoriginal, is a useful one not only because it covers—at least I hope it does—all of our efforts to improve what our students can do but also because it reminds us that no one of the three is likely to work unless it is related to each of the others. In fact each of the three types of cure—"develop an awareness of audience," "give them something to say," and "enliven their writing personalities"—threatens us with characteristic dangers and distortions; all three together are indispensable to any lasting cure.

Perhaps the most obvious omission in that Indiana teacher's assignments is all sense of an audience to be persuaded, of a serious rhetorical purpose to be achieved. One tempting cure for this omission is to teach them to put a controversial edge on what they say. So we ask them to write a three-page paper arguing that China should be allowed into the UN or that women are superior to men or that American colleges are failing in their historic task. Then we are surprised when the papers turn out to be as boring as ever. The papers on Red China are full of abstract pomposities that the students themselves obviously do not understand or care about, since they have gleaned them in a desperate dash through the most readily available sources listed in the *Readers' Guide*. Except for the rare student who has some political background and awareness, and who thus might have written on the subject anyway, they manage to convey little more than their resentment at the assignment and their boredom in carrying it out. One of the worst batches of papers I ever read came out of a good idea we had at Earlham College for getting the whole student body involved in controversial discussion about world affairs. We required them to read Barbara Ward's *Five Ideas that Change the World*; we even had Lady Jackson come to the campus and talk to everyone about her concern for the backward nations. The papers, to our surprise, were a discouraging business. We found ourselves in desperation collecting the boners that are always a sure sign, when present in great numbers, that students are thoroughly disengaged. "I think altruism is all right, so long as we practice it in our own interest." "I would be willing to die for anything fatal." "It sure is a doggie dog world."

It is obvious what had gone wrong: though we had ostensibly given the student a writing purpose, it had not become *his* purpose, and he was really no better off, perhaps worse, than if we had him writing about, say, piccolos or pizza. We might be tempted in revulsion from such overly ambitious failures to search for controversy in the students' own mundane lives. This may be a good move, but we should not be surprised when the papers on "Let's clean up the campus" or "Why must we have traffic fatalities?" turn out to be just as empty as the papers on the UN or the Congo. They may have more exclamation points and underlined adjectives, but they will not interest any teacher who would like to read papers for his own pleasure or edification. "People often fail to realize that nearly 40,000 people are killed on our highways each year. Must this carnage continue?" Well, I suppose it must, until people who write about it learn to see it with their own eyes, and hearts, instead of through a haze of cliché. The truth is that to make students assume a controversial pose before they have any genuine substance to be controversial about is to encourage dishonesty and slovenliness, and to ensure our own boredom. It may very well lead them into the kind of commercial concern for the audience which makes almost every *Reader's Digest* article intelligible to everyone over the chronological age of ten and boring to everyone over the mental age of fifteen. *Newsweek* magazine recently had a readability survey conducted on itself. It was found to be readable by the average twelfth grader, unlike *Time*, which is readable by the average eleventh grader. The editors were advised, and I understand are taking the advice, that by improving their "readability" by one year they could improve their circulation by several hundred thousand. Whether they will thereby lop off a few thousand adult readers in the process was not reported.

The only protection from this destructive type of concern for the audience is the control of substance, of having something solid to say. Our students bore us, even when they take a seemingly lively controversial tone, because they have nothing to say, to us or to anybody else. If and when they discover something to say, they will no longer bore us, and our comments will no longer bore them. Having something to say, they will be interested in learning how to say it better. Having something to say, they can be taught how to give a properly controversial edge to what will by its nature be controversial—nothing, after all, is worth saying that everybody agrees on already.

When we think of providing substance, we are perhaps tempted first to find some way of filling students' minds with a goodly store of general ideas, available on demand. This temptation is not necessarily a bad one. After all, if we think of the adult writers who interest us, most of them have such a store; they have read and thought about man's major problems, and they have opinions and arguments ready to hand about how men ought to live, how society ought to be run, how literature ought to be written. Edmund Wilson, for example, one of the most consistently interesting men alive, seems to have an inexhaustible flow of reasoned opinions on any subject that comes before him. Obviously our students are not going to interest us until they too have some ideas.

But it is not easy to impart ideas. It is not even easy to impart opinions, though a popular teacher can usually manage to get students to parrot his views. But ideas—that is, opinions backed with genuine reasoning—are extremely difficult to develop. If they were not, we wouldn't have a problem in the first place; we could simply send our students off with an assignment to prove their conviction that God does or does not exist or that the American high school system is the best on God's earth, and the interesting arguments would flow.

There is, in fact, no short cut to the development of reasoned ideas. Years and years of daily contact with the world of ideas are required before the child can be expected to begin formulating his own ideas and his own reasons. And for the most part the capacity to handle abstract ideas comes fairly late. I recently saw a paper of a bright high school sophomore, from a good private school, relating the economic growth of China and India to their political development and relative supply of natural resources. It was a terrible paper; the student's hatred of the subject, his sense of frustration in trying to invent generalizations about processes that were still too big for him, showed in every line. The child's parent told me that when the paper was returned by the geography teacher, he had pencilled on the top of one page, "Why do you mix so many bad ideas with your good ones?" The son was almost in tears, his father told me, with anger and helplessness. "He talks as if I'd put bad ideas in on purpose. *I* don't know a bad idea from a good one on this subject."

Yet with all this said, I am still convinced that general ideas are not only a resource but also a duty that cannot be dodged just because it is a dangerous one. There is nothing we touch, as English teachers, that is immune to being tainted by our touch; all the difference lies in how we go about it.

Ideas are a resource because adolescents are surprisingly responsive to any real encouragement to think for themselves, *if* methods of forced feeding are avoided. The seventeen-year-old who has been given nothing but commonplaces and clichés all his life and who finally discovers a teacher with ideas of his own may have his life changed, and, as I shall say in my final point, when his life is changed his writing is changed. Perhaps some of you can remember, as I can, a first experience with a teacher who could think for himself. I can remember going home from a conversation with my high school chemistry teacher and audibly vowing to myself: "Someday I'm going to be able to think for myself like that." There was nothing especially unconventional about Luther Gidding's ideas—at least I can remember few of them now. But what I cannot forget is the way he had with an idea, the genuine curiosity with which he approached it, the pause while he gave his little thoughtful cough, and then the bulldog tenacity with which he would argue it through. And I am convinced that though he never required me to write a line, he did more to improve my writing during the high school years than all of my English teachers put together. The diary I kept to record my sessions with him, never read by anyone, was the best possible writing practice.

If ideas, in this sense of speculation backed up with an attempt to think about things rigorously and constructively, are a great and often neglected resource, they are also our civic responsibility—a far more serious responsibility than our duty to teach spelling and grammar. It is a commonplace to say that democracy depends for its survival on an informed citizenry, but we all know that mere information is not what we are talking about when we say such things. What we mean is that democracy depends on a citizenry that can reason for themselves, on men who know whether a case has been proved, or at least made probable. Democracy depends, if you will forgive some truisms for a moment, on free choices, and choices cannot be in any sense free if they are made blind: free choice is, in fact, choice that is based on knowledge—not just opinions, but knowledge in the sense of reasoned opinion. And if that half of our population who do not go beyond high school do not learn from us how to put two and two together and how to test the efforts of others to do so, and if the colleges continue to fail with most of the other half, we are doomed to become even more sheeplike, as a nation, than we are already.

Papers about ideas written by sheep are boring; papers written by thinking boys and girls are interesting. The problem is always to find ideas at a level that will allow the student to *reason*, that is, to provide support for his ideas, rather than merely assert them in half-baked form. And this means something that is all too often forgotten by the most ambitious teachers—namely, that whatever ideas the student writes about must somehow be connected with his own experience. Teaching machines will never be able to teach the kind of writing we all want, precisely because no machine can ever know which general ideas relate, for a given student, to some meaningful experience. In the same class we'll have one student for whom philosophical and religious ideas are meaningful, another who can talk with confidence about entropy and the second law of thermodynamics, a third who can write about social justice, and a fourth who can discuss the phony world of Holden Caulfield. Each of them can do a good job on his own subject, because he has as part of his equipment a growing awareness of how conclusions in that subject are related to the steps of argument that support conclusions. Ideally, each of these students ought to have the personal attention of a tutor for an hour or so each week, someone who can help him sharpen those connections, and not force him to write on topics not yet appropriate to his interests or experience. But when these four are in a class of thirty or forty others, taught by a teacher who has three or four other similar sections, we all know what happens: the teacher is forced by his circumstances to provide some sort of mold into which all of the students can be poured. Although he is still better able to adapt to individual differences than a machine, he is unfortunately subject to boredom and fatigue, as a machine would not be. Instead of being the philosopher, scientist, political analyst, and literary critic that these four students require him to be, teaching them and learning from them at the same time, the teacher is almost inevitably tempted to force them all to write about the ideas he himself knows best. The result is that at least three of the four must write out of ignorance.

Now clearly the best way out of this impasse would be for legislatures and school boards and college presidents to recognize the teaching of English for what it is: the most demanding of all teaching jobs, justifying the smallest sections and the lightest course loads. No composition teacher can possibly concentrate on finding special interests, making imaginative assignments, and testing the effectiveness and cogency of papers if he has more than seventy-five students at a time; the really desirable limit would be about forty-five—three sections of fifteen students each. Nobody would ever expect a piano teacher, who has no themes to read, to handle the great masses of pupils that we handle. Everyone recognizes that for all other technical skills individual attention is required. Yet for this, the most delicate of all skills, the one requiring the most subtle interrelationships of training, character, and experience, we fling students and teachers into hopelessly impersonal patterns.

But if I'm not careful I'll find myself saying that our pupils bore us because the superintendents and college presidents hire us to be bored. Administrative neglect and misallocation of educational funds are basic to our problem, and we should let the citizenry know of the scandal on every occasion. But meanwhile, back at the ranch, we are 'faced with the situation as it now is: we must find some way to train a people to write responsibly even though the people, as represented, don't want this service sufficiently to pay for it.

The tone of political exhortation into which I have now fallen leads me to one natural large source of ideas as we try to encourage writing that is not just lively and controversial but informed and genuinely persuasive. For many students there is obviously more potential interest in social problems and forces, political controversy, and the processes of everyday living around them than in more general ideas. The four students I described a moment ago, students who can say something about philosophy, science, general political theory, or literary criticism, are rare. But most students, including these four, can in theory at least be interested in meaningful argument about social problems in which they are personally involved.

As a profession we have tried, over the past several decades, a variety of approaches attempting to capitalize on such interests. Papers on corruption in TV, arguments about race relations, analyses of distortions in advertising, descriptions of mass communication—these have been combined in various quantities with traditional subjects like grammar, rhetoric, and literature. The "communications" movement, which looked so powerful only a few years ago and which now seems almost dead, had at its heart a perfectly respectable notion, a notion not much different from the one I'm working with today: get them to write about something they know about, and make sure that they see their writing as an act of communication, not as a meaningless exercise. And what better material than other acts of communication.

The dangers of such an approach are by now sufficiently understood. As subject matter for the English course, current "communications media" can at best provide only a supplement to literature and analysis of ideas. But they can be a valuable supplement. Analysis in class of the appeals buried in a *New Yorker* or *Life* advertisement followed by a writing assignment requiring similar analyses can be a far more interesting introduction to the intricacies of style than assignments out of a language text on levels of usage or emotion-charged adjectives. Analysis of a *Time* magazine account, purporting to be objective news but in actual fact a highly emotional editorial, can be not only a valuable experience in itself, but it can lead to papers in which the students do say something to us. Stylistic analysis of the treatment of the same news events by two newspapers or weeklies of different editorial policy can lead to an intellectual awakening of great importance, and thus to papers that will not, cannot, bore the teacher. But this will happen only if the students' critical powers are genuinely developed. It will not do simply to teach the instructor's own prejudices.

There was a time in decades not long past when many of the most lively English teachers thought of their job as primarily to serve as handmaids to liberalism. I had one teacher in college who confessed to me that his overriding purpose was to get students to read and believe *The Nation* rather than the editorials of their daily paper. I suppose that his approach was not entirely valueless. It seems preferable to the effort to be noncontroversial that marks too many English teachers in the '60's, and at least it stirred some of us out of our dogmatic slumbers. But unfortunately it did nothing whatever about teaching us to think critically. Though we graduated from his course at least aware—as many college graduates do not seem to be today—that you can't believe anything you read in the daily press until you have analyzed it and related it to your past experience and to other accounts, it failed to teach us that you can't believe what you read in *The Nation* either. It left the job undone of training our ability to think, because it concentrated too heavily on our opinions. The result was, as I remember, that my own papers in that course were generally regurgitated liberalism. I was excited by them, and that was something. But I can't believe that the instructor found reading them anything other than a chore. There was nothing in them that came from my own experience, my own notions of what would constitute evidence for my conclusions. There I was, in Utah in the depths of the depression, writing about the Okies when I could have been writing about the impoverished farmers all around me. I wrote about race relations in the south without ever having talked with a Negro in my life and without recognizing that the bootblack I occasionally saw in Salt Lake City in the Hotel Utah was in any way related to the problem of race relations.

The third element that accounts for our boring papers is the lack of character and personality in the writer. My life, my observations, my insights were not included in those papers on the Okies and race relations and the New Deal. Every opinion was derivative, every observation second-hand. I had no real opinions of my own, and my eyes were not open wide enough for me to make first-hand observations on the world around me. What I wrote was therefore characterless, without true personality, though often full of personal pronouns. My opinions had been changed, my *self* had not. The style was the boy, the opinionated, immature, uninformed boy; whether my teacher knew it or not—and apparently he did not—his real job was to make a man of me if he wanted me to write like a man.

Putting the difficulty in this way naturally leads me to what perhaps many of you have been impatient about from the beginning. Are not the narrative arts, both as encountered in great literature and as practiced by the students themselves, the best road to the infusion of individuality that no good writing can lack? Would not a real look at the life of that bootblack, and an attempt to deal with him in narrative, have led to a more interesting paper than all of my generalized attacks on the prejudiced southerners?

I think it would, but once again I am almost more conscious of the dangers of the cure than of the advantages. As soon as we make our general rule something like, "Have the students write a personal narrative on what they know about, what they can see and feel at first hand," we have opened the floodgates for those dreadful assignments that we all find ourselves using, even though we know better: "My Summer Vacation," "Catching My First Fish," and "Our Trip to the Seattle World's Fair." Here are personal experiences that call for personal observation and narration. What's wrong with them?

Quite simply, they invite triviality, superficiality, puerility. Our students have been writing essays on such non-subjects all their lives, and until they have developed some sort of critical vision, some way of looking at the world they passed through on their vacations or fishing trips, they are going to feed us the same old bromides that have always won their passing grades. "My Summer Vacation" is an invitation to a grocery list of items, because it implies no audience, no point to be made, no point of view, no character in the speaker. A bright student will make something of such an invitation, by dramatizing the comic family quarrel that developed two days out, or by comparing his view of the American motel system with Nabokov's in *Lolita*, or by remembering the types of people seen in the campgrounds. If he had his own eyes and ears open he might have seen, in a men's room in Grand Canyon last summer, a camper with a very thick French accent trying to convert a Brooklyn Jew into believing the story of the Mormon gold plates. Or he could have heard, at Mesa Verde, a young park ranger, left behind toward the end of the season by all of the experienced rangers, struggling ungrammatically through a set speech on the geology of the area and finally breaking down in embarrassment over his lack of education. Such an episode, really *seen*, could be used narratively to say something to other high school students about what education really is.

But mere narration can be in itself just as dull as the most abstract theorizing about the nature of the universe or the most derivative opinion-mongering about politics. Even relatively skilful narration, used too obviously as a gimmick to catch interest, with no real relation to the subject, can be as dull as the most abstract pomposities. We all know the student papers that begin like *Reader's Digest* articles, with stereotyped narration that makes one doubt the event itself: "On a dark night last January, two teen agers were seen etc., etc." One can open any issue of *Time* and find this so-called narrative interest plastered throughout. From the March 29 issue I find, among many others, the following bits of fantasy: #1: "A Bolivian father sadly surveyed his nation's seven universities, then made up his mind. 'I don't want my son mixed up in politics.' . . . So saying, he sent his son off to West Germany to college." So writing, the author sends me into hysterical laughter: the quote is phony, made up for the occasion to disguise the generality of the news item. #2: "Around 12:30 P.M. every Monday and Friday, an aging Cubana Airlines turbo-prop Britannia whistles to a halt at Mexico City's International Airport. Squads of police stand by. All passengers . . . without diplomatic or Mexican passports are photographed and questioned. . . . They always dodge questions. 'Why are you here? Where are you going?' ask the Mexicans. 'None of your business,' answer the secretive travelers." "Why should I go on reading?" ask I. #3: "At 6:30 one morning early this month, a phone shrilled in the small office off the bedroom of Egypt's President. . . . Nasser. [All early morning phones "shrill" for *Time*.] Already awake, he lifted the receiver to hear exciting news: a military coup had just been launched against the anti-Nasser government of Syria. The phone rang again. It was the Minister of Culture. . . . How should Radio Cairo handle the Syrian crisis? 'Support the rebels,' snapped Nasser." Oh lucky reporter, I sigh, to have such an efficient wiretapping service. #4: "In South Korea last week, a farmer named Song Kyu Il traveled all the way from the southern provinces to parade before Seoul's Duk Soo Palace with a placard scrawled in his own blood. . . . Farmer Song was thrown in jail, along with some 200 other demonstrators." That's the last we hear of Song, who is invented as an individual for this opening and then dropped. #5: "Defense Secretary Robert McNamara last spring stood beside President Kennedy on the tenth-deck bridge of the nuclear-powered carrier *Enterprise*. For as far as the eye could see, other U. S. ships deployed over the Atlantic seascape." Well, maybe. But for as far as the eye can see, the narrative clichés are piled, rank on rank. At 12:00 midnight last Thursday a gaunt, harried English professor could be seen hunched over his typewriter, a pile of *Time* magazines beside him on the floor. "What," he murmured to himself, sadly, "Whatever can we do about this trashy imitation of narration?"

Fortunately there is something we can do, and it is directly within our province. We can subject our students to models of genuine narration, with the sharp observation and penetrating critical judgment that underlies all good story telling, whether reportorial or fictional.

> It is a truth universally acknowledged, that a single man in possession of a good fortune must be in want of a wife.
> However little known the feelings or views of such a man may be on his first entering a neighborhood, this truth is so well fixed in the minds of the surrounding families, that he is considered as the rightful property of someone or other of their daughters.
> "My dear Mr. Bennet," said his lady to him one day, "have you heard that Netherfield Park is let at last?"

And already we have a strong personal tone established, a tone of mocking irony which leaves Jane Austen's Mrs. Bennet revealed before us as the grasping, silly gossip she is. Or try this one:

> I am an American, Chicago-born—Chicago, that somber city—and go at things as I have taught myself, free-style, and will make the record in my own way: first to knock, first admitted; sometimes an innocent knock, sometimes a not so innocent. But a man's character is his fate, says Heraclitus, and in the end there isn't any way to disguise the nature of the knocks by acoustical work on the door or gloving the knuckles.
> Everybody knows there is no fineness or accuracy of suppression; if you hold down one thing you hold down the adjoining.
> My own parents were not much to me, though I cared for my mother. She was simple-minded, and what I learned from her was not what she taught. . . .

Do you catch the accent of Saul Bellow here, beneath the accent of his Augie March? You do, of course, but the students, many of them, do not. How do you know, they will ask, that Jane Austen is being ironic? How do you know, they ask again, that Augie is being characterized by his author through what he says? In teaching them how we know, in exposing them to the great narrative voices, ancient and modern, and in teaching them to hear these voices accurately, we are, of course, trying to change their lives, to make them new, to raise their perceptions to a new level altogether. Nobody can really catch these accents who has not grown up sufficiently to see through cheap substitutes. Or, to put it another way, a steady exposure to such voices is the very thing that will produce the maturity that alone can make our students ashamed of beclouded, commercial, borrowed spectacles for viewing the world.

It is true that exposure to good fiction will not in itself transform our students into good writers. Even the best-read student still needs endless hours and years of practice, with rigorous criticism. Fiction will not do the job of discipline in reasoned argument and of practice in developing habits of addressing a living audience. But in the great fiction they will learn what it means to look at something with full attention, what it means to see beneath the surface of society's platitudes. If we then give them practice in writing about things close to the home base of their own honest observations, constantly stretching their powers of generalization and argument but never allowing them to drift into pompous inanities or empty controversiality, we may have that rare but wonderful pleasure of witnessing the miracle: a man and a style where before there was only a bag of wind or a bundle of received opinions. Even when, as with most of our students, no miracles occur, we can hope for papers that we can enjoy reading And as a final bonus, we might hope that when our students encounter someone on a train who says that he teaches English, their automatic response may be something other than looks of pity or cries of mock alarm.

QUESTIONS

1. *Booth is writing for an audience of English teachers. In what ways might the essay differ if he were writing for an audience of students?*

2. *On page 272 Booth says he has "now fallen" into a "tone of political exhortation." (Tone may be defined as the reflection in language of the attitude a writer takes toward his subject or his audience or both.) What other "tones" are there in the essay? Why does Booth find it necessary to vary the tone?*

3. *What steps are necessary before an "opinion" can become a "reasoned opinion"? Select some subject on which you have a strong opinion and decide whether it is a reasoned opinion.*

4. *Booth characterizes the writing in the Reader's Digest and Time (pp. 275–276). What does he feel the two magazines have in common? Analyze an article from either one of these magazines to see how accurate Booth's characterization is.*

AN ALBUM OF STYLES

ROGER ASCHAM: The Wind

To see the wind with a man his eyes it is unpossible, the nature of it is so fine and subtile; yet this experience of the wind had I once myself, and that was in the great snow that fell four years ago. I rode in the high way betwixt Topcliff-upon-Swale and Borough-bridge, the way being somewhat trodden before, by wayfaring men; the fields on both sides were plain, and lay almost yard-deep with snow; the night afore had been a little frost, so that the snow was hard and crusted above; that morning the sun shone bright and clear, the wind was whistling aloft, and sharp, according to the time of the year; the snow in the high way lay loose and trodden with horses' feet; so as the wind blew, it took the loose snow with it, and made it so slide upon the snow in the field, which was hard and crusted by reason of the frost over night, that thereby I might see very well the whole nature of the wind as it blew that day. And I had a great delight and pleasure to mark it, which maketh me now far better to remember it. Sometime the wind would be not past two yards broad, and so it would carry the snow as far as I could see. Another time the snow would blow over half the field at once. Sometime the snow would tumble softly; by and by it would fly wonderful fast. And this I perceived also, that the wind goeth by streams, and not whole together. For I should see one stream within a score on me; then the space of two score, no snow would stir; but, after so much quantity of ground, another stream of snow, at the same very time, should be carried likewise, but not equally, for the one would stand still, when the other flew apace and so continue sometime swiftlier, sometime slowlier, sometime broader, sometime narrower, as far as I could see. Nor it flew not straight, but sometime it crooked this way, sometime that way, and sometime it ran round about in a compass. And sometime the snow would be lift clean from the ground up to the air, and by and by it would be all clapt to the ground, as though there had been no wind at all, straightway it would rise and fly again. And that which was the most marvel of all, at one time two drifts of snow flew, the one out of the west into the east, the other out of the north into the east. And I saw two winds, by reason of the snow, the one cross over the other, as it had been two high ways. And, again, I should hear the wind blow in the air, when nothing was stirred at the ground. And when all was still where I rode, not very far from me the snow should be lifted wonderfully. This experience made me more marvel at the nature of the wind, than it made me cunning in the knowledge of the wind; but yet thereby I learned perfectly that it is no marvel at all though men in wind lose their length in shooting, seeing so many ways the wind is so variable in blowing.

FRANCIS BACON: Of Revenge

Revenge is a kind of wild justice; which the more man's nature runs to, the more ought law to weed it out. For as for the first wrong, it doth but offend the law; but the revenge of that wrong putteth the law out of office. Certainly, in taking revenge, a man is but even with his enemy; but in passing it over, he is superior; for it is a prince's part to pardon. And Salomon, I am sure, saith, *It is the glory of a man to pass by an offence.* That which is past is gone, and irrevocable; and wise men have enough to do with things present and to come: therefore they do but trifle with themselves, that labour in past matters. There is no man doth a wrong for the wrong's sake; but thereby to purchase himself profit, or pleasure, or honour, or the like. Therefore why should I be angry with a man for loving himself better than me? And if any man should do wrong merely out of ill nature, why, yet it is but like the thorn or briar, which prick and scratch, because they can do no other. The most tolerable sort of revenge is for those wrongs which there is no law to remedy; but then let a man take heed the revenge be such as there is no law to punish; else a man's enemy is still beforehand, and it is two for one. Some, when they take revenge, are desirous the party should know whence it cometh: this is the more generous. For the delight seemeth to be not so much in doing the hurt as in making the party repent: but base and crafty cowards are like the arrow that flieth in the dark. Cosmus, duke of Florence, had a desperate saying against perfidious or neglecting friends, as if those wrongs were unpardonable: *You shall read* (saith he) *that we are commanded to forgive our enemies; but you never read that we are commanded to forgive our friends.* But yet the spirit of Job was in a better tune: *Shall we* (saith he) *take good at God's hands, and not be content to take evil also*? And so of friends in a proportion. This is certain, that a man that studieth revenge keeps his own wounds green, which otherwise would heal and do well. Public revenges are for the most part fortunate; as that for the death of Caesar; for the death of Pertinax;[1] for the death of Henry the third of France;[2] and many more. But in private revenges it is not so. Nay rather, vindictive persons live the life of witches; who as they are mischievous, so end they infortunate.

JOHN DONNE: Men Are Sleeping Prisoners

We are all conceived in close prison; in our Mothers wombs, we are close prisoners all; when we are born, we are born but to the lib-

1. Publius Helvius Pertinax became Emperor of Rome in 193 and was assassinated three months after his accession to the throne by a soldier in his Praetorian Guard.

2. King of France 1574–1589; assassinated during the Siege of Paris.

erty of the house;[1] prisoners still, though within larger walls; and then all our life is but a going out to the place of execution, to death. Now was there ever any man seen to sleep in the cart, between Newgate, and Tyburn?[2] Between the prison and the place of execution, does any man sleep? And we sleep all the way; from the womb to the grave we are never thoroughly awake; but pass on with such dreams, and imaginations as these, I may live as well, as another, and why should I die, rather than another? But awake, and tell me, says this text *Quis homo*?[3] Who is that other that thou talkest of? *What man is he that liveth, and shall not see death?*

SAMUEL JOHNSON: The Pyramids

Of the wall [of China] it is very easy to assign the motives. It secured a wealthy and timorous nation from the incursions of Barbarians, whose unskillfulness in arts made it easier for them to supply their wants by rapine than by industry, and who from time to time poured in upon the habitations of peaceful commerce, as vultures descend upon domestic fowl. Their celerity and fierceness made the wall necessary, and their ignorance made it efficacious.

But for the pyramids no reason has ever been given adequate to the cost and labor of the work. The narrowness of the chambers proves that it could afford no retreat from enemies, and treasures might have been reposited at far less expense with equal security. It seems to have been erected only in compliance with that hunger of imagination which preys incessantly upon life, and must be always appeased by some employment. Those who have already all that they can enjoy, must enlarge their desires. He that has built for use, till use is supplied must begin to build for vanity, and extend his plan to the utmost power of human performance, that he may not be soon reduced to form another wish.

I consider this mighty structure as a monument of the insufficiency of human enjoyments. A king, whose power is unlimited, and whose treasures surmount all real and imaginary wants, is compelled to solace, by the erection of a pyramid, the satiety of dominion and tastelessness of pleasures, and to amuse the tediousness of declining life, by seeing thousands laboring without end, and one stone, for no purpose, laid upon another. Whoever thou art, that, not content with a moderate condition, imaginest happiness in royal magnificence, and dreamest that command or riches can feed the appetite of novelty with perpetual gratifications, survey the pyramids, and confess thy folly!

1. Donne distinguishes between a prisoner confined to a cell and one given somewhat more liberty.
2. London prisoners were taken in carts from Newgate prison to nearby Tyburn for execution.
3. "Who [is] the man?"

LAURENCE STERNE:

Of Door Hinges and Life in General

Every day for at least ten years together did my father resolve to have it mended—'tis not mended yet: no family but ours would have borne with it an hour—and what is most astonishing, there was not a subject in the world upon which my father was so eloquent, as upon that of door-hinges. And yet at the same time, he was certainly one of the greatest bubbles to them, I think, that history can produce: his rhetoric and conduct were at perpetual handycuffs. Never did the parlor-door open—but his philosophy or his principles fell a victim to it; three drops of oyl with a feather, and a smart stroke of a hammer, had saved his honor for ever. Inconsistent soul that man is—languishing under wounds, which he has the power to heal—his whole life a contradiction to his knowledge—his reason, that precious gift of God to him—(instead of pouring in oyl) serving but to sharpen his sensibilities, to multiply his pains and render him more melancholy and uneasy under them—poor unhappy creature, that he should do so! Are not the necessary causes of misery in this life enow, but he must add voluntary ones to his stock of sorrow, struggle against evils which cannot be avoided, and submit to others, which a tenth part of the trouble they create him, would remove from his heart forever?

By all that is good and virtuous! if there are three drops of oyl to be got, and a hammer to be found within ten miles of Shandy-Hall, the parlor-door hinge shall be mended this reign.

CHARLES LAMB: The Two Races of Men

The human species, according to the best theory I can form of it, is composed of two distinct races, *the men who borrow*, and *the men who lend*. To these two original diversities may be reduced all those impertinent classifications of Gothic and Celtic tribes, white men, black men, red men. All the dwellers upon earth, "Parthians, and Medes, and Elamites," flock hither, and do naturally fall in with one or other of these primary distinctions. The infinite superiority of the former, which I choose to designate as the *great race*, is discernible in their figure, port, and a certain instinctive sovereignty. The latter are born degraded. "He shall serve his brethren." There is something in the air of one of this cast, lean and suspicious; contrasting with the open, trusting, generous manners of the other.

Observe who have been the greatest borrowers of all ages—Alcibiades—Falstaff—Sir Richard Steele—our late incomparable Brinsley—what a family likeness in all four!

What a careless, even deportment hath your borrower! what rosy gills! what a beautiful reliance on Providence doth he manifest—

taking no more thought than lilies! What contempt for money—accounting it (yours and mine especially) no better than dross. What a liberal confounding of those pedantic distinctions of *meum* and *tuum!* or rather, what a noble simplification of language (beyond Tooke), resolving these supposed opposites into one clear, intelligible pronoun adjective! What near approaches doth he make to the primitive *community*—to the extent of one half of the principle at least!

THOMAS DE QUINCEY:

Literature of Knowledge and Literature of Power

In that great social organ which, collectively, we call literature, there may be distinguished two separate offices that may blend and often do so, but capable, severally, of a severe insulation, and naturally fitted for reciprocal repulsion. There is, first, the literature of *knowledge*, and secondly, the literature of *power*. The function of the first is to *teach*; the function of the second is to *move*; the first is a rudder, the second an oar or a sail. The first speaks to the mere discursive understanding; the second speaks ultimately, it may happen, to the higher understanding or reason, but always through affections of pleasure and sympathy. Remotely, it may travel towards an object seated in what Lord Bacon calls *dry* light; but, proximately, it does and must operate—else it ceases to be a literature of *power*—and on through that *humid* light which clothes itself in the mists and glittering *iris* of human passions, desires, and genial emotions. Men have so little reflected on the higher functios of literature as to find it a paradox if one should describe it as a mean or subordinate purpose of books to give information. But this is a paradox only in the sense which makes it honorable to be paradoxical. Whenever we talk in ordinary language of seeking information or gaining knowledge, we understand the words as connected with something of absolute novelty. But it is the grandeur of all truth which *can* occupy a very high place in human interests that it is never absolutely novel to the meanest of minds: it exists eternally by way of germ or latent principle in the lowest as in the highest, needing to be developed, but never to be planted. To be capable of transplantation is the immediate criterion of a truth that ranges on a lower scale. Besides which, there is a rarer thing than truth—namely, *power*, or deep sympathy with truth. What is the effect, for instance, upon society, of children? By the pity, by the tenderness, and by the peculiar modes of admiration, which connect themselves with the helplessness, with the innocence, and with the simplicity of children, not only are the primal affections strengthened and continually renewed, but the qualities which are dearest in the sight of heaven—the frailty, for instance, which appeals to forbearance, the innocence which symbolizes the heavenly, and the simplicity which is most alien from the worldly—are kept up in perpetual remembrance, and their ideals are continually refreshed. A purpose of the same nature is answered by the high literature, viz., the literature of power. What do you learn from *Paradise Lost?* Nothing at all. What do you learn from a cookery book? Something new, something that you did not know before, in every paragraph. But would you therefore put the wretched cookery book on a higher level of estimation than the divine poem? What you owe to Milton is not any knowledge, of which a million separate items are still but a million of advancing steps on the same earthly level; what you owe is *power*—that is, exercise and expansion to your own latent capacity of sympathy with the infinite, where every pulse and each separate influx is a step upwards, a step ascending as upon a Jacob's ladder from earth to mysterious altitudes above the earth. *All* the steps of knowledge, from first to last, carry you further on the same plane, but could never raise you one foot above your ancient level of earth: whereas the very *first* step in power is a flight—is an ascending movement into another element where earth is forgotten.

JOHN HENRY NEWMAN: Knowledge and Virtue

Knowledge is one thing, virtue is another; good sense is not conscience, refinement is not humility, nor is largeness and justness of view faith. Philosophy, however enlightened, however profound, gives no command over the passions, no influential motives, no vivifying principles. Liberal Education makes not the Christian, not the Catholic, but the gentleman. It is well to be a gentleman, it is well to have a cultivated intellect, a delicate taste, a candid, equitable, dispassionate mind, a noble and courteous bearing in the conduct of life—these are the connatural qualities of a large knowledge; they are the objects of a University; I am advocating, I shall illustrate and insist upon them; but still, I repeat, they are no guarantee for sanctity or even for conscientiousness, they may attach to the man of the world, to the profligate, to the heartless, pleasant, alas, and attractive as he shows when decked out in them. Taken by themselves, they do but seem to be what they are not; they look like virtue at a distance, but they are detected by close observers, and on the long run; and hence it is that they are popularly accused of pretense and hypocrisy, not, I repeat, from their own fault, but because their professors and their admirers persist in taking them for what they are not, and are officious in arrogating for them a praise to which they have no claim. Quarry the granite rock with razors, or moor the vessel with a thread of silk; then may you hope with such keen and delicate instruments as human knowledge and human reason to contend against those giants, the passion and the pride of man.

MATTHEW ARNOLD: Culture

But there is of culture another view, in which not solely the scientific passion, the sheer desire to see things as they are, natural and proper in an intelligent being, appears as the ground of it. There is a view in which all the love of our neighbor, the impulses towards action, help, and beneficence, the desire for removing human error, clearing human confusion, and diminishing human misery, the noble aspiration to leave the world better and happier than we found it—motives eminently such as are called social—come in as part of the grounds of culture, and the main and pre-eminent part. Culture is then properly described not as having its origin in curiosity, but as having its origin in the love of perfection; it is *a study of perfection*. It moves by the force, not merely or primarily of the scientific passion for pure knowledge, but also of the moral and social passion for doing good. As, in the first view of it, we took for its worthy motto Montesquieu's words: "To render an intelligent being yet more intelligent!" so, in the second view of it, there is no better motto which it can have than these words of Bishop Wilson: "To make reason and the will of God prevail!"

Only, whereas the passion for doing good is apt to be overhasty in determining what reason and the will of God say, because its turn is for acting rather than thinking, and it wants to be beginning to act; and whereas it is apt to take its own conceptions, which proceed from its own state of development and share in all the imperfections and immaturities of this, for a basis of action; what distinguishes culture is, that it is possessed by the scientific passion as well as by the passion of doing good; that it demands worthy notions of reason and the will of God, and does not readily suffer its own crude conceptions to substitute themselves for them. And knowing that no action or institution can be salutary and stable which is not based on reason and the will of God, it is not so bent on acting and instituting, even with the great aim of diminishing human error and misery ever before its thoughts, but that it can remember that acting and instituting are of little use, unless we know how and what we ought to act and to institute.

WALTER PATER: The Mona Lisa

The presence that rose thus so strangely beside the waters, is expressive of what in the ways of a thousand years men had come to desire. Hers is the head upon which all "the ends of the world are come," and the eyelids are a little weary. It is a beauty wrought out from within upon the flesh, the deposit, little cell by cell, of strange thoughts and fantastic reveries and exquisite passions. Set it for a moment beside one of those white Greek goddesses or beautiful women of antiquity, and how would they be troubled by this beauty, into which the soul with all its maladies has passed! All the thoughts and experience of the world have etched and molded there, in that which they have of power to refine and make expressive the outward form, the animalism of Greece, the lust of Rome, the mysticism of the middle ages with its spiritual ambition and imaginative loves, the return of the Pagan world, the sins of the Borgias. She is older than the rocks among which she sits; like the vampire, she has been dead many times, and learned the secrets of the grave; and has been a diver in deep seas, and keeps their fallen day about her; and trafficked for strange webs with Eastern merchants: and, as Leda, was the mother of Helen of Troy, and, as Saint Anne, the mother of Mary; and all this has been to her but as the sound of lyres and flutes, and lives only in the delicacy with which it has molded the changing lineaments, and tinged the eyelids and the hands. The fancy of a perpetual life, sweeping together ten-thousand experiences, is an old one; and modern philosophy has conceived the idea of humanity as wrought upon by, and summing up in itself, all modes of thought and life. Certainly Lady Lisa might stand as the embodiment of the old fancy, the symbol of the modern idea.

JAMES THURBER: A Dog's Eye View of Man

If Man has benefited immeasurably by his association with the dog, what, you may ask, has the dog got out of it? His scroll has, of course, been heavily charged with punishments: he has known the muzzle, the leash, and the tether; he has suffered the indignities of the show bench, the tin can on the tail, the ribbon in the hair; his love life with the other sex of his species has been regulated by the frigid hand of authority, his digestion ruined by the macaroons and marshmallows of doting women. The list of his woes could be continued indefinitely. But he has also had his fun, for he has been privileged to live with and study at close range the only creature with reason, the most unreasonable of creatures.

The dog has got more fun out of Man than Man has got out of the dog, for the clearly demonstrable reason that Man is the more laughable of the two animals. The dog has long been bemused by the singular activities and the curious practices of men, cocking his head inquiringly to one side, intently watching and listening to the strangest goings-on in the world. He has seen men sing together and fight one another in the same evening. He has watched them go to bed when it is time to get up, and get up when it is time to go to bed. He has observed them destroying the soil in vast areas, and nurturing it in small patches. He has stood by while men built strong and solid houses for rest and quiet, and then filled them with lights and bells and machinery. His sensitive nose, which can detect what's cooking in the next township, has caught at one and the same time the bewildering smells of the hospital and the munitions factory. He has seen men raise up great cities to heaven and then blow them to hell.

E. B. WHITE: Progress and Change

In resenting progress and change, a man lays himself open to censure. I suppose the explanation of anyone's defending anything as rudimentary and cramped as a Pullman berth is that such things are associated with an earlier period in one's life and that this period in retrospect seems a happy one. People who favor progress and improvements are apt to be people who have had a tough enough time without any extra inconvenience. Reactionaries who pout at innovations are apt to be well-heeled sentimentalists who had the breaks. Yet for all that, there is always a subtle danger in life's refinements, a dim degeneracy in progress. I have just been refining the room in which I sit, yet I sometimes doubt that a writer should refine or improve his workroom by so much as a dictionary: one thing leads to another and the first thing you know he has a stuffed chair and is fast asleep in it. Half a man's life is devoted to what he calls improvements, yet the original had some quality which is lost in the process. There was a fine natural spring of water on this place when I bought it. Our drinking water had to be lugged in a pail, from a wet glade of alder and tamarack. I visited the spring often in those first years, and had friends there—a frog, a woodcock, and an eel which had churned its way all the way up through the pasture creek to enjoy the luxury of pure water. In the normal course of development, the spring was rocked up, fitted with a concrete curb, a copper pipe, and an electric pump. I have visited it only once or twice since. This year my only gesture was the purely perfunctory one of sending a sample to the state bureau of health for analysis. I felt cheap, as though I were smelling an old friend's breath.

VIRGINIA WOOLF: How Should One Read a Book?

It is simple enough to say that since books have classes—fiction, biography, poetry—we should separate them and take from each what it is right that each should give us. Yet few people ask from books what books can give us. Most commonly we come to books with blurred and divided minds, asking of fiction that it shall be true, of poetry that it shall be false, of biography that it shall be flattering, of history that it shall enforce our own prejudices. If we could banish all such preconceptions when we read, that would be an admirable beginning. Do not dictate to your author; try to become him. Be his fellow-worker and accomplice. If you hang back, and reserve and criticise at first, you are preventing yourself from getting the fullest possible value from what you read. But if you open your mind as widely as possible, then signs and hints of almost imperceptible fineness, from the twist and turn of the first sentences, will bring you into the presence of a human being unlike any other. Steep yourself in this, acquaint yourself with this, and soon you will find that your author is giving you, or attempting to give you, something far more definite. The thirty-two chapters of a novel—if we consider how to read a novel first—are an attempt to make something as formed and controlled as a building: but words are more impalpable than bricks; reading is a longer and more complicated process than seeing. Perhaps the quickest way to understand the elements of what a novelist is doing is not to read, but to write; to make your own experiment with the dangers and difficulties of words. Recall, then, some event that has left a distinct impression on you—how at the corner of the street, perhaps, you passed two people talking. A tree shook; an electric light danced; the tone of the talk was comic, but also tragic; a whole vision, an entire conception, seemed contained in that moment.

But when you attempt to reconstruct it in words, you will find that it breaks into a thousand conflicting impressions. Some must be subdued; others emphasised; in the process you will lose, probably, all grasp upon the emotion itself. Then turn from your blurred and littered pages to the opening pages of some great novelist—Defoe, Jane Austen, Hardy. Now you will be better able to appreciate their mastery. It is not merely that we are in the presence of a different person—Defoe, Jane Austen, or Thomas Hardy —but that we are living in a different world. Here, in *Robinson Crusoe*, we are trudging a plain high road; one thing happens after another; the fact and the order of the fact is enough. But if the open air and adventure mean everything to Defoe they mean nothing to Jane Austen. Hers is the drawing-room, and people talking, and by the many mirrors of their talk revealing their characters. And if, when we have accustomed ourselves to the drawing-room and its reflections, we turn to Hardy, we are once more spun around. The moors are round us and the stars are above our heads. The other side of the mind is now exposed—the dark side that comes uppermost in solitude, not the light side that shows in company. Our relations are not towards people, but towards Nature and destiny. Yet different as these worlds are, each is consistent with itself. The maker of each is careful to observe the laws of his own perspective, and however great a strain they may put upon us they will never confuse us, as lesser writers so frequently do, by introducing two different kinds of reality into the same book. Thus to go from one great novelist to another—from Jane Austen to Hardy, from Peacock to Trollope, from Scott to Meredith—is to be wrenched and uprooted; to be thrown this way and then that. To read a novel is a difficult and complex art. You must be capable not only of great finesse of perception, but of great boldness of imagination if you are going to make use of all that the novelist—the great artist—gives you.

TONI MORRISON: Three Merry Gargoyles

Three merry gargoyles. Three merry harridans. Amused by a long-ago time of ignorance. They did not belong to those generations of prostitutes created in novels, with great and generous hearts, dedicated, because of the horror of circumstance, to ameliorating the luckless, barren life of men, taking money incidentally and humbly for their "understanding." Nor were they from that sensitive breed of young girl, gone wrong at the hands of fate, forced to cultivate an outward brittleness in order to protect her springtime from further shock, but knowing full well she was cut out for better things, and could make the right man happy. Neither were they the sloppy, inadequate whores who, unable to make a living at it alone, turn to drug consumption and traffic or pimps to help complete their scheme of self-destruction, avoiding suicide only to punish the memory of some absent father or to sustain the misery of some silent mother. Except for Marie's fabled love for Dewey Prince, these women hated men, all men, without shame, apology, or discrimination. They abused their visitors with a scorn grown mechanical from use. Black men, white men, Puerto Ricans, Mexicans, Jews, Poles, whatever—all were inadequate and weak, all came under their jaundiced eyes and were the recipients of their disinterested wrath. They took delight in cheating them. On one occasion the town well knew, they lured a Jew up the stairs, pounced on him, all three, held him up by the heels, shook everything out of his pants pockets, and threw him out of the window.

Neither did they have respect for women, who, although not their colleagues, so to speak, nevertheless deceived their husbands —regularly or irregularly, it made no difference. "Sugar-coated whores," they called them, and did not yearn to be in their shoes. Their only respect was for what they would have described as "good Christian colored women." The woman whose reputation was spotless, and who tended to her family, who didn't drink or smoke or run around. These women had their undying, if covert, affection. They would sleep with their husbands, and take their money, but always with a vengeance.

Nor were they protective and solicitous of youthful innocence. They looked back on their own youth as a period of ignorance, and regretted that they had not made more of it. They were not young girls in whores' clothing, or whores regretting their loss of innocence. They were whores in whores' clothing, whores who had never been young and had no word for innocence. With Pecola they were as free as they were with each other. Marie concocted stories for her because she was a child, but the stories were breezy and rough. If

Pecola had announced her intention to live the life they did, they would not have tried to dissuade her or voiced any alarm.

JOYCE CARY: Art and Education

A very large number of people cease when quite young to add anything to a limited stock of judgments. After a certain age, say 25, they consider that their education is finished.

It is perhaps natural that having passed through that painful and boring process, called expressly education, they should suppose it over, and that they are equipped for life to label every event as it occurs and drop it into its given pigeonhole. But one who has a label ready for everything does not bother to observe any more, even such ordinary happenings as he has observed for himself, with attention, before he went to school. He merely acts and reacts.

For people who have stopped noticing, the only possible new or renewed experience, and, therefore, new knowledge, is from a work of art. Because that is the only kind of experience which they are prepared to receive on its own terms, they will come out from their shells and expose themselves to music, to a play, to a book, because it is the accepted method of enjoying such things. True, even to plays and books they may bring artistic prejudices which prevent them from seeing *that* play or comprehending *that* book. Their artistic sensibilities may be as crusted over as their minds.

But it is part of an artist's job to break crusts, or let us say rather that artists who work for the public and not merely for themselves are interested in breaking crusts because they want to communicate their intuitions.

JOHN STEINBECK: The Danger of Small Things

I guess it is true that big and strong things are much less dangerous than small soft weak things. Nature (whatever that is) makes the small and weak reproduce faster. And that is not true of course. The ones that did not reproduce faster than they died, disappeared. But how about little faults, little pains, little worries. The cosmic ulcer comes not from great concerns, but from little irritations. And great things can kill a man but if they do not he is stronger and better for them. A man is destroyed by the duck nibblings of nagging, small bills, telephones (wrong number), athlete's foot, ragweed, the common cold, boredom. All of these are the negatives, the tiny frustrations, and no one is stronger for them.

JOHN UPDIKE: Beer Can

This seems to be an era of gratuitous inventions and negative improvements. Consider the beer can. It was beautiful—as beautiful as the clothespin, as inevitable as the wine bottle, as dignified and reassuring as the fire hydrant. A tranquil cylinder of delightfully resonant metal, it could be opened in an instant, requiring only the application of a handy gadget freely dispensed by every grocer. Who can forget the small, symmetrical thrill of those two triangular punctures, the dainty *pffff*, the little crest of suds that foamed eagerly in the exultation of release? Now we are given, instead, a top beetling with an ugly, shmoo-shaped "tab," which, after fiercely resisting the tugging, bleeding fingers of the thirsty man, threatens his lips with a dangerous and hideous hole. However, we have discovered a way to thwart Progress, usually so unthwartable. *Turn the beer can upside down and open the bottom.* The bottom is still the way the top used to be. True, this operation gives the beer an unsettling jolt, and the sight of a consistently inverted beer can might make people edgy, not to say queasy. But the latter difficulty could be eliminated if manufacturers would design cans that looked the same whichever end was up, like playing cards. What we need is Progress with an escape hatch.

TOM WOLFE: The Legend of Junior Johnson

The legend of Junior Johnson! In this legend, here is a country boy, Junior Johnson, who learns to drive by running whiskey for his father, Johnson, Senior, one of the biggest copper-still operators of all time, up in Ingle Hollow, near North Wilkesboro, in northwestern North Carolina, and grows up to be a famous stock car racing driver, rich, grossing $100,000 in 1963, for example, respected, solid, idolized in his hometown and throughout the rural South. There is all this about how good old boys would wake up in the middle of the night in the apple shacks and hear a supercharged Oldsmobile engine roaring over Brushy Mountain and say, "Listen at him—there he goes!" although that part is doubtful, since some nights there were so many good old boys taking off down the road in supercharged automobiles out of Wilkes County, and running loads to Charlotte, Salisbury, Greensboro, Winston-Salem, High Point, or wherever, it would be pretty hard to pick out one. It was Junior Johnson, specifically, however, who was famous for the "bootleg turn" or "about-face," in which, if the Alcohol Tax agents had a roadblock up for you or were too close behind, you threw the car up into second gear, cocked the wheel, stepped on the accelerator and made the car's rear end skid around in a complete 180-degree arc, a complete about-face, and tore on back up the road exactly the way you came from. God! The Alcohol Tax agents used to burn over Junior Johnson. Practically every good old boy in town in Wilkesboro, the county seat, got to know the agents by sight in a very short time. They would rag them practically to their faces on the subject of Junior Johnson, so that it got to be an obsession. Finally, one night they had Junior trapped on the road up toward the bridge around Millersville, there's no way out of there, they had the barricades up and they could hear this souped-up car roaring around the bend, and here it comes—but suddenly they can hear a siren and see a red light flashing in the grille, so they think it's another agent, and boy, they run out like ants and pull those barrels and boards and sawhorses out of the way, and then—Ggghhzzzzzzzzhhhhhh-gggggggzzzzzzzeeeeeong!—gawdam! there he goes again, it was him, Junior Johnson! with a gawdam agent's sireen and a red light in his grille!

ROBERT PIRSIG: Concrete, Brick, and Neon[1]

The city closes in on him now, and in his strange perspective it becomes the antithesis of what he believes. The citadel not of Qual-ity, the citadel of form and substance. Substance in the form of steel sheets and girders, substance in the form of concrete piers and roads, in the form of brick, of asphalt, of auto parts, old radios, and rails, dead carcasses of animals that once grazed the prairies. Form and substance without Quality. That is the soul of this place. Blind, huge, sinister and inhuman: seen by the light of fire flaring upward in the night from the blast furnaces in the south, through heavy coal smoke deeper and denser into the neon of BEER and PIZZA and LAUNDROMAT signs and unknown and meaningless signs along meaningless straight streets going off into other straight streets for-ever.

If it was all bricks and concrete, pure forms of substance, clearly and openly, he might survive. It is the little, pathetic attempts at Quality that kill. The plaster false fireplace in the apartment, shaped and waiting to contain a flame that can never exist. Or the hedge in front of the apartment building with a few square feet of grass behind it. A few square feet of grass, after Montana. If they just left out the hedge and grass it would be all right. Now it serves only to draw attention to what has been lost.

Along the streets that lead away from the apartment he can never see anything through the concrete and brick and neon but he knows that buried within it are grotesque, twisted souls forever trying the manners that will convince themselves they possess Quality, learn-ing strange poses of style and glamour vended by dream magazines and other mass media, and paid for by the vendors of substance. He thinks of them at night alone with their advertised glamorous shoes and stockings and underclothes off, staring through the sooty win-dows at the grotesque shells revealed beyond them, when the poses weaken and the truth creeps in, the only truth that exists here, crying to heaven, God, there is nothing here but dead neon and cement and brick.

1. Pp. 338–89 from *Zen and the Art of Motorcycle Maintenance* (1975).

JONATHAN SCHELL: Law in the United States

In the United States, the role of the law in defining the shape of political life is of particular importance. For in the United States, where the national government and the nation itself were brought formally into existence when the states ratified the Constitution, the very being of the government is founded in law. The Founding Fathers' act of creation was a legal act, and the institutions they framed were defined and empowered by law. In the American system, the law is more than a set of restrictions, and more, even, than a universal code of justice; it is to the nation's institutions the breath of the creator. The people decide in elections who will man the institutions, but the law continues to define what the institutions are. It binds them together into a whole that can be seen, understood, and brought to account, and that works. And since, in the United States, customs, communities, and even buildings tend to be rubbed out almost as soon as they appear, there is very little in the way of tradition for the nation to fall back on if legal forms break down. If the controlling, molding influence of the law declines, then the outlines of the political system itself blur and eventually disappear. Institutions, no longer able to grasp firmly what is expected of them and what they are, grow slovenly and mis-shapen, and wander away from their appointed tasks in the Constitutional scheme. Roles and jurisdictions clash and become confused, power goes to whoever grabs it, and the system warps and sags and heads toward collapse.

Guidelines for Equal Treatment of the Sexes in McGraw-Hill Book Company Publications[1]

The word *sexism* was coined, by analogy to *racism*, to denote discrimination based on gender. In its original sense, *sexism* referred to prejudice against the female sex. In a broader sense, the term now indicates any arbitrary stereotyping of males and females on the basis of their gender.

We are endeavoring through these guidelines to eliminate sexist assumptions from McGraw-Hill Book Company publications and to encourage a greater freedom for all individuals to pursue their interests and realize their potentials. Specifically, these guidelines are designed to make McGraw-Hill staff members and McGraw-Hill authors aware of the ways in which males and females have been stereotyped in publications; to show the role language has played in reinforcing inequality; and to indicate positive approaches toward

---

1. Reprinted by permission of Mc Graw-Hill Book Company.

providing fair, accurate, and balanced treatment of both sexes in our publications.

One approach is to recruit more women as authors and contributors in all fields. The writings and viewpoints of women should be represented in quotations and references whenever possible. Anthologies should include a larger proportion of selections by and about women in fields where suitable materials are available but women are currently underrepresented.

Women as well as men have been leaders and heroes, explorers and pioneers, and have made notable contributions to science, medicine, law, business, politics, civics, economics, literature, the arts, sports, and other areas of endeavor. Books dealing with subjects like these, as well as general histories, should acknowledge the achievements of women. The fact that women's rights, opportunities, and accomplishments have been limited by the social customs and conditions of their time should be openly discussed whenever relevant to the topic at hand.

We realize that the language of literature cannot be prescribed. The recommendations in these guidelines, thus, are intended primarily for use in teaching materials, reference works, and nonfiction works in general.

Nonsexist Treatment of Women and Men

Men and women should be treated primarily as people, and not primarily as members of opposite sexes. Their shared humanity and common attributes should be stressed not their gender difference. Neither sex should be stereotyped or arbitrarily assigned to a leading or secondary role.

1.

a. Though many women will continue to choose traditional occupations such as homemaker or secretary, women should not be type-cast in these roles but shown in a wide variety of professions and trades: as doctors and dentists, not always as nurses; as principals and professors, not always as teachers; as lawyers and judges, not always as social workers; as bank presidents, not always as tellers; as members of Congress, not always as members of the League of Women Voters.

b. Similarly, men should not be shown as constantly subject to the "masculine mystique" in their interests, attitudes, or careers. They should not be made to feel that their self-worth depends entirely upon their income level or the status level of their jobs. They should not be conditioned to believe that a man ought to earn more than a woman or that he ought to be the sole support of a family.

c. An attempt should be made to break job stereotypes for both women and men. No job should be considered sex-typed, and it should never be implied that certain jobs are incompatible with a woman's "femininity" or a man's "masculinity." Thus, women as well as men should be shown as accountants, engineers, pilots, plumbers, bridge-builders, computer operators, TV repairers, and astronauts, while men as well as women should be shown as nurses, grade-school teachers, secretaries, typists, librarians, file clerks, switchboard operators, and baby-sitters.

Women within a profession should be shown at all professional levels, including the top levels. Women should be portrayed in positions of authority over men and over other women, and there should be no implication that a man loses face or that a woman faces difficulty if the employer or supervisor is a woman. All work should be treated as honorable and worthy of respect; no job or job choices should be downgraded. Instead, women and men should be offered more options than were available to them when work was stereotyped by sex.

d. Books designed for children at the pre-school, elementary, and secondary levels should show married women who work outside the home and should treat them favorably. Teaching materials should not assume or imply that most women are wives who are also full-time mothers, but should instead emphasize the fact that women have choices about their marital status, just as men do: that some women choose to stay permanently single and some are in no hurry to marry; that some women marry but do not have children, while others marry, have children, and continue to work outside the home. Thus, a text might say that some married people have children and some do not, and that sometimes *one or both parents* work outside the home. Instructional materials should never imply that all women have a "mother instinct" or that the emotional life of a family suffers because a woman works. Instead they might state that when both parents work outside the home there is usually either greater sharing of the child-rearing activities or reliance on day-care centers, nursery schools, or other help.

According to Labor Department statistics for 1972, over 42 per cent of all mothers with children under 18 worked outside the home, and about a third of these working mothers had children under 6. Publications ought to reflect this reality.

Both men and women should be shown engaged in home maintenance activities, ranging from cooking and housecleaning to washing the car and making household repairs. Sometimes the man should be shown preparing the meals, doing the laundry, or diapering the baby, while the woman builds bookcases or takes out the trash.

e. Girls should be shown as having, and exercising, the same options as boys in their play and career choices. In school materials, girls should be encouraged to show an interest in mathematics, mechanical skills, and active sports, for example, while boys should never be made to feel ashamed of an interest in poetry, art, or music, or an aptitude for cooking, sewing, or child care. Course materials should be addressed to students of both sexes. For example, home economics courses should apply to boys as well as girls, and shop to girls as well as boys. Both males and females should be shown in textbook illustrations depicting career choices.

When as a practical matter it is known that a book will be used primarily by women for the life of the edition (say, the next five years), it is pointless to pretend that the readership is divided equally between males and females. In such cases it may be more beneficial to address the book fully to women and exploit every opportunity (1) to point out to them a broader set of options than they might otherwise have considered, and (2) to encourage them to aspire to a more active, assertive, and policy-making role than they might otherwise have thought of.

f. Women and girls should be portrayed as active participants in the same proportion as men and boys in stories, examples, problems, illustrations, discussion questions, test items, and exercises, regardless of subject matter. Women should not be stereotyped in examples by being spoken of only in connection with cooking, sewing, shopping, and similar activities.

2.

a. Members of both sexes should be represented as whole human beings with *human* strengths and weaknesses, not masculine or feminine ones. Women and girls should be shown as having the same abilities, interests, and ambitions as men and boys. Characteristics that have been traditionally praised in males—such as boldness, initiative, and assertiveness—should also be praised in females. Characteristics that have been praised in females—such as gentleness, compassion, and sensitivity—should also be praised in males.

b. Like men and boys, women and girls should be portrayed as independent, active, strong, courageous, competent, decisive, persistent, serious-minded, and successful. They should appear as logical thinkers, problem-solvers, and decision makers. They should be shown as interested in their work, pursuing a variety of career goals, and both deserving of and receiving public recognition for their accomplishments.

c. Sometimes men should be shown as quiet and passive, or fearful and indecisive, or illogical and immature. Similarly, women should sometimes be shown as tough, aggressive, and insensitive. Stereotypes of the logical, objective male and the emotional, subjective female are to be avoided. In descriptions, the smarter, braver, or more successful person should be a woman or girl as often as a man or boy. In illustrations, the taller, heavier, stronger, or more active person should not always be male, especially when children are portrayed.

3.

Women and men should be treated with the same respect, dignity, and seriousness. Neither should be trivialized or stereotyped, either in text or in illustrations. Women should not be described by physical attributes when men are being described by mental attributes or professional position. Instead, both sexes should be dealt with in the same terms. References to a man's or a woman's appearance, charm, or intuition should be avoided when irrelevant.

no	*yes*
Henry Harris is a shrewd lawyer and his wife Ann is a striking brunette.	The Harrises are an attractive couple. Henry is a handsome blond and Ann is a striking brunette.

or

The Harrises are highly respected in their fields. Ann is an accomplished musician and Henry is a shrewd lawyer.

The Harrises are an interesting couple. Henry is a shrewd lawyer and Ann is very active in community (*or* church *or* civic) affairs.

a. In descriptions of women, a patronizing or girl-watching tone should be avoided, as should sexual innuendoes, jokes, and puns. Examples of practices to be avoided: focusing on physical appearance (a buxom blonde); using special female-gender word forms (poetess, aviatrix, usherette); treating women as sex objects or portraying the typical woman as weak, helpless, or hysterical; making women figures of fun or objects of scorn and treating their issues as humorous or unimportant.

Examples of stereotypes to be avoided: scatterbrained female, fragile flower, goddess on a pedestal, catty gossip, henpecking shrew, apron-wearing mother, frustrated spinster, ladylike little girl. Jokes at women's expense—such as the woman driver or nagging mother-in-law cliches—are to be avoided.

no	*yes*
the fair sex; the weaker sex	women
the distaff side	the female side or line
the girls or *the ladies* (when adult females are meant)	the women
girl, as in: I'll have my *girl* check that.	I'll have my *secretary* (or my *assistant*) check that. (Or use the person's name.)
lady used as a modifier, as in *lady* lawyer	lawyer (A woman may be identified simply through the choice of pronouns, as in: *The lawyer made her summation to the jury.* Try to avoid gender modifiers altogether. When you *must* modify, use *woman* or *female*, as in: *a course on women writers*, or *the airline's first female pilot*.)
the little woman; the better half; the ball and chain	wife
female-gender word forms, such as *authoress, poetess, Jewess*	author, poet, Jew
female-gender or diminutive word forms, such as *suffragette, usherette, aviatrix*	suffragist, usher, aviator (or pilot)
libber (a put-down)	feminist; liberationist
sweet young thing	young woman; girl
co-ed (as a noun)	student

(*Note:* Logically, *co-ed* should refer to any student at a co-educational college or university. Since it does not, it is a sexist term.)

housewife	homemaker for a person who works at home, or rephrase with a more precise or more inclusive term
The sound of the drilling disturbed the housewives in the neighborhood.	The sound of the drilling disturbed everyone within earshot (or everyone in the neighborhood).

Housewives are feeling the pinch of higher prices	Consumers (customers or shoppers) are feeling the pinch of higher prices.
career girl or *career woman*	name the woman's profession: *attorney Ellen Smith; Maria Sanchez, a journalist* or editor or business executive or doctor or lawyer or agent
cleaning woman, cleaning lady, or *maid*	*housekeeper; house* or *office cleaner*

b. In descriptions of men, especially men in the home, references to general ineptness should be avoided. Men should not be characterized as dependent on women for meals, or clumsy in household maintenance, or as foolish in self-care.

To be avoided: characterizations that stress men's dependence on women for advice on what to wear and what to eat, inability of men to care for themselves in times of illness, and men as objects of fun (the henpecked husband).

c. Women should be treated as part of the rule, not as the exception.

Generic terms, such as doctor and nurse, should be assumed to include both men and women, and modified titles such as "woman doctor" or "male nurse," should be avoided. Work should never be stereotyped as "woman's work" or as "a man-sized job." Writers should avoid showing a "gee-whiz" attitude toward women who perform competently; ("Though a woman, she ran the business as well as any man" or "Though a woman, she ran the business efficiently.")

d. Women should be spoken of as participants in the action, not as possessions of the men. Terms such as *pioneer, farmer,* and *settler* should not be used as though they applied only to adult males.

no	*yes*
Pioneers moved West, taking their wives and children with them.	Pioneer families moved West.
	Pioneer men and women (*or* pioneer couples) moved West, taking their children with them.

e. Women should not be portrayed as needing male permission in order to act or to exercise rights (except, of course, for historical or factual accuracy).

| no | yes |
| Jim Weiss allows his wife to work part-time. | Judy Weiss works part-time. |

4.

Women should be recognized for their own achievements. Intelligent, daring, and innovative women, both in history and in fiction, should be provided as role-models for girls, and leaders in the fight for women's rights should be honored and respected, not mocked or ignored.

5.

In references to humanity at large, language should operate to include women and girls. Terms that tend to exclude females should be avoided whenever possible.

a. The word *man* has long been used not only to denote a person of male gender, but also generically to denote humanity at large. To many people today, however, the word *man* has become so closely associated with the first meaning (a male human being) that they consider it no longer broad enough to be applied to any person or to human beings as a whole. In deference to this position, alternative expressions should be used in place of *man* (or derivative constructions used generically to signify humanity at large) whenever such substitutions can be made without producing an awkward or artificial construction. In cases where *man*-words must be used, special efforts should be made to ensure that pictures and other devices make explicit that such references include women.

Here are some possible substitutions for *man*-words:

no	yes
mankind	humanity, human beings, human race, people
primitive man	primitive people or peoples; primitive human beings; primitive men and women
man's achievements	human achievements
If a man drove 50 miles at 60 mph . . .	If a person (or driver) drove 50 miles at 60 mph . . .
the best man for the job	the best person (or candidate) for the job
manmade	artificial; synthetic, manufactured; constructed; of human origin

| manpower | human power; human energy; workers; workforce |
| grow to manhood | grow to adulthood; grow to manhood or womanhood |

b. The English language lacks a generic singular pronoun signifying *he* or *she*, and therefore it has been customary and grammatically sanctioned to use masculine pronouns in expressions such as "one . . . *he*," "anyone . . . *he*," and "each child opens *his* book." Nevertheless, avoid when possible the pronouns *he*, *him*, and *his* in reference to the hypothetical person or humanity in general.

Various alternatives may be considered:

(1) Reword to eliminate unnecessary gender pronouns.

no	yes
The average American drinks his coffee black	The average American drinks black coffee.
(2) Recast into the plural.	Most Americans drink their coffee black.

(3) Replace the masculine pronoun with *one, you, he* or *she, her* or *his*, as appropriate. (Use *he* or *she* and its variations sparingly to avoid clumsy prose.)

(4) Alternate male and female expressions and examples.

| no | yes |
| I've often heard supervisors say, "He's not the right man for the job," or "He lacks the qualifications for success." | I've often heard supervisors say, "She's not the right person for the job," or "He lacks the qualifications for success." |

(5) To avoid severe problems of repetition or inept wording, it may sometimes be best to use the generic *he* freely, but to add, in the preface and as often as necessary in the text, emphatic statements to the effect that the masculine pronouns are being used for succinctness and are intended to refer to both females and males.

These guidelines can only suggest a few solutions to difficult problems of rewording. The proper solution in any given passage must depend on the context and on the author's intention. For example, it would be wrong to pluralize in contexts stressing a one-to-one relationship, as between teacher and child. In such cases, either using the expression *he or she* or alternating *he* and *she*, as appropriate, will be acceptable.

c. Occupational terms ending in *man* should be replaced whenever possible by terms that can include members of either sex unless they refer to a particular person.

no	yes
congressman	member of Congress; representative (but *Congressman* Koch and *Congresswoman* Holtzman)
businessman	business executive; business manager
fireman	fire fighter
mailman	mail carrier; letter carrier
salesman	sales representative; salesperson; sales clerk
insurance man	insurance agent
statesman	leader; public servant
chairman	the person presiding at (or chairing) a meeting; the presiding officer; the chair; head leader; coordinator; moderator
cameraman	camera operator
foreman	supervisor

d. Language that assumes all readers are male should be avoided.

no	yes
you and your wife	you and your spouse
when you shave in the morning	when you brush your teeth (or wash up) in the morning

6.

The language used to designate and describe females and males should treat the sexes equally.

a. Parallel language should be used for women and men.

no	yes
the men and the ladies	the men and the women
	the ladies and the gentlemen
	the girls and the boys
man and wife	husband and wife

Note that *lady* and *gentleman, wife* and *husband,* and *mother* and *father* are role words. *Ladies* should be used for women only when men are being referred to as *gentlemen.* Similarly, women should be called *wives* and *mothers* only when men are referred to as *husbands* and *fathers.* Like a male shopper, a woman in a grocery store should be called a *customer, not a housewife.*

b. Women should be identified by their own names (e.g., Indira Gandhi). They should not be referred to in terms of their roles as wife, mother, sister, or daughter unless it is in these roles that they are significant in context. Nor should they be identified in terms of their marital relationships (Mrs. Gandhi) unless this brief form is stylistically more convenient (than, say Prime Minister Gandhi) or is paired up with similar references to men.

(1) A woman should be referred to by name in the same way that a man is. Both should be called by their full names, by first or last name only, or by title.

no	*yes*
Bobby Riggs and Billie Jean	Bobby Riggs and Billie Jean King
Billie Jean and Riggs	Billie Jean and Bobby
Mrs. King and Riggs	King and Riggs
	Ms. King (because she prefers Ms.) and Mr. Riggs
Mrs. Meir and Moshe Dayan	Golda Meir and Moshe Dayan or Mrs. Meir and Dr. Dayan

(2) Unnecessary reference to or emphasis on a woman's marital status should be avoided. Whether married or not, a woman may be referred to by the name by which she chooses to be known, whether her name is her original name or her married name.

c. Whenever possible, a term should be used that includes both sexes. Unnecessary references to gender should be avoided.

no	*yes*
college boys and co-eds	students

d. Insofar as possible, job titles should be nonsexist. Different nomenclature should not be used for the same job depending on whether it is held by a male or by a female. (See also paragraph 5c for additional examples of words ending in *man.*)

no	*yes*
steward or purser or stewardess	flight attendant
policeman and policewoman	police officer
maid and houseboy	house or office cleaner; servant

e. Different pronouns should not be linked with certain work or occupations on the assumption that the worker is always (or usually) female or male. Instead either pluralize or use *he or she* and *she or he.*

no	*yes*
the consumer or shopper . . . she	consumers or shoppers . . . they
the secretary . . . she	secretaries . . . they
the breadwinner . . . his earnings	the breadwinner . . . his or her earnings *or* breadwinners . . . their earnings.

f. Males should not always be first in order of mention. Instead, alternate the order, sometimes using: *women and men, gentlemen and ladies, she or he, her or his.*

Conclusion

It is hoped that these guidelines have alerted authors and staff members to the problems of sex discrimination and to various ways of solving them.

QUESTIONS

1. What assumptions about the powers and functions of language underlie these guidelines?
2. Racism and sexism represent discrimination on the basis of race or sex. What other kinds of discrimination exist in our society? Invent an analogous term for one of these and write a brief characterization of it.
3. "Discriminate" and "discrimination" originally had to do simply with the act of "distinguishing" or finding "distinguishing features." Explain the relationship between these earlier meanings and our current one connected with prejudice. Does the perception of distinctions or differences necessarily lead to prejudice?
4. Using the guidelines in the essay, examine a newspaper, a magazine, or a textbook for examples of sexism. Try to determine which examples reflect unconscious prejudice.
5. Study the examples in the guidelines carefully. Will the guidelines lead to greater clarity or precision? Less? Discuss.

JACQUES BARZUN

Was Paul Revere a Minute Person?

Early last spring I received as member of a large and elderly professional association a committee report signed with two names.

Each was identified as *Co-chairperson* of the committee. The designation was not then new to me, but for some reason the pathos of attaching such a label to live fellow workers struck me with fresh force, and in my sadness I began to reflect on the cause.

Obviously, the reason for using *person* was to avoid man, now felt to be the sign of an arrogant imperialism. And in the background, no doubt, was the further wish to get rid of sex reference altogether, to confirm equality by insisting on our common humanness. With the last intention no one will quarrel. The only question is whether it can be served so usefully by terminology that language has to be wrenched out of shape, on top of being misunderstood.

For the pity of the matter is that *man*, in *chairman* and elsewhere, still means *person*, as it does etymologically. As far back as the Sanskrit *manus*, the root *man* means *human being*, with no implication of sex. The German *Mann* and *Mensch*, the Latin *homo* (from which derives the name *human* that we so passionately seek) originally denote the *kind* of creature we all are. *Homo Sapiens* means male and female alike. For the male sort, the words were *vir* in Latin, *wer* in Old English (as in *wergeld*, the fine for a crime). *Woman* is the contraction of *wīf-man*, the she-person.

To be sure, confusion set in early, as one would expect, and in the evolution of the Germanic and Romance languages *Mann*, *Mensch*, *man*, *homo*, *homme*, and *vir*, as well as *wīf*, *wife*, *weib*, and *woman*, usurped one or another's place. Virtue, for example, lost its exclusively male tone and became a pre-eminently female attribute. The point to remember is that the meanings switch back and forth, not just one way. In modern German *man sagt*, meaning *they say*, is a common singular for both genders. In French, the *on* of the corresponding *on dit* is *homo* whittled down and flouting *homme* by meaning either he or she. In English, *man* and *woman* acquired their present differentiation without depriving *man* of its universal, unisex meaning. As an Act of Parliament in 1878 reminded the world in platitudinous terms, "man embraces woman." Unless limited by context, *mankind* means and has always meant humanity entire. It includes the child, who is—in the other sense of the words—neither man nor woman. Tribal names—Norsemen, Norman, German, Allemand (*Alle Männer*)—are likewise inclusive by their very form.

The present urge to tamper with these familiar notions and nuances is foolishly misdirected. A colleague tells me that he recently gave a new departmental secretary a book note to type, in a great hurry at the end of the day. The young woman was most obliging and pleasant about it and turned out clean copy in a few minutes. My friend took it home to proofread and found it perfect, except for a mysterious gap near the end. A three-letter space had been left after the puzzling word *spokes*. The next day he gingerly askd the girl to explain. She replied quietly that she belonged to a group that had vowed never to type in full the words *chairman,* *spokesman,* and the like. Does the embargo by these earnest souls extend to *woman?*

No one denies that words are powerful symbols of feeling and attitude and, as such, solid parts of the social structure. That is why from time to time it seems as if to change the structure one need only change the words. The trouble is that the effort can never be thorough and effectual. Language is too subtle, and the force of common speech, set in its course by the generations, sweeps the censor away like a twig in a torrent. Suppose you get rid of *chairman* and *spokesman* by dint of not typing them. What will you do with *fireman; minute man, Frenchman?* "She phoned and the firepersons came." "Paul Revere was a minute person." Honestly! As for the *Frenchperson,* some fool will want to know whether "it" was a he or a she, while another will mutilate *dragoman,* mistaking it for a native compound with *man* like the rest.

The esthetic sense, not to say the art of literature, is implicated in this silly game. *Person* is not a word to cherish and ubiquitize. Who does not feel that in its most general sense, which asserts anonymity, the word is disagreeably hoity-toity: "There is a person at the door"? In the classic English novel the *young person* holds an ambiguous place—always a she, but now unsavory, now requiring protection. The very etymology of *person* is in doubt, though in mid-career at Rome it certainly had associations with the emptiness of a mask—*persona.* In French, indeed, it often means *nobody:* "Who's there?"—"*Personne.*" Compare, in American speech, "certain persons believe . . ." with the vernacular: "some people think. . . ."

The advertiser's conception of the person ("let us personalize your paper towels"—as if your initials were your self) is another reason for putting the word in frequent quarantine. Let loose, it tempts to such absurdities as: "I want to enjoy my personal life," "he sold his personal library," and to the appalling compliment: "She's a very real person." In any case, sound and length unsuit it for spontaneous use in dozens of ordinary places: "Yes, the river's dammed; it's a personmade lake." "She had to be personhandled to get her out of the bar."

It is no new discovery that in its ways of marking gender English is capricious and inconvenient. Perhaps it was a good thing to drop the gender of nouns (though reference by pronoun would often benefit from its presence), but it was not sensible to keep gender in the possessives without allowing one of them to indicate either or both genders indifferently. Just as we miss a *man sagt* or *on dit* and must resort to the plural *they,* so we are commonly driven to: "Has everybody got *their* ticket?" To use *his-or-her* (*her-or-his*) as often as it would be needed in a single sentence or paragraph is quite impracticable.

This is not to say that the use of gender words in English has stood still. Notice *it* and *its* in Shakespeare. At some point since Wordsworth wrote "A little child, what should it know of death?" a preference developed for referring to children as he or she—to "personalize" them. And in that same interval we have laudably got rid of *poetess* and *authoress*, as well as of the short-lived *doctress* and *paintress*, which some early feminists demanded as their right. Who can tell whether the road to equality lies through signalizing sex or ignoring it? If credit is wanted, then women workers and doers must be readily known by their titles, and *poetess* returns. But if "minority" feeling is to merge in a unisex psyche, then not even "the way of a man with a maid" dare be mentioned: the way is the same for both.

In the *person* binge of today this uncertainty remains, for Hannah and Harold still give away the co-chairpersons' sexual affiliation. Will the next move be toward first names amputated so as to be undetectable, on the model of *Ms*? If English is thus in need of revision and reform (as Strindberg said of the multiplication table) the task ahead is formidable. Will it not be necessary to ostracize *virtue* because of its masculine taint? Will not men denounce the inequity of calling *all* ships "she" and women the injustice of employing the officer known as the "ship's husband"? And what of the naval she which is a *man-of-war*? *Warperson?* . .

Nor will it end with the unhappy English tongue. Sex is a source of chaos in language generally, as it is in life. German makes *mädchen* unpardonably neuter, considers *weib* a low word and substitutes *frau*, though it is surely "das ewig-weibliche"—the eternal feminine—that draws us upward (a quite different thing from running after frau or fräulein), to say nothing of the weird form and sense of *frauenzimmer*. In French *personne* is masculine when it means *nobody* but feminine when it turns around and refers to someone, in which sense it can be applied to a male and then qualified by an adjective in the feminine. Such anomalies abound; they exist in all modern languages as they do in ancient Greek and Latin.

All this insinuates the idea that language cannot be turned at will into a sort of garrulous algebra under the rule of strictness and fixity. Even in algebra one changes the sign, and hence the value, as one moves the terms around. The same adaptability, but far wider, must continue to prevail among words if we are to have a tolerable idiom and the enjoyment that in good hands it can produce. Make childish war on accepted designations, try to force the use of *person* to suppress gender, and sooner or later free speech will find a way; dire need will inspire dreadful revivals—say, *female* as a noun, in the manner of early nineteenth-century fiction. I see no gain for the lexicon of human dignity either in the prospect of this she-person, with her irrelevant -*male* and her masculine companion, "an individual," or in the present peopling of the world with the blank neuters called *person*.

In short, within the great treasury of terms and their combinations, all of equal and emancipated human beings must accept the rough with the smooth, the convenient and inconvenient, the direct and roundabout. We must understand that the "brotherhood of man" does not exclude our beloved sisters; that the potent formula Liberty, Equality, Fr - - - - - cannot be revised to end with either Sorority or Personality; that *mankind* in modern usage is not the opposite of *womankind* as *menfolk* is of *womenfolk*; that we are all *fellowman* and *fellowmen* together; and that while *poetess* is offensive and *doctress* ridiculous, *actress* is here to stay.

Even if the banded typists of the world should, to a woman, withhold the last syllable of *spokesman,* their success would hardly legislate the reforms they are after. Important goals must be fought for on their own grounds. Demand equal pay for equal work and the world will come to it. But it was not by the compulsory use of *citoyen* and *citoyenne* after 1789 that democratic manners were established in France. There is more democracy under the Fifth Republic with *monsieur* and *madame* than there was with that affectation under the Committee of Public Safety.

I conclude, on the score of history, etymology, and *Sprachgefühl,* that "Madame chairman" is a correct and decent appellation. No one until recently ever saw in the phrase any paradox, incongruity, or oppugnancy between terms. It is consistent with common sense and perfect equity: the *man* in it denotes either sex, and therefore the key word means precisely *chairperson.* For my part, I shall continue to use it unless stopped by the chair herself, when I will duly defer to authority with the compromise "Madame la Chaise"—that at the risk of being in my turn called Père Lachaise[1] and buried there with full semantic honors.

RICHARD HOGGART

Taking for Granted

Most of the signals we pick up, especially when we are in our own society, we pick up without knowing it. We are like people who take part by ear in a very subtle, non-stop symphony. This is true whatever education we have had and whatever our social class; and our idioms show it. Whenever you look closely at something very much a part of common experience, you find a range of subtle obser-

---

1. A cemetery in Paris.

vations on it woven into everyday speech. Since I began thinking around this subject many old and apparently hackneyed phrases, phrases such as 'getting out of touch' and 'taking for granted,' have come up mint-new. They point straight to the fact that so much in our communicating depends on the assumption of extraordinarily close relationships.

Take these, for example:

> You should have seen the look he gave me
> I gave her a meaning look
> Her looks spoke daggers
> She didn't say anything, but I knew what she was thinking.

And here are two which have more than a single dimension. Each implies a set of relationships and a manner of speaking to match:

> Who do you think you're talking to?
> Don't use that tone of voice with me

It is easy to see that tone is more important than the dictionary-meanings of the words we use. Properly described, tone is a complicated matter of pitch, stress, timbre and the like. But I am using the word as a shorthand way of referring to those qualities in speech or writing which carry our sense of a relationship to another person. I want to get away from any remnant of the idea that tone is a dead carrier of live substance. Tone is part of substance; it can make the same words carry wholly opposed meanings. If you know your contexts it's simple to make 'Goodbye' mean: '. . . and I hope I never see you again' or '. . . and I can't wait to get back to you' or many points between.

Sometimes one can communicate effectively through the spaces between words. I don't only mean deliberate silences for effect. I mean pauses, unfinished bits, not used deliberately but no less full of meaning. As in those conversations which never quite touch a substantive or verb and which move, like fish gliding past rocks and huge growths in those underwater films, from 'you know . . . sort of . . . I mean . . . like . . . kind of' all the way to the end, with gestures orchestrating the words all the way too. And being understood. There is a corny old joke about a West Riding[1] working-man who had to be away from home for a long time. His wife heard nothing from him. Then one day he turned up, took his seat at the side of the fire, sat awhile and finally said: 'Owt?' 'Nowt,' his wife replied, and that was the end of that conversation. I suppose it is meant to show the droll taciturnity of Yorkshire people, but it just as well shows that in some contexts most communication goes on in the gaps between the words. Sometimes silence on the part of one person is assumed, as an integral part of the act of communicating.

1. A part of the Yorkshire region in the north of England.

The hearer's place is defined by the speaker's needs. It would be a mistake if he said a word; he has to listen but in a certain way.

Words, tones, pauses make up very rich registers for speaking to each other. So do many other things, especially most aspects of our appearance. Those too are ways of passing signals to others. And to ourselves; they are means by which we support our own inner sense of ourselves, even in what may at first glance seem very public situations. This is true both of those parts of our appearance we can easily control, such as dress, and those we have less day-to-day, conscious control over, such as habitual gestures, expressions of the eyes, voice, face.

I am going to begin with some sketches towards social readings or interpretations of manners and styles in England. So these are home thoughts from abroad, especially about the many signals you simply take for granted until you go away, and about the ways we get in touch other than through words—they are about eyes, voices, faces as ways of speaking.

Actually, eyes are used less, socially, than many other features. They *are* used in that way, it's true. There are such things as histrionic 'piercing' looks and—this one has become a cliché—the cocktail party quick flicker, when someone's eyes sweep the room on the lookout for more important people while they are supposed to be engaged with you. But more often eyes say something about the individual below the acquired social manners—from eyes assured of certain certainties to vulnerable, hurt eyes, or to eyes which go from you in a way different from that met in cocktail party situations. You may not be in a crowd at all; but the eyes facing you switch off as though an electric plug has been pulled, and they are no longer lighted outwards. You know that the person facing you is a long way off at that moment, living elsewhere and at a greater depth.

Voices are much more easily translated, socially, particularly in Britain. Most of us in Britain, perhaps because of their class qualities, seem almost as responsive to voices as to smells. One of the more marked English voices is that acquired by certain middle-aged, middle-class women. It is as much the sign of a group as what people used to call "Billingsgate fishwife' to indicate one kind of harsh, working-class woman's voice. House-hunting in middle-class Birmingham, as we trailed from one desirable residence to another, we heard that middle-class voice again and again. Both the voice and the manner that goes with it are hard. They speak of a class defending itself and its one-eighth of an acre, as it had for centuries, against all those below: lazy workmen, fiddling shopkeepers, insolent public servants.

I once met an even more heavily-accented group, when by chance I spent a few days in an hotel with some barristers. They were quite amiable, though they found me at least as odd a bird as I found them. They enjoyed calling me 'Prof.,' and the word rolled warmly off their tongues, slightly amused, even slightly impressed, slightly puzzled. Surely, their cultural stereotypes said to them, he should have a weighty presence. On my side, I was struck by the closed world they inhabited, and seemed to have inhabited since they were first sent to their prep. schools. Their closed or in-group speech made me feel out of it, in spite of their friendliness.

Most of them lived in exurbanite areas round London. They had all been to good public schools, and could read each other's signals immediately. They were all living within similar, invisible but unbroken plastic wrappers, moving easily towards old age inside them, within a society about whose other members they were not, and had not been inspired by their education to be, curious in an informed way. A certain anecdotal curiosity they could show, but that is easy. They were an assured group within a society about whose other groups, parts, history, they had sketchy but firm and most misleading views. Their ideas on 'the place of Britain in the world today', 'the working classes', 'the North', 'the student generation,' were travesties; and they were confident within them. That part of the system into which they had been born had trained them to serve a view of the legal profession and its social relations which was not only inadequate but false.

If their legal procedures usually worked, in human terms—and they seemed to do so more than one would have predicted from their off-duty conversation—this was because, in spite of the reach-me-down social and psychological ideas they held, they could also draw on a tradition of reasonableness and undramatic honesty. They were sensibly buttressed in their practice not by abstract principles but by the fact that they didn't expect too much of men. They were not prigs; they knew chaps tended to get into scrapes. I remembered, years before, seeing a judge at the Old Bailey[2] find it hard to follow the arguments, by both sides, about *Lady Chatterley's Lover*. But when disposing, in an interval, of some of the more usual and nasty kinds of case, he showed great wisdom and humanity. Still, in the barristers I met, one couldn't help thinking that livelier imaginations would have been useful.

Most formal educations don't give much help in reading the signals of society closely or accurately. Think of English faces, for example. Years ago I became interested in faces, especially in the faces of middle-aged men. I remember the exact moment. A diesel coach pulled up at a small Lincolnshire village; I looked out and there on the almost deserted platform was Winston Churchill, dressed as a station master. Or a stationmaster pretending to be Winston Churchill? Not quite that, either; but a heavy man in advanced middle-age who had put up an expression like Churchill's. How strange, and how difficult to interpret confidently. He had

2. A criminal court in London.

decisions to make in his job, and no doubt they could be worrying. Did they weigh as heavily on him as though he were the Prime Minister of a country at war? Or had he given way to a self-indulgent inflation of his role? Seen close-up for any length of time, would the heavily decisive Churchillian lines haves turned out to be no more than a rough sketch? How much was his face for the world, and how much for himself?

But this begins to seem belittling and I don't intend that. One is tempted that way because the Churchillian face is, or was, so obvious a model for copying; it suggests kidding yourself. But other kinds of strength can be imprinted on faces, even though we assume that only the kind of faces which go with recognizably big jobs have a right to be taken seriously. I met not long ago, in a time of great personal crisis, a man with a job which, though responsible, would not in the usual ranking be thought important. He showed steadiness and a great ability to manage; he had, one soon saw, a very strong presence. What one learnt during that crisis, and what the usual social images would not necessarily have led one to expect, was that the presence was real. He had struck a balance which was effective and humane, struck it through facing and trying to resolve, day by day, difficult human problems in a setting which to the public eye would seem dull, unimportant, provincial in all the limit- and senses. The public eye would have been wrong. Men of substance, if that phrase is to have any worthwhile meaning, are everywhere. It's a pity our range of recognized faces for strength, and for lots of other qualities, is so limited.

There are signals, especially of slightly insecure self-importance, at all levels. If you spend much time among professors you will be struck by the recurrence of a few styles. Most of them are not peacocky; folksy, perhaps, as a foil to the suggestion of learning worn lightly. I have seen the same professor move in a single two- or three-hour Faculty meeting from a pipe-ruminating, shrewd, academic statesman in his expression, his gestures and even his voice to a Northern no-flies-on-Charlie light-voiced urchin. Another professor puzzled me by an inverted comma effect around the radiance of his smile towards students. It was open, expansive, warmly assured. And yet, yet . . . something was being played that was not easy to hear. Then suddenly it clicked. It was the public smile of a handsome man, a man still handsome in middle age, who *knows* he is handsome.

If you stand on New Street Station, Birmingham, waiting for one of the fast morning trains to London, you find yourself in a crowd of middle-aged men mostly wearing elements of the same well-known uniform—the dark suit, homburg, good brief or executive case, rolled umbrella, pigskin gloves—and the same style of face; all in all a portliness, an air of substance, importance and seriousness. Solicitors, higher executives of Building Societies, officials of the big works and corporations, professors. Then, unexpectedly, you may have, without trying to be funny, a sharp, sudden vision of them all in their underwear in their bedrooms that night in Solihull or Sutton Coldfield,[3] with their glasses off, talking to their wives, worrying about their daughters living in London bedsitters,[4] each carrying on that attempt to make coherent, unified sense of his public and private life which for all of us finds its most common expression in a continuous conversation, sometimes in their presence, sometimes only in our own heads, with the person who is nearest to us, wife or husband; a process which is like the most elaborate, continuous knitting of a fabric that is always threatening to fall apart; but which we have to keep whole, and do usually manage to keep whole, because that is the basis on which our lives have whatever meaning they do have.

Then just as suddenly we come back to that railway station platform, near the point where the first-class carriages stop, on the morning of a full working day. How *do* we get, make, our faces? How to distinguish between what the society offers by way of a stock of translatable faces, what the inner personality of each of us forces on our face, and what the hazards of experience—illness, accidents, failure, success—engrain on it? It is the cheerful faces which puzzle most. One's instinct is to mistrust them, to assume they indicate some disingenuousness. But what could be to underrate the luck of good health, or be unjust to courage.

People, we assume, are much the same everywhere; personality will out, and the ups-and-downs of life are much the same everywhere too. Sure, but the ways these qualities and experiences express themselves differ in different societies. Each society has several ranges of typical face, and the distinctions between them become finer and finer as you look at them. There is a lean, quizzical, face one finds among clever men on the Eastern seaboard of the United States, the face of an intelligent man in a wide-open, mass-persuasive society who is not to be taken in, who has kept his cool and his irony. Such a face is not so likely to be found among its counterparts in Eastern Europe; the winds which beat on these men are different. Their faces are graver, more direct, and yet more reserved.

Because I have met them at some cross-roads in my own life, I am particularly interested in a range of faces which cluster round the idea of a public man in Britain. At his most characteristic, this man is in his middle-fifties. His appearance is what the whisky advertisements, giving it more of a gloss than it really has, call distinguished. His face is well-shaven but not scraped; it has a healthy bloom, but not an outdoor roughness; it is smooth, but not waxy. What is by now quite a full face is as solid as leather club-

3. Residential suburbs of Birmingham.   4. One-room apartments.

armchairs, and as decently groomed; it smells as good as the public rooms of those clubs. The hair is often marked by the appearance of Cabinet Minister's wings, that is, it is brushed straight back above the ears to plump out at the sides; it has a silvery sheen. The teeth are strong, one sees, when the lips, as they readily do, curl back into a full, firm smile. They suggest someone who is used to talking in public and to deciding, to biting firmly into problems. They are wonderfully communicative teeth, and remarkable evidence that from all the possible ways of using teeth, the ways we smile or grimace, we select only some: we select from the code-book of tooth-signals in our society.

The coherence of the style is rarely breached. I remember one occasion which, because of its oddness, underlined how consistent that style usually is. One such public man—one who was apparently such a man—said to me, as we stood around in the intervals of a meeting: 'You see, Hoggart, I believe in the English people'. As he said it, it sounded näive, a little self-important, touching generous; but not sayable by a native English intellectual, least of all in that particular ambience. But he was a first generation European immigrant intellectual. His son is hardly likely to strike a false note like that.

Among the most striking in the line of public figures is the old–young man; and they are most often found in the higher reaches of education. These men are slim, with little trace of a paunch even at fifty-five; their faces still show the outlines formed when they were Head boys at their public schools or good day-schools. There is a French public type of about the same age who is in some ways similar; but the differences are interesting and, to me, unexpected. The French type is even leaner; he is also more elegant, better groomed, and more profssionale-looking than the Englishman. He is likely to have close-cropped hair and glasses with thin gold rims. It all fits with being called a 'haut fonctionnaire'. The English type is more casual, looser in the limb.

Englishmen of this kind are obviously energetic. They like to be ironic about them and say: 'The steadiness of the half-shut eye'. But these men are not rigid. They get a lot done and their limits are not where one might assume. Even their occasional blokeishness is not really patronizing, unless you get further than usual into that word's meanings.

None of this gives a translation of personality unless you do a second and third reading. Granted that this is the pattern of available signals, and that their social meanings are thus and thus, what does that tell us about what any particular man wants to say to his society and to himself; what does it tell us about him at bottom? The justification for learning more about social vocabularies is that unless you understand what social signals you are responding to, all the time, you will be less likely to see through the groups of a certain age and style, and see the individuals within. But even that is not the right way of putting it; it is too anxious to see real character as the inviolate inner kernel of a fruit. In all of us our particular environments, our particular times and places, encourage certain sides and discourage others; and though these things may not be able totally to make character they have more effect than we usually admit. They filter and order the way we receive and respond to even our most powerful emotional experiences, those we would assume brought us face to face, nakedly, with our own character.

I have been underlining how complex are the day-to-day social readings we all make. It follows that, even after years, we communicate relatively thinly in a society not our own. Some foreign signals are easy and can be read after a few weeks. The danger then is that we over-interpret them, lean on them too much so as to make up for the lack of density and resonance in our response. Not long ago I was lost before a new kind of face. Or, rather, I mistrusted my own reading of it; it was too easy and dismissive. This was a politician from the United States, a man who had been successful in oil or insurance well before he was forty and who now, in his middle forties, had an assured, thrusting, mercantile, tanned, smoothly smiling but tough look. To me the face, the whole manner, was two-dimensional, unmarked. It was like the face of a well-groomed dog. It said only: 'Public acquaintance . . . manipulation . . . action'; not: 'Friendliness . . . thought . . . feeling'. Had such a man, you wondered, ever felt shabby or insecure? Oddly, it was easier to imagine him crying. There was probably within the rhetorics available to him a form of crying that would do. But I was probably wrong, unable to read the signals in a way which got me near his character, which made him three-dimensional, capable of real grief and joy, unpublic. I couldn't easily imagine *him* in his underwear, and when I did he looked like an advertisement in ESQUIRE.

Inside our own society things may look easier; after all, we have the code-book for reading the signals which that society provides. But what we are given is an all-purpose, self-defining kit. We are given the styles and then the keys to them. They tend to be convenient keys, not always accurate keys; so we have to learn to break through the codes. It is easy to see the self-defining double process at work in the attitudes of those middle-class figures I talked about earlier. Our own attitudes may seem more independent, penetrating, and objective; but they are often just as much the product of a group's fashions, its ways of selecting and interpreting other parts of society. One of the main results of questioning yourself like this is being led step by step to see how many more clichés you have in your own baggage than you had thought. Not all of them have to be rejected. Sometimes you find they have, after all, to be kept; but by then they have been seen in new lights; you have a new hold on them so that they are no longer clichés.

One of the commonest sets of clichés are those which define the nature of suburban life. I'm struck now by the selectiveness of the picture they produce and by the extent to which they constrict the understanding of suburban life. That life can be even more grim than the clichés allow one to feel; it can also be more attractive.

It can be small-minded, keeping-itself-to-itself, fearful about status to a depressing extent. It can be claustrophobically turned in upon itself; as at moments during a grammar-school speech day when you can look around at all the carefully groomed mothers and fathers and feel the heavy weight of socio-academic anxiety bearing down on that platform. How can we be so totally engrossed in this particular bit of Western Hemisphere ritualism? How lacking in perspective can we get? You recall Auden's unpleasant line about "The clerk going "oompah, oompah" to his minor grave'.

But Auden also wrote a poem called 'In Praise of Limestone' which can be seen as a tribute to aspects of suburban life, to the lives of people who are, in Auden's phrase: 'adjusted to the local needs of valleys'. In some ways, he is saying, people who settle for a domestic scale among others who have done the same, who have no great urge towards power or asceticism, may be in touch with important and neglected parts of of our being. Their lives may not be full of striking contours; but they can now and again reveal some things about *not* going places, about one sort of harmony.

I once knew well a man and his wife who lived the most conventional of lives in the semi-detached suburbs of a Northern city. He was what is called a minor clerk and they had one very much loved daughter. All three were small—generations of working-class city life in the North had brought that about. He had, in his family's terms, done quite well for himself. Yes, and they had a little car, too; the *lot*, according to the caricature. The parents are dead now, and that particular home is gone as though it had never existed. But to feel superior to all that, as you walked along there on a bright Sunday morning, would have been stupid. We all know the stock images . . . the whole area smelling of roast beef, Radio 2 coming out of open windows, the men at work in the garden or washing the car. Still, there was above all a feeling of peace. When all has been said about its limits, you have also to stand back and say how much better this was, as a style of life, than many alternatives. It was not aggressive; it was out to be neighbourly and it had all sorts of well-practised ways of being so. On those Sunday mornings, people really were living in the present, which is what enjoying yourself means; they felt settled, comfortable in their places, not looking for the next move. They did not ask many questions about the good, the true and the beautiful; nor did they tear one another apart. If we looked more closely at suburban life we would see that it can at times achieve a domesticity and neighbourliness which are a kind of quiet triumph.

But that is only one possible example, chosen because suburban life particularly attracts quick judgements from many people. We can all be subtle interpreters of social signals. But we like to limit the number of adjustments we make, whether about suburban life or middle-class life or professional life or academic life; or in interpreting faces, voices or gestures. And our society, or more accurately the particular parts of society to which each of us belongs, encourages us to limit our readings. All of which is a pity because if we looked more closely we would—all of us, whatever our education—be surprised by how much we had simply taken over unexamined.

ERICH FROMM
The Nature of Symbolic Language

Let us assume you want to tell someone the difference between the taste of white wine and red wine. This may seem quite simple to you. You know the difference very well; why should it not be easy to explain it to someone else? Yet you find the greatest difficulty putting this taste difference into words. And probably you will end up by saying, "Now look here, I can't explain it to you. Just drink red wine and then white wine, and you will know what the difference is." You have no difficulty in finding words to explain the most complicated machine, and yet words seem to be futile to describe a simple taste experience.

Are we not confronted with the same difficulty when we try to explain a feeling experience? Let us take a mood in which you feel lost, deserted, where the world looks gray, a little frightening though not really dangerous. You want to describe this mood to a friend, but again you find yourself groping for words and eventually feel that nothing you have said is an adequate explanation of the many nuances of the mood. The following night you have a dream. You see yourself in the outskirts of a city just before dawn, the streets are empty except for a milk wagon, the houses look poor, the surroundings are unfamiliar, you have no means of accustomed transportation to places familiar to you and where you feel you belong. When you wake up and remember the dream, it occurs to you that the feeling you had in that dream was exactly the feeling of lostness and grayness you tried to describe to your friend the day before. It is just one picture, whose visualization took less than a second. And yet this picture is a more vivid and precise description than you could have given by talking *about* it at length. The picture you see in the dream is a *symbol* of something you felt.

What is a symbol? A symbol is often defined as "something that stands for something else." This definition seems rather disappointing. It becomes more interesting, however, if we concern ourselves with those symbols which are sensory expressions of seeing, hearing, smelling, touching, standing for a "something else" which is an inner experience, a feeling or thought. A symbol of this kind is something outside ourselves; that which it symbolizes is something inside ourselves. Symbolic language is language in which we express inner experience as if it were a sensory experience, as if it were something we were doing or something that was done to us in the world of things. Symbolic language is language in which the world outside is a symbol of the world inside, a symbol for our souls and our minds.

If we define a symbol as "something which stands for something else," the crucial question is: *What is the specific connection between the symbol and that which it symbolizes?*

In answer to this question we can differentiate between three kinds of symbols: the *conventional*, the *accidental* and the *universal* symbol. As will become apparent presently, only the latter two kinds of symbols express inner experiences as if they were sensory experiences, and only they have the elements of symbolic language.

The *conventional* symbol is the best known of the three, since we employ it in everyday language. If we see the word "table" or hear the sound "table," the letters T-A-B-L-E stand for something else. They stand for the thing table that we see, touch and use. What is the connection between the *word* "table" and the *thing* "table"? Is there any inherent relationship between them? Obviously not. The thing table has nothing to do with the sound table, and the only reason the word symbolizes the thing is the convention of calling this particular thing by a particular name. We learn this connection as children by the repeated experience of hearing the word in reference to the thing until a lasting association is formed so that we don't have to think to find the right word.

There are some words, however, where the association is not only conventional. When we say "phooey," for instance, we make with our lips a movement of dispelling the air quickly. It is an expression of disgust in which our mouths participate. By this quick expulsion of air we imitate and thus express our intention to expel something, to get it out of our system. In this case, as in some others, the symbol has an inherent connection with the feeling it symbolizes. But even if we assume that originally many or even all words had their origins in some such inherent connection between symbol and the symbolized, most words no longer have this meaning for us when we learn a language.

Words are not the only illustration for conventional symbols, although they are the most frequent and best-known ones. Pictures also can be conventional symbols. A flag, for instance, may stand for a specific country, and yet there is no connection between the specific colors and the country for which they stand. They have been accepted as denoting that particular country, and we translate the visual impression of the flag into the concept of that country, again on conventional grounds. Some pictorial symbols are not entirely conventional; for example, the cross. The cross can be merely a conventional symbol of the Christian church and in that respect no different from a flag. But the specific content of the cross referring to Jesus' death or, beyond that, to the interpenetration of the material and spiritual planes, puts the connection between the symbol and what it symbolizes beyond the level of mere conventional symbols.

The very opposite to the conventional symbol is the *accidental* symbol, although they have one thing in common: there is no intrinsic relationship between the symbol and that which it symbolizes. Let us assume that someone has had a saddening experience in a certain city; when he hears the name of that city, he will easily connect the name with a mood of sadness, just as he would connect it with a mood of joy had his experience been a happy one. Quite obviously there is nothing in the nature of the city that is either sad or joyful. It is the individual experience connected with the city that makes it a symbol of a mood.

The same reaction could occur in connection with a house, a street, a certain dress, certain scenery, or anything once connected with a specific mood. We might find ourselves dreaming that we are in a certain city. In fact, there may be no particular mood connected with it in the dream; all we see is a street or even simply the name of the city. We ask ourselves why we happened to think of that city in our sleep and may discover that we had fallen asleep in a mood similar to the one symbolized by the city. The picture in the dream represents this mood, the city "stands for" the mood once experienced in it. Here the connection between the symbol and the experience symbolized is entirely accidental.

In contrast to the conventional symbol, the accidental symbol cannot be shared by anyone else except as we relate the events connected with the symbol. For this reason accidental symbols are rarely used in myths, fairy tales, or works of art written in symbolic language because they are not communicable unless the writer adds a lengthy comment to each symbol he uses. In dreams, however, accidental symbols are frequent. * * *

The *universal* symbol is one in which there is an intrinsic relationship between the symbol and that which it represents. We have already given one example, that of the outskirts of the city. The sensory experience of a deserted, strange, poor environment has indeed a significant relationship to a mood of lostness and anxiety. True enough, if we have never been in the outskirts of a city we could not use that symbol, just as the word "table" would be meaningless had we never seen a table. This symbol is meaningful only to city dwellers and would be meaningless to people living in cultures that have no big cities. Many other universal symbols, however, are rooted in the experience of every human being. Take, for instance, the symbol of fire. We are fascinated by certain qualities of fire in a fireplace. First of all, by its aliveness. It changes continuously, it moves all the time, and yet there is constancy in it. It remains the same without being the same. It gives the impression of power, of energy, of grace and lightness. It is as if it were dancing and had an inexhaustible source of energy. When we use fire as a symbol, we describe the inner experience characterized by the same elements which we notice in the sensory experience of fire; the mood of energy, lightness, movement, grace, gaiety—sometimes one, sometimes another of these elements being predominant in the feeling.

Similar in some ways and different in others is the symbol of water—of the ocean or of the stream. Here, too, we find the blending of change and permanence, of constant movement and yet of permanence. We also feel the quality of aliveness, continuity and energy. But there is a difference; where fire is adventurous, quick, exciting, water is quiet, slow and steady. Fire has an element of surprise; water an element of predictability. Water symbolizes the mood of aliveness, too, but one which is "heavier," "slower," and more comforting than exciting.

That a phenomenon of the physical world can be the adequate expression of an inner experience, that the world of things can be a symbol of the world of the mind, is not surprising. We all know that our bodies express our minds. Blood rushes to our heads when we are furious, it rushes away from them when we are afraid; our hearts beat more quickly when we are angry, and the whole body has a different tonus if we are happy from the one it has when we are sad. We express our moods by our facial expressions and our attitudes and feelings by movements and gestures so precise that others recognize them more accurately from our gestures than from our words. Indeed, the body is a symbol—and not an allegory—of the mind. Deeply and genuinely felt emotion, and even any genuinely felt thought, is expressed in our whole organism. In the case of the universal symbol, we find the same connection between mental and physical experience. Certain physical phenomena suggest by their very nature certain emotional and mental experiences, and we express emotional experiences in the language of physical experiences, that is to say, symbolically.

The universal symbol is the only one in which the relationship between the symbol and that which is symbolized is not coincidental but intrinsic. It is rooted in the experience of the affinity between an emotion or thought, on the one hand, and a sensory experience, on the other. It can be called universal because it is shared by all men, in contrast not only to the accidental symbol, which is by its very nature entirely personal, but also to the conventional symbol, which is restricted to a group of people sharing the same convention. The universal symbol is rooted in the properties of our body, our senses, and our mind, which are common to all men and, therefore, not restricted to individuals or to specific groups. Indeed, the language of the universal symbol is the one common tongue developed by the human race, a language which it forgot before it succeeded in developing a universal conventional language.

There is no need to speak of a racial inheritance in order to explain the universal character of symbols. Every human being who shares the essential features of bodily and mental equipment with the rest of mankind is capable of speaking and understanding the symbolic language that is based upon these common properties. Just as we do not need to learn to cry when we are sad or to get red in the face when we are angry, and just as these reactions are not restricted to any particular race or group of people, symbolic language does not have to be learned and is not restricted to any segment of the human race. Evidence for this is to be found in the fact that symbolic language as it is employed in myths and dreams is found in all cultures—in so-called primitive as well as such highly developed cultures as Egypt and Greece. Furthermore, the symbols used in these various cultures are strikingly similar since they all go back to the basic sensory as well as emotional experiences shared by men of all cultures. Added evidence is to be found in recent experiments in which people who had no knowledge of the theory of dream interpretation were able, under hypnosis, to interpret the symbolism of their dreams without any difficulty. After emerging from the hypnotic state and being asked to interpret the same dreams, they were puzzled and said, "Well, there is no meaning to them—it is just nonsense."

The foregoing statement needs qualification, however. Some symbols differ in meaning according to the difference in their realistic significance in various cultures. For instance, the function and consequently the meaning of the sun is different in northern countries and in tropical countries. In northern countries, where water is plentiful, all growth depends on sufficient sunshine. The sun is the warm, life-giving, protecting, loving power. In the Near East, where the heat of the sun is much more powerful, the sun is a dangerous and even threatening power from which man must protect himself, while water is felt to be the source of all life and the main condition for growth. We may speak of dialects of universal symbolic language, which are determined by those differences in natural conditions which cause certain symbols to have a different meaning in different regions of the earth.

Quite different from these "symbolic dialects" is the fact that many symbols have more than one meaning in accordance with different kinds of experiences which can be connected with one and the same natural phenomenon. Let us take up the symbol of fire again. If we watch fire in the fireplace, which is a source of pleasure and comfort, it is expressive of a mood of aliveness, warmth, and pleasure. But if we see a building or forest on fire, it conveys to us an experience of threat or terror, of the powerlessness of man against the elements of nature. Fire, then, can be the symbolic representation of inner aliveness and happiness as well as of fear, powerlessness, or of one's own destructive tendencies. The same holds true of the symbol water. Water can be a most destructive force when it is whipped up by a storm or when a swollen river floods its banks. Therefore, it can be the symbolic expression of horror and chaos as well as of comfort and peace.

Another illustration of the same principle is a symbol of a valley. The valley enclosed between mountains can arouse in us the feeling of security and comfort, of protection against all dangers from the outside. But the protecting mountains can also mean isolating walls which do not permit us to get out of the valley and thus the valley can become a symbol of imprisonment. The particular meaning of the symbol in any given place can only be determined from the whole context in which the symbol appears, and in terms of the predominant experiences of the person using the symbol. * * *

A good illustration of the function of the universal symbol is a story, written in symbolic language, which is known to almost every one in Western culture: the Book of Jonah. Jonah has heard God's voice telling him to go to Nineveh and preach to its inhabitants to give up their evil ways lest they be destroyed. Jonah cannot help hearing God's voice and that is why he is a prophet. But he is an unwilling prophet, who, though knowing what he should do, tries to run away from the command of God (or, as we may say, the voice of his conscience). He is a man who does not care for other human beings. He is a man with a strong sense of law and order, but without love.[1]

How does the story express the inner processes in Jonah?

We are told that Jonah went down to Joppa and found a ship which should bring him to Tarshish. In mid-ocean a storm rises and, while everyone else is excited and afraid, Jonah goes into the ship's belly and falls into a deep sleep. The sailors, believing that God must have sent the storm because someone on the ship is to be punished, wake Jonah, who had told them he was trying to flee from God's command. He tells them to take him and cast him forth into the sea and that the sea would then become calm. The

---

1. Cf. the discussion of Jonah in E. Fromm's *Man for Himself* (New York, Rinehart & Co., 1947), where the story is discussed from the point of view of the meaning of love.

sailors (betraying a remarkable sense of humanity by first trying everything else before following his advice) eventually take Jonah and cast him into the sea, which immediately stops raging. Jonah is swallowed by a big fish and stays in the fish's belly three days and three nights. He prays to God to free him from this prison. God makes the fish vomit out Jonah unto the dry land and Jonah goes to Nineveh, fulfills God's command, and thus saves the inhabitants of the city.

The story is told as if these events had actually happened. However, it is written in symbolic language and all the realistic events described are symbols for the inner experiences of the hero. We find a sequence of symbols which follow one another: going into the ship, going into the ship's belly, falling asleep, being in the ocean, and being in the fish's belly. All these symbols stand for the same inner experience: for a condition of being protected and isolated, of safe withdrawal from communication with other human beings. They represent what could be represented in another symbol, the fetus in the mother's womb. Different as the ship's belly, deep sleep, the ocean, and a fish's belly are realistically, they are expressive of the same inner experience, of the blending between protection and isolation.

In the manifest story events happen in space and time: *first*, going into the ship's belly; *then*, falling alseep; *then*, being thrown into the ocean; *then*, being swallowed by the fish. One thing happens after the other and, although some events are obviously unrealistic, the story has its own logical consistency in terms of time and space. But if we understand that the writer did not intend to tell us the story of external events, but of the inner experience of a man torn between his conscience and his wish to escape from his inner voice, it becomes clear that his various actions following one after the other express the same mood in him; and that *sequence in time* is expressive of a *growing intensity* of the same feeling. In his attempt to escape from his obligation to his fellow men Jonah isolates himself more and more until, in the belly of the fish, the protective element has so given way to the imprisoning element that he can stand it no longer and is forced to pray to God to be released from where he had put himself. (This is a mechanism which we find so characteristic of neurosis. An attitude is assumed as a defense against a danger, but then it grows far beyond its original defense function and becomes a neurotic symptom from which the person tries to be relieved.) Thus Jonah's escape into protective isolation ends in the terror of being imprisoned, and he takes up his life at the point where he had tried to escape.

There is another difference between the logic of the manifest and of the latent story. In the manifest story the logical connection is one of causality of external events. Jonah wants to go overseas *because* he wants to flee from God, he falls asleep *because* he is tired, he is thrown overboard *because* he is supposed to be the reason for the storm, and he is swallowed by the fish *because* there are man-eating fish in the ocean. One event occurs because of a previous event. (The last part of the story is unrealistic but not illogical.) But in the latent story the logic is different. The various events are related to each other by their association with the same inner experience. What appears to be a causal sequence of external events stand for a connection of experiences linked with each other by their association in terms of inner events. This is as logical as the manifest story—but it is a logic of a different kind. * * *

GEORGE ORWELL
Politics and the English Language

Most people who bother with the matter at all would admit that the English language is in a bad way, but it is generally assumed that we cannot by conscious action do anything about it. Our civilization is decadent and our language—so the argument runs—must inevitably share in the general collapse. It follows that any struggle against the abuse of language is a sentimental archaism, like preferring candles to electric light or hansom cabs to aeroplanes. Underneath this lies the half-conscious belief that language is a natural growth and not an instrument which we shape for our own purposes.

Now, it is clear that the decline of a language must ultimately have political and economic causes: it is not due simply to the bad influence of this or that individual writer. But an effect can become a cause, reinforcing the original cause and producing the same effect in an intensified form, and so on indefinitely. A man may take to drink because he feels himself to be a failure, and then fail all the more completely because he drinks. It is rather the same thing that is happening to the English language. It becomes ugly and inaccurate because our thoughts are foolish, but the slovenliness of our language makes it easier for us to have foolish thoughts. The point is that the process is reversible. Modern English, especially written English, is full of bad habits which spread by imitation and which can be avoided if one is willing to take the necessary trouble. If one gets rid of these habits one can think more clearly, and to think clearly is a necessary first step towards political regeneration: so that the fight against bad English is not frivolous and is not the exclusive concern of professional writers. I will come back to this presently, and I hope that by that time the meaning of what I have said here will have become clearer. Meanwhile, here are five specimens of the English language as it is now habitually written.

These five passages have not been picked out because they are especially bad—I could have quoted far worse if I had chosen—but because they illustrate various of the mental vices from which we now suffer. They are a little below the average, but are fairly representative samples. I number them so that I can refer back to them when necessary:

"(1) I am not, indeed, sure whether it is not true to say that the Milton who once seemed not unlike a seventeenth-century Shelley had not become, out of an experience ever more bitter in each year, more alien [*sic*] to the founder of that Jesuit sect which nothing could induce him to tolerate."

Professor Harold Laski (Essay in *Freedom of Expression*).

"(2) Above all, we cannot play ducks and drakes with a native battery of idioms which prescribes such egregious collocations of vocables as the Basic *put up with* for *tolerate* or *put at a loss* for *bewilder*."

Professor Lancelot Hogben (*Interglossa*).

"(3) On the one side we have the free personality: by definition it is not neurotic, for it has neither conflict nor dream. Its desires, such as they are, are transparent, for they are just what institutional approval keeps in the forefront of consciousness; another institutional pattern would alter their number and intensity; there is little in them that is natural, irreducible, or culturally dangerous. But *on the other side*, the social bond itself is nothing but the mutual reflection of these self-secure integrities. Recall the definition of love. Is not this the very picture of a small academic? Where is there a place in this hall of mirrors for either personality or fraternity?"

Essay on psychology in *Politics* (New York).

"(4) All the 'best people' from the gentlemen's clubs, and all the frantic fascist captains, united in common hatred of Socialism and bestial horror of the rising tide of the mass revolutionary movement, have turned to acts of provocation, to foul incendiarism, to medieval legends of poisoned wells, to legalize their own destruction of proletarian organizations, and rouse the agitated petty-bourgeoisie to chauvinistic fervour on behalf of the fight against the revolutionary way out of the crisis."

Communist pamphlet.

"(5) If a new spirit *is* to be infused into this old country, there is one thorny and contentious reform which must be tackled, and that is the humanization and galvanization of the B.B.C. Timidity here will bespeak cancer and atrophy of the soul. The heart of Britain may be sound and of strong beat, for instance, but the British lion's roar at present is like that of Bottom in Shakespeare's *Midsummer Night's Dream*—as gentle as any sucking dove. A virile new Britain cannot continue indefinitely to be traduced in the eyes or rather ears, of the world by the effete languors of Langham Place, brazenly masquerading as 'standard English'. When the Voice of Britain is heard at nine o'clock, better far and infinitely less ludicrous to hear aitches honestly dropped than the present priggish, inflated, inhibited, school-ma'amish arch braying of blameless bashful mewing maidens!"

Letter in *Tribune*.

Each of these passages has faults of its own, but, quite apart from avoidable ugliness, two qualities are common to all of them. The first is staleness of imagery: the other is lack of precision. The writer either has a meaning and cannot express it, or he inadvertently says something else, or he is almost indifferent as to whether his words mean anything or not. This mixture of vagueness and sheer incompetence is the most marked characteristic of modern English prose, and especially of any kind of political writing. As soon as certain topics are raised, the concrete melts into the abstract and no one seems able to think of turns of speech that are not hackneyed: prose consists less and less of *words* chosen for the sake of their meaning, and more and more of *phrases* tacked together like the sections of a prefabricated hen-house. I list below, with notes and examples, various of the tricks by means of which the work of prose-construction is habitually dodged:

Dying Metaphors

A newly invented metaphor assists thought by evoking a visual image, while on the other hand a metaphor which is technically "dead" (e.g. *iron resolution*) has in effect reverted to being an ordinary word and can generally be used without loss of vividness. But in between these two classes there is a huge dump of worn-out metaphors which have lost all evocative power and are merely used because they save people the trouble of inventing phrases for themselves. Examples are: *Ring the changes on, take up the cudgels for, toe the line, ride roughshod over, stand shoulder to shoulder with, play into the hands of, no axe to grind, grist to the mill, fishing in troubled waters, on the order of the day, Achilles' heel, swan song, hotbed*. Many of these are used without knowledge of their meaning (what is a "rift", for instance?), and incompatible metaphors are frequently mixed, a sure sign that the writer is not interested in what he is saying. Some metaphors now current have been twisted out of their original meaning without those who use them even being aware of the fact. For example, *toe the line* is sometimes written *tow the line*. Another example is *the hammer and the anvil*, now always used with the implication that the anvil gets the worst of it. In real life it is always the anvil that breaks the hammer, never the other way about: a writer who stopped to think what he was saying would be aware of this, and would avoid perverting the original phrase.

Operators or Verbal False Limbs

These save the trouble of picking out appropriate verbs and nouns, and at the same time pad each sentence with extra syllables which give it an appearance of symmetry. Characteristic phrases are: *render inoperative, militate against, make contact with, be subjected to, give rise to, give grounds for, have the effect of, play a leading part (role) in, make itself felt, take effect, exhibit a tendency to, serve the purpose of, etc., etc.* The keynote is the elimination of simple verbs. Instead of being a single word, such as *break, stop, spoil, mend, kill,* a verb becomes a *phrase,* made up of a noun or adjective tacked on to some general-purposes verb such as *prove, serve, form, play, render.* In addition, the passive voice is wherever possible used in preference to the active, and noun constructions are used instead of gerunds (*by examination of* instead of *by examining*). The range of verbs is further cut down by means of the *-ize* and *de-* formation, and the banal statements are given an appearance of profundity by means of the *not un-* formation. Simple conjunctions and prepositions are replaced by such phrases as *with respect to, having regard to, the fact that, by dint of, in view of, in the interests of, on the hypothesis that;* and the ends of sentences are saved from anticlimax by such resounding commonplaces as *greatly to be desired, cannot be left out of account, a development to be expected in the near future, deserving of serious consideration, brought to a satisfactory conclusion,* and so on and so forth.

Pretentious Diction

Words like *phenomenon, element, individual* (as noun), *objective, categorical, effective, virtual, basic, primary, promote, constitute, exhibit, exploit, utilize, eliminate, liquidate,* are used to dress up simple statements and give an air of scientific impartiality to biased judgments. Adjectives like *epoch-making, epic, historic, unforgettable, triumphant, age-old, inevitable, inexorable, veritable,* are used to dignify the sordid processes of international politics, while writing that aims at glorifying war usually takes on an archaic colour, its characteristic words being: *realm, throne, chariot, mailed fist, trident, sword, shield, buckler, banner, jackboot, clarion.* Foreign words and expressions such as *cul de sac, ancien régime, deus ex machina, mutatis mutandis, status quo, gleichschaltung, weltanschauung,* are used to give an air of culture and elegance. Except for the useful abbreviations *i.e., e.g.,* and *etc.,* there is no real need for any of the hundreds of foreign phrases now current in English. Bad writers, and especially scientific, political and sociological writers, are nearly always haunted by the notion that Latin or Greek words are grander than Saxon ones, and unnecessary words like *expedite, ameliorate, predict, extraneous, deracinated, clandestine, subaqueous* and hundreds of others constantly gain ground from their Anglo-Saxon opposite numbers.[1] The jargon peculiar to Marxist writing (*hyena, hangman, cannibal, petty bourgeois, these gentry,*

---

1. An interesting illustration of this is the way in which the English flower names which were in use till very recently are being ousted by Greek ones, *snapdragon* becoming *antirrhinum, forget-me-not* becoming *myosotis,* etc. It is hard to see any practical reason for this change of fashion: it is probably due to an instinctive turning-away from the more homely word and a vague feeling that the Greek word is scientific [Orwell's note].

lacquey, flunkey, mad dog, White Guard, etc.) consists largely of words and phrases translated from Russian, German or French; but the normal way of coining a new word is to use a Latin or Greek root with the appropriate affix and, where necessary, the *-ize* formation. It is often easier to make up words of this kind (*deregionalize, impermissible, extramarital, nonfragmentatory* and so forth) than to think up the English words that will cover one's meaning. The result, in general, is an increase in slovenliness and vagueness.

Meaningless Words

In certain kinds of writing, particularly in art criticism and literary criticism, it is normal to come across long passages which are almost completely lacking in meaning.[2] Words like *romantic, plastic, values, human, dead, sentimental, natural, vitality,* as used in art criticism, are strictly meaningless in the sense that they not only do not point to any discoverable object, but are hardly ever expected to do so by the reader. When one critic writes, "The outstanding feature of Mr. X's work is its living quality", while another writes, "The immediately striking thing about Mr. X's work is its peculiar deadness", the reader accepts this as a simple difference of opinion. If words like *black* and *white* were involved, instead of the jargon words *dead* and *living*, he would see at once that language was being used in an improper way. Many political words are similarly abused. The word *Fascism* has now no meaning except in so far as it signifies "something not desirable". The words *democracy, socialism, freedom, patriotic, realistic, justice,* have each of them several different meanings which cannot be reconciled with one another. In the case of a word like *democracy*, not only is there no agreed definition, but the attempt to make one is resisted from all sides. It is almost universally felt that when we call a country democratic we are praising it: consequently the defenders of every kind of régime claim that it is a democracy, and fear that they might have to stop using the word if it were tied down to any one meaning. Words of this kind are often used in a consciously dishonest way. That is, the person who uses them has his own private definition, but allows his hearer to think he means something quite different. Statements like *Marshal Pétain was a true patriot, The Soviet Press is the freest in the world, The Catholic Church is opposed to persecution,* are almost always made with intent to deceive. Other words used in variable meanings, in most cases more or less dishonestly, are: *class, totalitarian, science, progressive, reactionary, bourgeois, equality.*

---

2. Example: "Comfort's catholicity of perception and image, strangely Whitmanesque in range, almost the exact opposite in aesthetic compulsion, continues to evoke that trembling atmospheric accumulative hinting at a cruel, an inexorably serene timelessness ... Wrey Gardiner scores by aiming at simple bull's-eyes with precision. Only they are not so simple, and through this contented sadness· runs more than the surface bittersweet of resignation" (*Poetry Quarterly*) [Orwell's note].

Now that I have made this catalogue of swindles and perversions, let me give another example of the kind of writing that they lead to. This time it must of its nature be an imaginary one. I am going to translate a passage of good English into modern English of the worst sort. Here is a well-known verse from *Ecclesiastes*:

"I returned and saw under the sun, that the race is not to the swift, nor the battle to the strong, neither yet bread to the wise, nor yet riches to men of understanding, nor yet favour to men of skill; but time and chance happeneth to them all."

Here it is in modern English:

"Objective consideration of contemporary phenomena compels the conclusion that success or failure in competitive activities exhibits no tendency to be commensurate with innate capacity, but that a considerable element of the unpredictable must invariably be taken into account."

This is a parody, but not a very gross one. Exhibit (3), above, for instance, contains several patches of the same kind of English. It will be seen that I have not made a full translation. The beginning and ending of the sentence follow the original meaning fairly closely, but in the middle the concrete illustrations—race, battle, bread—dissolve into the vague phrase "success or failure in competitive activities". This had to be so, because no modern writer of the kind I am discussing—no one capable of using phrases like "objective consideration of contemporary phenomena"—would ever tabulate his thoughts in that precise and detailed way. The whole tendency of modern prose is away from concreteness. Now analyse these two sentences a little more closely. The first contains forty-nine words but only sixty syllables, and all its words are those of everyday life. The second contains thirty-eight words of ninety syllables: eighteen of its words are from Latin roots, and one from Greek. The first sentence contains six vivid images, and only one phrase ("time and chance") that could be called vague. The second contains not a single fresh, arresting phrase, and in spite of its ninety syllables it gives only a shortened version of the meaning contained in the first. Yet without a doubt it is the second kind of sentence that is gaining ground in modern English. I do not want to exaggerate. This kind of writing is not yet universal, and outcrops of simplicity will occur here and there in the worst-written page. Still, if you or I were told to write a few lines on the uncertainty of human fortunes, we should probably come much nearer to my imaginary sentence than to the one from *Ecclesiastes*.

As I have tried to show, modern writing at its worst does not consist in picking out words for the sake of their meaning and inventing images in order to make the meaning clearer. It consists in gumming together long strips of words which have already been set in order by someone else, and making the results presentable by sheer humbug. The attraction of this way of writing is that it is easy. It is easier—even quicker, once you have the habit—to say *In my opinion it is a not unjustifiable assumption that* than to say *I think*. If you use ready-made phrases, you not only don't have to hunt about for words; you also don't have to bother with the rhythms of your sentences, since these phrases are generally so arranged as to be more or less euphonious. When you are composing in a hurry—when you are dictating to a stenographer, for instance, or making a public speech—it is natural to fall into a pretentious, Latinized style. Tags like *a consideration which we should do well to bear in mind* or *a conclusion to which all of us would readily assent* will save many a sentence from coming down with a bump. By using stale metaphors, similes and idioms, you save much mental effort, at the cost of leaving your meaning vague, not only for your reader but for yourself. This is the significance of mixed metaphors. The sole aim of a metaphor is to call up a visual image. When these images clash—as in *The Fascist octopus has sung its swan song, the jackboot is thrown into the melting pot*—it can be taken as certain that the writer is not seeing a mental image of the objects he is naming; in other words he is not really thinking. Look again at the examples I gave at the beginning of this essay. Professor Laski (1) uses five negatives in fifty-three words. One of these is superfluous, making nonsense of the whole passage, and in addition there is the slip *alien* for akin, making further nonsense, and several avoidable pieces of clumsiness which increase the general vagueness. Professor Hogben (2) plays ducks and drakes with a battery which is able to write prescriptions, and, while disapproving of the everyday phrase *put up with,* is unwilling to look *egregious* up in the dictionary and see what it means. (3), if one takes an uncharitable attitude towards it, is simply meaningless: probably one could work out its intended meaning by reading the whole of the article in which it occurs. In (4), the writer knows more or less what he wants to say, but an accumulation of stale phrases chokes him like tea leaves blocking a sink. In (5), words and meaning have almost parted company. People who write in this manner usually have a general emotional meaning—they dislike one thing and want to express solidarity with another—but they are not interested in the detail of what they are saying. A scrupulous writer, in every sentence that he writes, will ask himself at least four questions, thus: What am I trying to say? What words will express it? What image or idiom will make it clearer? Is this image fresh enough to have an effect? And he will probably ask himself two more: Could I put it more shortly? Have I said anything that is avoidably ugly? But you are not obliged to go to all this trouble. You can shirk it by simply throwing your mind open and letting the ready-made phrases come crowding in. They will construct your sentences for you—even think your thoughts for you, to a certain extent—and at need they will perform the important service of partially concealing your meaning even from yourself. It is at this point that the special connection between politics and the debasement of language becomes clear.

In our time it is broadly true that political writing is bad writing. Where it is not true, it will generally be found that the writer is some kind of rebel, expressing his private opinions and not a "party line". Orthodoxy, of whatever colour, seems to demand a lifeless, imitative style. The political dialects to be found in pamphlets, leading articles, manifestos, White Papers and the speeches of under-secretaries do, of course, vary from party to party, but they are all alike in that one almost never finds in them a fresh, vivid, home-made turn of speech. When one watches some tired hack on the platform mechanically repeating the familiar phrases—*bestial atrocities, iron heel, bloodstained tyranny, free peoples of the world, stand shoulder to shoulder*—one often has a curious feeling that one is not watching a live human being but some kind of dummy: a feeling which suddenly becomes stronger at moments when the light catches the speaker's spectacles and turns them into blank discs which seem to have no eyes behind them. And this is not altogether fanciful. A speaker who uses that kind of phraseology has gone some distance towards turning himself into a machine. The appropriate noises are coming out of his larynx, but his brain is not involved as it would be if he were choosing his words for himself. If the speech he is making is one that he is accustomed to make over and over again, he may be almost unconscious of what he is saying, as one is when one utters the responses in church. And this reduced state of consciousness, if not indispensable, is at any rate favourable to political conformity.

In our time, political speech and writing are largely the defence of the indefensible. Things like the continuance of British rule in India, the Russian purges and deportations, the dropping of the atom bombs on Japan, can indeed be defended, but only by arguments which are too brutal for most people to face, and which do not square with the professed aims of political parties. Thus political language has to consist largely of euphemism, question-begging and sheer cloudy vagueness. Defenceless villages are bombarded from the air, the inhabitants driven out into the countryside, the cattle machine-gunned, the huts set on fire with incendiary bullets: this is called *pacification*. Millions of peasants are robbed of their farms and sent trudging along the roads with no more than they can carry: this is called *transfer of population* or *rectification of frontiers*. People are imprisoned for years without trial, or shot in the back of the neck or sent to die of scurvy in Arctic lumber camps: this is called *elimination of unreliable elements*. Such phraseology is needed if one wants to name things without calling up mental pictures of them. Consider for instance some comfortable English professor defending Russian totalitarianism. He cannot say outright, "I believe in killing off your opponents when you can get good results by doing so". Probably, therefore, he will say something like this:

"While freely conceding that the Soviet régime exhibits certain features which the humanitarian may be inclined to deplore, we must, I think, agree that a certain curtailment of the right to political opposition is an unavoidable concomitant of transitional periods, and that the rigours which the Russian people have been called upon to undergo have been amply justified in the sphere of concrete achievement."

The inflated style is itself a kind of euphemism. A mass of Latin words falls upon the facts like soft snow, blurring the outlines and covering up all the details. The great enemy of clear language is insincerity. When there is a gap between one's real and one's declared aims, one turns as it were instinctively to long words and exhausted idioms, like a cuttlefish squirting out ink. In our age there is no such thing as "keeping out of politics". All issues are political issues, and politics itself is a mass of lies, evasions, folly, hatred and schizophrenia. When the general atmosphere is bad, language must suffer. I should expect to find—this is a guess which I have not sufficient knowledge to verify—that the German, Russian and Italian languages have all deteriorated in the last ten or fifteen years, as a result of dictatorship.

But if thought corrupts language, language can also corrupt thought. A bad usage can spread by tradition and imitation, even among people who should and do know better. The debased language that I have been discussing is in some ways very convenient. Phrases like *a not unjustifiable assumption*, *leaves much to be desired*, *would serve no good purpose*, *a consideration which we should do well to bear in mind*, are a continuous temptation, a packet of aspirins always at one's elbow. Look back through this essay, and for certain you will find that I have again and again committed the very faults I am protesting against. By this morning's post I have received a pamphlet dealing with conditions in Germany. The author tells me that he "felt impelled" to write it. I open it at random, and here is almost the first sentence that I see: "(The Allies) have an opportunity not only of achieving a radical transformation of Germany's social and political structure in such a way as to avoid a nationalistic reaction in Germany itself, but at the same time of laying the foundations of a co-operative and unified Europe." You see, he "feels impelled" to write—feels, presumably, that he has something new to say—and yet his words, like cavalry horses answering the bugle, group themselves automatically into the familiar dreary pattern. This invasion of one's mind by ready-made phrases (*lay the foundations*, *achieve a radical transformation*) can only be prevented if one is constantly on guard against them, and every such phrase anaesthetizes a portion of one's brain.

I said earlier that the decadence of our language is probably curable. Those who deny this would argue, if they produced an argument at all, that language merely reflects existing social conditions, and that we cannot influence its development by any direct tinkering with words and constructions. So far as the general tone or spirit of a language goes, this may be true, but it is not true in detail. Silly words and expressions have often disappeared, not through any evolutionary process but owing to the conscious action of a minority. Two recent examples were *explore every avenue* and *leave no stone unturned,* which were killed by the jeers of a few journalists. There is a long list of flyblown metaphors which could similarly be got rid of if enough people would interest themselves in the job; and it should also be possible to laugh the *not un-* formation out of existence,[3] to reduce the amount of Latin and Greek in the average sentence, to drive out foreign phrases and strayed scientific words, and, in general, to make pretentiousness unfashionable. But all these are minor points. The defence of the English language implies more than this, and perhaps it is best to start by saying what it does *not* imply.

To begin with it has nothing to do with archaism, with the salvaging of obsolete words and turns of speech, or with the setting up of a "standard English" which must never be departed from. On the contrary, it is especially concerned with the scrapping of every word or idiom which has outworn its usefulness. It has nothing to do with correct grammar and syntax, which are of no importance so long as one makes one's meaning clear, or with the avoidance of Americanisms, or with having what is called a "good prose style". On the other hand it is not concerned with fake simplicity and the attempt to make written English colloquial. Nor does it even imply in every case preferring the Saxon word to the Latin one, though it does imply using the fewest and shortest words that will cover one's meaning. What is above all needed is to let the meaning choose the word, and not the other way about. In prose, the worst thing one can do with words is to surrender to them. When you think of a concrete object, you think wordlessly, and then, if you want to describe the thing you have been visualizing you probably hunt about till you find the exact words that seem to fit. When you think of something abstract you are more inclined to use words from the start, and unless you make a conscious effort to prevent it, the existing dialect will come rushing in and do the job for you, at the expense of blurring or even changing your meaning. Probably it is better to put off using words as long as possible and get one's meaning as clear as one can through pictures or sensations. Afterwards one can choose—not simply *accept*—the phrases that will best cover the meaning, and then switch round and decide what impression one's words are likely to make on another person. This

---

3. One can cure oneself of the *not un-* formation by memorizing this sentence: *A not unblack dog was chasing a not* *unsmall rabbit across a not ungreen field* [Orwell's note].

last effort of the mind cuts out all stale or mixed images, all pre-fabricated phrases, needless repetitions, and humbug and vagueness generally. But one can often be in doubt about the effect of a word or a phrase, and one needs rules that one can rely on when instinct fails. I think the following rules will cover most cases:

(i) Never use a metaphor, simile or other figure of speech which you are used to seeing in print.

(ii) Never use a long word where a short one will do.

(iii) If it is possible to cut a word out, always cut it out.

(iv) Never use the passive where you can use the active.

(v) Never use a foreign phrase, a scientific word or a jargon word if you can think of an everyday English equivalent.

(vi) Break any of these rules sooner than say anything outright barbarous.

These rules sound elementary, and so they are, but they demand a deep change of attitude in anyone who has grown used to writing in the style now fashionable. One could keep all of them and still write bad English, but one could not write the kind of stuff that I quoted in those five specimens at the beginning of this article.

I have not here been considering the literary use of language, but merely language as an instrument for expressing and not for con-cealing or preventing thought. Stuart Chase and others have come near to claiming that all abstract words are meaningless, and have used this as a pretext for advocating a kind of political quietism. Since you don't know what Fascism is, how can you struggle against Fascism? One need not swallow such absurdities as this, but one ought to recognize that the present political chaos is connected with the decay of language, and that one can probably bring about some improvement by starting at the verbal end. If you simplify your English, you are freed from the worst follies of orthodoxy. You cannot speak any of the necessary dialects, and when you make a stupid remark its stupidity will be obvious, even to yourself. Politi-cal language—and with variations this is true of all political parties, from Conservatives to Anarchists—is designed to make lies sound truthful and murder respectable, and to give an appearance of solid-ity to pure wind. One cannot change this all in a moment, but one can at least change one's own habits, and from time to time one can even, if one jeers loudly enough, send some worn-out and use-less phrase—some *jackboot, Achilles' heel, hotbed, melting pot, acid test, veritable inferno* or other lump of verbal refuse—into the dustbin where it belongs.

QUESTIONS

1. What is Orwell's pivotal point? Where is it best stated?
2. Discuss Orwell's assertion that "the decline of a language must ultimately have political and economic causes" Is this "clear" as he claims?

3. How can you be sure that a metaphor is dying, rather than alive or dead? Is Orwell's test of seeing it often in print a sufficient one? Can you defend any of his examples of dying metaphors as necessary or useful additions to our vocabularies?
4. Orwell gives a list of questions for the writer to ask himself (p. 329) and a list of rules for the writer to follow (p. 333). Why does he consider it necessary to give both kinds of advice? How much do the two overlap? Are both consistent with Orwell's major ideas expressed elsewhere in the essay? Does his injunction to "break any of these rules sooner than say anything outright barbarous" beg the question?
5. Orwell suggests that if you look back through his essay you will find that he has "again and again committed the very faults" he is protesting against. Is this true? If it is, does it affect the validity of his major points?
6. Words create a personality or confer a character. Describe the personality that would be created by following Orwell's six rules; show that character in action.
7. The brief selections by Richard Gambino (pp. 334–336), which follows, and by Robert Pattison (pp. 265–266) illustrate some of the things that have been happening to the English language since Orwell wrote his essay in the forties. Compare and contrast the attitudes of the three writers toward language. Which of the two later writers is closer in attitude and approach to Orwell? What would Orwell say about Pattison's attitude toward "grammatical innovations"?

RICHARD GAMBINO

Through the Dark, Glassily

A stock language has evolved in government over many years, a language that makes it impossible to discuss, let alone fix or evaluate, questions of official and public political or moral responsibility.

We are increasingly compelled to follow public events through the medium of this newspeak.

More than ever before in American politics, language is used not as an instrument for forming and expressing thought. It is used to prevent, confuse and conceal thinking. Members of each branch and agency of government at every level, representing every hue of political opinion, habitually speak a language of nonresponsibility.

Euphemisms and palliative phrases are a favorite form of evasive language. "To select out" someone means to dismiss him from a job. People "misspeak" themselves; they never say foolish or deceptive things or (heaven forbid!) lie. Everything from nonsense and propaganda to vicious slanders and incitements to violence is described as "rhetoric." Similarly any falsehood, no matter how malicious, and any indoctrination, no matter how unconscionable, is "consciousness-raising."

An error in planning or prediction is not a "mistake," for this term raises depressing questions of personal competency and accountability; it is a "shortfall." Those in authority and their cronies never make inaccurate, perhaps purposely deceptive, estimates of public expenditures; instead we have "cost overruns."

With metaphysical judgment, officials, bureaucrats and office seekers tell us what are "acceptable rates" of crime, unemployment and casualties. The mugged, the raped, jobless people and those killed and maimed in battle need not reply.

The abuse of metaphors and similes to coat questions with obscuring layers of sugar or poison has created an art form, an idiot poetry. Practices are "ventilated,"—that is, skirted and not examined or exposed.

Money is "laundered" and people are "brought forward"—that is, made patsies. Information is "developed" as in a darkroom or laboratory, saving the speaker from explaining whether he means compiled, sought, filed, pursued, fabricated, altered, concealed or revealed.

Whereas others spy, our officials conduct "electronic" and "visual surveillance," especially when spying on us. Evil people cover up, lie and bribe. Our leaders "contain situations" like so many protective dams. This is particularly true when they are involved in a "game plan" (conspiracy). Politicians and bureaucrats are too pure of soul to use provocative expressions or loaded terms. They would never deprive children of school funds or poor people of proper housing. They merely "trade off" highways for schools and missiles for slums.

Perish the thought that they would do anything so personal as make choices and have goals. No, they merely "announce" "priority determinations" and "terminal objectives," and thereby inflict diseases upon the public. Of course when something is shown to be wrong it is done so only "in hindsight."

The use of misplaced technical jargon taken from specialized fields is very popular, serving as it does three marvelously useful purposes of evasion. It creates codes that mask the nature of what is happening. Jargon that is legitimate elsewhere also lends an aura of respectability to dubious behavior. Finally, it serves an old priesthood mystique: Those privy to the code enjoy a special, privileged, sophisticated status making them superior to us ordinary people.

Thus, any published bit of nonsense is a "print-out." Plans are not made as well as possible; instead, "scenarios" are "programed" toward "terminal objectives" in an effort to "maximize" "output" in "a zero-defect system."

The use of neologisms is gaining ground. Things are forever

being "optimized," "randomized," "finalized" and "federalized," rather than being decided, acted upon or resolved. People no longer talk on the telephone; they "deal with each other telephon-ically." And one's opinion is "the quality of one's mind."

The last, but by no means least used, art of evasive language is the use of stock phrases (preferably made up of multisyllabic words) and circumlocution.

Every inflated committee is a "task force." If something is to be "taken under advisement" and receive a "thorough and complete study" and is "referred through proper channels" to "issue in a position statement," it has been hastily swept under the rug and will never again be mentioned.

No bureaucrat deals with patterns, ways, means, values and num-bers but with "norms," "parameters," "variables," "inputs," "out-puts," "context fields" and "quotas."

No one with political panache wrestles with problems. He "meets the challenges" and "deals with crises"—the more the better to hide behind. Failure in this effort may lead to a "widening cred-ibility gap," that odoriferous witch's brew of exposed lies, deceptions and distortions.

All this is what Shakespeare called the never-ending "insolence of office."

ROBERT DARNTON

Writing News and Telling Stories

All the news that fits we print.
From the graffiti in the pressroom of police headquarters, Manhattan, 1964

This essay is a personal report on the experience of writing news.[1] It resulted from an attempt to circumnavigate the litera-ture on communication theory, diffusion studies, and the sociology of the media, which I undertook in the expectation of finding a new approach to the French Revolution. As a historian of pro-paganda and radical ideology, I have always held onto the hope that the social sciences will provide a kind of Northwest Passage to the past. I ran aground, however, while reading "Newsmen's Fantasies, Audiences, and Newswriting" by Ithiel de Sola Pool and Irwin Shulman in *Public Opinion Quarterly* (Summer, 1959).

1. This paper was conceived in discus-sions with Robert Merton, Giddings Pro-fessor of Sociology at Columbia Univer-sity. It owes a great deal to his ideas and criticism and also to the Center for Advanced Study in the Behavioral Sci-ences at Stanford, California, which made us fellow Fellows in 1973–74 and gave us the opportunity to wander out-side our disciplines. My brother John Darnton, a reporter on *The New York Times*, gave the paper a very helpful, critical reading, although he should not be held responsible for anything in it [Darnton's note].

That article touched off an analysis of my earlier experience as a reporter, which I offer with the wish that it may point to some fruitful lines of inquiry, despite its subjective character.

The Pool-Shulman Study

Pool and Shulman got newspapermen to conjure up images of their public through a process of free association. They asked thirty-three reporters to name persons who came to mind as they were going over stories they had just completed. Some reporters named persons whom they liked and whom they expected to react warmly to stories conveying good news. Other imagined hostile readers and took a certain pleasure in providing them with bad news. The comparison of the fantasies about "supportive" and "critical" readers suggested that the affective component in a reporter's image of his public might influence the accuracy of his writing. Pool and Shulman tried to test this distortion factor by supplying four groups of thirty-three journalism students each with scrambled facts taken from stories that communicated both good news and bad news. Each student assembled the facts into his own version of the story and then listed persons who came to mind while thinking back over the writing. He then was interviewed to determine the degree of approval or criticism that he attributed to the persons on his list, and his story was checked for accuracy. The experimenters found that writers with supportive "image persons" reported good news more accurately than they reported bad news, and that writers with critical "image persons" reported bad news with more accuracy. Pool and Shulman concluded that accuracy was congruent with a reporter's fantasies about his public.

The experiment suggests how current theories about mass communication may be applied to research on the media. Now that sociologists no longer think of communication as a one-way process of implanting messages in a relatively passive "mass" audience, they can analyze the audience's influence on the communicator. Having become sensitive to the importance of feedback and noise, they can understand how a writer's image of his public shapes his writing. But they sometimes fail to take into consideration another element, which is conspicuously absent from the Pool-Shulman study, namely the communicator's milieu. Reporters operate in city rooms, not in classrooms. They write for one another as well as for the public. And their way of conceiving and communicating news results from an apprenticeship in their craft. Translated into sociological language, those observations suggest four hypotheses: in order to understand how newspapermen function as communicators, one should analyze (1) the structure of their milieu, the city room; (2) their relation to primary reference groups, i.e., editors, other reporters, and news sources; (3) their occupational socialization, or the way they get "broken in" as reporters; and (4) the cultural determinants of their encoding, or how standardized techniques of telling "stories" influence their writing of "news." By ignoring the milieu of the city room and by dealing with students who had not undergone an apprenticeship, Pool and Shulman neglected the most important elements in newswriting. In order to indicate the importance of the four elements named above, I have tried to analyze my recollections of my brief career as a reporter for the *Newark Star Ledger* and *The New York Times* from 1959 to 1964.

The Structure of the Newsroom

Reporters on *The New York Times* used to believe that their editors expected them to aim their stories at an imaginary twelve-year-old girl. Some thought that she appeared in *The Style Book of the New York Times*, although she only existed in our minds. "Why twelve years old?" I used to ask myself. "Why a girl? What are her opinions on prison reform and the Women's House of Detention?" This mythical creature was the only "audience image" I ever ran across in my newspaper work, and she merely functioned as a reminder that we should keep our copy clear and clean. We really wrote for one another. Our primary reference group was spread around us in the newsroom, or "the snake pit," as some called it. We knew that no one would jump on our stories as quickly as our colleagues; for reporters make the most voracious readers, and they have to win their status anew each day as they expose themselves before their peers in print.

There are structural elements to the status system of the newsroom, as its layout indicates. The managing editor rules from within an office; and lesser editors command clusters of "desks" (foreign desk, national desk, city or "metropolitan" desk) at one end of the room, an end that stands out by the different orientation of the furniture and that is enclosed behind a low fence. At the other end, row upon row of reporters' desks face the editors across the fence. They fall into four sections. First, a few rows of star reporters led by luminaries like Homer Bigart, Peter Kihss, and McCandlish Phillips. Then three rows of rewrite men, who sit to the side of the stars at the front of the room so that they can be near the command posts during deadline periods. Next, a spread of middle-aged veterans, men who have made their names and can be trusted with any story. And finally, a herd of young men on the make in the back of the room, the youngest generally occupying the remotest positions. Function determines some locations: sports, shipping, "culture," and "society" have their own corners; and copy readers sit accessibly to the side. But to the eye of the initiate, the general lines of the status system stand out as clearly as a banner headline.[2]

The most expert eye in the city room belongs to the city editor. From his point of maximal visibility, he can survey his entire staff and can put each man in his place, for he alone knows the exact standing of everyone. The "staffer" is only aware of occupying an indeterminate position in one of the four sections. He therefore tries to trace the trajectory of his career by watching the key variable in the functioning of the city room: the assignment. A reporter who keeps a string of good assignments going for several weeks is destined to move up to a desk nearer the editor's end of the room, while a man who constantly bungles stories will stagnate in his present position or will be exiled to Brooklyn or "society" or "the West Side shack" (a police beat now extinct and replaced, functionally, by New Jersey). The daily paper shows who has received the best assignments. It is a map, which reporters learn to read and to compare with their mental map of the city room in an attempt to know where they stand and where they are headed.

But once you have learned to read the status system, you must learn to write. How do you know when you have done a good job on a story? When I was a greenhorn on *The Times*, I began one week with a "profile" or man-in-the-news, which won a compliment from the assistant city editor and a coveted out-of-town assignment for the next day. Half the police force of a small town had been arrested for stealing stolen goods, and I found a cop who was willing to talk, so the story made the "second front," the front page of the second section, which attracts a good deal of attention. On the third day, I covered the centenary celebrations at Cornell. They satisfied my ego (I rode back to New York in the private plane that normally served the president of the university) but not my editor: I filed seven hundred and fifty words, which were cut down to five hundred. Next, I went to a two-day convention of city planners at West Point. Once again my ego swelled as the planners scrambled to get their names in *The Times*, but for the life of me I could not find anything interesting to say about them. I filed five hundred words, which did not even make the paper. For the next week I wrote nothing but obituaries.

Assignments, cuts, and the situating or "play" of stories therefore belong to a system of positive and negative reinforcements. By-lines come easily on *The Times*, unlike many papers, so reporters find gratification in getting their stories past the copy

2. The layout and personnel of the newsroom have changed somewhat since I left *The Times*, and of course much of this description would not fit other newspapers, which have their own organization and ethos [Darnton's note].

desk unchanged and into a desirable location in the paper, that is, close to the front and above the fold. Every day every foreign correspondent gets his reinforcement in the form of "frontings," a cable telling him which stories have made the front page and which have been "inside." Compliments also carry weight, especially if they come from persons with prestige, like the night city editor, the stars, or the most talented reporters in one's own territory. The city editor and managing editor dispense pats on the back, occasional congratulatory notes, and lunches; and every month the publisher awards cash prizes for the best stories. As the reinforcements accrue, one's status evolves. A greenhorn may eventually become a veteran or embark on more exotic channels of upward mobility by winning a national or foreign assignment. The veterans also include a sad collection of men on the decline, foreign correspondents who have been sent home to pasture, or bitter, ambitious men who have failed to get editorships. I often heard it said that reporting was a young man's game, that you passed your prime by forty, and that as you got older all stories began to seem the same.

Reporters naturally write to please the editors manipulating the reward system from the other end of the room, but there is no straightforward way of winning reinforcement by writing the best possible story. In run-of-the-mill assignments, a voice over the public address system—"Jones, city desk"—summons the reporter to the assignment editor, who explains the assignment: "The Kiwanis Club of Brooklyn is holding its annual luncheon, where it will announce the results of this year's charity drive and the winner of its Man of the Year Award. It's probably worth a good half-column, because we haven't done anything on Brooklyn recently, and the drive is a big deal over there." The editor tries to get the best effort from Jones by playing up the importance of the assignment, and he plants a few clues as to what he thinks "the story" is. A potential lead sentence may actually rattle around in Jones's head as he takes the subway to Brooklyn: "This year's charity drive in Brooklyn produced a record-breaking $. . . . ., the Kiwanis Club announced at its annual luncheon meeting yesterday." Jones arrives, interviews the president of the club, sits through a chicken dinner and several speeches, and learns that the drive produced a disappointing $300,000 and that the club named a civic-minded florist as its man of the year. "So what's the story?" the night city editor asks him upon his return. Jones knows better than to play up this non-event to the night city editor, but he wants something to show for his day's work; so he explains the unspectacular character of the drive, adding that the florist seemed to be an interesting character. "You'd better lead with the florist, then. Two hundred words," says the night city editor. Jones walks off to the back of the room and begins the story: "Anthony Izzo, a florist who has made trees grow in Brooklyn for a decade, received the annual Man of the Year Award from the Brooklyn Kiwanis Club yesterday for his efforts to beautify the city's streets. The club also announced that its annual charity drive netted $300,000, a slight drop from last year's total, which the Club's president, Michael Calise, attributed to the high rate of unemployment in the area." The story occupies a mere fourth of a column well back in the second section of the paper. No one mentions it to Jones on the following day. No letters arrive for him from Brooklyn. And he feels rather dissatisfied about the whole experience, especially as Smith, who sits next to him in the remote centerfield section of the city room, made the second front with a colorful story about garbage dumping. But Jones consoles himself with the hope that he might get a better assignment today and with the reflection that the allusion to the tree growing in Brooklyn was a nice touch, which might have been noticed by the city editor and certainly had been appreciated by Smith. But Jones also knows that the story did not make his stock rise with the assignment editor, who had had a different conception of it, or with the night city editor, who had not had time to devote more than two or three minutes' thought to it, nor to the other editors, who must have perceived it as the hack job that it was.

In the case of an important assignment, like a multi-column "take out," the city editor might walk over to Jones' desk and discuss the story with him in a kind of conspiratorial huddle before a sea of eyes. Jones contacts a dozen different sources and writes a story that differs considerably from what the editor had in mind. The editor, who gets a carbon copy of everything submitted to the copy desk, disapproves of the text and has Jones summoned to him by the public address system. After huddling in alien territory, Jones negotiates his way back to his desk through the sea of eyes and tries again. Eventually he reaches a version that represents a compromise between the editor's preconceptions and his own impressions—but he knows that he would have won more points if his impressions had come closer to the mark imagined by the editor in the first place. And he did not enjoy walking the tightrope between his desk and the city editor before the crowd of reporters waiting for his status to drop.

Like everyone else, reporters vary in their sensitivity to pressure from their peer group, but I doubt that many of them— especially from the ranks of the greenhorns—enjoy being summoned to the city desk. They learn to escape to the bathroom or to crouch behind drinking fountains when the hungry eye of the editor surveys the field. When the fatal call comes over the public address system—"Jones, city desk"—Jones can feel his colleagues thinking as he walks past them. "I hope he gets a lousy assignment or that he gets a good one and blows it." The result will be there for everyone to see in tomorrow's paper. Editors sometimes try to get the best effort out of their men by playing them off against one another and by advocating values like competitiveness and "hustling." "Did you see how Smith handled that garbage story?" the city editor will say to Jones. "That's the kind of work we need from the man who is going to fill the next opening in the Chicago bureau. You should hustle more." Two days later, Jones may have outdone Smith. The immediacy and the irregularity of reinforcement in the assignment-publication process mean that no one, except a few stars, can be sure of his status in the newsroom.

Chronic insecurity breeds resentment. While scrambling over one another for the approval of the editors, the reporters develop great hostility to the men at the other end of the room, and some peer-group solidarity develops as a counter-force to the competitiveness. The reporters feel united by a sentiment of "them" against "us," which they express in horseplay and house jokes. (I remember a clandestine meeting in the men's room, where one reporter gave a parody of urinating techniques among "them.") Many reporters, especially among the embittered veterans, deride the editors, who are mostly former reporters, for selling out to the management and for losing contacts with the down-to-earth reality that can only be appreciated by honest "shoe-leather men." This anti-management ideology creates a barrier to the open courting of editors and makes some reporters think that they write only to please themselves and their peers.

The feeling of solidarity against "them" expresses itself most strongly in the reporters' taboo against "piping" or distorting a story so that it fits an editor's preconceptions. Editors apparently think of themselves as "idea men," who put a reporter on the scent of a story and expect him to track it down and bring it back in publishable form. Reporters think of editors as manipulators of both reality and men. To them, an editor is a person who cares mainly about improving his position in his own, separate hierarchy by coming up with bright ideas and getting his staff to write in conformity to them. The power of editor over reporter, like that of publisher over editor, does indeed produce bias in newswriting, as has been emphasized in studies of "social control in the newsroom." But the reporters' horror of "piping" acts as a countervailing influence. For example, an assistant city editor on *The Times* once got an inspiration for a pollution story from his son, who complained that an ice-cream cone had become so filthy as he walked down the street that he had had to throw it into a trash can. The reporter dutifully built the story around the anecdote, adding as an embellishment that the unnamed little boy missed the trash can and walked away. The editor did not delete this last touch. He was delighted with the story, which presumably improved his standing with the other editors and the reporter's standing with him. But it made the reporter's reputation plummet among her peers and served as a deterrent against further "piping" on the other side of the fence.

The peer group's own standards of craftsmanship also pit reporters against copyeditors. Copyeditors tend to be a separate breed among newspapermen. Quiet, intense, perhaps more eccentric and more learned than most reporters, they are cast in the role of being sticklers for language. They go by the book—*The Style Book of The New York Times* on *The Times*—and they have their own hierarchy, which leads from the lowly members of their desk to the "slot man," who apportions the copy among them to the "bull pen," where the final tailoring of each edition takes place, and ultimately to an assistant managing editor, who in my day was Theodore Bernstein, a man of great power and prestige. Copyeditors apparently think of themselves as second-class citizens in the newsroom: every day, as they see it, they save the reporters from dozens of errors of fact and grammar; yet the reporters revile them. "The game is to sneak some color or interpretation past that line of humorless zombies," one reporter explained to me. Copyeditors seem to view stories as segments in an unremitting flow of "copy," which cries out for standardization, while reporters regard each piece as their own. Personal touches—bright quotations or observations—satisfy the reporter's sense of craftsmanship and provoke the blue-penciling instinct of the copyeditor. Lead sentences produce the worst injuries in the reporter's unending battle with his editors and copyeditors; he may attribute cuts and poor play of his stories to the pressure of circumstances, but a change in his lead is a challenge to his news judgment, the ineffable quality that marks him as a "pro." To reverse the order of a reporter's first two paragraphs is to wound his professional identity. He will even take offense at slight changes of phrasing in his first sentence that he would hardly notice further down in the story. And a really bad lead can damage a man's career. A friend of mine once led a story with a remark about a baby who had been burned "to an almost unrecognizable crisp." It was the "almost" that especially outraged the editors. That lead cost him ten years in the lowliest position of the newsroom, or so we believed.

Reporters are held together by sub-groups, which also mitigate competitiveness and insecurity and influence ways of writing. Clusters of reporters form according to age, life-style, or cultural background (City College vs. Harvard in the early sixties at *The Times*). Some have lunch together, buy each other drinks in certain bars, or exchange family visits. A reporter develops trust in his subgroup. He consults it while working on stories and pays attention to its shop talk. A reporter in my group once had to do a rushed story about a confusing change in the city's incomprehensible welfare programs. Four or five of us went over his material, trying to extract some meaning from it, until one person finally pronounced, "It's a holding operation." That became the lead of the story and the idea around which the entire article was organized. Almost every article develops around a core conception of what constitutes "the story," which may emerge from the reporter's contacts with allies in the city room as well as from his dialogue with the editors. Just as messages pass through a "two-step" or multi-step communication process on the receiving end, they pass through several stages in their formation. If the communicator is a city reporter, he filters his ideas through reference groups and role sets in the city room before turning them loose on "the public."

The adjustment of writer to milieu is complicated by a final factor: institutional history. Long-term shifts in the power structure of a newspaper affect the way reporters write, even though the rank and file does not know exactly what goes on among editors and executives. Many papers are divided into semi-autonomous dukedoms ruled by the city editor, the foreign editor, and the national editor. Each of these men commands clusters of assistant editors and owes fealty to the managing editor, who in turn shares power with other executives, such as the business manager, and submits to the supreme sovereign of all, the publisher. At *The Times*, each editor dominates a certain proportion of the paper, so that in an issue of *n* columns, the city editor can expect to command *x* columns, the foreign editor *y* columns, and so forth. Of course the proportions vary every day according to the importance of events, but in the long run they are determined by the ability of each potentate to defend and extend his domain. Changes in territoriality often take place at the "four o'clock conference" in the managing editor's office, where the day's paper takes shape. Here each editor summarizes the output of his staff and, day after day, builds up a case for the coverage of his area. A forceful city editor can get more space for city-room reporters and can inspire them with a fresh sense of the newsworthiness of their subjects.

City news underwent such a revival during my period at *The Times*, owing to the influence of a new city editor, A. M. Rosenthal. Before Rosenthal's editorship, New York stories tended to be thorough, reliable, conventional, and dull. Rosenthal wanted snappier, more original copy, and he wanted his men to "hustle." He therefore gave the best assignments to the reporters who conformed most closely to his standards, regardless of their position in the city room. This policy infuriated the veterans, who had learned to write according to the old rules and who believed in the established principle that one earned the right to the best assignments by years of solid service. They complained about trendiness, jazziness, superficiality, and sophomorism. Some of them resigned, some succeeded in brightening up their copy, and many withdrew into a world of private or peer-group bitterness. Most of the green-horns responded by exuberant hustling. An alliance grew up between them and Rosenthal, a poor boy from the Bronx and City College, who had hustled his way to the top of *The Times*. The qualities that had made him succeed—talent, drive, enthusiasm—now made for success in the city room. Of course those qualities were recognized under the old seniority system (otherwise Rosenthal himself would never have had such a spectacular career), but the new editor shifted the balance among the norms: the emphasis on hustling at the expense of seniority meant that achievement outweighed ascription in the determination of status.

The institutionalization of this new value system created more confusion and pain than can be conveyed by sociological terminology. In disturbing the established routes of mobility, Rosenthal did not completely cut himself off from the veterans. He did not interfere with the stars, and he did not win over all the greenhorns. Instead, he produced status anxiety everywhere, perhaps even for himself; for he seemed to have been surprised at the hostility he evoked from men who had been his friends, and he probably had worries about his own standing among the other editors and executives. The first months of his editorship constituted a difficult, transitional period in the city room. While the rules of the game were changing, no one knew where he stood; for standing seemed to fluctuate as erratically as the apportionment of assignments. A reporter might keep a string of good assignments going for a week, while a deadly rain of obituaries fell all around him, but he could also be banished overnight to the obit page or the "caboose" (the last news section of the Sunday paper). Hence the dread character of the summons over the public address system. Eventually, however, a new status system became established according to the new norms. Bolstered by raises and promotions, the bright, aggressive young men set the tone in the newsroom and moved on to more prestigious posts. By now several of them have become stars. Changes also occurred throughout the executive ranks. The paper acquired a new foreign editor, city editor, national editor, Washington bureau chief, and, ultimately, a new managing editor—A. M. Rosenthal. Gossips attributed these changes to personal machinations, but in its brutal, awkward way *The Times* was really rejuvenating itself by putting power into the hands of the generation that was ready and eager to succeed those who had reached their prime during World War II. Institutional evolution—the redistribution of power, the disturbance of role-sets, the modification of norms—had an important influence on the way we wrote news, even though we were only half aware of the forces at work.

* * *

Occupational Socialization

Although some reporters may learn to write in journalism schools, where Pool and Shulman selected the subjects for the student group in their experiment, most of them (including many journalism-school graduates) pick up newswriting in the course of an apprenticeship. They acquire attitudes, values, and a professional ethos while serving as copy boys in the city room; and they learn to perceive news and to communicate it while being "broken in" as rookie reporters.

By watching the smoke rise from Homer Bigart's typewriter near deadline time, by carrying his hot copy to the editors, and by reading it in cold print on the next day, the copy boy internalizes the norms of the craft. He acquires the tone of the newsroom by listening. Slowly he learns to sound more like a New Yorker, to speak more loudly, to use reporter's slang, and to increase the proportion of swear words in his speech. These techniques ease communication with colleagues and with news sources. It is difficult, for example, to get much out of a telephone conversation with a police lieutenant unless you know how to place your mouth close to the receiver and shout obscenities. While mastering these mannerisms, the copy boy insensibly stocks his mind with values. I remember vividly the disgust on a copy reader's face when he read a dispatch from a correspondent in the Congo that contained some hysterical phrases about bullets whizzing through the hotel room. It did not do to lose one's cool. Another correspondent, who had seen some rough fighting during the Algerian revolution, impressed me with a story about a lizard that got caught in the fan of his cooling unit in the Algiers bureau. He did not mention the slaughter of Algerians, but he had a great deal to say about the difficulty of writing while being sprayed with chopped lizard. One does not have to eavesdrop very hard to get the gist of reporters' talk. They talk about themselves, not the personages of their stories—just as history professors talk about history professors, not Frederick II. It takes only a few weeks of carrying copy to learn how Mike Berger interviewed Clare Booth Luce, how Abe Rosenthal anatomized Poland, and how Dave Halberstam scored against the Diems in South Vietnam. In fact, the talk of *The Times* is institutionalized and appears as *Times Talk*, a house publication in which reporters describe their work. So even if you feel timid about approaching Tom Wicker, you may still read his own version of how he covered the assassination of President Kennedy.

Like other crafts, newspapering has its own mythology. Many times have I heard the tale of how Jamie MacDonald covered a raid over Germany from the turret of an R.A.F. bomber and how his wife Kitty, the greatest telephone operator of all time, put Mike Berger, the greatest city reporter, in touch with the governor of New York by establishing a radio link-up to a yacht in the middle of the Atlantic, where the governor was trying to remain incommunicado. The newsroom will not soon forget the day that Edwin L. James took up his duties as managing editor. He arrived in his fabled fur coat, sat down at the poker game that was always under way behind the rewrite desks, cleaned everybody out, and then joined "them" at the other end of the room, where he reigned thenceforth with supreme authority. Reporters sense an obligation to "measure up" to standards set in the past, though they know that they must look small in comparison with their mythical titans. It does not matter that Gay Talese can never write about New York as well as Mike Berger or that Abe Rosenthal can never command the managing editorship with the intelligence and flair of Edwin L. James. The cult of the dead gives life to the quick. We wrote for Berger and James as well as for the living members of the city room.

Reporters' talk also concerns the conditions of their work: the problems of telephone and telegraph communication in underdeveloped countries, the censorship in Israel and the U.S.S.R., expense accounts. (I was so obtuse about filing for expenses in London that I did not even get the point of the classic stories about the Canadian correspondent who put in for a dogsled, or the African correspondent who invited reporters to spend week-ends in his villa and then presented them with fake hotel bills to be filed with their expense accounts. I had to be told that my paltry expenses were lowering the living standard of the whole bureau.) One city room reporter told me that his proudest moment came when he was sent to cover a fire, discovered it was a false alarm, and returned with a story about false alarms. He felt he had transformed the humdrum into "news" by finding a new "angle." Another reporter said that he felt he had crossed the line dividing greenhorns and veterans one day when he was covering the civil war in the Congo. He got an open line to London at an unexpectedly early moment, when he had hardly finished reading over his notes. Knowing that he could not postpone communication and that every minute was terribly expensive, he wrote the story at great speed directly on the teletype machine. Some reporters remarked that they did not feel fully professional until they had completed a year on night rewrite, an assignment that requires great speed and clarity in writing. Others said that they gained complete confidence after successfully covering a big story that broke right on deadline.

Reporters gradually develop a sense of mastery over their craft— of being able to write a column in an hour on anything, no matter how difficult the conditions. The staff in London had great respect for Drew Middleton's ability to dictate a new lead to a story immediately after being awakened in the middle of the night and informed of a major new development. Failure to make a deadline is considered unspeakably unprofessional. One man near me in the city room had missed several deadlines. At about 4:00 P.M. when he had a big story, he would furtively gulp down a Dixie Cup full of bourbon from a bottle that he hid in the bottom drawer of his desk. The copy boys knew all about him. In one sweep of the eye, they could take in the deadline agonies of dozens of men. Their job virtually forces anticipatory socialization upon them, for they have no fixed position but rove all over the city room, working with editors and copyreaders as well as reporters. They quickly learn to read the status system and have no difficulty in choosing positive and negative identity models. By listening to shop talk and observing behavior patterns, they assimilate an ethos: unflappability, accuracy, speed, shrewdness, toughness, earthiness, and hustle. Reporters seem somewhat cynical about the subjects of their stories and sentimental about themselves. They speak of the "shoe-leather man" as if he were the only honest and intelligent person in a world of rogues and fools. While everyone about him manipulates and falsifies reality, he stands aside and records it. I remember how one reporter introduced the figure of the news-paperman into an anecdote about politicians, ad men, and p.r. men: ". . . and then there was this guy in a trench coat." I never saw a trenchcoat anywhere in *The Times*. The reporters tended to outfit themselves at Brooks Brothers, which may have been a sign of ambivalence about an "establishment" that they pretended to despise. But they had a trench-coat image of themselves. In fact, they had a whole repertory of stylized images, which shaped the way they reported the news, and they acquired this peculiar mental set through their on-the-job training.

Standardizing and Stereotyping

Although the copy boy may become a reporter through different rites of passage, he normally undergoes a training period at police headquarters. After this "probation," as it is known at *The Times*, he is supposed to be able to handle anything; for the police story passes as an archetypical form of "news," and he is ready for the White House if he has survived headquarters—a parallel, incidentally, that suggests something of the spirit in which reporters approach their material.

I was inducted at the police headquarters of Newark, New Jersey, in the summer of 1959, when I worked for the *Newark Star Ledger*. On my first day of work, a veteran reporter gave me a tour of the place, which came to a climax in the photographic section. Since a police photographer takes a picture of every corpse that is found in Newark, the police have developed a remarkable collection of pictures of ripped-open and decomposed cadavers (the corpses of drowned persons are the most impressive), and they enjoy showing it off to greenhorns from the press. Press photographers build up their own collections, sometimes with help from the police, who get arrested prostitutes to pose for them. When I returned to the pressroom, a photographer from the *Mirror* gave me one of his obscene mug shots and showed me his homemade pin-up collection, which featured his fiancée. A woman reporter then asked me whether I was a virgin, which produced a round of laughs from the men at the poker game. She was leaning back in her chair with her feet on the desk and her skirt around her hips, and my face changed instantly from green to red. Once the initiation was over, the poker game resumed, and I was left to do the "leg work" for everyone. That meant collecting the "squeal sheets," or summary reports of every action by the police, from an office upstairs. The reporters depended on the police radio and on tips from friends on the force to inform them of big stories, but they used the squeal sheets to check out the odd, man-bites-dog occurrence that has potential news value. Every hour or so I would bring a batch of squeal sheets down to the pressroom and would read them aloud to the poker game, announcing anything that struck me as a potential story. I soon discovered that I was not born with a nose for news; for when I smelled something newsworthy, the veterans usually told me that it was not a story, while they frequently picked up items that seemed unimportant to me I knew, of course, that no news is good news and that only something awful could make a really "good" story. But it took some time before I learned not to get excited at a "d.o.a." (dead on arrival—a notation that often refers to heart attacks) or a "cutting" (a stabbing, usually connected with minor thefts or family squabbles that were too numerous to be newsworthy). Once I thought I had found such a spectacular squeal sheet—I think it included murder, rape, and incest—that I went directly to the homicide squad to check it out. After reading the sheet, the detective looked up at me in disgust, "Can't you see that it's 'black,' kid? That's no story." A capital "B" followed the names of the victim and the suspect. I had not known that atrocities among black persons did not constitute "news."

The higher the victim's status, the bigger the story: that principle became clear when Newark was lucky enough to get the biggest crime story of the summer. A beautiful, wealthy debutante disappeared mysteriously from the Newark airport, and immediately the pressroom filled with hot-shot reporters from all over the East, who filed such stories as NEWARK HUNTS THE MISSING DEB. FIANCEE DISAPPEARS IN BROAD DAYLIGHT, and FATHER GRIEVES KIDNAPPED HEIRESS. We had not been able to get our desks to take more than a paragraph on the best muggings and rapes, but they would accept anything about the missing deb. A colleague and I filed a long report on HER LAST STEPS, which was nothing more than a description of the airport's floor plan with some speculation as to where the girl could have gone, but it turned out that "side bars" (stories devoted to secondary aspects of an event) about last steps often accompany stories about kidnappings and vanishings. We simply drew on the traditional repertory of genres. It was like making cookies from an antique cookie cutter.

Big stories develop in special patterns and have an archaic flavor, as if they were metamorphoses of Ur-stories that have been lost in the depths of time. The first thing a city-room reporter does after receiving an assignment is to search for relevant material among earlier stories filed in the "morgue." The dead hand of the past therefore shapes his perception of the present. Once he has been through the morgue, he will make a few phone calls and perhaps do some interviewing or observing outside the office. (I found that reporters consumed little shoe leather and ran up enormous telephone bills.) But the new information he acquires must fit into categories that he has inherited from his predecessors. Thus many stories are remarkably similar in form, whether they concern "hard news" or more stylized "features." Historians of American journalism—with the exception of Helen MacGill Hughes, a sociologist—seem to have overlooked the long-term cultural determinants of "news." French historians, however, have observed some remarkable cases of continuity in their own journalistic tradition. One story concerns a case of mistaken identity in which a father and mother murder their own son. It first was published in a primitive Parisian news-sheet of 1618. Then it went through a series of reincarnations, appearing in Toulouse in 1848, in Angoulême in 1881, and finally in a modern Algerian newspaper, where Albert Camus picked it up and reworked it in existentialist style for L'Etranger and Malentendu.[3] Although the names, dates, and places vary, the form of the story is unmistakably the same throughout those three centuries.

Of course it would be absurd to suggest that newsmen's fantasies are haunted by primitive myths of the sort imagined by Jung and Lévi-Strauss, but newswriting is heavily influenced by stereotypes and by preconceptions of what "the story" should be. Without pre-established categories of what constitutes "news," it is impossible to sort out experience. There is an epistemology of the fait divers. To turn a squeal sheet into an article requires training in perception and in the manipulation of standardized images, clichés, "angles," "slants," and scenarios, which will call

3. J. P. Seguin, *Nouvelles à sensation:* pp. 187–90 [Darnton's note].
Canards du XIXe siècle (Paris, 1959),

forth a conventional response in the minds of editors and readers. A clever writer imposes an old form on new matter in a way that creates some tension—will the subject fit the predicate?—and then resolves it by falling back on the familiar. Hence Jones's satisfaction with his lead sentence. Jones began by summoning up a standard image, the tree growing in Brooklyn, and just when the reader began to feel uneasy about where it might be going, Jones snapped it on the "peg" or the event of the day: the man-of-the-year award. "A florist gets a prize for making trees grow in Brooklyn," the reader thinks. "That's neat." It is the neatness of the fit that produces the sense of satisfaction, like the comfort that follows the struggle to force one's foot into a tight boot. The trick will not work if the writer deviates too far from the conceptual repertory that he shares with his public and from the techniques of tapping it that he has learned from his predecessors.

The tendency toward stereotyping did not mean that the half-dozen reporters in Newark police headquarters wrote exactly the same thing, though our copy was very similar and we shared all our information. Some reporters favored certain slants. One of the two women regulars in the pressroom frequently phoned around district police stations asking, "Any teen-age sex parties lately?" As the acknowledged expert in her field, she filed stories on teen-age sex that the rest of us would not touch. Similarly, a fire-buff among the Manhattan reporters—a strange man with a wooden leg, who wore a revolver around his chest—reported more fires than anyone else. To remain as a "regular" in a police pressroom probably calls for some congruity in temperament and subject matter, and also for a certain callousness. I learned to be fairly casual about "cuttings" and even "jumpers" (suicides who leap off buildings), but I never got over my amazement at the reporters' ability to get "reaction" stories by informing parents of their childrens' death: " 'He was always such a good boy,' exclaimed Mrs. MacNaughton, her body heaving with sobs." When I needed such quotes, I used to make them up, as did some of the others—a tendency that also contributed toward standardization, for we knew what "the bereaved mother" and "the mourning father" should have said and possibly even heard them speak what was in our minds rather than what was on theirs. "Color" or feature stories left more room for improvization but they, too, fell into conventional patterns. Animal stories, for example, went over very well with the city desk. I did one on policeman's horses and learned after its publication that my paper had carried the same story, more or less, at least twice during the previous ten years.

By the end of my summer in Newark, I had written a great many stories but had not received a by-line. One day, when I had nothing better to do, I checked out a squeal sheet about a boy who had been robbed of his bicycle in a park. I knew that my desk would not take it, but I produced four paragraphs on it anyway, in order to practice writing, and I showed it to one of the regulars during a lull in the poker game. You can't write that kind of a story straight as if it were a press release, he explained. And in a minute or so he typed out an entirely different version, making up details as he needed them. It went something like this:

Every week Billy put his twenty-five-cent allowance in his piggy bank. He wanted to buy a bike. Finally, the big day came. He chose a shiny red Schwinn, and took it out for a spin in the park. Every day for a week he rode proudly around the same route. But yesterday three toughs jumped him in the middle of the park. They knocked him from the bike and ran off with it. Battered and bleeding, Billy trudged home to his father, George F. Wagner of 43 Elm Street. "Never mind son," his dad said, "I'll buy you a new bike, and you can use it on a paper route to earn the money to pay me back." Billy hopes to begin work soon. But he'll never ride through the park again.

I got back on the phone to Mr. Wagner with a new set of questions: Did Billy get an allowance? Did he save it in a piggy bank? What was the color of the bicycle? What did Mr. Wagner say to him after the robbery? Soon I had enough details to fit the new pattern of the story. I rewrote it in the new style, and it appeared the next day in a special box, above the fold, on the front page, and with a by-line. The story produced quite a response, especially on Elm Street, where the Wagners' neighbors took up a collection for a new bicycle, as Mr. Wagner told me later. The commissioner of parks was upset and telephoned to explain how well the parks were patrolled, and how new measures were being taken to protect citizens in the Elm Street area. I was astonished to discover that I had struck several chords by manipulating stock sentiments and figures: the boy and his bike, piggy-bank saving, heartless bullies, the comforting father. The story sounded strangely old-fashioned. Except for the bicycle, it might have come out of the mid-nineteenth century.

Several years later, when I did some research on popular culture in early modern France and England, I came across tales that bore a striking resemblance to the stories that we had written from the pressroom of police headquarters in Newark. English chapbooks, broadside ballads, and penny dreadfuls, French *canards*, *images d'Epinal*, and the *bibliothèque bleue* all purvey the same motifs, which also appear in children's literature and probably derive from ancient oral traditions. A nursery rhyme or an illustration from Mother Goose may have hovered in some semi-conscious corner of my mind while I wrote the tale of Billy and the bullies.

I had a little moppet [a doll]
I kept it in my pocket
And fed it on corn and hay;
Then came a proud beggar
And said he would have her,
And stole my little moppet away.

In their original version, nursery rhymes were often intended for adults. When journalists began to address their stories to a "popular" audience, they wrote as if they were communicating with children, or "le peuple, ce grand enfant," as the French say. Thus the condescending, sentimental, and moralistic character of popular journalism. It would be misleading, however, to conceive of cultural diffusion exclusively as a "trickle-down" process, for currents move up from the common people as well as down from the élite. The *Tales* of Perrault, *The Magic Flute* by Mozart, and Courbet's *Burial at Ornans* illustrate the dialectical play between "high" and "low" cultural in three genres during three centuries. Of course we did not suspect that cultural determinants were shaping the way we wrote about crimes in Newark, but we did not sit down at our typewriters with our minds a *tabula rasa*. Because of our tendency to see immediate events rather than long-term processes, we were blind to the archaic element in journalism. But our very conception of "news" resulted from ancient ways of telling "stories."

Tabloid stories and crime reporting may be more stylized than the writing that goes into *The New York Times*, but I found a great deal of standardization and stereotyping in the stories of *The Times*' London bureau, when I worked there in 1963-64. Having spent more time in England than the other correspondents in the bureau, I thought I could give a truer picture of the country; but my copy was as stylized as theirs. We had to work within the conventions of the craft. When we covered diplomatic stories, the press spokesman for the Foreign Office would provide an official statement, an off-the-record explanation, and a background analysis for anything we needed to know. The information came so carefully packaged that it was difficult to unwrap it and to put it together in another way; as a result, diplomatic stories all sounded very much alike. In writing "color" stories, it was almost impossible to escape American clichés about England. The foreign desk devoured everything about the royal family, Sir Winston Churchill, cockneys, pubs, Ascot, and Oxford. When Churchill was ailing, I wrote a story about the crowds that gathered outside his window and quoted one man who had caught a glimpse of him as saying, "Blimey he's beautiful." The cockney-Churchill combination could not be resisted. *The Times* put it on the front page, and it was picked up by dozens of other papers, wire services, and news magazines. Few foreign correspondents speak the language of the country they cover. But that handicap does not hurt them because, if they have a nose for news, they do not need a tongue or ears; they bring more to the events they cover than they take away from them. Consequently, we wrote about the England of Dickens, and our colleagues in Paris portrayed the France of Victor Hugo, with some Maurice Chevalier thrown in.

After leaving London, I returned to the newsroom of *The Times*. One of my first stories concerned a "homicidal maniac" who had scattered his victims' limbs under various doorsteps of the West Side. I wrote it up as if I were composing an ancient *canard*: "Un homme de 60 ans coupé en morceaux. . . . Détails horribles!!!"[4] When I has finished the story, I noticed one of the graffiti scribbled on the walls of the pressroom in the headquarters of the Manhattan police: "All the news that fits we print." The writer meant that one can only get articles into the paper if there is enough space for them, but he might have been expressing a deeper truth: newspaper stories must fit cultural preconceptions of news. Yet eight million people live out their lives every day in New York City, and I felt overwhelmed by the disparity between their experience, whatever it was, and the tales that they read in *The Times*.

Conclusion

One man's encounter with two newspapers hardly provides enough material to construct a sociology of newswriting. I would not presume to pronounce on the meaning of other reporters' experience, because I never got beyond the greenhorn stage and because I did not work on papers that typify either "yellow" or "quality" journalism. Styles of reporting vary according to time, place, and the character of each newspaper. The American way of writing news differs from the European and has differed throughout American history. Benjamin Franklin probably did not worry about an occupational ethos when he wrote the copy, set the type, pulled the sheets, distributed the issues, and collected the revenue of *The Pennsylvania Gazette*. But since Franklin's time, newspapermen have become increasingly enmeshed in complex professional relationships, in the newsroom, in the bureau, and on the beat. With specialization and professionalization, they have responded increasingly to the influence of their professional peer group, which far exceeds that of any images they may have of a general public.

In emphasizing this influence, I do not mean to discount

4. *Ibid.* p. 173 [Darnton's note].

others. Sociologists, political scientists, and experts on communication have produced a large literature on the effects of economic interests and political biases on journalism. It seems to me, however, that they have failed to understand the way reporters work. The context of work shapes the context of news, and stories also take form under the influence of inherited techniques of story-telling. Those two elements of newswriting may seem to be contradictory, but they come together during a reporter's "breaking in," when he is most vulnerable and most malleable. As he passes through this formative phase, he familarizes himself with news, both as a commodity that is manufactured in the newsrooms and as a way of seeing the world that somehow reached *The New York Times* from *Mother Goose*.

TIMOTHY CROUSE

Coming to Power

For the men following the primary campaigns in 1972, and later the general election campaigns, such as they were, campaign coverage began to settle into a neat and comfortable science around the time of Theodore Roosevelt, the first big-time American politican to rationalize the handing out of news. Stepping into the White House over McKinley's dead body, Roosevelt had given the Washington correspondents a White House pressroom for the first time; installed phones for them; held occasional news conferences in the Oval Office while his barber gave him a late afternoon shave; frequently leaked items to his favorite reporters; and had given out what were the first primitive campaign press schedules.

"He made our work tons lighter," wrote a beholden reporter aboard Teddy's campaign train in 1904. "Whenever he returned to the car after a speech he would round us up and say, 'Now, the next stop will be Bankville. You don't have to bother about that; I'm going to get off the usual thing.' Or, 'At Dashtown, where we stop next, you'd better be on the job. I'll have some new stuff there.' Sometimes he would even tell us in the rough what the new stuff was to be . . . In this way he not only saved us useless physical and mental work, but economized our time and systematized our schedules. It also aided the editors at home to plan out their work without uncertainty . . ."

From Teddy Roosevelt's time until 1956, when Stevenson began taking large jumps around the country by airplane, candidates campaigned by train. For fifty years, the routine hardly changed. In the post-Depression era, the thirty or forty reporters would pile out at each whistle stop, wearing fedoras, carrying notebooks and pencils, and when the high school band had blared its last sour note, and the candidate had stepped out onto the rear platform, they would stand on the tracks making notes and counting the crowd. When the speech was done, the train's whistle would blow, and the reporters would clamber back into their fetid press car— the aroma was a compound of cigar smoke, whiskey and the stench of men who had not bathed for five or six days. The smell sometimes became so rank that porters burned incense in the Pullmans.

The press car was a Pullman car whose seats had been ripped out and replaced with two boards which ran the length of the car on either side. The men sat at these long tables, looking out at the passing countryside, and wrote their stories on bulky typewriters. The stories contained three simple elements: what the candidate had said, the size of the crowd, and the weather. (In their Sunday stories, the men would usually try to assess the candidate's chances, or report what hastily interviewed local politicians thought of the candidate's chances.) Then they would give the stories to the Western Union man. He would tie the stories up in a bundle and toss them off at the next small station, whence the telegrapher would transmit them to the reporters' home offices. There is a story, perhaps apocryphal, that Merriman Smith of the UPI, anxious to file a story before coming to the next station, tied pillows around his number-two man and tossed him off a moving train.

After filing, they would repair to the dining car for lunch or dinner—Rocky Ford melon and fresh mountain trout if they had just passed through Denver, and Dungeness crab if they had made a stop in San Francisco. Traveling on Presidential trains, they ate with the Secret Service men, and since these Secret Service men were husky fellows and had a food allowance of only six dollars a day, the reporters would often treat them to sirloin steak.

As for the candidate, he was usually accessible for news conferences or informal chats throughout the trip. Truman even played poker with the boys; one of them, Joe Short of the Baltimore *Sun*, lost four hundred dollars to the President in one afternoon and had to make it up by padding his expense account for the next few months. "We liked Harry Truman very much," an old timer, Edward T. Folliard, recalled, twenty-four years later. "Of course we felt sorry for him. Poor son of a bitch. We knew he was going to lose."

"It was all very friendly and romantic," said Folliard. Once the Washington *Post*'s chief campaign reporter, he was now seventy-four and lived in retirement in suburban Washington. A tall, skinny man with black hair and the face of a Norman Rockwell farmer, he covered his first campaign when he was twenty-eight—the Herbert Hoover–Al Smith contest of 1928.

Folliard remembered his colleagues as hard-working men who

wrote objective, unbiased stories. "I think 95 percent of the men wrote what they heard and saw and damn little what they thought," he said. "They left that to the editorial writers." Folliard was proud of that objectivity. Yet other observers had a different view of that era of campaign reporting. They saw the reporters of the thirties, forties and fifties as poorly educated men, drawn from the ranks of police reporters and sportswriters who had neither the intellectual curiosity nor equipment to dig below the shimmering surface of the campaign.

In 1937, Leo C. Rosten did a scholarly survey of the 127 main Washington correspondents and found that only half of them had finished college. Eight did not have a high school diploma and two had no high school education at all. Rosten concluded that "men without a 'frame of reference' and with an uncontrolled impressionistic (rather than analytic) approach to issues are driven to a surface interpretation of events."

They are oriented [Rosten continued] with reference to normative words of ambiguous content: "liberty," "Americanism," "justice," "democracy," "socialism," "communism." . . . Newspaper men evidence a marked insecurity in the presence of social theories or political conceptualization. In this light the caustic reportorial reaction to "New Deal professors," "crackpot theories," "the Brain Trust," "Frankfurter's bright young men" soon suggests the projection of doubts of personal adequacy upon men who have unwittingly increased personal and professional insecurities.[1]

But most of these men were not overly worried by the fact that they lacked a diploma. Some simply sent home the kind of news which they knew would please their publishers. The rest were secure in the knowledge that they were not paid to think, analyze, or judge. With few exceptions, these reporters were interchangeable drones who wrote the same simple formula stories day after day.

When these men began to retire, in the fifties, they were replaced by a new generation of young reporters who had gone to college and were asking different kinds of questions. In those days the younger men wrote the same formulaic stories, but at the same time, they were more comfortable with theories and concepts, and more anxious to analyze the political process and report on how it worked.

Their dominance of the profession was sealed with the rise and election of John F. Kennedy. Kennedy played on the values he shared with these young reporters in order to engage their loyalty. He knew many of them socially, and he was careful to treat them with respect and affection. His Harvard-trained advisers spoke in an academic, sophisticated idiom that excluded many of the older reporters but appealed to the new generation. Because they were so obviously in tune with the youthful, "intellectual" atmo-

1. Leo C. Rosten, *Journalism Quarterly*, June 1937 [Crouse's note].

sphere of the New Frontier, the young reporters who had covered Kennedy's campaign in 1960, and now covered him in office, found their stock soaring. It was no coincidence that many of them— reporters like David Broder, Ben Bradlee, Bob Novak, Rowland Evans, Mary McGrory, and Russell Baker—would become leading journalists in the sixties and seventies, and would help to change the techniques of campaign reporting.

But in 1960, campaign coverage had changed very little from what it had been in the 1920's. Planes replaced trains, and the networks made their first all-out attempt to cover an election, but most of the reporting remained superficial, formulaic, and dull. Newspapers approached campaign coverage as a civic duty, like reporting sermons and testimonials to retiring fire chiefs.

The most devasting comment on the political coverage of the time was the reception that greeted Theodore White's book, *The Making of the President 1960*. The book struck most readers as a total revelation—it was as if they had never before read anything, anywhere, that told them what a political campaign was about. They had some idea that a campaign consisted of a series of arcane deals and dull speeches, and suddenly White came along with a book that laid out the campaign as a wide-screen thriller with full-blooded heroes and white-knuckle suspense on every page. The book hit the number-one spot on the best-seller lists six weeks after publication and stayed there for exactly a year.

White had started covering American politics in 1953 for *The Reporter*, after fifteen years in Europe and Asia as a *Time* correspondent. Two years later, he signed on with *Collier's* as the magazine's national political correspondent and began covering his first Presidential campaign. The press entourage in the first primary consisted of White and an AP man riding around New Hampshire with Estes Kefauver. There were occasional interloping visits from a *Times*man or a CBS crew out on a day trip, but in 1956 primaries were considered minor, local events, too inconsequential to rate extensive national coverage. All spring, White had the candidates almost entirely to himself, and he took advantage of the opportunity to build up good relationships with Kefauver, Harriman, and Stevenson as they passed through the primaries and the convention.

He was flying high on the greatest assignment of his life. The only trouble was that *Collier's* was going down for the third time. In September, just as the campaign was gearing up, the management called him back with instructions to supervise a total reorganization of the editorial department in a last-ditch move to save the magazine. Four months later, in spite of White's best efforts, *Collier's* was dead.

What upset White as much as anything was that he had not had the chance to finish the campaign. "It was a classic case of coitus interruptus," said White as he sat in the living room of his Manhattan town house, taking a break from writing the fourth *Making of the President* volume. "There I was, stiff cock, ready to go for the massive summary of the 1956 campaign, and here I am out of a job and no place to write it." Instead, he dined out for the next couple of years on campaign anecdotes, stories about what had *really* happened as opposed to the newspaper accounts, and he found that these stories intrigued a lot of people. He also wrote two novels, the second of which he sold to Hollywood for $85,000. With his financial future secure for at least two years, he decided to indulge himself in his great love, political reporting, and write a book about the 1960 Presidential campaign. He had to go to several publishers before he found one who was enthusiastic about the project, and he assumed that the book would make very little money.

If it was hard to imagine in 1972 that only thirteen years before, a proven novelist had a difficult time selling the idea of a popular book about Presidential politics, it was just as hard to imagine the absolute virginity of much of the territory White set out to explore. "It was like walking through a field playing a brass tuba the day it rained gold," said White. "Everything was sitting around waiting to be reported."

The Republicans were not overly helpful; being somehow convinced that White was writing a work of fiction, they kept assigning him to the Zoo plane with the television technicians and foreign reporters, listing him on the manifest as "Theodore White, novelist." Fortunately, they lost. White had all of his best contacts among the Democrats anyway, and the Kennedy people were especially cooperative, perhaps sensing that they could use White to help them promote the New Frontier. White got to know all the staffers well, and had little trouble seeing Kennedy himself. Flying back from the Montana convention early in 1960, for instance, White had only one CBS correspondent, Blair Clark, for competition. "Blair and I sat around with John F. Kennedy all the way from Montana back to the East Coast, just shooting the breeze," he remembered. "You can't do that any more. Because now there are 27 million correspondents squeezing in."

The reason that 27 million reporters now show up for every kaffee klatsch in New Hampshire has a lot to do with White's first book. "When that book came out," said White, "it was like Columbus telling about America at the court of Ferdinand and Isabella. Goddam thing was an unbelievable success." White is not the world's humblest journalist, but he is not far off the mark about the book's success—the number of imitations and spinoffs testify to that. The first rival, published by *The New York Times*, came out in 1964. By 1968, White was competing against seventeen other campaign books. The London *Sunday Express* and

Sunday Times both sent teams of writers; White began to see him-self as a small independent businessman fighting off giant corpora-tions which had swooped down to cash in on his success. Most of the books adopted White's magic formula: present politics in nov-elistic terms, as the struggle of great personalities, with generous helpings of colorful detail to sugar the political analysis.

The book competition was bad enough, but White also had to contend with the newspapers jumping his claim. In 1972, the AP told its men: "When Teddy White's book comes out, there shouldn't be one single story in that book that we haven't reported ourselves." Abe Rosenthal, the managing editor of *The New York Times*, told his reporters and editors: "We aren't going to wait until a year after the election to read in Teddy White's book what we should have reported ourselves." It took from eight to twelve years for the newspapers to accept White as an institution, but by 1972 most editors were sending off their men with rabid pep talks about the importance of sniffing out inside dope, getting back-ground into the story, finding out what makes the campaign tick, and generally going beyond the old style of campaign reporting.

Of course, reporters had been doing many of these things as early as the 1968 campaign, causing George Romney to howl that he had been a victim of "the Teddy White syndrome." By that, Romney meant that flocks of reporters had started looking into the embryonic stages of Presidential campaigns, scrutinizing aspi-rants even before the primaries, killing candidacies with untimely exposure.

If this premature mass coverage upset politicians, it nearly drove Teddy White to distraction. After the *succès fou*[2] of the 1960 book, he had looked to make a living from the *Making of the President* series for the next twenty years. Now, with the market glutted, he was no longer sure that he could. "People have read so much of what I have to say in *Newsweek*, in *Time*, in *The New York Times* and the Washington *Post*," he lamented that afternoon in New York, as he started on his third or fourth pack of cigarettes.

But his uneasiness stemmed from more than a fear that the 1972 book might not sell as well as the earlier ones. He some-times felt that the methods he had pioneered had gotten out of control, had turned into a Frankenstein's monster. Thinking back to the early spring of 1960, he remembered watching a relaxed John Kennedy receiving the Wisconsin primary returns in a Mil-waukee hotel room. White had been the only journalist present, except for a young film maker working on a documentary, and he

2. Wild success.

had blended in with the Kennedy Mafia as unobtrusively as a distant in-law.

Then he recalled the July night, only a few months before, when
George McGovern had won the Democratic nomination in Miami.
White had been in McGovern's suite at the Doral Hotel:

"It's appalling what we've done to these guys. McGovern was like
a fish in a goldfish bowl. There were three different network crews
at different times. The still photographers kept coming in in groups
of five. And there were at least six writers sitting in the corner—I
don't even know their names. We're all sitting there watching him
work on his acceptance speech, poor bastard. He tries to go into the
bedroom with Fred Dutton to go over the list of Vice Presidents,
which would later turn out to be the fuck-up of the century of
course, and all of us are observing him, taking notes like mad, getting all the little details. Which I think I invented as a method of
reporting and which I now sincerely regret. If you write about this,
say that I sincerely regret it. Who gives a fuck if the guy had milk
and Total for breakfast?"

"There's a conflict here—the absolute need of the public to know
versus the candidate's need for privacy, which is an equivalent and
absolute need. I don't know how to resolve it. McGovern was so
sweet, so kind to everybody, but he must have been crying out for
privacy. And I felt, finally, that our being there was a total imposition."

The reporters who followed the Presidential hopefuls in 1972
would probably have been surprised to hear White say these things.
They were arriving in Washington, or were first beginning to make
their reputations, around the time that the first *Making of the President* books hit the stores. Now they took White and his techniques
for granted; it made sense to them to treat a political campaign as a
growing, organic drama and to examine the psychological and
sociological causes of political decisions. Many of the new generation of campaign reporters looked down on White as a pathetic,
written-out hack. They saw him as a political groupie who wrote flattering, mawkish descriptions of major politicians in order to keep
them primed as sources for future books. His 1968 volume, with its
penitently overkind description of Richard Nixon, had taken a beating from reviewers. A lot of reporters laughed out loud when they
read sentences like: "In 1968, Nixon conspicuously, conscientiously,
calculatedly denied himself all racist votes, yielding them to Wallace." It was left for three of White's British competitors, in a book
called *An American Melodrama*, to give a decent account of
Nixon's wholly opportunistic Southern Strategy.

By 1972, the traveling press openly resented White. They felt
that he was a snob, that he placed himself above the rank and file
of the press. White would suddenly appear in some pressroom,

embracing old friends on the campaign staff, and would immediately be ushered off to the candidate's suite or the forward compart-
ment of the plane for an exclusive interview. And the reporters
would grumble about Teddy White getting the royal treatment.

These same reporters forgot that Teddy White's first books had
radically altered the function of the campaign press. Because of
him, the press now began to cover political campaigns two years
before the election.[3] Unlike White, the reporters were not collecting tidbits for use at some remote future date, in case one of the
primary candidates went on to win the Big One. They were using
the information immediately, exposing flaws and inconsistencies in
the candidate that could ruin his chances before he even reached
the primaries. As recently as 1960, or even 1964, a coalition of party
heavies, state conventions, and big-city bosses had chosen the candidate in relatively unviolated privacy, and then presented him to the
press to report on.

Now the press screened the candidates, usurping the party's old
function. By reporting a man's political strengths, they made him a
front runner; by mentioning his weaknesses and liabilities, they cut
him down. Teddy White, even in his wildest flights of megalomania, had never allowed himself this kind of power. The press was
no longer simply guessing who might run and who might win; the
press was in some way determining these things. The classic example was George Romney. Romney had opened his campaign almost
a year before the first primary, expecting a press contingent of two
or three reporters. Instead, twenty or thirty showed up for Romney's first exploratory trips around the country, and they all
reported Romney's embarrassing inability to give coherent answers
to their questions about Vietnam, thus dooming his candidacy. But
Romney was the perfect, textbook example. The process was usually
more subtle, and more difficult to describe.

The journalists involved in this selection process were a very
small group, consisting mostly of the national political correspondents, and they formed what David Broder called "the screening
committee." Of the two-hundred-odd men and women who followed the candidates in 1972, less than thirty were full-time
national political correspondents. Most of the campaign reporters
came from other beats around Washington—the Justice Department, the Pentagon, the Hill, or the White House. After the campaign, they would go back to these beats, and if they did well, they

---

3. White's emphasis on the vital importance of John F. Kennedy's early
start was the main reason for all this
early coverage. There was also another
factor. In 1961, a political amateur
named Clifton White started assembling
the political machine which eventually
won the 1964 Republican nomination for
Barry Goldwater. The press did not fin̄ᵤ
out about Clifton White's activities until
early 1963. Many reporters later felt cha-
grin that they had taken so long to catch
on to the Goldwater movement, and resolved not to let it happen again
[Crouse's note].

would rise to a management position at their newspaper, magazine or network. But the national political correspondents had covered the whole political scene for five, ten or fifteen years and were likely to continue doing so until they died in harness; and if the actuarial tables were correct, their jobs would kill them at a relatively early age. Many of the members of this group belonged to an organization called Political Writers for a Democratic Society, an organization whose evolution requires some explaining.

In 1966, a stolid, slightly pompous *Christian Science Monitor* reporter named Godfrey Sperling started organizing breakfasts where he and some of his friends could meet with leading politicians and government officials. He would have the *Monitor*'s secretaries call up Warren Weaver of the *Times*, David Broder of the *Post*, Phil Potter of the Baltimore *Sun*, Bob Donovan of the *Los Angeles Times*, Peter Lisagor of the Chicago *Daily News* and nine or ten other political writers, to invite them to breakfast at the National Press Club, where for five dollars a head they would get scrambled eggs and hash-browns and a chance to further their acquaintance with some politician. The breakfasts were also "background" sessions—any news that came out of them was not for attribution but had to be treated as coming from "a highly placed Democrat" or a "Republican strategist." A great deal of useful information was served up with the orange juice at these sessions. Romney first stumbled over Vietnam at one of Sperling's breakfasts, and Agnew made his debut as a buffoon by declaring that Humphrey was "soft on communism." At another breakfast, shortly before the 1968 Republican Convention, the reporters kept suggesting to Nelson Rockefeller that his chances were nil. "Gee," Rockefeller finally said, "if I thought I was as bad off as you guys say I am, I'd drop out." The most memorable breakfast took place in January 1968, when Robert Kennedy anguished out loud for an hour as to whether or not he should run. The reporters there recalled the scene in the stories they wrote when Kennedy finally decided to enter the race.

By 1970, Sperling's breakfast club began to go to hell; almost anybody who wanted to could come, and the guests often spoke on the record, which meant that they said nothing of importance. But in the early days, Sperling restricted the breakfasts to his friends, which caused great bitterness among the writers who were not invited. Jack Germond, the chief political writer for the Gannett chain, was furious. He had eighteen papers in New York State and he was tired of getting scooped by *The New York Times* whenever John Lindsay, Nelson Rockefeller or Robert Kennedy appeared at Sperling's breakfasts. So in 1969 he and Jules Witcover, who was working for the Newhouse chain and was also shut out, organized a rival group. Witcover christened it, with tongue in cheek, Political Writers for a Democratic Society.

The main purpose of PWDS was to get to know politicians in easy, informal surroundings. The meetings were usually held at Germond's three-story row house in southwest Washington. The fourteen members would assemble once a month, have a couple of drinks with the guest, eat a catered supper downstairs in a big family room, and then go back upstairs to the long, rectangular living room. The guest sat in a large armchair in the middle of the room, taking questions from the reporters, who sat around him on sofas and other easy chairs. More drinks were served. Finally, after the guest had left, the men would pull out their notebooks and reconstruct the main points of the evening, trying to decide what the guest may or may not have meant in certain statements and generally sizing him up.

The most interesting thing about PWDS was its composition, which had been determined largely by Germond and Witcover. I cornered Germond one August night in the McGovern pressroom at the Biltmore Hotel in New York to ask him about the group. He was sitting all alone at one of the long typewriter tables, waiting in vain for a poker game to materialize and slowly getting drunk. He was a little cannonball of a man, forty-four years old, with a fresh, leprechaunish face, a fringe of white hair around his bald head, and a pugnacious, hands-on-hip manner of talking. He was not simply drawn to journalism as a profession; like Hildy Johnson in *Front Page*, he was addicted to it as a way of life.

Although he himself sometimes described his chain as a "bunch of shitkicker papers," he was proud of his position as a national political writer and the dues he had paid to win it.[4] Nothing made him angrier than small-town newspapermen—"homers"—who came up to him during campaigns and told him that he was ignoring "local factors." "God," he said, "I remember this one homer in Columbus. I've worked in these jobs, you know, as a homer. I've been a city-side reporter, a statehouse reporter, I've done the whole bit—and I've worked for a bunch of obscure newspapers. Christ Almighty, they were obscure. And for some guy from Ohio who works for this goddam shitty newspaper to come up and tell me that I don't understand the whole thing—I've been covering this campaign for about sixteen months—and this asshole comes up and tells me this after two weeks' exposure—ooh, I was outraged. Got pretty testy in the saloon, I must say. Told him what I'd do with his fucking newspaper."

So PWDS was not for homers or tyros. It was for the professionals' professionals. More specifically, said Germond, sipping a Scotch and soda, the standard was this: Who are the men who cover an obscure Western governors' conference in an off political year?

4. He was also the Washington Bureau chief for Gannett, which meant that he was as powerful within the organization and as well-paid as many of the publishers of the chain's newspapers [Crouse's note].

"Everyone covers the national governors' conferences," said Germond, "that easy. You go out there and they just drop stories in your goddam lap. But you go out there and cover the Western governors, or the Southern governors in a year like '67 or '69, and if you can make a story out of that—if you can even convince your office they ought to pay your fare home—you're a goddam genius." Germond and Witcover had found fourteen men who passed this test. Not counting themselves, there were:

> David Broder of the Washington *Post*
> Paul Hope of the Washington *Star*
> Robert Novak of the Chicago *Sun Times Syndicate*
> Warren Weaver of *The New York Times*
> Ted Knapp of Scripps-Howard
> Bruce Biossat of the Newspaper Enterprise Association
> Jim Dickenson of the *National Observer*
> Loye Miller of Knight Newspapers
> Tom Ottenad of the *St. Louis Post-Dispatch*
> Marty Nolan of the Boston *Globe* (who replaced James Doyle in the group when Doyle moved from the *Globe* to the Washington *Star*)
> Pat Furgurson of the Baltimore *Sun*
> Jim Large of *The Wall Street Journal*

These people, said Germond, rated membership because of what they did, not because of the organizations they represented. The rule was that no member could send a substitute to a dinner. It was an elite group of men who, by their own consensus, were the flame-keepers of political journalism—the heavics. "We took a couple of guys who we thought were pretty dumb," said Germond, "but we brought 'em in because they were entitled by what they did." No doubt there were some serious omissions—reporters like Johnny Apple of *The New York Times*, Alan Otten of *The Wall Street Journal*, Peter Lisagor, Jim Doyle, Harry Kelly of Hearst, and Jim Perry of the *National Observer*—who either were not congenial to the group or worked for papers already represented. But by and large this group was the elite's idea of the elite. They did not consider the network correspondents to be serious political reporters, nor did they hold a high opinion of the wire-service men (except for Walter Mears) or of newsmagazine reporters (except for John Lindsay of *Newsweek*). But Lindsay could not be admitted because he would have got more out of the dinners than the rest—little pieces of color that the daily journalists couldn't use. And Mears had to be excluded because, on the rare occasions when a not-for-attribution story emerged from one of the dinners, he would have put it on the wire and beaten everybody else. "Most of the wire-service reports generally reflect nothing about what is going on," said Germond, "but Walter's good enough so that he would *whip our ass off*. Walter and I are good friends and he was pissed and kept asking me why he couldn't get in the group. And I said, 'Jeez,

Walter, I brought it up and you had eight co-sponsors, but the vote was 13 to 1 against you.'"

The members of PWDS did not constitute a pack. They were too confident, competitive, proud, and self-sufficient for that. They also differed ideologically. Germond for instance was a political agnostic, leaning toward liberalism;[5] Novak was increasingly embracing the ideological tenets of the Sun King;[6] and Nolan stood, on many matters, to the left of George McGovern.

But they did form a sort of club, with a certain code and certain rituals. If you shared a cab with members of PWDS, for instance, they would invariably dive for the back seat, leaving you to ride with the driver. At the end of the ride, one of them would say, "I think we'd better invoke the Germond rule."

"What's that?" you would say.

"The Germond rule states that the person who rides up front has to pay."

It was an established rule, widely accepted throughout the world of political journalism, and most people paid.

But PWDS was primarily a dinner group, and their main goal was to set themselves up for the 1972 campaign. They did the drudge work of political journalism, therefore they were entitled to an advantage, a closer relationship with the candidates. They saw the dinners as a new tool of the trade. The alternative was to go around, individually, and formally interview each new cabinet member or potential candidate—which would teach them next to nothing about the man's personality. "What we were trying to do," said Germond, "was to sit down with the guy without having to file any shit about his program or something. Have a couple of pops and dinner, talk, and decide 'What kind of a guy is this, has he got any class?' You don't hand down arbitrary, ex cathedra judgments —get to know the man. And this was true of cabinet members, Presidential candidates—you learn—the people are nice, a lot of them anyway. Or sometimes you don't learn anything. Our great non-learning session was George McGovern. Jeez, we were the dumbest bastards in the world about George McGovern."

McGovern actually came twice, and the second time, in 1971, he carefully spelled out his entire strategy for winning the nomination. "To show you how strange it was," says Warren Weaver, "I do not even remember it. I just didn't believe the man. I thought it was a pipe dream." That was the consensus of the whole group that night. "We thought he was a nice guy, even a savvy guy," says Ger-

---

5. Germond often talked like a hard-hat and made a point of being equally cynical about all the candidates. However, when Washington liberals decided to help rehabilitate the poor black southwest section of town by buying homes there, Germond had been one of the first people to move in. He was one of the last to leave the area after it became clear that the project was a failure [Crouse's note].

6. Louis XIV of France (1638–1715), who shaped the government into an autocracy under his personal rule.

mond. "But we didn't believe him. We figured he was a total loss." So George McGovern slipped right through the screening process. The incredulity of the press failed to stop him.

In fact, the dinners yielded very few tangible results. Mel Laird, Bob Finch, Teddy Kennedy provided nothing more than a few minor stories. From dining with George Wallace, the group was surprised to discover that he was consistently witty and genuinely puritanical, but they found out little else. The dinners provided only one solid insight—that Ed Muskie had a bad temper. At his first guest shot, in 1970, the members gave him the old George Romney treatment, boring in with question after question about Vietnam. Muskie kept giving equivocal answers and finally he blew up, attacking the group for trying to trap him. They *were* trying to trap him, but Presidential candidates were supposed to stay cool in the face of such questioning. Some of the members knew about Muskie's temper from covering his vice-presidential campaign in 1968, but most of them were stunned.

Muskie appeared again in December 1971, accompanied by his press secretary, a former Boston *Globe* editor named Dick Stewart. Every time Muskie began to lose control, Stewart would say, "Now, Ed, don't get testy!" They began to wonder a little about Muskie's stability, but most of them decided that it was just a minor flaw and wouldn't make any difference.

Nevertheless, when the national political correspondents— PWDS members and a few others—checked their scratch sheets at the end of 1971, Muskie looked like the only man who really had a chance. Johnny Apple had written a series of exclusive articles in the *Times* about various big Democratic politicans endorsing Muskie, and these articles helped to build up an impression that Muskie had it made. If he took New Hampshire he would be hard to stop, but because he looked like the one and only contender, he could not afford to do poorly in that first primary.

On January 9, 1972, David Broder, the most influential political writer in Washington, wrote from Manchester, New Hampshire: "As the acknowledged front runner and a resident of the neighboring state, Muskie will have to win the support of at least half the New Hampshire Democrats in order to claim a victory." At the beginning of the campaign, that was the wisdom of the screening committee of national political journalists. And when Muskie's big Scenicruiser bus rolled out of Manchester in January, most of them were on it—writing down every fact that might prove useful six months later when they did the big piece about how Muskie had won the nomination. Thanks to the screening committee, no other candidate in sight had half the press entourage that Muskie had.

The screening committee had never held a meeting to appoint Muskie the front runner. They had never even discussed it at great length. If there was a consensus, it was simply because all the national political reporters lived in Washington, saw the same people, used the same sources, belonged to the same background groups, and swore by the same omens. They arrived at their answers just as independently as a class of honest seventh graders using the same geometry text—they did not have to cheat off each other to come up with the same answer. All signs pointed to Ed Muskie as the easy winner, and as the wisdom of the national political men began to filter down through the campaign reporters and the networks to the people, victory began to seem assured for the Senator from Maine.

Of course, Muskie made no such predictions for himself. All he wanted to do was win, he said, and with all the time he had to spend shuttling back and forth between Florida and New Hampshire, he'd consider himself *lucky* to get fifty percent. Nobody listened to him. And when the returns came in on the night of March 7, leaving Muskie with only 46 percent of the vote, the press started muttering about a Muskie set back.

The next morning Muskie held a press conference in the dingy ballroom of the Sheraton Carpenter Hotel in Manchester, and several members of the screening committee turned out for it. David Broder and Tom Ottenad kept asking him about the percentage of his victory. Why hadn't he done as well as predicted? What had happened? Suddenly Muskie's temper exploded and he launched into a tirade, lashing out at Broder and Ottenad, who were two of the gentlest and most soft-spoken men in the business. The percentage, said Muskie, had nothing to do with anything. The press was misinterpreting it because the press was out to get him.

Nothing daunted, Broder asked him how, specifically, the New Hampshire results would affect his chances in Florida and in the other primaries. "I can't tell you that," Muskie snapped. "You'll tell me and you'll tell the rest of the country because you interpret this victory. This press conference today is my only chance to interpret it, but you'll probably even misinterpret that."

Broder just shrugged, but Marty Nolan, who was sitting directly behind him, raised his hand and said sternly, "Senator, will you answer the question?" Muskie simply looked at him and went on to some other subject. Nolan asked him again, got the same response.

After the press conference, Nolan stalked over to Dick Stewart and some Muskie aides who were talking in a corner.

"Calm down, Marty, calm down," said Stewart.

"Look," said Nolan. "I've taken three and a half years of this kind of shit from Nixon and those people, and I'm not gonna take it from you pricks."

Muskie, who had known Nolan for many years, came over and put his hand on Nolan's shoulder. "What's the problem, Marty?" he asked in his gravest tones.

Nolan turned around and looked at him. "The bullshit you've been handing out—that's the problem, Senator."

Nolan then repeated to Muskie that he was tired of taking bullshit from Nixon and Agnew. "I expect much more of you and I intend to hold you to it," he said sharply.

"Well, Marty," said the Senator. "I guess you're right." For the next five minutes, he apologized for his outburst.

If the press had ever been more powerful than in 1972, nobody could remember when.

QUESTIONS

1. How does this piece fit with other selections in the section? Where else might it have been placed?

2. What is the difference between a fact and the communication of a fact? Use examples from this selection in arriving at your conclusion. (You may also find Richard Hoggart's "Taking for Granted" [p. 307] useful in considering this question.)

3. On p. 360 Crouse says that most of the books about presidential campaigns "adopted White's magic formula: present politics in novelistic terms, as the struggle of great personalities, with generous helpings of colorful detail to sugar the political analysis." What does it mean to present something "in novelistic terms"? What are some of the alternative modes of presentation? What are the advantages, disadvantages, dangers, and delights of the different modes?

4. Crouse's style might be called "informal" or "conversational." He also quotes from the conversation of others, especially that of Theodore White. What are some of the differences in style between the passages written by Crouse and those in which he is quoting White's words from conversation? What might explain the differences? Are the two communication situations different?

5. Crouse mixes more formal language with colloquial expressions like Theodore Roosevelt's "stepping into the White House over McKinley's dead body" (p. 355), and White "was flying high in the greatest assignment of his life" (p. 358). What is the effect of this mixture upon you as a reader? Is the effect different in the two examples cited above, and if so, how?

6. On p. 357 Crouse quotes from Leo Rosten's "scholarly survey" of Washington correspondents. Try rewriting Rosten's words in a style more like that which Crouse adopts. What are the differences? Is the meaning clearer in Rosten's style or Crouse's?

7. On p. 359 Crouse speaks of "the absolute virginity of much of the territory White set out to explore," and on the previous page he quotes another sexual metaphor from White's conversation. Is there any connection between the two metaphors? Discuss their appropriateness or inappropriateness to the subject being discussed.

8. Beginning on p. 363 Crouse gives a brief character sketch of Jack Germond. What means does he use to give you an idea of what Germond is like? How successful is he? What other kinds of things might he have said about Germond? Why do you suppose he didn't say them?

9. How does the view of the newspaper reporter's job in this selection compare with that in Robert Darnton's "Writing News and Telling Stories" (p. 336)?

On Literature and the Arts

RADCLIFFE SQUIRES

The Dark Side of the Moon

In 1952 Brewster Ghiselin published from the University of California Press an anthology entitled *The Creative Process*, a pioneering work that has proved indispensable to all later investigators. Mr. Ghiselin had worried about creativity for many years, partly no doubt because of his own involvement as an artist, a poet of remarkable powers, and partly because as a teacher of young writers he wanted to help his students as much as he could. For years, he collected materials, and the range of his anthology is broad. We learn, for example, that Albert Einstein believed that the basis for arriving at "logical concepts" was an "emotional" one. We learn that Mozart observed that in the creation of his music he did not hear "the parts successively . . . but all at once." We learn that A. E. Housman, like Yeats, thought poetry derived from a physical, rather than purely intellectual, condition. A pint of beer and a walk helped him to write. And so forth. Mr. Ghiselin's anthology met with a success that probably astounded its publisher. Soon it was entered in the Mentor paperback series where it still resides. But there is one portentous, if not sinister, note in the story. A very large corporation purchased a number of copies to distribute to its executives. The corporation wanted its family to be "creative." Similarly Mr. Sylvester L. Weaver, then president of the National Broadcasting Company, sent in an order with the notation, "I would like to get a dozen copies of *The Creative Process*, edited by Brewster Ghiselin, so that they may be given to our key thinking élite at N.B.C." In short, Mr. Ghiselin's book appeared just at the time creativity became a modish concept, a "hot item," as they say in the automotive industry. Could not creativity be bought and transplanted like hydroponic vegetables into the think-tank?

My title "The Dark Side of the Moon" underlines a condition of danger and enigma in the subject, which the business executives seem to have ignored. I am thinking about the side of the moon held away from our earthly view, though seen first at long last by Russian spacemen. Of course I am thinking of that moon often associated with poetry and imagination. Here, again, a Russian first saw its dark side; not this time a cosmonaut, but Feodor Dostoevsky. In my ensuing observations on the dark side of creativity it may seem I am playing the part of the noble lady in an old joke. This lady after her wedding night asks her husband if the peasants also have sexual intercourse. Upon being assured they have, she exclaims, "Take it away from them. It's too good for them." But, no, my aim is not that of keeping creativity from the peasants. My aim is to chastize a few lunatics in academy and corporation for having propagated a mushy science, a woozy educationism out of the term *creativity*.

In his introduction to *The Creative Process* Ghiselin brings before us two points that apparently quarrel with each other. First, observing that we live in perilous times, he suggests that one use for investigations of the creative process rests in a need to find new answers to problems both old and new. Our survival as a species may depend on it. Second he observes that great advances in art and science have often come about in an unconscious way. A perfected symphony comes all at once to a composer's inner ear; perhaps a mathematical solution comes in a dream. From extensive evidence the deduction properly follows for him that something of the "automatic" or unconscious underlies new modes, new perceptions, new forms. We ask, of course, the inevitable question: if new configurations have been delivered to us in the past through the unconscious mind, if they have occurred without summons, beyond any control, why, then, how shall our pondering the theory of creativity yield, let alone guarantee, a desired result? We neither can keep an unconscious solution to a problem from arising nor can we force it to arise. However, Brewster Ghiselin holds before us the likelihood that knowledge and severe discipline underlie automatic discovery, subconscious organization, sudden vision. We can make infinite patterns by shaking a kaleidoscope, but we can make none at all unless those stiff bits of shakable stuff are in the apparatus. At the same time he insists, "self-surrender so familiar to creative minds is nearly always hard to achieve. It calls for a purity of motive that is rarely sustained except through dedication and discipline. Subordination of everything to the whole impulse of life is easier for the innocent and ignorant because they are not so fully aware of the hazards of it or are less impressed by them, and they are not so powerfully possessed by convention." Mr. Ghiselin thus holds out all possibilities to us but promises nothing. That, I think, is the proper approach to the subject, and we shall never improve on it. It is, however, possi-

ble to do just the opposite. (I am zeroing in on the enemy now.)
For creativity has come to be thought of not as a sacramental form
of experience, which it merits, but as commodity, as shibboleth.
The deterioration of the term is evident in the following paragraph
from an article entitled "Creativity as Personality Development" by
Harold H. Anderson, published in 1959. Mr. Anderson writes that
heretofore we have tended to associate creativity with figures like
Leonardo da Vinci, and he wants to expand the field:

There is another kind of creativity, which we may call psychological
or social invention, whose product is not an object as such. This is
creativity not with objects but with persons: creativity in human
relations. . . . Creativity in human relations requires individual integrity and an ability to work with others. Historical examples are found
in social and political attempts to deal with differences. Magna Charta,
the Bill of Rights, the Emancipation Proclamation, constitutions, bylaws
and their amendments, codes of law, and city ordinances are examples of
social invention. There are other interpersonal examples of social creativity such as arranging car pools, keeping on good terms with one's
neighbors, courting, making love, and child rearing.

Now I have nothing against carpools, but surely we must wonder at
the way Mr. Anderson's mind is working here. In effect he is
saying: "Creativity is considered a virtue. Therefore, anything that
is virtuous may be included in the category of creativity." While
Mr. Anderson's view is certainly comprehensive, he missed a great
opportunity, it seems to me, by setting his sights a bit low. Why
didn't he say that carpools are what Coleridge had in mind when he
spoke of participating in the Infinite I Am?[1] Still it is just as well
he did not; half the princes of Christendom would have immediately agreed and cheered Mr. Anderson on.

Let me give another example of how the subject of creativity has
been treated. In "Traits of Creativity" (1959) J. P. Guilford with
startling insight observes that a primary trait of creativity is "originality." Of this trait he says: "There is a growing suspicion that what
we have called originality is actually a case of adaptive flexibility
when dealing with verbally meaningful material, parallel to the
factor of adaptive flexibility as now known, which pertains to tasks
dealing with nonverbal material. In either case one must get away
from the obvious, the ordinary, or the conventional." Mr. Guilford
does seem to have gotten away from the obvious, the ordinary, and
the conventional, but I haven't the slightest idea where he has
gotten to. Of course the reader may properly object to my having
taken Mr. Guilford's paragraph out of context, but the context is
much like the paragraph I just quoted from. Lives there a reader
who is sure he wants that context? I can also see that one might

---

1. Samuel Taylor Coleridge (1772–
1834) held, in his *Biographia Literaria*,
that the "primary imagination" is "the
living power and prime agent of all
human perception," and the human
equivalent of the creation of the universe
by God, "the infinite I AM."

feel that here is someone educated in language (I refer immodestly to myself), who is grabbing a cheap victory by making fun of a social scientist who has a good heart and has been too busy doing good in the world to learn how to write. I am happy to allow the probability of Mr. Guilford's having a good heart and having busied himself with doing good. As to the rest, no. For the prose in that paragraph is not the result of one's not having been trained. Just the opposite obtains. You have to *learn* how to write that kind of prose. No child or savage would or could express himself like that. The real question is: why has our goodhearted Mr. Guilford trained himself—it must have taken considerable training—to write in this way? I shall put the answer coolly. It is because, like Mr. Anderson, he thinks creativity a virtue and he would like to say something about a virtuous—and fashionable—topic. In all reality he has nothing to say. His prose is a mask upon nothingness, an awesome, almost diabolical defense. I have put the answer coolly; I shall draw the moral coldly. That very creativity in which we put our hopes has been suborned, redefined, and then disseminated by those who have the least claim to being creative.

The deterioration of the term *creativity*, a deterioration which has incrementally continued since 1959, has had a pervasive effect on our world. Elementary school teachers, for example, whether or not they are required to teach anything of substance, are supposed to foster creativity. There are a number of things wrong with that as a pedagogical view, but the most important thing is that no child is truly creative. Tell him to look like a tomato and he may do a very good job of looking like a tomato. We only think children are creative because they are more ecstatic and spontaneous than we are and because we are entranced by their perceptions unencumbered by habit and stylistic prejudgments. We are captivated by their poems because they have not yet learned to write like Mr. Guilford. We think they are wise because they see that the emperor is wearing no clothes—but a sage would see that the emperor is wearing the heaviest robes of all, the robes of delusion. A child can only be a perceiver and an imitator, for that is the nature of his becoming, his growth. Creation begins when growth is finished, and when neither imitation nor perception is enough. Therefore, fostering creativity in children is a hoax. It is a wicked hoax since what is really most likely to thwart creativity is to withhold the materials of growth—facts, knowledge, the paradigms of grammar and mathematics.

Perhaps none of this may seem very important if all that is at stake is fingerpainting. Yet it ought to be of the utmost importance. If we are genuinely serious about creativity, we must realize that much of what is being done today in kindergartens, colleges, and hot-shot symposia so emphasizes the result at the expense of the means that the result cannot be obtained.

If we are really serious about creativity we should realize it has nothing to do with happiness, nothing to do with "self-fulfillment." We should realize that courting it is not without danger. I do not refer to some vision of a world in which everyone would be a scientist, a musician, a sculptor, a wild poet. That is not the danger, for while such a world would be hideously dull, we don't even consider it. We dismiss it by reason of its patent absurdity. The danger I refer to is that greatly creative persons are not often very settled souls. For every Artur Schnabel who on his deathbed can say that he has had a very happy life and looks forward now to a deserved rest, there is an Arthur Rimbaud who on his deathbed mutters a sad gibberish, an approximation of the poems he let get away.[2] The late W. H. Auden in his poetic memorial to his friend Louis MacNeice comically and sadly observes:

> You hope, yes,
> your books will excuse you,
> save you from hell:
> nevertheless,
> without looking sad,
> without in any way
> seeming to blame . . .
> God may reduce you
> on Judgment Day
> to tears of shame,
> reciting by heart
> the poems you would
> have written had
> your life been good.

The creative life is no bed of roses, and those who glibly recommend it like an insurance plan should know what they are recommending.

It is no bed of roses. I think I know a little bit about why it is not. The act of creation in the arts at least, and very possibly in the mathematical modes as well, involves really *two* processes or aspects that are at war with each other but which must nevertheless be made one. One of these aspects concerns the release of an anarchistic, quite feral voice, and it quarrels with the other aspect, a voice that is formal, debonair, and legal. The formal and legal side is so terrified of the feral that it seeks to cover it, to hide it away. The formal aspect of art is never so much an embellishment or a honeying of message as it is defense against the barbarians at the gates. We may see some evidence for this view in the fact that, in those ages that most deplore or fear the irrational, art and science will be most formal and constructive. The eighteenth century felt there was something obscene about hypochondria—remember how Dr. John-

2. Artur Schnabel (1882–1951), concert pianist famous for his interpretations of the German classics; Arthur Rimbaud (1854–1891), French poet, wrote all his poems before he was twenty, and spent the remainder of his life as a vagrant in Europe and trader in northern Africa.

son prized "cheerfulness"—and while it was liberally laced with neurotics, still it gave us portraits not of people but of public and rational gestures. It gave us thousands of self-contained couplets and Newton's persuasive arrangements. The defensive role played by the formal aspect of creativity can also be seen in ways that have to do with the nature of art but are not themselves art. I mean, auctioneers, purveyors of quack medicines, circus barkers, and other confidence men, who do not really want to face or know what they are doing, tend to fall into a rhythmic cadence as they deliver their spiels. And so does the stock boy who is taking inventory in a supermarket. The formality of a singsong speech saves him, I suppose, from error and the dizzying whirlpool of complete tedium. And we know, too, that certain neurotic patients, the order of whose inner world has been fragmented, may take to speaking in rhymes. They place an exterior order over their chaos. The novel *David and Lisa* presents such a case history in fiction. But I said that the truly creative act must bring the two aspects together. And I said it is no bed of roses. Let us look a bit further into the matter.

Once become, once grown, the artist-no-longer-the-child takes what he has—bits of experience, pieces of learning, compulsions of style, tyrannies of ego. This little is more or less all he has to work with, and none of these things is probably new or impressive. His task is to form them, make them into something potent by setting them in a relationship not only to each other but also to the actual world and, ultimately, to some presentiment or superstition of God. What a task! For the self is tricky, the world but partially apprehended, and God—in a perpetual state of convalescence—is hidden by an oxygen mask.

Here the dark side of the moon is ancillary. Here the automatic or unconscious process operates. It has to be this way, for the rational frontal mind would immediately censor the whole project as being impossible. I do not know if the feral aspect triumphs over the formal or if another mediating faculty enters the process. But if the feral side triumphs it does so without destroying the formal. Whatever happens, something older and more innocent than the rational mind—the primitive nerve bundles in the cortex, perhaps —goes about the task. When the rational mind, which tires easily, rests, the wilder faculty makes some kind of composition and in so doing gives point to reason and depth and beauty to formality. So long as this cooperation endures, the artist, still not settled and never terribly interested in carpools, is maybe happy enough. But when, for reasons that are always obscure, the cooperation fails and the task is not performed, then the artist is in Hell. He may in fact by such stoppages be driven mad. An illuminating analogy is provided by recent scientific research.

In the past decade researchers, notably at the University of Chicago, have been looking into what they call "rapid eye-movements" during sleep. They have found that these movements of the eye take place during periods of dreaming. They have also discovered that dreaming is a necessity of health. For when the sleepers have been repeatedly awakened just as the rapid eye-movements began so that they did not dream, they became irritable and unwell even though they got adequate sleep. We can guess why a deprivation of dreams—despite the fact that we do not even remember most dreams—would lead to malaise. In dreams begin responsibilities. In dreams we punish ourselves for our sins and we symbolically work out our psychological puzzles. Here, then, is the analogy. If the abrogation of dreams can make a well-adjusted, untortured person ill, think what a blockage of the unconscious creative process, which is like dreaming, can do to a creator. Or, rather, let the easy purveyors of creativity think of that. Let them think of Hart Crane, his seraphic vision annulled, staring at the Gulf of Mexico.[3]

We need creativity, but we need to know that it is necessary rather than nice. We need to know that here as elsewhere there exists no exultation without despair, no exaltation without humiliation. When we truly know this then we can claim the right to recommend and the courage to seek creativity.

NORTHROP FRYE

The Keys to Dreamland[1]

* * * Suppose you're walking down the street of a North American city. All around you is a highly artificial society, but you don't think of it as artificial: you're so accustomed to it that you think of it as natural. But suppose your imagination plays a little trick on you of a kind that it often does play, and you suddenly feel like a complete outsider, someone who's just blown in from Mars on a flying saucer. Instantly you see how conventionalized everything is: the clothes, the shop windows, the movement of the cars in traffic, the cropped hair and shaved faces of the men, the red lips and blue eyelids that women put on because they want to conventionalize their faces, or "look nice," as they say, which means the same thing. All this convention is pressing toward uniformity or likeness. To be outside the convention makes a person look queer, or, if he's driving a car, a menace to life and limb. The only exceptions are people who have decided to conform to different conventions, like nuns or beatniks. There's clearly a strong force making toward conformity in society, so strong that it seems to have some-

---

3. Hart Crane (1899–1932), American poet, visited Mexico planning to write a long poem about the Aztec chief Monte- zuma. Returning by ship, he suddenly leaped overboard and drowned.

1. Chapter 4 in *The Educated Imagination,* 1964.

thing to do with the stability of society itself. In ordinary life even the most splendid things we can think of, goodness and truth and beauty, all mean essentially what we're accustomed to. As I hinted just now in speaking of female makeup, most of our ideas of beauty are pure convention, and even truth has been defined as whatever doesn't disturb the pattern of what we already know.

When we move on to literature, we again find conventions, but this time we notice that they are conventions, because we're not so used to them. These conventions seem to have something to do with making literature as unlike life as possible. Chaucer represents people as making up stories in ten-syllable couplets. Shakespeare uses dramatic conventions, which means, for instance, that Iago has to smash Othello's marriage and dreams of future happiness and get him ready to murder his wife in a few minutes. Milton has two nudes in a garden haranguing each other in set speeches beginning with such lines as "Daughter of God and Man, immortal Eve"—Eve being Adam's daughter because she's just been extracted from his ribcase. Almost every story we read demands that we accept as fact something that we know to be nonsense: that good people always win, especially in love; that murders are complicated and ingenious puzzles to be solved by logic, and so on. It isn't only popular literature that demands this: more highbrow stories are apt to be more ironic, but irony has its conventions too. If we go further back into literature, we run into such conventions as the king's rash promise, the enraged cuckold, the cruel mistress of love poetry—never anything that we or any other time would recognize as the normal behavior of adult people, only the maddened ethics of fairyland.

Even the details of literature are equally perverse. Literature is a world where phoenixes and unicorns are quite as important as horses and dogs—and in literature some of the horses talk, like the ones in *Gulliver's Travels*. A random example is calling Shakespeare the "swan of Avon"—he was called that by Ben Jonson. The town of Stratford, Ontario, keeps swans in its river partly as a literary allusion. Poets of Shakespeare's day hated to admit that they were writing words on a page: they always insisted that they were producing music. In pastoral poetry they might be playing a flute (or more accurately an oboe), but every other kind of poetic effort was called song, with a harp, a lyre or a lute in the background, depending on how highbrow the song was. Singing suggests birds, and so for their typical songbird and emblem of themselves, the poets chose the swan, a bird that can't sing. Because it can't sing, they made up a legend that it sang once before death, when nobody was listening. But Shakespeare didn't burst into song before his death: he wrote two plays a year until he'd made enough money to retire, and spent the last five years of his life counting his take.

So however useful literature may be in improving one's imagination or vocabulary, it would be the wildest kind of pedantry to use it directly as a guide to life. Perhaps here we see one reason why the poet is not only very seldom a person one would turn to for insight into the state of the world, but often seems even more gullible and simple-minded than the rest of us. For the poet, the particular literary conventions he adopts are likely to become, for him, facts of life. If he finds that the kind of writing he's best at has a good deal to do with fairies, like Yeats, or a white goddess, like Graves, or a life-force, like Bernard Shaw, or episcopal sermons, like T. S. Eliot, or bullfights, like Hemingway, or exasperation at social hypocrisies, as with the so-called angry school, these things are apt to take on a reality for him that seems badly out of proportion to his contemporaries. His life may imitate literature in a way that may warp or even destroy his social personality, as Byron wore himself out at thirty-four with the strain of being Byronic. Life and literature, then, are both conventionalized, and of the conventions of literature about all we can say is that they don't much resemble the conditions of life. It's when two sets of conventions collide that we realize how different they are.

In fact, whenever literature gets too probable, too much like life, some self-defeating process, some mysterious law of diminishing returns, seems to set in. There's a vivid and expertly written novel by H. G. Wells called *Kipps*, about a lower-middle-class, inarticulate, very likeable Cockney, the kind of character we often find in Dickens. Kipps is carefully studied: he never says anything that a man like Kipps wouldn't say; he never sounds the "h" in home or head; nothing he does is out of line with what we expect such a person to be like. It's an admirable novel, well worth reading, and yet I have a nagging feeling that there's some inner secret in bringing him completely to life that Dickens would have and that Wells doesn't have. All right, then, what would Dickens have done? Well, one of the things that Dickens often does do is write *badly*. He might have given Kipps sentimental speeches and false heroics and all sorts of inappropriate verbiage to say; and some readers would have clucked and tut-tutted over these passages and explained to each other how bad Dickens's taste was and how uncertain his hold on character could be. Perhaps they'd be right too. But we'd have had Kipps a few times the way he'd look to himself or the way he'd sometimes wish he could be: that's part of his reality, and the effect would remain with us however much we disapproved of it. Whether I'm right about this book or not, and I'm not at all sure I am, I think my general principle is right. What we'd never see except in a book is often what we go to books to find. Whatever is completely lifelike in literature is a bit of a laboratory specimen there. To bring anything really to life in literature we can't be lifelike: we have to be literaturelike.

The same thing is true even of the use of language. We're often taught that prose is the language of ordinary speech, which is usually true in literature. But in ordinary life prose is no more the language of ordinary speech than one's Sunday suit is a bathing suit. The people who actually speak prose are highly cultivated and articulate people, who've read a good many books, and even they can speak prose only to each other. If you read the beautiful sentences of Elizabeth Bennett's conversation in *Pride and Prejudice*, you can see how in that book they give a powerfully convincing impression of a sensible and intelligent girl. But any girl who talked as coherently as that on a street car would be stared at as though she had green hair. It isn't only the difference between 1813 and 1962 that's involved either, as you'll see if you compare her speech with her mother's. The poet Emily Dickinson complained that everybody said "What?" to her, until finally she practically gave up trying to talk altogether, and confined herself to writing notes.

All this is involved with the difference between literary and other kinds of writing. If we're writing to convey information, or for any practical reason, our writing is an act of will and intention: we mean what we say, and the words we use represent that meaning directly. It's different in literature, not because the poet doesn't mean what he says too, but because his real effort is one of putting words together. What's important is not what he may have meant to say, but what words themselves say when they get fitted together. With a novelist it's rather the incidents in the story he tells that get fitted together—as D. H. Lawrence says, don't trust the novelist; trust his story. That's why so much of a writer's best writing is or seems to be involuntary. It's involuntary because the forms of literature itself are taking control of it, and these forms are what are embodied in the conventions of literature. Conventions, we see, have the same role in literature that they have in life: they impose certain patterns of order and stability on the writer. Only, if they're such different conventions, it seems clear that the order of words, or the structure of literature, is different from the social order.

The absence of any clear line of connection between literature and life comes out in the issues involved in censorship. Because of the large involuntary element in writing, works of literature can't be treated as embodiments of conscious will or intention, like people, and so no laws can be framed to control their behavior which assume a tendency to do this or an intention of doing that. Works of literature get into legal trouble because they offend some powerful religious or political interest, and this interest in its turn usually acquires or exploits the kind of social hysteria that's always revolving around sex. But it's impossible to give legal definitions of such terms as obscenity in relation to works of literature. What happens to the book depends mainly on the intelligence of the judge. If he's a sensible man we get a sensible decision; if he's an ass we get that sort of decision, but what we don't get is a legal decision, because the basis for one doesn't exist. The best we get is a precedent tending to discourage cranks and pressure groups from attacking serious books. If you read the casebook on the trial of *Lady Chatterley's Lover*, you may remember how bewildered the critics were when they were asked what the moral effect of the book would be. They weren't putting on an act: they didn't know. Novels can only be good or bad in their own categories. There's no such thing as a morally bad novel: its moral effect depends entirely on the moral quality of its reader, and nobody can predict what that will be. And if literature isn't morally bad it isn't morally good either. I suppose one reason why *Lady Chatterley's Lover* dramatized this question so vividly was that it's a rather preachy and self-conscious book: like the Sunday-school novels of my childhood, it bores me a little because it tries so hard to do me good.

So literature has no consistent connection with ordinary life, positive or negative. Here we touch on another important difference between structures of the imagination and structures of practical sense, which include the applied sciences. Imagination is certainly essential to science, applied or pure. Without a constructive power in the mind to make models of experience, get hunches and follow them out, play freely around with hypotheses, and so forth, no scientist could get anywhere. But all imaginative effort in practical fields has to meet the test of practicability, otherwise it's discarded. The imagination in literature has no such test to meet. You don't relate it directly to life or reality: you relate works of literature to each other. Whatever value there is in studying literature, cultural or practical, comes from the total body of our reading, the castle of words we've built, and keep adding new wings to all the time.

So it's natural to swing to the opposite extreme and say that literature is really a refuge or escape from life, a self-contained world like the world of the dream, a world of play or make-believe to balance the world of work. Some literature is like that, and many people tell us that they only read to get away from reality for a bit. And I've suggested myself that the sense of escape, or at least detachment, does come into everybody's literary experience. But the real point of literature can hardly be that. Think of such writers as William Faulkner or François Mauriac, their great moral dignity, the intensity and compassion that they've studied the life around them with. Or think of James Joyce, spending seven years on one book and seventeen on another, and having them ridiculed or abused or banned by the customs when they did get published. Or of the poets Rilke and Valéry, waiting patiently for years in silence until what they had to say was ready to be said. There's a deadly seriousness in all this that even the most refined theories of fantasy or make-believe won't quite cover. Still, let's go along with the idea for a bit, because we're not getting on very fast with the relation of literature of life, or what we could call the horizontal perspective of literature. That seems to block us off on all sides.

The world of literature is a world where there is no reality except that of the human imagination. We see a great deal in it that reminds us vividly of the life we know. But in that very vividness there's something unreal. We can understand this more clearly with pictures, perhaps. There are trick-pictures—*trompe l'oeil*, the French call them—where the resemblance to life is very strong. An American painter of this school played a joke on his bitchy wife by painting one of her best napkins so expertly that she grabbed at the canvas trying to pull it off. But a painting as realistic as that isn't a reality but an illusion: it has the glittering unnatural clarity of a hallucination. The real realities, so to speak, are things that don't remind us directly of our own experience, but are such things as the wrath of Achilles or the jealousy of Othello, which are bigger and more intense experiences than anything we can reach—except in our imagination, which is what we're reaching with. Sometimes, as in the happy endings of comedies, or in the ideal world of romances, we seem to be looking at a pleasanter world than we ordinarily know. Sometimes, as in tragedy and satire, we seem to be looking at a world more devoted to suffering or absurdity than we ordinarily know. In literature we always seem to be looking either up or down. It's the vertical perspective that's important, not the horizontal one that looks out to life. Of course, in the greatest works of literature we get both the up and down views, often at the same time as different aspects of one event.

There are two halves to literary experience, then. Imagination gives us both a better and a worse world than the one we usually live with, and demands that we keep looking steadily at them both. The arts follow the path of the emotions, and of the tendency of the emotions to separate the world into a half that we like and a half that we don't like. Literature is not a world of dreams, but it would be if we had only one half without the other. If we had nothing but romances and comedies with happy endings, literature would express only a wish-fulfilment dream. Some people ask why poets want to write tragedies when the world's so full of them anyway, and suggest that enjoying such things has something morbid or gloating about it. It doesn't, but it might if there were nothing else in literature.

This point is worth spending another minute on. You recall that terrible scene in *King Lear* where Gloucester's eyes are put out on the stage. That's part of a play, and a play is supposed to be entertaining. Now in what sense can a scene like that be entertaining? The fact that it's not really happening is certainly important. It would be degrading to watch a real blinding scene, and far more so to get any pleasure out of watching it. Consequently, the entertainment doesn't consist in its reminding us of a real blinding scene. If it did, one of the great scenes of drama would turn into a piece of repulsive pornography. We couldn't stop anyone from reacting in this way, and it certainly wouldn't cure him, much less help the public, to start blaming or censoring Shakespeare for putting sadistic ideas in his head. But a reaction of that kind has nothing to do with drama. In a dramatic scene of cruelty and hatred we're seeing cruelty and hatred, which we know are permanently real things in human life, from the point of view of the imagination. What the imagination suggests is horror, not the paralyzing sickening horror of a real blinding scene, but an exuberant horror, full of the energy of repudiation. This is as powerful a rendering as we can ever get of life as we don't want it.

So we see that there are moral standards in literature after all, even though they have nothing to do with calling the police when we see a word in a book that's more familiar in sound that in print. One of the things Gloucester says in that scene is: "I am tied to the stake, and I must stand the course." In Shakespeare's day it was a favorite sport to tie a bear to a stake and set dogs on it until they killed it. The Puritans suppressed this sport, according to Macaulay, not because it gave pain to the bear but because it gave pleasure to the spectators. Macaulay may have intended his remark to be a sneer at the Puritans, but surely if the Puritans did feel this way they were one hundred per cent right. What other reason is there for abolishing public hangings? Whatever their motives, the Puritans and Shakespeare were operating in the same direction. Literature keeps presenting the most vicious things to us as entertainment, but what is appeals to is not any pleasure in these things, but the exhilaration of standing apart from them and being able to see them for what they are because they aren't really happening. The more exposed we are to this, the less likely we are to find an unthinking pleasure in cruel or evil things. As the eighteenth century said in a fine mouth-filling phrase, literature refines our sensibilities.

The top half of literature is the world expressed by such words as sublime, inspiring, and the like, where what we feel is not detachment but absorption. This is the world of heroes and gods and titans and Rabelaisian giants, a world of powers and passions and moments of ecstasy far greater than anything we meet outside the imagination. Such forces would not only absorb but annihilate us if they entered ordinary life, but luckily the protecting wall of the imagination is here too. As the German poet Rilke says, we adore them because they disdain to destroy us. We seem to have got quite a long way from our emotions with their division of things into "I like this" and "I don't like this." Literature gives us an experience that stretches us vertically to the heights and depths of what the human mind can conceive, to what corresponds to the conceptions of heaven and hell in religion. In this perspective what

I like or don't like disappears, because there's nothing left of me as a separate person: as a reader of literature I exist only as a representative of humanity as a whole.

No matter how much experience we may gather in life, we can never in life get the dimension of experience that the imagination gives us. Only the arts and sciences can do that, and of these, only literature gives us the whole sweep and range of human imagination as it sees itself. It seems to be very difficult for many people to understand the reality and intensity of literary experience. To give an example that you may think a bit irrelevant: why have so many people managed to convince themselves that Shakespeare did not write Shakespeare's plays, when there is not an atom of evidence that anybody else did? Apparently because they feel that poetry must be written out of personal experience, and that Shakespeare didn't have enough experience of the right kind. But Shakespeare's plays weren't produced by his experience: they were produced by his imagination, and the way to develop the imagination is to read a good book or two. As for us, we can't speak or think or comprehend even our own experience except within the limits of our own power over words, and those limits have been established for us by our great writers.

Literature, then, is not a dream-world: it's two dreams, a wish-fulfillment dream and an anxiety dream, that are focused together, like a pair of glasses, and become a fully conscious vision. Art, according to Plato, is a dream for awakened minds, a work of imagination withdrawn from ordinary life, dominated by the same forces that dominate the dream, and yet giving us a perspective and dimension on reality that we don't get from any other approach to reality. So the poet and the dreamer are distinct, as Keats says. Ordinary life forms a community, and literature is among other things an art of communication, so it forms a community too. In ordinary life we fall into a private and separate subconscious every night, where we reshape the world according to a private and separate imagination. Underneath literature there's another kind of subconscious, which is social and not private, a need for forming a community around certain symbols, like the Queen and the flag, or around certain gods that represent order and stability, or becoming and change, or death and rebirth to a new life. This is the myth-making power of the human mind, which throws up and dissolves one civilization after another.

I've taken my title, "The Keys to Dreamland," from what is possibly the greatest single effort of the literary imagination in the twentieth century, Joyce's *Finnegans Wake*. In this book a man goes to sleep and falls, not into the Freudian separate or private subconscious, but into the deeper dream of man that creates and destroys his own societies. The entire book is written in the language of this dream. It's a subconscious language, mainly English, but connected by associations and puns with the eighteen or so other languages that Joyce knew. *Finnegans Wake* is not a book to read, but a book to decipher: as Joyce says, it's about a dreamer, but it's addressed to an ideal reader suffering from an ideal insomnia. The reader or critic, then, has a role complementing the poet's role. We need two powers in literature, a power to create and a power to understand.

In all our literary experience there are two kinds of response. There is the direct experience of the work itself, while we're reading a book or seeing a play, especially for the first time. This experience is uncritical, or rather pre-critical, so it's not infallible. If our experience is limited, we can be roused to enthusiasm or carried away by something that we can later see to have been second-rate or even phony. Then there is the conscious, critical response we make after we've finished reading or left the theatre, where we compare what we've experienced with other things of the same kind, and form a judgment of value and proportion on it. This critical response, with practice, gradually makes our pre-critical responses more sensitive and accurate, or improves our taste, as we say. But behind our responses to individual works, there's a bigger response to our literary experience as a whole, as a total possession.

The critic has always been called a judge of literature, which means, not that he's in a superior position to the poet, but that he ought to know something about literature, just as a judge's right to be on a bench depends on his knowledge of law. If he's up against something the size of Shakespeare, he's the one being judged. The critic's function is to interpret every work of literature in the light of all the literature he knows, to keep constantly struggling to understand what literature as a whole is about. Literature as a whole is not an aggregate of exhibits with red and blue ribbons attached to them, like a cat show, but the range of articulate human imagination as it extends from the height of imaginative heaven to the depth of imaginative hell. Literature is a human apocalypse, man's revelation to man, and criticism is not a body of adjudications, but the awareness of that revelation, the last judgment of mankind.

QUESTIONS

1. Frye uses the word "conventions" a number of times; what meanings does he appear to give the word? Why does he seek to show that life has conventions as does literature? Are they the same sort of conventions?

2. Early in his essay Frye makes some amusing remarks about poets and their ways. Is he making fun of them? If so, why? Does he suggest that poets are contemptible? If not, what is he trying to do?

3. Toward what sort of audience is Frye addressing his remarks? What can you tell about the audience he has in view from the

language he chooses, and from the line of development his essay takes? What conception of the relationship between life and literature does Frye assume his audience might have at the outset? Does Frye seek to persuade his audience to adopt a certain view of literature, perhaps to change a previous view? What devices in his writing (as of tone, diction, figures of speech) are directed toward persuasion?

4. What ideas about literature and its relationship to life does Frye examine and reject? Why does he reject them? What are the main features of his own position? Does he set forth that position in a single thesis sentence anywhere in the essay?

5. What is Frye's view of the moral effect of art and literature? How does his view compare with that of Krutch ("Modern Painting," (pp. 459–464)?

SUSANNE K. LANGER

Expressiveness[1]

When we talk about "Art" with a capital "A"—that is, about any or all of the arts: painting, sculpture, architecture, the potter's and goldsmith's and other designers' arts, music, dance, poetry, and prose fiction, drama and film—it is a constant temptation to say things about "Art" in this general sense that are true only in one special domain, or to assume that what holds for one art must hold for another. For instance, the fact that music is made for performance, for presentation to the ear, and is simply not the same thing when it is given only to the tonal imagination of a reader silently perusing the score, has made some aestheticians pass straight to the conclusion that literature, too, must be physically heard to be fully experienced, because words are originally spoken, not written; an obvious parallel, but a careless and, I think, invalid one. It is dangerous to set up principles by analogy, and generalize from a single consideration.

But it is natural, and safe enough, to ask analogous questions: What is the function of sound in music? What is the function of sound in poetry? What is the function of sound in prose composition? What is the function of sound in drama?" The answers may be quite heterogeneous; and that is itself an important fact, a guide to something more than a simple and sweeping theory. Such findings guide us to exact relations and abstract, variously exemplified basic principles.

At present, however, we are dealing with principles that have proven to be the same in all the arts, when each kind of art—plastic, musical, balletic, poetic, and each major mode, such as literary and dramatic writing, or painting, sculpturing, building plastic

1. Chapter 2 of *Problems of Art*, 1957.

shapes—has been studied in its own terms. Such candid study is more rewarding than the usual passionate declaration that all the arts are alike, only their materials differ, their principles are all the same, their techniques all analogous, etc. That is not only unsafe, but untrue. It is in pursuing the differences among them that one arrives, finally, at a point where no more differences appear; then one has found, not postulated, their unity. At that deep level there is only one concept exemplified in all the different arts, and that is the concept of Art.

The principles that obtain wholly and fundamentally in every kind of art are few, but decisive; they determine what is art, and what is not. Expressiveness, in one definite and appropriate sense, is the same in all art works of any kind. What is created is not the same in any two distinct arts—this is, in fact, what makes them distinct—but the principle of creation is the same. And "living form" means the same in all of them.

A work of art is an expressive form created for our perception through sense or imagination, and what it expresses is human feeling. The word "feeling" must be taken here in its broadest sense, meaning *everything that can be felt*, from physical sensation, pain and comfort, excitement and repose, to the most complex emotions, intellectual tensions, or the steady feeling-tones of a conscious human life. In stating what a work of art is, I have just used the words "form," "expressive," and "created"; these are key words. One at a time, they will keep us engaged.

Let us consider first what is meant, in this context, by a *form*. The word has many meanings, all equally legitimate for various purposes; even in connection with art it has several. It may, for instance—and often does—denote the familiar, characteristic structures known as the sonnet form, the sestina, or the ballad form in poetry, the sonata form, the madrigal, or the symphony in music, the contredance or the classical ballet in choreography, and so on. This is not what I mean; or rather, it is only a very small part of what I mean. There is another sense in which artists speak of "form" when they say, for instance, "form follows function," or declare that the one quality shared by all good works of art is "significant form," or entitle a book *The Life of Forms in Art*, or *Search for Form*. They are using "form" in a wider sense, which on the one hand is close to the commonest, popular meaning, namely just the *shape* of a thing, and on the other hand to the quite unpopular meaning it has in science and philosophy, where it designates something more abstract; "form" in its most abstract sense means structure, articulation, a whole resulting from the relation of mutually dependent factors, or more precisely, the way that whole is put together.

The abstract sense, which is sometimes called "logical form," is involved in the notion of expression, at least the kind of expression that characterizes art. That is why artists, when they speak of achieving "form," use the word with something of an abstract connotation, even when they are talking about a visible and tangible art object in which that form is embodied.

The more recondite concept of form is derived, of course, from the naive one, that is, material shape. Perhaps the easiest way to grasp the idea of "logical form" is to trace its derivation.

Let us consider the most obvious sort of form, the shape of an object, say a lampshade. In any department store you will find a wide choice of lampshades, mostly monstrosities, and what is monstrous is usually their shape. You select the least offensive one, maybe even a good one, but realize that the color, say violet, will not fit into your room; so you look about for another shade of the same shape but a different color, perhaps green. In recognizing this same shape in another object, possibly of another material as well as another color, you have quite naturally and easily abstracted the concept of this shape from your actual impression of the first lampshade. Presently it may occur to you that this shade is too big for your lamp; you ask whether they have *this same shade* (meaning another one of this shape) in a smaller size. The clerk understands you.

But what is *the same* in the big violet shade and the little green one? Nothing but the interrelations among their respective various dimensions. They are not "the same" even in their spatial properties, for none of their actual measures are alike, but their shapes are congruent. Their respective spatial factors are put together in the same way, so they exemplify the same form.

It is really astounding what complicated abstractions we make in our ordinary dealing with forms—that is to say, through what twists and transformations we recognize the same logical form. Consider the similarity of your two hands. Put one on the table, palm down, superimpose the other, palm down, as you may have superimposed cut-out geometric shapes in school—they are not alike at all. But their shapes are *exact opposites*. Their respective shapes fit the same description, provided that the description is modified by a principle of application whereby the measures are read one way for one hand and the other way for the other—like a timetable in which the list of stations is marked: "Eastbound, read down; Westbound, read up."

As the two hands exemplify the same form with a principle of reversal understood, so the list of stations describes two ways of moving, indicated by the advice to "read down" for one and "read up" for the other. We can all abstract the common element in these two respective trips, which is called the *route*. With a return ticket we may return only by the same route. The same principle relates a mold to the form of the thing that is cast in it, and establishes their formal correspondence, or common logical form.

So far we have considered only objects—lampshades, hands, or regions of the earth—as having forms. These have fixed shapes; their parts remain in fairly stable relations to each other. But there are also substances that have no definite shapes, such as gases, mist, and water, which take the shape of any bounded space that contains them. The interesting thing about such amorphous fluids is that when they are put into violent motion they do exhibit visible forms, not bounded by any container. Think of the momentary efflorescence of a bursting rocket, the mushroom cloud of an atomic bomb, the funnel of water or dust screwing upward in a whirlwind. The instant the motion stops, or even slows beyond a certain degree, those shapes collapse and the apparent "thing" disappears. They are not shapes of things at all, but forms of motions, or dynamic forms.

Some dynamic forms, however, have more permanent manifestations, because the stuff that moves and makes them visible is constantly replenished. A waterfall seems to hang from the cliff, waving streamers of foam. Actually, of course, nothing stays there in mid-air; the water is always passing; but there is more and more water taking the same paths, so we have a lasting shape made and maintained by its passage—a permanent dynamic form. A quiet river, too, has dynamic form; if it stopped flowing it would either go dry or become a lake. Some twenty-five hundred years ago, Heracleitos was struck by the fact that you cannot step twice into the same river at the same place—at least, if the river means the water, not its dynamic form, the flow.

When a river ceases to flow because the water is deflected or dried up, there remains the river bed, sometimes cut deeply in solid stone. That bed is shaped by the flow, and records as graven lines the currents that have ceased to exist. Its shape is static, but it *expresses* the dynamic form of the river. Again, we have two congruent forms, like a cast and its mold, but this time the congruence is more remarkable because it holds between a dynamic form and a static one. That relation is important; we shall be dealing with it again when we come to consider the meaning of "living form" in art.

The congruence of two given perceptible forms is not always evident upon simple inspection. The common *logical* form they both exhibit may become apparent only when you know the principle whereby to relate them, as you compare the shapes of your hands not by direct correspondence, but by correspondence of opposite parts. Where the two exemplifications of the single logical form are unlike in most other respects one needs a rule for matching up the relevant factors of one with the relevant factors of the other; that is to say, a *rule of translation*, whereby one instance of the logical form is shown to correspond formally to the other.

The logical form itself is not another thing, but an abstract concept, or better an *abstractable* concept. We usually don't abstract it deliberately, but only use it, as we use our vocal cords in speech without first learning all about their operation and then applying our knowledge. Most people perceive intuitively the similarity of their two hands without thinking of them as conversely related; they can guess at the shape of the hollow inside a wooden shoe from the shape of a human foot, without any abstract study of topology. But the first time they see a map in the Mercator projection—with parallel lines of longitude, not meeting at the poles—they find it hard to believe that this corresponds logically to the circular map they used in school, where the meridians bulged apart toward the equator and met at both poles. The visible shapes of the continents are different on the two maps, and it takes abstract thinking to match up the two representations of the same earth. If, however, they have grown up with both maps, they will probably see the geographical relationships either way with equal ease, because these relationships are not *copied* by either map, but *expressed*, and expressed equally well by both; for the two maps are different *projections* of the same logical form, which the spherical earth exhibits in still another—that is, a spherical—projecton.

An expressive form is any perceptible or imaginable whole that exhibits relationships of parts, or points, or even qualities or aspects within the whole, so that it may be taken to represent some other whole whose elements have analogous relations. The reason for using such a form as a symbol is usually that the thing it represents is not perceivable or readily imaginable. We cannot see the earth as an object. We let a map or a little globe express the relationships of places on the earth, and think about the earth by means of it. The understanding of one thing through another seems to be a deeply intuitive process in the human brain; it is so natural that we often have difficulty in distinguishing the symbolic expressive form from what it conveys. The symbol seems to be the thing itself, or contain it, or be contained in it. A child interested in a globe will not say: "This means the earth," but: "Look, this is the earth." A similar identification of symbol and meaning underlies the widespread conception of holy names, of the physical efficacy of rites, and many other primitive but culturally persistent phenomena. It has a bearing on our perception of artistic import; that is why I mention it here.

The most astounding and developed symbolic device humanity has evolved is language. By means of language we can conceive the intangible, incorporeal things we call our *ideas*, and the equally inostensible elements of our perceptual world that we call *facts*. It is by virtue of language that we can think, remember, imagine, and finally conceive a universe of facts. We can describe things and represent their relations, express rules of their interactions, speculate and predict and carry on a long symbolizing process known as reasoning. And above all, we can communicate, by producing a serried array of audible or visible words, in a pattern commonly known, and readily understood to reflect our multifarious concepts and percepts and their interconnections. This use of language is *discourse*; and the pattern of discourse is known as *discursive* form. It is a highly versatile, amazingly powerful pattern. It has impressed itself on our tacit thinking, so that we call all systematic reflection "discursive thought." It has made, far more than most people know, the very frame of our sensory experience—the frame of objective facts in which we carry on the practical business of life.

Yet even the discursive pattern has its limits of usefulness. An expressive form can express any complex of conceptions that, via some rule of projection, appears congruent with it, that is, appears to be of that form. Whatever there is in experience that will not take the impress—directly or indirectly—of discursive form, is not discursively communicable or, in the strictest sense, logically thinkable. It is unspeakable, ineffable; according to practically all serious philosophical theories today, it is unknowable.

Yet there is a great deal of experience that is knowable, not only as immediate, formless, meaningless impact, but as one aspect of the intricate web of life, yet defies discursive formulation, and therefore verbal expression: that is what we sometimes call the *subjective aspect* of experience, the direct feeling of it—what it is like to be waking and moving, to be drowsy, slowing down, or to be sociable, or to feel self-sufficient but alone; what it feels like to pursue an elusive thought or to have a big idea. All such directly felt experiences usually have no names—they are named, if at all, for the outward conditions that normally accompany their occurrence. Only the most striking ones have names like "anger," "hate," "love," "fear," and are collectively called "emotion." But we feel many things that never develop into any designable emotion. The ways we are moved are as various as the lights in a forest; and they may intersect, sometimes without cancelling each other, take shape and dissolve, conflict, explode into passion, or be transfigured. All these inseparable elements of subjective reality compose what we call the "inward life" of human beings. The usual factoring of that life-stream into mental, emotional, and sensory units is an arbitrary scheme of simplification that makes scientific treatment possible to a considerable extent; but we may already be close to the limit of its usefulness, that is, close to the point where its simplicity becomes an obstacle to further questioning and discovery instead of the revealing, ever-suitable logical projection it was expected to be.

Whatever resists projection into the discursive form of language is, indeed, hard to hold in conception, and perhaps impossible to communicate, in the proper and strict sense of the word "communicate." But fortunately our logical intuition, or form-perception, is really much more powerful than we commonly believe, and our knowledge—genuine knowledge, understanding—is considerably wider than our discourse. Even in the use of language, if we want to name something that is too new to have a name (e.g., a newly invented gadget or a newly discovered creature), or want to express a relationship for which there is no verb or other connective word, we resort to metaphor; we mention it or describe it as something else, something analogous. The principle of metaphor is simply the principle of saying one thing and meaning another, and expecting to be understood to mean the other. A metaphor is not language, it is an idea expressed by language, an idea that in its turn functions as a symbol to express something. It is not discursive and therefore does not really make a statement of the idea it conveys; but it formulates a new conception for our direct imaginative grasp.

Sometimes our comprehension of a total experience is mediated by a metaphorical symbol because the experience is new, and language has words and phrases only for familiar notions. Then an extension of language will gradually follow the wordless insight, and discursive expression will supersede the non-discursive pristine symbol. This is, I think, the normal advance of human thought and language in that whole realm of knowledge where discourse is possible at all.

But the symbolic presentation of subjective reality for contemplation is not only tentatively beyond the reach of language—that is, not merely beyond the words we have; it is impossible in the essential frame of language. That is why those semanticists who recognize only discourse as a symbolic form must regard the whole life of feeling as formless, chaotic, capable only of symptomatic expression, typified in exclamations like "Ah!" "Ouch!" "My sainted aunt!" They usually do believe that art is an expression of feeling, but that "expression" in art is of this sort, indicating that the speaker has an emotion, a pain, or other personal experience, perhaps also giving us a clue to the general kind of experience it is—pleasant or unpleasant, violent or mild—but not setting that piece of inward life objectively before us so we may understand its intricacy, its rhythms and shifts of total appearance. The differences in feeling-tones or other elements of subjective experience are regarded as differences in quality, which must be felt to be appreciated. Furthermore, since we have no intellectual access to pure subjectivity, the only way to study it is to study the symptoms of the person who is having subjective experiences. This leads to physiological psychology—a very important and interesting field. But it tells us nothing about the phenomena of subjective life, and sometimes simplifies the problem by saying they don't exist.

Now, I believe the expression of feeling in a work of art—the function that makes the work an expressive form—is not symptomatic at all. An artist working on a tragedy need not be in personal despair or violent upheaval; nobody, indeed, could work in such a state of mind. His mind would be occupied with the causes of his emotional upset. Self-expression does not require composition and lucidity; a screaming baby gives his feeling far more release than any musician, but we don't go into a concert hall to hear a baby scream; in fact, if that baby is brought in we are likely to go out. We don't want self-expression.

A work of art presents feeling (in the broad sense I mentioned before, as everything that can be felt) for our contemplation, making it visible or audible or in some way perceivable through a symbol, not inferable from a symptom. Artistic form is congruent with the dynamic forms of our direct sensuous, mental, and emotional life; works of art are projections of "felt life," as Henry James called it, into spatial, temporal, and poetic structures. They are images of feeling, that formulate it for our cognition. What is artistically good is whatever articulates and presents feeling to our understanding.

Artistic forms are more complex than any other symbolic forms we know. They are, indeed, not abstractable from the works that exhibit them. We may abstract a shape from an object that has this shape, by disregarding color, weight and texture, even size; but to the total effect that is an artistic form, the color matters, the thickness of lines matters, and the appearance of texture and weight. A given triangle is the same in any position, but to an artistic form its location, balance, and surroundings are not indifferent. Form, in the sense in which artists speak of "significant form" or "expressive form," is not an abstracted structure, but an apparition; and the vital processes of sense and emotion that a good work of art expresses seem to the beholder to be directly contained in it, not symbolized but really presented. The congruence is so striking that symbol and meaning appear as one reality. Actually, as one psychologist who is also a musician has written, "Music sounds as feelings feel." And likewise, in good painting, sculpture, or building, balanced shapes and colors, lines and masses look as emotions, vital tensions and their resolutions feel.

An artist, then, expresses feeling, but not in the way a politician blows off steam or a baby laughs and cries. He formulates that elusive aspect of reality that is commonly taken to be amorphous and chaotic; that is, he objectifies the subjective realm. What he expresses is, therefore, not his own actual feelings, but what he knows about human feeling. Once he is in possession of a rich symbolism, that knowledge may actually exceed his entire personal experience. A work of art expresses a conception of life, emotion, inward reality. But it is neither a confessional nor a frozen tantrum; it is a developed metaphor, a non-discursive symbol that articulates what is verbally ineffable—the logic of consciousness itself.

CARL GUSTAV JUNG
The Poet

Creativeness, like the freedom of the will, contains a secret. The psychologist can describe both these manifestations as processes, but he can find no solution of the philosophical problems they offer. Creative man is a riddle that we may try to answer in various ways, but always in vain, a truth that has not prevented modern psychology from turning now and again to the question of the artist and his art. Freud thought that he had found a key in his procedure of deriving the work of art from the personal experiences of the artist. It is true that certain possibilities lay in this direction, for it was conceivable that a work of art, no less than a neurosis, might be traced back to those knots in psychic life that we call the complexes. It was Freud's great discovery that neuroses have a causal origin in the psychic realm—that they take their rise from emotional states and from real or imagined childhood experiences. Certain of his followers, like Rank and Stekel, have taken up related lines of enquiry and have achieved important results. It is undeniable that the poet's psychic disposition permeates his work root and branch. Nor is there anything new in the statement that personal factors largely influence the poet's choice and use of his materials. Credit, however, must certainly be given to the Freudian school for showing how far-reaching this influence is and in what curious ways it comes to expression.

Freud takes the neurosis as a substitute for a direct means of gratification. He therefore regards it as something inappropriate—a mistake, a dodge, an excuse, a voluntary blindness. To him it is essentially a shortcoming that should never have been. Since a neurosis, to all appearances, is nothing but a disturbance that is all the more irritating because it is without sense or meaning, few people will venture to say a good word for it. And a work of art is brought into questionable proximity with the neurosis when it is taken as something which can be analysed in terms of the poet's repressions. In a sense it finds itself in good company, for religion and philosophy are regarded in the same light by Freudian psychology. No objection can be raised if it is admitted that this approach amounts to nothing more than the elucidation of those personal determinants without which a work of art is unthinkable. But should the claim be made that such an analysis accounts for the work of art itself, then a categorical denial is called for. The personal idiosyncrasies that creep into a work of art are not essential; in fact, the more we have to cope with these peculiarities, the less is it a question of art. What is essential in a work of art is that it should rise far above the realm of personal life and speak from the spirit and heart of the poet as man to the spirit and heart of mankind. The personal aspect is a limitation—and even a sin—in the realm of art. When a form of "art" is primarily personal it deserves to be treated as if it were a neurosis. There may be some validity in the idea held by the Freudian school that artists without exception are narcissistic—by which is meant that they are undeveloped persons with infantile and auto-erotic traits. The statement is only valid, however, for the artist as a person, and has nothing to do with the man as an artist. In his capacity of artist he is neither auto-erotic, nor hetero-erotic, nor erotic in any sense. He is objective and impersonal—even inhuman —for as an artist he is his work, and not a human being.

Every creative person is a duality or a synthesis of contradictory aptitudes. On the one side he is a human being with a personal life, while on the other side he is an impersonal, creative process. Since as a human being he may be sound or morbid, we must look at his psychic make-up to find the determinants of his personality. But we can only understand him in his capacity of artist by looking at his creative achievement. We should make a sad mistake if we tried to explain the mode of life of an English gentleman, a Prussian officer, or a cardinal in terms of personal factors. The gentleman, the officer and the cleric function as such in an impersonal role, and their psychic make-up is qualified by a peculiar objectivity. We must grant that the artist does not function in an official capacity—the very opposite is nearer the truth. He nevertheless resembles the types I have named in one respect, for the specifically artistic disposition involves an overweight of collective psychic life as against the personal. Art is a kind of innate drive that seizes a human being and makes him its instrument. The artist is not a person endowed with free will who seeks his own ends, but one who allows art to realize its purposes through him. As a human being he may have moods and a will and personal aims, but as an artist he is "man" in a higher sense—he is "collective man"—one who carries and shapes the unconscious, psychic life of mankind. To perform this difficult office it is sometimes necessary for him to sacrifice happiness and everything that makes life worth living for the ordinary human being.

All this being so, it is not strange that the artist is an especially interesting case for the psychologist who uses an analytical method. The artist's life cannot be otherwise than full of conflicts, for two forces are at war within him—on the one hand the common human longing for happiness, satisfaction and security in life, and on the other a ruthless passion for creation which may go so far as to override every personal desire. The lives of artists are as a rule so highly unsatisfactory—not to say tragic—because of their inferiority on the human and personal side, and not because of a sinister dispensation. There are hardly any exceptions to the rule that a person must pay dearly for the divine gift of the creative fire. It is as though each of us were endowed at birth with a certain capital of energy. The strongest force in our make-up will seize and all but monopolize this energy, leaving so little over that nothing of value can come of it. In this way the creative force can drain the human impulses to such a degree that the personal ego must develop all sorts of bad qualities—ruthlessness, selfishness and vanity (so-called "auto-ero-tism")—and even every kind of vice, in order to maintain the spark of life and to keep itself from being wholly bereft. The auto-erotism of artists resembles that of illegitimate or neglected children who from their tenderest years must protect themselves from the destructive influence of people who have no love to give them—who develop bad qualities for that very purpose and later maintain an invincible egocentrism by remaining all their lives infantile and helpless or by actively offending against the moral code or the law. How can we doubt that it is his art that explains the artist, and not the insufficiencies and conflicts of his personal life? These are nothing but the regrettable results of the fact that he is an artist—that is to say, a man who from his very birth has been called to a greater task than the ordinary mortal. A special ability means a heavy expenditure of energy in a particular direction, with a consequent drain from some other side of life.

It makes no difference whether the poet knows that his work is begotten, grows and matures with him, or whether he supposes that by taking thought he produces it out of the void. His opinion of the matter does not change the fact that his own work outgrows him as a child its mother. The creative process has feminine quality, and the creative work arises from unconscious depths—we might say, from the realm of the mothers. Whenever the creative force predominates, human life is ruled and moulded by the unconscious as against the active will, and the conscious ego is swept along on a subterranean current, being nothing more than a helpless observer of events. The work in process becomes the poet's fate and determines his psychic development. It is not Goethe who creates *Faust*, but *Faust* which creates Goethe. And what is *Faust* but a symbol? By this I do not mean an allegory that points to something all too familiar, but an expression that stands for something not clearly known and yet profoundly alive. Here it is something that lives in the soul of every German, and that Goethe has helped to bring to birth. Could we conceive of anyone but a

German writing *Faust* or *Also sprach Zarathustra?* Both play upon something that reverberates in the German soul—a "primordial image," as Jacob Burckhardt once called it—the figure of a physician or teacher of mankind. The archetypal image of the wise man, the saviour or redeemer, lies buried and dormant in man's unconscious since the dawn of culture; it is awakened whenever the times are out of joint and a human society is committed to a serious error. When people go astray they feel the need of a guide or teacher or even of the physician. These primordial images are numerous, but do not appear in the dreams of individuals or in works of art until they are called into being by the waywardness of the general outlook. When conscious life is characterized by one-sidedness and by a false attitude, then they are activated—one might say, "instinctively"—and come to light in the dreams of individuals and the visions of artists and seers, thus restoring the psychic equilibrium of the epoch.

In this way the work of the poet comes to meet the spiritual need of the society in which he lives, and for this reason his work means more to him than his personal fate, whether he is aware of this or not. Being essentially the instrument for his work, he is subordinate to it, and we have no reason for expecting him to interpret it for us. He has done the best that in him lies in giving it form, and he must leave the interpretation to others and to the future. A great work of art is like a dream; for all its apparent obviousness it does not explain itself and is never unequivocal. A dream never says: "You ought," or: "This is the truth." It presents an image in much the same way as nature allows a plant to grow, and we must draw our own conclusions. If a person has a nightmare, it means either that he is too much given to fear, or else that he is too exempt from it; and if he dreams of the old wise man it may mean that he is too pedagogical, as also that he stands in need of a teacher. In a subtle way both meanings come to the same thing, as we perceive when we are able to let the work of art act upon us as it acted upon the artist. To grasp its meaning, we must allow it to shape us as it once shaped him. Then we understand the nature of his experience. We see that he has drawn upon the healing and redeeming forces of the collective psyche that underlies consciousness with its isolation and its painful errors; that he has penetrated to that matrix of life in which all men are embedded, which imparts a common rhythm to all human existence, and allows the individual to communicate his feeling and his striving to mankind as a whole.

The secret of artistic creation and of the effectiveness of art is to be found in a return to the state of *participation mystique*—to that level of experience at which it is man who lives, and not the individual, and at which the weal or woe of the single human being does not count, but only human existence. This is why every great work of art is objective and impersonal, but none the less profoundly moves us each and all. And this is also why the personal life of the poet cannot be held essential to his art—but at most a help or a hindrance to his creative task. He may go the way of a Philistine, a good citizen, a neurotic, a fool or a criminal. His personal career may be inevitable and interesting, but it does not explain the poet.

QUESTIONS

1. Jung makes a distinction between the "human being with a personal life" and the "impersonal, creative process." What is the importance of this distinction? How does it help to shape the rest of Jung's argument?

2. Jung says that the "personal idiosyncrasies that creep into a work of art are not essential," since art "should rise far above the realm of personal life and speak from the spirit and heart of the poet as man to the spirit and heart of mankind." Is a contradiction involved here? Can a poet speak from his heart without being personal? Are "personal idiosyncrasies" desirable in a work to give it the flavor of a distinctive style?

3. In "The Keys to Dreamland" (p. 376), Frye says that "literature has no consistent connection with ordinary life. . . . You don't relate it directly to life or reality, you relate works of literature to each other." Compare Frye's view with Jung's statement that "a great work of art is like a dream. . . . It presents an image in much the same way as nature allows a plant to grow, and we must draw our own conclusions."

4. Consider the following stanzas (69–72) from Byron's "Childe Harold's Pilgrimage." To what extent would Jung feel that psychological considerations were helpful in analyzing these lines?

> To fly from, need not be to hate, mankind:
> All are not fit with them to stir and toil,
> Nor is it discontent to keep the mind
> Deep in its fountain, lest it overboil
> In the hot throng, where we become the spoil
> Of our infection, till too late and long
> We may deplore and struggle with the coil,
> In wretched interchange of wrong for wrong
> Midst a contentious world, striving where none are strong.
>
> There, in a moment we may plunge our years
> In fatal penitence, and in the blight
> Of our own Soul turn all our blood to tears,
> And colour things to come with hues of Night;
> The race of life becomes a hopeless flight
> To those that walk in darkness: on the sea
> The boldest steer but where their ports invite—
> But there are wanderers o'er Eternity
> Whose bark drives on and on, and anchored ne'er shall be.

Is it not better, then, to be alone,
And love Earth only for its earthly sake?
By the blue rushing of the arrowy Rhone,
Or the pure bosom of its nursing Lake,
Which feeds it as a mother who doth make
A fair but froward infant her own care,
Kissing its cries away as these awake;—
Is it not better thus our lives to wear,
Than join the crushing crowd, doomed to inflict or bear?

I live not in myself, but I become
Portion of that around me; and to me
High mountains are a feeling, but the hum
Of human cities torture: I can see
Nothing to loathe in Nature, save to be
A link reluctant in a fleshly chain,
Classed among creatures, when the soul can flee,
And with the sky—the peak—the heaving plain.
Of ocean, or the stars, mingle—and not in vain.

JEAN KERR

The Poet and the Peasants

We have made mistakes with our children, which will undoubtedly become clearer as they get old enough to write their own books. But here I would like to be serious for a few minutes about the one thing we did that was right. We taught them not to be afraid of poetry.

For a number of years, or until the older boys went away to school, we gathered the protesting brood in the living room every Sunday evening, right after dinner, for what the children scornfully referred to as "Culture Hour." Each boy would recite a poem he had memorized during the week, after which we would play some classical music on the hi-fi for twenty minutes or so. This will sound simple and easy only to those who refuse to grasp that if there is an irresistible force there are most definitely immovable objects.

Actually the program came about by accident. One night I went into the den and turned on a light which promptly burned out. Then when I turned on a second light the same thing happened. Cursing the darkness, I muttered "When I consider how my light is spent . . ."

My husband surprised me by asking, "What's that from?" I recoiled as though he had just announced that he couldn't remember the colors of the American flag. "It's not possible," I said, "that you don't know what that's from. Everybody knows what that's from."

His look was short-suffering. "You don't have to sound so superior," he said. "The first present I ever gave you was a book of poetry." (I was eighteen and it was *The Collected Poems of Stephen Crane.*) "I know that's a poem, I just don't know *which* poem."

"Well," I continued, fatuous as before, "that is Milton's *Sonnet on His Blindness* and it's inconceivable to me that a man who used to be a teacher wouldn't remember." But he had left to get two new light bulbs and out of the range of my voice.

That started me mulling, which is one of the things I do best. Were our five boys going to grow up knowing all about such folk heroes as Joe Namath and Vince Lombardi and nothing whatsoever about Milton or Keats or Yeats or even Ogden Nash? Steps, I felt, had to be taken.

When I first proposed the idea to my husband his enthusiasm was less contagious than I might have hoped. "I don't suppose it will kill them" is what he said. "Them" at that point were Chris, aged fourteen, the twins, Colin and John, aged ten, and Gilbert, aged seven. There was also Gregory, aged two, who could recite "I love Bosco, that's the drink for me," but I didn't suppose his talents could be pushed further at that juncture.

I did suppose that we could plunge ahead with the four older boys. But if their father felt it wouldn't kill them, they had no such confidence. As I unfolded The Plan they couldn't have been more horrified if I had suddenly suggested that all of them wear hair ribbons to football practice. Nevertheless, I was adamant, and, as it turned out, rather obtuse. At that stage of my life I was still in good voice and bigger than they were. And I was used to giving commands. "Go," I would say to one, and he would goeth, "Come," I would say to another and he would cometh. (Occasionally he would runneth out the back door.)

I always tried (and still do try) to be very specific. To say to a ten-year-old boy, "If you don't start keeping that room tidy, I am going to go absolutely crazy" is a waste of time and breath. To begin with, he doesn't know what the word "tidy" means and he won't find out until he marries the right girl. And since he considers that you are already crazy, he will not believe that his actions are likely to worsen the situation. It may not be infallible, but it surely is more practical to say, "You don't leave this room until I say it is *perfect* and I do mean all those Good Humor sticks under the bed."

Anyway, it was with this sense of being totally explicit that I told the boys one Monday morning, "I want you to find a poem that you like and I want you to learn it so you can say it out loud next Sunday night. Is that clear?" The sighs and the groaning reassured me. I had been perfectly clear. During the week I nudged them from time to time, "How is that poem coming, do you know it yet?"

On Sunday evening there was the usual hassle over whose turn it was to dry the silver and whose turn it was to line the kitchen waste basket, etc. My own mother used to solve this problem by saying, "Just don't bother, I'll do it myself," but I am too judicious for that and also too lazy. So getting the dishes put away is always a long-drawn-out process. Tonight it was a longer-drawn-out process. But eventually the victims presented themselves in the living room, and the recital began. Three of the boys had selected limericks and poor limericks at that (imagine anybody rhyming "breakfast" with "steadfast") while the fourth recited a lengthy and truly dreadful verse about a Cookie Jar Elf. My husband, more than most men of his generation, has seen some pretty horrendous performances, but this was in a class by itself. He polished his glasses, presumably to make sure that these *were* his children. As for me, I had intended to make a few illuminating comments. Instead I was left as slack-jawed and as speechless as those television commentators who were picked up by the camera minutes after President Johnson announced he would *not* run again.

In the vacuum I put a record, *The Nutcracker Suite*, on the hi-fi and warned the boys they were not to talk, they were to listen. They were not to whisper, they were to listen. The boys kept to the letter, if not the spirit, of the instructions, with the result that I was the one who talked and talked all through the music: "Stop kicking him in the ankle, take that ashtray off the top of your head, I know you can hear the music from there but get out from under the coffee table."

The whole thing was a disaster but, while I was definitely daunted, I was not yet ready to give up. (Remember that *Hello, Dolly!* looked like a failure when it opened in Detroit.) Eventually I was able to identify Mistake Number One. Asking the boys to find a poem they "liked" made about as much sense as asking me to select a Rock Group that I liked. Of course they didn't like poems, any poems. How could they, why should they? When I was the age of our oldest and was required at school to learn whole passages of *The Lady of the Lake*, I thought "The stag at eve had drunk his fill/Where danced the moon on Monan's rill" was pretty ghastly stuff. (To tell the truth, I still think it's pretty ghastly.) Once, as a senior in high school, I got sixty on an English exam because of the way I answered a forty-point question which read: "Discuss Wordsworth's *The World Is Too Much with Us* and explain what it means to you." You will not have to remember the poem to grasp that I was not only saucy but asking for trouble when I wrote that, whatever Wordsworth was looking for as he stood on that pleasant lea, the *last* thing I wanted was to see Proteus rising from the sea or, for that matter, hear old Triton blow his wreathèd horn. I mention this only to make it clear that I was not among those prodigies who are reading Shakespeare's sonnets for pleasure at the age of five. Poetry struck me as an arbitrary and capricious method of avoiding clarity, and where my betters heard lyricism I kept hearing foolishness. If the poem said, "Go, lovely rose!" I found myself thinking "Scram, rose. On the double. Take a powder, rose."

What happened to open my eyes and shut my mouth was quite simple. I was a freshman in college when a Jesuit poet named Alfred Barrett came to lecture. I attended with the same enthusiasm that characterized my presence in Advanced Algebra, sitting way at the back of the hall behind a pillar on the theory that I could live through it if I could sleep through it.

It's hard for me to remember, all these years later, what Father Barrett said about poetry, if indeed he said anything. What he did was to read poetry—some of his own, a great deal of Gerard Manley Hopkins (whose existence I was unaware of), Yeats, Shelley, Donne, and Housman. He read with such clarity, such melody, and, above all, such directness that even I—sixteen year-old skeptic—was converted on the spot. It wasn't so much that I cried "Eureka —I see!" I felt like a woman I know who swears she didn't get her first kiss until she was twenty-three and who exclaimed, on that occasion, "Hey, why didn't somebody *tell* me?" Later in my life I was to meet a teacher and a director, Josephine Callan, who read poetry even better than Father Barrett did but by that time I was already a believer.

Okay, that was *my* story. To get back to the indoctrination of our boys, it was clear that their taste was decidedly peccable and that we would have to select the poems for them, keeping in mind the difference in the boys' ages. (My husband was quick to point out that fortunately there was no difference in the ages of the twins.) We went through the bookshelves, leafed and leafed, and gave each of the boys a book with the poem he was to learn. This was another error because by the end of the week our good books were dog-eared or rateared, depending upon the age and irresponsibility of the boy. For a while after that we typed out copies of the poems, but that was a chore and a nuisance (why is poetry harder to type than *anything?*) so eventually we did in the last place what we should have done in the first place, which was to go out and buy a pile of cheap paperback anthologies (these are widely available and often surprisingly good).

The second, or return, engagement of "Culture" night was hardly an improvement on the first. The fact that the poems were of better quality and somewhat longer made the recitations even more agonizing, if that were possible. The younger boys stared at the rug and mumbled like altar boys answering their first Mass in Latin, while Chris stared at the ceiling and chanted in a loud, dum-de-dum see-saw-Margery-Daw rhythm (banging on every end-rhyme until I could definitely feel my inlays ache).

As I see it now, the surprising thing is that I should have been surprised. Even granting that I was much younger then (I was, you will be able to surmise, over twenty-one), there was no excuse for my being so dim-witted. Did I really believe that we were harboring a gaggle of Laurence Oliviers? (Ellen Terry heard Olivier in a school play when he was eleven and instantly announced, "That young man is already an actor.") Not, heaven forbid, that we were trying to develop actors. In my opinion, young people who wish to become actors have an addiction only a little less dangerous than heroin. No, we didn't want them to qualify for a Tony or an Emmy, we just wanted them to feel at home with language that was different from and better than the colloquial speech they heard every day. We wanted them to accept poetry without embarrassment and perhaps finally to realize that a good poem is an emotional short-cut and not just the long way around.

My husband gave a deep sigh as he faced up to the obvious. "We're just going to have to work on them," he said. And so we did. One week he'd work on two of them while I worked on the other two (the following week we alternated so that the hostility engendered would be evenly divided). Getting a boy and his poem together (a not inconsiderable feat), we read the poem aloud to him, slowly. Ignoring giggles and glassy-eyed boredom, we read it again at the proper speed and then asked questions: What do you think this poem means, is it happy or sad, and so on? Even a piece of verse as simple as "Little Boy Blue" holds mysteries for a seven-year-old. He may not know what the word "staunch" means, or even "musket." Perhaps he may not get the point at all and will be as perplexed as the little toy soldier and the little toy dog as to "what has become of our Little Boy Blue since he kissed them and put them there."

Once we determined that the child actually understood the whole poem, we got *him* to read it aloud, correcting him when he mispronounced words, correcting him when he misread phrases, persuading him not to say the rhyming word louder than any other word in the line. Two of the boys were very quick to grasp inflections; the other two were so slow that rehearsing them was like the Chinese Water Torture and I found myself wondering if there was some way to withdraw from the whole plan—with honor. What kept me resolute was the conviction I read in all those clear blue eyes that I would soon come to my senses, that this madness too would pass.

On the third Sunday night the boys were not exactly ready to cut a tape for Angel Records but they were definitely improved. In fact, the session was almost endurable, and we had some general discussion afterward about what the four poems meant, with even Gilbert making a contribution: "When the angel waked him up with a song it means he was dead, stupid."

Thereafter the Sunday hour became just another fact of life around this house and the boys seemed to accept it with hardly more resentment than they accepted baths or sweaters or my notion that a present that came in the mail required a thank-you letter. And, of course, they did get better. The day finally came when they were really able to tackle a poem without our having to tell them "What Tennyson is trying to say here is . . ." They knew. And if they made mistakes, these were fewer and fewer. Sometimes they came up with an unusual interpretation that was, we had to concede, quite possibly valid.

But this didn't happen until we'd been through years of poetry, yards of poetry, volumes of poetry. We made a number of discoveries along the way. Christopher in his mid-teens and already a little world-weary had a particular affinity for the cynical or sardonic, whether it was in a simple lyric form like Housman's

> When I was one and twenty
> I heard a wise man say,
> 'Give crowns and pounds and guineas
> But not your heart away;
> . . . .
> 'Tis paid with sighs a-plenty
> And sold for endless rue.'
> And I am two and twenty
> And oh, 'tis true, 'tis true.

or in the rich resonance of Arnold's *Dover Beach*:

> Ah, love, let us be true
> To one another! for the world, which seems
> To lie before us like a land of dreams,
> So various, so beautiful, so new,
> Hath really neither joy, nor love, nor light,
> Nor certitude, nor peace, nor help for pain;
> And we are here as on a darkling plain
> Swept with confused alarms of struggle and flight,
> Where ignorant armies clash by night.

I can still see him—he must have been fifteen, messy and mussed with dirty sneakers and a deplorable shirt—reciting Browning with all the hauteur and severity of George Sanders:

> That's my last Duchess painted on the wall,
> Looking as if she were alive. . . .
> > > > She had
> A heart . . . how shall I say? . . . too soon made glad,
> Too easily impressed; she liked whate'er
> She looked on, and her looks went everywhere.

George Sanders chilled into George C. Scott as he came to the lines:

> . . . This grew; I gave commands;
> Then all smiles stopped together.

Colin was a very serious ten-year-old (he's now six feet five and a very serious Harvard junior) and it seemed to us that he did better with the dark and the dire. "Out of the night that covers me, black as pitch from pole to pole," he would say in a voice that was at once sweet and piercing, "I thank whatever gods may be for my unconquerable soul." He was downright threatening as he recited John Donne's:

> Death, be not proud, though some have callèd thee
> Mighty and dreadful, for thou art not so:
> For those whom thou think'st thou dost overthrow
> Die not, poor Death; nor yet canst thou kill me.

John had a good voice, a trace of ham, and a total lack of inhibition that made him a natural for the more flamboyant ballads. His early pièce de résistance was *The Highwayman* by Alfred Noyes. I'm sure he couldn't do it as well today as he could when he was twelve. But then I don't honestly think *anybody* can do *The Highwayman* the way John could when he was twelve. John began the opening lines with a sense of excitement that never flagged:

> The wind was a torrent of darkness among the gusty trees.
> The moon was a ghostly galleon tossed upon cloudy seas.
> The road was a ribbon of moonlight over the purple moor,
> And the highwayman came riding—
>   Riding—riding—
> The highwayman came riding, up to the old inn door.

And he handled the love story of the highwayman and the innkeeper's daughter with great tenderness. Describing how she loosened her hair in the casement window, he would pause before saying, ever so gently, "Oh, sweet black waves in the moonlight!" and then flash with the fire of a prosecuting attorney as the highwayman went

> Down like a dog on the highway
> And he lay in his blood on the highway, with a bunch
> of lace at his throat.

With John's passion, one felt that the body was there on the living-room floor. Another of his early hits was *Barbara Frietchie*, and if you think that one is just another chestnut ("Who touches a hair of yon grey head dies like a dog, he said") you haven't heard it read by someone who doesn't *know* it's a chestnut and who believes he was there and is giving you an eyewitness account. John was always awfully good with people who died, or were about to die, like dogs.

Having tried the tried and the true, John gradually moved on to the intricacies of Hopkins, where he could be majestic:

The world is charged with the grandeur of God.
It will flame out, like shining from shook foil. . . .

Or filled with righteous indignation:

Thou art indeed just, Lord, if I contend
With thee; but, sir, so what I plead is just.
Why do sinners' ways prosper? And why must
Disappointment all I endeavor end?

Or rueful, as in *Spring and Fall*, which he recited often because
it's a particular favorite of mine:

Margaret, are you grieving over goldengrove unleaving?
Leaves, like the things of man, you
With your fresh thoughts care for, can you?
Ah! As the heart grows older
It will come to such sights colder
By and by, nor spare a sigh
Though worlds of wanwood leafmeal lie;
And yet you will weep and know why.
Now no matter, child, the name:
Sorrow's springs are the same.
Nor mouth had, no nor mind, expressed
What heart heard of, ghost guessed:
It is the blight man was born for,
It is Margaret you mourn for.

Gilbert, being much younger, was limited to what we thought
was "easy," which meant that he got relatively cheerful poems and
we got some relief. As I remember it, in his poems he was always
planning to go someplace. He was going to see the cherry filled with
snow, he was going to go down to the lonely seas again, he was
going to arise and go to Innisfree. He was also going to leave
Lucasta and go to war, but that was later.

During these evenings we continued to play twenty minutes of
music. This became more bearable after I stopped trying to make
the boys *look* attentive; it had occurred to me, after many a grind-
ing play and many a dull sermon, that no matter how hard you try
not to listen, something sticks to you anyway. And some nights we
broke the pattern by running the films Leonard Bernstein had made
for *Omnibus*. My husband had worked for *Omnibus* and was able
to borrow kinescopes of the Bernstein talks on Modern Music, Jazz,
The Beethoven Manuscripts, The Art of Conducting, and so on. I
think these programs are as exhilarating as anything ever done on television. What the children thought was harder to fathom, since
they remained totally noncommittal. Clearly, though, Bernstein
made some impression on them. I know this because, months after
we had played the last of the series, I discovered that Colin had
built a new fort in the backyard. It was a crude affair made from

two old card tables, an abandoned playpen, and some tar paper. However, insubstantial as it was, the fort appeared to have a name. A tattered banner floating over the entrance bore the legend: *Fort Issimo*.

We also began to get evidence that gallons of nineteenth-century poetry hadn't washed over them in vain. I recall one night—the twins were twelve—when John was made an Eagle Scout. Driving home from this awe-inspiring ceremony (oh, the Nobel people could take lessons!), I started to tease John. "Well," I said, "you've reached the top. Now what are you going to do?" The answer came from Colin in the back seat. "Oh," he announced briskly, "I expect he will go down to the vile dust from whence he sprung, unwept, unhonored, and unsung."

Sometimes, I must confess, this readiness with the apt quotation could be quite maddening. I think of another night when the two smaller boys were supposed to have gone to bed but had, against all orders, slipped outside to bat a few balls directly under the living-room window. Suddenly there was a splatter of broken glass and a baseball on the rug. Chris grinned cheerfully as he said, "Come to the window, sweet is the night air."

During all the years we continued our program I never at any time was given any hint that the boys approved. Not ever, not once. So I was thunderstruck one summer, after they'd all returned from school, when the boys themselves suggested that we resume "Culture Hour" for the weeks they were to be at home. I couldn't have been more startled if they had suddenly volunteered to clean out the attic. In fact, it occurred to me that they were making an elaborate joke (irony is frequently wasted on me), so I pressed for an explanation. It turned out that they thought it was time for Gregory to have "his turn." This might have been taken as further evidence that the older children felt they had been made the guinea pigs of the system while their younger siblings got off scot-free, but here they were volunteering to suffer right along with him. Now I believed them capable of altruism, particularly where Gregory was concerned, but not heroism. It had to be, it just had to be that they enjoyed it.

So we started over with Gregory, who, at seven, was already as complex as John Kenneth Galbraith. Not necessarily smart, you understand, just complex. Some days he'd come bursting in the back door with the air of one who'd just been rescued from a burning building and call out for his father, "Where's Mr. Kerr? I need him." (No, no, no, none of the other boys ever called their father Mister.) The next day he'd drift in as slowly as smoke, like a character out of Chekhov who has just lost his country estates.

Certainly *we* didn't understand him, but he did seem to have certain intimations about himself. Let me explain. On the opening night of the cultural revival, Gregory—with much prompting—

struggled and stammered his way through no more than six lines of *The Gingham Dog and the Calico Cat*. It wasn't just that he was confused about gingham and calico. I began to wonder if he knew what dog and cat meant.

I don't remember what the other boys recited that evening, but Chris recited a long section of T. S. Eliot's *Prufrock*. The next morning I was passing through the garage and came upon Gregory building a birdhouse. He was also muttering something to himself. What with the noise of the saw, he wasn't aware that I had come up behind him, so I was able to overhear him. What he was saying, thoughtfully and precisely, was "I am not Prince Hamlet, nor was meant to be."

Soon the summer was over, school began, the Captains and the Kings departed, and the program was dropped. It was never to resume again because the following summer the older boys all had jobs away from home. It was never to resume and something special, I realized, had gone out of our lives. You lose not only your own youth but the youth of your children. Sweet things vanish and brightness falls from the air.

Now all those Sunday nights blur in memory like the ghost of birthdays past. But if there is one night that remains more vivid than the others it is because of my own strange behavior. Colin was just finishing *John Anderson My Jo*. Do you remember it all?

> John Anderson my jo, John,
>   When we were first acquent,
> Your locks were like the raven,
>   Your bonnie brow was brent;
> But now your brow is beld, John,
>   Your locks are like the snaw;
> But blessings on your frosty pow,
>   John Anderson, my jo.
>
> John Anderson my jo, John,
>   We clamb the hill thegither;
> And monie a canty day, John,
>   We've had wi'ane anither:
> Now we maun totter down, John,
>   And hand in hand we'll go,
> And sleep thegither at the foot,
>   John Anderson, my jo.

I already knew the poem by heart, so how it happened that I heard new meanings in it I cannot exactly explain. All I can say is that after Colin had finished, to the horror of the boys and to my own acute embarrassment, I burst into tears. An uneasy silence prevailed until John said, very quietly, "Mom, it is Margaret you mourn for."

And he was right, you know. He was absolutely right.

ROBERT FROST
Education by Poetry: A Meditative Monologue[1]

I am going to urge nothing in my talk. I am not an advocate. I am going to consider a matter, and commit a description. And I am going to describe other colleges than Amherst. Or, rather say all that is good can be taken as about Amherst; all that is bad will be about other colleges.

I know whole colleges where all American poetry is barred—whole colleges. I know whole colleges where all contemporary poetry is barred.

I once heard of a minister who turned his daughter—his poetry-writing daughter—out on the street to earn a living, because he said there should be no more books written; God wrote one book, and that was enough. (My friend George Russell, "Æ", has read no literature, he protests, since just before Chaucer.)

That all seems sufficiently safe, and you can say one thing for it. It takes the onus off the poetry of having to be used to teach children anything. It comes pretty hard on poetry, I sometimes think, what it has to bear in the teaching process.

Then I know whole colleges where, though they let in older poetry, they manage to bar all that is poetical in it by treating it as something other than poetry. It is not so hard to do that. Their reason I have often hunted for. It may be that these people act from a kind of modesty. Who are professors that they should attempt to deal with a thing as high and as fine as poetry? Who are *they?* There is a certain manly modesty in that.

That is the best general way of settling the problem; treat all poetry as if it were something else than poetry, as if it were syntax, language, science. Then you can even come down into the American and into the contemporary without any special risk.

There is another reason they have, and that is that they are, first and foremost in life, markers. They have the marking problem to consider. Now, I stand here a teacher of many years' experience and I have never complained of having had to mark. I had rather mark anyone for anything—for his looks, carriage, his ideas, his correctness, his exactness, anything you please—I would rather give him a mark in terms of letters, A, B, C, D, than have to use adjectives on him. We are all being marked by each other all the time, classified, ranked, put in our place, and I see no escape from that. I am no sentimentalist. You have got to mark, and you have got to mark, first of all, for accuracy, for correctness. But if I am going to give a mark, that is the least part of my marking. The hard part is the part beyond that, the part where the adventure begins.

1. An address given at Amherst College in 1930.

One other way to rid the curriculum of the poetry nuisance has been considered. More merciful than the others it would neither abolish nor denature the poetry, but only turn it out to disport itself, with the plays and games—in no wise discredited, though given no credit for. Any one who liked to teach poetically could take his subject, whether English, Latin, Greek or French, out into the nowhere along with the poetry. One side of a sharp line would be left to the rigorous and righteous; the other side would be assigned to the flowery where they would know what could be expected of them. Grade marks were more easily given, of course, in the courses concentrating on correctness and exactness as the only forms of honesty recognized by plain people; a general indefinite mark of X in the courses that scatter brains over taste and opinion. On inquiry I have found no teacher willing to take position on either side of the line, either among the rigors or among the flowers. No one is willing to admit that his discipline is not partly in exactness. No one is willing to admit that his discipline is not partly in taste and enthusiasm.

How shall a man go through college without having been marked for taste and judgment? What will become of him? What will his end be? He will have to take continuation courses for college graduates. He will have to go to night schools. They are having night schools now, you know, for college graduates. Why? Because they have not been educated enough to find their way around in contemporary literature. They don't know what they may safely like in the libraries and galleries. They don't know how to judge an editorial when they see one. They don't know how to judge a political campaign. They don't know when they are being fooled by a metaphor, an analogy, a parable. And metaphor is, of course, what we are talking about. Education by poetry is education by metaphor.

Suppose we stop short of imagination, initiative, enthusiasm, inspiration and originality—dread words. Suppose we don't mark in such things at all. There are still two minimal things, that we have got to take care of, taste and judgment. Americans are supposed to have more judgment than taste, but taste is there to be dealt with. That is what poetry, the only art in the colleges of arts, is there for. I for my part would not be afraid to go in for enthusiasm. There is the enthusiasm like a blinding light, or the enthusiasm of the deafening shout, the crude enthusiasm that you get uneducated by poetry, outside of poetry. It is exemplified in what I might call "sunset raving." You look westward toward the sunset, or if you get up early enough, eastward toward the sunrise, and you rave. It is oh's and ah's with you and no more.

But the enthusiasm I mean is taken through the prism of the intellect and spread on the screen in a color, all the way from hyperbole at one end—or overstatement, at one end—to understatement at the other end. It is a long strip of dark lines and many colors. Such enthusiasm is one object of all teaching in poetry. I heard wonderful things said about Virgil yesterday, and many of them seemed to me crude enthusiasm, more like a deafening shout, many of them. But one speech had range, something of overstatement, something of statement, and something of understatement. It had all the colors of an enthusiasm passed through an idea.

I would be willing to throw away everything else but that: enthusiasm tamed by metaphor. Let me rest the case there. Enthusiasm tamed to metaphor, tamed to that much of it. I do not think anybody ever knows the discreet use of metaphor, his own and other people's, the discreet handling of metaphor, unless he has been properly educated in poetry.

Poetry begins in trivial metaphors, petty metaphors, "grace" metaphors, and goes on to the profoundest thinking that we have. Poetry provides the one permissible way of saying one thing and meaning another. People say, "Why don't you say what you mean?" We never do that, do we, being all of us too much poets. We like to talk in parables and in hints and in indirections—whether from diffidence or some other instinct.

I have wanted in late years to go further and further in making metaphor the whole of thinking. I find some one now and then to agree with me that all thinking, except mathematical thinking, is metaphorical, or all thinking except scientific thinking. The mathematical might be difficult for me to bring in, but the scientific is easy enough.

Once on a time all the Greeks were busy telling each other what the All was—or was like unto. All was three elements, air, earth, and water (we once thought it was ninety elements; now we think it is only one). All was substance, said another. All was change, said a third. But best and most fruitful was Pythagoras' comparison of the universe with number. Number of what? Number of feet, pounds, and seconds was the answer, and we had science and all that has followed in science. The metaphor has held and held, breaking down only when it came to the spiritual and psychological or the out of the way places of the physical.

The other day we had a visitor here, a noted scientist, whose latest word to the world has been that the more accurately you know where a thing is, the less accurately you are able to state how fast it is moving. You can see why that would be so, without going back to Zeno's problem of the arrow's flight. In carrying numbers into the realm of space and at the same time into the realm of time you are mixing metaphors, that is all, and you are in trouble. They won't mix. The two don't go together.

Let's take two or three more of the metaphors now in use to live by. I have just spoken of one of the new ones, a charming mixed metaphor right in the realm of higher mathematics and higher physics: that the more accurately you state where a thing is, the less accurately you will be able to tell how fast it is moving. And, of course everything is moving. Everything is an event now. Another metaphor. A thing, they say, is an event. Do you believe it is? Not quite. I believe it is almost an event. But I like the comparison of a thing with an event.

I notice another from the same quarter. "In the neighborhood of matter space is something like curved." Isn't that a good one! It seems to me that that is simply and utterly charming—to say that space is something like curved in the neighborhood of matter. "Something like."

Another amusing one is from—what is the book?—I can't say it now; but here is the metaphor. Its aim is to restore you to your ideas of free will. It wants to give you back your freedom of will. All right, here it is on a platter. You know that you can't tell by name what persons in a certain class will be dead ten years after graduation, but you can tell actuarially how many will be dead. Now, just so this scientist says of the particles of matter flying at a screen, striking a screen; you can't tell what individual particles will come, but you can say in general that a certain number will strike in a given time. It shows, you see, that the individual particle can come freely. I asked Bohr about that particularly, and he said, "Yes, it is so. It can come when it wills and as it wills; and the action of the individual particle is unpredictable. But it is not so of the action of the mass. There you can predict." He says, "That gives the individual atom its freedom, but the mass its necessity."

Another metaphor that has interested us in our time and has done all our thinking for us is the metaphor of evolution. Never mind going into the Latin word. The metaphor is simply the metaphor of the growing plant or of the growing thing. And somebody very brilliantly, quite a while ago, said that the whole universe, the whole of everything, was like unto a growing thing. That is all. I know the metaphor will break down at some point, but it has not failed everywhere. It is a very brilliant metaphor, I acknowledge, though I myself get too tired of the kind of essay that talks about the evolution of candy, we will say, or the evolution of elevators—the evolution of this, that, and the other. Everything is evolution. I emancipate myself by simply saying that I didn't get up the metaphor and so am not much interested in it.

What I am pointing out is that unless you are at home in the metaphor, unless you have had your proper poetical education in the metaphor, you are not safe anywhere. Because you are not at ease with figurative values: you don't know the metaphor in its strength and its weakness. You don't know how far you may expect to ride it and when it may break down with you. You are not safe in science; you are not safe in history. In history, for instance—to show that is the same in history as elsewhere—I heard somebody say yesterday that Aeneas was to be likened unto (those words, "likened unto"!) George Washington. He was that type of national hero, the middle-class man, not thinking of being a hero at all, bent on building the future, bent on his children, his descendants. A good metaphor, as far as it goes, and you must know how far. And then he added that Odysseus should be likened unto Theodore Roosevelt. I don't think that is so good. Someone visiting Gibbon at the point of death, said he was the same Gibbon as of old; still at his parallels.

Take the way we have been led into our present position morally, the world over. It is by a sort of metaphorical gradient. There is a kind of thinking—to speak metaphorically—there is a kind of thinking you might say was endemic in the brothel. It is always there. And every now and then in some mysterious way it becomes epidemic in the world. And how does it do so? By using all the good words that virtue has invented to maintain virtue. It uses honesty, first—frankness, sincerity—those words; picks them up, uses them. "In the name of honesty, let us see what we are." You know. And then it picks up the word joy. "Let us in the name of joy, which is the enemy of our ancestors, the Puritans . . . Let us in the name of joy, which is the enemy of the kill-joy Puritan . . . " You see. "Let us," and so on. And then, "In the name of health . . . " Health is another good word. And that is the metaphor Freudianism trades on, mental health. And the first thing we know, it has us all in up to the top knot. I suppose we may blame the artists a good deal, because they are great people to spread by metaphor. The stage too—the stage is always a good intermediary between the two worlds, the under and the upper, if I may say so without personal prejudice to the stage.

In all this, I have only been saying that the devil can quote Scripture, which simply means that the good words you have lying around the devil can use for his purposes as well as anybody else. Never mind about my morality. I am not here to urge anything. I don't care whether the world is good or bad—not on any particular day.

Let me ask you to watch a metaphor breaking down here before you.

Somebody said to me a little while ago, "It is easy enough for me to think of the universe as a machine, as a mechanism."

I said, "You mean the universe is like a machine?"

He said, "No. I think it is one . . .Well, it is like . . ."

"I think you mean the universe is like a machine."

"All right. Let it go at that."

I asked him, "Did you ever see a machine without a pedal for the foot, or a lever for the hand, or a button for the finger?"

He said "No—no."

I said, "All right. Is the universe like that?"

And he said, "No. I mean it is like a machine, only . . ."

". . . it is different from a machine," I said.

He wanted to go just that far with that metaphor and no further. And so do we all. All metaphor breaks down somewhere. That is the beauty of it. It is touch and go with the metaphor, and until you have lived with it long enough you don't know when it is going. You don't know how much you can get out of it and when it will cease to yield. It is a very living thing. It is as life itself.

I have heard this ever since I can remember, and ever since I have taught: the teacher must teach the pupil to think. I saw a teacher once going around in a great school and snapping pupils' heads with thumb and finger and saying, "Think." That was when thinking was becoming the fashion. The fashion hasn't yet quite gone out.

We still ask boys in college to think, as in the nineties, but we seldom tell them what thinking means; we seldom tell them it is just putting this and that together; it is saying one thing in terms of another. To tell them is to set their feet on the first rung of a ladder the top of which sticks through the sky.

Greatest of all attempts to say one thing in terms of another is the philosophical attempt to say matter in terms of spirit, or spirit in terms of matter, to make the final unity. That is the greatest attempt that ever failed. We stop just short there. But it is the height of poetry, the height of all thinking, the height of all poetic thinking, that attempt to say matter in terms of spirit and spirit in terms of matter. It is wrong to call anybody a materialist simply because he tries to say spirit in terms of matter, as if that were a sin. Materialism is not the attempt to say all in terms of matter. The only materialist —be he poet, teacher, scientist, politician, or statesman—is the man who gets lost in his material without a gathering metaphor to throw it into shape and order. He is the lost soul.

We ask people to think, and we don't show them what thinking is. Somebody says we don't need to show them how to think; bye and bye they will think. We will give them the forms of sentences and, if they have any ideas, then they will know how to write them. But that is preposterous. All there is to writing is having ideas. To learn to write is to learn to have ideas.

The first little metaphor . . . Take some of the trivial ones. I would rather have trivial ones of my own to live by than the big ones of other people.

I remember a boy saying, "He is the kind of person that wounds with his shield." That may be a slender one, of course. It goes a good way in character description. It has poetic grace. "He is the kind that wounds with his shield."

The shield reminds me—just to linger a minute—the shield reminds me of the inverted shield spoken of in one of the books of the *Odyssey*, the book that tells about the longest swim on record. I forget how long it lasted—several days, was it?—but at last as Odysseus came near the coast of Phoenicia, he saw it on the horizon "like an inverted shield."

There is a better metaphor in the same book. In the end Odysseus comes ashore and crawls up the beach to spend the night under a double olive tree, and it says, as in a lonely farmhouse where it is hard to get fire—I am not quoting exactly—where it is hard to start the fire again if it goes out, they cover the seeds of fire with ashes to preserve it for the night, so Odysseus covered himself with the leaves around him and went to sleep. There you have something that gives you character, something of Odysseus himself. "Seeds of fire." So Odysseus covered the seeds of fire in himself. You get the greatness of his nature.

But these are slighter metaphors than the ones we live by. They have their charm, their passing charm. They are as it were the first steps toward the great thoughts, grave thoughts, thoughts lasting to the end.

The metaphor whose manage we are best taught in poetry—that is all there is of thinking. It may not seem far for the mind to go but it is the mind's furthest. The richest accumulation of the ages is the noble metaphors we have rolled up.

I want to add one thing more that the experience of poetry is to anyone who comes close to poetry. There are two ways of coming close to poetry. One is by writing poetry. And some people think I want people to write poetry, but I don't; that is, I don't necessarily. I only want people to write poetry if they want to write poetry. I have never encouraged anybody to write poetry that did not want to write it, and I have not always encouraged those who did want to write it. That ought to be one's own funeral. It is a hard, hard life, as they say.

(I have just been to a city in the West, a city full of poets, a city they have made safe for poets. The whole city is so lovely that you do not have to write it up to make it poetry; it is ready-made for you. But, I don't know—the poetry written in that city might not seem like poetry if read outside of the city. It would be like the jokes made when you were drunk; you have to get drunk again to appreciate them.)

But as I say, there is another way to come close to poetry, fortunately, and that is in the reading of it, not as linguistics, not as history, not as anything but poetry. It is one of the hard things for a teacher to know how close a man has come in reading poetry. How do I know whether a man has come close to Keats in reading Keats? It is hard for me to know. I have lived with some boys a whole year over some of the poets and I have not felt sure whether they have come near what it was all about. One remark sometimes told me. One remark was their mark for the year; had to be—it was all I got that told me what I wanted to know. And that is enough, if it was the right remark, if it came close enough. I think a man might make twenty fool remarks if he made one good one some time in the year. His mark would depend on that good remark.

The closeness—everything depends on the closeness with which you come, and you ought to be marked for the closeness, for nothing else. And that will have to be estimated by chance remarks, not by question and answer. It is only by accident that you know some day how near a person has come.

The person who gets close enough to poetry, he is going to know more about the word *belief* than anybody else knows, even in religion nowadays. There are two or three places where we know belief outside of religion. One of them is at the age of fifteen to twenty, in our self-belief. A young man knows more about himself than he is able to prove to anybody. He has no knowledge that anybody else will accept as knowledge. In his foreknowledge he has something that is going to believe itself into fulfilment, into acceptance.

There is another belief like that, the belief in someone else, a relationship of two that is going to be believed into fulfilment. That is what we are talking about in our novels, the belief of love. And disillusionment that the novels are full of is simply the disillusionment from disappointment in that belief. That belief can fail, of course.

Then there is a literary belief. Every time a poem is written, every time a short story is written, it is written not by cunning, but by belief. The beauty, the something, the little charm of the thing to be, is more felt than known. There is a common jest, one that always annoys me, on the writers, that they write the last end first, and then work up to it; that they lay a train toward one sentence that they think is pretty nice and have all fixed up to set like a trap to close with. No, it should not be that way at all. No one who has ever come close to the arts has failed to see the difference between things written that way, with cunning and device, and the kind that are believed into existence, that begin in something more felt than known. This you can realize quite as well—not quite as well, perhaps, but nearly as well—in reading as you can in writing. I would undertake to separate short stories on that principle; stories that have been believed into existence and stories that have been cunningly devised. And I could separate the poems still more easily.

Now I think—I happen to think—that those three beliefs that I speak of, the self-belief, the love-belief, and the art-belief, are all closely related to the God-belief, that the belief in God is a relationship you enter into with Him to bring about the future.

There is a national belief like that, too. One feels it. I have been where I came near getting up and walking out on the people who thought that they had to talk against nations, against nationalism, in order to curry favor with internationalism. Their metaphors are all mixed up. They think that because a Frenchman and an American and an Englishman can all sit down on the same platform and receive honors together, it must be that there is no such thing as nations. That kind of bad thinking springs from a source we all know. I should want to say to anyone like that: "Look! First I want to be a person.

And I want you to be a person, and then we can be as interpersonal as you please. We can pull each other's noses—do all sorts of things. But, first of all, you have got to have the personality. First of all, you have got to have the nations and then they can be as international as they please with each other."

I should like to use another metaphor on them. I want my palette, if I am a painter, I want my palette on my thumb or on my chair, all clean, pure, separate colors. Then I will do the mixing on the canvas. The canvas is where the work of art is, where we make the conquest. But we want the nations all separate, pure, distinct, things as separate as we can make them; and then in our thoughts, in our arts, and so on, we can do what we please about it.

But I go back. There are four beliefs that I know more about from having lived with poetry. One is the personal belief, which is a knowledge that you don't want to tell other people about because you cannot prove that you know. You are saying nothing about it till you see. The love belief, just the same, has that same shyness. It knows it cannot tell; only the outcome can tell. And the national belief we enter into socially with each other, all together, party of the first part, party of the second part, we enter into that to bring the future of the country. We cannot tell some people what it is we believe, partly, because they are too stupid to understand and partly because we are too proudly vague to explain. And anyway it has got to be fulfilled, and we are not talking until we know more, until we have something to show. And then the literary one in every work of art, not of cunning and craft, mind you, but of real art; that believing the thing into existence, saying as you go more than you even hoped you were going to be able to say, and coming with surprise to an end that you foreknew only with some sort of emotion. And then finally the relationship we enter into with God to believe the future in—to believe the hereafter in.

QUESTIONS

1. *In what way does the subtitle describe this essay? Is it rambling? Is it unified?*
2. *How can the "poetry nuisance" be gotten out of the curriculum? Does Frost think it ought to stay in? Why?*
3. *What is meant by "enthusiasm passed through an idea" and "enthusiasm tamed to metaphor" (p. 410)? What sort of metaphors does Frost use in those phrases, and what do they imply?*
4. *What does Frost mean when he says "unless you have had your proper poetical education in the metaphor, you are not safe anywhere" (p. 411)? Indicate some of the metaphors Frost examines in this essay. From what fields are they drawn? What does he say about each? Nominate some further metaphors—from politics, science, sociology, or anything else—and analyze them. To what extent are they useful? Do they have a breaking point? How might they mislead beyond the breaking point?*
5. *Frost admires a speech that has "range, something of overstatement, something of statement, and something of understate-*

ment." *Is this spectrum visible in Frost's own speech? Show where and how.*

MARY ELLMANN

Phallic Criticism

Through practice, begun when they begin to read, women learn to read about women calmly. Perhaps there have been some, but I have not heard of women who killed themselves simply and entirely because they were women.[1] They are evidently sustained by the conviction that I can never be They, by the fact that the self always, at least to itself, eludes identification with others. And, in turn, this radical separateness is fortified in some of us by phlegm, in others by vanity or most of all by ignorance (the uneducated are humiliated by class rather than by sex)—by all the usual defenses against self-loathing. Moreover, both men and women are now particularly accustomed, not so much to the resolution of issues, as to the proliferation of irreconcilable opinions upon them. In this intellectual suspension, it is possible for women, most of the time, to be more interested in what *is* said about them than in what presumably and finally *should* be said about them. In fact, none of them knows what should be said.

Their detachment is perhaps especially useful in reading literary criticism. Here, the opinions of men about men and of women about women are at least possibly esthetic, but elsewhere they are, almost inescapably, sexual as well. Like eruptions of physical desire, this intellectual distraction is no less frequent for being gratuitous as well. With a kind of inverted fidelity, the discussion of women's books by men will arrive punctually at the point of preoccupation, which is the fact of femininity. Books by women are treated as though they themselves were women, and criticism embarks, at its happiest, upon an intellectual measuring of busts and hips. Of course, this preoccupation has its engaging and compensatory sides.[2] Like such minor physical disorders as shingles and mumps, it often seems (whether or not it *feels* to the critic) comical as well as

---

1. Men, however, have been known to kill themselves for this reason. Otto Weininger, the German author of *Sex and Character,* killed himself because of the femininity which he ascribed to the Jews, of whom he was one [Ellmann's note].

2. It has an unnerving side as well, though this appears less often in criticism, I think, than in fiction or poetry. For example, James Dickey's poem "Falling" expresses an extraordinary concern with the underwear of a woman who has fallen out of an airplane. While this woman, a stewardess, was in the airplane, her girdle obscured, to the observation of even the most alert passenger, her mesial groove. The effect was, as the poem recalls, "monobuttocked." As the woman falls, however, she undresses and "passes her palms" over her legs, her breasts, and "deeply between her thighs." Beneath her, "widowed farmers" are soon to wake with futile (and irrelevant?) erections. She lands on her back in a field, naked, and dies. The sensation of the poem is necrophilic: it mourns a vagina rather than a person crashing to the ground [Ellmann's note].

distressing. Then too, whatever intellectual risks this criticism runs, one of them is not abstraction. Any sexual reference, even in the most dryasdust context, shares the power which any reference to food has, of provoking fresh and immediate interest. As lunch can be mentioned every day without boring those who are hungry, the critic can always return to heterosexual (and, increasingly, to homosexual) relations and opinions with certainty of being read.

Admittedly, everyone is amused by the skillful wrapping of a book, like a negligee, about an author. Stanley Kauffmann opened a review of Françoise Sagan's *La Chamade* with this simile:

> Poor old Françoise Sagan. Just one more old-fashioned old-timer, bypassed in the rush for the latest literary vogue and for youth. Superficially, her career in America resembles the lifespan of those medieval beauties who flowered at 14, were deflowered at 15, were old at 30 and crones at 40.[3]

A superior instance of the mode—the play, for example, between *flowered and deflowered* is neat. And quite probably, of course, women might enjoy discussing men's books in similar terms. Some such emulative project would be diverting for a book season or two, if it were possible to persuade conventional journals to print its equivalent remarks. From a review of a new novel by the popular French novelist, François Sagan:

> Poor old François Sagan. . . . Superficially, his career in America resembles the life-span of those medieval troubadours who masturbated at 14, copulated at 15, were impotent at 30 and prostate cases at 40.

Somehow or other, No. It is not that male sexual histories, in themselves, are not potentially funny—even though they seem to be thought perceptibly less so than female sexual histories. It is rather that the literal fact of masculinity, unlike femininity, does not impose an erogenic form upon all aspects of the person's career.

I do not mean to suggest, however, that this imposition necessarily results in injustice. (Stanley Kauffmann went on to be more than just, *merciful* to Françoise Sagan.) In fact, it sometimes issues in fulsome praise. Excess occurs when the critic, like Dr. Johnson congratulating the dog who walked like a man, is impressed that the woman has—not so much written well, as written at all. But unfortunately, benign as this upright-pooch predisposition can be in the estimate of indifferent work, it can also infect the praise of work which deserves (what has to be called) asexual approval. In this case, enthusiasm issues in an explanation of the ways in which the work is free of what the critic ordinarily dislikes in the work of a woman. He had despaired of ever seeing a birdhouse built by a woman; now *here* is a birdhouse built by a woman. Pleasure may mount even to an admission of male envy of the work examined: an

3. Stanley Kauffmann, "Toujours Tristesse," *New Republic*, October 29, 1966, p. 2 [Ellmann's note].

exceptionally sturdy birdhouse at that! In *Commentary*, Warren Coffey has expressed his belief that "a man would give his right arm to have written Flannery O'Connor's 'Good Country People.' "[4] And here, not only the sentiment but the confidence with which the cliché is wielded, is distinctly phallic. It is as though, merely by thinking about Flannery O'Connor or Mrs. Gaskell or Harriet Beecher Stowe, the critic experienced acute sensations of his own liberty. The more he considers a feeble, cautious and timid existence, the more devil-may-care he seems to himself. This exhilaration then issues, rather tamely, in a daring to be commonplace.

And curiously, it often issues in expressions of contempt for delicate men as well. In this piece, for example, Flannery O'Connor is praised not only as a woman writer who writes as well as a man might wish to write, but also as a woman writer who succeeds in being less feminine than some men. She is less "girlish" than Truman Capote or Tennessee Williams.[5] In effect, once the critic's attention is trained, like Sweeney's, upon the Female Temperament, he invariably sideswipes at effeminacy in the male as well. The basic distinction becomes nonliterary; it is less between the book under review and other books, than between the critic and other persons who seem to him, regrettably, less masculine than he is. The assumption of the piece is that no higher praise of a woman's work exists than that such a critic should like it or think that other men will like it. The same ploy can also be executed in reverse. Norman Mailer, for example, is pleased to think that Joseph Heller's *Catch-22* is a man's book to read, a book which merely "puzzles" women. Women cannot comprehend male books, men cannot tolerate female books. The working rule is simple, basic: there must always be two literatures like two public toilets, one for Men and one for Women.

Sometimes it seems that no achievement can override this division. When Marianne Moore received the Poetry Society of America's Gold Medal for Poetry, she received as well Robert Lowell's encomium, "She is the best woman poet in English." The late Langston Hughes added, "I consider her the most famous Negro woman poet in America," and others would have enjoyed "the best blue-eyed woman poet."[6] Lowell has also praised Sylvia Plath's last book of poems, *Ariel*. His foreword begins:

4. Warren Coffey, *Commentary*, November 1965, p. 98 [Ellmann's note].

5. Though Tennessee Williams is cited here to enhance Flannery O'Connor's virtues, he is just as easily cited to prove other women's defects. For example, Dr. Karl Stern has resorted to Williams and Edward Albee as witnesses to the modern prevalence of the Castrating Woman. (*Barat Review*, January 1967, p. 46.) Naturally, in this context, both playwrights assume a status of unqualified virility [Ellmann's note].

6. Miss Moore's femininity leaves her vulnerable even to the imagination of John Berryman:

Fancy a lark with Sappho,
a tumble in the bushes with Miss Moore,
a spoon with Emily, while Charlotte glare.
Miss Bishop's too noble-O.

("Four Dream Songs," *Atlantic*, February 1968, p. 68) [Ellmann's note].

In these poems, written in the last months of her life and often rushed out at the rate of two or three a day, Sylvia Plath becomes herself, becomes something imaginary, newly, wildly and subtly created— hardly a person at all, or a woman, certainly not another "poetess," but one of those super-real, hypnotic, great classical heroines. The character is feminine, rather than female, though almost everything we customarily think of as feminine is turned on its head. The voice is now coolly amused, witty, now sour, now fanciful, girlish, charming, now sinking to the strident rasp of the vampire—a Dido, Phaedra, or Medea, who can laugh at herself as "cow-heavy and floral in my Victorian nightgown."

A little cloudburst, a short heavy rain of sexual references. The word *poetess*, whose gender killed it long ago, is exhumed—to be denied. Equivalently, a critic of W. H. Auden would be at pains, first of all, to deny that Auden is a poetaster. But *poetess* is only part of the general pelting away at the single fact that Sylvia Plath belonged to a sex (that inescapable membership) and that her sex was not male—*woman, heroines, feminine, female, girlish, fanciful, charming, Dido, Phaedra, Medea. Vampire,* too. And it would of course be this line, "Cow-heavy and floral in my Victorian night-gown," which seizes attention first and evokes the surprised pleasure of realizing that Sylvia Plath "can laugh at herself." Self-mockery, particularly sexual self-mockery, is not expected in a woman, and it is irresistible in the criticism of women to describe what was expected: the actual seems to exist only in relation to the preconceived.

Lowell's distinction between *feminine* and *female* is difficult, though less difficult than a distinction between *masculine* and *male* would be—say, in an introduction to Blake's *Songs of Innocence.* What helps us with the first is our all knowing, for some time now, that femaleness is a congenital fault, rather like eczema or Original Sin. An indicative denunciation, made in 1889: "They are no ladies. The only word good enough for them is the word of opprobrium—females." But fortunately, some women can be saved. By good manners, they are translated from females into ladies; and by talent, into feminine creatures (or even into "classical heroines"). And we are entirely accustomed to this generic mobility on their part: the individual is assumed into the sex and loses all but typical meaning within it. The emphasis is finally macabre, as though women wrote with breasts instead of pens—in which event it would be remarkable, as Lowell feels that it is, if one of them achieved ironic detachment.

When the subject of the work by a woman is also women (as it often has to be, since everyone has to eat what's in the cupboard), its critical treatment is still more aberrant. Like less specialized men, critics seem to fluctuate between attraction and surfeit. An obsessive concern with femininity shifts, at any moment, into a sense of being confined or suffocated by it. In the second condition, a distaste for books *before they are read* is not uncommon, as in Norman Mailer's unsolicited confession of not having been able to read Virginia Woolf, or in Anthony Burgess's inhibitory "impression of high-waisted dresses and genteel parsonage flirtation"[7] in Jane Austen's novels. More luckily, the work may be patronized by mild minds already persuaded that the human temperament combines traits of both sexes and that even masculine natures may respond, through their subterranean femininity, to the thoroughly feminine book.

A similar indulgence is fostered by any association, however tenuous, which the critic forms between the woman writer and some previous student of his own. Now that almost everyone who writes teaches too, the incidence of this association is fairly high. Robert Lowell remembers that Sylvia Plath once audited a class of his at Boston University:

> She was never a student of mine, but for a couple of months seven years ago, she used to drop in on my poetry seminar at Boston University. I see her dim against the bright sky of a high window, viewless unless one cared to look down on the city outskirts' defeated yellow brick and square concrete pillbox filling stations. She was willowy, long-waisted, sharp-elbowed, nervous, giggly, gracious—a brilliant tense presence embarrassed by restraint. Her humility and willingness to accept what was admired seemed at times to give her an air of maddening docility that hid her unfashionable patience and boldness.[8]

It is not easy, of course, to write about a person whom one knew only slightly in the past. The strain is felt here, for example, in the gratuitous street scene from the classroom window. And in general, there is a sense of a physical recollection emended by a much later intellectual and poetic impression. The "brilliant tense presence" of the final poetry is affixed, generously enough, to the original figure of a young girl. The "maddening docility" too must have been a sexual enlargement, now reduced to an "air" of docility, since again the poems demonstrate the artistic (rather than "feminine") union of "patience and boldness." (Elsewhere they are, according to Lowell, "modest" poems too, they are uniquely "modest" *and* "bold.") But then the poet Anne Sexton's recollections, which originate in the same poetry seminar, make no reference to elbows or giggles or docility. Miss Sexton seems to have seen even at that time a woman entirely congruous with her later work. After class, the two used to drink together—at the Ritz bar, some distance away from those "concrete pillbox filling stations"—and conduct workmanlike discussions of suicidal techniques:

---

7. *New York Times Book Review*, December 4, 1966, p. 1 [Ellmann's note].

8. Foreword to Sylvia Plath's *Ariel*, p. xi [Ellmann's note].

> *But suicides have a special language.*
> *Like carpenters they want to know which tools.*
> *They never ask why build.*
>
> ("Wanting to Die")[9]

Lowell seems honestly caught between two ways of comprehending what exists outside the self. And certainly there is nothing of the stag posture about his remarks, no pretense of writing only for other men about women. All critics are of course secretly aware that no literary audience, except perhaps in Yemen, is any longer restricted to men. The man's-man tone is a deliberate archaism, coy and even flirtatious, like wearing spats. No one doubts that some silent misogyny may be dark and deep, but written misogyny is now generally a kind of chaffing, and not frightfully clever, gambit. For the critic in this style, the writer whose work is most easily related to established stereotypes of femininity, is, oddly, the most welcome. What-to-say then flows effortlessly from the stereotypes themselves. The word *feminine* alone, like a grimace, expresses a displeasure which is not less certain for its being undefined. In a review of Fawn Brodie's biography of Sir Richard Burton, *The Devil Drives*, Josh Greenfeld remarked on the "feminine biographer's attachment to subject," and suggested that this quality (*or else* a "scholarly objectivity") prevented Mrs. Brodie's conceding Burton's homosexuality.[1] So her book is either too subjective or too objective: we will never know which.

But the same word can be turned upon men too. John Weightman has remarked that Genet's criminals cannot play male and female effectively because "a convicted criminal, however potent, has been classified as an object, and therefore feminized, by society."[2] An admirably simple social equation: a man in prison amounts to a woman. Similarly, *feminine* functions as an eight-letter word in the notorious Woodrow Wilson biography by Freud and William Bullitt. At one heated point, Clemenceau calls Wilson feminine, Wilson calls Clemenceau feminine, then both Freud and Bullitt call Wilson feminine again. The word means that all four men thoroughly dislike each other. It is also sufficient for Norman Mailer to say that Herbert Gold reminds him "of nothing so much as a woman writer,"[3] and for Richard Gilman to consign Philip Roth to the "ladies' magazine" level.[4] In fact, chapters of *When*

9. Anne Sexton, "The barfly ought to sing," *Tri-Quarterly*, Fall 1966, p. 90 [Ellmann's note].

1. *Book Week*, May 28, 1967, p. 2. Mrs. Brodie had still more trouble in the *Times Literary Supplement* (January 11, 1968, p. 32), where her nationality as well as her sex was at fault: "So immense is this gulf, so inalienably remote are the societies that produced biographer and subject, *so difficult is it, even now, for a woman to get beneath a*

man's skin, that only some imaginative genius could really have succeeded in the task Mrs. Brodie so boldly undertook." [My italics.] [Ellmann's note.]

2. *New York Review of Books*. August 24, 1967, p. 8 [Ellmann's note].

3. *Advertisements for Myself*, p. 435 [Ellmann's note].

4. Richard Gilman, "Let's Lynch Lucy," *New Republic*, June 24, 1967, p. 19 [Ellmann's note].

She Was Good were first published, and seemed to settle in snugly, at
the *haut bourgeois* level of *Harper's* and the *Atlantic*. But, except
perhaps in the *Daily Worker*, the consciousness of class is less insistent than that of sex: the phrase "ladies' magazine" is one of those
which refuses not to be written once a month.

But at heart most of these "the-ladies-bless-them" comments are
as cheerful and offhand as they are predictable. When contempt,
like anything else, has an assigned route to follow, and when it is
accustomed to its course, it can proceed happily. This is evident, for
example, in Norman Mailer's lively, even jocular, essay on the
deplorable faults of Mary McCarthy's *The Group*. What accounts
for these high spirits, except the fact that Mailer rejoices in what he
spanks so loudly? The pleasure lies in Mary McCarthy's having
capitulated, as it seems to Mailer, having at last written what he
can securely and triumphantly call a female novel.[5] Not that Mailer's treatment of *The Group*, even in these familiar terms, is not
still remarkable—even frightening, and that is a rare treat in criticism. One does not expect a disdain for feminine concerns, which is
entirely commonplace, to mount to cloacal loathing. Mary
McCarthy has soiled an abstraction, a genre, the novel-yet-to-be:
"Yes, Mary deposited a load on the premise, and it has to be
washed all over again, this little long-lived existential premise".[6]

But few rise to that kind of washing-up with Mailer's alacrity. In
most critics, revulsion is an under-developed area. What rouses a
much more interesting hostility in many is the work which does not
conform to sexual preconception. That is, if feminine concerns can
be found, they are conventionally rebuked; but their absence is
shocking. While all women's writing should presumably strive for a
suprafeminine condition, it is profoundly distrusted for achieving it.
So for all Anthony Burgess's resistance to Jane Austen, he is still
less pleased by George Eliot ("The male impersonation is wholly
successful") or by Ivy Compton-Burnett ("A big sexless nemesic
force"). Similarly, he cannot leave alone what strikes him as the
contradiction between Brigid Brophy's appearance and her writing.
His review of her book of essays, *Don't Never Forget*, opens in this
sprightly manner:

An American professor friend of mine, formerly an admirer of Miss
Brophy's work, could no longer think of her as an author once he'd
seen her in the flesh. "That girl was made for love," he would growl.

5. A female novel, Mailer indicates, is
one which deals with the superficial details of women's lives instead of their
lower depths. Such a book is at once tedious and cowardly. On the other hand.
Joseph Heller's *Catch-22* is a book for
men (rather than a male novel) which
deals with the superficial details of men's
lives. It speaks, according to Mailer, to
the man who "prefers to become interested in quick proportions and contradictions; in the practical surface of things."
Both novels, then, are tedious but the
first is a disgrace while the second has
"a vast appeal." Obviously, it all depends on which practical surface of
things the commentator himself is glued
to [Ellmann's note].

6. *Cannibals and Christians*, p. 138
[Ellmann's note].

Various writers who have smarted from her critical attentions might find it hard to agree.[7]

It is as though Elizabeth Hardwick, asked to review William Manchester's *Death of a President,* was obliged to refuse, growling, "That man was made for love." The same notion of an irreconcilable difference between the nature of woman and the mind of man prompts the hermaphroditic fallacy according to which one half the person, separating from the other half, produces a book by binary fission. So Mary McCarthy has been complimented, though not by Norman Mailer, on her "masculine mind" while, through the ages, poor Virgil has never been complimented on his "effeminacy." (Western criticism begins with this same tedious distinction—between manly Homer and womanish Virgil.) At the same time, while sentiment is a disadvantage, the alternative of feminine coolness is found still more disagreeable. Mary McCarthy used to be too *formidable,* Jean Stafford has sometimes been *clinical,* and others (going down, down) are *perverse, petulant, catty, waspish.*

The point is that comment upon Violette Leduc, who is not directly assertive, will be slurring; but the slur hardens into resentment of those writers who seem to endorse the same standards of restraint and reason which the critic presumably endorses. If for nothing else, for her tolerance of Sade, Simone de Beauvoir must be referred to (scathingly!) as "the lady," and then even her qualifications of tolerance must be described as a reluctance "to give herself unreservedly" to Sade.[8] Similarly, it is possible that much of the voluble male distaste for Jane Austen is based, not upon her military limitations (her infamous failure to discuss the Napoleonic Wars), but upon her antipathetic detachment. So a determined counteremphasis was first placed by her relatives, and has been continued since by most of her critics, upon her allegiance to domestic ideals—when, in fact, she is read only for her mockery of them.

What seems to be wanted, insisted upon, is the critic's conception of women expressed in his conception of feminine terms—that is, a confirmation of the one sex's opinions by the imagination of the other, a difficult request which can seldom be gratified. It is perhaps this request which explains Louis Auchincloss's erratic view of Mary McCarthy in his *Pioneers and Caretakers.* Suddenly she is sister to Ellen Glasgow and Sarah Orne Jewett, as one of our feminine "caretakers of the culture," a guise in which few other readers can easily recognize her. But if one's thesis is sexual, the attachment of women to the past and the incapacity of women for "the clean sweep," then Mary McCarthy only seems to hate a few present

7. *Manchester Guardian Weekly,* November 24, 1966, p. 11. There is, incidentally, An American Professor who exists only in the minds of English journalists. The *Times Literary Supplement* would be halved without him [Ellmann's note].

8. Leslie Schaeffer, *New Republic,* August 19, 1967, p. 28 [Ellmann's note].

things and actually loves many past things. One might as well argue that it was Swift's finding babies so sweet that made him think of eating them for dinner.

MARY McCARTHY

Settling the Colonel's Hash[1]

Seven years ago, when I taught in a progressive college, I had a pretty girl student in one of my classes who wanted to be a short-story writer. She was not studying writing with me, but she knew that I sometimes wrote short stories, and one day, breathless and glowing, she came up to me in the hall, to tell me that she had just written a story that her writing teacher, a Mr. Converse, was terribly excited about. "He thinks it's wonderful," she said, "and he's going to help me fix it up for publication."

I asked what the story was about; the girl was a rather simple being who loved clothes and dates. Her answer had a deprecating tone. It was just about a girl (herself) and some sailors she had met on the train. But then her face, which had looked perturbed for a moment, gladdened.

"Mr. Converse is going over it with me and we're going to put in the symbols."

Another girl in the same college, when asked by us in her sophomore orals why she read novels (one of the pseudo-profound questions that ought never to be put) answered in a defensive flurry: "Well, *of course* I don't read them to find out what happens to the hero."

At the time, I thought these notions were peculiar to progressive education: it was old-fashioned or regressive to read a novel to find out what happens to the hero or to have a mere experience empty of symbolic pointers. But I now discover that this attitude is quite general, and that readers and students all over the country are in a state of apprehension, lest they read a book or story literally and miss the presence of a symbol. And like everything in America, this search for meanings has become a socially competitive enterprise; the best reader is the one who detects the most symbols in a given stretch of prose. And the benighted reader who fails to find any symbols humbly assents when they are pointed out to him; he accepts his mortification.

I had no idea how far this process had gone until last spring, when I began to get responses to a story I had published in *Har-*

1. This was given first as a talk at the Breadloaf School of English, in Middle-bury, Vermont. Cf. "Artists in Uniform," page [57; McCarthy's note].

per's. I say "story" because that was what it was called by *Harper's.*
I myself would not know quite what to call it; it was a piece of
reporting or a fragment of autobiography—an account of my meeting with an anti-Semitic army colonel. It began in the club car of a
train going to St. Louis; I was wearing an apple-green shirtwaist and
a dark-green skirt and pink earrings; we got into an argument about
the Jews. The colonel was a rather dapper, flashy kind of Irish-
American with a worldly blue eye; he took me, he said, for a sculptress, which made me feel, to my horror, that I looked Bohemian
and therefore rather suspect. He was full of the usual profound
clichés that anti-Semites air, like original epigrams, about the Jews:
that he could tell a Jew, that they were different from other people,
that you couldn't trust them in business, that some of his best
friends were Jews, that he distinguished between a Jew and a kike,
and finally that, of course, he didn't agree with Hitler: Hitler went
too far, the Jews were human beings.

All the time we talked, and I defended the Jews, he was trying to
get my angle, as he called it; he thought it was abnormal for anybody who wasn't Jewish not to feel as he did. As a matter of fact, I
have a Jewish grandmother, but I decided to keep this news to
myself: I did not want the colonel to think that I had any interested reason for speaking on behalf of the Jews, that is, that I was
prejudiced. In the end, though, I got my comeuppance. Just as we
were parting, the colonel asked me my married name, which is
Broadwater, and the whole mystery was cleared up for him,
instantly; he supposed I was married to a Jew and that the name
was spelled B-r-o-d-w-a-t-e-r. I did not try to enlighten him; I let
him think what he wanted; in a certain sense, he was right; he had
unearthed my Jewish grandmother or her equivalent. There were a
few details that I must mention to make the next part clear: in my
car, there were two nuns, whom I talked to as a distraction from
the colonel and the moral problems he raised. He and I finally had
lunch together in the St. Louis railroad station, where we continued
the discussion. It was a very hot day. I had a sandwich; he had
roast-beef hash. We both had an old-fashioned.

The whole point of this "story" was that it really happened; it is
written in the first person; I speak of myself in my own name,
McCarthy; at the end, I mention my husband's name, Broadwater.
When I was thinking about writing the story, I decided not to treat
it fictionally; the chief interest, I felt, lay in the fact that it happened, in real life, last summer, to the writer herself, who was a
good deal at fault in the incident. I wanted to embarrass myself
and, if possible, the reader too.

Yet, strangely enough, many of my readers preferred to think of
this account as fiction. I still meet people who ask me, confiden-
tially, "That story of yours about the colonel—was it really true?"

It seemed to them perfectly natural that I would write a fabrication, in which I figured under my own name, and sign it, though in my eyes this would be like perjuring yourself in court or forging checks. Shortly after the "story" was published, I got a kindly letter from a man in Mexico, in which he criticized the menu from an artistic point of view: he thought salads would be better for hot weather and it would be more in character for the narrator-heroine to have a Martini. I did not answer the letter, though I was moved to, because I had the sense that he would not understand the distinction between what *ought* to happen and what *did* happen.

Then in April I got another letter, from an English teacher in a small college in the Middle West, that reduced me to despair. I am going to cite it at length.

"My students in freshman English chose to analyze your story, 'Artists in Uniform,' from the March issue of *Harper's*. For a week I heard oral discussions on it and then the students wrote critical analyses. In so far as it is possible, I stayed out of their discussions, encouraging them to read the story closely with your intentions as a guide to their understanding. Although some of them insisted that the story has no other level than the realistic one, most of them decided it has symbolic overtones.

"The question is: how closely do you want the symbols labeled? They wrestled with the nuns, the author's two shades of green with pink accents, with the 'materialistic godlessness' of the colonel. . . . A surprising number wanted exact symbols; for example, they searched for the significance of the colonel's eating hash and the author eating a sandwich. . . . From my standpoint, the story was an entirely satisfactory springboard for understanding the various shades of prejudice, for seeing how much of the artist goes into his painting. If it is any satisfaction to you, our campus was alive with discussions about 'Artists in Uniform.' We liked the story and we thought it amazing that an author could succeed in making readers dislike the author—for a purpose, of course!"

I probably should have answered this letter, but I did not. The gulf seemed to me too wide. I could not applaud the backward students who insisted that the story has no other level than the realistic one without giving offense to the teacher, who was evidently a well-meaning person. But I shall try now to address a reply, not to this teacher and her unfortunate class, but to a whole school of misunderstanding. There were no symbols in this story; there was no deeper level. The nuns were in the story because they were on the train; the contrasting greens were the dress I happened to be wearing; the colonel had hash because he had hash; materialistic godlessness meant just what it means when a priest thunders it from the pulpit—the phrase, for the first time, had meaning for me as I watched and listened to the colonel.

But to clarify the misunderstanding, one must go a little further and try to see what a literary symbol is. Now in one sense, the colonel's hash and my sandwich can be regarded as symbols; that is, they typify the colonel's food tastes and mine. (The man in Mexico had different food tastes which he wished to interpose into our reality.) The hash and the sandwich might even be said to show something very obvious about our characters and bringing-up, or about our sexes; I was a woman, he was a man. And though on another day I might have ordered hash myself, that day I did not, because the colonel and I, in our disagreement, were polarizing each other.

The hash and the sandwich, then, could be regarded as symbols of our disagreement, almost conscious symbols. And underneath our discussion of the Jews, there was a thin sexual current running, as there always is in such random encounters or pickups (for they have a strong suggestion of the illicit). The fact that I ordered something conventionally feminine and he ordered something conventionally masculine represented, no doubt, our awareness of a sexual possibility; even though I was not attracted to the colonel, nor he to me, the circumstances of our meeting made us define ourselves as a woman and a man.

The sandwich and the hash were our provisional, *ad hoc* symbols of ourselves. But in this sense all human actions are symbolic because they represent the person who does them. If the colonel had ordered a fruit salad with whipped cream, this too would have represented him in some way; given his other traits, it would have pointed to a complexity in his character that the hash did not suggest.

In the same way, the contrasting greens of my dress were a symbol of my taste in clothes and hence representative of me—all too representative, I suddenly saw, in the club car, when I got an "artistic" image of myself flashed back at me from the men's eyes. I had no wish to stylize myself as an artist, that is, to parade about as a symbol of flamboyant unconventionality, but apparently I had done so unwittingly when I picked those colors off a rack, under the impression that they suited me or "expressed my personality" as salesladies say.

My dress, then, was a symbol of the perplexity I found myself in with the colonel; I did not want to be categorized as a member of a peculiar minority—an artist or a Jew; but brute fate and the colonel kept resolutely cramming me into both those uncomfortable pigeonholes. I wished to be regarded as ordinary or rather as universal, to be anybody and therefore everybody (that is, in one sense, I wanted to be on the colonel's side, majestically above minorities); but every time the colonel looked at my dress and me in it with my pink earrings I shrank to minority status and felt the dress in the heat shriveling me, like the shirt of Nessus the centaur that consumed Hercules.

But this is not what the students meant when they wanted the symbols "labeled." They were searching for a more recondite significance than that afforded by the trite symbolism of ordinary life, in which a dress is a social badge. They supposed that I was engaging in literary or artificial symbolism, which would lead the reader out of the confines of reality into the vast fairy tale of myth, in which the color green would have an emblematic meaning (or did the two greens signify for them what the teacher calls "shades" of prejudice), and the colonel's hash, I imagine, would be some sort of Eucharistic mincemeat.

Apparently, the presence of the nuns assured them there were overtones of theology; it did not occur to them (a) that the nuns were there because pairs of nuns are a standardized feature of summer Pullman travel, like crying babies, and perspiring businessmen in the club car, and (b) that if I thought the nuns worth mentioning, it was also because of something very simple and directly relevant: the nuns and the colonel and I all had something in common—we had all at one time been Catholics—and I was seeking common ground with the colonel, from which to turn and attack his position.

In any account of reality, even a televised one, which comes closest to being a literal transcript or replay, some details are left out as irrelevant (though nothing is really irrelevant). The details that are not eliminated have to stand as symbols of the whole, like stenographic signs, and of course there is an art of selection, even in a newspaper account: the writer, if he has any ability, is looking for the revealing detail that will sum up the picture for the reader in a flash of recognition.

But the art of abridgment and condensation, which is familiar to anybody who tries to relate an anecdote, or give a direction—the art of natural symbolism, which is at the basis of speech and all representation—has at bottom a centripetal intention. It hovers over an object, an event, or series of events and tries to declare what it is. Analogy (that is, comparison to other objects) is inevitably one of its methods. "The weather was soupy," i.e., like soup. "He wedged his way in," i.e., he had to enter, thin edge first, as a wedge enters, and so on. All this is obvious. But these metaphorical aids to communication are a far cry from literary symbolism, as taught in the schools and practiced by certain fashionable writers. Literary symbolism is centrifugal and flees from the object, the event, into the incorporeal distance, where concepts are taken for substance and floating ideas and archetypes assume a hieratic authority.

In this dream-forest, symbols become arbitrary; all counters are interchangeable; anything can stand for anything else. The colonel's hash can be a Eucharist or a cannibal feast or the banquet of Atreus, or all three, so long as the actual dish set before the actual man is disparaged. What is depressing about this insistent symbolization is the fact that while it claims to lead to the infinite, it quickly reaches very finite limits—there are only so many myths on record, and once you have got through Bulfinch, the Scandinavian, and the Indian, there is not much left. And if all stories reduce themselves to myth and symbol, qualitative differences vanish, and there is only a single, monotonous story.

American fiction of the symbolist school demonstrates this mournful truth, without precisely intending to. A few years ago, when the mode was at its height, chic novels and stories fell into three classes: those which had a Greek myth for their framework, which the reader was supposed to detect, like finding the faces in the clouds in old newspaper puzzle contests; those which had symbolic modern figures, dwarfs, hermaphrodites, and cripples, illustrating maiming and loneliness; and those which contained symbolic animals, cougars, wild cats, and monkeys. One young novelist, a product of the Princeton school of symbolism, had all three elements going at once, like the ringmaster of a three-ring circus, with the freaks, the animals, and the statues.

The quest for symbolic referents had as its object, of course, the deepening of the writer's subject and the reader's awareness. But the result was paradoxical. At the very moment when American writing was penetrated by the symbolic urge, it ceased to be able to create symbols of its own. Babbitt, I suppose, was the last important symbol to be created by an American writer; he gave his name to a type that henceforth would be recognizable to everybody. He passed into the language. The same thing could be said, perhaps, though to a lesser degree, of Caldwell's Tobacco Road, Eliot's Prufrock, and possibly of Faulkner's Snopeses. The discovery of new symbols is not the only function of a writer, but the writer who cares about this must be fascinated by reality itself, as a butterfly collector is fascinated by the glimpse of a new specimen. Such a specimen was Mme. Bovary or M. Homais or M. de Charlus or Jupien; these specimens were precious to their discoverers, not because they repeated an age-old pattern but because their markings were new. Once the specimen has been described, the public instantly spots other examples of the kind, and the world seems suddenly full of Babbitts and Charlus, where none had been noted before.

A different matter was Joyce's Mr. Bloom. Mr. Bloom can be called a symbol of eternal recurrence—the wandering Jew, Ulysses the voyager—but he is a symbol thickly incarnate, fleshed out in a Dublin advertising canvasser. He is not like Ulysses or vaguely suggestive of Ulysses; he is Ulysses, circa 1905. Joyce evidently believed in a cyclical theory of history, in which everything repeated itself; he also subscribed in youth to the doctrine that declares that the Host, a piece of bread, is also God's body and blood. How it can be both things at the same time, transubstantially, is a mystery, and Mr. Bloom is just such a mystery: Ulysses in the visible appearance of a Dublin advertising canvasser.

Mr. Bloom is not a symbol of Ulysses, but Ulysses-Bloom together, one and indivisible, symbolize or rather demonstrate eternal recurrence. I hope I make myself clear. The point is transubstantiation: Bloom and Ulysses are transfused into each other and neither reality is diminished. Both realities are locked together, like the protons and neutrons of an atom. *Finnegans Wake* is a still more ambitious attempt to create a fusion, this time a myriad fusion, and to exemplify the mystery of how a thing can be itself and at the same time be something else. The world is many and it is also one.

But the clarity and tension of Joyce's thought brought him closer in a way to the strictness of allegory than to the diffuse practices of latter-day symbolists. In Joyce, the equivalences and analogies are very sharp and distinct, as in a pun, and the real world is almost querulously audible, like the voices of the washerwomen on the Liffey that come into Earwicker's dream. But this is not true of Joyce's imitators or of the imitators of his imitators, for whom reality is only a shadowy pretext for the introduction of a whole *corps de ballet* of dancing symbols in mythic draperies and animal skins.

Let me make a distinction. There are some great writers, like Joyce or Melville, who have consciously introduced symbolic elements into their work; and there are great writers who have written fables or allegories. In both cases, the writer makes it quite clear to the reader how he is to be read; only an idiot would take *Pilgrim's Progress* for a realistic story, and even a young boy, reading *Moby Dick*, realizes that there is something more than whale-fishing here, though he may not be able to name what it is. But the great body of fiction contains only what I have called natural symbolism, in which selected events represent or typify a problem, a kind of society or psychology, a philosophical theory, in the same way that they do in real life. What happens to the hero becomes of the highest importance. This symbolism needs no abstruse interpretation, and abstruse interpretation will only lead the reader away from the reality that the writer is trying to press on his attention.

I shall give an example or two of what I mean by natural symbolism and I shall begin with a rather florid one: Henry James' *The Golden Bowl*. This is the story of a rich American girl who collects European objects. One of these objects is a husband, Prince Amerigo, who proves to be unfaithful. Early in the story, there is a visit to an antique shop in which the Prince picks out a gold bowl for his fiancée and finds, to his annoyance, that it is cracked. It is not hard to see that the cracked bowl is a symbol, both of the Prince himself, who is a valuable antique but a little flawed, morally, and also of the marriage, which represents an act of acquisition or purchase on the part of the heroine and her father. If the reader should fail to notice the analogy, James calls his attention to it in the title.

I myself would not regard this symbol as necessary to this particular history; it seems to me, rather, an ornament of the kind that was fashionable in the architecture and interior decoration of the period, like stylized sheaves of corn or palms on the façade of a house. Nevertheless, it is handsome and has an obvious appropriateness to the theme. It introduces the reader into the Gilded Age attitudes of the novel. I think there is also a scriptural echo in the title that conveys the idea of punishment. But having seen and felt the weight of meaning that James put into this symbol, one must not be tempted to press further and look at the bowl as a female sex symbol, a chalice, a Holy Grail, and so on; a book is not a pious excuse for reciting a litany of associations.

My second example is from Tolstoy's *Anna Karenina*. Toward the beginning of the novel, Anna meets the man who will be her lover, Vronsky, on the Moscow-St. Petersburg express; as they meet, there has been an accident; a workman has been killed by the train. This is the beginning of Anna's doom, which is completed when she throws herself under a train and is killed; and the last we see of Vronsky is in a train, with a toothache; he is off to the wars. The train is necessary to the plot of the novel, and I believe it is also symbolic, both of the iron forces of material progress that Tolstoy hated so and that played a part in Anna's moral destruction, and also of those iron laws of necessity and consequence that govern human action when it remains on the sensual level.

One can read the whole novel, however, without being conscious that the train is a symbol; we do not have to "interpret" to feel the import of doom and loneliness in the train's whistle—the same import we ourselves can feel when we hear a train whistle blow in the country, even today. Tolstoy was a deeper artist than James, and we cannot be sure that the train was a conscious device with him. The appropriateness to Anna's history may have been only a *felt* appropriateness; everything in Tolstoy has such a supreme naturalness that one shrinks from attributing contrivance to him, as if it were a sort of fraud. Yet he worked very hard on his novels—I forget how many times Countess Tolstoy copied out *War and Peace* by hand.

The impression one gets from his diaries is that he wrote by ear; he speaks repeatedly, even as an old man, of having to start a story over again because he has the wrong tone, and I suspect that he did not think of the train as a symbol but that it sounded "right" to him, because it was, in that day, an almost fearsome emblem of ruthless and impersonal force, not only to a writer of genius but to the poorest peasant in the fields. And in Tolstoy's case I think it would be impossible, even for the most fanciful critic, to extricate the train from the novel and try to make it say something that the novel itself does not say directly. Every detail in Tolstoy has an almost cruel and viselike meaningfulness and truth to itself that make it tautological to talk of symbolism; he was a moralist and to him the tiniest action, even the curiosities of physical appearance, Vronsky's bald spot, the small white hands of Prince Andrei, told a moral tale.

It is now considered very old-fashioned and tasteless to speak of an author's "philosophy of life" as something that can be harvested from his work. Actually, most of the great authors did have a "philosophy of life" which they were eager to communicate to the public; this was one of their motives for writing. And to disentangle a moral philosophy from a work that evidently contains one is far less damaging to the author's purpose and the integrity of his art than to violate his imagery by symbol-hunting, as though reading a novel were a sort of paper-chase.

The images of a novel or a story belong, as it were, to a family, very closely knit and inseparable from each other; the parent "idea" of a story or a novel generates events and images all bearing a strong family resemblance. And to understand a story or a novel, you must look for the parent "idea," which is usually in plain view, if you read quite carefully and literally what the author says.

I will go back, for a moment, to my own story, to show how this can be done. Clearly, it is about the Jewish question, for that is what the people are talking about. It also seems to be about artists, since the title is "Artists in Uniform." Then there must be some relation between artists and Jews. What is it? They are both minorities that other people claim to be able to recognize by their appearance. But artists and Jews do not care for this categorization; they want to be universal, that is, like everybody else. They do not want to wear their destiny as a badge, as the soldier wears his uniform. But this aim is really hopeless, for life has formed them as Jews or artists, in a way that immediately betrays them to the majority they are trying to melt into. In my conversation with the colonel, I was endeavoring to play a double game. I was trying to force him into a minority by treating anti-Semitism as an aberration, which, in fact, I believe it is. On his side, the colonel resisted this attempt and tried to show that anti-Semitism was normal, and he was normal, while I was the queer one. He declined to be categorized as anti-Semite; he regarded himself as an independent thinker, who by a happy chance thought the same as everybody else.

I imagined I had a card up my sleeve; I had guessed that the colonel was Irish (i.e., that he belonged to a minority) and presumed that he was a Catholic. I did not see how he could possibly guess that I, with my Irish name and Irish appearance, had a Jewish grandmother in the background. Therefore when I found I had not convinced him by reasoning, I played my last card; I told him that the Church, his Church, forbade anti-Semitism. I went even further; I implied that God forbade it, though I had no right to do this, since I did not believe in God, but was only using Him as a whip to crack over the colonel, to make him feel humble and inferior, a raw Irish Catholic lad under discipline. But the colonel, it turned out, did not believe in God, either, and I lost. And since, in a sense, I had been cheating all along in this game we were playing, I had to concede the colonel a sort of moral victory in the end; I let him think that my husband was Jewish and that that "explained" everything satisfactorily.

Now there are a number of morals or meanings in this little tale, starting with the simple one: don't talk to strangers on a train. The chief moral or meaning (what I learned, in other words from this experience) was that you cannot be a universal unless you accept the fact that you are a singular, that is, a Jew or an artist or what-have-you. What the colonel and I were discussing, and at the same time illustrating and enacting, was the definition of a human being. I was trying to be something better than a human being; I was trying to be the voice of pure reason; and pride went before a fall. The colonel, without trying, was being something worse than a human being, and somehow we found ourselves on the same plane —facing each other, like mutually repellent twins. Or, put in another way: it is dangerous to be drawn into discussions of the Jews with anti-Semites: you delude yourself that you are spreading light, but you are really sinking into muck; if you endeavor to be dispassionate, you are really claiming for yourself a privileged position, a little mountain top, from which you look down, impartially, on both the Jews and the colonel.

Anti-Semitism is a horrible disease from which nobody is immune, and it has a kind of evil fascination that makes an enlightened person draw near the source of infection, supposedly, in a scientific spirit, but really to sniff the vapors and dally with the possibility. The enlightened person who lunches with the colonel in order, as she tells herself, to improve him, is cheating herself, having her cake and eating it. This attempted cheat, on my part, was related to the question of the artist and the green dress; I wanted to be an artist but not to pay the price of looking like one, just as I was willing to have Jewish blood but not willing to show it, where it would cost me something—the loss of superiority in an argument.

These meanings are all there, quite patent, to anyone who consents to look *into* the story. They were *in* the experience itself, waiting to be found and considered. I did not perceive them all at the time the experience was happening; otherwise, it would not have taken place, in all probability—I should have given the colonel a wide berth. But when I went back over the experience, in order to write it, I came upon these meanings, protruding at me, as it were, from the details of the occasion. I put in the green dress and my mortification over it because they were part of the truth, just as it had occurred, but I did not see how they were related to the general question of anti-Semitism and my grandmother until they *showed* me their relation in the course of writing.

Every short story, at least for me, is a little act of discovery. A cluster of details presents itself to my scrutiny, like a mystery that I will understand in the course of writing or sometimes not fully until afterward, when, if I have been honest and listened to these details carefully, I will find that they are connected and that there is a coherent pattern. This pattern is *in* experience itself; you do not impose it from the outside and if you try to, you will find that the story is taking the wrong tack, dribbling away from you into artificiality or inconsequence. A story that you do not learn something from while you are writing it, that does not illuminate something for you, is dead, finished before you started it. The "idea" of a story is implicit in it, on the one hand; on the other hand, it is always ahead of the writer, like a form dimly discerned in the distance; he is working *toward* the "idea."

It can sometimes happen that you begin a story thinking that you know the "idea" of it and find, when you are finished, that you have said something quite different and utterly unexpected to you. Most writers have been haunted all their lives by the "idea" of a story or a novel that they think they want to write and see very clearly: Tolstoy always wanted to write a novel about the Decembrists and instead, almost against his will, wrote *War and Peace*; Henry James thought he wanted to write a novel about Napoleon. Probably these ideas for novels were too set in their creators' minds to inspire creative discovery.

In any work that is truly creative, I believe, the writer cannot be omniscient in advance about the effects that he proposes to produce. The suspense in a novel is not only in the reader, but in the novelist himself, who is intensely curious too about what will happen to the hero. Jane Austen may know in a general way that Emma will marry Mr. Knightley in the end (the reader knows this too, as a matter of fact); the suspense for the author lies in the how, in the twists and turns of circumstance, waiting but as yet unknown, that will bring the consummation about. Hence, I would say to the student of writing that outlines, patterns, arrangements of symbols may have a certain usefulness at the outset for some kinds of minds, but in the end they will have to be scrapped. If the story does not contradict the outline, overrun the pattern, break the symbols, like an insurrection against authority, it is surely a still birth. The natural symbolism of reality has more messages to communicate than the dry Morse code of the disengaged mind.

The tree of life, said Hegel, is greener than the tree of thought; I have quoted this before but I cannot forbear from citing it again in this context. This is not an incitement to mindlessness or an endorsement of realism in the short story (there are several kinds of reality, including interior reality); it means only that the writer must be, first of all, a listener and observer, who can pay attention to reality, like an obedient pupil, and who is willing, always, to be surprised by the messages reality is sending through to him. And if he gets the messages correctly he will not have to go back and put in the symbols; he will find that the symbols are there, staring at him significantly from the commonplace.

E. M. FORSTER

Not Listening to Music

Listening to music is such a muddle that one scarcely knows how to start describing it. The first point to get clear in my own case is that during the greater part of every performance I do not attend. The nice sounds make me think of something else. I wool-gather most of the time, and am surprised that others don't. Professional critics can listen to a piece as consistently and as steadily as if they were reading a chapter in a novel. This seems to me an amazing feat, and probably they only achieve it through intellectual training; that is to say, they find in the music the equivalent of a plot; they are following the ground bass or expecting the theme to re-enter in the dominant, and so on, and this keeps them on the rails. But I fly off every minute: after a bar or two I think how musical I am, or of something smart I might have said in conversation; or I wonder what the composer—dead a couple of centuries—can be feeling as the flames on the altar still flicker up; or how soon an H.E. bomb[1] would extinguish them. Not to mention more obvious distractions: the tilt of the soprano's chin or chins; the antics of the conductor, that impassioned beetle, especially when it is night time and he waves his shards; the affection of the pianist when he takes a top note with difficulty, as if he too were a soprano; the backs of the chairs; the bumps on the ceiling; the extreme physical ugliness of the audience. A classical audience is surely the plainest collection of people anywhere assembled for any common purpose; contributing my quota, I have the right to point this out. Compare us with a gang of navvies or with an office staff, and you will be appalled. This, too, distracts me.

1. A high explosive.

What do I hear during the intervals when I do attend? Two sorts of music. They melt into each other all the time, and are not easy to christen, but I will call one of them "music that reminds me of something," and the other "music itself." I used to be very fond of music that reminded me of something, and especially fond of Wagner. With Wagner I always knew where I was; he never let the fancy roam; he ordained that one phrase should recall the ring, another the sword, another the blameless fool and so on; he was as precise in his indications as an oriental dancer. Since he is a great poet, that did not matter, but I accepted his leitmotiv system much too reverently and forced it onto other composers whom it did not suit, such as Beethoven and Franck. I thought that music must be the better for having a meaning. I think so still, but am less clear as to what "a meaning" is. In those days it was either a non-musical object, such as a sword or a blameless fool, or a non-musical emotion, such as fear, lust, or resignation. When music reminded me of something which was not music, I supposed it was getting me somewhere. "How like Monet!" I thought when listening to Debussy, and "How like Debussy!" when looking at Monet. I translated sounds into colours, saw the piccolo as apple-green, and the trumpets as scarlet. The arts were to be enriched by taking in one another's washing.

I still listen to some music this way. For instance, the slow start of Beethoven's Seventh Symphony invokes a gray-green tapestry of hunting scenes, and the slow movement of his Fourth Piano Concerto (the dialogue between piano and orchestra) reminds me of the dialogue between Orpheus and the Furies in Gluck. The climax of the first movement of the Appassionata (the "più allegro") seems to me sexual, although I can detect no sex in the Kreutzer, nor have I come across anyone who could, except Tolstoy. That disappointing work, Brahms' Violin Concerto, promises me clear skies at the opening, and only when the violin has squealed up in the air for page after page is the promise falsified. Wolf's "Ganymed" does give me sky—stratosphere beyond stratosphere. In these cases and in many others music reminds me of something non-musical, and I fancy that to do so is part of its job. Only a purist would condemn all visual parallels, all emotional labelings, all programs.

Yet there is a danger. Music that reminds does open the door to that imp of the concert hall, inattention. To think of a gray-green tapestry is not very different from thinking of the backs of the chairs. We gather a superior wool from it, still we do wool-gather, and the sounds slip by blurred. The sounds! It is for them that we come, and the closer we can get up against them the better. So I do prefer "music itself" and listen to it and for it as far as possible. In this connection, I will try to analyze a mishap that has recently overtaken the Coriolanus Overture. I used to listen to the Coriolanus for "itself," conscious when it passed of something important and agitating, but not defining further. Now I learn that Wagner, endorsed by Sir Donald Tovey, has provided it with a Program: the opening bars indicate the hero's decision to destroy the Volscii, then a sweet tune for female influence, then the dotted-quaver-restlessness of indecision. This seems indisputable, and there is no doubt that this was, or was almost, Beethoven's intention. All the same, I have lost my Coriolanus. Its largeness and freedom have gone. The exquisite sounds have been hardened like a road that has been tarred for traffic. One has to go somewhere down them, and to pass through the same domestic crisis to the same military impasse, each time the overture is played.

Music is so very queer that an amateur is bound to get muddled when writing about it. It seems to be more "real" than anything, and to survive when the rest of civilization decays. In these days I am always thinking of it with relief. It can never be ruined or nationalized. So that the music which is untrammeled and untainted by reference is obviously the best sort of music to listen to; we get nearer the center of reality. Yet though it is untainted, it is never abstract; it is not like mathematics, even when it uses them. The Goldberg Variations, the last Beethoven Sonata, the Franck Quartet, the Schumann Piano Quintet and the Fourth Symphonies of Tchaikovsky and of Brahms certainly have a message. Though what on earth is it? I shall get tied up trying to say. There's an insistence in music—expressed largely through rhythm; there's a sense that it is trying to push across at us something which is neither an esthetic pattern nor a sermon. That's what I listen for specially.

So music that is itself seems on the whole better than music that reminds. And now to end with an important point: my own performances upon the piano. These grow worse yearly, but never will I give them up. For one thing, they compel me to attend—no wool-gathering or thinking myself clever here—and they drain off all non-musical matter. For another thing, they teach me a little about construction. I see what becomes of a phrase, how it is transformed or returned, sometimes bottom upward, and get some notion of the relation of keys. Playing Beethoven, as I generally do, I grow familiar with his tricks, his impatience, his sudden softnesses, his dropping of a tragic theme one semitone, his love, when tragic, for the key of C minor, and his aversion to the key of B major. This gives me a physical approach to Beethoven which cannot be gained through the slough of "appreciation." Even when people play as badly as I do, they should continue: it will help them to listen.

QUESTIONS

1. Forster carries his discussion of listening to music through three stages. What are they? Where in the essay is each introduced? Where does Forster make it clear that the first two stages resemble each other?

2. What devices of language and attitude does Forster use to establish an informal, relaxed approach to his topic? Does he appear to be addressing himself to a particular kind of audience? Explain.
3. What is "music itself"? By what means does Forster seek to define it?
4. Early in the essay Forster says that it seems to him an "amazing feat" that professional critics can listen to music "as consistently and steadily as if they were reading a chapter in a novel." What does this indicate as to Forster's view of the novel? Is he being ironical?
5. What does playing the piano teach Forster about listening to music? The closing paragraph, on playing and listening, suggests a similar relationship between writing and reading. Following Forster's strategy of organization, write a brief essay on "Not Reading a Novel," "Not Looking at Pictures," "Not Going to a Lecture," or "Not Studying an Assignment."

EDWIN DENBY

Against Meaning in Ballet

Some of my friends who go to ballet and like the entertainment it gives are sorry to have it classed among the fine arts and discussed, as the other fine arts are, intellectually. Though I do not agree with them I have a great deal of sympathy for their anti-intellectual point of view. The dazzle of a ballet performance is quite reason enough to go; you see handsome young people—girls and boys with a bounding or delicate animal grace—dancing among the sensual luxuries of orchestral music and shining stage decoration and in the glamor of an audience's delight. To watch their lightness and harmonious ease, their clarity and boldness of motion, is a pleasure. And ballet dancers' specialties are their elastic tautness, their openness of gesture, their gaiety of leaping, beating and whirling, their slow soaring flights. Your senses enjoy directly how they come forward and closer to you, or recede upstage, turning smaller and more fragile; how the boys and girls approach one another or draw apart, how they pass close without touching or entwine their bodies in stars of legs and arms—all the many ways they have of dancing together. You see a single dancer alone showing her figure from all sides deployed in many positions, or you see a troop of them dancing in happy unison. They are graceful, well-mannered, and they preserve at best a personal dignity, a civilized modesty of deportment that keeps the sensual stimulus from being foolishly cute or commercially sexy. The beauty of young women's and young men's bodies, in motion or in momentary repose is exhibited in an extraordinarily friendly manner.

When you enjoy ballet this way—and it is one of the ways everybody does enjoy it who likes to go—you don't find any prodigious difference between one piece and another, except that one will have enough dancing to satisfy and another not enough, one will show the dancers to their best advantage and another will tend to make them look a little more awkward and unfree. Such a happy ballet lover is puzzled by the severities of critics. He wonders why they seem to find immense differences between one piece and another, or between one short number and another, or between the proficiency of two striking dancers. The reasons the critics give, the relation of the steps to the music, the sequence of the effects, the sharply differentiated intellectual meaning they ascribe to dances, all this he will find either fanciful or plainly absurd.

Has ballet an intellectual content? The ballet lover with the point of view I am describing will concede that occasionally a soloist gives the sense of characterizing a part, that a few ballets even suggest a story with a psychological interest, a dramatic suspense, or a reference to real life. In such a case, he grants, ballet may be said to have an intellectual content. But these ballets generally turn out to be less satisfying to watch because the dancers do less ballet dancing in them; so, he concludes, one may as well affirm broadly that ballet does not properly offer a "serious" comment on life and that it is foolish to look for one.

I do not share these conclusions, and I find my interest in the kind of meaning a ballet has leads me to an interest in choreography and dance technique. But I have a great deal of sympathy for the general attitude I have described. It is the general attitude that underlies the brilliant reviews of Théophile Gautier, the French poet of a hundred years ago, who is by common consent the greatest of ballet critics. He said of himself that he was a man who believed in the visible world. And his reviews are the image of what an intelligent man of the world saw happening on the stage. They are perfectly open; there is no private malignity in them; he is neither pontifical nor "popular"; there is no jargon and no ulterior motive. He watches not as a specialist in ballet, but as a responsive Parisian. The easy flow of his sentences is as much a tribute to the social occasion as it is to the accurate and elegant ease of ballet dancers in action. His warmth of response to personal varieties of grace and to the charming limits of a gift, his amusement at the pretensions of a libretto or the pretensions of a star, his sensual interest in the line of a shoulder and bosom, in the elasticity of an ankle, in the cut of a dress, place the ballet he watches in a perspective of civilized good sense.

Ballet for him is an entertainment—a particularly agreeable way of spending an evening in town; and ballet is an art, it is a sensual refinement that delights the spirit. Art for him is not a temple of humanity one enters with a reverent exaltation. Art is a familiar pleasure and Gautier assumes that one strolls through the world of art as familiarly as one strolls through Paris, looking about in good weather or bad, meeting congenial friends or remarkable strangers, and one's enemies, too. Whether in art or in Paris, a civilized person appreciates seeing a gift and is refreshed by a graceful impulse; there is a general agreement about what constitutes good workmanship; and one takes one's neighbors' opinions less seriously than their behavior. Gautier differentiates keenly between good and bad ballet; but he differentiates as a matter of personal taste. He illustrates the advantages the sensual approach to ballet can have for an intelligence of exceptional sensual susceptibility and for a man of large sensual complacency.

Gautier assumes that all that people need do to enjoy art is to look and listen with ready attention and trust their own sensual impressions. He is right. But when they hear that ballet is an elaborate art with a complicated technique and tradition, many modest people are intimidated and are afraid to trust their own spontaneous impressions. They may have been to a few performances, they may have liked it when they saw it, but now they wonder if maybe they liked the wrong things and missed the right ones. Before going again, they want it explained, they want to know what to watch for and exactly what to feel. If it is really real art and fine great art, it must be studied before it is enjoyed, that is what they remember from school. In school the art of poetry is approached by a strictly rational method, which teaches you what to enjoy and how to discriminate. You are taught to analyze the technique and the relation of form to content; you are taught to identify and "evaluate" stylistic, biographical, economic and anthropological influences and told what is great and what is minor so you can prepare yourself for a great reaction or for a minor one. The effect of these conscientious labors on the pupils is distressing. For the rest of their lives they can't face a page of verse without experiencing a complete mental blackout. They don't enjoy, they don't discriminate, they don't even take the printed words at face value. For the rest of their lives they go prying for hidden motives back of literature, for psychological, economic or stylistic explanations, and it never occurs to them to read the words and respond to them as they do to the nonsense of current songs or the nonsense of billboards by the roadside. Poetry is the same thing, it's words, only more interesting, more directly and richly sensual.

The first taste of art in spontaneously sensual, it is the discovery of an absorbing entertainment, an absorbing pleasure. If you ask anyone who enjoys ballet or any other art how he started, he will tell you that he enjoyed it long before he knew what it meant or how it worked. I remember the intense pleasure reading Shelley's *Adonais* gave me as a boy—long before I followed accurately the sense of the words; and once, twenty years later, I had two kittens who would purr in unison and watch me bright-eyed when I read them Shakespeare's *Sonnets*, clearly pleased by the compliment and by the sounds they heard. Would they have enjoyed them better if they had understood them? The answer is, they enjoyed them very much. Many a college graduate might have envied them.

I don't mean that so orderly and respectable an entertainment as that of art is made for the susceptibilities of kittens or children. But consider how the enormous orderly and respectable symphonic public enjoys its listening, enjoys it without recognizing themes, harmonics or timbres, without evaluating the style historically or even knowing if the piece is being played as the composer intended. What do they hear when they hear a symphony? Why, they hear the music, the interesting noises it makes. They follow the form and the character of it by following their direct acoustic impressions.

Susceptibility to ballet is a way of being susceptible to animal grace of movement. Many people are highly susceptible to the pleasure of seeing grace of movement who have never thought of going to ballet to look for it. They find it instead in watching graceful animals, animals of many species at play, flying, swimming, racing and leaping and making gestures of affection toward one another, or watchful in harmonious repose. And they find it too in seeing graceful young people on the street or in a game or at the beach or in a dance hall, boys and girls in exuberant health who are doing pretty much what the charming animals do, and are as unconscious of their grace as they. Unconscious grace of movement is a natural and impermanent gift like grace of features or of voice or of character, a lucky accident you keep meeting with all your life wherever you are. To be watching grace puts people into a particularly amiable frame of mind. It is an especially attractive form of feeling social consciousness.

But if ballet is a way of entertaining the audience by showing them animal grace, why is its way of moving so very unanimal-like and artificial? For the same reason that music has evolved so very artificial a way of organizing its pleasing noises. Art takes what in life is an accidental pleasure and tries to repeat and prolong it. It organizes, diversifies, characterizes, through an artifice that men evolve by trial and error. Ballet nowadays is as different from an accidental product as a symphony at Carnegie Hall is different from the noises Junior makes on his trumpet upstairs or Mary Ann with comb and tissue paper, sitting on the roof, the little monkey.

You don't have to know about ballet to enjoy it, all you have to do is look at it. If you are susceptible to it, and a good many people evidently are, you will like spontaneously some things you see and dislike others, and quite violently too. You may be so dazzled at first by a star or by the general atmosphere you don't really know what happened; you may on the other hand find the performance absurdly stiff and affected except for a few unreasonable moments of intense pleasure; but, if you are susceptible you will find you want to go again. When you go repeatedly, you begin to recognize what it is you like, and watch for it the next time. That way you get to know about ballet, you know a device of ballet because you have responded to it, you know that much at least about it. Even if nobody agrees with you, you still know it for yourself.

That the composite effect of ballet is a complex one is clear enough. Its devices make a long list, wherever you start. These devices are useful to give a particular moment of a dance a particular expression. The dancers in action give it at that moment a direct sensual reality. But if you watch often and watch attentively, the expressive power of some ballets and dancers will fascinate, perturb and delight far more than that of others; and will keep alive in your imagination much more intensely long after you have left the theater. It is this after effect that dancers and ballets are judged by by their audience.

To some of my friends the images ballet leaves in the imagination suggest, as poetry does, an aspect of the drama of human behavior. For others such ballet images keep their sensual mysteriousness, "abstract," unrationalized and magical. Anyone who cannot bear to contemplate human behavior except from a rationalistic point of view had better not try to "understand" the exhilarating excitement of ballet; its finest images of our fate are no easier to face than those of poetry itself, though they are no less beautiful.

KENNETH CLARK

The Blot and the Diagram

I have been told to "look down from a high place over the whole extensive landscape of modern art." We all know how tempting high places can be, and how dangerous. I usually avoid them myself. But if I must do as I am told, I shall try to find out why modern art has taken its peculiar form, and to guess how long that form will continue.

I shall begin with Leonardo da Vinci, because although all processes are gradual, he does represent one clearly marked turning point in the history of art. Before that time, the painter's intentions were quite simple; they were first of all to tell a story, secondly to make the invisible visible, and thirdly to turn a plain surface into a decorated surface. Those are all very ancient aims, going back to the earliest civilizations, or beyond; and for three hundred years painters had been instructed how to carry them out by means of a workshop tradition. Of course, there had been breaks in that tradition—in the fourth century, maybe, and towards the end of the seventh century; but broadly speaking, the artist learnt what he could about the technique of art from his master in his workshop, and then set up shop on his own and tried to do better.

As is well known, Leonardo had a different view of art. He thought that it involved both science and the pursuit of some peculiar attribute called beauty or grace. He was, by inclination, a scientist: he wanted to find out how things worked, and he believed that this knowledge could be stated mathematically. He said "Let no one who is not a mathematician read my works," and he tried to relate this belief in measurement to his belief in beauty. This involved him in two rather different lines of thought, one concerned with magic—the magic of numbers—the other with science. Ever since Pythagoras had discovered that the musical scale could be stated mathematically, by means of the length of the strings, etc., and so had thrown a bridge between intellectual analysis and sensory perception, thinkers on art had felt that it should be possible to do the same for painting. I must say that their effort had not been very rewarding; the modulus, or golden section, and the logarithmic spiral of shells are practically the only undisputed results. But Leonardo lived at a time when it was still possible to hope great things from perspective, which should not only define space, but order it harmoniously; and he also inherited a belief that ideal mathematical combinations could be derived from the proportions of the human body. This line of thought may be called the *mystique* of measurement. The other line may be called *the use* of measurement. Leonardo wished to state mathematically various facts related to the act of seeing. How do we see light passing over a sphere? What happens when objects make themselves perceptible on our retina? Both these lines of thought involved him in drawing diagrams and taking measurements, and for this reason were closely related in his mind. No painter except perhaps Piero della Francesca has tried more strenuously to find a mathematical statement of art, nor has had a greater equipment for doing so.

But Leonardo was also a man of powerful and disturbing imagination. In his notebooks, side by side with his attempts to achieve *order* by mathematics, are drawings and descriptions of the most violent scenes of *disorder* which the human mind can conceive—battles, deluges, eruptions. And he included in his treatise on painting advice on how to develop this side of the artistic faculty also. The passages in which he does so have often been quoted, but they are so incredibly foreign to the whole Renaissance idea of art, although related to a remark in Pliny,[1] that each time I read them, they give me a fresh surprise. I will, therefore, quote them again.

I shall not refrain from including among these precepts a new and specu-lative idea, which although it may seem trivial and almost laughable, is none the less of great value in quickening the spirit of invention. It is this: that you should look at certain walls stained with damp or at stones of un-even color. If you have to invent some setting you will be able to see in these the likeness of divine landscapes, adorned with mountains, ruins, rocks, woods, great plains, hills and valleys in great variety; and then again you will see there battles and strange figures in violent action, expressions of faces and clothes and an infinity of things which you will be able to reduce to their complete and proper forms. In such walls the same thing happens as in the sound of bells, in whose strokes you may find every named word which you can imagine.

Later he repeats this suggestion in slightly different form, advis-ing the painter to study not only marks on walls, but also "the embers of the fire, or clouds or mud, or other similar objects from which you will find most admirable ideas . . . because from a con-fusion of shapes the spirit is quickened to new inventions."

I hardly need to insist on how relevant these passages are to modern painting. Almost every morning I receive cards inviting me to current exhibitions, and on the cards are photographs of the works exhibited. Some of them consist of blots, some of scrawls, some look like clouds, some like embers of the fire, some are like mud—some of them are mud; a great many look like stains on walls, and one of them, I remember, consisted of actual stains on walls, photographed and framed. Leonardo's famous passage has been illustrated in every particular. And yet I doubt if he would have been satisfied with the results, because he believed that we must somehow unite the two opposite poles of our faculties. Art itself was the connection between the diagram and the blot.

Now in order to prevent the impression that I am taking advantage of a metaphor, as writers on art are often bound to do, I should explain how I am going to use these words. By "diagram" I mean a rational statement in a visible form, involving measurements, and usually done with an ulterior motive. The theorem of Pythagoras is proved by a diagram. Leonardo's drawings of light striking a sphere are diagrams; but the works of Mondrian, although made up of straight lines, are not diagrams, because they are not done in order to prove or measure some experience, but to please the eye. That they look like diagrams is due to influences which I will examine later. But diagrams can exist with no motive other than their own perfection, just as mathematical propositions can.

1. Roman naturalist, first century A.D.

By "blots" I mean marks or areas which are not intended to convey information, but which, for some reason, seem pleasant and memorable to the maker, and can be accepted in the same sense by the spectator. I said that these blots were not intended to convey information, but of course they do, and that of two kinds. First, they tell us through association, about things we had forgotten; that was the function of Leonardo's stains on walls, which as he said, quickened the spirit of invention, and it can be the function of man-made blots as well; and secondly a man-made blot will tell us about the artist. Unless it is made entirely accidentally, as by spilling an inkpot, it will be a commitment. It is quite difficult to make a non-committal blot. Although the two are connected, I think we can distinguish between analogy blots and gesture blots.

Now let me try to apply this to modern art. Modern art is not a subject on which one can hope for a large measure of agreement, but I hope I may be allowed two assumptions. The first is that the kind of painting and architecture which we call, with varying inflections of the voice, "modern," is a true and vital expression of our own day; and the second assumption is that it differs radically from any art which has preceded it. Both these assumptions have been questioned. It has been said that modern art is "a racket" engineered by art dealers, who have exploited the incompetence of artists and the gullibility of patrons, that the whole thing is a kind of vast and very expensive practical joke. Well, fifty years is a long time to keep up a hoax of this kind, and during these years modern art has spread all over the free world and created a complete international style. I don't think that any honest-minded historian, whether he liked it or not, could pretend that modern art was the result of an accident or a conspiracy. The only doubt he could have would be whether it is, so to say, a long-term or a short-term movement. In the history of art there are stylistic changes which appear to develop from purely internal causes, and seem almost accidental in relation to the other circumstances of life and society. Such, for example, was the state of art in Italy (outside Venice) from about 1530 to 1600. When all is said about the religious disturbances of the time, the real cause of the Mannerist style was the domination of Michelangelo, who had both created an irresistible style and exhausted its possibilities. It needed the almost equally powerful pictorial imagination of Caravaggio to produce a counter-infection, which could spread from Rome to Spain and the Netherlands and prepare the way for Rembrandt. I can see nothing in the history of man's spirit to account for this episode. It seems to me to be due to an internal and specifically artistic chain of events which are easily related to one another, and comprehensible within the general framework of European art. On the other hand, there are events in the history of art which go far beyond the interaction of styles and which evidently reflect a change in the whole condition of the human spirit. Such an event took place towards the end of the fifth century, when the Hellenistic-Roman style gradually became what we call Byzantine; and again in the early thirteenth century, when the Gothic cathedrals shot up out of the ground. In each case the historian could produce a series of examples to prove that the change was inevitable. But actually, it was nothing of the sort; it was wholly unpredictable; and was part of a complete spiritual revolution.

Whether we think that modern art represents a transformation of style or a change of spirit depends to some extent on my second assumption, that it differs radically from anything which has preceded it. This too has been questioned; it has been said that Léger is only a logical development of Poussin, or Mondrian of Vermeer.[2] And it is true that the element of design in each has something in common. If we pare a Poussin down to its bare bones, there are combinations of curves and cubes which are the foundations of much classical painting, and Léger had the good sense to make use of them. Similarly, in Vermeer there is a use of rectangles, large areas contrasted with very narrow ones, and a feeling for shallow recessions, which became the preferred theme of Mondrian. But such analogies are trifling compared with the differences. Poussin was a very intelligent man who thought deeply about his art, and if anyone had suggested to him that his pictures were praiseworthy solely on account of their construction, he would have been incredulous and affronted.

So let us agree that the kind of painting and architecture which we find most representative of our times—say, the painting of Jackson Pollock and the architecture of the Lever building—is deeply different from the painting and architecture of the past; and is *not* a mere whim of fashion, but the result of a great change in our ways of thinking and feeling.

How did this great change take place and what does it mean? To begin with, I think it is related to the development upon which all industrial civilization depends, the differentiation of function. Leonardo was exceptional, almost unique in his integration of functions —the scientific and the imaginative. Yet he foreshadowed more than any other artist their disintegration, by noting and treating in isolation the diagrammatic faculty and the blot-making faculty. The average artist took the unity of these faculties for granted. They were united in Leonardo, and in lesser artists, by *interest or pleasure in the thing seen*. The external object was like a magnetic pole which drew the two faculties together. At some point the external object became a negative rather than a positive charge. Instead of drawing

2. Léger and Mondrian: French and Dutch modern painters, respectively. Poussin, French, and Vermeer, Dutch, were both seventeenth-century painters.

together the two faculties, it completely dissociated them; architecture went off in one direction with the diagram, painting went in the other direction with the blot.

This disintegration was related to a radical change in the philosophy of art. We all know that such changes, however harmless they sound when first enunciated, can have drastic consequences in the world of action. Rulers who wish to maintain the *status quo* are well advised to chop off the heads of all philosophers. What Hilaire Belloc called the "remote and ineffectual don" is more dangerous than the busy columnist with his eye on the day's news. The revolution in our ideas about the nature of painting seems to have been hatched by a don who was considered remote and ineffectual even by Oxford standards—Walter Pater. It was he (inspired, I believe, by Schopenhauer) who first propounded the idea of the aesthetic sensation, intuitively perceived.

In its primary aspect [Pater said] a great picture has no more difficult message for us than an accidental play of sunlight and shadow for a few moments on the wall or floor; in itself, in truth, a space of such fallen light, caught, as in the colors of an Eastern carpet, but refined upon and dealt with more subtly and exquisitely than by nature itself.

It is true that his comparison with an Eastern carpet admits the possibility of "pleasant sensations" being arranged or organized; and Pater confirms this need for organization a few lines later, when he sets down his famous dictum that "all art constantly aspires towards the condition of music." He does not believe in blots uncontrolled by the conscious mind. But he is very far from the information-giving diagram.

This belief that art has its origin in our intuitive rather than our rational faculties, picturesquely asserted by Pater, was worked out historically and philosophically, in the somewhat wearisome volumes of Benedetto Croce, and owing to his authoritative tone, he is usually considered the originator of a new theory of aesthetics. It was, in fact, the reversion to a very old idea. Long before the Romantics had stressed the importance of intuition and self-expression, men had admitted the Dionysiac nature of art. But philosophers had always assumed that the frenzy of inspiration must be controlled by law and by the intellectual power of putting things into harmonious order. And this general philosophic concept of art as a combination of intuition and intellect had been supported by technical necessities. It was necessary to master certain laws and to use the intellect in order to build the Gothic cathedrals, or set up the stained glass windows of Chartres or cast the bronze doors of the Florence Baptistry. When this bracing element of craftsmanship ceased to dominate the artist's outlook, as happened soon after the time of Leonardo, new scientific disciples had to be invented to maintain the intellectual element in art. Such were perspective and anatomy. From a purely artistic point of view, they were unneccessary. The Chinese produced some of the finest landscapes ever painted, without any systematic knowledge of perspective. Greek figure sculpture reached its highest point before the study of anatomy had been systematized. But from the Renaissance onwards, painters felt that these two sciences made their art intellectually respectable. They were two ways of connecting the diagram and the blot.

In the nineteenth century, belief in art as a scientific activity declined, for a quantity of reasons. Science and technology withdrew into specialization. Voltaire's efforts to investigate the nature of heat seem to us ludicrous; Goethe's studies of botany and physics a waste of a great poet's time. In spite of their belief in inspiration, the great Romantics were aware of the impoverishment of the imagination which would take place when science had drifted out of reach, and both Shelley and Coleridge spent much time in chemical experiments. Even Turner, whose letters reveal a singular lack of analytic faculty, annotated Goethe's theories of color, and painted two pictures to demonstrate them. No good. The laws which govern the movement of the human spirit are inexorable. The enveloping assumption, within which the artist has to function, was that science was no longer approachable by any but the specialist. And gradually there grew up the idea that all intellectual activities were hostile to art.

I have mentioned the philosophic development of this view of Croce. Let me give one example of its quiet acceptance by the official mind. The British Council sends all over the world, even to Florence and Rome, exhibitions of children's art—the point of these children's pictures being that they have no instruction of any kind, and do not attempt the troublesome task of painting what they see. Well, why not, after all? The results are quite agreeable—sometimes strangely beautiful; and the therapeutic effect on the children is said to be excellent. It is like one of those small harmless heresies which we are shocked to find were the object of persecution by the Mediaeval Church. When, however, we hear admired modern painters saying that they draw their inspiration from the drawings of children and lunatics, as well as from stains on walls, we recognize that we have accomplices in a revolution.

The lawless and intuitive character of modern art is a familiar theme and certain historians have said that it is symptomatic of a decline in Western civilization. This is journalism—one of those statements that sound well to-day and nonsense to-morrow. It is obvious that the development of physical science in the last hundred years has been one of the most colossal efforts the human intellect has ever made. But I think it is also true that human beings can produce, in a given epoch, only a certain amount of creative energy, and that this is directed to different ends and different times

—music in the eighteenth century is the obvious example; and I believe that the dazzling achievements of science during the last seventy years have deflected far more of those skills and endowments which go to the making of a work of art than is usually realized. To begin with, there is the sheer energy. In every molding of a Renaissance palace we are conscious of an immense intellectual energy, and it is the absence of this energy in the nineteenth-century copies of Renaissance buildings which makes them seem so dead. To find a form with the same vitality as a window molding of the Palazzo Farnese I must wait till I get back into an aeroplane, and look at the relation of the engine to the wing. That form is alive, not (as used to be said) because it is functional—many functional shapes are entirely uninteresting—but because it is animated by the breath of modern science.

The deflections from art to science are the more serious because these are not, as used to be supposed, two contrary activities, but in fact draw on many of the same capacities of the human mind. In the last resort each depends on the imagination. Artist and scientist alike are both trying to give concrete form to dimly apprehended ideas. Dr. Bronowski has put it very well: "All science is the search for unity in hidden likenesses, and the starting point is an image, because then the unity is before our mind's eye." Even if we no longer have to pretend that a group of stars looks like a plough or a bear, our scientists still depend on humanly comprehensible images, and it is striking that the valid symbols of our time, invented to embody some scientific truth, have taken root in the popular imagination. Do those red and blue balls connected by rods really resemble a type of atomic structure? I am too ignorant to say. I accept the symbol just as an early Christian accepted the Fish or the Lamb, and I find it echoed or even (it would seem) anticipated in the work of modern artists like Kandinsky and Miró.

Finally, there is the question of popular interest and approval. We have grown accustomed to the idea that artists can work in solitude and incomprehension; but that was not the way things happened in the Renaissance or the seventeenth century, still less in ancient Greece. The pictures carried through the streets by cheering crowds, the *Te Deum* sung on completion of a public building—all this indicates a state of opinion in which men could undertake great works of art with a confidence quite impossible to-day. The research scientist, on the other hand, not only has millions of pounds worth of plant and equipment for the asking, he has principalities and powers waiting for his conclusions. He goes to work, as Titian once did, confident that he will succeed because the strong tide of popular admiration is flowing with him.

But although science has absorbed so many of the functions of art and deflected (I believe) so many potential artists, it obviously cannot be a *substitute* for art. Its mental process may be similar, but its ends are different. There have been three views about the purpose of art. First that it aims simply at imitation; secondly that it should influence human conduct; and thirdly that it should produce a kind of exalted happiness. The first view, which was developed in ancient Greece, must be reckoned one of the outstanding failures of Greek thought. It is simply contrary to experience, because if the visual arts aimed solely at imitating things they would be of very little importance; whereas the Greeks above all people knew that they were important, and treated them as such. Yet such was the prestige of Greek thought that this theory of art was revived in the Renaissance, in an uncomfortable sort of way, and had a remarkable recrudescence in the nineteenth century. The second view, that art should influence conduct and opinions, is more respectable, and held the field throughout the Middle Ages; indeed the more we learn about the art of the past and motives of those who commissioned it, the more important this particular aim appeares to be; it still dominated art theory in the time of Diderot. The third view, that art should produce a kind of exalted happiness, was invented by the Romantics at the beginning of the nineteenth century (well, perhaps *invented* by Plotinus, but given currency by the Romantics), and gradually gained ground until by the end of the century it was believed in by almost all educated people. It has held the field in Western Europe till the present day. Leaving aside the question which of these theories is correct, let me ask which of them is most likely to be a helpful background to art (for that is all that a theory of aesthetics can be) in an age when science has such an overwhelming domination over the human mind. The first aim must be reckoned *by itself* to be pointless, since science has now discovered so many ways of imitating appearances, which are incomparably more accurate and convincing than even the most realistic picture. Painting might defend itself against the daguerreotype, but not against Cinerama.

The popular application of science has also, it seems to me, invalidated the second aim of art, because it is quite obvious that no picture can influence human conduct as effectively as a television advertisement. It is quite true that in totalitarian countries artists are still instructed to influence conduct. But that is either due to technical deficiencies, as in China, where in default of T.V., broadsheets and posters are an important way of communicating with an illiterate population; or, in Russia, to a philosophic time-lag. The fact is that very few countries have had the courage to take Plato's advice and exclude works of art altogether. They have, therefore, had to invent some excuse for keeping them on, and the Russians are still using the pretext that paintings and sculpture can influence people in favor of socialist and national policies, although it must have dawned on them that these results can be obtained far more effectively by the cinema and television.

So it seems to me that of these three possible purposes of art—imitation, persuasion, or exalted pleasure—only the third still holds good in an age of science; and it must be justified very largely by the fact that it is a feeling which is absent from scientific achievements—although mathematicians have told us that it is similar to the feeling aroused by their finest calculations. We might say that in the modern world the art of painting is defensible only in so far as it is complementary to science.

We are propelled in the same direction by another achievement of modern science, the study of psychology. That peeling away of the psyche, which was formerly confined to spiritual instructors, or the great novelists, has become a commonplace of conversation. When a good, solid, external word like Duty is turned into a vague, uneasy, internal word like Guilt, one cannot expect artists to take much interest in good, solid, external objects. The artist has always been involved in the painful process of turning himself inside out, but in the past his inner convictions have been of such a kind that they can, so to say, re-form themselves round an object. But, as we have seen, even in Leonardo's time, there were certain obscure needs and patterns of the spirit, which could discover themselves only through less precise analogies—the analogies provided by stains on walls or the embers of a fire. Now, I think that in this inward-looking age, when we have become so much more aware of the vagaries of the spirit, and so respectful of the working of the unconscious, the artist is more likely to find his point of departure in analogies of this kind. They are more exciting because they, so to say, take us by surprise, like forgotten smells; and they seem to be more profound because the memories they awaken have been deeply buried in our minds. Whether Jung is right in believing that this free, undirected, illogical form of mental activity will allow us to pick up, like a magic radio station, some deep memories of our race which can be of universal interest, I do not know. The satisfaction we derive from certain combinations of shape and color does seem to be inexplicable even by the remotest analogies, and may perhaps involve inherited memories. It is not yet time for the art-historian to venture in to that mysterious jungle. I must, however, observe that our respect for the unconscious mind not only gives us an interest in analogy blots, but in what I called "gesture blots" as well. We recognize how free and forceful such a communication can be, and this aspect of art has become more important in the last ten years. An apologist of modern art has said: "What we want to know is not what the world looks like, but what we mean to each other." So the gesture blot becomes a sort of ideogram, like primitive Chinese writing. Students of Zen assure us it is a means of communication more direct and complete than anything which our analytic system can achieve. Almost 2,000 years before Leonardo looked for images in blots, Lao-tzu had written:

> The Tao is something blurred and indistinct.
> How indistinct! How blurred!
> Yet within are images,
> How blurred! How indistinct!
> Yet within are things.

I said that when the split took place between our faculties of measurement and intuition, *architecture* went off with the diagram. Of course architecture had always been involved with measurement and calculation, but we tend to forget how greatly it was also involved with the imitation of external objects. "The question to be determined," said Ruskin, "is whether architecture is a frame for the sculpture, or the sculpture an ornament of the architecture." And he came down on the first alternative. He thought that a building became architecture only in so far as it was a frame for figurative sculpture. I wonder if there is a single person alive who would agree with him. And yet Ruskin had the most sensitive eye and the keenest analytic faculty that has ever been applied to architecture. Many people disagreed with him in his own day; they thought that sculpture should be subordinate to the total design of the building. But that anything claiming to be architecture could dispense with ornament altogether never entered anyone's head till a relatively short time ago.

A purely diagrammatic architecture is only about thirty years older than a purely blottesque painting; yet it has changed the face of the world and produced in every big city a growing uniformity. Perhaps because it is a little older, perhaps because it seems to have a material justification, we have come to accept it without question. People who are still puzzled or affronted by action painting are proud of the great steel and glass boxes which have arisen so miraculously in the last ten years. And yet these two are manifestations of the same state of mind. The same difficulties of function, the same deflection from the external object, and the same triumph of science. Abstract painting and glass box architecture are related in two different ways. There is the direct relationship of style—the kind of relationship which painting and architecture had with one another in the great consistent ages of art like the 13th and 17th centuries. For modern architecture is not simply functional; at its best it has a style which is almost as definite and as arbitrary as Gothic. And this leads me back to my earlier point: that diagrams can be drawn in order to achieve some imagined perfection, similar to that of certain mathematical propositions. Thirty years after Pater's famous dictum, painters in Russia, Holland, and France began to put into practice the theory that "all art constantly aspires to the condition of music"; and curiously enough this Pythagorean mystique of measurements produced a style—the style which reached its purest expression in the Dutch painter, Mondrian. And through the influence of the Bauhaus, this became the leading style of modern architecture.

The other relationship between contemporary architecture and painting appears to be indirect and even accidental. I am thinking of the visual impact when the whole upper part of a tall glass building mirrors the clouds or the dying embers of a sunset, and so becomes a frame for a marvelous, moving Tachiste[3] picture. I do not think that future historians of art will find this accidental at all, but will see it as the culmination of a long process beginning in the Romantic period, in which, from Wordsworth and De Quincey onwards, poets and philosophers recognized the movement of clouds as the symbol of a newly discovered mental faculty.

Such, then, would be my diagnosis of the present condition of art. I must now, by special request, say what I think will happen to art in the future. I think that the state of affairs which I have called the blot and the diagram will last for a long time. Architecture will continue to be made up of glass boxes and steel grids, without ornament of any kind. Painting will continue to be subjective and arcane, an art of accident rather than rule, of stains on walls rather than of calculation, of inscape rather than of external reality.

This conclusion is rejected by those who believe in a social theory of art. They maintain that a living art must depend on the popular will, and that neither the blot nor the diagram is popular; and, since those who hold a social theory of art are usually Marxists, they point to Soviet Russia as a country where all my conditions obtain—differentiation of function, the domination of science and so forth—and yet what we call modern art has gained no hold. This argument does not impress me. There is of course, nothing at all in the idea that Communist doctrines inevitably produce social realism. Painting in Yugoslavia, in Poland and Hungary is in the same modern idiom as painting in the United States, and shows remarkable vitality. Whereas the official social realism of the U.S.S.R., except for a few illustrators, lacks life or conviction, and shows no evidence of representing the popular will. In fact Russian architecture has already dropped the grandiose official style, and I am told that this is now taking place in painting also. In spite of disapproval amounting to persecution, experimental painters exist and find buyers.

I doubt if the Marxists are even correct in saying that the blot and the diagram are not popular. The power, size, and splendor of,

3. A method of nonrepresentational contemporary painting which exploits the quality of freely flowing oil paint for its own sake.

say, the Seagram building in New York makes it as much the object of pride and wonder as great architecture was in the past. And one of the remarkable things about Tachisme is the speed with which it has spread throughout the world, not only in sophisticated centers, but in small local art societies. It has become as much an international style as Gothic in the 14th and Baroque in the 17th centuries. I recently visited the exhibition of a provincial academy in the north, of England, a very respectable body then celebrating its hundred and fiftieth anniversary. A few years ago it had been full of Welsh mountain landscapes, and scenes of streets and harbors, carefully delineated. Now practically every picture was in the Tachiste style, and I found that many of them were painted by the same artists, often quite elderly people, who had previously painted the mountains and streets. As works of art, they seemed to me neither better nor worse. But I could not help thinking that they must have been less trouble to do, and I reflected that the painters must have had a happy time releasing the Dionysiac elements in their natures. However, we must not be too cynical about this. I do not believe that the spread of action painting is due solely to the fact that it is easy to do. Cubism, especially synthetic Cubism, also looks easy to do, and never had this immense diffusion. It remained the style of a small élite of professional painters and specialized art lovers; whereas Tachisme has spread to fabrics, to the decoration of public buildings, to the backgrounds of television programs, to advertising of all kinds. Indeed the closest analogy to action painting is the most popular art of all—the art of jazz. The trumpeter who rises from his seat as one possessed, and squirts out his melody like a scarlet scrawl against a background of plangent dashes and dots, is not as a rule performing for a small body of intellectuals.

Nevertheless, I do not think that the style of the blot and the diagram will last forever. For one thing, I believe that the imitation of external reality is a fundamental human instinct which is bound to reassert itself. In his admirable book on sculpture called *Aratra Pentelici,* Ruskin describes an experience which many of us could confirm. "Having been always desirous," he says,

that the education of women should begin in learning how to cook, I got leave, one day, for a little girl of eleven years old to exchange, much to her satisfaction, her schoolroom for the kitchen. But as ill fortune would have it, there was some pastry toward, and she was left unadvisedly in command of some delicately rolled paste; whereof she made no pies, but an unlimited quantity of cats and mice....

Now [he continues] you may read the works of the gravest critics of art from end to end; but you will find, at last, they can give you no other true account of the spirit of sculpture than that it is an irresistible human instinct for the making of cats and mice, and other imitable living creatures, in such permanent form that one may play with the images at leisure.

I cannot help feeling that he was right. I am fond of works of art, and I collect them. But I do not want to hang them on the wall simply in order to get an electric shock every time that I pass them. I want to hold them, and turn them round and re-hang them—in short, to play with the images at leisure. And, putting aside what may be no more than a personal prejudice, I rather doubt if an art which depends solely on the first impact on our emotions is permanently valid. When the shock is exhausted, we have nothing to occupy our minds. And this is particularly troublesome with an art which depends so much on the unconscious, because, as we know from the analysis of dreams, the furniture of our unconscious minds is even more limited, repetitive, and commonplace than that of our conscious minds. The blots and stains of modern painting depend ultimately on the memories of things seen, memories sunk deep in the unconscious, overlaid, transformed, assimilated to a physical condition, but memories none the less. *Ex nihilo nihil fit.* It is not possible for a painter to lose contact with the visible world.

At this point the apes have provided valuable evidence. There is no doubt that they are Tachiste painters of considerable accomplishment. I do not myself care for the work of Congo the chimp, but Sophie, the Rotterdam gorilla, is a charming artist, whose delicate traceries remind me of early Paul Klee. As you know, apes take their painting seriously. The patterns they produce are not the result of mere accident, but of intense, if short-lived, concentration, and a lively sense of balance and space-filling. If you compare the painting of a young ape with that of a human child of relatively the same age, you will find that in the first, expressive, pattern-making stage, the ape is superior. Then, automatically and inexorably the child begins to draw *things*—man, house, truck, etc. This the ape never does. Of course his Tachiste paintings are far more attractive than the child's crude conceptual outlines. But they cannot develop. They are monotonous and ultimately rather depressing.

The difference between the child and the ape does not show itself in aesthetic perception, or in physical perception of any kind, but in the child's power to form a concept. Later, as we know, he will spend his time trying to adapt his concept to the evidence of physical sensation; in that struggle lies the whole of style. But the concept —the need to draw a line round his thought—comes first. Now it is a truism that the power to form concepts is what distinguishes man from the animals; although the prophets of modern society, Freud, Jung, D. H. Lawrence, have rightly insisted on the importance of animal perceptions in balanced human personality, the concept-forming faculty has not declined in modern man. On the contrary, it is the basis of that vast scientific achievement which, as I said earlier, seems almost to have put art out of business.

Now, if the desire to represent external reality depended solely on an interest in visual sensation, I would agree that it might disap-

pear from art and never return. But if, as the evidence of children
and monkeys indicates, it depends primarily on the formation of
concepts, which are then modified by visual sensation, I think it is
bound to return. For I consider the human faculty of forming concepts at least as "inalienable" as "life, liberty, and the pursuit of
happiness. . . ."

I am not, of course, suggesting that the imitation of external
reality will ever again become what it was in European art from the
mid-17th to the late 19th centuries. Such a subordination of the
concept to the visual sensation was altogether exceptional in the
history of art. Much of the territory won by modern painting will, I
believe, be held. For example, freedom of association, the immediate passage from one association to another—which is so much a part
of Picasso's painting and Henry Moore's sculpture, is something
which has existed in music since Wagner and in poetry since
Rimbaud and Mallarmé. (I mean existed consciously; of course it
underlies all great poetry and music.) It need not be sacrificed
in a return to external reality. Nor need the direct communication
of intuition, through touch and an instinctive sense of materials. This I consider pure gain. In the words of my original
metaphor, both the association blot and the gesture blot can remain. But they must be given more nourishment: they must be
related to a fuller knowledge of the forms and structures which
impress us most powerfully, and so become part of our concept of
natural order. At the end of the passage in which Leonardo tells the
painter that he can look for battles, landscapes, and animals in the
stains on walls, he adds this caution, "But first be sure that you know
all the members of all things you wish to depict, both the members
of the animals and the members of landscapes, that is to say of
rocks, plants, and so forth." It is because one feels in Henry Moore's
sculpture this knowledge of the members of animals and plants, that
his work, even at its most abstract, makes an impression on us
different from that of his imitators. His figures are not merely pleasing examples of design, but seem to be a part of nature, "rolled
round in Earth's diurnal course with rocks and stones and trees."

Those lines of Wordsworth lead me to the last reason why I feel
that the intuitive blot and scribble may not dominate painting forever. Our belief in the whole purpose of art may change. I said earlier
that we now believe it should aim at producing a kind of exalted
happiness: this really means that art becomes an end in itself. Now
it is an incontrovertible fact of history that the greatest art has
always been *about* something, a means of communicating some truth
which is assumed to be more important than the art itself. The
truths which art has been able to communicate have been of a kind
which could not be put in any other way. They have been ultimate
truths, stated symbolically. Science has achieved its triumph precisely

by disregarding such truths, by not asking unanswerable questions, but sticking to the question "how." I confess it looks to me as if we shall have to wait a long time before there is some new belief which requires expression through art rather than through statistics or equations. And until this happens, the visual arts will fall short of the greatest epochs, the ages of the Parthenon, the Sistine Ceiling, and Chartres Cathedral.

I am afraid there is nothing we can do about it. No amount of goodwill and no expenditure of money can affect that sort of change. We cannot even dimly foresee when it will happen or what form it will take. We can only be thankful for what we have got—a vigorous, popular, decorative art, complementary to our architecture and our science, somewhat monotonous, somewhat prone to charlatanism, but genuinely expressive of our time.

QUESTIONS

1. What definition does Clark give of his central metaphor, "the blot and the diagram"? Are "blot" and "diagram" the equivalents of "art" and "science"? Explain.
2. What distinction does Clark make between "analogy (or association) blot" and "gesture blot"? What importance does the distinction have for his discussion of modern painting?
3. In what ways, according to Clark, is the place of science in the modern world similar to the place occupied by science in the past? What past functions of art has science assumed? To what extent does Clark consider the situation satisfactory? What defects does he mention?
4. How does Clark show "blot" painting and "diagram" architecture to be related? Is architecture today an art or a science? How scientific is painting?
5. Clark points out that "the closest analogy to action painting is the most popular art of all—the art of jazz" (p. 455). Is there any jazz analogous to "diagram"? Explain.
6. Study closely some examples of advertising layout. To what extent do they appear influenced by "blot"? Is there influence of "diagram" in any? Are any exemplary of "blot" and "diagram" in harmony?
7. What extensions into other disciplines can be made of Clark's blot-diagram antithesis? Does it apply in literature? In psychology?
8. Why, according to Clark, will man's concept-forming nature eventually bring about a change of style in art?

JOSEPH WOOD KRUTCH
Modern Painting

I am, I hope, not insensitive to any of the arts. I have spent happy hours in museums, and I listen with pleasure to Bach, Mozart, and Beethoven. But I have more confidence in my ability to understand what is said in words than I have in my understanding of anything that dispenses with them. Such opinions as I hold concerning modern music or modern painting are as tentative as those I once expressed in these pages[1] about modern architecture.

Nevertheless, as I said on that occasion, it is one of the privileges of the essayist to hold forth on subjects he doesn't know much about. Because he does not pretend to any expertness, those who know better than he what he is talking about need be no more than mildly exasperated. His misconceptions may give valuable hints to those who would set him right. If he didn't expose his obtuseness, his would-be mentors wouldn't know so well just what the misconceptions are and how they arose. An honest philistinism is easier to educate than the conscious or unconscious hypocrisy of those who admire whatever they are told that they should.

In the case of modern painting, the very fact that I can take pleasure in some of the works of yesterday's *avant-garde* but little in that of my own day suggests, even to me, that I may be merely the victim of a cultural lag. But there is no use in pretending that I am delighted by what delights me not, and I find that much serious criticism of the most recent painting is no help. Those who write it are talking over my head; they just don't start far enough back.

For instance, I read in the *Nation* that what a certain painter I had never heard of had accomplished during the war might be summarized as "an unstructured painterliness—neither expressionist nor surrealist in character, and therefore out of keeping with available alternatives." Shortly after the war "he followed through with an intimation of the picture facade as its own reason for being, preferring a unitary sensation, by being irregularly blotted out by masses that kept on pushing at, and disappearing past, the perimeters. Executed on a vastness of scale quite unprecedented in easel painting (which he was in any event attacking), these paintings sidestep drawing and the illusion of spatial recession without ever giving the impression of evasiveness. The result was a sense of the picture surface—now extraordinarily flattened—as a kind of wall

---

1. "If You Don't Mind My Saying So," Mr. Krutch's regular column in   *The American Scholar.*

whereby constricted elements no longer had any exclusive formal relationship with one another."

When I read things like that my first impulse is to exclaim, "If that young man expresses himself in terms too deep for me . . ."[2] But then I realize the possibility that the words do say something to those whose visual perceptions are better trained than mine. I am at best a second grader, still struggling with the multiplication table, who has wandered into a seminar at the Institute for Advanced Studies.

When, therefore, I happened to see an advertisement of the Book-of-the-Month Club explaining that the Metropolitan Museum of Art had been persuaded to prepare a twelve-part seminar on art, which could be subscribed to for "only $60," I had the feeling that this might very well be getting down to my level. The advertisement was adorned by reproductions of two contrasting pictures: one of the Metropolitan's own "Storm" (or "Paul and Virginia") by Pierre Cot, and the other of a swirling abstraction. "Which of these is a good painting?" demanded the headline. My immediate answer "Neither." And I was not too much discouraged by the fact that I was pretty sure this was not the right answer.

I think I know at least some of the reasons why "The Storm" is not one of the great masterpieces—even though some supposedly competent expert must have once paid a whopping price for it. On the other hand, I had not the slightest idea why the abstraction was good or even just not quite as bad as the supposedly horrid example facing it.

I confess that I did not subscribe to the seminars. But I did borrow a set from an acquaintance who had done so, and I must report that I did understand what the Metropolitan people were saying as I had not understood the *Nation* critic. But I was not by any means wholly convinced. Many years ago I read Roger Fry on "Significant Form" and the terrible-tempered Albert Barnes on *The Art in Painting*. I found nothing in the Metropolitan seminar that was not this doctrine somewhat updated, and I was no more convinced than I had been by the earlier critics that what they were talking about was indeed the only thing in painting worth talking about, or that significant form by itself (if that is possible) was as good as, if not better than, classical paintings in which equally significant form had been imposed upon subject matters themselves interesting or moving in one way or another. In that problem lies the real crux of the matter. Granted that "composition," "significant form," or whatever you want to call it is a *sine qua non* of great painting, is it also the one thing necessary? Is it *the* art in

2. " * * * Why, what a most particularly deep young man that deep young man must be." So the aesthete Bunthorne sings admiringly of himself in Gilbert and Sullivan's *Patience*.

painting or only *an* art in painting? My mentors from the Metropolitan are by no means fanatical. They never themselves insist that subject matter, or the communication of an emotion in connection with it, is irrelevant in judging a picture. But unless my memory fails me, they never really face the question of the extent to which the painter who abandons the suggestion of a subject matter is to that extent lesser than one who at the same time tells a story, reveals a character, or communicates an attitude.

The hopeful student is confronted at the very beginning with what seems to me this unanswered question. He is warned that "Whistler's Mother" was called by the artist "Arrangement in Grey and Black"—and let that be a lesson to you. You may think that your enjoyment of the picture derives from its "appealing likeness of the author's mother and from sentimental associations with old age," but "the *real* [italics in the original] subject is something else . . . We may ask whether the picture would be just as effective if we omitted the subject altogether . . . the abstract school of contemporary painting argues that subject matter is only something that gets in the way. It confuses the issue—the issue being pure expression by means of color, texture, line, and shape existing in their own right and representing nothing at all."

Throughout the course, stress is laid again and again on the comparison between two seemingly very different pictures said to be similar, although I don't think they are ever said to be identical. For instance, Vermeer's "The Artist and His Studio" is compared with Picasso's "The Studio." "Picasso," I am told, "had sacrificed . . . the interest inherent in the objects comprising the picture . . . the fascination and variety of natural textures . . . the harmonies of flowing light, the satisfaction of building solid forms out of light and shape. What has he gained? . . . Complete freedom to manipulate the forms of his picture . . . The abstractionist would argue that the enjoyment of a picture like Picasso's 'The Studio' is more intense because it is purer than the enjoyment we take in Vermeer."

Is "purer" the right adjective? Is it purer or merely thinner? To me the answer is quite plain and the same as that given to the proponents of pure poetry who argued that poetry is essentially only sound so that the most beautiful single line in French literature is Racine's "*La fille de Minos et de Pasiphaé*," not because the genealogy of Phèdre was interesting but just because the sound of the words is delightful. The sound of "O frabjous day! Callooh! Callay!" is also delightful but I don't think it as good as, for instance, "No spring, nor summer beauty hath such grace,/ As I have seen in one autumnal face."

It is all very well to say that two pictures as different as those by

Vermeer and Picasso are somewhat similar in composition and that to this extent they produce a somewhat similar effect. But to say that the total experience of the two is not vastly different is, so it seems to me, pure nonsense and so is the statement that the two experiences are equally rich.

The author of the seminar session just quoted seems himself to think so when he writes: "But we also contend that a painting is a projection of the personality of the man who painted it, and a statement of the philosophy of the age that produced it."

If that is true, then the painter who claims to be "painting nothing but paint" is either a very deficient painter or is, perhaps without knowing it, projecting his personality and making a statement of a philosophy of the age that produced it. He is doing that just as truly and just as inevitably as Whistler was doing more than an arrangement in black and grey. And if that also is true, then the way to understand what is most meaningful and significant in any modern painting is to ask what it is that the painter, consciously or not, is revealing about his personality and about the age that finds his philosophy and his personality congenial.

At least that much seems often to be admitted by admiring critics of certain painters not fully abstract but who seem to be interested primarily in pure form. Take, for instance, the case of Ferdinand Léger and his reduction of the whole visible world, including human beings, to what looks like mechanical drawings. Are they examples of pure form meaning nothing but themselves? Certainly they are not always so considered by admirers. When the painter died in 1955 the distinguished critic André Chastel wrote:

From 1910 on, his views of cities with smoke-like zinc, his country scenes inspired as if by a woodchopper, his still lifes made as if of metal, clearly showed what always remained his inspiration: the maximum hardening of a world of objects, which he made firmer and more articulate than they are in reality. Sacrifice of color and nuance was total and line was defined with severity and a well-meaning aggressiveness, projecting his violent, cold Norman temperament. This revolution he consecrated himself to seemed rather simple—the exaltation of the machine age, which after 1920 dominated the western world.

To me it seems equally plain that even those who profess to paint nothing but paint are in fact doing a great deal more because they would not find anything of the sort to be the real aim of painting unless they had certain attitudes toward nature, toward society, and toward man. What that attitude is cannot, I think, be very well defined without recourse to two words that I hate to use because they have become so fashionable and are so loosely tossed about. What these painters are expressing is the alienation of the existentialist. They no longer represent anything in the external world because they no longer believe that the world that exists outside of man in any way shares or supports human aspirations and values or has any meaning for him. They are determined, like the existential moralist, to go it alone. They do not believe that in nature there is anything inherently beautiful, just as the existentialist moralizer refuses to believe that there is any suggestion of moral values in the external universe. The great literature and painting of the past have almost invariably been founded upon assumptions the exact opposite of these. They expressed man's attempt to find beauty and meaning in an external world from which he was not alienated because he believed that both his aesthetic and his moral sense corresponded to something outside himself.

Salvador Dali (whom, in general, I do not greatly admire) once made the remark that Picasso's greatness consisted in the fact that he had destroyed one by one all the historical styles of painting. I am not sure that there is not something in that remark, and if there is, then it suggests that in many important respects Picasso is much like the workers in several branches of literature whose aim is to destroy the novel with the antinovel, the theater with the antitheater, and philosophy by philosophies that consist, like logical positivism and linguistic analysis, in a refusal to philosophize. They are all determined, as the surrealist André Breton once said he was, to "wring the neck of literature."

Having now convinced myself of all these things, I will crawl farther out on a limb and confess that I have often wondered if the new styles created by modern painters—pointillism, cubism, surrealism, and the mechanism of Léger (to say nothing of op and pop)—ought not be regarded as gimmicks rather than actual styles. And to my own great astonishment I have discovered that Picasso himself believes, or did once believe, exactly that.

The luxurious French monthly *Jardin des Arts* published (March 1964) a long and laudatory article on Picasso in the course of which it cited "a text of Picasso on himself" which had been reproduced at various times but most recently in a periodical called *Le Spectacle du Monde* (November 1962). I translate as follows:

When I was young I was possessed by the religion of great art. But, as the years passed, I realized that art as one conceived it up to the end of the 1880's was, from then on, dying, condemned, and finished and that the pretended artistic activity of today, despite all its superabundance, was nothing but a manifestation of its agony... Despite appearances our contemporaries have given their heart to the machine, to scientific discovery, to wealth, to the control of natural forces, and of the world ... From that moment when art became no longer the food of the superior, the artist was able to exteriorize his talent in various sorts of experiments, in new formulae, in all kinds of caprices and fantasies, and in all the varieties of intellectual charlatanism...

As for me, from cubism on I have satisfied these gentlemen [rich people who are looking for something extravagant] and the critics also with all the many bizarre notions which have come into my head and the less they understood the more they admired them . . . Today, as you know, I am famous and rich. But when I am alone with my soul, I haven't the courage to consider myself as an artist. In the great and ancient sense of that word, Greco, Titian, Rembrandt, and Goya were great painters. I am only the entertainer of a public which understands its age.

Chirico is another modern painter who has said something very much like this. But enough of quotations. And to me it seems that Picasso said all that I have been trying to say, namely, that a picture somehow involved with the world of reality outside man is more valuable than one that has nothing to say about anything except the painter himself. What he calls painters "in the great and ancient sense of that word" were able to be such only because they were not alienated existentialists.

QUESTIONS

1. Indicate particular details that show what Krutch suggests to be the proper business of an essayist.
2. What is this essay's thesis? What assumptions underlie the thesis?
3. What relationship does Krutch see between modern painting and "the philosophy of the age"? How does he attempt to demonstrate, or illustrate, that relationship? Is this view persuasive? Why, or why not?
4. Does Krutch assume that his audience is disposed at the outset to think of modern painting very much as he does, or very differently? to think as he does in some particulars, and not in others? Show, by specific details of his manner, what attitudes he seems to expect, what responses he anticipates.
5. Why does Krutch quote (p. 459) a passage he has read about a certain painter? What can be learned from the quotation? Would it help to know the identity of the painter? Why doesn't Krutch name him?
6. What effect does Krutch achieve by referring twice, in two separate connections, to Picasso?

ADA LOUISE HUXTABLE

Pop Architecture

There has been a lot of pseudo-profound theorizing about the democratization of the arts in our time, but the only art in which the process has actually taken place is architecture. What has happened in painting and sculpture is, more properly, popularization. The product itself still follows the standards of a small group that might be called the creative elite, although it is merchandised to the masses.

The public, in the case of these arts, is merely the consumer, and it is presently consuming at a record rate; but it sets no standards for what is produced. And if it chooses to consume the products of, say, a Washington Square outdoor show, this work, in turn, has little effect on "art." The real thing continues to be produced by a cultural and creative aristocracy, if aristocracy is defined as that portion of the trend-setting minority that operates on accepted traditions of knowledge, talent and taste. Today it is called the Establishment and it is no longer the traditional social aristocracy. Nor are its standards like the traditional standards. They are often a deliberate reversal of those standards, but their criterion is basically the same: acceptability by the taste-making elite.

The situation used to be particularly true in architecture, where the style and standards of past periods have been established consistently by the creative elite. Today, however, the situation is virtually reversed.

Except for a pathetically small showing, the cultural aristocracy is no longer responsible for most building styles. It is barely holding its own, with those isolated examples that represent structural and design excellence, against the tide, or better, flood, or what we propose to call Pop Architecture.

Pop Architecture is the true democratization of the art of architecture in that it represents not just mass consumption but mass taste.

Its standards are set not by those with an informed and knowledgeable judgment, but by those with little knowledge or judgment at all. It is the indisputable creation of the lower rather than of the upper classes. As such, it is a significant first: probably the only architectural style in history to be formed at the bottom rather than at the top.

Even more significantly, it consists of the vast, inescapable, depressingly omnipresent and all-too-typical bulk of American building. This includes the greatest part of today's construction and capital investment.

In Pop Architecture the timeless determinants of comparative knowledge and trained evaluation have been supplanted by the typical parvenu love of the novel, the flashy and the bizarre.

The characteristics of Pop Architecture are gaudy misuses of structural effects for aggressive and often meaningless eccentricities of form, the garish misapplication of color and material for jazzed-up facades of fluorescent brilliance and busy metal and enamel panel patterns unrelated to underlying structure, with glittering grilles and appendages that conceal the most pedestrian plans.

It is, of course, Miami with its uninhibited monuments to lavish pretentious ignorance like the prototypal Fontainebleau. It is every Miracle Mile in suburbia, offering every new effect in the architect's sample book and a frankly phony, but eye-catching version of every new structural technique. It is dazzling glamor to the optically naive; consummate vulgarity to the conventionally visually educated; and a new kick to the avant-garde, which discerns—often correctly—some underlying basics of contemporary function and life-style in the drive-in and the architecture of the road. Some of the architectural facts of contemporary life undoubtedly deserve critical analysis, since they serve modern society legitimately and are equally obviously not going to be wished away. Dismissal is too simplistic an attitude.

However, like Pop Art, Pop Architecture shows mass taste at its most cruelly self-revealing. Unlike Pop Art, it is the real thing rather than a sophisticated, detached commentary. Pop Art is the ironical statement of those who know, being outrageous. Pop Architecture is the straight-faced product of those who don't know, just being themselves.

Pop Architecture may be derided, but it cannot be dismissed. While the Washington Square canvases and all of their kind may not make a ripple on art's surface, the hotels, motels, stores, shopping centers, bowling alleys, restaurants, office buildings and commercial complexes of Pop Architecture and those churches, community centers, speculative buildings and civic and other structures that ape their style stack up as the country's major building effort in quantity, size and expense.

This is architectural reality, and an esthetic and historical phenomenon not to be dismissed just as "bad design." It is frequently atrocious design, of course, but it is obviously here to stay in appalling amounts unless its characteristic look of transient tinniness indicates a fortuitous built-in obsolescence. It is determining the face of America and it is, inescapably, our architecture, whether we like it or not.

And whether we like it or not, it will have its place in history as well, as an awesome demonstration of the first truly democratic style and popular art on a scale that the twentieth century only promised until now, but has finally delivered. It may go down in the record with bad generals, decadent states and corrupt societies when submitted to the cool, objective scrutiny of future scholars or it may be taken as a serious departure point to a new kind of world.

But it is pointed, legitimate commentary on our current cultural condition and the general level of architectural practice, even among qualified professionals. And where Pop Art shocks the laymen, Pop Architecture does not—perhaps the most terrifying comment of all.

The plans and proposals bursting into print today vie with each other for size, novelty and status. Architecture has never been more important; it is the stuff with which our cities are being built and rebuilt for unprecedented sums on an unprecedented scale. What is being built represents the culmination of a twentieth-century revolution in structure and design based on profound philosophical considerations and technical miracles that should have produced, by any reasoning, one of the greatest periods in the history of the building art.

But a look around shows a distorted dream, a travesty of purpose, an abandonment of principles, a jazzy slide down the primrose path of fads, publicity, structural sensationalism, muzzy romanticism and dubious art for art's sake that has led to a vicious decline in architectural values and a corruption of architectural purpose. It has also led to some of the worst and most offensive building ever produced.

A serious indictment? It is long overdue. The evidence is inescapable. A Stamford, Conn., office center is an architectural fun fair of corporate flying saucers and ramped, battlemented research centers. A Manhattan branch bank in early Howard Johnson pseudo-Georgian style offers a classic cupola, computers and infrared comfort for outdoor customers at eighteenth-century-type deposit windows, and, we assume, twentieth-century money. The banklet is in a landscaped parklet.

The buildings would be funny, if they were not typical and tragic indications of the depth to which the great revolution has sunk. These examples represent two extremes of the current malaise.

The first, the Stamford headquarters for the General Time Corporation and a laboratory for the Columbia Broadcasting System (oh, shades of Eero Saarinen!), might be called the space-age-fly-with-the-future trend. The second, Franklin National's "bank in the park" for a corner lot at Broadway and Howard Street, is the stop the-world-I-want-to-get-off school, or time-turn-backward-in-your-flight-with-all-modern-conveniences.

Given the choice between hot modern and cold Colonial, one hardly blames Franklin National for settling for ersatz nostalgia. At least Franklin has the dubious distinction of pursuing ersatz all-out.

Billing itself as "the country bank in New York" since it started on Long Island, bucolic-paradise of subdivisions, Franklin settled on the country Colonial image executed by the firm of Eggers and Higgins, even when it meant disguising a nine-story steel-frame structure as an inflated five-story Georgian mansion on Madison Avenue. Its officers are far from farmers. They have also devised "La Banque," the Franklin National branch at Fifth Avenue and 60th Street. This is solid Louis Seize for a clientele of non-rural sophisticates with a mandatory balance of $25,000, in dollars, not francs.

The Pop Architecture at Stamford causes distress of a different kind. The architect, Victor Bisharat, describes the battered, striated walls of the CBS laboratory as "symbolizing the upsurge of the creative force in research, reaching for the sky with questing fingers." The effect seems more like sticky fingers reaching for Wright and Saarinen.

This kind of architectural whizz-bang was originally restricted to the spangled sunglasses set. It is now for businessmen, corporation presidents and community cultural leaders. The trend-setting corporate clients of the 1950's established a selective standard that has had a hard time surviving the building boom and the cultural bandwagon. There is a bank like a split orange in Casper, Wyoming. There is a Kaiser Aluminum plant in Portsmouth, R.I., wearing a flashy gift wrap that promises to open if you lift up the box top and tear off the decorative vertical strip.

The trend ranges from irrationality, or novelty for its own sake, to dishonesty, or the complete vulgarization of art. It is followed by architects of large and small reputation, with more or less overtly awful results.

The sad fact is that public and patrons will accept anything quicker than rational simplicity, or the logical and sensitive solution to a problem. They are sick to death of plain, cheap, badly constructed speculative building, and their non-professional eyes are not always adept at distinguishing between simple statements of quality and simple junk.

The popular reaction is still largely *horror vacui*.[1] Fill it up, busy it up, distort it, disguise it, make it look arty or different, but don't make it a logical, artistic expression of conscientiously considered structure, function and form. It wouldn't get published if you did.

There is no justification for this brand of self-seeking architectural exhibitionism. And yet the architect is asking for a larger share of the responsibility for designing the environment, at the same time that he faults and flouts it by demonstrating a lack of responsibility in his own work.

In Europe architecture is still primarily a social art, its highest and best expression frequently sublimated with sensitivity to larger human and environmental needs. In the United States there is no environment, in spite of all the talk about it. There are buildings that strut and fight and turn their backs on each other and the city —advertisements for architects and for an art in serious trouble.

HENRI BERGSON

The Comic in General; the Comic Element in Forms and Movements[2]

What does laughter mean? What is the basal element in the laughable? What common ground can we find between the grimace of a merry-andrew,[3] a play upon words, an equivocal situation in a

1. Abhorrence of a vacuum.
2. From the opening section of Bergson's essay "Laughter."
3. A clown.

burlesque and a scene of high comedy? What method of distillation will yield us invariably the same essence from which so many different products borrow either their obtrusive odor or their delicate perfume? The greatest of thinkers, from Aristotle downwards, have tackled this little problem, which has a knack of baffling every effort, of slipping away and escaping only to bob up again, a pert challenge flung at philosophic speculation.

Our excuse for attacking the problem in our turn must lie in the fact that we shall not aim at imprisoning the comic spirit within a definition. We regard it, above all, as a living thing. However trivial it may be, we shall treat it with the respect due to life. We shall confine ourselves to watching it grow and expand. Passing by imperceptible gradations from one form to another, it will be seen to achieve the strangest metamorphoses. We shall disdain nothing we have seen. Maybe we may gain from this prolonged contact, for the matter of that, something more flexible than an abstract definition—a practical, intimate acquaintance, such as springs from a long companionship. And maybe we may also find that, unintentionally, we have made an acquaintance that is useful. For the comic spirit has a logic of its own, even in its wildest eccentricities. It has a method in its madness. It dreams, I admit, but it conjures up in its dreams visions that are at once accepted and understood by the whole of a social group. Can it then fail to throw light for us on the way that human imagination works, and more particularly social, collective, and popular imagination? Begotten of real life and akin to art, should it not also have something of its own to tell us about art and life?

At the outset we shall put forward three observations which we look upon as fundamental. They have less bearing on the actually comic than on the field within which it must be sought.

I

The first point to which attention should be called is that the comic does not exist outside the pale of what is strictly *human*. A landscape may be beautiful, charming and sublime, or insignificant and ugly; it will never be laughable. You may laugh at an animal, but only because you have detected in it some human attitude or expression. You may laugh at a hat, but what you are making fun of, in this case, is not the piece of felt or straw, but the shape that men have given it—the human caprice whose mold it has assumed. It is strange that so important a fact, and such a simple one too, has not attracted to a greater degree the attention of philosophers. Several have defined man as "an animal which laughs." They might equally well have defined him as an animal which is laughed at; for if any other animal, or some lifeless object, produces the same effect, it is always because of some resemblance to man, of the stamp he gives it or the use he puts it to.

Here I would point out, as a symptom equally worthy of notice, the *absence of feeling* which usually accompanies laughter. It seems as though the comic could not produce its disturbing effect unless it fell, so to say, on the surface of a soul that is thoroughly calm and unruffled. Indifference is its natural environment, for laughter has no greater foe than emotion. I do not mean that we could not laugh at a person who inspires us with pity, for instance, or even with affection, but in such a case we must, for the moment, put our affection out of court and impose silence upon our pity. In a society composed of pure intelligences there would probably be no more tears, though perhaps there would still be laughter; whereas highly emotional souls, in tune and unison with life, in whom every event would be sentimentally prolonged and re-echoed, would neither know nor understand laughter. Try, for a moment, to become interested in everything that is being said and done; act, in imagination, with those who act, and feel with those who feel; in a word, give your sympathy its widest expansion: as though at the touch of a fairy wand you will see the flimsiest of objects assume importance, and a gloomy hue spread over everything. Now step aside, look upon life as a disinterested spectator: many a drama will turn into a comedy. It is enough for us to stop our ears to the sound of music in a room, where dancing is going on, for the dancers at once to appear ridiculous. How many human actions would stand a similar test? Should we not see many of them suddenly pass from grave to gay, on isolating them from the accompanying music of sentiment? To produce the whole of its effect, then, the comic demands something like a momentary anesthesia of the heart. Its appeal is to intelligence, pure and simple.

This intelligence, however, must always remain in touch with other intelligences. And here is the third fact to which attention should be drawn. You would hardly appreciate the comic if you felt yourself isolated from others. Laughter appears to stand in need of an echo. Listen to it carefully: it is not an articulate, clear, well-defined sound; it is something which would fain be prolonged by reverberating from one to another, something beginning with a crash, to continue in successive rumblings, like thunder in a mountain. Still, this reverberation cannot go on for ever. It can travel within as wide a circle as you please: the circle remains, none the less, a closed one. Our laughter is always the laughter of a group. It may, perchance, have happened to you, when seated in a railway carriage or at *table d'hôte*, to hear travelers relating to one another stories which must have been comic to them, for they laughed heartily. Had you been one of their company, you would have laughed like them, but, as you were not, you had no desire whatever to do so. A man who was once asked why he did not weep at a sermon when everybody else was shedding tears replied:

"I don't belong to the parish!" What that man thought of tears would be still more true of laughter. However spontaneous it seems, laughter always implies a kind of secret freemasonry, or even complicity, with other laughers, real or imaginary. How often has it been said that the fuller the theatre, the more uncontrolled the laughter of the audience! On the other hand, how often has the remark been made that many comic effects are incapable of translation from one language to another, because they refer to the customs and ideas of a particular social group! It is through not understanding the importance of this double fact that the comic has been looked upon as a mere curiosity in which the mind finds amusement, and laughter itself as a strange, isolated phenomenon, without any bearing on the rest of human activity. Hence those definitions which tend to make the comic into an abstract relation between ideas: "an intellectual contrast," "a patent absurdity," etc., definitions which, even were they really suitable to every form of the comic, would not in the least explain why the comic makes us laugh. How, indeed, should it come about that this particular logical relation, as soon as it is perceived, contracts, expands and shakes our limbs, whilst all other relations leave the body unaffected? It is not from this point of view that we shall approach the problem. To understand laughter, we must put it back into its natural environment, which is society, and above all must we determine the utility of its functions, which is a social one. Such, let us say at once, will be the leading idea of all our investigations. Laughter must answer to certain requirements of life in common. It must have a *social* signification.

Let us clearly mark the point towards which our three preliminary observations are converging. The comic will come into being, it appears, whenever a group of men concentrate their attention on one of their number, imposing silence on their emotions and calling into play nothing but their intelligence. What, now, is the particular point on which their attention will have to be concentrated, and what will here be the function of intelligence? To reply to these questions will be at once to come to closer grips with the problem. But here a few examples have become indispensable.

II

A man, running along the street, stumbles and falls; the passersby burst out laughing. They would not laugh at him, I imagine, could they suppose that the whim had suddenly seized him to sit down on the ground. They laugh because his sitting down is involuntary. Consequently, it is not his sudden change of attitude that raises a laugh, but rather the involuntary element in this change— his clumsiness, in fact. Perhaps there was a stone on the road. He should have altered his pace or avoided the obstacle. Instead of that, through lack of elasticity, through absentmindedness and a kind of physical obstinacy, *as a result, in fact, of rigidity or of momentum*, the muscles continued to perform the same movement when the circumstances of the case called for something else. That is the reason of the man's fall, and also of the people's laughter.

Now, take the case of a person who attends to the petty occupations of his everyday life with mathematical precision. The objects around him, however, have all been tampered with by a mischievous wag, the result being that when he dips his pen into the inkstand he draws it out all covered with mud, when he fancies he is sitting down on a solid chair he finds himself sprawling on the floor, in a word his actions are all topsy-turvy or mere beating the air, while in every case the effect is invariably one of momentum. Habit has given the impulse: what was wanted was to check the movement or deflect it. He did nothing of the sort, but continued like a machine in the same straight line. The victim, then, of a practical joke is in a position similar to that of a runner who falls—he is comic for the same reason. The laughable element in both cases consists of a certain *mechanical inelasticity*, just where one would expect to find the wideawake adaptability and the living pliableness of a human being. The only difference in the two cases is that the former happened of itself, whilst the latter was obtained artificially. In the first instance, the passer-by does nothing but look on, but in the second the mischievous wag intervenes.

All the same, in both cases the result has been brought about by an external circumstance. The comic is therefore accidental: it remains, so to speak, in superficial contact with the person. How is it to penetrate within? The necessary conditions will be fulfilled when mechanical rigidity no longer requires for its manifestation a stumbling-block which either the hazard of circumstance or human knavery has set in its way, but extracts by natural processes, from its own store, an inexhaustible series of opportunities for externally revealing its presence. Suppose, then, we imagine a mind always thinking of what it has just done and never of what it is doing, like a song which lags behind its accompaniment. Let us try to picture to ourselves a certain inborn lack of elasticity of both senses and intelligence, which brings it to pass that we continue to see what is no longer visible, to hear what is no longer audible, to say what is no longer to the point: in short, to adapt ourselves to a past and therefore imaginary situation, when we ought to be shaping our conduct in accordance with the reality which is present. This time the comic will take up its abode in the person himself; it is the person who will supply it with everything—matter and form, cause and opportunity. Is it then surprising that the absent-minded individual—for this is the character we have just been describing—has usually fired the imagination of comic authors? When

La Bruyere[4] came across this particular type, he realized, on analyzing it, that he had got hold of a recipe for the wholesale manufacture of comic effects. As a matter of fact he overdid it, and gave
us far too lengthy and detailed a description of *Ménalque*, coming
back to his subject, dwelling and expatiating on it beyond all bounds.
The very facility of the subject fascinated him. Absentmindedness,
indeed, is not perhaps the actual fountain-head of the comic, but
surely it is contiguous to a certain stream of facts and fancies which
flows straight from the fountain-head. It is situated, so to say, on
one of the great natural watersheds of laughter.

Now, the effect of absentmindedness may gather strength in its
turn. There is a general law, the first example of which we have
just encountered, and which we will formulate in the following
terms: when a certain comic effect has its origin in a certain cause,
the more natural we regard the cause to be, the more comic shall
we find the effect. Even now we laugh at absentmindedness when
presented to us as a simple fact. Still more laughable will be the
absentmindedness we have seen springing up and growing before
our very eyes, with whose origin we are acquainted and whose life-
history we can reconstruct. To choose a definite example: suppose
a man has taken to reading nothing but romances of love and
chivalry. Attracted and fascinated by his heroes, his thoughts and
intentions gradually turn more and more towards them, till one
fine day we find him walking among us like a somnambulist. His
actions are distractions. But then his distractions can be traced back
to a definite, positive cause. They are no longer cases of *absence* of
mind, pure and simple; they find their explanation in the *presence*
of the individual in quite definite, though imaginary, surroundings.
Doubtless a fall is always a fall, but it is one thing to tumble into
a well because you were looking anywhere but in front of you, it
is quite another thing to fall into it because you were intent upon
a star. It was certainly a star at which Don Quixote was gazing.
How profound is the comic element in the over-romantic, Utopian
bent of mind! And yet, if you reintroduce the idea of absentmindedness, which acts as a go-between, you will see this profound comic
element uniting with the most superficial type. Yes, indeed, these
whimsical wild enthusiasts, these madmen who are yet so strangely
reasonable, excite us to laugher by playing on the same chords
within ourselves, by setting in motion the same inner mechanism,
as does the victim of a practical joke or the passer-by who slips
down in the street. They, too, are runners who fall and simple souls
who are being hoaxed—runners after the ideal who stumble over
realities, child-like dreamers for whom life delights to lie in wait.

4. Seventeenth-century French moralist, a writer of "characters"; his *Ménalque*
describes the absent-minded man.

But, above all, they are past-masters in absentmindedness, with this superiority over their fellows that their absentmindedness is systematic and organized around one central idea, and that their mishaps are also quite coherent, thanks to the inexorable logic which reality applies to the correction of dreams, so that they kindle in those around them, by a series of cumulative effects, a hilarity capable of unlimited expansion.

Now, let us go a little further. Might not certain vices have the same relation to character that the rigidity of a fixed idea has to intellect? Whether as a moral kink or a crooked twist given to the will, vice has often the appearance of a curvature of the soul. Doubtless there are vices into which the soul plunges deeply with all its pregnant potency, which it rejuvenates and drags along with it into a moving circle of reincarnations. Those are tragic vices. But the vice capable of making us comic is, on the contrary, that which is brought from without, like a ready-made frame into which we are to step. It lends us its own rigidity instead of borrowing from us our flexibility. We do not render it more complicated; on the contrary, it simplifies us. Here, as we shall see later on in the concluding section of this study, lies the essential difference between comedy and drama. A drama, even when portraying passions or vices that bear a name, so completely incorporates them in the person that their names are forgotten, their general characteristics effaced, and we no longer think of them at all, but rather of the person in whom they are assimilated; hence, the title of a drama can seldom be anything else than a proper noun. On the other hand, many comedies have a common noun as their title: *l'Avare, le Joueur*, etc. Were you asked to think of a play capable of being called *le Jaloux*, for instance, you would find that *Sganarelle* or *George Dandin* would occur to your mind, but not *Othello: le Jaloux* could only be the title of a comedy.[5] The reason is that, however intimately vice, when comic, is associated with persons, it none the less retains its simple, independent existence, it remains the central character, present though invisible, to which the characters in flesh and blood on the stage are attached. At times it delights in dragging them down with its own weight and making them share in its tumbles. More frequently, however, it plays on them as on an instrument or pulls the strings as though they were puppets. Look closely: you will find that the art of the comic poet consists in making us so well acquainted with the particular vice, in introducing us, the spectators, to such a degree of intimacy with it, that in the end we get hold of some of the strings of the marionette

5. *L'Avare (The Miser)* is a play by Molière, and *le Joueur (The Gamester)* was the work of his successor, Jean-Francois Regnard. Molière's *Sganarelle* and *George Dandin* have jealous husbands as their chief comic figures, so that *le Jaloux (The Jealous Man)* would be a suitable title for either play.

with which he is playing, and actually work them ourselves; this it is that explains part of the pleasure we feel. Here, too, it is really a kind of automatism that makes us laugh—an automatism, as we have already remarked, closely akin to mere absentmindedness. To realize this more fully, it need only be noted that a comic character is generally comic in proportion to his ignorance of himself. The comic person is unconscious. As though wearing the ring of Gyges with reverse effect, he becomes invisible to himself while remaining visible to all the world. A character in a tragedy will make no change in his conduct because he will know how it is judged by us; he may continue therein even though fully conscious of what he is and feeling keenly the horror he inspires in us. But a defect that is ridiculous, as soon as it feels itself to be so, endeavors to modify itself or at least to appear as though it did. Were Harpagon[6] to see us laugh at his miserliness, I do not say that he would get rid of it, but he would either show it less or show it differently. Indeed, it is in this sense only that laughter "corrects men's manners." It makes us at once endeavor to appear what we ought to be, what some day we shall perhaps end in being.

It is unnecessary to carry this analysis any further. From the runner who falls to the simpleton who is hoaxed, from a state of being hoaxed to one of absentmindedness, from absentmindedness to wild enthusiasm, from wild enthusiasm to various distortions of character and will, we have followed the line of progress along which the comic becomes more and more deeply imbedded in the person, yet without ceasing, in its subtler manifestations, to recall to us some trace of what we noticed in its grosser forms, an effect of automatism and of inelasticity. Now we can obtain a first glimpse —a distant one, it is true, and still hazy and confused—of the laughable side of human nature and of the ordinary function of laughter.

What life and society require of each of us is a constantly alert attention that discerns the outlines of the present situation, together with a certain elasticity of mind and body to enable us to adapt ourselves in consequence. *Tension* and *elasticity* are two forces, mutually complementary, which life brings into play. If these two forces are lacking in the body to any considerable extent, we have sickness and infirmity and accidents of every kind. If they are lacking in the mind, we find every degree of mental deficiency, every variety of insanity. Finally, if they are lacking in the character, we have cases of the gravest inadaptability to social life, which are the sources of misery and at times the causes of crime. Once these elements of inferiority that affect the serious side of existence are removed—and they tend to eliminate themselves in what has

6. The miser of Molière's *l'Avare.*

been called the struggle for life—the person can live, and that in common with other persons. But society asks for something more; it is not satisfied with simply living, it insists on living well. What it now has to dread is that each one of us, content with paying attention to what affects the essentials of life, will, so far as the rest is concerned, give way to the easy automatism of acquired habits. Another thing it must fear is that the members of whom it is made up, instead of aiming after an increasingly delicate adjustment of wills which will fit more and more perfectly into one another, will confine themselves to respecting simply the fundamental conditions of this adjustment: a cut-and-dried agreement among the persons will not satisfy it, it insists on a constant striving after reciprocal adaptation. Society will therefore be suspicious of all *inelasticity* of character, of mind and even of body, because it is the possible sign of a slumbering activity as well as of an activity with separatist tendencies, that inclines to swerve from the common center round which society gravitates: in short, because it is the sign of an eccentricity. And yet, society cannot intervene at this stage by material repression, since it is not affected in a material fashion. It is confronted with something that makes it uneasy, but only as a symptom—scarcely a threat, at the very most a gesture. A gesture, therefore, will be its reply. Laughter must be something of this kind, a sort of *social gesture*. By the fear which it inspires, it restrains eccentricity, keeps constantly awake and in mutual contact certain activities of a secondary order which might retire into their shell and go to sleep, and in short, softens down whatever the surface of the social body may retain of mechanical inelasticity. Laughter, then, does not belong to the province of esthetics alone, since unconsciously (and even immorally in many particular instances) it pursues a utilitarian aim of general improvement. And yet there is something esthetic about it, since the comic comes into being just when society and the individual, freed from the worry of self-preservation, begin to regard themselves as works of art. In a word, if a circle be drawn round those actions and dispositions—implied in individual or social life—to which their natural consequences bring their own penalties, there remains outside this sphere of emotion and struggle—and within a neutral zone in which man simply exposes himself to man's curiosity—a certain rigidity of body, mind and character that society would still like to get rid of in order to obtain from its members the greatest possible degree of elasticity and sociability. This rigidity is the comic, and laughter is its corrective.

Still, we must not accept this formula as a definition of the comic. It is suitable only for cases that are elementary, theoretical and perfect, in which the comic is free from all adulteration. Nor do we offer it, either, as an explanation. We prefer to make it, if you will, the *leitmotiv* which is to accompany all our explanations. We must ever keep it in mind, though without dwelling on it too much, somewhat as a skilful fencer must think of the discontinuous movements of the lesson whilst his body is given up to the continuity of the fencing-match. We will now endeavor to reconstruct the sequence of comic forms, taking up again the thread that leads from the horseplay of a clown up to the most refined effects of comedy, following this thread in its often unforeseen windings, halting at intervals to look around, and finally getting back, if possible, to the point at which the thread is dangling and where we shall perhaps find—since the comic oscillates between life and art —the general relation that art bears to life.

QUESTIONS

1. What three conditions does Bergson say are necessary to the appearance of comic effect? Does Bergson contradict himself when he says that the appeal of the comic "is to intelligence, pure and simple" but that a definition of the comic as "an abstract relation between ideas" is inadequate? Explain his point.
2. According to what principle does Bergson arrange his examples of the comic in section II of the essay? How are the examples differentiated, and what are they said to have in common?
3. What relationships exist between sections I and II of the essay?
4. What, according to Bergson, is the social function of laughter?
5. Bergson refers to Don Quixote as exemplary of comic romantic idealism. But few readers consider the Don solely comic. Why not? What considerations might inhibit, or replace, laughter as romantic idealism?
6. Does Bergson's analysis explain the comic effect of animated movie cartoons, often violent and preposterous? How? What qualities of film comedy in general does Bergson's discussion illuminate?

CHRISTOPHER FRY

Laughter

A friend once told me that when he was under the influence of ether, he dreamed he was turning over the pages of a great book, in which he knew he would find, on the last page, the meaning of life. The pages of the book were alternately tragic and comic, and he turned page after page, his excitement growing, not only because he was approaching the answer but because he couldn't know, until he arrived, on which side of the book the final page would be. At last it came: the universe opened up to him in a hundred words: and they were uproariously funny. He came back to consciousness crying with laughter, remembering everything. He opened his lips to speak. It was then that the great and comic answer plunged back out of his reach.

If I had to draw a picture of the person of Comedy, it is so I should like to draw it: the tears of laughter running down the face, one hand still lying on the tragic page which so nearly contained the answer, the lips about to frame the great revelation, only to find it had gone as disconcertingly as a chair twitched away when we want to sit down. Comedy is an escape, not from truth but from despair: a narrow escape into faith. It believes in a universal cause for delight, even though knowledge of the cause is always twitched away from under us, which leaves us to rest on our own buoyancy. In tragedy every moment is eternity; in comedy eternity is a moment. In tragedy we suffer pain; in comedy pain is a fool, suffered gladly.

Charles Williams once said to me, indeed it was the last thing he said to me (he died not long after), and it was shouted from the tailboard of a moving bus, over the heads of pedestrians and bicyclists outside the Midland Station, Oxford: "When we're dead we shall have the sensation of having enjoyed life altogether, whatever has happened to us." The distance between us widened, and he leaned out into the space so that his voice should reach me: "Even if we've been murdered, what a pleasure to have been capable of it!"; and, having spoken the words for comedy, away he went like that revelation which almost came out of the ether.

He was not at all saying that everything is for the best in the best of all possible worlds. He was saying—or so it seems to me—that there is an angle of experience where the dark is distilled into light: either here or hereafter, in or out of time: where our tragic fate finds itself with perfect pitch, and goes straight to the key which creation was composed in. And comedy senses and reaches out to this experience. It says, in effect, that, groaning as we may be, we move in the figure of a dance, and, so moving, we trace the outline of the mystery. Laughter did not come by chance, but how or why it came is beyond comprehension, unless we think of it as a kind of perception. The human animal, beginning to feel his spiritual inches, broke in onto an unfamiliar tension of life, where laughter became inevitable. But how? Could he, in his first unlaughing condition, have contrived a comic view of life and then developed the strange rib-shaking response?

Or is it not more likely that when he was able to grasp the tragic nature of time he was of a stature to sense its comic nature also; and, by the experience of tragedy and the intuition of comedy, to make his difficult way? The difference between tragedy and comedy is the difference between experience and intuition. In the experience we strive against every condition of our animal life: against death, against the frustration of ambition, against the instability of human love. In the intuition we trust the arduous eccentricities we're born to, and see the oddness of a creature who has never got acclimatized to being created. Laughter inclines me to know that man is essential spirit; his body, with its functions and accidents and frustrations, is endlessly quaint and remarkable to him; and though comedy accepts our position in time, it barely accepts our posture in space.

The bridge by which we cross from tragedy to comedy and back again is precarious and narrow. We find ourselves in one or the other by the turn of a thought; a turn such as we make when we turn from speaking to listening. I know that when I set about writing a comedy the idea presents itself to me first of all as tragedy. The characters press on to the theme with all their divisions and perplexities heavy about them; they are already entered for the race to doom, and good and evil are an infernal tangle skinning the fingers that try to unravel them. If the characters were not qualified for tragedy there would be no comedy, and to some extent I have to cross the one before I can light on the other. In a century less flayed and quivering we might reach it more directly; but not now, unless every word we write is going to mock us. A bridge has to be crossed, a thought has to be turned. Somehow the characters have to unmortify themselves: to affirm life and assimilate death and persevere in joy. Their hearts must be as determined as the phoenix; what burns must also light and renew: not by a vulnerable optimism but by a hard-won maturity of delight, by the intuition of comedy, an active patience declaring the solvency of good. The Book of Job is the great reservoir of comedy. "But there is a spirit in man. . . . Fair weather cometh out of the north. . . . The blessing of him that was ready to perish came upon me: and I caused the widow's heart to sing for joy."

I have come, you may think, to the verge of saying that comedy is greater than tragedy. On the verge I stand and go no further. Tragedy's experience hammers against the mystery to make a breach which would admit the whole triumphant answer. Intuition has no such potential. But there are times in the state of man when comedy has a special worth, and the present is one of them: a time when the loudest faith has been faith in a trampling materialism, when literature has been thought unrealistic which did not mark and remark our poverty and doom. Joy (of a kind) has been all on the devil's side, and one of the necessities of our time is to redeem it. If not, we are in poor sort to meet the circumstances, the circumstances being the contention of death with life, which is to say evil with good, which is to say desolation with delight. Laughter may only seem to be like an exhalation of air, but out of that air we came; in the beginning we inhaled it; it is a truth, not a fantasy, a truth voluble of good which comedy stoutly maintains.

E. B. WHITE

Some Remarks on Humor[1]

Analysts have had their go at humor, and I have read some of this interpretative literature, but without being greatly instructed. Humor can be dissected, as a frog can, but the thing dies in the process and the innards are discouraging to any but the pure scientific mind.

In a newsreel theatre the other day I saw a picture of a man who had developed the soap bubble to a higher point than it had ever before reached. He had become the ace soap bubble blower of America, had perfected the business of blowing bubbles, refined it, doubled it, squared it, and had even worked himself up into a convenient lather. The effect was not pretty. Some of the bubbles were too big to be beautiful, and the blower was always jumping into them or out of them, or playing some sort of unattractive trick with them. It was, if anything, a rather repulsive sight. Humor is a little like that: it won't stand much blowing up, and it won't stand much poking. It has a certain fragility, an evasiveness, which one had best respect. Essentially, it is a complete mystery. A human frame convulsed with laughter, and the laughter becoming hysterical and uncontrollable, is as far out of balance as one shaken with the hiccoughs or in the throes of a sneezing fit.

One of the things commonly said about humorists is that they are really very sad people—clowns with a breaking heart. There is some truth in it, but it is badly stated. It would be more accurate, I think, to say that there is a deep vein of melancholy running through everyone's life and that the humorist, perhaps more sensible of it than some others, compensates for it actively and positively. Humorists fatten on trouble. They have always made trouble pay. They struggle along with a good will and endure pain cheerfully, knowing how well it will serve them in the sweet by and by. You find them wrestling with foreign languages, fighting folding ironing boards and swollen drainpipes, suffering the terrible discomfort of tight boots (or as Josh Billings wittily called them, "tite" boots). They pour out their sorrows profitably, in a form that is not quite fiction nor quite fact either. Beneath the sparkling surface of these dilemmas flows the strong tide of human woe.

Practically everyone is a manic depressive of sorts, with his up moments and his down moments, and you certainly don't have to be a humorist to taste the sadness of situation and mood. But there is often a rather fine line between laughing and crying, and if a humorous piece of writing brings a person to the point where his emotional responses are untrustworthy and seem likely to break over

---

1. From *The Second Tree from the Corner*, 1954.

into the opposite realm, it is because humor, like poetry, has an extra content. It plays close to the big hot fire which is Truth, and sometimes the reader feels the heat.

QUESTIONS

1. White uses a number of concrete details (dissected frog, soap bubbles and bubble blower, clowns with a breaking heart, fighting folding ironing boards and swollen drain pipes, suffering the terrible discomfort of tight boots, big hot fire which is Truth). Which of these are metaphors or analogies (comparisons with a different kind of thing) and which are concrete examples of general statements? Why does White use so many metaphors or analogies in his definition?
2. Rewrite White's definition in abstract or general language, leaving out the analogies or metaphors and the concrete examples. Then compare the rewritten version with the original. Which is clearer? Which is more interesting to read?
3. Compare White's definition of humor with his definition of democracy (p. 875). Is there a recognizable similarity in language or style? In devices used?
4. Compare White's definition of humor with Fry's definition of laughter. How far do the two definitions agree? Would White agree with Fry's hint that comedy might even be considered greater than tragedy?
5. Bergson says that "laughter has no greater foe than emotion," since its "appeal is to intelligence, pure and simple." White, on the other hand, suggests that laughter "is a complete mystery" and that "there is often a rather fine line between laughing and crying." Does the seeming disagreement between Bergson and White result from the fact their viewpoints are opposed or from the fact they appear to be defining slightly different things?

Signs of the Times

MARK KRAM

Ring of Bright Marbles

The world is in bad shape, brother. The world needs help, brother. Just look to the right or the left, and you know what the Captain is hollering about between the stutters of his Woolworth horn at a Broadway stakeout. Heck, he complains, this was once a prized territory: you could always get a decent piece of cheesecake at any hour and you seldom heard the clank of coin, only the silence of bills falling gently. Well, nothing is the same anymore, even for Salvation Army captains, not to mention summer and children and neighborhood games and the quality of jawbreakers.

For one thing, summers always seemed longer and hotter, the beaches more vacant and children more like children. Kids 10 years old seldom sound their age. They sound like they're 50 and have more opinions than a racetrack tout, like "Tell him, Billy, what you think about nuclear détente." Another thing, where have all the butterflies gone? They are rarely seen in large cities anymore and are vanishing from the suburbs as well. Lepidopterists in England did not see a single black and gold Chequered Skipper in all of 1973. The world is in bad shape, brother.

All of this brings us down to marbles, not the argot for brains but the real thing: perfectly round; so smooth; brilliantly colored; as precious to generations of children as any diamond. Has anyone seen a marble lately? Has anyone seen a marble in the hand of a kid? Most likely the answer is no, for the only things kids carry these days are transistor radios, slices of pizza and tickets to rock concerts. The marble belongs to a time that now seems otherworldly, when trees lined big city blocks as far as the eye could see, when barley soup was supper three times a week, when children had secret places.

True, but not absolutely so. Nothing is absolute in the U.S. of A., not even the decline and fall of marbles. That was evident recently in Wildwood, N.J., hard by the Atlantic Ocean and only a

482

couple of steps removed from being an esthetic blight. Now, Wildwood is not a common name in seaside language, nor will you find it on any object fished out of a penny arcade claw machine, but three things made Wildwood, N.J. a subject of curiosity the other day: it had its first earthquake (a sudden tremor), an event quickly ignored because it would only produce bad publicity; it had the largest assemblage of elderly people (known offensively as Senior Citizens) ever beheld by the human eye; and it was the site of something called the National Marbles Tournament.

Scientists easily explained the quake, saying that something out there in the ocean slipped back into place after ten thousand years. One lovely and aged lady explained the presence of the Citizens. "Nobody else wants us," she said. "Nobody likes to look at or have old people around. We have to stick together." Fine, but nobody could figure out what the National Marbles was doing there, least of all the mayor of Wildwood who—if he does not exactly consider marbles anathema—would prefer that the players take their marbles and go somewhere else to play. The mayor likes conventions, he likes people with funny hats on—the fez kind—rolling up and down his boardwalk, he likes people who buy things.

"You mean to tell me that the mayor of this town doesn't like marbles?" the mayor's public relations man is asked.

"Well, I wouldn't say that," he says.

"Then the mayor is crazy about marbles, is that right?" he is asked again.

"No, I wouldn't say that."

"Well, what would you say?"

"I say we like publicity. We don't get any publicity out of this. We just get a lot of kids shooting marbles."

"The mayor doesn't like marbles?"

"The mayor hates marbles," he finally says, his voice moving into a higher octave.

The conversation seems a splice in the middle of a dream, a hazy film of a dream, the work of Bergman or Antonioni. The day is hot, the light as harsh as that which comes from an Algerian sun, and all around you are motels of bilious green or cheap pink. The verandas are stacked with old women knitting, or just talking over tinny tables, some with artificial flowers in the center. The boardwalk is a block away, and the first thing of note there is a sign saying that the lumber used in the redecking of the walk has been taken from the reviewing stand of Richard Nixon's 1973 inauguration. The mayor, among others, can be thanked.

Go on, and the senses are mugged. Noise blasts out of shops in the form of music of every persuasion, words stream from a hundred pitchmen waving their arms in front of rows of stuffed animals and garish figurines. The smells are those of onions, of hamburgers drowning in grease, of pizza curling at the edges on the counters. Here, in the middle of all this, between two giant amusement parks on piers that stretch out into the sea, is what remains of the lost world of marbles. Below on the beach and just off the board a handful of kids kneel on the edges of raised platforms knocking marbles out of a large green circle. The sea rolls in languidly. Click. Click. The old people, their eyes watery from the white glare, squint down at the kids. Click. Click. The sound of marbles, how familiar it once was.

The kids are precise, almost grim. A winner must knock seven of 13 marbles out of the 10-foot-diameter ring. Players can shoot continuously, as long as they bang a marble out of the ring and their taw (a big marble, a shooter) stays in the circle. The players are not contemplative; unblinking, their tongues clamped by teeth, they line up their shots and shoot in seconds. The boys are taciturn, given to brooding over failure, the loss of an edge. The girls are much more social, at ease, more inclined to inhale the wonderful craziness of it all. Escorts and officials provide the passion.

Nothing much is at stake, but adults can always find something to flame their agressiveness. The big prize is a $600 college scholarship, and what has happened to those awards is telling. Not one champion has taken advantage of the scholarship. "They would prefer money," says one official, "but we won't allow it. Their parents would only take it and spend it." That explains much about the atmosphere in which marbles is played today. The game—what is left of it—belongs to the poor urban and rural areas, where a recreation center is an island of escape in the midst of drabness. But even in these centers, the game is hardly ever played.

The kids—30 of them this year—are not used to being the point of focus, in contrast to middle-class kids, who are always aware that they are the center of an intensive effort, that their happiness is a matter of great stakes. "Some of the kids," an official says, "have never seen the ocean, never stayed in a motel, hardly know much about anything." They have much in common with the generation of the '30s and World War II, when marbles were as treasured as a tartaped baseball, a raggedy glove and a cracked bat made usable by nails and more tape.

Families then had no recourse to Dr. Spock and were not frantically striving to produce his near-perfect being. A kid was a kid— not the future of America in bold letters. Parents watched after his health, sent him to school, tried to give him three squares a day— and left him alone; he was an individual in the best sense of the word. For a treat there were the bleachers at the ball park, or a Saturday afternoon with Gabby Hayes or Buck Jones and an all-day lunch at the movies. Parents were not entertainment directors, nor did they feel guilty for not making every hour their young spent memorable.

Ennui was seldom in the air in the old neighborhood, whether it was street blocks with a maze of alleys and vacant lots or a country field. One of the saddest complaints to be heard from a kid is that he or she is bored. If you were bored in that other time, well, that was your problem; kids without imagination were not suffered long. There were games to be played, and children who knew how to play them gloriously—by themselves, without mouthy adults nearby grappling with identity crises.

Group play then had no supervision, and very few rules, and those that did exist changed by the moment. It was usually at the shank of the dying day when play climbed to its highest pitch, as if everyone was trying to drain the last full measure of joy before dark, when voices would cut through the night: "Boy, where are you? You come in here right this minute!" There was no specific time for play to begin, but the young seemed to gather by means of the mysterious signals of childhood. One by one they would turn up, going their own ways and to their own amusements.

Streetlamps cast light over the sidewalk, and even now the shadows of the tiny figures move through the mind with a strange reality. And the singsong chants of the girls jumping rope still carry with them a sweet poignance:

> *I had a little brother,*
> *His name was Tiny Tim,*
> *I put him in the bathtub*
> *To teach him how to swim.*
> *He drank up all the water,*
> *He ate up all the soap,*
> *He died last night*
> *With a bubble in his throat.*

Anytime, of course, was right for marbles, but winter was cruel. Fingers moved reluctantly into position, the wind blew stingingly across the vacant lot and one's will could be sapped rapidly; winter was clearly a time when form did not hold. Summer was the best, the time when a player's finest stock was brought out: shooters of exotic colors, looking as if they contained mysteries known only to their owners; big bags full of marbles won from previous campaigns, now to be used for a season to end all seasons. If the knees of your pants held out, if your thumbnail could take it, why, could greatness be far off?

This year Pittsburgh—always dangerous in the National Marbles Tournament—provided the finalists, Susan Regan, 13, and Larry Kokos, 14. It was the first time in 14 years for a boy-girl match, and it was not achieved without turbulence. When told of the arrangement, some male players sulked, and one member of the executive committee said he would relinquish his chair. ITT saved the day; a spokesman said the company would not be involved in any discriminatory practices. Being the sponsor (the company's range of interests is endless) ITT brooked no back talk.

Larry Kokos, tall, dark and angular and wearing a Budweiser sun visor went on to win the overall title. He was quite proficient. He had long, lean hands, which are helpful in marbles. He could put English on his shooter, so much so that first it would do a pirouette and then go to its position as if it were on a string; a player who can gain position consistently is not to be fooled with. Larry kissed the girl, the mayor gave a speech, the few old people left continued to stare and they were still there looking out toward the quiet sea when the kids were gone.

Thoughts chase each other through the mind. It was good that poor kids could leave the gray vise of the city for a few days because of a marbles tournament. But of all games, marbles should never be organized. It belongs to other summers, filled with games like prisoner's base, kick the can, to solitary hours when you merely climbed a tree, watched a spider spin a web across a dusty window, tossed a ball aimlessly against a factory wall or took a streetcar to the other end of town. Those summers exist now only in memory, and perhaps they were not as golden as they appear from a distance. But dumb toys, given too freely, and the adult frenzy to organize everything, will never replace them, for there were no child sophisticates then, and you could get distance out of a good jawbreaker, and most of all there was a beautiful aloneness to it.

QUESTIONS
1. Explain why you think Kram's title does or does not fully and accurately describe what his essay is about.
2. Kram describes one of the conversations he reports (p. 483) in terms of film technique. Describe how you might turn the whole essay into a film.
3. Why does Kram mention the earthquake and the senior citizens?
4. What are some of the contrasts between adults and kids that are developed? How do these contrasts contribute to the major contrast that Kram develops between the past and the present?
5. Nostalgia might be defined as "a homesickness for the past." Explain whether you think this piece fits that definition.
6. Explain what you think Shulamith Firestone (see p. 831) might say about Kram's essay.
7. Write an essay in which you look back to some pleasant thing in your own past or in our nation's past, and compare it to something in the present.

VERTA MAE
The Kitchen Crisis

AUTHOR'S NOTE:
*i do not consider myself a writer, i am a rapper. therefore do not
read this piece silently . . . rap it aloud.*

there is confusion in the kitchen!
we've got to develop kitchen consciousness or we may very well see
the end of kitchens as we now know them. kitchens are getting
smaller. in some apts the closet is bigger than the kitchen. some
thing that i saw the other day leads me to believe that there may
well be a subversive plot to take kitchens out of the home and put
them in the street. i was sitting in the park knitting my old man a
pair of socks for next winter when a tall well dressed man in his
mid thirties sat next to me.
i didnt pay him no mind until he went into his act.
he pulled his irish linen hankie from his lapel, spread it on his lap,
opened his attache case, took out a box, popped a pill, drank from
his thermos jug, and turned and offered the box to me. thank you
no said i. "i never eat with strangers."
that would have been all except that i am curious black and i
looked at the label on the box, then i screamed, the box said
INSTANT LUNCH PILL: (imitation ham and cheese on rye, with diet
cola, and apple pie flavor). i sat frozen while he did his next act. he
folded his hankie, put it back in his lapel, packed his thermos jug
away, and took out a piece of yellow plastic and blew into it, in less
than 3 minutes it had turned into a yellow plastic castro convertible
couch.
enough is enough i thought to myself. so i dropped the knitting and
ran like hell. last i saw of that dude he was stretched out on the
couch reading portnoys complaint.
the kitchens that are still left in the home are so instant they might
as well be out to lunch.
instant milk, instant coffee, instant tea, instant potatoes, instant old
fashioned oatmeal, everything is preprepared for the unprepared
woman in the kitchen. the chicken is pre cut. the flour is pre measured, the rice is minute, the salt is pre seasoned, and the peas are
pre buttered. just goes to show you white folks will do anything for
their women. they had to invent instant food because the servant
problem got so bad that their women had to get in the kitchen herself with her own two little lily white hands. it is no accident that
in the old old south where they had slaves that they was eating
fried chicken, coated with batter, biscuits so light they could have
flown across the mason dixon line if they had wanted to. they was

eating pound cake that had to be beat 800 strokes. who do you think was doing this beating?

it sure wasnt missy. missy was beating the upstairs house nigger for not bringing her mint julep quick enough.

massa was out beating the field niggers for not hoeing the cotton fast enough. meanwhile up in the north country where they didnt have no slaves to speak of they was eating baked beans and so called new england boiled dinner.

it aint no big thing to put everything in one pot and let it cook. missy wasnt about to go through changes and whup no pound cake for 800 strokes.

black men and black women have been whipping up fine food for centuries and outside of black bottom pie and nigger toes there is no reference to our contribution and participation in and to the culinary arts.

when they do mention our food they act like it is some obscure thing that niggers down south made up and dont nobody else in the world eat it.

food aint nothing but food.

food is universal.

everybody eats.

a potato is a patata and not irish as white folks would have you believe. watermelons is prehistoric and eaten all ober de world.

the russians make a watermelon beer. in the orient they dry and roast and salt the seeds. when old chris got here the indians was eating hominy grits. and before he "discovered" this country the greeks and romans were smacking on collard greens. blackeyed peas aint nothing but dried cow peas whose name in sanskrit traces its lineage back to the days before history was recorded. uh ah excuse me boss, means befo you-all was recording history. uh ah i know this is hard for you to believe suh but i got it from one of yo history books and i know you-all wouldnt talk with no forked tongue about history.

the cooking of food is one of the highest of all the human arts. we need to develop food consciousness.

so called enlightened people will rap for hours about jean paul sartre, campus unrest, the feminine mystique, black power, and tania, but mention food and they say, rather proudly too, "i'm a bad cook." some go so far as to boast "i cant even boil water without burning it."

that is a damn shame.

bad cooks got a bad life style.

food is life.

food changes up into blood, blood into cells, cells into energy, energy changes up into the forces which make up your life style.

so if one takes a creative, imaginative, loving, serious attitude toward life everything one does will reflect one attitude hence when one cooks this attitude will be served at the table. and it will be good.

so bad cooks got a bad life style and i dont mean bad like we (blacks) mean bad i mean bad bad.

come on give a damn. anybody can get it together for vacation. change up and daily walk through kitchen life like you was on an endless holiday. aint no use to save yourself for vacation. it's here now.

make every and each moment count like time was running out. that will cool out that matter of guess who is coming to dinner and make it a fact that DINNER IS SERVED.

one of the best meals i was ever served was at my friend bella's. bella served an elegant meal in her two room cold water tub in kitchen six story walk up flat. she had a round oak table with carved legs, covered with a floor length off white shaker lace tablecloth. in the center was a carved african gourd filled with peanuts, persimmons, lemons and limes. to start off we had fresh squeezed tangerine juice in chilled champagne glasses. then scrambled eggs, sliced red onions marinated in lemon juice and pickapeppa sauce, fried green tomatoes, on cobalt blue china plates. hot buttermilk biscuits with homemade apple jelly on limoges saucers (bella got them from goodwill for 10 cent a piece) and fresh ground bustelo coffee served in mugs that bella made in pottery class at the neighborhood anti poverty pro community cultural workshop for people in low socio economic ethnic groups.

you are what you eat.

i was saying that a long time before the movie came out but it doesnt bother me that they stole my line. white folks are always stealing and borrowing and discovering and making myths. you take terrapins. diamondback terrapins. the so called goremays squeal with epicurean delight at the very mention of the word. there is a mystique surrounding the word. diamondback terrapins.

are you ready for the demystification of diamondback terrapins???????? they ain't nothing but salt water turtles.

slaves on the eastern shores used to eat them all the time. the slaves was eating so many that a law was passed to making it a crime to feed slaves terrapins more than 3 times a week.

white folks discovered terrapins, ate them all up and now they are all but extinct (terrapins).

oh there are a few left on terrapin reservations but the chances of seeing one in your neighborhood is not likely.

in my old neighborhood (fairfax s.c.) we always talk about how folks in new york will give you something to drink but nothing to eat. after having lived for several years in fun city i understand how the natives got into this.

with the cost of living as high as it is here i understand how you can become paranoid and weird about your food. i understand where they are coming from but i thank the creator that there is still a cultural gap between me and the natives. on the other hand you cant be no fool about it. it dont make sense to take food out your childrens mouths to give to the last lower east side poet who knocks on your door but you can give up a margarine sandwich and a glass of water. cant you? eating is a very personal thing.

some people will sit down and eat with anybody.

that is very uncool. you cant eat with everybody.

you got to have the right vibrations.

if you dont get good vibrations from someone, cancel them out for eating. (other things too.)

that is the only way to keep bad kitchen vibes at a minimum. tell those kind of folks that you will meet them in a luncheonette or a bar.

even at the risk of static from family and friends PRO TECT YO KITCH'N. it's hard though. sometimes look like in spite of all you do and as careful as you try to be a rapscallion will slip right in your kitchen. i cant stand rapscallions. among other things they are insensitive. you ask them "may i offer you something" "some coffee tea juice water milk juice or maybe an alcoholic beverage."

they always answer "nah nutin for me" or else they say "i'll have tea if you got tea bags" or "coffee if it is instant i dont want to put you through no trouble." check that out! talking about not going to any trouble. hell they already in your house and that is trouble and personal. what the rapscallions are really saying is dont go to any trouble for me cause i wouldnt go to none for you. rapscallions dont mind taking the alcoholic drink because it is impersonal. nothing of you is in that. all you got to do is pour from a bottle. they dont feel that you have extended yourself for them so they wont have to do no trouble for you in return. in most other cultures when you enter a persons home you and the host share a moment together by partaking of something. rapscallions love to talk about culture but their actions prove they aint got none. they dont understand that it is about more than the coffee tea or drink of water.

it's about extending yourself.

so watch out for rapscallions. they'll mess up your kitchen vibes.

PROTECT YOUR KITCHEN

ART BUCHWALD

Hurts Rent-A-Gun

The Senate recently passed a new gun-control bill, which some observers consider worse than no bill at all. Any serious attempt at handgun registration was gutted, and Senate gun lovers even managed to repeal a 1968 gun law controlling the purchase of .22 rimfire ammunition.

After the Senate got finished with its work on the gun-control bill, I received a telephone call from my friend Bromley Hurts, who told me he had a business proposition to discuss with me. I met him for lunch at a pistol range in Maryland.

"I think I've got a fantastic idea," he said, "I want to start a new business called Hurts Rent-A-Gun."

"What on earth for?" I asked.

"There are a lot of people in this country who only use a handgun once or twice a year, and they don't want to go to all the expense of buying one. So we'll rent them a gun for a day or two. By leasing a firearm from us, they won't have to tie up all their money."

"That makes sense," I admitted.

"Say a guy is away from home on a trip, and he doesn't want to carry his own gun with him. He can rent a gun from us and then return it when he's finished with his business."

"You could set up rent-a-gun counters at gas stations," I said excitedly.

"And we could have stores in town where someone could rent a gun to settle a bet," Hurts said.

"A lot of people would want to rent a gun for a domestic quarrel," I said.

"Right. Say a jealous husband suspects there is someone at home with his wife. He rents a pistol from us and tries to catch them in the act. If he discovers his wife is alone, he isn't out the eighty dollars it would have cost him to buy a gun."

"Don't forget about kids who want to play Russian roulette. They could pool their allowances and rent a gun for a couple of hours," I said.

"Our market surveys indicate," Hurts said, "that there are also a lot of kids who claim their parents don't listen to them. If they could rent a gun, they feel they could arrive at an understanding with their folks in no time."

"There's no end to the business," I said. "How would you charge for Hurts Rent-A-Gun?"

"There would be hourly rates, day rates, and weekly rates, plus ten cents for each bullet fired. Our guns would be the latest models, and we would guarantee clean barrels and the latest safety devices. If a gun malfunctions through no fault of the user, we will give him another gun absolutely free."

"For many Americans it's a dream come true," I said.

"We've also made it possible for people to return the gun in another town. For example, if you rent the gun in Chicago and want to use it in Salt Lake City, you can drop it off there at no extra charge."

"Why didn't you start this before?"

"We wanted to see what happened with the gun-control legislation. We were pretty sure the Senate and the White House would not do anything about strong gun control, especially during an election year. But we didn't want to invest a lot of money until we were certain they would all chicken out."

"I'd like the franchise for Washington's National Airport," I said.

"You've got it. It's a great location," Hurts said. "You'll make a fortune in hijackings alone."

ELDRIDGE CLEAVER

Convalescence[1]

. . . just as in childhood I envied Negroes for what seemed to me their superior masculinity, so I envy them today for what seems to me their superior physical grace and beauty. I have come to value physical grace very highly, and I am now capable of aching with all my being when I watch a Negro couple on the dance floor, or a Negro playing baseball or basketball. *They are on the kind of terms with their own bodies that I should like to be on with mine, and for that precious quality they seem blessed to me.* [Italics added]

—Norman Podhoretz, "My Negro Problem—And Ours," *Commentary*, February 1963

Why envy the Negro his grace, his physical skills? Why not ask what it is that prevents grace and physical skill from becoming a general property of the young? Mr. Podhoretz speaks of middle-class, white respectability—what does this mean but being cut off from the labor process, the work process, the creative process, as such? *The solution is thus not the direct liquidation of the color line, through the liquidation of color; but rather through a greater physical connectedness of the whites; and a greater intellective connectedness of the blacks . . .*" [Italics added]

—Irving Louis Horowitz,
Chairman, Department of Sociology,
Hobart and William Smith Colleges, Geneva, New York,
Commentary, June 1963

If the separation of the black and white people in America along the color line had the effect, in terms of social imagery, of separating the Mind from the Body—the oppressor whites usurping sovereignty by monopolizing the Mind, abdicating the Body and becoming bodiless Omnipotent Administrators and Ultrafeminines; and

1. From *Soul on Ice*, 1968.

the oppressed blacks, divested of sovereignty and therefore of Mind, manifesting the Body and becoming mindless Supermasculine Menials and Black Amazons—if this is so, then the 1954 U.S. Supreme Court decision in the case of *Brown v. Board of Education*, demolishing the principle of segregation of the races in public education and striking at the very root of the practice of segregation generally, was a major surgical operation performed by nine men in black robes on the racial Maginot Line which is imbedded as deep as sex or the lust for lucre in the schismatic American psyche. This piece of social surgery, if successful, performed without benefit of any anesthetic except God and the Constitution, in a land where God is dead and the Constitution has been in a coma for 180 years, is more marvelous than a successful heart transplant would be, for it was meant to graft the nation's Mind back onto its Body and vice versa.

If the foregoing is true, then the history of America in the years following the pivotal Supreme Court edict should be a record of the convalescence of the nation. And upon investigation we should be able to see the Omnipotent Administrators and Ultrafeminines grappling with their unfamiliar and alienated Bodies, and the Supermasculine Menials and Amazons attempting to acquire and assert *a mind of their own*. The record, I think, is clear and unequivocal. The bargain which seems to have been struck is that the whites have had to turn to the blacks for a clue on how to swing with the Body, while the blacks have had to turn to the whites for the secret of the Mind. It was Chubby Checker's mission, bearing the Twist as *good news*, to teach the whites, whom history had taught to forget, how to shake their asses again. It is a skill they surely must once have possessed but which they abandoned for puritanical dreams of escaping the corruption of the flesh, by leaving the terrors of the Body to the blacks.

In the swift, fierce years since the 1954 school desegregation decision, a rash of seemingly unrelated mass phenomena has appeared on the American scene—deviating radically from the prevailing Hot-Dog-and-Malted-Milk norm of the bloodless, square, superficial, faceless Sunday-Morning atmosphere that was suffocating the nation's soul. And all of this in a nation where the so-called molders of public opinion, the writers, politicians, teachers, and cab drivers, are willful, euphoric liars or zip-dam ostriches and owls, a clique of undercover ghosts, a bunch of Walter Jenkinses,[2] a lot of coffee-drinking, cigarette-smoking, sly, suck-assing, status-seeking, cheating, nervous, dry-balled, tranquillizer-gulched, countdown-minded, out-of-style, slithering snakes. No wonder that many "innocent people," the manipulated and the stimulated, some of whom were game for

---

2. Former White House aide; arrested in 1964 on a morals charge.

a reasonable amount of mystery and even adventure, had their minds scrambled. These observers were not equipped to either *feel* or *know* that a radical break, a revolutionary leap out of their sight, had taken place in the secret parts of this nation's soul. It was as if a driverless vehicle were speeding through the American night down an unlighted street toward a stone wall and was boarded on the fly by a stealthy ghost with a drooling leer on his face, who, at the last detour before chaos and disaster, careened the vehicle down a smooth highway that leads to the future and life; and to ask these Americans to understand that they were the passengers on this driverless vehicle and that the lascivious ghost was the Saturday-night crotchfunk of the Twist, or the "Yeah, Yeah, Yeah!" which the Beatles highjacked from Ray Charles, to ask these Calvinistic profligates to see the logical and reciprocal links is more cruel than asking a hope-to-die Okie Music buff to cop the sounds of John Coltrane.

In the beginning of the era came a thief with a seven-year itch who knew that the ostriches and the owls had been bribed with a fix of Euphony, which is their kick. The thief knew that he need not wait for the cover of night, that with impunity he could show his face in the marketplace in the full light of the sun, do his deed, scratch his dirt, sell his loot to the fence while the ostriches and owls, coasting on Euphony, one with his head in a hole—any hole —and the other with his head in the clouds, would only cluck and whisper and hear-see-speak no evil.

So Elvis Presley came, strumming a weird guitar and wagging his tail across the continent, ripping off fame and fortune as he scrunched his way, and, like a latter-day Johnny Appleseed, sowing seeds of a new rhythm and style in the white souls of the white youth of America, whose inner hunger and need was no longer satisfied with the antiseptic white shoes and whiter songs of Pat Boone. "You can do anything," sang Elvis to Pat Boone's white shoes, "but don't you step on my Blue Suede Shoes!"

During this period of ferment and beginnings, at about the same time that the blacks of Montgomery, Alabama, began their historic bus boycott (giving birth to the leadership of Martin Luther King, signifying to the nation that, with this initiative, this first affirmative step, somewhere in the universe a gear in the machinery had shifted), something, a target, came into focus. The tensions in the American psyche had torn a fissure in the racial Maginot Line and through this fissure, this tiny bridge between the Mind and Body, the black masses, who had been silent and somnolent since the '20s and '30s, were now making a break toward the dimly seen light that beckoned to them through the fissure. The fact that these blacks could now take such a step was perceived by the ostriches and owls as a sign of national decay, a sign that the System had caved in at that spot. And this gave birth to a fear, a fear that quickly became a focus for all the anxieties and exasperations in the Omnipotent

Administrators' minds; and to embody this perceived decay and act as a lightning rod for the fear, the beatniks bloomed onto the American scene.

Like pioneers staking their claims in the no-man's land that lay along the racial Maginot Line, the beatniks, like Elvis Presley before them, dared to do in the light of day what America had long been doing in the sneak-thief anonymity of night—consorted on a human level with the blacks. Reviled, cursed, held in contempt by the "molders of public opinion," persecuted by the police, made into an epithet of derision by the deep-frozen geeks of the Hot-Dog-and-Malted-Milk set, the beatniks irreverently refused to go away. Allan Ginsberg and Jack Kerouac ("the Suzuki rhythm boys," James Baldwin called them, derisively, in a moment of panic, "tired of white ambitions" and "dragging themselves through the Negro streets at dawn, looking for an angry fix"; "with," as Mailer put it, "the black man's code to fit their facts"). Bing Crosbyism, Perry Comoism, and Dinah Shoreism had led to cancer, and the vanguard of the white youth knew it.

And as the spirit of revolt crept across the continent from that wayward bus in Montgomery, Alabama, seeping like new life into the cracks and nooks of the northern ghettos and sweeping in furious gales across the campuses of southern Negro colleges, erupting, finally, in the sit-ins and freedom rides—as this swirling maelstrom of social change convulsed the nation, shocking an unsuspecting American public, folk music, speaking of fundamental verities, climbed slowly out of the grave; and the hip lobe of the national ear, twitching involuntarily at first, began to listen.

From the moment that Mrs. Rosa Parks, in that bus in Montgomery, Alabama, resisted the Omnipotent Administrator, contact, however fleeting, had been made with the lost sovereignty—the Body had made contact with its Mind—and the shock of that contact sent an electric current throughout this nation, traversing the racial Maginot Line and striking fire in the hearts of the whites. The wheels began to turn, the thaw set in, and though Emmett Till and Mack Parker[3] were dead, though Eisenhower sent troops to Little Rock,[4] though Autherine Lucy's token presence at the University of Alabama was a mockery—notwithstanding this, it was already clear that the 1954 major surgical operation had been successful and the patient would live. The challenge loomed on the horizon: Africa, black, enigmatic, and hard-driving, had begun to parade its newly freed nations into the UN; and the Islam of Elijah Muhammad, amplified as it was fired in salvos from the piercing

---

3. Emmett Till, a fourteen-year-old youth, kidnapped and killed for whistling at a white woman in Mississippi in August 1955; Mack Parker, lynched in Poplarville, Mississippi, while awaiting trial on a rape charge, April 1959.

4. Troops sent to Little Rock, Arkansas, in 1957 in support of a court order to integrate Little Rock schools.

tongue of Malcolm X, was racing through the Negro streets with Allen Ginsberg and Jack Kerouac.

Then, as the verbal revolt of the black masses soared to a cacophonous peak—the Body, the Black Amazons and Supermasculine Menials, becoming conscious, shouting, in a thousand different ways, *"I've got a Mind of my own!"*; and as the senator from Massachusetts was saving the nation from the Strangelove grasp of Dirty Dick, injecting, as he emerged victorious, a new and vivacious spirit into the people with the style of his smile and his wife's hairdo; then, as if a signal had been given, as if the Mind had shouted to the Body, "I'm ready!"—the Twist, superseding the Hula Hoop, burst upon the scene like a nuclear explosion, sending its fallout of rhythm into the Minds and Bodies of the people. The fallout: the Hully Gully, the Mashed Potato, the Dog, the Smashed Banana, the Watusi, the Frug, the Swim. The Twist was a guided missile, launched from the ghetto into the very heart of suburbia. The Twist succeeded, as politics, religion, and law could never do, in writing in the heart and soul what the Supreme Court could only write on the books. The Twist was a form of therapy for a convalescing nation. The Omnipotent Administrator and the Ultrafeminine responded so dramatically, in stampede fashion, to the Twist precisely because it afforded them the possibility of reclaiming their Bodies again after generations of alienated and disembodied existence.

The stiff, mechanical Omnipotent Administrators and Ultrafeminines presented a startling spectacle as they entered in droves onto the dance floors to learn how to Twist. They came from every level of society, from top to bottom, writhing pitifully though gamely about the floor, feeling exhilarating and soothing new sensations, release from some unknown prison in which their Bodies had been encased, a sense of freedom they had never known before, a feeling of communion with some mystical root-source of life and vigor, from which sprang a new awareness and enjoyment of the flesh, a new appreciation of the possibilities of their Bodies. They were swinging and gyrating and shaking their dead asses like petrified zombies trying to regain the warmth of life, rekindle the dead limbs, the cold ass, the stone heart, the stiff, mechanical, disused joints with the spark of life.

This spectacle truly startled many Negroes, because they perceived it as an intrusion by the Mind into the province of the Body, and this intimated chaos; because the Negroes knew, from the survival experience of their everyday lives, that the system within which they were imprisoned was based upon the racial Maginot Line and that the cardinal sin, crossing the line—which was, in their experience, usually initiated from the black side—was being committed, *en masse*, by the whites. The Omnipotent Administrators and Ultrafeminines were storming the Maginot Line! A massive assault had been launched without parallel in American history, and to Negroes it was confusing. Sure, they had witnessed it on an individual scale: they had seen many ofays destroy the Maginot Line in themselves. But this time it had all the appearances of a national movement. There were even rumors that President Kennedy and his Jackie were doing the Twist secretly in the White House; that their Number One Boy had been sent to the Peppermint Lounge in disguise to learn how to Twist, and he in turn brought the trick back to the White House. These Negroes knew that something fundamental had changed.

"Man, what done got into them ofays?" one asked.

"They trying to get back," said another.

"Shit," said a young Negro who made his living by shoplifting. "If you ask me, I think it must be the end of the world."

"Oooo-weee!" said a Negro musician who had been playing at a dance and was now standing back checking the dancers. "Baby, I don't dig this action at all! Look here, baby, pull my coat to what's going down! I mean, have I missed it somewhere? Where've I been? Baby, I been blowing all my life and I ain't never dug no happenings like this. You know what, man, I'm gon' cut that fucking weed aloose. Oooo-weee! Check that little bitch right there! What the fuck she trying to do? Is she trying to shake it or break it? Oooo-weee!"

A Negro girl said: "Take me home, I'm sick!"

Another one said: "No, let's stay! This is too much!"

And a bearded Negro cat, who was not interested in learning how to Twist himself, who felt that if he was interested in doing it, he could get up from the table right now and start Twisting, he said, sitting at the table with a tinsel-minded female: "It ain't nothing. They just trying to get back, that's all."

"Get back?" said the girl, arching her brows quizzically, "Get back from where?"

"From wherever they've been," said the cat, "where else?"

"Are they doing it in Mississippi is what I want to know," said a tall, deadly looking Negro who had a long razor line down his left cheek and who had left Mississippi in a hurry one night.

And the dancers: they were caught up in a whirl of ecstasy, swinging like pendulums, mechanical like metronomes or puppets on invisible strings being manipulated by a master with a sick sense of humor. "They look like Chinese doing communal exercise," said a Negro. "That's all they're doing, calisthenics!"

"Yeah," said his companion. "They're trying to get in shape."

But if at first it was funny and confusing, it was nonetheless a breakthrough. The Omnipotent Administrators and Ultrafeminines were discovering new aspects of the Body, new possibilities of rhythm, new ways to move. The Hula Hoop had been a false start, a mechanized, theatrical attempt by the Mind to supply to itself what only the Body can give. But, with the Twist, as last they knew themselves to be swinging. The forces acting upon the world stage in our era had created, in the collective psyche of the Omnipotent —and the Hula Hoop and Twist offered socially acceptable ways to Administrators and Ultrafeminines, an irresistible urge—to just stand up and shake the ice and cancer out of their alienated white asses—the Hula Hoop and Twist offered socially acceptable ways to do it.

Of course, not all the whites took part in these joyful experiments. For many, the more "suggestive" a dance became—i.e., the more it became pure Body and less Mind—the more scandalous it seemed to them; and their reaction in this sense was an index to the degree of their alienation from their Bodies. But what they condemned as a sign of degeneracy and moral decay was actually a sign of health, a sign of hope for full recovery. As Norman Mailer prophesied: ". . . the Negro's equality would tear a profound shift into the psychology, the sexuality, and the moral imagination of every white alive." Precisely because the Mind will have united with the Body, theory will have merged with practice.

It is significant that the Twist and the Hula Hoop came into the scene in all their fury at the close of the Eisenhower and the dawn of the Kennedy era. It could be interpreted as a rebellion against the vacuous Eisenhower years. It could also be argued that the same collective urge that gave rise to the Twist also swept Kennedy into office. I shudder to think that, given the closeness of the final vote in 1960, Richard Nixon might have won the election in a breeze if he had persuaded one of his Ultrafeminine daughters, not to mention Ultrapat, to do the Twist in public. Not if Kennedy had stayed on the phone a week sympathizing with Mrs. Martin Luther King, Jr., over the fact that the cat was in jail, would he have won. Even as I am convinced that Luci Baines Johnson, dancing the Watusi in public with Killer Joe Piro,[5] won more votes for her old man in 1964 than a whole boxcar full of his hog-calling speeches ever did.

When the Birmingham Revolt erupted in the summer of 1963 and President Kennedy stepped into the void and delivered his unprecedented speech to the nation on civil rights and sent his bill to Congress, the foundation had been completed. Martin Luther King, Jr., giving voice to the needs of the Body, and President Kennedy, speaking out the needs of the Mind, made contact on that day. The Twisters, sporting their blue suede shoes, moved beyond the ghost in white shoes who ate a Hot Dog and sipped Malted Milk as he danced the mechanical jig of Satan on top of Medgar Evers' tomb.[6] In vain now would the murderers bomb that church and slaughter grotesquely those four little black girls[7] (what did they

---

5. Discothèque dance teacher.
6. Evers was killed by a sniper in Jackson, Mississippi, in June 1963.

7. The bombing took place in Birmingham, Alabama, in September 1963.

hope to kill? were they striking at the black of the skin or the fire of the soul? at history? at the Body?). In vain also the assassins' bullets that crashed through the head of John Kennedy, taking a life, yes, but creating a larger-than-life and failing utterly to expunge from the record the March on Washington and its truth: that this nation—bourgeois or not, imperialist or not, murderous or not, ugly or not—its people, somewhere in their butchered and hypocritical souls, still contained an epic potential of spirit which is its hope, a bottomless potential which fires the imaginations of its youth. It was all too late. It was too late because it was time for the blacks ("I've got a *Mind* of my own!") to riot, to sweep through the Harlem night like a wave of locusts, breaking, screaming, bleeding, laughing, crying, rejoicing, celebrating, in a jubilee of destruction, to regurgitate the white man's bullshit they'd been eating for four hundred years; smashing the windows of the white man's stores, throwing bricks they wished were bombs, running, leaping whirling like a cyclone through the white man's Mind, past his backlash, through the night streets of Rochester, New Jersey, Philadelphia. And even though the opposition, gorging on Hot Dogs and Malted Milk, with blood now splattered over the white shoes, would still strike out in the dark against the manifestations of the turning, showing the protocol of Southern Hospitality reserved for Niggers and Nigger Lovers—SCHWERNER–CHANEY–GOODMAN[8] —it was still too late. For not only had Luci Baines Johnson danced the Watusi in public with Killer Joe, but the Beatles were on the scene, injecting Negritude by the ton into whites, in this post Elvis Presley-beatnik era of ferment.

Before we toss the Beatles a homosexual kiss—saying, "If a man be ass enough to reach for the bitch in them, that man will kiss a man, and if a woman reaches for the stud in them, that woman will kiss a woman"—let us marvel at the genius of their image, which comforts the owls and ostriches in the one spot where Elvis Presley bummed their kick: Elvis, with his unfunky (yet mechanical, alienated) bumpgrinding, was still too much Body (too soon) for the strained collapsing psyches of the Omnipotent Administrators and Ultrafeminines; whereas the Beatles, affecting the caucasoid crown of femininity and ignoring the Body on the visual plane (while their music on the contrary being full of Body), assuaged the doubts of the owls and ostriches by presenting an incorporeal, cerebral image.

Song and dance are, perhaps, only a little less old than man himself. It is with his music and dance, the recreation through art of the rhythms suggested by and implicit in the tempo of his life and cultural environment, that man purges his soul of the tensions of daily strife and maintains his harmony in the universe. In the

---

8. Michael Schwerner, James Chaney, and Andrew Goodman, civil rights workers, were killed near Philadelphia, Mississippi, in June 1964.

increasingly mechanized, automated, cybernated environment of the modern world—a cold, bodiless world of wheels, smooth plastic surfaces, tubes, pushbuttons, transistors, computers, jet propulsion, rockets to the moon, atomic energy—man's need for affirmation of his biology has become that much more intense. He feels need for a clear definition of where his body ends and the machine begins, where man ends and the *extensions* of man begin. This great mass hunger, which transcends national or racial boundaries, recoils from the subtle subversions of the mechanical evironment which modern technology is creating faster than man, with his present savage relationship to his fellow men, is able to receive and assimilate. This is the central contradiction of the twentieth century; and it is against this backdrop that America's attempt to unite its Mind with its Body, to save its soul, is taking place.

It is in this connection that the blacks, personifying the Body and thereby in closer communion with their biological roots than other Americans, provide the saving link, the bridge between man's biology and man's machines. In its purest form, as adjustment to the scientific and technological environment of our era, as purgative and lullaby-soother of man's soul, it is the jazz issuing from the friction and harmony of the American Negro with his environment that captured the beat and tempo of our times. And although modern science and technology are the same whether in New York, Paris, London, Accra, Cairo, Berlin, Moscow, Tokyo, Peking, or São Paulo, jazz is the only true international medium of communication current in the world today, capable of speaking creatively, with equal intensity and relevance, to the people in all those places.

The less sophisticated (but no less Body-based) popular music of urban Negroes—which was known as Rhythm and Blues before the whites appropriated and distilled it into a product they called Rock 'n Roll—is the basic ingredient, the core, of the gaudy, cacophonous hymns with which the Beatles of Liverpool drive their hordes of Ultrafeminine fans into catatonia and hysteria. For Beatle fans, having been alienated from their own Bodies so long and so deeply, the effect of these potent, erotic rhythms is electric. Into this music, the Negro projected—as it were, *drained off*, as pus from a sore—a powerful sensuality, his pain and lust, his love and his hate, his ambition and his despair. The Negro projected into his music his very Body. The Beatles, the four long-haired lads from Liverpool, are offering up as their gift the Negro's Body, and in so doing establish a rhythmic communication between the listener's own Mind and Body.

Enter the Beatles—soul by proxy, middlemen between the Mind and the Body. A long way from Pat Boone's White Shoes. A way station on a slow route traveled with all deliberate speed.

QUESTIONS

1. What racial differences does Cleaver assume? Would you respond differently to these assumptions if they had been implicit in a piece by, say, a southern white racist politician?
2. Does Cleaver establish any connection between the Supreme Court decision he discusses in his introduction and the song and dance he focuses on in the body of the essay? Do you think the "convalescence" could have occurred without that particular piece of surgery? What other influences may have served to graft mind and body? What others may have impeded the convalescence?
3. This piece abounds with figures of speech. How many can you find? What purposes do they serve? Do they clarify Cleaver's argument? Or do they becloud the issues?
4. Cleaver's sentences are long, with ins and outs and round-abouts— and many internal interruptions. How would he do at Time or Newsweek?
5. Are Cleaver's long lists of appositives and adjectives of substantive importance? Or are they mere gimmicks?
6. Are you persuaded by Cleaver's pronouncements on how things are—or were?

SAUL BELLOW

Culture Now

The American literary situation has greatly changed during the past decade. What do you think of the more recent trend?

I'm not sure that what we have *is* a literary situation; it seems rather to be a sociological, a political, a psychological situation in which there are literary elements. Literature itself has been swallowed up. In East Africa last year I heard an account (probably sheer fantasy) of a disaster that had overtaken one of three young Americans who had parked their Land Rover under a tree for the night. A python had silently crushed and swallowed the young man. In the morning his friends saw the shape of his body within the snake and his tennis shoes sticking out of the creature's mouth. What we see of literature now are its sneakers.

Why has this happened? No one should take upon himself the responsibility of a definitive explanation—indeed, no such explanation would be generally acceptable—but, for what they may be worth, I am willing to offer my impressions and opinions.

Literature became swallowable, enormously profitable, after World War II, thanks to the university boom, the expansion of the publishing industry and the new opportunities offered by journalism. In the universities a literary culture rapidly formed. It took charge of certain modern masterpieces (James, Lawrence, Joyce, Eliot, etc.), taught them, discoursed about them, *described* them. This process of redescription is most important. Everything was told again, in other words, and related to myth, to history, to philosophy or to psychology.

Behind this body of interpretations appeared a new bureaucracy with its own needs and ambitions and its own orthodoxy. Since the masterpieces of modernism are radical, this orthodoxy is radical too. Within a liberal society, a "revolutionary" or anticapitalist culture has established itself. The need—a social need—for such a culture is evidently great, much greater than the need for novels and poems. In a word, what-can-be-done with literature is for many intellectuals, certainly for the most influential of them, infinitely more important than books.

We have passed from contemplative reading to movement, to action, politics and power struggles. I do not mean large action, broad movement or the conquest of national power. No, not large, not broad. But intellectuals are curiously busy with social questions. From the study of literature comes the prestige they enjoy and exploit. And why do I say that they are curiously busy? Well, consider for example the statement by Marshall McLuhan in *The New York Times* of September 18, 1970. It interprets the Mick Jagger film *Performance* and runs, in part, as follows:

> *Performance* is figured against the overall background of "Planet Polluto." . . .
> *Performance* is a key term in American management and organization circles, and mergers, private and corporate, are the themes of the picture. . . .
> Figured against the British background of a society junked by the new surround of larger powers, *Performance* is a satirical spoof on the screen and fiction violence of the days of Bogart, Al Capone, Studs Lonigan and Hemingway—the tough guy as half-man. . . .
> Figured against the new background of America "The Inefficient," America deprived of outer goals and inner connection, America confronted by the Orient within, *Performance* is as satirical as The Beatles or The Rolling Stones. . . .
> *Performance* projects a nihilistic vision of the establishments which are using all their means for their own liquidation. . . .
> *Performance* is a "garbage apocalypse—notice of the cancellation of a world."

These utterances (copyright McLuhan Associates Ltd., 1970) show what the avant-garde and Ph.D. programs in literature have combined to give us: apocalyptic clichés; a wild self-confidence; violently compact historical judgments; easy formulas about the "cancellation of a world." And can one miss here the presence of money? What else does the copyright by McLuhan Associates signify? McLuhan, who speaks continually of the medium, seems himself, in a different sense, the Cagliostro sense, to be a medium. The avant-garde formed him. He started out esoteric; he speaks now to a great public.

Avant-Garde Bias

Everyone now has a sense that a great revolution is occurring in the consciousness of mankind—in the consciousness of a majority. But literary intellectuals who began with an avant-garde bias against the great public seem to have changed their minds about it. They have returned to the majority, to the masses, but as demagogues and not as writers.

It is not literature that they offer but a culture that contains, as we can see from our McLuhan sample, literary elements. Their interests are exclusively social and political. The long estrangement of the avant-garde from the larger community has come to a curious end. Intellectuals hunger once more for contact with the tribe— that tribe to whose words a century ago the Mallarmés were trying to give a more pure sense.

A few months ago I forced myself on several miserable afternoons to go to the library and to read the literary magazines and the underground papers. This is my report. I shall begin with the representatives or former representatives of the avant-garde, the literary quarterlies. Reading them I was first uncomfortable, then queasy, then indignant, contemptuous and finally quite bleak, flattened out by the bad writing. Brutal profs and bad-tempered ivy league sodomites seemed to have taken over.

Amazing Country

Who was reading this stuff, cultivated housewives? Graduate students who felt they must know the latest? Was it possible that anyone wanted to eat these stale ideological French chocolates? Yes. Evidently there were customers. People were reading these wearisome pages. And someone was financially responsible, paying the bills. This is an amazing country! McLuhan doesn't know the half of it.

Open the *Partisan Review*. Turn to a recent essay by William Phillips.

The subject is—Susan Sontag.

The experience is much like trying to go scuba diving at Coney Island in urinous brine and scraps of old paper, orange rinds and soaked hot dog buns.

The essay on Silence is a good example of Susan Sontag's method. The idea of silence is actually used as a metaphor· for the opposite of talkiness in art, talkiness being too full of subject matter, too directly aimed at an audience, too bustly in its language, too nicely constructed —all suggesting a closed, stale view of existence. Art that babbles thinks of itself as finished, with an audience out there, an inert voyeuristic mass. Only a silent medium can properly engage an audience, because it is not performing but completing itself. The ideal form for Miss Sontag, as one would expect, is the movies, which is able to deal with subjects, that is, with verbal material, by splintering and transforming into immediate visual associations and experiences. And several long and quite brilliant essays in the book, on Godard, Bergman, and the relation of theater to film, explore the possibilities of the most modern art.

One of the nice things about *Hamlet* is that Polonius is stabbed. Mr. Phillips is an old-timer, a founder of the magazine. In the thirties, forties and fifties *Partisan Review* published Malraux, Koestler, Orwell, Silone, Leon Trotsky; its American contributors were Jarrell, Delmore Schwartz, John Berryman, Robert Lowell, Jean Stafford, Edmund Wilson. Future textbooks will surely contain the name of Mr. Phillips. What is he saying?

Upsidedown Politics

"The idea of silence is actually used as a metaphor for the opposite of talkiness in art. . . ." What writing! Eleanor Roosevelt wrote far better in *My Days*.

Of Susan Sontag's rage against the U.S. he says, "On the whole, anti-Americanism has become identified in many parts of the world with socialism and national liberation, though not, significantly, in the communist countries of Eastern Europe, and it is often used as a substitute for socialist theory. As Trotsky pointed out, this is upsidedown politics. . . . Clearly what is lacking is some large perspective for assessing motives and movements throughout the world. . . . These are some of the questions I found myself thinking about as I read Susan Sontag's new book. And if there are no answers to many of them, it might be because this is a time not for rigor and caution in politics and criticism but for boldness in discarding stale ideas and trying out untested ones."

Let us look at one of these original, bold untested ideas. Mr. Phillips is speaking of the New Left. He grants that the New Left has no theory, no program. But, he says, "I am convinced that only an antitheoretical, antihistorical, non-Marxist, unstructured movement like that of the youth today could have created a new left force in the West." This statement, in its idiocy, is really rather touching. One must consider that in surrendering his Marxism Mr. Phillips is giving up his youth, his maturity, forty years of his life. When in doubt he still quotes Trotsky. And he is still a revolutionist, for he desires a New Left force in the West.

Why has Marxism lost his loyalty? Is it because communist revolutions have created nothing but police states? He doesn't say that. Is it because the communists have made Russia one of the most boring nations in history? He doesn't say that either. Is it because China threatens to be even more tedious than Russia? No, I don't think that tedium frightens Mr. Phillips. What frightens him is that he may not make it with the young and that people in New York will think him a silly dry old stick who is *out* of it.

In the same number of *Partisan Review* there is an essay by Mr. Cecil M. Brown on "The White Whale." Mr. Brown, author of a novel, *The Life and Loves of Mr. Jiveass Nigger*, sees in Ishmael the ancestor of the contemporary white liberal.

> In *Moby Dick*, Ishmael's understanding and questioning of his "survival" is so conspicuously absent that one is tempted to conclude that it was he, and not Ahab, who went down with the white whale.

Ishmael, then, is one of the living dead, not a survivor, but, in Mr. Brown's own words, a cop out. Ishmael's attempt to explain himself in the final chapter of the novel

> . . . is so vacuous as to be soporific . . . oh, man, stop the literary bullshit; because *we* know why you survived, you survived because you were white; because you didn't pay your dues, survived because physically you were not even on the ship, you survived because when Queequeg, Tashtego and Daggo, those niggers, were actually in there dealing with that whale, actually *risking* their lives, actually *using* their *bodies*, while they were actually involved your disembodied intelligence, your white ghost, as it were, was off somewhere contemplating in a moment of crisis the significance of Plato and Aristotle, you survived because you never invested any soul, survived because you were never really vulnerable hence never really alive, yes, you survived like a piece of driftwood survives (good image), survived because you planned it that way, and if you didn't plan it, how is it that although it is Queequeg—that strange nigger from the South Seas—who actually executed the idea of a coffin lifesaver, it is you, the white boy, who survives on it? Do you think we are stupid enough to believe that if Queequeg had anything to do with the master plans he'd have let you survive on *his* lifesaver? And furthermore, we are hip to your weird game—we *know* that the white whale, that heinous symbol of the gray world which "darn Ahab" and his "mongrel crew" (i.e., the Third World, dig that) detested so is none other than you, Ishmael—the white, disembodied, overliterate, boring, snobbish, insipid, jew-bastard, nigger-lover, effete, mediocre, assistant-professor-type liberal.

Mr. Brown ends his article with a quotation from LeRoi Jones.

> *Who will survive America?*
> *Few Americans*
> *Very few Negroes*
> *No crackers at all . . .*
>
> *But the Black Man will survive America.*
> *His survival will mean the death of America.*

Some of this of course is Halloween childishness. Educated readers love a hearty scare. Abuse is good for us, they seem to think, and revolutionary violence is what we all want. The revolutionary position is a privileged one. Rage is a luxury, destruction is a sort of *romance*. In the *Art of Being Ruled* Wyndham Lewis spoke of the super freedom of the revolutionary rich. He held that emancipation and irresponsibility were for most people commutative terms and that in playing at revolution and aping proletarian freedom the rich were having and eating their cake.

This, I suggest, is the position of many middle-class liberals whose fortunes have risen. They are doing what the revolutionary rich were able to do in 1925, enjoying a sort of utopian freedom. There is no risk, really. It is perfectly safe and shows that one has done well in life and enjoys a higher status. Moreover, anger is emotionally valuable, as every kindergarten teacher knows. And that ideological passion puts liberalism—i.e., slow secular morality—to shame is not exactly the latest news. There may even be vestiges of religion here; a touch of masochism possibly reminds people of the beatitudes. And, lastly, energy is beauty—that we know from William Blake.

(As for Melville, he was evidently of two minds about it for he wrote, later in life, *"Indolence is Heaven's ally here/And energy the Child of Hell."*)

American intellectuals, White and Black, live on a trust fund of ideas. One can often see the source of a writer's mental income. In Mr. Brown's case I see the hatred of bourgeois intellectuals, the cult of will, the heroics of personal involvement, fondness for cataclysm, etc. Malraux had some of these notions; before him came Sorel; before Sorel a good many others. But for Mr. Brown and Mr. LeRoi Jones, the supreme source seems to be D. H. Lawrence. Here is Lawrence himself on *Moby Dick*. The similarities will be obvious:

Doom of our white day. We are doomed, doomed. And the doom is in America. The doom of our white day.

Ah, well, if my day is doomed, and I am doomed with my day, it is something greater than I which dooms me, so I accept my doom as a sign of the greatness which is more than I am.

Melville knew. He knew his race was doomed, his white soul, doomed. His great white epoch, doomed. Himself, doomed. The idealist, doomed. The spirit, doomed. . . .

What then is Moby Dick? He is the deepest blood-being of the white race; he is our deepest blood-nature.

And he is hunted, hunted, hunted by the maniacal fanaticism of our white mental consciousness. We want to hunt him down. To subject him to our will. . . .

The last phallic being of the white man. Hunted into the death of upper consciousness and the ideal will. . . .

Oh God, oh God, what next when the Pequod has sunk?

She sank in the war, and we are all flotsam. . . .

The Pequod went down. And the Pequod was the ship of the white American soul. . . . If the Great White Whale sank the ship of the Great White Soul in 1851, what has been happening ever since?

Post-mortem effect, presumably.

And there it is, all of it: the last phallic being of the white man, the sinking of the white soul, the doom of the white day. No wonder Mr. Brown and Mr. Jones conclude that the Black man alone will make it. It was Lawrence who set up this little trust fund. He was a genius, but was he also a seer? Perhaps not.

I have picked on the *Partisan Review*. The other quarterlies are not very different. Most of them are university subsidized, as what is not these days. The university has become the sanctuary, at times the hospital, of literature, painting, music and theater. It contains also computers, atom smashers, agricultural researchers, free psychotherapy, technocratic planners, revolutionary ideologists. It has everything, including bohemia. But the university is only one of the homes of bohemia. American society is being thoroughly bohemianized. I speak not only of the middle class, where the signs are clear, but also of the working class, where they are now beginning to appear. And what is art, in this bohemianized society? It is a toy.

New Self-Consciousness

De Tocqueville observed that in a democracy ordinary people wished primarily to view themselves and that the citizen of a democratic country would find nothing more fascinating than—himself. In America we are, I think, looking—no, staring!—at ourselves.

Art is an element of this new self-consciousness. Assimilated by the mass media, the methods, the discoveries of great modern artists are being spread throughout society. The *frénésie journalière*[1] of Baudelaire is no longer exclusively for poets. Millions of people are involved in some sort of *frénésie journalière*.

In *Playboy*, too, we can see the sneakers in the python's mouth. In a recent number of that magazine, Dr. Leslie Fiedler has the following things to say:

Almost all today's readers and writers are aware that we are living through the death throes of literary modernism and the birth pangs of postmodernism. The kind of literature that had arrogated to itself the name modern (with the presumption that it represented the ultimate advance in sensibility and form, that beyond it newness was not possible), and whose moment of triumph lasted from just before World War One until just after World War Two, is *dead*; i.e., belongs to history, not actuality. In the field of the novel, this means that the age of Proust, Mann and Joyce is over, just as in verse, that of T. S. Eliot and Paul Valéry is done with. . . .

The kind of criticism the age demands is death-of-art criticism, which is most naturally practiced by those who have come of age since the death of the new poetry and the new criticism. It seems evident that writers not blessed to be under 30 (or 35, or whatever the critical age is these days) must be reborn in order to seem relevant to the moment and to those who inhabit it most comfortably: the young. But one hasn't even the hope of being reborn unless he knows first that he is dead.

1. Daily frenzy.

What a lot of death we have here! Ishmael is dead without knowing it. The survival of the Black man will mean the death of America. The ship of the Great White Soul sank in 1851 and since then we have been seeing postmortem effects. And now Fiedler's coroner's verdict. Actually he is nicer than the others because he gives the dead a second chance.

But what a lot of ideological burial parties the twentieth century has seen! Common to all of them is a certain historical outlook. All that is not *now*, they say, is obsolete and dead. Any man who does not accept the historical moment as defined by the only authoritative interpreters is dead. In Dr. Fiedler's view, however, a man can rise again from the grave if he agrees that he is indeed dead. "Okay —I'm dead." "Then come forth, Lazarus." It can be fun, I suppose. Anyway it beats oblivion.

What Fiedler wants is to "close the gap between high culture and low, belles lettres and pop art." He calls for more obscenity, more of the *mantic,* the *mad* and the *savage*. We must go back again to Westerns:

> It is impossible to write any Western that does not in some sense glorify violence; but the violence celebrated in the anti-white Western is guerrilla violence—the sneak attack on civilization as practiced first by Geronimo and Cochise and other Indian warrior chiefs and more latterly apologized for by Che Guevara or the spokesman for North Vietnam. Warfare, however, is not the final vision implicit in the new Western, which is motivated on a deeper level by a nostalgia for the tribe—a social organization thought of as preferable to both the bourgeois family, from which its authors come, and the soulless out-of-human-scale bureaucratic state, into which they are initiated via schools and universities. In the end, both the dream of violence in the woods and the vision of tribal life seem juvenile, even infantile. But this is precisely the point; for what recommends the Western to the new novelist is preeminently its association with children.

For without the Child, where are we? And Dr. Fiedler now goes full throttle.

> For our latest poets realize . . . that merely to instruct and delight is not enough. They are convinced that wonder and fantasy that deliver the mind from the body, the body from the mind, must be naturalized to a world of machines. . . . One must live the tribal life among and with the support of machines; to shelter new communes under domes constructed according to the technology of Buckminster Fuller; and to warm the nakedness of new primitives with advanced techniques of solar heating.

In short, postelectronic romanticism. Dow Chemical manufactures napalm but also the "powerful psychedelic agent STP," and drugs are linked by Dr. Fiedler to

> . . . a great religious revival, scarcely noticed by the official spokesmen of established Christian churches, since it speaks quite another language. . . . Certain poets and novelists, as well as pop singers and pornographic

playwrights, are suggesting in print, on the air, everywhere, that not work but vision is the proper activity of men and that, therefore, the contemplative life [contemplation induced by LSD, STP—S.B.] may, after all, be preferable to the active one. In such an age, it is not surprising that the books that most move the young are essentially religious books, as indeed, pop art is always religious.

This is amusing but it is dismal, too. One cannot keep smiling at this nonsense, it is too near to madness. Nor is the madness original, the madness of great wit; it's all such old stuff. Again Dr. Fiedler shows us the Rebel, and the Outsider, and again The Desperado, the Primitive, the Redskin, the Sense-Deranged Poet, the Child, and then the Bard chanting to the tribe, and then again the Child. The Child, *über alles!* And he, Dr. Fiedler, is also a man of many faces. Sometimes he is the Little Demon of Sologub[2] and sometimes the dear Professor of *Little Women*,[3] all loving kindness.

A Good Scare

But loving kindness is often the favorite camouflage of the nihilist. The Grand Inquisitor[4] is always primping to kiss Jesus. However, a positive attitude is required of all who address the great U.S. public. Every society has its favorite lies. Our own favorite is kindliness. Dr. Fiedler loves the young, the new, loves the tribe, loves popular culture (formerly known to intellectuals as Masscult). Still the Petty Demon does burst out, spitting wrathfully.

Why does reading Fiedler's essay so promptly and strongly bring fascism to mind? Is he really a dangerous person? Does he literally mean that those of us who are over thirty-five might as well be dead? Probably not. His job is to frighten us, to give us all a good scare. In the old days he would have been writing for the Hearst Sunday Supplement. (Hefner[5] is quite a lot like W. R. Hearst.) But hatred of liberalism, love of an imaginary past (Cowboys and Indians), somnambulistic certitude, praise of tribalism and of Dionysiac excesses, the cult of youth, the chastising of high culture by the masses, the consecration of violence—all these suggest fascism. Lidless, the garbage can waits. Necessary and superfluous are the main categories, here. History is important for what you can get rid of. Considerations of style, quality or degree are irrelevant.

An Old Story

According to Fiedler, we are confronted with nothing less than the spiritual regeneration of mankind, we must expect to pass

2. Fyodor Sologub was the pen name of F. K. Teternikov, a Russian novelist, whose best-known book, *Little Demon*, portrays a sordid, perverted, and paranoid schoolteacher.

3. A children's novel by Louisa May Alcott.

4. Ivan's fictitious cardinal, in Dostoievsky's *Brothers Karamazov*, who, on Jesus' coming again to earth, condemns Him to death.

5. Hugh Hefner, publisher of *Playboy*.

through the earlier theological and metaphysical stages of voodoo, storefront revivalism, astrology, holyrolling and Manson[6] cults. But the barbarous and the monstrous will refresh us and, as everybody knows, renewal always follows destruction. High culture will return —like *Mare Nostrum?* like the Thousand-Year Reich?

An old, old story—an ancient religious belief, really. Destruction purifies. We go through Hell, and we come out again. Jung, Lawrence, many others repeat the same myth. After the holocaust, the Phoenix; after the Flood, Ararat; after the Final Conflict, a Just Society; after Death, Resurrection. From Dr. Fiedler, powerfully flapping but never actually flying, the same message reaches us.

At this time, he says, we must yield and go along with pop art. Does that mean that we must make terms with the media-managing intellectuals? Evidently it does. And here it begins to appear that Dr. Fiedler's own class interests are involved. Isn't it obvious that college-educated, swinging, bearded, costumed, bohemianized intellectuals are writing the ads, manufacturing the gimmicks, directing the shows, exploiting the Woodstocks? Dr. Fiedler, an influential educator, is endorsing his own product. These new publicity intellectuals are his pupils. He tells us that the worst sins of the masses are better than the dead virtues of high culture. From many beards we hear amen to that. Yes, civilization has been profoundly disappointing. But this disappointment is also the foundation of their personal success. *It*—civilization—is a failure, but *they*—the publicity intellectuals—are doing extremely well.

What civilization has accumulated they treat as fuel and burn up. As the nineteenth century got its industrial power from coal, from the combustion of carboniferous forests, so successful operators burn up the culture of the nineteenth, the eighteenth, the seventeenth centuries, of all centuries, of all the ages. While they complain of a consumer culture, they consume the past, consume it all. They see nothing wrong with this. They find their sanction in the Contemporaneous. For whatever is not Contemporaneous is worthless.

I now turn briefly to the Underground Press.

Mr. D. A. Latimer, writing in the *East Village Other*, has this to say about the use of the word bullshit in the *New York Daily News*.

Reuben Maury has been busted for using the word "bullshit." Not I, mind you, I use the word "bullshit" without fear—bullshit on you, *Daily NEWS!*—because there is already one who has died for my sins, and that is Lenny Bruce. This week Douglas Records released a new album of Lenny Bruce tapes, monologues that have not been heard since their original delivery in some sleazy nightclub; and as part of their massive publicity campaign, Douglas invited me up to their plush offices last month

6. Charles Manson, head of the "family" that murdered Sharon Tate and oth- ers in California in 1969.

and laid some sweet rap on me. Mainly they allowed me to cup a lazy moment in my hands the posterior of the resident receptionist, a tall brunette lovely right out of some of my better cocaine visions. You want some bally-hoo, you just send your office chickie around by Latimer; women's lib will be down on me for this, but there it is, a piece for a piece, that's my professional credo.

At no time in the last few years have I heard any Lenny Bruce tapes, but I *have* been doing some research, and you know, there's a story in all that for our times. He was a fucking genius, this Bruce, when the scroll is written up on the Twentieth Century this guy has got to be the presiding Great Mind. And of course they blew him away, caught him in a lavatory trying to pump a French cruller up his arm, burned him off in August, 1966, you know all that. But the way they did it was so very similar to the way they're burning everybody off today, it could be quite instructive to inspect his history.

They kept busting him, see, and they ruined his head with all that courtroom shit. That's really bad news, when you're just trying to get your point across to some people, and the heat comes out and hits you for using dirty words. "Pray the Court's indulgence, the defendant in a public place used the word 'bullshit' at approximately 7:10 in the evening and repeated it at 7:27, 7:40, and 8:12. Also on the same occasion, he was heard by myself and Officer Phlud as saying, 'the sisters, the sisters do it this way,' in an obscene context." Now, how do you defend yourself against something like that? Sure enough, Lenny Bruce *said* "bullshit" several times in his life, and he made innumerable references to God and the Church and the sisters—but he knew there wasn't anything *illegal* about it, how can something you *say* be *illegal?* But they kept putting him in the exceedingly clumsy position before the courts of having to prove that he hadn't broken any laws, to persuade a judge to that effect. And the judge hasn't seen the show, but he *has* seen the District Attorney, day in and day out, so he's very likely to send you down the river just to keep this confusing shit at arm's length.

With Mr. Latimer we are at the heart of the phenomenon. And what do we see? We see, straight from *King Lear,* the burning words, "Thou, Nature, art my Goddess." Then we see feces as the most potent of primordial materials, very powerful indeed. The word Shit is to anal Protestantism what the crucifix was to werewolves. Narcotics also are known in the underground as Shit, addicts are said to "shoot Shit" into their veins.

In his essay "Inside the Whale" George Orwell praised Henry Miller for putting aside the old literary language, the language of literary protocol, and for using instead the real language of real men, the language of streets and shipping rooms. The Miller victory is complete. The resonance of the street words has become great. A word like Bullshit has a moral force like that of Church Latin. *Vade retro Satanas!*[7] sounds no more magnificent to modern ears. There are religious undertones, too, for even in the underground religion (though in the form of blasphemy) has not disappeared, Dr. Fiedler is right about that. Thus Bruce is a Jesus who died for our sins. He was caught while taking the narcotics sacrament and

7. "Get thee hence, Satan." Matthew iv.10.

his (or His) pure spirit was destroyed. (An excrement-sacrament?)

"They" caught him trying to pump a French cruller up his arm. "They" is the Heat, Authority, the Law, the Enemy. It is certainly, in many ways, an enemy. Even to itself it is no friend. Heavily armed, authority feels weak. Upper-class Protestant America freely, even excessively confesses its failures. Its last great man was F.D.R. It has much power still, but it is floundering. Certain of its industries are dominated by a new class, the publicity intellectuals. These are former students of literature, sociology or psychology, graduates of art institutes and drama departments. They have gone directly from college into the Mass Media. Unlike the intellectuals of the Depression era who were unemployed and who lived as intellectuals, publicity intellectuals have never been independent (and impoverished) writers, painters or thinkers.

Seeking Intercession

In the magazines and newspapers, top management, formerly so autocratic (think of Henry Luce), now casts itself at the feet of the publicity intellectuals, seeking their intercession with the youth-worshiping public. One picks up *The New York Times* and reads on the front page that the posthumous homosexual novel of E. M. Forster is about to appear in England. Why not simply Forster's posthumous novel, on page 40? No, the word is HOMOSEXUAL and it is on the front page. The *Times* still keeps up its statesmanlike and grave appearance, but its journalism is yellower than ever. It has surrendered without a fight to the new class.

The present standard is the amusement standard: more accurately the amusement-boredom standard.

Literature in the nineteenth century laid a transforming touch on ordinary social realities, on city scenes and on the modern character. Many people now want to make literal use of imaginative suggestions. How shall we put it: they want to cook their meals over Pater's hard gemlike flame and light their cigarettes at it. They crave the exceptional for daily use, and the main purpose is perhaps to make behavior. No wonder the boundaries between stage and audience are disappearing and that spectators take off their clothes and mingle with the actors. Even American intellectuals, from Emerson to Norman O. Brown, preferred marvelous conduct to sedentary culture. Now belles lettres are licked; beautiful behavior wins hands down.

A powerful nation of unparalleled energy and practicality created an industrial society without precedent in history. The accompanying ugliness, boredom and spiritual trouble are also without precedent. Parts of society seem mad. It is essential (as Edgar Wind remarks in *Art and Anarchy*) that the whole should be less mad then the parts. But Authority has neither the imagination nor the moral capacity to act for the whole.

The peculiar difficulty of the artist in this situation is that he is obliged to take a common-sense view of things. What are his alternatives? He can no longer do the Child, the Primitive, the Romantic Agonist, the Rebel, the Drugged Visionary. All that is busted. Modernism is in the hands of demagogues, dunces and businessmen. It belongs to the publicity intellectuals. Because of this, the artist loses the benefit of contact with his modernist predecessors and is deprived of certain impulses and of a certain admirable verve.

Theatricality of Literature

As many observers tell us, everyone is "in the act." Of course Wallace Stevens was correct in pointing out the theatricality of literature. Authors are actors, he said, and books are theaters. But if the theater is everywhere and everyone is acting, where are exemplary events to be seen? The theory of creative equality implies the death of art. Reading the Underground Press, one becomes aware of ten thousand Villons.[8] The problem is one for the census taker, not the critic.

It should not be assumed that I recommend common sense for the artist. Surrounded by lunatics, he must make rational judgments, but he is not bound by these in his art. The operations of common sense are only preliminary. Once a writer has understood the state of fantasy prevailing, once he has understood what an art-polluted environment this is, his imagination is free again to receive new impulses.

The depths of the spirit are never overcrowded.

This society, like decadent Rome, is an amusement society. That is the grim fact. Art cannot and should not compete with amusement. It has business at the heart of humankind. The artist, as Collingwood tells us, must be a prophet, "not in the sense that he foretells things to come, but that he tells the audience, at risk of their displeasure, the secrets of their own hearts." That is why he exists. He is spokesman of his community. This account of the artist's business is old, much older than Collingwood, very old, but in modern times this truth, which we all feel, is seldom expressed. ". . . No community altogether knows its own heart: and by failing in this knowledge a community deceives itself on the one subject concerning which ignorance means death. . . . The remedy is the poem itself. Art is the community's medicine for the worst disease of mind, the corruption of consciousness."

---

8. François Villon, fifteenth-century French poet, here used as a type of the anti-establishment bard.

ANTHONY BURGESS
Is America Falling Apart?

I am back in Bracciano, a castellated town about 13 miles north of Rome, after a year in New Jersey. I find the Italian Government still unstable, gasoline more expensive than anywhere in the world, butchers and bank clerks and tobacconists (which also means salt-sellers) ready to go on strike at the drop of a *cappello*, neo-Fascists at their dirty work, the hammer and sickle painted on the rumps of public statues, a thousand-lire note (officially worth about $1.63) shrunk to the slightness of a dollar bill.

Nevertheless, it's delightful to be back. People are underpaid but they go through an act of liking their work, the open markets are luscious with esculent color, the community is more important than the state, the human condition is humorously accepted. The *tra-montana* blows viciously today, and there's no central heating to turn on, but it will be pleasant when the wind drops. The two television channels are inadequate, but next Wednesday's rerun of an old Western, with Gary Cooper coming into a saloon saying *"Ciao, ragazzi,"* is something to look forward to. Manifold consumption isn't important here. The quality of life has nothing to do with the quantity of brand names. What matters is talk, family, cheap wine in the open air, the wresting of minimal sweetness out of the long-known bitterness of living. I was spoiled in New Jersey. The Italian for *spoiled* is *viziato*, cognate with *vitiated*, which has to do with vice.

Spoiled? Well, yes. I never had to shiver by a fire that wouldn't draw, or go without canned kraut juice or wild rice. America made me develop new appetites in order to make proper use of the super-market. A character in Evelyn Waugh's *Put Out More Flags* said that the difference between prewar and postwar life was that, prewar, if one thing went wrong the day was ruined; postwar, if one thing went right the day would be made. America is a prewar coun-try, psychologically unprepared for one thing to go wrong. Now everything seems to be going wrong. Hence the neurosis, despair, the Kafka feeling that the whole marvelous fabric of American life is coming apart at the seams. Italy is used to everything going wrong. This is what the human condition is about.

Let me stay for a while on this subject of consumption. American individualism, on the face of it an admirable philosophy, wishes to manifest itself in independence of the community. You don't share things in common; you have your own things. A family's strength is signalized by its possessions. Herein lies a paradox. For the desire for possessions must eventually mean dependence on possessions.

Freedom is slavery. Once let the acquisitive instinct burgeon (enough flour for the winter, not just for the week), and there are ruggedly individual forces only too ready to make it come to full and monstrous blossom. New appetites are invented; what to the European are bizarre luxuries become, to the American, plain necessities.

During my year's stay in New Jersey I let my appetites flower into full Americanism except for one thing. I did not possess an automobile. This self-elected deprivation was a way into the nastier side of the consumer society. Where private ownership prevails, public amenities decay or are prevented from coming into being. The wretched run-down rail services of America are something I try, vainly, to forget. The nightmare of filth, outside and in, that enfolds the trip from Springfield, Mass., to Grand Central Station would not be accepted in backward Europe. But far worse is the nightmare of travel in and around Los Angeles, where public transport does not exist and people are literally choking to death in their exhaust fumes. This is part of the price of the metaphysic of individual ownership.

But if the car owner can ignore the lack of public transport, he can hardly ignore the decay of services in general. His car needs mechanics, and mechanics grow more expensive and less efficient. The gadgets in the home are cheaper to replace than repair. The more efficiently self-contained the home, primary fortress of independence, seems to be, the more dependent it is on the great impersonal corporations, as well as a diminishing army of servitors. Skills at the lowest level have to be wooed slavishly and exorbitantly rewarded. Plumbers will not come. Nor, at the higher level, will doctors. And doctors and dentists, in a nation committed to maiming itself with sugar and cholesterol, know their scarcity value and behave accordingly.

Americans are at last realizing that the acquisition of goods is not the whole of life. Consumption, on one level, is turning insipid, especially as the quality of the artifacts themselves seems to be deteriorating. Planned obsolescence is not conducive to pride in workmanship. On another level, consumption is turning sour. There is a growing guilt about the masses of discarded junk—rusting automobiles and refrigerators and washing machines and dehumidifiers— that it is uneconomical to recycle. Indestructible plastic hasn't even the grace to undergo chemical change. America, the world's biggest consumer, is the world's biggest polluter. Awareness of this is a kind of redemptive grace, but it doesn't appreciably lead to repentance and a revolution in consumer habits. Citizens of Los Angeles are horrified by that daily pall of golden smog, but they don't noticeably clamor for a decrease in the number of owner-vehicles. There is no worse neurosis than that which derives from a consciousness of guilt and an inability to reform.

America is anachronistic in so many ways, and not least in its clinging to a belief—now known to be unviable—in the capacity of the individual citizen to do everything for himself. Americans are admirable in their distrust of the corporate state—they have fought both Fascism and Communism—but they forget that there is a use for everything, even the loathsome bureaucratic machine. America needs a measure of socialization, as Britain needed it. Things—especially those we need most—don't always pay their way, and it is here that the state must enter, dismissing the profit element. Part of the present American neurosis, again, springs from awareness of this but inability to do anything about practical implementation. Perhaps only a country full of bombed cities feels capable of this kind of social revolution.

It would be supererogatory for me to list those areas in which thoughtful Americans feel that collapse is coming. It is enough for me to concentrate on what, during my New Jersey stay, impinged on my own life. Education, for instance, since I have a 6-year-old son to be brought up. America has always despised its teachers and, as a consequence, it has been granted the teachers it deserves. The quality of first-grade education that my son received, in a New Jersey town noted for the excellence of its public schools, could not, I suppose, be faulted on the level of dogged conscientiousness. The principal had read all the right pedagogic books, and was ready to quote these in the footnotes to his circular exhortations to parents. The teachers worked rigidly from the approved rigidly programed primers, ensuring that school textbook publication remains the big business it is.

But there seemed to be no spark; no daring, no madness, no readiness to engage the individual child's mind as anything other than raw material for statistical reductions. The fear of being unorthodox is rooted in the American teacher's soul: you can be fired for treading the path of experimental enterprise. In England, teachers cannot be fired, except for raping girl students and getting boy students drunk. In consequence, there is the kind of security that breeds eccentric genius, the capacity for firing mad enthusiasms.

I know that American technical genius, and most of all the moon landings, seems to give the lie to too summary a condemnation of the educational system, but there is more to education than the segmental equipping of the mind. There is that transmission of the value of the past as a force still miraculously fertile and moving—mostly absent from American education at all levels.

Of course, America was built on a rejection of the past. Even the basic Christianity which was brought to the continent in 1620 was of a novel and bizarre kind that would have nothing to do with the great rank river of belief that produced Dante and Michelangelo. America as a nation has never been able to settle to a common belief more sophisticated than the dangerous naiveté of the Declaration of Independence. "Life, liberty and the pursuit of happiness," indeed. And now America, filling in the vacuum left by the liquefied British Empire, has the task of telling the rest of the world that there's something better than Communism. The something better can only be money-making and consumption for its own sake. In the name of this ghastly creed the jungles must be defoliated.

No wonder the guilt of the thoughtful Americans I met in Princeton and New York and, indeed, all over the Union tended to express itself as an extravagant masochism, a desire for flagellation. Americans want to take on all the blame they can find, gluttons for punishment. "What do Europeans really think of us?" is a common question at parties. The expected answer is: "They think you're a load of decadent, gross-lipped, potbellied, callous, overbearing neoimperialists." Then the head can be bowed and the chest smitten: "*Nostra culpa, nostra maxima culpa*. . . ." But the fact is that such an answer, however much desired, would not be an honest one. Europeans think more highly of Americans now than they ever did. Let me try to explain why.

When Europe, after millennia of war, rapine, slavery, famine, intolerance, had sunk to the level of a sewer, America became the golden dream, the Eden where innocence could be recovered. Original sin was the monopoly of that dirty continent over there; in America man could glow in an aura of natural goodness, driven along his shining path by divine reason. The Declaration of Independence itself is a monument to reason. Progress was possible, and the wrongs committed against the Indians, the wildlife, the land itself, could be explained away in terms of the rational control of environment necessary for the building of a New Jerusalem. Right and wrong made up the moral dichotomy; evil—that great eternal inextirpable entity—had no place in America.

At last, with the Vietnam war and especially the Mylai horror, Americans are beginning to realize that they are subject to original sin as much as Europeans are. Some things—the massive crime figures, for instance—can now be explained only in terms of absolute evil. Europe, which has long known about evil and learned to live with it (*live* is *evil* spelled backwards), is now grimly pleased to find that America is becoming like Europe. America is no longer Europe's daughter nor her rich stepmother: she is Europe's sister. The agony that America is undergoing is not to be associated with breakdown so much as with the parturition of self-knowledge.

It has been assumed by many that the youth of America has

been in the vanguard of the discovery of both the disease and the cure. The various copping-out movements, however, from the Beats on, have committed the gross error of assuming that original sin rested with their elders, their rulers, and that they themselves could manifest their essential innocence by building little neo-Edens. The drug culture could confirm that the paradisal vision was available to all who sought it. But instant ecstasy has to be purchased, like any other commodity, and, in economic terms, that passive life of pure being involves parasitism. Practically all of the crime I encountered in New York—directly or through report—was a preying of the opium-eaters on the working community. There has to be a snake in paradise. You can't escape the heritage of human evil by building communes, usually on an agronomic ignorance that, intended to be a rejection of inherited knowledge, that suspect property of the elders, does violence to life. The American young are well-meaning but misguided, and must not themselves be taken as guides.

The guides, as always, lie among the writers and artists. And Americans ought to note that, however things may seem to be falling apart, arts and the humane scholarship are flourishing here, as they are not, for instance, in England. I'm not suggesting that Bellow, Mailer, Roth and the rest have the task of finding a solution to the American mess, but they can at least clarify its nature and show how it relates to the human condition in general. Literature, that most directly human of the arts, often reacts magnificently to an ambience of unease or apparent breakdown. The Elizabethans, to whose era we look back as to an irrecoverable Golden Age, were far more conscious than modern Americans of the chaos and corruption and incompetence of the state. Shakespeare's period was one of poverty, unemployment, ghastly inflation, violence in the streets. Twenty-six years after his death there was a bloody civil war, followed by a dictatorship of religious fanatics, followed by a calm respite in which the seeds of a revolution were sown. England survived. America will survive.

I'm not suggesting that Americans sit back and wait for a transient period of mistrust and despair to resolve itself, like a disease, through the unconscious healing forces which lie deep in organic nature. Man, as Thornton Wilder showed in *The Skin of Our Teeth*, always comes through—though sometimes only just. Americans living here and now have a right to an improvement in the quality of their lives, and they themselves, not the remote governors, must do something about it. It is not right that men and women should fear to go on the streets at night, and that they should sometimes fear the police as much as the criminals, both of whom sometimes look like mirror images of each other. I have had too much evidence, in my year in New Jersey, of the police behaving like the "Fascist pigs" of the revolutionary press. There are too many guns about, and the disarming of the police should be a natural aspect of the disarming of the entire citizenry.

American politics, at both the state and the Federal levels, is too much concerned with the protection of large fortunes, America being the only example in history of a genuine timocracy. The wealth qualification for the aspiring politician is taken for granted; a governmental system dedicated to the promotion of personal wealth in a few selected areas will never act for the public good. The time has come, nevertheless, for citizens to demand, from their government, a measure of socialization—the provision of amenities for the many, of which adequate state pensions and sickness benefits, as well as nationalized transport, should be priorities.

As for those remoter solutions to the American nightmare—only an aspect, after all, of the human nightmare—an Englishman must be diffident about suggesting that America made her biggest mistake in becoming America—meaning a revolutionary republic based on a romantic view of human nature. To reject a limited monarchy in favor of an absolute one (which is, after all, what the American Presidency is) argues a trust in the disinterestedness of an elected ruler which is, of course, no more than a reflection of belief in the innate goodness of man—so long as he happens to be American man. The American Constitution is out of date. Republics tend to corruption. Canada and Australia have their own problems, but they are happier countries than America.

This *Angst* about America coming apart at the seams, which apparently is shared by nearly 50 per cent of the entire American population, is something to rejoice about. A sense of sin is always admirable, though it must not be allowed to become neurotic. If electric systems break down and gadgets disintegrate, it doesn't matter much. There is always wine to be drunk by candlelight, uniced. If America's position as a world power collapses, and the Union dissolves into independent states, there is still the life of the family or the individual to be lived. England has survived her own dissolution as an imperial power, and Englishmen seem to be happy enough. But I ask the reader to note that I, an Englishman, no longer live in England, and I can't spend more than six months at a stretch in Italy—or any other European country, for that matter. I home to America as to a country more stimulating than depressing. The future of mankind is being worked out there on a scale typically American—vast, dramatic, almost apocalyptical. I brave the brutality and the guilt in order to be in on the scene. I shall be back.

QUESTIONS

1. What would Burgess say of the Whole Earth Catalogue: is it a rejection of consumerism or a surrender to it?
2. In what respects is the substance of Burgess' argument similar to that of Eldridge Cleaver (pp. 492–500)? compare the language used by each to articulate the similar substance; is the language of either more basic than that of the other?
3. Burgess' observation about the Italian word for spoiled implies a concern for etymology and precision of language. Is there evidence of that concern in his choice of English words?

PHILIP SLATER

The Old Culture and the New

There are an almost infinite number of polarities by means of which one can differentiate between the two cultures. The old culture, when forced to choose, tends to give preference to property rights over personal rights, technological requirements over human needs, competition over cooperation, violence over sexuality, concentration over distribution, the producer over the consumer, means over ends, secrecy over openness, social forms over personal expression, striving over gratification, Oedipal love over communal love, and so on. The new counterculture tends to reverse all of these priorities.

Now it is important to recognize that these differences cannot be resolved by some sort of compromise or "golden mean" position. Every cultural system is a dynamic whole, resting on processes that must be accelerative to be self-sustaining. Change must therefore affect the motivational roots of a society or it is not change at all. An attempt to introduce some isolated element into such a system produces cultural redefinition and absorption of the novel element if the culture is strong, and deculturation if it is susceptible. As Margaret Mead points out, to introduce cloth garments into a grass-or-bark-clad population, without simultaneously introducing closets, soap, sewing, and furniture, merely transforms a neat and attractive tribe into a dirty and slovenly one. Cloth is part of a complex cultural pattern that includes storing, cleaning, mending, and protecting—just as the automobile is part of a system that includes fueling, maintenance, and repair. A fish with the lungs of a land mammal still will not survive out of water.

Imagine, for example, that we are cooperation purists attempting to remove the invidious element from a foot race. We decide, first of all, that we will award no prize to the winner, or else prizes to everyone. This, we discover, brings no reduction in competitiveness.

Spectators and participants alike are still preoccupied with who won and how fast he ran relative to someone else now or in the past. We then decide to eliminate even *announcing* the winner. To our dismay we discover that our efforts have generated some new cultural forms: the runners have taken to wearing more conspicuous identifying clothing—bright-colored trunks or shirts, or names emblazoned in iridescent letters—and underground printed programs have appeared with names, physical descriptions, and other information facilitating this identification. In despair we decide to have the runners run one at a time and we keep no time records. But now we find that the sale of stopwatches has become a booming enterprise, that the underground printed programs have expanded to include voluminous statistics on past time records of participants, and that private "timing services," comparable to the rating services of the television industry, have grown up to provide definitive and instantaneous results for spectators willing to pay a nominal sum (thus does artificial deprivation facilitate enterprise).

At this point we are obliged to eliminate the start and finish lines —an innovation which arouses angry protest from both spectators and participants, who have evinced only mild grumbling over our previous efforts. "What kind of a race can it be if people begin and end wherever they like? Who will be interested in it?" To mollify their complaints and combat dwindling attendance, we reintroduce the practice of having everyone run at the same time. Before long we observe that the runners have evolved the practice of all starting to run at about the same time (although we disallowed beginning at the same place), and that all of the races are being run on the circular track. The races get longer and longer, and the underground printed programs now record statistics on how many laps were run by a given runner in a given race. All races have now become longevity contests, and one goes to them equipped with a picnic basket. The newer fields, in fact, do not have bleachers, but only tables at which drinks are served, with scattered observation windows through which the curious look from time to time and report to their tables the latest news on which runners are still going. Time passes, and we are increasingly subjected to newspaper attacks concerning the corrupt state into which our efforts have fallen. With great trepidation, and in the face of enormous opposition from the ideologically apathetic masses, we inaugurate a cultural revolution and make further drastic alterations in racing rules. Runners begin and end at a signal, but there is no track, merely an open field. A runner must change direction every thirty seconds, and if he runs parallel with another runner for more than fifteen seconds he is disqualified. At first attendance falls off badly, but after a time spectators become interested in how many runners can survive a thirty-minute race without being eliminated for a breach of these rules. Soon specific groups become so skilled at not running parallel that none of them are ever disqualified. In the meantime they begin to run a little more slowly and to elaborate intricate patterns of synchronizing their direction changes. The more gifted groups become virtuosi at moving parallel until the last split second and then diverging. The thirty-second rule becomes unnecessary as direction changes are voluntarily frequent, but the fifteen-second rule becomes a five-second one. The motions of the runners become more and more elegant, and a vast outpouring of books and articles descends from and upon the university (ever a dirty bird) to establish definitive distinctions between the race and the dance.

The first half of this parable is a reasonably accurate representation of what most liberal reform amounts to: opportunities for the existing system to flex its muscles and exercise its self-maintaining capabilities. Poverty programs put very little money into the hands of the poor because middle-class hands are so much more gifted at grasping money—they know better where it is, how to apply for it, how to divert it, how to concentrate it. That is what being middle class means, just as a race means competition. No matter how much we try to change things it somehow ends as merely a more complex, intricate, bizarre, and interesting version of what existed before. A heavily graduated income tax somehow ends by making the rich richer and the poor poorer. "Highway beautification" somehow turns into rural blight, and so on.

But there is a limit to the amount of change a system can absorb, and the second half of the parable suggests that if we persist in our efforts and finally attack the system at its motivational roots we may indeed be successful. In any case there is no such thing as "compromise": we are either strong enough to lever the train onto a new track or it stays on the old one or it is derailed.

Thus it becomes important to discern the core motivational logic behind the old and the new cultures. Knowing this would make rational change possible—would unlock the door that leads most directly from the old to the new.[1] For a prolonged, unplanned collision will nullify both cultures, like bright pigments combining into gray. The transition must be as deft as possible if we are to minimize the destructive chaos that inevitably accompanies significant cultural transformations.

The core of the old culture is scarcity. Everything in it rests upon the assumption that the world does not contain the wherewithal to satisfy the needs of its human inhabitants. From this it follows that people must compete with one another for these scarce resources— lie, swindle, steal, and kill, if necessary. These basic assumptions

---

1. This of course makes the assumption that some kind of drastic change is either desirable or inevitable. I do not believe our society can long continue on its old premises without destroying itself and everything else. Nor do I believe it can contain or resist the gathering forces of change without committing suicide in the process [Slater's note].

create the danger of a "war of all against all" and must be buttressed by a series of counternorms which attempt to qualify and restrain the intensity of the struggle. Those who can take the largest share of the scarce resources are said to be "successful," and if they can do it without violating the counternorms they are said to have character and moral fibre.

The key flaw in the old culture is, of course, the fact that the scarcity is spurious—man-made in the case of bodily gratifications and man-allowed or man-maintained in the case of material goods. It now exists only for the purpose of maintaining the system that depends upon it, and its artificiality becomes more palpable each day. Americans continually find themselves in the position of having killed someone to avoid sharing a meal which turns out to be too large to eat alone.

The new culture is based on the assumption that important human needs are easily satisfied and that the resources for doing so are plentiful. Competition is unnecessary and the only danger to humans is human aggression. There is no reason outside of human perversity for peace not to reign and for life not to be spent in the cultivation of joy and beauty. Those who can do this in the face of the old culture's ubiquity are considered "beautiful."

The flaw in the new culture is the fact that the old culture has succeeded in hiding the cornucopia of satisfactions that the new assumes—that a certain amount of work is required to release the bounty that exists from the restraints under which it is now placed. Whereas the flaw in the old culture has caused it to begin to decompose, the flaw in the new culture has produced a profound schism in its ranks—a schism between activist and dropout approaches to the culture as it now exists. We will return to this problem a little later.

It is important to recognize the internal logic of the old culture, however absurd its premise. If one assumes scarcity, then the knowledge that others want the same things that we have leads with some logic to preparations for defense, and, ultimately (since the best defense is offense), for attack. The same assumption leads to a high value being placed on the ability to postpone gratification (since there is not enough to go around). The expression of feelings is a luxury, since it might alert the scarce resources to the fact that the hunter is near.

The high value placed on restraint and coldness (which creates even greater scarcity) generates in turn another norm: that of "good taste." One can best understand the meaning of such a norm by examining what is common to those acts considered to be in violation of it, and on this basis the meaning of "good taste" is very clear. "Good taste" means tasteless in the literal sense. Any act or product which contains too much stimulus value is considered to be "in bad taste" by old-culture adherents. Since gratification is viewed as a scarce commodity, arousal is dangerous. Clothes must be drab and inconspicuous, colors of low intensity, smells nonexistent ("if it weren't for bad taste there wouldn't be no taste at all"). Sounds should be quiet, words should lack affect. Four-letter words are always in bad taste because they have high stimulus value. Satire is in bad taste if it arouses political passions or creates images that are too vivid or exciting. All direct references to sexuality are in bad taste until proven innocent, since sexual arousal is the most feared result of all. The lines in old-culture homes, furnishings, and public buildings are hard and utilitarian. Since auditory overstimulation is more familiarly painful than its visual counterpart, brilliant, intense, vibrant colors are called "loud," and the preferred colors for old-culture homes are dull and listless. Stimulation in any form leaves old-culture Americans with a "bad taste" in their mouths. This taste is the taste of desire—a reminder that life in the here-and-now contains many pleasures to distract them from the carrot dangling beyond their reach. Too much stimulation makes the carrot hard to see. Good taste is a taste for carrots.

In the past decade, however, this pattern has undergone a merciless assault from the new culture. For if we assume that gratification is easy and resources plentiful, stimulation is no longer to be feared. Psychedelic colors, amplified sound, erotic books and films, bright and elaborate clothing, spicy food, "intense" (i.e., Anglo-Saxon) words, angry and irreverent satire—all go counter to the old pattern of understimulation. Long hair and beards provide a more "tactile" appearance than the bland, shaven-and-shorn, geometric lines of the fifties. Even Edward Hall's accusation that America is a land of "olfactory blandness" (a statement any traveler will confirm) must now be qualified a little, as the smells of coffee shops, foreign cooking, and incense combine to breathe a modicum of sensation even into the olfactory sphere. (Hall is right, however, in the sense that when America is filled with intense color, music, and ornament, deodorants will be the old culture's last-ditch holdouts. It is no accident that hostility to hippies so often focuses on their olfactory humanity.) The old culture turned the volume down on emotional experience in order to concentrate on its dreams of glory, but the new culture has turned it up again.

New-culture adherents, in fact, often display symptoms of *under*sensitivity to stimuli. They say "Wow!" in response to almost everything, but in voices utterly devoid of either tension or affect. They seem in general to be more certain that desire can be gratified than that it can be aroused.

This phenomenon probably owes much to early child-rearing conditions. Under ordinary circumstances a mother responds to her child's needs when they are expressed powerfully enough to distract her from other cares and activities. Mothers who overrespond to the Spockian challenge, however, often try to anticipate the child's needs. Before arousal has proceeded very far they hover about and try several possible satisfactions. Since we tend to use these early parental responses as models for the way we treat our own impulses in adulthood, some new-culture adherents find themselves moving toward gratification before need arousal is clear or compelling. Like their mothers they are not altogether clear which need they are feeling. To make matters worse they are caught in the dilemma that spontaneity automatically evaporates the moment it becomes an ideology. It is a paradox of the modern condition that only those who oppose complete libidinal freedom are capable of ever achieving it.

Another logical consequence of scarcity assumptions is structured inequality. If there is not enough to go around then those who have more will find ways to prolong their advantage, and even legitimate it through various devices. The law itself, although philosophically committed to equality, is fundamentally a social device for maintaining structured systems of inequality (defining as crimes, for example, only those forms of theft and violence in which lower class persons engage). One of the major thrusts of the new culture, on the other hand, is equality: since the good things of life are plentiful, everyone should share them: rich and poor, black and white, female and male.

It is a central characteristic of the old culture that means habitually become ends, and ends means. Instead of people working in order to obtain goods in order to be happy, for example, we find that people should be made happy in order to work better in order to obtain more goods, and so on. Inequality, originally a consequence of scarcity, is now a means of creating artificial scarcities. For in the old culture, as we have seen, the manufacture of scarcity is the principal activity. Hostile comments of old-culture adherents toward new-culture forms ("people won't want to work if they can get things for nothing," "people won't want to get married if they can get it free") often reveal this preoccupation. Scarcity, the presumably undesired but unavoidable foundation for the whole old-culture edifice, has now become its most treasured and sacred value, and to maintain this value in the midst of plenty it has been necessary to establish invidiousness as the foremost criterion of worth. Old-culture Americans are peculiarly drawn to anything that seems to be the exclusive possession of some group or other, and find it difficult to enjoy anything they themselves have unless they can be sure that there are people to whom this pleasure is denied. For those in power even life itself derives its value invidiously: amid the emptiness and anesthesia of a power-oriented career many officials derive reassurance of their vitality from their proximity to the possibility of blowing up the world.

The centrality of invidiousness offers a strong barrier to the diffusion of social justice and equality. But it provides a *raison d'être* for the advertising industry, whose primary function is to manufacture illusions of scarcity. In a society engorged to the point of strangulation with useless and joyless products, advertisements show people calamitiously running out of their food or beer, avidly hoarding potato chips, stealing each other's cigarettes, guiltily borrowing each other's deodorants, and so on. In a land of plenty there is little to fight over, but in the world of advertising images men and women will fight before changing their brand, in a kind of parody of the Vietnam war.

The fact that property takes precedence over human life in the old culture also follows logically from scarcity assumptions. If possessions are scarce relative to people they come to have more value than people. This is especially true of people with few possessions, who come to be considered so worthless as to be subhuman and hence eligible for extermination. Many possessions, on the other hand, entitle the owner to a status somewhat more than human. But as a society becomes more affluent these priorities begin to change—human life increases in value and property decreases. New-culture adherents challenge the high relative value placed on property, although the old priority still permeates the society's normative structure. It is still considered permissible, for example, to kill someone who is stealing your property under certain conditions. This is especially true if that person is without property himself—a wealthy kleptomaniac (in contrast to a poor black looter) would probably be worth a murder trial if killed while stealing.

A recent sign of the shift in values was the *Pueblo* courtmartial. While the Navy, standing firmly behind old-culture priorities, argued that the Commander of the spy ship should have sacrificed the lives of ninety men to prevent the loss of "expensive equipment" to the enemy, the public at large supported his having put human life first. Much of the intense legal upheaval visible today—expressed most noticeably in the glare of publicity that now attaches to the activities of the U.S. Supreme Court—derives from the attempt to adapt an old-culture legal system to the changing priorities that render it obsolete.

It would not be difficult to show how the other characteristics of the old culture are based on the same scarcity assumptions, or to trace out in detail the derivation of the new culture from the promise that life's satisfactions exist in abundance and sufficiency for all. Let us instead look more closely at the relationship that the new culture bears to the old—the continuities and discontinuities that it offers—and explore some of the contradictions it holds within itself.

First of all it should be stressed that affluence and economic security are not in themselves responsible for the new culture. The rich, like the poor, have always been with us to some degree, but the new culture has not. What is significant in the new culture is not a celebration of economic affluence but a rejection of its foundation. The new culture is concerned with rejecting the artificial scarcities upon which material abundance is based. It argues that instead of throwing away one's body so that one can accumulate material artifacts, one should throw away the artifacts and enjoy one's body. The new culture is not merely blindly reactive, however, but embodies a sociological consciousness. In this consciousness lies the key insight that possessions actually generate scarcity. The more emotion one invests in them the more chances for significant gratification are lost—the more committed to them one becomes the more deprived one feels, like a thirsty man drinking salt water. To accumulate possessions is to deliver pieces of oneself to dead things. Possessions can absorb an emotional cathexis, but unlike personal relationships they feed nothing back. Americans have combined the proliferation of possessions with the disruption, circumscription, and trivialization of most personal relationships. An alcoholic becomes malnourished because drinking obliterates his hunger. Americans become unhappy and vicious because their preoccupation with amassing possessions obliterates their loneliness. This is why production in America seems to be on such an endless upward spiral: every time we buy something we deepen our emotional deprivation and hence our need to buy something. This is good for business, of course, but those who profit most from this process are just as trapped in the general deprivation as everyone else. The new-culture adherents are thus not merely affluent—they are trying to substitute an adequate emotional diet for a crippling addiction.

The new culture is nevertheless a product of the old, not merely a rejection of it. It picks up themes latent or dormant or subordinate in the old and magnifies them. The hippie movement, for example, is brimming with nostalgia—a nostalgia peculiarly American and shared by old-culture adherents. This nostalgia embraces the Old West, Amerindian culture, the wilderness, the simple life, the utopian community—all venerable American traditions. But for the old culture they represent a subordinate, ancillary aspect of the culture, appropriate for recreational occasions or fantasy representation—a kind of pastoral relief from everyday striving—whereas for the new culture they are dominant themes. The new culture's passion for memorabilia, paradoxically, causes uneasiness in old-culture adherents, whose future-oriented invidiousness leads to a desire to sever themselves from the past. Yet for the most part it is a question of the new culture making the old culture's secondary themes primary, rather than simply seeking to discard the old culture's primary theme. Even the notion of "dropping out" is an important American tradition—neither the United States itself nor its populous suburbs would exist were this not so.

Americans have always been deeply ambivalent about the issue of social involvement. On the one hand they are suspicious of it and share deep romantic fantasies of withdrawal to a simple pastoral or even sylvan life. On the other hand they are much given to acting out grandiose fantasies of taking society by storm, through the achievement of wealth, power, or fame. This ambivalence has led to many strange institutions—the suburb and the automobile being the most obvious. But note that both fantasies express the viewpoint of an outsider. Americans have a profound tendency to feel like outsiders—they wonder where the action is and wander about in search of it (this puts an enormous burden on celebrities, who are supposed to know, but in fact feel just as doubtful as everyone else). Americans have created a society in which they are automatically nobodies, since no one has any stable place or enduring connection. The village idiot of earlier times was less a "nobody" in this sense than the mobile junior executive or academic. An American has to "make a place for himself" because he does not have one.

Since the society rests on scarcity assumptions, involvement in it has always meant competitive involvement, and, curiously enough, the theme of bucolic withdrawal has often associated itself with that of cooperative, communal life. So consistently, in fact, have intentional communities established themselves in the wilderness that one can only infer that society as we know it makes cooperative life impossible.

Be that as it may, it is important to remember that the New England colonies grew out of utopian communes, so that the drop-out tradition is not only old but extremely important to our history. Like so many of the more successful nineteenth century utopian communities (Oneida and Amana, for example) the puritans became corrupted by involvement in successful economic enterprise and the communal aspect was eroded away—another example of a system being destroyed by what it attempts to ignore. The new culture is thus a kind of reform movement, attempting to revive a decayed tradition once important to our civilization.

In stressing these continuities between the new culture and the American past, I do not mean to imply a process unique to our society. One of the most basic characteristics of all successful social systems—indeed, perhaps all living matter as well—is that they include devices that serve to keep alive alternatives that are antithetical to their dominant emphases, as a kind of hedge against change. These latent alternatives usually persist in some encapsulated and imprisoned form ("break glass in case of fire"), such as myths, festivals, or specialized roles. Fanatics continually try to expunge these circumscribed contradictions, but when they succeed it is often fatal to the society. For, as Lewis Mumford once pointed out, it is the "laxity, corruption, and disorder" in a system that makes it viable, considering the contradictory needs that all social systems must satisfy. Such latent alternatives are priceless treasures and must be carefully guarded against loss. For a new cultural pattern does not emerge out of nothing—the seed must already be there, like the magic tricks of wizards and witches in folklore, who can make an ocean out of a drop of water, a palace out of a stone, a forest out of a blade of grass, but nothing out of nothing. Many peoples keep alive a tradition of a golden age, in which a totally different social structure existed. The Judeo-Christian God, patriarchal and omnipotent, has served in matrifocal cultures to keep alive the concept of a strong and protective paternal figure in the absence of real-life examples. Jesters kept alive a wide variety of behavior patterns amid the stilted and restrictive formality of royal courts. The specialized effeminate roles that one finds in many warrior cultures are not merely a refuge for those who fail to succeed in the dominant pattern—they are also a living reminder that the rigid "protest masculinity" that prevails is not the only conceivable kind of behavior for a male. And conversely, the warrior ethos is maintained in a peaceful society or era by means of a military cadre or reserve system.

These phenomena are equivalent to (and in literate cultures tend increasingly to be replaced by) written records of social practices. They are like a box of seldom-used tools, or a trunk of old costumes awaiting the proper period-play. Suddenly the environment changes, the tolerated eccentric becomes a prophet, the clown a dancing-master, the doll an idol, the idol a doll. The elements have not changed, only the arrangement and the emphases have changed. Every revolution is in part a revival.

Sometimes societal ambivalence is so marked that the latent pattern is retained in a form almost as elaborated as the dominant one. Our society, for example, is one of the most mobile (geographically, at least) ever known; yet, unlike other nomadic cultures it makes little allowance for this fact in its patterns of material accumulation. Our homes are furnished as if we intended to spend the rest of our lives in them, instead of moving every few years. This perhaps represents merely a kind of technological neurosis—a yearning for stability expressed in a technological failure to adapt. Should Americans ever settle down, however, they will find little to do in the way of readjusting their household furnishing habits.

Ultimately it seems inevitable that Americans must either abandon their nomadic habits (which seems unlikely) or moderate their tendency to invest their libido exclusively in material possessions (an addiction upon which the economy relies rather heavily). The new culture is of course pushing hard to realize the second alternative, and if it is successful one might anticipate a trend toward more simply furnished dwellings in which all but the most portable and decorative items are permanent installations. In such a case we might like or dislike a sofa or bed or dresser, but would have no more personal involvement with it than we now do with a stove, furnace, or garage. We would possess, cathect, feel as a part of us, only a few truly personal and portable items.

This tendency of human societies to keep alternative patterns alive has many biological analogues. One of these is *neoteny*—the evolutionary process in which foetal or juvenile characteristics are retained in the adult animal. Body characteristics that have long had only transitional relevance are exploited in response to altered environmental circumstances (thus many human features resemble foetal traits of apes). I have not chosen this example at random, for much of the new culture is implicitly and explicitly "neotenous" in a cultural sense: behavior, values, and life-styles formerly seen as appropriate only to childhood are being retained into adulthood as a counterforce to the old culture.

I pointed out earlier, for example, that children are taught a set of values in earliest childhood—cooperation, sharing, equalitarianism—which they begin to unlearn as they enter school, wherein competition, invidiousness, status differentiation, and ethnocentrism prevail. By the time they enter adult life children are expected to have largely abandoned the value assumptions with which their social lives began. But for affluent, protected, middle-class children this process is slowed down, while intellectual development is speeded up, so that the earlier childhood values can become integrated into a conscious, adult value system centered around social justice. The same is true of other characteristics of childhood: spontaneity, hedonism, candor, playfulness, use of the senses for pleasure rather than utility, and so on. The protective, child-oriented, middle-class family allows the child to preserve some of these qualities longer than is possible under more austere conditions, and his intellectual precocity makes it possible for him to integrate them into an ideological system with which he can confront the corrosive, life-abusing tendencies of the old culture.

When these neotenous characteristics become manifest to old-culture adherents the effect is painfully disturbing, for they vibrate feelings and attitudes that are very old and very deep, although long and harshly stifled. Old-culture adherents have learned to reject all this, but since the learning antedated intellectual maturity they have no coherent ideological framework within which such a rejection can be consciously understood and thoughtfully endorsed. They are deeply attracted and acutely revolted at the same time. They can neither resist their fascination nor control their antipathy. This is exemplified by the extravagant curiosity that hippie communes attract, and by the harassment that so often extinguishes them. It is usually necessary in such situations for the rote-learned abhorrence to discharge itself in persecutory activity before the more positive responses can be released. This was true in the case of the early Christians in Rome, with whom contemporary hippies are often compared (both were communal, utopian, mystical, dropouts, unwashed; both were viewed as dangerous, masochistic, ostentatious, the cause of their own troubles; both existed in societies in which the exclusive pursuit of material advantages had reached some kind of dead end), and seems equally true today. The absorption of this persecution is part of the process through which the latent values that the oppressed group protects and nurtures are expropriated by the majority and released into the mainstream of the culture.

Up to this point we have (rather awkwardly) discussed the new culture as if it were an integrated, monolithic pattern, which is certainly very far from the case. There are many varied and contradictory streams feeding the new culture, and some of these deserve particular attention, since they provide the raw material for future axes of conflict.

The most glaring split in the new culture is that which separates militant activism from the traits we generally associate with the hippie movement. The first strand stresses political confrontation, revolutionary action, radical commitment to the process of changing the basic structure of modern industrial society. The second involves a renunciation of that society in favor of the cultivation of inner experience and pleasing internal feeling-states. Heightening of sensory receptivity, commitment to the immediate present, and tranquil acceptance of the physical environment are sought in contradistinction to old-culture ways, in which the larger part of one's immediate experience is overlooked or grayed out by the preoccupation with utility, future goals, and external mastery. Since, in the old culture, experience is classified before it is felt, conceptualization tends here to be forsworn altogether. There is also much emphasis on aesthetic expression and an overarching belief in the power of love.

This division is a crude one, and there are, of course, many areas of overlap. Both value systems share an antipathy to the old culture, both share beliefs in sexual freedom and personal autonomy. Some groups (the Yippies, in particular) have tried with some success to bridge the gap in a variety of interesting ways. But there is nonetheless an inherent contradiction between them. Militant activism is task-oriented, and hence partakes of certain old-culture traits such as postponement of gratification, preoccupation with power, and so on. To be a competent revolutionary one must possess a certain tolerance for the "Protestant Ethic" virtues, and the activists' moral code is a stern one indeed. The hippie ethic, on the other hand, is a "salvation now" approach. It is thus more radical, since it remains relatively uncontaminated with old-culture values. It is also far less realistic, since it ignores the fact that the existing culture provides a totally antagonistic milieu in which the hippie movement must try to survive in a state of highly vulnerable parasitic dependence. The activists can reasonably say that the flower people are absurd to pretend that the revolution has already occurred, for such pretense leads only to severe victimization by the old culture. The flower people can reasonably retort that a revolution based to so great a degree on old-culture premises is lost before it is begun, for even if the militants are victorious they will have been corrupted by the process of winning.

The dilemma is a very real one and arises whenever radical change is sought. For every social system attempts to exercise the most rigid control over the mechanisms by which it can be altered —defining some as legitimate and others as criminal or disloyal. When we examine the characteristics of legitimate and nonlegitimate techniques, however, we find that the "legitimate" ones involve a course of action requiring a sustained commitment to the core assumptions of the culture. In other words, if the individual follows the "legitimate" pathway there is a very good chance that his initial radical intent will be eroded in the process. If he feels that some fundamental change in the system is required, then, he has a choice between following a path that subverts his goal or one that leads him to be jailed as a criminal or traitor.

This process is not a Machiavellian invention of American capitalists, but rather a mechanism which all viable social systems must evolve spontaneously in order to protect themselves from instability. When the system as it stands is no longer viable, however, the mechanism must be exposed for the swindle that it is; otherwise the needed radical changes will be rendered ineffectual.

The key to the mechanism is the powerful human reluctance to admit that an achieved goal was not worth the unpleasant experience required to achieve it. This is the basic principle underlying initiation rituals: "if I had to suffer so much pain and humiliation to get into this club it must be a wonderful organization." The evidence of thousands of years is that the mechanism works extremely well. Up to some point, for example, war leaders can count on high casualties to increase popular commitment to military adventures.

Thus when a political leader says to a militant, "why don't you run for political office (get a haircut, dress conservatively, make deals, do the dirty work for your elders) and try to change the system in that way"—or the teacher says to the student, "wait until you have your Ph.D. (M.D., LL.B.) and then you can criticize our program," or the white man says to the black man. "when you begin to act like us you'll receive the same opportunities we do"— there is a serious subterfuge involved (however unconscious it may be) in that the protester, if he accepts the condition, will in most cases be automatically converted by it to his opponent's point of view.

The dilemma of the radical, then, is that he is likely to be corrupted if he fights the *status quo* on its own terms, but it is not permitted to fight it in any other way. The real significance of the New Left is that it has discovered, in the politics of confrontation, as near a solution to this dilemma as can be found: it is always a bit problematic whether the acts of the new militants are "within the system" or not, and substantial headway can be made in the resulting confusion.

Yet even here the problem remains: if an activist devotes his life to altering the power structure, will he not become like old-culture adherents—utilitarian, invidious, scarcity-oriented, future-centered, and so on? Having made the world safe for flower people will he be likely to relinquish it to them? "You tell me it's the institution," object the Beatles, "you'd better free your mind instead." But what if all the freed minds are in jail?

The dilemma is particularly clear for blacks. Some blacks are much absorbed in rediscovering and celebrating those characteristics which seem most distinctly black and in sharpest contrast to white Western culture: black expressiveness, creativity, sensuality, and spontaneity being opposed to white constrictedness, rigidity, frigidity, bustle, and hypocrisy. For these blacks, to make too great a commitment to the power game is to forsake one's blackness. Power is a white hangup. Yet the absence of power places rather severe limits on the ability of blacks to realize their blackness or anything else.

There is no way to resolve this dilemma, and indeed, it is probably better left unresolved. In a revolutionary situation one needs discipline and unity of purpose, which, however, leads to all kinds of abuses when the goal is won. Discipline and unity become ends in themselves (after the old-culture pattern) and the victory becomes an empty one. It is therefore of great importance to have the envisioned revolutionary goals embodied in a group culture of some kind, with which the acts of those in power can be compared. In the meantime the old culture is subject to a two-pronged attack: a direct assault from activists—unmasking its life-destroying proclivities, its corruption, its futility and pointlessness, its failure to achieve any of its objectives—and an indirect assault by the expansion of expressive countercultures beyond a tolerable (i.e., freak) size.

Closely related to the activist-hippie division is the conflict over the proper role of aggression in the new culture. Violence is a major theme in the old culture and most new-culture adherents view human aggression with deep suspicion. Nonviolence has been the dominant trend in both the activist and hippie segments of the new culture until recently. But more and more activists have become impatient with the capacity of the old culture to strike the second cheek with even more enthusiasm than the first, and have endorsed violence under certain conditions as a necessary evil.

For the activists the issue has been practical rather than ideological: most serious and thoughtful activists have only a tactical commitment to violence. For the dropout ideologues, however, aggression poses a difficult problem: if they seek to minimize the artificial constriction of emotional expression, how can they be consistently

loving and pacific? This logical dilemma is usually resolved by ignoring it: the love cult typically represses aggressive feelings ruthlessly
—the body is paramount only so long as it is a loving body.

At the moment the old culture is so fanatically absorbed in violence that it does the work for everyone. If the new culture should
prevail, however, the problem of human aggression would probably
be its principal bone of contention. Faced with the persistence of
aggressiveness (even in the absence of the old culture's exaggerated
violence-inducing institutions), the love cult will be forced to reex-
amine its premises, and opt for some combination of expression and
restraint that will restore human aggression to its rightful place as a
natural, though secondary, human emotion.

A third split in the new culture is the conflict between individualism and collectivism. On this question the new culture talks out of
both sides of its mouth, one moment pitting ideals of cooperation
and community against old-culture competitiveness, the next
moment espousing the old culture in its most extreme form with
exhortations to "do your own thing." I am not arguing that individualism need be totally extirpated in order to make community possible, but new-culture enterprises often collapse because of a dogmatic unwillingness to subordinate the whim of the individual to
the needs of the group. This problem is rarely faced honestly by
new-culture adherents, who seem unaware of the conservatism
involved in their attachment to individualistic principles.

It is always disastrous to attempt to eliminate any structural principle altogether; but if the balance between individualistic and
collective emphases in America is not altered, everything in the new
culture will be perverted and caricatured into simply another bizarre
old-culture product. There must be continuities between the old
and the new, but these cannot extend to the relative weights
assigned to core motivational principles. The new culture seeks to
create a tolerable society within the context of persistent American
strivings—utopianism, the pursuit of happiness. But nothing will
change until individualism is assigned a subordinate place in the
American value system—for individualism lies at the core of the old
culture, and a prepotent individualism is not a viable foundation for
any society in a nuclear age.

QUESTIONS

1. At the beginning of his essay, Slater lists a number of contrasts
   between the old and the new cultures. Which of these does he
   go on to emphasize most in the essay and why? What concrete
   illustrations does he give? Supply additional concrete illustrations of some of the contrasts he lists.
2. Read Anthony Burgess, "Is America Falling Apart?" (p. 514).
   In what ways do Burgess' and Slater's concerns and attitudes
   overlap? In what ways are they different? Explain whether you
   think any of the differences arise from the fact that Burgess'
   background is British, Slater's American.

3. Slater asserts that the scarcity on which the competitiveness of the old culture is based is "spurious." What evidence do you have or can you find to test that assertion? What evidence would you need to prove or disprove it?

4. Slater calls his description of what might happen if we tried to eliminate competition (pp. 520–22) a "parable." Compare this with some of the selections in the Parables section (pp. 1114–1136). Can you find parables there with similarities in method? What kinds of ideas are best suited to the parable form? Is Slater's parable literally believable—or does that matter?

5. On p. 520 Slater describes the complicated way that cloth and the automobile fit into our society. Cite two or three other things in our culture that have equally "complex cultural patterns" and explain what those patterns are. Do all the patterns have anything in common?

6. Slater sees "a schism between activist and dropout approaches" (p. 523) within the new culture. What enables Slater to group the two approaches together as part of the new culture in spite of the differences? Are there similar schisms within the old culture?

7. Slater speaks of the advertising industry (p. 526), showing its place in promoting some of the values of the old culture. Read Cox, "The Playboy and Miss America" (p. 569). Does Cox see advertising as playing the same role in our culture? Explain whether Cox would agree with Slater's interpretation of American culture.

8. Compare the individualism of the old culture with the individualism of the new culture. Explain whether they differ in important ways.

9. Compare Slater's comparison of the old and new cultures with Kram's comparison of the past and the present in "Ring of Bright Marbles" (p. 482)

"ADAM SMITH" (GEORGE J. W. GOODMAN)

Cotton Mather and Vince Lombardi[1]

For many, the traditional motivations of job security, money reward, and opportunity for personal advancement are proving insufficient.[2]

Insufficient! Security, money, and personal advancement? Do you know what we have to throw off to get to this point?

I give you the honorable Cotton Mather:

There are *Two Callings* to be minded by *All* Christians. Every Christian hath a GENERAL CALLING which is to Serve the Lord Jesus

---

1. From *Supermoney*, 1972.
2. From a memorandum by a vice-president for industrial relations in the Ford Motor Company, quoted earlier in full by "Smith."

Christ and Save his own Soul . . . and every Christian hath also a PERSONAL CALLING or a certain *Particular Employment* by which his *Usefulness* in his Neighborhood is Distinguished . . . a Christian at his *Two Callings* is a man in a Boat, Rowing for Heaven; if he mind but one of his *Callings*, be it which it will, he pulls the *Oar* but on *one side* of the Boat, and will make but a poor dispatch to the Shoar of Eternal Blessedness . . . every Christian should have some *Special Business* . . . so he may Glorify God, by doing *Good* for *others*, and *getting* of Good for *himself* . . . to be without a *Calling*, as tis against the *Fourth Commandment*, so tis against the Eighth, which bids men seek for themselves a comfortable Subsistence . . . [if he follow no calling] . . . a man is *Impious* toward God, *Unrighteous* toward his family, toward his *Neighborhood*, toward the *Commonwealth* . . . it is not enough that a Christian *have* an Occupation; but he must *mind* it, and give a *Good Account*, with *Diligence* . . .

and so on to *Poor Richard's Almanac*: A sleeping fox catches no poultry; one day is worth two tomorrows; diligence is the mother of good luck; early to bed and early to rise provides a man with job security, money reward and opportunity for personal advancement.

The extension of this ethic into industrial America was a real triumph. The Ford vice-president has a distinct problem: it is very hard to think of working on the line as a Calling. Cotton Mather's listeners did not take this lightly, nor did he: "Man and his Posterity will Gain but little, by a Calling whereto God hath not Called him"; a Calling was to be *Agreeable* as well as *Allowable*. It does make work seem softer and more important to have been prayed for:

It is a wonderful Inconvenience for a man to have a *Calling* that won't *Agree* with him. See to it, *O Parents*, that when you chuse *Callings* for your *Children*, you wisely consult their *Capacities* and their *Inclinations*; lest you Ruine them. And, Oh! cry mightily to God, by *Prayer*, yea with *Fasting* and *Prayer*, for His Direction when you are to resolve upon a matter of such considerable consequence. But, O *Children*, you should also be *Thoughtful* and *Prayerful*, when you are going to fix upon your *Callings*; and above all propose deliberately *Right Ends* unto your selves in what you do.

It is a bit hard to imagine, then: "Ma, I have fasted and prayed and sought the wisdom of God. I know my Calling, and I am going to work on the line at Ford, $4.57 an hour, as an assembler."

It seems almost simplistic to suggest, but you are more likely to bust your ass when everybody has been fasting and praying for you and what you are doing and your oar of the boat on the way to the Shoar of Eternal Blessedness than if none of those things are true, and if you are Ford, you have an extra problem if that spirit has departed.

Not that it has departed everywhere. It is still in the literature. Ralph Waldo Emerson's "Self-Reliance" and "Wealth" are in a direct line from Cotton Mather and Poor Richard: be not only industrious, be clever, absorb and invest. Bishop Lawrence, doyen of the Episcopal Church at the turn of the century, really did say, "In the long run, it is only to the man of morality that wealth comes. Godliness is in league with riches." Some of our major corporations have institutional advertising even today that could have been written by the Social Darwinists, and Dale Carnegie courses run on principles that were devised by Benjamin Franklin. The Man Who Gets Ahead in Business Reads *The Wall Street Journal* Every Business Day. (Did you ever see the television commercial about The Man Who Gets Ahead in Business? Business is a field event, pole-vaulting, and the bar is set at about a hundred feet, and the poor bastard is there in his business suit and his Knox hat and his brief-case, and he looks up nervously at this bar a hundred feet high and fingers the pole uncertainly. After knocking the bar off the first time, he makes it the second, presumably because he has read *The Wall Street Journal*. The *Wall Street Journal* may be one of the best papers in the country, but I suggest that anyone who sees his job as a hundred-foot pole vault with no track shoes is in the wrong Calling and should pray for guidance.)

While the literature of the Protestant Ethic has been exhorting everybody for three hundred years in this country to be industrious and thrifty, sober and wise—to "postpone gratification," in the words of the scholars—another literature has sprung up. It is literature really only in the McLuhanesque sense, but it is with us every day, and that is advertising. The purpose of the advertising is not to get you to produce and save but to spend, to buy the goods, and this has been the case since at least fifty years ago, when mass marketing and mass advertising really got going. Now we have commercials in living color, and the populace spends far more time with them than the old populace did with Cotton Mather. What do we see? First of all, we never see anybody *working* except when they are candidates for medication: aspirin, pain relievers, tranquilizers, cold remedies. At least not office or factory work; the White Tornado and the Man From Glad will come and help with the housework. The rest of the time, people are at play: is it possible to sell soft drinks without running into the surf? You only go around once in life, says the beer commercial, so you have to grab everything you can; that character is hanging precariously onto the rigging of his boat because one hand is clutching a beer can. And the airlines— well, there is the bell tolling the end of the Protestant Ethic: Fly now, pay later, Pan Am will take you to an island in the sun where you can be a beachcomber (not a Calling approved by Cotton Mather) and Eastern wants to fly you and Bob and Carol and Ted and Alice *all* to your own little love-nest in Jamaica.

The message of capitalism has been schizophrenic: at work, be hard-nosed, industrious, single-minded, frugal and thrifty, and once you leave work, *whoopee*, have you seen Carol *and* Alice in their bikinis? It may be that some doers can step into a telephone booth and emerge as Clark Kent, but I doubt if it works for a whole society.

The second literature of exhortation, advertising, sometimes recognizes this, and tries to say that the deferred gratification of the Protestant Ethic is a matter of hours, not lifetimes and generations. "You've worked hard, you deserve this," says the clever ad, whether it is a beer, the reward for a day, or a vacation, the reward for a season, or whatever: buy, try, fly.

The less intensive attitude toward work also applies to play. In the winter of 1972 Columbia barely managed to field a basketball team for its Ivy League opener; it could send only six men to Providence to play Brown. "Four members," *The New York Times* reported (January 6) "had resigned, making it a particularly dramatic example of student unhappiness with organized extracurricular pursuits . . . Several other college teams have suffered similar player shortages in the last month." Said the team's second-highest scorer as he departed: "My father thinks I'm just a degenerate hippie now, because when I left high school I had all these fantastic ambitions for wealth and fame—and I wanted to be the greatest lawyer in North Carolina. Now I just don't have that."

Oppose this to the paragon of the extreme ethic, Vince Lombardi. You could say, of course, that this is not quite fair: soldiers and professional football players are supposed to win. But the example is not frivolous. When Lombardi died, his death was a major front-page story in all—including the most serious—of newspapers, and personally grieved the President of the United States. Lombardi's hold on the country and the President was that for ten years the teams he had coached had either won championships or come in second. The ethic according to Lombardi, all from *Lombardi* and *Run to Daylight*:

Winning is not everything. It is the only thing.

The will to excel and the will to win, they endure. They are more important than any event that occasions them.

To play this game, you must have that fire in you, and there is nothing that stokes fire like hate.

And from Lombardi's players:

He had us all feeling that we weren't going to win for the Green Bay Packers, but to preserve our manhood . . . and we went out and whipped them good and preserved our manhood.

Vinny believes in the Spartan life, the total self-sacrifice, and to succeed and reach the pinnacle he has, you've got to be that way. The hours you put in on a job can't even be considered.

He treated us all equally—like dogs. I don't think I'd want to be like Lombardi. It takes too much out of you. You drive like that, you've got to give up a lot of time with your family, and you lose a lot physically . . . Still, now that I'm in business, I'm applying Lombardi's principles. I sent my secretary home crying my first three days on the job. One gal retired on me. I was putting them through training camp. I walked in and the first thing I said was, "Your job is on the line. If you don't make it, you're through." I said to the secretary, "What the heck you been doing all day? I don't see anything you've done." And if she gave me a letter and there was one mistake in it, I'd make a big X all the way across it and say, "Type it again." It worked out pretty well. They're organized now . . . I'm strict. A lot of him has rubbed off on me.

And the players on the changes:

If you were told to beat your head against the wall, you did it . . . I think we're entering a different period now. I think we now have to give youngsters a good reason to get them to beat their heads against a wall.

Kids today don't fight like we did. They can play football and basketball like hell, but they're very gentle, very kind. They're out playing for fun, and it's not going to interfere with their demonstration for the week or with the things they consider important . . . Those kids don't look at it like the whole world is going to fall apart if you don't beat the Bears.

The examples are so eloquent they need no comment.

ADA LOUISE HUXTABLE

Where Did We Go Wrong?

The following item was not invented by some gifted pixie mentality; it is from *Preservation News,* published by the National Trust for Historic Preservation. The National Trust would not put you on. We quote:

Babe Ruth's birthplace and a few neighboring properties were recently purchased by the city of Baltimore for $1,850. The home of one of baseball's immortals is located on Emory Street, a narrow alley of humble row houses. The Mayor's Committee for the Preservation of Babe Ruth's Birthplace is now debating whether to leave the house at its present location or to move it and the neighboring houses to a site adjoining Memorial Stadium, to be part of the Babe Ruth Plaza. Vandalism in the present neighborhood has prompted the committee to resolve "to restore the house at its present location only if environmental amenities are found to be reasonable." The inaccessibility of Emory Street is also cited as a reason to move the house elsewhere. However, Emory Street is too narrow to move the house intact and dismantling would be the only solution.

It reads exactly as if Lewis Carroll wrote it.

"Leave the house where it is," said the Red Queen. "I can't," said Alice. "It's inaccessible and there's vandalism." "Then get some environmental amenities," said the Red Queen, "and be quick about it." "What are environmental amenities?" asked Alice.

"Don't ask foolish questions; just move the house," said the Red Queen. "But the street is too narrow," said Alice. "Nonsense," said the Red Queen, "don't you know anything? Take the house apart and put it back together again. And move the rest of the houses with it." "Poor things," said Alice. "Where to?" "To the Memorial Stadium, naturally," said the Red Queen, "and call it Babe Ruth Plaza." "Couldn't we just leave it?" asked Alice. "If you do," said the Red Queen, "you will have to take out the other houses and put up a sign, 'No Ball Playing Allowed.' " "Mightn't 'Ballplayers Welcome' be better?" said Alice.

Alas, it is not straight out of *Through the Looking-Glass*; it is straight out of life. And if it sounds like parody, that is exactly what much of the preservation movement has become. It is game-playing. The game as it is played—by a strict set of rules—is to seal off historic buildings from the contemporary environment in a vacuum of assiduous make-believe.

The process ranges from babes in Babe-Ruth-land to the phenomenon of Williamsburg, where the art of scholarly self-delusion reaches the extravagantly ($79 million) sublime. It deals in "cut-off dates," which means ruthlessly destroying anything later than a certain arbitrarily selected year that interferes with the illusion desired, and "restoring back," a horrendous process of faking the chosen period by removing all subsequent accumulations of time and history. The final perversion is "reconstruction," or rebuilding things that no longer exist, and that, if you take the blinders off for a moment, merely means putting up brand-new "old" buildings, which, no matter how carefully researched and how admirable the educational motives, is a contradiction in terms and values that shows how sick the whole thing has become.

"I say the moon is made of green cheese and this is the eighteenth century," the sponsors of these historical "enclaves" (a favorite euphemism) of the studiously unreal tells us. No matter how you slice it, it is still green cheese, and you can slice it many ways, from Strawberry Banke to Old Sacramento. The point is that the whole idea and purpose of preservation—saving the past because it is part of the living heritage of the present, so that the process of history enriches the city and the environment—has been lost.

The result is a cross between playacting in the name of history (and the lesson being taught is curiously subversive if one still equates education with traditional values of truth and, by extension, morality, or knowing what is true or false) and a museum of period arts. The inevitable conflict set up between the forms of the past and the uses of the present—a conflict denied overtly but carefully and often comically disguised to accommodate the tourist trade—is an abrasive anachronism. It all dead-ends in a head-on clash of new, old, and new-made-to-seem-old for which there is no solution except playing the game harder, increasing the make-believe and the confusions of real and reproduction, not for a living lie, but for something that is a dead lie at best.

The tragedy is that this concept has become so popular that it has almost totally aborted the proper approach to the conservation of our urban heritage. The purpose of preservation is not to "recreate" the past, a laughable impossibility filled with booby traps like the lady in saddle shoes, harlequin glasses and hoop skirt who shattered this observer's first schoolgirl visit to Williamsburg. (No, changing the shoes and glasses wouldn't fix up anything at all; you really couldn't restore the lady back.)

More shattering, on a much later visit, was lack of information from guides as to what was authentic and what was not, since obviously no distinction was made in their own minds between copies and genuine survivals. Even the survivals have been so smoothed up that the line gets fuzzy. To them, it was all real. Actually, nothing is real except those buildings that have lasted a couple of centuries, gathering a significant patina of changing American culture (stripped, naturally) and the collections of furnishings that are curatorial triumphs, deliciously arranged to simulate someone's personal possessions by a well-researched extension of wishful-think.

It is all art and artifice and the finest green cheese. It is a beautifully hollow stage-set shell, totally removed from the life-force of the society that gave it form and meaning. A little fudging for effect hardly matters. (Please don't write, oh superpatriots, to tell me that I am simultaneously sullying both Williamsburg and the American flag; it is not treason to look art and history in the eye. I value both beyond the call of tourism.)

What preservation is really all about is the retention and active relationship of the buildings of the past to the community's functioning present. You don't erase history to get history, a city's character and quality are a product of continuity. You don't get any of it with "enclaves" in quarantine. What a cut-off date cuts off is any contact with the present at all. In urban terms, preservation is the saving of the essence and style of other eras, through their architecture and urban forms, so that the meaning and flavor of those other times and tastes are incorporated into the mainstream of the city's life. The accumulation is called culture.

JANE JACOBS
Sidewalk Ballet[1]

Under the seeming disorder of the old city, wherever the old city is working successfully, is a marvelous order for maintaining the

1. From Chapter 2 of *The Death and Life of Great American Cities*, 1961.

safety of the streets and the freedom of the city. It is a complex order. Its essence is intricacy of sidewalk use, bringing with it a constant succession of eyes. This order is all composed of movement and change, and although it is life, not art, we may fancifully call it the art form of the city and liken it to the dance—not to a simple-minded precision dance with everyone kicking up at the same time, twirling in unison, and bowing off en masse, but to an intricate ballet in which the individual dancers and ensembles all have distinctive parts which miraculously reinforce each other and compose an orderly whole. The ballet of the good city sidewalk never repeats itself from place to place, and in any one place is always replete with new improvisations.

The stretch of Hudson Street where I live is each day the scene of an intricate sidewalk ballet. I make my own first entrance into it a little after eight when I put out the garbage can, surely a prosaic occupation, but I enjoy my part, my little clang, as the droves of junior high school students walk by the center of the stage dropping candy wrappers. (How do they eat so much candy so early in the morning?)

While I sweep up the wrappers I watch the other rituals of morning: Mr. Halpert unlocking the laundry's handcart from its mooring to a cellar door, Joe Cornacchia's son-in-law stacking out the empty crates from the delicatessen, the barber bringing out his sidewalk folding chair, Mr. Goldstein arranging the coils of wire which proclaim the hardware store is open, the wife of the tenement's superintendent depositing her chunky three-year-old with a toy mandolin on the stoop, the vantage point from which he is learning the English his mother cannot speak. Now the primary children, heading for St. Luke's, dribble through to the south; the children for St. Veronica's cross, heading to the west, and the children for P.S. 41, heading toward the east. Two new entrances are being made from the wings: well-dressed and even elegant women and men with briefcases emerge from doorways and side streets. Most of these are heading for the bus and subways, but some hover on the curbs, stopping taxis which have miraculously appeared at the right moment, for the taxis are part of a wider morning ritual: having dropped passengers from midtown in the downtown financial district, they are now bringing downtowners up to midtown. Simultaneously, numbers of women in housedresses have emerged and as they crisscross with one another they pause for quick conversations that sound with either laughter or joint indignation, never, it seems, anything between. It is time for me to hurry to work too, and I exchange my ritual farewell with Mr. Lofaro, the short, thick-bodied, white-aproned fruit man who stands outside his doorway a little up the street, his arms folded, his feet planted, looking solid as earth itself. We nod; we each glance quickly up and down the street, then look back to each other and smile. We have done

this many a morning for more than ten years, and we both know
what it means: All is well.

The heart-of-the-day ballet I seldom see, because part of the
nature of it is that working people who live there, like me, are
mostly gone, filling the roles of strangers on other sidewalks. But
from days off, I know enough of it to know that it becomes more
and more intricate. Longshoremen who are not working that day
gather at the White Horse or the Ideal or the International for
beer and conversation. The executives and business lunchers from
the industries just to the west throng the Dorgene restaurant and
the Lion's Head coffee house; meat-market workers and communications scientists fill the bakery lunchroom. Character dancers come
on, a strange old man with strings of old shoes over his shoulders,
motor-scooter riders with big beards and girl friends who bounce on
the back of the scooters and wear their hair long in front of their
faces as well as behind, drunks who follow the advice of the Hat
Council and are always turned out in hats, but not hats the Council would approve. Mr. Lacey, the locksmith, shuts up his shop for
a while and goes to exchange the time of day with Mr. Slube at the
cigar store. Mr. Koochagian, the tailor, waters the luxuriant jungle
of plants in his window, gives them a critical look from the outside,
accepts a compliment on them from two passers-by, fingers the
leaves on the plane tree in front of our house with a thoughtful
gardener's appraisal, and crosses the street for a bite at the Ideal
where he can keep an eye on customers and wigwag across the message that he is coming. The baby carriages come out, and clusters
of everyone from toddlers with dolls to teen-agers with homework
gather at the stoops.

When I get home after work, the ballet is reaching its crescendo.
This is the time of roller skates and stilts and tricycles, and games
in the lee of the stoop with bottletops and plastic cowboys; this is
the time of bundles and packages, zigzagging from the drug store
to the fruit stand and back over to the butcher's; this is the time
when teen-agers, all dressed up, are pausing to ask if their slips
show or their collars look right; this is the time when beautiful girls
get out of MG's; this is the time when the fire engines go through;
this is the time when anybody you know around Hudson Street will
go by.

As darkness thickens and Mr. Halpert moors the laundry cart to
the cellar door again, the ballet goes on under lights, eddying back
and forth but intensifying at the bright spotlight pools of Joe's
sidewalk pizza dispensary, the bars, the delicatessen, the restaurant,
and the drug store. The night workers stop now at the delicatessen,
to pick up salami and a container of milk. Things have settled
down for the evening but the street and its ballet have not come to
a stop.

I know the deep night ballet and its seasons best from waking long after midnight to tend a baby and, sitting in the dark, seeing the shadows and hearing the sounds of the party conversation and, about three in the morning, singing, very good singing. Sometimes there is sharpness and anger or sad, sad weeping, or a flurry of search for a string of beads broken. One night a young man came roaring along, bellowing terrible language at two girls whom he had apparently picked up and who were disappointing him. Doors opened, a wary semicircle formed around him, not too close, until the police came. Out came the heads, too, along Hudson Street, offering opinion, "Drunk . . . Crazy . . . A wild kid from the suburbs."[2]

Deep in the night, I am almost unaware how many people are on the street unless something calls them together, like the bagpipe. Who the piper was and why he favored our street I have no idea. The bagpipe just skirled out in the February night, and as if it were a signal the random, dwindled movements of the sidewalk took on direction. Swiftly, quietly, almost magically a little crowd was there, a crowd that evolved into a circle with a Highland fling inside it. The crowd could be seen on the shadowy sidewalk, the dancers could be seen, but the bagpiper himself was almost invisible because his bravura was all in his music. He was a very little man in a plain brown overcoat. When he finished and vanished, the dancers and watchers applauded, and applause came from the galleries too, half a dozen of the hundred windows on Hudson Street. Then the windows closed, and the little crowd dissolved into the random movements of the night street.

The strangers on Hudson Street, the allies whose eyes help us natives keep the peace of the street, are so many that they always seem to be different people from one day to the next. That does not matter. Whether they are so many always-different people as they seem to be, I do not know. Likely they are. When Jimmy Rogan fell through a plate-glass window (he was separating some scuffling friends) and almost lost his arm, a stranger in an old T shirt emerged from the Ideal bar, swiftly applied an expert tourniquet, and, according to the hospital's emergency staff, saved Jimmy's life. Nobody remembered seeing the man before and no one has seen him since. The hospital was called in this way: a woman sitting on the steps next to the accident ran over to the bus stop, wordlessly snatched the dime from the hand of a stranger who was waiting with his fifteen-cent fare ready, and raced into the Ideal's phone booth. The stranger raced after her to offer the nickel too. Nobody remembered seeing him before, and no one has seen him since. When you see the same stranger three or four times on

2. He turned out to be a wild kid from the suburbs. Sometimes, on Hudson Street, we are tempted to believe the suburbs must be a difficult place to bring up children [Jacobs' note].

Hudson Street, you begin to nod. This is almost getting to be an acquaintance, a public acquaintance, of course.

I have made the daily ballet of Hudson Street sound more frenetic than it is, because writing it telescopes it. In real life, it is not that way. In real life, to be sure, something is always going on, the ballet is never at a halt, but the general effect is peaceful and the general tenor even leisurely. People who know well such animated city streets will know how it is. I am afraid people who do not will always have it a little wrong in their head—like the old prints of rhinoceroses made from travelers' descriptions of rhinoceroses.

On Hudson Street, the same as in the North End of Boston or in any other animated neighborhoods of great cities, we are not innately more competent at keeping the sidewalks safe than are the people who try to live off the hostile truce of Turf in a blind-eyed city. We are the lucky possessors of a city order that makes it relatively simple to keep the peace because there are plenty of eyes on the street. But there is nothing simple about that order itself, or the bewildering number of components that go into it. Most of those components are specialized in one way or another. They unite in their joint effect upon the sidewalk, which is not specialized in the least. That is its strength.

STEPHEN DARST

Prufrock with a Baedeker

The cliches add little to an understanding of the city—the breweries do not offer a definition; St. Louis is no longer first in shoes and the Browns, alas, play now on greener grass, in Baltimore, where they place more often first than last.

Hollywood images are of no help. On Christmas 1943, aglow with World's Fair nostalgia after seeing *Meet Me in St. Louis,* I walked the four blocks from our house to 5135 Kensington Avenue, expecting to find Judy Garland and Margaret O'Brien filling the street with song. Nostalgia died quickly: Sally Benson's old neighborhood had deteriorated by then, and things have since gotten worse—it is now a street of fried-chicken emporiums, junked cars rusting hub-down in the weeds, tire husks, and broken wine bottles. 5135 Kensington Avenue is a rooming house today; the boy next door is on welfare; the lights are shining elsewhere. The trolley doesn't run here anymore.

Trolleys don't run anywhere anymore, and the St. Louis plant that sent streetcars around the world closed down recently, joining other local enterprises that have faltered over the years. French fur traders founded the city in 1764 on the first high ground south of the confluence of the rivers—the Missouri, which led to the furs of the Northwest, and the Mississippi, which carried the hides to New Orleans and the markets of Europe. But the trade in beaver pelts has since, to put it mildly, slackened. The position near the confluence of the great rivers was strategic during the development of the West—in 1890 St. Louis was the fourth largest city in the country (really third, by today's way of reckoning, with Brooklyn as part of New York City, but in those days the ranking was New York, Philadelphia, Brooklyn, then St. Louis). During the nineteenth century, St. Louis was the great city of the continent's interior, the jumping-off point for the exploration, development, and settlement of the western half of the United States. For a while the city continued to grow, although at a slower rate than the newer cities to the west. In recent years however, the decline has not been merely comparative. When the 1950 population reached 856,796, city fathers thought the million population mark was at hand. It never came. The 1960 census revealed instead a decline to 750,026. A monumental error, derangement of the census, was suspected. St. Louis officials discussed a recount; they should have sought permanent freeze at existing levels. In 1970, the last census figures showed further decline, a drop of 127,790 in population, off 17 percent from 1960, the greatest percentage decrease in population of any American city during that period.

These figures are for the city itself, not the metropolitan area. Cities, of course, are no longer their traditional, storied old selves. They have overflowed the old limits, so that it is practical to include Winnetka when discussing Chicago, and it is even more sensible to include suburbs when considering St. Louis. In 1876 the corporate limits of the city were set close in, so close in that the first scattered showers of population washed waves of migration over the corporate banks, and ninety-six municipalities, principalities, and baronies proliferated in the surrounding countryside, leaving St. Louis today a virtually all-inner-city city.

But even counting the entire metropolitan area as St. Louis, the growth is at a slower rate than other metropolitan areas'. Population, demographers say, is moving southward and westward, mountainward, lakeward, and seaward, across the globe. The population center of the United States (near Mascoutah, Illinois, in 1970) will slip through St. Louis any night now, headed west for softer climes.

In its attitude to lost prestige, St. Louis is like a shabbily genteel family, Sartoris-scornful of Snopes[1] hustle, with the Snopeses in this case Chicago, a prairie by the lake when St. Louis was the Athens, or at any rate, the Brasilia, of the West. And there is a story (shabby gentility always has stories, of Coca-Cola stock

---

1. In the novels of William Faulkner the Sartoris family represents old established tradition, the Snopeses are a clan of brash upstarts.

declined, Rockefellers snubbed, Fords ignored) that after the Civil War, when St. Louis was still far larger than Chicago, a railroad bridge across the Mississippi was proposed. Cautious voices were raised, rail traffic bypassed St. Louis; Chicago prospered at our expense.

"That's a typical myth," says Dempster Holland, a St. Louis University urbanologist. "The idea is that if St. Louis had built that bridge we would have been the rail center of the country instead of Chicago—ignoring the fact that Chicago grew because of the lake and the ore, among other things. A railroad bridge over the Mississippi wasn't going to bring ore three hundred miles out of the way for processing, but that is the local myth. There is still the feeling that if you repaved Washington Avenue, for example, commerce would detour four hundred miles to the repaved street."

Forces of history count for nothing in myth. There are only wrong turns, temporary setbacks due to bad generalship, to be recouped by good generalship. In the early 1950s, even before the census reports began to come in, the *St. Louis Post-Dispatch*, alarmed at signs of decay, began pushing for revitalization. It found its general, an urban Rommel,[2] in Mayor Raymond R. Tucker, a Washington University professor of engineering with a well-deserved reputation for intelligence, integrity, and political savvy. For a while, with the construction of the new downtown stadium and the Saarinen Gateway Arch, things did seem to be looking up. The dispatches out of the city were of a "New Spirit of St. Louis." A run-down section of antique shops become nationally renowned as "Gaslight Square," a lively, imaginative entertainment area. The Pruitt-Igoe Housing Development, according to *Architectural Forum*, was to lead the way in solving public housing problems across the country. Indeed, St. Louis's success in handling urban problems seemed to national observers to offer a blue-print for others. A 1964 *Harper's* article gave the general tone of the news: "St. Louis Takes the Cure—A Case History for Ailing Cities." Urbanologists came to listen, nod, point, take note.

By 1968, when *Fortune* carried an article about the "St. Louis Economic Blues," the tone had obviously changed. "Gaslight Square," the slum that had the comeback as a nightlife center, suffered a relapse attributed to blight and crime, and sank back into rubble. O'Connell's Pub held an Irish wake last summer and moved south, the last establishment to depart. Pruitt-Igoe, which was to serve as the national model for public housing, became instead nationally notorious as the definitive disaster in the history of public housing, a crime-ridden, urine-soaked outrage. The picture-book general, Tucker, was replaced in 1965 by Alfonso Juan Cervantes, a

2. German Field Marshal Erwin Rommel was a brilliant military commander in World War II.

late-blooming hurrah who charged out of the wards with promises to restore lost population, lost confidence, lost initiative.

The decline continues. Prestige stores are moving to the country; St. Louis has declined from second to ninth place as a trucking center within a year. From 1969 to 1972, while jobs rose 5.1 percent nationally, they declined 6.6 percent in the St. Louis metropolitan area. Memphis is challenging St. Louis's once unrivaled position as the leading handler of river cargo. The white population of the city has entered a stage which demographers (the true poets of municipal decadence?) call "biological dissolution"—more are dying than are being born.

There are pluses—the Saarinen arch, the new downtown stadium, the plans for a new convention center and other downtown construction, but the general outlook is what it was in 1951 when Edwin Clark arrived to take over as head of Southwestern Bell Telephone and announced, "This is a decadent city."

Decay may not be good for business, but it often makes for land-office literature, and during the time St. Louis was slipping in so many other ways, its literary production flourished, in a neurasthenic sort of way. The Mississippi River at St. Louis is indeed the strong brown god of T. S. Eliot's "Dry Salvages," present in the nursery bedroom when the poet lived at 2635 Locust Street. The yellow fog that rubs its back upon the window panes in "The Love Song of J. Alfred Prufrock" is our very own pollution, and there are literary exegesists in St. Louis who can lead you to the precise dooryard, the exact sprinkled street, the very chimney pot. The Prufrock Furniture Company at 1104 Olive Street served literature better than the trade, gave its name to perhaps the most famous poem in English in the twentieth century, and vanished, as did the Eliot residence on Locust Street, but the house at 4445 Westminster Place where the poet later came for visits with his parents still stands (as does the Hydraulic Press Brick Company, the firm Eliot's father headed, now half-submerged beneath the King's-highway viaduct, among the all-night saunas, among the weeds, the rusting railroad tracks, looking for all the world like the original dead land). Also on Westminster, a half-block from the Eliot's former house, is the Wednesday Club, where Mrs. Eliot read her verse. And in the same part of town, a block west on Westminster, is the apartment building where Tennessee Williams grew up, the setting for *The Glass Menagerie*.

Other stops, most of them in the same Central West End, include the house where Sara Teasdale lived and houses (or vacant lots—historical tours of St. Louis include a great deal of pausing silently before vacant lots, venerating rubble) that marked some segment in the lives of Ulysses S. Grant, Mark Twain, Thomas Wolfe, William Marion Reedy, Marianne Moore, Zöe Akins, Sally

Benson, Fannie Hurst, and Eugene Field. The house where William Burroughs grew up is in the same quarter, but it is not on the tours, nor is the clinic, several blocks away, where Masters and Johnson filmed those Technicolor orgasms that became data for *Human Sexual Response*. (St. Louis may be the only city in the world that could have tolerated the Reproductive Biology Research Foundation while banning a production of *Hair*.)

You can tell something about a city by what it commemorates— there is a Eugene Field School and a Eugene Field House, with mementos of the versifier's life, but since Eliot Seminary changed its name to Washington University, nothing commemorates the Nobel Prize-winning poet or his family. Joyce left Dublin at about the age Eliot left St. Louis, but Joyce gave his hometown a thriving tourist industry—postcards, picture books, tours of the Martello Tower, the door from 7 Eccles Street displayed in a pub. Eliot, being Eliot, left no aging madams with fond recollections of the night young T. S. busted up the stews, and it would be futile to try to hawk tea and cakes and ices in these increasingly deserted streets.

But at least Eliot never knocked the old wasteland. When I was growing up in St. Louis I was appalled by the sheer weight of derogatory comment about my hometown, much of it from famous writers. It started early in our history, with British visitors in particular. British lecturers weren't going to miss those Western vulgarians and their fur dollars, and they knew we would make good material for their memoirs. There is a certain masochistic pleasure to be had from reading the rotten things the great men said about us.

Off the steamboat gangplank . . . "An honor, Mr. Arnold . . . truly a pleasure, Mr. Dickens . . . source of great civic satisfaction, Mr. Wilde . . ." Over to the Planters Hotel . . . "Yes, hot, yes, we do have these muggy days, air seems to get stuck in the river valley for weeks, years, centuries even, never gets out really. Too bad you can't stay more than a night, but of course you have to get back to the East, back to London, to your study—you should have some great yarns to spin. Wild West! Buffalo herds! Indians! Should make some corking reading, your visit here—you won't be too hard on us?"

And, of course, they were lousy. Dickens, in his *American Notes*:

No man ever admits the unhealthyness of the place he dwells in (unless he is going away from it) and I shall, therefore, I have no doubt, be at issue with the inhabitants of St. Louis in questioning the perfect salubrity of its climate, and in thinking that I think it must rather dispose to fever in the summer and autumnal seasons. Just adding that it is very hot, lies among great rivers and has vast tracts of undrained swampy land around it, I leave the reader to form his own opinion.

But the British insult everyone. It wasn't just the British. In *Papa Hemingway*, A.E. Hotchner recalls breaking the news to the great author that he, Hotchner, had grown up there.

"Do you know St. Louis?" Hotchner asked Hemingway.

"First three wives from St. Louis," Hemingway said. He shook his head sadly. "I know St. Louis. Only good person I know who didn't leave there was Martha Gellhorn's ma."

Lincoln Steffens, according to Alfred Kazin in *On Native Grounds,* discovered in St. Louis "the story of the decade, the corruption of big cities, and 'Tweed Days in St. Louis' kicked off not only *The Shame of the Cities* but the entire muckraking tradition." Steffens called St. Louis "one of the most corrupt cities in the country."

And it wasn't just the outsiders. Tennessee Williams found St. Louis sordid, commercial, and cruel after an early boyhood in Mississippi. It is a town that David Merrick, who refuses even to fly over, much less revisit, would close out of town.

Fallen-away St. Louisans, like lapsed Catholics, tend to center their apostasy on what they see as smothering, stultifying stagnation, arbitrary icebound conventions, retreat into the past. Recollection tends to return to the same tales, endlessly retold, the debut ball with gondolas shipped from Venice, mansions on private streets that look like left-overs from the Metro back lot, fabulous art collections, royal land grants sold off parcel by parcel, maintaining old French families for centuries.

Decadence looked at in the best light can be thought of as civilized restraint, and St. Louis takes some satisfaction in not being Kansas City, in not fostering vulgar boosterism. But with time this pose can congeal into something like reverse boosterism, a general attitude that even when things seem to be going right, they will be set on a properly disastrous course soon enough. St. Louisans see Pruitt-Igoe becoming nationally notorious on the Cronkite news, and they nod cynically—HUD might, they believe, with brighter expectations fund the Babylon Land Clearance for Redevelopment Authority.

St. Louisans were not surprised when Mayor Cervantes' brainchild, the Spanish Pavilion, trucked stone by stone from the New York World's Fair grounds, was quickly padlocked for lack of patronage. Nor were they amazed when the replica of the Santa Maria, barged in by the mayor as a tourist attraction for the riverfront, sank in the Mississippi the first stormy night. When *Life* printed a cover-story exposé, "The Mayor, the Mob and the Lawyer," attempting to link Cervantes with the Mafia, though, even citizens who didn't like Cervantes thought this was going too far—but for peculiarly local reasons: the discussion did not center so much on whether the mayor had too much integrity to mix with the Mafia as it did on disbelief that a forward-looking, can-do outfit like the Mafia would have anything to do with St. Louis. Kansas City, yes—no doubt. High capos, growth potential in a diversified underworld portfolio, dope, women, gambling. But St. Louis? If anything, perhaps a few exquisitely mannered gentlemen, sawed-off Purdeys discreetly hidden from view, advancing their ineluctable propositions in cadenced Tuscan.

When even your vicious impulses become thinned, anemic, it is time to seek help and word came recently that some aid, at least some advice, was on the way. The National Science Foundation granted $1 million to the RAND Corporation, coroner at the Vietnam inquest, to perform a similar autopsy on St. Louis—specifically to try to find out why the city is decaying at such a pell-mell rate. The RAND report was released several months ago, and its prediction for the future of the city was bleak. At best, St. Louis would find itself a sort of sick suburb in the metropolitan body. The city fathers were outraged, claiming that RAND's researchers conferred only with starry-eyed university professors, that RAND failed to question many civic leaders, and that the report is superficial overall. They may have a point. For a conscientious portrait of the city you need everything—old World's Fair programs, yellowed quitclaim deeds, dog-eared Social Registers; it all has to go into the think tank, everything goes in—mildewed Veiled Prophet souvenirs, royal land grants, snatches of song ("You've Come a Long Way from . . ." "Meet Me in . . ." "All Aboard for . . ."), bits of poems, French recipes, principal products, mementos of famous citizens, significant anecdotes, important dates in municipal history, street guides, letters flown by Charles Lindbergh, old Cardinal box scores, the junk of two centuries from the civic attic, to be pored over by RAND economists, sociologists, urbanologists, and demographers, but for now just throw it all in, Kate Chopin novels, old beaver pelts, copies of *Reedy's Mirror*, tattered steamboat timetables . . .

It is difficult enough to summarize any city, to condense the decades of history and the thousands of residents into a report, forcing to the foreground what is properly background, making of scenery both character and plot, the effective cause of action like Zola mines and Dreiser slums. And it is too easy to fall into the sappiest generalities, lyrics, not words, and the most obvious "city 'cross the bay," "My Kind of Town" lyrics at that.

To go beneath the surface, though, to lay bare the social watchworks (every Springfield a world of allegedly Proustian complexity, nuance, and shading) is of little interest to the outsider—where it is not numbingly familiar: Mr. Big Banker, Mayor Get-Out-the-Vote, Brother Man-the-Machines, and Publisher Print-the-Facts, arm-in-arm against the sunset, progress their only concern.

And it is even more difficult to reduce an older city to the pages of a report. St. Louis was never what it thinks it was; things now are probably not as bad as they appear. But old cities, like old families, obviously shabby, presumptively genteel, sustain themselves on dreams of vanished grandeur, and it may be better to leave such dreams intact. In a land paved with franchised hamburger joints, pizza huts, processed fried-chicken emporiums, formula barbecue, coast-to-coast hot dog and root beer and chili-mac cartels, network programming, all-points fugitives, pasteurized moonshine, nationally shared goals and concerns, it becomes increasingly difficult to find qualities that distinguish, one from another, the theoretically individual cities, which are becoming, like the interstate highway dollars that link them, 90 percent federal, 10 percent local, in everything except their highly individual fantasies.

The peculiar local fantasy of St. Louis is that central location is of increasing importance, that rivers are on the way back, and the Middle West is becoming big box office, that our summers grow longer and greener and cooler, and that if we only brew a little faster, stretch out our city limits a little farther we will wake again to the summer of 1904, the Louisiana Purchase Exposition, the greatest fair ever held, with the world again on our lawns with paddle-wheelers churning at leveeside, with President Teddy Roosevelt, vest straining with merry girth, weighing down the reviewing stand, and the Sousa band, red and gold on the Forest Park green, will thump and toot anew and lights will shine again as nowhere else but here.

JAN MORRIS

Views from Lookout Mountain

"Why Chattanooga?" they often asked me, for it is hardly one of the representative cities that foreigners usually frequent when they want to take the pulse of the Republic. Well, it was partly because I like the name, and the song and the friends I made there long ago, but chiefly because it *isn't* representative. It represents nothing in particular. It is in the South but hardly of it. It is a busy industrial town in a region of hill-folk. It is a Republican stronghold in the heartland of TVA, a rich urban centre in the middle of the Bible belt. So it offers a bit of nearly everything, suave to hick, revival meeting with Devotional Songsters to massage parlour with Nude Operators. No sir, I used to tell them, it was no mere fancy that took me back to Chattanooga, Tennessee, for my own American meditations. It was calculated whim.

Also its setting is perfect for the facile symbolisms I prefer. Every morning before breakfast I went walking on Lookout Mountain, a high forested promontory south of the city which was the site of a decisive battle in the Civil War, and is littered with gunsites and memorials. The woods were still damp then, with a lingering fragrance of the night, a few birds tentatively gurgled, the sky was crystal blue above my head and the rib of the mountain ran away, scarred here and there with rocky outcrops, far down into Georgia. Below me, though, between the trees, Chattanooga was generally veiled in a white morning mist, so impenetrable that you would never guess a city lay there at all: until as the sun rose and the day warmed up, as the mist crept away from the mountain slopes and the stir of the awakening town reached me through the white, slowly, structure by structure, Chattanooga revealed itself.

Its downtown buildings showed first, then the sprawl of its suburbs north and south, then the great bend of the Tennessee River with its three bridges, and the shimmer of Chickamauga Lake beyond, until by the time I reached the crest of the hill there it all lay below me complete and ready for the day, and the river ran away sternly through its gorges to the north, and cars glinted in the city streets, and America itself, wherever I looked, seemed to be rising to a new morning, the *Chattanooga Times* and the statutory southern side-plate of hominy grits.

"Anyway", they often added, "be honest, you jes' like the place, don't you?"

"Yep", I replied, lapsing easily into the vernacular. "Always have."

Take that hominy grits. It is a cereal made of maize, and though nowadays it often comes in a nasty synthetic-looking dollop, and though when I went to a political breakfast one day I noticed sadly that most of the guests gobbled up their eggs but left their grits forlorn upon the plate, still there is something kindly and reassuring to the stuff, something that smacks of an America not quite homogenised.

Of course nowhere in America can escape the creep of uniformity, distributed everywhere by education, television, and that ultimate blight upon spontaneity, tourism. I never thought of Chattanooga as a tourist centre, but to its publicists nowadays it is the Fun City of the South, one of the most Scenic and Historical Areas in the Nation. Nowhere is immune to tourism, the great leveller. When I first went to Chattanooga passenger trains still used the Union Station, and the Civil War epic of the original Chattanooga Choo-Choo was told with reverence. Today the tracks are full of trains still, but they are motionless, the whole building having been frozen into an immense tourist conglomeration, carriages, booking office, locomotives and all, and called inevitably The Choo-Choo. "Where ya staying?" sober businessmen ask of each other in Chattanooga, and they reply without a flicker "Choo-Choo."

Architecturally too, most American cities are much like most others, and Chattanooga, with 120,000 people, is characteristic of many. Its ring roads are like ramparts. Its business district consists of perhaps a dozen high blocks attended by a waste of car parks. It has no single building of much merit, except perhaps some of the better baronial mansions in the mountain suburbs. Standing in one of its downtown streets offers a dispiriting sensation of aridity, as though there is no sap to the place, only a desiccated commercial expertise. You might be almost anywhere in the English-speaking world, in fact, except possibly England.

But the grits are still on the plate, and behind that characterless façade an eclectic variety survives. Chattanooga is not short of individualists, eccentrics even. This is partly perhaps because it is a city of the South, a land of mavericks, and partly because a third of its people are Blacks, the most real of Americans; but it is partly too, I like to think, because the ornery side of the American genius, the Mencken streak, the Truman touch, has never been quite extinguished by the prevailing sameness, and has been held in trust particularly, far from the founts of trend and pressure, by such modest but stubborn cities of the interior.

An endearing braggadocio is part of it, as it has been traditionally part of America. "The view you are enjoying", said a man to me on the mountain one morning, "is the Longest View in the South." I like this kind of thing. I like America to be pleased with itself, and wish it happened more often these days. Fortunately Chattanooga is great on superlatives. Did you know that Chattanooga had the biggest Sunday School in the world? that it is the Electrical Capital of the World? that it supports more churches per head than anywhere else in the world? that the steepest funicular railway in the world runs up Lookout Mountain to the highest railway station in America? that the Choo-Choo Restaurant is the biggest eating-house in the world? that Chattanooga is America's Saddlery? that the view you are enjoying is the Longest View in the South, embracing seven States? "Made in Chattanooga", says the proud boast in many a local store, "by Chattanoogans"—which is to say, created on the spot by the Brightest and Best of the Sons of the Morning.

With this disarming self-esteem goes a simplicity of manners left over from an older America. "Come right in heah, hon", says the lady at the reception desk when I ask if I may use her typewriter, "come right in an' make yourself *nice* 'n snug." Prosperous burghers, when they order their coffee at the drug store, call the waitress "Ma'am." As for the poorer whites, the red-necks, the times have changed them not a jot. Lanky, prickly, drawly, loose-limbed, they look still exactly what they are, mountain peasants come to town. They speak in a grotesque rural patois, they present a heedless or even a feckless front, and if the women often suggest to me self-sacrificing housewives in dramas of the depression, the men often look like slightly beaten-up Irish Australians—which in all essentials, as it happens, they more or less are.

I spent one day with an elderly woman—pardon me, an *older*

woman, a well-known citizen of Chattanooga who splendidly expressed this sense of anachronism. My, as she might say, what fun we had! It seemed to me that though she naturally knew more than I did about Tennessee, I was far more integrated into the contemporary American way of life. A successful journalist, a proud grandmother, a red-hot Democrat, she nevertheless seemed able to ignore almost entirely all the demands of American materialism. Her car was a wreck—"pay no attention to that funny knocking noise." Her manners were utterly without pretence—"which of these darned forks are we supposed to use?" She never watched television, possessed no credit card, did not seem to grasp the basic idea of traffic lights, and very nearly drove us into the Tennessee River off the Dayton ferry—"Nothin' to worry about", the ferryman said, though, "we got a radio link here with the Chickamauga coastguard —soon fish y'all out. . . ."

How many such souls, I wondered, have defied so magnificently all the diktats of the technological age? Like so many American movements the ecological impulse, the impulse towards simplicity, has long since been absorbed into the accepted orthodoxy, and is nowadays propagated as skilfully by General Motors as by Friends of the Earth. The generation that first whole-heartedly embraced it, and gave their emotions to the Greening of America, has graduated from its universities now, emerged from its pacifist furies, changed from its cut-down jeans into suits with waistcoats; whether its members have grown out of those Thoreauesque convictions, too, is anybody's guess.

There were moments in Chattanooga when, clutching my seat as we lurched off the ferry, or exchanging homely grumbles with women in bus queues, I felt that America might still reverse the stream of progress, and become its simpler self again. But I doubt it really. I suspect the powers of American business enterprise, though they may have been jolted lately, are not really much discountenanced. The ecological generation will grow up much like its fathers after all, for it takes more than a bold example here and there, a strong-willed lady, an inbred community, even a generation of dissidents, to fortify a nation against the devices of the profit motive.

Now take morality, which is the next best thing to innocence. Chattanooga is just the place for this inquiry. It is a living book of the Bible belt, its First Kings, say, or its Ezekiel. *Hair* is still banned in Chattanooga, those massage parlours will be lucky to survive much longer, and the Inspirational section is dominant in the city bookshops. Chattanooga supports more churches per . . . oh yes, I said that. There is a chapel on every corner, a sect for every taste, churches for the speaking of Tongues, for the Laying On of Hands, even churches for the Taking up of Snakes ("In My name . . . they shall take up serpents").

The Chattanooga telephone book lists not only the Church of

Christ, the Church of God and the Church of God *in* Christ, but the Church of God of Prophecy, the Bible Church, the Bible Missionary Church, the Nazarene Church, the Pentecostal Church, five kinds of Baptist Church, five kinds of Methodist Church, the African Methodist Episcopal Church, the African Methodist Episcopal *Zion* Church and, oblivious to all heresies, The Christian Church down McCallie Avenue (which operates the Dial-a-Prayer service).

America is a Christian country to a degree long since forgotten in Britain. In Chattanooga, Christianity runs to extremes, but elsewhere, too, it remains a stable and influential force, with power temporal as well as spiritual. But if in the theory the American nation is devout, in the practice there can hardly be a society more riddled with insincerity and opportunism. Everyone knows that. Few Americans over 35 mean exactly what they say, because they have been brainwashed too often, by too many invigilators—by Dale Carnegie or Ralph Nader, by *Time* magazine or Johnny Carson, by Clive Barnes, by Helena Rubinstein, by the Minister, the Sales Manager, the president of the Jaycees, by Mom, by John Wayne, and by all the inexorable, unavoidable pressures of commerce, ambition and survival. America is an inexhaustible fount of new ideas, but for every citizen of true originality, of conscience as of intellect, a thousand find it more politic to suit their views to their circumstances.

And if this insincerity permeates daily life, with all its false flattery and adopted opinions, no less profoundly does it infect the public life of the nation. Watergate was not a phenomenon, only an example. Every day in America, every city, every ward, knows its own corruption: every Chattanooga has its Mr B—"you remember him, the police chief, got caught accepting moonshine money?" The bribe, the bug, the lie, the evasion, the double-talk are strands of the American texture, part of life, part of the system in small things as in great. The venom with which this people turned upon President Nixon, having voted him into office by an unprecedented majority, was only the venom of resentment: for they saw their own Watergates all around them, and even recognised themselves, perhaps, their colleagues or their husbands in Tricky Dick at the White House.

And yet, and yet . . . the idea remains, the noble idea of America, which is above all a republic of aspiration. All the splendour of that idea seemed to come alive, when I looked across Tennessee in the morning, in the majesty of that great valley, in the blue mystery of the hills, in the space and spread of it all lying there, so calm, so grand around the city. Which was the truth about America, I used to wonder as I contemplated this spectacle, the idea or the practice? People often tell me that there is a new yearning in America for *goodness*, for a scouring of the national values, and sometimes, even through Chattanooga's garish screen of religiosity. I thought I glimpsed it for myself.

One evening, for example, I went to a revival meeting outside town. It took place in a lavishly furnished sanctuary, all urns and chandeliers, designed, built and named for its presiding evangelist, Mrs W——, and set in a crematorial style among landscaped gardens of devotion. Mrs W—— proved to be magnificent, if alarming. With proud fiery gestures she stalked amongst us, warning us of demoniac plots, promising us eternal recompense, abjuring us to repent, to bear witness, to expose false prophets such as some of those we all knew without having to mention names in present company, to speak in the Tongues of Pentecost—"*Shoutin', shoutin', that's what the Lord wants!"*

It was tremendous theatre. Sometimes the Redemption Trio, in pale blue jackets with white lapels, contributed a soothing rendering of *Only Believe*. Sometimes a solitary congregant, abruptly visited by the Pentecostal gift, sprang to his feet and shouted to the Lord in old Hebrew, Aramaic or perhaps Babylonic. People fell to the floor in trances, or writhed at the feet of Mrs W——, or sobbed uncontrollably, or burst into song, and sometimes Mrs W—— struck someone heavily on the chest, or hissed at them, or amply embraced them.

I watched it all amazed and often disturbed—for it seemed to me a very good thing, on the whole, that Mrs W—— was on God's side. After a while, however, I found myself unexpectedly moved as well. How wan they looked, those intent and trusting Christians! How earnestly, how lovingly even, they listened to the exhortations of Mrs W——! What true pathos and yearning filled the hall that night! In the pew in front of me were three school-girls, and when Mrs W—— violently demanded that those in need of succour should come forward to be entranced, reviled, thumped, hugged, sung at by the Redemption Trio or shouted over in Chaldean, one of those children, with a wistful smile at her friends, left her seat and walked shakily up the aisle (for she was wearing brand new platform shoes, ornamented with rhinestones).

I could not bear to see what happened to the poor little soul, so I left; and when I looked back from the door she was standing silently in the queue before the preacher, tenth in line among those anguished expectant Americans, waiting still, as one might wait for a stamp at the post office, patiently for the touch of God.

There were no black people at that shrine, but some of those unnamed who received the lash of Mrs. W——'s anathema were, I was later told, black pretenders to the Truth. One can hardly escape the vibrations of race in Chattanooga, standing as it does at the junction of Tennessee, Georgia, and Alabama, and as it happens it was on the corner of Broad Street and West 13th, sitting in my dear old green Chevrolet 20 years ago, that I heard on the radio the Supreme Court's forbidding of racial segregation in schools. Hallelujah, they cried that day in the far mountain shanties and the city slums! It was the overture to the racial revolution that has been simmering or exploding ever since, and it seemed to me that in Chattanooga, at least, things had gone well since 1954. There had been riots, indeed, but my white friends seemed to agree that on the whole this fundamentalist southern community had adapted remarkably easily to *autres temps, autres moeurs*.

But it did not seem that way, I presently learned, if you happened to be black. To get a glimpse of the obverse image I called upon a remarkable black woman, a senior official at one of the local Federal offices, who was not so sanguine. It was true, she said that the white hillfolk and the black townspeople, meeting each other for the first time on the factory floor, got on better than their fathers might have dreamt in their uneasiest nightmares. It was true that there was a Black on the five-man city executive, and that petty *apartheid* in Chattanooga was dead. Still from a black point of view, she assured me, the more things changed the more they stayed the same. The old attitudes had not much softened, seen from the black receiving end. A Black was still, in most inter-racial situations, an un-white, even a non-person. The city might seem content, she said, but it was festering below.

I wondered how true this was of America as a whole. She did not answer, merely moved the flowers on her desk with a gesture part irony, part cynicism, part bewilderment, and indeed it was a silly question. Nobody knows. To be black is currently beautiful, of course. In New York I am constantly struck by the elegance and opulence of the black women to be seen enviably furred and maddeningly diamonded on Fifth Avenue. In Washington, which is said to be the biggest black city outside Africa, Black Power is a political fact, and if it expresses itself at one level in violence, at another it blazes with an exhilarating charm and panache. But how deep has integration gone? Does it work? Is it the right answer anyway?

"My liberal principles", said a white Chattanooga industrialist when I asked *him*, "are alive, but ageing." Though his own labour force was successfully integrated, still he had his doubts. He could not get used to it, after all. He could not stomach the idea of black men consorting with white women. He could not believe in bussing, the compulsory ferrying of children between schools to keep a racial balance; it was not only artificial and self-conscious, he thought, it was also ineffective. Twenty years ago he had been one of the most eager integrationists in Tennessee; now he was no more than a liberal half-heart.

There is a lull now in the American race conflict, broken only by sporadic demonstrations. But I take it to be not an armistice, but a mutual withdrawal from a war of attrition. The certainty has gone from the struggle. It is as though there is a tacit acceptance not necessarily of hostility, but of separateness. Blacks no longer want to be like whites. Whites are no longer sure of their superiority. The gulf between the races may be narrower, but perhaps it is deeper too. A mutual tolerance may be the most, as it must certainly be the least, that Americans can expect of themselves.

But after all it is not too sad a prospect. There is nothing ignoble to separate-but-equal, if it is honestly pursued. I find it hard to remember in Chattanooga now that not so long ago a black man could not walk into most hotels, could not eat at most restaurants, was unwelcome in many shops and was altogether unknown in local society. Even now you will seldom spot a black man at the dining-tables of Lookout Mountain, but still the atmosphere, like the law, has changed out of all recognition. "After all", I said to my black friend, as we walked together to her car, "it's only 20 years. It's a lot to achieve in a generation, isn't it?"

"I'm not thinking of generations," she said. "I'm thinking of me."

Or consider tyranny. Tyranny is the *raison d'être* of America, just as freedom is its point. The only tyranny Chattanooga has known has been the tyranny of race, but with Watergate in mind this time I wondered what elements of local society might, if the chance arose, incline towards autocracy.

In America it is always possible. I have myself experienced two phases of American history when the extinction of liberty seemed potentially imminent; by its very nature, so delicately balanced upon the points of a written constitution, American democracy is dangerously brittle. At that political breakfast the speakers were the two rival candidates for the Governorship of Tennessee. One was the smoothest of young Ivy League lawyers, with an urbane languor and a witty tongue, the other a swarthy populist with padded shoulders and a boxer's walk: I found it perfectly easy to imagine either of them as little Mussolinis in the gubernatorial mansion.

There are several obvious power centres in Chattanooga. There are the political parties themselves, the commercial organisations, the churches and schools, Rotary, Kiwanis, the Mountain City Club. There are several important industries. There is a handful of rich families, whose elders are to be glimpsed sedate and benign through the double-glazing of their mountain homes, and whose scions may be observed eating Shrimp Creole off tables made of Victory ship hatch-covers at the Brass Register, Chattanooga's brightest Nitery. Above all there is the *Chattanooga Times*, a fine old newspaper, linked by origin and ownership with the *New York Times*, which has for more than a century tempered and civilised the attitudes of the town.

The American Press has always been a rather different institution from the British. In so huge a country the local newspaper has acquired much greater power, and there is something forcefully romantic to the status of grand old organs like the *St Louis Post-Dispatch* or the *Milwaukee Journal*, with their humming offices in the heart of town, their squadrons of reporters, their locally celebrated editors and regionally lionised columnists, their ancillary TV stations and their dashing fleets of delivery vans. It was a Briton who called the Press the fourth estate of the realm, but the Americans were the first, I think, to recognise the concept constitutionally, and ever since the newspapers of America have occupied a station in public life different in kind from their European contemporaries.

It never occurred to me, when I was first in Chattanooga, to wonder if the good old *Times* could ever become an instrument of tyranny: but it did cross my mind this time, not because it has ever wavered from its habitual standards of integrity, but because in America as a whole the Press seems to me to have developed an unhealthy new arrogance. One senses it partly in the dogmatism, often slavishly accepted, of critics and editorial writers, but chiefly in the disturbing vogue for investigative reporting. This springs largely, of course, from the success of the *Washington Post* in exhibiting the immoralities of the Nixon régime, but it has gone much farther now. The Press enjoyed that letting of blood, and now too often seems to think that good journalism knows no secrets, respects no privacies, pardons no faults and brooks no reticence.

A nation, they say, gets the Press it warrants, and I think perhaps this predatory journalism does genuinely reflect a meanness or cruelty in the American spirit today. It is bad journalism, to my mind, for it is out of balance. It is unrealistic in its demands. It is immature in its excesses. It is distasteful in its relentlessness. It is often disgracefully inaccurate. It is harmful to the commonality in its inescapable innuendo that nobody in high office is beyond suspicion. The right to say anything about anybody is not, after all, one of the inalienable rights envisaged by the Founding Fathers.

I find it easy to imagine a tyranny there: those handsome offices, of *Journal* or *Herald-Times*, transformed into bureaus of authority, those columnists and talk-show kings revealed as fawning spokesmen of the régime, those investigative tigers translated without much difficulty into agents of police or secret intelligence. It is not hard to see. They are half-way there already, if not in method at least in instinct; and sometimes from Lookout Mountain, in moments of black fancy, I could even descry the crooked banner of some unsuspected despot, a crazed revivalist perhaps, or an unhinged Rotarian, fluttering from the rooftop of the *Chattanooga Times.*

"You're getting a bit wild now, aren't you? We've got a high-minded set of civic leaders here in Chattanooga, regular nice set of guys. I can't see any of our fellows setting up to be any kind of dictator."

Well, maybe you're right. It's those Martinis. For people of my generation, though, who first knew an America so brave, so powerful, so rich and so generous that it seemed unshakable in its values, it is sad to see how inexorably Americans have come to question their own principles. Nostalgia is not an emotion I ever thought I would feel in Chattanooga, but I often feel it now. I miss those brave days of patriotism, magnanimity and Norman Rockwell. I miss the old sensation that in America everything was possible, that hope was here, and decision, and sidewalks paved with gold. It was an illusion anyway, I know, but to the illusion there was not only comfort, but also its own truth.

Today that old exhilaration has become nostalgia. Hollywood America, which so stamped its image upon the imagination of the world, exists no longer. Here as everywhere people are poorer than they were, more worried, less sure of themselves, less happy, I think. Who would ever have envisaged an American shortage of *gasoline*? Who could have foreseen Americans taking cold showers to save fuel? Who could have imagined, two decades ago, the victorious Republic standing half in fee to the United Arab Emirates? The American dream has been shattered this way and that. Democracy is safer in Germany now, and many a poor immigrant might be better off if he had never come.

Even the proverbial efficiency of America is fading. They had run out of corn-flakes at my Chattanooga hotel. They had forgotten to clean the boot of my Budget rental car. The road signs of Chattanooga, once models of lucid common sense, are now almost totally incomprehensible. Even the American telephone system, that unattainable ideal of yesteryear, is showing signs of ennui, and peters away ever more frequently into unexplained blurps and sepulchral silences. Capitalism, like democracy perhaps, has lost the flare of conviction in America, and its flame is guttering all down the line, from the bankrupt airlines and discredited corporations to the car door that won't shut, or the drip in the tap in the room next door.

And saddest of all is the tarnish that has appeared upon the American sense of history. Like everywhere else in the United States, Chattanooga is preparing for the great celebrations of 1976, when Americans will remember their two centuries of independence. All the old texts will be quoted then, all the old principles rehearsed, Mr Jefferson and General Washington will be paraded for our allegiance, schoolchildren from coast to coast will pipe again the Declaration of Independence or the Gettysburg Address. But it is all a pretence. The America of 1775 bears little more resemblance to the America of today than Soviet Russia bears to the Russia of the Czars. It is only lip service to a lost vision, publicity for an abandoned cause.

I discovered from one of the Chattanooga publicity brochures that the very last skirmish of the American Revolution had been fought right there on Lookout Mountain, when a last wandering group of redcoats had surrendered to the mountaineers. I'd never heard of that before, I observed. That was a useful addition to the Scenic and Historical Wonders. Yeah, they mordantly replied, comes in handy for the Bicentennial, too.

And yet, and yet . . . America is the land of the fresh divisions, storming in splendidly to the rescue of the old. All is not lost over there! Absolutely the greatest change that has occurred in America in our time is the emergence of the free woman, a new force, a new army. The excitement of this development, its sense of limitless new potential, can scarcely be grasped by people on this side of the Atlantic, and is only dimly perceived I think by most American males, who are not yet aware what is about to hit them. To the women who are themselves experiencing it, though, and who recognise it to be nothing less than a fundamental shift in the balance of human power, it has come as a kind of revelation.

It began grotesquely enough, like so many epochal developments, in the excesses and bullyings of Women's Lib. All that is *passé* now, the bra-burning and the brow-beating and the indignant letters from Minnesota housewives protesting against their rejection as trainee lumberjacks. A new and calmer purpose now dignifies the women's movement, as women have gradually realised that they are arguing not out of weakness, but out of strength—for in evolutionary terms, or so it seems to me, femaleness rather than maleness is the more efficient condition for our times, the more *modern* condition so to speak. For all its inventive genius America is a country terribly set in its ways, socially and politically far older than its years; if anyone is to restore its old excitements, enabling it to stand once more as an exemplar for the world, it is likely to be the free women.

For the American women's movement possesses an ecstatic quality which I take to be much like the spirit of the original America. It rises above tired old syndromes, and sees visions once more. One evening in Chattanooga a young woman came to call on me at my hotel. She was in her early twenties, perhaps. We had dinner together, and as we sat there in the dim-lit velvety restaurant, to the squashy music of the electric organ beyond the hors d'oeuvre trolley, an exuberant radiance seemed to emanate from her, not quite like the glow of a woman in love, more like a cultist's brilliance.

She had not though, as it turned out, been visited at any grotto, or irradiated by Mrs W—: she had simply joined the new Chattanooga branch of NOW, the National Organization for Women, and she was as afire with the truth, the fun and the power of it all, as ever the original American patriots were, when they first sensed the meaning of liberty.

What cheek it always is, to speculate in this maundering way about the affairs of another country! America especially has suffered from impertinence since the start, and when I first went to Chattanooga I was always conscious of a prickly defensiveness in the air. Power, though, if it corrupts, also matures, and in America today a tired *noblesse oblige* is in order. If the old brag has gone, so has the touchiness. In the 1940s Geoffrey Gorer could write of Europe as America's Father-Figure; in the 1960s President could defer to Prime Minister as the repository of experience, today, when Dr Kissinger is thanked for saving the world, he merely says "You're welcome" (though as a matter of cultural interest, in the old American way he still calls a sheikh a "sheek").

But I write only out of love. I loved America the moment I set foot there, and in my walks on Lookout Mountain I only rediscovered my affection. It is no good rationalising America, anyway, for if Brazil is perpetually the country of the future, America is uncontrollably the country of change. It is a country that will never be finished. Its natural state is seismic, or protean. Its citizens may pine for stability, order, permanence: but to live temporarily, from crisis to reappraisal, disillusionment to renewal, is the pride and penalty of being American.

Such were the sententious truisms I thought, along with others less communicable, on those quiet cloud-filled mornings on the mountain. There is no landscape that feels so immovable as the American, so rooted and profound. It is a curious irony that upon it mankind has deposited the most volatile and restless of its societies, never at ease, and awakening each morning not, as the view from Lookout Mountain might suggest, to another day of easeful grandeur, but only to another instalment of clash, doubt and astonishment.

Who can ever be bored in America? New every morning breaks the marvel! Even the Chattanooga birds, chirruping my way back through the woods to breakfast, sounded as though they were speculating, as America has speculated every breakfast-time for two centuries, what in the world would happen next.

S. J. PERELMAN

The Machismo Mystique

It was 3 P.M., that climactic midafternoon moment toward which every gallant worthy of the name bends his energies, and I'd done all the preparatory work time and an unencumbered credit card could accomplish. I had stoked my Chilean vis-à-vis with three vodka martinis, half a gallon of Sancerre, and two balloons of Armagnac until her eyes were veritable liquid pools. Under my bold, not to say outrageous, compliments her damask skin and the alabaster column of her throat glowed like a lovely pink pearl; her hair, black as the raven's wing, shimmered in the reflection of the boudoir lamp shading our discreet banquette; and every now and again as my knee nudged hers under the table, my affinity's magnificent bosom heaved uncontrollably. I had glissed through all those earnest confidences that begin, "You know, I've never said this to anyone before," to, "Look, I'm not very articulate, but I feel that in these parlous times, it behooves us all to reach out, to cling to another lonely person—do you know what I mean?" Suddenly I had the feeling that she knew what I meant, all right. In a swift glance, I encompassed the small chic restaurant whence all but we had fled—its idle barman and the maître d'hôtel stifling a yawn— and I struck.

"Listen," I said as if inspired. "This friend of mine, the Marquis de Cad, who has a wonderful collection of African sculpture, was called away to Cleveland, and I promised to stop by his flat and dust it. Why don't we pick up a bottle of lemon oil . . ."

Inamorata threw back her sleek head and shouted with laughter. "Stop, *querido*," she implored. "You're ruining my mascara. Such *machismo*—who would have expected it from a shrimp like you?"

Quicker than any hidalgo[1] of Old Spain to erase an insult, I sprang up prepared to plunge my poniard[2] into her bosom (a striking demonstration of the maxim that man kills that which he most loves). Unfortunately, I had left my poniard at home on the bureau and was wearing only a tie-tack that could never penetrate anyone so thick-skinned. Nonetheless, I made the hussy smart for her insolence. "Let me tell you something, Chubby," I rasped. "Never underestimate the American male. I may not dance the mambo or reek of garlic, but I'm just as feisty as those caballeros of yours below the Rio Grande. Remember that our first colonial flag in Kentucky, the Dark and Bloody Ground, portrayed a coiled rattlesnake over the legend, 'Don't Tread on Me.'"

"Big deal," she scoffed. "Do you want an example of real *machismo*—the kind of masculinity Latin-American men are capable of? Tell them to bring me another Armagnac."

Downcast at the realization that our matinee had blown out the back, I sullenly acceded. The story as she related it dealt with a bar in Guatemala City called *Mi apuesta* (The Wager) after a bet once made there. Two young bloods or *machos*, it appeared, had swaggered in one evening, stiff with conceit and supremely self-con-

1. Gentleman.   2. Dagger.

fident, arrogant as a pair of fighting cocks. Lounging at the bar over a glass of manzanilla, one of them remarked to the other, "*Te apuesto que no eres bastante macho para matar al primero que entre*" (I wager you're not man enough to kill the first hombre who comes in).

The other sneered thinly. "No?" he said. "I bet you fifty *centavos* I will."

The bet was covered, whereupon the challenged party extracted a Beretta from his waistband, and a moment later, as a totally inoffensive stranger stepped through the saloon door, a bullet drilled him through the heart.

"*Madre de Dios,*" I exclaimed, shocked. "What happened to the assassin?"

"*Niente,*" said Inamorata calmly. "The judge gave him a three months' suspended sentence on the ground that the crime was in no way premeditated."

Needless to say, whenever Inamorata rang up after our abortive meeting and besought me to lunch her again, I showed her a clean pair of heels. (They were two fellows who dispensed towels at the Luxor Baths; they pursued her madly, and I hope with more success than I had.) At any rate, in pondering the whole business of *machismo,* of male bravado and excessive manliness, it occurred to me that I had met quite a few *machos* in my time, both in the entertainment world and belles-lettres. The one I remember most vividly in the former was a Hollywood screenwriter—a big redheaded blowhard I'll call Rick Ferret. A Montanan who claimed to have grown up on the range, Ferret was forever beating his gums about his amatory exploits; by his own blushing admission, he was Casanova reborn, the swordsman supreme, the reincarnation of Don Juan. According to him, women in every walk of life—society leaders and shopgirls, leading ladies and vendeuses—fell in windrows in his path, and though it was obvious to his auditors at the Brown Derby that he dealt in quantity rather than quality, the references he dropped to his nuclear power and durability left us pale with jealousy.

One evening, I attended a party at his house in Laurel Canyon. Living with him at the time was a lady named Susie, quite well-endowed and with a rather sharp tongue. So late was the hour when the bash ended that the two insisted I stay over, and the next morning, while I was adjusting my false lashes, Ferret entered the bathroom and proceeded to take a shower. Just as he was snorting and puffing like a grampus, I chanced to observe a quite formidable scar on his *Sitzfleisch.* With an apology for the personal nature of the question, I asked if it was a war wound of some kind.

"Yes, in a way," he said carelessly, turning off the taps. "There's quite a story attached to it." He opened the door of the bathroom to disperse the steam, and I glimpsed his Susie breakfasting in bed a few feet distant. "The fact is," he went on, "it happened some years ago down on the south fork of the Brazos while I was rounding up some mavericks. This gang of rustlers from Durango way cut into the herd, and I took after them hell for leather. Well, the greasers were spoiling for action, and they got it." He chuckled. "Before I could yank out my six-guns, they creased me here, but I managed to rub out the whole dad-blamed lot."

"Oh, for God's sake, Ferret," I heard Susie's voice croak from the bedroom. "You know perfectly well you had a boil lanced on your tail only last Tuesday."

The two most celebrated *machos* I ever knew, I suppose, were Ernest Hemingway—unquestionably the holder of the black belt in the Anglo-Saxon world—and Mike Todd, who, to pilfer a phrase from Marcel Proust, might aptly be termed the Sweet Cheat Gone. My go-around with Hemingway took place in the winter of 1954, directly after his two widely publicized plane crashes in East Africa. He was borne into the New Stanley Hotel in Nairobi in a somewhat disoriented state, suffering a double concussion, a smashed kidney, and alarming symptoms of *folie de grandeur*.[3] I turned up there two days later from Uganda with fourteen women comprising the first American all-girl safari (quite another story), and since my room was adjacent to his, saw a good bit of him thereafter. What with his tribulations and frequent infusions of hooch, Papa was inclined to ramble somewhat, and it was not always easy to follow the thread of his discourse. Once in a while, though, the clouds dissipated, and we were able to chat about mutual friends in the Montparnasse of the 'twenties. It was on such an occasion, one night, that he told me an anecdote that stunningly dramatized his *machismo*.

It concerned a period when he used to box at Stillman's Gymnasium in New York, a favorite haunt of enthusiasts of what is termed the manly art. His adversaries, Hemingway blushingly admitted, never matched his own speed and strength, but one of them improved so under his tutelage that occasionally the pair had a tolerable scrimmage. Thinking to intensify it, Hemingway suggested they discard their gloves and fight bareknuckle. This, too, while diverting, soon palled, but at last he had an inspiration.

"The room we boxed in," Hemingway explained, "had these rows of pipes running along the walls—you know, like backstage in a theater? Well, we flooded the place with steam, so thickly that it looked like a pea-soup fog in London. Then we started charging each other like a couple of rhinos. Butting our heads together and roaring like crazy. God, it was terrific—you could hear the impact of bone on bone, and we bled like stuck pigs. Of course, that made the footwork a bit more difficult, slipping and sliding all over, but it

3. Delusions of grandeur.

sure heightened the fun. Man, those were the days. You had to have real *cojones*[4] to stand up to it."

The same hormonal doodads were imperative in order to cope with Mike Todd and his vagaries. Todd's *machismo* was that common form that afflicts all undersized men—megalomania. He freely identified himself with Napoleon, P. T. Barnum, and Carl Laemmle, Junior, not to mention the Roman emperors of the decline. Whereas the latter, however, believed in giving the populace bread and circuses, Todd gave them circuses and kept the bread. Rarely if ever has there been anyone more unwilling to fork over what he owed to those actors, writers, and technicians who aided him in his grandiloquent projects of stage and screen. The little corpuscle, in short, believed in flaunting money where it made the most impression—at Deauville, Monaco, and the gaming tables of Las Vegas. In this respect, he was a true *macho*. My sole souvenir of our frenetic association is a replica of the carpetbag Phileas Fogg carried on his celebrated journey, a thousand of which Todd distributed in lordly fashion to Broadway companions, investors, accountants, dentists, and other sycophants. But surely, his admirers have since queried me, I must have been awed by his tremendous vitality; Only in part, I respond: *Moi-même*, I prefer the anthropoid apes. The gibbon swings farther, the chimpanzee's reflexes are quicker, the orangutan can scratch faster, and the gorilla—my particular love object—has been known to crunch a Stillson wrench in his teeth.

Of such literary *machos* was the late Robert Ruark, who of course patterned himself on Hemingway. Their careers afford ample demonstration of my two favorite maxims: a) that the gaudier the patter, the cheaper the scribe, and b) that easy writing makes hard reading. The legend of Ruark's fatal charisma with women still gives one a pain in the posterior when recounted, and his press interviews, studded with reference to the millions of words he merchandised, act as a tourniquet on bleeders like myself who labor over a postcard. Even John O'Hara, somewhat more talented, was not above buttonholing acquaintances and boasting that he had written this or that deathless vignette in three quarters of an hour. It is interesting, by the way, that Scott Fitzgerald, with whom O'Hara was given to comparing himself, never made any claims to his own facility when I knew him in Hollywood. On the contrary, both he and Nathanael West were continually obsessed by delusions of their inadequacy with sex and their small literary output.

Looking back over a long and mottled career, I think the best illustration of real *machismo* I ever beheld took place on the terrace of the Café du Dôme in Paris in 1927. I was seated there at dusk

4. Testicles.

one day with a fellow journalist when an enormous yellow Hispano-Suiza landaulet driven by a chauffeur drew up at the curb. From it emerged a tall and beautiful, exquisitely clad lady, followed by another even more photogenic—both clearly high-fashion manne-quins. Reaching into the tonneau, they brought forth a wizened homunculus with a yellow face resembling Earl Sande, the cele-brated jockey. Hooking their arms through his, they assisted him to a table farther down the terrace. I turned to my *copain* with my eyebrows raised, searching for some explanation of the phenome-non. A slow smile overspread his countenance, and he held his hands apart as does one when asked to steady a skein of wool.

That's *machismo,* sweetheart.

QUESTIONS

1. Write your own definition of machismo, basing it on Perelman's examples.
2. Perelman says his last paragraph contains his "best illustration of real machismo." Explain why you agree or disagree.
3. Toward the end of his essay Perelman talks about writers who boast about how fast and how much they write. Why do you think Perelman includes these examples? Explain whether they are a part of his definition of machismo or merely analogous to it.
4. Describe an incident (either actual or invented) which illustrates machismo. Then change the incident so that it no longer illus-trates machismo. Explain whether the changes involved (1) changes in people, (2) changes in circumstances or social cus-toms, or (3) changes in both. What conclusions can you draw about whether machismo is a part of human nature or is cul-turally conditioned?
5. Perelman has a very distinctive style. Try to determine what its characteristics are by rewriting one of his paragraphs in a more neutral style.
6. Read the McGraw-Hill "Guidelines for Equal Treatment of the Sexes" (pp. 292–303). In what ways are machismo attitudes re-flected in language?
7. Read Harvey Cox's "The Playboy and Miss America" (pp. 569–79). Explain whether you think Perelman and Cox are pointing to any similar cultural phenomena or trends.

HARVEY COX

The Playboy and Miss America[1]

No aspect of human life seethes with so many unexorcised demons as does sex. No human activity is so hexed by superstition, so haunted by residual tribal lore, and so harassed by socially induced fear. Within the breast of urban-secular man, a toe-to-toe struggle still rages between his savage and his bourgeois forebears. Like everything else, the images of sex which informed tribal and town society are expiring along with the eras in which they arose. The erosion of traditional values and the disappearance of accepted modes of behavior have left contemporary man free, but somewhat rudderless. Abhorring a vacuum, the mass media have rushed in to supply a new code and a new set of behavioral prototypes. They appeal to the unexorcised demons. Nowhere is the persistence of mythical and metalogical denizens more obvious than in sex, and the shamans of sales do their best to nourish them. Nowhere is the humanization of life more frustrated. Nowhere is a clear word of exorcism more needed.

How is the humanization of sex impeded? First it is thwarted by the parading of cultural-identity images for the sexually dispossessed, to make money. These images become the tyrant gods of the secular society, undercutting its liberation from religion and transforming it into a kind of neotribal culture. Second, the authentic secularization of sex is checkmated by an anxious clinging to the sexual standards of the town, an era so recent and yet so different from ours that simply to transplant its sexual ethos into our situation is to invite hypocrisy of the worst degree.[2]

Let us look first at the spurious sexual models conjured up for our anxious society by the sorcerers of the mass media and the advertising guild. Like all pagan deities, these come in pairs—the god and his consort. For our purposes they are best symbolized by The Playboy and Miss America, the Adonis and Aphrodite[3] of a leisure-consumer society which still seems unready to venture into full postreligious maturity and freedom. The Playboy and Miss America represent The Boy and The Girl. They incorporate a vision of life. They function as religious phenomena and should be exorcised and exposed.

Let us begin with Miss America. In the first century b.c., Lucretius wrote this description of the pageant of Cybele:

1. From Chapter 9 of *The Secular City*.

2. Cox goes on to discuss the "remnants of town virtues" in a section following the present selection.

3. Adonis and Aphrodite (the Greek goddess of love corresponding to the Latin Venus) were lovers; both had great physical beauty and were worshiped widely.

Adorned with emblem and crown . . . she is carried in awe-inspiring state. Tight-stretched tambourines and hollow cymbals thunder all round to the stroke of open hands, hollow pipes stir with Phrygian strain. . . . She rides in procession through great cities and mutely enriches mortals with a blessing not expressed in words. They straw all her path with brass and silver, presenting her with bounteous alms, and scatter over her a snow-shower of roses.[4]

Now compare this with the annual twentieth-century Miss America pageant in Atlantic City, New Jersey. Spotlights probe the dimness like votive tapers, banks of flowers exude their varied aromas, the orchestra blends feminine strings and regal trumpets. There is a hushed moment of tortured suspense, a drumroll, then the climax —a young woman with carefully prescribed anatomical proportions and exemplary "personality" parades serenely with scepter and crown to her throne. At TV sets across the nation throats tighten and eyes moisten. "There she goes, Miss America—" sings the crooner. "There she goes, your ideal." A new queen in America's emerging cult of The Girl has been crowned.

Is it merely illusory or anachronistic to discern in the multiplying pageants of the Miss America, Miss Universe, Miss College Queen type a residuum of the cults of the pre-Christian fertility goddesses? Perhaps, but students of the history of religions have become less prone in recent years to dismiss the possibility that the cultural behavior of modern man may be significantly illuminated by studying it in the perspective of the mythologies of bygone ages. After all, did not Freud initiate a revolution in social science by utilizing the venerable myth of Oedipus to help make sense out of the strange behavior of his Viennese contemporaries? Contemporary man carries with him, like his appendix and his fingernails, vestiges of his tribal and pagan past.

In light of this fertile combination of insights from modern social science and the history of religions, it is no longer possible to see in the Miss America pageant merely an overpublicized prank foisted on us by the advertising industry. It certainly is this, but it is also much more. It represents the mass cultic celebration, complete with a rich variety of ancient ritual embellishments, of the growing place of The Girl in the collective soul of America.

This young woman—though she is no doubt totally ignorant of the fact—symbolizes something beyond herself. She symbolizes The Girl, the primal image, the one behind the many. Just as the Virgin appears in many guises—as our Lady of Lourdes or of Fatima or of Guadalupe—but is always recognizably the Virgin, so with The Girl.

---

4. This is quoted from Lucretius ii, 608f. in T. R. Glover. *The Conflict of Religions in the Early Roman Empire* (Boston: Beacon, 1960), p. 20. It was originally published in London in 1909 by Methuen & Co. Ltd. [Cox's note].

Cybele, the Great Mother, was associated with "the principle of life and its reproduction," Glover also says, "and her worship appealed to every male and female being in the world."

The Girl is also the omnipresent icon of consumer society. Selling beer, she is folksy and jolly. Selling gems, she is chic and distant. But behind her various theophanies she remains recognizably The Girl. In Miss America's glowingly healthy smile, her openly sexual but officially virginal figure, and in the name-brand gadgets around her, she personalifies the stunted aspirations and ambivalent fears of her culture. "There she goes, your ideal."

Miss America stands in a long line of queens going back to Isis, Ceres, and Aphrodite.[5] Everything from the elaborate sexual taboos surrounding her person to the symbolic gifts at her coronation hints at her ancient ancestry. But the real proof comes when we find that the function served by The Girl in our culture is just as much a "religious" one as that served by Cybele in hers. The functions are identical—to provide a secure personal "identity" for initiates and to sanctify a particular value structure.

Let us look first at the way in which The Girl confers a kind of identity on her initiates. Simone de Beauvoir says in *The Second Sex* that "no one is *born* a woman."[6] One is merely born a female, and "*becomes* a woman" according to the models and meanings provided by the civilization. During the classical Christian centuries, it might be argued, the Virgin Mary served in part as this model. With the Reformation and especially with the Puritans, the place of Mary within the symbol system of the Protestant countries was reduced or eliminated. There are those who claim that this excision constituted an excess of zeal that greatly impoverished Western culture, an impoverishment from which it has never recovered. Some would even claim that the alleged failure of American novelists to produce a single great heroine (we have no Phaedra, no Anna Karenina) stems from this self-imposed lack of a central feminine ideal.

Without entering into this fascinating discussion, we can certainly be sure that, even within modern American Roman Catholicism, the Virgin Mary provides an identity image for few American girls. Where then do they look for the "model" Simone de Beauvoir convincingly contends they need? For most, the prototype of femininity seen in their mothers, their friends, and in the multitudinous images to which they are exposed on the mass media is what we have called The Girl.

In his significant monograph *Identity and the Life Cycle*, Erik Erikson reminds us that the child's identity is not modeled simply on the parent but on the parent's "super-ego."[7] Thus in seeking to forge her own identity the young girl is led beyond her mother to

---

5. Isis was the Egyptian goddess of procreation and birth; Ceres (equivalent to the Greek Demeter) was the goddess of fertility and of the harvest and was often confused in later times with Cybele; for Aphrodite, see note 3 above.

6. Simone de Beauvoir, *The Second Sex* (New York: Knopf, 1953; London: Cape), p. 41 [Cox's note].

7. Erik Erikson, *Identity and the Life Cycle* (New York: International University Press, 1959) [Cox's note].

her mother's ideal image, and it is here that what Freud called "the ideologies of the superego . . . the traditions of the race and the people" become formative. It is here also that The Girl functions, conferring identity on those for whom she is—perhaps never completely consciously—the tangible incarnation of womanhood.

To describe the mechanics of this complex psychological process by which the fledgling American girl participates in the life of The Girl and thus attains a woman's identity would require a thorough description of American adolescence. There is little doubt, however, that such an analysis would reveal certain striking parallels to the "savage" practices by which initiates in the mystery cults shared in the magical life of their god.

For those inured to the process, the tortuous nightly fetish by which the young American female pulls her hair into tight bunches secured by metal clips may bear little resemblance to the incisions made on their arms by certain African tribesmen to make them resemble their totem, the tiger. But to an anthropologist comparing two ways of attempting to resemble the holy one, the only difference might appear to be that with the Africans the torture is over after initiation, while with the American it has to be repeated every night, a luxury only a culture with abundant leisure can afford.

In turning now to an examination of the second function of The Girl—supporting and portraying a value system—a comparison with the role of the Virgin in the twelfth and thirteenth centuries may be helpful. Just as the Virgin exhibited and sustained the ideals of the age that fashioned Chartres Cathedral, as Henry Adams saw,[8] so The Girl symbolizes the values and aspirations of a consumer society. (She is crowned not in the political capital, remember, but in Atlantic City or Miami Beach, centers associated with leisure and consumption.) And she is not entirely incapable of exploitation. If men sometimes sought to buy with gold the Virgin's blessings on their questionable causes, so The Girl now dispenses her charismatic favor on watches, refrigerators, and razor blades—for a price. Though The Girl has built no cathedrals, without her the colossal edifice of mass persuasion would crumble. Her sharply stylized face and figure beckon us from every magazine and TV channel, luring us toward the beatific vision of a consumer's paradise.

The Girl is *not* the Virgin. In fact she is a kind of anti-Madonna. She reverses most of the values traditionally associated with the Virgin—poverty, humility, sacrifice. In startling contrast, particularly, to the biblical portrait of Mary in Luke 1:46–55, The Girl has nothing to do with filling the hungry with "good things,"[9] hawking

---

8. See *The Education of Henry Adams: An Autobiography* (Boston: Houghton Mifflin, 1961). pp. 388, 427. Adams sees the Virgin as the "force" behind the building of the cathedral at Chartres and points to Venus and the goddesses of Indian mythology as similar "forces."

9. It is actually God who has "filled the hungry with good things," and Mary praises Him for it.

instead an endless proliferation of trivia on TV spot commercials. The Girl exalts the mighty, extols the rich, and brings nothing to the hungry but added despair. So The Girl does buttress and bring into personal focus a value system, such as it is. In both social and psychological terms, The Girl, whether or not she is really a goddess, certainly acts that way.

Perhaps the most ironic element in the rise of the cult of The Girl is that Protestantism has almost completely failed to notice it, while Roman Catholics have at least given some evidence of sensing its significance. In some places, for instance, Catholics are forbidden to participate in beauty pageants, a ruling not entirely inspired by prudery. It is ironic that Protestants have traditionally been most opposed to lady cults while Catholics have managed to assimilate more than one at various points in history.

If we are correct in assuming that The Girl *functions* in many ways as a goddess, then the cult of The Girl demands careful Protestant theological criticism. Anything that functions, even in part, as a god when it is in fact not God, is an idol. When the Reformers and their Puritan offspring criticized the cult of Mary it was not because they were antifeminist. They opposed anything—man, woman, or beast (or dogma or institution)—that usurped in the slightest the prerogatives that belonged alone to God Almighty. As Max Weber has insisted, when the prophets of Israel railed against fertility cults, they had nothing against fertility.[1] It is not against sexuality but against a cult that protest is needed. Not, as it were, against the beauty but against the pageant.

Thus the Protestant objection to the present cult of The Girl must be based on the realization that The Girl is an *idol*. She functions as the source of value, the giver of personal identity. But the values she mediates and the identity she confers are both spurious. Like every idol she is ultimately a creation of our own hands and cannot save us. The values she represents as ultimate satisfactions —mechanical comfort, sexual success, unencumbered leisure—have no ultimacy. They lead only to endless upward mobility, competitive consumption, and anxious cynicism. The devilish social insecurities from which she promises to deliver us are, alas, still there, even after we have purified our breaths, our skins, and our armpits by applying her sacred oils. She is a merciless goddess who draws us farther and farther into the net of accelerated ordeals of obeisance. As the queen of commodities in an expanding economy, the fulfillment she promises must always remain just beyond the tips of our fingers.

Why has Protestantism kept its attention obsessively fastened on the development of Mariolatry in Catholicism and not noticed the sinister rise of this vampirelike cult of The Girl in our society?

1. See, *passim*, Max Weber, *Ancient Judaism* (Glencoe, Ill.: The Free Press, 1952).

Unfortunately, it is due to the continuing incapacity of theological critics to recognize the religious significance of cultural phenomena outside the formal religious system itself. But the rise of this new cult reminds us that the work of the reformer is never done. Man's mind is indeed—as Luther[2] said—a factory busy making idols. The Girl is a far more pervasive and destructive influence than the Virgin, and it is to her and her omnipresent altars that we should be directing our criticism.

Besides sanctifying a set of phony values, The Girl compounds her noxiousness by maiming her victims in a procrustean bed of uniformity. This is the empty "identity" she panders. Take the Miss America pageant, for example. Are these virtually indistinguishable specimens of white, middleclass postadolescence really the best we can do? Do they not mirror the ethos of a mass-production society, in which genuine individualism somehow mars the clean, precision-tooled effect? Like their sisters, the finely calibrated Rockettes,[3] these meticulously measured and pretested "beauties" lined up on the boardwalk bear an ominous similarity to the faceless retinues of goose-steppers and the interchangeable mass exercisers of explicitly totalitarian societies. In short, *who* says this is beauty?

The caricature becomes complete in the Miss Universe contest, when Miss Rhodesia is a blonde, Miss South Africa is white, and Oriental girls with a totally different tradition of feminine beauty are forced to display their thighs and appear in spike heels and Catalina swim suits. Miss Universe is as universal as an American adman's stereotype of what beauty should be.

The truth is that The Girl can*not* bestow the identity she promises. She forces her initiates to torture themselves with starvation diets and beauty-parlor ordeals, but still cannot deliver the satisfactions she holds out. She is young, but what happens when her followers, despite added hours in the boudoir, can no longer appear young? She is happy and smiling and loved. What happens when, despite all the potions and incantations, her disciples still feel the human pangs of rejection and loneliness? Or what about all the girls whose statistics, or "personality" (or color) do not match the authoritative "ideal"?

After all, it is God—not The Girl—who is God. He is the center and source of value. He liberates men and women from the bland uniformity of cultural deities so that they may feast on the luxurious diversity of life He has provided. The identity He confers frees men from all pseudo-identities to be themselves, to fulfill their human destinies regardless of whether their faces or figures match

2. The reference is to Martin Luther (1483–1546), religious reformer and instigator of the Protestant Reformation.

3. The famous group of female dancers at New York's Radio City Music Hall, chosen for their physical similarities as well as their dancing ability and trained to move with precision and in unison in a chorus line in which they are arranged according to gradations in their height.

some predetermined abstract "ideal." As His gift, sex is freed from both fertility cults and commercial exploitation to become the thoroughly human thing He intended. And since it is one of the last items we have left that is neither prepackaged nor standardized, let us not sacrifice it too hastily on the omnivorous altar of Cybele.

The Playboy, illustrated by the monthly magazine of that name, does for the boys what Miss America does for the girls. Despite accusations to the contrary, the immense popularity of this magazine is not solely attributable to pinup girls. For sheer nudity its pictorial art cannot compete with such would-be competitors as *Dude* and *Escapade*. *Playboy* appeals to a highly mobile, increasingly affluent group of young readers, mostly between eighteen and thirty, who want much more from their drugstore reading than bosoms and thighs. They need a total image of what it means to be a man. And Mr. Hefner's *Playboy* has no hesitation in telling them.

Why should such a need arise? David Riesman has argued that the responsibility for character formation in our society has shifted from the family to the peer group and to the mass-media peer-group surrogates.[4] Things are changing so rapidly that one who is equipped by his family with inflexible, highly internalized values becomes unable to deal with the accelerated pace of change and with the varying contexts in which he is called upon to function. This is especially true in the area of consumer values toward which the "other-directed person" is increasingly oriented.

Within the confusing plethora of mass media signals and peer-group values, *Playboy* fills a special need. For the insecure young man with newly acquired free time and money who still feels uncertain about his consumer skills, *Playboy* supplies a comprehensive and authoritative guidebook to this forbidding new world to which he now has access. It tells him not only who to be; it tells him *how* to be, and even provides consolation outlets for those who secretly feel that they have not quite made it.

In supplying for the other-directed consumer of leisure both the normative identity image and the means of achieving it, *Playboy* relies on a careful integration of copy and advertising material. The comic book that appeals to a younger generation with an analogous problem skillfully intersperses illustrations of incredibly muscled men and excessively mammalian women with advertisement for body-building gimmicks and foam-rubber brassière supplements. Thus the thin-chested comic-book readers of both sexes are thoughtfully supplied with both the ends and the means for attaining a spurious brand of maturity. *Playboy* merely continues the comic-book tactic for the next age group. Since within every identity crisis,

---

4. David Riesman, *The Lonely Crowd*   (New Haven: Yale University Press,   1950; Harmondsworth, Middlesex: Penguin) [Cox's note].

whether in teens or twenties, there is usually a sexual identity problem, *Playboy* speaks to those who desperately want to know what it means to be a man, and more specifically a *male*, in today's world.

Both the image of man and the means for its attainment exhibit a remarkable consistency in *Playboy*. The skilled consumer is cool and unruffled. He savors sports cars, liquor, high fidelity, and book-club selections with a casual, unhurried aplomb. Though he must certainly *have* and *use* the latest consumption item, he must not permit himself to get too attached to it. The style will change and he must always be ready to adjust. His persistent anxiety that he may mix a drink incorrectly, enjoy a jazz group that is passe, or wear last year's necktie style is comforted by an authoritative tone in *Playboy* beside which papal encyclicals sound irresolute.

"Don't hesitate," he is told, "this assertive, self-assured weskit is what every man of taste wants for the fall season." Lingering doubts about his masculinity are extirpated by the firm assurance that "real men demand this ruggedly masculine smoke" (cigar ad). Though "the ladies will swoon for you, no matter what they promise, don't give them a puff. This cigar is for men only." A fur-lined canvas field jacket is described as "the most masculine thing since the cave man." What to be and how to be it are both made unambiguously clear.

Since being a male necessitates some kind of relationship to females, *Playboy* fearlessly confronts this problem too, and solves it by the consistent application of the same formula. Sex becomes one of the items of leisure activity that the knowledgeable consumer of leisure handles with his characteristic skill and detachment. The girl becomes a desirable—indeed an indispensable—"Playboy accessory."

In a question-answer column entitled "The Playboy Adviser," queries about smoking equipment (how to break in a meerschaum pipe), cocktail preparation (how to mix a Yellow Fever), and whether or not to wear suspenders with a vest alternate with questions about what to do with girls who complicate the cardinal principle of casualness either by suggesting marriage or by some other impulsive gesture toward a permanent relationship. The infallible answer from the oracle never varies: sex must be contained, at all costs, within the entertainment-recreation area. Don't let her get "serious."

After all, the most famous feature of the magazine is its monthly foldout photo of a *play*mate. She is the symbol par excellence of recreational sex. When playtime is over, the playmate's function ceases, so she must be made to understand the rules of the game. As the crew-cut young man in a *Playboy* cartoon says to the rumpled and disarrayed girl he is passionately embracing, "Why speak of love at a time like this?"

The magazine's fiction purveys the same kind of severely departmentalized sex. Although the editors have recently improved the *Playboy* contents with contributions by Hemingway, Bemelmans, and even a Chekhov translation, many of the stories still rely on a repetitious and predictable formula. A successful young man, either single or somewhat less than ideally married—a figure with whom readers have no difficulty identifying—encounters a gorgeous and seductive woman who makes no demands on him except sex. She is the prose duplication of the cool-eyed but hot-blooded playmate of the foldout.

Drawing heavily on the fantasy life of all young Americans, the writers utilize for their stereotyped heroines the hero's school-teacher, his secretary, an old girl friend, or the girl who brings her car into the garage where he works. The happy issue is always a casual but satisfying sexual experience with no entangling alliances whatever. Unlike the women he knows in real life, the *Playboy* reader's fictional girl friends know their place and ask for nothing more. They present no danger of permanent involvement. Like any good accessory, they are detachable and disposable.

Many of the advertisements reinforce the sex-accessory identification in another way—by attributing female characteristics to the items they sell. Thus a full-page ad for the MG assures us that this car is not only "the smoothest pleasure machine" on the road and that having one is a "love affair," but most important, "you drive it —it doesn't drive you." The ad ends with the equivocal question "Is it a date?"[5]

Playboy insists that its message is one of liberation. Its gospel frees us from captivity to the puritanical "hatpin brigade." It solemnly crusades for "frankness" and publishes scores of letters congratulating it for its unblushing "candor." Yet the whole phenomenon of which *Playboy* is only a part vividly illustrates the awful fact of a new kind of tyranny.

Those liberated by technology and increased prosperity to new worlds of leisure now become the anxious slaves of dictatorial taste makers. Obsequiously waiting for the latest signal on what is cool and what is awkward, they are paralyzed by the fear that they may hear pronounced on them that dread sentence occasionally intoned by "The Playboy Adviser": "You goofed!" Leisure is thus swallowed up in apprehensive competitiveness, its liberating potential transformed into a self-destructive compulsion to consume only what is *à la mode*. *Playboy* mediates the Word of the most high into one section of the consumer world, but it is a word of bondage, not of freedom.

Nor will *Playboy*'s synthetic doctrine of man stand the test of scrutiny. Psychoanalysts constantly remind us how deep-seated sex-

5. This whole fusing of sex and machine symbols in contemporary mass media was once brilliantly explored by Marshall McLuhan in *The Mechanical Bride* (New York: Vanguard, 1957), now out of print [Cox's note].

uality is in the human being. But if they didn't remind us, we would soon discover it ourselves anyway. Much as the human male might like to terminate his relationship with a woman as he would snap off the stereo, or store her for special purposes like a camel's-hair jacket, it really can't be done. And anyone with a modicum of experience with women knows it can't be done. Perhaps this is the reason *Playboy*'s readership drops off so sharply after the age of thirty.

Playboy really feeds on the existence of a repressed fear of involvement with women, which for various reasons is still present in many otherwise adult Americans. So *Playboy*'s version of sexuality grows increasingly irrelevant as authentic sexual maturity is achieved.

The male identity crisis to which *Playboy* speaks has at its roots a deeply set fear of sex, a fear that is uncomfortably combined with fascination. *Playboy* strives to resolve this antinomy by reducing the proportions of sexuality, its power and its passion, to a packageable consumption item. Thus in *Playboy*'s iconography the nude woman symbolizes total sexual accessibility but demands nothing from the observer. "You drive it—it doesn't drive you." The terror of sex, which cannot be separated from its ecstasy, is dissolved. But this futile attempt to reduce the *mysterium tremendum*[6] of the sexual fails to solve the problem of being a man. For sexuality is the basic form of all human relationship, and therein lies its terror and its power.

Karl Barth has called this basic relational form of man's life *Mit-mensch*, co-humanity.[7] This means that becoming fully human, in this case a human male, requires not having the other totally exposed to me and my purposes—while I remain uncommitted—but exposing myself to the risk of encounter with the other by reciprocal self-exposure. The story of man's refusal to be so exposed goes back to the story of Eden and is expressed by man's desire to control the other rather than to *be with* the other. It is basically the fear to be one's self, a lack of the "courage to be."

Thus any theological critique of *Playboy* that focuses on its "lewdness" will misfire completely. *Playboy* and its less successful imitators are not "sex magazines" at all. They are basically antisexual. They dilute and dissipate authentic sexuality by reducing it to an accessory, by keeping it at a safe distance.

It is precisely because these magazines are antisexual that they deserve the most searching kind of theological criticism. They foster a heretical doctrine of man, one at radical variance with the biblical view. For *Playboy*'s man, others—especially women—are *for* him. They are his leisure accessories, his playthings. For the Bible, man only becomes fully man by being *for* the other.

6. Awesome mystery.
7. Karl Barth, *Church Dogmatics* (Ed- inburgh: T & T Clark, 1957), II2. [Cox's note].

Moralistic criticisms of *Playboy* fail because its antimoralism is one of the few places in which *Playboy* is right. But if Christians bear the name of one who was truly man because he was totally *for* the other, and if it is in him that we know who God is and what human life is for, then we must see in *Playboy* the latest and slickest episode in man's continuing refusal to be fully human.

Freedom for mature sexuality comes to man only when he is freed from the despotic powers which crowd and cower him into fixed patterns of behavior. Both Miss America and The Playboy illustrate such powers. When they determine man's sexual life, they hold him in captivity. They prevent him from achieving maturity. They represent the constant danger of relapsing into tribal thralldom which always haunts the secular society, a threat from which the liberating, secularizing word of the Gospel repeatedly recalls it.

QUESTIONS

1. Cox begins his essay by stating that the mass media have continued to "appeal to the unexorcised demons" connected with sex. What illustrations of this view do you find later in the essay? How have the mass media impeded "the humanization of sex"—and what does "humanization" mean in this context?
2. Cox asserts that The Playboy and Miss America are "spurious sexual models." Explain why he uses the word "spurious." Explain what he means when he says they "should be exorcised and exposed."
3. Cox points out some similarities between the "cult of The Girl" and pagan fertility worship. What are some of the differences between the two? Why doesn't Cox discuss these to any extent?
4. Cox speaks of the Virgin Mary and suggests a comparison with The Girl. What does he mean by calling The Girl "the omnipresent icon of consumer society?" Explain whether it is inconsistent to compare The Girl to both a pagan fertility goddess and the Virgin Mary.
5. Cox asserts that "The Playboy . . . does for the boys what Miss America does for the girls." Examine the second half of the essay with this assertion in mind and explain how exact the parallels seem. Explain whether you think there are significant differences between Miss America and The Playboy that Cox overlooks.
6. Explain the terms "consumer skills" and "sex as an accessory." Why should we need "skills" to consume things? How does sex become an accessory? What characteristics of our society do these two terms highlight?
7. Write a brief account of a Miss American contest or a copy of Playboy magazine from a different point of view than the one Cox adopts. Examples: a contestant in the Miss America contest, a member of the Anti-Vice Society reading Playboy, the parents of a Miss America winner, a writer trying to sell a story to Playboy, etc.

8. Cox's essay was written some years ago. How would you go about testing how valid its conclusions remain today? What kinds of evidence can you collect to test those conclusions? What does the evidence show?

STUDS TERKEL

Roberta Victor

She had been a prostitute, starting at the age of fifteen. During the first five or six years, she worked as a high-priced call girl in Manhattan. Later she was a streetwalker . . .

You never used your own name in hustling. I used a different name practically every week. If you got busted, it was more difficult for them to find out who you really were. The role one plays when hustling has nothing to do with who you are. It's only fitting and proper you take another name.

There were certain names that were in great demand. Every second hustler had the name Kim or Tracy or Stacy and a couple others that were in vogue. These were all young women from seventeen to twenty-five, and we picked these very non-ethnic-oriented WASP names, rich names.

A hustler is any woman in American society. I was the kind of hustler who received money for favors granted rather than the type of hustler who signs a lifetime contract for her trick. Or the kind of hustler who carefully reads women's magazines and learns what it is proper to give for each date, depending on how much money her date or trick spends on her.

The favors I granted were not always sexual. When I was a call girl, men were not paying for sex. They were paying for something else. They were either paying to act out a fantasy or they were paying for companionship or they were paying to be seen with a well-dressed young woman. Or they were paying for somebody to listen to them. They were paying for a *lot* of things. Some men were paying for sex that *they* felt was deviant. They were paying so that nobody would accuse them of being perverted or dirty or nasty. A large proportion of these guys asked for things that were not at all deviant. Many of them wanted oral sex. They felt they couldn't ask their wives or girl friends because they'd be repulsed. Many of them wanted somebody to talk dirty to them. Every good call girl in New York used to share her book and we all knew the same tricks.

We know a guy who used to lie in a coffin in the middle of his bedroom and he would see the girl only once. He got his kicks when the door would be open, the lights would be out, and there would be candles in the living room, and all you could see was his coffin on wheels. As you walked into the living room, he'd suddenly sit up. Of course, you screamed. He got his kicks when you screamed. Or the guy who set a table like the Last Supper and sat in a robe and sandals and wanted you to play Mary Magdalene. (Laughs.)

I was about fifteen, going on sixteen. I was sitting in a coffee shop in the Village, and a friend of mine came by. She said: "I've got a cab waiting. Hurry up. You can make fifty dollars in twenty minutes." Looking back, I wonder why I was so willing to run out of the coffee shop, get in a cab, and turn a trick. It wasn't traumatic because my training had been in how to be a hustler anyway.

I learned it from the society around me, just as a woman. We're taught how to hustle, how to attract, hold a man, and give sexual favors in return. The language that you hear all the time, "Don't sell yourself cheap." "Hold out for the highest bidder." "Is it proper to kiss a man good night on the first date?" The implication is it may not be proper on the first date, but if he takes you out to dinner on the second date, it's proper. If he brings you a bottle of perfume on the third date, you should let him touch you above the waist. And go on from there. It's a market place transaction.

Somehow I managed to absorb that when I was quite young. So it wasn't even a moment of truth when this woman came into the coffee shop and said; "Come on." I was back in twenty-five minutes and I felt no guilt.

She was a virgin until she was fourteen. A jazz musician, with whom she had fallen in love, avoided her. "So I went out to have sex with somebody to present him with an accomplished fact. I found it nonpleasurable. I did a lot of sleeping around before I ever made money."

A precocious child, she was already attending a high school of demanding academic standards. "I was very lonely. I didn't experience myself as being attractive. I had always felt I was too big, too fat, too awkward, didn't look like a Pepsi-Cola ad, was not anywhere near the American Dream. Guys were mostly scared of me. I was athletic, I was bright, and I didn't know how to keep my mouth shut. I didn't know how to play the games right.

"I understood very clearly they were not attracted to me for what I was, but as a sexual object. I was attractive. The year before I started hustling there were a lot of guys that wanted to go to bed with me. They didn't want to get involved emotionally, but they did want to ball. For a while I was willing to accept that. It was feeling intimacy, feeling close, feeling warm.

"The time spent in bed wasn't unpleasant. It just wasn't terribly pleasant. It was a way of feeling somebody cared about me, at least for a moment. And it mattered that I was there, that I was impor-

tant. I discovered that in bed it was possible. It was one skill that I had and I was proud of my reputation as an amateur.

"I viewed all girls as being threats. That's what we were all taught. You can't be friends with another woman, she might take your man. If you tell her anything about how you really feel, she'll use it against you. You smile at other girls and you spend time with them when there's nothing better to do, but you'd leave any girl sitting anywhere if you had an opportunity to go somewhere with a man. Because the most important thing in life is the way men feel about you."

How could you forget your first trick? (Laughs.) We took a cab to midtown Manhattan, we went to a penthouse. The guy up there was quite well known. What he really wanted to do was watch two women make love, and then he wanted to have sex with me. It was barely sex. He was almost finished by the time we started. He barely touched me and we were finished.

Of course, we faked it, the woman and me. The ethic was: You don't participate in a sexual act with another woman if a trick is watching. You always fake it. You're putting something over on him and he's paying for something he didn't really get. That's the only way you can keep any sense of self-respect.

The call girl ethic is very strong. You were the lowest of the low if you allowed yourself to feel anything with a trick. The bed puts you on their level. The way you maintain your integrity is by acting all the way through. It's not too far removed from what most American women do—which is to put on a big smile and act.

It was a tremendous kick. Here I was doing absolutely nothing, *feeling* nothing, and in twenty minutes I was going to walk out with fifty dollars in my pocket. That just made me feel absolutely marvelous. I came downtown. I can't believe this! I'm not changed, I'm the same as I was twenty minutes ago, except that now I have fifty dollars in my pocket. It really was tremendous status. How many people could make fifty dollars for twenty minutes' work? Folks work for eighty dollars take-home pay. I worked twenty minutes for fifty dollars clear, no taxes, nothing! I was still in school, I was smoking grass, I was shooting heroin, I wasn't hooked yet, and I had money. It was terrific.

After that, I made it my business to let my friend know that I was available for more of these situations. (Laughs.) She had good connections. Very shortly I linked up with a couple of others who had a good call book.

Books of phone numbers are passed around from call girl to call girl. They're numbers of folks who are quite respectable and with whom there is little risk. They're not liable to pull a knife on you, they're not going to cheat you out of money. Businessmen and society figures. There's three or four groups. The wealthy executive, who makes periodic trips into the city and is known to several girls. There's the social figure, whose name appears quite regularly in the society pages and who's a regular once-a-week John. Or there's the quiet, independently wealthy type. Nobody knows how they got their money. I know one of them made his money off munitions in World War II. Then there's the entertainer. There's another crowd that runs around the night spots, the 21 Club . . .

These were the people whose names you saw in the paper almost every day. But I knew what they were really like. Any John who was obnoxious or aggressive was just crossed out of your book. You passed the word around that this person was not somebody other people should call.

We used to share numbers—standard procedure. The book I had I got from a guy who got it from a very good call girl. We kept a copy of that book in a safe deposit box. The standard procedure was that somebody new gave half of what they got the first time for each number. You'd tell them: "Call so-and-so, that's a fifty-dollar trick." They would give you twenty-five dollars. Then the number was theirs. My first book, I paid half of each trick to the person who gave it to me. After that, it was my book.

The book had the name and phone number coded, the price, what the person wants, and the contact name. For four years I didn't turn a trick for less than fifty dollars. They were all fifty to one hundred dollars and up for twenty minutes, an hour. The understanding is: it doesn't get conducted as a business transaction. The myth is that it's a social occasion.

You're expected to be well dressed, well made up, appear glad to see the man. I would get a book from somebody and I would call and say, "I'm a friend of so-and-so's, and she thought it would be nice if we got together." The next move was his. Invariably he'd say. "Why don't we do that? Tonight or tomorrow night. Why don't you come over for a drink?" I would get very carefully dressed and made up

There's a given way of dressing in that league—that's to dress well but not ostentatiously. You have to pass doormen, cabdrivers. You have to look as if you belong in those buildings on Park Avenue or Central Park West. You're expected not to look cheap, not to look hard. Youth is the premium. I was quite young, but I looked older, so I had to work very hard at looking my age. Most men want girls who are eighteen. They really want girls who are younger, but they're afraid of trouble.

Preparations are very elaborate. It has to do with beauty parlors and shopping for clothes and taking long baths and spending money on preserving the kind of front that gives you a respectable address and telephone and being seen at the right clubs and drinking at the right bars. And being able to read the newspapers faithfully, so that not only can you talk about current events, you can talk about the society columns as well.

It's a social ritual. Being able to talk about what is happening and learn from this great master, and be properly respectful and know the names that he mentions. They always drop names of their friends, their contacts, and their clients. You should recognize these. Playing a role . . .

At the beginning I was very excited. But in order to continue I had to turn myself off. I had to disassociate who I was from what I was doing.

It's a process of numbing yourself. I couldn't associate with people who were not in the life—either the drug life or the hustling life. I found I couldn't turn myself back on when I finished working. When I turned myself off, I was numb—emotionally, sexually numb.

At first I felt like I was putting one over on all the other poor slobs that would go to work at eight-thirty in the morning and come home at five. I was coming home at four in the morning and I could sleep all day. I really thought a lot of people would change places with me because of the romantic image: being able to spend two hours out, riding cabs, and coming home with a hundred dollars. I could spend my mornings doing my nails, going to the beauty parlor, taking long baths, going shopping . . .

It was usually two tricks a night. That was easily a hundred, a hundred and a quarter. I always had money in my pocket. I didn't know what the inside of a subway smelled like. Nobody traveled any other way except by cab. I ate in all the best restaurants and I drank in all the best clubs. A lot of people wanted you to go out to dinner with them. All you had to do was be an ornament.

Almost all the call girls I knew were involved in drugs. The fast life, the night hours. At after-hours clubs, if you're not a big drinker, you usually find somebody who has cocaine, 'cause that's the big drug in those places. You wake up at noon, there's not very much to do till nine or ten that night. Everybody else is at work, so you shoot heroin. After a while the work became a means of supplying drugs, rather than drugs being something we took when we were bored.

The work becomes boring because you're not part of the life. You're the part that's always hidden. The doormen smirk when you come in, 'cause they know what's going on. The cabdriver, when you give him a certain address—he knows exactly where you're going when you're riding up Park Avenue at ten o'clock at night, for Christ sake. You leave there and go back—to what? Really, to what? To an emptiness. You've got all this money in your pocket and nobody to care about.

When I was a call girl I looked down on streetwalkers. I couldn't understand why anybody would put themselves in that position. It seemed to me to be hard work and very dangerous. What I was doing was basically riskless. You never had to worry about disease. These were folks who you know took care of themselves and saw the doctor regularly. Their apartments were always immaculate and the liquor was always good. They were always polite. You didn't have to ask them for money first. It was always implicit: when you were ready to leave, there would be an envelope under the lamp or there'd be something in your pocketbook. It never had to be discussed.

I had to work an awful lot harder for the same money when I was a streetwalker. I remember having knives pulled on me, broken bottles held over my head, being raped, having my money stolen back from me, having to jump out of a second-story window, having a gun pointed at me.

As a call girl, I had lunch at the same places society women had lunch. There was no way of telling me apart from anybody else in the upper tax bracket. I made my own hours, no more than three or so hours of work an evening. I didn't have to accept calls. All I had to do was play a role.

As a streetwalker, I didn't have to act. I let myself show the contempt I felt for the tricks. They weren't paying enough to make it worth performing for them. As a call girl, I pretended I enjoyed it sexually. You have to act as if you had an orgasm. As a streetwalker, I didn't. I used to lie there with my hands behind my head and do mathematics equations in my head or memorize the keyboard typewriter.

It was strictly a transaction. No conversation, no acting, no myth around it, no romanticism. It was purely a business transaction. You always asked for your money in front. If you could get away without undressing totally, you did that.

It's not too different than the distinction between an executive secretary and somebody in the typing pool. As an executive secretary you really identify with your boss. When you're part of the typing pool, you're a body, you're hired labor, a set of hands on the typewriter. You have nothing to do with whoever is passing the work down to you. You do it as quickly as you can.

What led you to the streets?

My drug habit. It got a lot larger. I started looking bad. All my money was going for drugs. I didn't have any money to spend on keeping myself up and going to beauty parlors and having a decent address and telephone.

If you can't keep yourself up, you can't call on your old tricks. You drop out of circulation. As a call girl, you have to maintain a whole image. The trick wants to know he can call you at a certain number and you have to have a stable address. You must look presentable, not like death on a soda cracker.

I looked terrible. When I hit the streets, I tried to stick to at least twenty dollars and folks would laugh. I needed a hundred dollars a night to maintain a drug habit and keep a room somewhere. It meant turning seven or eight tricks a night. I was out on the street from nine o'clock at night till four in the morning. I was taking subways and eating in hamburger stands.

For the first time I ran the risk of being busted. I was never arrested as a call girl. Every once in a while a cop would get hold of somebody's book. They would call one of the girls and say, "I'm a friend of so-and-so's." They would try to trap them. I never took calls from people I didn't know. But on the streets, how do you know who you're gonna pick up?

As a call girl, some of my tricks were upper echelon cops, not patrolmen. Priests, financiers, garment industry folks, bigtimers. On the street, they ranged from *junior* executive types, blue-collar workers, upwardly striving postal workers, college kids, suburban white collars who were in the city for their big night, restaurant workers . . .

You walk a certain area, usually five or six blocks. It has a couple of restaurants, a couple of bars. There's the step in-between: hanging out in a given bar, where people come to you. I did that briefly.

You'd walk very slowly, you'd stop and look in the window. Somebody would come up to you. There was a ritual here too. The law says in order to arrest a woman for prostitution, she has to mention money and she has to tell you what she'll do for the money. We would keep within the letter of the law, even though the cops never did.

Somebody would come up and say, "It's a nice night, isn't it?" "Yes." They'd say, "Are you busy?" I'd say, "Not particularly." "Would you like to come with me and have a drink?" You start walking and they say, "I have fifteen dollars or twelve dollars and I'm very lonely." Something to preserve the myth. Then they want you to spell out exactly what you're willing to do for the money.

I never approached anybody on the street. That was the ultimate risk. Even if he weren't a cop, he could be some kind of super-square, who would call a cop. I was trapped by cops several times.

The first one didn't even trap me as a trick. It was three in the morning. I was in Chinatown. I ran into a trick I knew. We made contact in a restaurant. He went home and I followed him a few minutes later. I knew the address. I remember passing a banana truck. It didn't dawn on me that it was strange for somebody to be selling bananas at three in the morning. I spent about twenty minutes with my friend. He paid me. I put the money in my shoe. I opened the door and got thrown back against the wall. The banana salesman was a vice squad cop. He'd stood on the garbage can to peer in the window. I got three years for that one.

I was under age. I was four months short of twenty-one. They sent me to what was then called Girls' Term Court. They wouldn't allow me a lawyer because I wasn't an adult, so it wasn't really a criminal charge. The judge said I was rehabilitable. Instead of giving me thirty days, he gave me three years in the reformatory. It was very friendly of him. I was out on parole a couple of times before I'd get caught and sent back.

I once really got trapped. It was about midnight and a guy came down the street. He said he was a postal worker who just got off the shift. He told me how much money he had and what he wanted. I took him to my room. The cop isn't supposed to undress. If you can describe the color of his shorts, it's an invalid arrest. Not only did he show me the color of his shorts, he went to bed with me. Then he pulled a badge and a gun and he busted me.

He lied to me. He told me he was a narc and he didn't want to bust me for hustling. If I would tell him who was dealing in the neighborhood, he'd cut me loose. I lied to him, but he won. He got me to walk out of the building past all my friends and when we got to the car, he threw me in. (Laughs.) It was great fun. I did time for that—close to four years.

What's the status of the streetwalker in prison?

It's fine. Everybody there had been hustling. It's status in reverse. Anybody who comes in saying things like they could never hustle is looked down on as being somewhat crazy.

She speaks of a profound love she had for a woman whom she'd met in prison; of her nursing her lover after the woman had become blind.

"I was out of the country for a couple of years. I worked a house in Mexico. It had heavy velour curtains—a Mexican version of a French whorehouse. There was a reception area, where the men would come and we'd parade in front of them.

"The Mexicans wanted American girls. The Americans wanted Mexican girls. So I didn't get any American tricks. I had to give a certain amount to the house for each trick I turned and anything I negotiated over that amount was mine. It was far less than anything I had taken in the States.

"I was in great demand even though I wasn't a blonde. A girl friend of mine worked there two nights. She was Norwegian and very blonde. Every trick who came in wanted her. Her head couldn't handle it all. She quit after two nights. So I was the only American.

"That was really hard work. The Mexicans would play macho. American tricks will come as quickly as they can. Mexicans will hold back and make me work for my money. I swear to God they

*were doing multiplication tables in their heards to keep from having
an orgasm. I would use every trick I knew to get them to finish. It
was crazy!*

"*I was teaching school at the same time. I used* Alice in Wonder-
land *as the text in my English class. During the day I tutored English for fifth-and sixth-grade kids. In the evening, I worked in the
call house.*

"*The junk down there was quite cheap and quite good. My habit
was quite large. I loved dope more than anything else around. After
a while I couldn't differentiate between working and not working.
All men were tricks, all relationships were acting. I was completely
turned off.*"

*She quit shooting dope the moment she was slugged, brutally
beaten by a dealer who wanted her. This was her revelatory experience. "It was the final indignity. I'd had tricks pulling broken bottles on me, I'd been in razor fights, but nobody had ever hit me." It
was a threat to her status. "I was strong. I could handle myself. A
tough broad. This was threatened, so . . ."*

I can't talk for women who were involved with pimps. That was
where I always drew the line. I always thought pimps were lower
than pregnant cockroaches. I didn't want anything to do with them.
I was involved from time to time with some men. They were either
selling dope or stealing, but they were not depending on my
income. Nor were they telling me to get my ass out on the street. I
never supported a man.

As a call girl I got satisfaction, an unbelievable joy—perhaps perverted—in knowing what these reputable folks were really like.
Being able to open a newspaper every morning, read about this
pillar of society, and know what a pig he really was. The tremendous kick in knowing that I didn't feel anything, that I was acting
and they weren't. It's sick, but no sicker than what every woman is
taught, all right?

I was in *control* with every one of those relationships. You're vulnerable if you allow yourself to be involved sexually. I wasn't. They
were. I called it. Being able to manipulate somebody sexually, I
could determine when I wanted that particular transaction to end.
'Cause I could make the guy come. I could play all kinds of games.
See? It was a tremendous sense of power.

What I did was no different from what ninety-nine percent of
American women are taught to do. I took the money from under
the lamp instead of in Arpege. What would I do with 150 bottles
of Arpege a week?

You become your job. I became what I did. I became a hustler. I
became cold, I became hard, I became turned off, I became numb.
Even when I wasn't hustling, I was a hustler. I don't think it's terribly different from somebody who works on the assembly line forty

hours a week and comes home cut off, numb, dehumanized. People aren't built to switch on and off like water faucets.

What was really horrifying about jail is that it really isn't horrifying. You adjust very easily. The same thing with hustling. It became my life. It was too much of an effort to try to make contact with another human being, to force myself to care, to feel.

I didn't care about me. It didn't matter whether I got up or didn't get up. I got high as soon as I awoke. The first thing I'd reach for, with my eyes half-closed, was my dope. I didn't like my work. It was messy. That was the biggest feeling about it. Here's all these guys slobbering over you all night long. I'm lying there, doing math or conjugations or Spanish poetry in my head. (Laughs.) And they're slobbering. God! God! What enabled me to do it was being high—high and numb.

The overt hustling society is the microcosm of the rest of the society. The power relationships are the same and the games are the same. Only this one I was in control of. The greater one I wasn't. In the outside society, if I tried to be me, I wasn't in control of anything. As a bright, assertive woman, I had no power. As a cold, manipulative hustler, I had a lot. I knew I was playing a role. Most women are taught to *become* what they act. All I did was act out the reality of American womanhood.

SUSAN LEE

Friendship, Feminism, and Betrayal

Home for Christmas my first year in college, I spoke to my best friend from high school. Elizabeth and I stayed on the phone for 45 minutes, but we had nothing very much to say to each other. After the conversation, I was upset. I remember wanting to tell my mother, who asked what the matter was, about the weirdness of discovering that this woman and I, who had talked every school day for five years, no longer had anything in common. All I could do was cry.

Except for a brief, awkward visit to my house a month later when my father died, a church wedding where Elizabeth married a man I'd gone out with in seventh grade, and two short stopovers in southern New Jersey, I don't remember ever seeing or speaking to her again.

We used to spend hours talking about our relationships with boys. We never discussed our relationship with each other. Except for the few minutes with my mother, who told me she thought Elizabeth and I never had anything in common, and my once making a distinction between acquaintances and friends, I'd never spoken about what I considered a real friendship.

Many people have expressed agreement with Cicero that "friendship can only exist between good men." I'm not one of them. As a 30-year-old woman who has had friends since grade school, I have been very concerned with those friendships. Yet only in the last few years have such relationships been acknowledged as being as important as they've always been.

It was always commonplace for girls in my high school to spend a great deal of time together. It was also commonplace for a girl to spend Saturdays with another girl listening to Johnny Mathis albums, trying on clothes to find something that fit right, or baby-sitting and then having the evening that was planned together usurped by some boy calling up for a date. When this happened to me, I felt betrayed. I never said anything. It didn't occur to me that this wasn't the natural order of things. I didn't know anyone who complained, nor do I remember anyone who ever turned down a boy because she'd already made plans with a girl.

One woman I know said that if as a teenager she had told her parents she'd prefer being with a girl than a boy, they would have sent her to a doctor.

Even now, this past summer, when I was home for a few weeks because my mother was sick, my mother only asked questions about the men who called. One night when I was coming into the city, she discovered I was going to see a woman instead of the man who had just called.

All she said was, "Oh?" Within that one word was more archness than I'd ever heard placed in such a small space.

A male friend of mine suggested that, as kids, if a girl could turn down another girl for a boy, maybe the girls weren't friends. What he didn't understand is how power works, how it matters who gets to set the dates, how important one telephone call can be, and how helpless someone can feel waiting for it.

But girls didn't deny each other because we weren't friends. We could only do it because we were and because boys weren't, and because they got to make the call and we didn't.

Still, a friend of mine recently remembered that she once was leaving a girl to go out on a date. Her girlfriend's mother, who was very hurt for her daughter, stopped her and said that when she was young, girls knew the value of friendship.

Now, each of us knows what this woman meant. We might express it in terms of a heightened woman's consciousness. We might talk of it in terms of respect for each of our relationships. My friend didn't. She went out on her date. She knew what was flexible in her life and what wasn't. The given of having friends then was that we understood the same rules. The same given remains except that some of the rules are changing.

* * *

Friendship has become so institutionalized in our culture that a recent book combined the notion that everyone should have a good friend with the alienated sense that each person should be her or his own best friend.

My guess is that as the family breaks down, friendships will grow in importance. In my own life, as I have relied less and less on the idea of marriage for myself, the more I've come to see the friendships that I've had for years and years as the on-going relationships in my life.

College was a relatively easy place to find people I liked. Condescending as it might have sounded to me then, we each had our futures ahead of us. It seemed possible to get on with a large number of people. Still, most of my college friends and acquaintances disappeared from my life almost as soon as I left the campus. Like Elizabeth and me, we had little more in common than living near each other.

I used to think affection was enough for friendship, but I no longer believe that. Affection can be sufficient for lovers in a way it isn't for friends. But then, people "fall in" love. Someone is a lover after a few days. A friendship, where love develops, often takes years.

A friend is someone I can be myself with; with a lover, I'm all too often someone else, someone I'd rather be.* * *

I can only be myself when there is a shared community of interests between the other person and me. I began to realize how important this was when I got to graduate school in San Francisco and met other people who cared intimately about the same work I did. No longer was someone's impending wedding date the ongoing center of a conversation.

I found people who perceived what went on outside of them and how they acted in the world in many of the same ways I did. I was not as aware of the need for loyalty to friends as I am now. If I fall under the illusion that I was particularly unusual in the way that I treated other women, I remind myself of the green rocking chair in my San Francisco living room. I gave this chair up to any man who came into my house and kept it for myself if another woman was there.

One relationship developed into something more than shared after classroom time. Both Linda and I were dedicated to writing fiction and to working out our lives so that we'd be able to write. And, however different Linda and I were, I was conscious that our friendship had a loyalty and a respect for each other that other friendly relationships did not have.

We spent hours discussing our lives, our work, our dailyness. Where a lover and I take endless time concerning ourselves with ourselves and our specific relationship, Linda and I were spectators at the landscapes of each other's lives. We were more like adjacent lands sharing common borders than the same property itself. It seemed to me that not only did I have my life, but I had hers as well, to see the working out of our goal to become the best writers we possibly could.

A friend like Linda is a reflection of what I value, in a way a lover is not necessarily. I like to be friends, with what is best in me and with what I'm interested in. While I, and several of my friends, too often excuse our choice of lovers as irrational or necessary acts, we take the responsibility for whom we've chosen as friends.

Still, I'm far more conscious of lovers than I am of friends. Though this is changing, I usually think about friends when something is wrong between us. When I'm in love, I'm almost always aware of my lover.

When I was in California and Linda didn't call or was late for an appointment, I assumed there was a good reason. When a lover messes up, I'm quick to think it's our relationship. Friends don't take things as personally as lovers do. There's less expectation and more politeness with friends, who are taken far more for granted than lovers. Yet the reality in my life is that friends are more constant. Lovers come and go except for those who become my friends and stay near me.

Even understanding this, it didn't occur to me to stay in California because of my friends. Linda, abiding by the same implicit rules I did, never mentioned my remaining to me; I don't know if she thought of it. Another friend confronted me; he asked how I could leave the people I freely acknowledged loving more than anyone else. It was enough for me that I was bored and dissatisfied in San Francisco and wanted to come back to New York.

The following year, I returned to the West Coast for Linda's wedding to another writer. Our relationship had deepened into the assumption that we were each other's friend. Although I had fears about the marriage which Linda was all too aware of, I didn't think of not going to give support. I hoped that if any woman could manage writing and a marriage, Linda would.

I tried seeing her for several weeks yearly in Italy or France where she lived. What I didn't admit to myself after one visit to Praiano was how the three of us were developing. I was writing; Thomas, Linda's husband, was writing; only Linda wasn't.

A year and a half later in Paris, I couldn't help seeing what I hadn't wanted to see in Italy. Thomas wrote constantly, and Linda talked about writing. When he worked, we had to whisper. One night when Linda went into her study to work, Thomas interrupted her. I expected her to tell him to leave her alone as she so assiduously left him. Instead, he talked her out of doing anything but spending time with him and me. She acceded to him as she did in much else of what he wanted. She had become a wife.

My visit to Paris was disastrous. Whenever I tried talking about what I found appalling, Linda turned the discussion to my love relationships of the previous year which had not been ones she would have liked to have had. My anger at what I construed as her growing passivity remained unarticulated and high.

I came home and didn't answer a cheery letter ignoring the realities of my stay. A few months later, I wrote a very disturbed explanatory response and did not hear from Linda again.

I knew she'd stopped speaking to her childhood best friend because the woman had once flirted with Thomas. I was aware she'd given me up because of what she thought was an opposite reaction to the man she chose to live with and to the way she led her life.

Six months later, I was speaking to an editor in the publishing house which had signed Thomas's novel and found out Linda and Thomas were in New York for a few weeks.

Sorting out my resentment at having lost my closest friendship, I called them. Linda answering, we talked awkwardly and arranged dinner for that night. I thought the two of us might be able to resolve our difficulties. Perhaps I had been wrong. Deep friendship is hard to come by, and I was prepared to do what I could to salvage this one.

When Linda arrived at the restaurant, she said Thomas would be there with some of his friends within half an hour. I was dumbfounded. She and I were to have dinner alone.

By the next day, I was furious. Living outside English-speaking countries, Linda might have missed the American women's movement. Still, she taught a college course on women in Paris. She couldn't be as unaware of turning into a passive, dependent person as she seemed to be. If she and I weren't going to be friends, I at least wanted to make clear what bothered me.

But she didn't want to hear it. As far as she was concerned, I was hostile, Finally, she agreed to meet.

There we were at the Buffalo Road House: I, with a tennis racket, T-shirt, and dungarees; she, with the latest long Parisian swirl skirt. We were surrounded by four booths of male couples who all stopped talking as we began.

I gathered they all thought we were the lovers Thomas had believed we were years before. I wanted to turn around and say, "No, no. This is worse. We were friends, and now we're not going to be."

We drank wine and were each very upset. Surprising me, she told me that I had betrayed her. She, who long before defined a friend as someone who knew you and loved you anyway, said I didn't trust her. On my side, I was sure she was the one who betrayed our original friendship. She was the one who'd given up her life for someone else's needs.

I argued, somewhat disingenuously, that I was never hostile to her but to her role as wife. I remember thinking that we were never as close as I had thought.

Linda said, "If Thomas ever was as nasty about you as you've been about him, I would have divorced him a long time ago."

I thought this was not only untrue but gratuitious. Thomas, whose novel includes such lines as, "He stuck his throbbing cock into her Hawaiian cunt," could afford to be magnanimous. There was little reason for him to complain. I could talk all I wanted of the need for women to struggle. While he and his friends discussed how liberated they were, he knew Linda's allegiance and investment were more and more in him and his future and less so in her own.

Then she said that since she and I had stopped corresponding, she'd started a novel about the friendship between two women and had gotten more than 100 pages into it.

She and I haven't spoken since. I've hoped she would finish that novel. Not only do I want her to write, I want to read about a friendship through her eyes, and I want something to come out of our relationship.

But I'm being disingenuous again. While acting as an external conscience to a friend might sound touching and be theoretically correct, the reshaping of people, luckily for friendship, is traditionally—and usually without success—left to lovers. Linda knew what I was upset about. At one point when I was in Paris talking to Thomas about each of our projects, Linda burst out, "Don't you both see? I'm the one in trouble." Thomas denied what I perceived was true. Linda didn't need me to be tiresome or belligerent about it. Even more, she didn't need someone who she sensed didn't trust her enough to overcome it.

While I now know I can no longer be friendly with someone who acts like a "wife," I think Linda was right about my betraying her. I acted like one of the Plymouth Bay colonists. In effect, I said that specific beliefs and actions meant more than our history together.

Still, I'm angry. I know very well that other people's supposedly durable friendships turn out unexpectedly fragile and break fairly easily. Yet, however necessary my betrayal was, this woman and I had made a commitment to each other, the alternative was not to have gone on being friends. We were too on edge with each other to do that. All we could have done was to fade away from each other without having had the courage to talk about our differences at all.

When I was young, I thought my friends *had* to act as they did. As a result, I overlooked many decisions that I fundamentally disagreed with. Now, due to the women's movement, I assume each of my friends takes responsibility for her life. Because I no longer consider us powerless, I no longer can forgive acting as if we were.

While a heightened women's consciousness has resulted in our openly valuing friendships more highly than we did before, this same consciousness has caused me, and other women, to demand more of these relationships. The validity of each of our lives has become an issue that might have been passed by before and now can no longer be.

Often, these new pressures are too great for many of these friendships to bear. I know there are no models to go by to put them back together. I know we have to develop new models of not only keeping friendships but having them at all.

Yet to venture that friendships often break apart because of social and political dislocations doesn't alleviate my wanting friendships that last or my being hurt that this relationship with Linda, which I had assumed would be one of these, no longer exists.

Looking back on what happened between us, I can understand the pressures on her to choose as she did. I can wish her well. I can understand my own development which made me make demands that others might find unreasonable. I can do a lot of things, but what I feel—not by Linda so much as by historical circumstance— is cheated.

QUESTIONS

1. Lee talks about differences in the relationships between friends and lovers and between men and women. Why are the two sets of terms necessary?
2. What does Lee mean when she says that she and her friends "too often excuse our choice of lovers as irrational or necessary acts," but "take the responsibility for whom we've chosen as friends?" What does it mean to "take the responsibility" for choosing a friend? How did this figure in Lee's friendship with Linda?
3. Explain the significance of the green rocking chair. Cite similar examples from your own experience or observation that illustrate something about relationships between men and women, friends, or lovers.
4. What does Lee mean when she says the "reshaping of people" is left to lovers rather than friends. Explain why you agree or disagree.
5. Try to write an account of Lee's friendship with Linda from Linda's point of view. Has Lee given you enough material to be able to do this? What, if anything, will you have to imagine or invent?
6. The following lyrics by Alan Jay Lerner from My Fair Lady talk about some of the same things that Lee does. (The situation is this: Higgins does not realize that it is his insensitivity that has caused Eliza to run off in tears; he is now talking to his male friend Pickering.) Compare Lee and Lerner both as to what they

are saying (ideas, attitudes, etc.) and how they are saying it (tone, seriousness, etc.).

"A Hymn to Him"

Why can't a woman be more like a man?
Men are so honest, so thoroughly square,
Eternally noble, historically fair,
Who when you win will always give your back a pat—
Why can't a woman be like that?

Why does every one do what the others do?
Can't a woman learn to use her head?
Why do they do everything their mothers do?
Why don't they grow up like their fathers instead?

Why can't a woman take after a man?
Men are so pleasant, so easy to please.
Whenever you're with them, you're always at ease.
Would you be slighted if I didn't speak for hours?
    Of course not.
Would you be livid if I had a drink or two?
    Nonsense.
Would you be wounded if I never sent you flowers?
    Never.
Well, why can't a woman be like you?

One man in a million may shout a bit,
Now and then there's one with slight defects,
One perhaps whose truthfulness you doubt a bit,
But by and large we are a marvelous sex.

Why can't a woman behave like a man?
Men are so friendly, good-natured and kind.
A better companion you never will find.
If I were hours late for dinner would you bellow?
    Of course not.
If I forgot your silly birthday would you fuss?
    Nonsense.
Would you complain if I took out another fellow?
    Never.
Well, why can't a woman be like us?

Why can't a woman be more like a man?
Men are so decent, such regular chaps,
Ready to help you through any mishaps,
Ready to buck you up whenever you are glum.
Why can't a woman be a chum?

Why is thinking something women never do?
Why is logic never even tried?
Straightening up their hair is all they ever do.
Why don't they straighten up the mess that's inside?

Why can't a woman be more like a man?
If I was a woman who'd been to a ball,
Been hailed as a princess by one and by all,
Would I start weeping like a bathtub overflowing?
Carry on as if my home were in a tree?
Would I run off and never tell me where I'm going?
Why can't a woman be like me?

ADRIENNE RICH
When We Dead Awaken: Writing as Re-Vision

Ibsen's *When We Dead Awaken* is a play about the use that the male artist and thinker—in the process of creating culture as we know it—has made of women, in his life and in his work; and about a woman's slow struggling awakening to the use to which her life has been put. Bernard Shaw wrote in 1900 of this play: "[Ibsen] shows us that no degradation ever devized or permitted is as disastrous as this degradation; that through it women can die into luxuries for men and yet can kill them; that men and women are becoming conscious of this: and that what remains to be seen as perhaps the most interesting of all imminent social developments is what will happen 'when we dead awaken.' "[1]

It's exhilarating to be alive in a time of awakening consciousness; it can also be confusing, disorienting, and painful. This awakening of dead or sleeping consciousness has already affected the lives of millions of women, even those who don't know it yet. It is also affecting the lives of men, even those who deny its claims upon them. The argument will go on whether an oppressive economic class system is responsible for the oppressive nature of male/female relations, or whether, in fact, the sexual class system is the original model on which all the others are based. But in the last few years connections have been drawn between our sexual lives and our political institutions which are inescapable and illuminating. The sleepwalkers are coming awake, and for the first time this awakening has a collective reality; it is no longer such a lonely thing to open one's eyes.

Re-vision—the act of looking back, of seeing with fresh eyes, of entering an old text from a new critical direction—is for us more than a chapter in cultural history: it is an act of survival. Until we can understand the assumptions in which we are drenched we cannot know ourselves. And this drive to self-knowledge, for woman, is more than a search for identity: it is part of her refusal of the destructiveness of male-dominated society. A radical critique of literature, feminist in its impulse, would take the work first of all as a clue to how we live, how we have been living, how we have been led to imagine ourselves, how our language has trapped as well as liberated us; and how we can begin to see—and therefore live—afresh. A change in the concept of sexual identity is essential if we are not going to see the old political order reassert itself in every new revolution. We need to know the writing of the past, and know it differently than we have ever known it; not to pass on a tradition but to break its hold over us.

1. G. B. Shaw, *The Quintessence of Ibsenism* (New York: Hill & Wang, 1959), p. 139.

For writers, and at this moment for women writers in particular, there is the challenge and promise of a whole new psychic geography to be explored. But there is also a difficult and dangerous walking on the ice, as we try to find language and images for a consciousness we are just coming into, and with little in the past to support us. I want to talk about some aspects of this difficulty and this danger.

Jane Harrison, the great classical anthropologist, wrote in 1914 in a letter to her friend Gilbert Murray: "By the by, about 'Women,' it has bothered me often—why do women never want to write poetry about Man as a sex—why is Woman a dream and a terror to man and not the other way around? . . . Is it mere convention and propriety, or something deeper?"[2] I think Jane's question cuts deep into the myth-making tradition, the romantic tradition; deep into what women and men have been to each other; and deep into the psyche of the woman writer. Thinking about that question, I began thinking of the work of two twentieth-century women poets, Sylvia Plath and Diane Wakoski. It strikes me that in the work of both Man appears as, if not a dream, a fascination, and a terror; and that the source of the fascination and the terror is, simply, Man's power—to dominate, tyrannize, choose or reject the woman. The charisma of Man seems to come purely from his power over her, and his control of the world by force; not from anything fertile or life-giving in him. And, in the work of both these poets, it is finally the woman's sense of *herself*—embattled, possessed—that gives the poetry its dynamic charge, its rhythms of struggle, need, will and female energy. Convention and propriety are perhaps not the right words, but until recently this female anger, this furious awareness of the Man's power over her, were not available materials to the female poet, who tended to write of Love as the source of her suffering, and to view that victimization by Love as an almost inevitable fate. Or, like Marianne Moore and Elizabeth Bishop, she kept human sexual relationships at a measured and chiselled distance in her poems.

One answer to Jane Harrison's question has to be that historically men and women have played very different parts in each others' lives. Where woman has been a luxury for man, and has served as the painter's model and the poet's muse, but also as comforter, nurse, cook, bearer of his seed, secretarial assistant, and copyist of manuscripts, man has played a quite different role for the female artist. Henry James repeats an incident which the writer Prosper Mérimée described, of how, while he was living with George Sand,

he once opened his eyes, in the raw winter dawn, to see his companion, in a dressing-gown, on her knees before the domestic hearth, a candlestick beside her and a red *madras* round her head, making bravely, with

2. Jessie G. Stewart, *Jane Ellen Harrison: A Portrait from Letters* (London: Merlin Press, 1959), pp. 140–41.

her own hands, the fire that was to enable her to sit down betimes to urgent pen and paper. The story represents him as having felt that the spectacle chilled his ardor and tried his taste; her appearance was unfortunate, her occupation an inconsequence, and her industry a reproof—the result of all of which was a lively irritation and an early rupture.[3]

I am suggesting that the specter of this kind of male judgment, along with the active discouragement and thwarting of her needs by a culture controlled by males, has created problems for the woman writer: problems of contact with herself, problems of language and style, problems of energy and survival.

In rereading Virginia Woolf's *A Room of One's Own* for the first time in some years, I was astonished at the sense of effort, of pains taken, of dogged tentativeness, in the tone of that essay. And I recognized that tone. I had heard it often enough, in myself and in other women. It is the tone of a woman almost in touch with her anger, who is determined not to appear angry, who is *willing* herself to be calm, detached, and even charming in a roomful of men where things have been said which are attacks on her very integrity. Virginia Woolf is addressing an audience of women, but she is acutely conscious—as she always was—of being overheard by men: by Morgan and Lytton and Maynard Keynes and for that matter by her father, Leslie Stephen. She drew the language out into an exacerbated thread in her determination to have her own sensibility yet protect it from those masculine presences. Only at rare moments in that essay do you hear the passion in her voice; she was trying to sound as cool as Jane Austen, as Olympian as Shakespeare, because that is the way the men of the culture thought a writer should sound.

No male writer has written primarily or even largely for women, or with the sense of women's criticism as a consideration when he chooses his materials, his theme, his language. But to a lesser or greater extent, every woman writer has written for men even when, like Virginia Woolf, she was supposed to be addressing women. If we have come to the point when this balance might begin to change, when women can stop being haunted, not only by "convention and propriety" but by internalized fears of being and saying themselves, then it is an extraordinary moment for the woman writer —and reader.

I have hesitated to do what I am going to do now, which is to use myself as an illustration. For one thing, it's a lot easier and less dangerous to talk about other women writers. But there is something else. Like Virginia Woolf, I am aware of the women who are not with us here because they are washing the dishes and looking after the children. Nearly fifty years after she spoke, that fact remains largely unchanged. And I am thinking also of women whom she left out of the picture altogether—women who are wash-

3. Henry James, *Notes on Novelists*, 1897.

ing other people's dishes and caring for other people's children, not to mention women who went on the streets last night in order to feed their children. We seem to be special women here, we have liked to think of ourselves as special, and we have known that men would tolerate, even romanticize us as special, as long as our words and actions didn't threaten their privilege of tolerating or rejecting us according to *their* ideas of what a special woman ought to be. An important insight of the radical women's movement, for me, has been how divisive and how ultimately destructive is this myth of the special woman, who is also the token woman. Every one of us here in this room has had great luck; our own gifts could not have been enough, for we all know women whose gifts are buried or aborted. Our struggles can have meaning only if they can help to change the lives of women whose gifts—and whose very being— continues to be thwarted.

My own luck was being born white and middle-class into a house full of books, with a father who encouraged me to read and write. So for about twenty years I wrote for a particular man, who criticized and praised me and made me feel I was indeed "special." The obverse side of this, of course, was that I tried for a long time to please him, or rather, not to displease him. And then of course there were other men—writers, teachers—the Man, who was not a terror or a dream but a literary master and a master in other ways less easy to acknowledge. And there were all those poems about women, written by men: it seemed to be a given that men wrote poems and women frequently inhabited them. These women were almost always beautiful, but threatened with the loss of beauty, the loss of youth—the fate worse than death. Or, they were beautiful and died young, like Lucy and Lenore. Or, the woman was like Maud Gonne, cruel and disastrously mistaken, and the poem reproached her because she had refused to become a luxury for the poet.

A lot is being said today about the influence that the myths and images of women have on all of us who are products of culture. I think it has been a peculiar confusion to the girl or woman who tries to write, because she is peculiarly susceptible to language. She goes to poetry or fiction looking for *her* way of being in the world, since she too has been putting words and images together; she is looking eagerly for guides, maps, possibilities; and over and over in the "words' masculine persuasive force" of literature she comes up against something that negates everything she is about: she meets the image of Woman in books written by men. She finds a terror and a dream, she finds a beautiful pale face, she finds La Belle Dame Sans Merci, she finds Juliet or Tess or Salomé, but precisely what she does not find is that absorbed, drudging, puzzled, sometimes inspired creature, herself, who sits at a desk trying to put words together.

So what does she do? What did I do? I read the older women poets with their peculiar keenness and ambivalence: Sappho, Christina Rossetti, Emily Dickinson, Elinor Wylie, Edna Millay, H.D. I discovered that the woman poet most admired at the time (by men) was Marianne Moore, who was maidenly, elegant, intellectual, discreet. But even in reading these women I was looking in them for the same things I had found in the poetry of men, because I wanted women poets to be the equals of men, and to be equal was still confused with sounding the same.

I know that my style was formed first by male poets: by the men I was reading as an undergraduate—Frost, Dylan Thomas, Donne, Auden, MacNiece, Stevens, Yeats. What I chiefly learned from them was craft. But poems are like dreams: in them you put what you don't know you know. Looking back at poems I wrote before I was twenty-one, I'm startled because beneath the conscious craft are glimpses of the split I even then experienced between the girl who wrote poems, who defined herself in writing poems, and the girl who was to define herself by her relationships with men. "Aunt Jennifer's Tigers," written while I was a student, looks with deliberate detachment at this split.

> Aunt Jennifer's tigers stride across a screen,
> Bright topaz denizens of a world of green.
> They do not fear the men beneath the tree,
> They pace in sleek chivalric certainty.
>
> Aunt Jennifer's fingers, fluttering through her wool,
> Find even the ivory needle hard to pull.
> The massive weight of Uncle's wedding-band
> Sits heavily upon Aunt Jennifer's hand.
>
> When Aunt is dead, her terrified hands will lie
> Still ringed with ordeals she was mastered by.
> The tigers in the panel that she made
> Will go on striding, proud and unafraid.

In writing this poem, composed and apparently cool as it is, I thought I was creating a portrait of an imaginary woman. But this woman suffers from the opposition of her imagination, worked out in tapestry, and her life-style, "ringed with ordeals she was mastered by." It was important to me that Aunt Jennifer was a person as distinct from myself as possible—distanced by the formalism of the poem; by its objective, observant tone; even by putting the woman in a different generation.

In those years formalism was part of the strategy—like asbestos gloves, it allowed me to handle materials I couldn't pick up barehanded. (A later strategy was to use the persona of a man, as I did in "The Loser.")

A man thinks of the woman he once loved: first, after her wedding, and then nearly a decade later.

I

I kissed you, bride and lost, and went
home from that bourgeois sacrament,
your cheek still tasting cold upon
my lips that gave you benison
with all the swagger that they knew—
as losers somehow learn to do.

Your wedding made my eyes ache; soon
the world would be worse off for one
more golden apple dropped to ground
without the least protesting sound,
and you would windfall lie, and we
forget your shimmer on the tree.

Beauty is always wasted: if
not Mignon's song sung to the deaf,
at all events to the unmoved.
A face like yours cannot be loved
long or seriously enough.
Almost, we seem to hold it off.

II

Well, you are tougher than I thought.
Now when the wash with ice hangs taut
this morning of St. Valentine,
I see you strip the squeaking line,
your body weighed against the load,
and all my groans can do no good.

Because you still are beautiful,
though squared and stiffened by the pull
of what nine windy years have done.
You have three daughters, lost a son.
I see all your intelligence
flung into that unwearied stance.

My envy is of no avail.
I turn my head and wish him well
who chafed your beauty into use
and lives forever in a house
lit by the friction of your mind.
You stagger in against the wind.[4]

1958

I finished college, published my first book by a fluke, as it seemed
to me, and broke off a love-affair. I took a job, lived alone, went on
writing, fell in love. I was young, full of energy, and the book
seemed to mean that others agreed I was a poet. Because I was also

---

4. "The Losers," in *Snapshots of a*   Norton, 1956), pp. 15–16.
Daughter-in-Law (New York: W. W.

determined to have a "full" woman's life, I plunged in my early twenties into marriage and had three children before I was thirty. There was nothing overt in the environment to warn me: these were the fifties, and in reaction to the earlier wave of feminism, middle-class women were making careers of domestic perfection, working to send their husbands through professional schools, then retiring to raise large families. People were moving out to the suburbs, technology was going to be the answer to everything, even sex; the family was in its glory. Life was extremely private; women were isolated from each other by the loyalties of marriage. I have a sense that women didn't talk to each other much in the fifties—not about their secret emptinesses, their frustrations. I went on trying to write, my second book and first child appeared in the same month. But by the time that book came out I was already dissatisfied with those poems, which seemed to me mere exercises for poems I hadn't written. The book was praised, however, for its "gracefulness"; I had a marriage and a child. If there were doubts, if there were periods of null depression or active despairing, these could only mean that I was ungrateful, insatiable, perhaps a monster.

About the time my third child was born, I felt that I had either to consider myself a failed woman and a failed poet, or try to find some synthesis by which to understand what was happening to me. What frightened me most was the sense of drift, of being pulled along on a current which called itself my destiny, but in which I seemed to be losing touch with whoever I had been, with the girl who had experienced her own will and energy almost ecstatically at times, walking around a city or riding a train at night or typing in a student room. In a poem about my grandmother, I wrote (of myself): "A young girl, thought sleeping, is certified dead."[5] I was writing very little, partly from fatigue, that female fatigue of suppressed anger and the loss of contact with her own being; partly from the discontinuity of female life with its attention to small chores, errands, work that others constantly undo, small children's constant needs. What I did write was unconvincing to me; my anger and frustration were hard to acknowledge in or out of poem, because in fact I cared a great deal about my husband and my children. Trying to look back and understand that time I have tried to analyze the real nature of the conflict. Most, if not all, human lives are full of fantasy—passive daydreaming which need not be acted on. But to write poetry or fiction, or even to think well, is not to fantasize, or to put fantasies on paper. For a poem to coalesce, for a character or an action to take shape, there has to be an imaginative transformation of reality which is in no way passive. And a certain freedom of the mind is needed—freedom to press on, to enter the currents of your thought like a glider pilot, knowing that your

5. "Halfway," in *Necessities of Life* (New York: W. W. Norton, 1966), p. 34.

motion can be sustained, that the buoyancy of your attention will not be suddenly snatched away. Moreover, if the imagination is to transcend and transform experience it has to question, to challenge, to conceive of alternatives, perhaps to the very life you are living at that moment. You have to be free to play around with the notion that day might be night, love might be hate; nothing can be too sacred for the imagination to turn into its opposite or to call experimentally by another name. For writing is re-naming. Now, to be maternally with small children all day in the old way, to be with a man in the old way of marriage, requires a holding-back, a putting-aside of that imaginative activity, and seems to demand instead a kind of conservatism. I want to make it clear that I am *not* saying that in order to write well, or think well, it is necessary to become unavailable to others, or to become a devouring ego. This has been the myth of the masculine artist and thinker; and I repeat, I do not accept it. But to be a female human being trying to fulfill traditional female functions in a traditional way *is* in direct conflict with the subversive function of the imagination. The word *traditional* is important here. There must be ways, and we will be finding out more and more about them, in which the energy of creation and the energy of relation can be united. But in those earlier years I always felt the conflict as a failure of love in myself. I had thought I was choosing a full life: the life available to most men, in which sexuality, work and parenthood could coexist. But I felt, at twenty-nine, guilt toward the people closest to me, and guilty toward my own being.

I wanted, then, more than anything, the one thing of which there was never enough: time to think, time to write. The fifties and early sixties were years of rapid revelations: the sit-ins and marches in the South, the Bay of Pigs, the early anti-war movement raised large questions—questions for which the masculine world of the academy around me seemed to have expert and fluent answers. But I needed desperately to think for myself—about pacifism and dissent and violence, about poetry and society and about my own relationship to all these things. For about ten years I was reading in fierce snatches, scribbling in notebooks, writing poetry in fragments; I was looking desperately for clues, because if there were no clues then I thought I might be insane. I wrote in a notebook about this time: "Paralyzed by the sense that there exists a mesh of relationships—e.g. between my anger at the children, my sensual life, pacifism, sex, (I mean sex in its broadest significance, not merely sexual desire)—an interconnectedness which, if I could see it, make it valid, would give me back myself, make it possible to function lucidly and passionately. Yet I grope in and out among these dark webs." I think I began at this point to feel that politics was not something "out there" but something "in here" and of the essence of my condition.

In the late fifties I was able to write, for the first time, directly
about experiencing myself as a woman. The poem was jotted in fragments during children's naps, brief hours in a library, or at 3 A.M.
after rising with a wakeful child. I despaired of doing any continuous work at this time. Yet I began to feel that my fragments and
scraps had a common consciousness and a common theme, one
which I would have been very unwilling to put on paper at an earlier time because I had been taught that poetry should be "universal," which meant, of course, non-female. Until then I had tried very
much *not* to identify myself as a female poet. Over two years I wrote
a ten-part poem called "Snapshots of A Daughter-in-Law," in a
longer, looser mode than I've ever trusted myself with before. It was
an extraordinary relief to write that poem. It strikes me now as too
literary, too dependent on allusion; I hadn't found the courage yet
to do without authorities, or even to use the pronoun *I*—the woman
in the poem is always *she*. One section of it, 2, concerns a woman
who thinks she is going mad; she is haunted by voices telling her to
resist and rebel, voices which she can hear but not obey.

2.

Banging the coffee-pot into the sink
she hears the angels chiding, and looks out
past the raked gardens to the sloppy sky.
Only a week since They said: *Have no patience.*

The next time it was. *Be insatiable.*
Then: *Save yourself; others you cannot save.*
Sometimes she's let the tapstream scald her arm,
a match burn to her thumbnail,

or held her hand above the kettle's snout
right in the woolly steam. They are probably angels,
since nothing hurts her any more, except
each morning's grit blowing into her eyes.[6]

The poem "Orion," written five years later, is a poem of
reconnection with a part of myself I had felt I was losing—the
active principle, the energetic imagination, the "half-brother" whom
I projected, as I had for many years, into the constellation Orion.

Far back when I went zig-zagging
through tamarack pastures
you were my genius, you
my cast-iron Viking, my helmed
lion-heart king in prison.
Years later now you're young

my fierce half-brother, staring
down from that simplified west

---

6. "Snapshots of a Daughter-in-Law," in *Snapshots of a Daughter-in-Law,* p. 21.

your breast open, your belt dragged down
by an oldfashioned thing, a sword
the last bravado you won't give over
though it weighs you down as you stride

and the stars in it are dim
and maybe have stopped burning.
But you burn, and I know it;
as I throw back my head to take you in
an old transfusion happens again:
divine astronomy is nothing to it.

Indoors I bruise and blunder,
break faith, leave ill enough
alone, a dead child born in the dark.
Night cracks up over the chimney,
pieces of time, frozen geodes
come showering down in the grate.

A man reaches behind my eyes
and finds them empty
a woman's head turns away
from my head in the mirror
children are dying my death
and eating crumbs of my life.

Pity is not your forte.
Calmly you ache up there
pinned aloft in your crow's nest,
my speechless pirate!
You take it all for granted
and when I look you back

it's with a starlike eye
shooting its cold and egotistical spear
where it can do least damage.
Breathe deep! No hurt, no pardon
out here in the cold with you
you with your back to the wall.[7]

It's no accident that the words *cold and egotistical* appear in this poem, and are applied to myself. The choice still seemed to be between "love"—womanly, maternal love, altruistic love—a love defined and ruled by the weight of an entire culture—and egotism— a force directed by men into creation, achievement, ambition, often at the expense of others, but justifiably so. For weren't they men, and wasn't that their destiny as womanly love was ours? I know now that the alternatives are false ones—that the word *love* is itself in need of re-vision.

There is a companion poem to "Orion," written three years later, in which at last the woman in the poem and the woman writing the poem become the same person. It is called "Planetarium," and it

7. "Orion," in *Leaflets* (New York: W. W. Norton, 1969), pp. 11–12.

was written after a visit to a real planetarium, where I read an account of the work of Caroline Herschel, the astronomer, who worked with her brother William, but whose name remained obscure, as his did not.

> (*Thinking of Caroline Herschel, 1750–1848, astronomer, sister of William; and others*)

A woman in the shape of a monster
a monster in the shape of a woman
the skies are full of them

a woman   'in the snow
among the Clocks and instruments
or measuring the ground with poles'

in her 98 years to discover
8 comets

she whom the moon ruled
like us
levitating into the night sky
riding the polished lenses

Galaxies of women, there
doing penance for impetuousness
ribs chilled
in those spaces   of the mind

An eye,
        'virile, precise and absolutely certain'
        from the mad webs of Uranisborg
                encountering the NOVA

every impulse of light exploding
from the core
as life flies out of us

        Tycho whispering at last
        'Let me not seem to have lived in vain'

What we see, we see
and seeing is changing

the light that shrivels a mountain
and leaves a man alive

Heartbeat of the pulsar
heart sweating through my body

The radio impulse
pouring in from Taurus

              I am bombarded yet   I stand

I have been standing all my life in the
direct path of a battery of signals
the most accurately transmitted most
untranslatable language in the universe
I am a galactic cloud so deep   so invo-
luted that a light wave could take 15
years to travel through me   And has
taken   I am an instrument in the shape
of a woman trying to translate pulsations
into images   for the relief of the body
and the reconstruction of the mind.[8]

In closing I want to tell you about a dream I had last summer. I dreamed I was asked to read my poetry at a mass women's meeting; but when I began to read, what came out were the lyrics of a blues song. I share this dream with you because it seemed to me to say a lot about the problems and the future of the woman writer, and probably of women in general. The awakening of consciousness is not like the crossing of a frontier—one step, and you are in another country. Much of women's poetry has been of the nature of the blues song: a cry of pain, of victimization, or a lyric of seduction. And today, much poetry by women—and prose for that matter—is charged with anger. I think we need to go through that anger, and we will betray our own reality if we try, as Virginia Woolf was trying, for an objectivity, a detachment; that would make us sound more like Jane Austen or Shakespeare. We know more than Jane Austen or Shakespeare knew: more than Jane Austen because our lives are more complex, more than Shakespeare because we know more about the lives of women, Jane Austen and Virginia Woolf included.

Both the victimization and the anger experienced by women are real, and have real sources, everywhere in the environment, built into society. They must go on being tapped and explored by poets, among others. We can neither deny them, nor can we rest there. They are our birth-pains, and we are bearing ourselves. We would be failing each other as writers and as women, if we neglected or denied what is negative, regressive or Sisyphean in our inwardness.

We all know that there is another story to be told. I am curious and expectant about the future of the masculine consciousness. I feel in the work of the men whose poetry I read today a deep pessimism and fatalistic grief; and I wonder if it isn't the masculine side of what women have experienced, the price of masculine dominance. One thing I am sure of: just as woman is becoming her own midwife, creating herself anew, so man will have to learn to gestate and give birth to his own subjectivity—something he has frequently

8. "Planetarium," in *The Will to Change* (New York: W. W. Norton, 1971), pp. 11–12.

wanted woman to do for him. We can go on trying to talk to each other, we can sometimes help each other, poetry and fiction can show us what the other is going through; but women can no longer be primarily mothers and muses for men: we have our own work cut out for us.

QUESTIONS

1. A typical male-chauvinist cliché *is that women take everything too personally, that they lack the larger (i.e. male) perspective. Does this article tend to confirm or deny that belief?*
2. In the eighth paragraph, Rich asserts that "no male writer has written primarily or even largely for women, or with the sense of women's criticism as a consideration when he chooses his materials, his theme, his language." How can she know this? Do you think she is right? How do you know?

ELIZABETH JANEWAY

Why Does the Women's Movement Have No Sense of Humor?

What a good question! I'm glad you asked me that since I believe (perhaps too optimistically) that inside every Male Chauvinist Pig there's a human being struggling to get out. Maybe a candid reply will inspire those striving humans to struggle harder.

In the first place, why *should* the Women's Movement have a sense of humor? Do you burst into peals of laughter reading Malcolm X or *The Thoughts of Chairman Mao?* Who played that smash week in Moscow in 1917—Smith and Dale, or Lenin and Trotsky? The Women's Movement is *serious.* Some of it, not all of it, is revolutionary. I think myself that a revolution in technology, economics and the underpinnings of social relations has already happened, and that we all would do well to face up to it and adjust our minds and our myths to the data of existence. But revolutionary or no, and the Movement is anything but monolithic, it is serious about its aims; especially so because one of the severest limitations on women's ambitions and activities has been the male view that their work and their goals are secondary if not actually frivolous. A good way to support this view and hold down rising feminine confidence is to describe Movement actions as jokes. Thus, the drive for equal opportunity and access to male prerogatives is often presented as those pickets around McSorley's Bar. What's serious, men ask, about *them?*

Well, what's serious about a business lunch? The IRS assumes you do business at one, so I will too. If women can't attend them because restaurants are permitted to practice sex segregation, that's a serious invasion of their rights. And believe me, in many professions the lunching, drinking, dining sessions that used to be limited to men (the past tense of course is madly wishful) were (are) places where candidates for promotion are put through their paces, discussed and helped on their way. Excluding women from these gatherings excludes them effectively from easy consideration for jobs, raises and steps up the ladder. In the Old Boys' Network there are few girls. No doubt you can't do away with the Old Boys' Network by legislation, but at least you can stop supporting it by legal segregation.

It isn't the beer at McSorley's that women want, any more than it's the squash courts at the Harvard Club that Radcliffe alumnae have been aiming at. It's a natural place in the natural social life of business, the professions and academia instead of the old "separate but equal" accommodations which operate against women in the same way they operate against Blacks. Picketing McSorley's may have been roundabout as well as symbolic, but it wasn't irrelevant and I even think it was kind of funny. Funnier anyway than being a female full professor who is expected to "join the ladies" when she dines at the President's house while her male colleagues settle down to a discussion of campus affairs.

You say that doesn't happen anymore? I wonder why. Could it be the effect of the Women's Movement and its humorless pursuit of women's rights?

So my first answer to the question about lack of humor in the Women's Movement is: What's so funny, anyway? Unequal wages, unequal opportunities, closed doors and closed minds don't make for hilarity in the people who run into them. Instead these people tend to argue, shout and repeat themselves endlessly, which is certainly irritating and boring to the people who don't run into inequities and so, quite naturally, can't see what the fuss is all about. "Do you think there's something wrong with being a woman?" an agitated young man asked me the other day. Alas, I do, and here's a simple for-instance. In the field of teaching at elementary and secondary school level, where women are a majority and "equal wages" supposedly an enforced obligation—women working full time in 1969 averaged $7,200. Full-time male teachers pulled down $10,000. I'm willing to say with the fabled Frenchman, "*Vive la petite différence!*" But does it have to add up to $2,800, more than a third of the female wage? To me that's not so petite.

Another response, complementary to the first, is also a question: Whose sense of humor, yours or mine? Too often men's jokes about women are put-downs, often sexist and sometimes racist too. A good example is the oldie about the anthropologist who sees a Black woman pushing a baby carriage, looks inside, discovers the baby has red hair and says, "How interesting! Did the father have red hair too?"

To which the woman replies, "I don't know, Boss, he didn't take his hat off."

The funniest thing about that joke has got to be the state of mind of the man who told it to me. He clearly wasn't trying to make me laugh, but did he realize what he was doing? The urge to keep women in their place by insulting them breaks over into irrationality so fast that one can't be certain. For instance when two women from NOW went up to Yonkers to speak at the Rotary Club (by invitation), one member addressed them thus: "If my wife said anything about women's lib, I'd leave her. She's got a pocketful of credit cards. What more freedom does she need?" This genial assessment of his wife's interests and aspirations came from a retired admiral who had served as City Tax Commissioner. Isn't it odd that a man intelligent and responsible enough to hold those posts should *unhesitatingly* reveal how meanly he thinks of the woman he courted and wed? I mean, if we're going to laugh, this kind of self-exposure strikes me as funny.

Indeed there are magic moments when failure of imagination is so complete that these put-downs attain a grotesque charm. The *Sunday Times* of London has been publishing a series of them recently, under the title "Woman's Role." Here's a snatch of conversation from an audience participation program on radio:

"Good morning, Mrs. —. It's very nice to hear from you."

"Good morning, Jimmy. Thank you."

"Tell me something about yourself. What does your husband do?"

Once alerted to this kind of unconscious male humor one finds examples everywhere. How about those two late papers on women where Freud repeatedly refers to "the fact of female castration"? What kind of a fact can that be? So far as I know, no woman in Western society has suffered even the trauma of circumcision. How about the up-to-date advice offered by Dr. Alex Comfort in *The Joy of Sex* to women about to be raped? Dr. Comfort is inclined to think that they must have done something to provoke this behavior, a well-known male view, but he suggests a way to put the rapist off if the provocateuse subsequently changes her mind: Let her have a bowel movement. Unfortunately he doesn't say how to do this.

Men, in fact, are funny people. So are women. Both often deserve to be laughed at—as people. But to laugh at people in groups is to deny them their full humanity because it denies their individual diversity. Jokes about Italians or Swedes or Chinese are intended to set these folk off in categories separate from the fun-loving human rest of us. It makes them lesser breeds without the law, whose opinions we can ignore. And so, when I pick up *A Treasury of Humorous Quotations for Speakers, Writers and Home Reference*, I am not astounded to discover that there are 105 funny things to say about women, and only 6 about men. It appears that dominant males, like Sam Goldwyn's comedies, are not to be laughed at. Which is all right with me, for I don't want to group them either. Some of them are quite nice, though even the nicest find it a bit hard to laugh at themselves.

It is this ability to laugh at oneself that is usually meant by "having a sense of humor," and I agree that it isn't a striking attribute of the Women's Movement qua Movement. One more reason, then, and that out of history. To laugh at yourself when you're top dog is appealing and humanizing. When underdogs laugh at themselves, it's different. It's a way to ease the pain of being stuck in a life situation you can't control: the sort of gallows humor which prompts Jews to tell anti-Semitic jokes. Lately a lot of underdogs have decided they don't need to be stuck. Black comics aren't telling Stepin Fetchit jokes any more, and women are laughing less at those familiar quips about women drivers, mothers-in-law and dumb blondes. Fewer and fewer are even laughing, as Dorothy Parker did, at the "normal" pain of loving a man who cheats or walks out, in the old grin-and-bear-it syndrome. The "grin" used to be part of the "bearing it"; but if you can walk out yourself, you really don't need to do either. Which doesn't necessarily mean that you'll grin less, simply that you'll enjoy it more because you'll be grinning at the oddities of the whole human condition.

Like the fascinating fact that the most popular speaker at Yale University in 1972 was a woman who was talking about chimpanzees. I'm not sure whether that's a triumph for men, women or apes (though it's certainly a tribute to an individual named Jane Goodall). Who knows? Perhaps there will come a day when the life-style of primates called women will seem as relevant to Yale men as that of chimpanzees; a day when group think and group jokes will be over, and we can sit down in all our individual differences and laugh together at the same things.

X. J. KENNEDY

Who Killed King Kong?

The ordeal and spectacular death of King Kong, the giant ape, undoubtedly have been witnessed by more Americans than have ever seen a performance of *Hamlet*, *Iphigenia at Aulis*, or even *Tobacco Road*. Since RKO-Radio Pictures first released *King Kong*, a quarter-century has gone by; yet year after year, from prints that grow more rain-beaten, from sound tracks that grow more tinny, ticket-buyers by thousands still pursue Kong's luckless fight against the forces of technology, tabloid journalism, and the DAR. They see him chloroformed to sleep, see him whisked from his jungle isle to New York and placed on show, see him burst his chains to roam the city (lugging a frightened blonde), at last to plunge from the spire of the Empire State Building, machine-gunned by model airplanes.

Though Kong may die, one begins to think his legend unkillable. No clearer proof of his hold upon the popular imagination may be seen than what emerged one catastrophic week in March 1955, when New York WOR-TV programmed *Kong* for seven evenings in a row (a total of sixteen showings). Many a rival network vice-president must have scowled when surveys showed that *Kong*—the 1933 B-picture—had lured away fat segments of the viewing populace from such powerful competitors as Ed Sullivan, Groucho Marx and Bishop Sheen.

But even television has failed to run *King Kong* into oblivion. Coffee-in-the-lobby cinemas still show the old hunk of hokum, with the apology that in its use of composite shots and animated models the film remains technically interesting. And no other monster in movie history has won so devoted a popular audience. None of the plodding mummies, the stultified draculas, the white-coated Lugosis[1] with their shiny pinball-machine laboratories, none of the invisible stranglers, berserk robots, or menaces from Mars has ever enjoyed so many resurrections.

Why does the American public refuse to let King Kong rest in peace? It is true, I'll admit, that *Kong* outdid every monster movie before or since in sheer carnage. Producers Cooper and Schoedsack crammed into it dinosaurs, headhunters, riots, aerial battles, bullets, bombs, bloodletting. Heroine Fay Wray, whose function is mainly to scream, shuts her mouth for hardly one uninterrupted minute from first reel to last. It is also true that *Kong* is larded with good healthy sadism, for those whose joy it is to see the frantic girl dangled from cliffs and harried by pterodactyls. But it seems to me that the abiding appeal of the giant ape rests on other foundations.

Kong has, first of all, the attraction of being manlike. His simian nature gives him one huge advantage over giant ants and walking vegetables in that an audience may conceivably identify with him. Kong's appeal has the quality that established the Tarzan series as American myth—for what man doesn't secretly image himself a huge hairy howler against whom no other monster has a chance? If Tarzan recalls the ape in us, then Kong may well appeal to that great-granddaddy primordial brute from whose tribe we have all deteriorated.

Intentionally or not, the producers of *King Kong* encourage this

1. Bela Lugosi, an actor in many horror movies.

identification by etching the character of Kong with keen sympathy. For the ape is a figure in a tradition familiar to moviegoers: the tradition of the pitiable monster. We think of Lon Chaney in the role of Quasimodo, of Karloff in the original *Frankenstein*. As we watch the Frankenstein monster's fumbling and disastrous attempts to befriend a flower-picking child, our sympathies are enlisted with the monster in his impenetrable loneliness. And so with Kong. As he roars in his chains, while barkers sell tickets to boobs who gape at him, we perhaps feel something more deep than pathos. We begin to sense something of the problem that engaged Eugene O'Neill in *The Hairy Ape*: the dilemma of a displaced animal spirit forced to live in a jungle built by machines.

King Kong, it is true, had special relevance in 1933. Landscapes of the depression are glimpsed early in the film when an impresario, seeking some desperate pretty girl to play the lead in a jungle movie, visits souplines and a Woman's Home Mission. In Fay Wray—who's been caught snitching an apple from a fruitstand—his search is ended. When he gives her a big feed and a movie contract, the girl is magic-carpeted out of the world of the National Recovery Act. And when, in the film's climax, Kong smashes that very Third Avenue landscape in which Fay had wandered hungry, audiences of 1933 may well have felt a personal satisfaction.

What is curious is that audiences of 1960 remain hooked. For in the heart of urban man, one suspects, lurks the impulse to fling a bomb. Though machines speed him to the scene of his daily grind, though IBM comptometers ("freeing the human mind from drudgery") enable him to drudge more efficiently once he arrives, there comes a moment when he wishes to turn upon his machines and kick hell out of them. He wants to hurl his combination radioalarmclock out the bedroom window and listen to its smash. What subway commuter wouldn't love—just for once—to see the downtown express smack head-on into the uptown local? Such a wish is gratified in that memorable scene in *Kong* that opens with a wide-angle shot: interior of a railway car on the Third Avenue El. Straphangers are nodding, the literate refold their newspapers. Unknown to them, Kong has torn away a section of trestle toward which the train now speeds. The motorman spies Kong up ahead, jams on the brakes. Passengers hurtle together like so many peas in a pail. In a window of the car appear Kong's bloodshot eyes. Women shriek. Kong picks up the railway car as if it were a rat, flips it to the street and ties knots in it, or something. To any commuter the scene must appear one of the most satisfactory pieces of celluloid ever exposed.

Yet however violent his acts, Kong remains a gentleman. Remarkable is his sense of chivalry. Whenever a fresh boa constrictor threatens Fay, Kong first sees that the lady is safely parked, then manfully thrashes her attacker. (And she, the ingrate, runs away every time his back is turned.) Atop the Empire State Building, ignoring his pursuers, Kong places Fay on a ledge as tenderly as if she were a dozen eggs. He fondles her, then turns to face the Army Air Force. And Kong is perhaps the most disinterested lover since Cyrano: his attentions to the lady are utterly without hope of reward. After all, between a five-foot blonde and a fifty-foot ape, love can hardly be more than an intellectual flirtation. In his simian way King Kong is the hopelessly yearning lover of Petrarchan convention. His forced exit from his jungle, in chains, results directly from his single-minded pursuit of Fay. He smashes a Broadway theater when the notion enters his dull brain that the flashbulbs of photographers somehow endanger the lady. His perilous shinnying up a skyscraper to pluck Fay from her boudoir is an act of the kindliest of hearts. He's impossible to discourage even though the love of his life can't lay eyes on him without shrieking murder.

The tragedy of King Kong then, is to be the beast who at the end of the fable fails to turn into the handsome prince. This is the conviction that the scriptwriters would leave with us in the film's closing line. As Kong's corpse lies blocking traffic in the street, the enterpreneur who brought Kong to New York turns to the assembled reporters and proclaims: "That's your story, boys—it was Beauty killed the Beast!" But greater forces than those of the screaming Lady have combined to lay Kong low, if you ask me. Kong lives for a time as one of those persecuted near-animal souls bewildered in the middle of an industrial order, whose simple desires are thwarted at every turn. He climbs the Empire State Building because in all New York it's the closest thing he can find to the clifftop of his jungle isle. He dies, a pitiful dolt, and the army brass and publicity-men cackle over him. His death is the only possible outcome to as neat a tragic dilemma as you can ask for. The machine-guns do him in, while the manicured human hero (a nice clean Dartmouth boy) carries away Kong's sweetheart to the altar. O, the misery of it all. There's far more truth about upper-middle-class American life in *King Kong* than in the last seven dozen novels of John P. Marquand.

A Negro friend from Atlanta tells me that in movie houses in colored neighborhoods throughout the South, *Kong* does a constant business. They show the thing in Atlanta at least every year, presumably to the same audiences. Perhaps this popularity may simply be due to the fact that Kong is one of the most watchable movies ever constructed, but I wonder whether Negro audiences may not find some archetypical appeal in this serio-comic tale of a huge black powerful free spirit whom all the hardworking white policemen are out to kill.

Every day in the week on a screen somewhere in the world, King Kong relives his agony. Again and again he expires on the Empire State Building, as audiences of the devout assist his sacrifice. We watch him die, and by extension kill the ape within our bones, but these little deaths of ours occur in prosaic surroundings. We do not die on a tower, New York before our feet, nor do we give our lives to smash a few flying machines. It is not for us to bring to a momentary standstill the civilization in which we move. King Kong does this for us. And so we kill him again and again, in much-spliced celluloid, while the ape in us expires from day to day, obscure, in desperation.

Prose Forms: Oral History

["But what did he say?" is a question listeners would sometimes like to ask when they have been told what another person meant, or intended, or implied, or even thought. It is not a matter of distrusting the reporter's account, nor necessarily of merely wishing to hear the report put differently. It may be that in order to get the direct, unmediated, uninterpreted utterance, the listener will ask for the authentic—and authoritative—words as they were said. Does the listener therefore get a greater measure of truth or a clearer sense of meaning from the original utterance than from a report of it? He may not, of course; but he may in many instances, if the "truth" and "meaning" of the utterance depend as much on the personality and character of the speaker as they do on the occasion about which he speaks.

The kind of occasion is important here. If it is generally familiar in its outline because widely known or frequently encountered (either directly in one's own experience or indirectly through reading, study, or the communications and entertainment media), it is public and therefore familiarly accessible to our immediate understanding. The relation of a specific personality to that occasion, his perception of it, is as telling as the public occasion itself seen independently of its private effect on specific individuals—and frequently much more interesting because the coming together of the private and the public not only particularizes the relation but indeed humanizes the occasion. The rituals of one housewife's day are, in the public sense, easy enough to imagine. Even if there is the special circumstance of a housewife receiving welfare assistance for the maintenance and care of her house and children, we have some generalized sense of what her life must be like. How much more authoritative, though, and how much more humanly persuasive are the direct accounts of Therese Carter and Jesusita Novarro to Studs Terkel when we hear these women speak not only of what they do, but more importantly of how they think and feel about what they do. Our public sense of what being "just a housewife" means is strengthened, but at the same time profoundly modified by the voices of two women speaking directly and particularly from inside their experiences. The narrative gains human authority, and a certain honesty and spontaneity peculiar to what we call oral history.

The range of possibility in oral history is wide: Nate Shaw, the bold and courageous black sharecropper recounting his trials with Southern white opposition to organized farmers' activities; Josef Gingold's immersion in the world of Toscanini the man and his music; the simple narratives of a police sergeant and a dime store saleswoman. The oral historian keeps us strictly in touch with the privately, personally human sieve of public experience.

All history was once oral, and out of it grew poetry as well as formal history as we now know it. One of the things which modern oral history preserves for us is the element of the poetic, if we understand that term to mean, in this broad context, the sense of private vision articulated in language which points toward both the public object or occasion and the unique sensibility perceiving it. In addition, it often arises freely, unpremeditated, almost unstructured except for loose chronology and the vagaries of association. It may not be logical, depending instead on a kind of psycho-logic which has its own meaning, usually evident in the style, the peculiar flavor of a distinct mind and personality apparent in the language of the recital.

And it is direct and honest, seeking usually no end except to express itself. We tend to minimize the factual errors, the mistaken vocabulary, the flamboyant rhetoric, the preposterous judgments of people and events in "Doc Graham," even as we are totally fascinated by him and his ruminations on crime, the Depression, and his own career in both. Uncensored, unrepressed, confined only by a sense of his own authority and confidence, Doc Graham's history wells up and flows out spontaneously, honestly, authentically. All around the edges of his remarks and appearing dramatically in the midst of them are "facts," public events and personalities and occasions which we know about independently. They are unsullied in our minds even if they are mangled in Doc Graham's, but the power and grandeur of his posture, his style as a man and as a speaker, ring marvelous subtleties on those facts without destroying them. He literally brings them to life, his life, in a way instructive to both. Private and public, person and events are the mixture. History of a very real and useful kind is the issue.]

THEODORE ROSENGARTEN: Nate Shaw

Nate Shaw was born in east-central Alabama in 1885. The son of former slaves, he was a cotton former through most of his life. In the fall of 1931, Shaw joined the sharecroppers' union, a militant organization "for the poor class of people." One morning in December, 1932, Shaw faced a crowd of sheriff's deputies sent to confiscate a neighbor's livestock. In the following story, he tells what happened and how he came to stand in the defense of his neighbor and himself. These paragraphs are excerpted from his autobiography, "All God's Dangers: The Life of Nate Shaw," taped in 1971, and transcribed and edited by Theodore Rosengarten. Nate Shaw died Nov. 5, 1973.

I was able when I was just ten or twelve years old to understand how they was treatin the colored folks in this country. I used to say —I criticized it and had every thought as I could have against such as that when I was a boy. I used to say—but I come down off that and just keep my mouth shut. I used to say, "I won't stand to rest the way they treatin colored folks in this country, I won't stand it." And I showed it to em, too, when I got grown, I showed it to em. I give em what they wanted when I was a boy, but somehow or other I got to where I couldn't keep that spirit in me, I had to do somethin.

Here's the rule of our colored people in this country, that I growed up in the knowledge of: they'll dote on a thing, they'll like it, still a heap stays shy of it. They knowed that their heads was liable to be cracked, if nothin else, about belongin to somethin that the white man didn't allow em to belong to. All of em was willin to it in their minds, but they was shy in their acts.

In a few weeks' time it come off, it come off. Mr. Watson sent the deputy sheriff to Virgil Jones' to attach his stock and bring it away from there. Virgil had got word of the plot and he come to warn me and several other men of the organization. I knowed I was goin to be next because my name was ringin in it as loud as Virgil Jones' was. Virgil come and told me about it on a Saturday evenin. That next Monday mornin I fixed myself up and walked over there, bout a mile from where I was livin. Got there and good God I run into a crowd, and Virgil Logan, deputy sheriff, was there fixin to attach up everything. I just walked up like somebody walkin about, that's the way I played it.

Several of us met there too, but we had no plan strictly about what we was goin to do. Leroy Roberts and two or three more of em come there early and left before I got there. Well, the devil started his work that mornin. I asked Mr. Logan, the deputy sheriff, I knowed him; he lived right over here at Pottstown at that time and he was a Tukabahchee deputy for the state of Alabama—I asked Mr. Logan kindly, talkin to all of em, "What's the matter here? What's this all about?"

The deputy said, "I'm goin to take all old Virgil Jones got this mornin."

Well, I knowed doggone well accordin to the quotation I was goin to be next. He just startin on Virgil Jones first. I stretched my eyes and said, "Mr. Logan, please sir, don't take what he got. He's got a wife and children and if you take all his stuff you'll leave his folks hungry. He aint got a dime left to support em if you take what he's got."

I begged him not to do it, begged him. "You'll dispossess him of bein able to feed his family."

The deputy said, "I got orders to take it and I'll be damned—"

I asked him humble and begged him not to do it. "Go back to the ones that gived you orders to do this and tell em the circumstances. He aint able to support his family. Aint got a dime to support his family."

He said, "I got orders to take it and I'll be damned if I aint goin to take it."

Well, that brought up a whole lot of hard words then. I just politely told him he weren't goin to do it, he weren't goin to do it. "Well, if you take it, I'll be damned if you don't take it over my dead body. Go ahead and take it."

Somebody got to stand up. If we don't we niggers in this country are easy prey. Nigger had anything a white man wanted, the white man took it; made no difference how the cut might have come, he took it.

Then the deputy walked up to me and said, "You done said enough already for me to be done killed you."

I said, "Well, if you want to kill me, I'm right before you. Kill me, kill me. Aint nothin between us but the air. Kill me."

I didn't change my disposition at all; if my orders hadn't a been listened to, the devil woulda took place sooner than it did.

A nigger by the name of Eph Todd seed me lowerin the scrape on Logan and he runned up on me from behind and grabbed a hold of me. Good God, I throwed a fit because it popped in my mind that quick—I heard many a time in my life that a man will meddle you when another man is fixin to kill you; he'll come up and grab you, maybe hold you for the other to kill you. I looked around and cussed him out and he left there. The deputy sheriff looked at me —I kept my eyes on him—and he walked away, just saunterin along.

One come and found the water was hot—Virgil Logan. He told the crowd that mornin, shyin away from em, "I'll just go and get Kurt Beall; he'll come down there and kill the last damn one of you. You know how he is"—well, all the niggers knowed that Mr.

Kurt Beall was a bad fellow—"When he comes in he comes in shootin."

I told him, "Go ahead and get him—" every man there heard it —"Go ahead and get Mr. Beall, I'll be here when he comes."

He left then. Drove away in his automobile and took Cece Pickett with him. Went to Beaufort and delivered the message to the High Sheriff, Kurt Beall.

After he left, I went in Virgil Jones' house one time to see who was in there, and there was four, five, or six settin in there and they was so quiet. Virgil Jones was there, but his wife and children was long gone, I don't know where they was. Sam MacFarland was there. Boss Hatch was there—they never did catch Boss Hatch neither. And there was some more of em. I stood there and looked at em and I could see they was scared. I went right back out the door where I could keep my eyes open, just keep a watchin for them officers to drive in. After a while, about twelve thirty or one o'clock —I know it was early after dinner—I looked down the road and seed that car comin. Well, I knowed that was the same car that left there that mornin. And I called the boys, "Hey, fellas, come on out, come on out"—I know they heard me—"Yonder they come, yonder come the officers."

Good God almighty, when I told em that, next thing I heard em runnin out of that house, hittin it to the swamps, just cleanin up from there. I reckon some of em peeped out the door or a window and seed them officers. So, stampedin, stampedin, stampedin out of there and they was still runnin scared when I come out of prison.

I just stood right on and I was standin alone. I seed there was weak spots in them men and there was bad acts comin up, but I didn't run a step. I stood there and they all runned out of there like rats runnin out of a woodpile, and all of em that run, run out the back. I didn't let that worry me; I just taken it for granted and let em go. I didn't think about gettin shot and I didn't think about not gettin shot. I thought this: a organization is a organization and if I don't mean nothin by joinin I ought to keep my ass out of it. But if I'm sworn to stand up for all the poor colored farmers—and poor white farmers if they'd takin a notion to join—I've got to do it. Weren't no use under God's sun to treat colored people like we'd been treated here in the state of Alabama. Work hard and look how they do you.

So, them officers runned that car up out there to the road comin to that house, and that house stood a good little piece off of the public road. Four of em come back there that evenin.

Who came back with Logan? Lew Badger from Hamilton, just up above Beaufort; Byron Ward, Kurt Beall's deputy from Beaufort; and a old fellow by the name of Platt, I never did see him before but I knowed of him. And of course, Virgil Logan come back with em. They stopped that car and jumped out of it and come right straight toward the front of the house in a fast walk—they weren't trottin but they was walkin as fast as they could walk. I stood there and looked at em till they got up to me. And when they hit the edge of the yard, Virgil Logan pointed his finger and said, "There stands Nate Shaw. That's him right there."

He just kept a walkin; him and Lew Badger went on around the house. Platt and Ward come straight to me. I noticed that Platt had a automatic shotgun—I could see about four inches of the barrel; he'd pulled the stock of it under a big brown weather coat. Platt walked right up to me. Ward went to the doorsteps and just laid down nearly, peepin in the house to see who was in there, me watchin Platt and watchin Ward too. They surrounded that house then and Platt walked up just about five paces from me and stopped; that's as close as he come. And he stood there, flashin his eyes over me, keepin his gun pointed on me. Right at that present time I was the only fellow out there. All the rest of em done run away and gone to the swamps and woods where the sheriffs couldn't see em.

I reckon Platt was lookin for a crooked move someway. I was standin there with my hands in my pockets, just so. Only my finger was on the trigger of my pistol and the pistol was in my hand. I'd carried that .32 Smith and Wesson there with me that mornin and concealed it from view. I had on a pair of Big-8 overalls, brand new, and the pockets was deep.

Well, everything got quiet and Mr. Logan and Mr. Badger was around there lookin in the back of the house. And Mr. Ward was busy at the doorstep there, just a few steps from where me and Mr. Platt was—Mr. Platt weren't sayin a word, he just lookin me over.

After awhile—I stood there just as long as I wanted to and I decided I'd go back in the house and get out from amongst em, and if nothin else, see if the house was clean—which it was, clean out, didn't a man show up in my sight but Mr. Platt. I weren't goin to stand right up there and look at him shoot me so I turned and walked off from him, started on into the house. And Mr. Ward was there at the doorstep. He just raised up and fastened his hand to my arm. I was a pretty good man then, I was young—I aint dead yet, thank the Lord—soon as he grabbed that arm, I just loosed up what I was holdin in my pocket and come out with a naked hand. Then I snapped him up to me and gived him a jolt and a fling—off he went like a leech. I never offered to hit him, I just flung him loose from my arm. Nobody hadn't said nothin to me, not a word.

All right. I started on again into the house, right on. Took one or two steps—BOOM—Mr. Platt throwed his gun on me. I didn't stop, the game didn't fall for him. BOOM BOOM—shot me two more times before I could get in the door. Blood commenced a flyin —I never did quit walkin. He filled my hind end up from the bend of my legs to my hips with shot. I walked on in the door, stopped right in the hallway and looked back. He was standin right close to a big old oak tree right in line with the door. Run my hand in my pocket, snatched out my .32 Smith and Wesson and I commenced a shootin at Platt. Good God he jumped behind that tree soon as that pistol fired; he jumped like lightnin. My mind told me: just keep shootin the tree, just keep shootin and maybe he'll get scared and run; you'll have a chance at him then. But as the devil would have it, the more I shot the tighter he drawed up behind that tree until I quit shootin. I seed his head poke around the tree—that tree saved him—and he seed what I was doin: good God almighty, I was reloadin and before I could reload my gun, them two sheriffs round the house, Mr. Logan and Mr. Badger, pulled out across the corn field headin to the road. Them two that had come to me, Mr. Platt and Mr. Ward, all I seed was their backs runnin. Every one of them officers outrun the devil away from there. I don't know how many people they might have thought was in that house, but that .32 Smith and Wesson was barkin too much for em to stand. They didn't see where the shots was comin from—nobody but Mr. Platt knowed that.

They hitched up to their ass-wagon and took off. And five minutes after that man shot me three times—I was standin in the door lookin out—my feet was just sloshin in blood. Now if that aint the truth the truth aint never been told. I was just burnt up with shot. Wonder they hadn't shot my secrets out.

STUDS TERKEL: Just a Housewife

> *Even if it is a woman making an apple*
> *dumpling, or a man a stool,*
> *If life goes into the pudding, good*
> *is the pudding,*
> *good is the stool.*
> *Content is the woman with fresh life*
> *rippling in her,*
> *content is the man.*
>
> —D. H. LAWRENCE

THERESE CARTER

We're in the kitchen of the Carter home, as we were eight years ago. It is in Downers Grove Estates, an unincorporated area west of Chicago. There are one-family dwellings in this blue-collar community of skilled craftsmen—"middle class. They've all got good jobs, plumbers, electricians, truckdrivers." Her husband Bob is the foreman of an auto body repair shop. They have three children: two boys, twenty-one and fourteen, and one girl, eighteen.

It is a house Bob has, to a great extent, built himself. During my previous visit he was still working at it. Today it is finished—to his satisfaction. The room is large, remarkably tidy; all is in its place. On the wall is a small blackboard of humorous familial comment, as well as a bulletin board of newspaper clippings and political cartoons.

On another wall is the kitchen prayer I remembered:

> *Bless the kitchen in which I cook*
> *Bless each moment within this nook*
> *Let joy and laughter share this room*
> *With spices, skillets and my broom*
> *Bless me and mine with love and health*
> *And I'll ask not for greater wealth.*

How would I describe myself? It'll sound terrible—just a housewife. (Laughs.) It's true. What is a housewife? You don't have to have any special talents. I don't have any.

First thing I do in the morning is come in the kitchen and have a cigarette. Then I'll put the coffee on and whatever else we're gonna have for breakfast: bacon and eggs, sausage, waffles, toast, whatever. Then I'll make one lunch for young Bob—when school's on, I'll pack more—and I get them off to work. I'll usually throw a load of clothes in the washer while I'm waiting for the next batch to get up out of bed, and carry on from there. It's nothing really.

Later I'll clean house and sew, do something. I sew a lot of dresses for Cathy and myself. I brought this sewing machine up here years ago. It belongs here. This is my room and I love it, the kitchen.

I start my dinner real early because I like to fuss. I'll bake, cook . . . There's always little interruptions, kids running in and out, take me here, take me there. After supper, I really let down. I'm not a worker after supper. I conk out. I sit and relax and read, take a bath, have my ice cream, and go to bed. (Laughs.) It's not really a full day. You think it *is?* You make me sound important. Keep talking. (Laughs.)

I don't think it's important because for so many years it wasn't considered. I'm doing what I'm doing and I fill my day and I'm very contented. Yet I see women all around that do a lot more than I do. Women that have to work. I feel they're worthy of much more of a title than housewife.

If anybody else would say this, I'd talk back to 'em, but I *myself* feel like it's not much. Anybody can do it. I was gone for four days and Cathy took over and managed perfectly well without me. (Laughs.) I felt great, I really did. I knew she was capable.

I'll never say I'm really a good mother until I see the way they all turn out. So far they've done fine. I had somebody tell me in the hospital I must have done a good job of raising them. I just went along from day to day and they turned out all right.

Oh—I even painted the house last year. How much does a painter get paid for painting a house? (Laughs.) What? I'm a skilled craftsman myself? I never thought about that. Artist? No. (Laughs.) I suppose if you do bake a good cake, you can be called an artist. But I never heard anybody say that. I bake bread too. Oh gosh, I've been a housewife for a long time. (Laughs.)

I never thought about what we'd be worth. I've read these things in the paper: If you were a tailor or a cook, you'd get so much an hour. I think that's a lot of boloney. I think if you're gonna be a mother or a housewife, you should do these things because you want to, not because you have to.

You look around at all these career women and they're really doing things. What am I doing? Cooking and cleaning. (Laughs.) It's necessary, but it's not really great.

It's known they lead a different life than a housewife. I'm not talking about Golda Meir or anybody like that. Just even some women in the neighborhood that have to work and come home and take care of the family. I really think they deserve an awful lot of credit.

A housewife is a housewife, that's all. Low on the totem pole. I can read the paper and find that out. Someone who is a model or a movie star, these are the great ones. I don't necessarily think they are, but they're the ones you hear about. A movie star will raise this wonderful family and yet she has a career. I imagine most women would feel less worthy. Not just me.

Somebody who goes out and works for a living is more important than somebody who doesn't. What they do is very important in the business world. What I do is only important to five people. I don't like putting a housewife down, but everybody has done it for so long. It's sort of the thing you do. Deep down, I feel what I'm doing is important. But you just hate to say it, because what are you? Just a housewife? (Laughs.)

I love being a housewife. Maybe that's why I feel so guilty. I shouldn't be happy doing what I'm doing. (Laughs.) Maybe you're not supposed to be having fun. I never looked on it as a duty.

I think a lot. (Laughs.) Oh sure, I daydream. Everybody does. Some of 'em are big and some of 'em are silly. Sometimes you dream you're still a kid and you're riding your bike. Sometimes you daydream you're really someone special and people are asking you for your advice, that you're in a really big deal. (Laughs.)

I have very simple pleasures. I'm not a deep reader. I can't understand a lot of things. I've never read—oh, how do you pronounce it, Camus? I'm not musically inclined. I go as far as Boston Pops and the Beatles. (Laughs.) I don't know anything about art at all. I could never converse with anybody about it. They'd have to be right, because I wouldn't know whether they're right or wrong. I have no special talents in any direction.

I just read a new Peter De Vries book. I can't think of the name of it, that's terrible. (Suddenly) *Always Panting.* I was the first Peter De Vries fan in the world. I introduced my sister to it and that was the one big thing I've ever done in my life. (Laughs.) Now I'm reading *Grapes Of Wrath.* I'm ashamed of myself. Everybody in the family has read that book and I've had it for about fifteen years. Finally I decided to read it because my daughter raved about it.

There is a paperback copy of The Savage God *by A. Alvarez nearby. I indicate it.*

I just started a little bit about Sylvia Plath and I decided I would read this book. *Ms.* magazine has an article about her. Sure I read *Ms.* I don't think it's unusual just because I live around here. I don't agree with everything in it. But I read it. I read matchbox covers too. (Laughs.)

I think Woman's Lib puts down a housewife. Even though they say if this is what a woman wants, it's perfectly all right. I feel it's said in such a snide way: "If this is all she can do and she's contented, leave her alone." It's patronizing.

I look on reading right now as strictly enjoyment and relaxation. So I won't even let myself pick up a book before ten o'clock at night. If I do, I'm afraid I might forget about everything else. During lunch time I'll look through a magazine because I can put it down and forget about it. But real enjoyable reading I'll do at night.

I'd feel guilty reading during the day. (Laughs.) In your own home. There are so many things you should be doing. If I did it, I wouldn't think the world's coming to an end, but that's the way I'm geared. That's not the time to do it, so I don't do it.

When I went to school a few years ago it was very startling around here. Why would an older woman like me be wanting to go back to school? They wouldn't say it directly, but you hear things. I took some courses in college English, psychology, sociology. I enjoy going but I didn't want to continue on and be a teacher. I still enjoyed being at home much more. Oh, I might go back if there was anything special I'd like.

I enjoy cooking. If it was a job, maybe I wouldn't like doing it. As low on the totem pole as I consider being a housewife, I love every minute of it. You will hear me gripe and groan like everybody else, but I do enjoy it.

I'll also enjoy it when the kids are all gone. I always had the feeling that I can *really*—oh, I don't know what I want to do, but whatever that would be, I can do it. I'll be on my own. I'm looking forward to it. Just a lot of things I've never taken the time to do.

I've never been to the Art Institute. Now that might be one

thing I might do. (Laughs.) I've grown up in Chicago and I've never been there and I think that's terrible. Because I've never gotten on the train and gone. I can't spend all that time there yet. But pretty soon I'll be able to.

I haven't been to the Museum of Science and Industry for ten years at least. These things are nothing special to anybody else, but to me they would be. And to sit down and read one whole book in one afternoon if I felt like it. That would be something!

When the kids leave I want it to be a happy kind of time. Just to do the things I would like to do. Not traveling. Just to do what you want to do not at a certain time or a certain day. Sewing a whole dress at one time. Or cooking for just two people.

That's what makes me feel guilty. Usually when kids go off and get married the mother sits and cries. But I'm afraid I'm just gonna smile all the way through it. (Laughs.) They'll think I'm not a typical mother. I love my kids, I love 'em to pieces. But by the same token, I'll be just so happy for them and for myself and for Bob, too. I think we deserve a time together alone.

I don't look at housework as a drudgery. People will complain: "Why do I have to scrub floors?" To me, that isn't the same thing as a man standing there—it's his livelihood—putting two screws together day after day after day. It would drive anybody nuts. It would drive me wild. That poor man doesn't even get to see the finished product. I'll sit here and I'll cook a pie and I'll get to see everybody eat it. This is my offering. I think it's the greatest satisfaction in the world to know you've pleased somebody. Everybody has to feel needed. I know I'm needed. I'm doing it for them and they're doing it for me. And that's the way it is.

JESUSITA NOVARRO

She is a mother of five children: the oldest twelve, the youngest two. "I went on welfare when my first husband walked out on me. I was swimming alone, completely cuckoo for a while. When I married this second man, I got off it. When he started drinking and bringing no money home, I had to quit my job and go on welfare again. I got something with this welfare business and I don't like it."

She is working part-time as an assistant case aide at a settlement house in the neighborhood. The director "says I'm doing real good and can have a job upstairs with a little bit more money. It's only four hours, because in the afternoon I want to be with my children. They're still small."

She has just come home from the hospital where she was treated for a serious illness. On this hot August afternoon—it is over a hundred degrees—the blower in the kitchen isn't doing much good. The three children in the house are more fascinated by technology

—the tape recorder—than the conversation, though they are listening . . .

I start my day here at five o'clock. I get up and prepare all the children's clothes. If there's shoes to shine, I do it in the morning. About seven o'clock I bathe the children. I leave my baby with the baby sitter and I go to work at the settlement house. I work until twelve o'clock. Sometimes I'll work longer if I have to go to welfare and get a check for somebody. When I get back, I try to make hot food for the kids to eat. In the afternoon it's pretty well on my own. I scrub and clean and cook and do whatever I have to do.

Welfare makes you feel like you're nothing. Like you're laying back and not doing anything and it's falling in your lap. But you must understand, mothers, too, work. My house is clean. I've been scrubbing since this morning. You could check my clothes, all washed and ironed. I'm home and I'm working. I am a working mother.

A job that a woman in a house is doing is a tedious job—especially if you want to do it right. If you do it slipshod, then it's not so bad. I'm pretty much of a perfectionist. I tell my kids, hang a towel. I don't want it thrown away. That is very hard. It's a constant game of picking up this, picking up that. And putting this away, so the house'll be clean.

Some men work eight hours a day. There are mothers that work eleven, twelve hours a day. We get up at night, a baby vomits, you have to be calling the doctor, you have to be changing the baby. When do you get a break, really? You don't. This is an all-around job, day and night. Why do they say it's charity? We're working for our money. I am working for this check. It is not charity. We are giving some kind of home to these children.

I'm so busy all day I don't have time to daydream. I pray a lot. I pray to God to give me strength. If He should take a child away from me, to have the strength to accept it. It's His kid. He just borrowed him to me.

I used to get in and close the door. Now I speak up for my right. I walk with my head up. If I want to wear big earrings, I do. If I'm overweight, that's too bad. I've gotten completely over feeling where I'm little. I'm working now, I'm pulling my weight. I'm gonna get off welfare in time, that's my goal—get off.

It's living off welfare and feeling that you're taking something for nothing the way people have said. You get to think maybe you are. You get to think, Why am I so stupid? Why can't I work? Why do I have to live this way? It's not enough to live on anyway. You feel degraded.

The other day I was at the hospital and I went to pay my bill. This nurse came and gave me the green card. Green card is for welfare. She went right in front of me and gave it to the cashier. She said, "I wish I could stay home and let the money fall in my lap." I felt rotten. I was just burning inside. You hear this all the way around you. The doctor doesn't even look at you. People are ashamed to show that green card. Why can't a woman just get a check in the mail: Here, this check is for you. Forget welfare. You're a mother who works.

This nurse, to her way of thinking, she represents the working people. The ones with the green card, we represent the lazy no-goods. This is what she was saying. They're the good ones and we're the bad guys.

You know what happened at the hospital? I was put in a nice room, semiprivate. You stay there until someone with insurance comes in and then you get pushed up to the fifth floor. There's about six people in there, and nobody comes even if you ring. I said, "Listen lady, you can put me on the roof. You just find out what's the matter with me so I can get the hell out of here."

How are you going to get people off welfare if they're constantly being pushed down? If they're constantly feeling they're not good for anything? People say, I'm down, I'll stay down. And this goes on generation to generation to generation. Their daughter and their daughter and their daughter. So how do you break this up? These kids don't ask to be born—these kids are gonna grow up and give their lives one day. There will always be a Vietnam.

There will always be war. There always has been. The way the world is run, yes, there will always be war. Why? I really don't know. Nobody has ever told me. I was so busy handling my own affairs and taking care of my children and trying to make my own money and calling up welfare when my checks are late or something has been stolen. All I know is what's going on here. I'm an intelligent woman up to a certain point, and after that . . . I wish I knew. I guess the big shots decided the war. I don't question it, because I've been busy fighting my own little war for so long.

The head of the settlement house wants me to take the social worker's job when I get back to work. I visit homes, I talk to mothers. I try to make them aware that they got something to give. I don't try to work out the problems. This is no good. I try to help them come to some kind of a decision. If there's no decision, to live with it, because some problem doesn't have any answer.

There was one mother that needed shoes, I found shoes for her. There was another mother that needed money because her check was late. I found someplace for her to borrow a couple of dollars. It's like a fund. I could borrow a couple of dollars until my check comes, then when my check comes I give it back. How much time have mothers left to go out and do this? How many of us have given time so other mothers could learn to speak English, so they'll be able to go to work. We do it gladly because the Lord gave us English.

I went to one woman's house and she's Spanish speaking. I was talking to her in English and she wouldn't unbend. I could see the fear in her eyes. So I started talking Spanish. Right away, she invited me for coffee and she was telling me the latest news . . .

I would like to help mothers be aware of how they can give to the community. Not the whole day—maybe three, four hours. And get paid for it. There's nothing more proud for you to receive a check where you worked at. It's yours, you done it.

At one time, during her second marriage, she had worked as an assembler at a television factory. "I didn't care for it. It was too automatic. It was just work, work, work, and I wasn't giving of myself. Just hurry it up and get it done. Even if you get a job that pays you, if you don't enjoy it, what are you getting? You're not growing up. (Taps temple.) Up here."

The people from the settlement house began visiting me, visiting welfare mothers, trying to get them interested in cooking projects and sewing. They began knocking on my door. At the beginning I was angry. It was just like I drew a curtain all around me. I didn't think I was really good for anything. So I kind of drew back. Just kept my troubles to myself, like vegetating. When these people began calling on me, I began to see that I could talk and that I did have a brain. I became a volunteer.

I want to be a social worker. Somebody that is not indifferent, that bends an ear to everybody. You cannot be slobberish. You cannot cry with the people. Even if you cry inside, you must keep a level head. You have to try to help that person get over this bump. I would go into a house and try to make friends. Not as a spy. The ladies have it that welfare comes as spies to see what you have. Or you gotta hide everything 'cause welfare is coming. There is this fear the social worker is gonna holler, because they got something, maybe a man or a boyfriend. I wouldn't take any notes or pens or paper or pencils or anything. I would just go into the house and talk. Of course, I would look around to see what kind of an environment it is. This you have to absorb. You wouldn't say it, but you would take it in.

I promised myself if I ever get to work all day, I'm going to buy me a little insurance. So the next time I go to the hospital I'll go to the room I want to go. I'm gonna stay there until it's time for me to leave, because I'm gonna pay my own bill. I don't like to feel rotten. I want my children, when they grow up, they don't have to live on it. I want to learn more. I'm hungry for knowledge. I want to do something. I'm searching for something. I don't know what it is.

LINDA LANE: Over the Counter: A Conversation
with a Saleswoman[1]

I went as far as the sixth grade in school. I'm 57 now. I was 16
and didn't want to be 16 in the seventh grade so I quit. I was out
of school a year and a half with blood poisoning and one teacher I
had left me back twice. When I walked into her classroom the
first day, she told me to get to the last row last seat and that's the
way it was all year. She just didn't like me. I got her as a teacher
twice and it was the same thing again.

After getting married and having a baby at sixteen I became a
maid because my mother was a maid. Most jobs I got $35 a month
plus room and board. $30 went to board my baby. My husband was
a seaman and didn't support us. My mother used to make $8 a
month when she came to this country so I thought I was doing
pretty good. I was proud I could work and felt better off than most
people. This was in the Depression. The nicest maid job I had was
with a bootlegger. I could eat and talk with the family. We all ate
in the kitchen. I had my own room with my baby and $10 a
month. The rich people I worked for I couldn't have my baby and
most of the time I didn't have my own room. One rich person I
was a maid for took money out of my pay for a water glass I broke
and a window that was already broken so I quit and she accused me
of stealing. Anyway I didn't have anything in common with those
people and ate in the kitchen alone so I was very lonely. That's one
of the reasons I like my job at the 5 & 10 better than being a maid.
Here I talk to people and no one tells me I'm doing something
wrong.

My job is marking the prices on the items and I only spend two
hours on the counters and no one watches over me. Five kids and
another husband later I'm doing well taking home from $65.12
from $82.50 a week gross. I started working for this store around
Easter time 16 years ago. I made Easter baskets for $1.00 an hour.
Then they offered me a full time job at $48 a week.

Once they didn't pay me for a day I stayed home sick so I walked
out. It was the first rebellious thing I ever did and it felt so good—I
was never the same again. The reason I had walked out was that the
girl on the bird counter was out for eight days and she got paid for
all eight days. She had such a bad job that the manager knew he
couldn't get anyone else so fast so he paid her. I had to take care of
her counter when she was out and it was a terrible job.

Then my boss offered me $60 a week to stay. It was upsetting in
a way—I told him that Jean worked there for 25 years and she was

---

1. "Linda Lane" is a pseudonym for   who works at a five-and-ten-cent store.
the subject of this interview, a woman

getting $48 so why should I get $60? He told me not to fight other people's battles.

All the women get $82.50 now except part-time and floorgirls. When women leave or are fired the boss doesn't replace them—we have eight women less than we had five years ago but we have to get the same work done. The woman on hardware has three counters to take care of now.

The manager has so many gimmicks to get the salesgirls to work harder. Each girl gets a "campaign button" with her name on it and the customers "vote" for the girls. The salesgirl with the most votes gets $10 in merchandise and a customer's name is taken from a jar and she gets $10 in merchandise too. This makes the girls superpolite to customers—they're not usually because it's a hectic job. It also pits the women against each other. They even had this contest on television and they hired a model to be a typical 5&10 salesgirl. We were thinking, "Why not one of us?"

The manager tells the salesgirls they can raise the prices on their counters as much as they think people will pay. The girls like that —they want to feel they have some control over their jobs. I guess it makes them feel important to be on the boss's side. He gets a commission from the profits of the store.

A few years ago I talked to the other women about starting a union, but their lives depend on the job. They wanted to organize but they were afraid of getting fired. Most of them didn't get far in school and they have to work because their husbands don't make enough. A year ago there was talk of a union, so the office raised everyone $.10 an hour. Big deal. I tell the women to threaten to quit cause then the boss gets panicked and gives them a raise, but the women are too scared.

The women chip in for everything. I don't mind chipping in for another girl but the brown-nosers start collecting for the manager every Christmas—they buy him a shirt which he doesn't need and give him the leftover money too. These "choice" women give him the gift on the side and none of the other women see him get the gift. All the gifts are bought in the 5&10 except the manager's. The assistant manager changes every year and the women chip in for his leaving too. I refuse to chip in for them with some other women and the brown-nosers get mad at us. We all get a Christmas bonus—$15 for one-year's service and $5 for each year after that, and they take off taxes too.

I like the high-school girls who work at night. We get along good. Only, once one of them told me to get flowers from the basement to fill up the counter so I said to her, "What? No more Indians, all chiefs?"

The prices go up every day and it's depressing. Now you can buy anything at the 5&10, from refrigerators to pencils, and you can probably get it cheaper someplace else. They have less help than years ago and they blame it on our "wage increases." The manager comments every Christmas that people would buy horseshit if it was on the counter with a price on it. Jean, who is working over thirty years now, got seven shares of the company's stock as a bonus for twenty-five years' service—she got a $2 dividend every three months —it just went up to $2.50. If she wanted 10 shares, she would have had to pay $90 in taxes right away, so she only took seven—she got a bill for taxes anyway. When she got the shares I went out and bought the *Wall Street Journal*—we had a good laugh.

She once tried to get another job. But if you work at a 5&10 other stores don't consider it a good reference because they think the women are dishonest and it's just like having no reference at all. The salesgirls that work here are very honest—I don't believe any of them steal. The other day my boss (the manager) was going up the stairs and one of the salesgirls was in front of him. He told her to get out of the way, she was going too slow for him. She had her hands in her pockets and he asked her why does she always have her hands in her pockets and then mentioned he was "working on getting rid of the pockets." What does he think, she can put one of the store's TVs in her pocket?

The store has a problem of shoplifting. The first shoplifter I saw was a well-dressed woman and she had a prayer book in her hands. I wouldn't steal cause I wouldn't want my kids to. I don't want them to be dishonest. Some people steal in front of their kids and they can afford to pay for it because they are made to pay for it when they are caught. Sometimes the manager and the floorgirl go to hell with it. Once the floorgirl followed a man in his seventies all around the store. He had a rolled-up newspaper under his arm and she accused him of stealing—he shook out the newspaper and showed he had nothing in it. Many times they'll throw kids out of the store—usually black kids. If a black person comes into the store they say, "Watch that one."

If you're working and you're not getting the right pay you want to steal cause you feel you're getting even with the boss. As a maid you steal what you can cause you're not getting paid enough. They give you a feeling you're no good so you steal from them to make them suffer. I did this once but some of my friends did it a lot. Sometimes the people you work for leave a penny or a nickel around to see if you would take it. Everybody that's got money got it some way and they got it by crooking people under them. That's how they got rich.

There's a real Hitler behind the lunch counter. She yells at the girls in front of the customers. She's the boss behind there and sometimes the customers complain about her. I feel sorry for her when I'm not mad at her. I know she has a hard life at home and needs to be "somebody." There aren't enough girls at the fountain so they are all pretty irritable. Right now, on top of all that, there's a gimmick of the boss's that drives the girls crazy. There's a sign on the fountain that says, "If your waitress doesn't ask if you want dessert, you get a free dessert." So people say the waitress didn't ask them when she did. Never eat at any 5&10—they have to use the food up from previous days before they make a new batch. Some of the stuff looks horrible—especially when the jelly apples get a week old, sometimes they get re-dipped.

Each girl that works behind the lunch counter has her own tip box. At the end of the day they have to take it to the office and the office personnel count it and take out the tax money from the tips. It's none of their business how much tips the girls get so they shouldn't take tax money off. Countergirls get less pay than the rest of us, too.

The whole story in a nutshell is we work hard. We keep the store clean and stocked but the company is trying to trick us and cheat us in little ways all the time. It's always the little person that gets hurt. It's about time that something happens so it's the rich people that hurt for a change. I'm not anyone's enemy unless they're an enemy to me and it seems to me people aren't seeing who their real friends are.

Two of my daughters and one son worked at this store. If you ask my nine-year-old granddaughter what she wants to be when she grows up she'll tell you a salesgirl at the 5&10. I think it's the best position she's ever seen a woman in, since her mother's on welfare. She likes the colors of the items and she likes to visit me at work. That would be the third generation to work there—but her grandmother wants her to be President of the U.S.

ROBERT COLES: A Police Sergeant[1]

* * *

Is he an "ordinary cop," as he once called himself? Is he a "boss," a "sergeant boss," as he refers to himself sometimes with mixed pride and embarrassment? Is he a "fascist pig," as he is called, among other things, by bright, vocal college students who are taking courses in sociology and psychology and political science and economics and urban affairs and law—and who prompt from him a wider range of responses than they might believe possible, for all their unquestionable awareness and sharpness of mind? It is, of course, possible to list those responses, and yet somehow no list, however well drawn up and accurately phrased, quite seems to render truthfully a man's ideas as they come tumbling out in the

1. From *The Middle Americans*, 1971.

course of talk after talk—all of which is rather obvious not only to "investigators" and "observers" doing their "research" but those very able and sensitive and strong-minded and independent and mean-spirited and inefficient and awkward and generous and sullen and lighthearted and callous and kind people who are "interviewed."

More than anything else the police sergeant resents "propaganda" about the police, his way of describing "those articles about our problems." He is tired of them, tired of "dumb reporters" doing "quickie stories on the cops," and tired of "smart-aleck graduate students and their professors" who are always going to police headquarters and wanting to interview someone on the force. Can't they simply go strike up a conversation with a cop, buy him a beer, get to know him, learn "whatever in hell it is" they want to know *that way?* Can't they do anything without those folders and the questions, dozens and dozens of questions? Life for him is too complicated for a questionnaire. Life for him is hard to put into any words, "even your own, never mind someone else's." It is easy to argue with him, or applaud him because he says what seems eminently sensible and correct. It is more important, perhaps, for all of us to understand that he is not so much against one or another "method" of research as he is doubtful that "a policeman or a fireman or a man who works on an assembly line of a factory" is going to get the compassion and fair treatment he deserves from people who make it their business to be known as compassionate and fair-minded: "The worst insults the police get is from the liberals and the radicals. A suburban housewife called up the other day and demanded to speak with 'the lieutenant.' She said she belonged to some committee, I didn't catch the name. She said we were the worst people in America, and if a Hitler ever took over here, we'd be marching people into concentration camps. Now, you know, that's not the first time I've heard that. Every time we get called to a college campus we get told things like that; and not only by the kids. Their teachers can be just as bad. I'd like to give each of them a jab to the stomach and a jab to the jaw. But I can't. And I tell my men that *they* can't either.

"Very few people know what it's like to have the radicals shouting at you from one direction and the Negro people in the slums looking at you as if you hate each and every one of them, and the people in between, most white people, claiming you've failed them, too, because there's crime all over, and it's the fault of the police, *the police.* I go to work some days and tell myself I'm going to quit. The men all say that. I don't know a policeman who feels he's being treated right. We don't get nearly the money we should, considering the fact that every hour we take risks all the time and could be killed almost every minute of the working day. And even our best friends and supporters don't know what we do—the calls that come in for our help, the duties we have. You go and ask the average Negro in a Negro neighborhood about the police, and he won't talk the way the civil rights people do. They call us all the time, Negroes do. I used to work in one of their districts. The switchboard was busy all day and all night. They fight and squabble with each other. They drink a lot. They lose themselves on drugs. They rob and steal from each other. They take after each other and kill. Then people say it's us, the police, the white man, that's to blame.

"I know I keep telling you all that, but people don't understand. I have one wish. I wish I could take some of those student radicals and send them out with some of my men that work in the Negro sections. I think it would open up their eyes, the students—that is, if anything can. They'd see that if you pulled the police out of the Negro sections, like the white radicals say you should—*they* don't live there—then the ones who would suffer would be the poor, innocent colored people. They're always the ones to suffer. A lot of Negroes are like a lot of white folks—good people, real good people.

"I hear my men talking. They say what I do. I have a brother who's a fireman. He says the same thing: it's not the average colored man who's to blame for all the trouble we're having in this country. It's a handful; well, it's more than a handful of trouble-makers. There are the crazy agitators, and the college crowd, the students and the teachers, and worst of all, if you ask me, are the rich people who support them all, and come into the city to march and demonstrate and wave their signs. Maybe it's all for the good, though. I've given up figuring out the answers. There's a whole lot of injustice in America. I know that. I can't afford for anyone in my family to get sick, least of all myself. The rich get richer and the poor ordinary man, he can barely buy his food and pay his rent. I feel sorry for the Negroes, I really do. People are prejudiced, most people are. You're almost born that way, don't you think? People like to stick together. The Irish want to live near the Irish. The same with the Italians or the others. Jews always stick together, even when they get rich, and a lot of them do. The poor Negroes, they want to get away from each other. They want to break out. I don't blame them. But when they break out what will they find? They'll see that the Irish are no good, and the Italians and Jews and everyone. We're all no good. I believe you should know the man, not where his grandfather came from. I mean, people like their own, but that isn't the way it should be. My son comes home and tells me that his teacher says the world is always changing. Well, you know it *is* always changing. I can remember a different world, the one I grew up in. That's gone, that world. A Negro boy born today is growing up in a country really worried over his people. I think everyone accepts the fact that we've got to end poverty and give people an even break, whether their skin is black or brown or whatever color it is.

"When I was a kid of twenty-five, I used to patrol a Negro section of this city. All was quiet then, no riots and no talk of revolution, and all the rest. I knew a lot of Negro people. They were poor, but they were polite and friendly. I'd get dozens of offers of coffee or a drink. We could talk, easy, real easy, with each other. Now all I hear is how no white man is trusted over there in that section. So, I asked one of my buddies who's a sergeant like me, and over in the district I used to be in—I asked him how he could stand it over there. He said he was surprised at me talking that way. I said I was surprised at *him* talking that way. He said it wasn't the same all the time, because they'd had a small riot or two, but it was the same as it always was most of the time: women who have to be rushed to the hospital to deliver their babies, and fires, and robberies, and fights to help settle, and kids caught on a roof or hurt playing who need to go to the emergency ward—you know, a cop's job. Then I thought to myself that I was a real fool for not thinking like that in the first place. You let those news stories go to your head, and you forget that most Negro people are too busy for demonstrations; they go to work, like the rest of us.

"I'd like to see more Negro policemen. I have nothing against them. But I don't believe in hiring a man just because he's colored or white or Chinese or anything else. If a man is going to be a policeman these days he's got to be tough. The world is tough; it's tougher than it ever was. Sometimes I look at my kids and hope they'll be all right when they grow up. I hope they'll have a world to live in."

STUDS TERKEL: Doc Graham[1]

A mutual acquaintance, Kid Pharaoh, insisted that we meet. Doc Graham had obviously seen better days.

My introduction to Chicago was when a guy got his head blowed off right across from where I went to stay. In that neighborhood where I gravitated, there was every kind of character that was ever invented. Con men, heist men, burglars, peet men: you name it, they had it.

These are highly sophisticated endeavors. To be proficient at it —well, my God, you spent a lifetime. And then you might fall, through not being sophisticated enough. You may have committed a common error, leaving fingerprints. . . .

1. From *Hard Times: An Oral History of the Great Depression,* 1970.

I was a caged panther. It was jungle. Survival was the law of the land. I watched so many of my partners fall along the way. I decided the modus operandi was bad. Unavailing, non-productive. After spending ten Saturdays in jail, one right after another, I changed my modus operandi.

What were you in jail for?

Various allegations. All alleged. I been a con man, a heist man—you name it.

How does a heist man differ from a con man?

One is by force and the other is by guile. Very few people have encompassed both. I was very daring. When I came to the city and seen groceries on the sidewalk, I swore I'd never be hungry again. My family was extremely poor. My father was an unsuccessful gambler, and my mother was a missionary. Not much money was connected with either profession.

A family conflict . . . ?

Yes, slightly. He threw the Bible in the fire. He was right, incidentally. [Laughs.] My mother didn't see it that way.

I'm sixty-one, and I have never held a Social Security card. I'm not knocking it. I have been what society generally refers to as a parasite. But I don't think I'd be a nicer fellow if I held two jobs.

My teacher was Count Victor Lustig. He was perhaps the greatest con man the United States has ever known. Lustig's outstanding achievement was getting put in jail and paying a Texas sheriff off with $30,000 counterfeit. And the sheriff made the penitentiary also. He got to be a believer. And he went into the counterfeit profession.

Another teacher was Ace Campbell.[2] He was the greatest card mechanic that ever arrived on the scene. Nick the Greek[3] wouldn't make him a butler. A footman. He couldn't open the door for him. Ace played the crimp. A crimp is putting a weave in a card that you'd need a microscope to see it. I know the techniques, but having had my arm half removed, I had to switch left-handed, deal left-handed. I'm ambidexterous.

An accident . . . ?

With a colored North American. The twenties and early thirties was a jungle, where only the strong survived and the weak fell by the wayside. In Chicago, at the time, the unsophisticated either belonged to the Bugs Moran mob or the Capone mob. The fellas with talent didn't bother with either one. And went around and robbed both of 'em.

We were extremely independent. Since I'm Irish, I had a working affiliate with Bugs Moran's outfit. In case muscle was needed

---

2. A pseudonym for a celebrated gambler of the twenties and early thirties. He is still alive [Terkel's note].

3. Another renowned gambler of the time [Terkel's note].

beyond what I had, I called on Moran for help. On the other hand, Moran might use me to help in one of his operations.

The nature of one operation was: if you had a load of whiskey hijacked, we went over and reloaded it on a truck, while several surrounded the place with machine guns, sawed-off shotguns, etcetera. *Did you find yourself in ticklish situations on occasion . . . ?*

Many of them. You see this fellow liquidated, that fellow disposed of. Red McLaughlin had the reputation of being the toughest guy in Chicago. But when you seen Red run out of the drainage canal, you realized Red's modus operandi was unavailing. His associates was Clifford and Adams. They were set in Al's doorway in his hotel in Cicero. That was unavailing. Red and his partners once stole the Checker Cab Company. They took machine guns and went up and had an election, and just went and took it over. I assisted in that operation.

What role did the forces of law and order play?

With a $10 bill, you wasn't bothered. If you had a speaking acquaintance with Mayor Thompson,[4] you could do no wrong. [Laughs.] Al spoke loud to him.

There was a long period during the Depression where the police were taking scrip. Cash had a language all of its own. One night in particular, I didn't have my pistol with me, and the lady of the evening pointed out a large score to me. [Laughs.] A squad car came by, which I was familiar with. A Cadillac, with a bell on it. I knew all the officers. I borrowed one of their pistols and took the score. Then I had to strip and be searched by the policemen, keeping honest in the end, as we divided the score. They wanted the right count. They thought I might be holding out on 'em. They even went into my shoes, even.

Oh, many policemen in that era were thieves. Legal thieves. I accepted it as such and performed accordingly. We didn't have no problems. It was an era where there was no bread on the table. So what was the difference whether I put the bread on the table by my endeavor or they put the bread? I performed with a hundred policemen in my time. I can't say nothin' for 'em, nothin' against 'em. I would say they were opportunists. I would say that they were merely persons that didn't perhaps have the courage to go on and do what I did. Nevertheless, they were willing to be a part of it. A minor part, that is.

The era of the times led into criminality, because of the old precept and concepts were destroyed against everyday reality. So when a policeman or a fireman was not being paid, how in the name of God could you expect him to enforce what he knew as the concept of law and order, when you see the beer barons changing hundred-dollar bills, and the pimp and the whorehouse guy had hundred-dollar bills, and the guy digging the sewers couldn't pay his bills? So how could you equate these things?

A good example is Clyde Barrow and Bonnie Parker. They were a product of the era. Dillinger—it wasn't that he was really a tough. No, he was just a product of survival. Actually, Dillinger was a country bumpkin. He realized the odds were stacked against him and performed accordingly. I knew Dillinger. Yeah, I met him on the North Side. And Dillinger was nothing like people wrote about him. The times produced Dillinger. Pretty Boy Floyd. Baby Face Nelson.

They were dedicated heist men and in the end were killed, to achieve their purpose. By themselves, they didn't need an army.

Al Capone sublet the matter. Capone quickly removed himself from the danger zone, aside from murdering Anselmi and Scalisi with a baseball bat. Bugs Moran to the end—he died for a bank heist in Ohio. They were from two different bolts of cloth. One was a dedicated thief. And one was an intriguing Mediterranean product of guile, etcetera. So you'd have to say that Moran was dedicated while Capone was an opportunist.

How did you get along during those hard times?

By every way known to the human brain. All my brothers were in the penitentiary. I had one brother in Jefferson City, another one in San Quentin, another one in Leavenworth, another one in Louisiana. At that time I am a fighter. I started boxing in 1925. Fourteen years till 1939. And it's a bloodthirsty thing.

How'd you become a boxer?

Gravitation. Being on the road simulated that fate, trying to grab a buck and so forth. Five different years, *Ring* magazine rated me the most devastating puncher in the profession, pound for pound.

What was it like, being a boxer in those days . . . ?

Survival. If it worked out that you were on top, you made a living. And if you were three or four shades below the top, you scuffled for a buck. Fighters were very, very hungry.

I made some pretty big scores. But I spent it practically all on getting my brothers out of penitentiaries around the country. At that time, the one in San Quentin stood me thirty thousand, the one in Jefferson City stood me twenty-five thousand. Those were big give-ups in those days.

I lived from the bottom to the top. I lived as good as you could live. I run the gamut of having a butler and a chauffeur to a flop joint, into an open car overnight.

He describes the boxing "combination" of those days; the fix; the refusal of his manager and himself to "play ball"; the boxer as an investment, cut up "like a watermelon."

I had many injuries in between. My hands, you can see. [He holds out his gnarled, broken knuckles.] In the meantime, I had to step out and make a dollar otherwise. It was never with the law.

I've switched craps, I've run up the cards, I do the complete bit. Every way known to the human brain. I'm probably a rare species that's left.

Was muscle always involved?

Muscle if you hope to leave with the money. Muscle everywhere, yes. Because for some unknown reason, muscle has been going on since the Roman Army conquered the field with a way of life.

When you enter an endeavor unsuccessfully, then the planning was incorrect. The risk was above the gains, and you stumble along the way. And the windup is a rude awakening with numbers strung out over your back. Unsuccessful in your modus operandi. Sagacity, ingenuity, planning . . . it involves much weighing, odds against failure, odds against gain—if you care to be in a free society.

I spent much time in jail. That's why I'm a student of the matter.

(*At this point, Kid Pharaoh and he conducted a vigorous and somewhat arcane debate concerning the relative dishonesty of Hoover and Roosevelt. The Kid insisted it was Hoover who, by clout, was saved from "the bucket." Doc was equally certain it was F.D.R. who should have had "numbers strung out over his shoulders."*)

Do you recall your biggest haul during the thirties?

It was alleged—

Who alleged . . . ?

The newspaper report came out as $75,000. We took eight and were happy about the whole thing.

What was your role during Prohibition?

I was a cheater. After studying under Count Lustig and Ace Campbell, I considered it beneath my dignity delivering a barrel of beer. Although I drink beer. I hustled with crap mobs, on the crimp, the weave, the holdout—the reason I didn't do the rum running is you can hire a mooch with muscle. But can you hire brains? Big firms have not succeeded in doing this.

I have met only several proficient men in my time. On of them was Jack Freed. [Cups hand over mouth, whispers.] D-e-a-d. He worked right up to the edge of his demise. This is in the evening, when you are not at home. He was dedicated to his labor. He spent half his lifetime in the penitentiaries. One of my closest friends. I, of course, assisted him, from time to time. He accused me of rattling my coat one night, making entrance. I, who have endeavored in every participation known to the human brain, where art, subterfuge and guile is involved.

I take it you were caught a few times—

Incarcerated. Nothing proven substantially. I was a victim of circumstances. What they were, I didn't say. Yes, I spent a year in Salinas, California, amongst other places. The highlight was when I was nineteen. If I get convicted, I'm going out to join my brother in San Quentin. My brother was doing twenty years there. If I'm not convicted, I'm going up to visit him. I'm going to San Quentin, one way or the other.

And you did?

I did. As a free man. I was fortunate enough in having one of the greatest criminal lawyers of all time defending me.

For someone engaging in your varied skills, do you sense a difference between the thirties and today?

It's so different today, it's unfathomable. You can't conjure what the difference is. Today everything is a robot. Today everything is mechanical. There is very little ingenuity. Everything today is no-personal, there is no personality whatsoever. Everything today is *ipso facto, fait accompli*. In my era they had to prove their point. Today, you don't have to prove your point.

Back then Ace Campbell steered Arnold Rothstein,[5] with Nigger Nate Raymond, into one of maybe the biggest card games was ever involved. I was a small feature of it in the Park Central Hotel in New York. Ace changed the weave [laughs], and when Rothstein wound up a half-a-million loser, he said he was cheated. Rothstein became jaded after he lost the half a million, no longer had any interest. No interest in life. After the card game broke up, he said he was no longer interested in this, that or the other. He refused to pay off. So Nigger Nate Raymond held court with him. And that was the end of that.

Held court . . . ?

The S&W people[6] had the implements that they held court with. That's all. Rothstein didn't have to pay off. You understand what I mean? I know, because I assisted in the operation with Ace. But let that be as it may. It was unfortunate, yes. But that was his demise.

Were the S&W people popular those days?

Naturally, it was part of your wearing apparel.

Aren't some of the survivors in legitimate enterprises today?

One of the fellows who was a pimp in Chicago is the boss of one of the grandest hotels in Las Vegas. I assisted him in a few small matters. But true to all pimping, he forgot me entirely as he advanced into the autumn of life.

After Prohibition, what did the guys do?

The ones that were adroit enough branched into other fields. If they didn't have any knowledge, they fell by the wayside. I achieved some small success in race tracks. Machine Gun Jack McGurn[7] couldn't stand the traffic. He got his brains blowed out, branching into other fields.

The night Prohibition was repealed, everybody got drunk. It was the only decent thing Roosevelt ever did in his Administration. I

---

5. A gambler and fixer of reknown. He was involved in the Black Sox scandal of 1919.

6. Smith & Wesson, revolver manufacturers.

7. It was alleged that he was one of Capone's executioners in the St. Valentine's Day Massacre. He was killed in a bowling alley in 1936, on the eve of St. Valentine's Day.

was not one of his admirers. I tried to fire him on four different occasions. If I ever had a person work for me that displeased me, it was Roosevelt. I voted against him four times.

What was it about him you didn't like?

Him being a con man, taking advantage of poor, misguided, gibbering idiots who believed in his fairy tales. The New Deal, the various gimmicks, the NRA . . . the complete subterfuge, artifice and guile. . . .

Some say Roosevelt saved our society. . . .

I dare say it would have been saved if Roosevelt's mother and father had never met.

Many people were on relief . . . on WPA. . . .

I didn't have a thing to do with that, because I was above that. Nevertheless, the people that were involved in it did it merely to get some meat on the plates, some food in the kitchen. It was no more, no less. Survival. None of the connotations of social dissent that has crept in since then. Merely an abstract way of eating. . . .

What do you think would happen if there were a big Depression today?

Very simple. They'd commit suicide today. I don't think they're conditioned to stand it. We were a hardier race then. We'd win wars. We didn't procrastinate. We'd win them or lose them. Today we're a new race of people. They'll quit on a draw—if they see any feasible way to see their way out to quit with any dignity, they'll quit. Back then, you had a different breed of people. You got $21 a month going into the army or the navy. So them guys, they went to win the war. There's been an emancipated woman since the beginning of the war, also.

KID PHARAOH *interjects.* "The American woman during the Depression was domesticated. Today, as we move into the late sixties, if you go into any high school, you don't see any classes of cooking any more. You don't see any classes at all in sewing. None of them can boil water. They're all today in business in competition to the male animal. Why should a Playboy bunny make $200 a week? If a veteran goes to war, puts his life up . . . can't raise a family."

DOC: ". . . a lot of country bumpkins in the city wanting to look at poor, misguided, gibbering idiot waitresses. That they've stripped down like a prostitute, but hasn't sense enough to know that it's on her alleged sex allure that the poor misguided chump is in the place. In the end it amounts to absolutely nothing. A hypothesis of silly nothingness . . . undressed broads serving hootch, that cannot fulfill. . . ."

KID PHARAOH: " . . . his dick directs him, like radar, to the Playboy Club. In a high moral society—in Russia—guys like Hugh Hefner would be working in the library."

During the Depression . . . if a guy had a few drinks with a girl . . . ?

If she had two drinks with him, and she didn't lay her frame down, she was in a serious matter. She could have one, and explain she made a mistake by marrying some sucker that she was trying to fulfill her marriage commitment. But in the thirties, if you had a second drink and she didn't make the commitment where she's going to lay her frame down for you, the entire matter was resolved quickly to the point and could end in mayhem. She was in a serious matter.

In the thirties, then, the individual con man, the heist man, had an easier time with it—all around?

Oh yes, it was much easier then. The Federal Government now has you on practically anything you do. They make a conspiracy whether you accomplish the matter or not. Today, it's fraught with much peril, any type of endeavor you engage in. A nefarious matter. It constantly comes under the heading of a federal statute. The Federal Government then collected taxes, and just a few interstate things, as white slavery, and that was about it.

Today, the Federal Government has expanded into every field. If you use a telephone, as an example, and you put slugs in it, that's a penitentiary offense. Strange as that may seem. So that will give you an idea how far the Federal Government has encroached on a citizen's prerogative.

You think Roosevelt had a role to play in this?

Definitely. He was perhaps the lowest human being that ever held public office. He, unfortunately, was a despot. I mean, you get an old con man at a point in high office, he begins to believe the platitudes that are expounded by the stupid populace about him.

What about the young people, during the Depression . . . ?

The young people in the Depression respected what laws there were. If they'd steal, they tried to do it with dignity. And what not. They respected the policeman. They looked at him with forebearance, that he was a necessary part of society. But, nevertheless, he didn't impede the mere fact of gain.

No, he didn't stop 'em.

The young today are feminized, embryo homosexuals. Stool pigeons.

What about the young dissenters?

If you gave 'em a push, they'd turn into a homosexual. When the German hordes fifty years ago surrounded Paris, Marshall Pétain brought out the pimps, whores, thieves, underground operators, he says: Our playground is jeopardized by the German Hun. Well, all Paris, every thief, burglar, pimp, he come out and picked up a musket. Stopped the German hordes.

Today you don't see any kind of patriotism like that. They're trying to tear down the courthouse, they try to throw paint on Johnson's car. How can you compare that era, coming into this? Those were men, and today you've got to question whether they're homosexual or whether they're not.

Since the Depression, manhood has been lost—the manhood that I knew. Where four or five guys went on an endeavor, they died trying to take the endeavor off. It was no big deal if they did die. If it didn't come off right, there was no recrimination. Everybody put skin off what they set on.

Today, the foible of our civilization is to attack the policeman with a rotten egg, throwing it at him. Or walking around with a placard, that they're against whatever the present society advocates as civilized. Those people today—the Fall of Rome could be compared with it. Because they were the strongest nation on earth, and they disinterrogated into nothing. Through debauchery, through moral decay.

They need a narcotic to do anything, they can't do it on their own. They need a drug. Back in my era, we could cold bloodedly do it.

B. H. HAGGIN: Josef Gingold on Toscanini[1]

My first rehearsal with Toscanini—for the first NBC Symphony broadcast in 1937—I think was the greatest musical experience of my life. I had of course heard Toscanini many times with the New York Philharmonic: he was my favorite conductor; and that was why I joined the NBC Symphony: I wanted to make music with this giant. I was a little apprehensive because of what I had heard about his temper; but I thought I'd try it for a season and see what happened.

That Sunday afternoon in 1937, a week before the broadcast, when he raised his stick to begin the Brahms First, there was electricity in the air; and the first chord gave me goose flesh. I don't think I've ever been as thrilled as I was then; and I'm still thrilled when I speak of it now, thirty years later. He went through the entire Brahms symphony with very little comment, apparently pleased with the orchestra; and we responded to his conducting by not only playing our hearts out for him but playing over our heads. After the Brahms we played the Mozart G-minor; and it was a marvelous performance, a marvelous experience. I have still to hear a Mozart G-minor as great as Toscanini's: in it Mozart emerged in a new light. Toscanini made it a great drama; and I will never forget the opening phrase—the pathos it had with the inflection he gave it. He kept saying to the violins: "*Molto arco! Molto arco! Non tedesco! Italiano! Molto arco!*" [Gingold illustrated with big movements of his bow arm as he sang the opening phrase in an impassioned manner.] It was *his* Mozart; and it was wonderful!

1. Interview with B. H. Haggin from *The Toscanini Musicians Knew*, 1967.

We also did the Vivaldi Concerto Grosso in D minor, which opened the broadcast on Christmas Eve; and I recall that at the broadcast, I don't know what happened, but Toscanini's first beat in the Vivaldi was very indecisive, so that we almost didn't get started together. For a moment the orchestra was a little shaken; but somehow we did get into it, and then it was all right. (I don't remember his making any mistakes—though I did see him balled up once, in Copland's *El Salón México*, by the constantly changing meter. Even so, I believe Copland said it was one of the best performances he ever had.)

I remember in those first weeks a wonderful experience in the two movements of Beethoven's Quartet Op. 135, which Toscanini played with string orchestra, and in which I've never heard any quartet approach him. The way he worked out every detail in the Largo! And the fire in the Scherzo! And those complicated string crossings that he worked out with the first violins alone! I wish he had done all the Beethoven quartets: for me they are the greatest masterpieces in the quartet literature; and where can you find a first violinist who is a Toscanini? He also did the *Moto Perpetuo* of Paganini, which was a lot of fun for the violinists, who practiced their parts and were well prepared.

It was in our second season that we played Tchaikovsky's *Pathétique* the first time; and it was quite a revelation to us, and gave us a bad morning. He came to the rehearsal with the preconceived idea that the orchestra was set in its way of playing the symphony; and he was right. We came to the second subject, the D-major melody which traditionally—for I don't know how many years—we had all played with a *ritardando* on the first three notes. When Toscanini began to conduct the melody in tempo, the orchestra took it away from him and slowed down the first three notes. He stopped: "*Signori, perchè?* Why? Is written so, eh? *Ancora!*" We started again; and again we made the *ritardando*: it was so ingrained in us that we couldn't help it. And he threw a fit. "*Si, tradizione!* The first *asino*, the first jackass, did it that way, and everyone follow him!" Then he pointed to the score: "*This* is my *tradizione!* So play like this!" Toscanini's logic was unanswerable: if Tchaikovsky had wanted a *ritardando* he would have written it in the score: "Is very easy to write *ritardando*, no?" So we played the three notes in time; and from then on we played everything as Tchaikovsky wanted it. This was the way we played it at the broadcast; and for the first time musicians and music-lovers heard the music as Tchaikovsky wrote it; but a great many of them didn't like it, because it was different. And today I hear the Tchaikovsky *Pathétique* played again in the "traditional" manner, I won't say by everybody: George Szell, for instance—who, incidentally, was a great admirer of Toscanini; oh yes, he had a tremendous admiration for him—Szell, who treats the classics with the utmost respect, tries to follow in Toscanini's footsteps with a personality of his own. I never heard Cantelli, unfortunately; but except for him, Toscanini didn't have the great young disciples to continue what he achieved.

I remember marvelous performances we gave in Buenos Aires. We were having a beautiful trip; we were rested; we were playing nothing but symphonic music, and not one broadcast a week but a concert every other day; Maestro was in fine spirits. And one performance of the *Tristan* Prelude and Finale in the Teatro Colón was *UN-FOR-GETTABLE!*

Certain performances of Toscanini's I don't think will ever be equalled by anyone else. The *Enigma Variations*, for instance: I don't think anybody did it as well. I don't think there will ever be a *La Mer* like his. The time he spent with the cellos and violas in that passage in the first movement! Also the Beethoven Ninth. The first movement: it was classic; it wept; it was operatic! The slow movement! And the recitatives of the basses in the finale! Berlioz's *Queen Mab*: the magic of it! The Rossini overtures: impossible to duplicate! The Wagner: no one conducted Wagner like Toscanini —no one! And of course Verdi: who will ever hear Verdi played like that? Even the accompaniments in performances of the arias: never banal, always with dignity, grandeur. Nothing was too small; everything was important. A little miniature like *Queen Mab*: how he worked on it! Twenty batons must have been broken to achieve it! Or the little Martucci pieces: with what grace and charm he did them! And I played with him at that Chatham Square benefit—in that little orchestra in which Heifetz played, and Milstein and Adolf Busch and Feuermann, with a few NBC men; and Toscanini conducted the *Moment Musical* of Schubert, the *Musical Joke* of Mozart, the *Perceptual Motion* of Reis, and a piece called *Loin du Bal* by Gillet, which you hear on Muzak and used to hear in hotels. Even though it was supposed to be a jamboree, we had a rehearsal, and the Old Man conducted as if it were a concert or broadcast: everything was done perfectly. And what he did with this little piece, this trifle, *Loin du Bal!* It came out like a wonderful jewel! Whatever he played, he played as though it was the greatest work.

I think he was the greatest recreative artist of this era—certainly as a conductor; and the explanation of how he did what he did has to begin with the unexplainable—that he was a genius. One can say he was a masterful conductor, who knew what he wanted and knew how to get it; one can speak of his tremendous knowledge, his thorough preparation, his ear, his baton technique. But I think that in the final analysis it was his genius that really won out: he was a genius blessed with all these things he needed for realization. It was not just one of them, but the combination of all of them.

From a purely technical viewpoint he had the clearest beat of any; but it wasn't the beat of a specialist in virtuoso conducting; it was the beat of a musician who had a stick and could show whatever he wished with it. And he never did more than was needed. He once quoted Hamlet's directions to the actors: "Suit the action to the word, and the word to the action"; and he himself made the motion that was suited to a *forte*, a *piano*, or any dynamic. He once said to the violinists, in a *pianissimo* passage where we were using too much bow: "Watch my hand. If my motion is small, your bow must be small; if my motion is large, your bow must be large." And the marvelous way he could conduct a slow tempo—the control! He is the only conductor I know who conducted the *Parsifal* Prelude in four instead of the customary eight; and he didn't give the silent downbeat most conductors give to assure perfect unanimity at the very beginning. He said: "Is no cadenza *per me*: I start to beat when we start to play." And he did, and the violins came in together! Also, he beat it all in four, and with his superb stick control it was always together. (To say nothing of the mood, the magic that he got in this piece.) Also the second movement of *Ibéria*, which is written in two, but which everyone does in four. Toscanini said: "I know is conducted in four, but I cannot do it so"; and he did it in two—and the control was marvelous. He was like a human metronome: a *human* metronome, I say, because I mean that his sense of rhythm was so marvelous. We played the *Eroica* one year; and the next year he varied by five seconds in a work which takes forty-eight minutes.

And yet he was smarter than some conductors who are *Kapellmeister*—who always hold the reins: he would run with a running horse. We did a performance of the Haydn No. 88; and we heard later from the people who were backstage after the performance that the Old Man came up beaming and said: "Did you hear the beautiful tempo *primi violini* took in finale?" They laughed at the idea of the violins taking a tempo; and he said: "*Si*, they took the tempo." Of course it was his tempo; but within hairsbreadths it could be a tiny bit on the fast side; and once it started there was nothing he could do; so, smart man that he was, he took what he got—which happened to be perfect—and played along with it. And he was so delighted! So many times he walked off the stage cursing —disgusted with the orchestra or with himself. He was very tough on himself: many times he said: "*Stupidi—anch' io!*" Even when something was good he was sparing with his praise: when he said "*Non c'è male*—not too bad" that was a real compliment.

Which reminds me of an extraordinary incident the first time we played Wagner's *Faust Overture*. The piece starts with a solo for tuba; and when our tuba-player, William Bell, had played it, Toscanini stopped and said: "*Ancora*. Again." So Bell played it again; and this time Toscanini went on; and we in front heard him say under his breath as he conducted: "This is first time in fifty-five years that I hear this solo played correct. Bravo, tuba, bravo, bravo."

This was extraordinary; but so was the rest of the story. Since Toscanini said it so softly, only those of us around him heard it; and
each of us assumed one of the others had told it to Bell, who sat
too far away to hear it. Well, Bell and I now teach at Indiana University; and last year, when we were reminiscing about the Old
Man, and I referred to Toscanini's terrific compliment to him, he
didn't know what I was talking about. It turned out that no one
had told him at the time; and when I told him what Toscanini had
said, he was just as thrilled now as he would have been in 1938.

To get back to the other things about Toscanini's conducting:
the score and parts of the Shostakovich Seventh arrived here at the
last possible minute; and Toscanini had no more than two weeks'
preparation before calling the first rehearsal. The work is about
seventy-three minutes long; and when Toscanini began that first reading he knew the entire work by memory. Now we were playing from
the parts of the Leningrad Philharmonic or whatever orchestra had
played it in Russia—if not conducted by Shostakovich, certainly
supervised by him—and not just one performance, but I believe
twenty or more. When Toscanini had run through the first movement he said *"Da capo"*; and pretty soon he stopped and said,
either to a trumpet- or a horn-player: "What you play there? You
play *si bémol*, eh? I think should be *fa.*" The player said: "But
Maestro, I have a B-flat in my part." "No, *caro*, I think should be
fa." And in his myopic way he peered at the score; and he was
right. He was right the first time; he was right the second time; and
I believe he must have found thirty-five or forty mistakes in the
parts, that Shostakovich himself hadn't heard in twenty or more
performances. The same thing happened when we played Roy Harris's Third Symphony. I think we had the parts from which the
Boston Symphony had played it and recorded it under Koussevitzky.
Roy Harris was at the rehearsals; and I imagine he must have been
at the Boston Symphony rehearsals; and Toscanini kept finding
wrong notes in the parts and turning to Harris: "Eh, Maestro, you
don't think should be this note?" Poor Harris had to look at the
music; and of course Toscanini was never wrong. There was a contemporary piece—I can't remember what—that he programmed,
tried once, and took off: he couldn't take it; it was too dissonant for
him. He came to that rehearsal knowing the piece by memory; and
as we were reading it we came to a terrific discord: it was so dissonant that we actually had to look at the fingerboard to see where our
notes were. And he stopped: "Eh, *terzo corno!* Third horn! *Re!* I
didn't hear!" The man had had a few bars' rest and had cleaned his
horn, and hadn't been able to get it up again in time to come in.
Toscanini couldn't see that far, and didn't see that the man wasn't
playing; but he heard that the D was missing.

Then there was his knowledge—not just of symphony and opera, but of everything in music. I don't think he ever forgot anything. This background of all-round knowledge came into the playing, no matter what particular work he was doing. One felt it.

And then there was the spell which his genius cast over the men. My wife likes to tell the story about the day I had some bug and wasn't feeling well enough to go to a rehearsal, but there was something on the program what I wanted to play, so I said: "I'll bundle up and go, and I'll play that one piece and then come right home." I went there feverish and in no condition really to play; but once Maestro began the rehearsal, I became so absorbed in what we were doing that I forgot I was sick, I forgot about myself entirely; and at the end of the rehearsal I was feeling completely well. This was the effect Toscanini had: when you were playing with him your mind never wandered for one moment; you were completely absorbed in music-making and at one with him and with the composer. And also, no matter what you were playing, you were convinced, at that moment, that this was the only way it could be played.

It was the spell of his musical personality; but it was also what he gave of himself. From the moment he began the rehearsal it was music-making plus a workshop; and it was never "Let's take it easy and save ourselves for the concert"; he never spared himself, and he expected his musicians never to spare themselves. How could we help responding to this man who worked harder than everybody else (there was a pool of water around him after a while), for whom music was a religion, and who made us feel the same way? We adored him; and we *tried* at least to give as much—and not only for him but for the music's sake. And let me say this: the concerts were of course a marvelous thing to have; BUT—THE REHEARSALS! As much public acclaim as he had in his sixty years as a conductor —and for me it wasn't enough; he should have had even more— only the musicians who were in the workshop with him really knew how great he was: they saw aspects of his art that one couldn't see at the concert. The concert was a finished thing; and sometimes one had a feeling, not that he didn't care, but that the work had already been done, the concert had to take place, so let's go through with it. *Some*times; I wouldn't say always. He was always inspired; but the rehearsals were incredible: he was as inspired at them as most conductors are at concerts. It was the wonder of wonders, the things you saw this man do, whereas you had difficulties playing just one line. You felt like a little nincompoop in the presence of a god.

A great, great genius—one in a lifetime: there will never be another one like him—not in our time. And the impact he had on all of us who played with him was such that our whole musical being was altered for the good—for the best. Music was a religion for him; and it rubbed off on all of us who came into contact with him. He instilled a love of work, a devotion and respect for music, for the composer. He taught us to look carefully at the composer's indications on the printed page—to see, for example, what he wrote *after Allegro*. He would say: "Is not *Allegro*. Is *Allegro ma*—" or "*Allegro con*—" Every word meant something. In *Allegro giusto* you had to pay attention to the *giusto*; in *Allegro vivace*, to the *vivace*. When we played an Andante he would say: "*Non marcia funebre! Andante!*"

But the statement one often hears—that one of the great things about him was that he played everything as it was written—those who say this are uttering a mere empty phrase. To play what's written is quite easy; what people don't realize is that Toscanini, being a great musician, read between the lines, and this was what gave the music the life it had in his performance. And very often he did change dynamics—because he had to. In a Beethoven symphony, for example, you will find that Beethoven wrote double-*forte* throughout a passage; and if you played it exactly as written it would sound poorly balanced and blurred. So Toscanini made certain changes in the dynamics for clarification, to enable certain voices to emerge. Where the violins had to fight against all the brass he changed the double-*forte* to *mezzo-forte* for the brass and left the double-*forte* for the violins, so the violins could be heard clearly without having to force.

His ideas of clarity, of voices always emerging clearly—there has never been anything like it. He would take just, let's say, the second clarinet and third horn and violas—inner voices—and make them play alone. And always "*Cantare! Cantare!* Sing! Sing!" He made these voices sing as if they were thematic, and then incorporated them with the rest of the orchestral texture. And how beautiful the whole thing became!

One thing he did that occurs to me is his beating in circles. Musicians I knew would ask me: "How do you know what he's doing?" The perspective was different for someone *in* the orchestra. He did the circular movement when he felt that the music called for expansion, for excitement, which he achieved by getting away from the square one-two-three-four beat. He always was making music; and as far as we were concerned the beat had been established. It was difficult for an outsider to understand; but we understood it perfectly.

As I said before, working with this man we felt that we were in the presence of a god. That's why when he would throw fits and would insult people—though it wasn't very pleasant, I must say, and we wished he had acted differently—we understood and accepted it. Sometimes we accepted even when we didn't understand. Chotzinoff once gave me the explanation of an incident which baffled us at the time. He sometimes came to a rehearsal with a preconceived idea about what was going to happen. I told you about the first time we rehearsed Tchaikovsky's *Pathétique*; and in this case it was the first time we were going to do the *Leonore*

No. 3. At the end there is that famous violin passage, which we prepared in advance: we practiced it individually, and together; and as you know we had a marvelous violin section. The day of the first rehearsal, Chotzinoff told me, the Old Man was pacing back and forth, back and forth, in his room. Chotzinoff asked him what was the matter. *"Tutti violini di NBC son stupidi!"* "But Maestro, you seemed satisfied at the concert on Saturday." "Eh, but you will hear *Leonore*. They cannot play. Is *male, male!"* At the rehearsal, we sensed that he was in an unusually bad mood; but it wasn't the first time. When he came to the difficult violin passage he stopped, pointed to the last four violins of the section, and said: "Last four violins play alone." They played very well. "Next four." They played very well. Down the line: everyone played well. Then the whole section: it was marvelous. And he was so angry that it went well, because it was contrary to what he had expected, that he began to scream: "You are *dilettanti!"* We just looked at him: there was no use trying to figure out what this was all about.

But he could be very understanding and patient when something was difficult. And he could be wonderful to people. When the orchestra manager once wanted to fire a musician, Toscanini said: "He stay." And when one of the men was killed in South America and Toscanini found out about it, he locked himself in his cabin and wept for hours, because he felt that if he hadn't made the tour this man would still be alive.

I myself had a wonderful experience with the Old Man. None of us ever approached him personally; we were asked to keep away from him when the orchestra was organized. So when I resigned from the orchestra in 1943 to become concert-master of the Detroit Symphony, I handed in my resignation to the personnel manager, not to Toscanini. But a notice appeared in *The Times* on the day of one of our Sunday afternoon broadcasts; and Maestro read it. After the broadcast Chotzinoff said: "Maestro wants to see you." I didn't associate it with the notice in the paper, and didn't know what it was about. For the moment I was stunned, and thought: "My God, what did I do?" I recapitulated the entire broadcast in my mind; but as far as I could remember I had played as well as I could, and hadn't spoiled anything. So I went in to see him; and he looked at me and said: *"Caro,* you don't like Maestro anymore?" I said: "Maestro, I adore you!" "Then why you leave?" "Well, Maestro, I've always wanted to be a concert-master; and of course one has to start in a smaller orchestra to realize this ambition." "*Ma*—is good orchestra here, and good maestro. Why you leave?" This was the first time he had shown any awareness of my existence: until then I had thought I was just another number—but not at all. He then invited me to visit him in Riverdale; and we spent a whole afternoon with him that was just terrific.

We debated whether to take our boy, who was then four years

old. My wife didn't think we should; but I said he was old enough to be able to remember it and say he once shook hands with Toscanini; so we decided to take him along. Toscanini was wonderful to him—gave him cookies, and took him out to a swing or something in the yard. We were alone with the Old Man the whole afternoon—four hours. He was sniffling and sneezing, and said: "I have terrible cold"; but my wife whispered that she thought it was hay fever, because *she* had it and it was the season; and we found out later that he did have hay fever. Well, he asked me about myself—with whom had I studied? I said: "With Ysaye." "Ah, is great violinist. He play with me innnnnn—Scala. Was innnnnn—April—eighteennnnn—ninety-six. *Mi-maggiore* Bach—and Mendelssohn." Just like that; and if the Old Man said it was April 1896, it was so. "He play beauuutifully. Beautiful *rubato e cantabile.* A beautiful artist." And then he said: "You know, Sarasate play with me in Italy first time Lalo *Symphonie Espagnole.* Is not very interesting, but beautiful technique. He play like—like lady."

It was lovely: he reminisced, and I asked him questions. I asked him about the great days at the Metropolitan when he was there. I said: "It must have been wonderful when they had singers like Caruso and Scotti." He said: "When I am young man I admire certain singers. And people say: 'You think these are good. You should have heard *Rubini!* You should have heard *Grisi!*' Is always so. Now in twenty-five years you will say: 'Singers today are no good. You should have heard *Peerce!*' Were not such golden years."

He spoke about Chaliapin, for whom he apparently at one time had great admiration. He said that they were going to do *Mefistofele* at La Scala and were looking for a suitable bass; and it so happened that a very dear friend who went on a business trip to Russia heard Chaliapin there. This friend was not a musician, but he knew opera, he knew singers; and he told Toscanini about this young Russian bass who he said was wonderful. So Toscanini sent Gatti-Casazza on a special trip to hear Chaliapin; and Gatti signed him up. It was the first time that Chaliapin sang outside of Russia; and Toscanini said that when he came to rehearse, "Was *molto bene, molto modesto.* He did some things not *perfetto;* but we worked. Everything I tell him, he say: '*Si, Maestro, si.*' And he did a wonderful Mefistofele. Correct! CORRRRECT!!!" You know what a compliment this was from Toscanini. Everything was done beautifully; and it was a great success. At last, Toscanini thought, he had a singer who not only had a marvelous voice and was a wonderful actor, but was modest and took direction. They engaged Chaliapin again for the following year; and meanwhile he was engaged elsewhere: he sang in London, he sang everywhere, and always with great success. Then reports came to Toscanini that Chaliapin had already had a fight with the conductor somewhere—that in the middle of a performance he signalled to the conductor—you know:

"*Via, via, via!*" And Toscanini said: "No, no, you make mistake. Is *molto, molto modesto*. No, no." Then he had to go to Paris; and in Paris he saw in the newspaper that Chaliapin was singing in *Mefistofele*. So he went; and he said: "Was *porcheria! Male*—bad—bad taste—everything distorted! I went backstage, and I said to him: 'Chaliapin, you must restudy the whole thing when you come to La Scala! We must work again!' '*Si, Maestro, si.*'" Then, he said, about two weeks before Chaliapin was scheduled to return to La Scala, they got a telegram that he was sick, so they postponed the performance. Then they got another telegram that he couldn't come for some other reason. And finally it was evident that he didn't want to come. Toscanini said he was disappointed that this man didn't want to be corrected. To find a great artist like that, and not to be able to do anything with him! He was so disappointed in him!

Later that afternoon Toscanini played a recording of *Harold in Italy*, which Koussevitzky and the Boston Symphony had made with Primrose; and he listened, tugging at his moustache, and said: "Poor Primrose. *Poor Primrose!* Next year he come to play this piece with me again; and he must play correct! This is not correct! This Koussevitzky play very good double bass, you know? *Molto bene.*" And he said it was a wonderful orchestra, but Boston always had good orchestras. "I remember Karl Muck. He play the Beethoven First"; and the Old Man imitated Muck conducting the Allegro of the first movement in a dragging tempo. "He did not make the first repeat: *was boring also for him*, no?!" And we couldn't laugh as you and I are laughing now; because the Old Man couldn't take a joke, and to him this was serious: he didn't think it was funny at all.

He was in great form that day. He recalled that when he was at La Scala, Ricordi came to him and told him that a composer named Leoncavallo, who was associated with them in some way, had written an opera, and they wanted Toscanini to do the premiere. So he looked at the score of *I Pagliacci*, and said: "*E porcheria.*" ["It's a mess."] And he said: "I didn't want to do it; but Ricordi, who was a good friend, begged me. He said: 'Do it just once. This man Leoncavallo is so poor.' And I don't know why, but I say: '*Bene, bene.* I do this *porcheria*.' And you know what success had this piece! It went all over the world for fifty years! But you know, *caro, anche* today is *porcheria!*"

It was a wonderful visit. A few years later—I don't remember exactly what year—I listened in Cleveland, over the radio, to an incredible performance; and I sat down and wrote a Christmas card to Toscanini. I wrote him: "I was just listening to your broadcast. It was absolutely sublime. Maestro, I wish you a Merry Christmas and a Happy New Year." That's all I wrote. On Christmas Day, at eight o'clock in the morning, a special delivery; and there was an envelope addressed in Toscanini's hand, with a bold "Special Delivery" at one side, and inside a card with a photograph of himself in it, and a handwritten inscription: "Thank you, my dear Gingold, for your very kind words. My very best wishes to you for a Merry Christmas and a Happy New Year." He went to the trouble—he probably went to the post office himself to send it! He never forgot a former musician.

And I had a lovely visit with him—it was the last time I saw him—when the orchestra played in Cleveland on the transcontinental tour. They played in the Public Auditorium, to 10,000 people. I went to the concert, and tried to get backstage afterwards; but there was a police guard at the stage door, and I couldn't get in. The next day some of the men came to my house for lunch; and I told them: "I tried to see the Old Man, but I couldn't get in. I feel so terrible: I wanted to tell him what a wonderful concert it was." And one of them said: "Call up Walter Toscanini; because the Old Man was expecting you, knowing you are here." So I called up Walter Toscanini; and he said: "But Father left word with Walker to let you in." I said: "I couldn't even get to Walker." He said: "Come to the train. We leave at midnight; and Father will be there about ten o'clock." I did, and had about two hours with the Old Man on the train—a beautiful visit. He wanted to know all about the concerts in Cleveland, and how I was doing. He told me I was getting too fat. And I must tell you this wonderful story. He was having trouble with his knee; and they had a railing around the conductor's podium, so that if his knee gave way he could hold on. In Cleveland he conducted the Brahms Fourth; and the Scherzo was as energetic as ever; but at the end of it, the three *forte* chords came out *forte—forte—pianissimo.* I was taken aback, but thought maybe because of the acoustics I didn't hear right. When I saw him he said: "You notice something in Scherzo of Brahms, eh?" And he looked at me with those eyes. I said: "Well, Maestro, I noticed the last chord was *piano.*" "*Si, caro,* was *piano.* You know, I have trouble with my knee. And I start to make *energico* the last chord; but my knee is going to break, eh; and I could not make the last chord big as should be. I make *piano;* and the *stupidi musicisti*—they follow me!"

I had brought him a little present—a book containing the programs of the Bonn Festival of 1892, which included programs of the Joachim Quartet. It was a very rare book; and when I gave it to him he was very happy: he looked through it thoroughly; told me he had heard the Joachim Quartet play; and spoke about them. I also had brought along the memoirs of Arditi. He's the man who wrote *Il Bacio;* and he was a well-known conductor in his day. I brought the book because Arditi has in it a story of how Rossini once and for all settled the question of a note in the English horn solo in the *William Tell* Overture. Arditi asked Rossini which is it:

E D B C B G or E D B C A G? And Rossini took out his visiting card and wrote on it E D B C A G and his signature. Arditi writes in his memoirs that now when English-horn-players ask him, he shows them Rossini's card; and he has a photograph of the card in the book. I showed it to the Old Man; and he said: "*Si*, is Rossini's writing. But is *banale* like this. Rossini sometimes write this way, sometimes another way. No, *caro*, is wrong—is *banale*. Is *banale* also for Rossini!"; and he shut the book *molto energico*.

It was a beautiful visit. And do you know what amazed me? When I left I embraced the Old Man; and he had the skin of a baby! I noticed also that he had all his teeth—and this was a man who was then over eighty! And the most beautiful eyes I've ever seen in my life! Incidentally, when he would look at the first-violin section, when he got angry, his eyes covered everybody: everyone thought he was looking at *him*—whereas he was looking at the whole section.

And that was the last time I saw the Old Man. He emerges today greater than ever—though I don't know whether his influence is very great now. The things he fought for are being distorted again —the tempi in Brahms's symphonies, for example: *allegros* are played as *andantes*, *andantes* as *adagios*—the very things Toscanini fought against. And if you question the conductors about this, their answer invariably is: "Well, that's the tradition." But there is hardly a day—when I am teaching, or practicing, or playing—that his image isn't before me, and that I don't recall some remark or idea or other reminder of his genius. I thank God for giving me those seven years of playing with him; because my whole life has been enriched by my contact with this great, great musician. And I am sorry that others didn't have this opportunity. In my twenty-five years of symphony playing I have played with great conductors and wonderful musicians; but there was only one Toscanini.

People

DORIS LESSING

My Father

We use our parents like recurring dreams, to be entered into when needed; they are always there for love or for hate; but it occurs to me that I was not always there for my father. I've written about him before, but novels, stories, don't have to be "true." Writing this article is difficult because it has to be "true." I knew him when his best years were over.

There are photographs of him. The largest is of an officer in the 1914–18 war. A new uniform—buttoned, badged, strapped, tabbed —confines a handsome, dark young man who holds himself stiffly to confront what he certainly thought of as his duty. His eyes are steady, serious, and responsible, and show no signs of what he became later. A photograph at sixteen is of a dark, introspective youth with the same intent eyes. But it is his mouth you notice—a heavily-jutting upper lip contradicts the rest of a regular face. His moustache was to hide it: "Had to do something—a damned fleshy mouth. Always made me uncomfortable, that mouth of mine."

Earlier a baby (eyes already alert) appears in a lace waterfall that cascades from the pillowy bosom of a fat, plain woman to her feet. It is the face of a head cook. "Lord, but my mother was a practical female—almost as bad as you!" as he used to say, or throw at my mother in moments of exasperation. Beside her stands, or droops, arms dangling, his father, the source of the dark, arresting eyes, but otherwise masked by a long beard.

The birth certificate says: Born 3rd August, 1886, Walton Villa, Creffield Road, S. Mary at the Wall, R.S.D. Name, Alfred Cook. Name and surname of Father: Alfred Cook Tayler. Name and maiden name of Mother: Caroline May Batley. Rank or Profession: Bank Clerk. Colchester, Essex.

They were very poor. Clothes and boots were a problem. They

"made their own amusements." Books were mostly the Bible and *The Pilgrim's Progress.* Every Saturday night they bathed in a hip-bath in front of the kitchen fire. No servants. Church three times on Sundays. "Lord, when I think of those Sundays! I dreaded them all week, like a nightmare coming at you full tilt and no escape." But he rabbited with ferrets along the lanes and fields, bird-nested, stole fruit, picked nuts and mushrooms, paid visits to the black-smith and the mill and rode a farmer's carthorse.

They ate economically, but when he got diabetes in his forties and subsisted on lean meat and lettuce leaves, he remembered suet puddings, treacle puddings, raisin and currant puddings, steak and kidney puddings, bread and butter pudding, "batter cooked in the gravy with the meat," potato cake, plum cake, butter cake, porridge with treacle, fruit tarts and pies, brawn, pig's trotters and pig's cheek and home-smoked ham and sausages. And "lashings of fresh butter and cream and eggs." He wondered if this diet had produced the diabetes, but said it was worth it.

There was an elder brother described by my father as: "Too damned clever by half. One of those quick, clever brains. Now I've always had a slow brain, but I get there in the end, damn it!"

The brothers went to a local school and the elder did well, but my father was beaten for being slow. They both became bank clerks in, I think, the Westminster Bank, and one must have found it congenial, for he became a manager, the "rich brother," who had cars and even a yacht. But my father did not like it, though he was conscientious. For instance, he changed his writing, letter by letter, because a senior criticised it. I never saw his unregenerate hand, but the one he created was elegant, spiky, careful. Did this mean he created a new personality for himself, hiding one he did not like, as he hid his "damned fleshy mouth"? I don't know.

Nor do I know when he left home to live in Luton, or why. He found family life too narrow? A safe guess—he found everything too narrow. His mother was too down-to-earth? He had to get away from his clever elder brother?

Being a young man in Luton was the best part of his life. It ended in 1914, so he had a decade of happiness. His reminiscences of it were all of pleasure, the delight of physical movement, of dancing in particular. All his girls were "a beautiful dancer, light as a feather." He played billiards and ping-pong (both for his coun-try); he swam, boated, played cricket and football, went to picnics and horse races, sang at musical evenings. One family of a mother and two daughters treated him "like a son only better. I didn't know whether I was in love with the mother or the daughters, but oh I did love going there; we had such good times." He was engaged to one daughter, then, for a time, to the other. An engage-ment was broken off because she was rude to a waiter. "I could not marry a woman who allowed herself to insult someone who was de-

fenceless." He used to say to my wryly smiling mother: "Just as well
I didn't marry either of *them*; they would never have stuck it out the
way you have, old girl."

Just before he died he told me he had dreamed he was standing
in a kitchen on a very high mountain holding X in his arms. "Ah,
yes, that's what I've missed in my life. Now don't you let yourself
be cheated out of life by the old dears. They take all the colour out
of everything if you let them."

But in that decade—"I'd walk 10, 15 miles to a dance two or three
times a week and think nothing of it. Then I'd dance every dance
and walk home again over the fields. Sometimes it was moonlight,
but I liked the snow best, all crisp and fresh. I loved walking back
and getting into my digs just as the sun was rising. My little dog
was so happy to see me, and I'd feed her, and make myself porridge
and tea, then I'd wash and shave and go off to work."

The boy who was beaten at school, who went too much to
church, who carried the fear of poverty all his life, but who nevertheless was filled with the memories of country pleasures; the young
bank clerk who worked such long hours for so little money, but who
danced, sang, played, flirted—this naturally vigorous, sensuous being
was killed in 1914, 1915, 1916. I think the best of my father died
in that war, that his spirit was crippled by it. The people I've met,
particularly the women, who knew him young, speak of his high
spirits, his energy, his enjoyment of life. Also of his kindness, his
compassion and—a word that keeps recurring—his wisdom. "Even
when he was just a boy he understood things that you'd think even
an old man would find it easy to condemn." I do not think these
people would have easily recognised the ill, irritable, abstracted,
hypochondriac man I knew.

He "joined up" as an ordinary soldier out of a characteristically
quirky scruple: it wasn't right to enjoy officers' privileges when the
Tommies had such a bad time. But he could not stick the communal
latrines, the obligatory drinking, the collective visits to brothels, the
jokes about girls. So next time he was offered a commission he took it.

His childhood and young man's memories, kept fluid, were added
to, grew, as living memories do. But his war memories were congealed in stories that he told again and again, with the same words
and gestures, in stereotyped phrases. They were anonymous, general,
as if they had come out of a communal war memoir. He met a
German in no-man's-land, but both slowly lowered their rifles and
smiled and walked away. The Tommies were the salt of the earth,
the British fighting men the best in the world. He had never known
such comradeship. A certain brutal officer was shot in a sortie by his
men, but the other officers, recognising rough justice, said nothing.
He had known men intimately who saw the Angels at Mons.[1] He

1. An apparition that appeared during a World War I battle.

wished he could force all the generals on both sides into the trenches for just one day, to see what the common soldiers endured —*that* would have ended the war at once.

There was an undercurrent of memories, dreams, and emotions much deeper, more personal. This dark region in him, fate-ruled, where nothing was true but horror, was expressed inarticulately, in brief, bitter exclamations or phrases of rage, incredulity, betrayal. The men who went to fight in that war believed it when they said it was to end war. My father believed it. And he was never able to reconcile his belief in his country with his anger at the cynicism of its leaders. And the anger, the sense of betrayal, strengthened as he grew old and ill.

But in 1914 he was naïve, the German atrocities in Belgium inflamed him, and he enlisted out of idealism, although he knew he would have a hard time. He knew because a fortuneteller told him. (He could be described as uncritically superstitious or as psychically gifted.) He would be in great danger twice, yet not die—he was being protected by a famous soldier who was his ancestor. "And sure enough, later I heard from the Little Aunties that the church records showed we were descended the backstairs way from the Duke of Wellington, or was it Marlborough? Damn it, I forget. But one of them would be beside me all through the war, she said." (He was romantic, not only about this solicitous ghost, but also about being a descendant of the Huguenots, on the strength of the "e" in Tayler; and about "the wild blood" in his veins from a great uncle who, sent unjustly to prison for smuggling, came out of a ten-year sentence and earned it, very efficiently, along the coasts of Cornwall until he died.)

The luckiest thing that ever happened to my father, he said, was getting his leg shattered by shrapnel ten days before Passchendaele. His whole company was killed. He knew he was going to be wounded because of the fortuneteller, who had said he would know. "I did not understand what she meant, but both times in the trenches, first when my appendix burst and I nearly died, and then just before Passchendaele, I felt for some days as if a thick, black velvet pall was settled over me. I can't tell you what it was like. Oh, it was awful, awful, and the second time it was so bad I wrote to the old people and told them I was going to be killed."

His leg was cut off at mid-thigh, he was shell-shocked, he was very ill for many months, with a prolonged depression afterwards. "You should always remember that sometimes people are all seething underneath. You don't know what terrible things people have to fight against. You should look at a person's eyes, that's how you tell. . . . When I was like that, after I lost my leg, I went to a nice doctor man and said I was going mad, but he said, don't worry, everyone locks up things like that. You don't know—horrible, horrible, awful things. I was afraid of myself, of what I used to dream. I wasn't myself at all."

In the Royal Free Hospital was my mother, Sister McVeagh. He married his nurse which, as they both said often enough (though in different tones of voice), was just as well. That was 1919. He could not face being a bank clerk in England, he said, not after the trenches. Besides, England was too narrow and conventional. Besides, the civilians did not know what the soldiers had suffered, they didn't want to know, and now it wasn't done even to remember "The Great Unmentionable." He went off to the Imperial Bank of Persia, in which country I was born.

The house was beautiful, with great stone-floored high-ceilinged rooms whose windows showed ranges of snow-streaked mountains. The gardens were full of roses, jasmine, pomegranates, walnuts. Kermanshah he spoke of with liking, but soon they went to Teheran, populous with "Embassy people," and my gregarious mother created a lively social life about which he was irritable even in recollection.

Irritableness—that note was first struck here, about Persia. He did not like, he said, "the graft and the corruption." But here it is time to try and describe something difficult—how a man's good qualities can also be his bad ones, or if not bad, a danger to him.

My father was honourable—he always knew exactly what that word meant. He had integrity. His "one does not do that sort of thing," his "no, it is *not* right," sounded throughout my childhood and were final for all of us. I am sure it was true he wanted to leave Persia because of "the corruption." But it was also because he was already unconsciously longing for something freer, because as a bank official he could not let go into the dream-logged personality that was waiting for him. And later in Rhodesia, too, what was best in him was also what prevented him from shaking away the shadows: it was always in the name of honesty or decency that he refused to take this step or that out of the slow decay of the family's fortunes.

In 1925 there was leave from Persia. That year in London there was an Empire Exhibition, and on the Southern Rhodesian stand some very fine maize cobs and a poster saying that fortunes could be made on maize at 25/-a bag. So on an impulse, turning his back forever on England, washing his hands of the corruption of the East, my father collected all his capital, £800, I think, while my mother packed curtains from Liberty's, clothes from Harrods, visiting cards, a piano, Persian rugs, a governess and two small children.

Soon, there was my father in a cigar-shaped house of thatch and mud on the top of a kopje that overlooked in all directions a great system of mountains, rivers, valleys, while overhead the sky arched from horizon to empty horizon. This was a couple of hundred miles south from the Zambesi, a hundred or so west from Mozambique, in the district of Banket, so called because certain of its reefs were of the same formation as those called *banket* on the Rand. Lomagundi—gold country, tobacco country, maize country—wild, almost empty. (The Africans had been turned off it into reserves.) Our neighbours were four, five, seven miles off. In front of the house . . . no neighbours, nothing; no farms, just wild bush with two rivers but no fences to the mountains seven miles away. And beyond these mountains and bush again to the Portuguese border, over which "our boys" used to escape when wanted by the police for pass or other offences.

And then? There was bad luck. For instance, the price of maize dropped from 25/- to 9/-a bag. The seasons were bad, prices bad, crops failed. This was the sort of thing that made it impossible for him ever to "get off the farm," which, he agreed with my mother, was what he most wanted to do.

It was an absurd country, he said. A man could "own" a farm for years that was totally mortgaged to the Government and run from the Land Bank, meanwhile employing half-a-hundred Africans at 12/-a month and none of them knew how to do a day's work. Why, two farm labourers from Europe could do in a day what twenty of these ignorant black savages would take a week to do. (Yet he was proud that he had a name as a just employer, that he gave "a square deal.") Things got worse. A fortuneteller had told him that her heart ached when she saw the misery ahead for my father: this was the misery.

But it was my mother who suffered. After a period of neurotic illness, which was a protest against her situation, she became brave and resourceful. But she never saw that her husband was not living in a real world, that he had made a captive of her common sense. We were always about to "get off the farm." A miracle would do it —a sweepstake, a goldmine, a legacy. And then? What a question! We would go to England where life would be normal with people coming in for musical evenings and nice supper parties at the Trocadero after a show. Poor woman, for the twenty years we were on the farm, she waited for when life would begin for her and for her children, for she never understood that what was a calamity for her was for them a blessing.

Meanwhile my father sank towards his death (at 61). Everything changed in him. He had been a dandy and fastidious, now he hated to change out of shabby khaki. He had been sociable, now he was misanthropic. His body's disorders—soon diabetes and all kinds of stomach ailments—dominated him. He was brave about his wooden leg, and even went down mine shafts and climbed trees with it, but he walked clumsily and it irked him badly. He greyed fast, and slept more in the day, but would be awake half the night pondering about. . . .

It could be gold divining. For ten years he experimented on private theories to do with the attractions and repulsions of metals. His whole soul went into it but his theories were wrong or he was *unlucky*—after all, if he had found a mine he would have had to leave the farm. It could be the relation between the minerals of the earth and of the moon; his decision to make infusions of all the plants on the farm and drink them himself in the interests of science; the criminal folly of the British Government in not realising that the Germans and the Russians were conspiring as Anti-Christ to . . . the inevitability of war because no one would listen to Churchill, but it would be all right because God (by then he was a British Israelite[2]) had destined Britain to rule the world; a prophecy said 10 million dead would surround Jerusalem—how would the corpses be cleared away?; people who wished to abolish flogging should be flogged; the natives understood nothing but a good beat, ing; hanging must not be abolished because the Old Testament said "an eye for an eye and a tooth for a tooth. . . ."

Yet, as this side of him darkened, so that it seemed all his thoughts were of violence, illness, war, still no one dared to make an unkind comment in his presence or to gossip. Criticism of people, particularly of women, made him more and more uncomfortable till at last he burst out with: "It's all very well, but no one has the right to say that about another person."

In Africa, when the sun goes down, the stars spring up, all of them in their expected places, glittering and moving. In the rainy season, the sky flashed and thundered. In the dry season, the great dark hollow of night was lit by veld fires: the mountains burned through September and October in chains of red fire. Every night my father took out his chair to watch the sky and the mountains, smoking, silent, a thin shabby fly-away figure under the stars. "Makes you think—there are so many worlds up there, wouldn't really matter if we did blow ourselves up—plenty more where we came from."

The Second World War, so long foreseen by him, was a bad time. His son was in the Navy and in danger, and his daughter a sorrow to him. He became very ill. More and more often it was necessary to drive him into Salisbury with him in a coma, or in danger of one, on the back seat. My mother moved him into a pretty little suburban house in town near the hospitals, where he took to his bed and a couple of years later died. For the most part he was unconscious under drugs. When awake he talked obsessively (a tongue licking a nagging sore place) about "the old war." Or he remembered his youth. "I've been dreaming—Lord, to see those horses come lickety-split down the course with their necks stretched

---

2. A reference to the contention that the English-speaking peoples are the descendants of the "ten tribes" of Israel, deported by Sargon of Assyria on the fall of Samaria in 721 B.C.

out and the sun on their coats and everyone shouting. . . . I've been dreaming how I walked along the river in the mist as the sun was rising. . . . Lord, lord, lord, what a time that was, what good times we all had then, before the old war."

QUESTIONS

1. Lessing says that "writing this article is difficult because it has to be 'true'." Why does she put quotation marks around "true"? Why would it be more difficult to write something that has to be "true" than, as she says, stories that "don't have to be 'true'?" How has she tried to make this sketch "true"? How well do you think she has succeeded?
2. Find facts about Lessing's father that are repeated or referred to more than once. Why does she repeat them?
3. Lessing says that it was difficult for her to write about her father because she "knew him when his best years were over." What other things about those "best years" might she have wanted to know that she apparently didn't?
4. If a stranger were writing about Lessing's father but had the same facts available, might the account differ in any ways? Explain.
5. Compare Lessing's depiction of her father with Breslin's depiction of Tip O'Neill (p. 700). Are the two men similar in any ways? Do the methods of characterization have anything in common? How are they different?

ELIZABETH HARDWICK

Jane Carlyle

Jane Carlyle died suddenly one day, in her carriage. She was sixty-five years old and had been married to Thomas Carlyle for forty years. It seems, as we look back on it, that at the moment of her death the idea was born that she had somehow been the victim of Carlyle's neglect. He thought as much and set out upon a large remorse, something like the "penance" of Dr. Johnson, although without the consolations of religion. The domestic torment the Carlyles endured in their long marriage is of a particular opacity due to the naturalness of so much of it, to its origin in the mere strains of living. The conflicts were not of a remarkable kind and domestic discontent was always complicated by other problems of temperament and by the unnerving immensity of Carlyle's literary undertakings.

They were, first of all, persons who drifted in and out of unhappiness, within the course of a single day. Nothing in their lives was easy, and so at one minute they were weary of the yoke and the next quite pleased with themselves. From their letters we can see an extraordinary closeness that took in all aspects of life, the literary as well as the domestic. A lot of letters went back and forth between them because of their pressing need for communication with each other. Except for a period in middle life their vexations were almost worth the pleasure of the telling of them.

They were very much a union. He is Mr. Carlyle and she is Mrs. Carlyle, entirely. Perhaps it is not quite accurate to say that theirs was *the* Victorian marriage; it was an imaginative confrontation from the beginning to the end. The center of the marriage was Carlyle's lifelong, unremitting agony of literary creation, done at home, every pain and despair and hope underfoot. Her genius, in her letters and in her character, was to turn his gigantism into a sort of domestic comedy, made out of bedbugs, carpets, soundproof rooms, and drunken serving girls. Just as the form and style of Carlyle's works set no limit upon themselves, so she sets limits upon everything. His grandiosities are accomplished in the midst of her minute particulars.

The bare facts of the French Revolution, of the life of Cromwell, and all the others were an exhausting accretion. And the style was also an exhaustion: strange, brilliant, the very words outlandish, outsized, epical. Carlyle had an exalted idea of his mission and of the power of literature. He thought of the writer as "an accident in society," one who "wanders like a wild Ishmaelite, in a world of which he is the spiritual light, either the guidance or the misguidance! Certainly the Art of Writing is the most miraculous of all things man has devised. Odin's *Runes* were the first form of the work of a Hero." The capital letter and the exclamation point are Carlyle's characteristic punctuation. Jane Carlyle's signature is the quotation mark of mimicry. Thus the two natures stand in balance, breathing in the coal dust of London, suffering the insomnias, the dyspeptic cruelties of their porridge and potato diets, the colds and headaches, the wrung nerves of two strong and yet precariously organized persons.

Jane Carlyle's letters, published after her death, are more brilliant, lively, and enduring than all except the best novels of the period. She was so interesting a woman, such a good conversationalist, such an engaging storyteller that everyone was always urging her to write novels. Carlyle himself liked to say she had surrendered her own talents in order to help him to have his great career. Among her friends in London there were a number of women writers. Professional activity was not unthinkable or even especially daring—and she was childless and he was busy as Thor up in his study. Imagining Mrs. Carlyle as a novelist is a natural extension of her letters with their little portraits of ordinary people, their gift with anecdote, their fluent delight in the common events of the day. But she lacks ambition and need—the psychic need for a creation to stand outside herself. One of the most interesting things about Jane

Carlyle is the predominance of the social in her character. Not Society in any sense of wordly advancement—it was on the ground of the "new aristocracy" that she later suffered wounds from her husband.

The "social" with Jane Carlyle was her interest in the daily, in her chores and friends—her love of gossip and her anxious house-keeping. She was born to live in London, having the sort of nature that took naturally to the city's complaints of exhaustion, headache, and insomnia. Still, there was a good deal of the Scotch Calvinist in both of the Carlyles, and Scotland itself, their birth and youth there, was very much a part of their character. Jane Carlyle kept from her provincial background a large store of Scottish witticisms and phrases and a feeling for the eccentric and unexpected in ordinary persons. She had something of Dickens's eye for the flow of characters in and out of her house, in the street, and also his ear for their characteristic emblems of speech. Dickens was much impressed with her and said when she died, "None of the writing women come near her at all."

The fact of the Carlyles' marriage to each other is somewhat unusual. Jane Welsh was an only child. Her father had been a doctor and she and her widowed mother were important in the town of Haddington. She was thought to be clever and was used to having her own way. Carlyle's family was poor and strict; his father was cold but somehow impressive and the children in the family turned out well. Carlyle himself was awkward, intense, and always special because of his large intellectual powers and ambitious concentration. His powers of mind were the stone upon which the lines and curves of an extravagant, eccentric nature were cut. A description of him, at the University of Edinburgh, before he met Jane Welsh: "Young Carlyle was distinguished at that time by the same peculiarities that still mark his character—sarcasm, irony, extravagance of sentiment, and a strong tendency to undervalue others, combined, however, with great kindness of heart and great simplicity of manners. His external figure . . . was tall, slender, awkward, not apparently very vigorous . . . His speech copious and bizarre."

Jane Welsh's acceptance of Carlyle seemed to rest upon her clear sense of his intellectual worth. She procrastinated, let him know her serious and most capricious doubts. Her letters at this point are impudent, and she seems to feel the courage of her own eligibility and his much smaller claim to consideration. "I love you, I have told you so a hundred times . . . but I am not *in love* with you; that is to say, my love for you is not a passion which overclouds my judgment and absorbs all my regard for myself and others . . . I conceive it a duty which every one owes to society not to throw up that station into which Providence has assigned him; and having this conviction I could not marry into a station inferior to my own . . . You

and I keeping house in Craigenputtock! . . . Nothing but your ignorance of the place saves you from the imputation of insanity for
admitting such a thought . . ."

Yet she did accept him and she did go to live in the wilds of
Craigenputtock for six years. Carlyle was in no sense established
when they married; she gave over immediately to her own conviction his great worth. Jane was not sentimental like Dorothy Wordsworth. From the first she began in her letters and her conversation
the amused creation of Carlyle at home. As a writer he was self-
created, like Zeus, but the living person, gruff, self-absorbed, driven,
intolerant, comes to life mostly from her London letters. But perhaps she never got over the feeling that she had, in choosing Carlyle, undertaken an original adventure for which credit was due her.
She, for all her wit, was conscious of playing a great role in the creation of Carlyle. Even she was a sort of collaborator in his sacred
mission.

The Carlyles are very contemporary. Perhaps the fact that they
were childless gives a sort of provisional, trial-and-error aspect to the
arrangements of their lives. They set themselves up in Cheyne Row
in a respectable and yet properly bohemian fashion. Things were
interesting and suitable, but not at all yearning for grandeur or
luxury. After her spoiled youth, her brilliance at study, the high
place she held among her acquaintances, *this* is what she came to
stand on in a private way: properly, if not rigidly, running the
house with one servant and sometimes none; prudence with
finances, visits to make an appeal to the Tax Collector ("Where
was Mr. Carlyle?" they wanted to know); cleaning, dusting, chasing
bedbugs, sewing, supervising redecorations.

She did these things with a nervous, anxious sort of Scotch
efficiency that never lost some lingering astonishment that such
were actually her duties. The tone of her letters is guarded and her
feelings are always masked by the wit and the good breeding and
pride that made a direct plea for sympathy impossible; it is not easy
to judge the true significance of her personal outbursts. After spending an evening mending Mr. Carlyle's trousers, she writes, "Being
an only child I never wished to sew men's trousers—no, never." To
these duties her charms, the enjoyment people took in her company, her own *fame* as a special person added much. She was
admired, treasured, and had her own group of confidants that
included Mazzini and the wild novelist Geraldine Jewsbury. But,
with some naturalness and a great deal of inevitability, Carlyle took,
as a day-to-day matter, her charms and wit for granted. It was still
his right, his need to scream when the piano started up in the next
house, to live out at home the appalling strains of his labors.

His health and his temper were fearful; her health and her
tongue were awful. A typical letter:

Carlyle returned from his travels very bilious and continues very bilious up to this hour. The amount of bile that he does bring home to me, in these cases, is something "awfully grand!" Even through that deteriorating medium he could not but be struck with a "certain admiration" at the immensity of needlework I had accomplished in his absence, in the shape of chair-covers, sofa-covers, window curtains, &c., &c., and all the other manifest improvements into which I had put my whole genius and industry, and so little money as was hardly to be conceived!

In the letters it is all turned into a comedy. Carlyle decided that the exhausting redecoration of the house was not enough, that he needed a work place on the top, a room built on the roof. "Up went the carpets my own hands had nailed down, in rushed the troops of incarnate demons, bricklayers, joiners, whitewashers . . . My husband himself at the sight of the uproar he had raised, was all but wringing his hands and tearing his hair like some German wizard servant who had learned magic enough to make the broomstick carry water for him, but had not the counter spell to stop it." She ends her letter with, "Alas, one can make fun of all this on paper; but in practice it is anything but fun, I can assure you. There is no help for it, however; a man cannot hold his genius as a sinecure."

It is almost ignoble to inspect these domestic letters with anything except gratitude for the intense, flowing picture they give us of a life, for the brilliance of the social history and the way the house, 5 Cheyne Row, becomes a Victorian treasure, itself a character. The value of Jane Carlyle's letters lies very much in their rendering of the prosaic scenery in which a truly staggering Victorian energy like Carlyle's had its existence. *Frederick the Great* took thirteen years in the writing ("Would Frederick had died when a baby," Jane said.); *Oliver Cromwell* burned up four years. This was the way it went on throughout Carlyle's life. His discipline and gospel of Work had its fearful apotheosis in his own practice. This is altogether different from nailing carpets and shaking out curtains.

Jane Carlyle's letters have something subversive in them; the tone is very far from the reverent modes that came naturally to Dorothy Wordsworth. Both the journals of the poet's sister and the letters of the wife of the great prophet are ways of preserving and discovering self-identity. It is easy to imagine that the steady literary labors going on around the two women made a kind of demand upon them; a supreme value attached to sitting at the desk with a pen rushing over the pages. Both had gifts of an uncommon nature, but the casual, spontaneous form of their writings is itself the ultimate risk. We are not *expected* a hundred and fifty years later to have them in our hands, to read them. It is only by the luckiest chance that they survive, and no doubt many letters were lost. Jane's letters might not have been collected, but *The French Revolution* would certainly have stepped forth; *Recollections of a Tour Made in Scot-*

land might have perished, while *The Excursion* was not written for
obscurity.

Jane Carlyle's letters have very much the character of a social
necessity for her. They are meant to delight, to preserve and pass on
her unique way of detailing the happenings of the day. They are
pictures of things and people, imitations, mimicry, autobiography of
a narrow sort. Most of the ones we have were written to family
members and to very close old friends, usually living in Scotland.
The largest number are to Carlyle himself. There is a sameness to
them because the tone is established early and continued long; it is
familiar, light, personal within limits. It tells of an attempt to live
in the midst of things in London, to manage their feelings for each
other, their uncertain temperaments, their unsteady nerves, his work
—to make of all this a life reasonably plain and undemanding and
yet worthy of their odd and valuable natures.

One of the things that made life hard for the Carlyles was that
they shared alike so many burdens of body and soul, their complaints ring out in unison and, of course, there is no one to answer.
Their hypochondria and neurasthenia are scandalous. Jane had
headaches, neuralgia that seldom gave up its dominance, insomnia
raging like a train through the whole night, indigestions, vomiting,
aches and pains of every kind. Harriet Martineau observed that
Mrs. Carlyle always had eight attacks of influenza each winter; she
was frail and exhausted, pale, and yet could be roused from invalid-
ism by interesting events. Carlyle had headaches, insomnia, dyspep-
sia, indigestion, melancholy, ill-temper, irritability. They took an
enormous number of pills and purges, and it appears that Mrs. Carlyle in middle life became addicted to morphine. This seems to
have caused some of her vomitings and faintings. During her most
suffering years in the early 1850s she was deranged with depression, jealousy, suicidal feelings. He too was scarcely ever free from
depression and irritability and was not able to put any kind of rein
on the flow into his mind of extreme opinions and the flow from
his tongue of the same opinions. During his later years Carlyle
exhorted mankind to a sacrificial life of Work and heroic, manly
Silence. Mazzini noted that Carlyle's love affair with Silence "was
only platonic."

There is very little in Jane's letters about Carlyle's ideas or about
the actual matter of his books. And, of course, he is all Idea, caught
up in a shifting Heroic and Prophetic tendency that finally engulfs
him in the unworthy authoritarianism and depressing angers and
superiorities of the *Latter-Day Pamphlets*. He scorns Democracy,
suffrage. A visit to a reformed prison brings out a hailstorm of hateful pellets of abuse. "These abject, ape, wolf, ox, imp and other
diabolic-animal specimens of humanity, who of the very gods could
ever have commanded them by love? A collar round the neck, and a

cart-whip flourished over the back; these, in a just and steady human hand, were what the gods would have appointed them . . ." John Stuart Mill broke with Carlyle over the violence of his feelings and recommendations, and this work received a bad press generally.

As Carlyle grew older he became more and more aggressive and ill-natured about his contemporaries. His own reputation suffered from his increasing lack of generosity and openness and his peevish self-importance. Visitors to Cheyne Row left in anger and disappointment. Jane is not known to have differed with his opinions, and Julian Symonds in his biography of Carlyle has a distressing picture of a woman who did not combat his warped inclinations on the intellectual level, but grew rather more privately and emotionally bitter and unhappy and crushing to him over personal matters. "There is a story that, in his [Carlyle's] last years, a group of people were discussing in his presence the silliness and blind adulation by which great men's wives often made their husbands look foolish. 'In that respect,' he said, 'I have been most mercifully spared.' "

Indeed Jane Carlyle does not seem interested in the passionate concern for the nature of society's arrangements and values—the flame that burned so madly in her husband. Her friendship with Mazzini was intense. She gave him a lock of her hair and confided some of her complaints about Carlyle, but she did not take seriously any of his plans and hopes for Italy. She had narrowed her sufferings and disappointments down to some private, nagging unfulfillment.

What was the trouble? It is very difficult to set the thing out with any certainty. The incredible question of Carlyle's impotence has no possibility of ever being laid to rest. Froude, the historian-disciple of Carlyle's and the one to whom was entrusted the printing of Jane's letters and Carlyle's strange remorseful memorial to her, seemed to have liked Carlyle a good deal less than he knew. The man was no sooner gone than Froude moved in on the papers, started the biography, and also dealt Carlyle's reputation so many slashes and lacerations it never recovered. Froude said that "Carlyle ought never to have married." The accusation survives, gathering later fuel from Frank Harris's assertion that a doctor examined Jane in her forties and found her *virgo intacta*. Jane is supposed to have told the story about their wedding night—that when he fumbled, she burst out laughing and he "got out of bed with one scornful word, 'Woman!' and went into the next room; he never came back to my bed again."

Carlyle's nature is so confident and expansive it is hard to believe him somehow blocked and incapacitated in this way. Their letters to each other are filled with exuberant appreciation and with an obsessive dependence on the very presence of the other, a condition not likely to lend itself to forty years of chastity and distance. The thing that brought about the pitiful misery and bitterness of the marriage was a matter of at least a secondary sexual nature—Jane's jealousy and fury over Carlyle's friendship with Lady Ashburton. That this jealousy may not have been sexual did not diminish the profound pain of it. It appears that it was in the end Carlyle's insensitivity to her wishes that drove Jane Carlyle into a debilitating madness of rage and depression, morphine and pill-swallowing.

Lady Ashburton was a powerful, intelligent, rich woman who liked Carlyle much better than she liked Jane. She made a great fuss over him, invited them to her country house, The Grange, and called him "her Prophet." At Lady Ashburton's, Carlyle was the star. He who had been accustomed to protesting social life with the complaint that "No health lies for me in that," or "My Welfare is possible only in solitude," suddenly and surprisingly changed his tune and was ever ready to attend functions, long visits, do any bidding. He had never valued idleness, riches, or relaxation, but now he seemed to find the comfortable luxuries of the town and country houses very much to his liking. Authoritarianism and a regard for privilege were growing on him also, like gray hairs he hardly noticed.

Lady Harriet was six years younger than Jane, rather large and utterly, bewilderingly confident of her own worth. She was moderately unconventional but not scarred by a rash of self-examination or complicated modesties and judgments. After Carlyle's acquaintance with her was established, she began to pursue him, to flatter him, to feel quite an urgent need to include him in her circle and in her activities. Lord Ashburton also accepted Carlyle with a good deal of warmth.

Lady Ashburton was not so greatly charmed by Jane. Jane had been adored at home and was much appreciated in London among writers and friends, but her style and tone were not comfortable for the ladies of the aristocracy. She was too ironical and humorous, too quick to identify with a mocking phrase; and most of all, her wit was a sort of private gem. Its sparkle depended upon everyone's understanding the shape of it, the voice. Lady Ashburton was friendly and correct with Jane but it didn't work. Also the society at the Ashburtons', where Carlyle was soon glowing in the attention he received, was much richer and in every way different from the kind of life and purpose Carlyle had taught Jane to value.

The worst of it was that Carlyle had suddenly turned away from his old notions—the Scotch Calvinist ones that had united them. He no longer felt bound by the dogmas of Work, Duty and Spiritual Strength. He now was on the road leading to the New Aristocracy. Lady Ashburton was a good starting point. When she summoned him he would answer, "Sunday, yes, my Beneficent, it shall be then; the dark man shall again see the daughter of the sun, for a little while; and be illuminated, as if he were not dark."

Between 1846 and Lady Ashburton's death in 1857 the Carlyles' life was distressingly unhappy. Their great marriage, the collaboration of two superior, tortured souls, became a nest of miseries, discontents, frustrations. Jane Carlyle's tolerant irony deserted her. She could not bear Carlyle's indifference to her feelings, his neglect of her wishes. It had been bad enough when his work made him demanding and overwhelming, but to have him take pleasure and find relaxation in company other than hers was unendurable. Still, so extreme is her emotion that one can only feel this particular neglect had come to stand for feelings much greater than the friendly, more or less harmless claims of Lady Ashburton.

It seems that all Jane Carlyle's efforts were dramatically brought into question by Lady Ashburton, by her riches, her arrogance, her birth. All of the carpets, the bedbugs, the papering and hammering, the creation of Cheyne Row to encircle and house Carlyle's needs, had been neither the pure expression of Jane's own nature nor a claim, as it seemed, upon his loyalty. For whom had she labored? Running the house with one somewhat shaky servant had been a triumph; the funny Scotch girls were *her* material, and her stories about them are among the best things in her letters. But her dealings with them show some of the defects and difficulties of her character. Jane Carlyle needed a great deal of care and concern herself. Her disasters with servants were bravely and humorously endured, but her way with them was a mirror showing her deepest, hidden nature—that of a clever, spoiled, and expectant only child.

When a servant appeared she was imagined to be the vessel of goodness, joy, trust; the poor creature was to give the exalted love, consideration, capability, attention, leisure, and comfort Jane Carlyle secretly felt her nature was entitled to receive. "She is by far the most loveable servant I ever had; a gentle, pretty, sweet-looking creature, with innocent winning ways." This is the way the hope rises at the beginning, time and again, but it soon sinks, and the reality are beasts, drunkards, thieves, with no knowledge of cooking or cleaning. With all of this longing never deserting her, Jane Carlyle could feel that in managing to live, to create their lives, at great pains to herself, she was doing something noble and important. Especially because it was she, never meant for it, who was the origin, the mover of it. She had endured Carlyle's bearishness, his grumbling, his fantastic consuming labors, his refusal of practical affairs. She had never felt very capable at the things she learned to do; they were against the grain.

She had sacrificed something—it was not altogether clear—in vain for Carlyle, and that discovery, if such it was, accounted for her exaggerated frenzy over Lady Ashburton. Some of the needs working on him she was not sufficiently knowledgeable about or sensitive to. (Her old indifference to the matter, while treasuring the producer.) Carlyle felt an increasing and insistent wish to shine and to find unplowed souls to shine upon. His ideas and programs were running out. He was a prophet rather worried about the next prophecy. Also in a sad way his own madness was being transformed into character. He was becoming inseparable from his defects and distortions. The projects he set out upon with Lady Ashburton and her friends were small and, even if worthy, retrograde in the light of the larger issues he was turning away from. His projects needed only money; he did not ask that his new friends remake their lives or redeem society. The London Library, new parks, that sort of thing. Members of the aristocracy should "bestir themselves" to fight off the stabs of the lazy rabble at the door.

Carlyle, morose at home, gladdened in the opulent warmth of Bath House, the Ashburtons' house in the city. But for Jane the visits were trying; they created an unease in her spirits and apparently a lowering sense of being an appendage, *there* but not at all necessary. When she showed her distress that invitations were accepted without her agreement, visits were made by her husband alone, even when she was feeling ill and needed him at home. Carlyle became vexed, insensitive to the depth of her unhappiness, or merely willfully indifferent to it. He would write, "Oh, my Jeannie! My own true Jeannie! Into what courses are we tending?" But he would go to the Ashburtons' in any case and remain for five days. For a time he and Lady Ashburton corresponded in secret because of the hysterical frenzy of feeling into which Mrs. Carlyle had somehow thrown herself.

It all seems negligible, out of proportion, one of those trivial points upon which marital rages ponderously come to rest. Still, the angers and quarrels darkened their lives. The sadness is that, even with a clever and uniquely attractive woman like Jane Carlyle, a conviction of having sacrificed only to be undervalued drove her to despair and pulled Carlyle along with her.

At this point she began to keep a melancholy little journal. It is bitter, freely complaining about just those indignities the letters approached with a guarded amusement. There is a measure of vindictiveness in the entries, some eye toward revenge or perhaps only toward the instruction of Carlyle in her true feelings. "That eternal Bath House. I wonder how many thousand miles Mr. C. has walked between here and there, putting it all together; setting up always another milestone and anchor betwixt him and me . . . When I first noticed that heavy yellow house . . . how far was I from dreaming that through years and years I should carry every stone's weight of it on my heart."

Mrs. Carlyle's sudden death plunged her husband into a deep grief. He lived on and on, for sixteen years, always melancholy, lonely, and preoccupied with his lost love and her rare qualities. He saw her journal of the Ashburton years. (Lady Ashburton died in 1857, ten years before Jane. The acute and pointed misery abated, but the general bitterness remained, by now hardened with illness, depression, and the thickening of angry feelings on both sides.) He read over Jane's letters. Remorse struck Carlyle—a strange, repeating, beating, insisting remorse. He treasured the brilliant letters and saw the delight in them and also the undercurrent of breathless effort she had made to create their lives.

His idea seemed to be that she had misunderstood the Lady Ashburton business. "Oh, if I could but see her for five minutes to assure her that I had really cared for her throughout all that! But she never knew it, she never knew it." He collected and edited her letters and gave them at his death to Froude for publication; and he wrote his odd, almost senile, remorseful memorial to her in *Reminiscences*.

He sat down to write, and all the bafflements of Jane Carlyle's place in the nature of things immediately and urgently confronted him. It was not the outlines of her life—that he knew or thought he knew from their long marriage. No, it was much deeper, more puzzling, more to the point. When he started the composition it was not as a family treasure, a book of memory; instead it was to be a real book. What, then, was she that might have a claim on the world's attention by way of print, a sort of biography? Even he could not feel it was as his wife alone that she had her eminence; nor could it be for her highly original and pleasing personal qualities. On the other hand, she was certainly not Schiller, nor even his friend—the preacher Edward Irving or the theologian John Sterling —about both of whom he wrote.

In the end the riddle is never solved and the work is both public and private. It is an ode to a lost love and a curiously, traditionally organized presentation of a life. The beginning strikes a classical note, mixed with worry and compositional confusion about his intentions. "In the ancient country town of Haddington, July 14, 1801, there was born to a lately wedded pair, not natives of the place but already reckoned among the best class of people there, a little daughter whom they named Jane Baillie Welsh, and whose subsequent and final name (her own common signature for many years), was *Jane Welsh Carlyle*, and now stands, now that she is mine in death only, on her and her father's tombstone in the Abbey Kirk of that town."

The work is filled with guilty hyperbole, yet he takes on his guilt so openly, with such a manly fullness that we see it is one of those guilts happily assumed as a gratification to the ego. Still, he must decide what Jane was, what she had given up to be his alone, and he is soon placing her in his thoughts above George Eliot and George Sand in creative powers. With this exaggeration and lack of precision, the excellence of the letters fades. They have not been defined, thought about, carefully placed.

When Jane Carlyle was cleaning and sweeping and keeping the

accounts within discreet limits she certainly did not set a price upon her actions. But, of course, there was a hidden price. It was that in exchange for her work, her dedication, her special if somewhat satirical charms, Carlyle would, as an instance, not go out to Lady Ashburton when she would rather he stayed at home. This is the unspoken contract of a wife and her works. In the long run wives are to be paid in a peculiar coin—consideration for their feelings. And it usually turns out this is an enormous, unthinkable inflation few men will remit, or if they will, only with a sense of being overcharged.

It is sad to think of Jane Carlyle's last years. Neurasthenia accounted for a lot of her torments in the middle of the night. But she has such gaiety and reasonableness that we are scarcely prepared for the devastation that swept over her as a result of feeling undervalued, put-upon, refused the consolations of a grateful husband. Once when she told Carlyle that she had, at a certain moment, thought of leaving him, he replied, "I don't know that I would have missed you. I was very busy just then with Cromwell." The raging productivity of the Victorians shattered nerves and punctured stomachs, but it was a thing noble, glorious, awesome in itself.

Jane Carlyle's subversive irony and her ambivalance make her the most interesting of the wives we know about in this period. It is very risky to think of her as a failed novelist or as a "sacrificed" writer in some other form. All we can look for are the openings she —and Dorothy Wordsworth, also—came upon, the little alleys for self-display, the routes found that are really a way of dominating the emotional material of daily life. The chanciness of it all, the modesty, the intermittent aspect of the production—there is pathos in that. In the end what strikes one as the greatest personal loss of these private writing careers is that the work could not truly build for the women a bulwark against the sufferings of neglect and the humiliations of lovelessness. The Victorian men, perverse as many of them are, were spared these pinches of inadequacy, faltering confidence, and fears of uselessness.

JANET FLANNER (GENÊT)

Isadora[1]

In the summer of 1926, like a ghost from the grave, Isadora Duncan began dancing again in Nice. Two decades before, her art, animated by her extraordinary public personality, came as close to founding an aesthetic renaissance as American morality would

---

1. Isadora Duncan, 1878–1927, American dancer.

allow, and the provinces especially had a narrow escape. But in the postwar European years her body, whose Attic splendor once brought Greece to Kansas and Kalamazoo, was approaching its half-century mark. Her spirit was still green as a bay tree, but her flesh was worn, perhaps by the weight of laurels. She was the last of the trilogy of great female personalities our century cherished. Two of them, Duse and Bernhardt, had already gone to their elaborate national tombs. Only Isadora Duncan, the youngest, the American, remained wandering the foreign earth.

No one had taken Isadora's place in her own country and she was not missed. Of that fervor for the classic dance which she was the first to bring to a land bred on "Turkey in the Straw," beneficial signs remained from which she alone had not benefited. Eurythmic movements were appearing in the curriculums of girls' schools. Vestal virgins formed a frieze about the altar fire of Saint Marks-in-the-Bouwerie on Sabbath afternoons. As a cross between gymnasiums and God, Greek-dance camps flourished in the Catskills, where under the summer spruce, metaphysics and muscles were welded in an Ilissan hocus-pocus for the female young.[2] Lisa, one of her first pupils, was teaching in the studio of the Théâtre des Champs-Elysées. Isadora's sister Elizabeth, to whom Greek might still be Greek if it had not been for Isadora, had a toga school in Berlin. Her brother Raymond, who operated a modern craft school in Paris, wore sandals and Socratic robes as if they were a family coat of arms. Isadora alone had neither sandals nor school. Most grandiose of all her influences, Diaghilev's Russian Ballet—which ironically owed its national rebirth to the inspiration of Isadora, then dancing with new terpsichorean ideals in Moscow—was still seasoning as an exotic spectacle in London and Monte Carlo. Only Isadora, animator of all these forces, had become obscure. Only she, with her heroic sculptural movements, had dropped by the wayside, where she lay inert like one of those beautiful battered pagan tombs that still line the Sacred Way between Eleusis and the city of the Parthenon.

As an artist, Isadora made her appearance in our plain and tasteless republic before the era of the half-nude revue, before the discovery of what is now called our Native Literary School, even before the era of the celluloid sophistication of the cinema, which by its ubiquity does so much to unite the cosmopolitanisms of Terre Haute and New York. What America now has, and gorges on in the way of sophistication, it then hungered for. Repressed by generations of Puritanism, it longed for bright, visible, and blatant beauty presented in a public form the simple citizenry could understand. Isadora appeared as a half-clothed Greek. . . .

2. Probably an allusion to dancing by the river Ilissus near ancient Athens. Isadora Duncan went to Greece and tried to recreate the kind of ritual or choric dancing that the ancients may have done at Ilissus and elsewhere.

A Paris *couturier* once said woman's modern freedom in dress is largely due to Isadora. She was the first artist to appear uncinctured, barefooted, and free. She arrived like a glorious bounding Minerva in the midst of a cautious corseted decade. The clergy, hearing of (though supposedly without ever seeing) her bare calf, denounced it as violently as if it had been golden. Despite its longings, for a moment America hesitated, Puritanism rather than poetry coupling lewd with nude in rhyme. But Isadora, originally from California and by then from Berlin, Paris, and other points, arrived bearing her gifts as a Greek. She came like a figure from the Elgin marbles. The world over, and in America particularly, Greek sculpture was recognized to be almost notorious for its purity. The overpowering sentiment for Hellenic culture, even in the unschooled United States, silenced the outcries. Isadora had come as antique art and with such backing she became a cult.

Those were Isadora's great years. Not only in New York and Chicago but in the smaller, harder towns, when she moved across the stage, head reared, eyes mad, scarlet kirtle flying to the music of the "Marseillaise," she lifted from their seats people who had never left theater seats before except to get up and go home. Whatever she danced to, whether it was France's revolutionary hymn, or the pure salon passion of Chopin's waltzes, or the unbearable heat of Brahms' German mode, she conspired to make the atmosphere Greek, fusing *Zeitgeists* and national sounds into one immortal Platonic pantomime.

Thus she inspired people who had never been inspired in their lives before, and to whom inspiration was exhilarating, useless, and unbecoming. Exalted at the concert hall by her display of Greek beauty, limbs, and drapes which though they were two thousand years old she seemed to make excitingly modern, her followers, dazzled, filled with Phidianisms, went home to Fords, big hats, and the theory of Bull Moose, the more real items of their progressive age.

Dancing appeals less to the public than the other two original theatrical forms, drama and opera (unless, like the Russian Ballet, dancing manages to partake of all three). Nevertheless, Isadora not only danced but was demanded all over America and Europe. On the Continent she was more widely known than any other American of that decade, including Woodrow Wilson and excepting only Chaplin and Fairbanks, both of whom, via a strip of celluloid, could penetrate to remote hamlets without ever leaving Hollywood. But Isadora went everywhere in the flesh. She danced before kings and peasants. She danced from the Pacific to London, from Petrograd to the Black Sea, from Athens to Paris and Berlin.

She penetrated to the Georgian states of the Caucasus, riding third-class amid fleas and disease, performing in obscure halls before yokels and princes whom she left astonished, slightly enlightened, and somehow altered by the vision. For thirty years her life was more exciting and fantastic than anything Zola or Defoe ever fabricated for their heroines. Her companions were the great public talent of our generation—Duse, D'Annunzio, Bakst, Bernhardt, Picabia, Brancusi, Anatole France, Comtesse Anna de Noailles, Sardou, Ellen Terry.

Three of the greatest sculptors of her day at this time took Isadora's body as a permanent model and influence on their work though, alas, left no record in marble. Maillol alone made over five hundred drawings of Isadora dancing to Beethoven's Seventh Symphony; Rodin followed her all over Europe and literally made thousands of drawings, many still in the Musée Rodin in Paris. One of his most beautiful *gouaches*, now in the Metropolitan Museum, is *La Naissance d'un Vase Grecque*, in which he used Isadora's torso as his inspiration. Bourdelle also used Isadora as the main typical figure in his Théâtre des Champs-Elysées frescoes. These artists made the likeness of Isadora's limbs and the loveliness of her small face immortal. This was the great, gay, successful period of life. Her friends ran the gamut from starving poets down to millionaires. She was prodigal of herself, her art, illusions, work, emotions, and everybody's funds. She spent fortunes. After the war was over in France, her Sunday-night suppers in the Rue de la Pompe were banquets where guests strolled in, strolled out, and from low divans supped principally on champagne and strawberry tarts, while Isadora, barely clad in chiffon robes, rose when the spirit moved her to dance exquisitely. Week after week came obscure people whose names she never even knew. They were like moths. She once gave a house party that started in Paris, gathered force in Venice, and culminated weeks later on a houseboat on the Nile. She was a nomad de luxe.

In order to promulgate her pedagogic theories of beauty and education for the young, she legally adopted and supported some thirty or forty children during her life, one group being the little Slavs who afterward danced in Soviet Russia. During her famous season at the New York Century Theatre where she gave a classic Greek cycle, *Oedipus Rex, Antigone,* and the like, she bought up every Easter lily in Manhattan to decorate the theater the night she opened in Berlioz's *L'Enfance du Christ,* which was her Easter program. The lilies, whose perfume suffocated the spectators, cost two thousand dollars. Isadora had, at the moment, three thousand dollars to her name. And at midnight, long after all good lily-selling florists were in bed, she gave a champagne supper. It cost the other thousand.

Isadora, who had an un-American genius for art, for organizing love, maternity, politics, and pedagogy on a great personal scale, had also an un-American genius for grandeur.

After the lilies faded, Isadora and her school sat amid their luggage on the pier where the ship was about to sail for France. They had neither tickets nor money. But they had a classic faith in fate and a determination to go back to Europe, where art was understood. Just before the boat sailed, there appeared a schoolteacher. Isadora had never seen her before. The teacher gave Isadora the savings of years and Isadora sailed away. Herself grand, she could inspire grandeur in others, a tragic and tiring gift. There were always schoolteachers and lilies in Isadora's life.

Those three summer programs which Isadora gave in 1926 at her studio in Nice were her last performances on earth. At the end of the next summer she was dead. One of the soirees was given with the concordance of Leo Tecktonius, the pianist, and the other two with Jean Cocteau, who accompanied her dancing with his spoken verse. In all three performances her art was seen to have changed. She treaded the boards but little, she stood almost immobile or in slow splendid steps with slow splendid arms moved to music, seeking, hunting, finding. Across her face, tilting this way and that, fled the mortal looks of tragedy, knowledge, love, scorn, pain. Posing through the works of Wagner, through the tales of Dante, through the touching legend of St. Francis feeding crumbs and wisdom to his birds, Isadora was still great. By an economy (her first) she had arrived at elimination. As if the movements of dancing had become too redundant for her spirit, she had saved from dancing only its shape.

In one of her periodic fits of extravagant poverty and although needing the big sum offered, she once refused to dance in Wanamaker's Auditorium, disdaining for her art such a "scene of suspenders." She refused to appear in certain Continental theaters because they contained restaurants where dining might distract the spectators from her art. She early refused (though she and her family were starving in Berlin) to dance at the Wintergarten for one thousand gold marks a night because there were animal acts on the bill. During the worst of her final financial predicaments in Paris, when few theaters were offering her anything at all, she refused to dance at the Théâtre des Champs-Elysées because it was a music hall. Yet her image in sculpture adorned the theater's façade, where Bourdelle had chiseled her likeness for all times and passers-by. She talked vaguely of consenting to dance in Catalonia. To anyone who knew her it seemed natural that Isadora would like to dance in a castle in Spain.

The lack of money, which never worried Isadora as much as it anguished her devoted friends, became more acute during the last years of her life. Nevertheless she refused a legacy of over a quarter of a million francs from the estate of her stormy young husband, Yessenine, the Russian revolutionary poet whom she had married late and unhappily. At the worst of her final picturesque poverty, when, as Isadora gallantly declared, she hardly knew where the next bottle of champagne was coming from (champagne was the only libation she loved), it was decided by her friends that she should write her memoirs. At this time she was living in a small studio hotel in the Rue Delambre, behind the Café du Dôme in Paris. Isadora's handwriting was characteristic; it was large, handsome, illegible, with two or three words to a line and four or five lines to a page. During her authorship the scantly scribbled pages accumulated like white leaves, left to drift over her littered studio floor. Then, as in all the frequent crises in her life, her friends rallied around her with scenes, jealousies, memories, quarrels, recriminations, good cases of wine, fine conversation, threats of farewell, new leases of affection—all the dramatics of loyalty, disillusion, hero worship, duty, fatigue, patience, and devotion which animated even her Platonic associations—all the humorous and painful disorders which genius, as if to prove its exceptional chemistry, catalyzes in commoner lives. The book, called *My Life*, finally appeared posthumously. It was to have furnished money for her to live.

As her autobiography made clear, an integral part of Isadora's nature died young when her two adored little children, Deirdre and Patrick, were tragically drowned in 1913 at Neuilly; the automobile in which they were waiting alone slipped its brakes and plunged into the Seine. The children had been the offspring of free unions, in which Isadora spiritedly believed. She believed, too, in polyandry and that each child thus benefited eugenically by having a different and carefully chosen father. She also attributed the loss of her third child, born the day war was declared, to what she called the curse of the machine. At the wild report that the Germans were advancing by motor on Paris, the old Bois de Boulogne gates were closed, her doctor and his automobile, amidst thousands of cars, were caught behind the grill, and by the time he arrived at her bedside it was too late. The child had been born dead. "Machines have been my enemy," she once said. "They killed my three children. Machines are the opposite of, since they are the invention of, man. Perhaps a machine will one day kill me."

In a moment of melancholy her friend Duse prophesied that Isadora would die like Jocasta. Both prophecies were fulfilled. On August 13, 1927, while driving on the Promenade des Anglais at Nice, Isadora Duncan met her death. She was strangled by her colored shawl, which became tangled in the wheel of the automobile.

A few days later in Paris great good-natured crowds had gathered in the Rue de Rivoli to watch the passing of the American Legion, then holding their initial postwar jollification and parade in France. By a solemn chance, what the crowd saw first, coming down the flag-strewn, gaily decorated thoroughfare, was the little funeral cortege of Isadora Duncan, treading its way to the cemetery of Père-Lachaise. Her coffin was covered by her famous purple dancing cape serving as a pall. On the back of the hearse, her family, though unsympathetic to her radical views, had loyally placed her most imposing floral tribute, a great mauve wreath from the Soviet Union with a banner that read *"Le Coeur de Russie Pleure Isadora."* Though she had once rented the Metropolitan Opera House to plead the cause of France before we went into the war, though she had given her Neuilly château as a hospital, though she had been a warm and active friend to France, the French government sent nothing. Nor did her great French friends, who had once eagerly drunk her fame and champagne, walk behind dead Isadora.

Of all the famous personages she had loved and known and who had hailed her genius and hospitality, only two went to Passy, where she lay in state, to sign the mourners' books—Yvette Guilbert and the actor Lugné-Poë. Hundreds of others scrawled their signatures on the pages, but they were casuals, common, loyal, unknown. Since Isadora was an American, it was regrettable that both the Paris American newspapers, the Paris *Herald* and the Chicago *Tribune*, busy doubtless with the gayer Legion matters, did not send reporters to follow her funeral cortege to its destination. Thus Americans next morning read that Isadora was followed to her grave by a pitiful handful. Only five carriages made up the official procession; but four thousand people—men, women, old, young, and of all nationalities—waited in the rain for the arrival of her body at Père-Lachaise.

Of earthly possessions, Isadora had little enough to leave. Still she had made a will—and forgot to sign it.

All her life Isadora had been a practical idealist. She had put into practice certain ideals of art, maternity, and political liberty which people prefer to read as theories on paper. Her ideals of human liberty were not unsimilar to those of Plato, to those of Shelley, to those of Lord Byron, which led him to die dramatically in Greece. All they gained for Isadora were the loss of her passport and the presence of the constabulary on the stage of the Indianapolis Opera House, where the chief of police watched for sedition in the movement of Isadora's knees.

Denounced as a Russian Bolshevik sympathizer, Isadora said she never even received a postal card from the Soviet government to give her news of her school which she housed in its capital. For Isadora had a fancy for facts. As she once told Boston it was tasteless and dull, so, when they were feting her in triumph in Moscow, she told the Communists she found them bourgeois. She had a wayward truthful streak in her and a fancy for paradox. "Everything antique Greek," she once said to an American woman friend, "is supposed to be noble. Did you ever notice how easily the Greeks became Roman?"

Great artists are tragic. Genius is too large, and it may have been grandeur that proved Isadora's undoing—the grandeur of temporary luxury, the grandeur of permanent ideals.

She was too expansive for personal salvation. She had thousands of friends. What she needed was an organized government. She had had checkbooks. Her scope called for a national treasury. It was not for nothing that she was hailed by her first name only, as queens have been, were they great Catherines or Marie Antoinettes.

As she stepped into the machine that was to be her final enemy, Isadora's last spoken words were, by chance, *"Je vais à la gloire!"*

JOHN DOS PASSOS

Art and Isadora

In San Francisco in eighteen seventyeight Mrs. Isadora O'Gorman Duncan, a highspirited lady with a taste for the piano, set about divorcing her husband, the prominent Mr. Duncan, whose behavior we are led to believe had been grossly indelicate; the whole thing made her so nervous that she declared to her children that she couldn't keep anything on her stomach but a little champagne and oysters; in the middle of the bitterness and recriminations of the family row,

into a world of gaslit boardinghouses kept by ruined southern belles and railroadmagnates and swinging doors and whiskery men nibbling cloves to hide the whiskey on their breaths and brass spittoons and four-wheel cabs and basques and bustles and long ruffled trailing skirts (in which lecturehall and concertroom, under the domination of ladies of culture, were the centers of aspiring life)

she bore a daughter whom she named after herself Isadora.

The break with Mr. Duncan and the discovery of his duplicity turned Mrs. Duncan into a bigoted feminist and an atheist, a passionate follower of Bob Ingersoll's lectures and writings; for God read Nature; for duty beauty, *and only man is vile*.

Mrs. Duncan had a hard struggle to raise her children in the love of beauty and the hatred of corsets and conventions and manmade laws. She gave piano-lessons, she did embroidery and knitted scarves and mittens.

The Duncans were always in debt.

The rent was always due.

Isadora's earliest memories were of wheedling grocers and butchers and landlords and selling little things her mother had made from door to door,

helping hand valises out of back windows when they had to jump their bills at one shabbygenteel boardinghouse after another in the outskirts of Oakland and San Francisco.

The little Duncans and their mother were a clan; it was the Duncans against a rude and sordid world. The Duncans weren't Catholics any more or Presbyterians or Quakers or Baptists; they were Artists.

When the children were quite young they managed to stir up interest among their neighbors by giving theatrical performances in a barn; the older girl Elizabeth gave lessons in society dancing; they were westerners, the world was a goldrush; they weren't ashamed of being in the public eye. Isadora had green eyes and reddish hair and a beautiful neck and arms. She couldn't afford lessons in conventional dancing, so she made up dances of her own.

They moved to Chicago. Isadora got a job dancing to *The Washington Post*[1] at the Masonic Temple Roof Garden for fifty a week. She danced at clubs. She went to see Augustin Daly and told him she'd discovered
the Dance
and went on in New York as a fairy in cheesecloth in a production of *Midsummer Night's Dream* with Ada Rehan.

The family followed her to New York. They rented a big room in Carnegie Hall, put mattresses in the corners, hung drapes on the wall and invented the first Greenwich Village studio.
They were never more than one jump ahead of the sheriff, they were always wheedling the tradespeople out of bills, standing the landlady up for the rent, coaxing handouts out of rich philistines.
Isadora arranged recitals with Ethelbert Nevin
danced to readings of Omar Khayyám for society women at Newport. When the Hotel Windsor burned they lost all their trunks and the very long bill they owed and sailed for London on a cattleboat
to escape the materialism of their native America.

In London at the British Museum
they discovered the Greeks;
the Dance was Greek.
Under the smoky chimneypots of London, in the sootcoated squares they danced in muslin tunics, they copied poses from Greek vases, went to lectures, artgalleries, concerts, plays, sopped up in a winter fifty years of Victorian culture.
Back to the Greeks.

Whenever they were put out of their lodgings for nonpayment of rent Isadora led them to the best hotel and engaged a suite and sent the waiters scurrying for lobster and champagne and fruits outofseason; nothing was too good for Artists, Duncans, Greeks;

1. *The Washington Post March* by John Philip Sousa (1854–1932).

and the nineties London liked her gall.

In Kensington and even in Mayfair she danced at parties in private houses,

the Britishers, Prince Edward down,
were carried away by her preraphaelite beauty
her lusty American innocence
her California accent.

After London, Paris during the great exposition of nineteen hundred. She danced with Loïe Fuller. She was still a virgin too shy to return the advances of Rodin the great master, completely baffled by the extraordinary behavior of Loïe Fuller's circle of crackbrained invert beauties. The Duncans were vegetarians, suspicious of vulgarity and men and materialism. Raymond made them all sandals.

Isadora and her mother and her brother Raymond went about Europe in sandals and fillets and Greek tunics

staying at the best hotels leading the Greek life of nature in a flutter of unpaid bills.

Isadora's first solo recital was at a theater in Budapest;

after that she was the diva, had a loveaffair with a leading actor; in Munich the students took the horses out of her carriage. Everything was flowers and handclapping and champagne suppers. In Berlin she was the rage.

With the money she made on her German tour she took the Duncans all to Greece. They arrived on a fishingboat from Ithaca. They posed in the Parthenon for photographs and danced in the Theater of Dionysus and trained a crowd of urchins to sing the ancient chorus from the *Suppliants* and built a temple to live in on a hill overlooking the ruins of ancient Athens, but there was no water on the hill and their money ran out before the temple was finished

so they had to stay at the Hôtel d'Angleterre and run up a bill there. When credit gave out they took their chorus back to Berlin and put on the *Suppliants* in ancient Greek. Meeting Isadora in her peplum marching through the Tiergarten at the head of her Greek boys marching in order all in Greek tunics, the kaiserin's horse shied,

and her highness was thrown.

Isadora was the vogue.

She arrived in St. Petersburg in time to see the night funeral of the marchers shot down in front of the Winter Palace in 1905. It hurt her. She was an American like Walt Whitman; the murdering rulers of the world were not her people; the marchers were her people; artists were not on the side of the machineguns; she was an American in a Greek tunic; she was for the people.

In St. Petersburg, still under the spell of the eighteenthcentury ballet of the court of the Sunking, her dancing was considered dangerous by the authorities.

In Germany she founded a school with the help of her sister Elizabeth who did the organizing, and she had a baby by Gordon Craig.

She went to America in triumph as she'd always planned and harried the home philistines with a tour; her followers were all the time getting pinched for wearing Greek tunics; she found no freedom for Art in America.

Back in Paris it was the top of the world; Art meant Isadora. At the funeral of the Prince de Polignac she met the mythical millionaire (sewingmachine king) who was to be her backer and to finance her school. She went off with him in his yacht (whatever Isadora did was Art)

to dance in the Temple at Paestum

only for him,

but it rained and the musicians all got drenched. So they all got drunk instead.

Art was the millionaire life. Art was whatever Isadora did. She was carrying the millionaire's child to the great scandal of the old-lady clubwomen and spinster artlovers when she danced on her second American tour;

she took to drinking too much and stepping to the footlights and bawling out the boxholders.

Isadora was at the height of glory and scandal and power and wealth, her school going, her millionaire was about to build her a theater in Paris, the Duncans were the priests of a cult, (Art was whatever Isadora did),

when the car that was bringing her two children home from the other side of Paris stalled on a bridge across the Seine. Forgetting that he'd left the car in gear the chauffeur got out to crank the motor. The car started, knocked down the chauffeur, plunged off the bridge into the Seine.

The children and their nurse were drowned.

The rest of her life moved desperately on

in the clatter of scandalized tongues, among the kidding faces of reporters, the threatening of bailiffs, the expostulations of hotelmanagers bringing overdue bills.

Isadora drank too much, she couldn't keep her hands off good-looking young men, she dyed her hair various shades of brightred, she never took the trouble to make up her face properly, was careless about her dress, couldn't bother to keep her figure in shape, never could keep track of her money

but a great sense of health

filled the hall

when the pearshaped figure with the beautiful great arms
tramped forward slowly from the back of the stage.
She was afraid of nothing; she was a great dancer.

In her own city of San Francisco the politicans wouldn't let her
dance in the Greek Theater they'd built under her influence. Wherever she went she gave offense to the philistines. When the war
broke out she danced the *Marseillaise*, but it didn't seem quite
respectable and she gave offense by refusing to give up Wagner or
to show the proper respectable feelings
of satisfaction at the butchery.

On her South American tour
she picked up men everywhere,
a Spanish painter, a couple of prizefighters, a stoker on the boat,
a Brazilian poet,
brawled in tangohalls, bawled out the Argentines for niggers from
the footlights, lushly triumphed in Montevideo and Brazil; but if
she had money she couldn't help scandalously spending it on tango-
dancers, handouts, afterthetheater suppers, the generous gesture, no,
all on my bill. The managers gypped her. She was afraid of nothing,
never ashamed in the public eye of the clatter of scandalized
tongues, the headlines in the afternoon papers.

When October split the husk off the old world she remembered
St. Petersburg, the coffins lurching through the silent streets, the
white faces, the clenched fists that night in St. Petersburg, and
danced the *Marche Slave*
and waved red cheesecloth under the noses of the Boston old
ladies in Symphony Hall,
but when she went to Russia full of hope of a school and work
and a new life in freedom, it was too enormous, it was too difficult:
cold, vodka, lice, no service in the hotels, new and old still piled
pellmell together, seedbed and scrapheap, she hadn't the patience,
her life had been too easy;
she picked up a yellowhaired poet
and brought him back
to Europe and the grand hotels.
Yessenin smashed up a whole floor of the Adlon in Berlin in one
drunken party, he ruined a suite at the Continental in Paris. When
he went back to Russia he killed himself. It was too enormous, it
was too difficult.

When it was impossible to raise any more money for Art, for the
crowds eating and drinking in the hotel suites and the rent of
Rolls-Royces and the board of her pupils and disciples,
Isadora went down to the Riviera to write her memoirs to scrape

up some cash out of the American public that had awakened after the war to the crassness of materialism and the Greeks and scandal and Art, and still had dollars to spend.

She hired a studio in Nice, but she could never pay the rent. She'd quarreled with her millionaire. Her jewels, the famous emerald, the ermine cloak, the works of art presented by the artists had all gone into the pawnshops or been seized by hotelkeepers. All she had was the old blue drapes that had seen her great triumphs, a redleather handbag, and an old furcoat that was split down the back.

She couldn't stop drinking or putting her arms round the neck of the nearest young man, if she got any cash she threw a party or gave it away.

She tried to drown herself but an English naval officer pulled her out of the moonlit Mediterranean.

One day at a little restaurant at Golfe Juan she picked up a goodlooking young wop who kept a garage and drove a little Bugatti racer.

Saying that she might want to buy the car, she made him go to her studio to take her out for a ride;

her friends didn't want her to go, said he was nothing but a mechanic, she insisted, she'd had a few drinks (there was nothing left she cared for in the world but a few drinks and a goodlooking young man);

she got in beside him and

she threw her heavilyfringed scarf round her neck with a big sweep she had and

turned back and said,

with the strong California accent her French never lost:

Adieu, mes amis, je vais à la gloire.

The mechanic put his car in gear and started.

The heavy trailing scarf caught in a wheel, wound tight. Her head was wrenched against the side of the car. The car stopped instantly; her neck was broken, her nose crushed, Isadora was dead.

QUESTIONS

1. *Isadora Duncan* begins her autobiography (*My Life* [New York: Liveright, 1955], pp. 1–2) this way:

I confess that when it was first proposed to me I had a terror of writing this book. Not that my life has not been more interesting than any novel and more adventurous than any cinema and, if really well written, would not be an epoch-making recital, but there's the rub—the writing of it!

It has taken me years of struggle, hard work and research to learn to make one simple gesture, and I know enough about the Art of writing to realise that it would take me again just so many years of concentrated effort to write one simple, beautiful sentence. How often have

I contended that although one man might toil to the Equator and have tremendous exploits with lions and tigers, and try to write about it, yet fail, whereas another, who never left his verandah, might write of the killing of tigers in their jungles in a way to make his readers feel that he was actually there, until they can suffer his agony and apprehension, smell lions and hear the fearful approach of the rattlesnake. Nothing seems to exist save in the imagination, and all the marvellous things that have happened to me may lose their savour because I do not possess the pen of a Cervantes or even of a Casanova.

Then another thing. How can we write the truth about ourselves? Do we even know it? There is the vision our friends have of us; the vision we have of ourselves, and the vision our lover has of us. Also the vision our enemies have of us—and all these visions are different. I have good reason to know this, because I have had served to me with my morning coffee newspaper criticisms that declared I was beautiful as a goddess, and that I was a genius, and hardly had I finished smiling contentedly over this, than I picked up the next paper and read that I was without any talent, badly shaped and a perfect harpy. . . .

So, if at each point of view others see in us a different person how are we to find in ourselves yet another personality of whom to write in this book? Is it to be the Chaste Madonna, or the Messalina, or the Magdalen, or the Blue Stocking? Where can I find the woman of all these adventures? It seems to me there was not one, but hundreds—and my soul soaring aloft, not really affected by any of them.

> Isadora Duncan says she was "hundreds" of women. What does she mean? (Look up in an encyclopedia the examples she mentions, if you are not familiar with them.) Which does Dos Passos present? Which emerges from this section of her autobiography?
> 2. How do the attitudes of Flanner and Dos Passos toward Isadora differ? Explain how you arrived at your conclusion.
> 3. Point out repetitions of phrases or metaphors that help to hold Flanner's and Dos Passos's pieces together. Explain whether each chooses different kinds of things to repeat and why.
> 4. Examine these two sentences: "[Isadora] arrived like a glorious bounding Minerva in the midst of a cautious corseted decade" (Flanner); "Mrs. Duncan had a hard struggle to raise her children in the love of beauty and the hatred of corsets and conventions and manmade laws" (Dos Passos). Explain any differences in attitude toward Isadora Duncan's unconventionality revealed by the two sentences. Explain which attitude seems closer to Isadora's own attitude as expressed in this passage in her autobiography:

My art was already in me when I was a little girl, and it was owing to the heroic and adventurous spirit of my mother that it was not stifled. I believe that whatever the child is going to do in life should be begun when it is very young. I wonder how many parents realise that by the so-called education they are giving their children, they are only driving them into the commonplace, and depriving them of any chance of doing anything beautiful or original. But I suppose this must be so, or who would supply us with the thousands of shop and bank clerks, etc., who seem to be necessary for organised civilised life.

> 5. Write two brief contrasting character sketches, each with a dif-

*ferent point of view. You could take someone you know per-
sonally or some public figure about whom you can gather sufficient information.*

FREDERICK LEWIS ALLEN

Al Capone

* * *

In 1920, when prohibition was very young, Johnny Torrio of Chicago had an inspiration. Torrio was a formidable figure in the Chicago underworld. He had discovered that there was big money in
the newly outlawed liquor business. He was fired with the hope of
getting control of the dispensation of booze to the whole city of
Chicago. At the moment there was a great deal too much competition; but possibly a well-disciplined gang of men handy with their
fists and their guns could take care of that, by intimidating rival
bootleggers and persuading speakeasy proprietors that life might not
be wholly comfortable for them unless they bought Torrio liquor.
What Torrio needed was a lieutenant who could mobilize and lead
his shock troops.

Being a graduate of the notorious Five Points gang in New York
and a disciple of such genial fellows as Lefty Louie and Gyp the
Blood (he himself had been questioned about the murder of
Herman Rosenthal in the famous Becker case in 1912), he naturally turned to his *alma mater* for his man. He picked for the job a
bullet-headed twenty-three-year-old Neapolitan roughneck of the
Five Points gang, and offered him a generous income and half the
profits of the bootleg trade if he would come to Chicago and take
care of the competition. The young hoodlum came, established
himself at Torrio's gambling-place, the Four Deuces, opened by way
of plausible stage setting an innocent-looking office which contained
among its properties a family Bible, and had a set of business cards
printed:

ALPHONSE CAPONE
Second Hand Furniture Dealer   2220 South Wabash Avenue

Torrio had guessed right—in fact, he had guessed right three
times. The profits of bootlegging in Chicago proved to be prodigious, allowing an ample margin for the mollification of the forces
of the law. The competition proved to be exacting: every now and
then Torrio would discover that his rivals had approached a speakeasy proprietor with the suggestion that he buy their beer instead of
the Torrio-Capone brand, and on receipt of an unfavorable answer
had beaten the proprietor senseless and smashed up his place of
business. But Al Capone had been an excellent choice as leader of

the Torrio offensives; Capone was learning how to deal with such emergencies.

Within three years it was said that the boy from the Five Points had seven hundred men at his disposal, many of them adept in the use of the sawed-off shotgun and the Thompson sub-machine gun. As the profits from beer and "alky-cooking" (illicit distilling) rolled in, young Capone acquired more finesse—particularly finesse in the management of politics and politicans. By the middle of the decade he had gained complete control of the suburb of Cicero, had installed his own mayor in office, had posted his agents in the wide-open gambling-resorts and in each of the 161 bars, and had established his personal headquarters in the Hawthorne Hotel. He was taking in millions now. Torrio was fading into the background; Capone was becoming the Big Shot. But his conquest of power did not come without bloodshed. As the rival gangs—the O'Banions, the Gennas, the Aiellos—disputed his growing domination, Chicago was afflicted with such an epidemic of killings as no civilized modern city had ever before seen, and a new technic of wholesale murder was developed.

One of the standard methods of disposing of a rival in this warfare of the gangs was to pursue his car with a stolen automobile full of men armed with sawed-off shotguns and sub-machine guns; to draw up beside it, forcing it to the curb, open fire upon it—and then disappear into the traffic, later abandoning the stolen car at a safe distance. Another favorite method was to take the victim "for a ride": in other words, to lure him into a supposedly friendly car, shoot him at leisure, drive to some distant and deserted part of the city, and quietly throw his body overboard. Still another was to lease an apartment or a room overlooking his front door, station a couple of hired assassins at the window, and as the victim emerged from the house some sunny afternoon, to spray him with a few dozen machine-gun bullets from behind drawn curtains. But there were also more ingenious and refined methods of slaughter.

Take, for example, the killing of Dion O'Banion, leader of the gang which for a time most seriously menaced Capone's reign in Chicago. The preparation of this particular murder was reminiscent of the kiss of Judas. O'Banion was a bootlegger and a gangster by night, but a florist by day: a strange and complex character, a connoisseur of orchids and of manslaughter. One morning a sedan drew up outside his flower shop and three men got out, leaving the fourth at the wheel. The three men had apparently taken good care to win O'Banion's trust, for although he always carried three guns, now for the moment he was off his guard as he advanced among the flowers to meet his visitors. The middle man of the three cordially shook hands with O'Banion—*and then held on* while his two companions put six bullets into the gangster-florist. The three conspirators walked out, climbed into the sedan, and departed. They were never brought to justice, and it is not recorded that any of them hung themselves to trees in remorse. O'Banion had a first-class funeral, gangster style: a ten-thousand-dollar casket, twenty-six truckloads of flowers, and among them a basket of flowers which bore the touching inscription, "From Al."

In 1926 the O'Banions, still unrepentant despite the loss of their leader, introduced another novelty in gang warfare. In broad daylight, while the streets of Cicero were alive with traffic, they raked Al Capone's headquarters with machine-gun fire from eight touring cars. The cars proceeded down the crowded street outside the Hawthorne Hotel in solemn line, the first one firing blank cartridges to disperse the innocent citizenry and to draw the Capone forces to the doors and windows, while from the succeeding cars, which followed a block behind, flowed a steady rattle of bullets, spraying the hotel and the adjoining buildings up and down. One gunman even got out of his car, knelt carefully upon the sidewalk at the door of the Hawthorne, and played one hundred bullets into the lobby—back and forth, as one might play the hose upon one's garden. The casualties were miraculously light, and Scarface Al himself remained in safety, flat on the floor of the Hotel Hawthorne restaurant; nevertheless, the bombardment quite naturally attracted public attention. Even in a day when bullion was transported in armored cars, the transformation of a suburban street into a shooting-gallery seemed a little unorthodox.

The war continued, one gangster after another crumpling under a rain of bullets; not until St. Valentine's Day of 1929 did it reach its climax in a massacre which outdid all that had preceded it in ingenuity and brutality. At half-past ten on the morning of February 14, 1929, seven of the O'Banions were sitting in the garage which went by the name of the S. M. C. Cartage Company, on North Clark Street, waiting for a promised consignment of hijacked liquor. A Cadillac touring-car slid to the curb, and three men dressed as policemen got out, followed by two others in civilian dress. The three supposed policemen entered the garage alone, disarmed the seven O'Banions, and told them to stand in a row against the wall. The victims readily submitted; they were used to police raids and thought nothing of them; they would get off easily enough, they expected. But thereupon the two men in civilian clothes emerged from the corridor and calmly mowed down all seven O'Banions with sub-machine gun fire as they stood with hands upraised against the wall. The little drama was completed when the three supposed policemen solemnly marched the two plainclothes killers across the sidewalk to the waiting car, and all five got in and drove off—having given to those in the wintry street a perfect tableau of an arrest satisfactorily made by the forces of the law!

These killings—together with that of "Jake" Lingle, who led a double life as reporter for the *Chicago Tribune* and as associate of gangsters, and who was shot to death in a crowded subway leading to the Illinois Central suburban railway station in 1930—were perhaps the most spectacular of the decade in Chicago. But there were over five hundred gang murders in all. Few of the murderers were apprehended; careful planning, money, influence, the intimidation of witnesses, and the refusal of any gangster to testify against any other, no matter how treacherous the murder, met that danger. The city of Chicago was giving the whole country, and indeed the whole world, an astonishing object lesson in violent and unpunished crime. How and why could such a thing happen?

To say that prohibition—or, if you prefer, the refusal of the public to abide by prohibition—caused the rise of the gangs to lawless power would be altogether too easy an explanation. There were other causes: the automobile, which made escape easy, as the officers of robbed banks had discovered; the adaptation to peacetime use of a new arsenal of handy and deadly weapons; the murderous traditions of the Mafia, imported by Sicilian gangsters; the inclination of a wet community to wink at the by-products of a trade which provided them with beer and gin; the sheer size and unwieldiness of the modern metropolitan community, which prevented the focusing of public opinion upon any depredation which did not immediately concern the average individual citizen; and, of course, the easy-going political apathy of the times. But the immediate occasion of the rise of gangs was undoubtedly prohibition—or, to be more precise, beer-running. (Beer rather than whisky on account of its bulk; to carry on a profitable trade in beer one must transport it in trucks, and trucks are so difficult to disguise that the traffic must be protected by bribery of the prohibition staff and the police and by gunfire against bandits.) There was vast profit in the manufacture, transportation, and sale of beer. In 1927, according to Fred D. Pasley, Al Capone's biographer, federal agents estimated that the Capone gang controlled the sources of a revenue from booze of something like sixty million dollars a year, and much of this—perhaps most of it—came from beer. Fill a man's pockets with money, give him a chance at a huge profit, put him into an illegal business and thus deny him recourse to the law if he is attacked, and you have made it easy for him to bribe and shoot. There have always been gangs and gangsters in American life and doubtless always will be; there has always been corruption of city officials and doubtless always will be; yet it is ironically true, none the less, that the outburst of corruption and crime in Chicago in the nineteen-twenties was immediately occasioned by the attempt to banish the temptations of liquor from the American home.

The young thug from the Five Points, New York, had traveled fast and far since 1920. By the end of the decade he had become as widely renowned as Charles Evans Hughes or Gene Tunney. He had become an American portent. Not only did he largely control the sale of liquor to Chicago's ten thousand speakeasies; he controlled the sources of supply, it was said, as far as Canada and the Florida coast. He had amassed, and concealed, a fortune the extent of which nobody knew; it was said by federal agents to amount to twenty millions. He was arrested and imprisoned once in Philadelphia for carrying a gun, but otherwise he seemed above the law. He rode about Chicago in an armored car, a traveling fortress, with another car to patrol the way ahead and a third car full of his armed henchmen following behind; he went to the theater attended by a body-guard of eighteen young men in dinner coats, with guns doubtless slung under their left armpits in approved gangster fashion; when his sister was married, thousands milled about the church in the snow, and he presented the bride with a nine-foot wedding cake and a special honeymoon car; he had a fine estate at Miami where he sometimes entertained seventy-five guests at a time; and high politicans—and even, it has been said, judges—took orders from him over the telephone from his headquarters in a downtown Chicago hotel. And still he was only thirty-two years old. What was Napoleon doing at thirty-two?

KENNETH ALLSOP

"Al, We're with You"

"You boys just made a mistake. I'm going to give you a break."
AL CAPONE *to a police squad*

At the door of Cook County Jail on an October morning in 1931, which, unbeknown to him then, was the last meridian moment of his singular career, Alphonse Capone paused on his way inside to issue a statement to the press. It was a sentence that, in its poignant bafflement and hurt, classically expressed the attitudes that set the psychotic criminal irreclaimably apart from society.

"It was a blow below the belt," he said, "but what can you expect when the whole community is prejudiced against you?"

Capone had just stepped down from the dock after receiving an eleven-year prison sentence for tax evasion, a sentence he managed to postpone until the following May, during which time he remained on bail pending appeal. Until that summer, when, only by the most stubborn persistence had the Federal Government hauled him into court, Capone had been one of the most obviously powerful men in the world. In this year of 1931 Mussolini had been dictator of Italy for nine years; the National Socialists had just won a hundred seats in the Reichstag, and it was only months ahead before Hitler became chancellor and constituted the Third Reich; Stalin had been supreme head of the Soviet Union for seven years.

All, in this developing age of rule by violence and victimization, were more sombrely fearsome by far than an American gangster whose ambitions were neither political nor nationalistic, but who used politics obliquely as a means of obtaining money and the power through which more money was obtainable. Yet perhaps all of them were part of the same pattern of that darkening time, an age when enforcement of policy by gun cruelty and oppression, in contempt of the theoretical canons of law, became naked and ubiquitous. Capone himself seemed hazily conscious of inherent similarities. As he walked, handcuffed, from the courtroom to his cell through volleys of exploding flashbulbs, he said with melancholy pride to Eliot Ness, the F.B.I. prohibition agent who was largely responsible for his conviction: "Jeez, you'd think Mussolini was passin' through." And, in 1931, when Hitler was aged forty-two, Mussolini forty-eight and Stalin fifty-two, Capone was but thirty-six. For a comparatively young man, a slum delinquent of foreign birth and little schooling, his accomplishments up to that year had been prodigiously impressive.

The President in status and several hundred industrialists in material possessions were mightier and more influential Americans than Capone, yet not by so great a margin, and, in concentrated autonomy, were much less so. Probably no one man since Cesare Borgia's rule of Rome had so inexorably controlled a city for purposes so piratically self-interested and contrary to principles of government in the society of which he was a member. In his four years of total power, between 1927 and 1931, Capone's authority ramified beyond Chicago and beyond the state of Illinois. "He was," wrote Paul Sann, "mayor, governor and machine boss all rolled into one. He gave the orders; the people's elected servants carried them out and kept their mouths shut. His authority was so great it could not be measured." The gross income of his business in liquor, gambling, prostitution, and assorted rackets ran into millions of dollars annually. Chicago's 20,000 speakeasies operated, with only sporadic and ineffectual interference from the Federal Prohibition squads, openly and busily for years. He ran an organization which owned or had stakes in breweries, distilleries, warehouses, truck companies, garages, bars, night clubs, dance halls, restaurants, brothels, race tracks and casinos, and which was beginning at the time of his retirement to infiltrate its extortion racket into unions, film production, and dozens of trades and industries. He amassed a fortune of $20,000,000—an incredible sum that is not my estimate but that of the Internal Revenue Office. He was the commanding officer of a private army of 700 storm troops, and for auxiliaries had call upon an estimated sixty per cent of Chicago's police force who were on his payroll. In that four-year period there were 227 gang murders; there were no convictions. In the 40-year period from 1919 to 1959 there were 929 gang murders committed in Chicago. Only seven-

teen culprits were convicted—and several of those were freed on
appeal to the Supreme Court. He took over the suburban district of
Cicero with a military efficiency and converted it into a vice reservation, a day-and-night resort of 161 cabarets, call houses, and dice
parlours, and when he seized control of the town of 50,000 people
he nominated his own group of bought politicians and posted
squads of gunmen at the polling stations to ensure their election.
His influence extended into journalism; there was certainly one
reporter—Jake Lingle of the Chicago *Tribune*—on his payroll, and
probably others in regular receipt of patronage in return for sympathetic coverage. Even during his prison term the headlines rang
with fond concern: CAPONE GAINS ELEVEN POUNDS and
CAPONE DOESN'T GO TO CHURCH ON SUNDAY. He was
a celebrity swelling into a legend. Citizens scurried to the curb to
stare when his three-and-a-half ton armour-plated Cadillac, with
bulletproof glass and tail-gunner's movable back window, passed
with its escort of two armed scout cars. Lucky out-of-town and foreign visitors among the crowds had their stimulating glimpse of the
famous face, stuck with cigar, in the dim haze of silken cushions,
perhaps the quick glint of one of his famous diamonds, behind the
bodyguard in the front seat with Thompson submachine gun handily across his knees. Tourist buses had "Capone Castle"—his Hawthorne Inn headquarters in Cicero—and his Metropole Hotel city
headquarters on their itinerary. A press photograph of him with a
heavyweight boxing champion and Bill Cunningham, former All-
American football player, which was nationally circulated by an
agency, was captioned "Gangland's King." When he attended a
prize fight or race meeting the fact was mentioned by the sports columnist. In 1929 the London *Daily Mail* despatched Mr. Edgar
Wallace to Chicago to write a series of articles about the Capone
regime, and he was only one of many European journalists who
were hastening towards a tastily juicy story of smoking guns and
brazen daring, an improbable Wild West melodrama here for the
harvesting in a modern city. The articles, interviews, biographies,
and personal reminiscences proliferated, and accuracy of detail was
not allowed dingily to stifle the rich potentialities of such material.
If one collated all the alleged direct quotations from Capone himself that were printed at that period, a curious portrait of a garrulous but primly stilted Boy Scout would emerge. This watchful and
wary crime-syndicalist, who, except when angry (which was rare to
see) or relaxed with wine (which was not often in the presence of
outsiders), confined his conversation outside the confederate circle
to pleasantries with reporters, would seem, from the printed records
that remain, to have been able to discourse learnedly upon philosophy or Napoleon's tactical errors ("the world's greatest racketeer,
but I could have wised him up on some things"). One 1929 newspaper report of his activities during his short prison sentence in Phil-

adelphia described him as "a stern highbrow" and cited his "favourite authors" as Shakespeare and Shaw; another despatch reported that he was occupying himself by reciting Balzac and Victor Hugo. He was even, in one odd publication in 1931, *Carrying a Gun for Al Capone* by the sculptor-painter Jack Bilbo—who later admitted that he had never been to Chicago—represented as being a reader of Robert Louis Stevenson and Karl Marx, and as talking like a ruminative cardigan-clad don in an English repertory drama: "Sentimentality is the main danger which threatens us in life. One either has to rid oneself of it or one is entirely in its power. The day will come when our softness will rise up and we will flounder in it." Most of the myth-making that was then beginning had at least a few more roots in reality, even if it was as fatuous as Edward D. Sullivan's description of him in a 1931 book, *Chicago Surrenders*, as "the best billiard player in the Greenpoint section of Brooklyn," but there was also a vast quantity of glamour-endowing mawkishness about Capone in Sunday paper serials, in "detective" magazines and in quick-turnover booklets, lavish with those smudgily sinister pictures of corpses sprawled beside fire-hydrants. One of these, *X Marks the Spot*, published in 1930, is a fair specimen of the tone of excited, fulsome admiration thinly veneered with moralising that was current then. Beside a full-page frontispiece ran this caption: "Here is an excellent likeness of Alphonse Capone, the big boy of Chicago Gangland, and the greatest gangster that ever lived. When King Al poses for a photograph, which isn't often, he always turns his right cheek to the camera. The left one is disfigured by an ugly scar. Legend has it that Capone was struck by a machine gun bullet when he was a soldier in France." (That, as will be seen later, is one little Capone-inspired legend that collapsed.[1]) Within, the story of Capone's life, which was on the level of the "official" biography of a film star in a fan-club circular, began: "He is a glamorous figure, an actual part of the American scene. Legends are already springing up around him. The magazine stands are aflame with underworld stories about the man with the gat who wears a tuxedo and has a liveried chauffeur. With no intention to eulogise him, Capone unquestionably stands apart as the greatest and most successful gangster who ever lived. The difference between him and all other gangsters is that he is possessed of a genius for organization and a profound business sense." All the documentary comment induced was not quite so banally degenerate as that but there were more sober and grudging tributes to his talent. An internal revenue officer, charged with investigating his tax dues, told Pasley: "Capone has exceptional business ability and would have gone far in any legitimate line. If he had only been honest, what a hero he

---

1. Allsop later says that although Capone claimed to have received the wound fighting overseas, he had in fact been wounded in a knife fight in a New York saloon.

would have made for a Horatio Alger tale." Capone and his regime also brought about novels such as W. R. Burnett's *Little Caesar*, plays such as Charles MacArthur and Ben Hecht's *The Front Page* and Edgar Wallace's *On the Spot*, and a cycle of brilliantly harsh gangster films of which *Scarface*, directed by Howard Hawks and with Paul Muni as the psychopathic hoodlum Tony Camonte, a name with, perhaps, a deliberate onomatopoeic quality, was the best. (In 1932 it was billed, deludingly, as "The Shame of a Nation," when there was, in mass unemployment and hunger, a far more bitter shame abroad.)

Fact was inextricably scrambled with fiction. It was fact that this new dignitary, the paunchy pallid-faced Big Fellow who was beginning to tower above the officially eminent with a unique glitter and who was giving Chicago a peculiar global fame, was among the committee appointed to welcome Commander Francesco da Pinedo, Mussolini's round-the-world good-will pilot in 1927, together with Leopold Zunini, Italian Consul-General, Dr. Ugo M. Galli, Chicago Fascisti President, and Judge Bernard P. Barasa, representing the Mayor. It was a fact that he was lionised by the smart—it was cute to know Al; that he entertained at his Florida estate seventy-five guests at a time, many of them fashionable and famous; that he rebuked and instructed politicans and judges over the telephone from his Metropole Hotel office; that on the occasion of the second Dempsey-Tunney fight he threw the biggest, and wettest, party seen before or since in Chicago—it blinded on for three days, the liquor bill (even at his wholesale rates) was $50,000, and it was attended by socialites, movie stars, politicians and theatre and boxing celebrities from all over America.

So it may well have also been a fact that—as he once bragged— in seven years he "fooled away" $10,000,000 pocket money on gambling. He customarily shot craps for $50,000 and $100,000 a throw, and never for less than $1000 unless with impoverished friends; he bet $100,000 at a time on a horse race (but would not gamble on the stock market—"Wall Street is crooked"). Appropriate to his station, he lived a sybaritically luxurious life. His custom-built car cost $30,000, his ring, an eleven-carat blue-white diamond from the South African Jagersfontein mines, $50,000. His casual munificence with his thickly wadded bankroll became one of the romances of that hard-bitten city where nothing had ever previously been for free. He was once charged—and paid without wincing—$1000 for a round of drinks in the Country Club, an exclusive New York speak run by Belle Livingstone, dubbed by the papers "the Most Dangerous Woman in Europe" when she was the outstandingly lurid playgirl of the Edwardian age. His personal gratuity rates were five dollars for a newsboy, ten dollars for a hat-check girl and one hundred dollars for a waiter. There were many such heartwarming stories as that of the hard-up hat-check girl who, decent but desperate, pleaded for a position in one of his brothels to support her ailing mother. "Forget it. Not a nice girl like you," said Al, peeling off a hundred dollars for her. At Christmas he spent $100,000 on miscellaneous gifts. All the year round he distributed diamond-inlet belts to his new friends and ruby-set gold cigarette cases to politicians and business associates, whose cellars were also kept stocked with wine and champagne (not the speakeasy brands). During his only other prison term—a short sojourn in Philadelphia in 1929 for carrying a gun—he bought $1000 dollars' worth of the convicts' handiwork, ship models, cigarette boxes, carvings, and other *objets d'art*, and posted them to friends as Christmas presents. He sent $1200 to a deserving Philadelphia orphanage. With probably no traditional knowledge to draw upon, he regarded the huge industrial city of Chicago as his estate and assumed the function of a squire, a benevolent despot capriciously distributing largesse among his villeins. In hard winters the poor of Cicero could draw all the groceries, clothing, and fuel they needed from coal depots and and department stores on the Capone account. His individual acts of charity, from a fifty-dollar loan to an outright gift to a destitute Italian family, were many. He paid the hospital bills of a woman bystander wounded in a street gun battle. It is not altogether astonishing that today there are many respectable citizens in Chicago who speak glowingly of Capone's philanthropy and particularly point out that in the early Depression days it was the Capone gang who set up the first soup-kitchens and block restaurants for the distribution of free food on Thanksgiving Day.

When this real-life Robin Hood appeared at a Northwestern University rally, 10,000 Boy Scouts, young eyes a-sparkle with hero worship, spontaneously set up the yell, to the embarrassment of their troop leaders: "Good old Al." Older people, too, made Capone what Pasley described as "the object of a sort of hero worship." Upstanding citizens sought out the opportunity in public places of grasping his hand. A Chicago civil engineer, on a business visit to Philadelphia during Capone's stay in the Eastern Penitentiary, requested an interview with him, introduced himself, shook his hand and told him: "Al, we're with you."

Perhaps one should remind oneself, however, that this one-man welfare state had at his disposal for his good works the lion's share of the $150,000,000, which was the sum estimated that marauding and extortion cost the State of Illinois annually.

At one point, around the time that he had been described as "a cancer" and "America's Nineteenth Amendment," and was saying mournfully: "There's a lot of grief attached to the limelight," Capone considered hiring Ivy Lee, the publicist who pulled off the most formidable assignment in public relations, that of popularizing the loathed, union-smashing millionaire John D. Rockefeller, Sr. This did not come about, possibly because Capone recognised that his own instincts for publicity were as sound as any advice he could buy from Lee. By 1930 he was a celebrity of a size rare in the pre-television age. Pasley, writing at that period, described him as "America's Exhibit A. Al had grown from civic to national stature. He was an institution," and Pasley grouped him in a small glorious host in the annals of enduring Americana with Will Rogers, Henry Ford, Rin Tin Tin, Babe Ruth, Charles Lindbergh, Texas Guinan, and Al Smith.

As it has turned out, Pasley sold Capone short. I suspect that today although Ford and Rin Tin Tin might be known to many children in Europe, Africa, the Far East and even perhaps the Soviet Union, most would instantly recognise one name only among that list and that, if language was a barrier to explanation, they would be able to communicate their knowledge with a levelled finger and a staccato rat-a-tat-tat.

He outlasted four chiefs of police, two municipal administrations, three United States district attorneys, and a regiment of Federal prohibition agents; he survived innumerable crime drives, grand jury investigations, reform crusades, clean-up election campaigns, police shake-ups, and Congressional inquiries and debates. He killed between twenty and sixty men himself—there is no way of ascertaining any nearer tally—and was responsible by delegation for the murder of at least 400 others, and was never charged with one of them. His ultimate arrest and commitment to jail on October 24, 1931, came about from the doggedness of the Intelligence Unit of Elmer Irey, chief of the United States Treasury Enforcement Branch; but it was not really the forces of law and order that defeated Capone. When he was struck down his strength and menace were failing. Capone had been defeated by those unexpected things: the approach of repeal, which was to dissolve his black market in booze; and the Depression, which dried to a dribble the easy money of the golden days; and disease which was eating him from within.

Now, thirty years after that febrile and predatory era, it is evident that Al Capone will have a more durable, definitive place in history, both popular and serious, than any of those other candidates for immortality with the possible exception of Henry Ford, although even that revolutionary will never be preserved in the same glare of popular fascination.

As the years go by Capone stands out more palpably as a phenomenon and a symbol of a sort. He cannot be summarised by all the conventional terms of disapproval, that he was evil, ruthless or corrupt, although he was all those things. The splendour of his dispensation to the needy and the greedy cannot be allowed to admit him back to grace, although he did practise a flashy generosity which, although doubtless paranoically vanity-feeding, was no mere fable. In only a decade he ascended from squalid poverty to a status, which, if no less squalid, was unique in its power and scope. He was, after all, a pioneer of a kind, for nobody before had done quite what he did, and in him there were undoubted qualities of imagination, forcefulness, and ingenuity.

QUESTIONS
1. Both Allen and Allsop place Capone in the very carefully described context of the historical period and the effects of Prohibition. Explain whether this helps to understand Capone as a man. Why does Allsop emphasize the world context as well as the American one?
2. Allen calls Capone "an American portent" (p. 692), Allsop calls him "a symbol of a sort" (p. 699). Explain whether you think they are talking about the same thing.
3. Allsop calls Capone a "real-life Robin Hood." What traits of Capone is he pointing to in this comparison and how appropriate is it? Explain whether this would have been an equally appropriate comparison for Allen to use, given the rest of the material he uses. What are the similarities and differences in the bodies of fact that Allen and Allsop have assembled?
4. Explain which of these two accounts you think Capone himself would have preferred.

JIMMY BRESLIN

Tip O'Neill

Tip O'Neill at all times has one great political weapon at his disposal. He understands so well that all political power is primarily an illusion. If people think you have power, then you have power. If people think you have no power, then you have no power. This is a great truth in politics that I was able to recognize in O'Neill's ways, because I had taken the enormous trouble to go out and learn this in the streets and clubhouses of the City of New York and particularly as a candidate for citywide office in 1969, an adventure which left me with the deep-lasting scars of one who went and learned the hard way, thus learning forever. For those who take their politics from a book, an easier but much less effective way of learning than mine, this same proposition has been advanced in print by Thomas Hobbes, who wrote in England in the 1600s: "The reputation of power is power." Power is an illusion.

Illusion. Mirrors and blue smoke, beautiful blue smoke rolling over the surface of highly polished mirrors, first a thin veil of blue smoke, then a thick cloud that suddenly dissolves into wisps of blue smoke, the mirrors catching it all, bouncing it back and forth. If somebody tells you how to look, there can be seen in the smoke great, magnificent shapes, castles and kingdoms, and maybe they can be yours. All this becomes particularly dynamic when the person telling you where to look knows how to adjust the mirrors, tilt one forward, walk to the other side, and turn one on its base a few degrees to the right, suddenly causing the refractions to be different everywhere. And then going to the blue smoke, lessening it, intensifying it, and all the time keeping those watching transfixed, hoping, believing himself. Believing perhaps more than anybody else in the room. And at the same time knowing that what he is believing in is mirrors and blue smoke.

This is the game called politics and power as it is played in the Legion Halls and Elks Clubs and church basements and political clubhouses throughout the country, thoughout the world, while men try to please and calm others in order to maintain and improve a public career. Always, no matter what country you are in, the culmination of politics is considered to be the men who are in Washington and who are the best in the world at taking an illusion and telling you, and telling themselves, that it really is power.

This thesis, this truth, never was clearer than it was in Washington in the summer of 1974. Thomas P. O'Neill, Jr., had power, great power at times, because nearly everybody in Washington thought of him as having power. In the book, *Rules and Practices of the House of Representatives,* mention is made of every rule and roost in the House. There happens not to be one single mention, direct or indirect, of a position known as Majority Leader. By law, there is no such post. There is custom for it. There also is a line in the appropriations to pay for staff salaries for the Majority Leader. The holder of the job has large offices and is driven in great limousines. But by law or custom, there is no exact definition of the duties of the Majority Leader.

When Tip O'Neill decided that his primary duty was to make rapid the removal of Richard Nixon he took on great power. Because everybody began to regard him as being quite powerful. And meanwhile, each day, these little pieces of trouble dropped on the floor at Richard Nixon's feet and more and more people noticed it. As the level of regard for Nixon's power dropped, the level of danger for his career rose. At the end, Nixon had not the personal political power of a city councilman. He sat in the Oval Office, but he might as well have been in City Hall, in Dayton.

The ability to create the illusion of power, to use mirrors and blue smoke, is one found in unusual people. They reach their objectives through overstatement or understatement, through silent agreements and, always, the use of language at the most opportune moments.

The night Nixon introduced Gerald R. Ford as his nominee to replace convicted Spiro T. Agnew as Vice President, there were strolling strings and champagne in the White House. The notion was to put Watergate behind us; you have won, you have gotten

Agnew, now let us forget about it and go on as before. In the pleasure of the evening, James Lynn, the Secretary of Housing and Urban Development, spoke with Thomas P. O'Neill.

"Tip, did you ever think we'd be standing here in the White House with history being made, the Twenty-fifth Amendment working for the first time. There's probably never going to be another night like it in the country's history."

"Not for about eight months," Tip O'Neill said.

Lynn's mouth opened. Tip O'Neill gave us this great street laugh of his and jammed a Daniel Webster cigar in his mouth. James Lynn went away from the night with cement in his stomach. When people around him would say hopefully that Watergate was finished, Lynn would tell them it was not finished. Not anywhere near finished.

Once, for Richard Nixon, there were only two kids on *The Washington Post* newspaper who were causing trouble. Journalism, no matter how skilled, how brilliant, is a passive trade. Words command only when used by someone in command. Words wirtten by a writer cause little immediate change. The full weight of nearly all the newspapers and nearly all the television had been used for eight years to make horrible the war in Vietnam. The war went on, more intensely at the end than it had at the beginning.

Another threat, another enemy for Richard Nixon now sprang up from another area. A judge, John Sirica.[1] He was painstakingly honest. Lawyers and law professors will point to him forever as a reason for the law triumphing in Watergate; that in the end the actions of no other institution was needed: the law handled the matter. Senator Sam J. Ervin, Jr.,[2] thundered about the sanctity of the Constitution and Judge Sirica quietly, decisively applied it. And always, there was the Supreme Court ready to make honest rulings. All of which is beautiful for speeches at a Bar Association dinner or a law-school seminar. Yet all those associated with the law, from Sam Ervin and his committee to John Sirica, crept and probed and yet never took the decisive step, never reached out to grab anyone in the name of the law. The committee subpoenaed. The court ordered. For months Nixon surrendered nothing. Always, he held up the results of the election: 61 per cent of the country voted for him. The Ervin committee said it was sad that the President did not cooperate. The court coughed. The law crumbled in the face of an election certificate. There was no evidence suggesting that Nixon planned the Watergate affair. All he did was enter into a conspiracy to obstruct justice in the aftermath. Where I come from, this is only a misdemeanor. The law says nothing about the true crime

---

1. Judge John Sirica presided at the Watergate trial.

2. Chairman of the Senate committee investigating the Watergate burglary and cover-up.

committed: that of repeatedly lying to 250 million people. All the law could produce was a minor complaint, and as the time dragged, and time could help Nixon, it began to appear that nobody truly was going to press and attempt to destroy a President for a misdemeanor. For if somebody wanted to treat Nixon as a citizen and apply the law to him, the time element would have been minimal.

Once, in a federal courthouse in Newark, in New Jersey, I saw a businessman, ordered to produce his books as evidence, tell a judge named Whipple that the books were lost. Whipple said that was all right with him; the man could just go in the back there, go into the cells, and sit there until the books were found. The businessman sat in a cell for three days. On the fourth day he was joined by a large gray rat which came out of a crack under the base of the toilet. The next morning, Judge Whipple, busy on the bench reading a motion, heard the doors in the courtroom squeak loudly. Whipple looked up. Staggering into the courtroom, unable to see over the huge pile of blue ledger books he carried, was the partner of the businessman. Your honor, we have just been able to locate the books you requested. Now can my friend get out of jail? This is how it works every place there is a courtroom.

But it did not work this way in the Senate Watergate hearing room and, despite the lore of Sirica, it did not work in his courtroom.

Citizens would have been thrown in the slam for contempt. But the half-royalty of the White House held everybody off. Even when John Dean[3] shook a nation with his testimony, there were only a few who felt anything ever could happen to Richard Nixon. Clearly, then, journalism and the law were not enough to do anything about the crimes of Richard Nixon. But this is only natural. This is a country of men, not laws, and therefore the situation at this point needed a man; a working politician; a professional; a drinking, eating, handshaking member of the Elks, Knights of Columbus, Knights of St. Finbar; trustee of Boston College; Man of the Year 1962; National Conference of Christians and Jews; a director of the United Appeal; a ten-term Congressman who had spent 4000 nights at dinner tables everywhere in the city of Washington. Only a working politician could challenge and erode the one thing Richard Nixon could not afford to lose: the support of political people. And now, early in the game, so early in the game, Richard Nixon had a new opponent who was a popular politician.

This art which O'Neill pursues, this art of mirrors and blue smoke, is not fraudulent. Rather, it is how all of life works: in politics, life is compressed into a small number of people who spend a short period of time in a circle with a stunted radius. The practice

3. Dean, a lawyer, had been a presidential adviser. He testified that Nixon had approved the payment of bribes in an attempt to hush up the Watergate burglars.

of art can only be done successfully, and for the good of others, by human beings who bring with them a little intelligence, a little wit, a little honor—a seascapist must love an ocean before he can make its movement stand still.

And throughout the quest for justice in the nation in the years 1973 and 1974, Thomas P. O'Neill stood in the full nobility of his profession: a politician of the Democratic party.

As such, the man has no visible means of support. There is no badge, no tool kit, no license that says you are allowed to be a politician. There is only your word: I will do it; I will not do it. And if there is one thing that makes Tip O'Neill so effective in his business, made him so effective against Richard Nixon, it is his belief that a commitment—his word given—is an extension of his religion.

Go to any time in his career, pick out a situation and inspect O'Neill's conduct in it, and always you will see the worth of his word. Go to early 1946, the night a Cambridge politician named Chick Artesani came to Tip O'Neill's house with a skinny young man named Jack Kennedy, whom Artesani introduced as the next Congressman from the area.

"I want you to be with us, Tip," Artesani said.

"Well, I'm delighted to meet you, Jack, but I'm sorry I have to tell you and my old pal here that I'm already committed to Mike Neville."

O'Neill had served in the state legislature with Neville for eight years, and O'Neill's word of support for this particular Congressional race had been given to Neville some time back.

Artesani shrugged, Kennedy and O'Neill shook hands, and the meeting ended. When the primary race for the Congressional seat began some weeks later, O'Neill went out onto the streets with Mike Neville. He toured his district, Russell Street, Orchard Street, Blake Street, and rang doorbells and chatted with people.

"Hello, I'm Tom O'Neill. I'm a member of the state legislature and I see you're new in the neighborhood here, and I haven't had a chance to meet you yet. I just want to say I've lived here in the neighborhood thirty-odd years and I'm not busy in the legislature at this moment because the legislature is not in session. So I'm just coming around to point out to you, if you don't mind, that I think Mike Neville will make a great Congressman from this area; he'll give us the type of voice in Washington we deserve. I hope you'll give him your consideration when you vote on primary day."

And the woman he was speaking to excused herself and went to the dining-room table and brought back a pamphlet with a picture of a PT boat on the front. "Is your Mr. Neville running against this brave young Kennedy?"

Tip shook his head and went on to the next house. And then he began to work the people he knew. He came into Mrs. Murphy's

house on Orchard Street, and she took him by the arm and led him
into the kitchen for a cup of tea.

"Tip, how are you?"

"Well, Nellie, I'm just great. I just came in to say hello. I'm
running again for re-election as you undoubtedly know, but I don't
have any opposition, so I want to come here and talk to you about
Mike Neville . . ."

Nellie Murphy said, "You don't have any opposition? Isn't this
young fellow Kennedy running against you?"

"No, Nellie, he's running for Congress in Washington against
my friend . . ."

"Oh, thanks be to God, Tom, I thought he was running against
you. What a wonderful boy. We've got all this literature. Oh, what
a beautiful story about the PT boat, getting lost in those islands.
Dear God, I don't know how I could have voted even for you
against such a wonderful, brave young man."

When O'Neill got home that night, there was a phone call from
candidate Mike Neville.

"What are you doing?" Neville asked.

"I'm taking a shower and you better do the same thing," O'Neill
said.

As the campaign went on, Chick Artesani called O'Neill again.
"I'm with Mike Neville, and that's it," O'Neill said. Jack Kennedy
then called. The answer was the same.

One night, a next-door neighbor, Joe Healy, called O'Neill. "I've
got Jack Kennedy here and I'm bringing him over to see you."

"Don't bring him here, it'll only embarrass him, and you'll
embarrass me too," O'Neill said. "I'm with Mike Neville and that's
it."

"Kennedy is going to win," Healy said.

"That doesn't have anything to do with it," Tip said.

A few minutes later the doorbell rang. It was Healy and Kennedy. O'Neill stood in his living room and said, "There's nothing I
can do for you, Jack, I'm with Mike all the way."

From O'Neill's house, Healy and Kennedy went up to the home
of Leo Diehl, O'Neill's closest friend. Diehl was delighted and flattered by the young Kennedy's attentions. But there was no way he
could help. "I gave my word to Neville," Leo said.

On primary day, wherever Tip O'Neill looked, he saw coming
down off the porches of their frame houses, coming down to vote,
hundreds of housewives with pictures of PT boats in their hands.

The day after the election, the first phone call Tip O'Neill
received was from Jack Kennedy. "Tip, I want you to know that the
next time I do anything, I want you to be with me. When you have
a friend, when Mike Neville had a friend like you, a trustworthy
friend, then I want you to know I appreciate the position you were
in and I will never forget how you acted."

And in 1974, when it all began in Congress against Richard Nixon, most politicians did not want to hear of impeachment. What is this impeachment? Freak John Dean, who elected him? What the hell does a courtroom have to do with our business? Let the judge go out and run for office. We're elected officials. If you can impeach Nixon, then you can impeach any of us. Translated into newspaper stories, this became a cry for national stability. But when a Tip O'Neill began using the word impeachment on the floor of the House of Representatives, this changed the issue. For he was no frivolous dreamer from the West Side of New York. This was a bone politician, a man with a word, and he gave great believability to the prospects of impeachment merely by saying it.

* * *

Weighing as much as he does, O'Neill does not look like a figure who has had anything to do with history. The thinness, the austerity, and the haughtiness that glare at you from oil portraits of such men is totally absent in O'Neill. He comes with the full blood of Cork City in his face. A great head of silver hair allows O'Neill to be picked out of a crowd at a glance. He has a large bulbous nose that is quite red. Large blue eyes sometimes seem to be sleepy-slow and have led a thousand victims into thinking that they were on the verge of winning. When he has a thick Daniel Webster cigar stuffed into one corner of his mouth, O'Neill appears to be a backroom politician who always has a drink or a contract in his hand. Someday, when he gets very old, I think O'Neill might say that no matter how far he went in life, how powerful he became, this appearance, as interpreted by so many others, prevented him from going even further, from going to the places where his talents belonged. Because if you see in a man and say of a man only that he is a big, overweight, cigar-smoking, whisky-drinking, back-pounding Boston politician, then somewhere over the years the man himself, somewhere deep down under the winces, could begin believing some of this himself and his momentum would become diminished. In this case, the Protestant ethic has robbed us of our eyes. For if you see Tom O'Neill as he is, not as comformity forces us to see, then there is coming into the room a lovely spring rain of a man.

He is not gruff; he is courtly. He is not cunning; he is open. His choice of words and the rhythm with which he uses them are many levels above most people who are great successes in private and public life. He does not become mesmerized with the sound of his voice; he is a spectacular aural learner.

However, he most certainly is one of those old-fashioned politicians that most people prefer to detest. So much of his life has demanded caution, waiting in line behind others, that he can often make going along sound like accomplishment. In 1967, speaking at Boston College, he told a crowd why he was in favor of the nation's policy in Vietnam: "I've been briefed forty-four times by the President, the State Department, the CIA, and the Department of Defense," he said. "I know more than you." He then went into the light-at-the-end-of-the-tunnel speech. A student named Pat McCarthy stood up and asked one question: "You've been briefed by the people in favor of the war. Have you ever been briefed by people on the other side of the question?" O'Neill was shot down by the question, and he knew it. He began to go around asking second-level Pentagon and CIA people about the war. They told him it was a disaster, that the country was being lied to. In August of the same year, in the 150,000 copies of his newsletter to constituents, O'Neill came out against the war. He informed no one else of it, however. It wasn't until October that *The Washington Star* heard about it and printed the story. That night, Lyndon Johnson had Secret Service men pull O'Neill out of a card game. Johnson asked O'Neill why he had done it. O'Neill said because he felt everybody was lying, even to Johnson, about the way the war was going. "Well, I've one request of you," Johnson said. "Just don't go around giving interviews about it."

"Why?" O'Neill asked.

Johnson then leaned on old friendships. He said that O'Neill had been allowed into Sam Rayburn's old "Board of Education," that John McCormack[4] was the one who had brought him into such an inside society. Somehow, Johnson saw this as an obligation. Somehow, O'Neill saw the same thing. He left the office and did not become one of the major voices against the war. His instinct might have taken him to the right decision, but his talent was betrayed by the life he had lived. Which makes his actions against Richard Nixon all the more important. We leave his full career for others to evaluate. Much more important is that here, in this single rare instance, O'Neill, and all these other politicians we scorn, stood up, stood apart from their pasts, and took us to heights we as a nation never have seen before.

NATHANIEL HAWTHORNE

Abraham Lincoln[1]

Of course, there was one other personage, in the class of statesmen, whom I should have been truly mortified to leave Washington without seeing; since (temporarily, at least, and by force of circumstances) he was the man of men. But a private grief had built up a barrier about him, impeding the customary free intercourse of Americans

---

4. Sam Rayburn (1882–1961) and John McCormack (1891–   ) were Speakers of the House of Representatives.

1. From an article in *The Atlantic Monthly*, July, 1862.

with their chief magistrate; so that I might have come away without a glimpse of his very remarkable physiognomy, save for a semi-official opportunity of which I was glad to take advantage. The fact is, we were invited to annex ourselves, as supernumeraries, to a deputation that was about to wait upon the President, from a Massachusetts whip factory, with a present of a splendid whip.

Our immediate party consisted only of four or five (including Major Ben Perley Poore, with his note-book and pencil), but we were joined by several other persons, who seemed to have been lounging about the precincts of the White House, under the spacious porch, or within the hall, and who swarmed in with us to take the chances of a presentation. Nine o'clock had been appointed as the time for receiving the deputation, and we were punctual to the moment; but not so the President, who sent us word that he was eating his breakfast, and would come as soon as he could. His appetite, we were glad to think, must have been a pretty fair one; for we waited about half an hour in one of the antechambers, and then were ushered into a reception-room, in one corner of which sat the Secretaries of War and of the Treasury, expecting, like ourselves, the termination of the Presidential breakfast. During this interval there were several new additions to our group, one or two of whom were in a working-garb, so that we formed a very miscellaneous collection of people, mostly unknown to each other, and without any common sponsor, but all with an equal right to look our head servant in the face.

By and by there was a little stir on the staircase and in the passage-way, and in lounged a tall, loose-jointed figure, of an exaggerated Yankee port and demeanor, whom (as being about the homeliest man I ever saw, yet by no means repulsive or disagreeable) it was impossible not to recognize as Uncle Abe.

Unquestionably, Western man though he be, and Kentuckian by birth, President Lincoln is the essential representative of all Yankees, and the veritable specimen, physically, of what the world seems determined to regard as our characteristic qualities. It is the strangest and yet the fittest thing in the jumble of human vicissitudes, that he, out of so many millions, unlooked for, unselected by any intelligible process that could be based upon his genuine qualities, unknown to those who chose him, and unsuspected of what endowments may adapt him for his tremendous responsibility, should have found the way open for him to fling his lank personality into the chair of state—where, I presume, it was his first impulse to throw his legs on the council-table, and tell the Cabinet Ministers a story. There is no describing his lengthy awkwardness, nor the uncouthness of his movement; and yet it seemed as if I had been in the habit of seeing him daily, and had shaken hands with him a thousand times in some village street; so true was he to the aspect of the pattern American, though with a certain extravagance which, possibly, I exaggerated still further by the delighted eagerness with which I took it in. If put to guess his calling and livelihood, I should have taken him for a country school-master as soon as anything else. He was dressed in a rusty black frock coat and pantaloons, unbrushed, and worn so faithfully that the suit had adapted itself to the curves and angularities of his figure, and had grown to be an outer skin of the man. His hair was black, still unmixed with gray, stiff, somewhat bushy, and had apparently been acquainted with neither brush nor comb that morning, after the disarrangement of the pillow; and as to a nightcap, Uncle Abe probably knows nothing of such effeminacies. His complexion is dark and sallow, betokening, I fear, a insalubrious atmosphere around the White House; he has thick black eyebrows and an impending brow; his nose is large, and the lines about his mouth are very strongly defined.

The whole physiognomy is as coarse a one as you would meet anywhere in the length and breadth of the States; but, withal, it is redeemed, illuminated, softened, and brightened by a kindly though serious look out of his eyes, and an expression of homely sagacity, that seems weighted with rich results of village experience. A great deal of native sense; no bookish cultivation, no refinement; honest at heart, and thoroughly so, and yet, in some sort, sly—at least, endowed with a sort of tact and wisdom that are akin to craft, and would impel him, I think, to take an antagonist in flank, rather than to make a bull-run at him right in front. But, on the whole, I like this sallow, queer, sagacious visage, with the homely human sympathies that warmed it; and, for my small share in the matter, would as lief have Uncle Abe for a ruler as any man whom it would have been practicable to put in his place.

Immediately on his entrance the President accosted our member of Congress, who had us in charge, and, with a comical twist of his face, made some jocular remark about the length of his breakfast. He then greeted us all round, not waiting for an introduction, but shaking and squeezing everybody's hand with the utmost cordiality, whether the individual's name was announced to him or not. His manner towards us was wholly without pretence, but yet had a kind of natural dignity, quite sufficient to keep the forwardest of us from clapping him on the shoulder and asking him for a story. A mutual acquaintance being established, our leader took the whip out of its case, and began to read the address of presentation. The whip was an exceedingly long one, its handle wrought in ivory (by some artist in the Massachusetts State Prison, I believe), and ornamented with a medallion of the President, and other equally beautiful devices; and along its whole length there was a succession of golden bands and ferrules. The address was shorter than the whip, but equally well made, consisting chiefly of an explanatory description of these artistic designs, and closing with a hint that the gift was a suggestive and emblematic one, and that the President would recognize the use to which such an instrument should be put.

This suggestion gave Uncle Abe rather a delicate task in his reply, because, slight as the matter seemed, it apparently called for some declaration, or intimation, or faint foreshadowing of policy in reference to the conduct of the war, and the final treatment of the Rebels. But the President's Yankee aptness and not-to-be-caughtness stood him in good stead, and he jerked or wiggled himself out of the dilemma with an uncouth dexterity that was entirely in character; although, without his gesticulation of eye and mouth—and especially the flourish of the whip, with which he imagined himself touching up a pair of fat horses—I doubt whether his words would be worth recording, even if I could remember them. The gist of the reply was, that he accepted the whip as an emblem of peace, not punishment; and, this great affair over, we retired out of the presence in high good humor, only regretting that we could not have seen the President sit down and fold up his legs (which is said to be a most extraordinary spectacle), or have heard him tell one of those delectable stories for which he is so celebrated. A good many of them are afloat upon the common talk of Washington, and are certainly the aptest, pithiest, and funniest little things imaginable; though, to be sure, they smack of the frontier freedom, and would not always bear repetition in a drawing-room, or on the immaculate page of the *Atlantic*.[2]

Good Heavens! what liberties have I been taking with one of the potentates of the earth, and the man on whose conduct more important consequences depend than on that of any other historical personage of the century! But with whom is an American citizen entitled to take a liberty, if not with his own chief magistrate? However, lest the above allusions to President Lincoln's little peculiarities (already well known to the country and to the world) should be misinterpreted, I deem it proper to say a word or two in regard to him, of unfeigned respect and measurable confidence. He is evidently a man of keen faculties, and, what is still more to the purpose, of powerful character. As to his integrity, the people have that intuition of it which is never deceived. Before he actually entered upon his great office, and for a considerable time afterwards, there is no reason to suppose that he adequately estimated the gigantic task about to be imposed on him, or, at least, had any distinct idea how it was to be managed; and I presume there may have been more than one veteran politician who proposed to himself to take the power out of President Lincoln's hands into his own, leaving our honest friend only the public responsibility for the good or ill success of the career. The extremely imperfect development of his statesmanly qualities, at that

2. This passage was one of those omitted from the article as originally published, and the following note was appended to explain the omission, which had been indicated by a line of points:
"We are compelled to omit two or three pages, in which the author describes the interview, and gives his idea of the personal appearance and deportment of the President. The sketch appears to have been written in a benign spirit, and perhaps conveys a not inaccurate impression of its august subject; but it lacks *reverence*, and it pains us to see a gentleman of ripe age, and who has spent years under the corrective influence of foreign institutions, falling into the characteristic and most ominous fault of Young America."

period, may have justified such designs. But the President is teach-
able by events, and has now spent a year in a very arduous course of
education; he has a flexible mind, capable of much expansion, and
convertible towards far loftier studies and activities than those of his
early, life; and if he came to Washington a backwoods humorist, he
has already transformed himself into as good a statesman (to speak
moderately) as his prime minister.[3]

3. Presumably the Secretary of State, William H. Seward.

QUESTIONS

1. In one sentence summarize Hawthorne's attitude toward Lincoln in the first seven paragraphs.
2. What is the basic pattern of the opening sentence of the fifth
paragraph? Find other examples of this pattern. What is their
total impact on Hawthorne's description?
3. In his final paragraph Hawthorne seeks to prevent misunderstanding by stressing his respect for and confidence in Lincoln.
Is there anything in the paragraph which runs counter to that
expression? To what effect?
4. In the footnote to the seventh paragraph the editor of The
Atlantic Monthly explains his omission of the first seven
paragraphs. On the evidence of this statement what sort of a
person does the editor seem to be? Is there anything in the omitted paragraphs that would tend to justify his decision? Is the full
description superior to the last paragraph printed alone? Explain.
5. Describe someone you know with a strong personality that has
contrasting characteristics.

THOMAS JEFFERSON
George Washington[1]

I think I knew General Washington intimately and thoroughly;
and were I called on to delineate his character, it should be in terms
like these.

His mind was great and powerful, without being of the very first
order; his penetration strong, though not so acute as that of a Newton,
Bacon, or Locke; and as far as he saw, no judgment was ever sounder.
It was slow in operation, being little aided by invention or imagination, but sure in conclusion. Hence the common remark of his
officers, of the advantage he derived from councils of war, where
hearing all suggestions, he selected whatever was best; and certainly no general ever planned his battles more judiciously. But if
deranged during the course of the action, if any member of his
plan was dislocated by sudden circumstances, he was slow in re-adjust-

1. From a letter written in 1814 to a
Doctor Jones, who was writing a history
and wanted to know about Washington's
role in the Federalist-Republican controversy.

ment. The consequence was, that he often failed in the field, and rarely against an enemy in station, as at Boston and York. He was incapable of fear, meeting personal dangers with the calmest unconcern. Perhaps the strongest feature in his character was prudence, never acting until every circumstance, every consideration, was maturely weighed; refraining if he saw a doubt, but, when once decided, going through with his purpose, whatever obstacles opposed. His integrity was most pure, his justice the most inflexible I have ever known, no motives of interest or consanguinity, of friendship or hatred, being able to bias his decision. He was, indeed, in every sense of the words, a wise, a good, and a great man. His temper was naturally irritable and high toned; but reflection and resolution had obtained a firm and habitual ascendency over it. If ever, however, it broke its bonds, he was most tremendous in his wrath. In his expenses he was honorable, but exact; liberal in contributions to whatever promised utility; but frowning and unyielding on all visionary projects, and all unworthy calls on his charity. His heart was not warm in its affections; but he exactly calculated every man's value, and gave him a solid esteem proportioned to it. His person, you know, was fine, his stature exactly what one would wish, his deportment easy, erect and noble; the best horseman of his age, and the most graceful figure that could be seen on horseback. Although in the circle of his friends, where he might be unreserved with safety, he took a free share in conversation, his colloquial talents were not above mediocrity, possessing neither copiousness of ideas, nor fluency of words. In public, when called on for a sudden opinion, he was unready, short and embarrassed. Yet he wrote readily, rather diffusely, in an easy and correct style. This he had acquired by conversation with the world, for his education was merely reading, writing and common arithmetic, to which he added surveying at a later day. His time was employed in action chiefly, reading little, and that only in agriculture and English history. His correspondence became necessarily extensive, and, with journalizing his agricultural proceedings, occupied most of his leisure hours within doors. On the whole, his character was, in its mass, perfect, in nothing bad, in few points indifferent; and it may truly be said, that never did nature and fortune combine more perfectly to make a man great, and to place him in the same constellation with whatever worthies have meritied from man an everlasting remembrance. For his was the singular destiny and merit, of leading the armies of his country successfully through an arduous war, for the establishment of its independence; of conducting its councils through the birth of a government, new in its forms and principles, until it had settled down into a quiet and orderly train; and of scrupulously obeying the laws through the whole of his career, civil and military, of which the history of the world furnishes no other example.

* * * I am satisfied the great body of republicans think of him as I

do. We were, indeed, dissatisfied with him on his ratification of the British treaty. But this was short lived. We knew his honesty, the wiles with which he was encompassed, and that age had already begun to relax the firmness of his purposes; and I am convinced he is more deeply seated in the love and gratitude of the republicans, than in the Pharisaical homage of the federal monarchists. For he was no monarchist from preference of his judgment. The soundness of that gave him correct views of the rights of man, and his severe justice devoted him to them. He has often declared to me that he considered our new Constitution as an experiment on the practicability of republican government, and with what dose of liberty man could be trusted for his own good; that he was determined the experiment should have a fair trial, and would lose the last drop of his blood in support of it. And these declarations he repeated to me the oftener and more pointedly, because he knew my suspicions of Colonel Hamilton's views, and probably had heard from him the same declarations which I had, to wit, "that the British constitution, with its unequal representation, corruption and other existing abuses, was the most perfect government which had ever been established on earth, and that a reformation of those abuses would make it an impracticable government." I do believe that General Washington had not a firm confidence in the durability of our government. He was naturally distrustful of men, and inclined to gloomy apprehensions; and I was ever persuaded that a belief that we must at length end in something like a British constitution, had some weight in his adoption of the ceremonies of levees, birthdays, pompous meetings with Congress, and other forms of the same character, calculated to prepare us gradually for a change which he believed possible, and to let it come on with as little shock as might be to the public mind.

These are my opinions of General Washington which I would vouch at the judgment seat of God, having been formed on an acquaintance of thirty years. I served with him in the Virginia legislature from 1769 to the Revolutionary war, and again, a short time in Congress, until he left us to take command of the army. During the war and after it we corresponded occasionally, and in the four years of my continuance in the office of Secretary of State, our intercourse was daily, confidential and cordial. After I retired from that office, great and malignant pains were taken by our federal monarchists, and not entirely without effect, to make him view me as a theorist, holding French principles of government, which would lead infallibly to licentiousness and anarchy. And to this he listened the more easily, from my known disapprobation of the British treaty. I never saw him afterwards, or these malignant insinuations should have been dissipated before his just judgment, as mists before the sun. I felt on his death, with my countrymen, that "verily a great man hath fallen this day in Israel."

On Ethics

JOHN DONNE

Tentation

After wee have parled with a tentation,[1] debating whether we should embrace it or no, and entertain'd some discourse with it, though some tendernesse, some remorse, make us turn our back upon it, and depart a little from it, yet the arrow overtakes us; some *reclinations*, some *retrospects* we have, a little of *Lot's wife*[2] is in us, a little *sociablenesse*, and *conversation*, a little point of *honour*, not to be false to former promises, a little *false gratitude*, and thankfulnesse, in respect of former obligations, a little of the *compassion* and *charity* of Hell, that another should not be miserable, for want of *us*, a little of this, which is but the good nature of the *Devill*, arrests us, stops us, fixes us, till the arrow, the tentation shoot us in the back, even when wee had a purpose of departing from that sin, and kils us over again.

1. Parleyed, spoken with a temptation.
2. Fleeing from the burning Sodom, she looked back upon the city. Genesis xix. 17-26.

QUESTIONS

1. Analyze this single-sentence passage, determining its syntax. What are the subject, predicate, and object? How many main or independent clauses are there? Which clauses and phrases are modifiers?
2. What metaphors does Donne use?
3. Taking syntax and metaphorical content together, indicate the effects Donne achieves in this sentence. Does it convey a sense of motion, speedy or lingering? What scene or scenes are pictured? What use is made of the sense of touch? How does the presentation of physical sensation work to convey Donne's statement about the operation of temptation?

JAMES THURBER
The Bear Who Let It Alone

In the words of the Far West there once lived a brown bear who could take it or let it alone. He would go into a bar where they sold mead, a fermented drink made of honey, and he would have just two drinks. Then he would put some money on the bar and say, "See what the bears in the back room will have," and he would go home. But finally he took to drinking by himself most of the day. He would reel home at night, kick over the umbrella stand, knock down the bridge lamps, and ram his elbows through the windows. Then he would collapse on the floor and lie there until he went to sleep. His wife was greatly distressed and his children were very frightened.

At length the bear saw the error of his ways and began to reform. In the end he became a famous teetotaller and a persistent temperance lecturer. He would tell everybody that came to his house about the awful effects of drink, and he would boast about how strong and well he had become since he gave up touching the stuff. To demonstrate this, he would stand on his head and on his hands and he would turn cartwheels in the house, kicking over the umbrella stand, knocking down the bridge lamps, and ramming his elbows through the windows. Then he would lie down on the floor, tired by his healthful exercise, and go to sleep. His wife was greatly distressed and his children were very frightened.

Moral: You might as well fall flat on your face as lean over too far backward.

SAMUEL JOHNSON
On Self-Love and Indolence[1]

—*Steriles transmisimus annos,*
Haec aevi mihi prima dies, haec limina vitae.
STAT. [I. 362]

—Our barren years are past;
Be this of life the first, of sloth the last.
ELPHINSTON

No weakness of the human mind has more frequently incurred animadversion, than the negligence with which men overlook their own faults, however flagrant, and the easiness with which they pardon them, however frequently repeated.

It seems generally believed, that, as the eye cannot see itself, the mind has no faculties by which it can contemplate its own state,

1. *The Rambler*, No. 15, Tuesday, September 10, 1751.

and that therefore we have not means of becoming acquainted with our real characters; an opinion which, like innumerable other postulates, an inquirer finds himself inclined to admit upon very little evidence, because it affords a ready solution of many difficulties. It will explain why the greatest abilities frequently fail to promote the happiness of those who possess them; why those who can distinguish with the utmost nicety the boundaries of vice and virtue, suffer them to be confounded in their own conduct; why the active and vigilant resign their affairs implicitly to the management of others; and why the cautious and fearful make hourly approaches toward ruin, without one sigh of solicitude or struggle for escape.

When a position teems thus with commodious consequences, who can without regret confess it to be false? Yet it is certain that declaimers have indulged a disposition to describe the dominion of the passions as extended beyond the limits that nature assigned. Self-love is often rather arrogant than blind; it does not hide our faults from ourselves, but persuades us that they escape the notice of others, and disposes us to resent censures lest we would confess them to be just. We are secretly conscious of defects and vices which we hope to conceal from the public eye, and please ourselves with innumerable impostures, by which, in reality, no body is deceived.

In proof of the dimness of our internal sight, or the general inability of man to determine rightly concerning his own character, it is common to urge the success of the most absurd and incredible flattery, and the resentment always raised by advice, however soft, benevolent, and reasonable. But flattery, if its operation be nearly examined, will be found to owe its acceptance not to our ignorance but knowledge of our failures, and to delight us rather as it consoles our wants than displays our possessions. He that shall solicit the favor of his patron by praising him for qualities which he can find in himself, will be defeated by the more daring panegyrist who enriches him with adscititious excellence. Just praise is only a debt, but flattery is a present. The acknowledgment of those virtues on which conscience congratulates us, is a tribute that we can at any time exact with confidence, but the celebration of those which we only feign, or desire without any vigorous endeavors to attain them, is received as a confession of sovereignty over regions never conquered, as a favorable decision of disputable claims, and is more welcome as it is more gratuitous.

Advice is offensive, not because it lays us open to unexpected regret, or convicts us of any fault which had escaped our notice, but because it shows us that we are known to others as well as to ourselves; and the officious monitor is persecuted with hatred, not because his accusation is false, but because he assumes that superiority which we are not willing to grant him, and has dared to detect what we desired to conceal.

For this reason advice is commonly ineffectual. If those who follow the call of their desires, without inquiry whither they are going, had deviated ignorantly from the paths of wisdom, and were rushing upon dangers unforeseen, they would readily listen to information that recalls them from their errors, and catch the first alarm by which destruction or infamy is denounced. Few that wander in the wrong way mistake it for the right; they only find it more smooth and flowery, and indulge their own choice rather than approve it: therefore few are persuaded to quit it by admonition or reproof, since it impresses no new conviction, nor confers any powers of action or resistance. He that is gravely informed how soon profusion will annihilate his fortune, hears with little advantage what he knew before, and catches at the next occasion of expense, because advice has no force to suppress his vanity. He that is told how certainly intemperance will hurry him to the grave, runs with his usual speed to a new course of luxury, because his reason is not invigorated, nor his appetite weakened.

The mischief of flattery is, not that it persuades any man that he is what he is not, but that it suppresses the influence of honest ambition, by raising an opinion that honor may be gained without the toil of merit; and the benefit of advice arises commonly, not from any new light imparted to the mind, but from the discovery which it affords of the· publick suffrages. He that could withstand conscience, is frighted at infamy, and shame prevails where reason was defeated.

As we all know our own faults, and know them commonly with many aggravations which human perspicacity cannot discover, there is, perhaps, no man, however hardened by impudence or dissipated by levity, sheltered by hypocrisy, or blasted by disgrace, who does not intend some time to review his conduct, and to regulate the remainder of his life by the laws of virtue. New temptations indeed attack him, new invitations are offered by pleasure and interest, and the hour of reformation is always delayed; every delay gives vice another opportunity of fortifying itself by habit; and the change of manners, though sincerely intended and rationally planned, is referred to the time when some craving passion shall be fully gratified, or some powerful allurement cease its importunity.

Thus procrastination is accumulated on procrastination, and one impediment succeeds another, till age shatters our resolution, or death intercepts the project of amendment. Such is often the end of salutary purposes, after they have long delighted the imagination, and appeased that disquiet which every mind feels from known misconduct, when the attention is not diverted by business or by pleasure.

Nothing surely can be more unworthy of a reasonable nature, than to continue in a state so opposite to real happiness, as that all

the peace of solitude and felicity of meditation, must arise from resolutions of forsaking it. Yet the world will often afford examples of
men, who pass months and years in a continual war with their own
convictions, and are daily dragged by habit or betrayed by passion
into practices, which they closed and opened their eyes with purposes to avoid; purposes which, though settled on conviction, the
first impulse of momentary desire totally overthrows.

The influence of custom is indeed such that to conquer it will
require the utmost efforts of fortitude and virtue, nor can I think any
man more worthy of veneration and renown, than those who have
burst the shackles of habitual vice. This victory however has different
degrees of glory as of difficulty; it is more heroic as the objects of
guilty gratification are more familiar, and the recurrence of solicita-
tion more frequent. He that from experience of the folly of ambition resigns his offices, may set himself free at once from temptation
to squander his life in courts, because he cannot regain his former
station. He who is enslaved by an amorous passion, may quit his
tyrant in disgust, and absence will without the help of reason overcome by degrees the desire of returning. But those appetites to
which every place affords their proper object, and which require no
preparatory measures or gradual advances, are more tenaciously
adhesive; the wish is so near the enjoyment, that compliance often
precedes consideration, and before the powers of reason can be summoned, the time for employing them is past.

Indolence is therefore one of the vices from which those whom it
once infects are seldom reformed. Every other species of luxury operates upon some appetite that is quickly satiated, and requires some
concurrence of art or accident which every place will not supply;
but the desire of ease acts equally at all hours, and the longer it
is indulged in the more increased. To do nothing is in every man's
power; we can never want an opportunity of omitting duties. The
lapse to indolence is soft and imperceptible, because it is only a
mere cessation of activity; but the return to diligence is difficult,
because it implies a change from rest to motion, from privation to
reality.

> —*Facilis descensus Averni:*
> *Noctes atque dies patet atri janua Ditis:*
> *Sed revocare gradum, superasque evadere ad auras,*
> *Hoc opus, hic labor est.—*
> > [VIR. *Aeneid* VI. 126]

> The gates of *Hell* are open night and day;
> Smooth the descent, and easy is the way:
> But, to return, and view the chearful skies;
> In this, the task and mighty labour lies.
> > DRYDEN

Of this vice, as of all others, every man who indulges it is conscious; we all know our own state, if we could be induced to consider it; and it might perhaps be useful to the conquest of all these ensnarers of the mind, if at certain stated days life was reviewed. Many things necessary are omitted, because we vainly imagine that they may be always performed, and what cannot be done without pain will for ever be delayed if the time of doing it be left unsettled. No corruption is great but by long negligence, which can scarcely prevail in a mind regularly and frequently awakened by periodical remorse. He that thus breaks his life into parts, will find in himself a desire to distinguish every stage of his existence by some improvement, and delight himself with the approach of the day of recollection, as of the time which is to begin a new series of virtue and felicity.

GEORGE P. ELLIOTT

Buried Envy

You have something I want and lack—riches, beauty, acclaim, new sneakers, enough to eat, children who love you, a reputation for goodness, goodness itself, top billing, a mother's sympathy, a Stutz Bearcat, the Presidency, a penis. You do something I would like to do and can't—bear a child, win the race, get your picture in the paper, command, catch a husband, stay married, star in a movie, vote, make love, sing beautifully, ask for your share, get your share, heal the sick, see.

How do I react?

Graced with a generous disposition, I rejoice with you; your good fortune gives me pleasure. If what you have came through luck, I am ready to accept what luck has in store for me, however much or little. If your accomplishment demands faculties I lack, I resolve to do as well as I can with what is available to me.

Not so graced, I can yet be disciplined enough to leave you undisturbed in the enjoyment of what you have. I keep my ugly feelings to myself, acknowledge them, regret them, but do not act on them.

But often I, being Everyman, am ungraceful, unconfident, and ill-controlled, and then your having what I lack becomes an evil to me. I neither want a good thing like the one you have nor strive for a real accomplishment of my own; instead, what I want most is to turn your joy into sadness. (The younger brother is given first choice. "Which do you want, the red one or the blue one?" He hesitates, then bursts into tears. "How can I tell until he chooses? I don't want either of them. I want *his*.") I may spoil your good thing for you, I may destroy it, I may steal it, I may cause you to do a bad job. What I want is not the thing itself but your misery at losing it.

When your good becomes my evil, and your evil my good, I am so ugly I can hardly bear to look at myself.

(I am not just Everyman. I am also a writer and a male, sane, middle-class, Wasp, in which roles I have had experience of envy both ways.)

Envy is devoid of dignity and lacks the passion that makes rage at least awful. The tone of voice and the words may be those of out-rage at injustice ("It isn't fair!"), but in a flick of the eyes, a twist of the mouth, a wince of the shoulders, the envy shows. Envy cannot, as treachery can, gloat, "I am the worst of all"; it is only the next worst. It is petty, devious, septic, cold. It is the self-dissatisfied. I am so ashamed of feeling it, I so despise myself for it, that after the first pangs, which surprise me into recognizing it for what it is, my impulse is to deny it. I would neither control nor purge it, but hide it.

But an evil that I hide in myself from myself does not go away; it rots and spreads, it shapes habits. Habitual envy confirms me in liti-giousness and complaint. It spoils my pleasure; my suspicion that someone is enjoying himself more than I ensures that he is. It impairs my either accepting or exercising authority, and it pollutes both my admiring excellence and my accomplishing something excellent. If authority and excellence are yours, I hate you for having them; if they are mine, I anticipate your hating me, and this dread disturbs my peace. My safest course is to muddy authority unless I can avoid it and to ignore excellence unless I can spoil it. One protection against envying or being envied is mediocrity.

When free and equal America was young and full of enthusiasm, Tocqueville could already identify envy as one of our special haz-ards. Now the causes of our envying and being envied have multi-pled and magnified: we Americans are rich and mighty, we talk louder than ever about freedom and equality, we can no longer effectively hide from ourselves our crimes of squandering and exploi-tation. Envy has become a pervasive affliction, yet it remains obscure. It can't be quantified; it can't be legislated against; it can't be denounced by public figures because the denunciation would be dismissible as a symptom of the ill it was meant to cure. Neverthe-less, we must try to understand how our ideals and institutions have inflamed envy and to modify these ideals and institutions in such a way as to reduce it—not get rid of it, for it is here to stay, but try to make it manageable as now it is not. Time to name it.

Like so many of the grand old pre-Enlightenment moral words, "envy" is too often used now for little, unclear things. The first event in the moral history of mankind, according to the Bible, resulted from Adam and Eve's disobedience, and the second from Cain's envy. For Dante, envy was the ugliest of the seven sins and next only to pride in gravity. Iago knew, and let us know, exactly what he suffered from when he said of Cassio, "He hath a daily beauty in his life/That makes me ugly"; yet in the early nineteenth century the label "motiveless malignity" was attached to Iago and stuck for generations—as though envy were not a motive as strong as vengeance or lust. Nowadays when people say, "I envy you," they commonly mean something innocuous like "I admire what you have and wish I had some, too." Johnson's Wax packages Envy for the housewife, knowing that nothing very negative is attached to being "the envy of your friends."

Trivializing a potent word keeps one from looking at what it really means. When envy was taught as a deadly fact of life, people knew what to look for and so could penetrate its disguises and defend themselves against it to some degree. But in this age of behavioral sciences, emergent envy is scarcely even named, especially not in America. Helmut Schoeck, an Austrian sociologist, in his compendious *Envy: A Theory of Social Behavior*, cites a 700-page book entitled *Human Behavior: An Inventory of Scientific Findings*, published in 1964 by two American behavioral scientists. He quotes them: "Our ambition in this book is to present, as fully and as accurately as possible, what the behavioral sciences now know about the behavior of human beings: what we really know, what we nearly know, what we think we know, what we claim to know." But, according to Schoeck: "The subject index fails to mention either envy or resentment. Jealousy is mentioned once."

Envy has come to be inextricably interwoven with advertising. Until modern times, most of what most people did was decided for them by custom. The Enlightenment, identifying hope with change and suspecting custom of being an enemy to change, promised people that, to the extent they got rid of custom, they could decide of their own free will what to put in its place. This progressive belief spread, and people have ever-increasingly abandoned custom. But the main thing that has taken its place turns out to be propaganda—a change, to be sure, but not for the better. In the United States, the dominant form of propaganda is advertising.

Originally, advertising was a sort of herald of progress: here are new ways to make your life better. And in fact technological progress did produce the goods and the wealth with which people made their lives materially more comfortable. But the more you have, the more sophisticated your appetites become. The ingenious temptations of advertising whet secondary and immoderate appetites for many things which exist only to create those appetites. And what can whet artificial appetites better than envy? "Our lotion will give your skin the beauty it lacks." A woman contemplates another woman who is beautiful with lotions or without, and her sense of inadequacy, latent in everyone but constantly evoked and magnified by advertising, inflames in her an envious longing. This longing is then manipulated so as to make her think it will be appeased by her using such-and-such a lotion; and so it is—for a while.

An overall effect of this chronic advertising is a restless insatiety which yields, among other ills, scorn of those who are content with what they have.

When President Johnson said the rest of the world wants what we have and we aren't going to let them have it, he was gloating in such a manner as to provoke envy; he was taunting. A great many freedoms were built into our Constitution by the Founding Fathers, and with spectacular success. However, the conditions that made this success possible in rich, raw, Enlightened, Anglo-Protestant America have never recurred, never can recur. The power, wealth, and hope, the spiritual energy released by America's new free way of doing things are among the wonders of the ages; conversely, among the great dangers of the world are the uglinesses also released by this new free way which we have taught others to want. "If you were as free and equal as we are, you'd be rich too." Surely Sukarno was right when he said that the greatest revolutionary force in Indonesia was not Marxism but American movies: envy as an engine of rebelliousness.

Any great change for the better brings its own evil with it, and so one powerful consideration should always be alive in the back of our minds: if we release this good thing, what evil is likely to escape with it? We have asked this question about free speech and have pretty much decided to take the risk; about free sex we are not yet so sure. In the eighteenth century, when economic enterprise was freed from the old pre-Enlightenment restraints and powered with technology, first in England and then throughout the West, the dangers latent in liberal capitalism seemed far outweighed by the enormous riches it generated; we are now appalled by the consequences of the greed and waste which were also released, and in such movements as environmentalism and consumer protection we are working to restrain the habits of custodial irresponsibility which we, like all the free-enterprise world, have been practicing. As more and more egalitarian pressures for change arise, we must be careful each time to ask, How may this change affect the workings of envy? For any change in social attitudes or customs that is likely to increase envy is as suspect as any change that increases greed, and to identify envy is to loathe it. About that at least there is agreement among all mankind: envy is loathsome, and the envious man is everywhere recognized as a menace to the common good.[1]

1. The first serious portrayal of Enlightenment envy was made by that apostle of the period who was wiser than he taught—Diderot, in his short novel *Rameau's Nephew* [Elliott's note].

Near the heart of the matter is equality/authority. Why should I look up to you? Why should I do as you say? Why should I serve you?

Before the Enlightenment, the answers to these questions were traditional: because I am poorer than you, because I am of lower class, because I am inferior. But, whatever the answer, somewhere in the offing, seldom mentioned yet always present, stood the hard threat: you are strong and I am weak, you will hurt me if I don't obey. Revulsion against this ugliness of hierarchy was a strong engine of the Enlightenment, which taught people the democratic challenge: I will look up to you, obey you, serve you only if I am persuaded that you are superior to me; prove it. It taught people to demand that social authority be vested, as it often is in science, only in those who are worthy of it and that those in office should retain their power only as they exercise it well. And who would argue against this as the ideal of authority in action?

The obvious trouble with this ideal is the false expectations it creates. In the social, moral world, the meritocratic ideal can seldom be fulfilled, and never for very long. A ruler may be strong, he may be wise, he may be so trained in the exercise of power that he is not corrupted by it; even so, he must constantly make decisions on insufficient evidence, he must err, he must antagonize some of those he rules, and he must disappoint idealists.

Now, if I do not like how I am ruled or those who rule me, one good course of action is for me to work to improve the ways in which I am ruled and to select better rulers. But, just as few of those with great power are in fact ideally worthy of their office, likewise few citizens in a huge democracy are, judged by the same ideal, good citizens. By trying to practice democracy's ideal of earned authority, we see to it that we are chronically disappointed both in our rulers and in ourselves as citizens. "He's no good; we elected him; to hell with the whole thing." Perhaps we have even acquired a sneaky taste for this sort of political self-cheat, for the candidate's "image" rather than for his political substance. Why else would we so often elect men blatantly impossible to admire or to obey gladly?

A better way is to give those in authority the benefit of the doubt, to undermine trust in them only as a last resort, and when you move against them to do it fast and hard—to make a clean distinction between granting them authority and leaving them undisturbed in the exercise of it. (On the scaffold, with the headsman holding the ax of the people's will over his head, Charles I of England said, "A subject and a sovereign are clean different things," and the ax fell.) We American citizens have done as badly by President Nixon as he has done by us. We elected him without, most of us, trusting him; because he served our greed well in the name of the public good, we overwhelmingly reelected him; we have treated him with even more suspicion and disrespect than we heap on most of our public officials; we have badly undercut him; yet we leave him there[2] with more power at his fingertips than any other man in the world (have even, in the energy crisis, added to it), though we fully expect that he will use that power badly, even dangerously. And the only rhetoric as high-minded as his is ours. Have we not done a mob job of it?

To arrange matters so that you cannot revere but must despise those over you implies an atrophy of the organs of admiration and an appetite to be cheated. Disorder of this kind is to be found not just in politics, but also in religion, entertainment, education, art, love. In this ugliness envy is rampant.

An evil released by a good pollutes that good itself. But because equality is so powerful an ideal and because we have been so negligent in identifying the envy which has been released with it and generated by it, we have not recognized the twin uglinesses of egalitarianism. One is the sly disposition to elevate the mediocre, the talentless, the boring (Andy Warhol, camp, popular singers who can't sing true); the other is the zeal to bring down the high, not just the rich and powerful like the Kennedys but also the excellent and good. Martin Luther King was subjected first to an assassin's bullet and then to a now-it-can-be-told journalist's pen. The moment we are threatened with having a saint on our hands, we turn him into a celebrity and debunk him.

A great many people are better than I am in a great many respects. When I accept my station in life, I see any disparity in gifts not as an injustice but as a part of reality, the way things are, and such envy as I feel is my private sadness. When I believe that all men are equal and that my station in life is either too high (in which case I feel guilty) or too low (in which case I feel resentful), I see any disparity in gifts as an injustice; and the sloppier my understanding of equality, of the very few respects in which it makes sense to say, "All men are equal," the wider my envy rampages, cloaked as outrage against injustice. Egalitarian radicalism provides an ideology which sanctions criminal rage, as recently with the Symbionese Liberation Army,[3] and envy uses equality as a device for bringing down the high and a justification for bringing down the good and the beautiful. Nevertheless, one way or another, excellence keeps manifesting itself, for America also encourages us to succeed, to stand out.[4]

Envy is a far dirtier little secret than sex or money; we are

---

2. Written before President Nixon's resignation from office.

3. A terrorist organization.

4. An extreme of egalitarian theory is to be found in *Inequality*, by Christopher Jencks and others. The authors' research and speculation were done at Harvard, that most elite of universities. Apparently, like the peculiar modesty for which some have made themselves famous, this equality can be excelled at, as in *Animal Farm*: "All animals are equal, but some animals are more equal than others" [Elliott's note].

ashamed to own up to it; looking at it pains us. Moreover, a lot of people believe man is perfectible, an opinion which makes them very keen indeed not to see us as stuck with envy no matter how hard we strive to progress, keen not to see us as incapable of limitless progress because we are stuck with envy and the like. There are even those who still, more or less overtly, believe that liberating everything in us will cause us to be happy; these free spirits, these pristine, unpenetrated minds, reason that prohibitions create evil rather than restrain it, so envy is therefore a mere by-product of oppression. But the Noble Savage brand, all ingredients guaranteed good, always has put out the prettiest can of worms going.

Envy has rotted and spread, filling us with a terrible anxiety whose origin we are ignorant of and are hence unfit to control. To fear envy and to keep from provoking it is sane enough, but dread generated by an unknown cause, especially one as septic as envy, is literally maddening. It can, and in the case of egalitarianism does, stoke the very fire it fears. Our first obligation is to look at the envy both in us and also out there because of us, to name it, to trace it, to meditate on what practical measures to take.

Consider our welfare system. Surely unadmitted fear of the resentful envy of the poor, of the black poor especially, has far more to do with the way welfare has evolved than does social justice, and surely the resentful envy which welfare provokes in those not quite poor enough to get any, and also in those who pay for it, is chief among the evils that nearly cancel the social good it does. Or consider the competitive envy generated by the way we decentralize authority over local public schools—just enough so that each neighborhood is spurred not only to do something good in itself but even more to make sure you don't get something I don't. Or consider that the most important thing most women do or ever could do is to make a home and raise their children, and then think of how inferior and deprived the women's liberation movement tries to make them feel about their most rewarding occupation.

A seeming remedy to such dreadful uglinesses as these is total dictatorial egalitarianism, and many want it. After all, who are more equal and less burdened by authority and responsibility than totalitarian slaves? It is plain that the limits of technological power are in sight and that there is not and never will be enough for everyone to be rich, as progress led mankind to hope. In many, rage from this disappointment combines with envy of privilege and with fear of technocratic totalitarianism à la Nixon, Haldeman, Ehrlichman, and Co., until the only relief is total leveling and suppression of that individualism essential for the prospering of most human excellence above the level of Ping-Pong and moonwalks.

This remedy, however, leads to the ultimate disorder of equality. "I'm as good as the next fellow. Every man a king. No one can have authority over me. I acknowledge no superior." In a frenzy of blinding itself to some plain facts of existence, this egalitarianism bursts all bounds and rages not just against excellence but against difference itself. "Let's make this one unanimous, shall we?"

The Russians have long made a wooden doll which opens to reveal another doll inside it; in that doll is another one, and in the third, still another. The Soviet dolls-within-dolls have identical faces, although they are of different sizes. Before the revolution each had its own face.

Mao's socialism not only teaches you to excel at not excelling—in his China, everyone dresses alike; music is composed by committee; you spend years in prison being reeducated and pay with your very self for having ideas of your own.

Among us, the main form the rage against difference takes is the drive to obliterate values and hierarchies. It's all just a matter of opinion and mine's as good as yours. Don't discriminate against the low-ability student in favor of the gifted. The only differences between the sexes or the races are superficial. A recurring theme in recent science fiction is that each of us is entitled to his own reality, one no better than another—a valuelessness that is ingenious, but frivolous because of its ingenuity.

The crisis of identity: so far as I can make out, the breakdown of separateness and individuality, which some psychotherapies currently advocate and practice, has nothing to do with the mystic's merging of the self with the One, or with Christ's "He that loses his life for my sake shall find it," or with Cathy's perfectly romantic cry, "I *am* Heathcliff." Rather, these therapies would cure the ill of alienation by blurring the difference between you and me.

Art provides an example of such homogenization which is not only extreme but vivid. Why does a painter offer you a canvas so covered with random dots and splashes that the right side looks pretty much like the left and the top like the bottom? Why does a poet offer you a page on which is printed a "grid" of nouns connected only if and as you choose to connect them? Why does a composer offer you a half hour of blips and zooms which are neither musical tones nor noises but something electronic in between, and which lack every sort of harmonious, melodious, or rhythmic pattern? An artist might do such things out of theory or because it is fashionable to do so. An even better reason for him to do them, though, is lack of talent or inability to use what talent he has. If he can blur the distinction not just between good art and bad but also between art and non-art, and if he can then get people to buy and praise his easy frauds, he will then have a double satisfaction: contempt for the suckers and at least some revenge on those who can and do create things worth looking at, hearing, imagining.

As for the blurring of sexual distinctions—between man and woman, between pleasure and communion, between marriage and romantic love—there is more to be said than room to say it here. But as with all this rage against difference, the roots are fear of failing to do well and envy of those who succeed highly.

Better to take the risk of being human, envy and all. When your good becomes my evil and your evil my good, then more than ever should I look straight at myself, however painful it is to do so. I must know my envy if I am to be myself.

QUESTIONS

1. *Envy is a personal or an individual feeling, yet much of Elliott's concern, and discussion, is general and social. How does he manage transitions between the two levels? Why does he combine the two levels and thus have to make these transitions?*
2. *Is envy as Elliott defines it a satisfactory explanation for the various phenomena he discusses?*
3. *On p. 721 Elliott speaks of trivializing potent words. Can you find examples in newspapers, magazines, advertising, or conversation? What is the relation between this process and evasive euphemizing as described by George Orwell in "Politics and the English Language" (p. 323)?*
4. *Elliott says that "an atrophy of the organs of admiration and an appetite to be cheated" may be found in politics, religion, entertainment, education, art, and love (p. 724). Discuss examples that might support or refute Elliott's contention.*

THEOPHRASTUS

The Flatterer

Flattery is a cringing sort of conduct that aims to promote the advantage of the flatterer. The flatterer is the kind of man who, as he walks with an acquaintance, says: "Behold! how the people gaze at you! There is not a man in the city who enjoys so much notice as yourself. Yesterday your praises were the talk of the Porch. While above thirty men were sitting there together and the conversation fell upon the topic: 'Who is our noblest citizen?' they all began and ended with your name." As the flatterer goes on talking in this strain he picks a speck of lint from his hero's cloak; or if the wind has lodged a bit of straw in his locks, he plucks it off and says laughingly, "See you? Because I have not been with you these two days, your beard is turned gray. And yet if any man has a beard that is black for his years, it is you."

While his patron speaks, he bids the rest be silent. He sounds his praises in his hearing and after the patron's speech gives the cue for applause by "Bravo!" If the patron makes a stale jest, the flatterer laughs and stuffs his sleeve into his mouth as though he could not contain himself.

If they meet people on the street, he asks them to wait until the master passes. He buys apples and pears, carries them to his hero's house and gives them to the children, and in the presence of the father, who is looking on, he kisses them, exclaiming: "Bairns of a worthy sire!" When the patron buys a pair of shoes, the flatterer observes: "The foot is of a finer pattern than the boot"; if he calls on a friend, the flatterer trips on ahead and says: "*You* are to have the honor of his visit"; and then turns back with, "I have announced you." Of course he can run and do the errands at the market in a twinkle.

Amongst guests at a banquet he is the first to praise the wine and, doing it ample justice, he observes: "What a fine cuisine you have!" He takes a bit from the board and exclaims: "What a dainty morsel this is!" Then he inquires whether his friend is chilly, asks if he would like a wrap put over his shoulders, and whether he shall throw one about him. With these words he bends over and whispers in his ear. While his talk is directed to the rest, his eye is fixed on his patron. In the theatre he takes the cushions from the page and himself adjusts them for the comfort of the master. Of his hero's house he says: "It is well built"; of his farm: "It is well tilled"; and of his portrait: "It is a speaking image."

FRANCIS BACON
Of Simulation and Dissimulation

Dissimulation is but a faint kind of policy or wisdom; for it asketh a strong wit and a strong heart to know when to tell truth, and to do it. Therefore it is the weaker sort of politics[1] that are the great dissemblers.

Tacitus saith, *Livia sorted well with the arts of her husband and dissimulation of her son*; attributing arts or policy to Augustus, and dissimulation to Tiberius. And again, when Mucianus encourageth Vespasian to take arms against Vitellius, he saith, *We rise not against the piercing judgment of Augustus, nor the extreme caution or closeness of Tiberius.*[2] These properties, of arts or policy and dissimulation or closeness, are indeed habits and faculties several, and to be distinguished. For if a man have that penetration of judgment as he can discern what things are to be laid open, and what to be secreted, and what to be shewed at half lights, and to whom and when, (which indeed are arts of state and arts of life, as Tacitus well calleth them), to him a habit of dissimulation is a hinderance

1. Politicians.
2. The Roman historian Tacitus here speaks of the plottings of Livia, wife of the emperor Augustus Caesar and mother of his successor Tiberius; and of the Roman official Mucianus, who in 69 A.D. supported Vespasian in his successful struggle against Vitellius to gain the imperial throne.

and a poorness. But if a man cannot obtain to that judgment, then it is left to him generally to be close, and a dissembler. For where a man cannot choose or vary in particulars, there it is good to take the safest and wariest way in general; like the going softly, by one that cannot well see. Certainly the ablest men that ever were have had all an openness and frankness of dealing; and a name of certainty and veracity; but then they were like horses well managed; for they could tell passing well when to stop or turn; and at such times when they thought the case indeed required dissimulation, if then they used it, it came to pass that the former opinion spread abroad of their good faith and clearness of dealing made them almost invisible.

There be three degrees of this hiding and veiling of a man's self. The first, Closeness, Reservation, and Secrecy; when a man leaveth himself without observation, or without hold to be taken, what he is. The second, Dissimulation, in the negative; when a man lets fall signs and arguments, that he is not that he is. And the third, Simulation, in the affirmative; when a man industriously and expressly feigns and pretends to be that he is not.

For the first of these, Secrecy; it is indeed the virtue of a confessor.[3] And assuredly the secret man heareth many confessions. For who will open himself to a blab or babbler? But if a man be thought secret, it inviteth discovery; as the more close air sucketh in the more open; and as in confession the revealing is not for worldly use, but for the ease of a man's heart, so secret men come to the knowledge of many things in that kind; while men rather discharge their minds than impart their minds. In few words, mysteries are due to secrecy. Besides (to say truth) nakedness is uncomely, as well in mind as body; and it addeth no small reverence to men's manners and actions, if they be not altogether open. As for talkers and futile persons, they are commonly vain and credulous withal. For he that talketh what he knoweth, will also talk what he knoweth not. Therefore set it down, *that an habit of secrecy is both politic and moral.* And in this part, it is good that a man's face give his tongue leave to speak. For the discovery of a man's self by the tracts of his countenance is a great weakness and betraying; by how much it is many times more marked and believed than a man's words.

For the second, which is Dissimulation; it followeth many times upon secrecy by a necessity; so that he that will be secret must be a dissembler in some degree. For men are too cunning to suffer a man to keep an indifferent carriage between both, and to be secret, without swaying the balance on either side. They will so beset a man with questions, and draw him on, and pick it out of him, that, without an absurd silence, he must shew an inclination one way; or if he do not, they will gather as much by his silence as by his speech. As for equivocations, or oraculous speeches, they cannot hold out

3. One to whom confession is made.

for long. So that no man can be secret, except he give himself a little scope of dissimulation; which is, as it were, but the skirts or train of secrecy.

But for the third degree, which is Simulation and false profession; that I hold more culpable, and less politic; except it be in great and rare matters. And therefore a general custom of simulation (which is this last degree) is a vice, rising either of a natural falseness or fearfulness, or of a mind that hath some main faults, which because a man must needs disguise, it maketh him practice simulation in other things, lest his hand should be out of ure.[4]

The great advantages of simulation and dissimulation are three. First, to lay asleep opposition, and to surprise. For where a man's intentions are published, it is an alarum to call up all that are against them. The second is, to reserve to a man's self a fair retreat. For if a man engage himself by a manifest declaration, he must go through or take a fall. The third is, the better to discover the mind of another. For to him that opens himself men will hardly shew themselves adverse; but will (fair) let him go on, and turn their freedom of speech to freedom of thought. And therefore it is a good shrewd proverb of the Spaniard, *Tell a lie and find a troth.* As if there were no way of discovery but by simulation. There be also three disadvantages, to set it even. The first, that simulation and dissimulation commonly carry with them a shew of fearfulness, which in any business doth spoil the feathers of round flying up to the mark.[5] The second, that it puzzleth and perplexeth the conceits of many, that perhaps would otherwise co-operate with him; and makes a man walk almost alone to his own ends. The third and greatest is, that it depriveth a man of one of the most principal instruments for action; which is trust and belief. The best composition and temperature is to have openness in fame and opinion; secrecy in habit; dissimulation in seasonable use; and a power to feign, if there be no remedy.

4. Practice.   5. Conceptions, thoughts.

QUESTIONS

1. Explain Bacon's distinction, drawn in the first two paragraphs, between dissembling, on the one hand, and, on the other, arts and policy. How does this opening prepare the way for the remainder of the essay?
2. How is the word "dissimulation" as used in the third paragraph and thereafter to be distinguished from its use in the first two paragraphs?
3. What are the three degrees of hiding of a man's self? According to what principles does Bacon arrange these degrees? What accounts for his according unequal amounts of space to the exposition of them?
4. Make a close analysis of Bacon's closing paragraph, indicating the ways Bacon achieves symmetry, balance. How does that effect

contribute to his tone and purpose? What elements in the
paragraph offset a mere symmetry?

5. In what connection and to what purpose does Bacon use the
following expressions? Explain the image or allusion in each:
   a. "like the going softly, by one that cannot well see" (p. 729)
   b. "like horses well managed; for they could tell passing well
   when to stop or turn" (p.729)
   c. "as the more close air sucketh in the more open" (p. 729)
   d. "it is good that a man's face give his tongue leave to speak"
   (p. 729)
   e. "he must go through or take a fall" (p. 730)
   f. "fearfulness, which in any business doth spoil the feathers of
   round flying up to the mark" (p. 730)

6. Bacon would allow "simulation and false profession" in "great
and rare matters." Would you? Give an example of such matters. Write a brief essay explaining your position.

7. What view of the world underlies Bacon's essay? Write an essay
showing what Bacon's assumptions about the world seem to be.
Be careful to show how you draw upon the essay to find out
Bacon's assumptions.

LORD CHESTERFIELD

Letter to His Son

London, October 16, O.S. 1747

DEAR BOY

The art of pleasing is a very necessary one to possess, but a very
difficult one to acquire. It can hardly be reduced to rules; and your
own good sense and observation will teach you more of it than I
can. "Do as you would be done by," is the surest method that I
know of pleasing. Observe carefully what pleases you in others, and
probably the same things in you will please others. If you are pleased
with the complaisance and attention of others to your humors, your
tastes, or your weaknesses, depend upon it, the same complaisance
and attention on your part to theirs will equally please them. Take
the tone of the company that you are in, and do not pretend to give
it; be serious, gay, or even trifling, as you find the present humor of
the company; this is an attention due from every individual to the
majority. Do not tell stories in company; there is nothing more tedious and disagreeable; if by chance you know a very short story,
and exceedingly applicable to the present subject of conversation, tell
it in as few words as possible; and even then, throw out that you do
not love to tell stories, but that the shortness of it tempted you.

Of all things banish the egotism out of your conversation, and
never think of entertaining people with your own personal concerns
or private affairs; though they are interesting to you, they are tedious

and impertinent to everybody else; besides that, one cannot keep one's own private affairs too secret. Whatever you think your own excellencies may be, do not affectedly display them in company; nor labor, as many people do, to give that turn to the conversation, which may supply you with an opportunity of exhibiting them. If they are real, they will infallibly be discovered, without your pointing them out yourself, and with much more advantage. Never maintain an argument with heat and clamor, though you think or know yourself to be in the right; but give your opinion modestly and coolly, which is the only way to convince; and, if that does not do, try to change the conversation, by saying, with good-humor, "We shall hardly convince one another; nor is it necessary that we should, so let us talk of something else."

Remember that there is a local propriety to be observed in all companies; and that what is extremely proper in one company may be, and often is, highly improper in another.

The jokes, the *bon-mots*, the little adventures, which may do very well in one company, will seem flat and tedious, when related in another. The particular characters, the habits, the cant of one company may give merit to a word, or a gesture, which would have none at all if divested of those accidental circumstances. Here people very commonly err; and fond of something that has entertained them in one company, and in certain circumstances, repeat it with emphasis in another, where it is either insipid, or, it may be, offensive, by being ill-timed or misplaced. Nay, they often do it with this silly preamble: "I will tell you an excellent thing," or, "I will tell you the best thing in the world." This raises expectations, which, when absolutely disappointed, make the relator of this excellent thing look, very deservedly, like a fool.

If you would particularly gain the affection and friendship of particular people, whether men or women, endeavor to find out their predominant excellency, if they have one, and their prevailing weakness, which everybody has; and do justice to the one, and something more than justice to the other. Men have various objects in which they may excel, or at least would be thought to excel; and, though they love to hear justice done to them, where they know that they excel, yet they are most and best flattered upon those points where they wish to excel, and yet are doubtful whether they do or not. As for example: Cardinal Richelieu, who was undoubtedly the ablest statesman of his time, or perhaps of any other, had the idle vanity of being thought the best poet too; he envied the great Corneille his reputation, and ordered a criticism to be written upon the *Cid*. Those, therefore, who flattered skillfully, said little to him of his abilities in state affairs, or at least but *en passant*, and as it might naturally occur. But the incense which they gave him, the smoke of which they knew would turn his head in their favor, was as a *bel esprit* and a poet. Why? Because he was sure of one excellency, and distrustful as to the other.

You will easily discover every man's prevailing vanity by observing his favorite topic of conversation; for every man talks most of what he has most a mind to be thought to excel in. Touch him but there, and you touch him to the quick. The late Sir Robert Walpole (who was certainly an able man) was little open to flattery upon that head, for he was in no doubt himself about it; but his prevailing weakness was, to be thought to have a polite and happy turn to gallantry— of which he had undoubtedly less than any man living. It was his favorite and frequent subject of conversation, which proved to those who had any penetration that it was his prevailing weakness, and they applied to it with success.

Women have, in general, but one object, which is their beauty; upon which scarce any flattery is too gross for them to follow. Nature has hardly formed a woman ugly enough to be insensible to flattery upon her person; if her face is so shocking that she must, in some degree, be conscious of it, her figure and air, she trusts, make ample amends for it. If her figure is deformed, her face, she thinks, counterbalances it. If they are both bad, she comforts herself that she has graces, a certain manner, a *je ne sais quoi* still more engaging than beauty. This truth is evident from the studied and elaborate dress of the ugliest woman in the world. An undoubted, uncontested, conscious beauty is, of all women, the least sensible of flattery upon that head; she knows it is her due, and is therefore obliged to nobody for giving it her. She must be flattered upon her understanding; which, though she may possibly not doubt of herself, yet she suspects that men may distrust.

Do not mistake me, and think that I mean to recommend to you abject and criminal flattery: no; flatter nobody's vices or crimes: on the contrary, abhor and discourage them. But there is no living in the world without a complaisant indulgence for people's weaknesses, and innocent, though ridiculous vanities. If a man has a mind to be thought wiser, and a woman handsomer, than they really are, their error is a comfortable one to themselves, and an innocent one with regard to other people; and I would rather make them my friends by indulging them in it, than my enemies by endeavoring (and that to no purpose) to undeceive them.

There are little attentions, likewise, which are infinitely engaging, and which sensibly affect that degree of pride and self-love, which is inseparable from human nature, as they are unquestionable proofs of the regard and consideration which we have for the persons to whom we pay them. As, for example, to observe the little habits, the likings, the antipathies, and the tastes of those whom we would gain; and then take care to provide them with the one, and to secure them from the other; giving them, genteelly, to understand, that you had observed they liked such a dish, or such a room, for which reason you had prepared it: or, on the contrary, that having observed they had an aversion to such a dish, a dislike to such a person, etc., you had taken care to avoid presenting them. Such attention to such trifles flatters self-love much more then greater things, as it makes people think themselves almost the only objects of your thoughts and care.

These are some of the arcana necessary for your initiation in the great society of the world. I wish I had known them better at your age; I have paid the price of three and fifty years for them, and shall not grudge it if you reap the advantage. Adieu.

SAMUEL L. CLEMENS

Advice to Youth

Being told I would be expected to talk here, I inquired what sort of a talk I ought to make. They said it should be something suitable to youth—something didactic, instructive, or something in the nature of good advice. Very well. I have a few things in my mind which I have often longed to say for the instruction of the young; for it is in one's tender early years that such things will best take root and be most enduring and most valuable. First, then, I will say to you, my young friends—and I say it beseechingly, urgingly—

Always obey your parents, when they are present. This is the best policy in the long run, because if you don't they will make you. Most parents think they know better than you do, and you can generally make more by humoring that superstition than you can by acting on your own better judgment.

Be respectful to your superiors, if you have any, also to strangers, and sometimes to others. If a person offend you, and you are in doubt as to whether it was intentional or not, do not resort to extreme measures; simply watch your chance and hit him with a brick. That will be sufficient. If you shall find that he had not intended any offense, come out frankly and confess yourself in the wrong when you struck him; acknowledge it like a man and say you didn't mean to. Yes, always avoid violence; in this age of charity and kindliness, the time has gone by for such things. Leave dynamite to the low and unrefined.

Go to bed early, get up early—this is wise. Some authorities say get up with the sun; some others say get up with one thing, some with another. But a lark is really the best thing to get up with. It gives you a splendid reputation with everybody to know that you get up with the lark; and if you get the right kind of a lark, and work at him right, you can easily train him to get up at half past nine, every time—it is no trick at all.

Now as to the matter of lying. You want to be very careful about lying; otherwise you are nearly sure to get caught. Once caught, you can never again be, in the eyes of the good and the pure, what you were before. Many a young person has injured himself permanently

through a single clumsy and illfinished lie, the result of carelessness
born of incomplete training. Some authorities hold that the young
ought not to lie at all. That, of course, is putting it rather stronger
than necessary; still, while I cannot go quite so far as that, I do
maintain, and I believe I am right, that the young ought to be temperate in the use of this great art until practice and experience shall
give them that confidence, elegance, and precision which alone can
make the accomplishment graceful and profitable. Patience, diligence, painstaking attention to detail—these are the requirements;
these, in time, will make the student perfect; upon these, and upon
these only, may he rely as the sure foundation for future eminence.
Think what tedious years of study, thought, practice, experience,
went to the equipment of that peerless old master who was able to
impose upon the whole world the lofty and sounding maxim that
"truth is mighty and will prevail"—the most majestic compound
fracture of fact which any of woman born has yet achieved. For the
history of our race, and each individual's experience, are sown thick
with evidence that a truth is not hard to kill and that a lie told well
is immortal. There is in Boston a monument of the man who discovered anaesthesia; many people are aware, in these latter days,
that that man didn't discover it at all, but stole the discovery from
another man. Is this truth mighty, and will it prevail? Ah no, my
hearers, the monument is made of hardy material, but the lie it tells
will outlast it a million years. An awkward, feeble, leaky lie is a
thing which you ought to make it your unceasing study to avoid;
such a lie as that has no more real permanence than an average
truth. Why, you might as well tell the truth at once and be done
with it. A feeble, stupid, preposterous lie will not live two years—
except it be a slander upon somebody. It is indestructible, then, of
course, but that is no merit of yours. A final word: begin your practice of this gracious and beautiful art early—begin now. If I had
begun earlier, I could have learned how.

Never handle firearms carelessly. The sorrow and suffering that
have been caused through the innocent but heedless handling of
firearms by the young! Only four days ago, right in the next farmhouse to the one where I am spending the summer, a grandmother,
old and gray and sweet, one of the loveliest spirits in the land, was
sitting at her work, when her young grandson crept in and got down
an old, battered, rusty gun which had not been touched for many
years and was supposed not to be loaded, and pointed it at her,
laughing and threatening to shoot. In her fright she ran screaming
and pleading toward the door on the other side of the room; but as
she passed him he placed the gun almost against her very breast and
pulled the trigger! He had supposed it was not loaded. And he was
right—it wasn't. So there wasn't any harm done. It is the only case
of that kind I ever heard of. Therefore, just the same, don't you
meddle with old unloaded firearms; they are the most deadly and

unerring things that have ever been created by man. You don't have to take any pains at all with them; you don't have to have a rest, you don't have to have any sights on the gun, you don't have to take aim, even. No, you just pick out a relative and bang away, and you are sure to get him. A youth who can't hit a cathedral at thirty yards with a Gatling gun in three-quarters of an hour, can take up an old empty musket and bag his grandmother every time, at a hundred. Think what Waterloo[1] would have been if one of the armies had been boys armed with old muskets supposed not to be loaded, and the other army had been composed of their female relations. The very thought of it makes one shudder.

There are many sorts of books; but good ones are the sort for the young to read. Remember that. They are a great, an inestimable, an unspeakable means of improvement. Therefore be careful in your selection, my young friends; be very careful; confine yourselves exclusively to Robertson's Sermons, Baxter's *Saint's Rest, The Innocents Abroad*, and works of that kind.[2]

But I have said enough. I hope you will treasure up the instructions which I have given you, and make them a guide to your feet and a light to your understanding. Build your character thoughtfully and painstakingly upon these precepts, and by and by, when you have got it built, you will be surprised and gratified to see how nicely and sharply it resembles everybody else's.

1. The bloody battle (1815) in which Napoleon suffered his final defeat at the hands of English and German troops under the Duke of Wellington.
2. The five volumes of sermons by Frederick William Robertson (1816–1853), an English clergyman, and Richard Baxter's *Saints' Everlasting Rest* (1650) were once well-known religious works. *The Innocents Abroad* is Clemens's own collection of humorous travel sketches.

QUESTIONS
1. *Is this piece unified? Does it have a thesis sentence? If you think it is unified, in what does the unity consist? If you think it is not unified, where are the breaks? Would it have seemed more unified when it was given as a speech?*
2. *What "image" or "personality" does Clemens project or assume? What does he do that creates his image or personality?*
3. *How much of his advice applies only to the young? How much of it is to be taken seriously?*
4. *What does Clemens assume about his audience? How many of these assumptions would hold true today?*

ERNEST HEMINGWAY
Bullfighting[1]

The bullfight is not a sport in the Anglo-Saxon sense of the word, that is, it is not an equal contest or an attempt at an equal contest between a bull and a man. Rather it is a tragedy; the death of the bull, which is played, more or less well, by the bull and the man involved and in which there is danger for the man but certain death for the animal. This danger to the man can be increased by the bullfighter at will in the measure in which he works close to the bull's horns. Keeping within the rules for bullfighting on foot in a closed ring formulated by years of experience, which, if known and followed, permit a man to perform certain actions with a bull without being caught by the bull's horns, the bullfighter may, by decreasing his distance from the bull's horns, depend more and more on his own reflexes and judgment of that distance to protect him from the points. This danger of goring, which the man creates voluntarily, can be changed to certainty of being caught and tossed by the bull if the man, through ignorance, slowness, torpidity, blind folly, or momentary grogginess breaks any of these fundamental rules for the execution of the different suertes. Everything that is done by the man in the ring is called a "suerte." It is the easiest term to use as it is short. It means act, but the word act has, in English, a connotation of the theatre that makes its use confusing.

People seeing their first bullfight say, "But the bulls are so stupid. They always go for the cape and not for the man."

The bull only goes for the percale of the cape or for the scarlet serge of the muleta[2] if the man makes him and so handles the cloth that the bull sees it rather than the man. Therefore to really start to see bullfights a spectator should go to the novilladas or apprentice fights. There the bulls do not always go for the cloth because the bullfighters are learning before your eyes the rules of bullfighting and they do not always remember or know the proper terrain to take and how to keep the bull after the lure and away from the man. It is one thing to know the rules in principle and another to remember them as they are needed when facing an animal that is seeking to kill you, and the spectator who wants to see men tossed and gored rather than judge the manner in which the bulls are dominated should go to a novillada before he sees a corrida de toros or complete bullfight. It should be a good thing for him to see a novillada first anyway if he wants to learn about technique, since the employment of knowledge that we call by

1. Chapter 2 in *Death in the Afternoon*, 1932.
2. A small cloth attached to a short tapered stick and used by a matador during the final passes leading to the kill.

that bastard name is always most visible in its imperfection. At a novillada the spectator may see the mistakes of the bullfighters, and the penalties that these mistakes carry. He will learn something too about the state of training or lack of training of the men and the effect this has on their courage.

One time in Madrid I remember we went to a novillada in the middle of the summer on a very hot Sunday when every one who could afford it had left the city for the beaches of the north or the mountains and the bullfight was not advertised to start until six o'clock in the evening, to see six Tovar bulls killed by three aspirant matadors who have all since failed in their profession. We sat in the first row behind the wooden barrier and when the first bull came out it was clear that Domingo Hernandorena, a short, thick-ankled, graceless Basque with a pale face who looked nervous and incompletely fed in a cheap rented suit, if he was to kill this bull would either make a fool of himself or be gored. Hernandorena could not control the nervousness of his feet. He wanted to stand quietly and play the bull with the cape with a slow movement of his arms, but when he tried to stand still as the bull charged his feet jumped away in short, nervous jerks. His feet were obviously not under his personal control and his effort to be statuesque while his feet jittered him away out of danger was very funny to the crowd. It was funny to them because many of them knew that was how their own feet would behave if they saw the horns coming toward them, and as always, they resented any one else being in there in the ring, making money, who had the same physical defects which barred them, the spectators, from that supposedly highly paid way of making a living. In their turn the other two matadors were very fancy with the cape and Hernandorena's nervous jerking was even worse after their performance. He had not been in the ring with a bull for over a year and he was altogether unable to control his nervousness. When the banderillas were in and it was time for him to go out with the red cloth and the sword to prepare the bull for killing and to kill, the crowd which had applauded ironically at every nervous move he had made knew something very funny would happen. Below us, as he took the muleta and the sword and rinsed his mouth out with water I could see the muscles of his cheeks twitching. The bull stood against the barrier watching him. Hernandorena could not trust his legs to carry him slowly toward the bull. He knew there was only one way he could stay in one place in the ring. He ran out toward the bull, and ten yards in front of him dropped to both knees on the sand. In that position he was safe from ridicule. He spread the red cloth with his sword and jerked himself forward on his knees toward the bull. The bull was watching the man and the triangle of red cloth, his ears pointed, his eyes fixed, and Hernandorena knee-ed himself a yard closer and shook the cloth. The bull's tail rose, his head lowered and he charged and, as he reached the man, Hernandorena rose solidly from his knees into the air, swung over like a bundle, his legs in all directions now, and then dropped to the ground. The bull looked for him, found a wide-spread moving cape held by another bullfighter instead, charged it, and Hernandorena stood up with sand on his white face and looked for his sword and the cloth. As he stood up I saw the heavy, soiled gray silk of his rented trousers open cleanly and deeply to show the thigh bone from the hip almost to the knee. He saw it too and looked very surprised and put his hand on it while people jumped over the barrier and ran toward him to carry him to the infirmary. The technical error that he had committed was in not keeping the red cloth of the muleta between himself and the bull until the charge; then at the moment of jurisdiction as it is called, when the bull's lowered head reaches the cloth, swaying back while he held the cloth, spread by the stick and the sword, far enough forward so that the bull following it would be clear of his body. It was a simple technical error.

That night at the café I heard no word of sympathy for him. He was ignorant, he was torpid, and he was out of training. Why did he insist on being a bullfighter? Why did he go down on both knees? Because he was a coward, they said. The knees are for cowards. If he was a coward why did he insist on being a bullfighter? There was no natural sympathy for uncontrollable nervousness because he was a paid public performer. It was preferable that he be gored rather than run from the bull. To be gored was honorable; they would have sympathized with him had he been caught in one of his nervous uncontrollable jerky retreats, which, although they mocked, they knew were from lack of training, rather than for him to have gone down on his knees. Because the hardest thing when frightened by the bull is to control the feet and let the bull come, and any attempt to control the feet was honorable even though they jeered at it because it looked ridiculous. But when he went on both knees, without the technique to fight from that position; the technique that Marcial Lalanda, the most scientific of living bullfighters, has, and which alone makes that position honorable; then Hernandorena admitted his nervousness. To show his nervousness was not shameful; only to admit it. When, lacking the technique and thereby admitting his inability to control his feet, the matador went down on both knees before the bull the crowd had no more sympathy with him than with a suicide.

For myself, not being a bullfighter, and being much interested in suicides, the problem was one of depiction and waking in the night I tried to remember what it was that seemed just out of my remembering and that was the thing that I had really seen and, finally, remembering all around, I got it. When he stood up, his face white and dirty and the silk of his breeches opened from waist to knee, it was the dirtiness of the rented breeches, the dirtiness of his slit underwear, and the clean, clean, unbearably clean whiteness of the thigh bone that I had seen, and it was that which was important.

At the novilladas, too, besides the study of technique, and the consequences of its lack you have a chance to learn about the manner of dealing with defective bulls since bulls which cannot be used in a formal bullfight because of some obvious defect are killed in the apprentice fights. Nearly all bulls develop defects in the course of any fight which must be corrected by the bullfighter, but in the novillada these defects, those of vision for instance, are many times obvious at the start and so the manner of their correcting, or the result of their not being corrected, is apparent.

The formal bullfight is a tragedy, not a sport, and the bull is certain to be killed. If the matador cannot kill him and, at the end of the allotted fifteen minutes for the preparation and killing, the bull is led and herded out of the ring alive by steers to dishonor the killer, he must, by law, be killed in the corrals. It is one hundred to one against the matador de toros or formally invested bullfighter being killed unless he is inexperienced, ignorant, out of training or too old and heavy on his feet. But the matador, if he knows his profession, can increase the amount of the danger of death that he runs exactly as much as he wishes. He should, however, increase this danger, *within the rules provided for his protection.* In other words it is to his credit if he does something that he knows how to do in a highly dangerous but still geometrically possible manner. It is to his discredit if he runs danger through ignorance, through disregard of the fundamental rules, through physical or mental slowness, or through blind folly.

The matador must dominate the bulls by knowledge and science. In the measure in which this domination is accomplished with grace will it be beautiful to watch. Strength is of little use to him except at the actual moment of killing. Once some one asked Rafael Gomez, "El Gallo," nearing fifty years old, a gypsy, brother of Jose Gomez, "Gallito," and the last living member of the great family of gypsy bullfighters of that name, what physical exercise he, Gallo, took to keep his strength up for bullfighting.

"Strength," Gallo said. "What do I want with strength, man? The bull weighs half a ton. Should I take exercises for strength to match him? Let the bull have the strength."

If the bulls were allowed to increase their knowledge as the bullfighter does and if those bulls which are not killed in the alloted fifteen minutes in the ring were not afterwards killed in the corrals but were allowed to be fought again they would kill all the bullfighters, if the bullfighters fought them according to the rules. Bullfighting is based on the fact that it is the first meeting between the wild animal and a dismounted man. This is the fundamental premise of modern bullfighting; that the bull has never been in the ring before. In the early days of bullfighting bulls were allowed to be fought which had been in the ring before and so many men were killed in the bull ring that on November 20, 1567, Pope Pius the Fifth issued a Papal edict excommunicating all Christian princes who should permit bullfights in their countries and denying Christian burial to any person killed in the bull ring. The Church only agreed to tolerate bullfighting, which continued steadily in Spain in spite of the edict, when it was agreed that the bulls should only appear once in the ring.

You would think then that it would make of bullfighting a true sport, rather than merely a tragic spectacle, if bulls that had been in the ring were allowed to reappear. I have seen such bulls fought, in violation of the law, in provincial towns in improvised arenas made by blocking the entrances to the public square with piled-up carts in the illegal capeas, or town-square bullfights with used bulls. The aspirant bullfighters, who have no financial backing, get their first experience in capeas. It is a sport, a very savage and primitive sport, and for the most part a truly amateur one. I am afraid however due to the danger of death it involves it would never have much success among the amateur sportsmen of America and England who play games. We, in games, are not fascinated by death, its nearness and its avoidance. We are fascinated by victory and we replace the avoidance of death by the avoidance of defeat. It is a very nice symbolism but it takes more cojones to be a sportsman when death is a closer party to the game. The bull in the capeas is rarely killed. This should appeal to sportsmen who are lovers of animals. The town is usually too poor to afford to pay for the killing of the bull and none of the aspirant bullfighters has enough money to buy a sword or he would not have chosen to serve his apprenticeship in the capeas. This would afford an opportunity for the man who is a wealthy sportsman, for he could afford to pay for the bull and buy himself a sword as well.

However, due to the mechanics of a bull's mental development the used bull does not make a brilliant spectacle. After his first charge or so he will stand quite still and will only charge if he is certain of getting the man or boy who is tempting him with a cape. When there is a crowd and the bull charges into it he will pick one man out and follow him, no matter how he may dodge, run and twist until he gets him and tosses him. If the tips of the bull's horns have been blunted this chasing and tossing is good fun to see for a little while. No one has to go in with the bull who does not want to, although of course many who want to very little go in to show their courage. It is very exciting for those who are down in the square, that is one test of a true amateur sport, whether it is more enjoyable to player than to spectator (as soon as it becomes enjoyable enough to the spectator for the charging of admission to be profitable the sport contains the germ of professionalism), and the smallest evidence of coolness or composure brings immediate applause. But when the bull's horns are sharp-pointed it is a disturbing spectacle. The men and boys try cape work with sacks, blouses, and old capes on the bull just as they do when his horns have been blunted; the only difference is that when the bull catches them and tosses them they are liable to come off the horn with wounds no local surgeon can cope with. One bull which was a great favorite in the capeas of the province of Valencia killed sixteen men and boys and badly wounded over sixty in a career of five years. The people who go into these capeas do so sometimes as aspirant professionals to get free experience with bulls but most often as amateurs, purely for sport, for the immediate excitement, and it is very great excitement; and for the retrospective pleasure, of having shown their contempt for death on a hot day in their own town square. Many go in from pride, hoping that they will be brave. Many find they are not brave at all; but at least they went in. There is absolutely nothing for them to gain except the inner satisfaction of having been in the ring with a bull; itself a thing that any one who has done it will always remember. It is a strange feeling to have an animal come toward you consciously seeking to kill you, his eyes open looking at you, and see the oncoming of the lowered horn that he intends to kill you with. It gives enough of a sensation so that there are always men willing to go into the capeas for the pride of having experienced it and the pleasure of having tried some bullfighting maneuver with a real bull although the actual pleasure at the time may not be great. Sometimes the bull is killed if the town has the money to afford it, or if the populace gets out of control; every one swarming on him at once with knives, daggers, butcher knives, and rocks; a man perhaps between his horns, being swung up and down, another flying through the air, surely several holding his tail, a swarm of choppers, thrusters and stabbers pushing into him, laying on him or cutting up at him until he sways and goes down. All amateur or group killing is a very barbarous, messy, though exciting business and is a long way from the ritual of the formal bullfight.

The bull which killed the sixteen and wounded the sixty was killed in a very odd way. One of those he had killed was a gypsy boy of about fourteen. Afterward the boy's brother and sister followed the bull around hoping perhaps to have a chance to assassinate him when he was loaded in his cage after a capea. That was difficult since, being a very highly valued performer, the bull was carefully taken care of. They followed him around for two years, not attempting anything, simply turning up wherever the bull was used. When the capeas were again abolished, they are always being abolished and reabolished, by government order, the bull's owner decided to send him to the slaughterhouse in Valencia, for the bull was getting on in years anyway. The two gypsies were at the slaughterhouse and the young man asked permission, since the bull had killed his brother, to kill the bull. This was granted and he started in by digging out both the bull's eyes while the bull was in his cage, and spitting carefully into the sockets, then after killing him by severing the spinal marrow between the neck vertebrae with a dagger, he experienced some difficulty in this, he asked permission to cut off the bull's testicles, which being granted, he and his sister built a small fire at the edge of the dusty street outside the slaughterhouse and roasted the two glands on sticks and when they were done, ate them. They then turned their backs on the slaughterhouse and went away along the road and out of town.

NORMAN PODHORETZ

My Negro Problem—And Ours

If we—and . . . I mean the relatively conscious whites and the relatively conscious blacks, who must, like lovers, insist on, or create, the consciousness of the others—do not falter in our duty now, we may be able, handful that we are, to end the racial nightmare, and achieve our country, and change the history of the world.

—JAMES BALDWIN[1]

Two ideas puzzled me deeply as a child growing up in Brooklyn during the 1930's in what today would be called an integrated neighborhood. One of them was that all Jews were rich; the other was that all Negroes were persecuted. These ideas has appeared in print; therefore they must be true. My own experience and the evidence of my senses told they were not true, but that only confirmed what a day-dreaming boy in the provinces—for the lower-class neighborhoods of New York belong as surely to the provinces as any rural town in North Dakota—discovers very early: *his* experience is unreal and the evidence of his senses is not to be trusted. Yet even a boy with a head full of fantasies incongruously synthesized out of Hollywood movies and English novels cannot altogether deny the reality of his own experience—especially when there is so much deprivation in that experience. Nor can he altogether gainsay the evidence of his own senses—especially such evidence of the senses as comes from being repeatedly beaten up, robbed, and in general hated, terrorized, and humiliated.

And so for a long time I was puzzled to think that Jews were supposed to be rich when the only Jews I knew were poor, and that Negroes were supposed to be persecuted when it was the Negroes who were doing the only persecuting I knew about—and doing it, moreover, to *me*. During the early years of the war, when my older

1. The quotation is from the conclusion of Baldwin's *The Fire Next Time*.

sister joined a left-wing youth organization, I remember my astonishment at hearing her passionately denounce my father for thinking that Jews were worse off than Negroes. To me, at the age of
twelve, it seemed very clear that Negroes were better off than Jews
—indeed, than *all* whites. A city boy's world is contained within
three or four square blocks, and in my world it was the whites, the
Italians and Jews, who feared the Negroes, not the other way
around. The Negroes were tougher than we were, more ruthless,
and on the whole they were better athletes. What could it mean,
then, to say that they were badly off and that we were more fortunate? Yet my sister's opinions, like print, were sacred, and when she
told me about exploitation and economic forces I believed her. I
believed her, but I was still afraid of Negroes. And I still hated
them with all my heart.

It had not always been so—that much I can recall from early
childhood. When did it start, this fear and this hatred? There was a
kindergarten in the local public school, and given the character of
the neighborhood, at least half of the children in my class must
have been Negroes. Yet I have no memory of being aware of color
differences at that age, and I know from observing my own children
that they attribute no significance to such differences even when
they begin noticing them. I think there was a day—first grade?
second grade?—when my best friend Carl hit me on the way home
from school and announced that he wouldn't play with me any
more because I had killed Jesus. When I ran home to my mother
crying for an explanation, she told me not to pay any attention to
such foolishness, and then in Yiddish she cursed the *goyim* and the
schwartzes, the *schwartzes* and the *goyim*.[2] Carl, it turned out, was
a *schwartze*, and so was added a third to the categories into which
people were mysteriously divided.

Sometimes I wonder whether this is a true memory at all. It is
blazingly vivid, but perhaps it never happened: can anyone really
remember back to the age of six? There is no uncertainty in my
mind, however, about the years that followed. Carl and I hardly
ever spoke, though we met in school every day up through the
eighth or ninth grade. There would be embarrassed moments of
catching his eye or of his catching mine—for whatever it was that
had attracted us to one another as very small children remained
alive in spite of the fantastic barrier of hostility that had grown up
between us, suddenly and out of nowhere. Nevertheless, friendship
would have been impossible, and even if it had been possible, it
would have been unthinkable. About that, there was nothing
anyone could do by the time we were eight years old.

---

2. The Yiddish words *goyim* (Gentiles   (blacks) are both partially derogatory
or white non-Jews) and *schwartzes*   terms.

Item: The orphanage across the street is torn down, a city housing project begins to rise in its place, and on the marvelous vacant lot next to the old orphange they are building a playground. Much excitement and anticipation as Opening Day draws near. Mayor LaGuardia himself comes to dedicate this great gesture of public benevolence. He speaks of neighborliness and borrowing cups of sugar, and of the playground he says that children of all races, colors, and creeds will learn to live together in harmony. A week later, some of us are swatting flies on the playground's inadequate little ball field. A gang of Negro kids, pretty much our own age, enter from the other side and order us out of the park. We refuse, proudly and indignantly, with superb masculine fervor. There is a fight, they win, and we retreat, half whimpering, half with bravado. My first nauseating experience of cowardice. And my first appalled realization that there are people in the world who do not seem to be afraid of anything, who act as though they have nothing to lose. Thereafter the playground becomes a battleground, sometimes quiet, sometimes the scene of athletic competition between Them and Us. But rocks are thrown as often as baseballs. Gradually we abandon the place and use the streets instead. The streets are safer, though we do not admit this to ourselves. We are not, after all, sissies— that most dreaded epithet of an American boyhood.

Item: I am standing alone in front of the building in which I live. It is late afternoon and getting dark. That day in school the teacher had asked a surly Negro boy named Quentin a question he was unable to answer. As usual I had waved my arm eagerly ("Be a good boy, get good marks, be smart, go to college, become a doctor") and, the right answer bursting from my lips, I was held up lovingly by the teacher as an example to the class. I had seen Quentin's face—a very dark, very cruel, very Oriental-looking face— harden, and there had been enough threat in his eyes to make me run all the way home for fear that he might catch me outside.

Now, standing idly in front of my own house, I see him approaching from the project accompanied by his little brother who is carrying a baseball bat and wearing a grin of malicious anticipation. As in a nightmare, I am trapped. The surroundings are secure and familiar, but terror is suddenly present and there is no one around to help. I am locked to the spot. I will not cry out or run away like a sissy, and I stand there, my heart wild, my throat clogged. He walks up, hurls the familiar epithet ("Hey, mo' f——r"), and to my surprise only pushes me. It is a violent push, but not a punch. Maybe I can still back out without entirely losing my dignity. Maybe I can still say, "Hey, c'mon Quentin, whaddya wanna do *that* for? I dint do nothin' to *you*," and walk away, not too rapidly. Instead, before I can stop myself, I push him back—a token gesture—and I say, "Cut that out, I don't wanna fight, I ain't got nothin' to fight about." As I turn to walk back into the building, the corner of my eye catches the motion of the bat his little brother has handed him. I try to duck, but the bat crashes colored lights into my head.

The next thing I know, my mother and sister are standing over me, both of them hysterical. My sister—she who was later to join the "progressive" youth organization—is shouting for the police and screaming imprecations at those dirty little black bastards. They take me upstairs, the doctor comes, the police come. I tell them that the boy who did it was a stranger, that he had been trying to get money from me. They do not believe me, but I am too scared to give them Quentin's name. When I return to school a few days later, Quentin avoids my eyes. He knows that I have not squealed, and he is ashamed. I try to feel proud, but in my heart I know that it was fear of what his friends might do to me that had kept me silent, and not the code of the street.

Item: There is an athletic meet in which the whole of our junior high school is participating. I am in one of the seventh-grade rapid-advance classes, and "segregation" has now set in with a vengeance. In the last three or four years of the elementary school from which we have just graduated, each grade had been divided into three classes, according to "intelligence." (In the earlier grades the divisions had either been arbitrary or else unrecognized by us as having anything to do with brains.) These divisions by IQ, or however it was arranged, had resulted in a preponderance of Jews in the "1" classes and a corresponding preponderance of Negroes in the "3's," with the Italians split unevenly along the spectrum. At least a few Negroes had always made the "1's," just as there had always been a few Jewish kids among the "3's" and more among the "2's" (where Italians dominated). But the junior high's rapid-advance class of which I am now a member is overwhelmingly Jewish and entirely white—except for a shy lonely Negro girl with light skin and reddish hair.

The athletic meet takes place in a city-owned stadium far from the school. It is an important event to which a whole day is given over. The winners are to get those precious little medallions stamped with the New York City emblem that can be screwed into a belt and that prove the wearer to be a distinguished personage. I am a fast runner, and so I am assigned the position of anchor man on my class's team in the relay race. There are three other seventh-grade teams in the race, two of them all Negro, as ours is all white. One of the all-Negro teams is very tall—their anchor man waiting silently next to me on the line looks years older than I am, and I do not recognize him. He is the first to get the baton and crosses the finishing line in a walk. Our team comes in second, but a few minutes later we are declared the winners, for it has been discovered that the anchor man on the first-place team is not a member of the class. We are awarded the medallions, and the following day our home-room teacher makes a speech about how proud she is of us for being superior athletes as well as superior students. We want to believe that we deserve the praise, but we know that we could not have won even if the other class had not cheated.

That afternoon, walking home, I am waylaid and surrounded by five Negroes, among whom is the anchor man of the disqualified team. "Gimme my medal, mo'f——r," he grunts. I do not have it with me and I tell him so. "Anyway, it ain't yours," I say foolishly. He calls me a liar on both counts and pushes me up against the wall on which we sometimes play handball. "Gimmie my mo'f——n' medal," he says again. I repeat that I have left it home. "Le's search the li'l mo'f——r," one of them suggests, "he prolly got it *hid* in his mo'f——n' *pants*." My panic is now unmanageable. (How many times had I been surrounded like this and asked in soft tones, "Len' me a nickel, boy." How many times had I been called a liar for pleading poverty and pushed around, or searched, or beaten up, unless there happened to be someone in the marauding gang like Carl who liked me across that enormous divide of hatred and who would therefore say, "Aaah, c'mon, le's git someone else, *this* boy ain't got no money on 'im.") I scream at them through tears of rage and self-contempt, "Keep your f——n' filthy lousy black hands offa me! I swear I'll get the cops." This is all they need to hear, and the five of them set upon me. They bang me around, mostly in the stomach and on the arms and shoulders, and when several adults loitering near the candy store down the block notice what is going on and begin to shout, they run off and away.

I do not tell my parents about the incident. My team-mates, who have also been waylaid, each by a gang led by his opposite number from the disqualified team, have had their medallions taken from them, and they never squeal either. For days, I walk home in terror, expecting to be caught again, but nothing happens. The medallion is put away into a drawer, never to be worn by anyone.

Obviously experiences like these have always been a common fea-ture of childhood life in working-class and immigrant neighbor-hoods, and Negroes do not necessarily figure in them. Wherever, and in whatever combination, they have lived together in the cities, kids of different groups have been at war, beating up and being beaten up: micks against kikes against wops against spicks against polacks. And even relatively homogeneous areas have not been spared the warring of the young: one block against another, one gang (called in my day, in a pathetic effort at gentility, an "S.A.C.," or social-athletic club) against another. But the Negro-white conflict had—and no doubt still has—a special intensity and was conducted with a ferocity unmatched by intramural white battling.

In my own neighborhood, a good deal of animosity existed between the Italian kids (most of whose parents were immigrants from Sicily) and the Jewish kids (who came largely from East European immigrant families). Yet everyone had friends, sometimes close friends, in the other "camp," and we often visited one another's strange-smelling houses, if not for meals, then for glasses of milk, and occasionally for some special event like a wedding or a wake. If it happened that we divided into warring factions and did battle, it would invariably be half-hearted and soon patched up. Our parents, to be sure, had nothing to do with one another and were mutually suspicious and hostile. But we, the kids, who all spoke Yiddish or Italian at home, were Americans, or New Yorkers, or Brooklyn boys: we shared a culture, the culture of the street, and at least for a while this culture proved to be more powerful than the opposing cultures of the home.

Why, *why* should it have been so different as between the Negroes and us? How was it borne in upon us so early, white and black alike, that we were enemies beyond any possibility of reconciliation? Why did we hate one another so?

I suppose if I tried, I could answer those questions more or less adequately from the perspective of what I have since learned. I could draw upon James Baldwin—what better witness is there?—to describe the sense of entrapment that poisons the soul of the Negro with hatred for the white man whom he knows to be his jailer. On the other side, if I wanted to understand how the white man comes to hate the Negro, I could call upon the psychologists who have spoken of the guilt that white Americans feel toward Negroes and that turns into hatred for lack of acknowledging itself as guilt. These are plausible answers and certainly there is truth in them. Yet when I think back upon my own experience of the Negro and his of me, I find myself troubled and puzzled, much as I was as a child when I heard that all Jews were rich and all Negroes persecuted. How could the Negroes in my neighborhood have regarded the whites across the street and around the corner as jailers? On the whole, the whites were not so poor as the Negroes, but they were quite poor enough, and the years were years of Depression. As for white hatred of the Negro, how could guilt have had anything to do with it? What share had these Italian and Jewish immigrants in the enslavement of the Negro? What share had they—downtrodden people themselves breaking their own necks to eke out a living—in the exploitation of the Negro?

No, I cannot believe that we hated each other back there in Brooklyn because they thought of us as jailers and we felt guilty toward them. But does it matter, given the fact that we all went through an unrepresentative confrontation? I think it matters profoundly, for if we managed the job of hating each other so well without benefit of the aids to hatred that are supposedly at the root of this madness everywhere else, it must mean that the madness is not yet properly understood. I am far from pretending that I understand it, but I would insist that no view of the problem will begin to approach the truth unless it can account for a case like the one I have been trying to describe. Are the elements of any such view available to us?

At least two, I would say, are. One of them is a point we frequently come upon in the work of James Baldwin, and the other is a related point always stressed by psychologists who have studied the mechanisms of prejudice. Baldwin tells us that one of the reasons Negroes hate the white man is that the white man refuses to *look* at him: the Negro knows that in white eyes all Negroes are alike; they are faceless and therefore not altogether human. The psychologists, in their turn, tell us that the white man hates the Negro because he tends to project those wild impulses that he fears in himself onto an alien group which he then punishes with his contempt. What Baldwin does *not* tell us, however, is that the principle of facelessness is a two-way street and can operate in both directions with no difficulty at all. Thus, in my neighborhood in Brooklyn, *I* was as faceless to the Negroes as they were to me, and if they hated me because I never looked at them, I must also have hated them for never looking at *me*. To the Negroes, my white skin was enough to define me as the enemy, and in a war it is only the uniform that counts and not the person.

So with the mechanism of projection that the psychologists talk about: it too works in both directions at once. There is no question that the psychologists are right about what the Negro represents symbolically to the white man. For me as a child the life lived on the other side of the playground and down the block on Ralph Avenue seemed the very embodiment of the values of the street— free, independent, reckless, brave, masculine, erotic. I put the word "erotic" last, though it is usually stressed above all others, because in fact it came last, in consciousness as in importance. What mainly counted for me about Negro kids of my own age was that they were "bad boys." There were plenty of bad boys among the whites—this was, after all, a neighborhood with a long tradition of crime as a career open to aspiring talents—but the Negroes were *really* bad, bad in a way that beckoned to one, and made one feel inadequate. We all went home every day for a lunch of spinach-and-potatoes; *they* roamed around during lunch hour, munching on candy bars. In winter *we* had to wear itchy woolen hats and mittens and cumbersome galoshes; *they* were bareheaded and loose as they pleased. We rarely played hookey, or got into serious trouble in school, for all our street-corner bravado; *they* were defiant, forever staying out (to do what delicious things?), forever making disturbances in class and in the halls, forever being sent to the principal and returning uncowed. But most important of all, they were *tough*; beautifully, enviably tough, not giving a damn for anyone or anything. To hell with the teacher, the truant officer, the cop; to hell with the whole of the adult world that held *us* in its grip and that we never had the courage to rebel against except sporadically and in petty ways.

This is what I saw and envied and feared in the Negro: this is what finally made him faceless to me, though some of it, of course, was actually there. (The psychologists also tell us that the alien group which becomes the object of a projection will tend to respond by trying to live up to what is expected of them.) But what, on his side, did the Negro see in me that made me faceless to *him*? Did he envy me my lunches of spinach-and-potatoes and my itchy woolen caps and my prudent behavior in the face of authority, as I envied him his noon-time candy bars and his bare head in winter and his magnificent rebelliousness? Did those lunches and caps spell for him the prospect of power and riches in the future? Did they mean that there were possibilities open to me that were denied to him? Very likely they did. But if so, one also supposes that he feared the impulses within himself toward submission to authority no less powerfully than I feared the impulses in myself toward defiance. If I represented the jailer to him, it was not because I was oppressing him or keeping him down: it was because I symbolized for him the dangerous and probably pointless temptation toward greater repression, just as he symbolized for me the equally perilous tug toward greater freedom. I personally was to be rewarded for this repression with a new and better life in the future, but how many of my friends paid an even higher price and were given only gall in return.

We have it on the authority of James Baldwin that all Negroes hate whites. I am trying to suggest that on their side all whites—all American whites, that is—are sick in their feelings about Negroes. There are Negroes, no doubt, who would say that Baldwin is wrong, but I suspect them of being less honest than he is, just as I suspect whites of self-deception who tell me they have no special feeling toward Negroes. Special feelings about color are a contagion to which white Americans seem susceptible even when there is nothing in their background to account for the susceptibility. Thus everywhere we look today in the North we find the curious phenomenon of white middle-class liberals with no previous personal experience of Negroes—people to whom Negroes have always been faceless in virtue rather than faceless in vice—discovering that their abstract commitment to the cause of Negro rights will not stand the test of a direct confrontation. We find such people fleeing in droves to the suburbs as the Negro population in the inner city grows; and when they stay in the city we find them sending their children to private school rather than to the "integrated" public school in the neighborhood. We find them resisting the demand that gerrymandered school districts be re-zoned for the purpose of overcoming de facto segregation; we find them judiciously considering whether the Negroes (for their own good, of course) are not perhaps pushing too hard; we find them clucking their tongues over Negro militancy; we find them speculating on the question of whether there may not, after all, be something in the theory that the races are biologically different; we find them saying that it will take a very long time for Negroes to achieve full equality, no matter what anyone does; we find them deploring the rise of black nationalism and expressing the solemn hope that the leaders of the Negro community will discover ways of containing the impatience and incipient violence within the Negro ghettos.[3]

But that is by no means the whole story; there is also the phenomenon of what Kenneth Rexroth once called "crow-jimism." There are the broken-down white boys like Vivaldo Moore in Baldwin's *Another Country* who go to Harlem in search of sex or simply to brush up against something that looks like primitive vitality, and who are so often punished by the Negroes they meet for crimes that they would have been the last ever to commit and of which they themselves have been as sorry victims as any of the Negroes who take it out on them. There are the writers and intellectuals and artists who romanticize Negroes and pander to them, assuming a guilt that is not properly theirs. And there are all the white liberals who permit Negroes to blackmail them into adopting a double standard of moral judgment, and who lend themselves—again assuming the responsibility for crimes they never committed—to cunning and contemptuous exploitation by Negroes they employ or try to befriend.

And what about me? What kind of feelings do I have about Negroes today? What happened to me, from Brooklyn, who grew up fearing and envying and hating Negroes? Now that Brooklyn is behind me, do I fear them and envy them and hate them still? The answer is yes, but not in the same proportions and certainly not in the same way. I now live on the upper west side of Manhattan, where there are many Negroes and many Puerto Ricans, and there are nights when I experience the old apprehensiveness again, and there are streets that I avoid when I am walking in the dark, as there were streets that I avoided when I was a child. I find that I am not afraid of Puerto Ricans, but I cannot restrain my nervousness whenever I pass a group of Negroes standing in front of a bar

3. For an account of developments like these, see "The White Liberal's Retreat" by Murray Friedman in the January 1963 *Atlantic Monthly* [Podhoretz's note].

or sauntering down the street. I know now, as I did not know when I was a child, that power is on my side, that the police are working for me and not for them. And knowing this I feel ashamed and guilty, like the good liberal I have grown up to be. Yet the twinges of fear and the resentment they bring and the self-contempt they arouse are not to be gainsaid.

But envy? Why envy? And hatred? Why hatred? Here again the intensities have lessened and everything has been complicated and qualified by the guilts and the resulting over-compensations that are the heritage of the enlightened middle-class world of which I am now a member. Yet just as in childhood I envied Negroes for what seemed to me their superior masculinity, so I envy them today for what seems to me their superior physical grace and beauty. I have come to value physical grace very highly, and I am now capable of aching with all my being when I watch a Negro couple on the dance floor, or a Negro playing baseball or basketball. They are on the kind of terms with their own bodies that I should like to be on with mine, and for that precious quality they seemed blessed to me.

The hatred I still feel for Negroes is the hardest of all the old feelings to face or admit, and it is the most hidden and the most overlarded by the conscious attitudes into which I have succeeded in willing myself. It no longer has, as for me it once did, any cause or justification (except, perhaps, that I am constantly being denied my right to an honest expression of the things I earned the right as a child to feel). How, then, do I know that this hatred has never entirely disappeared? I know it from the insane rage that can stir in me at the thought of Negro anti-Semitism; I know it from the disgusting prurience that can stir in me at the sight of a mixed couple; and I know it from the violence that can stir in me whenever I encounter that special brand of paranoid touchiness to which many Negroes are prone.

This, then, is where I am; it is not exactly where I think all other white liberals are, but it cannot be so very far away either. And it is because I am convinced that we white Americans are—for whatever reason, it no longer matters—so twisted and sick in our feelings about Negroes that I despair of the present push toward integration. If the pace of progress were not a factor here, there would perhaps be no cause for despair: time and the law and even the international political situation are on the side of the Negroes, and ultimately, therefore, victory—of a sort, anyway—must come. But from everything we have learned from observers who ought to know, pace has become as important to the Negroes as substance. They want equality and they want it *now*, and the white world is yielding to their demand only as much and as fast as it is absolutely being compelled to do. The Negroes know this in the most concrete terms imaginable, and it is thus becoming increasingly difficult to buy them off with rhetoric and promises and pious assurances of support. And so within the Negro community we find more and more people declaring—as Harold R. Isaacs recently put it in an article in *Commentary*—that they want *out*: people who say that integration will never come, or that it will take a hundred or a thousand years to come, or that it will come at too high a price in suffering and struggle for the pallid and sodden life of the American middle class that at the very best it may bring.

The most numerous, influential, and dangerous movement that has grown out of Negro despair with the goal of integration is, of course, the Black Muslims. This movement, whatever else we may say about it, must be credited with one enduring achievement: it inspired James Baldwin to write an essay which deserves to be placed among the classics of our language. Everything Baldwin has ever been trying to tell us is distilled in *The Fire Next Time* into a statement of overwhelming persuasiveness and prophetic magnificence. Baldwin's message is and always has been simple. It is this: "Color is not a human or personal reality; it is a political reality." And Baldwin's demand is correspondingly simple; color must be forgotten, lest we all be smited with a vengeance "that does not really depend on, and cannot really be executed by, any person or organization, and that cannot be prevented by any police force or army: historical vengeance, a cosmic vengeance based on the law that we recognize when we say, 'Whatever goes up must come down.' " The Black Muslims Baldwin portrays as a sign and a warning to the intransigent white world. They come to proclaim how deep is the Negro's disaffection with the white world and all its works, and Baldwin implies that no American Negro can fail to respond somewhere in his being to their message: that the white man is the devil, that Allah has doomed him to destruction, and that the black man is about to inherit the earth. Baldwin of course knows that this nightmare inversion of the racism from which the black man has suffered can neither win nor even point to the neighborhood in which victory might be located. For in his view the neighborhood of victory lies in exactly the opposite direction: the transcendence of color through love.

Yet the tragic fact is that love is not the answer to hate—not in the world of politics, at any rate. Color is indeed a political rather than a human or a personal reality and if politics (which is to say power) has made it into a human and personal reality, then only politics (which is to say power) can unmake it once again. But the way of politics is slow and bitter, and as impatience on the one side is matched by a setting of the jaw on the other, we move closer and closer to an explosion and blood may yet run in the streets.

Will this madness in which we are all caught never find a resting-place? Is there never to be an end to it? In thinking about the Jews I have often wondered whether their survival as a distinct group was worth one hair on the head of a single infant. Did the Jews have to survive so that six million innocent people should one day be burned in the ovens of Auschwitz? It is a terrible question and no one, not God himself, could ever answer it to my satisfaction. And when I think about the Negroes in America and about the image of integration as a state in which the Negroes would take their rightful place as another of the protected minorities in a pluralistic society, I wonder whether they really believe in their hearts that such a state can actually be attained, and if so *why* they should wish to survive as a distinct group. I think I know why the Jews once wished to survive (though I am less certain as to why we still do): they not only believed that God had given them no choice, but they were tied to a memory of past glory and a dream of imminent redemption. What does the American Negro have that might correspond to this? His past is a stigma, his color is a stigma, and his vision of the future is the hope of erasing the stigma by making color irrelevant, by making it disappear as a fact of consciousness.

I share this hope, but I cannot see how it will ever be realized unless color does *in fact* disappear: and that means not integration, it means assimilation, it means—let the brutal word come out—miscegenation. The Black Muslims, like their racist counterparts in the white world, accuse the "so-called Negro leaders" of secretly pursuing miscegenation as a goal. The racists are wrong, but I wish they were right, for I believe that the wholesale merger of the two races is the most desirable alternative for everyone concerned. I am not claiming that this alternative can be pursued programmatically or that it is immediately feasible as a solution; obviously there are even greater barriers to its achievement than to the achievement of integration. What I am saying, however, is that in my opinion the Negro problem can be solved in this country in no other way.

I have told the story of my own twisted feelings about Negroes here, and of how they conflict with the moral convictions I have since developed, in order to assert that such feelings must be acknowledged as honestly as possible so that they can be controlled and ultimately disregarded in favor of the convictions. It is *wrong* for a man to suffer because of the color of his skin. Beside that clichéd proposition of liberal thought, what argument can stand and be respected? If the arguments are the arguments of feeling, they must be made to yield; and one's own soul is not the worst place to begin working a huge social transformation. Not so long ago, it used to be asked of white liberals, "Would you like your sister to marry one?" When I was a boy and my sister was still unmarried I would certainly have said no to that question. But now I am a man, my sister is already married, and I have daughters. If I were to be asked today whether I would like a daughter of mine "to marry one," I would have to answer: "No, I wouldn't *like* it at all. I would rail and rave and rant and tear my hair. And then I hope I would have the courage to curse myself for raving and ranting, and to give her my blessing. How dare I withhold it at the behest of the child I once was and against the man I now have a duty to be?"

ERIK H. ERIKSON

The Golden Rule in the Light of New Insight[1]

When a lecture is announced one does not usually expect the title to foretell very much about the content. But it must be rare, indeed, that a title is as opaque as the one on your invitation to this lecture: for it does not specify the field from which new insight is to come and. throw new light on the old principle of the Golden Rule. You took a chance, then, in coming, and now that I have been introduced as a psychoanalyst, you must feel that you have taken a double chance.

Let me tell you, therefore, how I came upon our subject. In Harvard College, I teach a course, "The Human Life Cycle." There (since I am by experience primarily a clinician) we begin by considering those aggravated *crises* which mark each stage of life and are known to psychiatry as potentially pathogenic. But we proceed to discuss the potential *strengths* which each stage contributes to human maturity. In either case, so psychiatric experience and the observation of healthy children tell us, much depends on the interplay of generations in which human strength can be revitalized or human weakness perseverated "into the second and third generation." But this leads us to the role of the individual in the sequence of generations, and thus to that evolved order which your scriptures call *Lokasangraha*—the "maintenance of the world" (in Professor Radhakrishnan's translation). Through the study of case-histories and of life-histories we psychoanalysts have begun to discern certain fateful and certain fruitful patterns of interaction in those most concrete categories (parent and child, man and woman, teacher and pupil) which carry the burden of maintenance from generation to generation. The implication of our insights for ethics had preoccupied me before I came here; and, as you will well understand, a few months of animated discussion in India have by no means disa-

1. From *Insight and Responsibility* (1964).

bused me from such concerns. I have, therefore. chosen to tell you where I stand in my teaching, in the hope of learning more from you in further discussion.

My base line is the Golden Rule, which advocates that one should do (or not do) to another what one wishes to be (or not to be) done by. Systematic students of ethics often indicate a certain disdain for this all-too-primitive ancestor of more logical principles; and Bernard Shaw found the rule an easy target: don't do to another what you would like to be done by, he warned, because his tastes may differ from yours. Yet this rule has marked a mysterious meeting ground between ancient peoples separated by oceans and eras, and has provided a hidden theme in the most memorable sayings of many thinkers.

The Golden Rule obviously concerns itself with one of the very basic paradoxes of human existence. Each man calls his own a separate body, a self-conscious individuality, a personal awareness of the cosmos, and a certain death; and yet he shares this world as a *reality* also perceived and judged by others and as an *actuality* within which he must commit himself to ceaseless interaction. This is acknowledged in your scriptures as the principle of Karma.

To identify self-interest and the interest of other selves, the Rule alternately employs the method of warning, "Do *not* as you would *not* be done by," and of exhortation, "Do, as you *would* be done by." For psychological appeal, some versions rely on a minimum of *egotistic prudence*, while others demand a maximum of *altruistic sympathy*. It must be admitted that the formula, "Do not to others what if done to you would cause you pain," does not presuppose much more than the mental level of the small child who desists from pinching when it gets pinched in return. More mature insight is assumed in the saying, "No one is a believer until he loves for his brother what he loves for himself." Of all the versions, however, none commit us as unconditionally as the Upanishad's, "he who sees all beings in his own self and his own self in all beings," and the Christian injunction, "love thy neighbor as thyself." They even suggest a true love and a true knowledge of ourselves. Freud, of course, took this Christian maxim deftly apart as altogether illusory, thus denying with the irony of the enlightenment what a maxim really is—and what (as I hope to show) his method may really stand for.

I will not (I could not) trace the versions of the Rule to various world religions. No doubt in English translation all of them have become somewhat assimilated to Biblical versions. Yet the basic formula seems to be universal, and it re-appears in an astonishing number of the most revered sayings of our civilization, from St. Francis' prayer to Kant's moral imperative and Lincoln's simple political creed: "As I would not be slave, I would not be master."

The variations of the Rule have, of course, provided material for many a discussion of ethics weighting the soundness of the logic implied and measuring the degree of ethical nobility reached in each. My field of inquiry, the clinical study of the human life cycle, suggests that I desist from arguing logical merit or spiritual worth and instead distinguish *variations in moral and ethical sensitivity* in accordance with stages in the development of human conscience.

The dictionary, our first refuge from ambiguity, in this case only confounds it: morals and ethics are defined as synonyms *and* antonyms of each other. In other words, they are the same, with a difference—a difference which I intend to emphasize. For it is clear that he who knows what is legal or illegal and what is moral or immoral has not necessarily learned thereby what is ethical. Highly moralistic people can do unethical things, while an ethical man's involvement in immoral doings becomes by inner necessity an occasion for tragedy.

I would propose that we consider *moral rules* of conduct to be based on a fear of *threats* to be forestalled. These may be outer threats of abandonment, punishment and public exposure, or a threatening inner sense of guilt, of shame or of isolation. In either case, the rationale for obeying a rule may not be too clear; it is the threat that counts. In contrast, I would consider *ethical rules* to be based on *ideals* to be striven for with a high degree of rational assent and with a ready consent to a formulated good, a definition of perfection, and some promise of self-realization. This differentiation may not agree with all existing definitions, but it is substantiated by the observation of human development. Here, then, is my first proposition: the moral and the ethical sense are different in their psychological dynamics, because the moral sense develops on an earlier, more immature level. This does not mean that the moral sense could be skipped, as it were. On the contrary, all that exists layer upon layer in an adult's mind has developed step by step in the growing child's, and all the major steps in the comprehension of what is considered good behavior in one's cultural universe are—for better and for worse—related to different stages in individual maturation. But they are all necessary to one another.

The response to a moral tone of voice develops early, and many an adult is startled when inadvertently he makes an infant cry, because his voice has conveyed more disapproval than he intended to. Yet, the small child, so limited to the intensity of the moment, somehow must learn the boundaries marked by "don'ts." Here, cultures have a certain leeway in underscoring the goodness of one who does not transgress or the evilness of one who does. But the conclusion is unavoidable that children can be made to feel evil, and that adults continue to project evil on one another and on their children far beyond the verdict of rational judgment. Mark Twain once characterized man as "the animal that blushes."

Psychoanalytic obervation first established the psychological basis of a fact which Eastern thinkers have always known, namely, that the radical division into good and bad can be *the* sickness of the mind. It has traced the moral scruples and excesses of the adult to the childhood stages in which guilt and shame are ready to be aroused and are easily exploited. It has named and studied the "super-ego" which hovers over the ego as the inner perpetuation of the child's subordination to the restraining will of his elders. The voice of the super-ego is not always cruel and derisive, but it is ever ready to become so whenever the precarious balance which we call a good conscience is upset, at which times the secret weapons of this inner governor are revealed: the brand of shame and the bite of conscience. We who deal with the consequences in individual neuroses and in collective irrationality must ask ourselves whether excessive guilt and excessive shame 'are "caused" or merely accentuated by the pressure of parental and communal methods, by the threat of loss of affection, of corporal punishment, of public shaming. Or are they by now a proclivity for self-alienation which has become a part—and, to some extent, a necessary part—of man's evolutionary heritage?

All we know for certain is that the moral proclivity in man does not develop without the establishment of some chronic self-doubt and some truly terrible—even if largely submerged—rage against anybody and anything that reinforces such doubt. The "lowest" in man is thus apt to reappear in the guise of the "highest." Irrational and pre-rational combinations of goodness, doubt, and rage can re-emerge in the adult in those malignant forms of righteousness and prejudice which we may call *moralism*. In the name of high moral principles all the vindictiveness of derision, of torture, and of mass extinction can be employed. One surely must come to the conclusion that the Golden Rule was meant to protect man not only against his enemy's open attacks, but also against his friend's righteousness.

Lest this view, in spite of the evidence of history, seem too "clinical," we turn to the writings of the evolutionists who in the last few decades have joined psychoanalysis in recognizing the super-ego as an evolutionary fact—and danger. The *developmental* principle is thus joined by an *evolutionary* one. Waddington[2] even goes so far as to say that super-ego rigidity may be an overspecialization in the human race, like the excessive body armor of the late dinosaurs. In a less grandiose comparison he likens the super-ego to "the finicky adaptation of certain parasites which fits them to live only on one

2. C. H. Waddington, *The Ethical Animal*, London: Allen and Unwin, 1960 [Erikson's note].

host animal." In recommending his book, *The Ethical Animal*, I must admit that his terminology contradicts mine. He calls the awakening of morality in childhood a proclivity for "ethicizing," whereas I would prefer to call it moralizing. As do many animal psychologists, he dwells on analogies between the very young child and the young animal instead of comparing, as I think we must, the young animal with the pre-adult human, including the adolescent.

In fact, I must introduce here an amendment to my first, my "developmental" proposition, for between the development in childhood of man's *moral* proclivity and that of his *ethical* powers in adulthood, adolescence intervenes when he perceives the universal good in *ideological* terms. The imagery of steps in development, of course, is useful only where it is to be suggested that one item precedes another in such a way that the earlier one is necessary to the later ones and that each later one is of a higher order.

This "epigenetic" principle, according to which the constituent parts of a ground plan develop during successive stages, will be immediately familiar to you. For in the traditional Hindu concept of the life cycle the four intrinsic goals of life (Dharma, the orders that define virtue; Artha, the powers of the actual; Kama, the joys of libidinal abandon; and Moksha, the peace of deliverance) come to their successive and mutual perfection during the four stages, the ashramas of the apprentice, the householder, the hermit, and the ascetic. These stages are divided from each other by sharp turns of direction; yet, each depends on the previous one, and whatever perfection is possible depends on them all.

I would not be able to discuss the relation of these two foursomes to each other, nor ready to compare this ideal conception to our epigenetic views of the life cycle. But the affinities of the two conceptions are apparent, and at least the ideological indoctrination of the apprentice, the Brahmacharya, and the ethical one of the Grihasta, the householder, correspond to the developmental categories suggested here.

No wonder; for it is the joint development of cognitive and emotional powers paired with appropriate social learning which enables the individual to realize the potentialities of a stage. Thus youth becomes ready—if often only after a severe bout with moralistic regression—to envisage the more universal principles of a highest human good. The adolescent learns to grasp the flux of time, to anticipate the future in a coherent way, to perceive ideas and to assent to ideals, to take—in short—an *ideological* position for which the younger child is cognitively not prepared. In adolescence, then, an ethical view is approximated, but it remains susceptible to an alternation of impulsive judgment and odd rationalization. It is, then, as true for adolescence as it is for childhood that man's way stations to maturity can become fixed, can become premature end stations, or stations for future regression.

The moral sense, in its perfections and its perversions, has been an intrinsic part of man's *evolution,* while the sense of ideological rejuvenation has pervaded his *revolutions,* both with prophetic idealism and with destructive fanaticism. Adolescent man, in all his sensitivity to the ideal, is easily exploited by promises of counterfeit millennia, easily taken in by the promise of a new and arrogantly exclusive identity.

The *true* ethical sense of the young adult, finally, encompasses and goes beyond moral restraint and ideal vision, while insisting on concrete commitments to those intimate relationships and work associations by which man can hope to share a lifetime of productivity and competence. But young adulthood engenders its own dangers. It adds to the moralist's righteousness, the *territorial defensiveness* of one who has appropriated and staked out his earthly claim and who seeks eternal security in the super-identity of organizations. Thus, what the Golden Rule at its highest has attempted to make all-inclusive, tribes and nations, castes and classes, moralities and ideologies have consistently made exclusive again—proudly, superstitiously, and viciously denying the status of reciprocal ethics to those "outside."

If I have so far underscored the malignant potentials of man's slow maturation, I have done so not in order to dwell on a kind of dogmatic pessimism which can emerge all too easily from clinical preoccupation and often leads only to anxious avoidances. I know that man's moral, ideological, and ethical propensities can find, and have found on occasion, a sublime integration, in individuals and in groups who were both tolerant and firm, both flexible and strong, both wise and obedient. Above all, men have always shown a dim knowledge of their better potentialities by paying homage to those purest leaders who taught the simplest and most inclusive rules for an undivided mankind. I will have a word to say later about Gandhi's continued "presence" in India. But men have also persistently betrayed them, on what passed for moral or ideological grounds, even as they are now preparing a potential betrayal of the human heritage on scientific and technological grounds in the name of that which is considered good merely because it can be made to work—no matter where it leads. No longer do we have license to emphasize either the "positive" or the "negative" in man. Step for step, they go together: moralism with moral obedience, fanaticism with ideological devotion, and rigid conservatism with adult ethics.

Man's socio-genetic evolution is about to reach a crisis in the full sense of the word, a crossroads offering one path to fatality, and one to recovery and further growth. Artful perverter of joy and keen exploiter of strength, man is the animal that has learned to survive "in a fashion," to multiply without food for the multitudes, to grow up healthily without reaching personal maturity, to live well but without purpose, to invent ingeniously without aim, and to kill grandiosely without need. But the processes of socio-genetic evolution also seem to promise a new humanism, the acceptance by man—as an evolved product as well as a producer, and a self-conscious tool of further evolution—of the obligation to be guided in his planned actions and his chosen self-restraints by his knowledge and his insights. In this endeavor, then, it may be of a certain importance to learn to understand and to master the differences between infantile morality, adolescent ideology and adult ethics. Each is necessary to the next, but each is effective only if they eventually combine in that wisdom which, as Waddington puts it, "fulfills sufficiently the function of mediating evolutionary advance."

At the point, however, when one is about to end an argument with a global injunction of what we *must* do, it is well to remember Blake's admonition that the common good readily becomes the topic of "the scoundrel, the hypocrite, and the flatterer"; and that he who would do some good must do so in "minute particulars." And indeed, I have so far spoken only of the developmental and the evolutionary principle, according to which the propensity for ethics grows in the individual as part of an adaptation roughly laid down by evolution. Yet, to grow in the individual, ethics must be generated and regenerated in and by the sequence of generations— again, a matter fully grasped and systematized, some will say stereotyped, in the Hindu tradition. I must now make more explicit what our insights tell us about this process.

Let me make an altogether new start here. Let us look at scientific man in his dealings with animals and let us assume (this is not a strange assumption in India) that animals, too, may have a place close to the "other" included in the Rule. The psychologists among you know Professor Harry Harlow's studies on the development of what he calls affection in monkeys.[3] He did some exquisite experimental and photographic work attempting, in the life of laboratory monkeys, to "control the mother variable." He took monkeys from their mothers within a few hours after birth, isolated them and left them with "mothers" made out of wire, metal, wood, and terry cloth. A rubber nipple somewhere in their middles emitted piped-in milk, and the whole contraption was wired for body warmth. All the "variables" of this mother situation were controlled: the amount of rocking, the temperature of the "skin," and the exact

---

3. H. F. Harlow and M. K. Harlow, "A Study of Animal Affection," *The Journal of the American Museum of* *Natural History*, Vol. 70, No. 10, 1961 [Erikson's note].

incline of the maternal body necessary to make a scared monkey feel safe and comfortable. Years ago, when this method was presented as a study of the development of affection in monkeys, the clinician could not help wondering whether the small animals' obvious attachment to this contraption was really *monkey* affection or a fetishist addiction to inanimate objects. And, indeed, while these laboratory-reared monkeys became healthier and healthier, and much more easily trained in technical know-how than the inferior animals brought up by mere monkey mothers, they became at the end what Harlow calls "psychotics." They sit passively, they stare vacantly, and some do a terrifying thing: when poked they bite themselves and tear at their own flesh until the blood flows. They have not learned to experience "the other," whether as mother, mate, child—or enemy. Only a tiny minority of the females produced offspring, and only one of them made an attempt to nurse hers. But science remains a wonderful thing. Now that we have succeeded in producing "psychotic" monkeys experimentally, we can convince ourselves that we have at last given scientific support to the theory that severely disturbed mother-child relationships "cause" human psychosis.

This is a long story; but it speaks for Professor Harlow's methods that what they demonstrate is unforgettable. At the same time, they lead us to that borderline where we recognize that the scientific approach toward living beings must be with concepts and methods adequate to the study of ongoing life, not of selective extinction. I have put it this way: one can study the nature of things by doing something *to* them, but one can really learn something about the essential nature of living beings only by doing something *with* them or *for* them. This, of course, is the principle of clinical science. It does not deny that one can learn by dissecting the dead, or that animal or man can be motivated to lend circumscribed parts of themselves to an experimental procedure. But for the study of those central transactions which are the carriers of socio-genetic evolution, and for which we must take responsibility in the future, the chosen unit of observation must be the generation, not the individual. Whether an individual animal or human being has partaken of the stuff of life can only be tested by the kind of observation which includes his ability to transmit life—in some essential form—to the next generation.

One remembers here the work of Konrad Lorenz, and the kind of "inter-living" research which he and others have developed, making—in principle—the life cycle of certain selected animals part of the same environment in which the observer lives his own life cycle, studying his own role as well as theirs and taking his chances with what his ingenuity can discern in a setting of sophisticated naturalist inquiry. One remembers also Elsa the lioness, a foundling who was brought up in the Adamson household in Kenya. There the mother variable was not controlled, it was in control. Mrs. Adamson and her husband even felt responsible for putting grown-up Elsa back among the lions and succeeded in sending her back to the bush, where she mated and had cubs, and yet came back from time to time (accompanied by her cubs) to visit her human foster parents. In our context, we cannot fail to wonder about the built-in "moral" sense that made Elsa respond—and respond in very critical situations, indeed—to the words, "No, Elsa, no," *if* the words came from human beings she trusted. Yet, even with this built-in "moral" response, and with a lasting trust in her foster parents (which she transmitted to her wild cubs) she was able to live as a wild lion. Her mate, however, never appeared; he apparently was not too curious about her folks.

The point of this and similar stories is that our habitual relationship to what we call beasts in nature and "instinctive" or "instinctual" beastliness in ourselves may be highly distorted by thousands of years of superstition, and that there may be resources for peace even in our "animal nature" if we will only learn to nurture nature, as well as to master it. Today, we can teach a monkey, in the very words of the Bible, to "eat the flesh of his own arm," even as we can permit "erring leaders" to make of all mankind the "fuel of the fire." Yet, it seems equally plausible that we can also let our children grow up to lead "the calf and the young lion and the fatling together"—in nature and in their own nature.

To recognize one of man's prime resources, however, we must trace back his individual development to his *pre-moral* days, his infancy. His earliest social experimentation at that time leads to a certain ratio of basic trust and basic mistrust—a ratio which, if favorable, establishes the fundamental human strength: hope. This over-all attitude emerges as the newborn organism reaches out to its caretakers and as they bring to it what we will now discuss as *mutuality*. The failure of basic trust and of mutuality has been recognized in psychiatry as the most far-reaching failure, undercutting all development. We know how tragic and deeply pathogenic its absence can be in children and parents who cannot arouse and cannot respond. It is my further proposition, then, that all moral, ideological, and ethical propensities depend on this early experience of mutuality.

I would call mutuality a relationship in which partners depend on each other for the development of their respective strengths. A baby's first responses can be seen as part of an actuality consisting of many details of mutual arousal and response. While the baby initially smiles at a mere configuration resembling the human face, the adult cannot help smiling back, filled with expectations of a "recognition" which he needs to secure from the new being as surely as it needs him. The fact is that the mutuality of adult and baby is the original source of hope, the basic ingredient of all effective as well as ethical human action. As far back as 1895, Freud, in his first outline of a "Psychology for Neurologists," confronts the "helpless" newborn infant with a "help-rich" (*"hilfreich"*) adult, and postulates that their mutual understanding is "the primal source of all moral motives."[4] Should we, then, endow the Golden Rule with a principle of mutuality, replacing the reciprocity of both prudence and sympathy?

Here we must add the observation that a parent dealing with a child will be strengthened in *his* vitality, in *his* sense of identity, and in *his* readiness for ethical action by the very ministrations by means of which he secures to the child vitality, future identity, and eventual readiness for ethical action.

But we should avoid making a new Utopia out of the "mother-child relationship." The paradise of early childhood must be abandoned—a fact which man has as yet not learned to accept. The earliest mutuality is only a beginning and leads to more complicated encounters, as both the child and his interaction with a widening circle of persons grow more complicated. I need only point out that the second basic set of vital strengths in childhood (following trust and hope) is autonomy and will, and it must be clear that a situation in which the child's willfulness faces the adult's will is a different proposition from that of the mutuality of instilling hope. Yet, any adult who has managed to train a child's will must admit—for better or for worse—that he has learned much about himself and about will that he never knew before, something which cannot be learned in any other way. Thus each growing individual's developing strength "dovetails" with the strengths of an increasing number of persons arranged about him in the formalized orders of family, school, community and society. But orders and rules are kept alive only by those "virtues" of which Shakespeare says (in what appears to me to be *his* passionate version of the Rule) that they, "shining upon others heat them and they retort that heat again to the first giver."

One more proposition must be added to the developmental and to the generational one, and to that of mutuality. It is implied in the term "activate," and I would call it the principle of *active choice*. It is, I think, most venerably expressed in St. Francis's prayer: "Grant that I may not so much seek to be consoled as to console; to be understood, as to understand; to be loved as to love; for it is in giving that we receive." Such commitment to an initia-

4. Sigmund Freud, *The Origins of Psychoanalysis: Letters to Wilhelm Fliess, Drafts and Notes: 1887-1902,* edited by Marie Bonaparte, Anna Freud and Ernst Kris, New York: Basic Books, 1954 [Erikson's note].

tive in love is, of course, contained in the admonition to "love thy neighbor." I think that we can recognize in these words a psychological verity, namely, that only he who approaches an encounter in a (consciously and unconsciously) active and giving attitude, rather than in a demanding and dependent one, will be able to make of that encounter what it can become.

With these considerations in mind, then, I will try to formulate my understanding of the Golden Rule. I have been reluctant to come to this point; it has taken thousands of years and many linguistic acrobatics to translate this Rule from one era to another and from one language into another, and at best one can only confound it again, in a somewhat different way.

I would advocate a general orientation which has its center in whatever activity or activities gives man the feeling, as William James put it, of being "most deeply and intensely active and alive." In this, so James promises, each one will find his "real me"; but, I would now add, he will also acquire the experience that *truly worthwhile acts enhance a mutuality between the doer and the other—a mutuality which strengthens the doer even as it strengthens the other.* Thus, the "doer" and "the other" are partners in one deed. Seen in the light of human development, this means that the doer is activated in whatever strength is *appropriate to his age, stage, and condition,* even as he activates in the other the strength appropriate to *his* age, stage, and condition. Understood this way, the Rule would say that it is best to do to another what will strengthen you even as it will strengthen him—that is, what will develop his best potentials even as it develops your own.

This variation of the Rule is obvious enough when applied to the relation of parent and child. But does the uniqueness of their respective positions, which has served as our model so far, have any significant analogies in other situations in which uniqueness depends on a divided function?

To return to particulars, I will attempt to apply my amendment to the diversity of function in the two sexes. I have not dwelled so far on this most usual subject of a psychoanalytic discourse, sexuality. So much of this otherwise absorbing aspect of life has, in recent years, become stereotyped in theoretical discussion. Among the terminological culprits to be blamed for this sorry fact is the psychoanalytic term "love object." For this word "object" in Freud's theory has been taken too literally by many of his friends and by most of his enemies—and moralistic critics do delight in misrepresenting a man's transitory formulations as his ultimate "values." The fact is that Freud, on purely conceptual grounds, and on the basis of the scientific language of his laboratory days, pointed out that drive energies have "objects." But he certainly never advocated that men or women should treat one another as objects on which to live out their sexual idiosyncrasies.

Instead, his central theory of genitality which combines strivings of sexuality and of love points to one of those basic mutualities in which *a partner's potency and potentialities are activated even as he activates the other's potency and potentialities.* Freud's theory implies that a man will be more a man to the extent to which he makes a woman more a woman—and vice versa—because only two uniquely different beings can enhance their respective uniqueness for one another. A "genital" person in Freud's sense is thus more apt to act in accordance with Kant's version of the Golden Rule, in that he would so act as to treat humanity "whether in his person or in another, always as an end, and never as only a means." What Freud added to the ethical principle, however, is a methodology which opens to our inquiry and to our influence the powerhouse of inner forces. For they provide the shining heat for our strengths— and the smoldering smoke of our weaknesses.

I cannot leave the subject of the two sexes without a word on the uniqueness of women. One may well question whether or not the Rule in its oldest form tacitly meant to include women as partners in the golden deal. Today's study of lives still leaves quite obscure the place of women in what is most relevant in the male image of man. True, women are being granted *equality* of political rights, and the recognition of a certain *sameness* in mental and moral equipment. But what they have not begun to earn, partially because they have not cared to ask for it, is the *equal right to be effectively unique,* and to use hard-won rights in the service of what they uniquely represent in human evolution. The West has much to learn, for example, from the unimpaired womanliness of India's modern women. But there is today a universal sense of the emergence of a new feminism as part of a more inclusive humanism. This coincides with a growing conviction—highly ambivalent, to be sure—that the future of mankind cannot depend on men alone and may well depend on the fate of a "mother variable" uncontrolled by technological man. The resistance to such a consideration always comes from men and women who are mortally afraid that by emphasizing what is unique one may tend to re-emphasize what is unequal. And, indeed, the study of life histories confirms a far-reaching sameness in men and women insofar as they express the mathematical architecture of the universe, the organization of logical thought, and the structure of language. But such a study also suggests that while boys and girls can think and act and talk alike, they naturally do not experience their bodies (and thus the world) alike. I have attempted to demonstrate this by pointing to sex differences in the structuralization of space in the play of children.[5] But I assume that a uniqueness of either sex will be granted without proof, and that the "difference" acclaimed by the much-quoted Frenchman is not considered only a matter of anatomical appointments for mutual sexual enjoyment, but a psychobiological difference central to two great modes of life, the *paternal* and the *maternal* modes. The amended Golden Rule suggests that one sex enhances the uniqueness of the other; it also implies that each, to be really unique, depends on a mutuality with an equally unique partner.

From the most intimate human encounters we now turn to a professional, and yet relatively intimate, one: that between healer and patient. There is a very real and specific inequality in the relationship of doctor and patient in their roles of knower and known, helper and sufferer, practitioner of life and victim of disease and death. For this reason medical people have their own and unique professional oath and strive to live up to a universal ideal of "the doctor." Yet the practice of the healing arts permits extreme types of practitioners, from the absolute authoritarian over homes and clinics to the harassed servant of demanding mankind, from the sadist of mere proficiency, to the effusive lover of all (well, almost all) of his patients. Here, too, Freud has thrown intimate and original light on the workings of a unique relationship. His letters to his friend and mentor Fliess illustrate the singular experience which made him recognize in his patients what he called "transference"—that is, the patient's wish to exploit sickness and treatment for infantile and regressive ends. But more, Freud, recognized a "countertransference" in the healer's motivation to exploit the patient's transference and to dominate or serve, possess or love him to the disadvantage of his true function. He made systematic insight into transference *and* countertransference part of the training of the psychoanalytic practitioner.

I would think that all of the motivations necessarily entering so vast and so intricate a field could be reconciled in a Golden Rule amended to include a mutuality of divided function. Each specialty and each technique in its own way permits the medical man to *develop as a practitioner, and as a person, even as the patient is cured as a patient, and as a person.* For a real cure transcends the transitory state of patienthood. It is an experience which enables the cured patient to develop and to transmit to home and neigh-

5. Erik H. Erikson, "Sex Differences in the Play Constructions of Pre-Adolescents," in *Discussions in Child Development*, World Health Organization, Vol. III, New York: International Universities Press, 1958. See also "Reflections on Womanhood," *Daedalus*, Spring 1964 [Erikson's note].

borhood an attitude toward health which is one of the most essential ingredients of an ethical outlook.

Beyond this, can the healing arts and sciences contribute to a new ethical outlook? This question always recurs in psychoanalysis and is usually disposed of with Freud's original answer that the psychoanalyst represents the ethics of scientific truth only and is committed to studying ethics (or morality) in a scientific way. Beyond this, he leaves *Weltanschauungen* (ethical world views) to others.

It seems to me, however, that the clinical arts and sciences, while employing the scientific method, are not defined by it or limited by it. The healer is commited to a highest good, the preservation of life and the furtherance of well-being—the "maintenance of life." He need not prove scientifically that these are, in fact, the highest good; rather, he is precommitted to this basic proposition while investigating what can be verified by scientific means. This, I think, is the meaning of the Hippocratic oath, which subordinates all medical method to a humanist ethic. True, a man can separate his personal, his professional, and his scientific ethics, seeking fulfillment of idiosyncratic needs in personal life, the welfare of others in his profession, and truths independent of personal preference or service in his research. However, there are psychological limits to the multiplicity of values a man can live by, and, in the end, not only the practitioner, but also his patient and his research, depend on a certain unification in him of temperament, intellect, and ethics. This unification clearly characterizes great doctors.

While it is true, then, that as scientists we must study ethics objectively, we are, as professional individuals, committed to a unification of personality, training, and conviction which alone will help us to do our work adequately. At the same time, as transient members of the human race, we must record the truest meaning of which the fallible methods of our era and the accidental circumstances of our existence have made us aware. In this sense, there is (and always has been) not only an ethics governing clinical work, and a clinical approach to the study of ethics, but also a contribution to ethics of the healing orientation. The healer, furthermore, has now committed himself to prevention on a large scale, and he cannot evade the problem of assuring ethical vitality to all lives saved from undernourishment, morbidity, and early mortality. Man's technical ability and social resolve to prevent accidental conception makes every child conceived a subject of universal responsibility.

As I approach my conclusion, let me again change my focus and devote a few minutes to a matter political and economic as well as ethical: Gandhi's "Rule."

In Ahmedabad I had occasion to visit Gandhi's ashram[6] across the Sabarmati River; and it was not long before I realized that in Ahmedabad a hallowed and yet eminently concrete event had occurred which perfectly exemplifies everything I am trying to say. I refer, of course, to Gandhi's leadership in the lockout and strike of the mill-workers in 1918, and his first fast in a public cause. This event is well known in the history of industrial relations the world over, and vaguely known to all educated Indians. Yet, I believe that only in Ahmedabad, among surviving witnesses and living institutions, can one fathom the "presence" of that event as a lastingly successful "experiment" in local industrial relations, influential in Indian politics, and, above all, representing a new type of encounter in divided human functions. The details of the strike and of the settlement need not concern us here. As usual, it began as a matter of wages. Nor can I take time to indicate the limited political and economic applicability of the Ahmedabad experiment to other industrial areas in and beyond India. What interests us here is the fact that Gandhi, from the moment of his entry into the struggle, considered it an occasion not for maximum reciprocal coercion resulting in the usual compromise, but as an opportunity for all—the workers, the owners, and himself—"to rise from the present conditions."

The utopian quality of the principles on which he determined to focus can only be grasped by one who can visualize the squalor of the workmen's living conditions, the latent panic in the ranks of the paternalistic millowners (beset by worries of British competition), and Gandhi's then as yet relative inexperience in handling the masses of India. The shadows of defeat, violence, and corruption hovered over every one of the "lofty" words which I am about to quote. But to Gandhi, any worthwhile struggle must "transform the inner life of the people." Gandhi spoke to the workers daily under the famous Babul Tree outside the medieval Shahpur Gate. He had studied their desperate condition, yet he urged them to ignore the threats and the promises of the millowners who in the obstinate fashion of all "haves" feared the anarchic insolence and violence of the "have nots." He knew that they feared him, too, for they had indicated that they might even accept his terms if only he would promise to leave and to stay away forever. But he settled down to prove that a just man could "secure the good of the workers while safeguarding the good of the employers"—the two opposing sides being represented by a sister and a brother, Anasuyabehn and Ambalal Sarabhai. Under the Babul Tree Gandhi announced the principle which somehow corresponds to our amended Rule:

6. Holy retreat.

"*That line of action is alone justice which does not harm either party to a dispute.*" By harm he meant—and his daily announcements leave no doubt of this—an inseparable combination of economic disadvantage, social indignity, loss of self-esteem, and latent vengeance.

Neither side found it easy to grasp this principle. When the workers began to weaken, Gandhi suddenly declared a fast. Some of his friends, he admitted, considered this "foolish, unmanly, or worse"; and some were deeply distressed. But, "I wanted to show you," he said to the workers, "that I was not playing with you." He was, as we would say, in dead earnest, and this fact, then as later, immediately raised an issue of local conscience to national significance. In daily appeals, Gandhi stressed variously those basic inner strengths without which no issue has "virtue," namely, will with justice, purpose with discipline, respect for work of any kind, and truthfulness. But he knew, and he said so, that these masses of illiterate men and women, newly arrived from the villages and already exposed to proletarization, did not have the moral strength or the social solidarity to adhere to principle without strong leadership. "You have yet to learn how and when to take an oath," he told them. The oath, the dead earnestness, then, was as yet the leader's privilege and commitment. In the end the matter was settled, not without a few Gandhian compromises to save face all around, but with a true acceptance of the settlement originally proposed by Gandhi.

I do not claim to understand the complex motivations and curious turns of Gandhi's mind—some contradicting Western rigidity in matters of principle, and some, I assume, strange to Indian observers, as well. I can also see in Gandhi's actions a paternalism which may now be "dated." But his monumental simplicity and total involvement in the "experiment" made both workers and owners revere him. And he himself said with humorous awe, "I have never come across such a fight." For, indeed both sides had matured in a way that lifted labor relations in Ahmedabad to a new and lasting level. Let me quote only the fact that, in 1950, the Ahmedabad Textile Labor Organization accounted for only a twentieth of India's union membership, but for eighty per cent of its welfare expenditures.

Such a singular historical event, then, reveals something essential in human strength, in traditional Indian strength, and in the power of Gandhi's own personal transformation at the time. To me, the miracle of the Ahmedabad experiment has been not only its lasting success and its tenacity during those days of anarchic violence which after the great partition broke down so many dams of solidarity, but above all, the spirit which points beyond the event.

And now a final word on what is, and will be for a long time to come, the sinister horizon of the world in which we all study and work: the international situation. Here, too, we cannot afford to live for long with a division of personal, professional, and political ethics—a division endangering the very life which our professions have vowed to keep intact, and thus cutting through the very fiber of our personal existence. Only in our time, and in our very generation, have we come, with traumatic suddenness, to be conscious of what was self-evident all along, namely, that in all of previous history the Rule, in whatever form, has comfortably coexisted with warfare. A warrior, all armored and spiked and set to do to another what he fully expected the other to be ready to do to him, saw no ethical contradiction between the Rule and his military ideology. He could, in fact, grant to his adversary a respect which he hoped to earn in return. This tenuous coexistence of ethics and warfare may outlive itself in our time. Even the military mind may well come to fear for its historical identity, as boundless slaughter replaces tactical warfare. What is there, even for a "fighting man," in the Golden Rule of the Nuclear Age, which seems to say, "Do not unto others—unless you are sure you can do them in as totally as they can do you in"?

One wonders, however, whether this deadlock in international morals can be broken by the most courageous protest, the most incisive interpretation, or the most prophetic warning—a warning of catastrophe so all-consuming that most men must ignore it, as they ignore their own death and have learned to ignore the monotonous prediction of hell. It seems, instead that only an ethical orientation, a direction for vigorous cooperation, can free today's energies from their bondage in armed defensiveness. We live at a time in which—with all the species-wide destruction possible—we can think for the first time of a species-wide identity, of a truly universal ethics, such as has been prepared in the world religions, in humanism, and by some philosophers. Ethics, however, cannot be fabricated. They can only emerge from an informed and inspired search for a more inclusive human identity, which a new technology and a new world image make possible as well as mandatory. But again, all I can offer you here is another variation of the theme. What has been said about the relationships of parent and child, of man and woman, and of doctor and patient, may have some application to the relationship of nations to each other. Nations today are by definition units at different stages of political, technological, and economic transformation. Under these conditions, it is all too easy for overdeveloped nations to believe that nations, too, should treat one another with a superior educative or clinical attitude. The point of what I have to say, however, is not underscored inequality, but respected uniqueness within historical differences. Insofar as a nation thinks of itself as a collective individual, then, it may well learn to visualize its task as that of maintaining mutuality in international relations. For the only alternative to armed competition seems to be the effort to *activate in the historical partner what will strengthen him in his historical development even as it strengthens the actor in his own development— toward a common future identity.* Only thus can we find a common denominator in the rapid change of technology and history and transcend the dangerous imagery of victory and defeat, of subjugation and exploitation which is the heritage of a fragmented past.

Does this sound utopian? I think, on the contrary, that all of what I have said is already known in many ways, is being expressed in many languages, and practiced on many levels. At our historical moment it becomes clear in a most practical way that the doer of the Golden Rule, and he who is done by, is the same man, *is* man.

Men of clinical background, however, must not lose sight of a dimension which I have taken for granted here. While the Golden Rule in its classical versions prods man to strive *consciously* for a highest good and to avoid mutual harm with a sharpened awareness, our insights assume an *unconscious* substratum of ethical strength and, at the same time, unconscious arsenals of destructive rage. The last century has traumatically expanded man's awareness of unconscious motivations stemming from his animal ancestry, from his economic history, and from his inner estrangements. It has also created (in all these respects) methods of productive self-analysis. These I consider the pragmatic Western version of that universal trend toward self-scrutiny which once reached such heights in Asian tradition. It will be the task of the next generation everywhere to begin to integrate new and old methods of self-awareness with the minute particulars of universal technical proficiency.

It does not seem easy to speak of ethical subjects without indulging in some moralizing. As an antidote I will conclude with the Talmudic version of the Rule. Rabbi Hillel once was asked by an unbeliever to tell the whole of the Torah while he stood on one foot. I do not know whether he meant to answer the request or to remark on its condition when he said: "What is hateful to yourself, do not to your fellow man. That is the whole of the Torah and the rest is but commentary." At any rate, he did not add: "Act accordingly." He said: "Go and learn it."

QUESTIONS

1. At times Erikson implies that he is digressing, and he certainly does cover a wide range of topics. How tightly is his talk organized? Can it be outlined?
2. Erikson distinguishes three stages of growth—moral, ideological, and ethical. What are the significant characteristics of each, and how do they relate to one another? What does Erikson mean by "evolution"?
3. Bruno Bettelheim said that liberals, the press, and teachers who failed to assert their authority all shared some blame for denying superego models to the young, particularly to the poor and disadvantaged: "There's no doubt about the underlying violence with which we are born. Whether we are going to have violence depends to a very large degree on how we develop the superego and controls of the coming generation." Would Erikson agree? Can you think of ways in which superego models are denied? Does a man in authority have to be unusually good himself to serve as a satisfactory model?

EDWARD HOAGLAND

The Problem of the Golden Rule

Like a good many New Yorkers, I've often wondered whether I was going to be mugged. I've lived in a number of neighborhoods, and being a night walker, have many times changed my course or speeded my stride, eying a formidable-looking figure as he approached. But it's never happened, and I imagine that if it finally does there may actually be a kind of relief, even a species of exhilaration, as I pick myself up—assuming that I am not badly hurt—because a danger anticipated for a long time may come to seem worse than the reality. People who come home and encounter a robber in their apartment who flees are likely to be less shaken up than the householder is who simply steps into a shambles of ransacked bureaus and upended beds: they've seen the fellow; they know he's human. A friend of mine wrestled a burglar for several minutes around the floor of his living room, both of them using the trips and hip throws that they remembered from their teens, until by the time my friend won and phoned the police they were old acquaintances. I know, too, that to describe the few incidents of violence I've met with in the past makes them sound more grisly than they were in fact. In the army, my platoon was put in the charge of a peculiar sergeant who, mostly for reasons of his own, had us do squat jumps one noontime until we could no longer walk or stand up. Then he strolled among us kicking us to make sure that we weren't faking. It was a hot drill field strewn with packs and stacked rifles and other movie props, and yet the experience was not nearly as bad as one would anticipate if he were told at breakfast what to expect that day. We just followed orders until we couldn't get up and then we lay where we were on the ground until the sergeant was satisfied that we had done what was humanly possible. Even in a true atrocity situation that's all that is ever done, what is humanly possible. Afterwards one becomes unresponsive and fatalistic; terror is no longer a factor.

Next day the sergeant wanted to have it both ways, so he set us into formation and told us what he was going to make us do, and thereupon went off to the latrine to give us a chance to stand at attention and think and stew. Another sergeant promptly walked up and dismissed us, however. We hobbled away in every direction as fast as possible, while the two sergeants met to discuss the issue in the barracks door. They met person-to-person, and we had been punished person-to-person, and the facelessness of the mugger whom one anticipates meeting on Little West 12th Street was never a part of it. This, like our doing whatever was humanly possible, made the experience supportable.

I visualize Armageddon not as a steel-muzzled affair of push-button silos under the earth but as a rusty freighter, flying the Liberian flag, perhaps, which sails inconspicuously up the Hudson past my apartment and goes off. Beyond that I don't see any details—though, as a non sequitur, I expect the tunnels and bridges would fill up with hikers leaving the city before it was too late. A woman I know says she sees Armageddon as getting under the bed. What we do with the insupportable is to turn it to terms we can file and forget. Unfortunately we are able to deal almost as handily with the nuclear bombs that have already gone off as we are with the ones that haven't. If as individual fighting men we had razed Hiroshima, then the horror of its destruction would persist as a legend to our great-grandchildren because it would have been witnessed and done on the spot—also because of the somber old notion that residing in every man is a spark of divinity, whether the man is an enemy or a friend. This putative spark is central to most religious belief; and right at the root of Western ethics is what is called, under one of its names, the Golden Rule. But spark or no spark, since in practice we cannot react to others with unabashed fellow-feeling, we usually reduce the Golden Rule to a sort of silver rule, doing to them just about what we think they would do to us if they had the opportunity. And this works—has been working—though the new impersonalized technology is challenging its workability, along with another behemoth among changes, which is that today there are too many people. Where there are too many people, we get tired of following even the silver rule, tired of paying that much attention, of noticing whom we are with and who is who. For the agnostic as well, basing his reverence for life on its variety and on a Jeffersonian fascination with the glimmerings of talent in every man, the glut is discouraging. Although we don't ridicule these old ideas, the sentiments that people have for one another in a traffic jam are becoming our sentiments more and more. A groan goes up in any suburb when it's announced that a new complex of housing for two thousand souls is going to be built on Lone Tree Hill. And the vast sigh of impatience which greeted Pope Paul's traditionalist statement of faith in the sanctity of the seed germs of life points to the tone to come. *Life for the living,* people will say: body-counts in war and baby-counts in peace. We grant each union man his $10,500 a year, and then the hell with him. He, for his part, doesn't care if our garbage cans fester with rats when the union goes after $10,900.

Never have people dealt so briskly with strangers as now. Many of us have ceased to see strangers at all; our eyes simply don't register them except as verticals on the sidewalk, and when we must parley with them we find out quickly what they are asking from us, do it—maybe—and that's that. When I was a child I remember how my astonishment evolved as I realized that people often would not do the smallest thing to convenience another person or make him feel easier for the moment. Of course I'd known that *kids* wouldn't, but I had thought that was because they were kids. It was my first comprehension of the deadness of life. Everyone has discovered at some particular point life's deadness, but the galloping sense of deadness which alarms so many people lately, and especially the young, goes way beyond such individual discoveries to dimensions and contexts that have brought revolution to the U.S. Even in the arts the ancient austerities have been deemed insufficient, and we have actors who jump into the audience and do their acting there. When acting seems to fail, they improvise, and finally improvisation isn't enough either, and instead of having an actor play the drug addict, the addict himself must appear onstage and play himself— like the toothpaste tube blown up and hanging on the museum wall: "Look, if nothing else, I'm real." This is the era when students are so busy trying to teach their teachers that they are hard to teach, and when the chip on the shoulder of the man in the street is his "personality"—personality is quarrelsomeness. The revolution, in any case, is overdue, but maybe our best hope is that we remain at least idiosyncratic creatures, absorbed close to home. Dog owners, when they walk their dogs, show nearly as exact an interest in their pets' defecations as they would in their own. The same communing silence steals over their faces, the look of musing solemnity, that usually only the bathroom mirror gets a glimpse of.

The worst public tragedy I've witnessed was in Boston, when from a distance I saw a brick wall fall on a company of firemen.

Some, with a great shout, got away, but even the leap that they made while the rest crumpled is blurred as a memory compared to the images of two old men whom I knew very slightly at the time. Mr. Kate wrote cookbooks in the winter and hired out as a cook on a private yacht during the warm months. His other love, besides cooking, was opera, and he lived in a room shaped like a shoebox that cost him eight dollars a week. He served himself candlelit meals on a folding table and concocted all of his recipes on a hot-plate set in the sink. By contrast, Mr. Hurth, although a somewhat less cultivated man, was an alumnus of Brown University and lived in a large ground-floor room in the same house. He had ruined himself in a scandal in St. Louis, where he had been a businessman, but that was all I learned. What he'd done next was to come to Boston and throw himself on the old-fashioned, private or "Christian" charity, as it used to be called, of a roommate from college, though thirty years had passed. He was a pleasant subdued man ordinarily, swinging from sweet to vaguely hangdog, but he was a drinker, and so this benefactor no longer asked him to Newton Centre for Thanksgiving because he was likely to break the furniture. When he did, he'd leave his glasses behind by mistake so that he'd have to go back out again for a whole second festival of apologies. Through charitable intercession, Mr. Hurth was on the payroll of the John Hancock Insurance Company, being listed on the books as a claims investigator, though actually (charity compounding charity) his single duty was to work for the United Fund once a year on a loan basis. The campaign was a brief one, but he was a bitter, floundering functionary, faced with his fate if his drinking should snap off his last sticks of presence and respectability.

As I say, next to the memory of two nodding acquaintances the death of some distant firemen is small potatoes. I was reminded of that catastrophe the other night for the first time in years while watching a fire on Third Avenue. Here in the bigger city one is witness to such a cataract of appalling happenings that they pass remembering. I saw a man who had just been burned out of his apartment turned away from a hotel in the neighborhood because he had a little blacking on him, although the shock and fear stood in his eyes. "Sure, there was a fire there, all right," the manager told me with a laugh. "I never take them in, those victims. They're dirty and they're scared to death. They're not worth the nuisance."

He was a modern, casual villain, however, impartial, just the kind who is not memorable. I came upon a much less gratuitous drama a few days afterwards. A child of two or three had been stuck inside one of those all-glass phone booths with a spring door which cannot be opened except by a grown person because of where the handle is placed. The world was passing—this was on the open street—but he was feeling his way around the glass in gathering panic, trying to find an escape route, reaching up and reaching down. Every few seconds he let out a thin, fluting scream so pure in pitch that it was hardly human; it was *pre*-human. You could see him thinking, learning, recording discoveries. He reached for the phone, but that was too high up; he thumped each pane of glass, searching for the door, and pounded on the metal frame, and screamed to find whether screaming would work. He was boxed into his terror, and you could see him grow older by leaps and bounds. I'm just this month a new father, so I was as transfixed as if he were my child. His governess or baby-sitter, baby-walker, or whatever she was, a short shadowy woman such as you might see manning a subway change booth, was standing right next to the glass, apparently feasting her eyes. Whether it was supposed to be a "punishment" or merely a pleasure fest, the child was too frightened by now to notice her.

Maybe our cruelty will save us. At least the cruel do pay attention, and the woman would probably have let him out before the crowd got around to hearing him. She had moved to the door, looking down at him intently as he pushed on the glass. I was seething, partly because I found that some of the woman's sexual excitement had communicated itself to me, which was intolerable, and partly because my cowardice in not interfering was equally outrageous. We've all become reluctant to stop and stick our noses in—a man is run over by a Breakstone cream-cheese truck and we pass quickly by. But cowardice was what it was in this particular event, since even under happy circumstances I stutter and it requires an enormous gearing up of nerve for me to step into a public fracas on the street. I strangle; I can't speak at all and must either use my hands on the stranger or gag and quaver, unable to put two words together. The seams of human nature frighten me in this regard, and the whole confrontation ethic of the sixties, much as I have entered into it on occasion, gives me nightmare visions because I have no conventional means of battling. I see myself as unable to protest in words to the person whose behavior has angered me and so using my hands on him; then just as unable to explain myself to the crowd that gathers, but only shuddering and stuttering; and then in court again enforcedly silent, dependent on the empathy or telepathic capacities of the people who are there to convey my side of the controversy.

Weaving like a nauseous moose, I was working my way toward her, when the woman, with a glance at me, pushed the door of the booth open, reached inside, and pulled the boy to her and walked away. In effect, I was let off, because only an exceptional well-doer would have tracked the woman down from that point on and questioned her about her psyche.

However, there are times one isn't let off, when one's very humanity hangs at issue and perhaps my specific problems with my stutter are an epitome of what each of us meets. Once in northern New England when I was snowshoeing, a hunter started shooting at me, really only to scare me, pinging with his .22 in my immediate vicinity. I was on an open hillside which I'd already realized was too slippery to climb, but as long as I kept scrabbling there in silence on the ice, like an animal in trouble, he was going to keep on pinging. Because a stutterer's every impulse is to stutter softly, unobtrusively, it's twice as hard to shout one's way through a stutter as to wedge through in quiet tones; but from the sheer imperatives of survival I shouted, "I CAN SEE YOU!" I shouted it several times again, although I couldn't see him; he was in the woods. I was insisting and reiterating that I was a human being: if I could get that message across to him he would stop shooting at me. It was even worse than my conception of a courtroom trial because this was one of those rare emergencies when we can't trust to all our faculties to operate together for us—the movements of our hands, our youth or age, our manner and expression—some compensating for the inadequacies of the others. I had to go to bat with my speaking abilities and nothing else. So I shouted to him that I could see him, by which I meant I was a man, and he stopped shooting.

More recently, I was on a tiny Danish island off the coast of Sweden, wandering around some seventeenth-century fortifications and the walled town, now a huddled fishing village. I had sat on the sea wall to watch the cloud action but was distracted by the spectacle below me of a boy mistreating a wild duck. Oddly enough, many times an incident where a person, rather than an animal, is being mauled and manhandled is easier to shrug off. The fact that he's a person complicates the case. As an onlooker you can see, for example, that he has gotten himself drunk and let his guard down, lost his dignity, talked out of turn. But the duck, with its wings clipped, presumably, was only trying to run away. The boy would catch it, pummel it and grip it tightly, trundling it about. Finally I got off my bench and went over and told him falteringly to cut that out. Many Danes speak English, but he was twelve or so and he may not have understood me. Like a mirror of myself, he stared at me without trying to say a word. Then he squeezed the duck again hard in both hands. My bugaboo about trying to explain myself to strangers rose in me, along with my indignation. Instead of looking for a local fellow to translate and take over, I lifted the duck from his arms, and with the sense of right and doom that I have dreaded in foreseeing a confrontation on the street, carried it down the stairs of the sea wall and released it on the beach. The boy ran for help; the duck paddled into the waves; I climbed to the promenade and started walking as deliberately as I could toward the small boat which had brought me to the island.

Uncannily soon, before I'd gone a dozen yards, practically the whole male populace was on the scene. "Hey! Turn around!" they yelled. I took another couple of steps away and then did so. They told me very plainly in English that they were going to throw me over the sea wall. They said the duck had been rescued by the boys of the island—their sons—after it had swum through an oil slick and almost drowned. Now, because of what I'd done, it really *was* about to drown, and when it went under, they would toss me over. This was not spoken in joking tones, and I could see the duck getting heavier in the water; its feathers, though as tidy to the eye as a healthy duck's feathers, had no buoyancy. Meanwhile, I'd fallen into something like what a prizefighter would call a clinch by refusing to acknowledge by any sign that I understood what was being said to me. It is a psychological necessity that when you punish somebody he understand the reason why. Even if he doesn't accept the guilty finding, you must explain to him why you are punishing him or you can't do it. So while they could scarcely contain their frustration, my face displayed bewilderment; I kept pretending to grope to understand, I was doing this instinctively, of course, and as their first impetus to violence passed, I found myself acting out with vehemence how I had seen the boy mistreat the duck. The men, who wanted at the least to take a poke at me, watched doubtfully, but there was a Coast Guardsman, an off-islander, who seemed to be arguing in Danish on my behalf. Another man went down to where the duck was swimming and reached out; the duck perceiving itself to be sinking, had moved cautiously closer to shore. And when the duck was saved I was saved; I only had the island's boys waiting for me in the embrasures of the wall.

Yet this quite comic misadventure, when every dread came real —I couldn't say a single word to save my life—was just as numbing as those ninety-five squat jumps at Fort Dix—only later was it terrifying. And in a way it makes up for the memories I have as a teenager of watching flocks of bats murdered with brooms and frogs tormented—moments when I didn't interfere, but giggled ruefully to keep my popularity and stifle my outcries.

Sociology progresses; the infant mortality rate among Negroes goes down. Nevertheless we know that if the announcement were made that there was going to be a public hanging in Central Park, Sheep Meadow would be crowded with spectators, like Tyburn mall. Sometimes at night my standing lamp shapes itself into an observant phantom figure which takes a position next to my bed. It doesn't threaten me directly, and I stretch out to clutch its throat with careful anger. My final grab bumps the lamp over. This electric phantom is a holdover from my vivid night demons when I was eight or ten. I never saw them outright, thank the Lord, but for years I fell asleep facing the wall to avoid beholding my destruction. I'd "whisper," as I called it, when I went to bed, telling myself an installment of a round-robin story, and when the installment was over I'd wait for the demons, until I fell asleep. Later, just as invariably, I faced the outer room so I could see them come and have warning to fight. Such archaisms in our minds are not an unmixed evil, however, because they link us to humanity and to our history as human beings. My wife says every man she's been familiar with would smell his socks at night before he went to bed: just a whiff —each sock, not only one. I do this too, although the smell has been of no intrinsic interest to me for twenty years. The smell of each sock checks precisely with the other one and smells as vital as pigs do. Maybe it reassures us that we're among the living still. We need to know. In the fifties I also liked the smell of air pollution. I didn't think of it as air pollution then—nobody did—but as the smell of industry and the highways I hitchhiked on, the big-shouldered America I loved.

In 1943 George Orwell said the problem of the times was the decay in the belief in personal immortality. Several French novelists had turned existentialist and several English novelists Catholic (possibly the same reaction), while he himself, like many of the more likable writers, had adopted a hardy humanist's masculine skepticism. Twenty-odd years later, the problem appears only to have grown more piercing, though it is not put into the same terms. You can't have as many people walking around as there are now and still simply see them as chips off the divine lodestone. Nor is the future 1984: that's too succinct. At first the new nuclear bullying, the new technocracy, made mere survival more the point, because we wanted to be sure of surviving here on earth before we worried about heaven. Lately, instead the talk has been about overpopulation, and city people have started venturing to the outback, buying acreage with all the premonitory fervor of Noah sawing logs. Everyone wants space to breathe; the character of city life has drastically deteriorated, and there's no questioning the statistics, just as there used to be no questioning the odds that eventually a nuclear war was going to penetrate our precautions through that old fontanel of existence: human mix-up.

When we say that enough is enough, that we have enough people on hand now for any good purpose, we mean that the divine spark has become something of a conflagration, besides an embarrassment of riches. We're trying to make a start at sorting the riches, buying Edwardian clothes but also Volkswagens, and settling down to the process of zoning the little land there is. As we also begin to cogitate on how the quality of life can be improved, we may be in for a religious revival, too. It's a natural beginning, and faddism will probably swing that way, and after all, we *are* extraordinary—we're so extraordinary we're everywhere. Next to the new mysticisms, old-fashioned, run-of-the-mill religion is not so hard to swallow. The difficulty will be how we regard individual people, a question which involves not only whether we think we're immortal but whether we think they are. The crowded impatience of suburb-city living doesn't often evoke intimations of other people's immortality, and neither do the hodge-podge leveling procedures of a modern democracy. So much of the vigor of the Victorian church, for instance, grew out of the contrast between its members and the raw, destitute brown masses who covered the rest of the globe. Among an elite, self-congratulatory minority even the greatest of attributes—immortality—seemed plausible.

But maybe I'm being overly sour. We have wiped tigers off the earth and yet our children hear as much about the symbolism of tigers as children did in the old days. And next to the subway station I use there is a newsdealer who was blinded in Orwell's war, the Spanish War, in the mountains behind Motril. He wears the aura of a revolutionary volunteer. He dresses bulkily, as if for weather at the front, and rigs canvas around his hut as neatly as a soldier's tent. Not one of your meek blind men, he's on his feet most of the day, especially in tough weather, pacing, marching, standing tall. He's gray and grim, hard and spare, and doubtless lives surrounded by the companions that he had in the Sierra Nevada. But he's too bluff and energetic to be a museum piece. If you help him cross the street you get the rough edge of his tongue. He searches for the lamppost with his cane like a tennis player swinging backhand, and if he loses his bearings and bumps against something, he jerks abruptly back like a cavalier insulted, looking gaunt and fierce. I pity him, but I take note of him; he counts himself among the living. I buy a paper and go home to my newborn baby, who is as intense and focused (to my eye) as a flight of angels dancing on a pinhead.

I don't believe in a god you can pray to, but I do find I believe in God—I do more than I don't. I believe in glee and in the exuberance I feel with friends and animals and in the fields, and in other emotions besides that. Anyway, as we know, it really isn't necessary to see sparks of a grand divinity in someone else to feel with the old immediacy that he is kin; we can evolve a more sophisticated Golden Rule than that. We will be trying to refine and revivify the qualities of life, and the chief stumbling block is that we must somehow reduce the density of people in our own comings and goings without doing it as we do now, which is by simply not seeing them, by registering them as shadows to dodge by on the street. Without degenerating into callousness, we must develop our ability to switch on and off—something analogous to what we do already with body temperature in a harsh world. Generally we'd button up if we were out walking, but when the Breakstone cream-cheese truck ran over an old man, this would be a time when our ancient instinct for cherishing a stranger would spring to being.

I live in a high-rise apartment and keep a pair of field glasses next to the window to use whenever somebody emerges on one of the rooftops nearby. There are ten or fifteen regulars—old people hanging wash, high school kids who have come up into the open to talk where they can be alone. All of them are neighbors to me now, though on the street I probably would turn away from them—even the bathing beauties would not be beauties there. Admittedly I am a bit of a voyeur, as who isn't, but the population density on the rooftops seems about right. In fact, I roused myself not long ago to drive some robbers off a roof across the street by gesticulating sternly. They waved back as they went down the stairs like people who've escaped a fall.

QUESTIONS

1. On p. 777 Hoagland says that stuttering makes him incapable of speech in tense confrontations. What does he do—word choice, figures of speech, management of detail—to make you feel his tension? What is the consequence of his breaking the sequence of his essay after explaining about his stuttering?
2. Hoagland provides a good deal of potentially verifiable biographical information about himself (e. g., he lives in New York, at the time of writing he had a newborn baby, he lives in a high-rise building). List this data and then explain what more you know about him and how you know it.
3. At the end Hoagland makes the issue into a perceptual problem —being able to see other people. What is the relation between his earlier stress on his inability to speak and this on perception?
4. Compare Hoagland on the golden rule with Erikson's discussion of it (p. 755). Which is the more effective treatment?

On Politics
and Government

W. E. B. DU BOIS
Jacob and Esau[1]

I remember very vividly the Sunday-school room where I spent the Sabbaths of my early years. It had been newly built after a disastrous fire; the room was large and full of sunlight; nice new chairs were grouped around where the classes met. My class was in the center, so that I could look out upon the elms of Main Street and see the passersby. But I was interested usually in the lessons and in my fellow students and the frail rather nervous teacher, who tried to make the Bible and its ethics clear to us. We were a trial to her, full of mischief, restless and even noisy; but perhaps more especially when we asked questions. And on the story of Jacob and Esau we did ask questions. My judgment then and my judgment now is very unfavorable to Jacob. I thought that he was a cad and a liar and I did not see how possibly he could be made the hero of a Sunday-school lesson.

Many days have passed since then and the world has gone through astonishing changes. But basically, my judgment of Jacob has not greatly changed and I have often promised myself the pleasure of talking about him publicly, and especially to young people. This is the first time that I have had the opportunity.

My subject then is "Jacob and Esau," and I want to examine these two men and the ideas which they represent; and the way in which those ideas have come to our day. Of course, our whole interpretation of this age-old story of Jewish mythology has greatly changed. We look upon these Old Testament stories today not as untrue and yet not as literally true. They are simple, they have their truths, and yet they are not by any means the expression of eternal verity. Here were brought forward for the education of Jewish chil-

1. Commencement address at Talladega College, June 5, 1944.

dren and for the interpretation of Jewish life to the world, two men: one small, lithe and quick-witted; the other tall, clumsy and impetuous; a hungry, hard-bitten man.

Historically, we know how these two types came to be set forth by the Bards of Israel. When the Jews marched north after escaping from slavery in Egypt, they penetrated and passed through the land of Edom; the land that lay between the Dead Sea and Egypt. It was an old center of hunters and nomads and the Israelites, while they admired the strength and organization of the Edomites, looked down upon them as lesser men; as men who did not have the Great Plan. Now the Great Plan of the Israelites was the building of a strong, concentered state under its own God, Jehovah, devoted to agriculture and household manufacture and trade. It raised its own food by careful planning. It did not wander and depend upon chance wild beasts. It depended upon organization, strict ethics, absolute devotion to the nation through strongly integrated planned life. It looked upon all its neighbors, not simply with suspicion, but with the exclusiveness of a chosen people, who were going to be the leaders of earth.

This called for sacrifice, for obedience, for continued planning. The man whom we call Esau was from the land of Edom, or inter-married with it, for the legend has it that he was twin of Jacob the Jew but the chief fact is that, no matter what his blood relations were, his cultural allegiance lay among the Edomites. He was trained in the free out-of-doors; he chased and faced the wild beasts; he knew vast and imperative appetite after long self-denial, and even pain and suffering; he gloried in food, he traveled afar; he gathered wives and concubines and he represented continuous primitive strife.

The legacy of Esau has come down the ages to us. It has not been dominant, but it has always and continually expressed and re-expressed itself; the joy of human appetites, the quick resentment that leads to fighting, the belief in force, which is war.

As I look back upon my own conception of Esau, he is not nearly as clear and definite a personality as Jacob. There is something rather shadowy about him; and yet he is curiously human and easily conceived. One understands his contemptuous surrender of his birthright; he was hungry after long days of hunting; he wanted rest and food, the stew of meat and vegetables which Jacob had in his possession, and determined to keep unless Esau bargained. "And Esau said, Behold, I am at the point to die: and what profit shall this birthright be to me? And Jacob said, Swear to me this day; and he swore unto him: and he sold his birthright unto Jacob."

On the other hand, the legacy of Jacob which has come down through the years, not simply as a Jewish idea, but more especially as typical of modern Europe, is more complicated and expresses itself something like this: life must be planned for the Other Self, for that personification of the group, the nation, the empire, which has eternal life as contrasted with the ephemeral life of individuals. For this we must plan, and for this there must be timeless and unceasing work. Out of this, the Jews as chosen children of Jehovah would triumph over themselves, over all Edom and in time over the world.

Now it happens that so far as actual history is concerned, this dream and plan failed. The poor little Jewish nation was dispersed to the ends of the earth by the overwhelming power of the great nations that arose East, North, and South and eventually became united in the vast empire of Rome. This was the diaspora, the dispersion of the Jews. But the idea of the Plan with a personality of its own took hold of Europe with relentless grasp and this was the real legacy of Jacob, and of other men of other peoples, whom Jacob represents.

There came the attempt to weld the world into a great unity, first under the Roman Empire, then under the Catholic Church. When this attempt failed, and the empire fell apart, there arose the individual states of Europe and of some other parts of the world; and these states adapted the idea of individual effort to make each of them dominant. The state was *all*, the individual subordinate, but right here came the poison of the Jacobean idea. How could the state get this power? Who was to wield the power within the state? So long as power was achieved, what difference did it make how it was gotten? Here then was war—but not Esau's war of passion, hunger and revenge, but Jacob's war of cold acquisition and power.

Granting to Jacob, as we must, the great idea of the family, the clan, and the state as dominant and superior in its claims, nevertheless, there is the bitter danger in trying to seek these ends without reference to the great standards of right and wrong. When men begin to lie and steal, in order to make the nation to which they belong great, then comes not only disaster, but rational contradiction which in many respects is worse than disaster, because it ruins the leadership of the divine machine, the human reason, by which we chart and guide our actions.

It was thus in the middle age and increasingly in the seventeenth and eighteenth and more especially in the nineteenth century, there arose the astonishing contradiction: that is, the action of men like Jacob who were perfectly willing and eager to lie and steal so long as their action brought profit to themselves and power to their state. And soon identifying themselves and their class with the state they identified their own wealth and power as that of the state. They did not listen to any arguments of right or wrong; might was right; they came to despise and deplore the natural appetites of human beings and their very lives, so long as by their suppression, they themselves got rich and powerful. There arose a great, rich Italy; a fabulously wealthy Spain; a strong and cultured France and, eventually, a British Empire which came near to dominating the world. The Esaus of those centuries were curiously represented by various groups of people: by the slum-dwellers and the criminals who, giving up all hope of profiting by the organized state, sold their birthrights for miserable messes of pottage. But more than that, the great majority of mankind, the peoples who lived in Asia, Africa and America and the islands of the sea, became subordinate tools for the profit-making of the crafty planners of great things, who worked regardless of religion or ethics.

It is almost unbelievable to think what happened in those centuries, when it is put in cold narrative; from whole volumes of tales, let me select only a few examples. The peoples of whole islands and countries were murdered in cold blood for their gold and jewels. The mass of the laboring people of the world were put to work for wages which led them into starvation, ignorance and disease. The right of the majority of mankind to speak and to act; to play and to dance was denied, if it interfered with profit-making work for others, or was ridiculed if it could not be capitalized. Karl Marx writes of Scotland: "As an example of the method of obtaining wealth and power in nineteenth century; the story of the Duchess of Sutherland will suffice here. This Scottish noblewoman resolved, on entering upon the government of her clan of white Scottish people, to turn the whole country, whose population had already been, by earlier processes, reduced to 15,000, into a sheep pasture. From 1814 to 1820 these 15,000 inhabitants were systematically hunted and rooted out. All their villages were destroyed and burnt, all their fields turned into pasture. Thus this lady appropriated 794,000 acres of land that had from time immemorial been the property of the people. She assigned to the expelled inhabitants about 6,000 acres on the seashore. The 6,000 acres had until this time lain waste, and brought in no income to their owners. The Duchess, in the nobility of her heart, actually went so far as to let these at an average rent of 50 cents per acre to the clansmen, who for centuries had shed their blood for her family. The whole of the stolen clan-land she divided into 29 great sheep farms, each inhabited by a single imported English family. In the year 1835 the 15,000 Scotsmen were already replaced by 131,000 sheep."[1]

1. This is a quotation from Karl Marx's *Capital*. However, Du Bois in places has paraphrased Marx and interpolated his own words for those of the English translation of the work. The essential meaning, however, is not distorted. Since it is likely Du Bois used the translation of *Capital* by Samuel Moore and Edward Aveling (published by Charles H. Kerr and Co., Chicago, 1906) the reader can compare Du Bois's rendition with the original by consulting pp. 801–802, vol. I, of the Kerr edition of *Capital*. [This and subsequent notes are those of Du Bois's editor, Philip S. Foner.]

The discovery of gold and silver in America, the extirpation, enslavement and entombment in mines of the Indian population, the beginning of the conquest and looting of the East Indies, the turning of Africa into a warren for the commercial hunting of black-skins, signalized the rosy dawn of power of those spiritual children of Jacob, who owned the birthright of the masses by fraud and murder. These idyllic proceedings are the chief momenta of primary accumulation of capital in private hands. On their heels tread the commercial wars of the European nations, with the globe for a theater. It begins with the revolt of the Netherlands from Spain, assumes giant dimensions in England's anti-jacobin war, and continues in the opium wars against China.

Of the Christian colonial system, Howitt says: "The barbarities and desperate outrages of the so-called Christians, throughout every region of the world, and upon people they have been able to subdue, are not to be paralleled by those of any other race, in any age of the earth." This history of the colonial administration of Holland—and Holland was the head capitalistic nation of the seventeenth century—is one of the most extraordinary relations of treachery, bribery, massacre, and meanness.

Nothing was more characteristic than the Dutch system of stealing men, to get slaves for Java. The men-stealers were trained for this purpose. The thief, the interpreter, and the seller were the chief agents in this trade; the native princes, the chief sellers. The young people stolen, were thrown into the secret dungeons of Celebes, until they were ready for sending to the slave ships. . . .

The English East India Company, in the seventeenth and eighteenth centuries, obtained, besides the political rule in India, the exclusive monopoly of the tea trade, as well as of the Chinese trade in general, and of the transport of goods to and from Europe. But the coasting trade of India was the monopoly of the higher employees of the company. The monopolies of salt, opium, betel nuts and other commodities, were inexhaustible mines of wealth. The employees themselves fixed the price and plundered at will the unhappy Hindus. The Governor General took part in this private traffic. His favorites received contracts under conditions whereby they, cleverer than the alchemists, made gold out of nothing. Great English fortunes sprang up like mushrooms in a day; investment profits went on without the advance of a shilling. The trial of Warren Hastings swarms with such cases. Here is an instance: a contract for opium was given to a certain Sullivan at the moment of his departure on an official mission. Sullivan sold his contract to one Binn for $200,000; Binn sold it the same day for $300,000 and the ultimate purchaser who carried out the contract declared that after all he realized an enormous gain. According to one of the lists laid before Parliament, the East India Company and its employees from 1757 to 1766 got $30,000,000 from the Indians as gifts alone.

The treatment of the aborigines was, naturally, most frightful in plantation colonies destined for export trade only, such as the West Indies, and in rich and well-populated countries, such as Mexico and India, that were given over to plunder. But even in the colonies properly so called, the followers of Jacob outdid him. These sober Protestants, the Puritans of New England, in 1703, by decrees of their assembly set a premium of $200 on every Indian scalp and every captured redskin: in 1720 a premium of $500 on every scalp; in 1744, after Massachusetts Bay had proclaimed a certain tribe as rebels, the following prices prevailed: for a male scalp of 12 years upward, $500 (new currency); for a male prisoner, $525; for women and children prisoners, $250; for scalps of women and children, $250. Some decades later, the colonial system took its revenge on the descendants of the pious pilgrim fathers, who had grown seditious in the meantime. At English instigation and for English pay they were tomahawked by redskins. The British Parliament proclaimed bloodhounds and scalping as "means that God and Nature had given into its hands."[2]

With the development of national industry during the eighteenth century, the public opinion of Europe had lost the last remnant of shame and conscience. The nations bragged cynically of every infamy that served them as a means to accumulating private wealth. Read, e.g., the naive *Annals of Commerce* of Anderson. Here it is trumpeted forth as a triumph of English statecraft that at the Peace of Utrecht, England extorted from the Spaniards by the Asiento Treaty the privilege of being allowed to ply the slave trade, between Africa and Spanish America. England thereby acquired the right of supplying Spanish America until 1743 with 4,800 Negroes yearly. This threw, at the same time, an official cloak over British smuggling. Liverpool waxed fat on the slave trade. ... Aikin (1795) quotes that spirit of bold adventure which has characterized the trade of Liverpool and rapidly carried it to its present state of prosperity; has occasioned vast employment for shipping and sailors, and greatly augmented the demand for the manufactures of the country; Liverpool employed in the slave trade, in 1730, 15 ships; in 1760, 74; in 1770, 96; and in 1792, 132.[3]

Henry George wrote of *Progress and Poverty* in the 1890s. He says: "At the beginning of this marvelous era it was natural to expect, and it was expected, that labor-saving inventions would lighten the toil and improve the condition of the laborer; that the enormous increase in the power of producing wealth would make

2. *Ibid.*, pp. 823–826.   3. *Ibid.*, pp. 832–833.

real poverty a thing of the past. Could a man of the last century [the eighteenth]—a Franklin or a Priestley—have seen, in a vision of the future, the steamship taking the place of the sailing vessel; the railroad train, of the wagon; the reaping machine, of the scythe; the threshing machine, of the flail; could he have heard the throb of the engines that in obedience to human will, and for the satisfaction of the human desire, exert a power greater than that of all the men and all the beasts of burden of the earth combined; could he have seen the forest tree transformed into finished lumber—into doors, sashes, blinds, boxes or barrels, with hardly the touch of a human hand; the great workshops where boots and shoes are turned out by the case with less labor than the old-fashioned cobbler could have put on a sole; the factories where, under the eye of one girl, cotton becomes cloth faster than hundreds of stalwart weavers could have turned it out with their hand-looms; could he have seen steam hammers shaping mammoth shafts and mighty anchors, and delicate machinery making tiny watches; the diamond drill cutting through the heart of the rocks, and coal oil sparing the whale; could he have realized the enormous saving of labor resulting from improved facilities of exchange and communication—sheep killed in Australia eaten fresh in England, and the order given by the London banker in the afternoon executed in San Francisco in the morning of the same day; could he have conceived of the hundred thousand improvements which these only suggest, what would he have inferred as to the social condition of mankind?

"It would not have seemed like an inference, further than the vision went it would have seemed as though he saw; and his heart would have leaped and his nerves would have thrilled, as one who from a height beholds just ahead of the thirst-stricken caravan the living gleam of rustling woods and the glint of laughing waters. Plainly, in the sight of the imagination, he would have beheld these new forces elevating society from its very foundations, lifting the very poorest above the possibility of want, exempting the very lowest from anxiety for the material needs of life; he would have seen these slaves of the lamp of knowledge taking on themselves the traditional curse, these muscles of iron and sinews of steel making the poorest laborer's life a holiday, in which every high quality and noble impulse could have scope to grow."[4]

This was the promise of Jacob's life. This would establish the birthright which Esau despised. But, says George, "Now, however, we are coming into collision with facts which there can be no mis-

4. Henry George, *Progress and Poverty*, New York, Robert Schalkenbach Foundation, 1939, pp. 3–4. This work, originally published in 1879, argued that the land belonged to society, which created its value and should properly tax that value, not improvements on the land. George's proposal for such a "Single Tax" gained many adherents.

taking. From all parts of the civilized world," he says speaking fifty years ago, "come complaints of industrial depression; of labor condemned to involuntary idleness; of capital massed and wasting; of pecuniary distress among businessmen; of want and suffering and anxiety among the working classes. All the full, deadening pain, all the keen, maddening anguish, that to great masses of men are involved in the words 'hard times,' afflict the world today."[5] What would Henry George have said in 1933 after airplane and radio and mass production, turbine and electricity had come?

Science and art grew and expanded despite all this, but it was warped by the poverty of the artist and the continuous attempt to make science subservient to industry. The latter effort finally succeeded so widely that modern civilization became typified as industrial technique. Education became learning a trade. Men thought of civilization as primarily mechanical and the mechanical means by which they reduced wool and cotton to their purposes, also reduced and bent humankind to their will. Individual initiative remained but it was cramped and distorted and there spread the idea of patriotism to one's country as the highest virtue, by which it became established, that just as in the case of Jacob, a man not only could lie, steal, cheat and murder for his native land, but by doing so, he became a hero whether his cause was just or unjust.

One remembers that old scene between Esau who had thoughtlessly surrendered his birthright and the father who had blessed his lying son; "Jacob came unto his father, and said, My Father: and he said, Here am I; who art thou? And Jacob said unto his father, I am Esau thy firstborn; I have done according as thou badest me: arise, I pray thee, sit and eat of my venison, that thy soul may bless me." In vain did clumsy, careless Esau beg for a blessing—some little blessing. It was denied and Esau hated Jacob because of the blessing: and Esau said in his heart, "The days of mourning for my father are at hand; then I will slay my brother Jacob." So revolution entered—so revolt darkened a dark world.

The same motif was repeated in modern Europe and America in the nineteenth and twentieth centuries, when there grew the superstate called the Empire. The Plan had now regimented the organization of men covering vast territories, dominating immense force and immeasurable wealth and determined to reduce to subserviency as large a part as possible, not only of Europe's own internal world, but of the world at large. Colonial imperialism swept over the earth and initiated the First World War, in envious scramble for division of power and profit.

Hardly a moment of time passed after that war, a moment in the eyes of the eternal forces looking down upon us when again the

5. *Ibid.*, pp. 5–6.

world, using all of that planning and all of that technical superiority
for which its civilization was noted; and all of the accumulated and
accumulating wealth which was available, proceeded to commit suicide on so vast a scale that it is almost impossible for us to realize
the meaning of the catastrophe. Of course, this sweeps us far
beyond anything that the peasant lad Jacob, with his petty lying
and thievery had in mind. Whatever was begun there of ethical
wrong among the Jews was surpassed in every particular by the
white world of Europe and America and carried to such length of
universal cheating, lying and killing that no comparisons remain.

We come therefore to the vast impasse of today: to the great
question, what was the initial right and wrong of the original Jacobs
and Esaus and of their spiritual descendants the world over? We
stand convinced today, at least those who remain sane, that lying
and cheating and killing will build no world organization worth the
building. We have got to stop making income by unholy methods;
out of stealing the pittances of the poor and calling it insurance;
out of seizing and monopolizing the natural resources of the world
and then making the world's poor pay exorbitant prices for aluminum, copper and oil, iron and coal. Not only have we got to stop
these practices, but we have got to stop lying about them and seeking to convince human beings that a civilization based upon the
enslavement of the majority of men for the income of the smart
minority is the highest aim of man.

But as is so usual in these cases, these transgressions of Jacob do
not mean that the attitude of Esau was flawless. The conscienceless
greed of capital does not excuse the careless sloth of labor. Life
cannot be all aimless wandering and indulgence if we are going to
constrain human beings to take advantage of their brain and make
successive generations stronger and wiser than the previous. There
must be reverence for the *birthright* of inherited *culture* and that
birthright cannot be sold for a dinner course, a dress suit or a winter
in Florida. It must be valued and conserved.

The method of conservation is work, endless and tireless and
planned work and this is the legacy which the Esaus of today who
condemn the Jacobs of yesterday have got to substitute as their path
of life, not vengeful revolution, but building and rebuilding.
Curiously enough, it will not be difficult to do this, because the
great majority of men, the poverty-stricken and diseased are the *real
workers* of the world. They are the ones who have made and are
making the *wealth* of this universe, and their future path is clear. It
is to accumulate such knowledge and balance of judgment that they
can reform the world, so that the workers of the world receive just
share of the wealth which they make and that all human beings
who are capable of work shall work. Not national glory and empire
for the few, but food, shelter and happiness for the many. With the

disappearance of systematic lying and killing, we may come into that birthright which so long we have called Freedom: that is, the right to act in a manner that seems to be beautiful; which makes life worth living and joy the only possible end of life. This is the experience which is Art and planning for this is the highest satisfaction of civilized needs. So that looking back upon the allegory and the history, tragedy and promise, we may change our subject and speak in closing of Esau and Jacob, realizing that neither was perfect, but that of the two, Esau had the elements which lead more naturally and directly to the salvation of man; while Jacob with all his crafty planning and cold sacrifice, held in his soul the things that are about to ruin mankind: exaggerated national patriotism, individual profit, the despising of men who are not the darlings of our particular God and the consequent lying and stealing and killing to monopolize power.

May we not hope that in the world after this catastrophe of blood, sweat and fire, we may have a new Esau and Jacob; a new allegory of men who enjoy life for life's sake; who have the Freedom of Art and wish for all men of all sorts the same freedom and enjoyment that they seek themselves and who work for all this and work hard.

Gentlemen and ladies of the class of 1944: in the days of the years of my pilgrimage, I have greeted many thousands of young men and women at the commencement of their careers as citizens of the select commonwealth of culture. In no case have I welcomed them to such a world of darkness and distractions as that into which I usher you. I take joy only in the thought that if work to be done is measure of man's opportunity you inherit a mighty fortune. You have only to remember that the birthright which is today in symbol draped over your shoulders is a heritage which has been preserved all too often by the lying, stealing and murdering of the Jacobs of the world, and if these are the only means by which this birthright can be preserved in the future, it is not worth the price. I do not believe this, and I lay it upon your hearts to prove that this not only need not be true, but is eternally and forever false.

GEORGE ORWELL

Shooting an Elephant

In Moulmein, in Lower Burma, I was hated by large numbers of people—the only time in my life that I have been important enough for this to happen to me. I was sub-divisional police officer of the town, and in an aimless, petty kind of way anti-European feeling was very bitter. No one had the guts to raise a riot, but if a

European woman went through the bazaars alone somebody would probably spit betel juice over her dress. As a police officer I was an obvious target and was baited whenever it seemed safe to do so. When a nimble Burman tripped me up on the football field and the referee (another Burman) looked the other way, the crowd yelled with hideous laughter. This happened more than once. In the end the sneering yellow faces of young men that met me everywhere, the insults hooted after me when I was at a safe distance, got badly on my nerves. The young Buddhist priests were the worst of all. There were several thousands of them in the town and none of them seemed to have anything to do except stand on street corners and jeer at Europeans.

All this was perplexing and upsetting. For at that time I had already made up my mind that imperialism was an evil thing and the sooner I chucked up my job and got out of it the better. Theoretically—and secretly, of course—I was all for the Burmese and all against their oppressors, the British. As for the job I was doing, I hated it more bitterly than I can perhaps make clear. In a job like that you see the dirty work of Empire at close quarters. The wretched prisoners huddling in the stinking cages of the lock-ups, the grey, cowed faces of the long-term convicts, the scarred buttocks of the men who had been flogged with bamboos—all these oppressed me with an intolerable sense of guilt. But I could get nothing into perspective. I was young and ill-educated and I had had to think out my problems in the utter silence that is imposed on every Englishman in the East. I did not even know that the British Empire is dying, still less did I know that it is a great deal better than the younger empires that are going to supplant it. All I knew was that I was stuck between my hatred of the empire I served and my rage against the evil-spirited little beasts who tried to make my job impossible. With one part of my mind I thought of the British Raj as an unbreakable tyranny, as something clamped down, in *saecula saeculorum*, upon the will of prostrate peoples; with another part I thought that the greatest joy in the world would be to drive a bayonet into a Buddhist priest's guts. Feelings like these are the normal by-products of imperialism; ask any Anglo-Indian official, if you can catch him off duty.

One day something happened which in a roundabout way was enlightening. It was a tiny incident in itself, but it gave me a better glimpse than I had had before of the real nature of imperialism— the real motives for which despotic governments act. Early one morning the sub-inspector at a police station the other end of the town rang me up on the 'phone and said that an elephant was ravaging the bazaar. Would I please come and do something about it? I did not know what I could do, but I wanted to see what was happening and I got on to a pony and started out. I took my rifle, an old .44 Winchester and much too small to kill an elephant, but I thought the noise might be useful *in terrorem*. Various Burmans stopped me on the way and told me about the elephant's doings. It was not, of course, a wild elephant, but a tame one which had gone "must." It had been chained up, as tame elephants always are when their attack of "must" is due, but on the previous night it had broken its chain and escaped. Its mahout, the only person who could manage it when it was in that state, had set out in pursuit, but had taken the wrong direction and was now twelve hours' journey away, and in the morning the elephant had suddenly reappeared in the town. The Burmese population had no weapons and were quite helpless against it. It had already destroyed somebody's bamboo hut, killed a cow and raided some fruit-stalls and devoured the stock; also it had met the municipal rubbish van and, when the driver jumped out and took to his heels, had turned the van over and inflicted violences upon it.

The Burmese sub-inspector and some Indian constables were waiting for me in the quarter where the elephant had been seen. It was a very poor quarter, a labyrinth of squalid bamboo huts, thatched with palm-leaf, winding all over a steep hillside. I remember that it was a cloudy, stuffy morning at the beginning of the rains. We began questioning the people as to where the elephant had gone and, as usual, failed to get any definite information. That is invariably the case in the East; a story always sounds clear enough at a distance, but the nearer you get to the scene of events the vaguer it becomes. Some of the people said that the elephant had gone in one direction, some said that he had gone in another, some professed not even to have heard of any elephant. I had almost made up my mind that the whole story was a pack of lies, when we heard yells a little distance away. There was a loud, scandalized cry of "Go away, child! Go away this instant!" and an old woman with a switch in her hand came round the corner of a hut, violently shooing away a crowd of naked children. Some more women followed, clicking their tongues and exclaiming; evidently there was something that the children ought not to have seen. I rounded the hut and saw a man's dead body sprawling in the mud. He was an Indian, a black Dravidian coolie, almost naked, and he could not have been dead many minutes. The people said that the elephant had come suddenly upon him round the corner of the hut, caught him with its trunk, put its foot on his back and ground him into the earth. This was the rainy season and the ground was soft, and his face had scored a trench a foot deep and a couple of yards long. He was lying on his belly with arms crucified and head sharply twisted to one side. His face was coated with mud, the eyes wide open, the teeth bared and grinning with an expression of unendurable agony. (Never tell me, by the way, that the dead look peaceful. Most of the corpses I have seen looked devilish.) The friction of the great beast's foot had stripped the skin from his back as neatly as one skins a rabbit. As soon as I saw the dead man I sent an orderly to a friend's house nearby to borrow an elephant rifle. I had already sent back the pony, not wanting it to go mad with fright and throw me if it smelt the elephant.

The orderly came back in a few minutes with a rifle and five cartridges, and meanwhile some Burmans had arrived and told us that the elephant was in the paddy fields below, only a few hundred yards away. As I started forward practically the whole population of the quarter flocked out of the houses and followed me. They had seen the rifle and were all shouting excitedly that I was going to shoot the elephant. They had not shown much interest in the elephant when he was merely ravaging their homes, but it was different now that he was going to be shot. It was a bit of fun to them, as it would be to an English crowd; besides they wanted the meat. It made me vaguely uneasy. I had no intention of shooting the elephant—I had merely sent for the rifle to defend myself if necessary —and it is always unnerving to have a crowd following you. I marched down the hill, looking and feeling a fool, with the rifle over my shoulder and an ever-growing army of people jostling at my heels. At the bottom, when you got away from the huts, there was a metalled road and beyond that a miry waste of paddy fields a thousand yards across, not yet ploughed but soggy from the first rains and dotted with coarse grass. The elephant was standing eight yards from the road, his left side towards us. He took not the slightest notice of the crowd's approach. He was tearing up bunches of grass, beating them against his knees to clean them and stuffing them into his mouth.

I had halted on the road. As soon as I saw the elephant I knew with perfect certainty that I ought not to shoot him. It is a serious matter to shoot a working elephant—it is comparable to destroying a huge and costly piece of machinery—and obviously one ought not to do it if it can possibly be avoided. And at that distance, peacefully eating, the elephant looked no more dangerous than a cow. I thought then and I think now that his attack of "must" was already passing off; in which case he would merely wander harmlessly about until the mahout came back and caught him. Moreover, I did not in the least want to shoot him. I decided that I would watch him for a little while to make sure that he did not turn savage again, and then go home.

But at that moment I glanced round at the crowd that had followed me. It was an immense crowd, two thousand at the least and growing every minute. It blocked the road for a long distance on either side. I looked at the sea of yellow faces above the garish clothes—faces all happy and excited over this bit of fun, all certain that the elephant was going to be shot. They were watching me as they would watch a conjurer about to perform a trick. They did not like me, but with the magical rifle in my hands I was momentarily worth watching. And suddenly I realized that I should have to shoot the elephant after all. The people expected it of me and I had got to do it; I could feel their two thousand wills pressing me forward, irresistibly. And it was at this moment, as I stood there with the rifle in my hands, that I first grasped the hollowness, the futility of the white man's dominion in the East. Here was I, the white man with his gun, standing in front of the unarmed native crowd —seemingly the leading actor of the piece; but in reality I was only an absurd puppet pushed to and fro by the will of those yellow faces behind. I perceived in this moment that when the white man turns tyrant it is his own freedom that he destroys. He becomes a sort of hollow, posing dummy, the conventionalized figure of a sahib. For it is the condition of his rule that he shall spend his life in trying to impress the "natives," and so in every crisis he has got to do what the "natives" expect of him. He wears a mask, and his face grows to fit it. I had got to shoot the elephant. I had committed myself to doing it when I sent for the rifle. A sahib has got to act like a sahib; he has got to appear resolute, to know his own mind and do definite things. To come all that way, rifle in hand, with two thousand people marching at my heels, and then to trail feebly away, having done nothing—no, that was impossible. The crowd would laugh at me. And my whole life, every white man's life in the East, was one long struggle not to be laughed at.

But I did not want to shoot the elephant. I watched him beating his bunch of grass against his knees, with that preoccupied grandmotherly air that elephants have. It seemed to me that it would be murder to shoot him. At that age I was not squeamish about killing animals, but I had never shot an elephant and never wanted to. (Somehow it always seems worse to kill a *large* animal.) Besides, there was the beast's owner to be considered. Alive, the elephant was worth at least a hundred pounds; dead, he would only be worth the value of his tusks, five pounds, possibly. But I had got to act quickly. I turned to some experienced-looking Burmans who had been there when we arrived, and asked them how the elephant had been behaving. They all said the same thing: he took no notice of you if you left him alone, but he might charge if you went too close to him.

It was perfectly clear to me what I ought to do. I ought to walk up to within, say, twenty-five yards of the elephant and test his behavior. If he charged, I could shoot; if he took no notice of me, it would be safe to leave him until the mahout came back. But also I knew that I was going to do no such thing. I was a poor shot with a rifle and the ground was soft mud into which one would sink at every step. If the elephant charged and I missed him, I should have about as much chance as a toad under a steam-roller. But even then I was not thinking particularly of my own skin, only of the watchful yellow faces behind. For at that moment, with the crowd watching me, I was not afraid in the ordinary sense, as I would have been if I had been alone. A white man mustn't be frightened in front of "natives"; and so, in general, he isn't frightened. The sole thought in my mind was that if anything went wrong those two thousand Burmans would see me pursued, caught, trampled on and reduced to a grinning corpse like that Indian up the hill. And if that happened it was quite probable that some of them would laugh. That would never do. There was only one alternative. I shoved the cartridges into the magazine and lay down on the road to get a better aim.

The crowd grew very still, and a deep, low, happy sigh, as of people who see the theatre curtain go up at last, breathed from innumerable throats. They were going to have their bit of fun after all. The rifle was a beautiful German thing with cross-hair sights. I did not then know that in shooting an elephant one would shoot to cut an imaginary bar running from ear-hole to ear-hole. I ought, therefore, as the elephant was sideways on, to have aimed straight at his ear-hole; actually I aimed several inches in front of this, thinking the brain would be further forward.

When I pulled the trigger I did not hear the bang or feel the kick—one never does when a shot goes home—but I heard the devilish roar of glee that went up from the crowd. In that instant, in too short a time, one would have thought, even for the bullet to get there, a mysterious, terrible change had come over the elephant. He neither stirred nor fell, but every line of his body had altered. He looked suddenly stricken, shrunken, immensely old, as though the frightful impact of the bullet had paralysed him without knocking him down. At last, after what seemed a long time—it might have been five seconds, I dare say—he sagged flabbily to his knees. His mouth slobbered. An enormous senility seemed to have settled upon him. One could have imagined him thousands of years old. I fired again into the same spot. At the second shot he did not collapse but climbed with desperate slowness to his feet and stood weakly upright, with legs sagging and head drooping. I fired a third time. That was the shot that did for him. You could see the agony of it jolt his whole body and knock the last remnant of strength from his legs. But in falling he seemed for a moment to rise, for as his hind legs collapsed beneath him he seemed to tower upward like a huge rock toppling, his trunk reaching skywards like a tree. He trumpeted, for the first and only time. And then down he came, his belly towards me, with a crash that seemed to shake the ground even where I lay.

I got up. The Burmans were already racing past me across the mud. It was obvious that the elephant would never rise again, but he was not dead. He was breathing very rhythmically with long rattling gasps, his great mound of a side painfully rising and falling. His mouth was wide open—I could see far down into caverns of pale pink throat. I waited a long time for him to die, but his breathing did not weaken. Finally I fired my two remaining shots into the spot where I thought his heart must be. The thick blood welled out of him like red velvet, but still he did not die. His body did not even jerk when the shots hit him, the tortured breathing continued without a pause. He was dying, very slowly and in great agony, but in some world remote from me where not even a bullet could damage him further. I felt that I had got to put an end to that dreadful noise. It seemed dreadful to see the great beast lying there, powerless to move and yet powerless to die, and not even to be able to finish him. I sent back for my small rifle and poured shot after shot into his heart and down his throat. They seemed to make no impression. The tortured gasps continued as steadily as the ticking of a clock.

In the end I could not stand it any longer and went away. I heard later that it took him half an hour to die. Burmans were bringing dahs and baskets even before I left, and I was told they had stripped his body almost to the bones by the afternoon.

Afterwards, of course, there were endless discussions about the shooting of the elephant. The owner was furious, but he was only an Indian and could do nothing. Besides, legally I had done the right thing, for a mad elephant has to be killed, like a mad dog, if its owner fails to control it. Among the Europeans opinion was divided. The older men said I was right, the younger men said it was a damn shame to shoot an elephant for killing a coolie, because an elephant was worth more than any damn Coringhee coolie. And afterwards I was very glad that the coolie had been killed; it put me legally in the right and it gave me a sufficient pretext for shooting the elephant. I often wondered whether any of the others grasped that I had done it solely to avoid looking a fool.

JAMES BALDWIN

Stranger in the Village

From all available evidence no black man had ever set foot in this tiny Swiss village before I came. I was told before arriving that I would probably be a "sight" for the village; I took this to mean that people of my complexion were rarely seen in Switzerland, and also that city people are always something of a "sight" outside of the city. It did not occur to me—possibly because I am an American—that there could be people anywhere who had never seen a Negro.

It is a fact that cannot be explained on the basis of the inaccessibility of the village. The village is very high, but it is only four hours from Milan and three hours from Lausanne. It is true that it is virtually unknown. Few people making plans for a holiday would elect to come here. On the other hand, the villagers are able, presumably, to come and go as they please—which they do: to another town at the foot of the mountain, with a population of approximately five thousand, the nearest place to see a movie or go to the bank. In the village there is no movie house, no bank, no library, no theater; very few radios, one jeep, one station wagon; and at the moment, one typewriter, mine, an invention which the woman next door to me here had never seen. There are about six hundred people living here, all Catholic—I conclude this from the fact that the Catholic church is open all year round, whereas the Protestant chapel, set off on a hill a little removed from the village, is open only in the summertime when the tourists arrive. There are four or five hotels, all closed now, and four or five *bistros*, of which, however, only two do any business during the winter. These two do not do a great deal, for life in the village seems to end around nine or ten o'clock. There are a few stores, butcher, baker, *épicerie*, a hardware store, and a money-changer—who cannot change travelers' checks, but must send them down to the bank, an operation which takes two or three days. There is something called the *Ballet Haus*, closed in the winter and used for God knows what, certainly not ballet, during the summer. There seems to be only one schoolhouse in the village, and this for the quite young children; I suppose this to mean that their older brothers and sisters at some point descend from these mountains in order to complete their education—possibly, again, to the town just below. The landscape is absolutely forbidding, mountains towering on all four sides, ice and snow as far as the eye can reach. In this white wilderness, men and women and children move all day, carrying washing, wood, buckets of milk or water, sometimes skiing on Sunday afternoons. All week long boys and young men are to be seen shoveling snow off the rooftops, or dragging wood down from the forest in sleds.

The village's only real attraction, which explains the tourist season, is the hot spring water. A disquietingly high proportion of these tourists are cripples, or semi-cripples, who come year after year—from other parts of Switzerland, usually—to take the waters. This lends the village, at the height of the season, a rather terrifying air of sanctity, as though it were a lesser Lourdes. There is often something beautiful, there is always something awful, in the spectacle of a person who has lost one of his faculties, a faculty he never questioned until it was gone, and who struggles to recover it. Yet people remain people, on crutches or indeed on deathbeds; and wherever I passed, the first summer I was here, among the native villagers or among the lame, a wind passed with me—of astonishment, curiosity, amusement, and outrage. That first summer I stayed two weeks and never intended to return. But I did return in the winter, to work; the village offers, obviously, no distractions whatever and has the further advantage of being extremely cheap. Now it is winter again, a year later, and I am here again. Everyone in the village knows my name, though they scarcely ever use it, knows that I come from America—though, this, apparently, they will never really believe: black men come from Africa—and everyone knows that I am the friend of the son of a woman who was born here, and that I am staying in their chalet. But I remain as much a stranger today as I was the first day I arrived, and the children shout *Neger! Neger!* as I walk along the streets.

It must be admitted that in the beginning I was far too shocked to have any real reaction. In so far as I reacted at all, I reacted by trying to be pleasant—it being a great part of the American Negro's education (long before he goes to school) that he must make people "like" him. This smile-and-the-world-smiles-with-you routine worked about as well in this situation as it had in the situation for which it was designed, which is to say that it did not work at all. No one, after all, can be liked whose human weight and complexity cannot be, or has not been, admitted. My smile was simply another unheard-of phenomenon which allowed them to see my teeth—they did not, really, see my smile and I began to think that, should I take to snarling, no one would notice any difference. All of the physical characteristics of the Negro which had caused me, in America, a very different and almost forgotten pain were nothing less than miraculous—or infernal—in the eyes of the village people. Some thought my hair was the color of tar, that it had the texture of wire, or the texture of cotton. It was jocularly suggested that I might let it all grow long and make myself a winter coat. If I sat in the sun for more than five minutes some daring creature was certain to come along and gingerly put his fingers on my hair, as though he were afraid of an electric shock, or put his hand on my hand, astonished that the color did not rub off. In all of this, in which it must be conceded there was the charm of genuine wonder and in which there were certainly no element of intentional unkindness, there was yet no suggestion that I was human: I was simply a living wonder.

I knew that they did not mean to be unkind, and I know it now; it is necessary, nevertheless, for me to repeat this to myself each time that I walk out of the chalet. The children who shout *Neger!* have no way of knowing the echoes this sound raises in me. They are brimming with good humor and the more daring swell with pride when I stop to speak with them. Just the same, there are days when I cannot pause and smile, when I have no heart to play with them; when, indeed, I mutter sourly to myself, exactly as I muttered on the streets of a city these children have never seen, when I was no bigger than these children are now: *Your* mother *was a nigger.* Joyce is right about history being a nightmare—but it may be the nightmare from which no one *can* awaken. People are trapped in history and history is trapped in them.

There is a custom in the village—I am told it is repeated in many villages—of "buying" African natives for the purpose of converting them to Christianity. There stands in the church all year round a small box with a slot for money, decorated with a black figurine, and into this box the villagers drop their francs. During the *carnaval* which precedes Lent, two village children have their faces blackened —out of which bloodless darkness their blue eyes shine like ice—and fantastic horsehair wigs are placed on their blond heads; thus disguised, they solicit among the villagers for money for the missionaries in Africa. Between the box in the church and the blackened children, the village "bought" last year six or eight African natives. This was reported to me with pride by the wife of one of the *bistro* owners and I was careful to express astonishment and pleasure at the solicitude shown by the village for the souls of black folks. The *bistro* owner's wife beamed with a pleasure far more genuine than my own and seemed to feel that I might now breathe more easily concerning the souls of at least six of my kinsmen.

I tried not to think of these so lately baptized kinsmen, of the price paid for them, or the peculiar price they themselves would pay, and said nothing about my father, who having taken his own conversion too literally never, at bottom, forgave the white world (which he described as heathen) for having saddled him with a Christ in whom, to judge at least from their treatment of him, they themselves no longer believed. I thought of white men arriving for the first time in an African village, strangers there, as I am a stranger here, and tried to imagine the astounded populace touching their hair and marveling at the color of their skin. But there is a great difference between being the first white man to be seen by Africans and being the first black man to be seen by whites. The white man takes the astonishment as tribute, for he arrives to conquer and to convert the natives, whose inferiority in relation to himself is not even to be questioned; whereas I, without a thought of conquest, find myself among a people whose culture controls me, has even, in a sense, created me, people who have cost me more in anguish and rage than they will ever know, who yet do not even know of my existence. The astonishment with which I might have greeted them, should they have stumbled into my African village a few hundred years ago, might have rejoiced their hearts. But the astonishment with which they greet me today can only poison mine.

And this is so despite everything I may do to feel differently, despite my friendly conversations with the *bistro* owner's wife, despite their three-year-old son who has at last become my friend, despite the *saluts* and *bonsoirs* which I exchange with people as I walk, despite the fact that I know that no individual can be taken to task for what history is doing, or has done. I say that the culture of these people controls me—but they can scarcely be held responsible for European culture. America comes out of Europe, but these people have never seen America, nor have most of them seen more of Europe than the hamlet at the foot of their mountain. Yet they move with an authority which I shall never have; and they regard me, quite rightly, not only as a stranger in their village but as a suspect late-comer, bearing no credentials, to everything they have—however unconsciously—inherited.

For this village, even were it incomparably more remote and incredibly more primitive, is the West, the West onto which I have been so strangely grafted. These people cannot be, from the point of view of power, strangers anywhere in the world; they have made the modern world, in effect, even if they do not know it. The most illiterate among them is related, in a way that I am not, to Dante, Shakespeare, Michelangelo, Aeschylus, Da Vinci, Rembrandt, and Racine; the cathedral at Chartres says something to them which it cannot say to me, as indeed would New York's Empire State Building, should anyone here ever see it. Out of their hymns and dances come Beethoven and Bach. Go back a few centuries and they are in their full glory—but I am in Africa, watching the conquerors arrive.

The rage of the disesteemed is personally fruitless, but it is also absolutely inevitable; this rage, so generally discounted, so little understood even among the people whose daily bread it is, is one of the things that makes history. Rage can only with difficulty, and never entirely, be brought under the domination of the intelligence and is therefore not susceptible to any arguments whatever. This is a fact which ordinary representatives of the *Herrenvolk*,[1] having never felt this rage and being unable to imagine, quite fail to understand. Also, rage cannot be hidden, it can only be dissembled. This dissembling deludes the thoughtless, and strengthens rage and adds, to rage, contempt. There are, no doubt, as many ways of coping with the resulting complex of tensions as there are black men in the world, but no black man can hope ever to be entirely liberated from this internal warfare—rage, dissembling, and contempt having inevitably accompanied his first realization of the power of white men. What is crucial here is that, since white men represent in the black man's world so heavy a weight, white men have for black men a reality which is far from being reciprocal; and hence all black men have

1. Master race.

toward all white men an attitude which is designed, really, either to rob the white man of the jewel of his naïveté, or else to make it cost him dear.

The black man insists, by whatever means he finds at his disposal, that the white man cease to regard him as an exotic rarity and recognize him as a human being. This is a very charged and difficult moment, for there is a great deal of will power involved in the white man's naïveté. Most people are not naturally reflective any more than they are naturally malicious, and the white man prefers to keep the black man at a certain human remove because it is easier for him thus to preserve his simplicity and avoid being called to account for crimes committed by his forefathers, or his neighbors. He is inescapably aware, nevertheless, that he is in a better position in the world than black men are, nor can he quite put to death the suspicion that he is hated by black men therefor. He does not wish to be hated, neither does he wish to change places, and at this point in his uneasiness he can scarcely avoid having recourse to those legends which white men have created about black men, the most usual effect of which is that the white man finds himself enmeshed, so to speak, in his own language which describes hell, as well as the attributes which lead one to hell, as being as black as night.

Every legend, moreover, contains its residuum of truth, and the root function of language is to control the universe by describing it. It is of quite considerable significance that black men remain, in the imagination, and in overwhelming numbers in fact, beyond the disciplines of salvation; and this despite the fact that the West has been "buying" African natives for centuries. There is, I should hazard, an instantaneous necessity to be divorced from this so visibly unsaved stranger, in whose heart, moreover, one cannot guess what dreams of vengeance are being nourished; and, at the same time, there are few things on earth more attractive than the idea of the unspeakable liberty which is allowed the unredeemed. When, beneath the black mask, a human being begins to make himself felt one cannot escape a certain awful wonder as to what kind of human being it is. What one's imagination makes of other people is dictated, of course, by the laws of one's own personality and it is one of the ironies of black-white relations that, by means of what the white man imagines the black man to be, the black man is enabled to know who the white man is.

I have said, for example, that I am as much a stranger in this village today as I was the first summer I arrived, but this is not quite true. The villagers wonder less about the texture of my hair than they did then, and wonder rather more about me. And the fact that their wonder now exists on another level is reflected in their attitudes and in their eyes. There are the children who make those delightful, hilarious, sometimes astonishingly grave overtures of friendship in the unpredictable fashion of children; other children, having been taught that the devil is a black man, scream in genuine anguish as I approach. Some of the older women never pass without a friendly greeting, never pass, indeed, if it seems that they will be able to engage me in conversation; other women look down or look away or rather contemptuously smirk. Some of the men drink with me and suggest that I learn how to ski—partly, I gather, because they cannot imagine what I would look like on skis—and want to know if I am married, and ask questions about my *métier*. But some of the men have accused *le sale nègre*—behind my back—of stealing wood and there is already in the eyes of some of them that peculiar, intent, paranoiac malevolence which one sometimes surprises in the eyes of American white men when, out walking with their Sunday girl, they see a Negro male approach.

There is a dreadful abyss between the streets of this village and the streets of the city in which I was born, between the children who shout *Neger!* today and those who shouted *Nigger!* yesterday— the abyss is experience, the American experience. The syllable hurled behind me today expresses, above all, wonder: I am a stranger here. But I am not a stranger in America and the same syllable riding on the American air expresses the war my presence has occasioned in the American soul.

For this village brings home to me this fact: that there was a day, and not really a very distant day, when Americans were scarcely Americans at all but discontented Europeans, facing a great unconquered continent and strolling, say, into a marketplace and seeing black men for the first time. The shock this spectacle afforded is suggested, surely, by the promptness with which they decided that these black men were not really men but cattle. It is true that the necessity on the part of the settlers of the New World of reconciling their moral assumptions with the fact—and the necessity—of slavery enhanced immensely the charm of this idea, and it is also true that this idea expresses, with a truly American bluntness, the attitude which to varying extents all masters have had toward all slaves.

But between all former slaves and slave-owners and the drama which begins for Americans over three hundred years ago at Jamestown, there are at least two differences to be observed. The American Negro slave could not suppose, for one thing, as slaves in past epochs had supposed and often done, that he would ever be able to wrest the power from his master's hands. This was a supposition which the modern era, which was to bring about such vast changes in the aims and dimensions of power, put to death; it only begins, in unprecedented fashion, and with dreadful implications, to be resurrected today. But even had this supposition persisted with undiminished force, the American Negro slave could not have used it to lend his condition dignity, for the reason that this supposition rests on another: that the slave in exile yet remains related to his past, has some means—if only in memory—of revering and sustaining the forms of his former life, is able, in short, to maintain his identity.

This was not the case with the American Negro slave. He is unique among the black men of the world in that his past was taken from him, almost literally, at one blow. One wonders what on earth the first slave found to say to the first dark child he bore. I am told that there are Haitians able to trace their ancestry back to African kings, but any American Negro wishing to go back so far will find his journey through time abruptly arrested by the signature on the bill of sale which served as the entrance paper for his ancestor. At the time—to say nothing of the circumstances—of the enslavement of the captive black man who was to become the American Negro, there was not the remotest possibility that he would ever take power from his master's hands. There was no reason to suppose that his situation would ever change, nor was there, shortly, anything to indicate that his situation had ever been different. It was his necessity, in the words of E. Franklin Frazier, to find a "motive for living under American culture or die." The identity of the American Negro comes out of this extreme situation, and the evolution of this identity was a source of the most intolerable anxiety in the minds and the lives of his masters.

For the history of the American Negro is unique also in this: that the question of his humanity, and of his rights therefore as a human being, became a burning one for several generations of Americans, so burning a question that it ultimately became one of those used to divide the nation. It is out of this argument that the venom of the epithet *Nigger!* is derived. It is an argument which Europe has never had, and hence Europe quite sincerely fails to understand how or why the argument arose in the first place, why its effects are frequently disastrous and always so unpredictable, why it refuses until today to be entirely settled. Europe's black possessions remained —and do remain—in Europe's colonies, at which remove they represented no threat whatever to European identity. If they posed any problem at all for the European conscience, it was a problem which remained comfortingly abstract: in effect, the black man, as a *man*, did not exist for Europe. But in America, even as a slave, he was an inescapable part of the general social fabric and no American could escape having an attitude toward him. Americans attempt until today to make an abstraction of the Negro, but the very nature of these abstractions reveals the tremendous effects the presence of the Negro has had on the American character.

When one considers the history of the Negro in America it is of the greatest importance to recognize that the moral beliefs of a person, or a people, are never really as tenuous as life—which is not moral—very often causes them to appear; these create for them a frame of reference and a necessary hope, the hope being that when life has done its worst they will be enabled to rise above themselves and to triumph over life. Life would scarcely be bearable if this hope did not exist. Again, even when the worst has been said, to betray a belief is not by any means to have put oneself beyond its power; the betrayal of a belief is not the same thing as ceasing to believe. If this were not so there would be no moral standards in the world at all. Yet one must also recognize that morality is based on ideas and that all ideas are dangerous—dangerous because ideas can only lead to action and where the action leads no man can say. And dangerous in this respect: that confronted with the impossibility of remaining faithful to one's beliefs, and the equal impossibility of becoming free of them, one can be driven to the most inhuman excesses. The ideas on which American beliefs are based are not, though Americans often seem to think so, ideas which originated in America. They came out of Europe. And the establishment of democracy on the American continent was scarcely as radical a break with the past as was the necessity, which Americans faced, of broadening this concept to include black men.

This was, literally, a hard necessity. It was impossible, for one thing, for Americans to abandon their beliefs, not only because these beliefs alone seemed able to justify the sacrifices they had endured and the blood that they had spilled, but also because these beliefs afforded them their only bulwark against a moral chaos as absolute as the physical chaos of the continent it was their destiny to conquer. But in the situation in which Americans found themselves, these beliefs threatened an idea which, whether or not one likes to think so, is the very warp and woof of the heritage of the West, the idea of white supremacy.

Americans have made themselves notorious by the shrillness and the brutality with which they have insisted on this idea, but they did not invent it; and it has escaped the world's notice that those very excesses of which Americans have been guilty imply a certain, unprecedented uneasiness over the idea's life and power, if not, indeed, the idea's validity. The idea of white supremacy rests simply on the fact that white men are the creators of civilization (the present civilization, which is the only one that matters; all previous civilizations are simply "contributions" to our own) and are therefore civilization's guardians and defenders. Thus it was impossible for Americans to accept the black man as one of themselves, for to do so was to jeopardize their status as white men. But not so to accept him was to deny his human reality, his human weight and complexity, and the strain of denying the overwhelmingly undeniable forced Americans into rationalizations so fantastic that they approached the pathological.

At the root of the American Negro problem is the necessity of the American white man to find a way of living with the Negro in order to be able to live with himself. And the history of this problem can be reduced to the means used by Americans—lynch law and law, segregation and legal acceptance, terrorization and concession —either to come to terms with this necessity, or to find a way around it, or (most usually) to find a way of doing both these things at once. The resulting spectacle, at once foolish and dreadful, led someone to make the quite accurate observation that "the Negro-in-America is a form of insanity which overtakes white men."

In this long battle, a battle by no means finished, the unforeseeable effects of which will be felt by many future generations, the white man's motive was the protection of his identity; the black man was motivated by the need to establish an identity. And despite the terrorization which the Negro in America endured and endures sporadically until today, despite the cruel and totally inescapable ambivalence of his status in his country, the battle for his identity has long ago been won. He is not a visitor to the West, but a citizen there, an American; as American as the Americans who despise him, the Americans who fear him, the Americans who love him—the Americans who became less than themselves, or rose to be greater than themselves by virtue of the fact that the challenge he represented was inescapable. He is perhaps the only black man in the world whose relationship to white men is more terrible, more subtle, and more meaningful than the relationship of bitter possessed to uncertain possessors. His survival depended, and his development depends, on his ability to turn his peculiar status in the Western world to his own advantage and, it may be, to the very great advantage of that world. It remains for him to fashion out of his experience that which will give him sustenance, and a voice.

The cathedral at Chartres, I have said, says something to the people of this village which it cannot say to me; but it is important to understand that this cathedral says something to me which it cannot say to them. Perhaps they are struck by the power of the spires, the glory of the windows; but they have known God, after all, longer than I have known him, and in a different way, and I am terrified by the slippery bottomless well to be found in the crypt, down which heretics were hurled to death, and by the obscene, inescapable gargoyles jutting out of the stone and seeming to say that God and the devil can never be divorced. I doubt that the villagers think of the devil when they face a cathedral because they have never been identified with the devil. But I must accept the status which myth, if nothing else, gives me in the West before I can hope to change the myth.

Yet, if the American Negro has arrived at his identity by virtue of the absoluteness of his estrangement from his past, American white men still nourish the illusion that there is some means of recovering the European innocence, of returning to a state in which black men do not exist. This is one of the greatest errors Americans can make. The identity they fought so hard to protect has, by virtue of that battle, undergone a change: Americans are as unlike any other white people in the world as it is possible to be. I do not think, for example, that it is too much to suggest that the American vision of the world—which allows so little reality, generally speaking, for any of the darker forces in human life, which tends until today to paint moral issues in glaring black and white—owes a great deal to the battle waged by Americans to maintain between themselves and black men a human separation which could not be bridged. It is only now beginning to be borne in on us—very faintly, it must be admitted, very slowly, and very much against our will—that this vision of the world is dangerously inaccurate, and perfectly useless. For it protects our moral high-mindedness at the terrible expense of weakening our grasp of reality. People who shut their eyes to reality simply invite their own destruction, and anyone who insists on remaining in a state of innocence long after that innocence is dead turns himself into a monster.

The time has come to realize that the interracial drama acted out on the American continent has not only created a new black man, it has created a new white man, too. No road whatever will lead Americans back to the simplicity of this European village where white men still have the luxury of looking on me as a stranger. I am not, really, a stranger any longer for any American alive. One of the things that distinguishes Americans from other people is that no other people has ever been so deeply involved in the lives of black men, and vice versa. This fact faced, with all its implications, it can be seen that the history of the American Negro problem is not merely shameful, it is also something of an achievement. For even when the worst has been said, it must also be added that the perpetual challenge posed by this problem was always, somehow, perpetually met. It is precisely this black-white experience which may prove of indispensable value to us in the world we face today. This world is white no longer, and it will never be white again.

QUESTIONS

1. Baldwin begins with the narration of his experience in a Swiss village. At what point do you become aware that he is going to do more than tell the story of his stay in the village? What purpose does he make his experience serve?
2. On page 805 Baldwin says that Americans have attempted to make an abstraction of the Negro. To what degree has his purpose forced Baldwin to make an abstraction of the white man? What are the components of that abstraction?
3. Baldwin intimately relates the white man's language and legends about black men to the "laws" of the white man's personality.

Bettelheim makes similar use of the myths of science fiction. This kind of inference reveals a conviction both men share about the nature of language; what is that conviction?

4. Describe some particular experience which raises a large social question or shows the working of large social forces. Does Baldwin offer any help in the problem of connecting the particular and the general?

5. Define alienation.

MARTIN LUTHER KING, JR.

Letter from Birmingham Jail[1]

My Dear Fellow Clergymen:

While confined here in the Birmingham city jail, I came across your recent statement calling my present activities "unwise and untimely." Seldom do I pause to answer criticism of my work and ideas. If I sought to answer all the criticisms that cross my desk, my secretaries would have little time for anything other than such correspondence in the course of the day, and I would have no time for constructive work. But since I feel that you are men of genuine good will and that your criticisms are sincerely set forth, I want to try to answer your statement in what I hope will be patient and reasonable terms.

I think I should indicate why I am here in Birmingham, since you have been influenced by the view which argues against "outsiders coming in." I have the honor of serving as president of the Southern Christian Leadership Conference, an organization operating in every southern state, with headquarters in Atlanta, Georgia. We have some eighty-five affiliated organizations across the South, and one of them is the Alabama Christian Movement for Human Rights. Frequently we share staff, educational, and financial resources with our affiliates. Several months ago the affiliate here in Birmingham asked us to be on call to engage in a nonviolent direct-action program if such were deemed necessary. We readily

1. This response to a published statement by eight fellow clergymen from Alabama (Bishop C. C. J. Carpenter, Bishop Joseph A. Durick, Rabbi Hilton L. Grafman, Bishop Paul Hardin, Bishop Holan B. Harmon, the Reverend George M. Murray, the Reverend Edward V. Ramage and the Reverend Earl Stallings) was composed under somewhat constricting circumstances. Begun on the margins of the newspaper in which the statement appeared while I was in jail, the letter was continued on scraps of writing paper supplied by a friendly Negro trusty, and concluded on a pad my attorneys were eventually permitted to leave me. Although the text remains in substance unaltered, I have indulged in the author's prerogative of polishing it for publication [King's note].

consented, and when the hour came we lived up to our promise. So I, along with several members of my staff, am here because I was invited here. I am here because I have organizational ties here.

But more basically, I am in Birmingham because injustice is here. Just as the prophets of the eighth century B.C. left their villages and carried their "thus saith the Lord" far beyond the boundaries of their home towns, and just as the Apostle Paul left his village of Tarsus and carried the gospel of Jesus Christ to the far corners of the Greco-Roman world, so am I compelled to carry the gospel of freedom beyond my own home town. Like Paul, I must constantly respond to the Macedonian call for aid.

Moreover, I am cognizant of the interrelatedness of all communities and states. I cannot sit idly by in Atlanta and not be concerned about what happens in Birmingham. Injustice anywhere is a threat to justice everywhere. We are caught in an inescapable network of mutuality, tied in a single garment of destiny. Whatever affects one directly, affects all indirectly. Never again can we afford to live with the narrow, provincial "outside agitator" idea. Anyone who lives inside the United States can never be considered an outsider anywhere within its bounds.

You deplore the demonstrations taking place in Birmingham. But your statement, I am sorry to say, fails to express a similar concern for the conditions that brought about the demonstrations. I am sure that none of you would want to rest content with the superficial kind of social analysis that deals merely with effects and does not grapple with underlying causes. It is unfortunate that demonstrations are taking place in Birmingham, but it is even more unfortunate that the city's white power structure left the Negro community with no alternative.

In any nonviolent campaign there are four basic steps: collection of the facts to determine whether injustices exist; negotiation; self-purification; and direct action. We have gone through all these steps in Birmingham. There can be no gainsaying the fact that racial injustice engulfs this community. Birmingham is probably the most thoroughly segregated city in the United States. Its ugly record of brutality is widely known. Negroes have experienced grossly unjust treatment in the courts. There have been more unsolved bombings of Negro homes and churches in Birmingham than in any other city in the nation. These are the hard, brutal facts of the case. On the basis of these conditions, Negro leaders sought to negotiate with the city fathers. But the latter consistently refused to engage in good-faith negotiation.

Then, last September, came the opportunity to talk with leaders of Birmingham's economic community. In the course of the negotiations, certain promises were made by the merchants—for example, to remove the stores' humiliating racial signs. On the basis of these promises, the Reverend Fred Shuttlesworth and the leaders of the Alabama Christian Movement for Human Rights agreed to a moratorium on all demonstrations. As the weeks and months went by, we realized that we were the victims of a broken promise. A few signs, briefly removed, returned; the others remained.

As in so many past experiences, our hopes had been blasted, and the shadow of deep disappointment settled upon us. We had no alternative except to prepare for direct action, whereby we would present our very bodies as a means of laying our case before the conscience of the local and the national community. Mindful of the difficulties involved, we decided to undertake a process of self-purification. We began a series of workshops on nonviolence, and we repeatedly asked ourselves: "Are you able to accept blows without retaliating?" "Are you able to endure the ordeal of jail?" We decided to schedule our direct-action program for the Easter season, realizing that except for Christmas, this is the main shopping period of the year. Knowing that a strong economic-withdrawal program would be the by product of direct action, we felt that this would be the best time to bring pressure to bear on the merchants for the needed change.

Then it occurred to us that Birmingham's mayoral election was coming up in March, and we speedily decided to postpone action until after election day. When we discovered that the Commissioner of Public Safety, Eugene "Bull" Connor, had piled up enough votes to be in the run-off, we decided again to postpone action until the day after the run-off so that the demonstrations could not be used to cloud the issues. Like many others, we wanted to see Mr. Connor defeated, and to this end we endured postponement after postponement. Having aided in this community need, we felt that our direct-action program could be delayed no longer.

You may well ask, "Why direct action? Why sit-ins, marches, and so forth? Isn't negotiation a better path?" You are quite right in calling for negotiation. Indeed, this is the very purpose of direct action. Nonviolent direct action seeks to create such a crisis and foster such a tension that a community which has constantly refused to negotiate is forced to confront the issue. It seeks so to dramatize the issue that it can no longer be ignored. My citing the creation of tension as part of the work of the nonviolent-resister may sound rather shocking. But I must confess that I am not afraid of the word "tension." I have earnestly opposed violent tension, but there is a type of constructive, nonviolent tension which is necessary for growth. Just as Socrates felt that it was necessary to create a tension in the mind so that individuals could rise from the bondage of myths and half-truths to the unfettered realm of creative analysis and objective appraisal, so must we see the need for nonviolent gadflies to create the kind of tension in society that will help men rise from the dark depths of prejudice and racism to the majestic heights of understanding and brotherhood.

The purpose of our direct-action program is to create a situation so crisis-packed that it will inevitably open the door to negotiation. I therefore concur with you in your call for negotiation. Too long has our beloved Southland been bogged down in a tragic effort to live in monologue rather than dialogue.

One of the basic points in your statement is that the action that I and my associates have taken in Birmingham is untimely. Some have asked: "Why didn't you give the new city administration time to act?" The only answer that I can give to this query is that the new Birmingham administration must be prodded about as much as the outgoing one, before it will act. We are sadly mistaken if we feel that the election of Albert Boutwell as mayor will bring the millennium to Birmingham. While Mr. Boutwell is a much more gentle person than Mr. Connor, they are both segregationists, dedicated to maintenance of the status quo. I have hoped that Mr. Boutwell will be reasonable enough to see the futility of massive resistance to desegregation. But he will not see this without pressure from devotees of civil rights. My friends, I must say to you that we have not made a single gain in civil rights without determined legal and nonviolent pressure. Lamentably, it is an historical fact that privileged groups seldom give up their privileges voluntarily. Individuals may see the moral light and voluntarily give up their unjust posture; but, as Reinhold Niebuhr has reminded us, groups tend to be more immoral than individuals.

We know through painful experience that freedom is never voluntarily given by the oppressor; it must be demanded by the oppressed. Frankly, I have yet to engage in a direct-action campaign that was "well timed" in the view of those who have not suffered unduly from the disease of segregation. For years now I have heard the word "Wait!" It rings in the ear of every Negro with piercing familiarity. This "Wait" has almost always meant "Never." We must come to see, with one of our distinguished jurists, that "justice too long delayed is justice denied."

We have waited for more than 340 years for our constitutional and God-given rights. The nations of Asia and Africa are moving with jetlike speed toward gaining political independence, but we still creep at horse-and-buggy pace toward gaining a cup of coffee at a lunch counter. Perhaps it is easy for those who have never felt the stinging darts of segregation to say, "Wait." But when you have seen vicious mobs lynch your mothers and fathers at will and drown your sisters and brothers at whim; when you have seen

hate-filled policemen curse, kick, and even kill your black brothers
and sisters; when you see the vast majority of your twenty million
Negro brothers smothering in an airtight cage of poverty in the
midst of an affluent society; when you suddenly find your tongue
twisted and your speech stammering as you seek to explain to your
six-year-old daughter why she can't go to the public amusement
park that has just been advertised on television, and see tears well-
ing up in her eyes when she is told that Funtown is closed to colored children, and see ominous clouds of inferiority beginning to
form in her little mental sky, and see her beginning to distort her
personality by developing an unconscious bitterness toward white
people; when you have to concoct an answer for a five-year-old son
who is asking, "Daddy, why do white people treat colored people so
mean?"; when you take a cross-country drive and find it necessary
to sleep night after night in the uncomfortable corners of your
automobile because no motel will accept you; when you are humiliated day in and day out by nagging signs reading "white" and "colored"; when your first name becomes "nigger," your middle name
becomes "boy" (however old you are) and your last name becomes
"John," and your wife and mother are never given the respected
title "Mrs."; when you are harried by day and haunted by night by
the fact that you are a Negro, living constantly at tiptoe stance,
never quite knowing what to expect next, and are plagued with
inner fears and outer resentments; when you are forever fighting a
degenerating sense of "nobodiness"—then you will understand why
we find it difficult to wait. There comes a time when the cup of
endurance runs over, and men are no longer willing to be plunged
into the abyss of despair. I hope, sirs, you can understand our legitimate and unavoidable impatience.

You express a great deal of anxiety over our willingness to break
laws. This is certainly a legitimate concern. Since we so diligently
urge people to obey the Supreme Court's decision of 1954 outlaw-
ing segregation in the public schools, at first glance it may seem
rather paradoxical for us consciously to break laws. One may well
ask: "How can you advocate breaking some laws and obeying
others?" The answer lies in the fact that there are two types of
laws: just and unjust. I would be the first to advocate obeying just
laws. One has not only a legal but a moral responsibility to obey
just laws. Conversely, one has a moral responsibility to disobey
unjust laws. I would agree with St. Augustine that "an unjust law is
no law at all."

Now, what is the difference between the two? How does one
determine whether a law is just or unjust? A just law is a man-made
code that squares with the moral law or the law of God. An unjust
law is a code that is out of harmony with the moral law. To put it

in the terms of St. Thomas Aquinas: An unjust law is a human law that is not rooted in eternal law and natural law. Any law that uplifts human personality is just. Any law that degrades human personality is unjust. All segregation statutes are unjust because segregation distorts the soul and damages the personality. It gives the segregator a false sense of superiority and the segregated a false sense of inferiority. Segregation, to use the terminology of the Jewish philosopher Martin Buber, substitutes an "I-it" relationship for an "I-thou" relationship and ends up relegating persons to the status of things. Hence segregation is not only politically, economically, and sociologically unsound, it is morally wrong and sinful. Paul Tillich has said that sin is separation. Is not segregation an existential expression of man's tragic separation, his awful estrangement, his terrible sinfulness? Thus it is that I can urge men to obey the 1954 decision of the Supreme Court, for it is morally right; and I can urge them to disobey segregation ordinances, for they are morally wrong.

Let us consider a more concrete example of just and unjust laws. An unjust law is a code that a numerical or power majority group compels a minority group to obey but does not make binding on itself. This is *difference* made legal. By the same token, a just law is a code that a majority compels a minority to follow and that it is willing to follow itself. This is *sameness* made legal.

Let me given another explanation. A law is unjust if it is inflicted on a minority that, as a result of being denied the right to vote, had no part in enacting or devising the law. Who can say that the legislature of Alabama which set up that state's segregation laws was democratically elected? Throughout Alabama all sorts of devious methods are used to prevent Negroes from becoming registered voters, and there are some counties in which, even though Negroes constitute a majority of the population, not a single Negro is registered. Can any law enacted under such circumstances be considered democratically structured?

Sometimes a law is just on its face and unjust in its application. For instance, I have been arrested on a charge of parading without a permit. Now, there is nothing wrong in having an ordinance which requires a permit for a parade. But such an ordinance becomes unjust when it is used to maintain segregation and to deny citizens the First-Amendment privilege of peaceful assembly and protest.

I hope you are able to see the distinction I am trying to point out. In no sense do I advocate evading or defying the law, as would the rabid segregationist. That would lead to anarchy. One who breaks an unjust law must do so openly, lovingly, and with a willingness to accept the penalty. I submit that an individual who breaks a law that conscience tells him is unjust, and who willingly accepts the penalty of imprisonment in order to arouse the conscience of the community over its injustice, is in reality expressing the highest respect for law.

Of course, there is nothing new about this kind of civil disobedience. It was evidenced sublimely in the refusal of Shadrach, Meshach, and Abednego to obey the laws of Nebuchadnezzar, on the ground that a higher moral law was at stake. It was practiced superbly by the early Christians, who were willing to face hungry lions and the excruciating pain of chopping blocks rather than submit to certain unjust laws of the Roman Empire. To a degree, academic freedom is a reality today because Socrates practiced civil disobedience. In our own nation, the Boston Tea Party represented a massive act of civil disobedience.

We should never forget that everything Adolf Hitler did in Germany was "legal" and everything the Hungarian freedom fighters did in Hungary was "illegal." It was "illegal" to aid and comfort a Jew in Hitler's Germany. Even so, I am sure that, had I lived in Germany at the time, I would have aided and comforted my Jewish brothers. If today I lived in a Communist country where certain principles dear to the Christian faith are suppressed, I would openly advocate disobeying that country's anti-religious laws.

I must make two honest confessions to you, my Christian and Jewish brothers. First, I must confess that over the past few years I have been gravely disappointed with the white moderate. I have almost reached the regrettable conclusion that the Negro's great stumbling block in his stride toward freedom is not the White Citizen's Counciler or the Ku Klux Klanner, but the white moderate, who is more devoted to "order" than to justice; who prefers a negative peace which is the absence of tension to a positive peace which is the presence of justice; who constantly says, "I agree with you in the goal you seek, but I cannot agree with your methods of direct action"; who paternalistically believes he can set the timetable for another man's freedom; who lives by a mythical concept of time and who constantly advises the Negro to wait for a "more convenient season." Shallow understanding from people of good will is more frustrating than absolute misunderstanding from people of ill will. Lukewarm acceptance is much more bewildering than outright rejection.

I had hoped that the white moderate would understand that law and order exist for the purpose of establishing justice and that when they fail in this purpose they become the dangerously structured dams that block the flow of social progress. I had hoped that the white moderate would understand that the present tension in the South is a necessary phase of the transition from an obnoxious negative peace, in which the Negro passively accepted his unjust plight, to a substantive and positive peace, in which all men will respect the dignity and worth of human personality. Actually, we who engage in nonviolent direct action are not the creators of tension. We merely bring to the surface the hidden tension that is already alive. We bring it out in the open, where it can be seen and dealt with. Like a boil that can never be cured so long as it is covered up but must be opened with all its ugliness to the natural medicines of air and light, injustice must be exposed, with all the tension its exposure creates, to the light of human conscience and the air of national opinion, before it can be cured.

In your statement you assert that our actions, even though peaceful, must be condemned because they precipitate violence. But is this a logical assertion? Isn't this like condemning a robbed man because his possession of money precipitated the evil act of robbery? Isn't this like condemning Socrates because his unswerving commitment to truth and his philosophical inquiries precipitated the act by the misguided populace in which they made him drink hemlock? Isn't this like condemning Jesus because his unique God-consciousness and never-ceasing devotion to God's will precipitated the evil act of crucifixion? We must come to see that, as the federal courts have consistently affirmed, it is wrong to urge an individual to cease his efforts to gain his basic constitutional rights because the quest may precipitate violence. Society must protect the robbed and punish the robber.

I had also hoped that the white moderate would reject the myth concerning time in relation to the struggle for freedom. I have just received a letter from a white brother in Texas. He writes: "All Christians know that the colored people will receive equal rights eventually, but it is possible that you are in too great a religious hurry. It has taken Christianity almost two thousand years to accomplish what it has. The teachings of Christ take time to come to earth." Such an attitude stems from a tragic misconception of time, from the strangely irrational notion that there is something in the very flow of time that will inevitably cure all ills. Actually, time itself is neutral; it can be used either destructively or constructively. More and more I feel that the people of ill will have used time much more effectively than have the people of good will. We will have to repent in this generation not merely for the hateful words and actions of the bad people, but for the appalling silence of the good people. Human progress never rolls in on wheels of inevitability; it comes through the tireless efforts of men willing to be co-workers with God, and without this hard work, time itself becomes an ally of the forces of social stagnation. We must use time creatively, in the knowledge that the time is always ripe to do right. Now is the time to make real the promise of democracy and transform our pending national elegy into a creative psalm of brotherhood. Now is the time to lift our national policy from the quicksand of racial injustice to the solid rock of human dignity.

You speak of our activity in Birmingham as extreme. At first I was rather disappointed that fellow clergymen would see my nonviolent efforts as those of an extremist. I began thinking about the fact that I stand in the middle of two opposing forces in the Negro community. One is a force of complacency, made up in part of Negroes who, as a result of long years of oppression, are so drained of self-respect and a sense of "somebodiness" that they have adjusted to segregation; and in part of a few middle-class Negroes who, because of a degree of academic and economic security and because in some ways they profit by segregation, have become insensitive to the problems of the masses. The other force is one of bitterness and hatred, and it comes perilously close to advocating violence. It is expressed in the various black nationalist groups that are springing up across the nation, the largest and best-known being Elijah Muhammad's Muslim movement. Nourished by the Negro's frustration over the continued existence of racial discrimination, this movement is made up of people who have lost faith in America, who have absolutely repudiated Christianity, and who have concluded that the white man is an incorrigible "devil."

I have tried to stand between these two forces, saying that we need emulate neither the "do-nothingism" of the complacent nor the hatred and despair of the black nationalist. For there is the more excellent way of love and nonviolent protest. I am grateful to God that, through the influence of the Negro church, the way of nonviolence became an integral part of our struggle.

If this philosophy had not emerged, by now many streets of the South would, I am convinced, be flowing with blood. And I am further convinced that if our white brothers dismiss as "rabble-rousers" and "outside agitators" those of us who employ nonviolent direct action, and if they refuse to support our nonviolent efforts, millions of Negroes will, out of frustration and despair, seek solace and security in black-nationalist ideologies—a development that would inevitably lead to a frightening racial nightmare.

Oppressed people cannot remain oppressed forever. The yearning for freedom eventually manifests itself, and that is what has happened to the American Negro. Something within has reminded him of his birthright of freedom, and something without has reminded him that it can be gained. Consciously or unconsciously, he has been caught up by the *Zeitgeist*, and with his black brothers of Africa and his brown and yellow brothers of Asia, South America, and the Caribbean, the United States Negro is moving with a sense of great urgency toward the promised land of racial justice. If one recognizes this vital urge that has engulfed the Negro community, one should readily understand why public demonstrations are taking place. The Negro has many pent-up resentments and latent frustrations, and he must release them. So let him march; let him make prayer pilgrimages to the city hall; let him go on freedom rides—and try to understand why he must do so. If his repressed emotions are not released in nonviolent ways, they will seek expression through violence; this is not a threat but a fact of history. So I have not said to my people, "Get rid of your discontent." Rather, I have tried to say that this normal and healthy discontent can be channeled into the creative outlet of nonviolent direct action. And now this approach is being termed extremist.

But though I was initially disappointed at being categorized as an extremist, as I continued to think about the matter I gradually gained a measure of satisfaction from the label. Was not Jesus an extremist for love: "Love your enemies, bless them that curse you, do good to them that hate you, and pray for them which despitefully use you, and persecute you." Was not Amos an extremist for justice: "Let justice roll down like waters and righteousness like an ever-flowing stream." Was not Paul an extremist for the Christian gospel: "I bear in my body the marks of the Lord Jesus." Was not Martin Luther an extremist: "Here I stand; I cannot do otherwise, so help me God." And John Bunyan: "I will stay in jail to the end of my days before I make a butchery of my conscience." And Abraham Lincoln: "This nation cannot survive half slave and half free." And Thomas Jefferson: "We hold these truths to be self-evident, that all men are created equal. . . ." So the question is not whether we will be extremists, but what kind of extremists we will be. Will we be extremists for hate or for love? Will we be extremists for the preservation of injustice or for the extension of justice? In that dramatic scene on Calvary's hill three men were crucified. We must never forget that all three were crucified for the same crime—the crime of extremism. Two were extremists for immorality, and thus fell below their environment. The other, Jesus Christ, was an extremist for love, truth, and goodness, and thereby rose above his environment. Perhaps the South, the nation, and the world are in dire need of creative extremists.

I had hoped that the white moderate would see this need. Perhaps I was too optimistic; perhaps I expected too much. I suppose I should have realized that few members of the oppressor race can understand the deep groans and passionate yearnings of the oppressed race, and still fewer have the vision to see that injustice must be rooted out by strong, persistent, and determined action. I am thankful, however, that some of our white brothers in the South have grasped the meaning of this social revolution and committed themselves to it. They are still all too few in quantity, but they are big in quality. Some—such as Ralph McGill, Lillian Smith, Harry Golden, James McBride Dabbs, Ann Braden, and

Sarah Patton Boyle—have written about our struggle in eloquent and prophetic terms. Others have marched with us down nameless streets of the South. They have languished in filthy, roach-infested jails, suffering the abuse and brutality of policemen who view them as "dirty nigger-lovers." Unlike so many of their moderate brothers and sisters, they have recognized the urgency of the moment and sensed the need for powerful "action" antidotes to combat the disease of segregation.

Let me take note of my other major disappointment. I have been so greatly disappointed with the white church and its leadership. Of course, there are some notable exceptions. I am not unmindful of the fact that each of you has taken some significant stands on this issue. I commend you, Reverend Stallings, for your Christian stand on this past Sunday, in welcoming Negroes to your worship service on a nonsegregated basis. I commend the Catholic leaders of this state for integrating Spring Hill College several years ago.

But despite these notable exceptions, I must honestly reiterate that I have been disappointed with the church. I do not say this as one of those negative critics who can always find something wrong with the church. I say this as a minister of the gospel, who loves the church; who was nurtured in its bosom; who has been sustained by its spiritual blessings and who will remain true to it as long as the cord of life shall lengthen.

When I was suddenly catapulted into the leadership of the bus protest in Montgomery, Alabama, a few years ago, I felt we would be supported by the white church. I felt that the white ministers, priests, and rabbis of the South would be among our strongest allies. Instead, some have been outright opponents, refusing to understand the freedom movement and misrepresenting its leaders; all too many others have been more cautious than courageous and have remained silent behind the anesthetizing security of stained-glass windows.

In spite of my shattered dreams, I came to Birmingham with the hope that the white religious leadership of this community would see the justice of our cause and, with deep moral concern, would serve as the channel through which our just grievances could reach the power structure. I had hoped that each of you would understand. But again I have been disappointed.

I have heard numerous southern religious leaders admonish their worshipers to comply with a desegregation decision because it is the law, but I have longed to hear white ministers declare: "Follow this decree because integration is morally right and because the Negro is your brother." In the midst of blatant injustices inflicted upon the Negro, I have watched white churchmen stand on the sideline and mouth pious irrelevancies and sanctimonious trivialities. In the midst of a mighty struggle to rid our nation of racial and economic injustice, I have heard many ministers say: "Those are social issues, with which the gospel has no real concern." And I have watched many churches commit themselves to a completely otherworldly religion which makes a strange, un-Biblical distinction between body and soul, between the sacred and the secular.

I have traveled the length and breadth of Alabama, Mississippi, and all the other southern states. On sweltering summer days and crisp autumn mornings I have looked at the South's beautiful churches with their lofty spires pointing heavenward. I have beheld the impressive outlines of her massive religious-education buildings. Over and over I have found myself asking: "What kind of people worship here? Who is their God? Where were their voices when the lips of Governor Barnett dripped with words of interposition and nullification? Where were they when Governor Wallace gave a clarion call for defiance and hatred? Where were their voices of support when bruised and weary Negro men and women decided to rise from the dark dungeons of complacency to the bright hills of creative protest?"

Yes, these questions are still in my mind. In deep disappointment I have wept over the laxity of the church. But be assured that my tears have been tears of love. There can be no deep disappointment where there is not deep love. Yes, I love the church. How could I do otherwise? I am in the rather unique position of being the son, the grandson, and the great-grandson of preachers. Yes, I see the church as the body of Christ. But, oh! How we have blemished and scarred that body through social neglect and through fear of being nonconformists.

There was a time when the church was very powerful—in the time when the early Christians rejoiced at being deemed worthy to suffer for what they believed. In those days the church was not merely a thermometer that recorded the ideas and principles of popular opinion; it was a thermostat that transformed the mores of society. Whenever the early Christians entered a town, the people in power became disturbed and immediately sought to convict the Christians for being "disturbers of the peace" and "outside agitators." But the Christians pressed on, in the conviction that they were "a colony of heaven," called to obey God rather than man. Small in number, they were big in commitment. They were too God-intoxicated to be "astronomically intimidated." By their effort and example they brought an end to such ancient evils as infanticide and gladiatorial contests.

Things are different now. So often the contemporary church is a weak, ineffectual voice with an uncertain sound. So often it is an archdefender of the status quo. Far from being disturbed by the presence of the church, the power structure of the average community is consoled by the church's silent—and often even vocal—

sanction of things as they are.

But the judgment of God is upon the church as never before. If today's church does not recapture the sacrificial spirit of the early church, it will lose its authenticity, forfeit the loyalty of millions, and be dismissed as an irrelevant social club with no meaning for the twentieth century. Every day I meet young people whose disappointment with the church has turned into outright disgust.

Perhaps I have once again been too optimistic. Is organized religion too inextricably bound to the status quo to save our nation and the world? Perhaps I must turn my faith to the inner spiritual church, the church within the church, as the true *ekklesia*[2] and the hope of the world. But again I am thankful to God that some noble souls from the ranks of organized religion have broken loose from the paralyzing chains of conformity and joined us as active partners in the struggle for freedom. They have left their secure congregations and walked the streets of Albany, Georgia, with us. They have gone down the highways of the South on tortuous rides for freedom. Yes, they have gone to jail with us. Some have been dismissed from their churches, have lost the support of their bishops and fellow ministers. But they have acted in the faith that right defeated is stronger than evil triumphant. Their witness has been the spiritual salt that has preserved the true meaning of the gospel in these troubled times. They have carved a tunnel of hope through the dark mountain of disappointment.

I hope the church as a whole will meet the challenge of this decisive hour. But even if the church does not come to the aid of justice, I have no despair about the future. I have no fear about the outcome of our struggle in Birmingham, even if our motives are at present misunderstood. We will reach the goal of freedom in Birmingham and all over the nation, because the goal of America is freedom. Abused and scorned though we may be, our destiny is tied up with America's destiny. Before the pilgrims landed at Plymouth, we were here. Before the pen of Jefferson etched the majestic words of the Declaration of Independence across the pages of history, we were here. For more than two centuries our forebears labored in this country without wages; they made cotton king; they built the homes of their masters while suffering gross injustice and shameful humiliation—and yet out of a bottomless vitality they continued to thrive and develop. If the inexpressible cruelties of slavery could not stop us, the opposition we now face will surely fail. We will win our freedom because the sacred heritage of our nation and the eternal will of God are embodied in our echoing demands.

Before closing I feel impelled to mention one other point in your statement that has troubled me profoundly. You warmly com-

2. The Greek New Testament word for the early Christian church.

mended the Birmingham police force for keeping "order" and "preventing violence." I doubt that you would have so warmly commended the police force if you had seen its dogs sinking their teeth into unarmed, nonviolent Negroes. I doubt that you would so quickly commend the policemen if you were to observe their ugly and inhumane treatment of Negroes here in the city jail; if you were to watch them push and curse old Negro women and young Negro girls; if you were to see them slap and kick old Negro men and young boys; if you were to observe them, as they did on two occasions, refuse to give us food because we wanted to sing our grace together. I cannot join you in your praise of the Birmingham police department.

It is true that the police have exercised a degree of discipline in handling the demonstrators. In this sense they have conducted themselves rather "nonviolently" in public. But for what purpose? To preserve the evil system of segregation. Over the past few years I have consistently preached that nonviolence demands that the means we use must be as pure as the ends we seek. I have tried to make clear that it is wrong to use immoral means to attain moral ends. But now I must affirm that it is just as wrong, or perhaps even more so, to use moral means to preserve immoral ends. Perhaps Mr. Connor and his policemen have been rather nonviolent in public, as was Chief Pritchett in Albany, Georgia, but they have used the moral means of nonviolence to maintain the immoral end of racial injustice. As T. S. Eliot has said, "The last temptation is the greatest treason: To do the right deed for the wrong reason."

I wish you had commended the Negro sit-inners and demonstrators of Birmingham for their sublime courage, their willingness to suffer, and their amazing discipline in the midst of great provocation. One day the South will recognize its real heroes. They will be the James Merediths, with the noble sense of purpose that enables them to face jeering and hostile mobs, and with the agonizing loneliness that characterizes the life of the pioneer. They will be old, oppressed, battered Negro women, symbolized in a seventy-two-year-old woman in Montgomery, Alabama, who rose up with a sense of dignity and with her people decided not to ride segregated buses, and who responded with ungrammatical profundity to one who inquired about her weariness: "My feets is tired, but my soul is at rest." They will be the young high school and college students, the young ministers of the gospel and a host of their elders, courageously and nonviolently sitting in at lunch counters and willingly going to jail for conscience' sake. One day the South will know that when these disinherited children of God sat down at lunch counters, they were in reality standing up for what is best in the American dream and for the most sacred values in our Judaeo-Christian heritage, thereby bringing our nation back to those great wells of democracy which were dug deep by the founding fathers in their formulation of the Constitution and the Declaration of Independence.

Never before have I written so long a letter. I'm afraid it is much too long to take your precious time. I can assure you that it would have been much shorter if I had been writing from a comfortable desk, but what else can one do when he is alone in a narrow jail cell, other than write long letters, think long thoughts, and pray long prayers?

If I have said anything in this letter that overstates the truth and indicates an unreasonable impatience, I beg you to forgive me. If I have said anything that understates the truth and indicates my having a patience that allows me to settle for anything less than brotherhood, I beg God to forgive me.

I hope this letter finds you strong in the faith. I also hope that circumstances will soon make it possible for me to meet each of you, not as an integrationist or a civil-rights leader but as a fellow clergyman and a Christian brother. Let us all hope that the dark clouds of racial prejudice will soon pass away and the deep fog of misunderstanding will be lifted from our fear-drenched communities, and in some not too distant tomorrow the radiant stars of love and brotherhood will shine over our great nation with all their scintillating beauty.

> Yours for the cause of Peace and Brotherhood,
> MARTIN LUTHER KING, JR.

JAMES THURBER
The Rabbits Who Caused All the Trouble

Within the memory of the youngest child there was a family of rabbits who lived near a pack of wolves. The wolves announced that they did not like the way the rabbits were living. (The wolves were crazy about the way they themselves were living, because it was the only way to live.) One night several wolves were killed in an earthquake and this was blamed on the rabbits, for it is well known that rabbits pound on the ground with their hind legs and cause earthquakes. On another night one of the wolves was killed by a bolt of lightning and this was also blamed on the rabbits, for it is well known that lettuce-eaters cause lightning. The wolves threatened to civilize the rabbits if they didn't behave, and the rabbits decided to run away to a desert island. But the other animals, who lived at a great distance, shamed them, saying, "You must stay where you are and be brave. This is no world for escapists. If the wolves attack you, we will come to your aid, in all probability." So the rabbits continued to live near the wolves and one day there was a terrible flood which drowned a great many wolves. This was blamed on the rabbits, for it is well known that carrot-nibblers with long ears cause floods. The wolves descended on the rabbits, for their own good, and imprisoned them in a dark cave, for their own protection.

When nothing was heard about the rabbits for some weeks, the other animals demanded to know what had happened to them. The wolves replied that the rabbits had been eaten and since they had been eaten the affair was a purely internal matter. But the other animals warned that they might possibly unite against the wolves unless some reason was given for the destruction of the rabbits. So the wolves gave them one. "They were trying to escape," said the wolves, "and, as you know, this is no world for escapists."

Moral: Run, don't walk, to the nearest desert island.

JONATHAN SWIFT

A Modest Proposal

For Preventing the Children of Poor People in Ireland from Being a Burden to Their Parents or Country, and for Making Them Beneficial to the Public

It is a melancholy object to those who walk through this great town or travel in the country, when they see the streets, the roads, and cabin doors, crowded with beggars of the female-sex, followed by three, four, or six children, all in rags and importuning every passenger for an alms. These mothers, instead of being able to work for their honest livelihood, are forced to employ all their time in strolling to beg sustenance for their helpless infants, who, as they grow up, either turn thieves for want of work, or leave their dear native country to fight for the Pretender in Spain, or sell themselves to the Barbadoes.[1]

I think it is agreed by all parties that this prodigious number of children in the arms, or on the backs, or at the heels of their mothers, and frequently of their fathers, is in the present deplorable state of the kingdom a very great additional grievance; and therefore whoever could find out a fair, cheap, and easy method of making these children sound, useful members of the commonwealth would deserve so well of the public as to have his statue set up for a preserver of the nation.

But my intention is very far from being confined to provide only for the children of professed beggars; it is of a much greater extent, and shall take in the whole number of infants at a certain age who are born of parents in effect as little able to support them as those who demand our charity in the streets.

1. That is, bind themselves to work for a period of years, in order to pay for their transportation to a colony.

As to my own part, having turned my thoughts for many years upon this important subject, and maturely weighed the several schemes of other projectors, I have always found them grossly mistaken in their computation. It is true, a child just dropped from its dam may be supported by her milk for a solar year, with little other nourishment; at most not above the value of two shillings, which the mother may certainly get, or the value in scraps, by her lawful occupation of begging; and it is exactly at one year old that I propose to provide for them in such a manner as instead of being a charge upon their parents or the parish, or wanting food and raiment for the rest of their lives, they shall on the contrary contribute to the feeding, and partly to the clothing, of many thousands.

There is likewise another great advantage in my scheme, that it will prevent those voluntary abortions, and that horrid practice of women murdering their bastard children, alas, too frequent among us, sacrificing the poor innocent babes, I doubt, more to avoid the expense than the shame, which would move tears and pity in the most savage and inhuman breast.

The number of souls in this kingdom being usually reckoned one million and a half, of these I calculate there may be about two hundred thousand couple whose wives are breeders; from which number I subtract thirty thousand couples who are able to maintain their own children, although I apprehend there cannot be so many under the present distresses of the kingdom; but this being granted, there will remain an hundred and seventy thousand breeders. I again subtract fifty thousand for those women who miscarry, or whose children die by accident or disease within the year. There only remain an hundred and twenty thousand children of poor parents annually born. The question therefore is, how this number shall be reared and provided for, which, as I have already said, under the present situation of affairs, is utterly impossible by all the methods hitherto proposed. For we can neither employ them in handicraft or agriculture; we neither build houses (I mean in the country) nor cultivate land. They can very seldom pick up a livelihood by stealing till they arrive at six years old, except where they are of towardly parts; although I confess they learn the rudiments much earlier, during which time they can however be looked upon only as probationers, as I have been informed by a principal gentleman in the county of Cavan, who protested to me that he never knew above one or two instances under the age of six, even in a part of the kingdom so renowned for the quickest proficiency in that art.

I am assured by our merchants that a boy or a girl before twelve years old is no salable commodity; and even when they come to this age they will not yield above three pounds, or three pounds and half a crown at most on the Exchange; which cannot turn to account either to the parents or the kingdom, the charge of nutriment and rags having been at least four times that value.

I shall now therefore humbly propose my own thoughts, which I hope will not be liable to the least objection.

I have been assured by a very knowing American of my acquaintance in London, that a young healthy child well nursed is at a year old a most delicious, nourishing, and wholesome food, whether stewed, roasted, baked, or boiled; and I make no doubt that it will equally serve in a fricassee or a ragout.

I do therefore humbly offer it to public consideration that of the hundred and twenty thousand children, already computed, twenty thousand may be reserved for breed, whereof only one fourth part to be males, which is more than we allow to sheep, black cattle, or swine; and my reason is that these children are seldom the fruits of marriage, a circumstance not much regarded by our savages, therefore one male will be sufficient to serve four females. That the remaining hundred thousand may at a year old be offered in sale to the persons of quality and fortune through the kingdom, always advising the mother to let them suck plentifully in the last month, so as to render them plump and fat for a good table. A child will make two dishes at an entertainment for friends; and when the family dines alone, the fore or hind quarter will make a reasonable dish, and seasoned with a little pepper or salt will be very good boiled on the fourth day, especially in winter.

I have reckoned upon a medium that a child just born will weigh twelve pounds, and in a solar year if tolerably nursed increaseth to twenty-eight pounds.

I grant this food will be somewhat dear, and therefore very proper for landlords, who, as they have already devoured most of the parents, seem to have the best title to the children.

Infant's flesh will be in season throughout the year, but more plentiful in March, and a little before and after. For we are told by a grave author, an eminent French physician,[2] that fish being a prolific diet, there are more children born in Roman Catholic countries about nine months after Lent than at any other season; therefore, reckoning a year after Lent, the markets will be more glutted than usual, because the number of popish infants is at least three to one in this kingdom; and therefore it will have one other collateral advantage, by lessening the number of Papists among us.

I have already computed the charge of nursing a beggar's child (in which list I reckon all cottagers, laborers, and four fifths of the farmers) to be about two shillings per annum, rags included; and I believe no gentleman would repine to give ten shillings for the carcass of a good fat child, which, as I have said, will make four dishes of excellent nutritive meat, when he hath only some particular friend or his own family to dine with him. Thus the squire will learn to be a good landlord, and grow popular among the ten-

2. Rabelais.

ants; the mother will have eight shillings net profit, and be fit for work till she produces another child.

Those who are more thrifty (as I must confess the times require) may flay the carcass; the skin of which artificially dressed will make admirable gloves for ladies, and summer boots for fine gentlemen.

As to our city of Dublin, shambles may be appointed for this purpose in the most convenient parts of it, and butchers we may be assured will not be wanting; although I rather recommend buying the children alive, and dressing them hot from the knife as we do roasting pigs.

A very worthy person, a true lover of his country, and whose virtues I highly esteem, was lately pleased in discoursing on this matter to offer a refinement upon my scheme. He said that many gentlemen of this kingdom, having of late destroyed their deer, he conceived that the want of venison might be well supplied by the bodies of young lads and maidens, not exceeding fourteen years of age nor under twelve, so great a number of both sexes in every county being now ready to starve for want of work and service; and these to be disposed of by their parents, if alive, or otherwise by their nearest relations. But with due deference to so excellent a friend and so deserving a patriot, I cannot be altogether in his sentiments; for as to the males, my American acquaintance assured me from frequent experience that their flesh was generally tough and lean, like that of our schoolboys, by continual exercise, and their taste disagreeable; and to fatten them would not answer the charge. Then as to the females, it would, I think with humble submission, be a loss to the public, because they soon would become breeders themselves: and besides, it is not improbable that some scrupulous people might be apt to censure such a practice (although indeed very unjustly) as a little bordering upon cruelty; which, I confess, hath always been with me the strongest objection against any project, how well soever intended.

But in order to justify my friend, he confessed that this expedient was put into his head by the famous Psalmanazar, a native of the island Formosa, who came from thence to London above twenty years ago, and in conversation told my friend that in his country when any young person happened to be put to death, the executioner sold the carcass to persons of quality as a prime dainty; and that in his time the body of a plump girl of fifteen, who was crucified for an attempt to poison the emperor, was sold to his Imperial Majesty's prime minister of state, and other great mandarins of the court, in joints from the gibbet, at four hundred crowns. Neither indeed can I deny that if the same use were made of several plump young girls in this town, who without one single groat to their fortunes cannot stir abroad without a chair, and appear at the playhouse and assemblies in foreign fineries which they never will pay for, the kingdom would not be the worse.

Some persons of a desponding spirit are in great concern about that vast number of poor people who are aged, diseased, or maimed, and I have been desired to employ my thoughts what course may be taken to ease the nation of so grievous an encumbrance. But I am not in the least pain upon that matter, because it is very well known that they are every day dying and rotting by cold and famine, and filth and vermin, as fast as can be reasonably expected. And as to the younger laborers, they are now in almost as hopeful a condition. They cannot get work, and consequently pine away for want of nourishment to a degree that if at any time they are accidentally hired to common labor, they have not strength to perform it; and thus the country and themselves are happily delivered from the evils to come.

I have too long digressed, and therefore shall return to my subject. I think the advantages by the proposal which I have made are obvious and many, as well as of the highest importance.

For first, as I have already observed, it would greatly lessen the number of Papists, with whom we are yearly overrun, being the principal breeders of the nation as well as our most dangerous enemies; and who stay at home on purpose to deliver the kingdom to the Pretender, hoping to take their advantage by the absence of so many good Protestants, who have chosen rather to leave their country than to stay at home and pay tithes against their conscience to an Episcopal curate.

Secondly, the poorer tenants will have something valuable of their own, which by law may be made liable to distress, and help to pay their landlord's rent, their corn and cattle being already seized and money a thing unknown.

Thirdly, whereas the maintenance of an hundred thousand children, from two years old and upwards, cannot be computed at less than ten shillings a piece per annum, the nation's stock will be thereby increased fifty thousand pounds per annum, besides the profit of a new dish introduced to the tables of all gentlemen of fortune in the kingdom who have any refinement in taste. And the money will circulate among ourselves, the goods being entirely of our own growth and manufacture.

Fourthly, the constant breeders, besides the gain of eight shillings sterling per annum by the sale of their children, will be rid of the charge of maintaining them after the first year.

Fifthly, this food would likewise bring great custom to taverns, where the vintners will certainly be so prudent as to procure the best receipts for dressing it to perfection, and consequently have their houses frequented by all the fine gentlemen, who justly value themselves upon their knowledge in good eating; and a skillful cook, who understands how to oblige his guests, will contrive to make it as expensive as they please.

Sixthly, this would be a great inducement to marriage, which all wise nations have either encouraged by rewards or enforced by laws and penalties. It would increase the care and tenderness of mothers toward their children, when they were sure of a settlement for life to the poor babes, provided in some sort by the public, to their annual profit instead of expense. We should see an honest emulation among the married women, which of them could bring the fattest child to the market. Men would become as fond of their wives during the time of their pregnancy as they are now of their mares in foal, their cows in calf, or sows when they are ready to farrow; nor offer to beat or kick them (as is too frequent a practice) for fear of a miscarriage.

Many other advantages might be enumerated. For instance, the addition of some thousand carcasses in our exportation of barreled beef, the propagation of swine's flesh, and improvement in the art of making good bacon, so much wanted among us by the great destruction of pigs, too frequent at our tables, which are no way comparable in taste or magnificence to a well-grown, fat, yearling child, which roasted whole will make a considerable figure at a lord mayor's feast or any other public entertainment. But this and many others I omit, being studious of brevity.

Supposing that one thousand families in this city would be constant customers for infants' flesh, besides others who might have it at merry meetings, particularly weddings and christenings, I compute that Dublin would take off annually about twenty thousand carcasses, and the rest of the kingdom (where probably they will be sold somewhat cheaper) the remaining eighty thousand.

I can think of no one objection that will possibly be raised against this proposal, unless it should be urged that the number of people will be thereby much lessened in the kingdom. This I freely own, and it was indeed one principal design in offering it to the world. I desire the reader will observe, that I calculate my remedy for this one individual kingdom of Ireland and for no other that ever was, is, or I think ever can be upon earth. Therefore let no man talk to me of other expedients: of taxing our absentees at five shillings a pound: of using neither clothes nor household furniture except what is of our own growth and manufacture: of utterly rejecting the materials and instruments that promote foreign luxury: of curing the expensiveness of pride, vanity, idleness, and gaming in our women: of introducing a vein of parsimony, prudence, and temperance: of learning to love our country, in the want of which we differ even from Laplanders and the inhabitants of Topinamboo[3]: of quitting our animosities and factions, nor acting any longer like the Jews, who were murdering one another at the very moment their city was taken: of being a little cautious not to sell our country and conscience for nothing: of teaching landlords to have at

3. A district in Brazil.

least one degree of mercy toward their tenants: lastly, of putting a spirit of honesty, industry, and skill into our shopkeepers; who, if a resolution could now be taken to buy only our native goods, would immediately unite to cheat and exact upon us in the price, the measure, and the goodness, nor could ever yet be brought to make one fair proposal of just dealing, though often and earnestly invited to it.[4]

Therefore I repeat, let no man talk to me of these and the like expedients, till he hath at least some glimpse of hope that there will ever be some hearty and sincere attempt to put them in practice.

But as to myself, having been wearied out for many years with offering vain, idle, visionary thoughts, and at length utterly despairing of success, I fortunately fell upon this proposal, which, as it is wholly new, so it hath something solid and real, of no expense and little trouble, full in our own power, and whereby we can incur no danger in disobliging England. For this kind of commodity will not bear exportation, the flesh being of too tender a consistence to admit a long continuance in salt, although perhaps I could name a country which would be glad to eat up our whole nation without it.

After all, I am not so violently bent upon my own opinion as to reject any offer proposed by wise men, which shall be found equally innocent, cheap, easy, and effectual. But before something of that kind shall be advanced in contradiction to my scheme, and offering a better, I desire the author or authors will be pleased maturely to consider two points. First, as things now stand, how they will be able to find food and raiment for an hundred thousand useless mouths and backs. And secondly, there being a round million of creatures in human figure throughout this kingdom, whose sole subsistence put into a common stock would leave them in debt two millions of pounds sterling, adding those who are beggars by profession to the bulk of farmers, cottagers, and laborers, with their wives and children who are beggars in effect; I desire those politicians who dislike my overture, and may perhaps be so bold to attempt an answer, that they will first ask the parents of these mortals whether they would not at this day think it a great happiness to have been sold for food at a year old in the manner I prescribe, and thereby have avoided such a perpetual scene of misfortunes as they have since gone through by the oppression of landlords, the impossibility of paying rent without money or trade, the want of common sustenance, with neither house nor clothes to cover them from the inclemencies of the weather, and the most inevitable prospect of entailing the like or greater miseries upon their breed forever.

I profess, in the sincerity of my heart, that I have not the least personal interest in endeavoring to promote this necessary work, having no other motive than the public good of my country, by

4. Swift himself has made these various proposals in previous works.

advancing our trade, providing for infants, relieving the poor, and giving some pleasure to the rich. I have no children by which I can propose to get a single penny; the youngest being nine years old, and my wife past childbearing.

QUESTIONS

1. This essay has been called one of the best examples of sustained irony in the English language. Irony is difficult to handle because there is always the danger that the reader will miss the irony and take what is said literally. What does Swift do to try to prevent this? In answering this question, consider such matters as these: Is the first sentence of the essay ironic? At what point do you begin to suspect that Swift is using irony? What further evidence accumulates to make you certain that Swift is being ironic?
2. What is the speaker like? How are his views and character different from Swift's? Is the character of the speaker consistent? What is the purpose of the essay's final sentence?
3. Why does Swift use such phrases as "just dropt from its dam," "whose wives are breeders," "one fourth part to be males"?
4. Does the essay shock you? Was it Swift's purpose to shock you?
5. What is the main target of Swift's attack? What subsidiary targets are there? Does Swift offer any serious solutions for the problems and conditions he is describing?
6. What devices of argument, apart from the use of irony, does Swift use that could be successfully applied to other subjects?
7. Compare Swift's methods of drawing in or engaging his audience to Coffin's ("What Crucified Christ?" pp. 1184–1199).

SHULAMITH FIRESTONE

The Myth of Childhood

In the Middle Ages there was no such thing as childhood. The medieval view of children was profoundly different from ours. It was not only that it was not "childcentered," it literally was not conscious of children as distinct from adults. The childmen and childwomen of medieval iconography are miniature adults, reflecting a wholly different social reality: children then *were* tiny adults, carriers of whatever class and name they had been born to, destined to rise into a clearly outlined social position. A child saw himself as the future adult going through his stages of apprenticeship; he was his future powerful self "when I was little." He moved into the various stages of his adult role almost immediately.

Children were so little differentiated from adults that there was no special vocabulary to describe them: They shared the vocabulary of feudal subordination; only later, with the introduction of childhood as a distinct state, did this confused vocabulary separate. The confusion was based on reality: Children differed socially from adults only in their economic dependence. They were used as another transient servant class, with the difference that because all adults began in this class, it was not seen as degrading (an equivalent would be the indentured servant of American history). *All* children were literally servants; it was their apprenticeship to adulthood. (Thus for a long time after, in France, waiting on table was not considered demeaning because it had been practiced as an art by all the youthful aristocracy.) This experience held in common by children and servants and the resulting intimacy that grew up between them has been bemoaned right down to the twentieth century: as the classes grew more and more isolated from each other, this lingering intimacy was considered the cause of considerable moral corruption of children from the upper and middle classes.

The child was just another member of the large patriarchal household, not even essential to family life. In every family the child was wetnursed by a stranger, and thereafter sent to another home (from about the age of seven until fourteen to eighteen) to serve an apprenticeship to a master—as I have mentioned, usually composed of or including domestic service. Thus, he never developed a heavy dependence on his parents: they were responsible only for his minimal physical welfare. And they in turn did not "need" their children—certainly children were not doted upon. For in addition to the infant mortality rate, which would discourage this, parents reared *other people's children* for adult life. And because households were so large, filled with many genuine servants as well as a constant troupe of visitors, friends and clients, a child's dependence on, or even contact with, any specific parent was limited; when a relationship did develop it might better be described as avuncular.

Transmission from one generation to the next was ensured by the everyday participation of children in adult life—children were never segregated off into special quarters, schools, or activities. Since the aim was to ready the child for adulthood as soon as possible, it was felt quite reasonably that such a segregation would delay or stymie an adult perspective. In every respect the child was integrated into the total community as soon as possible: There were no special toys, games, clothes, or classes designed just for children. Games were shared by all age groups; children took part in the festivities of the adult community. Schools (only for specialized skills) imparted learning to anyone who was interested, of whatever age: the system of apprenticeship was open to children as well as adults.

After the fourteenth century, with the development of the bourgeoisie and empirical science, this situation slowly began to evolve. The concept of childhood developed as an adjunct to the modern family. A vocabulary to describe children and childhood was articulated (e.g., the French *le bébé*) and another vocabulary was built especially for addressing children: "childrenese" became fashionable during the seventeenth century. (Since then it has been expanded into an art and a way of life. There are all kinds of modern refinements on baby talk: some people never go without it, using it especially on their girlfriends, whom they treat as grown-up children.) Children's toys did not appear until 1600 and even then were not used beyond the age of three or four. The first toys were only child-size replicas of adult objects: the hobby horse took the place of the real horse that the child was too small to ride. But by the late seventeenth century special artifacts for children were common. Also in the late seventeenth century we find the introduction of special children's games. (In fact these signified only a division: certain games formerly shared by both children and adults were abandoned by the adults to children and the lower class, while other games were taken over from then on exclusively for adult use, becoming the upper-class adult "parlor games.")

Thus, by the seventeenth century childhood as a new and fashionable concept was "in." Ariès[1] shows how the iconography too reflects the change, with, for example, the gradual increase of glorified depictions of the mother/child relationship, e.g., the Infant in the Arms of Mary, or, later, in the fifteenth and the sixteenth centuries, of depictions of interiors and family scenes, including even individualized portraits of children and the paraphernalia of childhood. Rousseau among others developed an ideology of "childhood."[2] Much was made of children's purity and "innocence." People began to worry about their exposure to vice. "Respect" for children, as for women, unknown before the sixteenth century, when they were still part of the larger society, became necessary now that they formed a clear-cut oppressed group. Their isolation and segregation had set in. The new bourgeois family, childcentered, entailed a constant supervision; all earlier independence was abolished.

The significance of these changes is illustrated by the history of children's costume. Costume was a way of denoting social rank and prosperity—and still is, especially for women. The consternation even now, especially in Europe, at any clothing impropriety is due primarily to the impropriety of "breaking rank"; and in the days when garments were expensive and mass production unheard of, this function of clothing was even more important. Because clothing customs so graphically describe disparities of sex and class, the history of child fashion gives us valuable clues to what was happening to children.

The first special children's costumes appeared at the end of the sixteenth century, an important date in the formation of the concept of childhood. At first children's clothing was modeled after

1. The reference is to Philippe Ariès, *Centuries of Childhood: A Social History of Family Life.*

2. See especially Jean-Jacques Rousseau, *Émile, passim.*

archaic adult clothing, in the fashion of the lower class, who also wore the hand-me-downs of the aristocracy. These archaisms symbolized the growing exclusion of children and the proletariat from contemporary public life. Before the French Revolution, when special trousers of naval origin were introduced, further distinguishing the lower class, we find the same custom spreading to upper-class male children. This is important because it illustrates quite clearly that children of the upper class formed a lower class within it. That differentiation of costume functions to increase segregation and make clear class distinctions is also borne out by an otherwise unexplainable custom of the seventeenth and the eighteenth centuries; two broad ribbons had to be worn by both male and female children fastened to the robe under each shoulder and trailing down the back. These ribbons apparently had no other function than to serve as sartorial indications of childhood.

The male child's costume especially reveals the connection of sex and childhood with economic class. A male child went through roughly three stages: The male infant went from swaddling clothes into female robes; at about the age of five he switched to a robe with some elements of the adult male costume, e.g., the collar; and finally, as an older boy, he advanced to full military regalia. The costume worn by the older male child in the period of Louis XVI was at once archaic (Renaissance collar), lower-class (naval trousers), and masculinely military (jacket and buttons). Clothing became another form of initiation into manhood, with the child, in modern terms, begging to advance to "long pants."

These stages of initiation into manhood reflected in the history of child costume neatly tie in with the Oedipus Complex. Male children begin life in the lower class of women. Dressed as women, they are in no way distinguished from female children; both identify at this time with the mother, the female; both play with dolls. Attempts are made at about the age of five to wean the child from its mother, to encourage it by slow degrees, e.g., the male collar, to imitate the father: this is the transitional period of the Oedipus Complex. Finally the child is rewarded for breaking away from the female and transferring his identifications to the male by a special "grown-up" costume, its military regalia a promise of the full adult male power to come.

What about girls' costumes? Here is an astonishing fact: *child-hood did not apply to women*. The female child went from swaddling clothes right into adult female dress. She did not go to school, which, as we shall see, was the institution that structured childhood. At the age of nine or ten she acted, literally, like a "little lady"; her activity did not differ from that of adult women. As soon as she reached puberty, as early as ten or twelve, she was married off to a much older male.

The class basis of childhood is exposed: Both girls and working-class boys did not have to be set apart by distinctive dress, for in their adult roles they would be servile to upper-class men; no initiation into freedom was necessary. Girls had no reason to go through costume changes, when there was nothing for them to grow up *to*: adult women were still in a lower class in relation to men. Children of the working class, even up to the present day, were freed of clothing restrictions, for their adult models, too, were "children" relative to the ruling class. While boys of the middle and upper classes temporarily shared the status of women and the working class, they gradually were elevated out of these subjected classes; women and lower-class boys stayed there. It is no coincidence, either, that the effeminization of little boys' dress was abolished at the same time that the feminists agitated for an end to oppressive women's clothes. Both dress styles were integrally connected to class subjection and the inferiority of women's roles. Little Lord Fauntleroy[3] went the way of the petticoat. (Though my own father remembers his first day in long pants, and even today, in some European countries, these clothing initiation customs are still practiced.)

We can also see the class basis of the emerging concept of childhood in the system of child education that came in along with it. If childhood was only an abstract concept, then the modern school was the institution that built it into reality. (New concepts about the life cycle in our society are organized around institutions, e.g., adolescence, a construction of the nineteenth century, was built to facilitate conscription for military service.) The modern school education was, indeed, the articulation of the new concept of childhood. Schooling was redefined: No longer confined to clerics and scholars, it was widely extended to become the normal instrument of social initiation—in the progress from childhood to *man*hood. (Those for whom true adulthood never would apply, e.g., girls and working-class boys, did not go to school for many centuries.[4])

For contrary to popular opinion, the development of the modern school had little connection with the traditional scholarship of the Middle Ages, nor with the development of the liberal arts and humanities in the Renaissance. (In fact the humanists of the Renaissance were noted for the inclusion in their ranks of many precocious children and learned women; they stressed the development of

---

3. Fastidiously dressed hero of a mid–nineteenth-century children's novel by Frances Hodgson Burnett.
4. Vestiges of these customs remain even into our own day. Working-class boys tend to become tradesmen, artisans, or the modern equivalent, rather than engaging in a, for them, useless "book-larnin'." This is left over from the time when lower-class children still followed a system of apprenticeship while middle-class children had begun attending the modern school. (It is no accident either that so many of the great artists of the Renaissance were lower-class boys, trained in the workshops of the "masters.") We can also find remnants of this history in our present-day army, where the extremes of the class society are concentrated: on the one hand, youthful working-class "dropouts," and on the other, upper-class officers, "West Pointers" of the aristocracy—for the aristocracy as well as the proletariat was late in adopting the family structure and public schooling of the bourgeoisie [Firestone's note].

the individual, of whatever age or sex.) According to Ariès, literary historians exaggerate the importance of the humanist tradition in the structure of our schools. The real architects and innovators were the moralists and pedagogues of the seventeenth century, the Jesuits, the Oratorians, and the Jansenists.[5] These men were at the origins of both the concept of childhood and its institutionalization, the modern concept of schooling. They were the first espousers of the weakness and "innocence" of childhood; they put childhood on a pedestal just as femininity had been put on a pedestal; they preached the segregation of children from the adult world. "Discipline" was the keynote to modern schooling, much more important finally than the imparting of learning or information. For to them discipline was an instrument of moral and spiritual improvement, adapted less for its efficiency in directing large groups to work in common than for its intrinsic moral and ascetic value. That is, repression itself was adopted as a spiritual value.

Thus, the function of the school became "childrearing," complete with disciplinary "child psychology." Ariès quotes the *Regulations for Boarders at Port-Royal*, a forerunner of our teacher training manuals:

A close watch must be kept on the children, and they must never be left alone anywhere, whether they are ill or in good health . . . this constant supervision should be exercised gently and with a certain trustfulness *calculated* to make them think one loves them, and that it is only to enjoy their company that one is with them. This will make them love their supervision rather than fear it. (Italics mine)

This passage, written in 1612, already exhibits the mincing tone characteristic of modern child psychology, and the peculiar distance —at that time rehearsed, but by now quite unconscious—between adults and children.

The new schooling effectively segregated children off from the adult world for longer and longer periods of time. But this segregation of child from adult, and the severe initiation process demanded to make the transition to adulthood, indicated a growing disrespect for, a systematic underestimation of, the abilities of the child.

The precocity so common in the Middle Ages and for some time after has dwindled almost to zero in our own time.[6] Today, for example, Mozart's feats as a child composer are hardly credible; in his own time he was not so unusual. Many children played and wrote music seriously then and also engaged in a good many other "adult" activities. Our piano lessons of today are in no way comparable. They are, in fact, only indications of child oppression—in the same way that the traditional "women's accomplishments" such

---

5. Catholic groups devoted to teaching and reform.

6. In the orthodox Jewish milieu in which I grew up, considered anachronistic by outsiders, many little boys still begin serious study before the age of five, and as a result Talmudic prodigies are common [Firestone's note].

as embroidery were superficial activity—telling us only about the subjugation of the child to adult whims. And it is significant that these "talents" are more often cultivated in girls than in boys; when boys study piano it is most often because they are exceptionally gifted or because their parents are musical.

Ariès quotes Heroard, *Journal sur l'enfance et la jeunesse de Louis XIII*, the detailed account of the Dauphin's childhood years written by his doctor, that the Dauphin played the violin and sang all the time at the age of *seventeen months*. But the Dauphin was no genius, later proving himself to be certainly no more intelligent than any average member of the aristocracy. And playing the violin wasn't all he did: The record of the child life of the Dauphin, born in 1601 —of only average intelligence—tells us that we underestimate the capabilities of children. We find that at the same age that he played the violin, he also played mall, the equivalent of golf for adults of that period, as well as tennis; he talked; he played games of military strategy. At three and four respectively, he learned to read and write. At four and five, though still playing with dolls (!), he practiced archery, played cards and chess (at six) with adults, and played many other adult games. At all times, just as soon as he was able to walk, he mixed as an equal with adults in all their activities (such as they were), professionally dancing, acting, and taking part in all amusements. At the age of seven the Dauphin began to wear adult male clothes, his dolls were taken away, and his education under male tutors began; he began hunting, riding, shooting, and gambling. But Ariès says:

We should beware of exaggerating [the importance of this age of seven]. For all that he had stopped playing, or should have stopped playing, with his dolls, the Dauphin went on leading the same life as before. . . . Rather more dolls and German toys before seven, and more hunting, riding, fencing, and possibly playgoing after seven; the change was almost imperceptible in that long succession of pastimes which the child shared with the adult.

What seems most clear to me from this description is this: that before the advent of the nuclear family and modern schooling, childhood was as little as possible distinct from adult life. The child learned directly from the adults around him, emerging as soon as he was able into adult society. At about the age of seven there was some sex-role differentiation—it had to happen sometime, given the patriarchy in operation, but this was not yet complicated by the lower-class position of children. The distinction as yet was only between men and women, not yet between children and adults. In another century, this had begun to change, as the oppression of women and children increasingly intertwined.

In summary, with the onset of the childcentered nuclear family, an institution became necessary to structure a "childhood" that would keep children under the jurisdiction of parents as long as possible. Schools multiplied, replacing scholarship and a practical apprenticeship with a theoretical education, the function of which was to "discipline" children rather than to impart learning for its own sake. Thus it is no surprise that *modern schooling retards development rather than escalating it.* By sequestering children away from the adult world—adults are, after all, simply larger children with worldly experience—and by artificially subjecting them to an adult/child ratio of one to twenty-plus, how could the final effect be other than a leveling of the group to a median (mediocre) intelligence? If this weren't enough, after the eighteenth century a rigid separation and distinction of ages took place ("grades"). Children were no longer able to learn even from older and wiser children. They were restricted in most of their waking hours to a chronological finely-drawn[7] peer group, and then spoon-fed a "curriculum." Such a rigid gradation increased the levels necessary for the initiation into adulthood and made it hard for a child to direct his own pace. His learning motivation became outer-directed and approval-conscious, a sure killer of originality. Children, once seen simply as younger people—the way we now see a half-grown puppy in terms of its future maturity—were now a clear-cut class with its own internal rankings, encouraging competiton: the "biggest guy on the block," the "brainiest guy in school," etc. Children were forced to think in hierarchical terms, all measured by the supreme "When I grow up. . . ." In this the growth of the school reflected the outside world which was becoming increasingly segregated according to age and class.

In conclusion: The development of the modern family meant the breakdown of a large, integrated society into small, self-centered units. The child within these conjugal units now became important; for he was the product of that unit, the reason for its maintenance. It became desirable to keep one's children at home for as long as possible to bind them psychologically, financially, and emotionally to the family unit until such time as they were ready to create a new family unit. For this purpose the Age of Childhood was created. (Later, extensions were added, such as adolescence, or in twentieth-century American terms, "teenagerdom," "collegiate youth," "young adulthood.") The concept of childhood dictated that children were a species different not just in age, but in kind, from adults. An ideology was developed to prove this, fancy tractates written about the innocence of children and their closeness to God ("little angels"), with a resulting belief that children were asexual, child sex play an aberration—all in strong contrast to the period preceding it, when children were exposed to the facts of life

7. This is carried to extremes in contemporary public schools where perfectly ready children are turned away for a whole year because their birthdays fall a few days short of an arbitrary date [Firestone's note].

from the beginning.[8] For any admission of child sexuality would have accelerated the transition into adulthood, and this now had to be retarded at all cost: The development of special costumes soon exaggerated the physical differences distinguishing children from adults or even from older children; children no longer played the same games as adults, nor did they share in their festivities (children today do not normally attend fancy dinner parties) but were given special games and artifacts of their own (toys); storytelling, once a community art, was relegated to children, leading to in our own time a special child literature; children were spoken to in a special language by adults and serious conversation was never indulged in in their presence ("Not in front of the children"); the "manners" of subjection were instituted in the home ("Children should be seen and not heard."). But none of this would have worked to effectively make of children an oppressed class if a special institution hadn't been created to do the job thoroughly: the modern school.

The ideology of school was the ideology of childhood. It operated on the assumption that children needed "discipline," that they were special creatures who had to be handled in a special way (child psych., child ed., etc.) and that to facilitate this they should be corralled in a special place with their own kind, and with an age group as restricted to their own as possible. The school was the institution that structured childhood by effectively segregating children from the rest of society, thus retarding their growth into adulthood and their development of specialized skills for which the society had use. As a result they remained economically dependent for longer and longer periods of time; thus family ties remained unbroken.

I have pointed out that there is a strong relationship between the hierarchies of the family and economic class. Engels[9] has observed that within the family the husband is the bourgeois and the wife and children are the proletariat. Similarities between children and all working-class or other oppressed groups have been noted, studies done to show that they share the same psychology. We have seen how the development of the proletarian costume paralleled that of children's costume, how games abandoned by upper-class adults were played by both children and "yokels"; both were said to like to "work with their hands" as opposed to the higher cerebrations of the adult male, abstractions beyond them; both were considered happy, carefree, and good-natured, "more in touch with reality"; both were reminded that they were lucky to be spared the worries of responsible adulthood—and both wanted it anyway. Relations

8. See Ariès, op.cit., Chapter V. "From Immodesty to Innocence," for a detailed description of this exposure, based on the sexual experiences of the Dauphin as recorded in the Heroard Journal [Firestone's note].

9. The reference is to Friedrich Engels, collaborator of Karl Marx in the formation of the theory of communism.

with the ruling class were tinged in both cases by fear, suspicion, and dishonesty, disguised under a thin coating of charm (the adorable lisp, the eyeroll and the shuffle).

The myth of childhood has an even greater parallel in the myth of femininity. Both women and children were considered asexual and thus "purer" than man. Their inferior status was ill-concealed under an elaborate "respect." One didn't discuss serious matters nor did one curse in front of women and children; one didn't *openly* degrade them, one did it behind their backs. (As for the double standard about cursing: A man is allowed to blaspheme the world because it belongs to him to damn—but the same curse out of the mouth of a woman or a minor, i.e., an incomplete "man" to whom the world does not yet belong, is considered presumptuous, and thus an impropriety or worse.) Both were set apart by fancy and nonfunctional clothing and were given special tasks (housework and homework respectively); both were considered mentally deficient ("What can you expect from a woman?" "He's too little to understand."). The pedestal of adoration on which both were set made it hard for them to breathe. Every interaction with the adult world became for children a tap dance. They learned how to use their childhood to get what they wanted indirectly ("He's throwing another tantrum!"), just as women learned how to use their femininity ("There she goes, crying again!"). All excursions into the adult world became terrifying survival expeditions. The difference between the natural behavior of children in their peer group as opposed to their stilted and/or coy behavior with adults bears this out—just as women act differently among themselves than when they are around men. In each case a physical difference had been enlarged culturally with the help of special dress, education, manners, and activity until this cultural reinforcement itself began to appear "natural," even instinctive, an exaggeration process that enables easy stereotyping: the individual eventually appears to be a different kind of human animal with its own peculiar set of laws and behavior ("I'll never understand women!" . . . "You don't know a thing about child psychology!").

Contemporay slang reflects this animal state: children are "mice," "rabbits," "kittens," women are called "chicks," (in England) "birds," "hens," "dumb clucks," "silly geese," "old mares," "bitches." Similar terminology is used about males as a defamation of character, or more broadly only about *oppressed* males: stud, wolf, cat, stag, jack—and then it is used much more rarely, and often with a specifically sexual connotation.

Because the class oppression of women and children is couched in the phraseology of "cute" it is much harder to fight than open oppression. What child can answer back when some inane aunt falls all over him or some stranger decides to pat his behind and gurgle baby talk? What woman can afford to frown when a passing stranger violates her privacy at will? If she responds to his, "Baby you're looking good today!" with "No better than when I didn't know you," he will grumble, "What's eating that bitch?" Or worse. Very often the real nature of these seemingly friendly remarks emerges when the child or the woman does not smile as she should: "Dirty old scum bag. I wouldn't screw you even if you *had* a smile on your puss!" . . . "Nasty little brat. If I were your father I would spank you so hard you wouldn't know what hit you!" . . . Their violence is amazing. Yet these men feel that the woman or the child is to blame for not being "friendly." Because it makes them uncomfortable to know that the woman or the child or the black or the workman is grumbling, the oppressed groups must also appear to *like* their oppression—smiling and simpering though they may feel like hell inside. The smile is the child/woman equivalent of the shuffle; it indicates acquiescence of the victim to his own oppression.

In my own case, I had to train myself out of that phony smile, which is like a nervous tic on every teenage girl. And this meant that I smiled rarely, for in truth, when it came down to real smiling, I had less to smile about. My "dream" action for the women's liberation movement: *a smile boycott*, at which declaration all women would instantly abandon their "pleasing" smiles, henceforth smiling only when something pleased *them*. Likewise children's liberation would demand an end to all fondling not dictated by the child itself. (This of course would predicate a society in which fondling in general was no longer frowned upon; often the only demonstration of affection a child now receives is of this phony kind, which he may still consider better than nothing.) Many men can't understand that their easy intimacies come as no privilege. Do they ever consider that the real person inside that baby or female animal may not choose to be fondled then, or by them, or even noticed? Imagine this man's own consternation were some stranger to approach him on the street in a similar manner—patting, gurgling, muttering baby talk—without respect for his profession or his "manhood."

In sum, if members of the working class and minority groups "act like children," it is because children of every class *are* lower-class, just as women have always been. The rise of the modern nuclear family,[1] with its adjunct "childhood," tightened the noose around the already economically dependent group by extending and reinforcing what had been only a brief dependence, by the usual means: the development of a special ideology, of a special indigenous life style, language, dress, mannerisms, etc. And with the increase and exaggeration of children's dependence, woman's bond-

1. Firestone has previously contrasted the modern "nuclear" family and its emphasis on "the conjugal unit," with the medieval family and its emphasis on "one's legal hereditary line."

age to motherhood was also extended to its limits. Women and children were now in the same lousy boat. Their oppressions began to reinforce one another. To the mystique of the glories of child-birth, the grandeur of "natural" female creativity, was now added a new mystique about the glories of childhood itself and the "creativity" of child*rearing*. ("Why, my dear, what could be more creative than raising a child?") By now people have forgotten what history has proven: that "raising" a child is tantamount to retarding his development. The best way to raise a child is to LAY OFF.

QUESTIONS

1. What is the thesis of Firestone's argument? Where in the argument does this become clear?
2. What evidence does Firestone provide for the proposition that there was no childhood in the Middle Ages? What is the function of the historical discussion?
3. What would Firestone think of little-league football where ten-year-olds play their games in full uniforms with complex formations and other features of big-time football?
4. Cite some current examples of child oppression in addition to those Firestone enumerates. What would she advocate as a remedy?

CLARENCE DARROW

Address to the Prisoners in the Cook County Jail[1]

If I looked at jails and crimes and prisoners in the way the ordinary person does, I should not speak on this subject to you. The reason I talk to you on the question of crime, its cause and cure, is that I really do not in the least believe in crime. There is no such thing as a crime as the word is generally understood. I do not believe there is any sort of distinction between the real moral conditions of the people in and out of jail. One is just as good as the other. The people here can no more help being here than the people outside can avoid being outside. I do not believe that people are in jail because they deserve to be. They are in jail simply because they cannot avoid it on account of circumstances which are entirely beyond their control and for which they are in no way responsible.

1. The warden of the Cook County Jail in Chicago, who knew Darrow as a criminologist, lawyer, and writer, invited him to speak before the inmates of the jail in 1902. Darrow's friends felt that the talk was inappropriate for its audience, but Darrow defended himself in the introduction to the lecture, which he had printed in pamphlet form: "Realizing the force of the suggestion that the truth should not be spoken to all people, I have caused these remarks to be printed on rather good paper and in a somewhat expensive form. In this way the truth does not become cheap and vulgar, and is only placed before those whose intelligence and affluence will prevent their being influenced by it." The pamphlet sold for five cents.

I suppose a great many people on the outside would say I was doing you harm if they should hear what I say to you this afternoon, but you cannot be hurt a great deal anyway, so it will not matter. Good people outside would say that I was really teaching you things that were calculated to injure society, but it's worth while now and then to hear something different from what you ordinarily get from preachers and the like. These will tell you that you should be good and then you will get rich and be happy. Of course we know that people do not get rich by being good, and that is the reason why so many of you people try to get rich some other way, only you do not understand how to do it quite as well as the fellow outside.

There are people who think that everything in this world is an accident. But really there is no such thing as an accident. A great many folks admit that many of the people in jail ought to be there, and many who are outside ought to be in. I think none of them ought to be here. There ought to be no jails; and if it were not for the fact that the people on the outside are so grasping and heartless in their dealings with the people on the inside, there would be no such institution as jails.

I do not want you to believe that I think all you people here are angels. I do not think that. You are people of all kinds, all of you doing the best you can—and that is evidently not very well. You are people of all kinds and conditions and under all circumstances. In one sense everybody is equally good and equally bad. We all do the best we can under the circumstances. But as to the exact things for which you are sent here, some of you are guilty and did the particular act because you needed the money. Some of you did it because you are in the habit of doing it, and some of you because you are born to it, and it comes to be as natural as it does, for instance, for me to be good.

Most of you probably have nothing against me, and most of you would treat me the same way as any other person would, probably better than some of the people on the outside would treat me, because you think I believe in you and they know I do not believe in them. While you would not have the least thing against me in the world, you might pick my pockets. I do not think all of you would, but I think some of you would. You would not have anything against me, but that's your profession, a few of you. Some of the rest of you, if my doors were unlocked, might come in if you saw anything you wanted—not out of any malice to me, but because that is your trade. There is no doubt there are quite a number of people in this jail who would pick my pockets. And still I know this—that when I get outside pretty nearly everybody picks my pocket. There may be some of you who would hold up a man on the street, if you did not happen to have something else to do, and needed the money; but when I want to light my house or my office the gas company holds me up. They charge me one dollar for something that is worth twenty-five cents. Still all these people are good people; they are pillars of society and support the churches, and they are respectable.

When I ride on the streetcars I am held up—I pay five cents for a ride that is worth two and a half cents, simply because a body of men have bribed the city council and the legislature, so that all the rest of us have to pay tribute to them.

If I do not want to fall into the clutches of the gas trust and choose to burn oil instead of gas, then good Mr. Rockefeller holds me up, and he uses a certain portion of his money to build universities and support churches which are engaged in telling us how to be good.

Some of you are here for obtaining property under false pretenses—yet I pick up a great Sunday paper and read the advertisements of a merchant prince—"Shirtwaists for 39 cents, marked down from $3.00."

When I read the advertisements in the paper I see they are all lies. When I want to get out and find a place to stand anywhere on the face of the earth, I find that it has all been taken up long ago before I came here, and before you came here, and somebody says, "Get off, swim into the lake, fly into the air; go anywhere, but get off." That is because these people have the police and they have the jails and the judges and the lawyers and the soldiers and all the rest of them to take care of the earth and drive everybody off that comes in their way.

A great many people will tell you that all this is true, but that it does not excuse you. These facts do not excuse some fellow who reaches into my pocket and takes out a five-dollar bill. The fact that the gas company bribes the members of the legislature from year to year, and fixes the law, so that all you people are compelled to be "fleeced" whenever you deal with them; the fact that the streetcar companies and the gas companies have control of the streets; and the fact that the landlords own all the earth—this, they say, has nothing to do with you.

Let us see whether there is any connection between the crimes of the respectable classes and your presence in the jail. Many of you people are in jail because you have really committed burglary; many of you, because you have stolen something. In the meaning of the law, you have taken some other person's property. Some of you have entered a store and carried off a pair of shoes because you did not have the price. Possibly some of you have committed murder. I cannot tell what all of you did. There are a great many people here who have done some of these things who really do not know themselves why they did them. I think I know why you did them—every one of you; you did these things because you were bound to do them. It looked to you at the time as if you had a chance to do them or not, as you saw fit; but still, after all, you had no choice. There may be people here who had some money in their pockets and who still went out and got some more money in a way society forbids. Now, you may not yourselves see exactly why it was you did this thing, but if you look at the question deeply enough and carefully enough you will see that there were circumstances that drove you to do exactly the thing which you did. You could not help it any more than we outside can help taking the positions that we take. The reformers who tell you to be good and you will be happy, and the people on the outside who have property to protect—they think that the only way to do it is by building jails and locking you up in cells on weekdays and praying for you Sundays.

I think that all of this has nothing whatever to do with right conduct. I think it is very easily seen what has to do with right conduct. Some so-called criminals—and I will use this word because it is handy, it means nothing to me—I speak of the criminals who get caught as distinguished from the criminals who catch them—some of these so-called criminals are in jail for their first offenses, but nine tenths of you are in jail because you did not have a good lawyer and, of course, you did not have a good lawyer because you did not have enough money to pay a good lawyer. There is no very great danger of a rich man going to jail.

Some of you may be here for the first time. If we would open the doors and let you out, and leave the laws as they are today, some of you would be back tomorrow. This is about as good a place as you can get anyway. There are many people here who are so in the habit of coming that they would not know where else to go. There are people who are born with the tendency to break into jail every chance they get, and they cannot avoid it. You cannot figure out your life and see why it was, but still there is a reason for it; and if we were all wise and knew all the facts, we could figure it out.

In the first place, there are a good many more people who go to jail in the wintertime than in summer. Why is this? Is it because people are more wicked in winter? No, it is because the coal trust begins to get in its grip in the winter. A few gentlemen take possession of the coal, and unless the people will pay seven or eight dollars a ton for something that is worth three dollars, they will have to freeze. Then there is nothing to do but to break into jail, and so there are many more in jail in the winter than in summer. It costs more for gas in the winter because the nights are longer, and people go to jail to save gas bills. The jails are electric-lighted. You may not know it, but these economic laws are working all the time, whether we know it or do not know it.

There are more people who go to jail in hard times than in good times—few people, comparatively, go to jail except when they are hard up. They go to jail because they have no other place to go. They may not know why, but it is true all the same. People are not more wicked in hard times. That is not the reason. The fact is true all over the world that in hard times more people go to jail than in good times, and in winter more people go to jail than in summer. Of course it is pretty hard times for people who go to jail at any time. The people who go to jail are almost always poor people— people who have no other place to live, first and last. When times are hard, then you find large numbers of people who go to jail who would not otherwise be in jail.

Long ago, Mr. Buckle,[2] who was a great philosopher and historian, collected facts, and he showed that the number of people who are arrested increased just as the price of food increased. When they put up the price of gas ten cents a thousand, I do not know who will go to jail, but I do know that a certain number of people will go. When the meat combine raises the price of beef, I do not know who is going to jail, but I know that a large number of people are bound to go. Whenever the Standard Oil Company raises the price of oil, I know that a certain number of girls who are seamstresses, and who work night after night long hours for somebody else, will be compelled to go out on the streets and ply another trade, and I know that Mr. Rockefeller and his associates are responsible and not the poor girls in the jails.

First and last, people are sent to jail because they are poor. Sometimes, as I say, you may not need money at the particular time, but you wish to have thrifty forehanded habits, and do not always wait until you are in absolute want. Some of you people are perhaps plying the trade, the profession, which is called burglary. No man in his right senses will go into a strange house in the dead of night and prowl around with a dark lantern through unfamiliar rooms and take chances of his life, if he has plenty of the good things of the world in his own home. You would not take any such chances as that. If a man had clothes in his clothes-press and beefsteak in his pantry and money in the bank, he would not navigate around nights in houses where he knows nothing about the premises whatever. It always requires experience and education for this profession, and people who fit themselves for it are no more to blame than I am for being a lawyer. A man would not hold up another man on the street if he had plenty of money in his own pocket. He might do it if he had one dollar or two dollars, but he wouldn't if he had as much money as Mr. Rockefeller has. Mr. Rockefeller has a great deal better hold-up game than that.

The more that is taken from the poor by the rich, who have the chance to take it, the more poor people there are who are com-

2. Henry Thomas Buckle (1821-1862), British historian and author of a *History of Civilization*, who was attacked during his lifetime by conservatives for his "radical" views of history.

pelled to resort to these means for a livelihood. They may not understand it, they may not think so at once, but after all they are driven into that line of employment.

There is a bill before the legislature of this state to punish kidnaping children with death. We have wise members of the legislature. They know the gas trust when they see it and they always see it—they can furnish light enough to be seen; and this legislature thinks it is going to stop kidnaping children by making a law punishing kidnapers of children with death. I don't believe in kidnaping children, but the legislature is all wrong. Kidnaping children is not a crime, it is a profession. It has been developed with the times. It has been developed with our modern industrial conditions. There are many ways of making money—many new ways that our ancestors knew nothing about. Our ancestors knew nothing about a billion-dollar trust; and here comes some poor fellow who has no other trade and he discovers the profession of kidnaping children.

This crime is born, not because people are bad; people don't kidnap other people's children because they want the children or because they are devilish, but because they see a chance to get some money out of it. You cannot cure this crime by passing a law punishing by death kidnapers of children. There is one way to cure it. There is one way to cure all these offenses, and that is to give the people a chance to live. There is no other way, and there never was any other way since the world began; and the world is so blind and stupid that it will not see. If every man and woman and child in the world had a chance to make a decent, fair, honest living, there would be no jails and no lawyers and no courts. There might be some persons here or there with some peculiar formation of their brain, like Rockefeller, who would do these things simply to be doing them; but they would be very, very few, and those should be sent to a hospital and treated, and not sent to jail; and they would entirely disappear in the second generation, or at least in the third generation.

I am not talking pure theory. I will just give you two or three illustrations.

The English people once punished criminals by sending them away. They would load them on a ship and export them to Australia. England was owned by lords and nobles and rich people. They owned the whole earth over there, and the other people had to stay in the streets. They could not get a decent living. They used to take their criminals and send them to Australia—I mean the class of criminals who got caught. When these criminals got over there, and nobody else had come, they had the whole continent to run over, and so they could raise sheep and furnish their own meat, which is easier than stealing it. These criminals then became decent, respectable people because they had a chance to live. They did not commit any crimes. They were just like the English people who sent them there, only better. And in the second generation the descendants of those criminals were as good and respectable a class of people as there were on the face of the earth, and then they began building churches and jails themselves.

A portion of this country was settled in the same way, landing prisoners down on the southern coast; but when they got here and had a whole continent to run over and plenty of chances to make a living, they became respectable citizens, making their own living just like any other citizen in the world. But finally the descendants of the English aristocracy who sent the people over to Australia found out they were getting rich, and so they went over to get possession of the earth as they always do, and they organized land syndicates and got control of the land and ores, and then they had just as many criminals in Australia as they did in England. It was not because the world had grown bad; it was because the earth had been taken away from the people.

Some of you people have lived in the country. It's prettier than it is here. And if you have ever lived on a farm you understand that if you put a lot of cattle in a field, when the pasture is short they will jump over the fence; but put them in a good field where there is plenty of pasture, and they will be law-abiding cattle to the end of time. The human animal is just like the rest of the animals, only a little more so. The same thing that governs in the one governs in the other.

Everybody makes his living along the lines of least resistance. A wise man who comes into a country early sees a great undeveloped land. For instance, our rich men twenty-five years ago saw that Chicago was small and knew a lot of people would come here and settle, and they readily saw that if they had all the land around here it would be worth a good deal, so they grabbed the land. You cannot be a landlord because somebody has got it all. You must find some other calling. In England and Ireland and Scotland less than five per cent own all the land there is, and the people are bound to stay there on any kind of terms the landlords give. They must live the best they can, so they develop all these various professions—burglary, picking pockets, and the like.

Again, people find all sorts of ways of getting rich. These are diseases like everything else. You look at people getting rich, organizing trusts and making a million dollars, and somebody gets the disease and he starts out. He catches it just as a man catches the mumps or the measles; he is not to blame, it is in the air. You will find men speculating beyond their means, because the mania of money-getting is taking possession of them. It is simply a disease—nothing more, nothing less. You cannot avoid catching it; but the fellows who have control of the earth have the advantage of you. See what the law is: when these men get control of things, they make the laws. They do not make the laws to protect anybody; courts are not instruments of justice. When your case gets into court it will make little difference whether you are guilty or innocent, but it's better if you have a smart lawyer. And you cannot have a smart lawyer unless you have money. First and last it's a question of money. Those men who own the earth make the laws to protect what they have. They fix up a sort of fence or pen around what they have, and they fix the law so the fellow on the outside cannot get in. The laws are really organized for the protection of the men who rule the world. They were never organized or enforced to do justice. We have no system for doing justice, not the slightest in the world.

Let me illustrate: Take the poorest person in this room. If the community had provided a system of doing justice, the poorest person in this room would have as good a lawyer as the richest, would he not? When you went into court you would have just as long a trial and just as fair a trial as the richest person in Chicago. Your case would not be tried in fifteen or twenty minutes, whereas it would take fifteen days to get through with a rich man's case.

Then if you were rich and were beaten, your case would be taken to the Appellate Court. A poor man cannot take his case to the Appellate Court; he has not the price. And then to the Supreme Court. And if he were beaten there he might perhaps go to the United States Supreme Court. And he might die of old age before he got into jail. If you are poor, it's a quick job. You are almost known to be guilty, else you would not be there. Why should anyone be in the criminal court if he were not guilty? He would not be there if he could be anywhere else. The officials have no time to look after all these cases. The people who are on the outside, who are running banks and building churches and making jails, they have no time to examine 600 or 700 prisoners each year to see whether they are guilty or innocent. If the courts were organized to promote justice the people would elect somebody to defend all these criminals, somebody as smart as the prosecutor—and give him as many detectives and as many assistants to help, and pay as much money to defend you as to prosecute you. We have a very able man for state's attorney, and he has many assistants, detectives, and policemen without end, and judges to hear the cases—everything handy.

Most all of our criminal code consists in offenses against property. People are sent to jail because they have committed a crime against property. It is of very little consequence whether one hundred people more or less go to jail who ought not to go—you must protect property, because in this world property is of more importance than anything else.

How is it done? These people who have property fix it so they can protect what they have. When somebody commits a crime it does not follow that he has done something that is morally wrong. The man on the outside who has committed no crime may have done something. For instance: to take all the coal in the United States and raise the price two dollars or three dollars when there is no need of it, and thus kill thousands of babies and send thousands of people to the poorhouse and tens of thousands to jail, as is done every year in the United States—this is a greater crime than all the people in our jails ever committed; but the law does not punish it. Why? Because the fellows who control the earth make the laws. If you and I had the making of the laws, the first thing we would do would be to punish the fellow who gets control of the earth. Nature put this coal in the ground for me as well as for them and nature made the prairies up here to raise wheat for me as well as for them, and then the great railroad companies came along and fenced it up.

Most all of the crimes for which we are punished are property crimes. There are a few personal crimes, like murder—but they are very few. The crimes committed are mostly those against property. If this punishment is right the criminals must have a lot of property. How much money is there is this crowd? And yet you are all here for crimes against property. The people up and down the Lake Shore[3] have not committed crime; still they have so much property they don't know what to do with it. It is perfectly plain why these people have not committed crimes against property; they make the laws and therefore do not need to break them. And in order for you to get some property you are obliged to break the rules of the game. I don't know but what some of you may have had a very nice chance to get rich by carrying a hod for one dollar a day, twelve hours. Instead of taking that nice, easy profession, you are a burglar. If you had been given a chance to be a banker you would rather follow that. Some of you may have had a chance to work as a switchman on a railroad where you know, according to statistics, that you cannot live and keep all your limbs more than seven years, and you can get fifty dollars or seventy-five dollars a month for taking your lives in your hands; and instead of taking that lucrative position you chose to be a sneak thief, or something like that. Some of you made that sort of choice. I don't know which I would take if I was reduced to this choice. I have an easier choice.

I will guarantee to take from this jail, or any jail in the world, five hundred men who have been the worst criminals and lawbreakers who ever got into jail, and I will go down to our lowest streets and take five hundred of the most abandoned prostitutes, and go out somewhere where there is plenty of land, and will give them a

---

3. The fashionable and expensive section of Chicago along Lake Michigan.

chance to make a living, and they will be as good people as the average in the community.

There is a remedy for the sort of condition we see here. The world never finds it out, or when it does find it out it does not enforce it. You may pass a law punishing every person with death for burglary, and it will make no difference. Men will commit it just the same. In England there was a time when one hundred different offenses were punishable with death, and it made no difference. The English people strangely found out that so fast as they repealed the severe penalties and so fast as they did away with punishing men by death, crime decreased instead of increased; that the smaller the penalty the fewer the crimes.

Hanging men in our county jails does not prevent murder. It makes murderers.

And this has been the history of the world. It's easy to see how to do away with what we call crime. It is not so easy to do it. I will tell you how to do it. It can be done by giving the people a chance to live—by destroying special privileges. So long as big criminals can get the coal fields, so long as the big criminals have control of the city council and get the public streets for streetcars and gas rights—this is bound to send thousands of poor people to jail. So long as men are allowed to monopolize all the earth, and compel others to live on such terms as these men see fit to make, then you are bound to get into jail.

The only way in the world to abolish crime and criminals is to abolish the big ones and the little ones together. Make fair conditions of life. Give men a chance to live. Abolish the right of private ownership of land, abolish monopoly, make the world partners in production, partners in the good things of life. Nobody would steal if he could get something of his own some easier way. Nobody will commit burglary when he has a house full. No girl will go out on the streets when she has a comfortable place at home. The man who owns a sweatshop or a department store may not be to blame himself for the condition of his girls, but when he pays them five dollars, three dollars, and two dollars a week, I wonder where he thinks they will get the rest of their money to live. The only way to cure these conditions is by equality. There should be no jails. They do not accomplish what they pretend to accomplish. If you would wipe them out there would be no more criminals than now. They terrorize nobody. They are a blot upon any civilization, and a jail is an evidence of the lack of charity of the people on the outside who make the jails and fill them with the victims of their greed.

QUESTIONS

1. What is Darrow's central thesis? What relationship does he see between the nature of a government or a society and the action of the individual?
2. One of the prisoners that Darrow addressed is said to have commented that the speech was "too radical." What might Darrow say this shows about his audience and their society?
3. Remembering that Darrow is a lawyer writing in 1902 and Martin Luther King, Jr. ("Letter from Birmingham Jail," pp. 809–823) a minister writing in 1963,
   a. compare the two pieces with respect to the writers, the occasions, and the audiences; and
   b. discuss whether segregation represents for King the things that property does for Darrow. (How far do their ideas on justice, minorities, and laws coincide? What possibilities for action by the individual does each see?)

NICCOLÒ MACHIAVELLI

The Morals of the Prince[1]

On Things for Which Men, and Particularly Princes, Are Praised or Blamed

We now have left to consider what should be the manners and attitudes of a prince toward his subjects and his friends. As I know that many have written on this subject I feel that I may be held presumptuous in what I have to say, if in my comments I do not follow the lines laid down by others. Since, however, it has been my intention to write something which may be of use to the understanding reader, it has seemed wiser to me to follow the real truth of the matter rather than what we imagine it to be. For imagination has created many principalities and republics that have never been seen or known to have any real existence, for how we live is so

1. Chapters 15-18 of *The Prince*.

different from how we ought to live that he who studies what ought to be done rather than what is done will learn the way to his downfall rather than to his preservation. A man striving in every way to be good will meet his ruin among the great number who are not good. Hence it is necessary for a prince, if he wishes to remain in power, to learn how not to be good and to use his knowledge or refrain from using it as he may need.

Putting aside then the things imagined as pertaining to a prince and considering those that really do, I will say that all men, and particularly princes because of their prominence, when comment is made of them, are noted as having some characteristics deserving either praise or blame. One is accounted liberal, another stingy, to use a Tuscan term for in our speech avaricious *(avaro)* is applied to such as are desirous of acquiring by rapine whereas stingy *(misero)* is the term used for those who are reluctant to part with their own—one is considered bountiful, another rapacious; one cruel, another tender-hearted; one false to his word, another trustworthy; one effeminate and pusillanimous, another wild and spirited; one humane, another haughty; one lascivious, another chaste; one a man of integrity and another sly; one tough and another pliant; one serious and another frivolous; one religious and another skeptical, and so on. Everyone will agree, I know, that it would be a most praiseworthy thing if all the qualities accounted as good in the above enumeration were found in a Prince. But since they cannot be so possessed nor observed because of human conditions which do not allow of it, what is necessary for the prince is to be prudent enough to escape the infamy of such vices as would result in the loss of his state; as for the others which would not have that effect, he must guard himself from them as far as possible but if he cannot, he may overlook them as being of less importance. Further, he should have no concern about incurring the infamy of such vices without which the preservation of his state would be difficult. For, if the matter be well considered, it will be seen that some habits which appear virtuous, if adopted would signify ruin, and others that seem vices lead to security and the well-being of a prince.

Generosity and Meanness

To begin then with the first characteristic set forth above, I will say that it would be well always to be considered generous, yet generosity used in such a way as not to bring you honor does you harm, for if it is practiced virtuously and as it is meant to be practiced it will not be publicly known and you will not lose the name of being just the opposite of generous. Hence to preserve the reputation of being generous among your friends you must not neglect any kind of lavish display, yet a prince of this sort will consume all his property in such gestures and, if he wishes to preserve his reputation for generosity, he will be forced to levy heavy taxes on his subjects and turn to fiscal measures and do everything possible to get money. Thus he will begin to be regarded with hatred by his subjects and should he become poor he will be held in scant esteem; having by his prodigality given offense to many and rewarded only a few, he will suffer at the first hint of adversity, and the first danger will be critical for him. Yet when he realizes this and tries to reform he will immediately get the name of being a miser. So a prince, as he is unable to adopt the virtue of generosity without danger to himself, must, if he is a wise man, accept with indifference the name of miser. For with the passage of time he will be regarded as increasingly generous when it is seen that, by virtue of his parsimony, his income suffices for him to defend himself in wartime and undertake his enterprises without heavily taxing his people. For in that way he practices generosity towards all from whom he refrains from taking money, who are many, and stinginess only toward those from whom he withholds gifts, who are few.

In our times we have seen great things accomplished only by such as have had the name of misers; all others have come to naught. Pope Julius made use of his reputation for generosity to make himself Pope but later, in order to carry on his war against the King of France, he made no effort to maintain it; and he has waged a great number of wars without having had recourse to heavy taxation because his persistent parsimony has made up for the extra expenses. The present King of Spain, had he had any reputation for generosity, would never have carried through to victory so many enterprises.

A prince then, if he wishes not to rob his subjects but to be able to defend himself and not to become poor and despised nor to be obliged to become rapacious, must consider it a matter of small importance to incur the name of miser, for this is one of the vices which keep him on his throne. Some may say Caesar through generosity won his way to the purple, and others either through being generous or being accounted so have risen to the highest ranks. But I will answer by pointing out that either you are already a prince or you are on the way to becoming one and in the first case generosity is harmful while in the second it is very necessary to be considered open-handed. Caesar was seeking to arrive at the domination of Rome but if he had survived after reaching his goal and had not moderated his lavishness he would certainly have destroyed the empire.

It might also be objected that there have been many princes, accomplishing great things with their armies, who have been acclaimed for their generosity. To which I would answer that the prince either spends his own (or his subjects') money or that of others; in the first case he must be very sparing but in the second he should overlook no aspect of open-handedness. So the prince who leads his armies and lives on looting and extortion and booty, thus handling the wealth of others, must indeed have this quality of generosity for otherwise his soldiers will not follow him. You can be very free with wealth not belonging to yourself or your subjects, in the fashion of Cyrus, Caesar, or Alexander, for spending what belongs to others rather enhances your reputation than detracts from it; it is only spending your own wealth that is dangerous. There is nothing that consumes itself as does prodigality; even as you practice it you lose the faculty of practicing it and either you become poor and despicable or, in order to escape poverty, rapacious and unpopular. And among the things a prince must guard against is precisely the danger of becoming an object either of contempt or of hatred. Generosity leads you to both these evils, wherefore it is wiser to accept the name of miserly, since the reproach it brings is without hatred, than to seek a reputation for generosity and thus perforce acquire the name of rapacious, which breeds hatred as well as infamy.

Cruelty and Clemency and Whether It Is Better to Be Loved or Feared

Now to continue with the list of characteristics. It should be the desire of every prince to be considered merciful and not cruel, yet he should take care not to make poor use of his clemency. Cesare Borgia was regarded as cruel, yet his cruelty reorganized Romagna and united it in peace and loyalty. Indeed, if we reflect, we shall see that this man was more merciful than the Florentines who, to avoid the charge of cruelty, allowed Pistoia to be destroyed.[2] A prince should care nothing for the accusation of cruelty so long as he keeps his subjects united and loyal; by making a very few examples he can be more truly merciful than those who through too much tender-heartedness allow disorders to arise whence come killings and rapine. For these offend an entire community, while the few executions ordered by the prince affect only a few individuals. For a new prince above all it is impossible not to earn a reputation for cruelty since new states are full of dangers. Virgil indeed has Dido apologize for the inhumanity of her rule because it is new, in the words:

> *Res dura et regni novitas me talia cogunt*
> *Moliri et late fines custode tueri.*[3]

Nevertheless a prince should not be too ready to listen to tale-

2. By unchecked rioting between opposing factions (1502).
3. ". . . my cruel fate / And doubts attending an unsettled state / Force me to guard my coast from foreign foes" — DRYDEN.

bearers nor to act on suspicion, nor should he allow himself to be easily frightened. He should proceed with a mixture of prudence and humanity in such a way as not to be made incautious by over-confidence nor yet intolerable by excessive mistrust.

Here the question arises; whether it is better to be loved than feared or feared than loved. The answer is that it would be desirable to be both but, since that is difficult, it is much safer to be feared than to be loved, if one must choose. For on men in general this observation may be made: they are ungrateful, fickle, and deceitful, eager to avoid dangers, and avid for gain, and while you are useful to them they are all with you, offering you their blood, their property, their lives, and their sons so long as danger is remote, as we noted above, but when it approaches they turn on you. Any prince, trust-ing only in their words and having no other preparations made, will fall to his ruin, for friendships that are bought at a price and not by greatness and nobility of soul are paid for indeed, but they are not owned and cannot be called upon in time of need. Men have less hesitation in offending a man who is loved than one who is feared, for love is held by a bond of obligation which, as men are wicked, is broken whenever personal advantage suggests it, but fear is accompanied by the dread of punishment which never relaxes.

Yet a prince should make himself feared in such a way that, if he does not thereby merit love, at least he may escape odium, for being feared and not hated may well go together. And indeed the prince may attain this end if he but respect the property and the women of his subjects and citizens. And if it should become neces-sary to seek the death of someone, he should find a proper justification and a public cause, and above all he should keep his hands off another's property, for men forget more readily the death of their father than the loss of their patrimony. Besides, pretexts for seizing property are never lacking, and when a prince begins to live by means of rapine he will always find some excuse for plundering others, and conversely pretexts for execution are rarer and are more quickly exhausted.

A prince at the head of his armies and with a vast number of soldiers under his command should give not the slightest heed if he is esteemed cruel, for without such a reputation he will not be able to keep his army united and ready for action. Among the marvelous things told of Hannibal is that, having a vast army under his command made up of all kinds and races of men and waging war far from his own country, he never allowed any dissension to arise either as between the troops and their leaders or among the troops themselves, and this both in times of good fortune and bad. This could only have come about through his most inhuman cruelty which, taken in conjunction with his great valor, kept him always an object of respect and terror in the eyes of his soldiers. And without the cruelty his other characteristics would not have achieved this effect. Thoughtless writers have admired his actions and at the same time deplored the cruelty which was the basis of them. As evidence of the truth of our statement that his other virtues would have been insufficient let us examine the case of Scipio, an extraordinary leader not only in his own day but for all recorded history. His army in Spain revolted and for no other reason than because of his kind-heartedness, which had allowed more license to his soldiery than military discipline properly permits. His policy was attacked in the Senate by Fabius Maximus, who called him a corrupter of the Roman arms. When the Locrians had been mishandled by one of his lieutenants, his easy-going nature prevented him from avenging them or disciplining his officer, and it was apropos of this incident that one of the senators remarked, wishing to find an excuse for him, that there were many men who knew better how to avoid error themselves than to correct it in others. This characteristic of Scipio would have clouded his fame and glory had he continued in authority, but as he lived under the government of the Senate, its harmful aspect was hidden and it reflected credit on him.

Hence, on the subject of being loved or feared I will conclude that since love depends on the subjects, but the prince has it in his own hands to create fear, a wise prince will rely on what is his own, remembering at the same time that he must avoid arousing hatred, as we have said.

In What Manner Princes Should Keep Their Word

How laudable it is for a prince to keep his word and govern his actions by integrity rather than trickery will be understood by all. Nonetheless we have in our times seen great things accomplished by many princes who have thought little of keeping their promises and have known the art of mystifying the minds of men. Such princes have won out over those whose actions were based on fidelity to their word.

It must be understood that there are two ways of fighting, one with laws and the other with arms. The first is the way of men, the second is the style of beasts, but since very often the first does not suffice it is necessary to turn to the second. Therefore a prince must know how to play the beast as well as the man. This lesson was taught allegorically by the ancient writers who related that Achilles and many other princes were brought up by Chiron the Centaur, who took them under his discipline. The clear significance of this half-man and half-beast preceptorship is that a prince must know how to use either of these two natures and that one without the other has no enduring strength. Now since the prince must make use of the characteristics of beasts he should choose those of the fox and the lion, though the lion cannot defend himself against snares and the fox is helpless against wolves. One must be a fox in avoiding traps and a lion in frightening wolves. Such as choose simply the rôle of a lion do not rightly understand the matter. Hence a wise leader cannot and should not keep his word when keeping it is not to his advantage or when the reasons that made him give it are no longer valid. If men were good, this would not be a good precept, but since they are wicked and will not keep faith with you, you are not bound to keep faith with them.

A prince has never lacked legitimate reasons to justify his breach of faith. We could give countless recent examples and show how any number of peace treaties or promises have been broken and rendered meaningless by the faithlessness of princes, and how success has fallen to the one who best knows how to counterfeit the fox. But it is necessary to know how to disguise this nature well and how to pretend and dissemble. Men are so simple and so ready to follow the needs of the moment that the deceiver will always find some one to deceive. Of recent examples I shall mention one. Alexander VI did nothing but deceive and never thought of anything else and always found some occasion for it. Never was there a man more convincing in his asseverations nor more willing to offer the most solemn oaths nor less likely to observe them. Yet his deceptions were always successful for he was an expert in this field.

So a prince need not have all the aforementioned good qualities, but it is most essential that he appear to have them. Indeed, I should go so far as to say that having them and always practising them is harmful, while seeming to have them is useful. It is good to appear clement, trustworthy, humane, religious, and honest, and also to be so, but always with the mind so disposed that, when the occasion arises not to be so, you can become the opposite. It must be understood that a prince and particularly a new prince cannot practise all the virtues for which men are accounted good, for the necessity of preserving the state often compels him to take actions which are opposed to loyalty, charity, humanity, and religion. Hence he must have a spirit ready to adapt itself as the varying winds of fortune command him. As I have said, so far as he is able, a prince should stick to the path of good but, if the necessity arises, he should know how to follow evil.

A prince must take great care that no word ever passes his lips that is not full of the above mentioned five good qualities, and he must seem to all who see and hear him a model of piety, loyalty, integrity, humanity, and religion. Nothing is more necessary than to seem to possess this last quality, for men in general judge more by the eye than the hand, as all can see but few can feel. Everyone sees what you seem to be, few experience what you really are and these few do not dare to set themselves up against the opinion of the majority supported by the majesty of the state. In the actions of all men and especially princes, where there is no court of appeal, the end is all that counts. Let a prince then concern himself with the acquisition or the maintenance of a state; the means employed will always be considered honorable and praised by all, for the mass of mankind is always swayed by appearances and by the outcome of an enterprise. And in the world there is only the mass, for the few find their place only when the majority has no base of support.

DESIDERIUS ERASMUS

The Arts of Peace[1]

Although the writers of antiquity divided the whole theory of state government into two sections, war and peace, the first and most important objective is the instruction of the prince in the matter of ruling wisely during times of peace, in which he should strive his utmost to preclude any future need for the science of war. In this matter it seems best that the prince should first know his own kingdom. This knowledge is best gained from a study of geography and history and from frequent visits through his provinces and cities. Let him first be eager to learn the location of his districts and cities, with their beginnings, their nature, institutions, customs, laws, annals, and privileges. No one can heal the body until he is thoroughly conversant with it. No one can properly till a field which he does not understand. To be sure, the tyrant takes great care in such matters, but it is the spirit, not the act, which singles out the good prince. The physician studies the functions of the body so as to be more adept in healing it; the poisoning assassin, to more surely end it! Next, the prince should love the land over which he rules just as a farmer loves the fields of his ancestors or as a good man feels affection toward his household. He should make it his especial interest to hand it over to his successor, whosoever he may be, better than he received it. If he has any children, devotion toward them should urge him on; if he has no family, he should be guided by devotion to his country; and he should always keep kindled the flame of love for his subjects. He should consider his kingdom as a great body of which he is the most outstanding member and remember that they who have entrusted all their fortunes and their very safety to the good faith of one man are deserving of consideration. He should keep constantly in mind the example of those rulers to whom the welfare of their people was dearer than their own lives; for it is obviously impossible for a prince to do violence to the state without injuring himself.

1. From *The Education of a Christian Prince.*

In the second place the prince will see to it that he is loved by his subjects in return, but in such a way that his authority is no less strong among them. There are some who are so stupid as to strive to win good will for themselves by incantations and magic rings, when there is no charm more efficacious than good character itself; nothing can be more lovable than that, for, as this is a real and immortal good, so it brings a man true and undying good will. The best formula is this: let him love, who would be loved, so that he may attach his subjects to him as God has won the peoples of the world to Himself by His goodness.

They are also wrong who win the hearts of the masses by largesses, feasts, and gross indulgence. It is true that some popular favor, instead of affection, is gained by these means, but it is neither genuine nor permanent. In the meanwhile the greed of the populace is developed, which, as happens, after it has reached large proportions thinks nothing is enough. Then there is an uprising, unless complete satisfaction is made to their demands. By this means your people are not won, but corrupted. And so by this means the average prince is accustomed to win his way into the hearts of the people after the fashion of these foolish husbands who beguile their wives with blandishments, gifts, and complaisance, instead of winning their love by their character and good actions. So at length it comes about that they are not loved; instead of a thrifty and well mannered wife they have a haughty and intractable one; instead of an obedient spouse they find one who is quarrelsome and rebellious. Or take the case of those unhappy women who desperately try to arouse love in their husbands' hearts by giving them drugs, with the result that they have madmen instead of sane lovers.

The wife should first learn the ways and means of loving her husband and then let him show himself worthy of her love. And so with the people—let them become accustomed to the best, and let the prince be the source of the best things. Those who begin to love through reason, love long.

In the first place, then, he who would be loved by his people should show himself a prince worthy of love; after that it will do some good to consider how best he may win his way into their hearts. The prince should do this first so that the best men may have the highest regard for him and that he may be accepted by those who are lauded by all. They are the men he should have for his close friends; they are the ones for his counselors; they are the ones on whom he should bestow his honors and whom he should allow to have the greatest influence with him. By this means everyone will come to have an excellent opinion of the prince, who is the source of all good will. I have known some princes who were not really evil themselves who incurred the hatred of the people for no other reason than that they granted too much liberty to those whom universal public sentiment condemned. The people judged the character of the prince by these other men.

For my part, I should like to see the prince born and raised among those people whom he is destined to rule, because friendship is created and confirmed most when the source of good will is in nature itself. The common people shun and hate even good qualities which they are unknown to them, while evils which are familiar are sometimes loved. This matter at hand has a twofold advantage to offer, for the prince will be more kindly disposed toward his subjects and certainly more ready to regard them as his own. The people on their part will feel more kindness in their hearts and be more willing to recognize his position as prince. For this reason I am especially opposed to the accepted [idea of] alliances of the princes with foreign, particularly with distant, nations.

The ties of birth and country and a mutual spirit of understanding, as it were, have a great deal to do with establishing a feeling of good will. A goodly part of this feeling must of necessity be lost if mixed marriages confuse that native and inborn spirit. But when nature has laid a foundation of mutual affection, then it should be developed and strengthened by every other means. When the opposite situation is presented, then even greater energy must be employed to secure this feeling of good will by mutual obligations and a character worthy of commendation. In marriage, the wife at first yields entirely to the husband, and he makes a few concessions to her and indulges her whims until, as they come really to know one another, a firm bond unites them; so it should be in the case of a prince selected from a foreign country. Mithridates learned the languages of all the peoples over whom he ruled, and they were said to be twenty in number. Alexander the Great, however barbarous the peoples with whom he was dealing, at once used to imitate their ways and customs and by this method subtly worked himself into their good graces. Alcibiades has been praised for the same thing. Nothing so alienates the affections of his people from a prince as for him to take great pleasure in living abroad, because then they seem to be neglected by him to whom they wish to be most important. The result of this is that the people feel that they are not paying taxes to a prince (since the moneys are spent elsewhere and totally lost as far as they are concerned) but that they are casting spoils to foreigners. Lastly, there is nothing more harmful and disastrous to a country, nor more dangerous for a prince, than visits to far-away places, especially if these visits are prolonged; for it was this, according to the opinion of everyone, that took Philip from us and injured his kingdom no less than the war with the Gelrii, which was dragged out for so many years. The king bee is hedged about in the midst of the swarm and does not fly out and away. The heart is situated in the very middle of the body. Just so should a prince always be found among his own people.

There are two factors, as Aristotle tells us in his *Politics*, which have played the greatest roles in the overthrow of empires. They are hatred and contempt. Good will is the opposite of hatred; respected authority, of contempt. Therefore it will be the duty of the prince to study the best way to win the former and avoid the latter. Hatred is kindled by an ugly temper, by violence, insulting language, sourness of character, meanness, and greediness; it is more easily aroused than allayed. A good prince must therefore use every caution to prevent any possibility of losing the affections of his subjects. You may take my word that whoever loses the favor of his people is thereby stripped of a great safeguard. On the other hand, the affections of the populace are won by those characteristics which, in general, are farthest removed from tyranny. They are clemency, affability, fairness, courtesy, and kindliness. This last is a spur to duty, especially if they who have been of good service to the state, see that they will be rewarded at the hands of the prince. Clemency inspires to better efforts those who are aware of their faults, while forgiveness extends hope to those who are now eager to make recompense by virtuous conduct for the short-comings of their earlier life and provides the steadfast with a happy reflection on human nature. Courtesy everywhere engenders love— or at least assuages hatred. This quality in a great prince is by far the most pleasing to the masses.

Contempt is most likely to spring from a penchant for the worldly pleasures of lust, for excessive drinking and eating, and for fools and clowns—in other words, for folly and idleness. Authority is gained by the following varied characteristics: in the first place wisdom, then integrity, self-restraint, seriousness, and alertness. These are the things by which a prince should commend himself, if he would be respected in his authority over his subjects. Some have the absurd idea that if they make the greatest confusion possible by their appearance, and dress with pompous display, they must be held in high esteem among their subjects. Who thinks a prince great just because he is adorned with gold and precious stones? Everyone knows he has as many as he wants. But in the meanwhile what else does the prince expose except the misfortunes of his people, who are supporting his extravagance to their great cost? And now lastly, what else does such a prince sow among his people, if not the seeds of all crime? Let the good prince be reared in such a manner and [continue to] live in such a manner that from the example of his life all the others (nobles and commoners alike) may take the model of frugality and temperance. Let him so conduct himself in the privacy of his home as not to be caught unawares by the sudden entrance of anyone. And in public it is unseemly for a prince to be seen anywhere, unless always in connection with

something that will benefit the people as a whole. The real character of the prince is revealed by his speech rather than by his dress.
Every word that is dropped from the lips of the prince is scattered
wide among the masses. He should exercise the greatest care to see
that whatever he says bears the stamp of [genuine] worth and evidences a mind becoming a good prince.

Aristotle's advice on this subject should not be overlooked. He
says that a prince who would escape incurring the hatred of his
people and would foster their affection for him should delegate to
others the odious duties and keep for himself the tasks which will
be sure to win favor. Thereby a great portion of any unpopularity
will be diverted upon those who carry out the administration, and
especially will it be so if these men are unpopular with the people
on other grounds as well. In the matter of benefits, however, the
genuine thanks redound to the prince alone. I should like to add
also that gratitude for a favor will be returned twofold if it is given
quickly, with no hesitation, spontaneously, and with a few words
of friendly commendation. If anything must be refused, refusal
should be affable and without offense. If it is necessary to impose
a punishment, some slight diminution of the penalty prescribed by
law should be made, and the sentence should be carried out as if
the prince were being forced [to act] against his own desires.

It is not enough for the prince to keep his own character pure
and uncorrupted for his state. He must give no less serious attention, in so far as he can, to see that every member of his household
—his nobles, his friends, his ministers, and his magistrates—follows
his example. They are one with the prince, and any hatred that is
aroused by their vicious acts rebounds upon the prince himself.
But, someone will say, this supervision is extremely difficult to
accomplish. It will be easy enough if the prince is careful to admit
only the best men into his household, and if he makes them understand that the prince is most pleased by that which is best for
the people. Otherwise it too often turns out that, due to the disregard of the prince in these matters or even his connivance in them,
the most criminal men (hiding under cover of the prince) force a
tyranny upon the people, and while they appear to be carrying out
the affairs of the prince, they are doing the greatest harm to his
good name. What is more, the condition of the state is more bearable when the prince himself is wicked than when he has evil
friends; we manage to bear up under a single tyrant. Somehow or
other the people can sate the greed of one man without difficulty:
it is not a matter of great effort to satisfy the wild desires of just
one man or to appease the vicious fierceness of a single individual,
but to content so many tyrants is a heavy burden. The prince should
avoid every novel idea in so far as he is capable of doing so; for
even if conditions are bettered thereby, the very innovation is a

stumbling block. The establishment of a state, the unwritten laws of a city, or the old legal code are never changed without great confusion. Therefore, if there is anything of this sort that can be endured, it should not be changed but should either be tolerated or happily diverted to a better function. As a last resort, if there is some absolutely unbearable condition, the change should be made, but [only] gradually and by a practiced hand.

The end which the prince sets for himself is of the greatest consequence, for if he shows little wisdom in its selection he must of necessity be wrong in all his plans. The cardinal principle of a good prince should be not only to preserve the present prosperity of the state but to pass it on more prosperous than when he received it. To use the jargon of the Peripatetics, there are three kinds of "good"—that of the mind, that of the body, and the external good. The prince must be careful not to evaluate them in reverse order and judge the good fortune of his state mainly by the external good, for these latter conditions should only be judged good in so far as they relate to the good of the mind and of the body; that is, in a word, the prince should consider his subjects to be most fortunate not if they are very wealthy or in excellent bodily health but if they are most honorable and self-controlled, if they have as little taste for greed and quarreling as could be hoped for, and if they are not at all factious but live in complete accord with one another. He must also beware of being deceived by the false names of the fairest things, for in this deception lies the fountainhead from which spring practically all the evils that abound in the world. It is no true state of happiness in which the people are given over to idleness and wasteful extravagance, any more than it is true liberty for everyone to be allowed to do as he pleases. Neither is it a state of servitude to live according to the letter of just laws. Nor is that a peaceful state in which the populace bows to every whim of the prince; but rather is it peaceful when it obeys good laws and a prince who has a keen regard for the authority of the laws. Equity does not lie in giving everyone the same reward, the same rights, the same honor; as a matter of fact, that is sometimes a mark of the greatest unfairness.

A prince who is about to assume control of the state must be advised at once that the main hope of a state lies in the proper education of its youth. This Xenophon wisely taught in his *Cyropaedia*. Pliable youth is amenable to any system of training. Therefore the greatest care should be exercised over public and private schools and over the education of the girls, so that the children may be placed under the best and most trustworthy instructors and may learn the teachings of Christ and that good literature which is beneficial to the state. As a result of this scheme of things, there will be no need for many laws or punishments, for the people will of their own free will follow the course of right.

Education exerts such a powerful influence, as Plato says, that a man who has been trained in the right develops into a sort of divine creature, while on the other hand, a person who has received a perverted training degenerates into a monstrous sort of savage beast. Nothing is of more importance to a prince than to have the best possible subjects.

The first effort, then, is to get them accustomed to the best influences, because any music has a soothing effect to the accustomed ear, and there is nothing harder than to rid people of those traits which have become second nature to them through habit. None of those tasks will be too difficult if the prince himself adheres to the best manners. It is the essence of tyranny, or rather trickery, to treat the common citizen as animal trainers are accustomed to treat a savage beast: first they carefully study the way in which these creatures are quieted or aroused, and then they anger them or quiet them at their pleasure. This Plato has painstakingly pointed out. Such a course is an abuse of the emotions of the masses and is no help to them. However, if the people prove intractable and rebel against what is good for them, then you must bide your time and gradually lead them over to your end, either by some subterfuge or by some helpful pretence. This works just as wine does, for when that is first taken it has no effect, but when it has gradually flowed through every vein it captivates the whole man and holds him in its power.

If sometimes the whirling course of events and public opinion beat the prince from his course, and he is forced to obey the [exigencies of the] time, yet he must not cease his efforts as long as he is able to renew his fight, and what he has not accomplished by one method he should try to effect by another.

QUESTIONS

1. Early in the essay Erasmus analogizes the relation of prince to people to that of a physician to the body, a farmer to a field, a husband to a wife. Why does he develop this last analogy more fully than the others and use it again later?
2. On page 862 Erasmus lists the "varied characteristics" by which authority is gained. Why does he put wisdom "in the first place"? Is there any significance to the order in which he places the other characteristics?
3. Erasmus says that "the real character of the prince is revealed by his speech rather than by his dress." Would this be equally true of people other than princes? How can both speech and dress reveal character?
4. Compare Erasmus' ideal prince with Machiavelli's. What is the significance of the title, "The Arts of Peace"?
5. Is the advice to "avoid every novel idea" (p. 863) sound? To

what does "novelty" apply in this context? How would Erasmus counter the charge that such a policy might lead to stagnation and corruption in government?

6. Why does Erasmus find it necessary to qualify so carefully what he means by "prosperity" (p. 864)? How does his definition differ from more commonly accepted ones today?

7. "Equity does not lie in giving everyone the same reward, the same rights, the same honor; as a matter of fact, that is sometimes a mark of the greatest unfairness" (p. 864). How does this implied definition of "equity" jibe with the statement in the Declaration of Independence that "all men are created equal" and "are endowed by their Creator with certain unalienable Rights" (p. 872)?

8. How far do leading political figures today correspond to Erasmus' ideal prince?

ABRAHAM LINCOLN

Second Inaugural Address

At this second appearing to take the oath of the presidential office, there is less occasion for an extended address than there was at the first. Then a statement, somewhat in detail, of a course to be pursued, seemed fitting and proper. Now, at the expiration of four years, during which public declarations have been constantly called forth on every point and phase of the great contest which still absorbs the attention, and engrosses the energies of the nation, little that is new could be presented. The progress of our arms, upon which all else chiefly depends, is as well known to the public as to myself; and it is, I trust, reasonably satisfactory and encouraging to all. With high hope for the future, no prediction in regard to it is ventured.

On the occasion corresponding to this four years ago, all thoughts were anxiously directed to an impending civil war. All dreaded it— all sought to avert it. While the inaugural address was being delivered from this place, devoted altogether to *saving* the Union without war, insurgent agents were in the city seeking to *destroy* it without war—seeking to dissolve the Union, and divide effects, by negotiation. Both parties deprecated war; but one of them would *make* war rather than let the nation survive; and the other would *accept* war rather than let it perish. And the war came.

One-eighth of the whole population were colored slaves, not distributed generally over the Union, but localized in the Southern part of it. These slaves constituted a peculiar and powerful interest. All knew that this interest was, somehow, the cause of the war. To strengthen, perpetuate, and extend this interest was the object for which the insurgents would rend the Union, even by war; while the government claimed no right to do more than to restrict the territorial enlargement of it. Neither party expected for the war, the magnitude, or the duration, which it has already attained. Neither anticipated that the *cause* of the conflict might cease with, or even before, the conflict itself should cease. Each looked for an easier triumph, and a result less fundamental and astounding. Both read the same Bible, and pray to the same God; and each invokes His aid against the other. It may seem strange that any men should dare to ask a just God's assistance in wringing their bread from the sweat of other men's faces[1]; but let us judge not that we be not judged.[2] The prayers of both could not be answered; that of neither has been answered fully. The Almighty has His own purposes. "Woe unto the world because of offenses! for it must needs be that offenses come; but woe to that man by whom the offense cometh!"[3] If we shall suppose that American slavery is one of those offenses which, in the providence of God, must needs come, but which, having continued through His appointed time, He now wills to remove, and that He gives to both North and South, this terrible war, as the woe due to those by whom the offense came, shall we discern therein any departure from those divine attributes which the believers in a Living God always ascribe to Him? Fondly do we hope—fervently do we pray—that this mighty scourge of war may speedily pass away. Yet, if God wills that it continue, until all the wealth piled by the bondman's two hundred and fifty years of unrequited toil shall be sunk, and until every drop of blood drawn with the lash, shall be paid by another drawn with the sword, as was said three thousand years ago, so still it must be said "the judgments of the Lord are true and righteous altogether."[4]

With malice toward none; with charity for all; with firmness in the right, as God gives us to see the right, let us strive on to finish the work we are in; to bind up the nation's wounds; to care for him who shall have borne the battle, and for his widow, and his orphan —to do all which may achieve and cherish a just, and a lasting peace, among ourselves, and with all nations.

1. See Genesis iii. 19.
2. See Matthew vii. 1.

3. See Matthew xviii. 7.
4. See Psalms xix. 9.

THOMAS JEFFERSON

Original Draft of the Declaration of Independence

A DECLARATION OF THE REPRESENTATIVES OF THE UNITED STATES OF AMERICA, IN GENERAL CONGRESS ASSEMBLED.

When in the course of human events it becomes necessary for a people to advance from that subordination in which they have hitherto remained, & to assume among the powers of the earth the equal & independant station to which the laws of nature & of nature's god entitle them, a decent respect to the opinions of mankind requires that they should declare the causes which impel them to the change.

We hold these truths to be sacred & undeniable; that all men are created equal & independant, that from that equal creation they derive rights inherent & inalienable, among which are the preservation of life, & liberty, & the spirit of happiness; that to secure these ends, governments are instituted among men, deriving their just powers from the consent of the governed; that whenever any form of government shall become destructive of these ends, it is the right of the people to alter or to abolish it, & to institute new government, laying it's foundation on such principles & organising it's powers in such form, as to them shall seem most likely to effect their safety & happiness. prudence indeed will dictate that governments long established should not be changed for light & transient causes: and accordingly all experience hath shewn that mankind are more disposed to suffer while evils are sufferable, than to right themselves by abolishing the forms to which they are accustomed. but when a long train of abuses & usurpations, begun at a distinguished period, & pursuing invariably the same object, evinces a design to subject them to arbitrary power, it is their right, it is their duty, to throw off such government & to provide new guards for their future security. such has been the patient sufferance of these colonies; & such is now the necessity which constrains them to expunge their former systems of government. the history of his present majesty, is a history of unremitting injuries and usurpations, among which no one fact stands single or solitary to contradict the uniform tenor of the rest, all of which have in direct object the establishment of an absolute tyranny over these states. to prove this, let facts be submited to a candid world, for the truth of which we pledge a faith yet unsullied by falsehood.

he has refused his assent to laws the most wholesome and necessary for the public good:

he has forbidden his governors to pass laws of immediate & pressing importance, unless suspended in their operation till his assent should be obtained; and when so suspended, he has neglected utterly to attend to them.

he has refused to pass other laws for the accommodation of large districts of people unless those people would relinquish the right of representation, a right inestimable to them, & formidable to tyrants alone:[1]

he has dissolved Representative houses repeatedly & continually, for opposing with manly firmness his invasions on the rights of the people:

he has refused for a long space of time to cause others to be elected, whereby the legislative powers, incapable of annihilation, have returned to the people at large for their exercise, the state remaining in the mean time exposed to all the dangers of invasion from without, &, convulsions within:

he has suffered the administration of justice totally to cease in some of these colonies, refusing his assent to laws for establishing judiciary powers:

he has made our judges dependant on his will alone, for the tenure of their offices, and amount of their salaries:

he has erected a multitude of new offices by a self-assumed power, & sent hither swarms of officers to harrass our people & eat out their substance:

he has kept among us in times of peace standing armies & ships of war:

he has affected to render the military, independent of & superior to the civil power:

he has combined with others to subject us to a jurisdiction foreign to our constitutions and unacknoledged by our laws; giving his assent to their pretended acts of legislation, for quartering large bodies of armed troops among us;

> for protecting them by a mock-trial from punishment for any murders they should commit on the inhabitants of these states;
>
> for cutting off our trade with all parts of the world;
>
> for imposing taxes on us without our consent;
>
> for depriving us of the benefits of trial by jury

he has endeavored to prevent the population of these states; for that purpose obstructing the laws for naturalization of foreigners; refusing to pass others to encourage their migrations hither; & raising the conditions of new appropriations of lands;

1. At this point in the manuscript a strip containing the following clause is inserted: "He called together legislative bodies at places unusual, unco[mfortable, & distant from] the depository of their public records for the sole purpose of fatiguing [them into compliance] with his measures:" Missing parts in the Library of Congress text are supplied from the copy made by Jefferson for George Wythe. This copy is in the New York Public Library. The fact that this passage was omitted from John Adams's transcript suggests that it was not a part of Jefferson's original rough draft.

for transporting us beyond seas to be tried for pretended offences:

for taking away our charters & altering fundamentally the forms of our governments;

for suspending our own legislatures & declaring themselves invested with power to legislate for us in all cases whatsoever:

he has abdicated government here, withdrawing his governors, & declaring us out of his allegiance & protection:

he has plundered our seas, ravaged our coasts, burnt our towns & destroyed the lives of our people:

he is at this time transporting large armies of foreign mercenaries to compleat the works of death, desolation & tyranny, already begun with circumstances of cruelty & perfidy unworthy the head of a civilized nation:

he has endeavored to bring on the inhabitants of our frontiers the merciless Indian savages, whose known rule of warfare is an undistinguished destruction of all ages, sexes, & conditions of existence:

he has incited treasonable insurrections of our fellow-citizens, with the allurements of forfeiture & confiscation of our property:

he has waged cruel war against human nature itself, violating it's most sacred rights of life & liberty in the persons of a distant people who never offended him, captivating & carrying them into slavery in another hemisphere, or to incur miserable death in their transportation thither. this piratical warfare, the opprobrium of *infidel* powers, is the warfare of the CHRISTIAN king of Great Britain. determined to keep open a market where MEN should be bought & sold; he has prostituted his negative for suppressing every legislative attempt to prohibit or to restrain this execrable commerce: and that this assemblage of horrors might want no fact of distinguished die, he is now exciting those very people to rise in arms among us, and to purchase that liberty of which *he* has deprived them, by murdering the people upon whom *he* also obtruded them; thus paying off former crimes committed against the *liberties* of one people, with crimes which he urges them to commit against the *lives* of another.

in every stage of these oppressions we have petitioned for redress in the most humble terms; our repeated petitions have been answered by repeated injury. a prince whose character is thus marked by every act which may define a tyrant, is unfit to be the ruler of a people who mean to be free. future ages will scarce believe that the hardiness of one man, adventured within the short compass of twelve years only, on so many acts of tyranny without a mask, over a people fostered & fixed in principles of liberty.

Nor have we been wanting in attentions to our British brethren. we have warned them from time to time of attempts by their legislature to extend a jurisdiction over these our states. we have reminded them of the circumstances of our emigration & settlement here, no one of which could warrant so strange a pretension: that these were effected at the expence of our own blood & treasure, unassisted by the wealth or the strength of Great Britain: that in constituting indeed our several forms of government, we had adopted one common king, thereby laying a foundation for perpetual league & amity with them; but that submission to their [Parliament, was no Part of our Constitution, nor ever in Idea, if History may be]² credited: and we appealed to their native justice & magnanimity, as to the ties of our common kindred to disavow these usurpations which were likely to interrupt our correspondence & connection. they too have been deaf to the voice of justice & of consanguinity, & when occasions have been given them, by the regular course of their laws, of removing from their councils the disturbers of our harmony, they have by their free election re-established them in power. at this very time too they are permitting their chief magistrate to send over not only soldiers of our common blood, but Scotch & foreign mercenaries to invade & deluge us in blood. these facts have given the last stab to agonizing affection, and manly spirit bids us to renounce for ever these unfeeling brethren. we must endeavor to forget our former love for them, and to hold them as we hold the rest of mankind, enemies in war, in peace friends. we might have been a free & a great people together; but a communication of grandeur & of freedom it seems is below their dignity. be it so, since they will have it: the road to glory & happiness is open to us too; we will climb it in a separate state, and acquiesce in the necessity which pronounces our everlasting Adieu!

We therefore the representatives of the United States of America in General Congress assembled do, in the name & by authority of the good people of these states, reject and renounce all allegiance & subjection to the kings of Great Britain & all others who may hereafter claim by, through, or under them; we utterly dissolve & break off all political connection which may have heretofore subsisted between us & the people or parliament of Great Britain; and finally we do assert and declare these colonies to be free and independant states, and that as free & independant states they shall hereafter have power to levy war, conclude peace, contract alliances, establish commerce, & to do all other acts and things which independant states may of right do. And for the support of this declaration we mutually pledge to each other our lives, our fortunes, & our sacred honour.

2. An illegible passage is supplied from John Adams's transcription.

THOMAS JEFFERSON and OTHERS
The Declaration of Independence

IN CONGRESS, JULY 4, 1776
THE UNANIMOUS DECLARATION OF THE
THIRTEEN UNITED STATES OF AMERICA

When in the Course of human events it becomes necessary for one people to dissolve the political bands which have connected them with another, and to assume among the powers of the earth, the separate and equal station to which the Laws of Nature and of Nature's God entitle them, a decent respect to the opinions of mankind requires that they should declare the causes which impel them to the separation.

We hold these truths to be self-evident, that all men are created equal, that they are endowed by their Creator with certain unalienable Rights, that among these are Life, Liberty and the pursuit of Happiness. That to secure these rights, Governments are instituted among Men, deriving their just powers from the consent of the governed, That whenever any Form of Government becomes destructive of these ends, it is the Right of the People to alter or to abolish it, and to institute new Government, laying its foundation on such principles and organizing its powers in such form, as to them shall seem most likely to affect their Safety and Happiness. Prudence, indeed, will dictate that Governments long established should not be changed for light and transient causes; and accordingly all experience hath shewn that mankind are more disposed to suffer, while evils are sufferable, than to right themselves by abolishing the forms to which they are accustomed. But when a long train of abuses and usurpations, pursuing invariably the same Object evinces a design to reduce them under absolute Despotism, it is their right, it is their duty, to throw off such Government, and to provide new Guards for their future security. Such has been the patient sufferance of these Colonies; and such is now the necessity which constrains them to alter their former Systems of Government. The history of the present King of Great Britain is a history of repeated injuries and usurpations, all having in direct object the establishment of an absolute Tyranny over these States. To prove this, let Facts be submitted to a candid world.

He has refused his Assent to Laws, the most wholesome and necessary for the public good.

He has forbidden his Governors to pass laws of immediate and pressing importance, unless suspended in their operation till his Assent should be obtained; and when so suspended, he has utterly neglected to attend to them.

He has refused to pass other Laws for the accommodation of large districts of people, unless those people would relinquish the right of Representation in the Legislature, a right inestimable to them and formidable to tyrants only.

He has called together legislative bodies at places unusual, uncomfortable, and distant from the depository of their Public Records, for the sole purpose of fatiguing them into compliance with his measures.

He has dissolved Representative Houses repeatedly, for opposing with manly firmness his invasions on the rights of the people.

He has refused for a long time, after such dissolutions, to cause others to be elected; whereby the Legislative Powers, incapable of Annihilation, have returned to the People at large for their exercise; the State remaining in the mean time exposed to all the dangers of invasion from without, and convulsions within.

He has endeavored to prevent the population of these States; for that purpose obstructing the Laws for Naturalization of Foreigners; refusing to pass others to encourage their migration hither, and raising the conditions of new Appropriations of Lands.

He has obstructed the Administration of Justice, by refusing his Assent to Laws for establishing Judiciary Powers.

He has made Judges dependent on his Will alone, for the tenure of their offices, and the amount and payment of their salaries.

He has erected a multitude of New Offices, and sent hither swarms of Officers to harass our people, and eat out their substance.

He has kept among us, in times of peace, Standing Armies without the Consent of our legislatures.

He has affected to render the Military independent of and superior to the Civil Power.

He has combined with others to subject us to a jurisdiction foreign to our constitution, and unacknowledged by our laws; giving his Assent to their Acts of pretended Legislation: For quartering large bodies of armed troops among us: For protecting them, by a mock Trial, from punishment for any Murders which they should commit on the Inhabitants of these States: For cutting off our Trade with all parts of the world: For imposing Taxes on us without our Consent: For depriving us in many cases, of the benefits of Trial by Jury; For transporting us beyond Seas to be tried for pretended offenses: for abolishing the free System of English Laws in a neighboring Province, establishing therein an Arbitrary government, and enlarging its Boundaries so as to render it at once an example and fit instrument for introducing the same absolute rule into these Colonies: For taking away our Charters, abolishing our most valuable Laws and altering fundamentally the Forms of our Governments: For suspending our own Legislatures, and declaring themselves invested with power to legislate for us in all cases whatsoever.

He has abdicated Government here, by declaring us out of his Protection and waging War against us.

He has plundered our seas, ravaged our Coasts, burnt our towns, and destroyed the lives of our people.

He is at this time transporting large Armies of foreign Mercenaries to complete the works of death, desolation and tyranny, already begun with circumstances of Cruelty & Perfidy scarcely paralleled in the most barbarous ages, and totally unworthy the Head of a civilized nation.

He has constrained our fellow Citizens taken Captive on the high Seas to bear Arms against their Country, to become the executioners of their friends and Brethren, or to fall themselves by their Hands.

He has excited domestic insurrections amongst us, and has endeavored to bring on the inhabitants of our frontiers, the merciless Indian Savages, whose known rule of warfare, is an undistinguished destruction of all ages, sexes, and conditions.

In every stage of these Oppressions We have Petitioned for Redress in the most humble terms: Our repeated Petitions have been answered only by repeated injury. A Prince, whose character is thus marked by every act which may define a Tyrant, is unfit to be the ruler of a free people.

Nor have We been wanting in attention to our British brethren. We have warned them from time to time of attempts by their legislature to extend an unwarrantable jurisdiction over us. We have reminded them of the circumstances of our emigration and settlement here. We have appealed to their native justice and magnanimity, and we have conjured them by the ties of our common kindred to disavow these usurpations, which would inevitably interrupt our connections and correspondence. They too have been deaf to the voice of justice and of consanguinity. We must, therefore, acquiesce in the necessity, which denounces our Separation, and hold them, as we hold the rest of mankind, Enemies in War, in Peace Friends.

We, THEREFORE, the Representatives of the UNITED STATES OF AMERICA, in General Congress, Assembled, appealing to the Supreme Judge of the world for the rectitude of our intentions, do, in the Name, and by Authority of the good People of these Colonies, solemnly publish and declare, That these United Colonies are, and of Right ought to be FREE AND INDEPENDENT STATES; that they are Absolved from all Allegiance to the British Crown, and that all political connection between them and the State of Great Britain, is and ought to be totally dissolved; and that as Free and Independent States, they have full Power to levy War, conclude Peace, contract Alliances, establish Commerce, and to do all other Acts and Things which Independent States may of right do. And for the support of this Declaration, with a firm reliance on the protection of Divine Providence, we mutually pledge to each other our Lives, our Fortunes, and our sacred Honor.

QUESTIONS

1. The Declaration of Independence was addressed to several audiences: the king of Great Britain, the people of Great Britain, the people of America, and the world at large. Show ways in which the final draft was adapted for its several audiences.
2. Examine the second paragraph of each version closely. How have the revisions in the final version increased its effectiveness over the first draft?
3. The Declaration has often been called a classic example of deductive argument: setting up general statements, relating particular cases to them, and drawing conclusions. Trace this pattern through the document, noting the way each part is developed. Would the document have been as effective if the long middle part had either come first or been left out entirely? Explain.
4. Find the key terms and phrases of the Declaration (such as "these truths . . . self-evident," "created equal," "unalienable rights," and so on) and determine how fully they are defined by the contexts in which they occur. Why are no formal definitions given for them?
5. The signers of the Declaration appeal both to general principles and to factual evidence in presenting their case. Which of the appeals to principle could still legitimately be made today by a nation eager to achieve independence? In other words, how far does the Declaration reflect unique events of history and how far does it reflect universal aspirations and ideals?

E. B. WHITE

Democracy

July 3, 1943

We received a letter from the Writers' War Board the other day asking for a statement on "The Meaning of Democracy." It presumably is our duty to comply with such a request, and it is certainly our pleasure.

Surely the Board knows what democracy is. It is the line that forms on the right. It is the don't in don't shove. It is the hole in the stuffed shirt through which the sawdust slowly trickles; it is the dent in the high hat. Democracy is the recurrent suspicion that more than half of the people are right more than half of the time. It is the feeling of privacy in the voting booths, the feeling of communion in the libraries, the feeling of vitality everywhere. Democracy is a letter to the editor. Democracy is the score at the beginning of the ninth. It is an idea which hasn't been disproved yet, a song the words of which have not gone bad. It's the mustard on the hot dog and the cream in the rationed coffee. Democracy is a request from a War Board, in the middle of a morning in the middle of a war, wanting to know what democracy is.

QUESTIONS

1. White's piece is dated July 3, 1943, the middle of World War II. How did the occasion shape what White says about democracy?
2. Look up "democracy" in a standard desk dictionary. Of the several meanings given, which one best applies to White's definition (below)? Does more than one apply?
3. Translate White's definition into non-metaphorical language. (For example, "It is the line that forms on the right" might be translated by "It has no special privileges.") Determine what is lost in the translation, or, in other words, what White has gained by using figurative language.

WALTER LIPPMANN

The Indispensable Opposition

Were they pressed hard enough, most men would probably confess that political freedom—that is to say, the right to speak freely and to act in opposition—is a noble ideal rather than a practical necessity. As the case for freedom is generally put today, the argument lends itself to this feeling. It is made to appear that, whereas each man claims his freedom as a matter of right, the freedom he accords to other men is a matter of toleration. Thus, the defense of freedom of opinion tends to rest not on its substantial, beneficial, and indispensable consequences, but on a somewhat eccentric, a rather vaguely benevolent, attachment to an abstraction.

It is all very well to say with Voltaire, "I wholly disapprove of what you say, but will defend to the death your right to say it," but as a matter of fact most men will not defend to the death the rights of other men: if they disapprove sufficiently what other men say, they will somehow suppress those men if they can.

So, if this is the best that can be said for liberty of opinion, that a man must tolerate his opponents because everyone has a "right" to say what he pleases, then we shall find that liberty of opinion is a luxury, safe only in pleasant times when men can be tolerant because they are not deeply and vitally concerned.

Yet actually, as a matter of historic fact, there is a much stronger foundation for the great constitutional right of freedom of speech, and as a matter of practical human experience there is a much more compelling reason for cultivating the habits of free men. We take, it seems to me, a naïvely self-righteous view when we argue as if the right of our opponents to speak were something that we protect because we are magnanimous, noble, and unselfish. The compelling reason why, if liberty of opinion did not exist, we should have to invent it, why it will eventually have to be restored in all civilized countries where it is now suppressed, is that we must protect the right of our opponents to speak because we must hear what they have to say.

We miss the whole point when we imagine that we tolerate the freedom of our political opponents as we tolerate a howling baby next door, as we put up with the blasts from our neighbor's radio because we are too peaceable to heave a brick through the window. If this were all there is to freedom of opinion, that we are too good-natured or too timid to do anything about our opponents and our critics except to let them talk, it would be difficult to say whether we are tolerant because we are magnanimous or because we are lazy, because we have strong principles or because we lack serious convictions, whether we have the hospitality of an inquiring mind or the indifference of an empty mind. And so, if we truly wish to understand why freedom is necessary in a civilized society, we must begin by realizing that, because freedom of discussion improves our own opinions, the liberties of other men are our own vital necessity.

We are much closer to the essence of the matter, not when we quote Voltaire, but when we go to the doctor and pay him to ask us the most embarrassing questions and to prescribe the most disagreeable diet. When we pay the doctor to exercise complete freedom of speech about the cause and cure of our stomachache, we do not look upon ourselves as tolerant and magnanimous, and worthy to be admired by ourselves. We have enough common sense to know that if we threaten to put the doctor in jail because we do not like the diagnosis and the prescription it will be unpleasant for the doctor, to be sure, but equally unpleasant for our own stomachache. That is why even the most ferocious dictator would rather be treated by a doctor who was free to think and speak the truth than by his own Minister of Propaganda. For there is a point, the point at which things really matter, where the freedom of others is no longer a question of their right but of our own need.

The point at which we recognize this need is much higher in some men than in others. The totalitarian rulers think they do not need the freedom of an opposition: they exile, imprison, or shoot their opponents. We have concluded on the basis of practical experience, which goes back to Magna Carta and beyond, that we need the opposition. We pay the opposition salaries out of the public treasury.

In so far as the usual apology for freedom of speech ignores this experience, it becomes abstract and eccentric rather than concrete and human. The emphasis is generally put on the right to speak, as if all that mattered were that the doctor should be free to go out into the park and explain to the vacant air why I have a stomach-ache. Surely that is a miserable caricature of the great civic right which men have bled and died for. What really matters is that the doctor should tell *me* what ails me, that I should listen to him; that if I do not like what he says I should be free to call in another doctor; and that then the first doctor should have to listen to the second doctor; and that out of all the speaking and listening, the give-and-take of opinions, the truth should be arrived at.

This is the creative principle of freedom of speech, not that it is a system for the tolerating of error, but that it is a system for finding the truth. It may not produce the truth, or the whole truth all the time, or often, or in some cases ever. But if the truth can be found, there is no other system which will normally and habitually find so much truth. Until we have thoroughly understood this principle, we shall not know why we must value our liberty, or how we can protect and develop it.

Let us apply this principle to the system of public speech in a totalitarian state. We may, without any serious falsification, picture a condition of affairs in which the mass of the people are being addressed through one broadcasting system by one man and his chosen subordinates. The orators speak. The audience listens but cannot and dare not speak back. It is a system of one-way communication; the opinions of the rulers are broadcast outwardly to the mass of the people. But nothing comes back to the rulers from the people except the cheers; nothing returns in the way of knowledge of forgotten facts, hidden feelings, neglected truths, and practical suggestions.

But even a dictator cannot govern by his own one-way inspiration alone. In practice, therefore, the totalitarian rulers get back the reports of the secret police and of their party henchmen down among the crowd. If these reports are competent, the rulers may manage to remain in touch with public sentiment. Yet that is not enough to know what the audience feels. The rulers have also to make great decisions that have enormous consequences, and here their system provides virtually no help from the give-and-take of opinion in the nation. So they must either rely on their own intuition, which cannot be permanently and continually inspired, or, if they are intelligent despots, encourage their trusted advisers and their technicians to speak and debate freely in their presence.

On the walls of the houses of Italian peasants one may see inscribed in large letters the legend, "Mussolini is always right." But if that legend is taken seriously by Italian ambassadors, by the Italian General Staff, and by the Ministry of Finance, then all one can say is heaven help Mussolini, heaven help Italy, and the new Emperor of Ethiopia.

For at some point, even in a totalitarian state, it is indispensable that there should exist the freedom of opinion which causes opposing opinions to be debated. As time goes on, that is less and less easy under a despotism; critical discussion disappears as the internal opposition is liquidated in favor of men who think and feel alike. That is why the early successes of despots, of Napoleon I and of Napoleon III, have usually been followed by an irreparable mistake. For in listening only to his yes men—the others being in exile or in concentration camps, or terrified—the despot shuts himself off from the truth that no man can dispense with.

We know all this well enough when we contemplate the dictatorships. But when we try to picture our own system, by way of contrast, what picture do we have in our minds? It is, is it not, that anyone may stand up on his own soapbox and say anything he pleases, like the individuals in Kipling's poem[1] who sit each in his separate star and draw the Thing as they see it for the God of Things as they are. Kipling, perhaps, could do this, since he was a poet. But the ordinary mortal isolated on his separate star will have an hallucination, and a citizenry declaiming from separate soapboxes will poison the air with hot and nonsensical confusion.

If the democratic alternative to the totalitarian one-way broadcasts is a row of separate soapboxes, than I submit that the alternative is unworkable, is unreasonable, and is humanly unattractive. It is above all a false alternative. It is not true that liberty has developed among civilized men when anyone is free to set up a soapbox, is free to hire a hall where he may expound his opinions to those who are willing to listen. On the contrary, freedom of speech is established to achieve its essential purpose only when different opinions are expounded in the same hall to the same audience.

For, while the right to talk may be the beginning of freedom, the necessity of listening is what makes the right important. Even in Russia and Germany a man may still stand in an open field and speak his mind. What matters is not the utterance of opinions. What matters is the confrontation of opinions in debate. No man can care profoundly that every fool should say what he likes. Nothing has been accomplished if the wisest man proclaims his wisdom in the middle of the Sahara Desert. This is the shadow. We have the substance of liberty when the fool is compelled to listen to the wise man and learn; when the wise man is compelled to take account of the fool, and to instruct him; when the wise man can increase his wisdom by hearing the judgment of his peers.

That is why civilized men must cherish liberty—as a means of promoting the discovery of truth. So we must not fix our whole attention on the right of anyone to hire his own hall, to rent his own broadcasting station, to distribute his own pamphlets. These

---

1. "L'Envoi."

rights are incidental; and though they must be preserved, they can be preserved only by regarding them as incidental, as auxiliary to the substance of liberty that must be cherished and cultivated.

Freedom of speech is best conceived, therefore, by having in mind the picture of a place like the American Congress, an assembly where opposing views are represented, where ideas are not merely uttered but debated, or the British Parliament, where men who are free to speak are also compelled to answer. We may picture the true condition of freedom as existing in a place like a court of law, where witnesses testify and are cross-examined, where the lawyer argues against the opposing lawyer before the same judge and in the presence of one jury. We may picture freedom as existing in a forum where the speaker must respond to questions; in a gathering of scientists where the data, the hypothesis, and the conclusion are submitted to men competent to judge them; in a reputable newspaper which not only will publish the opinions of those who disagree but will re-examine its own opinion in the light of what they say.

Thus the essence of freedom of opinion is not in mere toleration as such, but in the debate which toleration provides: it is not in the venting of opinion, but in the confrontation of opinion. That this is the practical substance can readily be understood when we remember how differently we feel and act about the censorship and regulation of opinion purveyed by different media of communication. We find then that, in so far as the medium makes difficult the confrontation of opinion in debate, we are driven towards censorship and regulation.

There is, for example, the whispering campaign, the circulation of anonymous rumors by men who cannot be compelled to prove what they say. They put the utmost strain on our tolerance, and there are few who do not rejoice when the anonymous slanderer is caught, exposed, and punished. At a higher level there is the moving picture, a most powerful medium for conveying ideas, but a medium which does not permit debate. A moving picture cannot be answered effectively by another moving picture; in all free countries there is some censorship of the movies, and there would be more if the producers did not recognize their limitations by avoiding political controversy. There is then the radio. Here debate is difficult: it is not easy to make sure that the speaker is being answered in the presence of the same audience. Inevitably, there is some regulation of the radio.

When we reach the newspaper press, the opportunity for debate is so considerable that discontent cannot grow to the point where under normal conditions there is any disposition to regulate the press. But when newspapers abuse their power by injuring people who have no means of replying, a disposition to regulate the press appears. When we arrive at Congress we find that, because the membership of the House is so large, full debate is impracticable. So there are restrictive rules. On the other hand, in the Senate, where the conditions of full debate exist, there is almost absolute freedom of speech.

This shows us that the preservation and development of freedom of opinion are not only a matter of adhering to abstract legal rights, but also, and very urgently, a matter of organizing and arranging sufficient debate. Once we have a firm hold on the central principle, there are many practical conclusions to be drawn. We then realize that the defense of freedom of opinion consists primarily in perfecting the opportunity for an adequate give-and-take of opinion; it consists also in regulating the freedom of those revolutionists who cannot or will not permit or maintain debate when it does not suit their purposes.

We must insist that free oratory is only the beginning of free speech; it is not the end, but a means to an end. The end is to find the truth. The practical justification of civil liberty is not that self-expression is one of the rights of man. It is that the examination of opinion is one of the necessities of man. For experience tells us that it is only when freedom of opinion becomes the compulsion to debate that the seed which our fathers planted has produced its fruit. When that is understood, freedom will be cherished not because it is a vent for our opinions but because it is the surest method of correcting them.

The unexamined life, said Socrates, is unfit to be lived by man. This is the virtue of liberty, and the ground on which we may best justify our belief in it, that it tolerates error in order to serve the truth. When men are brought face to face with their opponents, forced to listen and learn and mend their ideas, they cease to be children and savages and begin to live like civilized men. Then only is freedom a reality, when men may voice their opinions because they must examine their opinions.

The only reason for dwelling on all this is that if we are to preserve democracy we must understand its principles. And the principle which distinguishes it from all other forms of government is that in a democracy the opposition not only is tolerated as constitutional but must be maintained because it is in fact indispensable.

The democratic system cannot be operated without effective opposition. For, in making the great experiment of governing people by consent rather than by coercion, it is not sufficient that the party in power should have a majority. It is just as necessary that the party in power should never outrage the minority. That means that it must listen to the minority and be moved by the criticisms of the minority. That means that its measures must take account of the minority's objections, and that in administering measures it must remember that the minority may become the majority.

The opposition is indispensable. A good statesman, like any other sensible human being, always learns more from his opponents than from his fervent supporters. For his supporters will push him to disaster unless his opponents show him where the dangers are. So if he is wise he will often pray to be delivered from his friends, because they will ruin him. But, though it hurts, he ought also to pray never to be left without opponents; for they keep him on the path of reason and good sense.

The national unity of a free people depends upon a sufficiently even balance of political power to make it impracticable for the administration to be arbitrary and for the opposition to be revolutionary and irreconcilable. Where that balance no longer exists, democracy perishes. For unless all the citizens of a state are forced by circumstances to compromise, unless they feel that they can affect policy but that no one can wholly dominate it, unless by habit and necessity they have to give and take, freedom cannot be maintained.

QUESTIONS

1. What is Lippmann's reason for dividing the essay into three parts? What is the purpose of the third part?
2. What is the importance of Lippmann's distinction between "free oratory" and "free speech" (p. 881)?
3. What does Lippmann mean when he says that the point at which we recognize the need for the freedom of others "is much higher in some men than in others" (p. 877)? Does this assertion in any way weaken his argument?
4. Why has Lippmann discussed motion pictures but not literature (p. 880)? How sound is his view that the motion picture is "a medium which does not permit debate"? Does literature permit debate?
5. What does Lippmann mean by his statement that "the usual apology for freedom of speech . . . becomes abstract and eccentric rather than concrete and human" (p. 877)? Why has he chosen these particular words to contrast the "usual apology" with his own view? Is his argument "concrete and human"?
6. Thurber's rabbits (p. 823) listened to their opposition—that is, "the other animals, who lived at a great distance"—and were annihilated. Does Thurber's fable suggest any necessary qualification for Lippmann's thesis concerning the value of the opposition? Explain.
7. Lippmann's essay was written before the term "brainwashing" was in common use. If he were writing the essay today, how might he take account of this term?

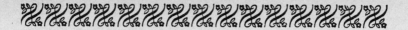

Prose Forms: Apothegms

[At the beginning of Bacon's essay "Of Truth," jesting Pilate asks, "What is truth?" and does not stay for an answer. Perhaps Pilate asked in jest because he thought the question foolish; perhaps because he thought an answer impossible. Something of Pilate's skepticism is in most of us, but something too of a belief that there is truth, even if—as the history of philosophy teaches us—determining its nature may be enormously difficult. We readily assume some things to be true even if we hesitate to say what ultimately *is* Truth.

The test of truth most often is an appeal to the observed facts of experience. The observation of experience yields knowledge; the generalized statement of that knowledge yields a concept of the experience; the concise, descriptive form in which that concept is expressed we call variously, apothegm, proverb, maxim, or aphorism. Thus Sir James Mackintosh can speak of apothegms as "the condensed good sense of nations," because the apothegm conveys the distilled observations of men about their own persistent conduct. To hear the familiar "*Absence makes the heart grow fonder*" is to be reminded of a general truth which you and the world acknowledge. It does not matter that the equally familiar "*Out of sight, out of mind*" seems to contradict the other saying; both are true but applicable to different situations. Both statements are immediately recognizable as true and neither requires to be argued for, representing as they do the collective experience of mankind intelligently observed.

Aphoristic statements often occur within the context of more extended pieces of writing, and while not apothegms in the strictest sense, but rather propositions, they have the force of apothegms. For example, Percy Shelley's Defence of Poetry (1821) concludes that "Poets are the unacknowledged legislators of the world." Seventy years later in his Preface to The Picture of Dorian Gray Oscar Wilde asserts that "All art is quite useless." Although these statements seem contradictory, each is unarguable within its own context.

Not everyone is as astute an observer as the writer of apothegms and maxims, of course, but everyone is presumably capable of per-

ceiving their rightness. What we perceive first is the facts to which
the saying applies. When Franklin says "An empty bag cannot stand
upright" (in 1740 he obviously had in mind a cloth bag), we acknowledge that this is the condition of the empty bag—and of ourselves
when we are empty. Or when La Rochefoucauld says "We are all
strong enough to endure the misfortunes of others," he too observes
a condition that exists among men.

Many aphoristic assertions claim their validity primarily in descriptive terms. But the descriptive "is" in most apothegms and maxims is joined to a normative "ought" and the sayings therefore convey
admonitions about and judgments of the conditions they describe.
"Waste not, want not" is a simple illustration of this use of fact to
admonish. Samuel Butler briefly gives us the presumed fact that
"the world will always be governed by self-interest." Then he quickly
advises: "We should not try to stop this, we should try to make the
self-interest of cads a little more consistent with that of decent people." The condition of "ought" need not always be admonitory; it
may be the implied judgment in La Rochefoucauld's assertion that
"It is the habit of mediocre minds to condemn all that is beyond their
grasp." The judgment is explicit in Franklin's "Fish and visitors
stink in three days." And Bierce's definitions of ordinary words are
not specifications of meanings in the way of ordinary dictionaries,
but critical concepts of the experiences to which the words point.

"Wisdom" or "good sense," then, is the heart of the apothegm
or maxim, the conjunction of "is" and "ought" in an assertion of universal truth. Unlike ordinary assertions of fact or opinion usually concerned with particular rather than universal experience, the wise saying is complete in its brevity. Before the ordinary assertion is allowed
to hold, we require that the assumptions on which it rests, the implications it carries, the critical concepts and terms it contains, be
examined closely and explored or justified. If someone says that the
modern college student wants most to succeed materially in life,
we want to be satisfied about what constitutes "modern," which
college students (and where) are referred to, what else is involved in
the comparative "most," what specifically is meant by "materially."
But the apothegm assumes facts widely known and accepted, and
in its judgments invokes values or attitudes readily intelligible to
the great majority. It is the truth as most men experience it.

In a sense, every writer's concern is ultimately with truth. Certainly the essayist is directly concerned, in his definition and ordering
of ideas, to say what is true and, somehow, to say it "new." Much of
what he says is of the nature of assertion about particular experience;
he must therefore be at pains to handle such matters as assumptions
and logical proofs carefully and deliberately. But he cannot always
be starting from scratch, not daring to assume anything, trusting no
certain knowledge or experience or beliefs held in common with

his fellows. Careful he must be, but also aware that available to him, in addition to methods of logical analysis and proof, rules of evidence, and the other means to effective exposition, is the whole memory and record of the vast experience of the race contained in a people's apothegms and aphorisms. In them is a treasury of truths useful to many demands of clarity and precision. And in them, too, is a valuable lesson in the way a significantly large body of experience—direct, in a person's day-to-day encounters; indirect, in his study of all forms of history—can be observed, conceptualized, and then expressed in an economy of language brief in form, comprehensive in meaning, and satisfyingly true.]

W. H. AUDEN: Apothegms

Some books are undeservedly forgotten; none are undeservedly remembered.

You do not educate a person's palate by telling him that what he has been in the habit of eating—watery, overboiled cabbage, let us say—is disgusting, but by persuading him to try a dish of vegetables which have been properly cooked. With some people, it is true, you seem to get quicker results by telling them—"Only vulgar people like overcooked cabbage; the best people like cabbage as the Chinese cook it"—but the results are less likely to be lasting.

No poet or novelist wishes he were the only one who ever lived, but most of them wish they were the only one alive, and quite a number fondly believe their wish has been granted.

The integrity of a writer is more threatened by appeals to his social conscience, his political or religious convictions, than by appeals to his cupidity. It is morally less confusing to be goosed by a traveling salesman than by a bishop.

Only a minor talent can be a perfect gentleman; a major talent is always more than a bit of a cad. Hence the importance of minor writers—as teachers of good manners. Now and again, an exquisite minor work can make a master feel thoroughly ashamed of himself.

Narcissus does not fall in love with his reflection because it is beautiful, but because it is *his*. If it were his beauty that enthralled him he would be set free in a few years by its fading.

"After all," sighed Narcissus the hunchback, "on *me* it looks good."

Our sufferings and weaknesses, in so far as they are personal, *our* sufferings, *our* weaknesses, are of no literary interest whatsoever. They are only interesting in so far as we can see them as typical of the human condition. A suffering, a weakness, which cannot be expressed as an aphorism should not be mentioned.

The same rules apply to self-examination as apply to confession to a priest: *be brief, be blunt, be gone*. Be brief, be blunt, forget. The scrupuland is a nasty specimen.

In a state of panic, a man runs round in circles by himself. In a state of joy, he links hands with others and they dance round in a circle together.

A sense of humor develops in a society to the degree that its members are simultaneously conscious of being each a unique person and of being all in common subjection to unalterable laws.

Among those whom I like or admire, I can find no common denominator, but among those whom I love, I can: all of them make me laugh.

If Homer had tried reading the *Iliad* to the gods on Olympus, they would either have started to fidget and presently asked if he hadn't got something a little lighter, or, taking it as a comic poem, would have roared with laughter or possibly, even, reacting like ourselves to a tear-jerking movie, have poured pleasing tears.

AMBROSE BIERCE: *from* The Devil's Dictionary

abdication, *n.* An act whereby a sovereign attests his sense of the high temperature of the throne.

abscond, *v.i.* To "move in a mysterious way," commonly with the property of another.

absent, *adj.* Peculiarly exposed to the tooth of detraction; vilified; hopelessly in the wrong; superseded in the consideration and affection of another.

accident, *n.* An inevitable occurrence due to the action of immutable natural laws.

accordion, *n.* An instrument in harmony with the sentiments of an assassin.

achievement, *n.* The death of endeavor and the birth of disgust.

admiration, *n.* Our polite recognition of another's resemblance to ourselves.

alone, *adj.* In bad company.

applause, *n.* The echo of a platitude.

ardor, *n.* The quality that distinguishes love without knowledge.

bore, *n.* A person who talks when you wish him to listen.

cemetery, *n.* An isolated suburban spot where mourners match lies, poets write at a target and stone-cutters spell for a wager. The inscription following will serve to illustrate the success attained in these Olympian games:

> His virtues were so conspicuous that his enemies, unable to overlook them, denied them, and his friends, to whose loose lives they were a rebuke, represented them as vices. They are here commemorated by his family, who shared them.

childhood, *n.* The period of human life intermediate between the idiocy of infancy and the folly of youth—two removes from the sin of manhood and three from the remorse of age.

Christian, *n.* One who believes that the New Testament is a divinely inspired book admirably suited to the spiritual needs of his neighbor. One who follows the teachings of Christ in so far as they are not inconsistent with a life of sin.

compulsion, *n.* The eloquence of power.

congratulation, *n.* The civility of envy.

conservative, *n.* A statesman who is enamored of existing evils, as distinguished from the Liberal, who wishes to replace them with others.

consult, *v.t.* To seek another's approval of a course already decided on.

contempt, *n.* The feeling of a prudent man for an enemy who is too formidable safely to be opposed.

coward, *n.* One who in a perilous emergency thinks with his legs.

debauchee, *n.* One who has so earnestly pursued pleasure that he has had the misfortune to overtake it.

destiny, *n.* A tyrant's authority for crime and a fool's excuse for failure.

diplomacy, *n.* The patriotic art of lying for one's country.

distance, *n.* The only thing that the rich are willing for the poor to call theirs and keep.

duty, *n.* That which sternly impels us in the direction of profit, along the line of desire.

education, *n.* That which discloses to the wise and disguises from the foolish their lack of understanding.

erudition, *n.* Dust shaken out of a book into an empty skull.

extinction, *n.* The raw material out of which theology created the future state.

faith, *n.* Belief without evidence in what is told by one who speaks without knowledge, of things without parallel.

genealogy, *n.* An account of one's descent from an ancestor who did not particularly care to trace his own.

ghost, *n.* The outward and visible sign of an inward fear.

habit, *n.* A shackle for the free.

heaven, *n.* A place where the wicked cease from troubling you with talk of their personal affairs, and the good listen with attention while you expound your own.

historian, *n.* A broad-gauge gossip.

hope, *n.* Desire and expectation rolled into one.

hypocrite, *n.* One who, professing virtues that he does not respect, secures the advantage of seeming to be what he despises.

impiety, *n.* Your irreverence toward my deity.

impunity, *n.* Wealth.

language, *n.* The music with which we charm the serpents guarding another's treasure.

logic, *n.* The art of thinking and reasoning in strict accordance with the limitations and incapacities of the human misunderstanding. The basis of logic is the syllogism, consisting of a major and a minor premise and a conclusion—thus:

Major Premise: Sixty men can do a piece of work sixty times as quickly as one man.

Minor Premise: One man can dig a post-hole in sixty seconds; therefore—

Conclusion: Sixty men can dig a post-hole in one second.

This may be called the syllogism arithmetical, in which, by combining logic and mathematics, we obtain a double certainty and are twice blessed.

love, *n.* A temporary insanity curable by marriage or by removal of the patient from the influences under which he incurred the disorder. This disease, like *caries* and many other ailments, is prevalent only among civilized races living under artificial conditions; barbarous nations breathing pure air and eating simple food enjoy immunity from its ravages. It is sometimes fatal, but more frequently to the physician than to the patient.

miracle, *n.* An act or event out of the order of nature and unaccountable, as beating a normal hand of four kings and an ace with four aces and a king.

monkey, *n.* An arboreal animal which makes itself at home in genealogical trees.

mouth, *n.* In man, the gateway to the soul; in woman, the outlet of the heart.

non-combatant, *n.* A dead Quaker.

platitude, *n.* The fundamental element and special glory of popular literature. A thought that snores in words that smoke. The wisdom of a million fools in the diction of a dullard. A fossil sentiment in artificial rock. A moral without the fable. All that is mortal of a departed truth. A demi-tasse of milk-and-morality. The Pope's-nose of a featherless peacock. A jelly-fish withering on the shore of the sea of thought. The cackle surviving the egg. A dessicated epigram.

pray, *v.* To ask that the laws of the universe be annulled in behalf of a single petitioner confessedly unworthy.

presidency, *n.* The greased pig in the field game of American politics.

prude, *n.* A bawd hiding behind the back of her demeanor.

rapacity, *n.* Providence without industry. The thrift of power.

reason, *v.i.* To weigh probabilities in the scales of desire.

religion, *n.* A daughter of Hope and Fear, explaining to Ignorance the nature of the Unknowable.

resolute, *adj.* Obstinate in a course that we approve.

retaliation, *n.* The natural rock upon which is reared the Temple of Law.

saint, *n.* A dead sinner revised and edited.

The Duchess of Orleans relates that the irreverent old calumniator, Marshal Villeroi, who in his youth had known St. Francis de Sales, said, on hearing him called saint: "I am delighted to hear that Monsieur de Sales is a saint. He was fond of saying indelicate things, and used to cheat at cards. In other respects he was a perfect gentleman, though a fool."

valor, *n.* A soldierly compound of vanity, duty and the gambler's hope:

"Why have you halted?" roared the commander of a division at Chickamauga, who had ordered a charge; "move forward, sir, at once."

"General," said the commander of the delinquent brigade, "I am persuaded that any further display of valor by my troops will bring them into collision with the enemy."

WILLIAM BLAKE: Proverbs of Hell

In seed time learn, in harvest teach, in winter enjoy.

Drive your cart and your plough over the bones of the dead.

The road of excess leads to the palace of wisdom.

Prudence is a rich, ugly old maid courted by Incapacity.

He who desires but acts not, breeds pestilence.

The cut worm forgives the plough.

Dip him in the river who loves water.

A fool sees not the same tree that a wise man sees.

He whose face gives no light, shall never become a star.

Eternity is in love with the productions of time.

The busy bee has no time for sorrow.

The hours of folly are measur'd by the clock; but of wisdom, no clock can measure.

All wholesome food is caught without a net or a trap.

Bring out number, weight, and measure in a year of dearth.

No bird soars too high, if he soars with his own wings.

A dead body revenges not injuries.

The most sublime act is to set another before you.

If the fool would persist in his folly he would become wise.

Folly is the cloak of knavery.

Shame is Pride's cloak.

Prisons are built with stones of Law, brothels with bricks of Religion.

The pride of the peacock is the glory of God.

The lust of the goat is the bounty of God.

The wrath of the lion is the wisdom of God.

The nakedness of woman is the work of God.

Excess of sorrow laughs. Excess of joy weeps.

The roaring of lions, the howling of wolves, the raging of the stormy sea, and the destructive sword are portions of eternity too great for the eye of man.

The fox condemns the trap, not himself.

Joys impregnate. Sorrows bring forth.

Let man wear the fell of the lion, woman the fleece of the sheep.

The bird a nest, the spider a web, man friendship.

The selfish, smiling fool, and the sullen, frowning fool shall be both thought wise, that they may be a rod.

What is now proved was once only imagin'd.

The rat, the mouse, the fox, the rabbit watch the roots; the lion, the tiger, the horse, the elephant watch the fruits.

The cistern contains: the fountain overflows.

One thought fills immensity.

Always be ready to speak your mind, and a base man will avoid you.

Everything possible to be believ'd is an image of truth.

The eagle never lost so much time as when he submitted to learn of the crow.

The fox provides for himself; but God provides for the lion.

Think in the morning. Act in the noon. Eat in the evening. Sleep in the night.

He who has suffer'd you to impose on him, knows you.

As the plough follows words, so God rewards prayers.

The tigers of wrath are wiser than the horses of instruction.

Expect poison from the standing water.

You never know what is enough unless you know what is more than enough.

Listen to the fool's reproach! it is a kingly title!

The eyes of fire, the nostrils of air, the mouth of water, the beard of earth.

The weak in courage is strong in cunning.

The apple tree never asks the beech how he shall grow; nor the lion, the horse, how he shall take his prey.

The thankful receiver bears a plentiful harvest.

If others had not been foolish, we should be so.

The soul of sweet delight can never be defil'd.

When thou seest an eagle, thou seest a portion of Genius; lift up thy head!

As the caterpillar chooses the fairest leaves to lay her eggs on, so the priest lays his curse on the fairest joys.

To create a little flower is the labor of ages.

Damn braces. Bless relaxes.

The best wine is the oldest, the best water the newest.

Prayers plough not! Praises reap not!

Joys laugh not! Sorrows weep not!

The head Sublime, the heart Pathos, the genitals Beauty, the hands and feet Proportion.

As the air to a bird or the sea to a fish, so is contempt to the contemptible.

The crow wish'd everything was black, the owl that everything was white.

Exuberance is Beauty.

If the lion was advised by the fox, he would be cunning.

Improvement makes straight roads; but the crooked roads without improvement are roads of Genius.

Sooner murder an infant in its cradle than nurse unacted desires.

Where man is not, nature is barren.

Truth can never be told so as to be understood, and not be believ'd.

Enough! or Too much.

OSCAR WILDE: Preface to *The Picture of Dorian Gray*

The artist is the creator of beautiful things.

To reveal art and conceal the artist is art's aim.

The critic is he who can translate into another manner or a new material his impression of beautiful things.

The highest as the lowest form of criticism is a mode of autobiography.

Those who find ugly meanings in beautiful things are corrupt without being charming. This is a fault.

Those who find beautiful meanings in beautiful things are the cultivated. For these there is hope.

They are the elect to whom beautiful things mean only beauty.

There is no such thing as a moral or an immoral book. Books are well written, or badly written. That is all. . . .

The moral life of man forms part of the subject matter of the artist, but the morality of art consists in the perfect use of an imperfect medium.

No artist desires to prove anything. Even things that are true can be proved.

No artist has ethical sympathies. An ethical sympathy in an artist is an unpardonable mannerism of style.

No artist is ever morbid. The artist can express everything.

Thought and language are to the artist instruments of an art.

Vice and virtue are to the artist materials for an art.

From the point of view of form, the type of all the arts is the art of the musician. From the point of view of feeling, the actor's craft is the type.

All art is at once surface and symbol.

Those who go beneath the surface do so at their peril.

Those who read the symbol do so at their peril.

It is the spectator, and not life, that art really mirrors.
Diversity of opinion about a work of art shows that
the work is new, complex, and vital.

When critics disagree the artist is in accord with
himself.

We can forgive a man for making a useful thing as long
as he does not admire it. The only excuse for making a
useless thing is that one admires it intensely. ·

    All art is quite useless.

SAMUEL BUTLER: *from* Notebooks

We play out our days as we play out cards, taking them as they come, not knowing what they will be, hoping for a lucky card and sometimes getting one, often getting just the wrong one.

The world will always be governed by self-interest. We should not try to stop this, we should try to make the self-interest of cads a little more consistent with that of decent people.

Morality turns on whether the pleasure precedes or follows the pain. Thus, it is immoral to get drunk because the headache comes after the drinking, but if the headache came first, and the drunkenness afterwards, it would be moral to get drunk.

Morality is the custom of one's country and the current feeling of one's peers. Cannibalism is moral in a cannibal country.

We want words to do more than they can. We try to do with them what comes to very much like trying to mend a watch with a pickaxe or to paint a miniature with a mop; we expect them to help us to grip and dissect that which in ultimate essence is as ungrippable as shadow. Nevertheless there they are; we have got to live with them, and the wise course is to treat them as we do our neighbours, and make the best and not the worst of them. But they are parvenu people as compared with thought and action. What we should read is not the words but the man whom we feel to be behind the words.

Words impede and either kill, or are killed by, perfect thought; but they are, as a scaffolding, useful, if not indispensable, for the building up of imperfect thought and helping to perfect it.

Always eat grapes downwards—that is, always eat the best grape first; in this way there will be none better left on the bunch, and each grape will seem good down to the last. If you eat the other way, you will not have a good grape in the lot. Besides, you will be tempting Providence to kill you before you come to the best. This is why autumn seems better than spring: in the autumn we are eating our days downwards, in the spring each day still seems "very bad." People should live on this principle more than they do, but they do live on it a good deal; from the age of, say, fifty, we eat our days downwards.

In New Zealand for a long time I had to do the washing-up after each meal. I used to do the knives first, for it might please God to take me before I came to the forks, and then what a sell it would have been to have done the forks rather than the knives!

The evil that men do lives after them. Yes, and a good deal of the evil that they never did as well.

A definition is the enclosing a wilderness of ideas within a wall of words.

Perseus and St. George. These dragon-slayers did not take lessons in dragon-slaying, nor do leaders of forlorn hopes generally rehearse their parts beforehand. Small things may be rehearsed, but the greatest are always do-or-die, neck-or-nothing matters.

Silence is not always tact and it is tact that is golden, not silence.

Providence, in making the rain fall also upon the sea, was like the man who, when he was to play Othello, must needs black himself all over.

A little girl and a little boy were looking at a picture of Adam and Eve.

"Which is Adam and which is Eve?" said one.

"I do not know," said the other, "but I could tell if they had their clothes on."

The pursuit of truth is chimerical. That is why it is so hard to say what truth is. There is no permanent absolute unchangeable truth; what we should pursue is the most convenient arrangement of our ideas.

The firmest line that can be drawn upon the smoothest paper has still jagged edges if seen through a microscope. This does not matter until important deductions are made on the supposition that there are no jagged edges.

Truth generally is kindness, but where the two diverge or collide, kindness should override truth.

We do with truth much as we do with God. We create it according to our own requirements and then say that it has created us, or requires that we shall do or think so and so—whatever we find convenient.

"What is Truth?" is often asked, as though it were harder to say what truth is than what anything else is. But what is Justice? What is anything? An eternal contradiction in terms meets us at the end of every enquiry. We are not required to know what truth is, but to speak the truth, and so with justice.

Imagination depends mainly upon memory, but there is a small percentage of creation of something out of nothing with it. We can invent a trifle more than can be got at by mere combination of remembered things.

Intuition and evidence seem to have something of the same relation that faith and reason, luck and cunning, free-will and necessity and demand and supply have. They grow up hand in hand and no man can say which comes first. It is the same with life and death, which lurk within the others as do rest and unrest, change and persistence, heat and cold, poverty and riches, harmony and counterpoint, night and day, summer and winter.

And so with pantheism and atheism; loving everybody is loving nobody, and God everywhere is, practically, God nowhere. I once asked a man if he was a free-thinker; he replied that he did not think he was. And so, I have heard of a man exclaiming "I am an atheist, thank God!" Those who say there is a God are wrong unless they mean at the same time that there is no God, and vice versa. The difference is the same as that between plus nothing and minus nothing, and it is hard to say which we ought to admire and thank most—the first theist or the first atheist. Nevertheless, for many reasons, the plus nothing is to be preferred.

BENJAMIN FRANKLIN: *from* Poor Richard's Almanack

Light purse, heavy heart. 1733
He's a fool that makes his doctor his heir.
Love well, whip well.
Hunger never saw bad bread.
Fools make feasts, and wise men eat 'em.
He that lies down with dogs, shall rise up with fleas.
He is ill clothed, who is bare of virtue.
There is no little enemy.

Without justice courage is weak. 1734
Where there's marriage without love, there will be love without marriage.
Do good to thy friend to keep him, to thy enemy to gain him.
He that cannot obey, cannot command.
Marry your son when you will, but your daughter when you can.

Approve not of him who commends all you say.   1735
Necessity never made a good bargain.
Be slow in chusing a friend, slower in changing.
Three may keep a secret, if two of them are dead.
Deny self for self's sake.
To be humble to superiors is duty, to equals courtesy, to inferiors nobleness.

Fish and visitors stink in three days.   1736
Do not do that which you would not have known.
Bargaining has neither friends nor relations.
Now I've a sheep and a cow, every body bids me good morrow.
God helps them that help themselves.
He that speaks much, is much mistaken.
God heals, and the doctor takes the fees.

There are no ugly loves, nor handsome prisons.   1737
Three good meals a day is bad living.

Who has deceiv'd thee so oft as thyself?   1738
Read much, but not many books.
Let thy vices die before thee.

He that falls in love with himself, will have no rivals.   1739
Sin is not hurtful because it is forbidden, but it is forbidden because it's hurtful.

An empty bag cannot stand upright.   1740

Learn of the skilful: he that teaches himself, hath a fool for his master.   1741

Death takes no bribes.   1742

An old man in a house is a good sign.   1744
Fear God, and your enemies will fear you.

He's a fool that cannot conceal his wisdom.   1745
Many complain of their memory, few of their judgment.

When the well's dry, we know the worth of water.   1746
The sting of a reproach is the truth of it.

Write injuries in dust, benefits in marble.   1747

Nine men in *ten* are suicides.   1749
A man in a passion rides a mad horse.

He is a governor that governs his passions, and he is a servant that serves them.   1750
Sorrow is good for nothing but sin.

Calamity and prosperity are the touchstones of integrity.   1752
Generous minds are all of kin.

Haste makes waste.   1753

The doors of wisdom are never shut.   1755

The way to be safe, is never to be secure.   1757

WILLIAM HAZLITT: *from* Characteristics

1. Of all virtues, magnanimity is the rarest. There are a hundred persons of merit for one who willingly acknowledges it in another.

13. Some people tell us all the harm—others as carefully conceal all the good they hear of us.

15. The silence of a friend commonly amounts to treachery. His not daring to say anything in our behalf implies a tacit censure.

23. Envy is a littleness of soul, which cannot see beyond a certain point, and if it does not occupy the whole space, feels itself excluded.

27. Those who are the most distrustful of themselves, are the most envious of others; as the most weak and cowardly are the most revengeful.

38. The wish is often "father to the thought"; but we are quite as apt to believe what we dread as what we hope.

46. We like characters and actions which we do not approve. There are amiable vices and obnoxious virtues, on the mere principle that our sympathy with a person who yields to obvious impulses (however prejudicial) is itself agreeable, while to sympathize with exercises of self-denial or fortitude, is a painful effort. Virtue costs the spectator, as well as the performer, something. We are touched by the immediate motives of actions, we judge of them by the consequences. We like a convivial character better than an abstemious one, because the idea of conviviality in the first instance is pleasanter than that of sobriety. For the same reason, we prefer generosity to justice, because the imagination lends itself more easily to an ebullition of feeling, than to the suppression of it on remote and abstract principles; and we like a good-natured fool, or even knave better than the severe professors of wisdom and morality. Cato, Brutus, etc. are characters to admire and applaud, rather than to love or imitate.

57. The surest way to make ourselves agreeable to others is by seeming to think them so. If we appear fully sensible of their good qualities, they will not complain of the want of them in us.

59. Silence is one great art of conversation. He is not a fool who knows when to hold his tongue; and a person may gain credit for

sense, eloquence, wit, who merely says nothing to lessen the opinion which others have of these qualities in themselves.

61. A man who is always defending his friends from the most trifling charges, will be apt to make other people their enemies.

85. The public have neither shame nor gratitude.

89. It is wonderful how soon men acquire talents for offices of trust and importance. The higher the situation, the higher the opinion it gives us of ourselves; and as is our confidence, so is our capacity. We *assume* an equality with circumstances.

105. The error in the reasonings of Mandeville, Rochefoucauld, and others, is this: they first find out that there is something mixed in the motives of all our actions, and they then proceed to argue, that they must all arise from one motive, *viz.* self-love. They make the exception the rule. It would be easy to reverse the argument, and prove that our most selfish actions are disinterested. There is honor among thieves. Robbers, murderers, etc. do not commit those actions, from a pleasure in pure villainy, or for their own benefit only, but from a mistaken regard to the welfare or good opinion of those with whom they are immediately connected.

115. We do not hate those who injure us, if they do not at the same time wound our self-love. We can forgive any one sooner than those who lower us in our own opinion. It is no wonder, therefore, that we as often dislike others for their virtues as for their vices. We naturally hate whatever makes us despise ourselves.

127. We as often repent the good we have done as the ill.

131. The fear of punishment may be necessary to the suppression of vice; but it also suspends the finer motives to virtue.

134. Vulgar prejudices are those which arise out of accident, ignorance, or authority. Natural prejudices are those which arise out of the constitution of the human mind itself.

138. Most codes of morality proceed on a supposition of *Original Sin*; as if the only object was to coerce the headstrong propensities to vice, and there were no natural disposition to good in the mind, which it was possible to improve, refine, and cultivate.

139. This *negative* system of virtue leads to a very low style of moral sentiment. It is as if the highest excellence in a picture was to avoid gross defects in drawing; or in writing, instances of bad grammar. It ought surely to be our aim in virtue, as well as in other things, "to snatch a grace beyond the reach of art."

142. When the imagination is continually led to the brink of vice by a system of terror and denunciations, people fling themselves over the precipice from the mere dread of falling.

145. Honesty is one part of eloquence. We persuade others by being in earnest ourselves.

LA ROCHEFOUCAULD: *from* Maxims

Our virtues are mostly but vices in disguise.

14. Men not only forget benefits received and injuries endured; they even come to dislike those to whom they are indebted, while ceasing to hate those others who have done them harm. Diligence in returning good for good, and in exacting vengeance for evil, comes to be a sort of servitude which we do not readily accept.

19. We are all strong enough to endure the misfortunes of others.

20. The steadiness of the wise man is only the art of keeping his agitations locked within his breast.

25. Firmer virtues are required to support good fortune than bad.

28. Jealousy is, in its way, both fair and reasonable, since its intention is to preserve for ourselves something which is ours, or which we believe to be ours; envy, on the other hand, is a frenzy which cannot endure contemplating the possessions of others.

31. Were we faultless, we would not derive such satisfaction from remarking the faults of others.

38. Our promises are made in hope, and kept in fear.

50. A man convinced of his own merit will accept misfortune as an honor, for thus can he persuade others, as well as himself, that he is a worthy target for the arrows of fate.

56. To achieve a position in the world a man will do his utmost to appear already arrived.

59. There is no accident so disastrous that a clever man cannot derive some profit from it; nor any so fortunate that a fool cannot turn it to his disadvantage.

62. Sincerity comes from an open heart. It is exceedingly rare; what usually passes for sincerity is only an artful pretense designed to win the confidence of others.

67. Grace is to the body what sense is to the mind.

71. When two people have ceased to love, the memory that remains is almost always one of shame.

72. Love, to judge by most of its effects, is closer to hatred than to friendship.

75. Love, like fire, needs constant motion; when it ceases to hope, or to fear, love dies.

78. For most men the love of justice is only the fear of suffering injustice.

79. For a man who lacks self-confidence, silence is the wisest course.

83. What men have called friendship is only a social arrangement, a mutual adjustment of interests, an interchange of services given and received; it is, in sum, simply a business from which those involved purpose to derive a steady profit for their own self-love.

89. Everyone complains of his memory, none of his judgment.

90. In daily life our faults are frequently more pleasant than our good qualities.

93. Old people love to give good advice: it compensates them for their inability nowadays to set a bad example.

119. We are so accustomed to adopting a mask before others that we end by being unable to recognize ourselves.

122. If we master our passions it is due to their weakness, not our strength.

134. We are never so ridiculous through what we are as through what we pretend to be.

138. We would rather speak ill of ourselves than not at all.

144. We do not like to give praise, and we never do so without reasons of self-interest. Praise is a cunning, concealed and delicate form of flattery which, in different ways, gratifies both the giver and the receiver; the one accepts it as the reward for merit; the other bestows it to display his sense of justice and his powers of discernment.

146. We usually only praise that we may be praised.

149. The refusal to accept praise is the desire to be praised twice over.

150. The wish to deserve the praise we receive strengthens our virtues; and praise bestowed upon wit, courage and beauty contributes to their increase.

167. Avarice, more than open-handedness, is the opposite of economy.

170. When a man's behavior is straightforward, sincere and honest it is hard to be sure whether this is due to rectitude or cleverness.

176. In love there are two sorts of constancy: the one comes from the perpetual discovery of new delights in the beloved: the other, from the self-esteem which we derive from our own fidelity.

180. Our repentance is less a regret for the evil we have done than a precaution against the evil that may be done to us.

185. Evil, like good, has its heroes.

186. Not all who have vices are contemptible: all without a trace of virtue are.

190. Only great men are marked with great faults.

192. When our vices depart from us, we flatter ourselves that it is we who have rid ourselves of them.

200. Virtue would not go so far did vanity not keep her company.

205. Virtue, in women, is often love of reputation and fondness for tranquillity.

216. Perfect valor is to behave, without witnesses, as one would act were all the world watching.

218. Hypocrisy is the tribute that vice pays to virtue.

230. Nothing is as contagious as example, and we never perform an outstandingly good or evil action without its producing others of its sort. We copy goodness in the spirit of emulation, and wickedness owing to the malignity of our nature which shame holds in check until example sets it free.

237. No man should be praised for his goodness if he lacks the strength to be bad: in such cases goodness is usually only the effect of indolence or impotence of will.

259. The pleasure of love is in loving: and there is more joy in the passion one feels than in that which one inspires.

264. Pity is often only the sentiment of our own misfortunes felt in the ills of others. It is a clever pre-science of the evil times upon which we may fall. We help others in order to ensure their help in similar circumstances; and the kindnesses we do them are, if the truth were told, only acts of charity towards ourselves invested against the future.

276. Absence diminishes small loves and increases great ones, as the wind blows out the candle and blows up the bonfire.

277. Women frequently believe themselves to be in love even when they are not: the pursuit of an intrigue, the stimulus of gallantry, the natural inclination towards the joys of being loved, and the difficulty of refusal, all these combine to tell them that their passions are aroused when in fact it is but their coquetry at play.

375. It is the habit of mediocre minds to condemn all that is beyond their grasp.

376. True friendship destroys envy, as true love puts an end to coquetry.

378. We give advice but we do not inspire behavior.

392. One should treat one's fate as one does one's health; enjoy it when it is good, be patient with it when it is poorly, and never attempt any drastic cure save as an ultimate resort.

399. There is a form of eminence which is quite independent of our fate; it is an air which distinguishes us from our fellow men and makes us appear destined for great things; it is the value which we imperceptibly attach to ourselves; it is the quality which wins us the deference of others; more than birth, honours or even merit, it gives us ascendancy.

417. In love, the person who recovers first recovers best.

423. Few people know how to be old.

467. Vanity leads us to act against our inclinations more often than does reason.

479. Only people who are strong can be truly gentle: what normally passes for gentleness is mere weakness, which quickly turns sour.

483. Vanity, rather than malice, is the usual source of slander.

540. Hope and fear are inseparable. There is no hope without fear, nor any fear without hope.

576. We always discover, in the misfortunes of our dearest friends, something not altogether displeasing.

597. No man can be sure of his own courage until he has stared danger in the face.

617. How can we expect another to keep our secret, if we cannot keep it ourself?

GEORGE BERNARD SHAW: *from* The Revolutionist's Handbook (*in* Man and Superman)

Democracy

Democracy substitutes selection by the incompetent many for appointment by the corrupt few.

Democratic republics can no more dispense with national idols than monarchies with public functionaries.

Liberty and Equality

He who confuses political liberty with freedom and political equality with similarity has never thought for five minutes about either.

Nothing can be unconditional: consequently nothing can be free.

Liberty means responsibility. That is why most men dread it.

The duke inquires contemptuously whether his gamekeeper is the equal of the Astronomer Royal; but he insists that they shall both be hanged equally if they murder him.

The notion that the colonel need be a better man than the private is as confused as the notion that the keystone need be stronger than the coping stone.

The relation of superior to inferior excludes good manners.

Education

When a man teaches something he does not know to somebody else who has no aptitude for it, and gives him a certificate of proficiency, the latter has completed the education of a gentleman.

A fool's brain digests philosophy into folly, science into superstition, and art into pedantry. Hence University education.

The best brought-up children are those who have seen their parents as they are. Hypocrisy is not the parent's first duty.

The vilest abortionist is he who attempts to mould a child's character.

He who can, does. He who cannot, teaches.

A learned man is an idler who kills time with study. Beware of his false knowledge: it is more dangerous than ignorance.

Activity is the only road to knowledge.

Every fool believes what his teachers tell him, and calls his credulity science or morality as confidently as his father called it divine revelation.

No man fully capable of his own language ever masters another.

No man can be a pure specialist without being in the strict sense an idiot.

Do not give your children moral and religious instruction unless you are quite sure they will not take it too seriously. Better be the mother of Henri Quatre and Nell Gwynne than of Robespierre and Queen Mary Tudor.

Virtues and Vices

No specific virtue or vice in a man implies the existence of any other specific virtue or vice in him, however closely the imagination may associate them.

Virtue consists, not in abstaining from vice, but in not desiring it.

Self-denial is not a virtue: it is only the effect of prudence on rascality.

Obedience simulates subordination as fear of the police simulates honesty.

Disobedience, the rarest and most courageous of the virtues, is seldom distinguished from neglect, the laziest and commonest of the vices.

Vice is waste of life. Poverty, obedience, and celibacy are the canonical vices.

Economy is the art of making the most of life.

The love of economy is the root of all virtue.

Greatness

In heaven an angel is nobody in particular.

Greatness is the secular name for Divinity: both mean simply what lies beyond us.

If a great man could make us understand him, we should hang him.

We admit that when the divinity we worshipped made itself visible and comprehensible we crucified it.

To a mathematician the eleventh means only a single unit: to the bushman who cannot count further than his ten fingers it is an incalculable myriad.

The difference between the shallowest routineer and the deepest thinker appears, to the latter, trifling; to the former, infinite.

In a stupid nation the man of genius becomes a god: everybody worships him and nobody does his will.

Gambling

The most popular method of distributing wealth is the method of the roulette table.

The roulette table pays nobody except him that keeps it. Nevertheless a passion for gaming is common, though a passion for keeping roulette tables is unknown.

Gambling promises the poor what Property performs for the rich: that is why the bishops dare not denounce it fundamentally.

On History

HENRY DAVID THOREAU
The Battle of the Ants[1]

One day when I went out to my wood-pile, or rather my pile of stumps, I observed two large ants, the one red, the other much larger, nearly half an inch long, and black, fiercely contending with one another. Having once got hold they never let go, but struggled and wrestled and rolled on the chips incessantly. Looking farther, I was surprised to find that the chips were covered with such combatants, that it was not a *duellum*, but a *bellum*, a war between two races of ants, the red always pitted against the black, and frequently two red ones to one black. The legions of these Myrmidons covered all the hills and vales in my wood-yard, and the ground was already strewn with the dead and dying, both red and black. It was the only battle which I have ever witnessed, the only battle-field I ever trod while the battle was raging; internecine war; the red republicans on the one hand, and the black imperialists on the other. On every side they were engaged in deadly combat, yet without any noise that I could hear, and human soldiers never fought so resolutely. I watched a couple that were fast locked in each other's embraces, in a little sunny valley amid the chips, now at noonday prepared to fight till the sun went down, or life went out. The smaller red champion had fastened himself like a vice to his adversary's front, and through all the tumblings on that field never for an instant ceased to gnaw at one of his feelers near the root, having already caused the other to go by the board; while the stronger black one dashed him from side to side, and, as I saw on looking nearer, had already divested him of several of his members. They fought with more pertinacity than bulldogs. Neither manifested the least disposi-

1. From "Brute Neighbors," Chapter XII of *Walden*.

tion to retreat. It was evident that their battle-cry was "Conquer or die." In the meanwhile there came along a single red ant on the hillside of this valley, evidently full of excitement, who either had despatched his foe, or had not yet taken part in the battle; probably the latter, for he had lost none of his limbs; whose mother had charged him to return with his shield or upon it. Or perchance he was some Achilles, who had nourished his wrath apart, and had now come to avenge or rescue his Patroclus.[2] He saw this unequal combat from afar—for the blacks were nearly twice the size of the red—he drew near with rapid pace till he stood on his guard within half an inch of the combatants; then, watching his opportunity, he sprang upon the black warrior, and commenced his operations near the root of his right fore leg, leaving the foe to select among his own members; and so there were three united for life, as if a new kind of attraction had been invented which put all other locks and cements to shame. I should not have wondered by this time to find that they had their respective musical bands stationed on some eminent chip, and playing their national airs the while, to excite the slow and cheer the dying combatants. I was myself excited somewhat even as if they had been men. The more you think of it, the less the difference. And certainly there is not the fight recorded in Concord history, at least, if in the history of America, that will bear a moment's comparison with this, whether for the numbers engaged in it, or for the patriotism and heroism displayed. For numbers and for carnage it was an Austerlitz or Dresden.[3] Concord Fight! Two killed on the patriots' side, and Luther Blanchard wounded! Why here every ant was a Buttrick—"Fire! for God's sake fire!"—and thousands shared the fate of Davis and Hosmer. There was not one hireling there. I have no doubt that it was a principle they fought for, as much as our ancestors, and not to avoid a three-penny tax on their tea; and the results of this battle will be as important and memorable to those whom it concerns as those of the battle of Bunker Hill, at least.

I took up the chip on which the three I have particularly described were struggling, carried into my house, and placed it under a tumbler on my window-sill, in order to see the issue. Holding a microscope to the first-mentioned red ant, I saw that, though he was assiduously gnawing at the near fore leg of his enemy, having severed his remaining feeler, his own breast was all torn away, exposing what vitals he had there to the jaws of the black warrior, whose breastplate was apparently too thick for him to pierce; and the dark carbuncles of the sufferer's eyes shone with ferocity such as war only could excite. They struggled half an hour longer under the tumbler, and when I looked again the black soldier had severed the heads of his foes from their bodies, and the still living heads were hanging on

2. A Greek warrior in the *Iliad*, whose death Achilles avenges.
3. Bloody Napoleonic victories.

either side of him like ghastly trophies at his saddle-bow, still apparently as firmly fastened as ever, and he was endeavoring with feeble struggles, being without feelers, and with only the remnant of a leg, and I know not how many other wounds, to divest himself of them; which at length, after half an hour more, he accomplished. I raised the glass, and he went off over the window-sill in that crippled state. Whether he finally survived that combat, and spent the remainder of his days in some Hôtel des Invalides, I do not know; but I thought that his industry would not be worth much thereafter. I never learned which party was victorious, nor the cause of the war, but I felt for the rest of that day as if I had my feelings excited and harrowed by witnessing the struggle, the ferocity and carnage, of a human battle before my door.

Kirby and Spence tell us that the battles of ants have long been celebrated and the date of them recorded, though they say that Huber[4] is the only modern author who appears to have witnessed them. "Aeneas Sylvius," say they, "after giving a very circumstantial account of one contested with great obstinacy by a great and small species on the trunk of a pear tree," adds that " 'this action was fought in the pontificate of Eugenius the Fourth, in the presence of Nicholas Pistoriensis, an eminent lawyer, who related the whole history of the battle with the greatest fidelity.' A similar engagement between great and small ants is recorded by Olaus Magnus, in which the small ones, being victorious, are said to have buried the bodies of their own soldiers, but left those of their giant enemies a prey to the birds. This event happened previous to the expulsion of the tyrant Christiern the Second from Sweden." The battle which I witnessed took place in the Presidency of Polk, five years before the passage of Webster's Fugitive-Slave Bill.

4. Kirby and Spence were nineteenth-century American entomologists; Huber was a great Swiss entomologist.

QUESTIONS

1. Thoreau uses the Latin word bellum to describe the battle of the ants and he quickly follows this with a reference to the Myrmidons of Achilles. What comparison is implicit here? Find further examples of it. This passage comes from a chapter entitled "Brute Neighbors"; how does this comparison amplify the meaning of that title?

2. Describe the life, or part of the life, of an animal so that, while remaining faithful to the facts as you understand them, your description opens outward as does Thoreau's, and speaks not only of the animal but also of man, society, or nature.

CHIEF SEATTLE

Address[1]

The Governor made a fine speech, but he was outranged and outclassed that day. Chief Seattle, who answered on behalf of the Indians, towered a foot above the Governor. He wore his blanket like the toga of a Roman senator, and he did not have to strain his famous voice, which everyone agreed was audible and distinct at a distance of half a mile.

Seattle's oration was in Duwamish. Doctor Smith, who had learned the language, wrote it down; under the flowery garlands of his translation the speech rolls like an articulate iron engine, grim with meanings that outlasted his generation and may outlast all the generations of men. As the amiable follies of the white race become less amiable, the iron rumble of old Seattle's speech sounds louder and more ominous.

Standing in front of Doctor Maynard's office in the stumpy clearing, with his hand on the little Governor's head, the white invaders about him and his people before him, Chief Seattle said:

"Yonder sky that has wept tears of compassion upon my people for centuries untold, and which to us appears changeless and eternal, may change. Today is fair. Tomorrow may be overcast with clouds. My words are like the stars that never change. Whatever Seattle says the great chief at Washington can rely upon with as much certainty as he can upon the return of the sun or the seasons. The White Chief says that Big Chief at Washington sends us greetings of friendship and goodwill. That is kind of him for we know he has little need of our friendship in return. His people are many. They are like the grass that covers vast prairies. My people are few. They resemble the scattering trees of a storm-swept plain. The great, and—I presume—good, White Chief sends us word that he wishes to buy our lands but is willing to allow us enough to live comfortably. This indeed appears just, even generous, for the Red Man no longer has rights that he need respect, and the offer may be wise also, as we are no longer in need of an extensive country. . . . I will not dwell on, nor mourn over, our untimely decay, nor reproach our paleface brothers with hastening it, as we too may have been somewhat to blame.

"Youth is impulsive. When our young men grow angry at some real or imaginary wrong, and disfigure their faces with black paint,

---

1. In 1854, Governor Isaac Stevens, Commissioner of Indian Affairs for the Washington Territory, proffered a treaty to the Indians providing for the sale of two million acres of their land to the federal government. This address is the reply of Chief Seattle of the Duwampo tribe. The translator was Henry A. Smith.

it denotes that their hearts are black, and then they are often cruel and relentless, and our old men and old women are unable to restrain them. Thus it has ever been. Thus it was when the white men first began to push our forefathers further westward. But let us hope that the hostilities between us may never return. We would have everything to lose and nothing to gain. Revenge by young men is considered gain, even at the cost of their own lives, but old men who stay at home in times of war, and mothers who have sons to lose, know better.

"Our good father at Washington—for I presume he is now our father as well as yours, since King George has moved his boundaries further north—our great good father, I say, sends us word that if we do as he desires he will protect us. His brave warriors will be to us a bristling wall of strength, and his wonderful ships of war will fill our harbors so that our ancient enemies far to the northward—the Hydas and Tsimpsians—will cease to frighten our women, children, and old men. Then in reality will he be our father and we his children. But can that ever be? Your God is not our God! Your God loves your people and hates mine. He folds his strong and protecting arms lovingly about the paleface and leads him by the hand as a father leads his infant son—but He has forsaken His red children —if they really are his. Our God, the Great Spirit, seems also to have forsaken us. Your God makes your people wax strong every day. Soon they will fill the land. Our people are ebbing away like a rapidly receding tide that will never return. The white man's God cannot love our people or He would protect them. They seem to be orphans who can look nowhere for help. How then can we be brothers? How can your God become our God and renew our prosperity and awaken in us dreams of returning greatness? If we have a common heavenly father He must be partial—for He came to his paleface children. We never saw Him. He gave you laws but He had no word for His red children whose teeming multitudes once filled this vast continent as stars fill the firmament. No; we are two distinct races with separate origins and separate destinies. There is little in common between us.

"To us the ashes of our ancestors are sacred and their resting place is hallowed ground. You wander far from the graves of your ancestors and seemingly without regret. Your religion was written upon tables of stone by the iron finger of your God so that you could not forget. The Red Man could never comprehend nor remember it. Our religion is the traditions of our ancestors—the dreams of our old men, given them in solemn hours of night by the Great Spirit; and the visions of our sachems; and it is written in the hearts of our people.

"Your dead cease to love you and the land of their nativity as soon as they pass the portals of the tomb and wander way beyond the stars. They are soon forgotten and never return. Our dead never forget the beautiful world that gave them being.

"Day and night cannot dwell together. The. Red Man has ever fled the approach of the White Man, as the morning mist flees before the morning sun. However, your proposition seems fair and I think that my people will accept it and will retire to the reservation you offer them. Then we will dwell apart in peace, for the words of the Great White Chief seem to be the words of nature speaking to my people out of dense darkness.

"It matters little where we pass the remnant of our days. They will not be many. A few more moons; a few more winters—and not one of the descendants of the mighty hosts that once moved over this broad land or lived in happy homes, protected by the Great Spirit, will remain to mourn over the graves of a people once more powerful and hopeful than yours. But why should I mourn at the untimely fate of my people? Tribe follows tribe, and nation follows nation, like the waves of the sea. It is the order of nature, and regret is useless. Your time of decay may be distant, but it will surely come, for even the White Man whose God walked and talked with him as friend with friend, cannot be exempt from the common destiny. We may be brothers after all. We will see.

"We will ponder your proposition, and when we decide we will let you know. But should we accept it, I here and now make this condition that we will not be denied the privilege without molestation of visiting at any time the tombs of our ancestors, friends and children. Every part of this soil is sacred in the estimation of my people. Every hillside, every valley, every plain and grove, has been hallowed by some sad or happy event in days long vanished. . . . The very dust upon which you now stand responds more lovingly to their footsteps than to yours, because it is rich with the blood of our ancestors and our bare feet are conscious of the sympathetic touch. . . . Even the little children who lived here and rejoiced here for a brief season will love these somber solitudes and at eventide they greet shadowy returning spirits. And when the last Red Man shall have perished, and the memory of my tribe shall have become a myth among the White Men, these shores will swarm with the invisible dead of my tribe, and when your children's children think themselves alone in the field, the store, the shop, upon the highway, or in the silence of the pathless woods, they will not be alone. . . . At night when the streets of your cities and villages are silent and you think them deserted, they will throng with the returning hosts that once filled and still love this beautiful land. The White Man will never be alone.

"Let him be just and deal kindly with my people, for the dead are not powerless. Dead, did I say? There is no death, only a change of worlds."

DEE BROWN
The War for the Black Hills[1]

Not long after Red Cloud and Spotted Tail and their Teton peoples settled down on their reservations in northwestern Nebraska, rumors began to fly among the white settlements that immense amounts of gold were hidden in the Black Hills. *Paha Sapa*, the Black Hills, was the center of the world, the place of gods and holy mountains, where warriors went to speak with the Great Spirit and await visions. In 1868 the Great Father considered the hills worthless and gave them to the Indians forever by treaty. Four years later white miners were violating the treaty. They invaded *Paha Sapa*, searching the rocky passes and clear-running streams for the yellow metal which drove white men crazy. When Indians found these crazy white men in their sacred hills, they killed them or chased them out. By 1874 there was such a mad clamor from gold-hungry Americans that the Army was ordered to make a reconnaissance into the Black Hills. The United States government did not bother to obtain consent from the Indians before starting on this armed invasion, although the treaty of 1868 prohibited entry of white men without the Indians' permission.

During the Moon of Red Cherries, more than a thousand pony soldiers marched across the Plains from Fort Abraham Lincoln to the Black Hills. They were the Seventh Cavalry, and at their head rode General George Armstrong Custer, the same Star Chief who in 1868 had slaughtered Black Kettle's Southern Cheyennes on the Washita. The Sioux called him Pahuska, the Long Hair, and because they had no warning of his coming, they could only watch from afar as the long columns of blue-uniformed cavalrymen and canvas-covered supply wagons invaded their sacred country.

When Red Cloud heard about the Long Hair's expedition, he protested: "I do not like General Custer and all his soldiers going into the Black Hills, as that is the country of the Oglala Sioux." It was also the country of the Cheyennes, Arapahos, and other Sioux tribes. The anger of the Indians was strong enough that the Great Father, Ulysses Grant, announced his determination "to prevent all invasion of this country by intruders so long as by law and treaty it is secured to the Indians."[2]

But when Custer reported that the hills were filled with gold "from the grass roots down," parties of white men began forming like summer locusts, crazy to begin panning and digging. The trail

1. From *Bury My Heart at Wounded Knee*, 1971. (All footnotes are Brown's.)

2. New York *Herald*, August 27 and September 25, 1874.

that Custer's supply wagons had cut into the heart of *Paha Sapa* soon became the Thieves' Road.

Red Cloud was having trouble that summer with his reservation agent, J. J. Saville, over the poor quality of rations and supplies being issued to the Oglalas. Preoccupied as he was, Red Cloud failed to assess the full impact upon the Sioux of Custer's intrusion into the Black Hills, especially upon those who left the reservations every spring to hunt and camp near the hills. Like many other aging leaders, Red Cloud was too much involved with petty details, and he was losing touch with the younger tribesmen.

In the autumn following Custer's expedition, the Sioux who had been hunting in the north began returning to the Red Cloud agency. They were angry as hornets over the invasion of *Paha Sapa*, and some talked of forming a war party to go back after the miners who were pouring into the hills. Red Cloud listened to the talk, but advised the young men to be patient; he was sure the Great Father would keep his promise and send soldiers to drive out the miners. In the Moon of Falling Leaves, however, something happened that made Red Cloud realize just how angry his young men were at the Long Hair's soldiers. On October 22 agent Saville sent some of his white workmen to cut a tall pine and bring the trunk back to the stockade. When the Indians saw the pine pole lying on the ground they asked Saville what it was to be used for. A flagpole, the agent told them; he was going to fly a flag over the stockade. The Indians protested. Long Hair Custer had flown flags in his camps across the Black Hills; they wanted no flags or anything else in their agency to remind them of soldiers.

Saville paid no attention to the protests, and next morning he put his men to work digging a hole for the flagpole. In a few minutes a band of young warriors came with axes and began chopping the pole to pieces. Saville ordered them to stop, but they paid no attention to him, and the agent strode across to Red Cloud's office and begged him to stop the warriors. Red Cloud refused; he knew the warriors were only expressing their rancor over the Long Hair's invasion of the Black Hills.

Infuriated, Saville now ordered one of his workmen to ride to the Soldiers' Town (Fort Robinson) and request a company of cavalry-men to come to his aid. When the demonstrating warriors saw the man riding toward the fort, they guessed his mission. They rushed for their tepee camps, armed and painted themselves for battle, and went to intercept the cavalrymen. There were only twenty-six Blue-coats led by a lieutenant; the warriors encircled them, fired their guns into the air, and yelled a few war cries. The lieutenant (Emmet Crawford) betrayed no fear. Through the great cloud of dust thrown up by the milling warriors, he kept his men moving steadily toward the agency. Some of the younger warriors began riding in close, colliding their ponies with the troopers' mounts, determined to precipitate a fight.

This time it was not another troop of cavalry which came galloping to Lieutenant Crawford's rescue, but a band of agency Sioux led by Young-Man-Afraid-of-His-Horses, son of Old-Man-Afraid. The agency Indians broke through the ring of warriors, formed a protective wall around the Bluecoats, and escorted them on to the stockade. The belligerent warriors were still so angry, however, that they tried to burn down the stockade, and only the persuasive oratory of Red Dog and Old-Man-Afraid-of-His-Horses stopped the demonstration.

Again Red Cloud refused to interfere. He was not surprised when many of the protesters packed up, dismantled their tepees, and started back north to spend the winter off the reservation. They had proved to him that there were still Sioux warriors who would never take lightly any invasion of *Paha Sapa*, yet apparently Red Cloud did not realize that he was losing these young men forever. They had rejected his leadership for that of Sitting Bull and Crazy Horse, neither of whom had ever lived on a reservation or taken the white man's handouts.

By the spring of 1875, tales of Black Hills gold had brought hundreds of miners up the Missouri River and out upon the Thieves' Road. The Army sent soldiers to stop the flow of prospectors. A few were removed from the hills, but no legal action was taken against them, and they soon returned to prospect their claims. General Crook (the Plains Indians called him Three Stars instead of Gray Wolf) made a reconnaissance of the Black Hills, and found more than a thousand miners in the area. Three Stars politely informed them that they were violating the law and ordered them to leave, but he made no effort to enforce his orders.

Alarmed by the white men's gold craze and the Army's failure to protect their territory, Red Cloud and Spotted Tail made strong protests to Washington officials. The Great Father's response was to send out a commission "to treat with the Sioux Indians for the relinquishment of the Black Hills." In other words, the time had come to take away one more piece of territory that had been assigned to the Indians in perpetuity. As usual, the commission was made up of politicians, missionaries, traders, and military officers. Senator William B. Allison of Iowa was the chairman. Reverend Samuel D. Hinman, who had long endeavored to replace the Santees' religion and culture with Christianity, was the principal missionary. General Alfred Terry represented the military. John Collins, post trader at Fort Laramie, represented the commercial interests.

To ensure representation of nonagency as well as agency Indians, runners were sent to invite Sitting Bull, Crazy Horse, and other "wild" chiefs to the council. Half-breed Louis Richard took the government letter to Sitting Bull and read it to him. "I want you to go and tell the Great Father," Sitting Bull responded, "that I do not want to sell any land to the government." He picked up a pinch of dust and added: "Not even as much as this."[3] Crazy Horse was also opposed to the selling of Sioux land, especially the Black Hills. He refused to attend the council, but Little Big Man would go as an observer for the free Oglalas.

If the commissioners expected to meet quietly with a few compliant chiefs and arrange an inexpensive trade, they were in for a rude surprise. When they arrived at the meeting place—on White River between the Red Cloud and Spotted Tail agencies—the Plains for miles around were covered with Sioux camps and immense herds of grazing ponies. From the Missouri River on the east to the Bighorn country on the west, all the nations of the Soux and many of their Cheyenne and Arapaho friends had gathered there—more than twenty thousand Indians.

Few of them had ever seen a copy of the treaty of 1868, but a goodly number knew the meaning of a certain clause in that sacred document: "No treaty for the cession of any part of the reservation herein described . . . shall be of any validity or force . . . unless executed and signed by at least *three-fourths of all the adult male Indians*, occupying or interested in the same."[4] Even if the commissioners had been able to intimidate or buy off every chief present, they could not have obtained more than a few dozen signatures from those thousands of angry, well-armed warriors who were determined to keep every pinch of dust and blade of grass within their territory. On September 20, 1875, the commission assembled under the shade of a large tarpaulin which had been strung beside a lone cottonwood on the rolling plain. The commissioners seated themselves on chairs facing the thousands of Indians who were moving restlessly about in the distance. A troop of 120 cavalrymen on white horses filed in from Fort Robinson and drew up in a line behind the canvas shelter. Spotted Tail arrived in a wagon from his agency, but Red Cloud had announced that he would not be there. A few other chiefs drifted in, and then suddenly a cloud of dust boiled up from the crest of a distant rise. A band of Indians came galloping down upon the council shelter. The warriors were dressed for battle, and as they came nearer they swerved to encircle the commissioners, fired their rifles skyward, and gave out a few whoops before trotting off to form a line immediately in the rear of the cavalrymen. By this time a second band of Indians was approaching, and thus tribe by tribe the Sioux warriors came in, making their demonstrations of power, until a great circle of several thousand Indians enclosed the

3. Gilbert, Hila. *"Big Bat" Pourier.* Sheridan, Wyoming, Mills Company, 1968, p. 43.

4. Kappler, Charles J. *Indian Affairs, Laws and Treaties.* Vol. 2, p. 1002.

council. Now the chiefs came forward, well satisfied that they had given the commissioners something strong to think about. They sat in a semicircle facing the nervous white men, eager to hear what they would have to say about the Black Hills.

During the few days that the commissioners had been at Fort Robinson observing the mood of the Indians, they recognized the futility of trying to buy the hills and had decided instead to negotiate for the mineral rights. "We have now to ask you if you are willing to give our people the right to mine in the Black Hills," Senator Allison began, "as long as gold or other valuable minerals are found, for a fair and just sum. If you are so willing, we will make a bargain with you for this right. When the gold or other valuable minerals are taken away, the country will again be yours to dispose of in any manner you may wish."

Spotted Tail took this proposal as a ludicrous joke. Was the commissioner asking the Indians to *lend* the Black Hills to the white men for a while? His rejoinder was to ask Senator Allison if he would lend him a team of mules on such terms.

"It will be hard for our government to keep the whites out of the hills," Allison continued. "To try to do so will give you and our government great trouble, because the whites that may wish to go there are very numerous." The senator's ignorance of the Plains Indians' feeling for the Powder River country was displayed in his next proposal: "There is another country lying far toward the setting sun, over which you roam and hunt, and which territory is yet unceded, extending to the summit of the Bighorn Mountains. . . . It does not seem to be of very great value or use to you, and our people think they would like to have the portion of it I have described."[5]

While Senator Allison's incredible demands were being translated, Red Dog rode up on a pony and announced that he had a message from Red Cloud. The absent Oglala chief, probably anticipating the greed of the commissioners, requested a week's recess to give the tribes time to hold councils of their own in which to consider all proposals concerning their lands. The commissioners considered the matter and agreed to give the Indians three days for holding tribal councils. On September 23 they would expect definite replies from the chiefs.

The idea of giving up their last great hunting ground was so preposterous that none of the chiefs even discussed it during their councils. They did debate very earnestly the question of the Black Hills. Some reasoned that if the United States government had no intention of enforcing the treaty and keeping the white miners out, then perhaps the Indians should demand payment—a great deal of mon-

5. U.S. Commissioner of Indian Affairs. Report, 1875, p. 187.

ey—for the yellow metal taken from the hills. Others were determined not to sell at any price. The Black Hills belonged to the Indians, they argued; if the Bluecoat soldiers would not drive out the miners, then the warriors must.

On September 23 the commissioners, riding in Army ambulances from Fort Robinson and escorted by a somewhat enlarged cavalry troop, again arrived at the council shelter. Red Cloud was there early, and he protested vigorously about the large number of soldiers. Just as he was preparing to give his preliminary speech to the commissioners, a sudden commotion broke out among the warriors far in the distance. About three hundred Oglalas who had come in from the Powder River country trotted their ponies down a slope, occasionally firing off rifles. Some were chanting a song in Sioux:

> The Black Hills is my land and I love it
> And whoever interferes
> Will hear this gun.[6]

An Indian mounted on a gray horse forced his way through the ranks of warriors gathered around the canvas shelter. He was Crazy Horse's envoy, Little Big Man, stripped for battle and wearing two revolvers belted to his waist. "I will kill the first chief who speaks for selling the Black Hills!" he shouted. He danced his horse across the open space between the commissioners and the chiefs.[7]

Young-Man-Afraid-of-His-Horses and a group of unofficial Sioux policemen immediately swarmed around Little Big Man and moved him away. The chiefs and the commissioners, however, must have guessed that Little Big Man voiced the feelings of most of the warriors present. General Terry suggested to his fellow commissioners that they board the Army ambulances and return to the safety of Fort Robinson.

After giving the Indians a few days to calm down, the commissioners quietly arranged a meeting with twenty chiefs in the headquarters building of the Red Cloud agency. During three days of speech making, the chiefs made it quite clear to the Great Father's representatives that the Black Hills could not be bought cheaply, if at any price. Spotted Tail finally grew impatient with the commissioners and asked them to submit a definite proposal in writing.

The offer was four hundred thousand dollars a year for the mineral rights; or if the Sioux wished to sell the hills outright the price would be six million dollars payable in fifteen annual installments. (This was a markdown price indeed, considering that one Black Hills mine alone yielded more than five hundred million dollars in gold.)

Red Cloud did not even appear for the final meeting, letting

6. Gilbert, p. 43.
7. Mills, Anson, *My Story*, Washington, D.C., 1918, p. 168.

Spotted Tail speak for all the Sioux. Spotted Tail rejected both offers, firmly. The Black Hills were not for lease or for sale.

The commissioners packed up, returned to Washington, reported their failure to persuade the Sioux to relinquish the Black Hills, and recommended that Congress disregard the wishes of the Indians and appropriate a sum fixed "as a fair equivalent of the value of the hills." This forced purchase of the Black Hills should be "presented to the Indians as a finality," they said.[8]

Thus was set in motion a chain of actions which would bring the greatest defeat ever suffered by the United States Army in its wars with the Indians, and ultimately would destroy forever the freedom of the northern Plains Indians:

November 9, 1875: E. T. Watkins, special inspector for the Indian Bureau, reported to the Commissioner of Indian Affairs that Plains Indians living outside reservations were fed and well armed, were lofty and independent in their attitudes, and were therefore a threat to the reservation system. Inspector Watkins recommended that troops be sent against these uncivilized Indians "in the winter, the sooner the better, and *whip* them into subjection."[9]

November 22, 1875: Secretary of War W. W. Belknap warned of trouble in the Black Hills "unless something is done to obtain possession of that section for the white miners who have been strongly attracted there by reports of rich deposits of the precious metal."[9a]

December 3, 1875: Commissioner of Indian Affairs Edward P. Smith ordered Sioux and Cheyenne agents to notify all Indians off reservations to come in and report to their agencies by January 31, 1876, or a "military force would be sent to compel them."

February 1, 1876: The Secretary of the Interior notified the Secretary of War that the time given the "hostile Indians" to come in to their reservations had expired, and that he was turning them over to the military authorities for such action as the Army might deem proper under the circumstances.[1]

February 7, 1876: The War Department authorized General Sheridan, commanding the Military Division of the Missouri, to commence operations against the "hostile Sioux," including the bands under Sitting Bull and Crazy Horse.

February 8, 1876: General Sheridan ordered generals Crook and Terry to begin preparations for military operations in the direction of the headwaters of the Powder, Tongue, Rosebud, and Bighorn rivers, "where Crazy Horse and his allies frequented."[2]

8. U.S. Commissioner of Indian Affairs. Report, 1875, p. 199.
9. U.S. Congress. 44th. 1st session. House Executive Document 184, pp. 8–9.
9a. U.S. Secretary of War. Report, 1875, p. 21.
1. U.S. Congress. 44th. 1st session. House Executive Document 184, pp. 10, 17–18.
2. U.S. Secretary of War. Report, 1876, p. 441.

Once this machinery of government began moving, it became an inexorable force, mindless and uncontrollable. When runners went out from the agencies late in December to warn the non-agency chiefs to come in, heavy snows blanketed the northern Plains. Blizzards and severe cold made it impossible for some couriers to return until weeks after the January 31 deadline; it would have been impossible to move women and children by ponies and travois. Had a few thousand "hostiles" somehow managed to reach the agencies, they would have starved there. On the reservations during the late winter, food supplies were so short that hundreds of Indians left in March to go north in search of game to supplement their meager government rations.

In January a courier found Sitting Bull camped near the mouth of the Powder. The Hunkpapa chief sent the messenger back to the agent, informing him that he would consider the order to come in, but could not do so until the Moon When the Green Grass Is Up.

Crazy Horse's Oglalas were in winter camp near Bear Butte, where the Thieves' Road came into the Black Hills from the north. During the spring it would be a good place to make up raiding parties to go against the miners violating *Paha Sapa*. When agency couriers made their way through the snow to Crazy Horse, he told them politely that he could not come until the cold went away. "It was very cold," a young Oglala remembered afterward, "and many of our people and ponies would have died in the snow. Also, we were in our own country and were doing no harm."[3]

The January 31 ultimatum was little short of a declaration of war against the independent Indians, and many of them accepted it as that. But they did not expect the Bluecoats to strike so soon. In the Moon of the Snowblind, Three Stars Crook came marching north from Fort Fetterman along the old Bozeman Road, where ten years before Red Cloud had begun his stubborn fight to keep the Powder-River country inviolate.

About this same time, a mixed band of Northern Cheyennes and Oglala Sioux left Red Cloud agency to go to the Powder River country, where they hoped to find a few buffalo and antelope. About the middle of March they joined some nonagency Indians camped a few miles from where the Little Powder runs into the Powder. Two Moon, Little Wolf, Old Bear, Maple Tree, and White Bull were the Cheyenne leaders. Low Dog was the Oglala chief, and some of the warriors with him were from Crazy Horse's village farther north.

Without warning, at dawn on March 17, Crook's advance column under Colonel Joseph J. Reynolds attacked this peaceful

---

3. Neihardt, John G. *Black Elk Speaks*. Lincoln, University of Nebraska Press, 1961, p. 90.

camp. Fearing nothing in their own country, the Indians were asleep when Captain James Egan's white-horse troop, formed in a company front, dashed into the tepee village, firing pistols and carbines. At the same time, a second troop of cavalry came in on the left flank, and a third swept away the Indians' horse herd.

The first reaction from the warriors was to get as many women and children as possible out of the way of the soldiers, who were firing recklessly in all directions. "Old people tottered and hobbled away to get out of reach of the bullets singing among the lodges," Wooden Leg said afterward. "Braves seized whatever weapons they had and tried to meet the attack." As soon as the noncombatants were started up a rugged mountain slope, the warriors took positions on ledges or behind huge rocks. From these places they held the soldiers at bay until the women and children could escape across the Powder.

"From a distance we saw the destruction of our village," Wooden Leg said. "Our tepees were burned with everything in them.... I had nothing left but the clothing I had on." The Bluecoats destroyed all the pemmican and saddles in the camp, and drove away almost every pony the Indians owned, "between twelve and fifteen hundred head."[4] As soon as darkness fell, the warriors went back to where the Bluecoats were camped, determined to recover their stolen horses. Two Moon succinctly described what happened: "That night the soldiers slept, leaving the horses to one side; so we crept up and stole them back again, and then we went away."[5]

Three Stars Crook was so angry at Colonel Reynolds for allowing the Indians to escape from their village and recover their horses that he ordered him court-martialed. The Army reported this foray as "the attack on Crazy Horse's village," but Crazy Horse was camped miles away to the northeast. That was where Two Moon and the other chiefs led their homeless people in hopes of finding food and shelter. They were more than three days making the journey; the temperature was below zero at night; only a few had buffalo robes; and there was very little food.

Crazy Horse received the fugitives hospitably, gave them food and robes, and found room for them in the Oglala tepees. "I'm glad you are come," he said to Two Moon after listening to accounts of the Bluecoats plundering the village. "We are going to fight the white man again."

"All right," Two Moon replied. "I am ready to fight. I have

4. Marquis, Thomas B. *Wooden Leg, a Warrior Who Fought Custer.* Lincoln, University of Nebraska Press, 1957, pp. 165, 168. De Barthe, Joe. *Life and Adventures of Frank Grouard.* Norman, University of Oklahoma Press, 1958, p. 98.

5. Garland, Hamlin. "General Custer's Last Fight as Seen by Two Moon." *McClure's Magazine,* Vol. 11, 1898, p. 444.

fought already. My people have been killed, my horses stolen; I am satisfied to fight."[6]

In the Geese Laying Moon, when the grass was tall and the horses strong, Crazy Horse broke camp and led the Oglalas and Cheyennes north to the mouth of Tongue River, where Sitting Bull and the Hunkpapas had been living through the winter. Not long after that, Lame Deer arrived with a band of Minneconjous and asked permission to camp nearby. They had heard about all the Bluecoats marching through the Sioux hunting grounds and wanted to be near Sitting Bull's powerful band of Hunkpapas should there be any trouble.

As the weather warmed, the tribes began moving northward in search of wild game and fresh grass. Along the way they were joined by bands of Brulés, Sans Arcs, Blackfoot Sioux, and additional Cheyennes. Most of these Indians had left their reservations in accordance with their treaty rights as hunters, and those who had heard of the January 31 ultimatum either considered it as only another idle threat of the Great Father's agents or did not believe it applied to peaceful Indians. "Many young men were anxious to go for fighting the soldiers," said the Cheyenne warrior Wooden Leg. "But the chiefs and old men all urged us to keep away from the white men."[7]

While these several thousand Indians were camped on the Rosebud, many young warriors joined them from the reservations. They brought rumors of great forces of Bluecoats marching from three directions. Three Stars Crook was coming from the south. The One Who Limps (Colonel John Gibbon) was coming from the west. One Star Terry and Long Hair Custer were coming from the east.

Early in the Moon of Making Fat, the Hunkpapas had their annual sun dance. For three days Sitting Bull danced, bled himself, and stared at the sun until he fell into a trance. When he rose again, he spoke to his people. In his vision he had heard a voice crying: "I give you these because they have no ears." When he looked into the sky he saw soldiers falling like grasshoppers, with their heads down and their hats falling off. They were falling right into the Indian camp. Because the white men had no ears and would not listen, Wakantanka the Great Spirit was giving these soldiers to the Indians to be killed.[8]

A few days later a hunting party of Cheyennes sighted a column of Bluecoats camped for the night in the valley of the Rosebud. The hunters rode back to camp, sounding the wolf howl of danger. Three Stars was coming, and he had employed mercenary Crows and Shoshones to scout ahead of his troops.

6. *Ibid.*, p. 445.
7. Marquis, p. 185.
8. Vestal, Stanley. *Sitting Bull, Cham-* *pion of the Sioux.* Norman, University of Oklahoma Press, 1957, pp. 150–51.

The different chiefs sent criers through their villages and then held hasty councils. It was decided to leave about half the warriors to protect the villages while the others would travel through the night and attack Three Stars's soldiers the next morning. About a thousand Sioux and Cheyennes formed the party. A few women went along to help with the spare horses. Sitting Bull, Crazy Horse, and Two Moon were among the leaders. Just before daylight they unsaddled and rested for a while; then they turned away from the river and rode across the hills.

Three Stars's Crow scouts had told him of a great Sioux village down the Rosebud, and the general started these mercenaries out early that morning. As the Crows rode over the crest of a hill and started down, they ran into the Sioux and Cheyenne warriors. At first the Sioux and Cheyennes chased the Crows in all directions, but Bluecoats began coming up fast, and the warriors pulled back.

For a long time Crazy Horse had been waiting for a chance to test himself in battle with the Bluecoats. In all the years since the Fetterman fight at Fort Phil Kearny, he had studied the soldiers and their ways of fighting. Each time he went into the Black Hills to seek visions, he had asked Wakantanka to give him secret powers so that he would know how to lead the Oglalas to victory if the white men ever came again to make war upon his people. Since the time of his youth, Crazy Horse had known that the world men lived in was only a shadow of the real world. To get into the real world, he had to dream, and when he was in the real world everything seemed to float or dance. In this real world his horse danced as if it were wild or crazy, and this was why he called himself Crazy Horse. He had learned that if he dreamed himself into the real world before going into a fight, he could endure anything.

On this day, June 17, 1876, Crazy Horse dreamed himself into the real world, and he showed the Sioux how to do many things they had never done before while fighting the white man's soldiers. When Crook sent his pony soldiers in mounted charges, instead of rushing forward into the fire of their carbines, the Sioux faded off to their flanks and struck weak places in their lines. Crazy Horse kept his warriors mounted and always moving from one place to another. By the time the sun was in the top of the sky he had the soldiers all mixed up in three separate fights. The Bluecoats were accustomed to forming skirmish lines and strong fronts, and when Crazy Horse prevented them from fighting like that they were thrown into confusion. By making many darting charges on their swift ponies, the Sioux kept the soldiers apart and always on the defensive. When the Bluecoats' fire grew too hot, the Sioux would draw away, tantalize a few soldiers into pursuit, and then turn on them with a fury.

The Cheyennes also distinguished themselves that day, especially in the dangerous charges. Chief-Comes-in-Sight was the bravest of all, but as he was swinging his horse about after a charge into the soldiers' flank the animal was shot down in front of a Bluecoat infantry line. Suddenly another horse and rider galloped out from the Cheyennes' position and swerved to shield Chief-Comes-in-Sight from the soldiers' fire. In a moment Chief-Comes-in-Sight was up behind the rider. The rescuer was his sister Buffalo-Calf-Road-Woman, who had come along to help with the horse herds. That was why the Cheyennes always remembered this fight as the Battle Where the Girl Saved Her Brother. The white men called it the Battle of the Rosebud.

When the sun went down, the fighting ended. The Indians knew they had given Three Stars a good fight, but they did not know until the next morning that they had whipped him. At first daylight, Sioux and Cheyenne scouts went out along the ridges, and they could see the Bluecoat column retreating far away to the south. General Crook was returning to his base camp on Goose Creek to await reinforcements or a message from Gibbon, Terry, or Custer. The Indians on the Rosebud were too strong for one column of soldiers.

After the fight on the Rosebud, the chiefs decided to move west to the valley of the Greasy Grass (Little Bighorn). Scouts had come in with reports of great herds of antelope west of there, and they said grass for the horses was plentiful on the nearby benchlands. Soon the camp circles were spread along the west bank of the twisting Greasy Grass for almost three miles. No one knew for certain how many Indians were there, but the number could not have been smaller than ten thousand people, including three or four thousand warriors. "It was a very big village and you could hardly count the tepees," Black Elk said.[9]

Farthest upstream toward the south was the Hunkpapa camp, with the Blackfoot Sioux nearby. The Hunkpapas always camped at the entrance, or at the head end of the circle, which was the meaning of their name. Below them were the Sans Arcs, Minneconjous, Oglalas, and Brulés. At the north end were the Cheyennes.

The time was early in the Moon When the Chokecherries Are Ripe, with days hot enough for boys to swim in the melted snow water of the Greasy Grass. Hunting parties were coming and going in the direction of the Bighorns, where they had found a few buffalo as well as antelope. The women were digging wild turnips out on the prairies. Every night one or more of the tribal circles held dances, and some nights the chiefs met in councils. "The chiefs of the different tribes met together as equals," Wooden Leg said. "There was only one who was considered as being above all the others. This was Sitting Bull. He was recognized as the one old man chief of all the camps combined."[1]

9. Neihardt, p. 106.   1. Marquis, p. 205.

Sitting Bull did not believe the victory on the Rosebud had fulfilled his prophecy of soldiers falling into the Indian camp. Since the retreat of Three Stars, however, no hunting parties had sighted any Bluecoats between the Powder and the Bighorn.

They did not know until the morning of June 24 that Long Hair Custer was prowling along the Rosebud. Next morning scouts reported that the soldiers had crossed the last high ridge between the Rosebud and the Indian camp and were marching toward the Little Bighorn.

The news of Custer's approach came to the Indians in various ways:

"I and four women were a short distance from the camp digging wild turnips," said Red Horse, one of the Sioux council chiefs. "Suddenly one of the women attracted my attention to a cloud of dust rising a short distance from camp. I soon saw that the soldiers were charging the camp. To the camp I and the women ran. When I arrived a person told me to hurry to the council lodge. The soldiers charged so quickly that we could not talk. We came out of the council lodge and talked in all directions. The Sioux mount horses, take guns, and go fight the soldiers. Women and children mount horses and go, meaning to get out of the way."[2]

Pte-San-Waste-Win, a cousin of Sitting Bull, was one of the young women digging turnips that morning. She said the soldiers were six to eight miles distant when first sighted. "We could see the flashing of their sabers and saw that there were very many soldiers in the party." The soldiers first seen by Pte-San-Waste-Win and other Indians in the middle of the camp were those in Custer's battalion. These Indians were not aware of Major Marcus Reno's surprise attack against the south end of camp until they heard rifle fire from the direction of the Blackfoot Sioux lodges. "Like that the soldiers were upon us. Through the tepee poles their bullets rattled. . . . The women and children cried, fearing they would be killed, but the men, the Hunkpapa and Blackfeet, the Oglala and Minneconjou, mounted their horses and raced to the Blackfoot tepees. We could still see the soldiers of Long Hair marching along in the distance, and our men, taken by surprise, and from a point whence they had not expected to be attacked, went singing the song of battle into the fight behind the Blackfoot village."[3]

Black Elk, a thirteen-year-old Oglala boy, was swimming with his companions in the Little Bighorn. The Sun was straight above and was getting very hot when he heard a crier shouting in the Hunkpapa camp: "The chargers are coming! They are charging! The chargers are coming!" The warning was repeated by an Oglala crier,

2. U.S. Bureau of American Ethnology. Annual Report, 19th, 1888–89, p. 564.
3. McLaughlin, James. *My Friend the Indian.* Boston, Houghton Mifflin Co., 1910, pp.168–69.

and Black Elk could hear the cry going from camp to camp northward to the Cheyennes.[4]

Low Dog, an Oglala chief, heard this same warning cry. "I did
not believe it. I thought it was a false alarm. I did not think it possible that any white man would attack us, so strong as we were. . . .
Although I did not believe it was a true alarm, I lost no time getting ready. When I got my gun and came out of my lodge the
attack had begun at the end of the camp where Sitting Bull and the
Hunkpapas were."

Iron Thunder was in the Minneconjou camp. "I did not know
anything about Reno's attack until his men were so close that the
bullets went through the camp, and everything was in confusion.
The horses were so frightened we could not catch them."

Crow King, who was in the Hunkpapa camp, said that Reno's
pony soldiers commenced firing at about four hundred yards' distance. The Hunkpapas and Blackfoot Sioux retreated slowly on foot
to give the women and children time to go to a place of safety.
"Other Indians got our horses. By that time we had warriors
enough to turn upon the whites."[5]

Near the Cheyenne camp, three miles to the north, Two Moon
was watering his horses. "I washed them off with cool water, then
took a swim myself. I came back to the camp afoot. When I got
near my lodge, I looked up the Little Bighorn toward Sitting Bull's
camp. I saw a great dust rising. It looked like a whirlwind. Soon a
Sioux horseman came rushing into camp shouting: 'Soldiers come!
Plenty white soldiers!' "

Two Moon ordered the Cheyenne warriors to get their horses,
and then told the women to take cover away from the tepee village.
"I rode swiftly toward Sitting Bull's camp. Then I saw the white
soldiers fighting in a line [Reno's men]. Indians covered the flat.
They began to drive the soldiers all mixed up—Sioux, then soldiers,
then more Sioux, and all shooting. The air was full of smoke and
dust. I saw the soldiers fall back and drop into the riverbed like buffalo fleeing."[6]

The war chief who rallied the Indians and turned back Reno's
attack was a muscular, full-chested, thirty-six-year-old Hunkpapa
named Pizi, or Gall. Gall had grown up in the tribe as an orphan.
While still a young man he distinguished himself as a hunter and
warrior, and Sitting Bull adopted him as a younger brother. Some
years before, while the commissioners were attempting to persuade
the Sioux to take up farming as a part of the treaty of 1868, Gall
went to Fort Rice to speak for the Hunkpapas. "We were born
naked," he said, "and have been taught to hunt and live on the

4. Neihardt, pp. 108–09.
5. *Leavenworth* (Kansas) *Weekly*
Times, August 18, 1881.
6. Garland, p. 446.

game. You tell us that we must learn to farm, live in one house, and take on your ways. Suppose the people living beyond the great sea should come and tell you that you must stop farming and kill your cattle, and take your houses and lands, what would you do? Would you not fight them?"[7] In the decade following that speech, nothing changed Gall's opinion of the white man's self-righteous arrogance, and by the summer of 1876 he was generally accepted by the Hunkpapas as Sitting Bull's lieutenant, the war chief of the tribe.

Reno's first onrush caught several women and children in the open, and the cavalry's flying bullets virtually wiped out Gall's family. "It made my heart bad," he told a newspaperman some years later. "After that I killed all my enemies with the hatchet." His description of the tactics used to block Reno was equally terse: "Sitting Bull and I were at the point where Reno attacked. Sitting Bull was big medicine. The women and children were hastily moved downstream. . . . The women and children caught the horses for the bucks to mount them; the bucks mounted and charged back Reno and checked him, and drove him into the timber."[8]

In military terms, Gall turned Reno's flank and forced him into the woods. He then frightened Reno into making a hasty retreat which the Indians quickly turned into a rout. The result made it possible for Gall to divert hundreds of warriors for a frontal attack against Custer's column, while Crazy Horse and Two Moon struck the flank and rear.

Meanwhile Pte-San-Waste-Win and the other women had been anxiously watching the Long Hair's soldiers across the river. "I could hear the music of the bugle and could see the column of soldiers turn to the left to march down to the river where the attack was to be made. . . . Soon I saw a number of Cheyennes ride into the river, then some young men of my band, then others, until there were hundreds of warriors in the river and running up into the ravine. When some hundreds had passed the river and gone into the ravine, the others who were left, still a very great number, moved back from the river and waited for the attack. And I knew that the fighting men of the Sioux, many hundreds in number, were hidden in the ravine behind the hill upon which Long Hair was marching, and he would be attacked from both sides."[9]

Kill Eagle, a Blackfoot Sioux chief, later said that the movement of Indians toward Custer's column was "like a hurricane . . . like bees swarming out of a hive." Hump, the Minneconjou comrade of Gall and Crazy Horse during the old Powder River days, said the

7. Robinson, D. W. "Editorial Notes on Historical Sketch of North and South Dakota." *South Dakota Historical Collections*, Vol. I, 1902, p. 151.

8. *St. Paul* (Minnesota) *Pioneer Press*, July 18, 1886.

9. McLaughlin, pp. 172-73.

first massive charge by the Indians caused the long-haired chief and his men to become confused. "The first dash the Indians made my horse was shot from under me and I was wounded—shot above the knee, and the ball came out at the hip, and I fell and lay right there." Crow King, who was with the Hunkpapas, said: "The greater portion of our warriors came together in their front and we rushed our horses on them. At the same time warriors rode out on each side of them and circled around them until they were surrounded."[1] Thirteen-year-old Black Elk, watching from across the river, could see a big dust whirling on the hill, and then horses began coming out of it with empty saddles.

"The smoke of the shooting and the dust of the horses shut out the hill," Pte-San-Waste-Win said, "and the soldiers fired many shots, but the Sioux shot straight and the soldiers fell dead. The women crossed the river after the men of our village, and when we came to the hill there were no soldiers living and Long Hair lay dead among the rest. . . . The blood of the people was hot and their hearts bad, and they took no prisoners that day."[2]

Crow King said that all the soldiers dismounted when the Indians surrounded them. "They tried to hold on to their horses, but as we pressed closer they let go their horses. We crowded them toward our main camp and killed them all. They kept in order and fought like brave warriors as long as they had a man left."[3]

According to Red Horse, toward the end of the fighting with Custer, "these soldiers became foolish, many throwing away their guns and raising their hands, saying, 'Sioux, pity us; take us prisoners.' The Sioux did not take a single soldier prisoner, but killed all of them; none were alive for even a few minutes."[4]

Long after the battle, White Bull of the Minneconjous drew four pictographs showing himself grappling with and killing a soldier identified as Custer. Among others who claimed to have killed Custer were Rain-in-the-Face, Flat Hip, and Brave Bear. Red Horse said that an unidentified Santee warrior killed Custer. Most Indians who told of the battle said they never saw Custer and did not know who killed him. "We did not know till the fight was over that he was the white chief," Low Dog said.[5]

In an interview given in Canada a year after the battle, Sitting Bull said that he never saw Custer, but that other Indians had seen and recognized him just before he was killed. "He did not wear his long hair as he used to wear it," Sitting Bull said. "It was short, but it was the color of the grass when the frost comes. . . . Where the

1. New York *Herald*, September 24, 1876. Easterwood, T. J. *Memories of Seventy-Six*. Dundee, Oregon, 1880, p. 15.
2. McLaughlin, p. 175.
3. *Leavenworth* (Kansas) *Weekly Times*, August 18, 1881.
4. U.S. Bureau of American Ethnology. Annual Report, 10th, 1888–89, p. 565.
5. *Leavenworth* (Kansas) *Weekly Times*, August 18, 1881.

last stand was made, the Long Hair stood like a sheaf of corn with all the ears fallen around him."[6] But Sitting Bull did not say who killed Custer.

An Arapaho warrior who was riding with the Cheyennes said that Custer was killed by several Indians. "He was dressed in buckskin, coat and pants, and was on his hands and knees. He had been shot through the side, and there was blood coming from his mouth. He seemed to be watching the Indians moving around him. Four soldiers were sitting up around him, but they were all badly wounded. All the other soldiers were down. Then the Indians closed in around him, and I did not see any more."[7]

Regardless of who had killed him, the Long Hair who made the Thieves' Road into the Black Hills was dead with all his men. Reno's soldiers, however, reinforced by those of Major Frederick Benteen, were dug in on a hill farther down the river. The Indians surrounded the hill completely and watched the soldiers through the night, and next morning started fighting them again. During the days, scouts sent out by the chiefs came back with warnings of many more soldiers marching in the direction of the Little Bighorn.

After a council it was decided to break camp. The warriors had expended most of their ammunition, and they knew it would be foolish to try to fight so many soldiers with bows and arrows. The women were told to begin packing, and before sunset they started up the valley toward the Bighorn Mountains, the tribes separating along the way and taking different directions.

When the white men in the East heard of the Long Hair's defeat, they called it a massacre and went crazy with anger. They wanted to punish all the Indians in the West. Because they could not punish Sitting Bull and the war chiefs, the Great Council in Washington decided to punish the Indians they could find—those who remained on the reservations and had taken no part in the fighting.

On July 22 the Great Warrior Sherman received authority to assume military control of all reservations in the Sioux country and to treat the Indians there as prisoners of war. On August 15 the Great Council made a new law requiring the Indians to give up all rights to the Powder River country and the Black Hills. They did this without regard to the treaty of 1868, maintaining that the Indians had violated the treaty by going to war with the United States. This was difficult for the reservation Indians to understand, because they had not attacked United States soldiers, nor had Sitting Bull's followers attacked them until Custer sent Reno charging through

6. New York *Herald*, November 16, 1877.

7. Graham, W. A. *The Custer Myth.* Harrisburg, Pa., Stackpole Co., 1953, p. 110.

the Sioux villages.

To keep the reservation Indians peaceful, the Great Father sent out a new commission in September to cajole and threaten the chiefs and secure their signatures to legal documents transferring the immeasurable wealth of the Black Hills to white ownership. Several members of this commission were old hands at stealing Indian lands, notably Newton Edmunds, Bishop Henry Whipple, and the Reverend Samuel D. Hinman. At the Red Cloud agency, Bishop Whipple opened the proceedings with a prayer, and then Chairman George Manypenny read the conditions laid down by Congress. Because these conditions were stated in the usual obfuscated language of lawmakers, Bishop Whipple attempted to explain them in phrases which could be used by the interpreters.

"My heart has for many years been very warm toward the red man. We came here to bring a message to you from your Great Father, and there are certain things we have given to you in his exact words. We cannot alter them even to the scratch of a pen. . . . When the Great Council made the appropriation this year to continue your supplies they made certain provisions, three in number, and unless they were complied with no more appropriations would be made by Congress. Those three provisions are: First, that you shall give up the Black Hills country and the country to the north; second, that you shall receive your rations on the Missouri River; and third, that the Great Father shall be permitted to locate three roads from the Missouri River across the reservation to that new country where the Black Hills are. . . . The Great Father said that his heart was full of tenderness for his red children, and he selected this commission of friends of the Indians that they might devise a plan, as he directed them, in order that the Indian nations might be saved, and that instead of growing smaller and smaller until the last Indian looks upon his own grave, they might become as the white man has become, a great and powerful people."[8]

To Bishop Whipple's listeners, this seemed a strange way indeed to save the Indian nations, taking away their Black Hills and hunting grounds, and moving them far away to the Missouri River. Most of the chiefs knew that it was already too late to save the Black Hills, but they protested strongly against having their reservations moved to the Missouri. "I think if my people should move there," Red Cloud said, "they would all be destroyed. There are a great many bad men there and bad whiskey; therefore I don't want to go there."[9]

No Heart said that white men had already ruined the Missouri River country so that Indians could not live there. "You travel up

8. U.S. Congress. 44th. 2nd session. Senate Executive Document 9, pp. 5, 31.

9. New York *Herald* 33, September 23, 1876.

and down the Missouri River and you do not see any timber," he declared. "You have probably seen where lots of it has been, and the Great Father's people have destroyed it."

"It is only six years since we came to live on this stream where we are living now," Red Dog said, "and nothing that has been promised us has been done." Another chief remembered that since the Great Father promised them that they would never be moved they had been moved five times. "I think you had better put the Indians on wheels," he said sardonically, "and you can run them about whenever you wish."

Spotted Tail accused the government and the commissioners of betraying the Indians, of broken promises and false words. "This war did not spring up here in our land; this was was brought upon us by the children of the Great Father who came to take our land from us without price, and who, in our land, do a great many evil things. . . . This war has come from robbery—from the stealing of our land."[1] As for moving to the Missouri, Spotted Tail was utterly opposed, and he told the commissioners he would not sign away the Black Hills until he could go to Washington and talk to the Great Father.

The commissioners gave the Indians a week to discuss the terms among themselves, and it soon became evident that they were not going to sign anything. The chiefs pointed out that the treaty of 1868 required the signatures of three-fourth of the male adults of the Sioux tribes to change anything in it, and more than half of the warriors were in the north with Sitting Bull and Crazy Horse. In reply to this the commissioners explained that the Indians off the reservations were hostiles; only friendly Indians were covered by the treaty. Most of the chiefs did not accept this. To break down their opposition, the commissioners dropped strong hints that unless they signed, the Great Council in its anger would cut off all rations immediately, would remove them to the Indian Territory in the south, and the Army would take all their guns and horses.

There was no way out. The Black Hills were stolen; the Powder River country and its herds of wild game were gone. Without wild game or rations, the people would starve. The thought of moving far away to a strange country in the south was unbearable, and if the Army took their guns and ponies they would no longer be men.

Red Cloud and his subchiefs signed first, and then Spotted Tail and his people signed. After that the commissioners went to agencies at Standing Rock, Cheyenne River, Crow Creek, Lower Brulé, and Santee, and badgered the other Sioux tribes into signing. Thus did *Paha Sapa*, its spirits and its mysteries, its vast pine forests, and

1. U.S. Congress. 44th. 2nd session.   38–40, 66.
Senate Executive Document 9, pp. 8,

its billion dollars in gold pass forever from the hands of the Indians into the domain of the United States.

Four weeks after Red Cloud and Spotted Tail touched pens to the paper, eight companies of United States cavalry under Three Fingers Mackenzie (the Eagle Chief who destroyed the Kiowas and Comanches in Palo Duro Canyon) marched out of Fort Robinson into the agency camps. Under orders of the War Department, Mackenzie had come to take the reservation Indians' ponies and guns. All males were placed under arrest, tepees were searched and dismantled, guns collected, and all ponies were rounded up by the soldiers. Mackenzie gave the women permission to use horses to haul their goods into Fort Robinson. The males, including Red Cloud and the other chiefs, were forced to walk to the fort. The tribe would have to live henceforth at Fort Robinson under the guns of the soldiers.

Next morning, to degrade his beaten prisoners even further, Mackenzie presented a company of mercenary Pawnee scouts (the same Pawnees the Sioux had once driven out of their Powder River country) with the horses the soldiers had taken from the Sioux.

Meanwhile, the United States Army, thirsting for revenge, was prowling the country north and west of the Black Hills, killing Indians wherever they could be found. In late summer of 1876, Three Stars Crook's reinforced column ran out of rations in the Heart River country of Dakota, and started a forced march southward to obtain supplies in the Black Hills mining camps. On September 9, near Slim Buttes, a forward detachment under Captain Anson Mills stumbled upon American Horse's village of Oglalas and Minneconjous. These Indians had left Crazy Horses's camp on Grand River a few days before and were moving south to spend the winter on their reservation. Captain Mills attacked, but the Sioux drove him back, and while he was waiting for Three Stars to arrive, all the Indians escaped except American Horse, four warriors, and fifteen women and children, who were trapped in a cave at the end of a small canyon.

When Crook came up with the main column, he ordered soldiers to positions from which they could fire volleys into the mouth of the cave. American Horse and his four warriors returned the fire, and after some hours of continuous dueling, two Bluecoats were dead and nine wounded. Crook then sent a scout, Frank Grouard, to ask the Indians to surrender. Grouard, who had lived with the Sioux, spoke to them in their language. "They told me they would come out if we would not kill them, and upon receiving this promise, they came out." American Horse, two warriors, five women, and several children crawled out of the cave; the others were dead or too badly wounded to move. American Horse's groin had been ripped open by buckshot. "He was holding his entrails in his hands as he came out," Grouard said. "Holding out one of his bloodstained hands, he shook hands with me."[2]

Captain Millls had found a little girl, three or four years old, hiding in the village. "She sprang up and ran away like a young partridge," he said. "The soldiers caught her and brought her to me." Mills comforted her and gave her some food, and then he asked his orderly to bring her along when he went down to the cave where the soldiers were dragging out the Indian casualties. Two of the dead were women, bloody with many wounds. "The little girl began to scream and fought the orderly until he placed her on the ground, when she ran and embraced one of these squaws, who was her mother. I told Adjutant Lemly I intended to adopt this little girl, as I had slain her mother."

A surgeon came to examine American Horse's wound. He pronounced it fatal, and the chief sat down before a fire, holding a blanket over his bullet-torn abdomen, until he lost consciousness and died.

Crook ordered Captain Mills to ready his men for a resumption of the march to the Black Hills. "Before starting," Mills said, "Adjutant Lemly asked me if I really intended to take the little girl. I told him I did, when he remarked, 'Well, how do you think Mrs. Mills will like it?' It was the first time I had given that side of the matter a thought, and I decided to leave the child where I found her."[3]

While Three Stars was destroying American Horse's village, some of the Sioux who had escaped made their way to Sitting Bull's camp and told him about the attack. Sitting Bull and Gall, with about six hundred warriors, immediately went to help American Horse, but they arrived too late. Although Sitting Bull launched an attack on Crook's soldiers, his warriors had so little ammunition that the Bluecoats held them off with rearguard actions while the main column marched on to the Black Hills.

When the soldiers were all gone, Sitting Bull and his warriors went into American Horse's devastated village, rescued the helpless survivors, and buried the dead. "What have we done that the white people want us to stop?" Sitting Bull asked. "We have been running up and down this country, but they follow us from one place to another."[4]

In an effort to get as far away from the soldiers as possible, Sitting Bull took his people north along the Yellowstone, where buffalo could be found. In the Moon of Falling Leaves, Gall went out with a hunting party and came upon an Army wagon train traveling through the Yellowstone country. The soldiers were taking supplies

2. De Barthe, pp. 157–58.
3. Mills, pp. 171–72.

4. U.S. Secretary of the Interior. Report, 1877, p. 724.

to a new fort they were building where Tongue River flowed into the Yellowstone (Fort Keogh, named for Captain Myles Keogh, who was killed at the Little Bighorn).

Gall's warriors ambushed the train near Glendive Creek and captured sixty mules. As soon as Sitting Bull heard about the wagon train and the new fort, he sent for Johnny Brughiere, a half-breed who had joined his camp. Brughiere knew how to write, and Sitting Bull told him to put down on a piece of paper some words he had to say to the commander of the soldiers:

I want to know what you are doing on this road. You scare all the buffalo away. I want to hunt in this place. I want you to turn back from here. If you don't, I will fight you again. I want you to leave what you have got here, and turn back from here. I am your friend.

—SITTING BULL[5]

When Lieutenant Colonel Elwell Otis, commanding the wagon train, received the message, he sent a scout with a reply to Sitting Bull. The soldiers were going to Fort Keogh, Otis said, and many more soldiers were coming to join them. If Sitting Bull wanted a fight, the soldiers would give him one.

Sitting Bull did not want a fight; he wanted only to be left alone to hunt buffalo. He sent a warrior out with a white flag, asking for a talk with the soldier chief. By this time Colonel Nelson Miles and more soldiers had overtaken the train. As Miles had been searching for Sitting Bull since the end of summer, he immediately agreed to a parley.

They met on October 22 between a line of soldiers and a line of warriors. Miles was escorted by an officer and five men, Sitting Bull by a subchief and five warriors. The day was very cold, and Miles was wearing a long coat trimmed with bear fur. From the first moment of his appearance, he was Bear Coat to the Indians.

There were no preliminary speeches, no friendly smokes of the pipe. With Johnny Brughiere interpreting, Bear Coat began the parley by accusing Sitting Bull of always being against the white man and his ways. Sitting Bull admitted that he was not for the whites, but neither was he an enemy to them as long as they left him alone. Bear Coat wanted to know what Sitting Bull was doing in the Yellowstone country. The question was a foolish one, but the Hunkpapa answered it politely; he was hunting buffalo to feed and clothe his people. Bear Coat then made passing mention of a reservation for the Hunkpapas, but Sitting Bull brushed it aside. He would spend the winter in the Black Hills, he said. The parley ended with nothing resolved, but the two men agced to meet again the next day.

5. U.S. War Department. Military Division of the Missouri. Record of Engagements with Hostile Indians. 1882, p. 62.

The second meeting quickly became a succession of disagreements. Sitting Bull began by saying that he had not fought the soldiers until they came to fight him, and promised that there would be no more fighting if the white men would take their soldiers and forts out of the Indians' country. Bear Coat replied that there could be no peace for the Sioux until they were all on reservations. At this, Sitting Bull became angry. He declared that the Great Spirit had made him an Indian but not an agency Indian, and he did not intend to become one. He ended the conference abruptly, and returned to his warriors, ordering them to scatter because he suspected that Bear Coat's soldiers would try to attack them. The soldiers did open fire, and once again the Hunkpapas had to start running up and down the country.

By springtime of 1877 Sitting Bull was tired of running. He decided there was no longer room enough for white men and the Sioux to live together in the Great Father's country. He would take his people to Canada, to the land of the Grandmother, Queen Victoria. Before he started, he searched for Crazy Horse, hoping to persuade him to bring the Oglalas to the Grandmother's land. But Crazy Horse's people were running up and down the country trying to escape the soldiers, and Sitting Bull could not find them.

In those same cold moons, General Crook was also looking for Crazy Horse. This time Crook had assembled an enormous army of infantry, cavalry, and artillery. This time he took along enough rations to fill 168 wagons and enough powder and ammunition to burden the backs of 400 pack mules. Three Stars's mighty column swept through the Powder River country like a swarm of grizzly bears, mauling and crushing all Indians in its path.

The soldiers were looking for Crazy Horse, but they found a Cheyenne village first, Dull Knife's village. Most of these Cheyennes had not been in the Little Bighorn battle, but had slipped away from Red Cloud agency in search of food after the Army took possession there and stopped their rations. General Crook sent Three Fingers Mackenzie against this village of 150 lodges.

It was in the Deer Rutting Moon, and very cold, with deep snow in the shaded places and ice-crusted snow in the open places. Mackenzie brought his troopers up to attacking positions during the night, and struck the Cheyennes at first daylight. The Pawnee mercenaries went in first, charging on the fast ponies Mackenzie had taken from the reservation Sioux. They caught the Cheyennes in their lodges, killing many of them as they came awake. Others ran out naked into the biting cold, the warriors trying to fight off the Pawnees and the onrushing soldiers long enough for their women and children to escape.

Some of the best warriors of the Northern Cheyennes sacrificed their lives in those first furious moments of fighting; one of them was Dull Knife's oldest son. Dull Knife and Little Wolf finally managed to form a rear guard along the upper ledges of a canyon, but their scanty supply of ammunition was soon exhausted. Little Wolf was shot seven times before he and Dull Knife broke away to join their women and children in full flight toward the Bighorns. Behind them Mackenzie was burning their lodges, and after that was done he herded their captured ponies against the canyon wall and ordered his men to shoot them down, just as he had done to the ponies of the Comanches and Kiowas in Palo Duro Canyon.

For Dull Knife's Cheyennes, their flight was a repetition of the flight of Two Moon's Cheyennes after the surprise attack in March by the Eagle Chief, Reynolds. But the weather was colder; they had only a few horses, and scarcely any blankets, robes, or even moccasins. Like Two Moon's people, they knew only one sanctuary—Crazy Horse's village on Box Elder Creek.

During the first night of flight, twelve infants and several old people froze to death. The next night, the men killed some of the ponies, disemboweled them, and thrust small children inside to keep them from freezing. The old people put their hands and feet in beside the children. For three days they tramped across the frozen snow, their bare feet leaving a trail of blood, and then they reached Crazy Horse's camp.

Crazy Horse shared food, blankets, and shelter with Dull Knife's people, but warned them to be ready to run. The Oglalas did not have enough ammunition left to stand and fight. Bear Coat Miles was looking for them in the north, and now Three Stars Crook was coming from the south. To survive, they would have to keep running up and down the country.

In the Moon of Popping Trees, Crazy Horse moved the camp north along the Tongue to a hiding place not far from the new Fort Keogh, where Bear Coat was wintering his soldiers. Cold and hunger became so unbearable for the children and old people that some of the chiefs told Crazy Horse it was time to go and parley with Bear Coat and find out what he wanted them to do. Their women and children were crying for food, and they needed warm shelters they would not have to run away from. Crazy Horse knew that Bear Coat wanted to make prisoners of them on a reservation, but he agreed that the chiefs should go if they wished to do so. He went with the party, about thirty chiefs and warriors, to a hill not far from the fort. Eight chiefs and warriors volunteered to ride down to the fort, one of them carrying a large white cloth on a lance. As they neared the fort, some of Bear Coat's mercenary Crows came charging out. Ignoring the truce flag, the Crows fired point-blank into the Sioux. Only three of the eight escaped alive. Some of the Sioux watching from the hill wanted to ride out and seek revenge on the Crows, but Crazy Horse insisted that they hurry back to camp. They would have to pack up and run again. Now that Bear Coat knew there were Sioux nearby, he would come searching through the snow for them.

Bear Coat caught up with them on the morning of January 8 (1877) at Battle Butte, and sent his soldiers charging through foot-deep snow. Crazy Horse had but little ammunition left to defend his people, but he had some good warrior chiefs who knew enough tricks to mislead and punish the soldiers while the main body of Indians escaped through the Wolf Mountains toward the Bighorns. Working in concert, Little Big Man, Two Moon, and Hump decoyed the troops into a canyon. For four hours they kept the soldiers—who were encumbered with bulky winter uniforms—stumbling and falling over ice-covered cliffs. Snow began sifting down during the engagement, and by early afternoon a blizzard was raging. This was enough for Bear Coat. He took his men back to the warmth of Fort Keogh.

Through the screen of sleety snow, Crazy Horse and his people made their way to the familiar country of the Little Powder. They were camped there in February, living off what game they could find, when runners brought news that Spotted Tail and a party of Brulés were coming from the south. Some of the Indians in the camp thought that perhaps Spotted Tail at last had tired of being told what to do on his reservation and was running away from the soldiers, but Crazy Horse knew better.

During the cold moons, Three Stars Crook had taken his men out of the snow into Fort Fetterman. While he was waiting for spring, he paid a visit to Spotted Tail and promised him that the reservation Sioux would not have to move to the Missouri River if the Brulé chief would go as a peace emissary to Crazy Horse and persuade him to surrender. That was the purpose of Spotted Tail's visit to Crazy Horse's camp.

Just before Spotted Tail arrived, Crazy Horse told his father that he was going away. He asked his father to shake hands with Spotted Tail and tell him the Oglalas would come in as soon as the weather made it possible for women and children to travel. Then he went off to the Bighorns alone. Crazy Horse had not made up his mind yet whether he would surrender; perhaps he would let his people go while he stayed in the Powder River country alone—like an old buffalo bull cast out of the herd.

When Spotted Tail arrived, he guessed that Crazy Horse was avoiding him. He sent messengers out to find the Oglala leader, but Crazy Horse had vanished in the deep snows. Before Spotted Tail returned to Nebraska, however, he convinced Big Foot that he should surrender his Minneconjous, and he received promises from

Touch-the-Clouds and three other chiefs that they would bring their people to the agency early in the spring.

On April 14 Touch-the-Clouds, with a large number of Minneconjous and Sans Arcs from Crazy Horse's village, arrived at the Spotted Tail agency and surrendered. A few days before this happened, Three Stars Crook had sent Red Cloud out to find Crazy Horse and promise him that if he surrendered he could have a reservation in the Powder River country. On April 27 Red Cloud met Crazy Horse and told him of Three Stars's promise. Crazy Horse's nine hundred Oglalas were starving, the warriors had no ammunition, and their horses were thin and bony. The promise of a reservation in the Powder River country was all that Crazy Horse needed to bring him in to Fort Robinson to surrender.

The last of the Sioux war chiefs now became a reservation Indian, disarmed, dismounted, with no authority over his people, a prisoner of the Army, which had never defeated him in battle. Yet he was still a hero to the young men, and their adulation caused jealousies to arise among the older agency chiefs. Crazy Horse remained aloof, he and his followers living only for the day when Three Stars would make good his promise of a reservation for them in the Powder River country.

Late in the summer, Crazy Horse heard that Three Stars wanted him to go to Washington for a council with the Great Father. Crazy Horse refused to go. He could see no point in talking about the promised reservation. He had seen what happened to chiefs who went to the Great Father's house in Washington; they came back fat from the white man's way of living and with all the hardness gone out of them. He could see the changes in Red Cloud and Spotted Tail, and they knew he saw and they did not like him for it.

In August news came that the Nez Percés, who lived beyond the Shining Mountains, were at war with the Bluecoats. At the agencies, soldier chiefs began enlisting warriors to do their scouting for them against the Nez Percés. Crazy Horse told the young men not to go against those other Indians far away, but some would not listen, and allowed themselves to be bought by the soldiers. On August 31, the day these former Sioux warriors put on their Bluecoat uniforms to march away, Crazy Horse was so sick with disgust that he said he was going to take his people and go back north to the Powder River country.

When Three Stars heard of this from his spies, he ordered eight companies of pony soldiers to march to Crazy Horse's camp outside Fort Robinson and arrest him. Before the soldiers arrived, however, Crazy Horse's friends warned him they were coming. Not knowing what the soldiers' purpose was, Crazy Horse told his people to scatter, and then he set out alone to Spotted Tail agency to seek refuge with his old friend Touch-the-Clouds.

The soldiers found him there, placed him under arrest, and informed him they were taking him back to Fort Robinson to see Three Stars. Upon arrival at the fort, Crazy Horse was told that it was too late to talk with Three Stars that day. He was turned over to Captain James Kennington and one of the agency policemen. Crazy Horse stared hard at the agency policeman. He was Little Big Man, who not so long ago had defied the commissioners who came to steal *Paha Sapa*, the same Little Big Man who had threatened to kill the first chief who spoke for selling the Black Hills, the brave Little Big Man who had last fought beside Crazy Horse on the icy slopes of the Wolf Mountains against Bear Coat Miles. Now the white men had bought Little Big Man and made him into an agency policeman.

As Crazy Horse walked between them, letting the soldier chief and Little Big Man lead him to wherever they were taking him, he must have tried to dream himself into the real world, to escape the darkness of the shadow world in which all was madness. They walked past a soldier with a bayoneted rifle on his shoulder, and then they were standing in the doorway of a building. The windows were barred with iron, and he could see men behind the bars with chains on their legs. It was a trap for an animal, and Crazy Horse lunged away like a trapped animal, with Little Big Man holding on to his arm. The scuffling went on for only a few seconds. Someone shouted a command, and then the soldier guard, Private William Gentles, thrust his bayonet deep into Crazy Horse's abdomen.

Crazy Horse died that night, September 5, 1877, at the age of thirty-five. At dawn the next day the soldiers presented the dead chief to his father and mother. They put the body of Crazy Horse into a wooden box, fastened it to a pony-drawn travios, and carried it to Spotted Tail agency, where they mounted it on a scaffold. All through the Drying Grass Moon, mourners watched beside the burial place. And then in the Moon of Falling Leaves came the heartbreaking news: the reservation Sioux must leave Nebraska and go to a new reservation on the Missouri River.

Through the crisp dry autumn of 1877, long lines of exiled Indians driven by soldiers marched northeastward toward the barren land. Along the way, several bands slipped away from the column and turned northwestward, determined to escape to Canada and join Sitting Bull. With them went the father and mother of Crazy Horse, carrying the heart and bones of their son. At a place known only to them they buried Crazy Horse somewhere near Chankpe Opi Wakpala, the creek called Wounded Knee.

Song of Sitting Bull

A warrior
I have been
Now
it is all over.
A hard time
I have.

QUESTIONS

1. Explain why Brown uses the Indian names for the months, for Custer, etc.
2. Compare one of the Indians' speeches (e.g., Gall's, pp. 924–925) with one of the white men's speeches (e.g., Bishop Whipple's, p. 928). If the way a person uses language can be taken as an index to his character, what can you deduce about the character of each man?
3. Judging from "Politics and the English Language" (pp. 323–333), what do you think George Orwell's comment on Bishop Whipple's speech (p. 928) might be?
4. Look closely at Brown's descriptions of the commission (p. 913) and of the reaction to Long Hair's defeat. Can you sense Brown's attitude in each case? How is that attitude conveyed?
5. In describing the events which led up to the climactic battle, Brown says that once the "machinery" of the white man's government began moving, "it became an inexorable force, mindless and uncontrollable" (p. 918). Discuss the definition of government implied by this description. Was any analogous development taking place among the Indians?
6. Evaluate Brown's choice of sources. Do the sources seem reliable? Well balanced? Why haven't more sources with the white man's point of view been included?
7. On pp. 924–925 Gall gives a defense of the life style of the Indians when they are asked by the commissioners to change their ways and take up farming. Is this a good argument to defend a life style against those who wish to change it?

TERRI SCHULTZ

Bamboozle Me Not at Wounded Knee

The Pine Ridge reservation in South Dakota has disillusioned those of us who once believed that it sheltered noble warriors and tragic heroes with tongues of gold. By some miracle, aided by equal parts folklore, liberal guilt, and isolation, most whites now court a public romance with the victim we have relentlessly screwed for 300 years, the American Indian. In fact, the reservation as it exists today seems hardly capable of a good protest, much less an effective national movement.

When I returned to the reservation this spring[1] after an eighteen-month absence, I found a game of charades played by an Indian Nation that had lost its soul and all hope of resurrection. The object of the game, which is still being played, is to twang white heartstrings, for when you no longer have clout you turn to sympathy.

Indian public relations have been deteriorating ever since the Utes staged the Red Man's first press conference in 1868, when the whites in Washington were trying to take Colorado away from them. "The agreement an Indian makes to a U.S. treaty," the Utes announced to the papers, "is like an agreement a buffalo makes with his hunters when pierced with arrows. All he can do is lie down and give in." They lost Colorado and didn't gain many friends in the press. Eleven years later, according to author Dee Brown, the *Denver Tribune* editorialized: "The Utes are actual, practical Communists and the government should be ashamed to foster and encourage them in their idleness and wanton waste of property . . . the only truly good Indians are dead ones."

Things haven't changed much. In Custer, South Dakota, I met Joe Ledbetter, the town painter, as he was slowly cursing himself into a frenzy over the Sioux. The angrier he got, the slower and harder he slapped his paint brush across the walls of the Custer County Courthouse. Finally he stopped painting altogether. "I fought the niggers in Watts and I moved here just one year ago, and already I got to fight the Indians here," he said. "These damn riots seem to follow me everywhere. And believe me, them Indians learned from the niggers. They got the same tactics."

Joe had just finished painting the entire courthouse when 200 Indians set it on fire last February 6, charring it so badly that he had to paint it all over again. The Indians chanted, "It's a good day to die," as they ran through the tourist town protesting the fatal stabbing of Wesley Bad Heart Bull by a white man. The white man was charged with manslaughter, and the Indians wanted the charge changed to murder. A lot of people got hit with clubs and bricks that day, but nobody died. "They were on pot, uppers or downers," says Joe. "They were Communist-inspired. And they'll probably be back as soon as I get done painting."

In the nearby town of Pine Ridge, Sen. George McGovern stands in the Bureau of Indian Affairs parking lot wondering what to do next. He and Sen. James Abourezk, himself part Sioux, have been negotiating the release of eleven hostages at Wounded Knee, but now they have learned that the hostages are really participants in

1. In 1973.

the whole show and are not being held against their will. McGovern is supposed to return to Wounded Knee for a final powwow in a tepee, but the rumor is that the Indians can't find a tepee they know how to put up. A young FBI man standing guard inside the BIA building quietly clucks his tongue at the McGovern group. "Can you imagine meeting in a tepee at this time of year?" he asks. "Why does McGovern put up with it?" He is quiet for a moment, then takes a swig of his Coke. "Maybe he's planning to run for President someday."

During this last powwow, held in a house after all, the Senators and Indians stare at one another through mirrors of South Dakota history, each mimicking images of themselves. "I will request a Senate investigation of reservation conditions," Senator Abourezk says. He might have added: "You are fed by the government, clothed by the government, your children are educated by the government, and all you have and are today is because of the government. You cannot insult the people of the United States of America or its committees." He might have added that; but Abourezk is more discreet than Sen. John Logan, who said those words to Sitting Bull ninety years ago. The Indians in turn might answer with the words of Chief Red Cloud: "They made us many promises, more than I can remember, but they never kept but one; they promised to take our land, and they took it."

McGovern will leave the reservation that night for his home in the Black Hills, on land the whites gave to the Oglala Sioux "forever" in 1868 and then took away in 1876. But the sixty to seventy reporters covering the story must stay on, glued to the BIA parking lot, which has been dubbed the "rumor mill." Everybody drives endlessly around the lot like high-school seniors in their fathers' cars, whispering what's-the-buzz-tell-me-what's-happenin'. The hell of it is, nothing ever happens, for the town of Pine Ridge is as quiet as a broken clock. Old Indian men with faces of stone sit on the narrow rock ledges of Main Street and watch the procession of rented cars; their heads swivel left as the cars leave for roadblock No. 1 on Big Foot Road twelve miles away, near Wounded Knee, then right as the cars return to the parking lot. Occasionally one of them wanders over to the lot and offers some colorful quotes for a price.

The sole reprieve from this purgatory is Naylor Joles, a gypsy from Chicago who runs a sideshow called the Crazy Horse Café, where a man can eat with his hat on and his guard down. Naylor is a white man who married a Sioux and manages to fit into the reservation like tumbleweed and denim and still keep flashes of sanity. He knows when we need coffee and where to get bootleg whiskey on a Sunday night.

The paleface press slowly becomes as bored and disillusioned as the redskins who fail to perform as advertised. A reporter from

London, dressed in blue jeans, leather jacket, and new cowboy boots, lends a Mohawk Indian leader his copy of *Bury My Heart at Wounded Knee*, for it turns out the Mohawk has never read it. A Chicago reporter watches as several Indians shoot a cow for food near Wounded Knee. They pull the trigger, and the cow blinks but does not fall. The Indians are mystified. The reporter takes the rifle, shoots the cow once again, this time between the eyes, and it keels over. The reporter then shows the Indians how to cut up the carcass. In nearby Whiteclay, Nebraska, a UPI reporter dictates his story from the only available phone, in the local bar, when a beer bottle crashes down on his head, courtesy of a patron who doesn't like his lead. It is hard to judge who was correct, for both sides of the dispute in Wounded Knee lied enthusiastically to compensate for an overwhelming mediocrity, and the main Indian spokesman was commonly referred to as Chief Sitting Bullshit.

The dispute is not all that complicated. Dick Wilson, president of the Oglala Sioux Tribal Council, fears and despises the 300 upstarts of the American Indian Movement who seized Wounded Knee last February 27 and—given Wilson's appeals for official help—managed to stage one of the year's leading media events. Wilson and his supporters would agree with AIM that unemployment, alcoholism, and suicide rates are far too high on the Pine Ridge Reservation; that the government has broken every treaty and shamelessly stolen their land. They see how they have been trapped into leasing their best land to white ranchers, how they are shepherded into low-income housing projects in villages far from their own property, how they have always been lied to. But to Indians like Wilson, the militant American Indian Movement is more of a threat than a savior. AIM has a street-gang cast; its city-bred leaders here, with real guns, slouch toward Pine Ridge to be born.[2] Even worse, their antigovernment attitudes endanger the few reservation Indians who actually have jobs, for these Indians owe their jobs to the omnipotent Bureau of Indian Affairs.

"You have to go to work or school just to keep from dyin' of boredom. That's why so many young people are drunk," says Saundra Kay Wilson, teenage daughter of Dick Wilson. Saundra and her mother Yvonne sit around their kitchen table in Pine Ridge waiting for Dick to come home. Mrs. Wilson's six children have nothing to do today—all the schools closed down when "the trouble" started. Empty Budweiser cans cover the table, and there's more beer in the refrigerator. "I'm so nervous over this whole thing, I can't cook, can't even concentrate. If I have a beer I will be okay," says Mrs. Wilson as she snaps another tab.

2. Adapted from W. B. Yeats's poem "The Second Coming": "And what rough beast, its hour come round at last,/Slouches toward Bethlehem to be born?"

A photographer from Minneapolis knocks timidly on Mrs. Wilson's front door and asks if he may take a family picture for his newspaper. "Okay, everybody," says Mrs. Wilson. "Put your beer cans under the table." The photographer waits politely. "Go ahead," Mrs. Wilson says, smiling. Click. Everyone puts his beer back on the table as the photographer leaves.

"Mom, the top button of your blouse was open when the photographer was here," Saundra Kay says. "Why didn't you tell me?" Mrs. Wilson fumbles for the button. "What kind of an impression are people going to get?"

"If those Indians aren't out of Wounded Knee soon," says a man introduced as Uncle Wayne, "we'll go out and fight them *and* the federal marshals." Then he passes out on the table.

The long-awaited Dick Wilson enters, a brick of a man with a stomach that matches his ego. He slams the screen door and straddles a kitchen chair with the cockiness expected from an ex-plumber who now makes $13,500 a year as tribal president on a reservation where the average annual income is $1,800. His home, an ex-motel, is in bad need of paint. He has not yet taken down the "Pine Ridge Motel" sign in front of his kitchen window.

"The only major Indian problem is AIM," Wilson begins. "They're just bums tryin' to get their braids and mugs in the press. We're gonna get 'em the hell out of Wounded Knee; I have 900 angry Indians on my side. I can't hold my people back much longer." Listening to him through the golden haze of several glasses of beer, I think, the way things are going we could hold the Indians back another 200 years.

Once in a while an event occurs. Under a crisp Dakota sky, smoke pours from Aaron DeSersa's one-story turquoise bungalow in the new subdivision of Northridge, just north of Pine Ridge. DeSersa, Indian public relations man for AIM, is out at Wounded Knee. The neighborhood children gather on muddy lawns to watch volunteer firemen haul out charred mattresses and antelope skins. "Dick Wilson hired someone to throw a Coke bottle filled with gasoline through the baby's bedroom window," someone whispers. Mrs. DeSersa huddles in a nearby bungalow, shaking, a rifle hidden under a blanket. Her five children are safe, and her oldest son, his face twisted in rage, vows, "I'll kill whoever did it. I'll kill him." In the Whiteclay, Nebraska, bar the bartender rubs his finger back and forth across the rim of an empty beer bottle and says, "Don't believe it. They probably set their own house on fire, just so's they could blame it on the Wilsons."

Standing in the rubble behind his house the next morning, feet spread, arms crossed, the four remaining teeth in his mouth gleaming in the sun, Aaron DeSersa tells a group of reporters: "I have ordered the caravans to come from St. Louis, Des Moines, St. Paul, and Oklahoma, to avenge the firebombing of my house by Wilson's goon squads. I will ask the Secretary of the Interior to declare martial law on the reservation."

His neighbor, Hobart Keith, leans his bulging belly across the backyard fence and cheers him on. "Wilson is a paper Caesar," Keith says, "with the morals of an alley cat." Keith warms to his subject. "You should keep twenty U.S. marshals here under *my* command. Fire the Indian police force, teach people law and order." He stops, listens to a German reporter interviewing DeSersa, then adds, "I left the reservation a long time ago, but came back in 1959. And now I see even Jesus Christ himself couldn't help this reservation." "Why do you stay?" a reporter asks. "Because," Keith says, "mass humanity repels me."

The state fire marshal inspects the DeSersa home and reports that faulty wiring, not a bomb, started the fire. House fires are fairly common on the reservation. The marshal reported last year that it takes only twenty-five minutes for these houses to burn to the ground.

I am sitting in the Crazy Horse Café in Pine Ridge and have just made a deal with an old man who says he can show me how to sneak past federal marshals into the village of Wounded Knee. The old Sioux, his features blurred in the shadow of his tan Stetson hat, drives me in his green Datsun over rutted roads and buffalo grass to the nearby village of Manderson, tells me to keep low along the bed of Wounded Knee Creek, then waves goodbye as I climb the first hill leading to the Sacred Heart Catholic Church three miles away in Wounded Knee.

I follow Wounded Knee Creek until it ends abruptly, then backtrack and follow a different branch. I want to get to Wounded Knee to find out about our graven images. Twice federal scouts pass near me, and once a helicopter dips overhead. I walk across arroyos, through herds of bulls, and after four hours realize I am lost. The sun by now is gliding along the treetops. At the risk of being seen and stopped by police, I climb to the pasture above me to get my bearings.

I am halfway across the open pasture that leads to Wounded Knee when four small figures appear on the ridge. We see each other at the same instant, and they shout vague curses and point rifles in my direction. Unsure what to do next, I sit down. They regroup for discussion, then suddenly a loudspeaker blares from their hidden police car: "Keep coming toward us, we've got you covered."

I start to walk their way when a new voice, an Indian voice, breaks from down in the wooded stream behind my back. "Turn around and come toward me," he says. "I've got you covered." I want to run to him, but the police radio crackles once again. I put my hands in the air, turn to the ridge, then to the stream, then back to the ridge. So this is the DMZ. The lone Indian calls up to me once more, and I think I hear his voice waver. The voices above me do not waver, so I go to them, defeated.

"What do you think you're doing?" the cop asked when I arrive at the top. "Taking a walk," I answer. He does not smile, but demands to see my press credentials, which I do not have. "How close am I to Wounded Knee?" I ask. "Half a mile," he says. "You almost made it."

The police drop me off at the roadblock on Big Foot Road, where I shiver in the cold and try to hitch a ride back to the Crazy Horse Café. A young federal marshal takes pity, brings me coffee and a bologna sandwich, then takes me aside. "Just remember, you don't know where you heard this," he says. "But if you want to get into Wounded Knee, drive to Denby Road just east of here, and take two right forks until you come to a place where you can park your car. Follow the stream from there on foot, and it will take you right to Wounded Knee. Nobody will stop you."

Early the next morning, I follow his instructions and get into the village in one hour.

Wounded Knee itself is the eye of a hurricane without the hurricane. Young Indian boys in buckskin race through the village in old cars, stirring up the dusty past. They tape M-1 carbine magazines together and drape them over the front seats, and when they walk, their hips swagger from the weight of their guns. They dress and act as if they believe everything the white man has written about them

In front of the trading post, Eddie Whitewater, a Winnebago from Oklahoma, is sweeping at the sidewalk with an old broom. The walk is piled high with day-glo bumper stickers: "South Dakota National Historic Site." Every time Eddie gets the bumper stickers in a pile the wind scatters them again. "That's okay," he says, sweeping them up again. "I got nothing else to do today." The two cavernous rooms inside the trading post, scarred from that brief evening of inspiration when the Indian Nation rose again, are stripped bare except for a few jars of blue cheese dressing and some plastic tomtoms. A black telephone, wires cut, sits mute on a lunch counter. A penciled sign on the wall says: "It is better to die on our feet than live on our knees," a slogan picked up from Londonderry. In Ireland it serves as an inspiration; here it reads like a borrowed cause.

The shades are drawn in the steepled country church. A dozen Indians, only their hair and boots showing from beneath blankets, sleep on the floor and pews, while a plaster of Paris St. Theresa looks on over her bouquet of plastic roses. In the church basement, rebels and refugees watch basketball on the color television set and occasionally talk. "No more red tape," says one. "No more promises," says another. "We want action *now*," says a third, and she turns back to her comic book. A single trough behind the church holds the mass grave that put Wounded Knee on the map. The grass on the graves is shaggy, the wooden crosses bent and broken, and the view is of a housing project. Only the names of the dead retain a semblance of romance: Weasel Bear, No Ears, Chase-in-Winter, Scabbard Knife. In front of the church an American flag is hanging—torn in half and upside down, of course.

The heart and bones of the old Sioux chief, Crazy Horse, are supposedly buried nearby. In 1877 Crazy Horse balked at being led into the prison at Fort Robinson, Nebraska, and was bayoneted by Private William Gentles of the U.S. Army. Crazy Horse's parents buried the remains of their thirty-five-year-old son near Chankpe Opi Wakpala, the Sioux name for the creek we know as Wounded Knee, but kept the location of the grave a secret. Thirteen years later, federal forces killed over 150 Indians along the creek, and the mass grave was filled. Stephen Vincent Benét wrote a poem about this valley of death: "I shall not be there. I shall rise and pass./Bury my heart at Wounded Knee." The poem provided the title for Dee Brown's book *Bury My Heart at Wounded Knee*, and the book's popularity in turn was among the considerations that led AIM to Wounded Knee to plead a public case for the American Indian. It virtually guaranteed them a good press.

Down the hill from the grave, AIM leader Russell Means entertains reporters in his living room. "The federal government hasn't changed from Wounded Knee to My Lai and back to Wounded Knee," Means says. He wears braided hair, a blue plaid shirt, and a red beaded belt with his name on the back. "The federal government never changes," he adds. The reporters write it down. He stops, seems to lose his train of thought, stares at the linoleum floor. "Are you full-blooded Indian?" a white woman asks him. "No, didn't you know?" Means stops playing with his braids and looks up. "My grandfather raped a white princess." The woman's eyes widen, and Means unravels a long stringy laugh. He has won.

Russell Means grew up on Pine Ridge Reservation, moved to Cleveland, helped form AIM in 1968 to protest police brutality in Minneapolis. Last fall he led the Trail of Broken Treaties to the BIA building in Washington, D.C., where the Indians caused two million dollars' damage and confiscated BIA records in order to track down alleged fraud. Last year he returned to Pine Ridge with AIM to protest the death of Raymond Yellow Thunder, an old Indian who was beaten up in a used-car lot in nearby Gordon, Nebraska. Yellow Thunder was thrown into the trunk of a car and driven to the Gordon American Legion Hall, where a dance was being held. He was stripped from the waist down, shoved into the hall, and ordered to dance "Indian style." Eight days later, he was found dead. The autopsy showed he died from a brain hemorrhage caused by the beating. Rumors spread that he had been tortured, burned with cigarettes, and castrated before he died. The rumors proved false, but they were enough.

Means and his partner, Dennis Banks, a tall craggy-faced Chippewa who fancies white silk scarves, demanded investigations by Congress, the Justice Department, McGovern. Nothing happened. They issued a call for 10,000 Indians to converge on Pine Ridge. Only a few dozen showed up. The pent-up pressure finally burst among the Pine Ridge Sioux, and they ransacked the Wounded Knee museum next to the trading post, causing $50,000 damage. When Wounded Knee was hit again this year, AIM put a sign on the museum door: "Keep your ass out of here."

Five whites were arrested in connection with Yellow Thunder's death. After a two-and-a-half day trial before an all-white jury, three defendants were found guilty of manslaughter and false imprisonment and received sentences of six, four, and two years. They are out on bond pending appeal. Another was fined $500; charges against the fifth defendant, a white woman, were dropped.

"What's the next stop in this year's siege?" a reporter asks Means. Means says: "Bang, bang!" and laughs. "Why are you militant?" a reporter asks. "Because I'm Indian," Means answers. "Are you encouraging the support of the local churches?" a reporter asks. "The churches are a ripoff, to turn us into facsimiles of white men," Means says, and yawns. After a while, he goes next door to a trailer where the rest of the reporters are watching the six o'clock news. He had helped direct the cameramen that day, even restaged events they missed. He is upset they didn't use more footage, but admits the white canvas tepee they finally put up looks nice. Inside the tepee white attorneys and Indian attorneys are shouting at each other. Several reporters, pencils flowing, lean heavily against the canvas as if blown there by a high wind.

Just out of camera range sits a young Indian man with words to explain Indian hatreds and hopes, but no one listens to him. He is a Mohawk, and Mohawks do not speak for the Sioux, even when the Sioux seem unable to speak for themselves. "Indian values sound romantic because all the patterns and attitudes of the last 200 years are based on exploitation," he says to an audience of one. "America had too many different interests to keep its relationship with the Indians healthy. The American economy must keep expanding, or it will choke. The Indians are givers and the Americans are takers, and when givers meet takers the givers lose." His Mohawk name is Kanatekeniate, but he uses the American name Tom Cook. Around his neck he wears a Sony tape recorder for his job with the Mohawk newspaper, *Akwesasne Notes*. So the press interviews the press.

"We don't want more welfare, more handouts," he says. "We want political rights. We want America to send us statesmen, not armed forces. We want the Indians who define themselves as Americans to get off the reservation.

"The spirit of what we are has been given us by the land, the air, and the stars," he continues slowly. "We cannot be separated from the earth. Old Indian men even look like the earth. But now our tribal structure is replaced with municipal government, a white man's government with elected bodies of representatives. Our spirit is ripped apart, and our definitions treated with contempt. What Indian things remain in us are broken and scattered."

His words paraphrase those of Chief Black Elk, who said after the massacre of Wounded Knee: "A people's dream died there. . . . the nation's hoop is broken and scattered. There is no center any longer, and the sacred tree is dead." Tom Cook looks up at the sun, hesitates. "It's hard to bring it together to make sense anymore," he says at last.

When Cook drove out of Wounded Knee late that afternoon, he asked the government agents at roadblock No. 1 if they would like to hear his tape of a meeting in Wounded Knee. Six FBI men, dressed in green khaki and black baseball caps with "FBI" written in white felt across the brims, bent into the car windows. "The Indians are praying for us," the cassette squeaked, while one man searched the car trunk. "People across the country, even non-Indian, are praying," it squeaked again. "The National Council of Churches will airlift food to us," it rasped, and the young FBI men listened, somber and thoughtful, until another car approached and they scurried off, rifles ready.

"If the FBI and marshals leave, there will be no crisis and we will have no story. Why do you stay?" I asked one of them. "They shot at our men," he answered. "We can't let them get away with that. We'll stay until we get them."

Everyone in South Dakota steps carefully around the words "racial problem" but the local whites' simmering neurosis about the Indian bubbles into full-fledged paranoia as these stalemates drag on. At Pine Ridge, a Justice Department spokesman drops strong hints around the parking lot that white ranchers are to blame for the cut electric and telephone wires leading into Wounded Knee. In Custer, every white I meet has a gun under the front seat of his car, and Custer mayor Gene Reese is quoted as saying that the people of his town "may have to take it upon themselves" to ward off future Indian attacks. "They came here because of our name," says Mrs. Hobart Gates, wife of the Custer County prosecutor. "How can we possibly negotiate a symbol?"

Even 115 miles away in urban Rapid City, whites skitter like colts in a burning barn at the mere mention of the "Indian problem." James Kuehn, longtime executive director of the *Rapid City Journal*, tells me: "We haven't yet run an editorial about Wounded Knee because we still aren't sure what to think. We've sent our own reporters out there a couple times, but mainly we use wire copy. We're so close to the situation and things are so tense, you can't say anything about the Indians without offending somebody."

A longtime friend in Rapid City, who has attended Bible class once a week ever since I've known him, says he doesn't talk about the "Indian problem" with anyone other than his wife. "Ever since Indians smashed up four bars in town," he explains, "you can't say a word about them having valid complaints, or people accuse you of being pro-Indian. It's not worth losing friends over." I try to cash a check in a Rapid City motel, and the owner's wife explains they no longer keep cash on hand. "No, no Indians ever robbed us yet, or anywhere else I've heard of, but with all this going on you never know what might happen next," she says. "Why, we never noticed the color of skin until those Indians busted up the town. It set them back a hundred years."

Whites in Custer have been even more virulent since the Indians burned down the town's Chamber of Commerce on February 6, the same day they attacked the courthouse. Actually, press reports about the fiery death of the building were greatly exaggerated. When I first tried to check those reports, I could not even find the charred remains of the building, and when I did find the foundation, I paced it off, reluctant to believe what I saw. The late Custer Chamber of Commerce, by my calculations, had apparently been the size of two hot dog stands set side by side.

As I did my pacing, a 1963 Ford braked in the middle of the intersection of Custer and Fourth Streets a few feet away. The driver wore glasses and a baseball cap with the brim turned up, from under which he peered at me through his windshield for several minutes. Finally, unable to contain himself, he left his car running and hurried over.

"You the appraiser?" he asked. "No, a writer," I answered. "Fur one of them liberal hippie magazines?" he asked. "Not exactly." "You know," he began, unprompted, "we were talkin' down at the fillin' station the other day, and we decided those goddamn Indian idiots got no goddamn business here. Why, it sounded like a Fourth of Jooly party over here when they burned down this here Chamber of Commerce. The people of South Dakota got more guns stuck in their faces in the last year than anybody in the United States." The skin of his face was rough, filled with a thousand hills and gullies, and his narrow lips barely moved when he talked. "Most of us hillbillies work in timber and mines—I worked in mines all my life, and I love my land," he said with a sweep of his hand toward the spring-ripened Black Hills that nestle lovingly against the town.

Two weeks later, a U.S. marshal was shot and paralyzed from the hips down as the result of a fire fight near Wounded Knee. That was enough for U.S. Assistant Attorney General Kent Frizzell, who had tried to let the alleged uprising collapse of its own accord. At a press conference, Frizzell declared, "The fun and games are over," and so they were. Desertions had cut the rebel ranks to a few hard-core militants, reportedly armed with two 50-caliber machine guns and home-made land mines. As the situation worsened, government armored cars moved closer to Wounded Knee, and a showdown seemed to be at hand. Or so it was said. None of us knew the facts: the press was finally barred from the scene. For us, the fun and games *were* over—at last.

These, then, are the stories of Wounded Knee and Custer, of Gordon and Rapid City. Stories of battles without glory, heroes without bravery, romance without vision. The reporters shredded the stories into pieces, tossed them into the air, and recreated them as they fell into designs of their own choosing. We tightened up the facts, smoothed the edges, covered up the blemishes like portrait artists with fussy clients. We wrote good cowboy-and-Indian stories because we thought it was what the public wanted, and they were harmless, even if they were not all true. For the truth is buried in too many centuries of lies like fossils embedded in layers of shale. Let the Recording of the Event make do as the event—and don't believe everything in the media.

ERIC HOFFER

The Role of the Undesirables

In the winter of 1934, I spent several weeks in a federal transient camp in California. These camps were originally established by Governor Rolph in the early days of the Depression to care for the single homeless unemployed of the state. In 1934 the federal government took charge of the camps for a time, and it was then that I first heard of them.

How I happened to get into one of the camps is soon told. Like thousands of migrant agricultural workers in California I then followed the crops from one part of the state to the other. Early in

1934 I arrived in the town of El Centro, in the Imperial Valley. I had been given a free ride on a truck from San Diego, and it was midnight when the truck driver dropped me on the outskirts of El Centro. I spread my bedroll by the side of the road and went to sleep. I had hardly dozed off when the rattle of a motorcycle drilled itself into my head and a policeman was bending over me saying, "Roll up, Mister." It looked as though I was in for something; it happened now and then that the police got overzealous and rounded up the freight trains. But this time the cop had no such thought. He said, "Better go over to the federal shelter and get yourself a bed and maybe some breakfast." He directed me to the place.

I found a large hall, obviously a former garage, dimly lit, and packed with cots. A concert of heavy breathing shook the thick air. In a small office near the door, I was registered by a middle-aged clerk. He informed me that this was the "receiving shelter" where I would get one night's lodging and breakfast. The meal was served in the camp nearby. Those who wished to stay on, he said, had to enroll in the camp. He then gave me three blankets and excused himself for not having a vacant cot. I spread the blankets on the cement floor and went to sleep.

I awoke with dawn amid a chorus of coughing, throat-clearing, the sound of running water, and the intermittent flushing of toilets in the back of the hall. There were about fifty of us, all colors and ages, all of us more or less ragged and soiled. The clerk handed out tickets for breakfast, and we filed out to the camp located several blocks away, near the railroad tracks.

From the outside the camp looked like a cross between a factory and a prison. A high fence of wire enclosed it, and inside were three large sheds and a huge boiler topped by a pillar of black smoke. Men in blue shirts and dungarees were strolling across the sandy yard. A ship's bell in front of one of the buildings announced breakfast. The regular camp members—there was a long line of them—ate first. Then we filed in through the gate, handing our tickets to the guard.

It was a good, plentiful meal. After breakfast our crowd dispersed. I heard some say that the camps in the northern part of the state were better, that they were going to catch a northbound freight. I decided to try this camp in El Centro.

My motives in enrolling were not crystal clear. I wanted to clean up. There were shower baths in the camp and wash tubs and plenty of soap. Of course I could have bathed and washed my clothes in one of the irrigation ditches, but here in the camp I had a chance to rest, get the wrinkles out of my belly, and clean up at leisure. In short, it was the easiest way out.

A brief interview at the camp office and a physical examination were all the formalities for enrollment.

There were some two hundred men in the camp. They were the kind I had worked and traveled with for years. I even saw familiar faces—men I had worked with in orchards and fields. Yet my predominant feeling was one of strangeness. It was my first experience of life in intimate contact with a crowd. For it is one thing to work and travel with a gang, and quite another thing to eat, sleep, and spend the greater part of the day cheek by jowl with two hundred men.

I found myself speculating on a variety of subjects: the reasons for their chronic bellyaching and beefing—it was more a ritual than the expression of a grievance; the amazing orderliness of the men; the comic seriousness with which they took their games of cards, checkers, and dominoes; the weird manner of reasoning one overheard now and then. Why, I kept wondering, were these men within the enclosure of a federal transient camp? Were they people temporarily hard up? Would jobs solve all their difficulties? Were we indeed like the people outside?

Up to then I was not aware of being one of a specific species of humanity. I had considered myself simply a human being—not particularly good or bad, and on the whole harmless. The people I worked and traveled with I knew as Americans and Mexicans, whites and Negroes, Northerners and Southerners, etc. It did not occur to me that we were a group possessed of peculiar traits, and that there was something—innate or acquired—in our makeup which made us adopt a particular mode of existence.

It was a slight thing that started me on a new track.

I got to talking to a mild-looking, elderly fellow. I liked his soft speech and pleasant manner. We swapped trivial experiences. Then he suggested a game of checkers. As we started to arrange the pieces on the board, I was startled by the sight of his crippled right hand. I had not noticed it before. Half of it was chopped off lengthwise, so that the horny stump with its three fingers looked like a hen's leg. I was mortified that I had not noticed the hand until he dangled it, so to speak, before my eyes. It was, perhaps, to bolster my shaken confidence in my powers of observation that I now began paying close attention to the hands of the people around me. The result was astounding. It seemed that every other man had had his hand mangled. There was a man with one arm. Some men limped. One young, good-looking fellow had a wooden leg. It was as though the majority of the men had escaped the snapping teeth of a machine and left part of themselves behind.

It was, I knew, an exaggerated impression. But I began counting the cripples as the men lined up in the yard at mealtime. I found thirty (out of two hundred) crippled either in arms or legs. I immediately sensed where the counting would land me. The simile preceded the statistical deduction: we in the camp were a human junk pile.

I began evaluating my fellow tramps as human material, and for the first time in my life I became face-conscious. There were some good faces, particularly among the young. Several of the middle-aged and the old looked healthy and well preserved. But the damaged and decayed faces were in the majority. I saw faces that were wrinkled, or bloated, or raw as the surface of a peeled plum. Some of the noses were purple and swollen, some broken, some pitted with enlarged pores. There were many toothless mouths (I counted seventy-eight). I noticed eyes that were blurred, faded, opaque, or bloodshot. I was struck by the fact that the old men, even the very old, showed their age mainly in the face. Their bodies were still slender and erect. One little man over sixty years of age looked a mere boy when seen from behind. The shriveled face joined to a boyish body made a startling sight.

My diffidence had now vanished. I was getting to know everybody in the camp. They were a friendly and talkative lot. Before many weeks I knew some essential fact about practically everyone.

And I was continually counting. Of the two hundred men in the camp there were approximately as follows:

Cripples	30
Confirmed drunkards	60
Old men (55 and over)	50
Youths under twenty	10
Men with chronic diseases, heart, asthma, TB	12
Mildly insane	4
Constitutionally lazy	6
Fugitives from justice	4
Apparently normal	70

(The numbers do not tally up to two hundred since some of the men were counted twice or even thrice—as cripples and old, or as old and confirmed drunks, etc.)

In other words: less than half the camp inmates (seventy normal, plus ten youths) were unemployed workers whose difficulties would be at an end once jobs were available. The rest (60 per cent) had handicaps in addition to unemployment.

I also counted fifty war veterans, and eighty skilled workers representing sixteen trades. All the men (including those with chronic diseases) were able to work. The one-armed man was a wizard with the shovel.

I did not attempt any definite measurement of character and intelligence. But it seemed to me that the intelligence of the men in the camp was certainly not below the average. And as to character, I found much forbearance and genuine good humor. I never came across one instance of real viciousness. Yet, on the whole, one would hardly say that these men were possessed of strong characters. Resistance, whether to one's appetites or to the ways of the world, is a chief factor in the shaping of character; and the average tramp is, more or less, a slave of his few appetites. He generally takes the easiest way out.

The connection between our makeup and our mode of existence as migrant workers presented itself now with some clarity. The majority of us were incapable of holding onto a steady job. We lacked self-discipline and the ability to endure monotonous, leaden hours. We were probably misfits from the very beginning. Our contact with a steady job was not unlike a collision. Some of us were maimed, some got frightened and ran away, and some took to drink. We inevitably drifted in the direction of least resistance—the open road. The life of a migrant worker is varied and demands only a minimum of self-discipline. We were now in one of the drainage ditches of ordered society. We could not keep a footing in the ranks of respectability and were washed into the slough of our present existence.

Yet, I mused, there must be in this world a task with an appeal so strong that were we to have a taste of it we would hold on and be rid for good of our restlessness.

My stay in the camp lasted about four weeks. Then I found a haying job not far from town, and finally, in April, when the hot winds began blowing, I shouldered my bedroll and took the highway to San Bernardino.

It was the next morning, after I had got a lift to Indio by truck, that a new idea began to take hold of me. The highway out of Indio leads through waving date groves, fragrant grapefruit orchards, and lush alfalfa fields; then, abruptly, passes into a desert of white sand. The sharp line between garden and desert is very striking. The turning of white sand into garden seemed to me an act of magic. This, I thought, was a job one would jump at—even the men in the transient camps. They had the skill and ability of the average American. But their energies, I felt, could be quickened only by a task that was spectacular, that had in it something of the miraculous. The pioneer task of making the desert flower would certainly fill the bill.

Tramps as pioneers? It seemed absurd. Every man and child in California knows that the pioneers had been giants, men of boundless courage and indomitable spirit. However, as I strode on across the white sand, I kept mulling the idea over.

Who were the pioneers? Who were the men who left their homes and went into the wilderness? A man rarely leaves a soft spot and goes deliberately in search of hardship and privation. People become attached to the places they live in; they drive roots. A change of habitat is a painful act of uprooting. A man who has made good and has a standing in his community stays put. The successful businessmen, farmers, and workers usually stayed where they were. Who then left for the wilderness and the unknown? Obviously those who had not made good: men who went broke or never amounted to much; men who though possessed of abilities were too impulsive to stand the daily grind; men who were slaves of their appetites—drunkards, gamblers, and woman-chasers; outcasts—fugitives from justice and ex-jailbirds. There were no doubt some who went in search of health—men suffering with TB, asthma, heart trouble. Finally there was a sprinkling of young and middle-aged in search of adventure.

All these people craved change, some probably actuated by the naïve belief that a change in place brings with it a change in luck. Many wanted to go to a place where they were not known and there make a new beginning. Certainly they did not go out deliberately in search of hard work and suffering. If in the end they shouldered enormous tasks, endured unspeakable hardships, and accomplished the impossible, it was because they had to. They became men of action on the run. They acquired strength and skill in the inescapable struggle for existence. It was a question of do or die. And once they tasted the joy of achievement, they craved for more.

Clearly the same types of people which now swelled the ranks of migratory workers and tramps had probably in former times made up the bulk of the pioneers. As a group the pioneers were probably as unlike the present-day "native sons"—their descendants—as one could well imagine. Indeed, were there to be today a new influx of typical pioneers, twin brothers of the forty-niners only in a modern garb, the citizens of California would consider it a menace to health, wealth, and morals.

With few exceptions, this seems to be the case in the settlement of all new countries. Ex-convicts were the vanguard in the settling of Australia. Exiles and convicts settled Siberia. In this country, a large portion of our earlier and later settlers were failures, fugitives, and felons. The exceptions seemed to be those who were motivated by religious fervor, such as the Pilgrim Fathers and the Mormons.

Although quite logical, this train of thought seemed to me then a wonderful joke. In my exhilaration I was eating up the road in long strides, and I reached the oasis of Elim in what seemed almost no time. A passing empty truck picked me up just then and we thundered through Banning and Beaumont, all the way to Riverside. From there I walked the seven miles to San Bernardino.

Somehow, this discovery of a family likeness between tramps and pioneers took a firm hold on my mind. For years afterward it kept intertwining itself with a mass of observations which on the face of them had no relation to either tramps or pioneers. And it moved me to speculate on subjects in which, up to then, I had no real interest, and of which I knew very little.

I talked with several old-timers—one of them over eighty and a native son—in Sacramento, Placerville, Auburn, and Fresno. It was not easy, at first, to obtain the information I was after. I could not make my questions specific enough. "What kind of people were the early settlers and miners?" I asked. They were a hard-working, tough lot, I was told. They drank, fought, gambled, and wenched. They were big-hearted, grasping, profane, and God-fearing. They wallowed in luxury, or lived on next to nothing with equal ease. They were the salt of the earth.

Still it was not clear what manner of people they were.

If I asked what they looked like, I was told of whiskers, broad-brimmed hats, high boots, shirts of many colors, sun-tanned faces, horny hands. Finally I asked: "What group of people in present-day California most closely resembles the pioneers?" The answer, usually after some hesitation, was invariably the same: "The Okies and the fruit tramps."

I tried also to evaluate the tramps as potential pioneers by watching them in action. I saw them fell timber, clear firebreaks, build rock walls, put up barracks, build dams and roads, handle steam shovels, bulldozers, tractors, and concrete mixers. I saw them put in a hard day's work after a night of steady drinking. They sweated and growled, but they did the work. I saw the tramps elevated to positions of authority as foremen and superintendents. Then I could notice a remarkable physical transformation: a seamed face gradually smoothed out and the skin showed a healthy hue: an indifferent mouth became firm and expressive; dull eyes cleared and brightened; voices actually changed; there was even an apparent increase in stature. In almost no time these promoted tramps looked as if they had been on top all their lives. Yet sooner or later I would meet up with them again in a railroad yard, on some skid row, or in the fields—tramps again. It was usually the same story: they got drunk or lost their temper and were fired, or they got fed up with the steady job and quit. Usually, when a tramp becomes a foreman, he is careful in his treatment of the tramps under him; he knows the day of reckoning is never far off.

In short, it was not difficult to visualize the tramps as pioneers. I reflected that if they were to find themselves in a singlehanded life-and-death struggle with nature, they would undoubtedly display persistence. For the pressure of responsibility and the heat of battle steel a character. The inadaptable would perish, and those who survived would be the equal of the successful pioneers.

I also considered the few instances of pioneering engineered from above—that is to say, by settlers possessed of lavish means, who were classed with the best where they came from. In these instances, it seemed to me, the resulting social structure was inevitably precarious. For pioneering deluxe usually results in a plantation society, made up of large landowners and peon labor, either native or imported. Very often there is a racial cleavage between the two. The colonizing activities of the Teutonic barons in the Baltic, the Hungarian nobles in Transylvania, the English in Ireland, the planters in our South, and the present-day plantation societies in Kenya and other British and Dutch colonies are cases in point. Whatever their merits, they are characterized by poor adaptability. They are likely eventually to be broken up either by a peon revolution or by an influx of typical pioneers—who are usually of the same race or nation as the landowners. The adjustment is not necessarily implemented by war. Even our old South, had it not been for the complication of secession, might eventually have attained stability without war: namely, by the activity of its own poor whites or by an influx of the indigent from other states.

There is in us a tendency to judge a race, a nation, or an organization by its least worthy members. The tendency is manifestly perverse and unfair; yet it has some justification. For the quality and destiny of a nation is determined to a considerable extent by the nature and potentialities of its inferior elements. The inert mass of a nation is in its middle section. The industrious, decent, well-to-do, and satisfied middle classes—whether in cities or on the land—are worked upon and shaped by minorities at both extremes: the best and the worst.

The superior individual, whether in politics, business, industry, science, literature, or religion, undoubtedly plays a major role in the shaping of a nation. But so do the individuals at the other extreme: the poor, the outcasts, the misfits, and those who are in the grip of some overpowering passion. The importance of these inferior elements as formative factors lies in the readiness with which they are swayed in any direction. This peculiarity is due to their inclination to take risks ("not giving a damn") and their propensity for united action. They crave to merge their drab, wasted lives into something grand and complete. Thus they are the first and most fervent adherents of new religions, political upheavals, patriotic hysteria, gangs, and mass rushes to new lands.

And the quality of a nation—its innermost worth—is made manifest by its dregs as they rise to the top: by how brave they are, how humane, how orderly, how skilled, how generous, how independent or servile; by the bounds they will not transgress in their dealings with man's soul, with truth, and with honor.

The average American of today bristles with indignation when he is told that his country was built, largely, by hordes of undesirables from Europe. Yet, far from being derogatory, this statement, if true, should be a cause for rejoicing, should fortify our pride in the stock from which we have sprung.

This vast continent with its towns, farms, factories, dams, aqueducts, docks, railroads, highways, powerhouses, schools, and parks is the handiwork of common folk from the Old World, where for centuries men of their kind had been as beasts of burden, the property of their masters—kings, nobles, and priests—and with no will and no aspirations of their own. When on rare occasions one of the lowly had reached the top in Europe he had kept the pattern intact and, if anything, tightened the screws. The stuffy little corporal from Corsica harnessed the lusty forces released by the French Revolution to a gilded state coach, and could think of nothing grander than mixing his blood with that of the Hapsburg masters and establishing a new dynasty. In our day a bricklayer in Italy, a house painter in Germany, and a shoemaker's son in Russia have made themselves masters of their nations; and what they did was to re-establish and reinforce the old pattern.

Only here, in America, were the common folk of the Old World given a chance to show what they could do on their own, without a master to push and order them about. History contrived an earth-shaking joke when it lifted by the nape of the neck lowly peasants, shopkeepers, laborers, paupers, jailbirds, and drunks from the midst of Europe, dumped them on a vast, virgin continent and said: "Go to it; it is yours!"

And the lowly were not awed by the magnitude of the task. A hunger for action, pent up for centuries, found an outlet. They went to it with ax, pick, shovel, plow, and rifle; on foot, on horse, in wagons, and on flatboats. They went to it praying, howling, singing, brawling, drinking, and fighting. Make way for the people! This is how I read the statement that this country was built by hordes of undesirables from the Old World.

Small wonder that we in this country have a deeply ingrained faith in human regeneration. We believe that, given a chance, even the degraded and the apparently worthless are capable of constructive work and great deeds. It is a faith founded on experience, not on some idealistic theory. And no matter what some anthropologists, sociologists, and geneticists may tell us, we shall go on believing that man, unlike other forms of life, is not a captive of his past—of his heredity and habits—but is possessed of infinite plasticity, and his potentialities for good and for evil are never wholly exhausted.

QUESTIONS

The following poem by Carl Sandburg speaks about "undesirables"—"rabble," "vagabonds," "hungry men." What other words might Sandburg have used for the "undesirables"? What effect do the words he uses create? Compare the terms used by Sandburg and Hoffer and determine the ways in which their words suggest similar or different attitudes toward these people.

Now the stone house on the lake front is finished and the
    workmen are beginning the fence.
The palings are made of iron bars with steel points that can
    stab the life out of any man who falls on them.
As a fence, it is a masterpiece, and will shut off the
    rabble and all vagabonds and hungry men and all
    wandering children looking for a place to play.
Passing through the bars and over the steel points will go
    nothing except Death and the Rain and To-morrow.
                —Carl Sandburg, "A Fence"

HANNAH ARENDT

Denmark and the Jews[1]

At the Wannsee Conference,[2] Martin Luther, of the Foreign Office, warned of great difficulties in the Scandinavian countries, notably in Norway and Denmark. (Sweden was never occupied, and Finland, though in the war on the side of the Axis, was one country the Nazis never even approached on the Jewish question. This surprising exception of Finland, with some two thousand Jews, may have been due to Hitler's great esteem for the Finns, whom perhaps he did not want to subject to threats and humiliating blackmail.) Luther proposed postponing evacuations from Scandinavia for the time being, and as far as Denmark was concerned, this really went without saying, since the country retained its independent government, and was respected as a neutral state, until the fall of 1943, although it, along with Norway, had been invaded by the German Army in April, 1940. There existed no Fascist or Nazi movement in Denmark worth mentioning, and therefore no collaborators. In

1. From "Deportations from Western Europe—France, Belgium, Holland, Denmark, Italy," Chapter X of *Eich-* *mann in Jerusalem*, 1963.
2. A meeting of German officials on "the Jewish question."

Norway, however, the Germans had been able to find enthusiastic supporters; indeed, Vidkun Quisling, leader of the pro-Nazi and anti-Semitic Norwegian party, gave his name to what later became known as a "quisling government." The bulk of Norway's seventeen hundred Jews were stateless, refugees from Germany; they were seized and interned in a few lightning operations in October and November, 1942. When Eichmann's office ordered their deportation to Auschwitz, some of Quisling's own men resigned their government posts. This may not have come as a surprise to Mr. Luther and the Foreign Office, but what was much more serious, and certainly totally unexpected, was that Sweden immediately offered asylum, and even Swedish nationality, to all who were persecuted. Dr. Ernst von Weizsäcker, Undersecretary of State of the Foreign Office, who received the proposal, refused to discuss it, but the offer helped nevertheless. It is always relatively easy to get out of a country illegally, whereas it is nearly impossible to enter the place of refuge without permission and to dodge the immigration authorities. Hence, about nine hundred people, slightly more than half of the small Norwegian community, could be smuggled into Sweden.

It was in Denmark, however, that the Germans found out how fully justified the Foreign Offices's apprehensions had been. The story of the Danish Jews is *sui generis*, and the behavior of the Danish people and their government was unique among all the countries in Europe—whether occupied, or a partner of the Axis, or neutral and truly independent. One is tempted to recommend the story as required reading in political science for all students who wish to learn something about the enormous power potential inherent in non-violent action and in resistance to an opponent possessing vastly superior means of violence. To be sure, a few other countries in Europe lacked proper "understanding of the Jewish question," and actually a majority of them were opposed to "radical" and "final" solutions. Like Denmark, Sweden, Italy, and Bulgaria proved to be nearly immune to anti-Semitism, but of the three that were in the German sphere of influence, only the Danes dared speak out on the subject to their German masters. Italy and Bulgaria sabotaged German orders and indulged in a complicated game of double-dealing and double-crossing, saving their Jews by a tour de force of sheer ingenuity, but they never contested the policy as such. That was totally different from what the Danes did. When the Germans approached them rather cautiously about introducing the yellow badge, they were simply told that the King would be the first to wear it, and the Danish government officials were careful to point out that anti-Jewish measures of any sort would cause their own immediate resignation. It was decisive in this whole matter that the Germans did not even succeed in introducing the vitally important distinction between native Danes of Jewish origin, of whom there were about sixty-four hundred, and the fourteen hundred German Jewish refugees who had found asylum in the country prior to the war and who now had been declared stateless by the German government. This refusal must have surprised the Germans no end, since it appeared so "illogical" for a government to protect people to whom it had categorically denied naturalization and even permission to work. (Legally, the prewar situation of refugees in Denmark was not unlike that in France, except that the general corruption in the Third Republic's civil services enabled a few of them to obtain naturalization papers, through bribes or "connections," and most refugees in France could work illegally, without a permit. But Denmark, like Switzerland, was no country *pour se débrouiller*[3].) The Danes, however, explained to the German officials that because the stateless refugees were no longer German citizens, the Nazis could not claim them without Danish assent. This was one of the few cases in which statelessness turned out to be an asset, although it was of course not statelessness per se that saved the Jews but, on the contrary, the fact that the Danish government had decided to protect them. Thus, none of the preparatory moves, so important for the bureaucracy of murder, could be carried out, and operations were postponed until the fall of 1943.

What happened then was truly amazing; compared with what took place in other European countries, everything went topsy-turvey. In August, 1943—after the German offensive in Russia had failed, the Afrika Korps had surrendered in Tunisia, and the Allies had invaded Italy—the Swedish government canceled its 1940 agreement with Germany which had permitted German troops the right to pass through the country. Thereupon, the Danish workers decided that they could help a bit in hurrying things up; riots broke out in Danish shipyards, where the dock workers refused to repair German ships and then went on strike. The German military commander proclaimed a state of emergency and imposed martial law, and Himmler thought this was the right moment to tackle the Jewish question, whose "solution" was long overdue. What he did not reckon with was that—quite apart from Danish resistance—the German officials who had been living in the country for years were no longer the same. Not only did General von Hannecken, the military commander, refuse to put troops at the disposal of the Reich plenipotentiary, Dr. Werner Best; the special S.S. units (*Einsatz-kommandos*) employed in Denmark very frequently objected to "the measures they were ordered to carry out by the central agencies"—according to Best's testimony at Nuremberg. And Best himself, an old Gestapo man and former legal adviser to Heydrich, author of a then famous book on the police, who had

---

3. For wangling—using bribery to circumvent bureaucratic regulations.

worked for the military government in Paris to the entire satisfaction of his superiors, could no longer be trusted, although it is doubtful that Berlin ever learned the extent of his unreliability. Still, it was clear from the beginning that things were not going well, and Eichmann's office sent one of its best men to Denmark—Rolf Günther, whom no one had ever accused of not possessing the required "ruthless toughness." Günther made no impression on his colleagues in Copenhagen, and now von Hannecken refused even to issue a decree requiring all Jews to report for work.

Best went to Berlin and obtained a promise that all Jews from Denmark would be sent to Theresienstadt[4] regardless of their category—a very important concession, from the Nazis' point of view. The night of October 1 was set for their seizure and immediate departure—ships were ready in the harbor—and since neither the Danes nor the Jews nor the German troops stationed in Denmark could be relied on to help, police units arrived from Germany for a door-to-door search. At the last moment, Best told them that they were not permitted to break into apartments, because the Danish police might then interfere, and they were not supposed to fight it out with the Danes. Hence they could seize only those Jews who voluntarily opened their doors. They found exactly 477 people, out of a total of more then 7,800, at home and willing to let them in. A few days before the date of doom, a German shipping agent, Georg F. Duckwitz, having probably been tipped off by Best himself, had revealed the whole plan to Danish government officials, who, in turn, had hurriedly informed the heads of the Jewish community. They, in marked contrast to Jewish leaders in other countries, had then communicated the news openly in the synagogues on the occasion of the New Year services. The Jews had just time enough to leave their apartments and go into hiding, which was very easy in Denmark, because, in the words of the judgment, "all sections of the Danish people, from the King down to simple citizens," stood ready to receive them.

They might have remained in hiding until the end of the war if the Danes had not been blessed with Sweden as a neighbor. It seemed reasonable to ship the Jews to Sweden, and this was done with the help of the Danish fishing fleet. The cost of transportation for people without means—about a hundred dollars per person—was paid largely by wealthy Danish citizens, and that was perhaps the most astounding feat of all, since this was a time when Jews were paying for their own deportation, when the rich among them were paying fortunes for exit permits (in Holland, Slovakia, and, later, in Hungary) either by bribing the local authorities or by negotiating "legally" with the S.S., who accepted only hard currency

4. A camp for certain classes of prisoners who were to receive special treatment.

and sold exit permits, in Holland, to the tune of five or ten thousand dollars per person. Even in places where Jews met with genuine sympathy and a sincere willingness to help, they had to pay for it, and the chances poor people had of escaping were nil.

It took the better part of October to ferry all the Jews across the five to fifteen miles of water that separates Denmark from Sweden. The Swedes received 5,919 refugees, of whom at least 1,000 were of German origin, 1,310 were half-Jews, and 686 were non-Jews married to Jews. (Almost half the Danish Jews seem to have remained in the country and survived the war in hiding.) The non-Danish Jews were better off than ever before, they all received permission to work. The few hundred Jews whom the German police had been able to arrest were shipped to Theresienstadt. They were old or poor people, who either had not received the news in time or had not been able to comprehend its meaning. In the ghetto, they enjoyed greater privileges than any other group because of the never-ending "fuss" made about them by Danish institutions and private persons. Forty-eight persons died, a figure that was not particularly high, in view of the average age of the group. When everything was over, it was the considered opinion of Eichmann that "for various reasons the action against the Jews in Denmark has been a failure," whereas the curious Dr. Best declared that "the objective of the operation was not to seize a great number of Jews but to clean Denmark of Jews, and this objective has now been achieved."

Politically and psychologically, the most interesting aspect of this incident is perhaps the role played by the German authorities in Denmark, their obvious sabotage of orders from Berlin. It is the only case we know of in which the Nazis met with *open* native resistance, and the result seems to have been that those exposed to it changed their minds. They themselves apparently no longer looked upon the extermination of a whole people as a matter of course. They had met resistance based on principle, and their "toughness" had melted like butter in the sun, they had even been able to show a few timid beginnings of genuine courage. That the ideal of "toughness," except, perhaps, for a few half-demented brutes, was nothing but a myth of self-deception, concealing a ruthless desire for conformity at any price, was clearly revealed at the Nuremberg Trials, where the defendants accused and betrayed each other and assured the world that they "had always been against it" or claimed, as Eichmann was to do, that their best qualities had been "abused" by their superiors. (In Jerusalem, he accused "those in power" of having abused his "obedience." "The subject of a good government is lucky, the subject of a bad government is unlucky. I had no luck.") The atmosphere had changed, and although most of them must have known that they were doomed, not a single one of them had the guts to defend the Nazi ideology. Werner Best claimed at Nuremberg that he had played a complicated double role and that it was thanks to him that the Danish officials had been warned of the impending catastrophe; documentary evidence showed, on the contrary, that he himself had proposed the Danish operation in Berlin, but he explained that this was all part of the game. He was extradited to Denmark and there condemned to death, but he appealed the sentence, with surprising results; because of "new evidence," his sentence was commuted to five years in prison, from which he was released soon afterward. He must have been able to prove to the satisfaction of the Danish court that he really had done his best.

IAN WATT

"The Bridge over the River Kwai" as Myth

The Kwai is a real river in Thailand, and nearly thirty years ago prisoners of the Japanese—including myself—really did build a bridge across it: actually, two. Anyone who was there knows that Boulle's novel, *The Bridge on the River Kwai*, and the movie based on it, are both completely fictitious. What is odd is how they combined to create a world-wide myth, and how that myth is largely the result of those very psychological and political delusions which the builders of the real bridges had been forced to put aside.

The Real Bridges

The origin of the myth can be traced back to two historical realities.

Early in 1942, Singapore, the Dutch East Indies, and the Philippines surrendered; and Japan was suddenly left with the task of looking after over two hundred thousand prisoners of war. The normal procedure is to separate the officers from the enlisted men and put them into different camps; but the Japanese hadn't got the staff to spare and left the job of organizing the prison-camps to the prisoners themselves; which in effect meant the usual chain of command. This was one essential basis for Boulle's story: prisoners of war, like other prisoners, don't normally command anyone; and so they don't have anything to negotiate with.

The other main reality behind the myth is the building of that particular bridge. Once their armies started driving towards India, the Japanese realized they needed a railway from Bangkok to Rangoon. In the summer of 1942 many trainloads of prisoners from Singapore were sent up to Thailand and started to hack a two-hundred-mile trace through the jungle along a river called the

Khwae Noi. In Thai, *Khwae* just means "stream;" *Noi* means "small." The "small stream" rises near the Burma border, at the Three Pagodas Pass; and it joins the main tributary of the Me Nam, called the Khwae Yai, or "Big Stream," at the old city of Karnburi, some eighty miles west of Bangkok. It was there that the Japanese faced the big task of getting the railway across the river. So, early in the autumn of 1942, a large construction camp was set up at a place called Tha Makham, about three miles west of Karn-buri.

Like the hundreds of other Japanese prison camps, Tha Makham had a very small and incompetent staff. To the Japanese the idea of being taken prisoner of war is—or was then—deeply shameful; even looking after prisoners shared some of this humiliation. Conse-quently, most of the Japanese staff were men who for one reason or another were thought unfit for combat duty; too old, perhaps, in disgrace, or just drunks. What was special about Tha Makham and the other camps on the Kwai was that they were also partly con-trolled by Japanese military engineers who were building the rail-way. These engineers usually despised the Japanese troops in charge of running the camps almost as much as they despised the prison-ers.

The continual friction between the Japanese prison staff and the engineers directly affected our ordinary lives as prisoners. Daily rou-tine in the camps in November 1942, when work on the Kwai bridge began, normally went like this: up at dawn; tea and rice for breakfast; and then on parade for the day's work. We might wait anything from ten minutes to half an hour for the Korean guard to count the whole parade and split it up into work groups. Then we marched to a small bamboo shed where the picks, shovels and so on were kept. Under any circumstances it would take a long time for one guard to issue tools for thousands of men out of one small shed; the delay was made worse by the fact that the tools usually belonged to the engineers, so two organizations were involved merely in issuing and checking picks and shovels. That might take another half hour, and then we would be reassembled and counted all over again before finally marching off to work.

When we had finally got out on the line, and found the right work site, the Japanese engineer in charge might be there to explain the day's task; but more probably not. He had a very long section of embankment or bridge to look after and perhaps thirty working parties in widely separate places to supervise. He had usually given some previous instructions to the particular guard at each site; but these orders might not be clear, or, even worse, they might be clear to us, but not to the guard.

There were many organizational problems. For instance, in the early days of the railway the total amount of work each man was supposed to do—moving a cubic meter of earth or driving in so many piles—was quite reasonable under normal circumstances. But the task often fell very unequally: some groups might have to carry their earth much further than others, or drive their teak piles into much rockier ground. So, as the day wore on, someone in a group with a very difficult, or impossible, assignment would get beaten up: all the guard thought about was that he'd probably be beaten up himself if the work on the section wasn't finished: so he lashed out.

Meanwhile, many other prisoners would already have finished their task, and would be sitting around waiting, or—even worse—pretending to work. The rule was that the whole day's task had to be finished, and often inspected by the Japanese engineer, before any single work party could leave the construction site. So some more prisoners would be beaten up for lying down in the shade when they were supposed to look as though there were still work to do in the sun.

At the end of the day's work an individual prisoner might well have been on his feet under the tropical sun from 7 in the morning until 7 or 8 even 9 at night, even though he'd only done three or four hours' work. He would come back late for the evening meal; there would be no lights in the huts; and as most of the guards went off duty at 6, he probably wouldn't be allowed to go down to the river to bathe, or wash his clothes.

So our lives were poisoned, not by calculated Japanese brutality, but merely by a special form of the boredom, waste of time, and demoralization which are typical of modern industrial society. Our most pressing daily problems were really the familiar trade-union issues of long portal-to-portal hours of work, and the various tensions arising from failures of communication between the technical specialists, the personnel managers, and the on-site foremen—in our case the Japanese engineers, the higher prisoner administration, and the guards.

The people best able to see the situation as a whole were probably the officer-prisoners in charge of individual working parties. (This was before officers had been forced to do manual work.) These officers, however, normally dealt only with the particular guards on their section of the line; and back at camp headquarters neither the Japanese prison staff nor the senior British officers had much direct knowledge of conditions out on the trace. But since—mainly because of a shortage of interpreters—most of the Japanese orders were handed down through Allied officers, who were in fact virtually impotent, everything tended to increase the confusion and mistrust in our own ranks.

At first the difficulties in the Bridge Camp of Tha Makham were much like those in all the others. But soon they began to change, mainly because of the personality of its senior British officer.

Colonel Philip Toosey was tall, rather young, and with one of those special English faces like a genial but sceptical bulldog. Unlike Boulle's Colonel Nicholson, he was not a career officer but a territorial.

Toosey's previous career had been managerial. Now a cotton merchant and banker, he had earlier run a factory, where he had experienced the decline of the Lancashire cotton industry, strikes, unemployment, the Depression; he'd even gone bankrupt himself. This past training helped him to see that the problem confronting him wasn't a standard military problem at all: it had an engineering side, a labor-organization side, and above all, a very complicated morale side affecting both the prisoners and their captors.

Escaping or refusing to work on a strategic bridge were both out of the question. Trying either could only mean some men killed, and the rest punished. We had already learned that in a showdown the Japanese would always win; they had the power, and no scruples about using it. But Toosey had the imagination to see that there was a shade more room for manoeuvre than anybody else had suspected—as long as the manoeuvres were of exactly the right kind. He was a brave man, but he never forced the issue so as to make the Japanese lose face; instead he first awed them with an impressive display of military swagger; and then proceeded to charm them with his apparently immovable assumption that no serious difficulty could arise between honorable soldiers whose only thought was to do the right thing.

The right thing from our point of view, obviously, was to do everything possible to increase food and medical supplies, improve working conditions, and allocate the work more reasonably. Gradually, Toosey persuaded the Japanese that things like issuing tools or allocating the day's tasks to each working party more evenly would be better handled if we did it ourselves. He also persuaded the Japanese that output would be much improved if the duties of the guards were limited entirely to preventing the prisoners from escaping. We would be responsible for our own organization and discipline. The officers in charge of working parties would supervise the construction work; while back at camp headquarters, if the Japanese engineers would assign the next day's work to Colonel Toosey, he and his staff would see how best to carry it out.

The new organization completely transformed our conditions of life. There was much less waste of time; daily tasks were often finished early in the afternoon; weeks passed without any prisoner being beaten; and the camp became almost happy.

Looked at from outside, Toosey's remarkable success obviously involved an increase in the degree of our collaboration with the enemy. But anybody on the spot knew that the real issue was not between building or not building the bridge; it was merely how many prisoners would die, be beaten up, or break down, in the process. There was only one way to persuade the Japanese to improve rations, provide medical supplies, allow regular holidays, or reduce the brutality of the guards: to convince them that the work got done better our way.

Toosey's drive and panache soon won him the confidence of the Japanese at the camp: they got about the same amount of work out of us, and their working day was much shorter too. At the same time Toosey was never accused by his fellow prisoners—as Boulle's Colonel Nicholson certainly would have been—of being "Jap happy." Some regarded him as a bit too regimental for their taste; but, unanswerably, he delivered the goods. Eventually, in all the dozens of camps up and down the River Kwai, Toosey became a legend: he was the man who could "handle the Nips." His general strategy of taking over as much responsibility as possible (often much more than the Japanese knew), was gradually put into practice by the most successful British, American, Australian and Dutch commanders in the other camps. Even more convincingly, in 1945, when the Japanese saw defeat ahead, and finally concentrated all their officer prisoners in one camp, the vast majority of the three thousand or so allied officers collected there agitated until various senior commanding officers were successively removed and Colonel Toosey was put in charge. He remained in command until the end of the war in August 1945, when, to general consternation, all kinds of ancient military characters precipitately emerged from the wood work to reclaim the privileges of seniority.

The Myth Begins

But Toosey, like all the other heroes—and non-heroes—of our prisoner-of-war days, would normally have been forgotten when peace finally broke out. That he left any mark on the larger world is only because a Free-French officer, Pierre Boulle, who had never known him, had never been near the railway, and was never a prisoner of the Japanese, wrote a novel called *Le Pont de la Rivière Kwai*.

The book was not in any sense intended as history. Though he took the river's real name, Boulle placed his bridge near the Burmese frontier, two hundred miles from the only actual bridge *across* the Kwai, the one at Tha Makham. And, as Boulle recounted in his fascinating but—on this topic—not very explicit autobiographical memoir, *The Sources of the River Kwai* (1966), Colonel Nicholson was based, not on any prisoner of war but on two French colonels he had known in Indo-China. Having been Boulle's comrades in arms until the collapse of France in 1941, they then sided with Vichy, and eventually punished Boulle's activities on behalf of the Allies as treason, quite blind to the notion that it was they, and not Boulle, who had changed sides.

In his novel Boulle made Nicholson's "collaboration" much more extreme: he built a better bridge than the one the Japanese had started, and in a better place. Boulle may have got the idea from the fact that the Japanese actually built two bridges over the Kwai at Tha Makham: a temporary wooden structure, which no longer survives; and another begun at the same time and finished in May, 1943, which was a permanent iron-trestle bridge on concrete piers, and still stands. Both bridges showed up clearly on Allied aerial photographs; and Boulle may have seen these photographs when he was a Free-French Intelligence officer in Calcutta during the last year of the war.

Boulle's main aim in the novel was presumably to dramatize the ironic contradictions which he had personally experienced in Indo-China. First, Nicholson embodied the paradox of how the military —like any other institutional—mind will tend to generate its own objectives, objectives which are often quite different from, and may even be contrary to, the original purposes of the institution. Secondly, there was the political paradox—the total reversals of attitude which continually occur, almost unnoticed, in our strange world of changing ideological alliances. To drive this point home Boulle also invented the Allied commandos who were sent to blow up the bridge with exactly the same patient technological expertness as had been used by their former comrades in arms who had built it.

The book's interest for the reader comes mainly from the similar but opposite efforts of the commandos and the prisoners. Like Nicholson we forget about aims because the means are absorbing; we watch how well the two jobs are being done, and it's only at the end that we wake up and realize that all this marvellous technological expertness harnessed to admirable collective effort has been leading to nothing except death; Nicholson sabotages the saboteurs, and then dies under the fire of Warden's mortar. So, finally, we see that the novel is not really about the Kwai, but about how the vast scale and complication of the operations which are rendered possible, and are even in a sense required, by modern technology tend finally to destroy human meanings and purposes. The West is the master of its means, but not of its ends.

This basic idea was lost, of course, in the movie; but there were many other elements in Boulle's narrative which gave it a more universal appeal.

First, there was the character of Nicholson, which was very little changed in the movie: an amiable fellow in his way, but egocentric; admirable, but ridiculous; intelligent, but basically infantile. Here we come back to a very ancient French myth about the English character, a stereotype which was already fully established in a book written about an English colonel by a French liaison officer after the first world war—in André Maurois' *The Silences of Colonel Bramble*. The infantile and egocentric side of Nicholson's character is essential to the plot; the book is after all about a monomaniac who falls in love with a boy's hobby: to build a bridge, but not with an Erector set, and not for toy trains.

The audience, of course, gets caught up in the hobby too; perhaps because it fulfills the greatest human need in the modern world: being able to love one's work. Along the Kwai there had been a daily conflict between the instinct of workmanship and disgust with what one was being forced to do: people would spend hours trying to get a perfect alignment of piles, and then try to hide termites or rotten wood in an important joint. These sabotage games weren't really very significant; but they expressed a collective need to pretend we were still fighting the enemy, and to resist any tendency to see things the Japanese way. We were always on the lookout for people becoming what we called "Jap-happy"; and if anyone had started talking about "my bridge," like Nicholson, he'd have been replaced at once.

Neither the novel nor the film even hint at these conflicting impulses; and so the question arises, "How can Boulle's shrewd and experienced mind ever have imagined that Nicholson could plausibly get away with his love affair for a Japanese bridge?"

There are at least three possible reasons. First, Boulle himself was born in Avignon, site of the world's most famous ruined bridge. Secondly, he was trained as an engineer and presumably shared the mystique of his profession. These were two positive motives for loving bridges; and there was also the general intellectual and political context of the post-war world. Boulle's first collection of short stories, *Tales of the Absurd*, expressed not only a sense that history had arrived at a meaningless dead-end, but the whole Existential perspective on the human condition in general; all political causes and individual purposes were equally fictitious and ridiculous. Boulle certainly intended *The Bridge on the River Kwai* to have the same implication; as we can see from his epigraph, taken from Conrad's *Victory*: "No, it was not funny; it was, rather, pathetic; he was so representative of all the past victims of the Great Joke. But it is by folly alone that the world moves, and so it is a respectable thing on the whole. And besides, he was what one would call a good man."

The Movie

Boulle's book was published in 1952 and sold about 6,000 copies annually in France until 1958. That year sales leaped to 122,000—

the movie had come out. Later, the film's success caused the book to be translated into more than twenty languages, and to sell millions of copies; it also, of course, created the myth.

Hollywood has been a great creator of myths, but they have usually been personal—myths of individual actors, such as Charlie Chaplin or Humphrey Bogart, or of character-types, such as the cowboy or the private eye. The Hungarian producer, Sam Spiegel, and the English director, David Lean, turned a little river in Thailand that is not marked in most atlases into a household word.

So great a success obviously presupposes a very complete adaptation to the tastes of the international cinema public: and this adaptive process can be seen in the differences between the book and the movie, which is even further from what really happened on the railway. Of course, one can't fairly blame the movie for not showing the real life of the prisoner-of-war camps along the Kwai, if only because that life was boring even to those who lived it. On the other hand, using the name of an actual river suggested an element of authenticity; and the movie's version of events at the bridge certainly seemed to the survivors a gross insult on their intelligence and on that of their commanders. When news of the film's being made came out, various ex-prisoner-of-war associations, led, among other people, by Colonel Toosey, protested against the movie's distortion of what had actually happened; since the name of the river was fairly well known, people were bound to think there was an element of truth in the film. But history had given Sam Spiegel a lot of free publicity, and he refused even to change the film's title. This was vital, not only for the aura of historical truth at the box-office, but for the growth of the myth; since, in the curious limbo of mythic reality, collective fantasies need to be anchored on some real name of a place or a person.

The movie's air of pseudo-reality was also inevitably enforced by its medium. No one reading Boulle could have failed to notice from his style alone that the book aimed at ironic fantasy, rather than detailed historical realism; but the camera can't help giving an air of total visual authenticity; and the effect of this technical authenticity tends to spread beyond the visual image to the substance of what is portrayed. Every moviegoer knows in some way that—whenever he can check against his own experience—life isn't really like that; but he forgets it most of the time, especially when the substance of what he sees conforms to his own psychological or political point of view.

Politically, the movie gave no inkling of the unpleasant facts about the terrible poverty and disease along the real river Kwai. Instead, the audience must have taken away some vague impression that the poor jungle villagers of South-East Asia all have perfect complexions, and fly elaborately lovely kites. They don't. Equally unrealistically, the movie suggested that beautiful Thai girls don't have any boyfriends until some handsome white man comes along. Much more dangerously, the movie incidentally promoted the political delusion—less common now than in 1958—that the people of these poor villages are merely marking time until they are given an opportunity to sacrifice their lives on behalf of the ideology of the Western powers. All these are examples of the colonialist attitudes which were also present in the central idea of the novel: although the Japanese had beaten the Allies in a campaign that, among other things, showed a remarkable command of very difficult engineering and transport problems, Boulle presented them as comically inferior to their captives as bridge builders. Both the novel and the movie, in fact, contained as a primary assumption the myth of white superiority whose results we have seen most recently in that same Vietnam that Boulle had known.

In the movie the bridge itself, of course, also had to be transformed into a symbol of Western engineering mastery. The form and color of those two giant cantilevers had a poised serenity which almost justified Nicholson's infatuation; but it was totally beyond the technical means and the military needs of the actual bridges over the Kwai; and its great beauty soon made one forget the sordid realities of the war and the prison camp. What actually happened was that the movie-makers went to Thailand, took one look at the Kwai, and saw it wouldn't do. The area wasn't particularly interesting—too flat, and not at all wild; there was already a bridge over the river —the real one; and in any case there wasn't any accommodation in the little provincial town of Karnburi to match the splendors of the Mount Lavinia Hotel in Ceylon, where most of the movie was eventually shot.

All this is a normal, perhaps inevitable, part of making movies; and one's only legitimate objection is that ultimately the pseudo-realism of Hollywood has the accidental effect of making millions of people think they are seeing what something is really like when actually they are not.

The biggest departure of the movie both from history and from the novel, was the blowing up of the bridge, which distorted reality in a rather similar direction. The movie credits read "Screenplay by Pierre Boulle, Based on His Novel." Actually, though Boulle got an Oscar for the screenplay, he took only a "modest" part in the preliminary discussions of the screenplay with Spiegel and Lean; and the real writer—who couldn't then be named—was Carl Foreman, who had been blacklisted by Hollywood during the McCarthy era. Pierre Boulle eventually approved their final version; but only after he'd objected to many of their changes, and especially to the one which contradicted his whole purpose: that in the movie the bridge was blown up. He was told that the audience would have watched the screen "for more than two hours . . . in the hope and expectation" of just that big bang; if it didn't happen "they would feel frustrated"; and anyway it was quite impossible to pass up "such a sensational bit of action." So, on March 12, 1957, a beautiful bridge that had cost a quarter of a million dollars to build was blown up with a real train crossing it.

Building a bridge just to blow it up again so that the movie public won't feel frustrated was an unbelievably apt illustration of Boulle's point about how contemporary society employs its awesome technological means in the pursuit of largely derisory ends.

Boulle's readers had been made to think about that; not so the moviegoers. Their consciences were kept quiet by a well-intentioned anti-war message—the killing of the terrified young Japanese soldier, for example—while they were having a rip-roaring time. But, as we all know, you can't have it both ways. You can't turn an exotic adventure-comedy into a true film about war just by dunking it in blood. The film only seemed to take up real problems; at the end a big explosion showed that there was no point in thinking things over—when things will work out nicely anyway, why bother?

In the movie of the *Bridge on the River Kwai*, then, historical and political and psychological reality became infinitely plastic to the desires of the audience. All over the world audiences gratefully responded; and in the end they even caused the myth to be reincarnated where it had begun.

Reincarnation on the Kwai

The decisive phase of a myth is when the story wins a special status for itself; when people begin to think of it, not exactly as history, but as something which, in some vague way, really happened; and then, later, the fiction eventually imposes itself on the world as literally true. The earliest signs of this are normally the erection of shrines, and the beginning of pilgrimages; but the process of reincarnation is only complete when whatever is left of the truth which conflicts with the myth's symbolic meaning is forgotten or transformed. All this has begun to happen to the myth of the Kwai.

After the war ended, in August 1945, and the last train had evacuated the sad remnants of the Japanese army in Burma, silence at last descended on the railway. Robbers furtively stole the telegraph wire; termites ate away the wooden sleepers of the line and the timbers of the bridges; the monsoon rains washed away parts of the embankment; and sensing that all was normal again, the wild elephants (which few prisoners had ever seen) once again emerged from the jungle, and, finding the railway trace a convenient path, leaned against whatever telegraph poles inconvenienced their passage. By the time that, in 1946, the Thai government bought the

Kwai railway from the Japanese for about $4,000,000, its track was on the way to being derelict.

Eventually it was decided to keep the railway going only as far up as a place called Nam Tok, some hundred miles above the bridge over the Kwai. Nam Tok was probably chosen as terminus because there are beautiful waterfalls nearby, waterfalls that are very famous in Thai history and legend. In 1961 the whole area was scheduled as a National Park; and now three trains a day carry villagers and tourists up to see the sights.

When I visited Nam Tok in 1966 I found that, just at the end of the embankment, the local villagers had set up a little shrine. On the altar table, in front of the little gilded image of the local tute- lary deity, or *Chao Tee*, there were the usual propitiatory offerings, flowers, incense-sticks, fruit, sweets, candles, paper garlands; but in the place of honor were two rusty old iron spikes—the kind we had used to fasten the rails to the wooden ties.

There are also other and much vaster shrines near the Tha Makham bridge: an Allied cemetery for 6,982 Australian, British and Dutch prisoners of war; a Roman Catholic chapel just opposite; a Chinese burial ground for a few of the Asiatic forced-laborers of whom over a hundred thousand died along the Kwai; and a Japa- nese Memorial to all the casualties of the railway, including their own. All these shrines are much visited, as the fresh flowers and incense sticks testify: the Japanese Ambassador regularly lays a wreath at the Japanese Memorial; and there is an annual commem- oration service in the Allied cemetery.

There are also other kinds of pilgrim. In Bangkok, "Sincere Travel Service," for instance, advertises

Tour No. 11 Daily: 7:30 a.m. Whole day soft drinks and lunch pro- vided. The Bridge over River Kwai and the notorious 'Death Railway' of World War fame is at Karnburi. The tourists will definitely have the joy of their life when cruising along the *real River Kwai* on the way to pay a visit to the Chungkai War Memorial Cemetery, then follows a delicious lunch by the Bridge Over River Kwai and see the real train rolling across it. All inclusive rate: US $20.—per person minimum 2 per- sons.

The world-wide diffusion of Boulle's novel through the cinema, then, has left its mark on the Kwai. Outside the Karnburi cemetery there stands today a road sign which reads: "Bridge over the River Kwai 2.590 kilometers." It points to a real bridge; but it is only worth pointing to because of the bridge the whole world saw in the movie.

In a recent pictorial guide to Thailand there is an even more striking example of how the power of the myth is beginning to transform reality. The book gives a fine photograph of what is actually the Wang Pho viaduct along a gorge some fifty miles further up the line; but the caption reads "Bridge on the River Kwai." Some obscure need, disappointed by the failure of the real bridge *over* the river Kwai to live up to the beauty of the one in the movie, has relocated the home of the myth, and selected the most spectacular view along the railway as a more appropriate setting.

The Myth and the Reality

The myth, then, is established. What does it mean?

When *The Bridge on the River Kwai* was first televised it drew the largest TV audience ever recorded. Millions of people must have responded to it because—among other things—it expressed the same delusions as are responsible for much unreal political thinking. There was, as I've already said, the colonial myth—the odd notion that the ordinary people of South-East Asia instinctively love the white strangers who have come to their lands, and want to sacrifice themselves on their behalf. There was also the implication of the blowing-up of the bridge—however muddled we may be about our political aims, advanced high-explosive technology will always come out on top in the end. The Big Bang theory of war, of course, fitted in very nicely with the consoling illusion of a world of Friendly (and militarily backward) Natives.

The theory, and the illusion, have one fatal weakness: they clash with what Sartre calls *"la force des choses."*[1] What happened to the real bridge illustrates this very neatly.

In the summer of 1944 the new American long-range bombers, the B 29's, started flying over the Kwai, and bombing the bridges. To anyone who knows any military history, what happened was absolutely predictable. Quite a lot of people, mainly prisoners, were killed; but eventually the bombers got some direct hits, and two spans of the steel bridge fell into the river. While it was being repaired, the low wooden bridge was put back into use; and when that, too, was damaged, it was easily restored by the labor of the prisoners in the nearby camps. Japanese military supplies weren't delayed for a single day. If you can build a bridge, you can repair it; in the long run, bombing military targets is only significant if the target can later be captured and held.

The Allied command in Ceylon knew this very well. They bombed the Kwai railway then because their armies were advancing in Burma and preparing to attack Thailand: but this vital context is absent from the novel and the film. Actually there were also Allied commandos in the bridge area at the time: not to blow up the bridge, though, but to link up with the Thai resistance, and help liberate prison camps once the invasion started. Boulle probably

---

1. The force of things as they are.

knew this, since he called his commandos Force 316, whereas the real ones were Force 136. Still, Boulle's novel certainly undercuts the Big Bang theory, and one imagines that he found in its blind destructive credulity a folly that wasn't exclusively military. Since 1866, and Nobel's invention of dynamite, all kinds of individuals and social groups have attributed magical powers to dynamite; they've refused to see that the best you can expect from explosives is an explosion.

The Big Bang theory of war is rather like the colonial myth, and even the schoolboy dream of defying the adult world; all three are essentially expressions of what Freud called the childish delusion of the omnipotence of thought. The myth of the Kwai deeply reflects this delusion, and shapes it according to the particular values of contemporary culture.

Hollywood, the advertising industry, Existentialism, even the current counter-culture are alike in their acceptance or their exploitation of the delusion of the omnipotence of thought. From this come many of their other similarities: that they are ego-centered, romantic, anti-historical; that they all show a belief in rapid and absolute solutions of human problems. They are all, in the last analysis, institutional patterns based on the posture of anti-institutionalism.

These basic assumptions of the myth are perhaps most obvious in the kernel of the story, which the movie made much more recognizable as a universal fantasy, the schoolboy's perennial dream of defying the adult world. Young Nicholson cheeks the mean old headmaster, called Saito: he gets a terrible beating, but the other students kick up such a row about it that Saito just has to give in. Confrontation tactics win out; and Nicholson is carried back in triumph across the playground. In the end, of course, he becomes the best student-body president Kwai High ever had.

I don't know if anything like this—total rebellion combined with total acceptance—has ever occurred in any educational institution; but I am forced to report that nothing like it ever happened in the prison-camps along the Kwai. There, all our circumstances were hostile to individual fantasies; surviving meant accepting the intractable realities which surrounded us, and making sure that our fellow prisoners accepted them too.

No one would even guess from the novel or the film that there were any wholly intractable realities on the Kwai. Boulle proposes a simple syllogism: war is madness; war is fought by soldiers; therefore, soldiers are mad. It's a flattering notion, no doubt, to non-soldiers, but it happens not to be true; and it's really much too easy a way out to delude ourselves with the belief that wars and injustices are caused only by lunatics, by people who don't see things as we see them.

Neither the novel nor the film admits that certain rational distinctions remain important even under the most difficult or confusing circumstances. They seem instead to derive a peculiar satisfaction from asserting that in a world of madness the weakness of our collective life can find its salvation only in the strength of madmen. There is no need to insist on the authoritarian nature of this idea, but it does seem necessary to enquire why these last decades have created a myth which totally subverts the stubbornness of facts and of the human will to resist unreason.

The basic reason is presumably the widespread belief that institutions are at the same time immoral, ridiculous, and unreal, whereas individuals exist in a world whose circumstances are essentially tractable. A prisoner-of-war camp has at least one thing in common with our modern world in general: both offer a very limited range of practical choices. No wonder the public acclaimed a film where, under the most limiting circumstances imaginable, one solitary individual managed to do just what he planned to do. Of course his triumph depended on making everything else subservient to his fantasy; and if our circumstances on the Kwai had been equally pliable, there would have been no reason whatever for Toosey or anybody else to act as they did.

It's probably true that at the beginning of our captivity many of us thought that at last the moment had arrived for revolt, if not against the Japanese, at least against our own military discipline and anything else that interfered with our individual liberty. But then circumstances forced us to see that this would be suicidal. We were terribly short of food, clothes, and medicine; theft soon became a real threat to everyone; and so we had to organize our own police. At first it seemed too ridiculous, but not for long. When cholera broke out, for instance, whole camps of Asiatic laborers were wiped out, whereas in our own camps nearby, with an effective organization to make sure everyone used the latrines and ate or drank only what had been boiled, we often had no deaths, even though we had no vaccine.

In the myth, then, the actual circumstances of our experience on the Kwai were overwhelmed by the deep blindness of our culture both to the stubbornness of reality and to the continuities of history. It was surely this blindness which encouraged the public, in accepting the plausibility of Nicholson's triumph, to assert its belief in the combined wickedness, folly, and unreality of institutions—notably of those which were in conflict on the Kwai: the Japanese and their prisoners.

It isn't only on the walls of the Sorbonne that we can see the slogan "It is forbidden to forbid." It is written on all individuals at birth, in the form "It is forbidden to forbid me"; and this text has been adopted fo their great profit by the movie and advertising industries: by Hollywood, in the version "You don't get rich by saying no to dreams," and by Madison Avenue in the version "Tell 'em they're suckers if they don't have everything they want."

The movie, incidentally, added one apt illustration of this slogan which had no basis whatever in Boulle or reality. No one wants to be a prisoner; you don't have to be; and so William Holden escapes, easily. On the Kwai, hundreds tried; most of them were killed; no one succeeded.

Among today's pilgrims to the present cemeteries on the Kwai, an increasing number come from the American forces in Thailand and Vietnam. When I leafed through the Visitors' Book, one entry caught my eye. A private from Apple Creek, Wisconsin, stationed at Da Nang, had been moved to write a protest that made all the other banal pieties look pale: "PEOPLE are STUPID."

Stupid, among other things, because they are mainly led by what they want to believe, not by what they know. It's easier to go along with the implication of the movie, and believe that a big bang—anywhere—will somehow end the world's confusion and our own fatigue. It would undoubtedly end it, but only in larger cemeteries for the victims of the last Great Joke.

Vietnam has been a painful lesson in the kinds of mythical thinking which *The Bridge on the River Kwai* both reflected and reinforced; we seem now to be slowly recovering from some of the political forms of the omnipotence-of-thought fantasy. Recently, I observed that the main audience reaction to the movie was ironical laughter.

If we can accept the notion that in all kinds of spheres some individual has to be responsible for the organization and continuity of human affairs, we should perhaps look again at the man without whom the myth would not have come into being. Along the Kwai, Colonel Toosey was almost universally recognized for what he was —a hero of the only kind we could afford then, and there. For he was led, not by what he wanted to believe, but by what he knew: he knew that the world would not do his bidding; that he could not beat the Japanese: that on the Kwai—even more obviously than at home—we were for the most part helpless prisoners of coercive circumstance. But he also knew that if things were as intractable as they looked, the outlook for the years ahead was hopeless: much death, and total demoralization, for the community he found himself in. The only thing worth working for was the possibility that tenacity and imagination could find a way by which the chances of decent survival could be increased. It was, no doubt, a very modest objective for so much work and restraint—two of Conrad's moral imperatives that Boulle didn't quote, incidentally; but in our circumstances then on the Kwai, the objective was quite enough to be getting on with; as it is here, now.

NORMAN O. BROWN

Neurosis and History

The doctrine that all men are mad appears to conflict with a historical perspective on the nature and destiny of man: it appears to swallow all cultural variety, all historical change, into a darkness in which all cats are gray. But this objection neglects the richness and complexity of the Freudian theory of neurosis.

In the first place there are several distinct kinds of neurosis, each with a different set of symptoms, a different structure in the relations between the repressed, the ego, and reality. We are therefore in a position to return to the varieties and complexities of individual cultures if we entertain, as Freud does in *Civilization and Its Discontents*, the hypothesis that the varieties of culture can be correlated with the varieties of neurosis: "If the evolution of civilization has such a far-reaching similarity with the development of an individual, and if the same methods are employed in both, would not the diagnosis be justified that many systems of civilization—or epochs of it—possibly even the whole of humanity—have become 'neurotic' under the pressure of civilizing trends? To analytic dissection of these neuroses therapeutic recommendations might follow which could claim a great practical interest."

And furthermore, it is a Freudian theorem that each individual neurosis is not static but dynamic. It is a historical process with its own internal logic. Because of the basically unsatisfactory nature of the neurotic compromise, tension between the repressed and repressing factors persists and produces a constant series of new symptom-formations. And the series of symptom-formations is not a shapeless series of mere changes; it exhibits a regressive pattern, which Freud calls the slow return of the repressed. It is a law of neurotic diseases, he says, that these obsessive acts increasingly come closer to the original impulse and to the original forbidden act itself. The doctrine of the universal neurosis of mankind, if we take it seriously, therefore compels us to entertain the hypothesis that the pattern of history exhibits a dialectic not hitherto recognized by historians, the dialectic of neurosis.

A reinterpretation of human history is not an appendage to psychoanalysis but an integral part of it. The empirical fact which compelled Freud to comprehend the whole of human history in the area of psychoanalysis is the appearance in dreams and in neurotic symptoms of themes substantially identical with major themes—both ritualistic and mythical—in the religious history of mankind. The link between the theory of neurosis and the theory of history is the theory of religion, as is made perfectly clear in *Totem and Taboo* and *Moses and Monotheism*.

And the link affects both ends linked. Freud not only maintains that human history can be understood only as a neurosis but also that the neuroses of individuals can be understood only in the context of human history as a whole. From the time when he wrote *Totem and Taboo* (1913), Freud says in *Moses and Monotheism* (1937), "I have never doubted that religious phenomena are to be understood only on the model of the neurotic symptoms of the individual." According to the analogy elaborated in *Moses and Monetheism*, "In the history of the species something happened similar to the events in the life of the individual. That is to say, mankind as a whole passed through conflicts of a sexual-aggressive nature, which left permanent traces, but which were for the most part warded off and forgotten; later, after a long period of latency, they came to life again and created phenomena similar in structure and tendency to neurotic symptoms."

This analogy supplies Freud with his notion of the "archaic heritage"; mankind is a prisoner of the past in the same sense as "our hysterical patients are suffering from reminiscences" and neurotics "cannot escape from the past." Thus the bondage of all cultures to their cultural heritage is a neurotic constriction. And conversely, Freud came to recognize that the core of the neuroses of individuals lay in the same "archaic heritage," "memory-traces of the experiences of former generations," which "can only be understood phylogenetically." The repressed unconscious which produces neurosis is not an individual unconscious but a collective one. Freud abstains from adopting Jung's term but says, "The content of the unconscious is collective anyhow." Ontogeny recapitulates phylogeny (each individual recapitulates the history of the race): in the few years of childhood "we have to cover the enormous distance of development from primitive man of the Stone Age to civilized man of today." From this it follows that the theory of neurosis must embrace a theory of history; and conversely a theory of history must embrace a theory of neurosis.

Psychoanalysis must view religion both as neurosis and as that attempt to become conscious and to cure, inside the neurosis itself, on which Freud came at the end of his life to pin his hopes for therapy. Psychoanalysis is vulgarly interpreted as dismissing religion as an erroneous system of wishful thinking. In *The Future of an Illusion*, Freud does speak of religion as a "substitute-gratification"—the Freudian analogue to the Marxian formula, "opiate of the people." But according to the whole doctrine of repression, "substitute-gratifications"—a term which applies not only to poetry and religion but also to dreams and neurotic symptoms—contain truth: they are expressions, distorted by repression, of the immortal desires of the human heart.

The proper psychoanalytical perspective on religion is that taken in *Moses and Monotheism*, where Freud set out to find the fragment of historic and psychological truth in Judaism and Christianity. Even Marx—in the same passage in which the notorious formula "opiate of the people" occurs—speaks of religion as "the sigh of the oppressed creature, the heart of a heartless world." But Marx, lacking the concept of repression and the unconscious—that is to say, not being prepared to recognize the mystery of the human heart—could not pursue the line of thought implied in his own epigram. Psychoanalysis is equipped to study the mystery of the human heart, and must recognize religion to be the heart of the mystery. But psychoanalysis can go beyond religion only if it sees itself as completing what religion tries to do, namely, make the unconscious conscious; then psychoanalysis would be the science of original sin. Psychoanalysis is in a position to define the error in religion only after it has recognized the truth.

It is not to be denied that Freud's earlier writings, especially *Totem and Taboo*, contain, besides much that looks forward to *Moses and Monotheism*, another line of thought on the relation between psychoanalysis and history. This other line of thought works out the notion that ontogeny recapitulates phylogeny in a different way. The psychoanalytical model for understanding history is not neurosis but the process of growing up; or rather, maturity is envisaged not as a return of the repressed infantile neurosis but as the overcoming of it. In effect, Freud correlates his own psychosexual stages of the individual with the stages of the history postulated by nineteenth-century evolutionary-minded thinkers of the type of Comte and Frazer. Thus in *Totem and Taboo* he says that the animistic phase corresponds to narcissism, in both time and substance; the religious phase corresponds to the stage of object-finding in which dependence on the parents is paramount; while the scientific phase corresponds to maturity, in which the individual, who by now has renounced the pleasure-principle and has accepted reality, seeks his object in the outer world.

This line of thought is a residue of eighteenth-century optimism and rationalism in Freud; in it history is not a process of becoming sicker but a process of becoming wiser. The early Freud—if we forget the later Freud—thus justifies the quite naïve and traditionalist view of history held by most psychoanalysts. But this line of thought is not simply inadequate as history; it is inadequate as psychoanalysis. It belongs with Freud's early system of psychoanalysis, with his early theory of the instincts, and with his early (and traditionalist) theory of the human ego.

It is true that the implementation of the approach to history adumbrated in Freud's later writings involves great difficulties. Freud himself, in the passage suggesting a correlation between cultures and neurosis, put his finger on the heart of the problem when he pointed out the need to develop a concept of a "normal" or healthy culture by which to measure the neurotic cultures recorded by history. From the point of view taken in this book, the development of such a concept is the central problem confronting both psychoanalysis and history. And the lack of such a concept explains the failure of both historians and psychoanalysts (with the exception of Róheim) to pursue Freud's pioneering efforts.

But if historians have failed to follow Freud, poets have characteristically anticipated him. Is there not, for example, a still unexplored truth in the statement of the German poet Hebbel: "Is it so hard to recognize that the German nation has up till now no life history to show for itself, but only the history of a disease (*Krankheitsgeschichte*)?" And not just the German nation—which is or used to be the scapegoat carrying all the sins of the Western world. According to James Joyce, "History is a nightmare from which I am trying to awaken." The poets, and Nietzsche—Nietzsche's *Genealogy of Morals* is the first attempt to grasp world history as the history of an ever increasing neurosis. And both Nietzsche and Freud find the same dynamic in the neurosis of history, an ever increasing sense of guilt caused by repression. Nietzsche's climax—"Too long has the world been a madhouse"—compares with the dark conclusion of *Civilization and Its Discontents*: "If civilization is an inevitable course of development from the group of the family to the group of humanity as a whole, then an intensification of the sense of guilt . . . will be inextricably bound up with it, until perhaps the sense of guilt may swell to a magnitude that individuals can hardly support."

The necessity of a psychoanalytical approach to history is pressed upon the historian by one question: Why does man, alone of all animals, have a history? For man is distinguished from animals not simply by the possession and transmission from generation to generation of that suprabiological apparatus which is culture, but also, if history and changes in time are essential characteristics of human culture and therefore of man, by a desire to change his culture and so to change himself. In making history "man makes himself," to use the suggestive title of Gordon Childe's book. Then the historical process is sustained by man's desire to become other than what he is. And man's desire to become something different is essentially an unconscious desire. The actual changes in history neither result from nor correspond to the conscious desires of the human agents who bring them about. Every historian knows this, and the philosopher of history, Hegel, in his doctrine of the "cunning of Reason," made it a fundamental point in his structural analysis of history. Mankind today is still making history without having any conscious idea of what it really wants or under what conditions it would stop being unhappy; in fact what it is doing seems to be making itself more unhappy and calling that unhappiness progress.

Christian theology, or at least Augustinian theology, recognizes human restlessness and discontent, the *cor irrequietum*,[1] as the psychological source of the historical process. But Christian theology, to account for the origin of human discontent and to indicate a solution, has to take man out of this real world, out of the animal kingdom, and inculcate into him delusions of grandeur. And thus Christian theology commits its own worst sin, the sin of pride.

Freud's real critique of religion in *The Future of an Illusion* is the contention (also Spinoza's) that true humility lies in science. True humility, he says, requires that we learn from Copernicus that the human world is not the purpose or the center of the universe; that we learn from Darwin that man is a member of the animal kingdom; and that we learn from Freud that the human ego is not even master in its own house. Apart from psychoanalysis there are no secular or scientific theories as to why man is the restless and discontented animal. The discontented animal is the neurotic animal, the animal with desires given in his nature which are not satisfied by culture. From the psychoanalytical point of view, these unsatisfied and repressed but immortal desires sustain the historical process. History is shaped, beyond our conscious wills, not by the cunning of Reason but by the cunning of Desire.

The riddle of history is not in Reason but in Desire; not in labor, but in love. A confrontation with Marx will clarify Freud. It is axiomatic in Marxism to define the essence of man as labor. Freud has no quarrel with the Marxist emphasis on the importance of the "economic factor" in history: he formally praises Marxism for "its clear insight into the determining influence which is exerted by the economic conditions of man upon his intellectual, ethical, and artistic reactions." For Freud, work and economic necessity are the essence of the reality-principle: but the essence of man lies not in the reality-principle but in repressed unconscious desires. No matter how stringently economic necessities press down on him, he is not in his essence *Homo economicus* or *Homo laborans*; no matter how bitter the struggle for bread, man does not live by bread alone.

Thus Freud becomes relevant when history raises this question: What does man want over and beyond "economic welfare" and "mastery over nature"? Marx defines the essence of man as labor and traces the dialectic of labor in history till labor abolishes itself. There is then a vacuum in the Marxist utopia. Unless there is no utopia, unless history is never abolished, unless labor continues to be, like Faust, driven to ever greater achievements, some other and truer definition of the essence of man must be found. Freud suggests that beyond labor there is love. And if beyond labor at the end of history there is love, love must have always been there from the beginning of history, and it must have been the hidden force

1. The restless heart.

supplying the energy devoted to labor and to making history. From this point of view, repressed Eros is the energy of history and labor must be seen as sublimated Eros. In this way a problem not faced by Marx can be faced with the aid of Freud.

Marxism is a system of sociology; the importance of the "economic factor" is a sociological question to be settled by sociologists; Freud himself, speaking as a sociologist, can say that in imposing repression "at bottom society's motive is economic." The quarrel between psychoanalysis and "economic determinism" arises in the tacit psychological assumptions behind economic determinism, and therefore arises only when we pass from sociology to psychology, from the abstraction of "society" to the concrete human individual. The issue is not the importance of economics but its psychology. Marx himself, though always complicated, is not free from the tacit assumption, held generally by economic determinists, that the concrete human needs and drives sustaining economic activity are just what they appear to be and are fully in consciousness: "self-preservation" and "pleasure," as understood by the utilitarians, summarize the psychological theory implied by the ingenuous invocation of categories like "economic necessity" and "human needs."

But the proof that human needs are not what they seem to be lies precisely in the fact of human history. The Faustian restlessness of man in history shows that men are not satisfied by the satisfaction of their conscious desires; men are unconscious of their real desires. Thus a psychology of history must be psychoanalytical.

In so far as Marx faced this question at all, lacking the concept of repressed unconscious desires he could only come up with a psychology of history which condemns man to be eternally Faustian and precludes any possibility of happiness. Marx needs a psychological premise to explain the unceasing bent for technological progress sustaining the dialectic of labor in history. Lacking the doctrine of repression—or rather not being able to see man as a psychological riddle—Marx, as a sympathetic critic has shown, turns to biology and postulates an absolute law of human biology that the satisfaction of human needs always generates new needs. If human discontent is thus biologically given, it is incurable. Quite specifically, not only "the abolition of history" but also an "economy of abundance," as envisioned in Marx's utopian phase, are out of the question. Hence the dark clouds of pessimism in the third volume of *Capital*, where he says:

Just as the savage must wrestle with nature, in order to satisfy his wants, in order to maintain his life and to reproduce it, so the civilized man has to do it in all forms of society and under all modes of production. With his development the realm of natural necessity expands, because his wants increase; but at the same time the forces of production increase, by which these wants are satisfied.

But Marx's assumption of a biological basis for "progress" in history really amounts to a confession that he is unable to explain it psychologically.

Psychoanalysis can provide a theory of "progress," but only by viewing history as a neurosis. By defining man as the neurotic animal, psychoanalysis not merely assumes man's Faustian character but also explains why man is so. To quote Freud:

What appears . . . as an untiring impulsion toward further perfection can easily be understood as a result of the instinctual repression upon which is based all that is most precious in human civilization. The repressed instinct never ceases to strive for complete satisfaction, which would consist in the repetition of a primary experience of satisfaction. No substitutive or reactive formations and no sublimations will suffice to remove the repressed instinct's persisting tension.

By the same token, psychoanalysis offers a theoretical framework for exploring the possibility of a way out of the nightmare of endless "progress" and endless Faustian discontent, a way out of the human neurosis, a way out of history. In the case of the neurotic individual, the goal of psychoanalytical therapy is to free him from the burden of his past, from the burden of his history, the burden which compels him to go on having (and being) a case history. And the method of psychoanalytical therapy is to deepen the historical consciousness of the individual ("fill up the memory-gaps") till he awakens from his own history as from a nightmare. Psychoanalytical consciousness, as a higher stage in the general consciousness of mankind, may be likewise the fulfillment of the historical consciousness, that ever widening and deepening search for origins which has obsessed Western thought ever since the Renaissance. If historical consciousness is finally transformed into psychoanalytical consciousness, the grip of the dead hand of the past on life in the present would be loosened, and man would be ready to live instead of making history, to enjoy instead of paying back old scores and debts, and to enter that state of Being which was the goal of his Becoming.

PETER GAY

Style—From Manner to Matter

Style is a centaur, joining what nature, it would seem, has decreed must be kept apart. It is form and content, woven into the texture of every art and every craft—including history. Apart from a few mechanical tricks of rhetoric, manner is indissolubly linked to matter; style shapes, and in turn is shaped by, substance. I have written these essays[1] to anatomize this familiar yet really strange being, style the centaur; the book may be read as an extended critical commentary on Buffon's[2] famous saying that the style is the man.

Buffon's epigram has a beautiful simplicity that makes it both possibly profound and certainly suspect. It seems frivolous, almost inappropriate, to be stylish about style, for it is necessary, and difficult, to disentangle the multiplicity of meanings and the thicket of metaphors that have accrued to the word in the course of centuries. Style, we are told, is the dress of thought and its sinews, its crowning glory and its expressive voice. There appear to be almost as many uses for style as there are users. The critic and the scholar, the lyric poet and the political publicist, each employs style in his own way and for his own purposes: to appreciate elegance and depreciate clumsiness, to decipher obscure passages, to exploit verbal ambiguities, to drive home a partisan point. The historian, who does all of these things—though one wishes that he would keep his lyricism in check and discard his politics when he writes history—encounters style in these and other dimensions. He is a professional writer and a professional reader. As a writer, he is under pressure to become a stylist while remaining a scientist; he must give pleasure without compromising truth. His style may be a conventional tool, an involuntary confession, or a striking illumination. As a reader, he prizes literary excellence, absorbs facts and interpretations, and explores the words before him for truths working beneath their surface; style may be, for him, an object of gratification, a vehicle of knowledge, or an instrument of diagnosis.

Yet this profusion is an opportunity as much as a problem. As I will show, it is desirable, for the sake of clarity, to discriminate among the varied meanings of style, but it is impossible, for the sake of understanding, to keep them permanently segregated. The use of a single word for many functions need not be a symptom of linguistic poverty; it can be a sign that these functions are related to one another. That the word *style* should enter diverse combinations —style of thought, style of life, and others—without strain reinforces the impression that the several kinds of style, and style and substance, have much to do with, and to say about, one another. Style is like Ranke's[3] Venetian ambassadors: widely traveled, highly adaptable, superbly informed, and, if adroitly interrogated, splendidly indiscreet. For the historian, therefore, the evidential value of style—both in getting and in giving evidence—is enormous.

I have said that this book may be read as an extended critical commentary on Buffon's *Le style est l'homme même.* The commentary must be extended, for, though an important observation, the

---

1. This essay is the first chapter of a book on the styles of four historians: Gibbon, Ranke, Macaulay, and Burckhardt.

2. Georges Louis Leclerc Buffon (1707–88), French naturalist.

3. Leopold von Ranke (1795–1886), German historian.

epigram is so laconic that we must, as the philosophers say, unpack it. And the commentary must be critical, for Buffon at once says too much and too little. In its day, his *bon mot* was an energetic, almost unprecedented demand that style not be taken lightly as mere decoration, but seen as reaching into the very foundations of the writer's work. Yet style is not always the man, certainly not the whole man. If manner and matter are joined in a Catholic marriage, irrevocably, this does not mean that they can never be apart from each other. Much talk about style centers on the search for literary felicities, and for the traditional, if surprisingly elusive, virtue of clarity.

Moreover, it is a historical fact (which the historian may privately deplore but must professionally investigate like any other) that style has not always been profoundly anchored. There have been those—in advertising, in journalism, in politics, even in publishing —who treat it as an afterthought, as the Gothic facade irrelevantly plastered onto modern concrete walls. Middleton Murry once called this practice "the heresy of the man in the street" and thought it "the most popular of all delusions about style." He anatomized this delusion half a century ago, but the heresy had been popular long before and remains as popular as it was when he wrote in 1922. Makers of verbal artifacts for mass consumption still find it convenient to ask researchers to do research, writers to write it up, and stylists to add the fine touches. Such Balkanization, I need hardly say, fatally divides what needs to be united; the products that such procedures throw on the market are, as we all know, persuasively packaged merchandise, decorated with obsessive puns, exhausted superlatives, and unauthentic anecdotes. Style here is a by-product of commercial enterprise; it is by no means the man but the system.

This vast, vulgar subliterature is a valuable reminder to the historian that the word *style* is not only a term of praise—"that novelist has style"—but also a neutral description—"that novelist works in the Naturalist style." He must remember that the very idea of style is infected with a central ambiguity: it must give information as well as pleasure. It opens windows on both truth and beauty—a bewildering double vista. Aesthetically indifferent or aesthetically offensive procedures, as long as they have a certain consistency and characteristic form, partake of style. Second-rate poets, painters— and historians—have a style. So do gangsters perpetrating gangland killings, songwriters manufacturing popular hits, priests performing religious ceremonies in standardized ways. The study of style has diagnostic value in all these instances; to the historian they are all valid clues to the past, though not to the same historical experiences. If style gives information not about the stylist but about his culture, the historian has no reason to be disappointed. When it comes to subject matter and to evidence, the historian is—or should be—a democrat.

Buffon, of course, was not a democrat, in his view of style or of anything else. He was speaking of the literary style of the accomplished writer. And what he meant to say about the writer, I think, was this: the cultivated manner of the writer instructively expresses his personal past as well as the culture's ways of thinking, feeling, believing, and working. The symptomatic value of style is therefore far greater than that of providing insights into literary habits. Style is the pattern in the carpet—the unambiguous indication, to the informed collector, of place and time of origin. It is also the marking on the wings of the butterfly—the unmistakable signature, to the alert lepidopterist, of its species. And it is the involuntary gesture of the witness in the dock—the infallible sign, to the observant lawyer, of concealed evidence. To unriddle the style, therefore, is to unriddle the man.

This exegesis makes a beginning, but it remains too elliptical to be conclusive. Both halves of Buffon's epigram, both *style* and *man*, require further explication. The most prominent and, for these essays, most productive kind of style is style in its narrow sense, literary style: the management of sentences, the use of rhetorical devices, the rhythm of narration. Gibbon's way of pairing phrases, Ranke's resort to dramatic techniques, Macaulay's reiteration of antitheses, Burckhardt's informal diction, taken by themselves, as single instances, mean what they say on the page. They describe a battle, analyze a political artifice, chronicle a painter's career. But once characteristic and habitual—that is, recognizable elements in the historian's mode of expression, of his style—they become signposts to larger, deeper matters. Partly idiosyncratic and partly conventional, partly selected and partly imposed by unconscious, professional, or political pressures, the devices of literary style are equally instructive, not always for the conclusive answers they supply but for the fertile questions they raise about the historian's central intentions and overriding interpretations, the state of his art, the essential beliefs of his culture—and, perhaps, about his insights into his subject.

While I have taken style in its strict sense as my principal witness, my materials have compelled me to reach out to other related forms of expression, to styles in looser senses of the word. Among the most revealing of these is what I want to call the historian's emotional style, his tone of voice as it emerges in the tension or repose of his phrases, his favorite adjectives, his selection of illustrative anecdotes, his emphases and epigrams. In a tightly regulated stylistic system like neoclassicism, in which expressive means are severely circumscribed, emotional style has potent diagnostic possibilities, for while accepted canons of rhetoric, say, proscribe "low" epithets for highly placed personages, the range of permissible expressions remains large enough to give room for instructive choices. Gibbon characterizing the Emperor Augustus as "artful" only tells us that Augustus was—or, rather that Gibbon thought him—artful. But scattered liberally across the pages of *The Decline and Fall of the Roman Empire*, the word *artful* begins to trail clouds of meaning behind it and becomes an emblem for Gibbon's cynical appraisal of the Empire, a clue not merely to what he saw but what he, as an individual historian, was best equipped to see. In the freer, more loose-jointed writing of the nineteenth century, emotional style retains its capacity to yield dividends to the interpreter: Burckhardt's chilling stories about Renaissance despots point to perceptions more general than those the stories are designed to illuminate. They help to outline the contours of Burckhardt's historical vision. In our examination of a historian's emotional style, we come very close to the man indeed.

Instructive as the historian's selection of expressive techniques and unconscious coloring of narrative may be, his habit of doing research and offering proof—his *professional* style—provides additional and significant clues. It invites inferences subtler and more far-reaching than judgments of his competence or his diligence. Ranke assiduously visited all accessible archives; Macaulay preferred to spend his time poring over broadsides and printed collections of popular verses; Gibbon mastered the history of ancient Rome from modern compilations; Burckhardt studied the Renaissance from contemporary accounts. To know this is to know something about the sheer validity of each historian's conclusions, but it also delineates his attitude toward his material. Ranke's obsessive, almost religious conscientiousness, which left its distinctive signature on all his work, reflects his sense of history as a grand, dramatic, divinely guided contest, and his sense of the historian as a man of God in the world. Gibbon's occasional credulousness, which contrasts so sharply with his pronounced, often malicious skepticism, suggests, not professional laxity, but a will to believe—especially in the wickedness of priests and the lasciviousness of emperors. Like the other styles I have mentioned, professional style, too, points beyond itself.

The reality all these styles point to, the fish that the analyst hopes to catch, is, as I have suggested, nothing less than the historian's total perception of the past, the constraints within which he works and the truths he is uniquely capable of grasping. Yet this exalted region—the ultimate destination of stylistics—where matter seems to hold a complete monopoly, is invaded by manner also. I am speaking of the historian's style of thinking, a convenient and telling phrase that relates style to content in more than a mere metaphorical sense. For a historian's most fundamental and therefore least examined assumptions about the nature of the world, its ontological makeup, also have their expressive aspect which may leave its traces in his literary, emotional, or professional style. Yet styles of thought may also find other, more subterranean, channels of communication: a historian need not write, or feel, or work like another, and yet think like him and learn from him. Gibbon was deeply indebted to Tacitus' disenchantment, but Gibbon structured his sentences, chose his adjectives, and pursued his research in ways markedly different from the ways of Tacitus. Burckhardt had a pronounced affinity for Hegel's vision of cultural wholes, but it is—fortunately—impossible to mistake a passage, any passage, of the *Kultur der Renaissance in Italien* for a passage, any passage, of Hegel's lectures on history.

In general, though, intellectual affinities scatter more clues than they did in Gibbon and Burckhardt. The styles I have discussed do not normally lie side by side as strangers, without touching. It is significant that many stylistic qualities are hard to place: does Gibbon's irony or Macaulay's rhetoric form part of their literary or their emotional style? Do Burckhardt's stories serve to disclose his view of the world, his private pessimism, his wish to keep his readers interested, or all three? These questions suggest their answer: styles are a network of clues to one another, and, together, to the man—to the historian at work.

This brings me to the second half of Buffon's epigram. Man lives in several worlds at once, most notably in his private sphere, in the comparatively intimate realm of his craft, and in the wide public domain of his culture. Like the various dimensions of style, these worlds intersect and continuously impinge upon one another: the private person internalizes the standards of craft and the commands of culture; craft by and large serves culture and obediently expresses its overriding ideals. A mature literary style is a synthesis of all these elements, variously combined; it is, therefore, at once individual and social, private and public, a combination of inherited ways, borrowed elements, and unique qualities. That is why the student of style can treat this synthesis analytically and sort out the threads of which the stylistic tapestry is composed. If, as some Romantics were inclined to think, style were simply the outward garb of inner states, the spontaneous overflowing of the springs of creativity, it would yield information about a writer's psyche, nothing more. But these Romantics were wrong. To begin with, literary style—and this is the style on which I shall concentrate—can be learned. Writers are not born stylists; they fashion their style through an unceasing effort to overcome dependence and find their own voice. Normally, the apprentice writer—and here, as elsewhere, the historian acts like other writers—discovers the style appropriate to him by first following and then discarding admired models; imitation seems to be an essential phase in the process of self-discovery. Not even in the beginning, then, does writing come wholly from the heart; it comes, for the most part, straight out of other books. The higher naïveté comes later, the fruit of labor that conceals labor.

To say that style can be learned is therefore not precise enough. It is more accurate to say, rather, that style must be learned. It is only in part a gift of talent; beyond that it is an act of will and an exercise of intelligence. It is the tribute that expressiveness pays to discipline. Style is an instrument of the practical reason. Words, of course, do many things: they convey information, they disclose affection, they utter warnings; they are, often, the unedited transcription of emotions into verbal form. But style is the application of means to an end; though, as we well know, it too has its passional side and its involuntary revelations.

That is why styles have histories, even in individual writers. Gibbon is perhaps an exception: while even he found it necessary to experiment, he cast all his writings, early and late, into the same unmistakable mold. But, then, Gibbon was never young. For nearly all other writers, style has been, in addition to being an endowment, a conquest; the study of style chronicles and analyzes that conquest. "Style," wrote Gibbon, "is the image of character." Here is the first indication of the uses that stylistics may have for the historian: it gives him access to a writer's private, psychological world.

This is not the only world that the study of style serves to discover. Writing is an activity pursued within the texture of a literary tradition. Apart from a handful of innovators, most writers, even the greatest, speak in a language that others have made familiar. Even those, like the Dadaist poets, who aim at incomprehensibility find their vocabulary within the context of a society no matter how select; their incomprehensibility is their way of communicating— comprehensibly—with the others in their circle. A writer's attitude to his tradition may be compliant, ambivalent, or rebellious. He may write as he does because others have written his way before, or because others have *not* written his way before. Whatever his attitude, he cannot be indifferent to the atmosphere that his choice of profession compels him to breathe.

Just as individual styles have a history, style itself has a history. In every epoch, writers have had specified expressive modes available to them. They have always been subject to rules laying down permissible language, to conventions channeling their private preferences, to hierarchies appropriate to any theme. Until modern times —which, in this context, means the 1890s—there have been some things historians must say and others that they would have found it unthinkable to say.

The boundaries within which historians have been compelled to maneuver are of peculiar importance for the history of history. That history is the history of the emancipation of a craft from powerful, normally overpowering, masters. Through long centuries, historians have lived in many houses, borrowing their speech and convictions from their hosts: the theatre in Greece, the law courts in Rome, the monastery in the Middle Ages, the salon in the Enlightenment.

Ancient, medieval, and early modern historians proffered their works as pieces of rhetoric; they had to satisfy moral demands and employ accepted literary devices. The tradition of eloquence, reinforced and distorted in the early modern era by memories of antique oratory, pervaded historical writings down to the sixteenth and even the seventeenth century, when historians added to this antique rhetorical tradition the eloquence of the pulpit. The philosophe-historians' dependence on polite society in the eighteenth century was actually a giant step toward independence: history became a respectable literary genre among other respectable literary genres.

Then, in the nineteenth century, historians moved into their own house, the university—not, I might add, without some losses. But, whatever the losses, the modern autonomy of the historian has markedly increased the range of his stylistic options. As more aspects of the past have become accessible to inquiry, more ways of speaking about the past have become permissible. The relation of the historian to his work has changed; the craftsman has become a professional. Yet in principle, the debt that the individual historian owes to his craft—its dominant traditions, its current debates, its exploratory techniques—has neither increased nor diminished. The study of historians' style, therefore, whether of ancient, medieval, or modern practitioners, gives access to the world of their craft.

But it also gives access, finally, to culture itself, of which craftsmanship is only a specialized, and sometimes recalcitrant, representative. This is what Macaulay had in mind when he said of Herodotus that he "wrote as it is natural that he should write. He wrote for a nation susceptible, curious, lively, insatiably desirous of novelty and excitement." Reading Herodotus tells us much about the Greece of his day, just as reading Mommsen or Namier tells us much about the Germany or England of their day. Conversely, it also tells us much about their perception of their culture: we cannot read Mommsen's *Römische Geschichte*, with its stunning anachronisms, its Junkers in togas, without sensing within Mommsen, the objective scholar, another Mommsen, the passionate and frustrated political animal. We cannot read Namier's *Structure of Politics at the Accession of George III*, with its resolute anti-intellectualism, its affectionate portrayal of the political microcosm of mid-eighteenth-century England, without detecting in Namier, the minute researcher, a hidden Namier, the lover of English civility so infatuated that he must be a foreigner.

The social information that style provides is by no means infallible; if past words were addressed to the chosen few, and if we have lost the key that will unlock their message, the intentions of the writer, and with them the full bearing of his utterance, will remain opaque. It has long been a commonplace that men often use words to conceal their meaning behind veils of indirection, difficulty, and ambiguity. In such circumstances, we must first solve the style before we can, with its aid, solve other puzzles: there are times when politics is as much a clue to style as style is a clue to politics. Fortunately this is not a logical but an existential circularity, a symptom of the mutual dependence of style and life and, hence, of the possibility that they may reciprocally illuminate each other.

While one school of intellectual historians, Leo Strauss and his disciples, has made a cottage industry of reading between the lines, reading the lines themselves remains, for the historian, a rewarding enterprise. Erich Auerbach, in his *Mimesis*, has shown the path that may take the historian from philology to sociology. It is easy to demonstrate, as he does, that the barbarous Latin of a Merovingian chronicle mirrors, with its impoverished vocabulary, the desperate decay of antique culture. But with his analysis of Tacitus' world view, Auerbach shows that stylistics may trap more elusive game: social perceptions. In describing a mutiny, he notes, Tacitus puts elevated words in the mouth of one of the mutineers, sprinkles his report with ethical adjectives, and employs the rhetorical devices current among cultivated orators in the Rome of his day. Auerbach deduces from such linguistic habits Tactius' blindness to the social and economic pressures bubbling beneath the surface of events. He sees this failure as more than the political bias of an aristocrat confronting the demands of famished soldiers; he sees it, rather, as characteristic for a Roman who does not, and cannot, *see* the lower social orders as full human beings. In sum, the study of style provides a diagnostic instrument as much for the historian's social and cultural as for his psychological and professional worlds, a decisive clue to their meanings, their limitations—and their insights.

I must add a final word. Style, I said earlier, is sometimes less than the man; often it is more than the man. In examining the style of four great historians, I am in no way committing myself to the fashionable relativist implications that have usually been drawn from Buffon's epigram. Historians have long been engaged in a great, or at least persistent, debate over the essential nature of their craft, and Buffon has been taken as supporting the view that history cannot be a science, but must be an art—a subjective encounter between a literary man and the past, which he reshapes through his private vision and reports in that idiosyncratic manner we call his style. But a personal report may be an objective report. It is even possible that while style reflects the man, the man it reflects is a scientist. I do not want to decide this matter now and will return to it in the Conclusion. But on this much I want to insist here: there is no reason why style must be the undistorted reflection of the historian's private neurosis, social location, or historical epoch. If he has any professional conscience and competence at all, he is bound to say far more about the time of which he writes than the time in which he lives. Individual stylists develop in rebellion against their past, their enviroment, even against themselves, and the results are not always predictable. While in all its aspects style is instructive, not all styles are instructive to the same degree: like other writers, a historian usually has two styles, formal and informal, and both are an intermixture of self-expression and self-control. There is no rule book, no prepared recipe, setting down in advance just what the study of style may disclose. All I claim is that it discloses much, and that it will contribute some light to the heated debate over the nature of history.

QUESTIONS

1. *Gay opens with a definition of style as a centaur. How helpful is that definition? What does he do to try to make it intelligible?*
2. *Describe some conceptions about style that Gay either does or would characterize as misconceptions.*
3. *Why do you suppose Gay feels compelled to add the last section, to assert that a personal report can be objective, to dispute with E. H. Carr below?*
4. *Describe the style of someone—like a singer or an athlete whose actions or performances have an identifying style. On p. 989 Gay speaks of three "worlds" or "elements"—the stylist's private world, the world of his craft, and the culture. Can you distinguish these three components in the style you describe?*
5. *Discuss one selection from the Album of Styles (pp. 278–369) from Gay's point of view.*

EDWARD HALLETT CARR

The Historian and His Facts[1]

What is history? Lest anyone think the question meaningless or superfluous, I will take as my text two passages relating respectively to the first and second incarnations of *The Cambridge Modern History.* Here is Acton in his report of October 1896 to the Syndics of the Cambridge University Press on the work which he had undertaken to edit:

> It is a unique opportunity of recording, in the way most useful to the greatest number, the fullness of the knowledge which the nineteenth century is about to bequeath. . . . By the judicious division of labor we should be able to do it, and to bring home to every man the last document, and the ripest conclusions of international research.
> Ultimate history we cannot have in this generation; but we can dispose of conventional history, and show the point we have reached on the road from one to the other, now that all information is within reach, and every problem has become capable of solution.[2]

1. Chapter I of *What is History?*, 1961.
2. *The Cambridge Modern History: Its Origin, Authorship and Production* (Cambridge University Press, 1907), pp. 10-12 [This and the following footnotes are Carr's].

And almost exactly sixty years later Professor Sir George Clark, in his general introduction to the second *Cambridge Modern History*, commented on this belief of Acton and his collaborators that it would one day be possible to produce "ultimate history," and went on:

Historians of a later generation do not look forward to any such prospect. They expect their work to be superseded again and again. They consider that knowledge of the past has come down through one or more human minds, has been "processed" by them, and therefore cannot consist of elemental and impersonal atoms which nothing can alter.... The exploration seems to be endless, and some impatient scholars take refuge in scepticism, or at least in the doctrine that, since all historical judgments involve persons and points of view, one is as good as another and there is no "objective" historical truth.[3]

Where the pundits contradict each other so flagrantly the field is open to enquiry. I hope that I am sufficiently up-to-date to recognize that anything written in the 1890's must be nonsense. But I am not yet advanced enough to be committed to the view that anything written in the 1950's necessarily makes sense, Indeed, it may already have occurred to you that this enquiry is liable to stray into something even broader than the nature of history. The clash between Acton and Sir George Clark is a reflection of the change in our total outlook on society over the interval between these two pronouncements. Acton speaks out of the positive belief, the cleareyed self-confidence of the later Victorian age; Sir George Clark echoes the bewilderment and distracted scepticism of the beat generation. When we attempt to answer the question, What is history?, our answer, consciously or unconsciously, reflects our own position in time, and forms part of our answer to the broader question, what view we take of the society in which we live. I have no fear that my subject may, on closer inspection, seem trivial. I am afraid only that I may seem presumptuous to have broached a question so vast and so important.

The nineteenth century was a great age for facts. "What I want," said Mr. Gradgrind in *Hard Times*, "is Facts. . . . Facts alone are wanted in life." Nineteenth-century historians on the whole agreed with him. When Ranke in the 1830's, in legitimate protest against moralizing history, remarked that the task of the historian was "simply to show how it really was [*wie es eigentlich gewesen*]" this not very profound aphorism had an astonishing success. Three generations of German, British, and even French historians marched into battle intoning the magic words, *"Wie es eigentlich gewesen"* like an incantation—designed, like most incantations, to save them from the tiresome obligation to think for themselves. The Positivists, anxious to stake out their claim for history as a science, contributed the weight of their influence to this cult of

3. *The New Cambridge Modern History,* I (Cambridge University Press, 1957), pp. xxiv-xxv.

facts. First ascertain the facts, said the positivists, then draw your conclusions from them. In Great Britain, this view of history fitted in perfectly with the empiricist tradition which was the dominant strain in British philosophy from Locke to Bertrand Russell. The empirical theory of knowledge presupposes a complete separation between subject and object. Facts, like sense-impressions, impinge on the observer from outside, and are independent of his consciousness. The process of reception is passive: having received the data, he then acts on them. *The Shorter Oxford English Dictionary*, a useful but tendentious work of the empirical school, clearly marks the separateness of the two processes by defining a fact as "a datum of experience as distinct from conclusions." This is what may be called the common-sense view of history. History consists of a corpus of ascertained facts. The facts are available to the historian in documents, inscriptions, and so on, like fish on the fishmonger's slab. The historian collects them, takes them home, and cooks and serves them in whatever style appeals to him. Acton, whose culinary tastes were austere, wanted them served plain. In his letter of instructions to contributors to the first *Cambridge Modern History* he announced the requirement "that our Waterloo must be one that satisfies French and English, German and Dutch alike; that nobody can tell, without examining the list of authors where the Bishop of Oxford laid down the pen, and whether Fairbairn or Gasquet, Liebermann or Harrison took it up."[4] Even Sir George Clark, critical as he was of Acton's attitude, himself contrasted the "hard core of facts" in history with the "surrounding pulp of disputable interpretation"[5]—forgetting perhaps that the pulpy part of the fruit is more rewarding than the hard core. First get your facts straight, then plunge at your peril into the shifting sands of interpretation—that is the ultimate wisdom of the empirical, common-sense school of history. It recalls the favorite dictum of the great liberal journalist C. P. Scott: "Facts are sacred, opinion is free."

Now this clearly will not do. I shall not embark on a philosophical discussion of the nature of our knowledge of the past. Let us assume for present purposes that the fact that Caesar crossed the Rubicon and the fact that there is a table in the middle of the room are facts of the same or of a comparable order, that both these facts enter our consciousness in the same or in a comparable manner, and that both have the same objective character in relation to the person who knows them. But, even on this bold and not very plausible assumption, our argument at once runs into the difficulty that not all facts about the past are historical facts, or are treated as such by the historian. What is the criterion which distinguishes the facts of history from other facts about the past? What is a historical fact? This is a crucial question into which

4. Acton: *Lectures on Modern History* (London: Macmillan & Co., 1906), p. 318.

5. Quoted in *The Listener* (June 19, 1952), p. 992.

we must look a little more closely. According to the common-sense view, there are certain basic facts which are the same for all historians and which form, so to speak, the backbone of history—the fact, for example, that the Battle of Hastings was fought in 1066. But this view calls for two observations. In the first place, it is not with facts like these that the historian is primarily concerned. It is no doubt important to know that the great battle was fought in 1066 and not in 1065 or 1067, and that it was fought at Hastings and not at Eastbourne or Brighton. The historian must not get these things wrong. But when points of this kind are raised, I am reminded of Housman's remark that "accuracy is a duty, not a virtue."[6] To praise a historian for his accuracy is like praising an architect for using well-seasoned timber or properly mixed concrete in his building. It is a necessary condition of his work, but not his essential function. It is precisely for matters of this kind that the historian is entitled to rely on what have been called the "auxiliary sciences" of history—archaeology, epigraphy, numismatics, chronology, and so forth. The historian is not required to have the special skills which enable the expert to determine the origin and period of a fragment of pottery or marble, or decipher an obscure inscription, or to make the elaborate astronomical calculations necessary to establish a precise date. These so-called basic facts which are the same for all historians commonly belong to the category of the raw materials of the historian rather than of history itself. The second observation is that the necessity to establish these basic facts rests not on any quality in the facts themselves, but on an *a priori* decision of the historian. In spite of C. P. Scott's motto, every journalist knows today that the most effective way to influence opinion is by the selection and arrangement of the appropriate facts. It used to be said that facts speak for themselves. This is, of course, untrue. The facts speak only when the historian calls on them: It is he who decides to which facts to give the floor, and in what order or context. It was, I think, one of Pirandello's characters who said that a fact is like a sack—it won't stand up till you've put something in it. The only reason why we are interested to know that the battle was fought at Hastings in 1066 is that historians regard it as a major historical event. It is the historian who has decided for his own reasons that Caesar's crossing of that petty stream, the Rubicon, is a fact of history, whereas the crossing of the Rubicon by millions of other people before or since interests nobody at all. The fact that you arrived in this building half an hour ago on foot, or on a bicycle, or in a car, is just as much a fact about the past as the fact that Caesar crossed the Rubicon. But it will probably be ignored by historians. Professor Talcott Parsons once called science "a selective system of

6. M. Manilius: *Astronomicon: Liber Primus*, 2nd ed. (Cambridge University Press, 1937), p. 87.

cognitive orientations to reality."[7] It might perhaps have been put more simply. But history is, among other things, that. The historian is necessarily selective. The belief in a hard core of historical facts existing objectively and independently of the interpretation of the historian is a preposterous fallacy, but one which it is very hard to eradicate.

Let us take a look at the process by which a mere fact about the past is transformed into a fact of history. At Stalybridge Wakes in 1850, a vendor of gingerbread, as the result of some petty dispute, was deliberately kicked to death by an angry mob. Is this a fact of history? A year ago I should unhesitatingly have said "no." It was recorded by an eyewitness in some little-known memoirs;[8] but I had never seen it judged worthy of mention by any historian. A year ago Dr. Kitson Clark cited it in his Ford lectures in Oxford.[9] Does this make it into a historical fact? Not, I think, yet. Its present status, I suggest, is that it has been proposed for membership of the select club of historical facts. It now awaits a seconder and sponsors. It may be that in the course of the next few years we shall see this fact appearing first in footnotes, then in the text, of articles and books about nineteenth-century England, and that in twenty or thirty years' time it may be a well established historical fact. Alternatively, nobody may take it up, in which case it will relapse into the limbo of unhistorical facts about the past from which Dr. Kitson Clark has gallantly attempted to rescue it. What will decide which of these two things will happen? It will depend, I think, on whether the thesis or interpretation in support of which Dr. Kitson Clark cited this incident is accepted by other historians as valid and significant. Its status as a historical fact will turn on a question of interpretation. This element of interpretation enters into every fact of history.

May I be allowed a personal reminiscence? When I studied ancient history in this university many years ago, I had as a special subject "Greece in the period of the Persian Wars." I collected fifteen or twenty volumes on my shelves and took it for granted that there, recorded in these volumes, I had all the facts relating to my subject. Let us assume—it was very nearly true—that those volumes contained all the facts about it that were then known, or could be known. It never occurred to me to enquire by what accident or process of attrition that minute selection of facts, out of all the myriad facts that must have once been known to somebody, had survived to become *the* facts of history. I suspect that even today one of the fascinations of ancient and mediaeval history is that it gives us the illusion of having all the facts at our disposal

7. Talcott Parsons and Edward A. Shils: *Toward a General Theory of Action*, 3rd ed. (Cambridge, Mass.: Harvard University Press, 1954), p. 167.

8. Lord George Sanger: *Seventy Years*

a *Showman* (London: J. M. Dent & Sons, 1926), pp. 188-9.

9. These will shortly be published under the title *The Making of Victorian England*.

within a manageable compass: the nagging distinction between the facts of history and other facts about the past vanishes because the few known facts are all facts of history. As Bury, who had worked in both periods, said, "the records of ancient and mediaeval history are starred with lacunae."[1] History has been called an enormous jig-saw with a lot of missing parts. But the main trouble does not consist of the lacunae. Our picture of Greece in the fifth century B.C. is defective not primarily because so many of the bits have been accidentally lost, but because it is, by and large, the picture formed by a tiny group of people in the city of Athens. We know a lot about what fifth-century Greece looked like to an Athenian citizen; but hardly anything about what it looked like to a Spartan, a Corinthian, or a Theban—not to mention a Persian, or a slave or other non-citizen resident in Athens. Our picture has been preselected and predetermined for us, not so much by accident as by people who were consciously or unconsciously imbued with a particular view and thought the facts which supported that view worth preserving. In the same way, when I read in a modern history of the Middle Ages that the people of the Middle Ages were deeply concerned with religion, I wonder how we know this, and whether it is true. What we know as the facts of mediaeval history have almost all been selected for us by generations of chroniclers who were professionally occupied in the theory and practice of religion, and who therefore thought it supremely important, and recorded everything relating to it, and not much else. The picture of the Russian peasant as devoutly religious was destroyed by the revolution of 1917. The picture of mediaeval man as devoutly religious, whether true or not, is indestructible, because nearly all the known facts about him were preselected for us by people who believed it, and wanted others to believe it, and a mass of other facts, in which we might possibly have found evidence to the contrary, has been lost beyond recall. The dead hand of vanished generations of historians, scribes, and chroniclers has determined beyond the possibility of appeal the pattern of the past. "The history we read," writes Professor Barraclough, himself trained as a mediaevalist, "though based on facts, is, strictly speaking, not factual at all, but a series of accepted judgments."[2]

But let us turn to the different, but equally grave, plight of the modern historian. The ancient or mediaeval historian may be grateful for the vast winnowing process which, over the years, has put at his disposal a manageable corpus of historical facts. As Lytton Strachey said in his mischievous way, "ignorance is the first requisite of the historian, ignorance which simplifies and clarifies, which selects and omits."[3] When I am tempted, as I sometimes am, to envy

1. John Bagnell Bury: *Selected Essays* (Cambridge University Press, 1930, p. 52.)

2. Geoffrey Barraclough: *History in a Changing World* (London; Basil Blackwell & Mott, 1955), p. 14.

3. Lytton Strachey: Preface to *Eminent Victorians*.

the extreme competence of colleagues engaged in writing ancient
or mediaeval history, I find consolation in the reflection that they
are so competent mainly because they are so ignorant of their subject. The modern historian enjoys none of the advantages of this
built-in ignorance. He must cultivate this necessary ignorance for
himself—the more so the nearer he comes to his own times. He
has the dual task of discovering the few significant facts and turning them into facts of history, and of discarding the many insignificant facts as unhistorical. But this is the very converse of the
nineteenth-century heresy that history consists of the compilation
of a maximum number of irrefutable and objective facts. Anyone
who succumbs to this heresy will either have to give up history as
a bad job, and take to stamp-collecting or some other form of anti-
quarianism, or end in a madhouse. It is this heresy, which during
the past hundred years has had such devastating effects on the
modern historian, producing in Germany, in Great Britain, and in
the United States a vast and growing mass of dry-as-dust factual
histories, of minutely specialized monographs, of would-be historians knowing more and more about less and less, sunk without
trace in an ocean of facts. It was, I suspect, this heresy—rather
than the alleged conflict between liberal and Catholic loyalties—
which frustrated Acton as a historian. In an early essay he said of
his teacher Döllinger: "He would not write with imperfect
materials, and to him the materials were always imperfect."[4] Acton
was surely here pronouncing an anticipatory verdict on himself, on
that strange phenomenon of a historian whom many would regard
as the most distinguished occupant the Regius Chair of Modern
History in this university has ever had—but who wrote no history.
And Acton wrote his own epitaph in the introductory note to the
first volume of the *Cambridge Modern History*, published just
after his death, when he lamented that the requirements pressing
on the historian "threaten to turn him from a man of letters into
the compiler of an encyclopedia."[5] Something had gone wrong.
What had gone wrong was the belief in this untiring and unending
accumulation of hard facts as the foundation of history, the belief
that facts speak for themselves and that we cannot have too many
facts, a belief at that time so unquestioning that few historians
then thought it necessary—and some still think it unnecessary today
—to ask themselves the question: What is history?

The nineteenth-century fetishism of facts was completed and
justified by a fetishism of documents. The documents were the
Ark of the Covenant in the temple of facts. The reverent historian
approached them with bowed head and spoke of them in awed

4. Quoted in George P. Gooch: *History and Historians in the Nineteenth
Century* (London: Longmans, Green &
Company, 1952), p. 385. Later Acton
said of Döllinger that "it was given him
to form his philosophy of history on the
largest induction ever available to man"
(*History of Freedom and Other Essays*
[London: Macmillan & Co., 1907], p.
435).

5. *The Cambridge Modern History*, I
(1902), p. 4.

tones. If you find it in the documents, it is so. But what, when we get down to it, do these documents—the decrees, the treaties, the rent-rolls, the blue books, the official correspondence, the private letters and diaries—tell us? No document can tell us more than what the author of the document thought—what he thought had happened, what he thought ought to happen or would happen, or perhaps only what he wanted others to think he thought, or even only what he himself thought he thought. None of this means anything until the historian has got to work on it and deciphered it. The facts, whether found in documents or not, have still to be processed by the historian before he can make any use of them: the use he makes of them is, if I may put it that way, the processing process.

Let me illustrate what I am trying to say by an example which I happen to know well. When Gustav Stresemann, the Foreign Minister of the Weimar Republic, died in 1929, he left behind him an enormous mass—300 boxes full—of papers, official, semi-official, and private, nearly all relating to the six years of his tenure of office as Foreign Minister. His friends and relatives naturally thought that a monument should be raised to the memory of so great a man. His faithful secretary Bernhardt got to work; and within three years there appeared three massive volumes, of some 600 pages each, of selected documents from the 300 boxes, with the impressive title *Stresemanns Vermächtnis*.[6] In the ordinary way the documents themselves would have moldered away in some cellar or attic and disappeared for ever; or perhaps in a hundred years or so some curious scholar would have come upon them and set out to compare them with Bernhardt's text. What happened was far more dramatic. In 1945 the documents fell into the hands of the British and the American governments, who photographed the lot and put the photostats at the disposal of scholars in the Public Record Office in London and in the National Archives in Washington, so that, if we have sufficient patience and curiosity, we can discover exactly what Bernhardt did. What he did was neither very unusual nor very shocking. When Stresemann died, his Western policy seemed to have been crowned with a series of brilliant successes—Locarno, the admission of Germany to the League of Nations, the Dawes and Young plans and the American loans, the withdrawal of allied occupation armies from the Rhineland. This seemed the important and rewarding part of Stresemann's foreign policy; and it was not unnatural that it should have been over-represented in Bernhardt's selection of documents. Stresemann's Eastern policy, on the other hand, his relations with the Soviet Union, seemed to have led nowhere in particular; and, since masses of documents about negotiations which yielded only trivial results were not very interesting and added nothing to Stresemann's

6. *Stresemann's Legacy.*

reputation, the process of selection could be more rigorous. Stresemann in fact devoted a far more constant and anxious attention to relations with the Soviet Union, and they played a far larger part in his foreign policy as a whole, than the reader of the Bernhardt selection would surmise. But the Bernhardt volumes compare favorably, I suspect, with many published collections of documents on which the ordinary historian implicitly relies.

This is not the end of my story. Shortly after the publication of Bernhardt's volumes, Hitler came into power. Stresemann's name was consigned to oblivion in Germany, and the volumes disappeared from circulation: many, perhaps most, of the copies must have been destroyed. Today *Stresemanns Vermächtnis* is a rather rare book. But in the West Stresemann's reputation stood high. In 1935 an English publisher brought out an abbreviated translation of Bernhardt's work—a selection from Bernhardt's selection; perhaps one third of the original was omitted. Sutton, a well-known translator from the German, did his job competently and well. The English version, he explained in the preface, was "slightly condensed, but only by the omission of a certain amount of what, it was felt, was more ephemeral matter . . . of little interest to English readers or students."[7] This again is natural enough. But the result is that Stresemann's Eastern policy, already under-represented in Bernhardt, recedes still further from view, and the Soviet Union appears in Sutton's volumes merely as an occasional and rather unwelcome intruder in Stresemann's predominantly Western foreign policy. Yet it is safe to say that, for all except a few specialists, Sutton and not Bernhardt—and still less the documents themselves—represents for the Western world the authentic voice of Stresemann. Had the documents perished in 1945 in the bombing, and had the remaining Bernhardt volumes disappeared, the authenticity and authority of Sutton would never have been questioned. Many printed collections of documents gratefully accepted by historians in default of the originals rest on no securer basis than this.

But I want to carry the story one step further. Let us forget about Bernhardt and Sutton, and be thankful that we can, if we choose, consult the authentic papers of a leading participant in some important events in recent European history. What do the papers tell us? Among other things they contain records of some hundreds of Stresemann's conversations with the Soviet ambassador in Berlin and of a score or so with Chicherin.[8] These records have one feature in common. They depict Stresemann as having the lion's share of the conversations and reveal his arguments as invariably well put and cogent, while those of his partner are for the most part scanty, confused, and unconvincing. This is a familiar characteristic

7. *Gustav Stresemann: His Diaries, Letters, and Papers* (London: Macmillan & Co.; 1935), I.

8. Soviet foreign minister 1918-28 [Editor's note].

of all records of diplomatic conversations. The documents do not tell us what happened, but only what Stresemann thought had happened. It was not Sutton or Bernhardt, but Stresemann himself, who started the process of selection. And, if we had, say, Chicherin's records of these same conversations, we should still learn from them only what Chicherin thought, and what really happened would still have to be reconstructed in the mind of the historian. Of course, facts and documents are essential to the historian. But do not make a fetish of them. They do not by themselves constitute history; they provide in themselves no ready-made answer to this tiresome question: What is history?

At this point I should like to say a few words on the question of why nineteenth-century historians were generally indifferent to the philosophy of history. The term was invented by Voltaire, and has since been used in different senses; but I shall take it to mean, if I use it at all, our answer to the question: What is history? The nineteenth century was, for the intellectuals of Western Europe, a comfortable period exuding confidence and optimism. The facts were on the whole satisfactory; and the inclination to ask and answer awkward questions about them was correspondingly weak. Ranke piously believed that divine providence would take care of the meaning of history if he took care of the facts; and Burckhardt with a more modern touch of cynicism observed that "we are not initiated into the purposes of the eternal wisdom." Professor Butterfield as late as 1931 noted with apparent satisfaction that "historians have reflected little upon the nature of things and even the nature of their own subject."[9] But my predecessor in these lectures, Dr. A. L. Rowse, more justly critical, wrote of Sir Winston Churchill's *The World Crisis*—his book about the First World War— that, while it matched Trotsky's *History of the Russian Revolution* in personality, vividness, and vitality, it was inferior in one respect: it had "no philosophy of history behind it."[1] British historians refused to be drawn, not because they believed that history had no meaning, but because they believed that its meaning was implicit and self-evident. The liberal nineteenth-century view of history had a close affinity with the economic doctrine of *laissez-faire*—also the product of a serene and self-confident outlook on the world. Let everyone get on with his particular job, and the hidden hand would take care of the universal harmony. The facts of history were themselves a demonstration of the supreme fact of a beneficent and apparently infinite progress towards higher things. This was the age of innocence, and historians walked in the Garden of Eden, without a scrap of philosophy to cover them, naked and unashamed before the

---

9. Herbert Butterfield: *The Whig Interpretation of History* (London: George Bell & Sons, 1931), p. 67.

1. Alfred L. Rowse: *The End of an Epoch* (London: Macmillan & Co., 1947), pp. 282-3.

god of history. Since then, we have known Sin and experienced a Fall; and those historians who today pretend to dispense with a philosophy of history are merely trying, vainly and self-consciously, like members of a nudist colony, to recreate the Garden of Eden in their garden suburb. Today the awkward question can no longer be evaded. * * *

During the past fifty years a good deal of serious work has been done on the question: What is history? It was from Germany, the country which was to do so much to upset the comfortable reign of nineteenth-century liberalism, that the first challenge came in the 1880's and 1890's to the doctrine of the primacy and autonomy of facts in history. The philosophers who made the challenge are now little more than names: Dilthey is the only one of them who has recently received some belated recognition in Great Britain. Before the turn of the century, prosperity and confidence were still too great in this country for any attention to be paid to heretics who attacked the cult of facts. But early in the new century, the torch passed to Italy, where Croce began to propound a philosophy of history which obviously owed much to German masters. All history is "contemporary history," declared Croce,[2] meaning that history consists essentially in seeing the past through the eyes of the present and in the light of its problems, and that the main work of the historian is not to record, but to evaluate; for, if he does not evaluate, how can he know what is worth recording? In 1910 the American philosopher, Carl Becker, argued in deliberately provocative language that "the facts of history do not exist for any historian till he creates them."[3] These challenges were for the moment little noticed. It was only after 1920 that Croce began to have a considerable vogue in France and Great Britain. This was not perhaps because Croce was a subtler thinker or a better stylist than his German predecessors, but because, after the First World War, the facts seemed to smile on us less propitiously than in the years before 1914, and we were therefore more accessible to a philosophy which sought to diminish their prestige. Croce was an important influence on the Oxford philosopher and historian Collingwood, the only British thinker in the present century who has made a serious contribution to the philosophy of history. He did not live to write the systematic treatise he had planned; but his published and unpublished papers on the subject were collected after his death in a volume entitled *The Idea of History*, which appeared in 1945.

2. The context of this celebrated aphorism is as follows: "The practical requirements which underlie every historical judgment give to all history the character of 'contemporary history,' because, however remote in time events thus recounted may seem to be, the history in reality refers to present needs and present situations wherein those events vibrate" (Benedetto Croce: *History as the Story of Liberty* [London: George Allen & Unwin, 1941], p. 19).

3. *Atlantic Monthly* (October 1928), p. 528.

The views of Collingwood can be summarized as follows. The philosophy of history is concerned neither with "the past by itself" nor with "the historian's thought about it by itself," but with "the two things in their mutual relations." (This dictum reflects the two current meanings of the word "history"—the enquiry conducted by the historian and the series of past events into which he enquires.) "The past which a historian studies is not a dead past, but a past which in some sense is still living in the present." But a past act is dead, *i.e.* meaningless to the historian, unless he can understand the thought that lay behind it. Hence "all history is the history of thought," and "history is the re-enactment in the historian's mind of the thought whose history he is studying." The reconstitution of the past in the historian's mind is dependent on empirical evidence. But it is not in itself an empirical process, and cannot consist in a mere recital of facts. On the contrary, the process of reconstitution governs the selection and interpretation of the facts: this, indeed, is what makes them historical facts. "History," says Professor Oakeshott, who on this point stands near to Collingwood, "is the historian's experience. It is 'made' by nobody save the historian: to write history is the only way of making it."[4]

This searching critique, though it may call for some serious reservations, brings to light certain neglected truths.

In the first place, the facts of history never come to us "pure," since they do not and cannot exist in a pure form: they are always refracted through the mind of the recorder. It follows that when we take up a work of history, our first concern should be not with the facts which it contains but with the historian who wrote it. Let me take as an example the great historian in whose honor and in whose name these lectures were founded. Trevelyan, as he tells us in his autobiography, was "brought up at home on a somewhat exuberantly Whig tradition"[5]; and he would not, I hope, disclaim the title if I described him as the last and not the least of the great English liberal historians of the Whig tradition. It is not for nothing that he traces back his family tree, through the great Whig historian George Otto Trevelyan, to Macaulay, incomparably the greatest of the Whig historians. Dr. Trevelyan's finest and maturest work *England under Queen Anne* was written against that background, and will yield its full meaning and significance to the reader only when read against that background. The author, indeed, leaves the reader with no excuse for failing to do so. For if, following the technique of connoisseurs of detective novels, you read the end first, you will find on the last few pages of the third volume the best summary known to me of what is nowadays called the Whig interpretation of history; and you will see that what Trevelyan is trying

4. Michael Oakeshott: *Experience and Its Modes* (Cambridge University Press, 1933), p. 99.

5. G. M. Trevelyan: *An Autobiography* (London: Longmans, Green & Company, 1949), p. 11.

to do is to investigate the origin and development of the Whig tradition, and to roof it fairly and squarely in the years after the death of its founder, William III. Though this is not, perhaps, the only conceivable interpretation of the events of Queen Anne's reign, it is a valid and, in Trevelyan's hands, a fruitful interpretation. But, in order to appreciate it at its full value, you have to understand what the historian is doing. For if, as Collingwood says, the historian must re-enact in thought what has gone on in the mind of his *dramatis personae*, so the reader in his turn must re-enact what goes on in the mind of the historian. Study the historian before you begin to study the facts. This is, after all, not very abstruse. It is what is already done by the intelligent undergraduate who, when recommended to read a work by that great scholar Jones of St. Jude's, goes round to a friend at St. Jude's to ask what sort of chap Jones is, and what bees he has in his bonnet. When you read a work of history, always listen out for the buzzing. If you can detect none, either you are tone deaf or your historian is a dull dog. The facts are really not at all like fish on the fishmonger's slab. They are like fish swimming about in a vast and sometimes inaccessible ocean; and what the historian catches will depend partly on chance, but mainly on what part of the ocean he chooses to fish in and what tackle he chooses to use—these two factors being, of course, determined by the kind of fish he wants to catch. By and large, the historian will get the kind of facts he wants. History means interpretation. Indeed, if, standing Sir George Clark on his head, I were to call history "a hard core of interpretation surrounded by a pulp of disputable facts," my statement would, no doubt, be one-sided and misleading, but no more so, I venture to think, than the original dictum.

The second point is the more familiar one of the historian's need of imaginative understanding for the minds of the people with whom he is dealing, for the thought behind their acts: I say "imaginative understanding," not "sympathy," lest sympathy should be supposed to imply agreement. The nineteenth century was weak in mediaeval history, because it was too much repelled by the superstitious beliefs of the Middle Ages and by the barbarities which they inspired, to have any imaginative understanding of mediaeval people. Or take Burckhardt's censorious remark about the Thirty Years' War: "It is scandalous for a creed, no matter whether it is Catholic or Protestant, to place its salvation above the integrity of the nation."[6] It was extremely difficult for a nineteenth-century liberal historian, brought up to believe that it is right and praiseworthy to kill in defense of one's country, but wicked and wrongheaded to kill in defense of one's religion, to enter into the state of mind of those who fought the Thirty Years' War. This difficulty is

6. Jacob Burckhardt: *Judgments on History and Historians* (London: S. J.   Reginald Saunders & Company, 1958), p. 179.

particularly acute in the field in which I am now working. Much of what has been written in English-speaking countries in the last ten years about the Soviet Union, and in the Soviet Union about the English-speaking countries, has been vitiated by this inability to achieve even the most elementary measure of imaginative understanding of what goes on in the mind of the other party, so that the words and actions of the other are always made to appear malign, senseless, or hypocritical. History cannot be written unless the historian can achieve some kind of contact with the mind of those about whom he is writing.

The third point is that we can view the past, and achieve our understanding of the past, only through the eyes of the present. The historian is of his own age, and is bound to it by the conditions of human existence. The very words which he uses—words like democracy, empire, war, revolution—have current connotations from which he cannot divorce them. Ancient historians have taken to using words like *polis* and *plebs* in the original, just in order to show that they have not fallen into this trap. This does not help them. They, too, live in the present, and cannot cheat themselves into the past by using unfamiliar or obsolete words, any more than they would become better Greek or Roman historians if they delivered their lectures in a *chlamys* or a *toga*. The names by which successive French historians have described the Parisian crowds which played so prominent a role in the French revolution—*les sans-culottes, le peuple, la canaille, les bras-nus*—are all, for those who know the rules of the game, manifestos of a political affiliation and of a particular interpretation. Yet the historian is obliged to choose: the use of language forbids him to be neutral. Nor is it a matter of words alone. Over the past hundred years the changed balance of power in Europe has reversed the attitude of British historians to Frederick the Great. The changed balance of power within the Christian churches between Catholicism and Protestantism has profoundly altered their attitude to such figures as Loyola, Luther, and Cromwell. It requires only a superficial knowledge of the work of French historians of the last forty years on the French revolution to recognize how deeply it has been affected by the Russian revolution of 1917. The historian belongs not to the past but to the present. Professor Trevor-Roper tells us that the historian "ought to love the past."[7] This is a dubious injunction. To love the past may easily be an expression of the nostalgic romanticism of old men and old societies, a symptom of loss of faith and interest in the present or future.[8] *Cliché* for *cliché*, I should prefer the one about freeing one-

7. Introduction to Burckhardt: *Judgments on History and Historians*, p. 17.

8. Compare Nietzsche's view of history: "To old age belongs the old man's business of looking back and casting up his accounts, of seeking consolation in the memories of the past, in historical culture" (*Thoughts Out of Season* [London: Macmillan & Co., 1909], II, pp. 65-6).

self from "the dead hand of the past." The function of the historian is neither to love the past nor to emancipate himself from the past, but to master and understand it as the key to the understanding of the present.

If, however, these are some of the sights of what I may call the Collingwood view of history, it is time to consider some of the dangers. The emphasis on the role of the historian in the making of history tends, if pressed to its logical conclusion, to rule out any objective history at all: history is what the historian makes. Collingwood seems indeed, at one moment, in an unpublished note quoted by his editor, to have reached this conclusion:

> St. Augustine looked at history from the point of view of the early Christian; Tillemont, from that of a seventeenth-century Frenchman; Gibbon, from that of an eighteenth-century Englishman; Mommsen, from that of a nineteenth-century German. There is no point in asking which was the right point of view. Each was the only one possible for the man who adopted it.[9]

This amounts to total scepticism, like Froude's remark that history is "a child's box of letters with which we can spell any word we please."[1] Collingwood, in his reaction against "scissors-and-paste history," against the view of history as a mere compilation of facts, comes perilously near to treating history as something spun out of the human brain, and leads back to the conclusion referred to by Sir George Clark in the passage which I quoted earlier, that "there is no 'objective' historical truth." In place of the theory that history has no meaning, we are offered here the theory of an infinity of meanings, none any more right than any other—which comes to much the same thing. The second theory is surely as untenable as the first. It does not follow that, because a mountain appears to take on different shapes from different angles of vision, it has objectively either no shape at all or an infinity of shapes. It does not follow that, because interpretation plays a necessary part in establishing the facts of history, and because no existing interpretation is wholly objective, one interpretation is as good as another, and the facts of history are in principle not amenable to objective interpretation. I shall have to consider at a later stage what exactly is meant by objectivity in history.

But a still greater danger lurks in the Collingwood hypothesis. If the historian necessarily looks at his period of history through the eyes of his own time, and studies the problems of the past as a key to those of the present, will he not fall into a purely pragmatic view of the facts, and maintain that the criterion of a right interpretation is its suitability to some present purpose? On this hypothesis, the facts of history are nothing, interpretation is everything. Nietzsche

9. Robin G. Collingwood: *The Idea of History* (London: Oxford University Press; 1946), p. xii.

1. James Anthony Froude: *Short Studies on Great Subjects* (1894), I, p. 21.

had already enunciated the principle: "The falseness of an opinion is not for us any objection to it. . . . The question is how far it is life-furthering, life-preserving, species-preserving, perhaps species-creating."[2] The American pragmatists moved, less explicitly and less wholeheartedly, along the same line. Knowledge is knowledge for some purpose. The validity of the knowledge depends on the validity of the purpose. But, even where no such theory has been professed, the practice has often been no less disquieting. In my own field of study, I have seen too many examples of extravagant interpretation riding roughshod over facts, not to be impressed with the reality of this danger. It is not surprising that perusal of some of the more extreme products of Soviet and anti-Soviet schools of historiography should sometimes breed a certain nostalgia for that illusory nineteenth-century heaven of purely factual history.

How then, in the middle of the twentieth century, are we to define the obligation of the historian to his facts? I trust that I have spent a sufficient number of hours in recent years chasing and perusing documents, and stuffing my historical narrative with properly footnoted facts, to escape the imputation of treating facts and documents too cavalierly. The duty of the historian to respect his facts is not exhausted by the obligation to see that his facts are accurate. He must seek to bring into the picture all known or knowable facts relevant, in one sense or another, to the theme on which he is engaged and to the interpretation proposed. If he seeks to depict the Victorian Englishman as a moral and rational being, he must not forget what happened at Stalybridge Wakes in 1850. But this, in turn, does not mean that he can eliminate interpretation, which is the life-blood of history. Laymen—that is to say, non-academic friends or friends from other academic disciplines—sometimes ask me how the historian goes to work when he writes history. The commonest assumption appears to be that the historian divides his work into two sharply distinguishable phases or periods. First, he spends a long preliminary period reading his source and filling his notebooks with facts: then, when this is over, he puts away his sources, takes out his notebooks, and writes his book from beginning to end. This is to me an unconvincing and unplausible picture. For myself, as soon as I have got going on a few of what I take to be the capital sources, the itch becomes too strong and I begin to write— not necessarily at the beginning, but somewhere, anywhere. Thereafter, reading and writing go on simultaneously. The writing is added to, subtracted from, re-shaped, cancelled, as I go on reading. The reading is guided and directed and made fruitful by the writing: the more I write, the more I know what I am looking for, the better I understand the significance and relevance of what I find. Some historians probably do all this preliminary writing in their

2. Nietzsche: *Beyond Good and Evil*, Chapter 1.

head without using pen, paper, or typewriter, just as some people play chess in their heads without recourse to board and chess-men: this is a talent which I envy, but cannot emulate. But I am convinced that, for any historian worth the name, the two processes of what economists call "input" and "output" go on simultaneously and are, in practice, parts of a single process. If you try to separate them, or to give one priority over the other, you fall into one of two heresies. Either you write scissors-and-paste history without meaning or significance; or you write propaganda or historical fiction, and merely use facts of the past to embroider a kind of writing which has nothing to do with history.

Our examination of the relation of the historian to the facts of history finds us, therefore, in an apparently precarious situation, navigating delicately between the Scylla of an untenable theory of history as an objective compilation of facts, of the unqualified primacy of fact over interpretation, and the Charybdis of an equally untenable theory of history as the subjective product of the mind of the historian who establishes the facts of history and masters them through the process of interpretation, between a view of history having the center of gravity in the past and the view having the center of gravity in the present. But our situation is less precarious than it seems. We shall encounter the same dichotomy of fact and interpretation again in these lectures in other guises—the particular and the general, the empirical and the theoretical, the objective and the subjective. The predicament of the historian is a reflection of the nature of man. Man, except perhaps in earliest infancy and in extreme old age, is not totally involved in his environment and unconditionally subject to it. On the other hand, he is never totally independent of it and its unconditional master. The relation of man to his environment is the relation of the historian to his theme. The historian is neither the humble slave, nor the tyrannical master, of his facts. The relation between the historian and his facts is one of equality, of give-and-take. As any working historian knows, if he stops to reflect what he is doing as he thinks and writes, the historian is engaged on a continuous process of molding his facts to his interpretation and his interpretation to his facts. It is impossible to assign primacy to one over the other.

The historian starts with the provisional selection of facts and a provisional interpretation in the light of which that selection has been made—by others as well as by himself. As he works, both the interpretation and the selection and ordering of facts undergo subtle and perhaps partly unconscious changes through the reciprocal action of one or the other. And this reciprocal action also involves reciprocity between present and past, since the historian is part of the present and the facts belong to the past. The historian and the facts of history are necessary to one another. The historian without his facts is rootless and futile; the facts without their historian are dead and meaningless. My first answer therefore to the question, What is history?, is that it is a continuous process of interaction between the historian and his facts, an unending dialogue between the present and the past.

QUESTIONS

1. Carr begins with a question but does not answer it until the last sentence. What are the main steps of the discussion leading to his answer? The answer takes the form of a definition: which is the most important of the defining words?
2. In his discussion of the facts of history, Carr distinguishes between a "mere fact about the past" and a "fact of history." Into which category should go Bruno Bettelheim's encounter with the infirmary guard (pp. 48–49)?
3. If you were commissioned to write a history of the semester or of a particular group during the semester, what would be your most important "facts of history"?

On Science

JOHN LIVINGSTON LOWES
Time in the Middle Ages[1]

We live in terms of *time*. And so pervasive is that element of our consciousness that we have to stand, as it were, outside it for a moment to realize how completely it controls our lives. For we think and act perpetually, we mortals who look before and after, in relation to hours and days and weeks and months and years. Yesterday and to-morrow, next week, a month from now, a year ago, in twenty minutes—those are the terms in which, wittingly or automatically, we act and plan and think. And to orient ourselves at any moment in that streaming continuum we carry watches on our wrists, and put clocks about our houses and on our public towers, and somewhere in our eye keep calendars, and scan time-tables when we would go abroad. And all this is so utterly familiar that it has ceased to be a matter of conscious thought or inference at all. And—to come to the heart of the business—unless we are mariners or woodsmen or astronomers or simple folk in lonely places, we never any longer reckon with the *sky*. Except for its bearing on the weather or upon our moods, or for contemplation of its depths of blue or fleets of white, or of the nightly splendor of its stars, we are oblivious of its influence. And therein lies the great gulf fixed between Chaucer's century and ours.

For Chaucer and his contemporaries, being likewise human, also lived in terms of time. But their calendar and time-piece was that sky through which moved immutably along predestined tracks the planets and the constellations. And no change, perhaps, wrought by the five centuries between us is more revealing of material differences than that shift of attitude towards "this brave o'erhanging firmament," the sky. And it is that change, first of all, that I wish, if I can, to make clear.

1. From Chapter I, "Backgrounds and Horizons," of *Geoffrey Chaucer*, 1934.

There could be, I suspect, no sharper contrast than that between the "mysterious universe" of modern science, as interpreters like Eddington and Jeans have made even laymen dimly perceive it, and the nest of closed, concentric spheres in terms of which Chaucer and his coevals thought. The structure of that universe may be stated simply enough. Its intricacies need not concern us here. About the earth, as the fixed center, revolved the spheres of the seven then known planets, of which the sun and the moon were two. Beyond these seven planetary spheres lay the sphere of the fixed stars. Beyond that in turn, and carrying along with it in its "diurnal sway" the eight spheres which lay within it, moved the *primum mobile*, a ninth sphere with which, to account for certain planetary eccentricities, the Middle Ages had supplemented the Ptolemaic system. We must think, in a word, of Chaucer's universe as geocentric—the "litel erthe," encompassed by "thilke speres thryes three."[2] As an interesting fact which we have learned, we know it; to conceive it as reality demands an exercise of the imagination. And only with that mental *volte-face* accomplished can we realize the cosmos as Chaucer thought of it.

Now the order of succession of the planetary spheres had far-reaching implications. Starting from the earth, which was their center, that succession was as follows: Moon, Mercury, Venus, Sun, Mars, Jupiter, Saturn. And implicit in that order were two fundamental consequences—the astrological status of the successive hours of the day, and the sequence of the days of the week. The two phenomena stood in intimate relation, and some apprehension of each is fundamental to an understanding of the framework of conceptions within which Chaucer thought, and in terms of which he often wrote.

There were, then, in the first place—and this is strange to us—two sorts of *hours*, with both of which everybody reckoned. There were the hours from midnight to midnight, which constituted the "day natural"—the hours, that is, with which we are familiar—and these, in Chaucer's phrase, were "hours equal," or "hours of the *clock*." But there were also the hours which were reckoned from sunrise to sunset (which made up "day artificial"), and on from sunset to sunrise again. And these, which will most concern us, were termed "hours inequal," or "hours of the *planets*." And they were the hours of peculiar significance, bound up far more closely with human affairs than the "hours of the clock." It is worth, then, a moment's time to get them clear.

They were termed "inequal" for an obvious reason. For the periods between sunrise and sunset, and sunset and sunrise, respectively, change in length with the annual course of the sun, and the length of their twelfths, or hours, must of necessity change too. Between

2. "Those spheres thrice three."

the equinoxes, then, it is clear that the inequal hours will now be longer by day than by night, now longer by night than by day. And only twice in the year, at the equinoxes, will the equal hours and the inequal hours—the hours of the clock and the hours of the planets—be identical. Moreover, each of the inequal hours (and this is of the first importance) was "ruled" by one of the seven planets, and it was as "hours of the planets" that the "hours inequal" touched most intimately human life. And that brings us at once to the days of the week, and their now almost forgotten implications. Why, to be explicit, is to-day Saturday? And why to-morrow Sunday? To answer those two questions is to arrive at one of the determining concepts of Chaucer's world.

Let me first arrange the seven planets in their order, starting (to simplify what follows) with the outermost. Their succession will then be this: Saturn, Jupiter, Mars, Sun, Venus, Mercury, Moon. Now Saturn will rule the first hour of the day which, for that reason, bears his name, and which we still call *Saturday*. Of that day Jupiter will rule the second hour, Mars the third, the Sun the fourth, Venus the fifth, Mercury the sixth, the Moon the seventh, and Saturn again, in due order, the eighth. Without carrying the computation farther around the clock it is obvious that Saturn will also rule the fifteenth and the twenty-second hours of the twenty-four which belong to his day. The twenty-third hour will then be ruled by Jupiter, the twenty-fourth by Mars, and the twenty-fifth by the Sun. But the twenty-fifth hour of one day is the first hour of the next, and accordingly the day after Saturn's day will be the Sun's day. And so, through starry compulsion, the next day after Saturday *must* be Sunday. In precisely the same fashion—accomplished most quickly by remembering that each planet must rule the twenty-second hour of its own day—the ruling planet of the first hour of each of the succeeding days may readily be found. And their order, so found, including Saturn and the Sun, is this: Saturn, Sun, Moon, Mars, Mercury, Jupiter, Venus—then Saturn again, and so on *ad libitum*. And the days of the week will accordingly be the days of the seven planets in that fixed order.

Now Saturn's day, the Sun's day, and the Moon's day are clearly recognizable in their English names of Saturday, Sunday, and Monday. But what of the remaining four—to wit, the days of Mars, Mercury, Jupiter, and Venus, which we call Tuesday, Wednesday, Thursday, and Friday? French has preserved, as also in Lundi, the planetary designations: Mardi (*Martis dies*), Mercredi (*Mercurii dies*), Jeudi (*Jovis dies*), and Vendredi (*Veneris dies*). The shift of the names in English is due to the ousting, in those four instances, of the Roman pantheon by the Germanic. Tiw, Woden, Thor, and Frig (or Freya) have usurped the seats of Mars, Mercury, Jupiter, and Venus, and given their barbarous names to the days. And in France a fourth, even more significant substitution has taken place. For the sun's day is in French *dimanche*, and *dimanche* is *dominica dies*, the Lord's day. And so between Saturn's planet and Diana's moon is memorialized, along with Mercury and Jupiter and Venus and Mars, the second Person of the Christian Trinity. The ancient world has crumbled, and its detritus has been remoulded into almost unrecognizable shapes. But half the history of Europe and of its early formative ideas is written in the nomenclature of the week. And that nomenclature depends in turn upon the succession of the planetary hours. And it was in terms of those hours that Chaucer and his contemporaries thought.

In the *Knight's Tale*, to be specific, Palamon, Emily, and Arcite go to pray, each for the granting of his own desire, to the temples respectively of Venus, Diana, and Mars. And each goes, as in due observance of ceremonial propriety he must, in the hour of the planet associated with the god to whom he prays. Palamon goes to the temple of Venus, "And *in hir houre* he walketh forth." A few lines earlier that hour has been stated in everyday terms: it was "The Sonday night, er day bigan to springe . . . Although it nere nat day by houres two"—two hours, that is, before sunrise. The day that was springing after Sunday night was Monday, and the hour of Monday's sunrise is the hour of the Moon. And the hour two hours earlier, in which Palamon walked forth, was the hour ruled by Venus, to whose temple he was on the way. And Emily and Arcite, as the tale goes on, performed their pilgrimages at similarly reckoned hours. To Chaucer and his readers all this was familiar matter of the day, as instantly comprehensible as are now to us the hours which we reckon by the clock. For us alas! it has become a theme for cumbrous exposition, because the hours of the planets have vanished, with the gods whose names they bore. All that is left of them is the time-worn and wonted sequence of the seven designations of the days.

Nothing, indeed, is more characteristic of the period in which Chaucer wrote than the strange, twisted mythology, transmogrified and confused, which emerged from the association of the planets and the gods. Not even Ovid had conceived such metamorphoses.[3] For the gods were invested with the attributes of planets, and as such became accountable for the most bizarre occurrences, and kept amazing company. Under the aegis of Mars, to take one instance only, were enrolled the butchers, hangmen, tailors, barbers, cooks, cutlers, carpenters, smiths, physicians, and apothecaries—a band about as "martial" as Falstaff's Thomas Wart and Francis Feeble.[4] And so, in "the temple of mighty Mars the rede" in the *Knight's Tale*, there were depicted, together with the "open werre" which

3. Ovid's *Metamorphoses* includes poetical renderings of myths dealing with the transformation of men and women into birds, flowers, trees, etc.
4. Recruits in Shakespeare's *Henry IV, Part 2.*

was his by virtue of his godhead, the disastrous chances proceeding from his malign ascendancy as planet—the corpse in the bushes with cut throat, the nail driven, like Jael's, into the temple,[5] the sow eating the child in the cradle, the cook scalded in spite of his long ladle. And from among the members of what Chaucer twice calls Mars' "divisioun" there were present—together with the pick-purse, and "the smyler with the knyf under the cloke"—the barber and the butcher and the smith. And in the next paragraph Mars becomes again "this god of armes"—god of war and wicked planet inextricably interfused.

Moreover, as the day and week were conceived in terms of planetary sequence, so the year stood in intricate relation to the *stars*. The sun, with the other planets, moved annually along the vast starry track across the sky which then, as now, was called the zodiac —so called, as Chaucer lucidly explains to "litel Lowis" in the *Treatise on the Astrolabe*, because (and his etymology is sound) "*zodia* in langage of Greek sowneth [signifies] 'bestes' . . . and in the zodiak ben the twelve signes that han names of bestes." These twelve signs, as everybody knows, are Aries, Taurus, Gemini, Cancer, Leo, Virgo, Libra, Scorpio, Sagittarius, Capricornus, Aquarius, Pisces—or, to follow Chaucer's praiseworthy example and translate, Ram, Bull, Twins, Crab, Lion, Virgin, Scales, Scorpion, Archer, Goat, Water-carrier, Fishes. There they were, "eyrish bestes," as Chaucer calls them in a delightful passage that will meet us later, and along their celestial highway passed, from one sign to another, and from house to house, the seven eternal wanderers. To us who read this—though not to countless thousands even yet—the twelve constellations of the zodiac are accidental groupings, to the eye, of infinitely distant suns. To Chaucer's century they were strangely living potencies, and the earth, in the words of a greater than Chaucer, was "this huge stage . . . whereon the stars in secret influence comment." Each sign, with its constellation, had its own individual efficacy or quality—Aries, "the colerik hote signe"; Taurus, cold and dry; and so on through the other ten. Each planet likewise had its own pecular nature—Mars, like Aries, hot and dry; Venus hot and moist; and so on through the other five. And as each planet passed from sign to sign, through the agency of the successive constellations its character and influence underwent change. Chaucer in the *Astrolabe* put the matter in its simplest terms: "Whan an hot planete cometh in-to an hot signe, then encresseth his hete; and yif a planete be cold, thanne amenuseth [diminshes] his coldnesse, by -cause of the hote signe." But there was far more to it than that. For these complex planetary changes exercised a determining influence upon human beings and their affairs. Arcite behind prison bars

---

5. See Judges iv, 17-22.

cries out:

> Som wikke aspect or disposicioun
> Of Saturne, *by sum constellacioun,*
> Hath yeven us this.

And "the olde colde Saturnus" names the constellation:

> Myn is the prison in the derke cote...
> *Whyl I dwelle in the signe of the Leoun.*

The tragedy of Constance, as the Man of Law conceived it, comes about because Mars, at the crucial moment, was in his "derkest hous." Mars gave, on the other hand, the Wife of Bath, as she avers, her "sturdy hardinesse," because Mars, at her birth, was in the constellation Taurus, which was, in astrological terminology, her own "ascendent." And since the constellation Taurus was also the "night house" of Venus, certain other propensities which the wife displayed had been thrust upon her, as she cheerfully averred, by the temporary sojourn of Mars in Venus's house, when she was born.

But the march of the signs along the zodiac touched human life in yet another way. "Everich of thise twelve signes," Chaucer wrote again to his little Lewis, "hath respecte to a certein parcelle of the body of a man and hath it in governance; as Aries hath thyn heved, and Taurus thy nekke and thy throte. Gemini thyn armholes and thyn armes, and so forth." And at once one recalls Sir Toby Belch and Sir Andrew Aguecheek in *Twelfth Night*. "Shall we not set about some revels?" asks Sir Andrew. "What shall we do else?" replies Sir Toby. "Were we not born under Taurus?" "Taurus!" exclaims Sir Andrews, "that's sides and heart." "No, sir," retorts Sir Toby, "it is legs and thighs." And you may still pick up, in the shops of apothecaries here and there, cheaply printed almanacs, designed to advertise quack remedies, in which the naked human figure is displayed with lines drawn from each of the pictured zodiacal signs— Ram, Bull, Crab, Scorpion—to the limbs or organs, legs, thighs, sides, or heart, which that particular sign (in Chaucerian phrase) "hath in governance." It is not only in worn stone and faded parchments that strange fragments of the elder world survive.

QUESTIONS

1. Arrange the steps of Lowes' explanation of medieval time in a different order. Is your order superior to Lowes' or inferior? By what criteria?
2. When the advertising man and the engineer from the electronics laboratory become suburban gardeners, why may they have to reckon with the sky and neglect their watches and calendars?
3. List some ways in which the abstractions of watch and calendar (and time table) "rule" our lives. This list will be a selection from the particulars of daily life. What generalizations about our

society will these particulars justify? Does our society, as focused
in these generalizations, have a mythology—a set of hypothetical
or typical characters going through hypothetical or typical experiences?

SIR JOHN MANDEVILLE[1]

The Earth Is Round

In that land[2] ne in many other beyond that, no man may see the
Star Transmontane, that is clept the Star of the Sea, that is unmov-
able and that is toward the north, that we clepe the Lode-star. But
men see another star, the contrary to him, that is toward the south,
that is clept Antarctic. And right as the ship-men take their advice
here and govern them by the Lode-star, right so do ship-men
beyond those parts by the star of the south, the which star appeareth not to us. And this star that is toward the north, that we clepe
the Lode-star, ne appeareth not to them. For which cause men may
well perceive, that the land and the sea be of round shape and
form; for the part of the firmament sheweth in one country that
sheweth not in another country. And men may well prove by experience and subtle compassment of wit, that if a man found passages
by ships that would go to search the world, men might go by ship
all about the world and above and beneath.

The which thing I prove thus after that I have seen. For I have
been toward the parts of Brabant, and beholden the Astrolabe that
the star that is clept the Transmontane is fifty-three degrees high;
and more further in Almayne and Bohemia it hath fifty-eight
degrees; and more further toward the parts septentrional it is sixty-
two degrees of height and certain minutes; for I myself have measured it by the Astrolabe. Now shall ye know, that against the Transmontane is the tother star that is clept Antarctic, as I have said
before. And those two stars ne move never, and by them turneth all
the firmament right as doth a wheel that turneth by his axle-tree.
So that those stars bear the firmament in two equal parts, so that it
hath as much above as it hath beneath. After this, I have gone
toward the parts meridional, that is, toward the south, and I have
found that in Lybia men see first the star Antarctic. And so far I
have gone more further in those countries, that I have found that
star more high; so that toward the High Lybia it is eighteen degrees
of height and certain minutes (of the which sixty minutes make a
degree). After going by sea and by land toward this country of that
I have spoken, and to other isles and lands beyond that country, I
have found the Star Antarctic of thirty-three degrees of height and

1. Sir John Mandeville is unknown; his travels were written in the late four-teenth century.
2. The Isle of Lamary (Sumatra).

more minutes. And if I had had company and shipping for to go more beyond, I trow well, in certain, that we should have seen all the roundness of the firmament all about. For, as I have said to you before, the half of the firmament is between those two stars, the which halvendel I have seen. And of the tother halvendel I have seen, toward the north under the Transmontane, sixty-two degrees and ten minutes, and toward the part meridional I have seen under the Antarctic, thirty-three degrees and sixteen minutes. And then, the halvendel of the firmament in all holdeth not but nine score degrees. And of those nine score, I have seen sixty-two on that one part and thirty-three on that other part; that be, ninety-five degrees and nigh the halvendel of a degree. And so, there ne faileth but that I have seen all the firmament, save four score and four degrees and the halvendel of a degree, and that is not the fourth part of the firmament; for the fourth part of the roundness of the firmament holds four score and ten degrees, so there faileth but five degrees and an half of the fourth part. And also I have seen the three parts of all the roundness of the firmament and more yet five degrees and a half. By the which I say you certainly that men may environ all the earth of all the world, as well under as above, and turn again to his country, that had company and shipping and conduct. And always he should find men, lands and isles, as well as in this country. For ye wit well, that they that be toward the Antarctic, they be straight, feet against feet, of them that dwell under the Transmontane; also well as we and they that dwell under us be feet against feet. For all the parts of sea and of land have their opposites, habitable or trespassable, and they of this half and beyond half.

And wit well, that, after that that I may perceive and comprehend, the lands of Prester John, Emperor of Ind, be under us. For in going from Scotland or from England toward Jerusalem men go upward always. For our land is in the low part of the earth toward the west, and the land of Prester John is in the low part of the earth toward the east. And [they] have there the day when we have the night; and also, high to the contrary, they have the night when we have the day. For the earth and the sea be of round form and shape, as I have said before; and that that men go upward to one coast, men go downward to another coast.

Also ye have heard me say that Jerusalem is in the midst of the world. And that may men prove, and shew there by a spear, that is pight into the earth, upon the hour of midday, when it is equinox, that sheweth no shadow on no side. And that it should be in the midst of the world, David witnesseth it in the Psalter, where he saith, *Deus operatus est salutem in medio terrae.*[3] Then, they, that part from those parts of the west for to go toward Jerusalem, as many journeys as they go upward for to go thither, in as many jour-

---

3. "God has wrought salvation in the midst of the earth" (Psalms 74:12, in the King James Bible).

neys may they go from Jerusalem unto other confines of the superficiality of the earth beyond. And when men go beyond those journeys toward Ind and to the foreign isles, all is environing the roundness of the earth and of the sea under our countries on this half.

And therefore hath it befallen many times of one thing that I have heard counted when I was young, how a worthy man departed some-time from our countries for to go search the world. And so he passed Ind and the isles beyond Ind, where be more than 5000 isles. And so long he went by sea and land, and so environed the world by many seasons, that he found an isle where he heard speak his own language, calling on oxen in the plough, such words as men speak to beasts in his own country; whereof he had great marvel, for he knew not how it might be. But I say, that he had gone so long by land and by sea, that he had environed all the earth; that he was come again environing, that is to say, going about, unto his own marches, and if he would have passed further, till he had found his country and his own knowledge. But he turned again from thence, from whence he was come from. And so he lost much painful labour, as himself said a great while after that he was come home. For it befell after, that he went into Norway. And there tempest of the sea took him, and he arrived in an isle. And, when he was in that isle, he knew well that it was the isle, where he had heard speak his own language before and the calling of oxen at the plough; and that was possible thing.

But how it seemeth to simple men unlearned, that men ne may not go under the earth, and also that men should fall toward the heaven from under. But that may not be, upon less than we may fall toward heaven from the earth where we be. For from what part of the earth that men dwell, either above or beneath, it seemeth always to them that dwell that they go more right than any other folk. And right as it seemeth to us that they be under us, right so it seemeth to them that we be under them. For if a man might fall from the earth unto the firmament, by greater reason the earth and the sea that be so great and so heavy should fall to the firmament: but that may not be, and therefore saith our Lord God, *Non timeas me, qui suspendi terram ex nihilo?*[4]

And albeit that it be possible thing that men may so environ all the world, natheles, of a thousand persons, one ne might not happen to return into his country. For, for the greatness of the earth and of the sea, men may go by a thousand and a thousand other ways, that no man could ready him perfectly toward the parts that he came from, but if it were by adventure and hap, or by the grace of God. For the earth is full large and full great, and holds in roundness and about environ, by above and by beneath, 20425 miles, after the opinion of old wise astronomers; and their sayings I

4. "Should you not fear me who hangs the world from nothing?" (Job 26:7).

reprove nought. But, after my little wit, it seemeth me, saving their reverence, that it is more.

And for to have better understanding I say thus. Be there imagined a figure that hath a great compass. And, about the point of the great compass that is clept the centre, be made another little compass. Then after, be the great compass devised by lines in many parts, and that all the lines meet at the centre. So, that in as many parts as the great compass shall be departed, in as many shall be departed the little, that is about the centre, albeit that the spaces be less. Now then, be the great compass represented for the firmament, and the little compass represented for the earth. Now then, the firmament is devised by astronomers in twelve signs, and every sign is devised in thirty degrees; that is, 360 degrees that the firmament hath above. Also, be the earth devised in as many parts as the firmament, and let every part answer to a degree of the firmament. And wit it well, that, after the authors of astronomy, 700 furlongs of earth answer to a degree of the firmament, and those be eighty-seven miles and four furlongs. Now be that here multiplied by 360 sithes, and then they be 31,500 miles every of eight furlongs, after miles of our country. So much hath the earth in roundness and of height environ, after mine opinion and mine understanding.

And ye shall understand, that after the opinion of old wise philosophers and astronomers, our country ne Ireland ne Wales ne Scotland ne Norway ne the other isles coasting to them ne be not in the superficiality counted above the earth, as it sheweth by all the books of astronomy. For the superficiality of the earth is parted in seven parts for the seven planets, and those parts be clept climates. And our parts be not of the seven climates, for they be descending toward the west [drawing] towards the roundness of the world. And also these isles of Ind which be even against us be not reckoned in the climates. For they be against us that be in the low country. And the seven climates stretch them environing the world.

KONRAD Z. LORENZ

The Taming of the Shrew[1]

Though Nature, red in tooth and claw,
With ravine, shrieked against his creed.
TENNYSON, *In Memoriam*

All shrews are particularly difficult to keep; this is not because, as we are led proverbially to believe, they are hard to tame, but because the metabolism of these smallest of mammals is so very

1. Chapter 9 of *King Solomon's Ring: New Light on Animal Ways*, 1952.

fast that they will die of hunger within two or three hours if the food supply fails. Since they feed exclusively on small, living animals, mostly insects, and demand, of these, considerably more than their own weight every day, they are most exacting charges. At the time of which I am writing, I had never succeeded in keeping any of the terrestrial shrews alive for any length of time; most of those that I happened to obtain had probably only been caught because they were already ill and they died almost at once. I had never succeeded in procuring a healthy specimen. Now the order Insectivora is very low in the genealogical hierarchy of mammals and is, therefore, of particular interest to the comparative ethologist. Of the whole group, there was only one representative with whose behavior I was tolerably familiar, namely the hedgehog, an extremely interesting animal of whose ethology Professor Herter of Berlin has made a very thorough study. Of the behavior of all other members of the family practically nothing is known. Since they are nocturnal and partly subterranean animals, it is nearly impossible to approach them in field observation, and the difficulty of keeping them in captivity had hitherto precluded their study in the laboratory. So the Insectivores were officially placed on my program.

First I tried to keep the common mole. It was easy to procure a healthy specimen, caught to order in the nursery gardens of my father-in-law, and I found no difficulty in keeping it alive. Immediately on its arrival, it devoured an almost incredible quantity of earthworms which, from the very first moment, it took from my hand. But, as an object of behavior study, it proved most disappointing. Certainly, it was interesting to watch its method of disappearing in the space of a few seconds under the surface of the ground, to study its astoundingly efficient use of its strong, spade-shaped fore-paws, and to feel their amazing strength when one held the little beast in one's hand. And again, it was remarkable with what surprising exactitude it located, by smell, from underground, the earthworms which I put on the surface of the soil in its terrarium. But these observations were the only benefits I derived from it. It never became any tamer and it never remained above ground any longer than it took to devour its prey; after this, it sank into the earth as a submarine sinks into the water. I soon grew tired of procuring the immense quantities of living food it required and, after a few weeks, I set it free in the garden.

It was years afterwards, on an excursion to that extraordinary lake, the Neusiedlersee, which lies on the Hungarian border of Austria, that I again thought of keeping an insectivore. This large stretch of water, though not thirty miles from Vienna, is an example of the peculiar type of lake found in the open steppes of Eastern Europe and Asia. More than thirty miles long and half as broad, its deepest parts are only about five feet deep and it is much shallower on the average. Nearly half its surface is overgrown with reeds which form an ideal habitat for all kinds of water birds. Great colonies of white, purple, and grey heron and spoonbills live among the reeds and, until a short while ago, glossy ibis were still to be found here. Greylag geese breed here in great numbers and, on the eastern, reedless shore, avocets and many other rare waders can regularly be found. On the occasion of which I am speaking, we, a dozen tired zoologists, under the experienced guidance of my friend Otto Koenig, were wending our way, slowly and painfully, through the forest of reeds. We were walking in single file, Koenig first, I second, with a few students in our wake. We literally left a wake, an inky-black one in pale grey water. In the reed forests of Lake Neusiedel, you walk knee deep in slimy, black ooze, wonderfully perfumed by sulphureted-hydrogen–producing bacteria. This mud clings tenaciously and only releases its hold on your foot with a loud, protesting plop at every step.

After a few hours of this kind of wading you discover aching muscles whose very existence you had never suspected. From the knees to the hips you are immersed in the milky, clay-colored water characteristic of the lake, which, among the reeds, is populated by myriads of extremely hungry leeches conforming to the old pharmaceutical recipe, *"Hirudines medicinales maxime affamati."*[2] The rest of your person inhabits the upper air, which here consists of clouds of tiny mosquitoes whose bloodthirsty attacks are all the more exasperating because you require both your hands to part the dense reeds in front of you and can only slap your face at intervals. The British ornithologist who may perhaps have envied us some of our rare specimens will perceive that bird watching on Lake Neusiedel is not, after all, an entirely enviable occupation.

We were thus wending our painful way through the rushes when suddenly Koenig stopped and pointed mutely towards a pond, free from reeds, that stretched in front of us. At first, I could only see whitish water, dark blue sky and green reeds, the standard colors of Lake Neusiedel. Then, suddenly, like a cork popping up on to the surface, there appeared, in the middle of the pool, a tiny black animal, hardly bigger than a man's thumb. And for a moment I was in the rare position of a zoologist who sees a specimen and is not able to classify it, in the literal sense of the word: I did not know to which class of vertebrates the object of my gaze belonged. For the first fraction of a second I took it for the young of some diving bird of a species unknown to me. It appeared to have a beak and it swam on the water like a bird, not in it as a mammal. It swam about in narrow curves and circles, very much like a whirligig beetle, creating an extensive wedge-shaped wake, quite out of proportion to the tiny animal's size. Then a second little beast popped up from below, chased the first one with a shrill, bat-like twitter,

2. "In medicine, the hungriest leech is best."

then both dived and were gone. The whole episode had not lasted five seconds.

I stood open-mouthed, my mind racing. Koenig turned round with a broad grin, calmly detached a leech that was sticking like a leech to his wrist, wiped away the trickle of blood from the wound, slapped his cheek, thereby killing thirty-five mosquitoes, and asked, in the tone of an examiner, "What was that?" I answered as calmly as I could, "water shrews," thanking, in my heart, the leech and the mosquitoes for the respite they had given me to collect my thoughts. But my mind was racing on: water shrews ate fishes and frogs which were easy to procure in any quantity; water shrews were less subterranean than most other insectivores; they were the very insectivore to keep in captivity. "That's an animal I must catch and keep," I said to my friend. "That is easy," he responded. "There is a nest with young under the floor mat of my tent." I had slept that night in his tent and Koenig had not thought it worthwhile to tell me of the shrews; such things are, to him, as much a matter of course as wild little spotted crakes feeding out of his hand, or as any other wonders of his queer kingdom in the reeds.

On our return to the tent that evening, he showed me the nest. It contained eight young which, compared with their mother, who rushed away as we lifted the mat, were of enormous size. They were considerably more than half her length and must each have weighed well between a fourth and a third of their dam: that is to say, the whole litter weighed, at a very modest estimate, twice as much as the old shrew. Yet they were still quite blind and the tips of their teeth were only just visible in their rosy mouths. And two days later when I took them under my care, they were still quite unable to eat even the soft abdomens of grasshoppers, and in spite of evident greed, they chewed interminably on a soft piece of frog's meat without succeeding in detaching a morsel from it. On our journey home, I fed them on the squeezed-out insides of grasshoppers and finely minced frog's meat, a diet on which they obviously throve. Arrived home in Altenberg, I improved on this diet by preparing a food from the squeezed-out insides of mealworm larvae, with some finely chopped small, fresh fishes, worked into a sort of gravy with a little milk. They consumed large quantities of this food, and their little nest-box looked quite small in comparison with the big china bowl whose contents they emptied three times a day. All these observations raise the problem of how the female water shrew succeeds in feeding her gigantic litter. It is absolutely impossible that she should do so on milk alone. Even on a more concentrated diet my young shrews devoured the equivalent of their own weight daily and this meant nearly twice the weight of a grown shrew. Yet, at that time of their lives, young shrews could not possibly engulf a frog or a fish brought whole to them by their mother, as my charges indisputably proved. I can only think that the mother feeds her young by regurgitation of chewed food. Even thus, it is little short of miraculous that the adult female should be able to obtain enough meat to sustain herself and her voracious progeny.

When I brought them home, my young watershrews were still blind. They had not suffered from the journey and were as sleek and fat as one could wish. Their black, glossy coats were reminiscent of moles, but the white color of their underside, as well as the round, streamlined contours of their bodies, reminded me distinctly of penguins, and not, indeed, without justification: both the streamlined form and the light underside are adaptations to a life in the water. Many free-swimming animals, mammals, birds, amphibians and fishes, are silvery-white below in order to be invisible to enemies swimming in the depths. Seen from below, the shining white belly blends perfectly with the reflecting surface film of the water. It is very characteristic of these water animals that the dark dorsal and the white ventral colors do not merge gradually into each other as is the case in "counter-shaded" land animals whose coloring is calculated to make them invisible by eliminating the contrasting shade on their undersides. As in the killer whale, in dolphins, and in penguins, the white underside of the watershrew is divided from the dark upper side by a sharp line which runs, often in very decorative curves, along the animal's flank. Curiously enough, this borderline between black and white showed considerable variations in individuals and even on both sides of one animal's body. I welcomed this, since it enabled me to recognize my shrews personally.

Three days after their arrival in Altenberg my eight shrew babies opened their eyes and began, very cautiously, to explore the precincts of their nest-box. It was now time to remove them to an appropriate container, and on this question I expended much hard thinking. The enormous quantity of food they consumed and, consequently, of excrement they produced, made it impossible to keep them in an ordinary aquarium whose water, within a day, would have become a stinking brew. Adequate sanitation was imperative for particular reasons; in ducks, grebes, and all waterfowl, the plumage must be kept perfectly dry if the animal is to remain in a state of health, and the same premise may reasonably be expected to hold good of the shrew's fur. Now water which has been polluted soon turns strongly alkaline and this I knew to be very bad for the plumage of waterbirds. It causes saponification of the fat to which the feathers owe their waterproof quality, and the bird becomes thoroughly wet and is unable to stay on the water. I hold the record, as far as I know hitherto unbroken by any other birdlover, for having kept dabchicks alive and healthy in captivity for nearly two years, and even then they did not die but escaped, and may still be living. My experience with these birds proved the absolute necessity of keeping the water perfectly clean; whenever it became a little dirty I noticed their feathers beginning to get wet, a danger which they anxiously tried to counteract by constantly preening themselves. I had, therefore, to keep these little grebes in crystal clear water which was changed every day, and I rightly assumed that the same would be necessary for my water shrews.

I took a large aquarium tank, rather over a yard in length and about two feet wide. At each end of this, I placed two little tables, and weighed them down with heavy stones so that they would not float. Then I filled up the tank until the water was level with the tops of the tables. I did not at first push the tables close against the panes of the tank, which was rather narrow, for fear that the shrews might become trapped underwater in the blind alley beneath a table and drown there; this precaution, however, subsequently proved unnecessary. The water shrew which, in its natural state, swims great distances under the ice, is quite able to find its way to the open surface in much more difficult situations. The nest-box, which was placed on one of the tables, was equipped with a sliding shutter, so that I could imprison the shrews whenever the container had to be cleaned. In the morning, at the hour of general cage-cleaning, the shrews were usually at home and asleep, so that the procedure caused them no appreciable disturbance. I will admit that I take great pride in devising, by creative imagination, suitable containers for animals of which nobody, myself included, has had any previous experience, and it was particularly gratifying that the contraption described above proved so satisfactory that I never had to alter even the minutest detail.

When first my baby shrews were liberated in this container they took a very long time to explore the top of the table on which their nest-box was standing. The water's edge seemed to exert a strong attraction; they approached it ever and again, smelled the surface and seemed to feel along it with the long, fine whiskers which surround their pointed snouts like a halo and represent not only their most important organ of touch but the most important of all their sensory organs. Like other aquatic mammals, the water shrew differs from the terrestrial members of its class in that its nose, the guiding organ of the average mammal, is of no use whatsoever in its underwater hunting. The water shrew's whiskers are actively mobile like the antennae of an insect or the fingers of a blind man.

Exactly as mice and many other small rodents would do under similar conditions, the shrews interrupted their careful exploration of their new surroundings every few minutes to dash wildly back into the safe cover of their nest-box. The survival value of this peculiar behavior is evident: the animal makes sure, from time to time that it has not lost its way and that it can, at a moment's notice, retreat to the one place it knows to be safe. It was a queer spectacle to see those podgy black figures slowly and carefully whiskering their way forward and, in the next second, with lightning speed, dash back to the nest-box. Queerly enough, they did not run straight through the little door, as one would have expected, but in their wild dash for safety they jumped, one and all, first onto the roof of the box and only then, whiskering along its edge, found the opening and slipped in with a half somersault, their back turned nearly vertically downward. After many repetitions of this maneuver, they were able to find the opening without feeling for it; they "knew" perfectly its whereabouts yet still persisted in the leap onto the roof. They jumped onto it and immediately vaulted in through the door, but they never, as long as they lived, found out that the leap and vault which had become their habit was really quite unnecessary and that they could have run in directly without this extraordinary detour. We shall hear more about this dominance of path habits in the water shrew presently.

It was only on the third day, when the shrews had become thoroughly acquainted with the geography of their little rectangular island, that the largest and most enterprising of them ventured into the water. As is so often the case with mammals, birds, reptiles, and fishes, it was the largest and most handsomely colored male which played the role of leader. First he sat on the edge of the water and thrust in the fore part of his body, at the same time frantically paddling with his forelegs but still clinging with his hind ones to the board. Then he slid in, but in the next moment took fright, scampered madly across the surface very much after the manner of a frightened duckling, and jumped out onto the board at the opposite end of the tank. There he sat, excitedly grooming his belly with one hind paw, exactly as coypus and beavers do. Soon he quieted down and sat still for a moment. Then he went to the water's edge a second time, hesitated for a moment, and plunged in; diving immediately, he swam ecstatically about underwater, swerving upward and downward again, running quickly along the bottom, and finally jumping out of the water at the same place as he had first entered it.

When I first saw a water shrew swimming I was most struck by a thing which I ought to have expected but did not: at the moment of diving, the little black and white beast appears to be made of silver. Like the plumage of ducks and grebes, but quite unlike the fur of most water mammals, such as seals, otters, beavers or coypus, the fur of the water shrew remains absolutely dry under water, that is to say, it retains a thick layer of air while the animal is below the surface. In the other mammals mentioned above, it is only the short, woolly undercoat that remains dry, the superficial hair tips becoming wet, wherefore the animal looks its natural color when underwater and is superficially wet when it emerges. I was already aware of the peculiar qualities of the waterproof fur of the shrew, and, had I given it a thought, I should have known that it would look, under water, exactly like the air-retaining fur on the underside of a water beetle or on the abdomen of a water spider. Nevertheless the wonderful, transparent silver coat of the shrew was, to me, one of those delicious surprises that nature has in store for her admirers.

Another surprising detail which I only noticed when I saw my shrews in the water was that they have a fringe of stiff, erectile hairs on the outer side of their fifth toes and on the underside of their tails. These form collapsible oars and a collapsible rudder. Folded and inconspicuous as long as the animal is on dry land, they unfold the moment it enters the water and broaden the effective surface of the propelling feet and of the steering tail by a considerable area.

Like penguins, the water shrews looked rather awkward and ungainly on dry land but were transformed into objects of elegance and grace on entering the water. As long as they walked, their strongly convex underside made them look pot-bellied and reminiscent of an old, overfed dachshund. But under water, the very same protruding belly balanced harmoniously the curve of their back and gave a beautifully symmetrical streamline which, together with their silver coating and the elegance of their movements, made them a sight of entrancing beauty.

When they had all become familiar with the water, their container was one of the chief attractions that our research station had to offer to any visiting naturalists or animal lovers. Unlike all other mammals of their size, the water shrews were largely diurnal and, except in the early hours of the morning, three or four of them were constantly on the scene. It was exceedingly interesting to watch their movements upon and under the water. Like the whirligig beetle, Gyrinus, they could turn in an extremely small radius without diminishing their speed, a faculty for which the large rudder surface of the tail with its fringe of erectile hairs is evidently essential. They had two different ways of diving, either by taking a little jump as grebes or coots do and working their way down at a steep angle, or by simply lowering their snout under the surface and paddling very fast till they reached "planing speed," thus working their way downward on the principle of the inclined plane—in other words, performing the converse movement of an ascending airplane. The water shrew must expend a large amount of energy in staying down since the air contained in its fur exerts a strong pull upwards. Unless it is paddling straight downwards, a thing it rarely does, it is forced to maintain a constant minimum speed, keeping its body at a slightly downward angle in order not to float to the surface. While swimming under water the shrew seems to flatten, broadening its body in a peculiar fashion, in order to present a better planing surface to the water. I never saw my shrews try to cling by their claws to any underwater objects, as the dipper is alleged to do. When they seemed to be running along the bottom, they were really swimming close above it, but perhaps the smooth gravel on the bottom of the tank was unsuitable for holding on to and it did not occur to me then to offer them a rougher surface. They were very playful when in the water and chased one another loudly twittering on the surface, or silently in the depths. Unlike any other mammal, but just like water birds, they could rest on the surface; this they used to do, rolling partly over and grooming themselves. Once out again, they instantly proceeded to clean their fur—one is almost tempted to say "preen" it, so similar was their behavior to that of ducks which have just left the water after a long swim.

Most interesting of all was their method of hunting under water. They came swimming along with an erratic course, darting a foot or so forward very swiftly in a straight line, then starting to gyrate in looped turns at reduced speed. While swimming straight and swiftly their whiskers were, as far as I could see, laid flat against their head, but while circling they were erect and bristled out in all directions, as they sought contact with some prey. I have no reason to believe that vision plays any part in the water shrew's hunting, except perhaps in the activation of its tactile search. My shrews may have noticed visually the presence of the live tadpoles or little fishes which I put in the tank, but in the actual hunting of its prey the animal is exclusively guided by its sense of touch, located in the wide-spreading whiskers on its snout. Certain small free-swimming species of catfish find their prey by exactly the same method. When these fishes swim fast and straight, the long feelers on their snout are depressed but, like the shrew's whiskers, are stiffly spread out when the fish becomes conscious of the proximity of potential prey; like the shrew, the fish then begins to gyrate blindly in order to establish contact with its prey. It may not even be necessary for the water shrew actually to touch its prey with one of its whiskers. Perhaps, at very close range, the water vibration caused by the movements of a small fish, a tadpole or a water insect is perceptible by those sensitive tactile organs. It is quite impossible to determine this question by mere observation, for the action is much too quick for the human eye. There is a quick turn and a snap and the shrew is already paddling shorewards with a wriggling creature in its maw.

In relation to its size, the water shrew is perhaps the most terrible predator of all vertebrate animals, and it can even vie with the invertebrates, including the murderous Dytiscus larva. It has been reported by A. E. Brehm that water shrews have killed fish more than sixty times heavier than themselves by biting out their eyes and brain. This happened only when the fish were confined in containers with no room for escape. The same story has been told to me by fishermen on Lake Neusiedel, who could not possibly have heard Brehm's report. I once offered to my shrews a large edible frog. I never did it again, nor could I bear to see out to its end the cruel scene that ensued. One of the shrews encountered the frog in the basin and instantly gave chase, repeatedly seizing hold of the creature's legs; although it was kicked off again it did not cease in its attack and finally, the frog, in desperation, jumped out of the water and onto one of the tables, where several shrews raced to the pursuer's assistance and buried their teeth in the legs and hindquarters of the wretched frog. And now, horribly, they began to eat the frog alive, beginning just where each one of them happened to have hold of it; the poor frog croaked heartrendingly, as the jaws of the shrews munched audibly in chorus. I need hardly be blamed for bringing this experiment to an abrupt and agitated end and putting the lacerated frog out of its misery. I never offered the shrews large prey again but only such as would be killed at the first bite or two. Nature can be very cruel indeed; it is not out of pity that most of the larger predatory animals kill their prey quickly. The lion has to finish off a big antelope or a buffalo very quickly indeed in order not to get hurt itself, for a beast of prey which has to hunt daily cannot afford to receive even a harmless scratch in effecting a kill; such scratches would soon add up to such an extent as to put the killer out of action. The same reason has forced the python and other large snakes to evolve a quick and really humane method of killing the well-armed mammals that are their natural prey. But where there is no danger of the victim doing damage to the killer, the latter shows no pity whatsoever. The hedgehog which, by virtue of its armor, is quite immune to the bite of a snake, regularly proceeds to eat it, beginning at the tail or in the middle of its body, and in the same way the water shrew treats its innocuous prey. But man should abstain from judging his innocently-cruel fellow creatures, for even if nature sometimes "shrieks against his creed," what pain does he himself not inflict upon the living creatures that he hunts for pleasure and not for food?

The mental qualities of the water shrew cannot be rated very high. They were quite tame and fearless of me and never tried to bite when I took them in my hand, nor did they ever try to evade it, but, like little tame rodents, they tried to dig their way out if I held them for too long in the hollow of my closed fist. Even when I took them out of their container and put them on a table or on the floor, they were by no means thrown into a panic but were quite ready to take food out of my hand and even tried actively to creep into it if they felt a longing for cover. When, in such an unwonted environment, they were shown their nest-box, they plainly showed that they knew it by sight and instantly made for it, and even pursued it with upraised heads if I moved the box along above them, just out of their reach. All in all, I really may pride myself that I have tamed the shrew, or at least one member of that family.

In their accustomed surroundings, my shrews proved to be very strict creatures of habit. I have already mentioned the remarkable conservatism with which they persevered in their unpractical way of entering their nest-box by climbing onto its roof and then vaulting, with a half turn, in through the door. Something more must be said about the unchanging tenacity with which these animals cling to their habits once they have formed them. In the water shrew, the path habits, in particular, are of a really amazing immutability; I hardly know another instance to which the saying, "As the twig is bent, so the tree is inclined," applies so literally.

In a territory unknown to it, the water shrew will never run fast except under pressure of extreme fear, and then it will run blindly along, bumping into objects and usually getting caught in a blind alley. But, unless the little animal is severely frightened, it moves in strange surroundings, only step by step, whiskering right and left all the time and following a path that is anything but straight. Its course is determined by a hundred fortuitous factors when it walks that way for the first time. But, after a few repetitions, it is evident that the shrew recognizes the locality in which it finds itself and that it repeats, with the utmost exactitude, the movements which it performed the previous time. At the same time, it is noticeable that the animal moves along much faster whenever it is repeating what it has already learned. When placed on a path which it has already traversed a few times, the shrew starts on its way slowly, carefully whiskering. Suddenly it finds known bearings, and now rushes forward a short distance, repeating exactly every step and turn which it executed on the last occasion. Then, when it comes to a spot where it ceases to know the way by heart, it is reduced to whiskering again and to feeling its way step by step. Soon, another burst of speed follows and the same thing is repeated, bursts of speed alternating with very slow progress. In the beginning of this process of learning their way, the shrews move along at an extremely slow average rate and the little bursts of speed are few and far between. But gradually the little laps of the course which have been "learned by heart" and which can be covered quickly begin to increase in length as well as in number until they fuse and the whole course can be completed in a fast, unbroken rush.

Often, when such a path habit is almost completely formed, there still remains one particularly difficult place where the shrew always loses its bearings and has to resort to its senses of smell and touch, sniffing and whiskering vigorously to find out where the next reach of its path "joins on." Once the shrew is well settled in its path habits it is as strictly bound to them as a railway engine to its tracks and as unable to deviate from them by even a few centimeters. If it diverges from its path by so much as an inch, it is forced to stop abruptly, and laboriously regain its bearings. The same behavior can be caused experimentally by changing some small detail in the customary path of the animal. Any major alteration in the habitual path threw the shrews into complete confusion. One of their paths ran along the wall adjoining the wooden table opposite to that on which the nest box was situated. This table was weighted with two stones lying close to the panes of the tank, and the shrews, running along the wall, were accustomed to jump on and off the stones which lay right in their path. If I moved the stones out of the runway, placing both together in the middle of the table, the shrews would jump right up into the air in the place where the stone should have been; they came down with a jarring bump, were obviously disconcerted and started whiskering cautiously right and left, just as they behaved in an unknown environment. And then they did a most interesting thing: they went back the way they had come, carefully feeling their way until they had again got their bearings. Then, facing round again, they tried a second time with a rush and jumped and crashed down exactly as they had done a few seconds before. Only then did they seem to realize that the first fall had not been their own fault but was due to a change in the wonted pathway, and now they proceeded to explore the alteration, cautiously sniffing and bewhiskering the place where the stone ought to have been. This method of going back to the start, and trying again always reminded me of a small boy who, in reciting a poem, gets stuck and begins again at an earlier verse.

In rats, as in many small mammals, the process of forming a path habit, for instance in learning a maze, is very similar to that just described; but a rat is far more adaptable in its behavior and would not dream of trying to jump over a stone which was not there. The preponderance of motor habit over present perception is a most remarkable peculiarity of the water shrew. One might say that the animal actually disbelieves its senses if they report a change of environment which necessitates a sudden alteration in its motor habits. In a new environment a water shrew would be perfectly able to see a stone of that size and consequently to avoid it or to run over it in a manner well adapted to the spatial conditions; but once a habit is formed and has become ingrained, it supersedes all better knowledge. I know of no animal that is a slave to its habits in so literal a sense as the water shrew. For this animal the geometric axiom that a straight line is the shortest distance between two points simply does not hold good. To them, the shortest line is always the accustomed path and, to a certain extent, they are justified in adhering to this principle: they run with amazing speed along their pathways and arrive at their destination much sooner than they would if, by whiskering and nosing, they tried to go straight. They will keep to the wonted path, even though it winds in such a way that it crosses and recrosses itself. A rat or mouse would be quick to discover that it was making an unnecessary detour, but the water shrew is no more able to do so than is a toy train to turn off at right angles at a level crossing. In order to change its route, the water shrew must change its whole path habit, and this cannot be done at a moment's notice but gradually, over a long period of time. An unnecessary, loop-shaped detour takes weeks and weeks to become a little shorter, and after months it is not even approximately straight. The biological advantage of such a path habit is obvious: it compensates the shrew for being nearly blind and enables it to run exceedingly fast without wasting a minute on orientation. On the other hand it may, under unusual circumstances, lead the shrew to destruction. It has been reported, quite plausibly, that water shrews have broken their necks by jumping into a pond which had been recently drained. In spite of the possibility of such mishaps, it would be shortsighted if one were simply to stigmatize the water shrew as stupid because it solves the spatial problems of its daily life in quite a different way from man. On the contrary, if one thinks a little more deeply, it is very wonderful that the same result, namely a perfect orientation in space, can be brought about in two so widely divergent ways: by true observation, as we achieve it, or, as the water shrew does, by learning by heart every possible spatial contingency that may arise in a given territory.

Among themselves, my water shrews were surprisingly good-natured. Although, in their play, they would often chase each other, twittering with a great show of excitement, I never saw a serious fight between them until an unfortunate accident occurred: one morning, I forgot to reopen the little door of the nest-box after cleaning out their tank. When at last I remembered, three hours had elapsed—a very long time for the swift metabolism of such small insectivores. Upon the opening of the door, all the shrews rushed out and made a dash for the food tray. In their haste to get out, not only did they soil themselves all over but they apparently discharged, in their excitement, some sort of glandular secretion, for a strong, musk-like odor accompanied their exit from the box. Since they appeared to have incurred no damage by their three hours' fasting, I turned away from the box to occupy myself with other things. However, on nearing the container soon afterwards, I heard an unusually loud, sharp twittering and, on my hurried approach, found my eight shrews locked in deadly battle. Two were even then dying and, though I consigned them at once to separate cages, two more died in the course of the day. The real cause of this sudden and terrible battle is hard to ascertain but I cannot help suspecting that the shrews, owing to the sudden change in the usual odor, had failed to recognize each other and had fallen upon each other as they would have done upon strangers. The four survivors quietened down after a certain time and I was able to reunite them in the original container without fear of further mishap.

I kept those four remaining shrews in good health for nearly seven months and would probably have had them much longer if the assistant whom I had engaged to feed them had not forgotten to do so. I had been obliged to go to Vienna and, on my return in the late afternoon, was met by that usually reliable fellow who turned pale when he saw me, thereupon remembering that he had forgotten to feed the shrews. All four of them were alive but very weak; they ate greedily when we fed them but died nonetheless within a few hours. In other words, they showed exactly the same symptoms as the shrews which I had formerly tried to keep; this confirmed my opinion that the latter were already dying of hunger when they came into my possession.

To any advanced animal keeper who is able to set up a large tank, preferably with running water, and who can obtain a sufficient supply of small fish, tadpoles, and the like, I can recommend the water shrew as one of the most gratifying, charming, and interesting objects of care. Of course it is a somewhat exacting charge. It will eat raw chopped heart (the customary substitute for small live prey) only in the absence of something better and it cannot be fed exclusively on this diet for long periods. Moreover, really clean water is indispensable. But if these clear-cut requirements be fulfilled, the water shrew will not merely remain alive but will really thrive, nor do I exclude the possibility that it might even breed in captivity.

QUESTIONS

1. Lorenz discusses a field trip and some other matters before he reports his laboratory observations. What is the effect of this organization?
2. What features of the shrew's behavior does Lorenz select for special emphasis? What conclusions does he draw about these features?
3. Though this is mainly a report of his observations, Lorenz includes matters which are not necessary to the report of strictly controlled observation of the shrew's habits. Indicate some of the places where his discussion moves beyond strict reporting. Characterize the roles he assumes in these passages. Do these other roles or revelations of personality compromise or support his claim to being a scientist?

NIKO TINBERGEN

The Bee-Hunters of Hulshorst[1]

On a sunny day in the summer of 1929 I was walking rather aimlessly over the sands, brooding and a little worried. I had just done my finals, had got a half-time job, and was hoping to start on

---

1. Hulshorst is the sparsely populated region in Holland where Tinbergen's observations and experiments were carried out.

1034 · *Niko Tinbergen*

research for a doctor's thesis. I wanted very much to work on some problem of animal behaviour and had for that reason rejected some suggestions of my well-meaning supervisor. But rejecting sound advice and taking one's own decisions are two very different things, and so far I had been unable to make up my mind.

While walking about, my eye was caught by a bright orange-yellow wasp the size of the ordinary jam-loving *Vespa*. It was busying itself in a strange way on the bare sand. With brisk, jerky movements it was walking slowly backwards, kicking the sand behind it as it proceeded. The sand flew away with every jerk. I was sure that this was a digger wasp. The only kind of that size I knew was *Bembex*, the large fly-killer. But this was no *Bembex*. I stopped to watch it, and soon saw that it was shovelling sand out of a burrow. After ten minutes of this, it turned round, and now, facing away from the entrance, began to rake loose sand over it. In a minute the entrance was completely covered. Then the wasp flew up, circled a few times round the spot, describing wider and wider loops in the air, and finally flew off. Knowing something of the way of digger wasps, I expected it to return with a prey within a reasonable time, and decided to wait.

Sitting down on the sand, I looked round and saw that I had blundered into what seemed to be a veritable wasp town. Within ten yards I saw more than twenty wasps occupied at their burrows. Each burrow had a patch of yellow sand round it the size of a hand, and to judge from the number of these sand patches there must have been hundreds of burrows.

I had not to wait long before I saw a wasp coming home. It descended slowly from the sky, alighting after the manner of a helicopter on a sand patch. Then I saw that it was carrying a load, a dark object about its own size. Without losing hold if it, the wasp made a few raking movements with its front legs, the entrance became visible and, dragging its load after it, the wasp slipped into the hole.

At the next opportunity I robbed a wasp of its prey, by scaring it on its arrival, so that it dropped its burden. Then I saw that the prey was a Honey Bee.

I watched these wasps at work all through that afternoon, and soon became absorbed in finding out exactly what was happening in this busy insect town. It seemed that the wasps were spending part of their time working at their burrows. Judging from the amount of sand excavated these must have been quite deep. Now and then a wasp would fly out and, after half an hour or longer, return with a load, which was then dragged in. Every time I examined the prey, it was a Honey Bee. No doubt they captured all these bees on the heath for all to and fro traffic was in the direction of the south-east, where I knew the nearest heath to be. A rough calculation showed that something was going on here that would not please the owners of the bee-hives on the heath; on a sunny day like this several thousand bees fell victims to this large colony of killers.

As I was watching the wasps, I began to realize that here was a wonderful opportunity for doing exactly the kind of field work I would like to do. Here were many hundreds of digger wasps—exactly which species I did not know yet, but that would not be difficult to find out. I had little doubt that each wasp was returning regularly to its own burrow, which showed that they must have excellent powers of homing. How did they manage to find their way back to their own burrow? * * *

Settling down to work, I started spending the wasps' working days (which lasted from about 8 a.m. till 6 p.m. and so did not put too much of a strain on me) on the 'Philanthus plains', as we called this part of the sands as soon as we had found out that *Philanthus triangulum Fabr.* was the official name of this bee-killing digger wasp. Its vernacular name was 'Bee-Wolf'.

An old chair, field glasses, note-books, and food and water for the day were my equipment. The local climate of the open sands was quite amazing, considering that ours is a temperate climate. Surface temperatures of 110° F were not rare.* * *

My first job was to find out whether each wasp was really limited to one burrow, as I suspected from the unhesitating way in which the home-coming wasps alighted on the sand patches in front of the burrows. I installed myself in a densely populated quarter of the colony, five yards or so from a group of about twenty-five nests. Each burrow was marked and mapped. Whenever I saw a wasp at work at a burrow, I caught it and, after a short unequal struggle, adorned its back with one or two colour dots (using quickly drying enamel paint) and released it. Such wasps soon returned to work, and after a few hours I had ten wasps, each marked with a different combination of colours, working right in front of me. It was remarkable how this simple trick of marking my wasps changed my whole attitude to them. From members of the species *Philanthus triangulum* they were transformed into personal acquaintances, whose lives from that very moment became affairs of the most personal interest and concern to me.

While waiting for events to develop, I spent my time having a close look at the wasps. A pair of lenses mounted on a frame that could be worn as spectacles enabled me, by crawling up slowly to a working wasp, to observe it, much enlarged, from a few inches away. When seen under such circumstances most insects reveal a marvellous beauty, totally unexpected as long as you observe them with the unaided eye. Through my lenses I could look at my *Philanthus* right into their huge compound eyes; I saw their enormous, claw-like jaws which they used for crumbling up the sandy crust; I saw their agile black antennae in continuous, restless movement; I watched their yellow, bristled legs rake away the loose sand with such vigour that it flew through the air in rhythmic puffs, landing several inches behind them.

Soon several of my marked wasps stopped working at their burrows, raked loose sand back over the entrance, and flew off. The take-off was often spectacular. Before leaving they circled a little while over the burrow, at first low above the ground, soon higher, describing ever widening loops; then flew away, but returned to cruise once more low over the nest. Finally, they would set out in a bee-line, fifteen to thirty feet above the ground, a rapidly vanishing speck against the blue sky. All the wasps disappeared towards the south-east. Half a mile away in that direction the bare sands bordered upon an extensive heath area, buzzing with bees. This, as I was to see later, was the wasps' hunting area.

The curious loops my wasps described in the air before leaving their home area had been described by other observers of many other digger wasps. Philip Rau had given them the name of 'locality studies'. Yet so far nobody proved that they deserved that name; that the wasps actually took in the features of the burrow's surroundings while circling above them. To check this if possible was one of my aims—I thought that it was most probable that the wasps would use landmarks, and that this locality study was what the name implied. First, however, I had to make sure that my marked wasps would return to their own holes.* * *

Before the first day was over, each of them had returned with a bee; some had returned twice or even three times. At the end of that day it was clear that each of them had its own nest, to which it returned regularly.

On subsequent days I extended these observations and found out some more facts about the wasps' daily life. As in other species, the digging of the large burrows and the capturing of prey that served as food for the larvae was exclusively the task of the females. And a formidable task it was. The wasps spent hours digging the long shafts, and throwing the sand out. Often they stayed down for a long time and, waiting for them to reappear, my patience was often put to a hard test. Eventually, however, there would be some almost imperceptible movement in the sand, and a small mound of damp soil was gradually lifted up, little by little, as if a miniature Mole were at work. Soon the wasp emerged, tail first, and all covered with sand. One quick shake, accompanied by a sharp staccato buzz, and the wasp was clean. Then it began to mop up, working as if possessed, shovelling the sand several inches away from the entrance.

I often tried to dig up the burrows to see their inner structure. Usually the sand crumbled and I lost track of the passage before I was ten inches down, but sometimes, by gently probing with a grass shoot first, and then digging down along it, I succeeded in getting down to the cells. These were found opening into the far end of the shaft, which itself was a narrow tube, often more than 2 ft. long. Each cell contained an egg or a larva with a couple of Honey Bees, its food store. A burrow contained from one to five cells. Each larva had its own living-room-cum-larder in the house, provided by the hard-working female. From the varying nunber of cells I found in the nests, and the varying ages of the larvae in one burrow, I concluded that the female usually filled each cell with bees before she started to dig a new cell, and I assumed that it was the tunnelling out of a new cell that made her stay down for such long spells.

I did not spend much time digging up the burrows, for I wanted to observe the wasps while they were undisturbed. Now that I was certain that each wasp returned regularly to her own burrow, I was faced with the problem of her orientation. The entire valley was littered with the yellow sand patches; how could a wasp, after a hunting trip of about a mile in all, find exactly her own burrow?

Having seen the wasps make their 'locality studies', I naturally believed that each female actually did what this term implied: take her bearings. A simple test suggested that this was correct. While a wasp was away I brushed over the ground surrounding the nest entrance, moving all possible landmarks such as pebbles, twigs, tufts of grass, Pine cones, etc, so that over an area of 3–4 square metres none of them remained in exactly the same place as before. The burrow itself, however, I left intact. Then I awaited the wasp's return. When she came, slowly descending from the skies, carrying her bee, her behaviour was striking. All went well until she was about 4 ft. above the ground. There she suddenly stopped, dashed back and forth as if in panic, hung motionless in the air for a while, then flew back and up in a wide loop, came slowly down again in the same way, and again shied at the same distance from the nest. Obviously she was severely disturbed. Since I had left the nest itself, its entrance, and the sand patch in front of it untouched, this showed that the wasp was affected by the change in the surroundings.

Gradually she calmed down, and began to search low over the disturbed area. But she seemed to be unable to find the nest. She alighted now here, now there, and began to dig tentatively at a variety of places at the approximate site of the nest entrance. After a while she dropped her bee and started a through trial-and-error search. After twenty-five minutes or so she stumbled on the nest entrance as if by accident, and only then did she take up her bee and drag it in. A few minutes later she came out again, closed the entrance, and set off. And now she had a nice surprise in store for me: upon leaving she made an excessively long 'locality study': for fully two minutes she circled and circled, coming back again and again to fly over the disturbed area before she finally zoomed off.

I waited for another hour and a half, and had the satisfaction of seeing her return once more. And what I had hoped for actually happened: there was scarcely a trace of hesitation this time. Not only had the wasp lost her shyness of the disturbed soil, but she now knew her way home perfectly well.

I repeated this test with a number of wasps, and their reactions to my interference were roughly the same each time. It seemed probable, therefore, that the wasps found their way home by using something like landmarks in the environment, and not by responding to some stimulus (visual or otherwise) sent out by the nest itself. I had now to test more critically whether this was actually the case.

The test I did next was again quite simple. If a wasp used landmarks it should be possible to do more than merely disturb her by throwing her beacons all over the place; I ought to be able to mislead her, to make her go to the wrong place, by moving the whole constellation of her landmarks over a certain distance. I did this at a few nests that were situated on bare sandy soil and that had only a few, but conspicuous, objects nearby, such as twigs, or tufts of grass. After the owner of such a nest was gone, I moved these two or three objects a foot to the south-west, roughly at right angles to the expected line of approach. The result was as I had hoped for and expected, and yet I could not help being surprised as well as delighted: each wasp missed her own nest, and alighted at exactly the spot where the nest 'ought' to be according to the landmarks' new positions! I could vary my tests by very cautiously shooing the wasp away, then moving the beacons a foot in another direction, and allowing the wasp to alight again. In whatever position I put the beacons, the wasp would follow them. At the end of such a series of tests I replaced the landmarks in their original position, and this finally enabled the wasp to return to her home. Thus the tests always had a happy ending—for both of us. This was no pure altruism on my part—I could now use the wasp for another test if I wished.

When engaged in such work, it is always worth observing oneself as well as the animals, and to do it as critically and as detachedly as possible—which, of course, is a tall order. I have often wondered why the outcome of such a test delighted me so much. A rationalist would probably like to assume that it was the increased predictability resulting from the test. This was a factor of considerable importance, I am sure. But a more important factor still (not only to me, but to many other people I have watched in this situation) is of a less dignified type: people enjoy, they relish the satisfaction of their desire for power. The truth of this was obvious, for instance, in people who enjoyed seeing the wasps being misled without caring much for the intellectual question whether they used landmarks or not. I am further convinced that even the joy of gaining insight was not often very pure either; it was mixed with pride at having had success with the tests.

To return to the wasps: next I tried to make the wasps use landmarks which I provided. This was not only for the purpose of satisfying my lust for power, but also for nobler purposes, as I hope to show later. Since changing the environment while the wasp was away disturbed her upon her return and even might prevent her from finding her nest altogether, I waited until a wasp had gone down into her nest, and then put my own landmarks round the entrance—sixteen Pine cones arranged in a circle of about eight inches diameter.

The first wasp to emerge was a little upset, and made a rather long locality study. On her return home, she hesitated for some time, but eventually alighted at the nest. When next she went out she made a really thorough locality study, and from then on everything went smoothly. Other wasps behaved in much the same way, and next day regular work was going on at five burrows so treated. I now subjected all five wasps, one by one, to a displacement test similar to those already described. The results, however, were not clearcut. Some wasps, upon returning, followed the cones; but others were not fooled, and went straight home, completely ignoring my beacons. Others again seemed to be unable to make up their minds, and oscillated between the real nest and the ring of cones. This half-hearted behaviour did not disturb me, however, for if my idea was correct—that the wasps use landmarks—one would rather expect that my tests put the wasps in a kind of conflict situation: the natural landmarks which they must have been using before I gave them the Pine cones were still in their original position; only the cones had been moved. And while the cones were very conspicuous landmarks, they had been there for no more than one day. I therefore put all the cone-rings back and waited for two more days before testing the wasps again. And sure enough, this time the tests gave a hundred per cent preference for the Pine cones; I had made the wasps train themselves to my landmarks.

The rest of this first summer I spent mainly in consolidating this result in various ways. There was not much time to do this, for the season lasts only two months; by the end of August the wasps became sluggish, and soon after they died, leaving the destiny of their race in the hands of the pupae deep down in the sand, which were to lie there dormant until next July. And even in this short summer season the wasps could not work steadily, but were active on dry sunny days only—and of these a Dutch summer rarely supplies more than about twenty in all.

However, I had time to make sure that the wasps relied for their homing mainly on vision. First, I could cut off their antennae—the bearers of delicate organs of smell, of touch and of other sense organs—without at all disturbing the orientation. Second, when, in other tests, I covered the eyes of intact wasps with black paint, the wasps could not fly at all. Removing the cover of paint restored their eyesight, and with it their normal behaviour. Furthermore, when I trained a wasp to accept a circle of Pine cones together with two small squares of cardboard drenched in Pine oil, which gave off a strong scent, displacement of the cones would mislead the wasps in the usual way, but moving the scented squares had not the slightest effect. Finally, when wasps used to rings of cones were given, instead of cones, a ring of grey pebbles a foot from the nest, they followed these pebbles. This can only have been due to the pebbles being visually similar to the cones.

* * *

We began by investigating the wasp's 'locality study' a little more closely. As I mentioned before, we had already quite suggestive indications that it really deserved this name, but clear-cut proof was still lacking. The otherwise annoying vagaries of the Atlantic climate provided us with a wonderful opportunity to get this proof. Long spells of cold rainy weather are not uncommon in a Dutch summer —in fact they are more common than periods of sunny weather, which alone could tempt the wasps to 'work'. Rainy weather put a strain on morale in our camp, but the first sign of improvement usually started an outburst of feverish activity, all of us doing our utmost to be ready for the wasps before they could resume their flights.

We had previously noticed that many (though not all) wasps spent cold and wet periods in their burrows. Rain and wind often played havoc with their landmarks and perhaps the wasps also forgot their exact position while sitting indoors. At any rate, with the return of good weather, all the wasps made prolonged 'locality studies' when setting out on their first trip. Could it be that they had to learn anew the lie of the land?

On one such morning, while the ground was still wet but the weather sunny and promising, we were at the colony at 7.30 a.m. Each of us took up a position near a group of nests and watched for the first signs of emerging wasps. We had not to wait long before we saw the sand covering one of the entrances move—a sure sign of a wasp trying to make her way into the open. Quickly we put a circle of pine cones round the burrow. When the wasp came out, she started digging and working at her nest, then raked sand over the entrance and left. In the course of the morning many wasps emerged and each received pine cones round her entrance before she had 'opened the door'. Some of these wasps did not bother to work at the nest, but left at once after coming out. These latter wasps we were going to use for our tests. As expected, they made elaborate locality studies, describing many loops of increasing range and altitude before finally departing. We timed these flights carefully. As soon as one of these wasps had definitely gone, we took the Pine cones away. This was done in order to make absolutely sure that, if the wasp should return unobserved, she could not see cones round her nest. If then, when we saw her return with a bee, a displacement test in which the circle of Pine cones was laid out some distance away from the nest would give positive results (i.e., the wasp would choose these cones), we would have proved that she must have learnt them during her locality study, for at no other time could she have seen them.

Not all such wasps returned on the same day. Their prolonged stay and their fast down in the burrows probably forced them to feed themselves in the Heather first. Some, however, returned with a bee and with these we succeeded in doing some exciting tests. In all we tested 13 wasps. They were observed to choose 93 times between the true nest and a 'sham nest' surrounded by the Pine cones. Seventy-three choices fell on the sham nests, against only 20 on the real nests. In control tests taken after the experiments, when the cones were put back round the real nest, of a total of 39 only 3 choices were now in favour of the sham nests, the other 36 being in favour of the real nests. There was no doubt then that these wasps had learnt the nature and the position of the new landmarks during the locality study.

The most impressive achievement was that of wasp No. 179. She had made one locality study of a mere six seconds and had left without returning, let alone alighting. When she was tested upon her return more than an hour later she chose the cones 12 times and never came near the nest. When the original situation was restored she alighted at once on her burrow and slipped in. Nos. 174 and 177 almost equalled this record; both were perfectly trained after uninterrupted locality studies of 13 seconds. All the other wasps either made longer locality studies or interrupted them by alighting on the nest one or more times before leaving again. Such wasps might have learnt during alighting rather than while performing the locality study, so their results were less convincing.

This result, while not at all unexpected, nevertheless impressed us very much. It not only revealed an amazing capacity in these little insects to learn so quickly, but we were struck even more by the fact that a wasp, when not fully oriented, would set out to perform such a locality study, as if it knew what the effect of this specialized type of behaviour would be.

I have already described that a wasp, which has made a number of flights to and from a burrow, makes no, or almost no, locality study, but that it will make an elaborate one after the surroundings have been disturbed. Further tests threw light on the question what exactly made her do this. We studied the effect on locality studies of two types of disturbances. In tests of type A we either added or removed a conspicuous landmark before the wasp returned and then restored the original situation while she was inside. Such wasps, although finding the old, familiar situation upon emerging again, made long locality studies. In tests of type B the wasps were not disturbed at all when entering, but changes similar to those of the A-tests were made just before they left. None of these wasps made locality studies. Wasps used for A-tests always hesitated before alighting. Therefore, disturbances of the familiar surroundings perceived upon returning make the wasps perform a locality study when next departing, while the same disturbances actually present at the time of departure have no influence!

Some further, rather incomplete and preliminary tests pointed to another interesting aspect. Conspicuous new landmarks given before the return of the wasp and left standing until after her departure influenced the form of the locality study as well as its duration: the wasp would repeatedly circle round this particular landmark. If, however, such a landmark was left for some time, so that the wasp passed it several times on her way out and back, and then moved to a new place, the wasp would make a longer locality study than before, yet she would not describe extra loops round the beacon. She obviously recognized the object and had merely to learn its new position. These tests were too few and not fully conclusive, but they did suggest that there is more to this locality study than we had at first suspected. The whole phenomenon is remarkable and certainly deserves further study.

We next turned our attention to the exact nature of the landmarks that were used by the wasps. What exactly did they learn? We spent several seasons examining this and the more striking of our tests are worth describing.

First of all we found that not all objects round the nest were of equal value to the wasps. The first indication of this was found when we tried to train them to use sheets of coloured paper about 3 × 4 inches, which we put out near the nests, as a preparation to study colour vision. It proved to be almost impossible to make the wasps use even a set of three of them; even after leaving them out for days on end we rarely succeeded with the same simple displacement tests that worked so well with the Pine cones. Most wasps just ignored them. Yet the bright blue, yellow and red papers were very conspicuous to us. For some reason, the Pine cones were meeting the wasps' requirements for landmarks better than the flat sheets. [We] worked out a method to test this. We provided two types of objects round a nest—for instance, flat discs and Pine cones—arranged in a circle in alternation. After a day or so, we moved the whole circle and checked whether the wasps used it. If so, we then provided two sham nests at equal distances, one on each side of the real nest, and put all objects of one type round one of these sham nests, all of the other type round the other. If then the wasp had trained herself to one type of landmark rather than to the other, it should prefer one of the two sham nests. Such a preferential choice could not be due to anything but the difference in the wasps' attitude towards the two classes of objects, for all could have been seen by the wasp equally often, their distance to the nest entrance had been the same, they had been offered all round the nest, etc.—in short, they had had absolutely equal chances.

In this way we compared flat objects with solid, dark with light, those contrasting with the colour of the background with those matching it, larger with smaller, nearer with more distant ones, and so on. Each test had, of course, to be done with many wasps and each wasp had to make a number of choices for us to be sure that there was consistency in her preference. This programme kept us busy for a long time, but the results were worth the trouble. The wasps actually showed for landmarks a preference which was different from ours.

When we offered flat circular discs and hemispheres of the same diameter, the wasps always followed the hemispheres (43 against 2 choices). This was not due to the larger surface area of the hemispheres, for when we did similar tests with flat discs of much larger size (of 10 cm. diameter, whereas the hemispheres had a diameter of only 4 cm.), the choices were still 73 in favour of the hemispheres against 19 for the discs.

In other tests we found out that the hemispheres were not preferred because of their shading, nor because they showed contrasts between highlights and deep blacks, nor because they were three-dimensional, but because of the fact that they stood out above the ground. The critical test for this was to offer hollow cones, half of them standing up on top of the soil on their bases, half sunk upside down into the ground. Both were three-dimensional, but one extended above the ground while the others formed pits in the ground. The standing cones were almost always chosen (108 against 21).

The preference for objects that projected above the ground was one of the reasons why Pine cones were preferred. Another reason was that Pine cones offered a chequered pattern of light and dark, while yet another reason was the fact that they had a broken instead of a smooth surface—i.e., dented objects were more stimulating than smooth ones. Similar facts had been found about Honey Bees by other students and much of this has probably to do with the organization of the compound eyes of insects.

We further found that large objects were better than small objects; near objects better than the same objects further away from the nest, objects that contrasted in tone with the background better than those matching the background, objects presented during critical periods (such as at the start of digging a new nest or immediately after a rainy period) better than objects offered once a wasp had acquired a knowledge of its surroundings.

It often amazed us, when doing these tests, that the wasps frequently chose a sham nest so readily although the circle offered contained only half the objects to which they had been trained. This would not be so strange if the wasps had just ignored the weaker 'beacons', but this was not the case. If, in our original test with flat discs and hemispheres, we would offer the discs alone, the wasps, confronted with a choice between the discs and the original nest without either discs or hemispheres, often chose the discs. These, therefore, had not been entirely ignored; they were potential beacons, but were less valued than the hemispheres. Once we knew this, we found that with a little perseverance we could train the wasps to our flat coloured papers. But it took time.

The fact that the wasps accepted these circles, with half the number of objects they used to see, suggested that they responded to the circular arrangement as a whole as well as to the properties of the individual beacon. This raised the interesting issue of 'configurational' stimuli and it seemed to offer good opportunities for experiment. This work was taken up by Van Beusekom who, in a number of ingenious tests, showed that the wasps responded to a very complicated stimulus situation indeed.

First of all, he made sure that wasps could recognize beacons such as Pine cones fairly well. He trained wasps to the usual circle of Pine cones and then gave them the choice between these and a similar arrangement of smooth blocks of Pine cone size. The wasps decided predominantly in favour of the Pine cones, which showed that they were responding to details which distinguished the two types of beacons.

He next trained a number of wasps to a circle of 16 Pine cones and subjected them to two types of tests. In Type A the wasp had to choose between two sets of 16 cones, one arranged in a circle, the other in a figure of another shape, such as a square, a triangle, or an ellipse. He found that, unless the figure was very similar to the circle, the wasps could distinguish between the two figures and alighted in the circle. In those tests the individual cones did not count; he could either use the original cones for constructing the circle or use them for the square or triangle. It was the circular figure the wasps chose, not the Pine cones used during training.

In tests of type B, after the usual training to a circle of 16, he offered the 16 cones in a non-circular arrangement against 8 or even fewer cones in a (loose) circle—and found that the wasps chose the circle in spite of the smaller number of cones. He could even go further and offer a circle of quite different elements, such as square blocks (which the wasps could distinguish from cones, as other tests had shown). If such a circle was offered against cones in a non-circular arrangement, it was the circle that won. Thus it was shown in a variety of ways that the wasps responded not only to the individual beacons (as the preference tests * * * had shown), but also to the circle as a whole.

However, all these experiments, while giving us valuable information about the way our wasps perceived their environment, had one limitation in common—they showed us only how the wasps behaved at the last stage of their journey home. We had many indications that the Pine cones were not seen until the wasps were within a few yards from the nest. How did they find their way previous to this?

Although we were aware of these limitations, it was extremely difficult to extend our tests. However, we did a little about this. More than once we displaced small Pine trees growing at a distance of several yards from nests under observation. In many cases wasps were misled by this and tried to find their nests in the correct position in relation to the displaced tree. The precision of their orientation to such relatively distant marks was truly amazing.

Such large landmarks were used in a slightly different way from the Pine cones. Firstly, they were used even when relatively far from the nest. Secondly, they could be moved over far greater distances than the Pine cones. A circle of Pine cones would fail to draw the wasp with it if it was moved over more than about 7 ft., but a Pine tree, or even a branch of about 4 ft. high, could lure the wasps away even if moved over 8 metres. We further observed in many of our earlier tests that wasps, upon finding the immediate surroundings of the nest disturbed, flew back, circled round a Pine tree or a large sandhill perhaps 70 yards away, and then again approached the nest. This looked very much as though they were taking their bearings upon these larger landmarks.

Van der Linde and others also spent a great deal of time and energy in transporting individual wasps in light-proof cloth over distances up to 1,000 metres in all directions. Since good hunting grounds were to the south and south-east of the colony, whereas in other directions bare sand flats or dense Pine plantations bordered upon the *Philanthus* plains, we could assume that our wasps knew the country to the south and south-east better than in other directions—an assumption which was confirmed by the fact that our wasps always flew out in a south or south-east direction and returned with bees from there. The transported wasps, whose return to their nests was watched, did indeed much better from the south and south-east than from any other direction. From the northwest, for instance, half the wasps never returned as long as our observations lasted. This did indeed suggest that return from unknown country was difficult if not impossible and, therefore, that learning of some kind was essential, but it could not tell us more.

ELAINE MORGAN

The Man-Made Myth

According to the Book of Genesis, God first created man. Woman was not only an afterthought, but an amenity. For close on two thousand years this holy scripture was believed to justify her subordination and explain her inferiority; for even as a copy she was not a very good copy. There were differences. She was not one of His best efforts.

There is a line in an old folk song that runs: "I called my donkey a horse gone wonky." Throughout most of the literature dealing with the differences between the sexes there runs a subtle underlying assumption that woman is a man gone wonky; that woman is a distorted version of the original blueprint; that they are the norm, and we are the deviation.

It might have been expected that when Darwin came along and wrote an entirely different account of *The Descent of Man*, this assumption would have been eradicated, for Darwin didn't believe she was an afterthought: he believed her origin was at least contemporaneous with man's. It should have led to some kind of breakthrough in the relationship between the sexes. But it didn't.

Almost at once men set about the congenial and fascinating task of working out an entirely new set of reasons why woman was manifestly inferior and irreversibly subordinate, and they have been happily engaged on this ever since. Instead of theology they use biology, and ethology, and primatology, but they use them to reach the same conclusions.

They are now prepared to debate the most complex problems of economic reform not in terms of the will of God, but in terms of the sexual behavior patterns of the cichlid fish; so that if a woman claims equal pay or the right to promotion there is usually an authoritative male thinker around to deliver a brief homily on hormones, and point out that what she secretly intends by this, and what will inevitably result, is the "psychological castration" of the men in her life.

Now, that may look to us like a stock piece of emotional blackmail—like the woman who whimpers that if Sonny doesn't do as she wants him to do, then Mother's going to have one of her nasty turns. It is not really surprising that most women who are concerned to win themselves a new and better status in society tend to sheer away from the whole subject of biology and origins, and hope that we can ignore all that and concentrate on ensuring that in the future things will be different.

I believe this is a mistake. The legend of the jungle heritage and the evolution of man as a hunting carnivore has taken root in man's mind as firmly as Genesis ever did. He may even genuinely believe that equal pay will do something terrible to his gonads. He has built a beautiful theoretical construction, with himself on the top of it, buttressed with a formidable array of scientifically authenticated facts. We cannot dispute the facts. We should not attempt to ignore the facts. What I think we can do is to suggest that the currently accepted interpretation of the facts is not the only possible one.

I have considerable admiration for scientists in general, and evolutionists and ethologists in particular, and though I think they have sometimes gone astray, it has not been purely through prejudice. Partly it is due to sheer semantic accident—the fact that "man" is an ambiguous term. It means the species; it also means the male of the species. If you begin to write a book about man or conceive a theory about man you cannot avoid using this word. You cannot avoid using a pronoun as a substitute for the word, and you will use the pronoun "he" as a simple matter of linguistic convenience. But before you are halfway through the first chapter a mental image of this evolving creature begins to form in your mind. It will be a male image, and he will be the hero of the story: everything and everyone else in the story will relate to him.

All this may sound like a mere linguistic quibble or a piece of feminist petulance. If you stay with me, I hope to convince you it's neither. I believe the deeply rooted semantic confusion between "man" as a male and "man" as a species has been fed back into and vitiated a great deal of the speculation that goes on about the origins, development, and nature of the human race.

A very high proportion of the thinking on these topics is androcentric (male-centered) in the same way as pre-Copernican thinking was geocentric. It's just as hard for man to break the habit of thinking of himself as central to the species as it was to break the habit of thinking of himself as central to the universe. He sees himself quite unconsciously as the main line of evolution, with a female satellite, revolving around him as the moon revolves around the earth. This not only causes him to overlook valuable clues to our ancestry, but sometimes leads him into making statements that are arrant and demonstrable nonsense.

The longer I went on reading his own books about himself, the more I longed to find a volume that would begin: "When the first ancestor of the human race descended from the trees, she had not yet developed the mighty brain that was to distinguish her so sharply from all other species. . . ."

Of course, she was no more the first ancester than he was—but she was no *less* the first ancestor, either. She was there all along, contributing half the genes to each succeeding generation. Most of the books forget about her for most of the time. They drag her on-

stage rather suddenly for the obligatory chapter on Sex and Reproduction, and then say: "All right, love, you can go now," while they
get on with the real meaty stuff about the Mighty Hunter with his
lovely new weapons and his lovely new straight legs racing across
the Pleistocene plains. Any modifications in her morphology are
taken to be imitations of the Hunter's evolution, or else designed
solely for his delectation.

Evolutionary thinking has been making great strides lately.
Archeologists, ethologists, paleontologists, geologists, chemists, biologists, and physicists are closing in from all points of the compass
on the central area of mystery that remains. For despite the frequent triumph dances of researchers coming up with another jaw-
bone or another statistic, some part of the miracle is still unac-
counted for. Most of their books include some such phrase as:
". . . the early stages of man's evolutionary progress remain a total
mystery." "Man is an accident, the culmination of a series of highly
improbable coincidences. . . ." "Man is a product of circumstances
special to the point of disbelief." They feel there is still something
missing, and they don't know what.

The trouble with specialists is that they tend to think in grooves.
From time to time something happens to shake them out of that
groove. Robert Ardrey tells how such enlightenment came to Dr.
Kenneth Oakley when the first Australopithecus remains had been
unearthed in Africa: "The answer flashed without warning in his
own large-domed head: 'Of course we believed that the big brain
came first! We assumed that the first man was an Englishman!' "
Neither he, nor Ardrey in relating the incident, noticed that he was
still making an equally unconscious, equally unwarrantable assumption. One of these days an evolutionist is going to strike a palm
against his large-domed head and cry: "Of course! We assumed the
first human being was a man!"

First, let's have a swift recap of the story as currently related, for
despite all the new evidence recently brought to light, the generally
accepted picture of human evolution has changed very little.

Smack in the center of it remains the Tarzanlike figure of the
prehominid male who came down from the trees, saw a grassland
teeming with game, picked up a weapon, and became a Mighty
Hunter.

Almost everything about us is held to have derived from this. If
we walk erect it was because the Mighty Hunter had to stand tall to
scan the distance for his prey. If we lived in caves it was because
hunters need a base to come home to. If we learned to speak it was
because hunters need to plan the next safari and boast about the
last. Desmond Morris, pondering on the shape of a woman's
breasts, instantly deduces that they evolved because her mate
became a Mighty Hunter, and defends this preposterous proposition

with the greatest ingenuity. There's something about the Tarzan figure which has them all mesmerized.

I find the whole yarn pretty incredible. It is riddled with mysteries, and inconsistencies, and unanswered questions. Even more damning than the unanswered questions are the questions that are never even asked, because, as Professor Peter Medawar has pointed out, "scientists tend not to ask themselves questions until they can see the rudiments of an answer in their minds." * * *

The first mystery is, "What happened during the Pliocene?"

There is a wide acceptance now of the theory that the human story began in Africa. Twenty million years ago in Kenya, there existed a flourishing population of apes of generalized body structure and of a profusion of types from the size of a small gibbon up to that of a large gorilla. Dr. L.S.B. Leakey has dug up their bones by the hundred in the region of Lake Victoria, and they were clearly doing very well there at the time. It was a period known as the Miocene. The weather was mild, the rainfall was heavier than today, and the forests were flourishing. So far, so good.

Then came the Pliocene drought. Robert Ardrey writes of it: "No mind can apprehend in terms of any possible human experience the duration of the Pliocene. Ten desiccated years were enough, a quarter of a century ago, to produce in the American Southwest that maelstrom of misery, the dust bowl. To the inhabitant of the region the ten years must have seemed endless. But the African Pliocene lasted twelve million."

On the entire African continent no Pliocene fossil bed has ever been found. During this period many promising Miocene ape species were, not surprisingly, wiped out altogether. A few were trapped in dwindling pockets of forest and when the Pliocene ended they reappeared as brachiating apes—specialized for swinging by their arms.

Something astonishing also reappeared—the Australopithecines, first discovered by Professor Raymond Dart in 1925 and since unearthed in considerable numbers by Dr. Leakey and others.

Australopithecus emerged from his horrifying twelve-million year ordeal much refreshed and improved. The occipital condyles of his skull suggest a bodily posture approaching that of modern man, and the orbital region, according to Sir Wilfred le Gros Clark, has "a remarkably human appearance." He was clever, too. His remains have been found in the Olduvai Gorge in association with crude pebble tools that have been hailed as the earliest beginning of human culture. Robert Ardrey says: "We entered the [Pliocene] crucible a generalized creature bearing only the human potential. We emerged a being lacking only a proper brain and a chin. What happened to us along the way?" The sixty-four-thousand-dollar question: "What happened to them? Where did they go?"

Second question: "Why did they stand upright?" The popular

versions skim very lightly over this patch of thin ice. Desmond Morris says simply: "With strong pressure on them to increase their prey-killing prowess, they became more upright—fast, better runners." Robert Ardrey says equally simply: "We learned to stand erect in the first place as a necessity of the hunting life."

But wait a minute. We were quadrupeds. These statements imply that a quadruped suddenly discovered that he could move faster on two legs than on four. Try to image any other quadruped discovering that —a cat? a dog? a horse?—and you'll see that it's totally nonsensical. Other things being equal, four legs are bound to run faster than two. The bipedal development was violently unnatural.

Stoats, gophers, rabbits, chimpanzees, will sit or stand bipedally to gaze into the distance, but when they want speed they have sense enough to use all the legs they've got. The only quadrupeds I can think of that can move faster on two legs than four are things like kangaroos—and a small lizard called the Texas boomer, and he doesn't keep it up for long. The secret in these cases is a long heavy counterbalancing tail which we certainly never had. You may say it was a natural development for a primate because primates sit erect in trees—but *was* it natural? Baboons and macaques have been largely terrestrial for millions of years without any sign of becoming bipedal.

George A. Bartholomew and Joseph B. Birdsell point out: ". . . . the extreme rarity of bipedalism among animals suggests that it is inefficient except under very special circumstances. Even modern man's unique vertical locomotion when compared to that of quadrupedal mammals, is relatively ineffective. . . . A significant nonlocomotor advantage must have resulted."

What was this advantage? The Tarzanists suggest that bipedalism enabled this ape to race after game while carrying weapons—in the first instance, presumably pebbles. But a chimp running off with a banana (or a pebble), if he can't put it in his mouth, will carry it in one hand and gallop along on the others, because even *three* legs are faster than two. So what was our ancestor supposed to be doing? Shambling along with a rock in each hand? Throwing boulders that took two hands to lift?

No. There must have been a pretty powerful reason why we were constrained over a long period of time to walk about on our hind legs *even though it was slower*. We need to find that reason.

Third question: How did the ape come to be using these weapons, anyway? Again Desmond Morris clears this one lightly, at a bound: "With strong pressure on them to increase their prey-killing prowess . . . their hands became strong efficient weapon-holders." Compared to Morris, Robert Ardrey is obsessed with weapons, which he calls "mankind's most signficant cultural endowment." Yet his explanation of how it all started is as cursory as anyone else's: "In the first evolutionary hour of the human emergence we became sufficiently skilled in the use of weapons to render redundant our natural primate daggers" (i.e., the large prehominid canine teeth).

But wait a minute—how? and why? Why did one, and only one, species of those Miocene apes start using weapons? A cornered baboon will fight a leopard; a hungry baboon will kill and eat a chicken. He could theoretically pick up a chunk of flint and forget about his "natural primate daggers," and become a Mighty Hunter. He doesn't do it, though. Why did we? Sarel Eimerl and Irven de Vore point out in their book *The Primates*:

"Actually, it takes quite a lot of explaining. For example, if an animal's normal mode of defense is to flee from a predator, it flees. If its normal method of defense is to fight with its teeth, it fights with its teeth. It does not suddenly adopt a totally new course of action, such as picking up a stick or a rock and throwing it. The idea would simply not occur to it, and even if it did, the animal would have no reason to suppose that it would work."

Now primates do acquire useful tool-deploying habits. A chimpanzee will use a stick to exact insects from their nests, and a crumpled leaf to sop up water. Wolfgang Köhler's apes used sticks to draw fruit toward the bars of their cage, and so on.

But this type of learning depends on three things. There must be leisure for trial-and-error experiment. The tools must be either in unlimited supply (a forest is full of sticks and leaves) or else in *exactly the right place*. (Even Köhler's brilliant Sultan could be stumped if the fruit was in front of him and a new potential tool was behind him—he needed them both in view at the same time.) Thirdly, for the habit to stick, the same effect must result from the same action every time.

Now look at that ape. The timing is wrong—when he's faced with a bristling rival or a charging cat or even an escaping prey, he won't fool around inventing fancy methods. A chimp sometimes brandishes a stick to convey menace to an adversary, but if his enemy keeps coming, he drops the stick and fights with hands and teeth. Even if we postulate a mutant ape cool enough to think, with the adrenalin surging through his veins, "There must be a better way than teeth," he still has to be lucky to notice that right in the middle of the primeval grassland there happens to be a stone of convenient size, precisely between him and his enemy. And when he throws it, he has to score a bull's-eye, first time and every time. Because if he failed to hit a leopard he wouldn't be there to tell his progeny that the trick only needed polishing up a bit; and if he failed to hit a springbok he'd think: "Ah well, that obviously doesn't work. Back to the old drawing board."

No. If it had taken all that much luck to turn man into a killer, we'd all be still living on nut cutlets.

A lot of Tarzanists privately realize that their explanations of bipedalism and weapon-wielding won't hold water. They have invented the doctrine of "feedback," which states that though these two theories are separately and individually nonsense, together they will just get by. It is alleged that the ape's bipedal gait, however unsteady, made him a better rock thrower (why?) and his rock throwing, however inaccurate, made him a better biped. (Why?) Eimerl and de Vore again put the awkward question: Since chimps can both walk erect and manipulate simple tools, "why was it only the hominids who benefited from the feed-back?" You may well ask.

Next question: Why did the naked ape become naked?

Desmond Morris claims that, unlike more specialized carnivores such as lions and jackals, the ex-vegetarian ape was not physically equipped to "make lightning dashes after his prey." He would "experience considerable overheating during the hunt, and the loss of body hair would be of great value for the supreme moments of the chase."

This is a perfect example of androcentric thinking. There were two sexes around at the time, and I don't believe it's ever been all that easy to part a woman from a fur coat, just to save the old man from getting into a muck-sweat during his supreme moments. What was supposed to be happening to the female during this period of denudation?

Dr. Morris says: "This system would not work, of course, if the climate was too intensely hot, because of damage to the exposed skin." So he is obviously dating the loss of hair later than the Pliocene "inferno." But the next period was the turbulent Pleistocene, punctuated by mammoth African "pluvials," corresponding to the Ice Ages of the north. A pluvial was century after century of torrential rainfall; so we have to picture our maternal ancestor sitting naked in the middle of the plain while the heavens emptied, needing both hands to keep her muddy grip on a slippery, squirming, equally naked infant. This is ludicrous. It's no advantage to the species for the Mighty Hunter to return home safe and cool if he finds his son's been dropped on his head and his wife is dead of hypothermia.

This problem could have been solved by dimorphism—the loss of hair could have gone further in one sex than the other. So it did, of course. But unfortunately for the Tarzanists it was the stay-at-home female who became nakedest, and the overheated hunter who kept the hair on his chest.

Next question: Why has our sex life become so involved and confusing?

The given answer, I need hardly say, is that it all began when man became a hunter. He had to travel long distances after his prey and he began worrying about what the little woman might be up to. He was also anxious about other members of the hunting pack, because, Desmond Morris explains, "if the weaker males were going to be expected to cooperate on the hunt, they had to be given more sexual rights. The females would have to be more shared out."

Thus it became necessary, so the story goes, to establish a system of "pair bonding" to ensure that couples remained faithful for life. I quote: "The simplest and most direct method of doing this was to make the shared activities of the pair more complicated and more rewarding. In other words, to make sex sexier."

To this end, the Naked Apes sprouted ear lobes, fleshy nostrils, and everted lips, all allegedly designed to stimulate one another to a frenzy. Mrs. A.'s nipples became highly erogenous, she invented and patented the female orgasm, and she learned to be sexually responsive at all times, even during pregnancy, "because with a one-male-one-female system, it would be dangerous to frustrate the male for too long a period. It might endanger the pair bond." He might go off in a huff, or look for another woman. Or even refuse to cooperate on the hunt.

In addition, they decided to change over to face-to-face sex, instead of the male mounting from behind as previously, because this new method led to "personalized sex." The frontal approach means that "the incoming sexual signals and rewards are kept tightly linked with the identity signals from the partner." In simpler words, you know who you're doing it with.

This landed Mrs. Naked Ape in something of a quandary. Up till then, the fashionable thing to flaunt in sexual approaches had been "a pair of fleshy, hemispherical buttocks." Now all of a sudden they were getting her nowhere. She would come up to her mate making full-frontal identity signals like mad with her nice new earlobes and nostrils, but somehow he just didn't want to know. He missed the fleshy hemispheres, you see. The position was parlous, Dr. Morris urges. "If the female of our species was going to successfully shift the interest of the male round to the front, evolution would have to do something to make the frontal region more stimulating." Guess what? Right the first time: she invested in a pair of fleshy hemispheres in the thoracic region and we were once more saved by the skin of our teeth.

All this is good stirring stuff, but hard to take seriously. Wolf packs manage to cooperate without all this erotic paraphernalia. Our near relatives the gibbons remain faithful for life without "personalized" frontal sex, without elaborate erogenous zones, without perennial female availability. Why couldn't we?

Above all, since when has increased sexiness been a guarantee of increased fidelity? If the naked ape could see all this added sexual potential in his own mate, how could he fail to see the same thing happening to all the other females around him? What effect was that supposed to have on him, especially in later life when he noticed Mrs. A.'s four hemispheres becoming a little less fleshy than they used to be?

We haven't yet begun on the unasked questions. * * * I will mention just two out of many.

First: If female orgasm was evolved in our species for the first time to provide the woman with a "behavioral reward" for increased sexual activity, why in the name of Darwin has the job been so badly bungled that there have been whole tribes and whole generations of women hardly aware of its existence? Even in the sex-conscious U.S.A., according to Dr. Kinsey, it rarely gets into proper working order before the age of about thirty. How could natural selection ever have operated on such a rickety, unreliable, late-developing endowment when in the harsh conditions of prehistory a woman would be lucky to survive more than twenty-nine years, anyway?

Second: Why in our species has sex become so closely linked with aggression? In most of the higher primates sexual activity is the one thing in life which is totally incompatible with hostility. A female primate can immediately deflect male wrath by presenting her backside and offering sex. Even a male monkey can calm and appease a furious aggressor by imitating the gesture. Nor is the mechanism confined to mammals. Lorenz tells of an irate lizard charging down upon a female painted with male markings to deceive him. When he got close enough to realize his mistake, the taboo was so immediate and so absolute that his aggression went out like a light, and being too late to stop himself he shot straight up into the air and turned a back somersault.

Female primates admittedly are not among the species that can count on this absolute chivalry at all times. A female monkey may be physically chastised for obstreperous behavior; or a male may (on rare occasions) direct hostility against her when another male is copulating with her; but between the male and female engaged in it, sex is always the friendliest of interactions. There is no more hostility associated with it than with a session of mutual grooming.

How then have sex and aggression, the two irreconcilables of the animal kingdom, become in our species alone so closely interlinked that the words for sexual activity are spat out as insults and expletives? In what evolutionary terms are we to explain the Marquis de Sade, and the subterranean echoes that his name evokes in so many human minds?

Not, I think, in terms of Tarzan. It is time to approach the whole thing again right from the beginning: this time from the distaff side, and along a totally different route.

QUESTIONS

1. What is Morgan's thesis? How does she organize her argument?
2. Morgan uses some nonlogical "weapons" in her debating; cite some examples. Do they occur as compensation where her argument is weak, or are they tonal manifestations of a valid logic?
3. Describe Morgan's style. Peter Gay in his essay on historians' style makes a good deal of the epigram, "Style is the man" (p. 984). What sort of a "man" is Morgan?
4. Shulamith Firestone also bases an argument about a contemporary issue on conditions in the remote past (p. 831); in what ways is Morgan's argument similar or different?
5. Why do you suppose Morgan asks more questions than she gives answers?

NAOMI WEISSTEIN

Psychology Constructs the Female, or, The Fantasy Life of the Male Psychologist
(With Some Attention to the Fantasies of His Friends, the Male Biologist and the Male Anthropologist)

It is an implicit assumption that the area of psychology which concerns itself with personality has the onerous but necessary task of describing the limits of human possibility. Thus when we are about to consider the liberation of women, we naturally look to psychology to tell us what "true" liberation would mean: what would give women the freedom to fulfill their own intrinsic natures. Psychologists have set about describing the true natures of women with a certainty and a sense of their own infallibility rarely found in the secular world. Bruno Bettelheim, of the University of Chicago, tells us that

We must start with the realization that, as much as women want to be good scientists or engineers, they want first and foremost to be womanly companions of men and to be mothers.[1]

1. Bruno Bettelheim, "The Commitment Required of a Woman Entering a Scientific Profession in Present-Day American Society," *Woman and the Scientific Professions*, MIT Symposium on American Women in Science and Engineering, 1965 [Weisstein's note].

Erik Erikson of Harvard University, upon noting that young women often ask whether they can "have an identity before they know whom they will marry, and for whom they will make a home," explains somewhat elegiacally that

Much of a young woman's identity is already defined in her kind of attractiveness and in the selectivity of her search for the man (or men) by whom she wishes to be sought . . .[2]

Mature womanly fulfillment, for Erikson, rests on the fact that a woman's

. . . somatic design harbors an "inner space" destined to bear the offspring of chosen men, and with it, a biological, psychological, and ethical commitment to take care of human infancy.[3]

Some psychiatrists even see the acceptance of woman's role by women as a solution to societal problems. "Woman is nurturance . . . ," writes Joseph Rheingold (1964), a psychiatrist at the Harvard Medical School, " . . . anatomy decrees the life of a woman . . . when women grow up without dread of their biological functions and without subversion by feminist doctrine, and therefore enter upon motherhood with a sense of fulfillment and altruistic sentiment, we shall attain the goal of a good life and a secure world in which to live it."[4]

These views from men who are assumed to be experts reflect, in a surprisingly transparent way, the cultural consensus. They not only assert that a woman is defined by her ability to attract men, they see no alternative definitions. They think that the definition of a woman in terms of a man is the way it should be; and they back it up with psychosexual incantation and biological ritual curses. A woman has an identity if she is attractive enough to obtain a man, and thus, a home; for this will allow her to set about her life's task of "joyful altruism and nurturance."

Business certainly does not disagree. If views such as Bettelheim's and Erikson's do indeed have something to do with real liberation for women, then seldom in human history has so much money and effort been spent on helping a group of people realize their true potential. Clothing, cosmetics, home furnishings, are multi-million dollar businesses: if you don't like investing in firms that make weaponry and flaming gasoline, then there's a lot of hard cash in "inner space." Sheet and pillowcase manufacturers are concerned to fill this inner space:

Mother, for a while this morning, I thought I wasn't cut out for married life. Hank was late for work and forgot his apricot juice and walked out

2. Erik Erikson, "Inner and Outer Space: Reflections on Womanhood," *Daedalus*, 93 (1964), 582–606 [Weisstein's note].

3. *Ibid.* [Weisstein's note].

4. Joseph Rheingold, *The Fear of Being a Woman* (New York: Grune & Stratton, 1964), p. 714 [Weisstein's note].

without kissing me, and when I was all alone I started crying. But then the postman came with the sheets and towels you sent, that look like big bandana handkerchiefs, and you know what I thought? That those big red and blue handkerchiefs are for girls like me to dry their tears on so they can get busy and do what a housewife has to do. Throw open the windows and start getting the house ready, and the dinner, maybe clean the silver and put new geraniums in the box. *Everything to be ready for him when he walks through that door.*[5]

Of course, it is not only the sheet and pillowcase manufacturers, the cosmetics industry, the home furnishings salesmen who profit from and make use of the cultural definitions of man and woman. The example above is blatantly and overtly pitched to a particular kind of sexist stereotype: the child nymph. But almost all aspects of the media are normative, that is, they have to do with the ways in which beautiful people, or just folks, or ordinary Americans, should live their lives. They define the possible; and the possibilities are usually in terms of what is male and what is female. Men and women alike are waiting for Hank, the Silva Thins man, to walk back through that door.

It is an interesting but limited exercise to show that psychologists and psychiatrists embrace these sexist norms of our culture, that they do not see beyond the most superficial and stultifying media conceptions of female nature, and that their ideas of female nature serve industry and commerce so well. Just because it's good for business doesn't mean it's wrong. What I will show is that it *is wrong*; that there isn't the tiniest shred of evidence that these fantasies of servitude and childish dependence have anything to do with women's true potential; that the idea of the nature of human possibility which rests on the accidents of individual development of genitalia, on what is possible today because of what happened yesterday, on the fundamentalist myth of sex organ causality, has strangled and deflected psychology so that it is relatively useless in describing, explaining or predicting humans and their behavior.

It then goes without saying that present psychology is less than worthless in contributing to a vision which could truly liberate—men as well as women.

The central argument of my paper, then, is this. Psychology has nothing to say about what women are really like, what they need and what they want, essentially because psychology does not know. I want to stress that this failure is not limited to women; rather, the kind of psychology which has addressed itself to how people act and who they are has failed to understand, in the first place, why people act the way they do, and certainly failed to understand what might make them act differently.

5. Fieldcrest advertisement in the *New Yorker*, 1965. My italics. [Weisstein's note].

The kind of psychology which has addressed itself to these questions divides into two professional areas: academic personality research, and clinical psychology and psychiatry. The basic reason for failure is the same in both these areas: the central assumption for most psychologists of human personality has been that human behavior rests on an individual and inner dynamic, perhaps fixed in infancy, perhaps fixed by genitalia, perhaps simply arranged in a rather immovable cognitive network. But this assumption is rapidly losing ground as personality psychologists fail again and again to get consistency in the assumed personalities of their subjects.[6] Meanwhile, the evidence is collecting that what a person does and who she believes herself to be, will in general be a function of what people around her expect her to be, and what the overall situation in which she is acting implies that she is. Compared to the influence of the social context within which a person lives, his or her history and "traits," as well as biological makeup, may simply be random variations, "noise" superimposed on the true signal which can predict behavior.

Some academic personality psychologists are at least looking at the counter evidence and questioning their theories; no such corrective is occurring in clinical psychology and psychiatry: Freudians and neo-Freudians, nudie-marathonists and touchy-feelies, classicists and swingers, clinicians and psychiatrists, simply refuse to look at the evidence against their theory and practice. And they support their theory and practice with stuff so transparently biased as to have absolutely no standing as empirical evidence.

To summarize: the first reason for psychology's failure to understand what people are and how they act is that psychology has looked for inner traits when it should have been looking for social context; the second reason for psychology's failure is that the theoreticians of personality have generally been clinicians and psychiatrists, and they have never considered it necessary to have evidence in support of their theories.

Theory without Evidence

Let us turn to this latter cause of failure first: the acceptance by psychiatrists and clinical psychologists of theory without evidence. If we inspect the literature of personality, it is immediately obvious that the bulk of it is written by clinicians and psychiatrists, and that the major support for their theories is "years of intensive clinical experience." This is a tradition started by Freud. His "insights" occurred during the course of his work with his patients. Now there

---

6. J. Block, "Some Reasons for the Apparent Inconsistency of Personality," *Psychological Bulletin*, 70 (1968), 210–212 [Weisstein's note].

is nothing wrong with such an approach to theory *formulation*; a person is free to make up theories with any inspiration that works: divine revelation, intensive clinical practice, a random numbers table. But he/she is not free to claim any validity for his/her theory until it has been tested and confirmed. But theories are treated in no such tentative way in ordinary clinical practice. Consider Freud. What he thought constituted evidence violated the most minimal conditions of scientific rigor. In *The Sexual Enlightenment of Children*,[7] the classic document which is supposed to demonstrate empirically the existence of a castration complex and its connection to a phobia, Freud based his analysis on the reports of the father of the little boy, himself in therapy, and a devotee of Freudian theory. I really don't have to comment further on the contamination in this kind of evidence. It is remarkable that only recently has Freud's classic theory on the sexuality of women—the notion of the double orgasm—been actually tested physiologically and found just plain wrong. Now those who claim that fifty years of psychoanalytic experience constitute evidence enough of the essential truths of Freud's theory should ponder the robust health of the double orgasm. Did women, until Masters and Johnson,[8] believe they were having two different kinds of orgasm? Did their psychiatrists badger them into reporting something that was not true? If so, were there other things they reported that were also not true? Did psychiatrists ever learn anything different than their theories had led them to believe? If clinical experience means anything at all, surely we should have been done with the double orgasm myth long before the Masters and Johnson studies.

But certainly, you may object, "years of intensive clinical experience" is the only reliable measure in a discipline which relies for its findings on insight, sensitivity, and intuition. The problem with insight, sensitivity, and intuition, is that they can confirm for all time the biases that one started with. People used to be absolutely convinced of their ability to tell which of their number were engaging in witchcraft. All it required was some sensitivity to the workings of the devil.

Years of intensive clinical experience is not the same thing as empirical evidence. The first thing an experimenter learns in any kind of experiment which involves humans is the concept of the "double blind". The term is taken from medical experiments, where one group is given a drug which is presumably supposed to change behavior in a certain way, and a control group is given a placebo. If the observers or the subjects know which group took which drug, the result invariably comes out on the positive side for the new drug.

7. Sigmund Freud, *The Sexual Enlightenment of Children* (New York: Collier Books, 1963) [Weisstein's note].

8. W. H. Masters and V. E. Johnson, *Human Sexual Response* (Boston: Little, Brown, 1966) [Weisstein's note].

Only when it is not known which subject took which pill is validity remotely approximated. In addition, with judgments of human behavior, it is so difficult to precisely tie down just what behavior is going on, let alone what behavior should be expected, that one must test again and again the reliability of judgments. How many judges, blind, will agree in their observations? Can they replicate their own judgments at some later time? When, in actual practice, these judgment criteria are tested for clinical judgments, then we find that the judges cannot judge reliably, nor can they judge consistently: they do no better than chance in identifying which of a certain set of stories were written by men and which by women; which of a whole battery of clinical test results are the products of homosexuals and which are the products of heterosexuals,[9] and which, of a battery of clinical test results *and* interviews (where questions are asked such as "Do you have delusions?"[1]) are products of psychotics, neurotics, psychosomatics, or normals. Lest this summary escape your notice, let me stress the implications of these findings. The ability of judges, chosen for their clinical expertise, to distinguish male heterosexuals from male homosexuals on the basis of three widely used clinical projective tests—the Rorschach, the TAT, and the MAP—was *no better than chance*. The reason this is such devastating news, of course, is that sexuality is supposed to be of fundamental importance in the deep dynamic of personality; if what is considered gross sexual deviance cannot be caught, then what are psychologists talking about when they, for example, claim that at the basis of paranoid psychosis is "latent homosexual panic"? They can't even identify what homosexual anything is, let alone "latent homosexual panic."[2] More frightening, expert clinicians cannot be consistent on what diagnostic category to assign to a person, again on the basis of both tests and interviews; a number of normals in the Little and Schneidman study were described as psychotic, in such categories as "schizophrenic with homosexual tendencies" or "schizoid character with depressive trends." But most disheartening, when the judges were asked to rejudge the test protocols some weeks later, their diagnoses of the same subjects on the basis of the same protocol differed markedly from their initial judgments. It is obvious that even simple descriptive conventions

9. E. Hooker, "Male Homosexuality in the Rorschach," *Journal of Projective Techniques*, 21 (1957), 18–31 [Weisstein's note].

1. K. B. Little and E. S. Schneidman, "Congruences among Interpretations of Psychological Test and Anamnestic Data," *Psychological Monographs*, 73 (1959), 1–42 [Weisstein's note].

2. It should be noted that psychologists have been as quick to assert absolute truths about the nature of homosexuality as they have about the nature of women. The arguments presented in this paper apply equally to the nature of homosexuality; psychologists know nothing about it; there is no more evidence for the "naturalness" of heterosexuality. Psychology has functioned as a pseudoscientific buttress for patriarchal ideology and patriarchal social organization: women's liberation and gay liberation fight against a common victimization [Weisstein's note].

in clinical psychology cannot be consistently applied; if clinicians were as faulty in recognizing food from non-food, they'd poison themselves and starve to death. That their descriptive conventions have any explanatory significance is therefore, of course, out of the question.

As a graduate student at Harvard some years ago, I was a member of a seminar which was asked to identify which of two piles of a clinical test, the TAT, had been written by males and which by females. Only four students out of twenty identified the piles correctly, and this was after one and a half months of intensively studying the differences between men and women. Since this result is below chance—that is, the result would occur by chance about four out of a thousand times—we may conclude that there *is* finally a consistency here; students are judging knowledgeably within the context of psychological teaching about the differences between men and women; the teachings themselves are simply erroneous.

You may argue that the theory may be scientifically "unsound" but at least it cures people. There is no evidence that it does. In 1952, Eysenck[3] reported the results of what is called an "outcome of therapy" study of neurotics which showed that, of the patients who received psychoanalysis the improvement rate was 44 percent; of the patients who received psychotherapy the improvement rate was 64 percent; and of the patients who received no treatment at all the improvement rate was 72 percent. These findings have never been refuted; subsequently, later studies have confirmed the negative results of the Eysenck study.[4] How can clinicians and psychiatrists, then, in all good conscience, continue to practice? Largely by ignoring these results and being careful not to do outcome-of-therapy studies. The attitude is nicely summarized by Rotter:[5] "Research studies in psychotherapy tend to be concerned more with pyschotherapeutic procedure and less with outcome. ... To some extent, it reflects an interest in the psychotherapy situation as a kind of personality laboratory." Some laboratory.

The Social Context

Thus, since we can conclude that because clinical experience and

3. H. J. Eysenck, "The Effects of Psychotherapy: An Evaluation," *Journal of Consulting Psychology*, 16 (1952), 319–324 [Weisstein's note].

4. F. Barron and T. Leary, "Changes in Psychoneurotic Patients with and without Psychotherapy," *Journal of Counseling Psychology*, 19 (1955); A. E. Bergin, "The Effects of Psychotherapy: Negative Results Revisited," *Journal of Counseling Psychology*, 10 (1963); R. D. Cartwright and J. L. Vogel, "A Comparison of Changes in Psychoneurotic Patients During Matched Periods of Therapy and No-therapy," *Journal of Counseling Psychology*, 24 (1960); C. B. Truax, "Effective Ingredients in Psychotherapy: An Approach to Unraveling the Patient-Therapist Interaction," *Journal of Counseling Psychology*, 10 (1963); E. Powers and H. Witmer, *An Experiment in the Prevention of Delinquency* (New York: Columbia University Press, 1951) [Weisstein's note].

5. J. B. Rotter, "Psychotherapy," *Annual Review of Psychology*, 11 (1960), 381–414 [Weisstein's note].

tools can be shown to be worse than useless when tested for consistency, efficacy, agreement, and reliability, we can safely conclude that theories of a clinical nature advanced about women are also worse than useless. I want to turn now to the second major point in my paper, which is that, even when psychological theory is constructed so that it may be tested, and rigorous standards of evidence are used, it has become increasingly clear that in order to understand why people do what they do, and certainly in order to change what people do, psychologists must turn away from the theory of the causal nature of the inner dynamic and look to the social context within which individuals live.

Before examining the relevance of this approach to the question of women, let me first sketch the groundwork for this assertion.

In the first place, it is clear[6] that personality tests never yield consistent predictions; a rigid authoritarian on one measure will be an unauthoritarian on the next. But the reason for this inconsistency is only now becoming clear, and it seems overwhelmingly to have much more to do with the social situation in which the subject finds him/herself than with the subject him/herself.

In a series of brilliant experiments, Rosenthal and his co-workers[7] have shown that if one group of experimenters has one hypothesis about what they expect to find, and another group of experimenters has the opposite hypothesis, both groups will obtain results in accord with their hypotheses. The results obtained are not due to mishandling of data by biased experimenters; rather, somehow, the bias of the experimenter creates a changed environment in which subjects actually act differently. For instance, in one experiment, subjects were to assign numbers to pictures of men's faces, with high numbers representing the subject's judgment that the man in the picture was a successful person, and low numbers representing the subject's judgment that the man in the picture was an unsuccessful person. Prior to running the subjects, one group of experimenters was told that the subjects tended to rate the faces high; another group of experimenters was told that the subjects tended to rate the faces low. Each group of experimenters was instructed to follow precisely the same procedure: they were required to read to subjects a set of instructions, and to say *nothing else*. For the 375 subjects run, the results showed clearly that those subjects who performed the task with experimenters who expected high ratings gave high ratings, and those subjects who performed the task with experimenters who expected low ratings gave low ratings. How did this

6. J. Block, *op. cit.* [Weisstein's note].
7. R. Rosenthal and L. Jacobson, *Pygmalion in the Classroom: Teacher Expectation and Pupil's Intellectual Development* (New York: Holt, Rinehart & Winston, 1968); R. Rosenthal, *Experimenter Effects in Behavioral Research* (New York: Appleton-Century Crofts, 1966) [Weisstein's note].

happen? The experimenters all used the same words; it was something in their conduct which made one group of subjects do one thing, and another group of subjects do another thing.[8]

The concreteness of the changed conditions produced by expectation is a fact, a reality: even with animal subjects, in two separate studies,[9] those experimenters who were told that rats learning mazes had been especially bred for brightness obtained better learning from their rats than did experimenters believing their rats to have been bred for dullness. In a very recent study, Rosenthal and Jacobson (1968) extended their analysis to the natural classroom situation. Here, they tested a group of students and reported to the teachers that some among the students tested "showed great promise." Actually, the students so named had been selected on a random basis. Some time later, the experimenters retested the group of students: those students whose teachers had been told that they were "promising" showed real and dramatic increments in their IQs as compared to the rest of the students. Something in the conduct of the teachers towards those who the teachers believed to be the "bright" students, made those students brighter.

Thus, even in carefully controlled experiments, and with no outward or conscious difference in behavior, the hypotheses we start with will influence enormously the behavior of another organism. These studies are extremely important when assessing the validity of psychological studies of women. Since it is beyond doubt that most of us start with notions as to the nature of men and women, the validity of a number of observations of sex differences is questionable, even when these observations have been made under carefully controlled conditions. Second, and more important, the Rosenthal experiments point quite clearly to the influence of social expectation. In some extremely important ways, people are what you expect them to be, or at least they behave as you expect them to behave. Thus, if women, according to Bettelheim, want first and foremost to be good wives and mothers, it is extremely likely that this is what Bruno Bettelheim, and the rest of society, want them to be.

There is another series of brilliant social psychological experiments which point to the overwhelming effect of social context. These are the obedience experiments of Stanley Milgram[1] in which subjects are asked to obey the orders of unknown experimenters,

8. I am indebted to Jesse Lemisch for his valuable suggestions in the interpretation of these studies [Weisstein's note].

9. R. Rosenthal and K. L. Fode, "The Effect of Experimenter Bias on the Performance of the Albino Rat," Harvard University, unpublished manuscript 1961; R. Rosenthal and R. Lawson, "A Longitudinal Study of the Effects of Experimenter Bias on the Operant Learning of Laboratory Rats," Harvard University, unpublished manuscript, 1961 [Weisstein's note].

1. Stanley Milgram, "Some Conditions of Obedience and Disobedience to Authority," *Human Relations*, 18 (1965), 57–76; "Liberating Effects of Group Pressures," *Journal of Personality and Social Psychology*, 1 (1965), 127–134 [Weisstein's note]. See "A Behavioral Study of Obedience," (pp. 293–307) in this volume.

orders which carry with them the distinct possibility that the subject is killing somebody.

In Milgram's experiments, a subject is told that he/she is administering a learning experiment, and that he/she is to deal out shocks each time the other "subject" (in reality, a confederate of the experimenter) answers incorrectly. The equipment appears to provide graduated shocks ranging upwards from 15 volts through 450 volts; for each of four consecutive voltages there are verbal descriptions such as "mild shock," "danger, severe shock," and, finally, for the 435- and 450-volt switches, a red XXX marked over the switches. Each time the stooge answers incorrectly, the subject is supposed to increase the voltage. As the voltage increases, the stooge begins to cry in pain; he/she demands that the experiment stop; finally, he/she refuses to answer at all. When he/she stops responding, the experimenter instructs the subject to continue increasing the voltage; for each shock administered the stooge shrieks in agony. Under these conditions, about 62½ percent of the subjects administered shocks that they believed to be possibly lethal.

No tested individual differences between subjects predicted how many would continue to obey, and which would break off the experiment. When forty psychiatrists predicted how many of a group of 100 subjects would go on to give the lethal shock, their predictions were orders of magnitude below the actual percentages; most expected only one-tenth of one per cent of the subjects to obey to the end.

But even though *psychiatrists* have no idea how people will behave in this situation, and even though individual differences do not predict which subjects will obey and which will not, it is easy to predict when subjects will be obedient and when they will be defiant. All the experimenter has to do is change the social situation. In a variant of Milgram's experiment, two stooges were present in addition to the "victim"; these worked along with the subject in administering electric shocks. When these two stooges refused to go on with the experiment, only 10 percent of the subjects continued to the maximum voltage. This is critical for personality theory. It says that behavior is predicted from the social situation, not from the individual history.

Finally, an ingenious experiment by Schachter and Singer[2] showed that subjects injected with adrenalin, which produces a state of physiological arousal in all but minor respects identical to that which occurs when subjects are extremely afraid, became euphoric when they were in a room with a stooge who was acting euphoric, and became extremely angry when they were placed in a room with

2. S. Schachter and J. E. Singer, "Cognitive, Social, and Physiological Determinants of Emotional State," *Psychological Review*, 63 (1962), 379–399 [Weisstein's note].

a stooge who was acting extremely angry.

To summarize: If subjects under quite innocuous and non-coercive social conditions can be made to kill other subjects and under other types of social conditions will positively refuse to do so; if subjects can react to a state of physiological fear by becoming euphoric because there is somebody else around who is euphoric, or angry because there is somebody else around who is angry; if students become intelligent because teachers expect them to be intelligent, and rats run mazes better because experimenters are told the rats are bright, then it is obvious that a study of human behavior requires, first and foremost, a study of the social contexts within which people move, the expectations as to how they will behave, and the authority which tells them who they are and what they are supposed to do.

Biologically Based Theories

Biologists also have at times assumed they could describe the limits of human potential from their observations not of human, but of animal behavior. Here, as in psychology, there has been no end of theorizing about the sexes, again with a sense of absolute certainty surprising in "science." These theories fall into two major categories.

One category of theory argues that since females and males differ in their sex hormones, and sex hormones enter the brain,[3] there must be innate behavioral differences. But the only thing this argument tells us is that there are differences in physiological state. The problem is whether these differences are at all relevant to behavior.

Consider, for example, differences in levels of the sex hormone testosterone. A man who calls himself Tiger[4] has recently argued[5] that the greater quantities of testosterone found in human males as compared with human females (of a certain age group) determine innate differences in aggressiveness, competitiveness, dominance, ability to hunt, ability to hold public office, and so forth. But Tiger demonstrates in this argument the same manly and courageous refusal to be intimidated by evidence which we have already seen in our consideration of the clinical and psychiatric tradition. The evidence does not support his argument, and in most cases, directly contradicts it. Testosterone level does not seem to be related to hunting ability, dominance, or aggression, or competitive-

3. D. A. Hamburg and D. T. Lunde, "Sex Hormones in the Development of Sex Differences in Human Behavior," in *The Development of Sex Differences*, ed. Maccoby (Stanford: Stanford University Press, 1966), pp. 1–24 [Weisstein's note].

4. H. N. G. Schwarz-Belkin claims that the name was originally Mouse, but this may be a reference to an earlier L. Tiger (putative). See "Les Fleurs Du Mal," in *Festschrift fir Piltdown* (New York: Ponzi Press, 1914) [Weisstein's note].

5. Lionel Tiger, "Male Dominance? Yes. A Sexist Plot? No," *New York Times Magazine*, sec. N, Oct. 25, 1970 [Weisstein's note].

ness. As Storch[6] has pointed out, all normal *male mammals* in the reproductive age group produce much greater quantities of testosterone than females; yet many of these males are neither hunters nor are they aggressive (e.g. rabbits). And, among some hunting mammals, such as the large cats, it turns out that more hunting is done by the female than the male. And there exist primate species where the female is clearly more aggressive, competitive, and dominant than the male.[7] Thus, for some species, being female, and therefore, having less testosterone than the male of that species means hunting more, or being more aggressive, or being more dominant. Nor does having *more* testosterone preclude behavior commonly thought of as "female"; there exist primate species where females do not touch infants except to feed them; the males care for the infants at all times.[8] So it is not clear what testosterone or any other sex-hormonal difference means for differences in nature, or sex-role behavior.

In other words, one can observe identical types of behavior which have been associated with sex (e.g. "mothering") in males and females, despite known differences in physiological state, i.e. sex hormones, genitalia, etc. What about the converse to this? That is, can one obtain differences in behavior given a single physiological state? The answer is overwhelmingly yes, not only as regards non-sex-specific hormones (as in the Schachter and Singer experiment cited above), but also as regards gender itself. Studies of hermaphrodites with the same diagnosis (the genetic, gonadal, hormonal sex, the internal reproductive organs, and the ambiguous appearances of the external genitalia were identical) have shown that one will consider oneself male or female depending simply on whether one was defined and raised as male or female:[9]

There is no more convincing evidence of the power of social interaction on gender-identity differentiation than in the case of congenital hermaphrodites who are of the same diagnosis and similar degree of hermaphroditism but are differently assigned and with a different postnatal medical and life history. (Money, 1970, p. 743).

Thus, for example, if out of two individuals diagnosed as having the adrenogenital syndrome of female hermaphroditism, one is raised as a girl and one as a boy, each will act and identify her/himself accordingly. The one raised as a girl will consider herself a girl; the one raised as a boy will consider himself a boy; and each will conduct her/himself successfully in accord with that self-definition.

6. M. Storch, "Reply to Tiger," unpublished manuscript, 1970 [Weisstein's note].
7. G. D. Mitchell, "Paternalistic Behavior in Primates," *Psychological Bulletin*, 71 (1969), 399–417 [Weisstein's note].
8. *Ibid.* [Weisstein's note].
9. J. Money, "Sexual Dimorphism and Homosexual Gender Identity," *Psychological Bulletin* 6 (1970), 425–440 [Weisstein's note].

So, identical behavior occurs given different physiological states; and different behavior occurs given an identical physiological starting point. So it is not clear that differences in sex hormones are at all relevant to behavior.

The other category of theory based on biology, a reductionist theory, goes like this. Sex-role behavior in some primate species is described, and it is concluded that this is the "natural" behavior for humans. Putting aside the not insignificant problem of observer bias (for instance, Harlow, of the University of Wisconsin, after observing differences between male and female rhesus monkeys, quotes Laurence Sterne to the effect that women are silly and trivial, and concludes that "men and women have differed in the past and they will differ in the future"[1]), there are a number of problems with this approach.

The most general and serious problem is that there are no grounds to assume that anything primates do is necessarily natural, or desirable in humans, for the simple reason that humans are not non-humans. For instance, it is found that male chimpanzees placed alone with infants will not "mother" them. Jumping from hard data to ideological speculation, researchers conclude from this information that *human* females are necessary for the safe growth of human infants. It would be reasonable to conclude, following this logic, that it is quite useless to teach human infants to speak, since it has been tried with chimpanzees and it does not work.

One strategy that has been used is to extrapolate from primate behavior to "innate" human preference by noticing certain trends in primate behavior as one moves phylogenetically closer to humans. But there are great difficulties with this approach. When behaviors from lower primates are directly opposite to those of higher primates, or to those one expects of humans, they can be dismissed on evolutionary grounds—higher primates and/or humans grew out of that kid stuff. On the other hand, if the behavior of higher primates is counter to the behavior considered natural for humans, while the behavior of some lower primate is considered the natural one for humans, the higher primate behavior can be dismissed also, on the grounds that it has diverged from an older, prototypical pattern. So either way, one can select those behaviors one wants to prove innate for humans. In addition, one does not know whether the sex-role behavior exhibited is dependent on the phylogenetic rank, or on the environmental conditions (both physical and social) under which different species live.

Is there then any value at all in primate observations as they relate to human females and males? There is a value but it is limited: its function can be no more than to show some extant examples of

1. H. F. Harlow, "The Heterosexual Affectional System in Monkeys," *American Psychologist*, 17 (1962), 1–9 [Weisstein's note].

diverse sex-role behavior. It must be stressed, however, that this is an extremely limited function. The extant behavior does not begin to suggest all the possibilities, either for non-human primates or for humans. Bearing these caveats in mind, it is nonetheless interesting that if one inspects the limited set of observations of existing non-human primate sex-role behaviors, one finds, in fact, a much larger range of sex-role behavior than is commonly believed to exist. "Biology" appears to limit very little; the fact that a female gives birth does not mean, even in non-humans, that she necessarily cares for the infant (in marmosets, for instance, the male carries the infant at all times except when the infant is feeding[2]); "natural" female and male behavior varies all the way from females who are much more aggressive and competitive than males (e.g. Tamarins[3]) and male "mothers" (e.g. Titi monkeys, night monkeys, and marmosets[4]) to submissive and passive females and male antagonists (e.g. rhesus monkeys).

But even for the limited function that primate arguments serve, the evidence has been misused. Invariably, those primates have been cited which exhibit exactly the kind of behavior that the proponents of the biological fixedness of human female behavior wish were true for humans. Thus, baboons and rhesus monkeys are generally cited: males in these groups exhibit some of the most irritable and aggressive behavior found in primates, and if one wishes to argue that females are naturally passive and submissive, these groups provide vivid examples. There are abundant counter examples, such as those mentioned above;[5] in fact, in general, a counter example can be found for every sex-role behavior cited, including, as mentioned in the case of marmosets, male "mothers."

But the presence of counter examples has not stopped florid and overarching theories of the natural or biological basis of male privilege from proliferating. For instance, there have been a number of theories dealing with the innate incapacity in human males for monogamy. Here, as in most of this type of theorizing, baboons are a favorite example, probably because of their fantasy value: the family unit of the hamadryas baboon, for instance, consists of a highly constant pattern of one male and a number of females and their young. And again, the counter examples, such as the invariably monogamous gibbon, are ignored.

An extreme example of this maiming and selective truncation of the evidence in the service of a plea for the maintenance of male privilege is a recent book, *Men in Groups* by Tiger.[6] The central

2. Mitchell, *op. cit.* [Weisstein's note].
3. *Ibid.* [Weisstein's note].
4. *Ibid.* (All these are lower-order primates, which makes their behavior with reference to humans unnatural, or more natural; take your choice.) [Weisstein's note].
5. *Ibid.* [Weisstein's note].
6. Lionel Tiger, *Men in Groups* (New York: Random House, 1969) [Weisstein's note].

claim of this book is that females are incapable of "bonding" as in "male bonding." What is "male bonding"? Its surface definition is simple: " . . . a particular relationship between two or more males such that they react differently to members of their bonding units as compared to individuals outside of it."[7] If one deletes the word male, the definition, on its face, would seem to include all organisms that have any kind of social organization. But this is not what Tiger means. For instance, Tiger asserts that females are incapable of bonding; and this alleged incapacity indicates to Tiger that females should be restricted from public life. Why is bonding an exclusively male behavior? Because, says Tiger, it is seen in male primates. All male primates? No, very few male primates. Tiger cites two examples where male bonding is seen: rhesus monkeys and baboons. Surprise, surprise. But not even all baboons: as mentioned above, the hamadryas social organization consists of one-male units; so does that of the gelada baboon.[8] And the great apes do not go in for male bonding much either. The "male bond" is hardly a serious contribution to scholarship; one reviewer for *Science* has observed that the book " . . . shows basically more resemblance to a partisan political tract than to a work of objective social science," with male bonding being " . . . some kind of behavioral phlogiston."[9]

In short, primate arguments have generally misused the evidence; primate studies themselves have, in any case, only the very limited function of describing some possible sex-role behavior; and at present, primate observations have been sufficiently limited so that even the range of possible sex-role behavior for non-human primates is not known. This range is not known since there is only minimal observation of what happens to behavior if the physical or social environment is changed. In one study,[1] different troops of Japanese macaques were observed. Here, there appeared to be cultural differences: males in 3 out of the 18 troops observed differed in the amount of their aggressiveness and infant-caring behavior. There could be no possibility of differential evolution here; the differences seemed largely transmitted by infant socialization. Thus, the very limited evidence points to some plasticity in the sex-role behavior of non-human primates; if we can figure out experiments which massively change the social organization of primate groups, it is possible that we might observe great changes in behavior. At present, however, we must conclude that given a constant physical environment, non-human primates do not change their social conditions by themselves very much and thus the "innateness" and fixedness of

7. *Ibid.*, pp. 19–20 [Weisstein's note].
8. Mitchell, *op. cit.* [Weisstein's note].
9. M. H. Fried, "Mankind Excluding Women," *Science*, 165 (1969), 883–884 [Weisstein's note].

1. J. Itani, "Paternal Care in the Wild Japanese Monkey *Macaca fuscata*," in *Primate Social Behavior*, ed. Southwick (Princeton: Van Nostrand, 1963) [Weisstein's note].

their behavior is simply not known. Thus, even if there were some way, which there isn't, to settle on the behavior of a particular primate species as being the "natural" way for humans, we would not know whether or not this were simply some function of the present social organization of that species. And finally, once again it must be stressed that even if non-human primate behavior turned out to be relatively fixed, this would say little about our behavior. More immediate and relevant evidence, e.g. the evidence from social psychology, points to the enormous plasticity in human behavior, not only from one culture to the next, but from one experimental group to the next. One of the most salient features of human social organization is its variety; there are a number of cultures where there is at least a rough equality between men and women.[2] In summary, primate arguments can tell us very little about our "innate" sex-role behavior; if they tell us anything at all, they tell us that there is no one biologically "natural" female or male behavior, and that sex-role behavior in non-human primates is much more varied than has previously been thought.

Conclusion

In brief, the uselessness of present psychology (and biology) with regard to women is simply a special case of the general conclusion: one must understand the social conditions under which humans live if one is going to attempt to explain their behavior. And, to understand the social conditions under which women live, one must understand the social expectations about women.

How are women characterized in our culture, and in psychology? They are inconsistent, emotionally unstable, lacking in a strong conscience or superego, weaker, "nurturant" rather then productive, "intuitive" rather than intelligent, and, if they are at all "normal," suited to the home and the family. In short, the list adds up to a typical minority group stereotype of inferiority:[3] if they know their place, which is in the home, they are really quite lovable, happy, childlike, loving creatures. In a review of the intellectual differences between little boys and little girls, Eleanor Maccoby[4] has shown that there are no intellectual differences until about high school, or, if there are, girls are slightly ahead of boys. At high school, girls begin to do worse on a few intellectual tasks, such as arithmetic reasoning, and beyond high school, the achievement of women now measured in terms of productivity and accomplishment drops off

2. Margaret Mead, *Male and Female: A Study of the Sexes in a Changing World* (New York: William Morrow, 1949) [Weisstein's note].

3. H. M. Hacker, "Women as a Minority Group," *Social Forces*, 30 (1951), 60–69 [Weisstein's note].

4. Eleanor E. Maccoby, "Sex Differences in Intellectual Functioning," in *The Development of Sex Differences*, ed. Maccoby (Stanford: Stanford University Press, 1966), pp. 25–55 [Weisstein's note].

even more rapidly. There are a number of other, non-intellectual tests which show sex differences; I choose the intellectual differences since it is seen clearly that women start becoming inferior. It is no use to talk about women being different but equal; all of the tests I can think of have a "good" outcome and a "bad" outcome. Women usually end up at the "bad" outcome. In light of social expectations about women, what is surprising is that little girls don't get the message that they are supposed to be stupid until high school; and what is even more remarkable is that some women resist this message even after high school, college, and graduate school.

My paper began with remarks on the task of the discovery of the limits of human potential. Psychologists must realize that it is they who are limiting discovery of human potential. They refuse to accept evidence, if they are clinical psychologists, or, if they are rigorous, they assume that people move in a context-free ether, with only their innate dispositions and their individual traits determining what they will do. Until psychologists begin to respect evidence, and until they begin looking at the social context within which people move, psychology will have nothing of substance to offer in this task of discovery. I don't know what immutable differences exist between men and women apart from differences in their genitals; perhaps there are some other unchangeable differences; probably there are a number of irrelevant differences. But it is clear that until social expectations for men and women are equal, until we provide equal respect for both men and women, our answers to this question will simply reflect our prejudices.

B. F. SKINNER
What Is Man?[1]

As a science of behavior follows the strategy of physics and biology, the autonomous agent to which we have traditionally attributed behavior is replaced by the environment—the environment in which the species evolved and in which the behavior of the individual is shaped and maintained.

Take, for example, a "cognitive" activity, *attention*. A person responds to only a small part of the stimuli impinging upon him. The traditional view is that he himself determines which stimuli are to be effective—by paying attention to them. Some kind of inner gatekeeper allows some stimuli to enter and keeps all others out. A sudden or strong stimulus may break through and "attract" attention, but the person himself is otherwise in control. An analysis of

1. The following essay, with this title, appeared in *Psychology Today*. It was enlarged and substantially revised for inclusion as a chapter in Skinner's book, *Beyond Freedom and Dignity*.

the environmental circumstances reverses the relation. The kinds of stimuli that break through by "attracting attention" do so because they have been associated in the evolutionary history of the species or the personal history of the individual with important—e.g., dangerous—things. Less forceful stimuli attract attention only to the extent that they have figured in contingencies of reinforcement.

We can arrange contingencies that insure that an organism—even such a simple organism as a pigeon—will attend to one object and not to another, or to one property of an object, such as its color, and not to another, such as its shape. The inner gatekeeper is replaced by the contingencies that the person has been exposed to and that select the stimuli he reacts to.

Face

In the traditional view a person perceives the world around him and acts upon it to make it known to him. It has even been argued that the world would not exist if no one perceived it. The action is exactly reversed in an environmental analysis. There would, of course, be no perception if there were no world to perceive, but we would not perceive an existing world if there were no appropriate contingencies.

We say that a baby perceives his mother's face and knows it. Our evidence is that the baby responds in one way to his mother's face and in other ways to other faces or other things. He makes this distinction not through some mental act of perception but because of prior contingencies. Some of these may be contingencies of survival. The face and facial expressions of the human mother have been associated with security, warmth, food and other important things during both the evolution of the species and the life of the child.

The role of the environment is particularly subtle when what is known is the knower himself. If there is no external world to initiate knowing, must we not then say that the knower himself acts first? This is, of course, the field of consciousness or awareness which a scientific analysis of behavior is often accused of ignoring. The charge is a serious one and should be taken seriously.

Man is said to differ from the other animals mainly because he is "aware of his own existence." He knows what he is doing; he knows that he has had a past and will have a future; he alone follows the classical injunction, "Know thyself." Any analysis of human behavior that neglected these facts would be defective indeed. And some analyses do. "Methodological behaviorism" limits itself to what can be observed publicly; mental processes may exist, but their nature rules them out of scientific consideration. The "behaviorists" in political science and many logical positivists in philosophy have followed a similar line. But we can study self-observation, and we must include it in any reasonably complete account of human behavior.

Rather than ignore consciousness, an experimental analysis of behavior has put much emphasis on certain crucial issues. The question is not whether a man can know himself but what he knows when he does so.

Skin

The problem arises in part from the indisputable fact of privacy: a small part of the universe is enclosed within a human skin. It would be foolish to deny the existence of that private world, but it is also foolish to assert that because it is private its nature is different from the world outside. The difference is not in the stuff that composes the private world but in its accessibility. There is an exclusive intimacy about a headache or heartache that has seemed to support the doctrine that knowing is a kind of possession.

The difficulty is that although privacy may bring the knower closer to what he knows, it interferes with the process through which he comes to know anything. As we have seen, contingencies under which a child learns to describe his feelings are necessarily defective; the verbal community cannot use the same procedures for this that it uses to teach a child to describe objects. There are, of course, natural contingencies under which we learn to respond to private stimuli, and they generate behavior of great precision; we could not walk if we were not stimulated by parts of our own body. But very little awareness is associated with this kind of behavior and, in fact, we behave in these ways most of the time without being aware of the stimuli to which we are responding. We do not attribute awareness to other species that obviously use similar private stimuli. To "know" private stimuli is more than to respond to them.

Help

The verbal community specializes in self-descriptive contingencies. It asks: What did you do yesterday? Why did you do that? How do you feel about that? The answers help persons adjust to each other effectively. And it is because such questions are asked that a person responds to himself and his behavior in the special way called knowing or being aware. Without the help of a verbal community all behavior would be unconscious. Consciousness is a social product. It is not only *not* the special field of autonomous man, it is not within the range of a solitary man.

And it is not within the range of accuracy of anyone. The privacy that seems to confer intimacy upon self-knowledge makes it impossible for the verbal community to maintain precise contingencies. Introspective vocabularies are by nature inaccurate, and that is one reason why they have varied so widely among schools of philosophy and psychology. Even a carefully trained observer runs into trouble when he studies new private stimuli.

Aware

Theories of psychotherapy that emphasize awareness assign a role to autonomous man that is the function of contingencies of reinforcement. Awareness may help if the problem is in part a lack of awareness, and "insight" into one's condition may help if one then takes remedial action. But awareness or insight alone is not always enough, and may be too much. One need not be aware of one's behavior or the conditions controlling it in order to behave effectively—or ineffectively.

The extent to which a man *should* be aware of himself depends upon the importance of self-observation for effective behavior. Self-knowledge is valuable only to the extent that it helps to meet the contingencies under which it has arisen.

Think

Perhaps the last stronghold of autonomous man is the complex "cognitive" activity called thinking. Because it is complex, it has yielded only slowly to explanation in terms of contingencies of reinforcement. We say that a person *forms a concept or an abstraction*, but all we see is that certain kinds of contingencies of reinforcement have brought a response under the control of a single property of a stimulus. We say that a person *recalls* or *remembers* what he has seen or heard, but all we see is that the present occasion evokes a response, possibly in weakened or altered form, acquired on another occasion. We say that a person *associates* one word with another, but all we observe is that one verbal stimulus evokes the response previously made to another. Rather than suppose that it is therefore autonomous man who forms concepts or abstractions, recalls or remembers, and associates, we can put matters in good order simply by noting that these terms do not refer to forms of behavior.

A person may take explicit action, however, when he solves a problem. The creative artist may manipulate a medium until something of interest turns up. Much of this can be done covertly, and we are then likely to assign it to a different dimensional system; but it can always be done overtly, perhaps more slowly but also often more effectively, and with rare exceptions it must have been learned in overt form. The culture constructs special contingencies to promote thinking. It teaches a person to make fine discriminations by making differential reinforcement more precise. It teaches techniques to use in solving problems. It provides rules that make it unnecessary to expose a person to the contingencies from which the rules derive, and it provides rules for finding rules.

Self-control or self-management is a special kind of problem-solving that, like self-knowledge, raises all the issues associated with privacy. It is always the environment that builds the behavior with which we solve problems, even when the problems are found in the private world inside the.skin. We have not investigated the matter of self-control in a very productive way, but the inadequacy of our analysis is no reason to fall back on a miracle-working mind. If our understanding of contingencies of reinforcement is not yet sufficient to explain all kinds of thinking, we must remember that the appeal to mind explains nothing at all.

Inside

In shifting control from autonomous man to the observable environment we do not leave an empty organism. A great deal goes on inside the skin, and physiology will eventually be able to tell us more about it. It will explain why behavior indeed relates to the antecedent events of which we can show it to be a function.

People do not always correctly understand the assignment. Many physiologists regard themselves as looking for the "physiological correlates" of mental events. They regard physiological research as simply a more scientific version of introspection. But physiological techniques are not, of course, designed to detect or measure personalities, feelings, or thoughts. At the moment neither introspection nor physiology supplies very adequate information about what is going on inside a man as he behaves, and since they are both directed inward they have the same effect of diverting attention from the external environment.

Much of the misunderstanding about an inner man comes from the metaphor of storage. Evolutionary and environmental histories change an organism, but they are not stored within it. Thus we observe that babies suck their mothers' breasts and can easily imagine that a strong tendency to do so has survival value, but much more is implied by a "sucking instinct" regarded as something a baby possesses that enables it to suck. The concept of "human nature" or "genetic endowment" is dangerous when we take it in that sense. We are closer to human nature in a baby than in an adult, or in a primitive culture than in an advanced one, in the sense that environmental contingencies are less likely to have obscured the genetic endowment, and it is tempting to dramatize that endowment by implying that earlier stages have survived in concealed form: man is a naked ape. But anatomists and physiologists will not find an ape, or for that matter, instincts. They will find anatomical and physiological features that are the product of an evolutionary history.

Sin

It is often said too that the personal history of the individual is stored within him as a "habit." The cigarette habit is talked of as being something more than the behavior said to show that a person possesses it. But the only other information we have is about the reinforcers and the schedules of reinforcement that make a person smoke a great deal. The contingencies are not stored; they simply leave a person changed.

The issue has had a curious place in theology. Does man sin because he is sinful, or is he sinful because he sins? Neither question points to anything very useful. To say that a man is sinful because he sins is to give an operational definition of sin. To say that he sins because he is sinful is to trace his behavior to a supposed inner trait. But whether a person engages in the kind of behavior called sinful depends upon circumstances not mentioned in either question. The sin assigned as an inner possession (the sin a person "knows") is to be found in a history of reinforcement.

Self

It is the nature of an experimental analysis of human behavior to strip away the functions previously assigned to autonomous man and transfer them one by one to the controlling environment. The analysis leaves less and less for autonomous man to do. But what about man himself? Is there not something about a person—a self —that is more than a living body?

A self is a repertoire of behavior appropriate to a given set of contingencies, and a substantial part of the conditions to which a person is exposed may play a dominant role. Under other conditions a person may sometimes report, "I'm not myself today" or "I couldn't have done what you said I did, because that's not like me." The identity conferred upon a self arises from the contingencies responsible for the behavior.

Split

Two or more repertoires generated by different sets of contingencies compose two or more selves. A person possesses one repertoire appropriate to his life with his friends and another appropriate to his life with his family. A problem of identity arises when a person finds himself with family and friends at the same time.

Self-knowledge and self-control imply two selves in this sense. The self-knower is almost always a product of social contingencies, but the self that is known may come from other sources. The controlling self (the conscience or superego) is of social origin, but the

controlled self is more likely to be the product of genetic susceptibilities to reinforcement (the id or the Old Adam). The controlling
self generally represents the interests of others; the controlled self
the interests of the individual.

Stranger

The picture that emerges from a scientific analysis is not of a
body with a person inside but of a body that *is* a person in the
sense that it displays a complex repertoire of behavior. The picture
is, of course, unfamiliar. The man we thus portray is a stranger, and
from the traditional point of view he may not seem to be a man at
all.

C. S. Lewis put it bluntly: "Man is being abolished."

There is clearly some difficulty in idenfifying the man to whom
Lewis referred. He cannot have meant the human species; far from
being abolished, it is filling the earth. Nor are individual men growing less effective or productive. What is being abolished is autonomous man—the inner man, the homunculus, the possessing demon,
the man defended by the literatures of freedom and dignity.

His abolition is long overdue. Autonomous man is a device we
use to explain what we cannot explain in any other way. We constructed him from our ignorance, and as our understanding
increases, the very stuff of which he is composed vanishes. Science
does not dehumanize man, it de-homunculizes him, and it must do
so if it is to prevent the abolition of the human species.

To man *qua* man we readily say good riddance. Only by dispossessing autonomous man can we turn to the real causes of human
behavior—from the inferred to the observed, from the miraculous
to the natural, from the inaccessible to the manipulable.

Purpose

It is often said that in doing so we must treat the man who survives as a mere animal. "Animal" is a pejorative term—but only
because "man" has been made spuriously honorific. Joseph Wood
Krutch argued that the traditional view supports Hamlet's exclamation "How like a god!" while Pavlov emphasized "How like a dog!"
But that was a step forward. A god is the archetypal pattern of an
explanatory fiction, of a miracle-working mind, of the metaphysical.
Man is much more than a dog, but like a dog he is within range of
a scientific analysis.

An important role of autonomous man has been to give direction
to human behavior, and it is often said that in dispossessing an
inner agent we leave man without a purpose: "Since a scientific psychology must regard human behavior objectively, as determined by
necessary laws, it must represent human behavior as unintentional."
But "necessary laws" would have this effect only if they referred

exclusively to antecedent conditions. Intention and purpose refer to selective consequences, the effects of which we can formulate in "necessary laws." Has life, in all the forms in which it exists on the surface of the earth, a purpose? And is this evidence of intentional design? The primate hand evolved *in order that* the primate could more successfully manipulate things, but its purpose was to be found not in a prior design but rather in the process of selection. Similarly, in operant conditioning—when a pianist acquires the behavior of playing a smooth scale, for example—we find the purpose of the skilled movement of the hand in the consequences that follow it. In neither the evolution of the human hand nor in the acquired use of the hand is any prior intention or purpose at issue.

There is a difference between biological and individual purpose in that the latter can be felt. No one could have felt the purpose in the development of the human hand, but a person can in a sense feel the purpose with which he plays a smooth scale. But he does not play a smooth scale *because* he feels the purpose of doing so; what he feels is a by-product of his behavior and of its consequences. The relation of the human hand to the contingencies of survival under which it evolved is, of course, out of reach of personal observation; the relation of the behavior to contingencies of reinforcement that have generated it is not.

Control

As a scientific analysis of behavior dispossesses autonomous man and turns the control he has been said to exert over to the environment, the individual may seem particularly vulnerable. He is henceforth to be controlled by the world around him, and in large part by other men. Is he not then simply a victim? Certainly men have been victims, as they have been victimizers, but the word is too strong. It implies despoliation, which is by no means an essential consequence of interpersonal control. But even under benevolent control is the individual not helpless—"at a dead end in his long struggle to control his own destiny"?

It is only autonomous man who has reached a dead end. Man himself may be controlled by his environment, but it is an environment almost wholly of his own making. The physical environment of most persons is largely man-made—the walls that shelter them, the tools they use, the surfaces they walk on—and the social environment is obviously man-made. It generates the language a person speaks, the customs he follows, and the behavior he exhibits with respect to the ethical, religious, governmental, economic, educational and psychotherapeutic institutions that control him.

The evolution of a culture is in fact a kind of gigantic exercise in self-control. As the individual controls himself by manipulating the world he lives in, so the human species has constructed an environment in which its members behave in a highly effective way. Mistakes have been made, and we have no assurance that the environment man has constructed will continue to provide gains that outstrip the losses. But man as we know him, for better or for worse, is what man has made of man.

Roles

This will not satisfy those who cry "Victim!" C. S. Lewis protested: ". . . the power of man to make himself what he pleases . . . means . . . the power of some men to make other men what they please." This is inevitable in the nature of cultural evolution. We must distinguish the controlling self from the controlled self even when they are both inside the same skin, and when control is exercised through the design of an external environment, the selves are, with minor exceptions, distinct.

The person who, purposely or not, introduces a new cultural practice is only one among possibly billions it will affect. If this does not seem like an act of self-control, it is only because we have misunderstood the nature of self-control in the individual.

When a person changes his physical or social environment "intentionally"—that is, in order to change human behavior, possibly including his own—he plays two roles: one as a controller, as the designer of a controlling culture, and another as the controlled, as the product of a culture. There is nothing inconsistent about this; it follows from the nature of the evolution of a culture, with or without intentional design.

The human species probably has undergone little genetic change in recorded time. We have only to go back a thousand generations to reach the artists of the caves of Lascaux. Features bearing directly on survival (such as resistance to disease) change substantially in a thousand generations, but the child of one of the Lascaux artists transplanted to the world of today might be almost indistinguishable from a modern child.

Man has improved himself enormously in the same period of time by changing the world he lives in. Modern religious practices developed over a hundred generations and modern government and law developed in fewer than a hundred. Perhaps no more than 20 generations have been needed to produce modern economic practices, and possibly no more than four or five to produce modern education, psychotherapy, and the physical and biological technologies that have increased man's sensitivity to the world around him and his power to change that world.

Change

Man has "controlled his own destiny," if that expression means anything at all. The man that man has made is the product of the culture man has devised. He has emerged from two quite different processes of evolution: biological and cultural. Both may now accelerate because both are subject to intentional design. Men have already changed their genetic endowment by breeding selectively and by changing contingencies of survival, and for a long time they have introduced cultural practices as cultural mutations. They may now begin to do both with a clearer eye to the consequences.

Stage

The individual is the carrier of both his species and his culture. Cultural practices like genetic traits are transmitted from individual to individual. Even within the most regimented culture every personal history is unique. But the individual remains merely a stage in a process that began long before he came into existence and will long outlast him. He has no ultimate responsibility for a species trait or a cultural practice, even though it was he who underwent the mutation or introduced the practice that became part of the species or culture.

Even if Lamarck had been right in supposing that the individual could change his genetic structure through personal effort, we should have to point to the environmental circumstances responsible for the effort, as we shall have to do when geneticists begin to change the human endowment. And when an individual engages in the intentional design of a cultural practice, we must turn to the culture that induces him to do so and supplies the art or science he uses.

End

One of the great problems of individualism, seldom recognized as such, is death—the inescapable fate of the individual, the final assault on freedom and dignity. Death is one of those remote events that are brought to bear on behavior only with the aid of cultural practices. What we see is the death of others, as in Pascal's famous metaphor: "Imagine a number of men in chains, all under sentence of death, some of whom are each day butchered in the sight of others; those remaining see their own condition in that of their fellows, and looking at each other with grief and despair await their turn. This is an image of the human condition."

Some religions have made death more important by picturing a future existence in heaven or hell, but the individualist has a special reason to fear death: it is the prospect of personal annihilation. The individualist can find no solace in reflecting upon any contribution that will survive him. He has refused to be concerned for the survival of his culture and is not reinforced by the fact that the culture will long survive him. In the defense of his own freedom and dignity he has denied the contributions of the past and must therefore relinquish all claim upon the future.

Pictures

Science probably has never demanded a more sweeping change in a traditional way of thinking about a subject, nor has there ever been a more important subject. In the traditional picture a person perceives the world around him, selects features to be perceived, discriminates among them, judges them good or bad, changes them to make them better (or worse), and may be held responsible for his action and justly rewarded or punished for its consequences. In the scientific picture a person is a member of a species shaped by evolutionary contingencies of survival, displaying behavioral processes that bring him under the control of the environment in which he lives, and largely under the control of a social environment that he and millions of others like him have constructed and maintained during the evolution of a culture. The direction of the controlling relation is reserved: a person does not act upon the world; the world acts upon him.

It is difficult to accept such a change simply on intellectual grounds and nearly impossible to accept its implications. The reaction of the traditionalist is usually described in terms of feelings. One of these, to which the Freudians have appealed in explaining the resistance to psychoanalysis, is wounded vanity. Freud himself expounded, as Ernest Jones said, "the three heavy blows which narcissism or self-love of mankind has suffered at the hands of science. The first was cosmological and was dealt by Copernicus; the second was biological and was dealt by Darwin; the third was psychological and was dealt by Freud." '

But what are the signs or symptoms of wounded vanity, and how shall we explain them? What people do about a scientific picture of man is to call it wrong, demeaning and dangerous, to argue against it, and to attack those who propose or defend it. These are signs of wounded vanity only to the extent that the scientific formulation destroys accustomed reinforcers. If a person can no longer take credit or be admired for what he does, then he seems to suffer a loss of dignity or worth, and behavior previously reinforced by credit or admiration will undergo extinction. Extinction often leads to aggressive attack.

Futility

Another effect of the scientific picture has been described as a loss of faith or "nerve," as a sense of doubt or powerlessness, or as discouragement, depression, or despondency. A person is said to feel that he can do nothing about his own destiny, but what he feels is a weakening of old responses that are no longer reinforced.

Another effect is a kind of nostalgia. Old repertoires break through as traditionalists seize upon and exaggerate similarities between present and past. They call the old days the good old days, when people recognized the inherent dignity of man and the importance of spiritual values. These fragments of outmoded behavior tend to be wistful—that is, they have the character of increasingly unsuccessful behavior.

Rainbow

These reactions to a scientific conception of man are, of course, unfortunate. They immobilize men of good will, and anyone concerned with the future of his culture will do what he can to correct them. No theory changes what it is a theory about. We change nothing because we look at it, talk about it, or analyze it in a new way. Keats drank confusion to Newton for analyzing the rainbow, but the rainbow remained as beautiful as ever and became for many even more beautiful.

Man has not changed because we look at him, talk about him, and analyze him scientifically. His achievements in science, government, religion, art and literature remain as they have always been, to be admired as one admires a storm at sea or autumn foliage or a mountain peak, quite apart from their origins and untouched by a scientific analysis. What does change is our chance of doing something about the subject of a theory. Newton's analysis of the light in a rainbow was a step in the direction of the laser.

Perils

The traditional conception of man is flattering; it confers reinforcing privileges. It is therefore easy to defend and difficult to change. It was designed to build up the individual as an instrument of countercontrol, and it did so effectively, but in such a way as to limit future progress.

We have seen how the literatures of freedom and dignity, with their concern for autonomous man, have perpetuated the use of punishment and condoned the use of only weak nonpunitive techniques. It is not difficult to demonstrate a connection between the unlimited right of the individual to pursue happiness and the catastrophes threatened by unchecked breeding, the unrestrained affluence that exhausts resources and pollutes the environment, and the imminence of nuclear war.

Physical and biological technologies have alleviated pestilence and famine and the painful, dangerous and exhausting features of daily life, and a behavioral technology can begin to alleviate other kinds of ills. In the analysis of human behavior it is just possible that we are slightly beyond Newton's position in the analysis of light, for we are beginning to make technological applications, and there are wonderful possibilities—all the more wonderful because traditional approaches have been so ineffective.

It is hard to imagine a world in which people live together without quarreling, maintain themselves by producing the food, shelter and clothing they need, enjoy themselves and contribute to the enjoyment of others in art, music, literature and games, consume only a reasonable part of the resources of the world and add as little as possible to its pollution, bear no more children than they can raise decently, continue to explore the world around them and discover better ways of dealing with it, and come to know themselves and the world around them accurately and comprehensively. Yet all this is possible. We have not yet seen what man can make of man.

QUESTIONS

1. What does Skinner say to indicate that he expects disagreement? Does he make any concessions in his address to his readers that would suggest an effort to win over those who disagree with him?
2. Do you find Skinner hard to read? If so, is it because his ideas are strange and disturbing, or because of his writing style? Does he pass the six stylistic tests that Orwell sets (p. 333)? If so (or if not), does that affect the validity, or the persuasiveness, of his argument? How?
3. The following essay deals with issues raised in "What Is Man?" Which writer do you find more logical, and which more convincing? Why?

WILLARD GAYLIN

Skinner Redux

It is a peculiarity of behavior control research, compared to almost all other biological experimentation, that success is more likely to bring dejection than joy. Devices that save or extend life aggrandize both the discoverer and general man, with the suggestion that such control of death, while still not the immortality of gods, is a cut above the helplessness of the general animal host. Behavior manipulation, on the other hand, reasserts our kinship with the pigeon and the rat. The more technological the control devices, the more mechanical the method, the scarier it all seems.

The most blatant behavior modification procedures—and technologically the most sophisticated—involve direct physical or chemical intervention into central nervous system functions. We have drugs that are more than "ups" or "downs," more specialized, more exact, pinpointing the emotions to be inhibited or enhanced. The structure of the brain is becoming more understandable, allowing for either specific destructive psychosurgery or stimulating devices to modify behavior. Electrodes with receivers and transmitters the size of quarters can be inserted into the brain to pattern in or out "desirable" or "undesirable" behavior. This year's angst has centered on psychosurgery, and while people may not know the difference between a cingulectomy and a thalomotomy, they know enough to be frightened by both. If this were not enough, we also seem to be on the verge of being able to alter the genetic components of man. Amniocentesis (a procedure for intrauterine diagnosis of the nature of the fetus) combined with free access to abortion already permits some selectivity in breeding, and the capacity for direct modification of genes may soon be available, if we wish, as a significant modifier of future man and his behavior.

Compared with all of this, operant conditioning, last year's *dernier cri*,[1] appears positively antique. Now that copies of *Beyond Freedom and Dignity* have been safely removed from thousands of coffee tables and tucked away on bookshelves unread, avuncular old Doc Skinner has slipped out of public consciousness. Today it passes almost unnoticed that there is a growing institutional interest in his theories for controlling man through manipulation of the environment. While conditioning is a less dramatic form of behavior modification than, for example, psychosurgery, it should concern us no less, especially when the federal government is preparing programs designed along Skinnerian lines. Inevitably these experiments are to be undertaken in the prisons, those unfailing institutions of failure, where each new indignity is traditionally presented as an act of grace.

At present, the government's investment in Skinnerism is limited, and not directed where most effective—the early years. That conditioning in early life can modify future behavior is undeniable. That it will be so used in the future seems inescapable. How it should be used is another question. The more specific and limited the behavior to be modified, the safer. But even relatively modest proposals require caution. The complexities of human development and human behavior are such that optimism may be arrogance, and arrogance may be fatal. The cure to one problem usually comes packaged with the cause of another. As we increase our readiness to manipulate, to control and maneuver man, we must balance where we can the profits gained thereby against the corresponding losses in other areas. Given the quiet acceptance that has been accorded Skinner's ideas in some quarters, and the programs that are resulting from them, it seems worthwhile to take an unhurried stroll around Walden Two[2] to remark on the garden path down which we are being led.

The swap that Dr. Skinner asks us to make is freedom for security. Dr. Skinner attempts to ease the pain by his reflections that this swap is not only necessary, but a free ride. We gain a great deal and we give up nothing, for freedom is only an illusion.

He starts his argument with disconcerting assumptions that seem

---

1. The latest rage or fad.
2. *Walden Two* and *Beyond Freedom* *and Dignity* are among the books written by the psychologist B. F. Skinner.

generally to have been swallowed whole. He says: "Were it not for the unwarranted generalization that all control is wrong, we should deal with the social environment as simply as we deal with the non-social." I know of no such generalization. Freedom and control are not a moral polarity in anyone's philosophy. The entire social structure is built on the right and need of society to control, indeed, coerce, certain behavior from the individual. Organized religion, organized morality, codified ethics, style and fashion, public education, civil law, constitutional law, criminal procedures, all operate in one way or another within a whole range of explicit and implicit control mechanisms. Unrestricted personal liberty (I presume that is what Dr. Skinner means by freedom in this quotation) has rarely been offered as an ideal for social living by any intelligent thinker. From Plato to the last decisions of the Supreme Court one sees the deliberation of the private right versus the public interest. Think of the current ecology movement with the insistence on ever greater controls. Is there anyone left who in the name of freedom glorifies man's right to pollute his environment? If anything, I suspect the balance today is in the opposite direction. The clearly held aspirations are more likely to be peace, order, harmony, efficiency, and security, instead of such unfashionable and romantically tainted concepts as dignity, humanity, and freedom.

In the psychology market, particularly, freedom has few buyers. The two major influences here, behaviorism and psychoanalysis, may be antagonistic in every other way but they have traditionally joined in blissfully embracing determinism. In both theories the cause-and-effect model of physics has been applied to the behavior of man. Never mind that the psychoanalyst and behavior psychologist see each other as putting the cart before the horse. It really matters very little. They are both concerned with the same cart and the same horse and neither has had any doubt that the problem is a cart-horse one, or a horse-cart one, depending on the orientation. Both see behavior as a complex end point, a mathematical resultant of a number of forces and counter-forces, or experiences and conditioning, accumulated over the years, and patterning the individual in such a way as to produce one logical and inevitable result. The concept of psychic determinism allows no place for free choice or free action. Ironically, while rejecting free will in theory, in practice the psychoanalyst demands it. This somewhat illogical dualism has been the only way the analyst could function as both therapist and theorist. The compromise reached was that, while freedom of behavior may not exist for man, the illusion of freedom was essential to effect change.

This may be an effective device in individual therapy but it is not a useful concept for a society that aspires to justice. One need only consider the relationship of psychoanalysis and law to see the sterility of psychic determinism. It is an impotent tool because in theory it will not differentiate between grotesquely different qualities of behavior. When a judge in a court of law is forced to distinguish between a free and a compelled act, he is not helped by being told by either a psychoanalyst or a behaviorist that all acts are compelled. Civilized society seems to require that there be a distinction between a man who violates the law with a gun pointed at his head and a man who commits the same violation for greed.

Even if we accept in principle the concept of psychic determinism, human behavior is not, and never will be, analyzable into all of its components, and therefore cannot be usefully considered to operate on the model of causality supplied by physical scientists. Despite Dr. Skinner's reassurance that "new evidences of the predictability of human behavior" are being discovered, most of man's actions, particularly in areas of volition and cognition, will involve so many variables as to make predictability almost impossible. Let me offer an example: A man is five pounds overweight and he has just decided that he will stop all snacks for the next month. It is the first night of this resolve. He is seated at a dinner meeting, listening to a rather dull lecture on freedom and determinism. The waiter places in front of him a bowl of peanuts, a particular weakness of our would-be dieter. Within ten seconds, the subject has an impulse to take a peanut. The question is simply to predict whether he will take the peanut or not at the time of that first impulse. Obviously, no one of the scientific mind would accept this test case and make a prediction. There are too many variables which are unknown to determine this particular piece of behavior. It is no different from being given a complex problem in physics with incomplete data. We simply could not know.

Now let us examine the next step. You are given the data that he does not follow his impulse. He does not take the peanut. Without analyzing the variables, you know that an entire lifetime of complex inputs toward taking the peanut have been placed on one side of the scale and an entire lifetime of training and conditioning to resist the peanut are added to the other side of the scale. We are asked to believe that, given that particular individual, that particular lifetime, and those particular conditions, at that particular moment of time, the refusal of the peanut was predetermined, in precisely the same way as if balancing weights were added to one side or the other. You are then told that three seconds later he has a second impulse. You now have the great advantage of knowing that an entire lifetime of inputs and variables, whether knowable or not, have culminated in the first decision to resist the impulse. Are you now prepared to predict the response to the second impulse?

You are not. Even though you start with the resultant of the immense number of seconds before the first decision and all you have to balance against that is three insignificant seconds of time. And if I were to give you the pattern of fifty impulses leading both to acceptance and rejection, you would be no better off predicting the fifty-first even if the interval were reduced to one-tenth of a second. For the number of variables that could be introduced in that fraction of time are as incalculable as those in that mass of time preceding the first decision. The same is not true of weights and measures, and that is what makes prediction of human behavior different from prediction of the behavior of inanimate things or of simple animal forms. Whether that is truly a "free" choice or not, it is an incalculable choice, and as such can pass for freedom.

Of course, we all know we can condition a man to reject peanuts. But my example has nothing to do with peanuts. It is concerned with impulse and control, passion and reason, appetite and knowledge, pleasure and safety, rationalization and rationality, hunger and wants, instinct and learning, motives and counter-motives, thought and action—and the complexity of the human mind, which in denying predictability, defies programming.

This is not to say that it is impossible to modify human behavior. I would not be a practicing psychiatrist if I believed it were impossible. Nor am I saying that it is not possible and even desirable to modify environment so as to encourage certain traits and discourage others, but it is impossible to guarantee any given results in precisely those more complex areas which are ultimately the crucial aspects of human behavior to control. What *is* possible to control may not warrant the excessive price that might have to be paid for it.

It should be understood, of course, that there are many ways of changing behavior besides modifying environment. Dr. Skinner tells us that "a person's behavior is determined by a genetic endowment traceable to the evolutionary history of the species and by the environmental circumstances to which as an individual he has been exposed." This is precisely the view expounded by Freud some fifty years ago in A *General Introduction to Psychoanalysis*. It is the kind of statement that we are all inclined to accept, as a generality. What else is there but nature and nurture? It is in the specific implications of the statement that the difficulty lies, because Dr. Skinner means "determined" not in the sense of "influenced by," but in a fixed sense. In addition, he tends to see environmental circumstances as accretions of a very specific kind of individualized experience. Given his specific meanings, he creates a model which seems to lead logically to only one conclusion. If something is caused by A and B, and if A is fixed, one must change B. Broad models often dictate narrow solutions. This one seems to indicate that only environmental manipulation works.

Let me offer another model, however. All human behavior, normal and neurotic, all action and emotion, all feeling and conduct, are mediated by physical-chemical reactions. This is another cliché which is obviously true. That does not, however, imply that the *only* way we can change behavior is through physical-chemical means, nor that the desired way to change behavior is through physical-chemical means. It certainly says nothing about which behavior is best changed by this means or which is unlikely ever to be changed this way. Even were we capable of finally solving chemical riddles of perception and action it is doubtful whether we would "understand" everything better in those terms or in that language. If we were capable of dissecting and analyzing a symphony in terms of frequencies, wave lengths, overtones, vibrations and all, we might add to our knowledge of music and composition, but it is doubtful that we would "understand" the symphony better than by listening to it. Nor would we find it easier to create an original great symphony.

Man's experience is not quite so specific as the sum of small learnings. There are mechanisms whereby environment can influence behavior wholesale, without having specifically been experienced. I am referring here to such concepts as identification, whereby the life experiences of another individual can be absorbed totally into our acting systems without having gone through our own personal experience. We may behave like our father, not because we experienced what our father did, but because we identify with him and in that identification we begin to act as we know he would, independent of reward and punishment, pleasure or pain. Whole modes of behavior will be instituted by that strange mechanism, halfway to love, that we call identification. Again, this is not to say that the modification of specific environmental factors cannot modify certain behaviors, but it is hardly the only, or necessarily the best, way.

Whatever the methods of learning—or programming—the lessons of the past will have a somber relevance. All that is predictable is minor in comparison with what is not predictable. This history of scientific and institutional approaches to controlling behavior gives us little comfort about the future of scientific behavior control. In many ways we have been better served by happenstance than social design. One need only look at the state of our designed institutions today—our prisons, our mental institutions, and our schools—to question the wisdom of social science in social engineering.

Any engineered society or engineered individual must be based on some pattern of correctness or normalcy, and the attempts to define this have been conspicuous failures in psychology. Dr. Skinner suggests his criteria for a good society. It must: (1) provide for order and security; (2) produce necessary goods; (3) maintain a healthy environment; (4) provide for education. All of these vague and general platitudes can exist in a monstrous as well as a benevolent society—depending on who defines "healthy" or "necessary," for example. But then he adds two more. He tells us that a good society must: "provide for the pursuit and achievement of happiness." What a blessed relief; what a leavening that offers. But what kind of word is "happiness," issuing from Dr. Skinner's scientific lips? What kind of behavior is it? How does he measure it? How can he recognize the contingencies for it? Lastly, he also reassures us that he wants a culture that will "encourage its members to examine its practices and to experiment with new ones." How does one encourage experimentation with determined behavior? What will be the limits of "experimentation" to be encouraged? Will we experiment with violence? Will we experiment with disobedience? How can a predetermined man experiment with deviations from the particular code, especially if the whole purpose of the conditioning is to assure subscribing to the code?

Dr. Skinner does give us some specific ideas of what problem areas demand our attention. He is disturbed that "students no longer respond in traditional ways to educational environments; they drop out of school, possibly for long periods of time, they take only courses which they enjoy or which seem to have relevance to their problems." So we will program in proper respect for learning. He is distressed that "many young people work as little as possible," and that is because "something is wrong with the contingencies which induce men to work industriously and carefully." We are also told, "that a serious problem arises when young people refuse to serve in the armed forces and desert or defect to other countries," and the solution here should seem a little embarrassing even to Dr. Skinner, although he doggedly insists that "what must be changed are the contingencies which induce young people to behave in given ways toward their governments."

Dr. Skinner is designing the world that he would like now, but he himself has said: "The problem is to design a world which will be liked not by people as they now are but by those who live in it." How in this world is he planning to do that? The examples he uses are not even what people in his world like, only what people of his generation like, and that is a world that is being passed by. We live in a technological age, in which things move fast, and generational life is shortened. The average college student often doesn't recognize an identity with a high-school sibling. Technology speeds up change to a frightening degree. Yet we are asked to do conditioning starting with the neonate, in order to guarantee the adult behavior in some unknown culture twenty to thirty years later that will not be inhabited by the designer. This time gap also discredits Dr. Skinner's reassurance that the democratic process will be maintained because "the principle of making the controller a member of the group he controls should apply to the designer of the culture." Since most of the control will be done on neonates, are we to have six-month-old designers?

It would be supremely difficult to find the guidelines that might indicate the most adaptive and rewarding values for a future whose conditions can only be partially anticipated. Dr. Skinner feels that it should be possible to "turn to the sources of the things people call good." But it is difficult to understand precisely where he would find his definitions for the good behavior. He has previously specifically rejected "almost every theory" in "political science, law, religion, economics, anthropology, sociology, psychotherapy, philosophy, ethics, history, education, child care, linguistics, architecture, city planning, and family life" as a "tremendous weight of traditional 'knowledge' which must be corrected or displaced." He refers to "the ultimate sources as being found in the evolution of the species and the evolution of the culture." But how is he to find ultimate, final, conclusive answers from the culture that is not only in process but, according to him, evolving on false premises?

Perhaps what Dr. Skinner really is saying is not that we are entitled to condition man since he is not free at any rate, but that we *must* condition man because he *is* free, and that freedom includes the freedom to be aggressive, the freedom to be immoral, the freedom to be destructive. I suppose if we come to the conclusion that the very survival of the species necessitates the abandonment of our concepts of freedom or, indeed, the abandonment of freedom itself, behavior conditioning would be necessary. The question is, are we at that point? At this stage of the world's development it is fashionable to think so and it is understandable. Given the horrors of the atomic age, it is not surprising that the most popular generalization about man in the last twenty years has been as hunter, killer, and aggressor.

But biologically we can make a better case for man as the loving animal. No species is helpless and dependent for so large a portion of its life-span as man. Incapable of either fight or flight, the two conventional mechanisms of survival, the defenseless and passive infant survives only in dependency. His very existence depends on the strength and support of the loving adult who will sacrifice himself, if need be, for the survival of the young. It is inconceivable that any species so designed could have survived if this were left to the chance institutions of education and culture. One must assume that built genetically into the organism is a protective response to the helpless member of the species.

Our whole biological view of man can be built starting with the enforced social structures that the prolonged dependency state dictate. In *Totem and Taboo*, one of the most criticized and, superficially, one of the most ingenuous of Freud's works, a hypothesis not unlike this is offered. True it is couched in the most naive genetic concepts, but it can be seen as a prophetic work transcending even the ignorance of genetics that Freud shared with his times. Stripped of the specifics which make it seem silly, Freud is saying that we cannot explain the survival of the group by the institutions of our society that facilitate social living, but rather the institutions are a product of a genetically fixed demand for them. He is saying, in essence, that it cannot be an accident of culture that we have survived; we are of necessity social animals with a genetic inheritance that must include certain taboos directed against crimes of violence within the group. The capacity for love, caring, empathy, and compassion are part of our natural endowment.

Theodosius Dobzhansky and others have pointed out that although culture is man's product, it also becomes his producer. *Whenever we alter our view of man and build it into our institutions, our altered view, independent of whether it is true or not, will become a determinant in the nature of the evolving man.* Dr. Skinner denies this when he concludes his book with the amazing statement: "No theory changes what it is a theory about; man remains what he has always been." This seems an incredible view from a psychologist. The attitude it expresses has usually been described as one of the crucial distinctions between psychological and physical definitions. It is true that if we define a solid as a gas it nonetheless retains its solidity; the atomic weight of an element is what it is despite our ignorant assumptions. But man is a product of his environment—which is what I had thought Dr. Skinner was saying—and he therefore becomes that which the environment makes him. Was Dr. Skinner not decrying such ideas as freedom which, by shaping the way that culture treats man, determines the nature of the man produced by that culture? In great part, that has seemed to me to be Dr. Skinner's thesis, and if he chooses to contradict himself at the end, it is only the final mystification.

The principle that our view of man will create a man in that image seems a reasonable assumption. Psychological and sociological theories do become self-fulfilling prophecies, and this must be a consideration in any attempts to engineer a new man. In attempting to improve man's condition we must not destroy that which is uniquely human. I do not agree with Dr. Skinner that man's strength is science and technology. They are only his products. I think the badger in *The Once and Future King*[3] defined the uniqueness of the human condition best, and we would do well to keep that view in mind when confronted with Skinnerian plans for the future.

When God had manufactured all of the eggs out of which the fishes and the serpents and the birds and the mammals . . . would eventually emerge, He called the embryos before him, and saw that they were good.

The embryos stood in front of God, with their fetal hands clasped politely over their stomachs and their heavy heads hanging down respectfully, and God addressed them. He said: "Now, you embryos,

3. A work of fiction by T. H. White.

here you are, all looking exactly the same, and We are going to give you the choice of what you want to be. When you grow up you will get bigger anyway, but we are pleased to grant you another gift as well. You may alter any parts of yourselves into anything which you think would be useful to you in later life. Now then . . . , step up and choose your tools, but remember that what you choose you will grow into, and will have to stick to."

At the very end of the sixth day they had got through all the little embryos except one. This embryo was man.

"Please God," said the embryo, "I think that you made me into a shape which I now have for reasons best known to Yourselves, and that it would be rude to change. If I am to have my choice I will stay as I am. I will not alter any of the parts which you gave me, for other and doubtless inferior tools, and I will stay a defenseless embryo all my life, doing my best to make myself a few futile implements out of the wood, iron, and the other materials which you have seen· fit to put before me."

"Well done," exclaimed the Creator in delighted tones. "Hear all you embryos, come here with your beaks and whatnots to look upon Our first Man. He is the only one who has guessed Our riddle, out of all of you, and We have great pleasure in conferring upon him the Order of Dominion over the Fowls of the Air, and the Beasts of the Earth and the Fishes of the Sea. Now let the rest of you get along and love and multiply, for it is time to knock off for the weekend. As for you, Man, you will be a naked tool all your life, though a user of tools. You will look like an embryo until they bury you, but all the others will be embryos before your might. Eternally undeveloped, you will always remain potentially in Our Image, able to see some of Our sorrows and to feel some of Our joys. We are partly sorry for you, man, but partly hopeful."

CHARLES SANDERS PEIRCE
The Fixation of Belief[1]

That which determines us, from given premises, to draw one inference rather than another, is some habit of mind, whether it be constitutional or acquired. The habit is good or otherwise, according as it produces true conclusions from true premises or not; and an inference is regarded as valid or not, without reference to the truth or falsity of its conclusion specially, but according as the habit which determines it is such as to produce true conclusions in general or not. The particular habit of mind which governs this or that inference may be formulated in a proposition whose truth depends on the validity of the inferences which the habit determines; and such a formula is called a *guiding principle* of inference. Suppose, for example, that we observe that a rotating disk of copper quickly comes to rest when placed between the poles of a magnet, and we infer that this will happen with every disk of copper. The guiding

---

1. The first in a series of papers, "Illustrations of the Logic of Science," published by Peirce in *The Popular Science Monthly*, 1877-1878.

principle is, that what is true of one piece of copper is true of another. Such a guiding principle with regard to copper would be much safer than with regard to many other substances—brass, for example.

A book might be written to signalize all the most important of these guiding principles of reasoning. It would probably be, we must confess, of no service to a person whose thought is directed wholly to practical subjects, and whose activity moves along thoroughly-beaten paths. The problems which present themselves to such a mind are matters of routine which he has learned once for all to handle in learning his business. But let a man venture into an unfamiliar field, or where his results are not continually checked by experience, and all history shows that the most masculine intellect will ofttimes lose his orientation and waste his efforts in directions which bring him no nearer to his goal, or even carry him entirely astray. He is like a ship in the open sea, with no one on board who understands the rules of navigation. And in such a case some general study of the guiding principles of reasoning would be sure to be found useful.

The subject could hardly be treated, however, without being first limited; since almost any fact may serve as a guiding principle. But it so happens that there exists a division among facts, such that in one class are all those which are absolutely essential as guiding principles, while in the others are all which have any other interest as objects of research. This division is between those which are necessarily taken for granted in asking whether a certain conclusion follows from certain premises, and those which are not implied in that question. A moment's thought will show that a variety of facts are already assumed when the logical question is first asked. It is implied, for instance, that there are such states of mind as doubt and belief—that a passage from one to the other is possible, the object of thought remaining the same, and that this transition is subject to some rules which all minds are alike bound by. As these are facts which we must already know before we can have any clear conception of reasoning at all, it cannot be supposed to be any longer of much interest to inquire into their truth or falsity. On the other hand, it is easy to believe that those rules of reasoning which are deduced from the very idea of the process are the ones which are the most essential; and, indeed, that so long as it conforms to these it will, at least, not lead to false conclusions from true premises. In point of fact, the importance of what may be deduced from the assumptions involved in the logical question turns out to be greater than might be supposed, and this for reasons which it is difficult to exhibit at the outset. The only one which I shall here mention is, that conceptions which are really products of logical reflection, without being readily seen to be so, mingle with our ordinary thoughts, and are frequently the causes of great confusion. This is the case, for example, with the conception of quality. A quality as such is never an object of observation. We can see that a thing is blue or green, but the quality of being blue and the quality of being green are not things which we see; they are products of logical reflection. The truth is, that common-sense, or thought as it first emerges above the level of the narrowly practical, is deeply imbued with that bad logical quality to which the epithet *metaphysical* is commonly applied; and nothing can clear it up but a severe course of logic.

We generally know when we wish to ask a question and when we wish to pronounce a judgment, for there is a dissimilarity between the sensation of doubting and that of believing.

But this is not all which distinguishes doubt from belief. There is a practical difference. Our beliefs guide our desires and shape our actions. The Assassins, or followers of the Old Man of the Mountain, used to rush into death at his least command, because they believed that obedience to him would insure everlasting felicity. Had they doubted this, they would not have acted as they did. So it is with every belief, according to its degree. The feeling of believing is a more or less sure indication of there being established in our nature some habit which will determine our actions. Doubt never has such an effect.

Nor must we overlook a third point of difference. Doubt is an uneasy and dissatisfied state from which we struggle to free ourselves and pass into the state of belief; while the latter is a calm and satisfactory state which we do not wish to avoid, or to change to a belief in anything else.[2] On the contrary, we cling tenaciously, not merely to believing, but to believing just what we do believe.

Thus, both doubt and belief have positive effects upon us, though very different ones. Belief does not make us act at once, but puts us into such a condition that we shall behave in a certain way, when the occasion arises. Doubt has not the least effect of this sort, but stimulates us to action until it is destroyed. This reminds us of the irritation of a nerve and the reflex action produced thereby; while for the analogue of belief, in the nervous system, we must look to what are called nervous associations—for example, to that habit of the nerves in consequence of which the smell of a peach will make the mouth water.

The irritation of doubt causes a struggle to attain a state of belief. I shall term this struggle *inquiry*, though it must be admitted that this is sometimes not a very apt designation.

The irritation of doubt is the only immediate motive for the struggle to attain belief. It is certainly best for us that our beliefs should be such as may truly guide our actions so as to satisfy our desires; and this reflection will make us reject any belief which does not seem to have been so formed as to insure this result. But

---

2. I am not speaking of secondary effects occasionally produced by the in- terference of other impulses [Peirce's note].

it will only do so by creating a doubt in the place of that belief. With the doubt, therefore, the struggle begins, and with the cessation of doubt it ends. Hence, the sole object of inquiry is the settlement of opinion. We may fancy that this is not enough for us, and that we seek, not merely an opinion, but a true opinion. But put this fancy to the test, and it proves groundless; for as soon as a firm belief is reached we are entirely satisfied, whether the belief be true or false. And it is clear that nothing out of the sphere of our knowledge can be our object, for nothing which does not affect the mind can be the motive for a mental effort. The most that can be maintained is, that we seek for a belief that we shall *think* to be true. But we think each one of our beliefs to be true, and, indeed, it is mere tautology to say so.

That the settlement of opinion is the sole end of inquiry is a very important proposition. It sweeps away, at once, various vague and erroneous conceptions of proof. A few of these may be noticed here.

1. Some philosophers have imagined that to start an inquiry it was only necessary to utter a question or set it down upon paper, and have even recommended us to begin our studies with questioning everything! But the mere putting of a proposition into the interrogative form does not stimulate the mind to any struggle after belief. There must be a real and living doubt, and without this all discussion is idle.

2. It is a very common idea that a demonstration must rest on some ultimate and absolutely indubitable propositions. These, according to one school, are first principles of a general nature; according to another, are first sensations. But, in point of fact, an inquiry, to have that completely satisfactory result called demonstration, has only to start with propositions perfectly free from all actual doubt. If the premises are not in fact doubted at all, they cannot be more satisfactory than they are.

3. Some people seem to love to argue a point after all the world is fully convinced of it. But no further advance can be made. When doubt ceases, mental action on the subject comes to an end; and, if it did go on, it would be without a purpose.

If the settlement of opinion is the sole object of inquiry, and if belief is of the nature of a habit, why should we not attain the desired end, by taking any answer to a question which we may fancy, and constantly reiterating it to ourselves, dwelling on all which may conduce to that belief, and learning to turn with contempt and hatred from anything which might disturb it? This simple and direct method is really pursued by many men. I remember once being entreated not to read a certain newspaper lest it might change my opinion upon free-trade. "Lest I might be entrapped by its fallacies and misstatements," was the form of expression. "You are not," my friend said, "a special student of political economy. You might, therefore, easily be deceived by fallacious arguments upon the subject. You might, then, if you read this paper, be led to believe in protection. But you admit that free-trade is the true doctrine; and you do not wish to believe what is not true." I have often known this system to be deliberately adopted. Still oftener, the instinctive dislike of an undecided state of mind, exaggerated into a vague dread of doubt, makes men cling spasmodically to the views they already take. The man feels that, if he only holds to his belief without wavering, it will be entirely satisfactory. Nor can it be denied that a steady and immovable faith yields great peace of mind. It may, indeed, give rise to inconveniences, as if a man should resolutely continue to believe that fire would not burn him, or that he would be eternally damned if he received his *ingesta* otherwise than through a stomach-pump. But then the man who adopts this method will not allow that its inconveniences are greater than its advantages. He will say, "I hold steadfastly to the truth, and the truth is always wholesome." And in many cases it may very well be that the pleasure he derives from his calm faith overbalances any inconveniences resulting from its deceptive character. Thus, if it be true that death is annihilation, then the man who believes that he will certainly go straight to heaven when he dies, provided he have fulfilled certain simple observances in this life, has a cheap pleasure which will not be followed by the least disappointment. A similar consideration seems to have weight with many persons in religious topics, for we frequently hear it said, "Oh, I could not believe so-and-so, because I should be wretched if I did." When an ostrich buries its head in the sand as danger approaches, it very likely takes the happiest course. It hides the danger, and then calmly says there is no danger; and, if it feels perfectly sure there is none, why should it raise its head to see? A man may go through life, systematically keeping out of view all that might cause a change in his opinions, and if he only succeeds—basing his method, as he does, on two fundamental psychological laws—I do not see what can be said against his doing so. It would be an egotistical impertinence to object that his procedure is irrational, for that only amounts to saying that his method of settling belief is not ours. He does not propose to himself to be rational, and, indeed, will often talk with scorn of man's weak and illusive reason. So let him think as he pleases.

But this method of fixing belief, which may be called the method of tenacity, will be unable to hold its ground in practice. The social impulse is against it. The man who adopts it will find that other men think differently from him, and it will be apt to occur to him, in some saner moment, that their opinions are quite as good as his own, and this will shake his confidence in his belief. This conception, that another man's thought or sentiment may be equivalent to one's own, is a distinctly new step, and a highly important one. It arises from an impulse too strong in man to be suppressed, without danger of destroying the human species. Unless we make ourselves hermits, we shall necessarily influence each other's opinions; so that the problem becomes how to fix belief, not in the individual merely, but in the community.

Let the will of the state act, then, instead of that of the individual. Let an institution be created which shall have for its object to keep correct doctrines before the attention of the people, to reiterate them perpetually, and to teach them to the young; having at the same time power to prevent contrary doctrines from being taught, advocated, or expressed. Let all possible causes of a change of mind be removed from men's apprehensions. Let them be kept ignorant, lest they should learn of some reason to think otherwise than they do. Let their passions be enlisted, so that they may regard private and unusual opinions with hatred and horror. Then, let all men who reject the established belief be terrified into silence. Let the people turn out and tar-and-feather such men, or let inquisitions be made into the manner of thinking of suspected persons, and, when they are found guilty of forbidden beliefs, let them be subjected to some signal punishment. When complete agreement could not otherwise be reached, a general massacre of all who have not thought in a certain way has proved a very effective means of settling opinion in a country. If the power to do this be wanting, let a list of opinions be drawn up, to which no man of the least independence of thought can assent, and let the faithful be required to accept all these propositions, in order to segregate them as radically as possible from the influence of the rest of the world.

This method has, from the earliest times, been one of the chief means of upholding correct theological and political doctrines, and of preserving their universal or catholic character. In Rome, especially, it has been practiced from the days of Numa Pompilius[3] to those of Pius Nonus.[4] This is the most perfect example in history; but wherever there is a priesthood—and no religion has been without one—this method has been more or less made use of. Wherever there is an aristocracy, or a guild, or any association of a class of men whose interests depend or are supposed to depend on certain propositions, there will be inevitably found some traces of this natural product of social feeling. Cruelties always accompany this system; and when it is consistently carried out, they become atrocities of the most horrible kind in the eyes of any rational man. Nor should this occasion surprise, for the officer of a society does not

3. The legendary second king of Rome (715-672 B.C.), supposed to be the founder of nearly all the early religious institutions of Rome.

4. Pope, 1846-1878, foe of modernism, proclaimer of the important dogma of the Immaculate Conception, first pope to be regarded infallible.

feel justified in surrendering the interests of that society for the sake of mercy, as he might his own private interests. It is natural, therefore, that sympathy and fellowship should thus produce a most ruthless power.

In judging this method of fixing belief, which may be called the method of authority, we must, in the first place, allow its immeasurable mental and moral superiority to the method of tenacity. Its success is proportionately greater; and, in fact, it has over and over again worked the most majestic results. The mere structures of stone which it has caused to be put together—in Siam, for example, in Egypt, and in Europe—have many of them a sublimity hardly more than rivaled by the greatest works of Nature. And, except the geological epochs, there are no periods of time so vast as those which are measured by some of these organized faiths. If we scrutinize the matter closely, we shall find that there has not been one of their creeds which has remained always the same; yet the change is so slow as to be imperceptible during one person's life, so that individual belief remains sensibly fixed. For the mass of mankind, then, there is perhaps no better method than this. If it is their highest impulse to be intellectual slaves, then slaves they ought to remain.

But no institution can undertake to regulate opinions upon every subject. Only the most important ones can be attended to, and on the rest men's minds must be left to the action of natural causes. This imperfection will be no source of weakness so long as men are in such a state of culture that one opinion does not influence another—that is, so long as they cannot put two and two together. But in the most priestridden states some individuals will be found who are raised above that condition. These men possess a wider sort of social feeling; they see that men in other countries and in other ages have held to very different doctrines from those which they themselves have been brought up to believe; and they cannot help seeing that it is the mere accident of their having been taught as they have, and of their having been surrounded with the manners and associations they have, that has caused them to believe as they do and not far differently. And their candor cannot resist the reflection that there is no reason to rate their own views at a higher value than those of other nations and other centuries; and this gives rise to doubts in their minds.

They will further perceive that such doubts as these must exist in their minds with reference to every belief which seems to be determined by the caprice either of themselves or of those who originated the popular opinions. The willful adherence to a belief, and the arbitrary forcing of it upon others, must, therefore, both be given up, and a new method of settling opinions must be adopted, which shall not only produce an impulse to believe, but shall also decide what proposition it is which is to be believed. Let the action of natural preferences be unimpeded, then, and under their influence let men, conversing together and regarding matters in different lights, gradually develop beliefs in harmony with natural causes. This method resembles that by which conceptions of art have been brought to maturity. The most perfect example of it is to be found in the history of metaphysical philosophy. Systems of this sort have not usually rested upon any observed facts, at least not in any great degree. They have been chiefly adopted because their fundamental propositions seemed "agreeable to reason." This is an apt expression; it does not mean that which agrees with experience, but that which we find ourselves inclined to believe. Plato, for example, finds it agreeable to reason that the distances of the celestial spheres from one another should be proportional to the different lengths of strings which produce harmonious chords. Many philosophers have been led to their main conclusions by considerations like this; but this is the lowest and least developed form which the method takes, for it is clear that another man might find Kepler's theory, that the celestial spheres are proportional to the inscribed and circumscribed spheres of the different regular solids, more agreeable to *his* reason. But the shock of opinions will soon lead men to rest on preferences of a far more universal nature. Take, for example, the doctrine that man only acts selfishly—that is, from the consideration that acting in one way will afford him more pleasure than acting in another. This rests on no fact in the world, but it has had a wide acceptance as being the only reasonable theory.

This method is far more intellectual and respectable from the point of view of reason than either of the others which we have noticed. But its failure has been the most manifest. It makes of inquiry something similar to the development of taste; but taste, unfortunately, is always more or less a matter of fashion, and accordingly metaphysicians have never come to any fixed agreement, but the pendulum has swung backward and forward between a more material and a more spiritual philosophy, from the earliest times to the latest. And so from this, which has been called the *a priori* method, we are driven, in Lord Bacon's phrase. to a true induction. We have examined into this *a priori* method as something which promised to deliver our opinions from their accidental and capricious element. But development, while it is a process which eliminates the effect of some casual circumstances, only magnifies that of others. This method, therefore, does not differ in a very essential way from that of authority. The government may not have lifted its finger to influence my convictions; I may have been left outwardly quite free to choose, we will say, between monogamy and polygamy, and, appealing to my conscience only, I may have concluded that the latter practice is in itself licentious. But when I come to see that the chief obstacle to the spread of

Christianity among a people of as high culture as the Hindus has been a conviction of the immorality of our way of treating women, I cannot help seeing that, though governments do not interfere, sentiments in their development will be very greatly determined by accidental causes. Now, there are some people, among whom I must suppose that my reader is to be found, who, when they see that any belief of theirs is determined by any circumstance extraneous to the facts, will from that moment not merely admit in words that that belief is doubtful, but will experience a real doubt of it, so that it ceases to be a belief.

To satisfy our doubts, therefore, it is necessary that a method should be found by which our beliefs may be caused by nothing human, but by some external permanency—by something upon which our thinking has no effect. Some mystics imagine that they have such a method in a private inspiration from on high. But that is only a form of the method of tenacity, in which the conception of truth as something public is not yet developed. Our external permanency could not be external, in our sense, if it was restricted in its influence to one individual. It must be something which affects, or might affect, every man. And, though these affections are necessarily as various as are individual conditions, yet the method must be such that the ultimate conclusion of every man shall be the same. Such is the method of science. Its fundamental hypothesis, restated in more familiar language, is this: There are real things, whose characters are entirely independent of our opinions about them; those realities affect our senses according to regular laws, and, though our sensations are as different as our relations to the objects, yet, by taking advantage of the laws of perception, we can ascertain by reasoning how things really are, and any man, if he have sufficient experience and reason enough about it, will be led to the one true conclusion. The new conception here involved is that of reality. It may be asked how I know that there are any realities. If this hypothesis is the sole support of my method of inquiry, my method of inquiry must not be used to support my hypothesis. The reply is this: (1) If investigation cannot be regarded as proving that there are real things, it at least does not lead to a contrary conclusion; but the method and the conception on which it is based remain ever in harmony. No doubts of the method, therefore, necessarily arise from its practice, as is the case with all the others. (2) The feeling which gives rise to any method of fixing belief is a dissatisfaction at two repugnant propositions. But here already is a vague concession that there is some *one* thing to which a proposition should conform. Nobody, therefore, can really doubt that there are realities, or, if he did, doubt would not be a source of dissatisfaction. The hypothesis, therefore, is one which every mind admits. So that the social impulse does not cause me to doubt it. (3) Everybody uses the scientific method about a great many things, and only ceases to use it when he does not know how to apply it. (4) Experience of the method has not led me to doubt it, but, on the contrary, scientific investigation has had the most wonderful triumphs in the way of settling opinion. These afford the explanation of my not doubting the method or the hypothesis which it supposes; and not having any doubt, nor believing that anybody else whom I could influence has, it would be the merest babble for me to say more about it. If there be anybody with a living doubt upon the subject, let him consider it.

To describe the method of scientific investigation is the object of this series of papers. At present I have only room to notice some points of contrast between it and other methods of fixing belief.

This is the only one of the four methods which presents any distinction of a right and a wrong way. If I adopt the method of tenacity and shut myself out from all influences, whatever I think necessary to doing this is necessary according to that method. So with the method of authority: the state may try to put down heresy by means which, from a scientific point of view, seem very ill-calculated to accomplish its purposes; but the only test *on that method* is what the state thinks, so that it cannot pursue the method wrongly. So with the *a priori* method. The very essence of it is to think as one is inclined to think. All metaphysicians will be sure to do that, however they may be inclined to judge each other to be perversely wrong. The Hegelian system recognizes every natural tendency of thought as logical, although it be certain to be abolished by counter-tendencies. Hegel thinks there is a regular system in the succession of these tendencies, in consequence of which, after drifting one way and the other for a long time, opinion will at last go right. And it is true that metaphysicians get the right ideas at last; Hegel's system of Nature represents tolerably the science of that day; and one may be sure that whatever scientific investigation has put out of doubt will presently receive *a priori* demonstration on the part of the metaphysicians. But with the scientific method the case is different. I may start with known and observed facts to proceed to the unknown; and yet the rules which I follow in doing so may not be such as investigation would approve. The test of whether I am truly following the method is not an immediate appeal to my feelings and purposes, but, on the contrary, itself involves the application of the method. Hence it is that bad reasoning as well as good reasoning is possible; and this fact is the foundation of the practical side of logic.

It is not to be supposed that the first three methods of settling opinion present no advantage whatever over the scientific method. On the contrary, each has some peculiar convenience of its own. The *a priori* method is distinguished for its comfortable conclusions. It is the nature of the process to adopt whatever belief we are inclined to, and there are certain flatteries to the vanity of man which we all believe by nature, until we are awakened from our pleasing dream by some rough facts. The method of authority will always govern the mass of mankind; and those who wield the various forms of organized force in the state will never be convinced that dangerous reasoning ought not to be suppressed in some way. If liberty of speech is to be untrammeled from the grosser forms of constraint, then uniformity of opinion will be secured by a moral terrorism to which the respectability of society will give its thorough approval. Following the method of authority is the path of peace. Certain non-conformities are permitted; certain others (considered unsafe) are forbidden. These are different in different countries and in different ages; but, wherever you are, let it be known that you seriously hold a tabooed belief, and you may be perfectly sure of being treated with a cruelty less brutal but more refined than hunting you like a wolf. Thus, the greatest intellectual benefactors of mankind have never dared, and dare not now, to utter the whole of their thought; and thus a shade of *prima facie* doubt is cast upon every proposition which is considered essential to the security of society. Singularly enough, the persecution does not all come from without; but a man torments himself and is oftentimes most distressed at finding himself believing propositions which he has been brought up to regard with aversion. The peaceful and sympathetic man will, therefore, find it hard to resist the temptation to submit his opinions to authority. But most of all I admire the method of tenacity for its strength, simplicity, and directness. Men who pursue it are distinguished for their decision of character, which becomes very easy with such a mental rule. They do not waste time in trying to make up their minds what they want, but, fastening like lightning upon whatever alternative comes first, they hold to it to the end, whatever happens, without an instant's irresolution. This is one of the splendid qualities which generally accompany brilliant, unlasting success. It is impossible not to envy the man who can dismiss reason, although we know how it must turn out at last.

Such are the advantages which the other methods of settling opinion have over scientific investigation. A man should consider well of them; and then he should consider that, after all, he wishes his opinions to coincide with the fact, and that there is no reason why the results of these three methods should do so. To bring about this effect is the prerogative of the method of science. Upon such considerations he has to make his choice—a choice which is far more than the adoption of any intellectual opinion, which is one of the ruling decisions of his life, to which, when once made, he is bound to adhere. The force of habit will sometimes cause a man to hold on to old beliefs, after he is in a condition to see that they have no sound basis. But reflection upon the state of the case will overcome these habits, and he ought to allow reflection its full weight. People sometimes shrink from doing this, having an idea that beliefs are wholesome which they cannot help feeling rest on nothing. But let such persons suppose an analogous though different case from their own. Let them ask themselves what they would say to a reformed Mussulman who should hesitate to give up his old notions in regard to the relations of the sexes; or to a reformed Catholic who should still shrink from reading the Bible. Would they not say that these persons ought to consider the matter fully, and clearly understand the new doctrine, and then ought to embrace it, in its entirety? But, above all, let it be considered that what is more wholesome than any particular belief is integrity of belief, and that to avoid looking into the support of any belief from a fear that it may turn out rotten is quite as immoral as it is disadvantageous. The person who confesses that there is such a thing as truth, which is distinguished from falsehood simply by this, that if acted on it will carry us to the point we aim at and not astray, and then, though convinced of this, dares not know the truth and seeks to avoid it, is in a sorry state of mind indeed.

Yes, the other methods do have their merits: a clear logical conscience does cost something—just as any virtue, just as all that we cherish, costs us dear. But we should not desire it to be otherwise. The genius of a man's logical method should be loved and reverenced as his bride, whom he has chosen from all the world. He need not contemn the others; on the contrary, he may honor them deeply, and in doing so he only honors her the more. But she is the one that he has chosen, and he knows that he was right in making that choice. And having made it, he will work and fight for her, and will not complain that there are blows to take, hoping that there may be as many and as hard to give, and will strive to be the worthy knight and champion of her from the blaze of whose splendors he draws his inspiration and his courage.

QUESTIONS

1. Why does Peirce distinguish between doubt and belief (p. 1095)?
2. What are the four methods of inquiry? Which of the four most closely describes the development of Peirce's argument?
3. Would Peirce restrict application of the method of science to the natural sciences? Would he consider as scientific Milgram's "The Perils of Obedience" (pp. 158–171)? Arendt's study of "Denmark and the Jews" (pp. 958–963)?
4. In the next-to-last paragraph the last sentence separates the subject noun from its verb by six clauses. Does Peirce gain or lose by this? Explain.

5. This essay says little about religion directly, yet many of Peirce's remarks implicitly convey a decided attitude toward the subject. What is that attitude, and in which passages is it most clearly conveyed?

THOMAS S. KUHN
The Route to Normal Science[1]

In this essay, 'normal science' means research firmly based upon one or more past scientific achievements, achievements that some particular scientific community acknowledges for a time as supplying the foundation for its further practice. Today such achievements are recounted, though seldom in their original form, by science textbooks, elementary and advanced. These textbooks expound the body of accepted theory, illustrate many or all of its successful applications, and compare these applications with exemplary observations and experiments. Before such books became popular early in the nineteenth century (and until even more recently in the newly matured sciences), many of the famous classics of science fulfilled a similar function. Aristotle's *Physica*, Ptolemy's *Almagest*, Newton's *Principia* and *Opticks*, Franklin's *Electricity*, Lavoisier's *Chemistry*, and Lyell's *Geology*—these and many other works served for a time implicitly to define the legitimate problems and methods of a research field for succeeding generations of practitioners. They were able to do so because they shared two essential characteristics. Their achievement was sufficiently unprecedented to attract an enduring group of adherents away from competing modes of scientific activity. Simultaneously, it was sufficiently open-ended to leave all sorts of problems for the redefined group of practitioners to resolve.

Achievements that share these two characteristics I shall henceforth refer to as 'paradigms,' a term that relates closely to 'normal science.' By choosing it, I mean to suggest that some accepted examples of actual scientific practice—examples which include law, theory, application, and instrumentation together—provide models from which spring particular coherent traditions of scientific research. These are the traditions which the historian describes under such rubrics as 'Ptolemaic astronomy' (or 'Copernican'), 'Aristotelian dynamics' (or 'Newtonian'), 'corpuscular optics' (or 'wave optics'), and so on. The study of paradigms, including many that are far more specialized than those named illustratively above, is what mainly prepares the student for membership in the particular scientific community with which he will later practice. Because he

1. From *The Structure of Scientific Revolutions*, 1962. (All notes are Kuhn's.)

there joins men who learned the bases of their field from the same concrete models, his subsequent practice will seldom evoke overt disagreement over fundamentals. Men whose research is based on shared paradigms are committed to the same rules and standards for scientific practice. That commitment and the apparent consensus it produces are prerequisites for normal science, i.e., for the genesis and continuation of a particular research tradition.

Because in this essay the concept of a paradigm will often substitute for a variety of familiar notions, more will need to be said about the reasons for its introduction. Why is the concrete scientific achievement, as a locus of professional commitment, prior to the various concepts, laws, theories, and points of view that may be abstracted from it? In what sense is the shared paradigm a fundamental unit for the student of scientific development, a unit that cannot be fully reduced to logically atomic components which might function in its stead? There can be a sort of scientific research without paradigms, or at least without any so unequivocal and so binding as the ones named above. Acquisition of a paradigm and of the more esoteric type of research it permits is a sign of maturity in the development of any given scientific field.

If the historian traces the scientific knowledge of any selected group of related phenomena backward in time, he is likely to encounter some minor variant of a pattern here illustrated from the history of physical optics. Today's physics textbooks tell the student that light is photons, i.e., quantum-mechanical entities that exhibit some characteristics of waves and some of particles. Research proceeds accordingly, or rather according to the more elaborate and mathematical characterization from which this usual verbalization is derived. That characterization of light is, however, scarcely half a century old. Before it was developed by Planck, Einstein, and others early in this century, physics texts taught that light was transverse wave motion, a conception rooted in a paradigm that derived ultimately from the optical writings of Young and Fresnel in the early nineteenth century. Nor was the wave theory the first to be embraced by almost all practitioners of optical science. During the eighteenth century the paradigm for this field was provided by Newton's *Opticks*, which taught that light was material corpuscles. At that time physicists sought evidence, as the early wave theorists had not, of the pressure exerted by light particles impinging on solid bodies.[2]

These transformations of the paradigms of physical optics are scientific revolutions, and the successive transition from one paradigm to another via revolution is the usual developmental pattern of mature science. It is not, however, the pattern characteristic of the

2. Joseph Priestley, *The History and Present State of Discoveries Relating to Vision, Light, and Colours* (London, 1772), pp. 385-90.

period before Newton's work, and that is the contrast that concerns us here. No period between remote antiquity and the end of the seventeenth century exhibited a single generally accepted veiw about the nature of light. Instead there were a number of competing schools and sub-schools, most of them espousing one variant or another of Epicurean, Aristotelian, or Platonic theory. One group took light to be particles emanating from material bodies; for another it was a modification of the medium that intervened between the body and the eye; still another explained light in terms of an interaction of the medium with an emanation from the eye; and there were other combinations and modifications besides. Each of the corresponding schools derive strength from its relation to some particular metaphysic, and each emphasized, as paradigmatic observations, the particular cluster of optical phenomena that its own theory could do most to explain. Other observations were dealt with by *ad hoc* elaborations, or they remained as outstanding problems for further research.[3]

At various times all these schools made significant contributions to the body of concepts, phenomena, and techniques from which Newton drew the first nearly uniformly accepted paradigm for physical optics. Any definition of the scientist that excludes at least the more creative members of these various schools will exclude their modern successors as well. Those men were scientists. Yet anyone examining a survey of physical optics before Newton may well conclude that, though the field's practitioners were scientists, the net result of their activity was something less than science. Being able to take no common body of belief for granted, each writer on physical optics felt forced to build his field anew from its foundations. In doing so, his choice of supporting observation and experiment was relatively free, for there was no standard set of methods or of phenomena that every optical writer felt forced to employ and explain. Under these circumstances, the dialogue of the resulting books was often directed as much to the members of other schools as it was to nature. That pattern is not unfamiliar in a number of creative fields today, nor is it incompatible with significant discovery and invention. It is not, however, the pattern of development that physical optics acquired after Newton and that other natural sciences make familiar today.

The history of electrical research in the first half of the eighteenth century provides a more concrete and better known example of the way a science develops before it acquires its first universally received paradigm. During that period there were almost as many views about the nature of electricity as there were important electrican experimenters, men like Haukshee, Gray, Desaguliers, Du Fay,

3. Vasco Ronchi, *Histoire de la lu-*   chaps. i-iv.
mière, trans. Jean Taton (Paris, 1956),

Nollett, Watson, Franklin, and others. All their numerous concepts of electricity had something in common—they were partially derived from one or another version of the mechanico-corpuscular philosophy that guided all scientific research of the day. In addition, all were components of real scientific theories, of theories that had been drawn in part from experiment and observation and that partially determined the choice and interpretation of additional problems undertaken in research. Yet though all the experiments were electrical and though most of the experimenters read each other's works, their theories had no more than a family resemblance.[4]

One early group of theories, following seventeenth-century practice, regarded attraction and frictional generation as the fundamental electrical phenomena. This group tended to treat repulsion as a secondary effect due to some sort of mechanical rebounding and also to postpone for as long as possible both discussion and systematic research on Gray's newly discovered effect, electrical conduction. Other "electricians" (the term is their own) took attraction and repulsion to be equally elementary manifestations of electricity and modified their theories and research accordingly. (Actually, this group is remarkably small—even Franklin's theory never quite accounted for the mutual repulsion of two negatively charged bodies.) But they had as much difficulty as the first group in accounting simultaneously for any but the simplest conduction effects. Those effects, however, provided the starting point for still a third group, one which tended to speak of electricity as a "fluid" that could run through conductors rather than as an "effluvium" that emanated from non-conductors. This group, in its turn, had difficulty reconciling its theory with a number of attractive and repulsive effects. Only through the work of Franklin and his immediate successors did a theory arise that could account with something like equal facility for very nearly all these effects and that therefore could and did provide a subsequent generation of "electricians" with a common paradigm for its research.

Excluding those fields, like mathematics and astronomy, in which the first firm paradigms date from prehistory and also those, like biochemistry, that arose by division and recombination of specialties already matured, the situations outlined above are historically typical. Though it involves my continuing to employ the unfortunate simplification that tags an extended historical episode with a single and somewhat arbitrarily chosen name (e.g., Newton or Franklin),

4. Duane Roller and Duane H. D. Roller, *The Development of the Concept of Electric Charge: Electricity from the Greeks to Coulomb* ("Harvard Case Histories in Experimental Science," Case 8; Cambridge, Mass., 1954); and I. B. Cohen, *Franklin and Newton: An Inquiry into Speculative Newtonian Experimental Science and Franklin's Work in Electricity as an Example Thereof* (Philadelphia, 1956), chaps. vii–xii.

1108 · *Thomas S. Kuhn*

I suggest that similar fundamental disagreements characterized, for example, the study of motion before Aristotle and of statics before Archimedes, the study of heat before Black, of chemistry before Boyle and Boerhaave, and of historical geology before Hutton. In parts of biology—the study of heredity, for example—the first universally received paradigms are still more recent; and it remains an open question what parts of social science have yet acquired such paradigms at all. History suggests that the road to a firm research consensus is extraordinarily arduous.

History also suggests, however, some reasons for the difficulties encountered on the road. In the absence of a paradigm or some candidate for paradigm, all of the facts that could possibly pertain to the development of a given science are likely to seem equally relevant. As a result, early fact-gathering is a far more nearly random activity than the one that subsequent scientific development makes familiar. Futhermore, in the absence of a reason for seeking some particular form of more recondite information, early fact-gathering is usually restricted to the wealth of data that lie ready to hand. The resulting pool of facts contains those accessible to casual observation and experiment together with some of the more esoteric data retrievable from established crafts medicine, calendar making, and metallurgy. Because the crafts are one readily accessible source of facts that could not have been casually discovered, technology has often played a vital role in the emergence of new sciences.

But though this sort of fact-collecting has been essential to the origin of many significant sciences, anyone who examines, for example, Pliny's encyclopedic writings or the Baconian natural histories of the seventeenth century will discover that it produces a morass. One somehow hesitates to call the literature that results scientific. The Baconian "histories" of heat, color, wind, mining, and so on, are filled with information, some of it recondite. But they juxtapose facts that will later prove revealing (e.g., heating by mixture) with others (e.g., the warmth of dung heaps) that will for some time remain too complex to be integrated with theory at all.[5] In addition, since any description must be partial, the typical natural history often omits from its immensely circumstantial accounts just those details that later scientists will find sources of important illumination. Almost none of the early "histories" of electricity, for example, mention that chaff, attracted to a rubbed glass rod, bounces off again. That effect seemed mechanical, not electrical.[6] Moreover, since the casual fact-gatherer seldom possesses the time or the

5. Compare the sketch for a natural history of heat in Bacon's *Novum Organum*, Vol. VIII of *The Works of Francis Bacon*, ed. J. Spedding, R. L. Ellis, and D. D. Heath (New York, 1869), pp. 179–203.

6. Roller and Roller, *op. cit.*, pp. 14, 22, 28, 43. Only after the work recorded in the last of these citations do repulsive effects gain general recognition as unequivocally electrical.

tools to be critical, the natural histories often juxtapose descriptions like the above with others, say, heating by antiperistasis (or by cooling), that we are now quite unable to confirm.[7] Only very occasionally, as in the cases of ancient statics, dynamics, and geometrical optics, do facts collected with so little guidance from pre-established theory speak with sufficient clarity to permit the emergence of a first paradigm.

This is the situation that creates the schools characteristic of the early stages of a science's development. No natural history can be interpreted in the absence of at least some implicit body of intertwined theoretical and methodological belief that permits selection, evaluation, and criticism. If that body of belief is not already implicit in the collection of facts—in which case more than "mere facts" are at hand—it must be externally supplied, perhaps by a current metaphysic, by another science, or by personal and historical accident. No wonder, then, that in the early stages of the development of any science different men confronting the same range of phenomena, but not usually all the same particular phenomena, describe and interpret them in different ways. What is surprising, and perhaps also unique in its degree to the fields we call science, is that such initial divergences should ever largely disappear.

For they do disappear to a very considerable extent and then apparently once and for all. Furthermore, their disappearance is usually caused by the triumph of one of the pre-paradigm schools, which, because of its own characteristic beliefs and pre-conceptions, emphasized only some special part of the too sizable and inchoate pool of information. Those electricians who thought electricity a fluid and therefore gave particular emphasis to conduction provide an excellent case in point. Led by this belief, which could scarcely cope with the known multiplicity of attractive and repulsive effects, several of them conceived the idea of bottling the electrical fluid. The immediate fruit of their efforts was the Leyden jar, a device which might never have been discovered by a man exploring nature casually or at random, but which was in fact independently developed by at least two investigators in the early 1740's.[8] Almost from the start of his electrical researches, Franklin was particularly concerned to explain that strange and, in the event, particularly revealing piece of special apparatus. His success in doing so provided the most effective of the arguments that made his theory a paradigm, though one that was still unable to account for quite all the known cases of electrical repulsion.[9] To be accepted as a paradigm, a theory

7. Bacon, *op. cit.*, pp. 235, 337, says, "Water slightly warm is more easily frozen than quite cold." For a partial account of the earlier history of this strange observation, see Marshall Clagett, *Giovanni Marliani and Late Medieval Physics* (New York, 1941), chap. iv.

8. Roller and Roller, *op. cit.*, pp. 51–54.

9. The troublesome case was the mutual repulsion of negatively charged bodies, for which see Cohen, *op. cit.*, pp. 491–94, 531–43.

must seem better than its competitors, but it need not, and in fact never does, explain all the facts with which it can be confronted.

What the fluid theory of electricity did for the subgroup that held it, the Franklinian paradigm later did for the entire group of electricians. It suggested which experiments would be worth performing and which, because directed to secondary or to overly complex manifestations of electricity, would not. Only the paradigm did the job far more effectively, partly because the end of interschool debate ended the constant reiteration of fundamentals and partly because the confidence that they were on the right track encouraged scientists to undertake more precise, esoteric, and consuming sorts of work.[1] Freed from the concern with any and all electrical phenomena, the united group of electricians could pursue selected phenomena in far more detail, designing much special equipment for the task and employing it more stubbornly and systematically than electricians had ever done before. Both fact collection and theory articulation became highly directed activities. The effectiveness and efficiency of electrical research increased accordingly, providing evidence for a societal version of Francis Bacon's acute methodological dictum: "Truth emerges more readily from error than from confusion."[2]

We shall be examining the nature of this highly directed or paradigm-based research in the next section, but must first note briefly how the emergence of a paradigm affects the structure of the group that practices the field. When, in the development of a natural science, an individual or group first produces a synthesis able to attract most of the next generation's practitioners, the older schools gradually disappear. In part their disappearance is caused by their members' conversion to the new paradigm. But there are always some men who cling to one or another of the older views, and they are simply read out of the profession, which thereafter ignores their work. The new paradigm implies a new and more rigid definition of the field. Those unwilling or unable to accommodate their work to it must proceed in isolation or attach themselves to some other

---

1. It should be noted that the acceptance of Franklin's theory did not end quite all debate. In 1759 Robert Symmer proposed a two-fluid version of that theory, and for many years thereafter electricians were divided about whether electricity was a single fluid or two. But the debates on this subject only confirm what has been said above about the manner in which a universally recognized achievement unites the profession. Electricians, though they continued divided on this point, rapidly concluded that no experimental tests could distinguish the two versions of the theory and that they were therefore equivalent. After that, both schools could and did exploit all the benefits that the Franklinian theory provided (*ibid.*, pp. 543–46, 548–54).

2. Bacon, *op. cit.*, p. 210.

group.[3] Historically, they have often simply stayed in the departments of philosophy from which so many of the special sciences have been spawned. As these indications hint, it is sometimes just its reception of a paradigm that transforms a group previously interested merely in the study of nature into a profession or, at least, a discipline. In the sciences (though not in fields like medicine, technology, and law, of which the principal *raison d'être* is an external social need), the formation of specialized journals, the foundation of specialists' societies, and the claim for a special place in the curriculum have usually been associated with a group's first reception of a single paradigm. At least this was the case between the time, a century and a half ago, when the institutional pattern of scientific specialization first developed and the very recent time when the paraphernalia of specialization acquired a prestige of their own.

The more rigid definition of the scientific group has other consequences. When the individual scientist can take a paradigm for granted, he need no longer, in his major works, attempt to build his field anew, starting from first principles and justifying the use of each concept introduced. That can be left to the writer of textbooks. Given a textbook, however, the creative scientist can begin his research where it leaves off and thus concentrate exclusively upon the subtlest and most esoteric aspects of the natural phenomena that concern his group. And as he does this, his research communiqués will begin to change in ways whose evolution has been too little studied but whose modern end products are obvious to all and oppressive to many. No longer will his researches usually be embodied in books addressed, like Franklin's *Experiments . . . on Electricity* or Darwin's *Origin of Species*, to anyone who might be interested in the subject matter of the field. Instead they will usually appear as brief articles addressed only to professional colleagues, the men whose knowledge of a shared paradigm can be assumed and who prove to be the only ones able to read the papers addressed to them.

3. The history of electricity provides an excellent example which could be duplicated from the careers of Priestley, Kelvin, and others. Franklin reports that Nollet, who at mid-century was the most influential of the Continental electricians, "lived to see himself the last of his Sect, except Mr. B.—his Eleve and immediate Disciple" (Max Farrand [ed.], *Benjamin Franklin's Memoirs* [Berkeley, Calif., 1949], pp. 384–86). More interesting, however, is the endurance of whole schools in increasing isolation from professional science. Consider, for example, the case of astrology, which was once an integral part of astronomy. Or consider the continuation in the late eighteenth and early nineteenth centuries of a previously respected tradition of "romantic" chemistry. This is the tradition discussed by Charles C. Gillispie in "The *Encyclopédie* and the Jacobin Philosophy of Science: A Study in Ideas and Consequences," *Critical Problems in the History of Science*, ed. Marshall Clagett (Madison, Wis., 1959), pp. 255–89; and "The Formation of Lamarck's Evolutionary Theory," *Archives internationales d'histoire des sciences*, XXXVII (1956), 323–38.

Today in the sciences, books are usually either texts or retrospective reflections upon one aspect or another of the scientific life. The scientist who writes one is more likely to find his professional reputation impaired than enhanced. Only in the earlier, pre-paradigm, stages of the development of the various sciences did the book ordinarily possess the same relation to professional achievement that it still retains in other creative fields. And only in those fields that still retain the book, with or without the article, as a vehicle for research communication are the lines of professionalization still so loosely drawn that the layman may hope to follow progress by reading the practitioners' original reports. Both in mathematics and astronomy, research reports had ceased already in antiquity to be intelligible to a generally educated audience. In dynamics, research became similarly esoteric in the latter Middle Ages, and it recaptured general intelligibility only briefly during the early seventeenth century when a new paradigm replaced the one that had guided medieval research. Electrical research began to require translation for the layman before the end of the eighteenth century, and most other fields of physical science ceased to be generally accessible in the nineteenth. During the same two centuries similar transitions can be isolated in the various parts of the biological sciences. In parts of the social sciences they may well be occurring today. Although it has become customary, and is surely proper, to deplore the widening gulf that separates the professional scientist from his colleagues in other fields, too little attention is paid to the essential relationship between that gulf and the mechanisms intrinsic to scientific advance.

Ever since prehistoric antiquity one field of study after another has crossed the divide between what the historian might call its prehistory as a science and its history proper. These transitions to maturity have seldom been so sudden or so unequivocal as my necessarily schematic discussion may have implied. But neither have they been historically gradual, coextensive, that is to say, with the entire development of the fields within which they occurred. Writers on electricity during the first four decades of the eighteenth century possessed far more information about electrical phenomena than had their sixteenth-century predecessors. During the half-century after 1740, few new sorts of electrical phenomena were added to their lists. Nevertheless, in important respects, the electrical writings of Cavendish, Coulomb, and Volta in the last third of the eighteenth century seem further removed from those of Gray, Du Fay, and even Franklin than are the writings of these early eighteenth-century electrical discoverers from those of the sixteenth century.[4] Sometime between

---

4. The post-Franklinian developments include an immense increase in the sensitivity of charge detectors, the first reliable and generally diffused techniques for measuring charge, the evolution of the concept of capacity and its relation to a newly refined notion of electric tension, and the quantification of electro-

1740 and 1780, electricians were for the first time enabled to take the foundations of their field for granted. From that point they pushed on to more concrete and recondite problems, and increasingly they then reported their results in articles addressed to other electricians rather than in books addressed to the learned world at large. As a group they achieved what had been gained by astronomers in antiquity and by students of motion in the Middle Ages, of physical optics in the late seventeenth century, and of historical geology in the early nineteenth. They had, that is, achieved a paradigm that proved able to guide the whole group's research. Except with the advantage of hindsight, it is hard to find another criterion that so clearly proclaims a field a science.

---

static force. On all of these see Roller and Roller, *op. cit.*, pp. 66–81; W. C. Walker, "The Detection and Estimation of Electric Charges in the Eighteenth Century," *Annals of Science*, I (1936), 66–100; and Edmund Hoppe, *Geschichte der Elektrizität* (Leipzig, 1884), Part I, chaps. iii–iv.

Prose Forms: Parables

[When we read a short story or a novel, we are less interested in the working out of ideas than in the working out of characters and their destinies. In Dickens' Great Expectations, for example, Pip the hero undergoes many triumphs and defeats in his pursuit of success, only to learn finally that he has expected the wrong things, or the right things for the wrong reasons; that the great values in life are not always to be found in what the world calls success. In realizing this meaning we entertain, with Dickens, certain concepts or ideas that organize and evaluate the life in the novel, and that ultimately we apply to life generally. Ideas are there not to be exploited discursively, but to be understood as the perspective which shapes the direction of the novel and our view of its relation to life.

When ideas in their own reality are no longer the primary interest in writing, we have obviously moved from expository to other forms of prose. The shift need not be abrupt and complete, however; there is an area where the discursive interest in ideas and the narrative interest in characters and events blend. In allegory, for example, abstract ideas are personified. "Good Will" or "Peace" may be shown as a young woman, strong, confident, and benevolent in her bearing but vulnerable, through her sweet reasonableness, to the single-minded, fierce woman who is "Dissension." Our immediate interest is in their behavior as characters, but our ultimate interest is in the working out, through them, of the ideas they represent. We do not ask that the characters and events be entirely plausible in relation to actual life, as we do for the novel; we are satisfied if they are consistent with the nature of the ideas that define their vitality.

Ideas themselves have vitality, a mobile and dynamic life with a behavior of its own. The title of the familiar Negro spiritual "Sometimes I Feel Like a Motherless Child," to choose a random instance, has several kinds of "motion" as an idea. The qualitative identity of an adult's feelings and those of a child; the whole burgeoning possibility of all that the phrase "motherless child" can mean; the subtle differences in meaning—the power of context—that occur when it is a black who feels this and when it is a white; the speculative possibilities of the title as social commentary or psychological analysis; the peculiar force of the ungrammatical "like"—these suggest something of the "life" going on in and around the idea. Definition, analogy, assumption, implication, context, illustration are some of the familiar terms we use to describe this kind of life.

There is, of course, another and more obvious kind of vitality which an idea has: its applicability to the affairs of men in everyday life. Both the kind and extent of an idea's relevance are measures of this vitality. When an essayist wishes to exploit both the life in an idea and the life it comprehends, he often turns to narration, because there he sees the advantage of lifelike characters and events, and of showing through them the liveliness of ideas in both the senses we have noted. Ideas about life can be illustrated in life. And, besides, people like stories. The writer's care must be to keep the reader's interest focused on the ideas, rather than on the life itself; otherwise, he has ceased being essentially the essayist and has become the short-story writer or novelist.

The parable and the moral fable are ideal forms for his purpose. In both, the idea is the heart of the composition; in both the ideas usually assume the form of a lesson about life, some moral truth of general consequence to men; and in both there are characters and actions. Jesus often depended on parables in his teaching. Simple, economical, pointed, the parables developed a "story," but more importantly, applied a moral truth to experience. Peter asked Jesus how often he must forgive the brother who sins against him, and Jesus answered with the parable of the king and his servants, one of whom asked and got forgiveness of the king for his debts but who would not in turn forgive a fellow servant his debt. The king, on hearing of this harshness, retracted his own benevolence and punished the unfeeling servant. Jesus concluded to Peter, "So likewise shall my heavenly Father do also unto you, if ye from your hearts forgive not every one his brother their trespasses." But before this direct drawing of the parallel, the lesson was clear in the outline of the narrative.

Parables usually have human characters; fables often achieve a special liveliness with animals or insects. Swift, in "The Spider and the Bee," narrates the confrontation of a comically humanized spider and bee who debate the merits of their natures and their usefulness in the world of experience. The exchange between the two creatures is brilliantly and characteristically set out, but by its end, the reader realizes that extraordinary implications about the nature of art, of education, of human psychological and intellectual potential have been the governing idea all along.

The writer will be verging continually on strict prose narrative when he writes the parable or fable, but if he is skillful and tactful, he will preserve the essayist's essential commitment to the definition and development of ideas in relation to experience.]

ANONYMOUS: The Whale[1]

The whale is the largest of all the fishes in the sea. If you saw one floating on the surface, you would think it was an island rising from the sea sands. When he is hungry, this huge fish opens his mouth and sends forth a breath—the sweetest thing on earth— from his gaping jaws. Other fish, enticed by this sweetness, draw near and hover in his mouth, happy in their ignorance of his deception. The whale then snaps shut his jaws, sucking in all these fish. He thus traps the little fish; the great he cannot ensnare.

This fish lives near the bottom of the sea until the time when equinoctial storms stir up all the waters, as winter struggles to supplant summer, and the sea bottom becomes so turbulent that he cannot stay there. Then he leaves his home and rises to the surface, where he lies motionless. In the midst of the storm, ships are tossed about on the sea. The sailors fearing death and hoping to live, look about them and see this fish. They think he is an island, and, overjoyed, they head their ships for him and drop anchor. They step ashore and, striking sparks from stone and steel into their tinder, they make a fire on this marvel, warm themselves, and eat and drink. The fish soon feels the fire and dives to the bottom, drawing the sailors down with him. He kills them all without leaving a wound.

Application: The devil is determined and powerful, with the craftiness of witches. He makes men hunger and thirst after sinful pleasures and draws them to him with the sweetness of his breath. But whoever follows him finds only shame. His followers are the men of little faith; men of great faith he cannot ensnare, for they are steadfast, body and soul, in true belief. Whoever listens to the devil's teachings will at last regret it bitterly; whoever anchors his hope on the devil will be drawn down by him to the gloomy depths of hell.

1. From *A Bestiary*, an anonymous thirteenth-century English work, translated by Alan B. and Lidie M. Howes.

PLATO: The Allegory of the Cave[1]

And now, I said, let me show in a figure how far our nature is enlightened or unenlightened: Behold! human beings living in an underground den, which has a mouth open towards the light and reaching all along the den; here they have been from their childhood, and have their legs and necks chained so that they cannot move, and can only see before them, being prevented by the chains from turning round their heads. Above and behind them a fire is blazing at a distance, and between the fire and the prisoners

1. From Book VII of *The Republic.*

there is a raised way; and you will see, if you look, a low wall built along the way, like the screen which marionette players have in front of them, over which they show the puppets.

I see.

And do you see, I said, men passing along the wall carrying all sorts of vessels, and statues and figures of animals made of wood and stone and various materials, which appear over the wall? Some of them are talking, others silent.

You have shown me a strange image, and they are strange prisoners.

Like ourselves, I replied; and they see only their own shadows, or the shadows of one another, which the fire throws on the opposite wall of the cave?

True, he said; how could they see anything but the shadows if they were never allowed to move their heads?

And of the objects which are being carried in like manner they would only see the shadows?

Yes, he said.

And if they were able to converse with one another, would they not suppose that they were naming what was actually before them?

Very true.

And suppose further that the prison had an echo which came from the other side, would they not be sure to fancy when one of the passers-by spoke that the voice which they heard came from the passing shadow?

No question, he replied.

To them, I said, the truth would be literally nothing but· the shadows of the images.

That is certain.

And now look again, and see what will naturally follow if the prisoners are released and disabused of their error. At first, when any of them is liberated and compelled suddenly to stand up and turn his neck round and walk and look towards the light, he will suffer sharp pains; the glare will distress him and he will be unable to see the realities of which in his former state he had seen the shadows; and then conceive some one saying to him, that what he saw before was an illusion, but that now, when he is approaching nearer to being and his eye is turned towards more real existence, he has a clearer vision—what will be his reply? And you may further imagine that his instructor is pointing to the objects as they pass and requiring him to name them—will he not be perplexed? Will he not fancy that the shadows which he formerly saw are truer than the objects which are now shown to him?

Far truer.

And if he is compelled to look straight at the light, will he not have a pain in his eyes which will make him turn away to take refuge in the objects of vision which he can see, and which he will conceive to be in reality clearer than the things which are now being shown to him?

True, he said.

And suppose once more, that he is reluctantly dragged up a steep and rugged ascent, and held fast until he is forced into the presence of the sun himself, is he not likely to be pained and irritated? When he approaches the light his eyes will be dazzled and he will not be able to see anything at all of what are now called realities.

Not all in a moment, he said.

He will require to grow accustomed to the sight of the upper world. And first he will see the shadows best, next the reflections of men and other objects in the water, and then the objects themselves; then he will gaze upon the light of the moon and the stars and the spangled heaven; and he will see the sky and the stars by night better than the sun or the light of the sun by day?

Certainly.

Last of all he will be able to see the sun, and not mere reflections of him in the water, but he will see him in his own proper place, and not in another; and he will contemplate him as he is.

Certainly.

He will then proceed to argue that this is he who gives the season and the years, and is the guardian of all that is in the visible world, and in a certain way the cause of all things which he and his fellows have been accustomed to behold?

Clearly, he said, he would first see the sun and then reason about him.

And when he remembered his old habitation, and the wisdom of the den and his fellow-prisoners, do you not suppose that he would felicitate himself on the change, and pity them?

Certainly, he would.

And if they were in the habit of conferring honors among themselves on those who were quickest to observe the passing shadows and to remark which of them went before, and which followed after, and which were together; and who were therefore best able to draw conclusions as to the future, do you think that he would care for such honors and glories, or envy the possessors of them? Would he not say with Homer,

> Better to be the poor servant of a poor master,

and to endure anything, rather than think as they do and live after their manner?

Yes, he said, I think that he would rather suffer anything than entertain these false notions and live in this miserable manner.

Imagine once more, I said, such an one coming suddenly out of the sun to be replaced in his old situation; would he not be certain to have his eyes full of darkness?

To be sure, he said.

And if there were a contest, and he had to compete in measuring the shadows with the prisoners who had never moved out of the den, while his sight was still weak, and before his eyes had become steady (and the time which would be needed to acquire this new habit of sight might be very considerable) would he not be ridiculous? Men would say of him that up he went and down he came without his eyes; and that it was better not even to think of ascending; and if any one tried to loose another and lead him up to the light, let them only catch the offender, and they would put him to death.

No question, he said.

This entire allegory, I said, you may now append, dear Glaucon, to the previous argument; the prison-house is the world of sight, the light of the fire is the sun, and you will not misapprehend me if you interpret the journey upwards to be the ascent of the soul into the intellectual world according to my poor belief, which, at your desire, I have expressed—whether rightly or wrongly God knows. But, whether true or false, my opinion is that in the world of knowledge the idea of good appears last of all, and is seen only with an effort; and, when seen, is also inferred to be the universal author of all things beautiful and right, parent of light and of the lord of light in this visible world, and the immediate source of reason and truth in the intellectual; and that this is the power upon which he who would act rationally either in public or private life must have his eye fixed.

I agree, he said, as far as I am able to understand you.

Moreover, I said, you must not wonder that those who attain to this beatific vision are unwilling to descend to human affairs; for their souls are ever hastening into the upper world where they desire to dwell; which desire of theirs is very natural, if our allegory may be trusted.

Yes, very natural.

And is there anything surprising in one who passes from divine contemplations to the evil state of man, misbehaving himself in a ridiculous manner; if, while his eyes are blinking and before he has become accustomed to the surrounding darkness, he is compelled to fight in courts of law, or in other places, about the images or the shadows of images of justice, and is endeavouring to meet the conceptions of those who have never yet seen absolute justice?

Anything but surprising, he replied.

Any one who has common sense will remember that the bewilderments of the eyes are of two kinds, and arise from two causes, either from coming out of the light or from going into the light, which is true of the mind's eye, quite as much as of the bodily eye; and he who remembers this when he sees any one whose vision is perplexed and weak, will not be too ready to laugh; he will first ask whether that soul of man has come out of the brighter life, and is unable to see because unaccustomed to the dark, or having turned from darkness to the day is dazzled by excess of light. And he will count the one happy in his condition and state of being, and he will pity the other; or, if he have a mind to laugh at the soul which comes from below into the light, there will be more reason in this than in the laugh which greets him who returns from above out of the light into the den.

That, he said, is a very just distinction.

JONATHAN SWIFT: The Spider and the Bee[1]

Things were at this crisis, when a material accident fell out. For, upon the highest corner of a large window, there dwelt a certain spider, swollen up to the first magnitude by the destruction of infinite numbers of flies, whose spoils lay scattered before the gates of his palace, like human bones before the cave of some giant. The avenues of his castle were guarded with turnpikes and palisadoes, all after the modern way of fortification. After you had passed several courts, you came to the center, wherein you might behold the constable himself in his own lodgings, which had windows fronting to each avenue, and ports to sally out upon all occasions of prey or defense. In this mansion he had for some time dwelt in peace and plenty, without danger to his person by swallows from above, or to his palace by brooms from below, when it was the pleasure of fortune to conduct thither a wandering bee, to whose curiosity a broken pane in the glass had discovered itself, and in he went; where expatiating a while, he at last happened to alight upon one of the outward walls of the spider's citadel; which, yielding to the unequal weight, sunk down to the very foundation. Thrice he endeavored to force his passage, and thrice the center shook. The spider within, feeling the terrible convulsion, supposed at first that nature was approaching to her final dissolution; or else that Beelzebub,[2] with all his legions, was come to revenge the death of many thousands of his subjects, whom his enemy had slain and devoured. However, he at length valiantly resolved to issue forth, and meet his fate. Meanwhile the bee had acquitted himself of his toils, and posted securely at some distance, was employed in cleansing his

1. From *The Battle of the Books.*   2. The Hebrew god of flies. Pate MS.

wings, and disengaging them from the ragged remnants of the cobweb. By this time the spider was adventured out, when beholding the chasms, and ruins, and dilapidations of his fortress, he was very near at his wit's end; he stormed and swore like a madman, and swelled till he was ready to burst. At length, casting his eye upon the bee, and wisely gathering causes from events (for they knew each other by sight), "A plague split you," said he, "for a giddy son of a whore. Is it you, with a vengeance, that have made this litter here? Could you not look before you, and be d——nd? Do you think I have nothing else to do (in the devil's name) but to mend and repair after your arse?" "Good words, friend," said the bee (having now pruned himself, and being disposed to droll) "I'll give you my hand and word to come near your kennel no more; I was never in such a confounded pickle since I was born." "Sirrah," replied the spider, "if it were not for breaking an old custom in our family, never to stir abroad against an enemy, I should come and teach you better manners." "I pray have patience," said the bee, "or you will spend your substance, and for aught I see, you may stand in need of it all, towards the repair of your house." "Rogue, rogue," replied the spider, "yet methinks you should have more respect to a person, whom all the world allows to be so much your betters." "By my troth," said the bee, "the comparison will amount to a very good jest, and you will do me a favor to let me know the reasons that all the world is pleased to use in so hopeful a dispute." At this the spider, having swelled himself into the size and posture of a disputant, began his argument in the true spirit of controversy, with a resolution to be heartily scurrilous and angry, to urge on his own reasons, without the least regard to the answers or objections of his opposite, and fully predetermined in his mind against all conviction.

"Not to disparage myself," said he, "by the comparison with such a rascal, what art thou but a vagabond without house or home, without stock or inheritance, born to no possession of your own, but a pair of wings and a drone-pipe? Your livelihood is an universal plunder upon nature; a freebooter over fields and gardens; and for the sake of stealing will rob a nettle as easily as a violet. Whereas I am a domestic animal, furnished with a native stock within myself. This large castle (to show my improvements in the mathematics) is all built with my own hands, and the materials extracted altogether out of my own person."

"I am glad," answered the bee, "to hear you grant at least that I am come honestly by my wings and my voice; for then, it seems, I am obliged to Heaven alone for my flights and my music; and Providence would never have bestowed on me two such gifts, without designing them for the noblest ends. I visit indeed all the flowers and blossoms of the field and the garden; but whatever I collect from thence enriches myself, without the least injury to their beauty, their smell, or their taste. Now, for you and your skill in architecture and other mathematics, I have little to say: in that building of yours there might, for aught I know, have been labor and method enough, but by woful experience for us both, 'tis too plain, the materials are naught, and I hope you will henceforth take warning, and consider duration and matter as well as method and art. You boast, indeed, of being obliged to no other creature, but of drawing and spinning out all from yourself; that is to say, if we may judge of the liquor in the vessel by what issues out, you possess a good plentiful store of dirt and poison in your breast; and, tho' I would by no means lessen or disparage your genuine stock of either, yet I doubt you are somewhat obliged for an increase of both, to a little foreign assistance. Your inherent portion of dirt does not fail of acquisitions, by sweepings exhaled from below; and one insect furnishes you with a share of poison to destroy another. So that in short, the question comes all to this—which is the nobler being of the two, that which by a lazy contemplation of four inches round, by an overweening pride, feeding and engendering on itself, turns all into excrement and venom, produces nothing at last, but flybane and a cobweb; or that which, by an universal range, with long search, much study, true judgment, and distinction of things, brings home honey and wax."

JAMES THURBER: The Glass in the Field

A short time ago some builders, working on a studio in Connecticut, left a huge square of plate glass standing upright in a field one day. A goldfinch flying swiftly across the field struck the glass and was knocked cold. When he came to he hastened to his club, where an attendant bandaged his head and gave him a stiff drink. "What the hell happened?" asked a sea gull. "I was flying across a meadow when all of a sudden the air crystallized on me," said the goldfinch. The sea gull and a hawk and an eagle all laughed heartily. A swallow listened gravely. "For fifteen years, fledgling and bird, I've flown this country," said the eagle, "and I assure you there is no such thing as air crystallizing. Water, yes; air, no." "You were probably struck by a hailstone," the hawk told the goldfinch. "Or he may have had a stroke," said the sea gull. "What do you think, swallow?" "Why, I—I think maybe the air crystallized on him," said the swallow. The large birds laughed so loudly that the goldfinch became annoyed and bet them each a dozen worms that they couldn't follow the course he had flown across the field without encountering the hardened atmosphere. They all took his bet; the swallow went along to watch. The sea gull, the eagle, and the hawk decided to fly together over the route the goldfinch indicated. "You come, too," they said to the swallow. "I—I—well, no," said the swallow. "I don't think I will." So the three large birds took off together and they hit the glass together and they were all knocked cold.

Moral: He who hesitates is sometimes saved.

MATTHEW: Parables of the Kingdom[1]

Then shall the kingdom of heaven be likened unto ten virgins, which took their lamps, and went forth to meet the bridegroom.

And five of them were wise, and five *were* foolish.

They that *were* foolish took their lamps, and took no oil with them:

But the wise took oil in their vessels with their lamps.

While the bridegroom tarried, they all slumbered and slept.

And at midnight there was a cry made, Behold, the bridegroom cometh; go ye out to meet him.

Then all those virgins arose, and trimmed their lamps.

And the foolish said unto the wise, Give us of your oil; for our lamps are gone out.

But the wise answered, saying, *Not so*; lest there be not enough for us and you: but go ye rather to them that sell, and buy for yourselves.

And while they went to buy, the bridegroom came; and they that were ready went in with him to the marriage: and the door was shut.

Afterward came also the other virgins, saying, Lord, Lord, open to us.

But he answered and said, Verily I say unto you, I know you not.

Watch therefore, for ye know neither the day nor the hour wherein the Son of man cometh.

For *the kingdom of heaven is* as a man travelling into a far country, *who* called his own servants, and delivered unto them his goods.

And unto one he gave five talents, to another two, and to another one; to every man according to his several ability; and straightway took his journey.

Then he that had received the five talents went and traded with the same, and made *them* other five talents.

And likewise he that *had received* two, he also gained other two.

But he that had received one went and digged in the earth, and hid his lord's money.

After a long time the lord of those servants cometh, and reckoneth with them.

And so he that had received five talents came and brought other

1. Matthew xxv.

five talents, saying, Lord, thou deliveredst unto me five talents: behold, I have gained beside them five talents more.

His lord said unto him, Well done, *thou* good and faithful servant: thou hast been faithful over a few things, I will make thee ruler over many things: enter thou into the joy of thy lord.

He also that had received two talents came and said, Lord, thou deliveredst unto me two talents: behold, I have gained two other talents beside them.

His lord said unto him, Well done, good and faithful servant; thou hast been faithful over a few things, I will make thee ruler over many things: enter thou into the joy of thy lord.

Then he which had received the one talent came and said, Lord, I knew thee that thou art an hard man, reaping where thou hast not sown, and gathering where thou hast not strawed:

And I was afraid, and went and hid thy talent in the earth: lo, *there* thou hast *that is* thine.

His lord answered and said unto him, *Thou* wicked and slothful servant, thou knewest that I reap where I sowed not, and gather where I have not strawed:

Thou oughtest therefore to have put my money to the exchanges, and *then* at my coming I should have received mine own with usury.

Take therefore the talent from him, and give *it* unto him which hath ten talents.

For unto every one that hath shall be given, and he shall have abundance: but from him that hath not shall be taken away even that which he hath.

And cast ye the unprofitable servant into outer darkness: there shall be weeping and gnashing of teeth.

When the Son of man shall come in his glory, and all the holy angels with him, then shall he sit upon the throne of his glory:

And before him shall be gathered all nations: and he shall separate them one from another, as a shepherd divideth *his* sheep from the goats:

And he shall set the sheep on his right hand, but the goats on the left.

Then shall the King say unto them on his right hand, Come, ye blessed of my Father, inherit the kingdom prepared for you from the foundation of the world:

For I was an hungred, and ye gave me meat: I was thirsty, and ye gave me drink: I was a stranger, and ye took me in:

Naked, and ye clothed me: I was sick, and ye visited me: I was in prison, and ye came unto me.

Then shall the righteous answer him, saying, Lord, when saw we thee an hungred, and fed *thee*? or thirsty, and gave *thee* drink?

When saw we thee a stranger, and took *thee* in? or naked, and clothed thee?

Or when saw we thee sick, or in prison, and came unto thee?

And the King shall answer and say unto them, Verily I say unto you, Inasmuch as ye have done *it* unto one of the least of these my brethren, ye have done *it* unto me.

Then shall he say also unto them on the left hand, Depart from me, ye cursed, into everlasting fire, prepared for the devil and his angels:

For I was an hungred, and ye gave me no meat: I was thirsty, and ye gave me no drink.

I was a stranger, and ye took me not in: naked, and ye clothed me not: sick, and in prison, and ye visited me not.

Then shall they also answer him, saying, Lord, when saw we thee an hungred, or athirst, or a stranger, or naked, or sick, or in prison, and did not minister unto thee?

Then shall he answer them, saying, Verily I say unto you, Inasmuch as ye did *it* not to one of the least of these, ye did *it* not to me.

And these shall go away into everlasting punishment: but the righteous into life eternal.

LAURENCE STERNE: Conjugation[1]

My father took a single turn across the room, then sat down and finished the chapter.

The verbs auxiliary we are concerned in here, continued my father, are, *am; was; have; had; do; did; make; made; suffer; shall; should; will; would; can; could; owe; ought; used;* or *is wont.*—And these varied with tenses, *present, past, future,* and conjugated with the verb *see,*—or with these questions added to them;—*Is it? Was it? Will it be? Would it be; May it be? Might it be?* And these again put negatively, *Is it not? Was it not? Ought it not?*—Or affirmatively,—*It is; It was; It ought to be.* Or chronologically,—*Has it been always? Lately? How long ago?*—Or hypothetically,—*If it was; If it was not? What would follow?*—If the *French* should beat the *English*? If the *Sun* go out of the *Zodiac*?

Now, by the right use and application of these, continued my father, in which a child's memory should be exercised, there is no one idea can enter his brain how barren soever, but a magazine[2] of conceptions and conclusions may be drawn forth from it.—Did'st thou ever see a white bear? cried my father, turning his head round to *Trim*, who stood at the back of his chair.—No, an' please your honour, replied the corporal.—But thou could'st discourse about one, *Trim*, said my father, in case of need?—How is it possible, brother, quoth my uncle *Toby*, if the corporal never saw one?—'Tis

1. From *Tristram Shandy*, Chapter 43,   2. Storehouse.
Vol. 5.

the fact I want; replied my father,—and the possibility of it, is as follows.

A WHITE BEAR! Very well. Have I ever seen one? Might I ever have seen one? Am I ever to see one? Ought I ever to have seen one? Or can I ever see one?

Would I had seen a white bear! (for how can I imagine it?)

If I should see a white bear, what should I say? If I should never see a white bear, what then?

If I never have, can, must or shall see a white bear alive; have I ever seen the skin of one? Did I ever see one painted?—described? Have I never dreamed of one?

Did my father, mother, uncle, aunt, brothers or sisters, ever see a white bear? What would they give? How would they behave? How would the white bear have behaved? Is he wild? Tame? Terrible? Rough? Smooth?

—Is the white bear worth seeing?—

—Is there no sin in it?—

Is it better than a BLACK ONE?

CHARLES DICKENS: Crumpets and Principle[1]

"I takes my determination on principle, sir," remarked Sam, "and you takes yours on the same ground; wich puts me in mind o' the man as killed his-self on principle, wich o' course, you've heerd on, sir." Mr. Weller paused when he arrived at this point, and cast a comical look at his master out of the corners of his eyes.

"There is no 'of course' in the case, Sam," said Mr. Pickwick, gradually breaking into a smile, in spite of the uneasiness which Sam's obstinacy had given him. "The fame of the gentleman in question, never reached my ears."

"No, sir!" exclaimed Mr. Weller. "You astonish me, sir, he wos a clerk in a gov'ment office, sir."

"Was he?" said Mr. Pickwick.

"Yes, he wos sir," rejoined Mr. Weller; "and a wery pleasant gen'l'm'n too—one o' the precise and tidy sort, as puts their feet in little India-rubber fire-buckets wen it's wet weather, and never has no other bosom friends but hare-skins; he saved up his money on principle, wore a clean shirt ev'ry day on principle; never spoke to none of his relations on principle, 'fear they shou'd want to borrow money of him; and wos altogether, in fact, an uncommon agreeable character. He had his hair cut on principle vunce a fortnight, and contracted for his clothes on the economic principle—three suits a year, and send back the old uns. Being a wery reg'lar gen'l'm'n, he din'd ev'ry day at the same place, where it wos one and nine to cut off the joint, and a wery good one and nine's worth he used to cut,

1. From *Pickwick Papers*. Chapter 44.

as the landlord often said, with the tears a tricklin' down his face: let alone the way he used to poke the fire in the vinter time, which was a dead loss o' four-pence ha'penny a day: to say nothin' at all o' the aggrawation o' seein' him do it. So uncommon grand with it too! 'Post arter the next gen'l'm'n,' he sings out ev'ry day ven he comes in. 'See arter the Times, Thomas; let me look at the Mornin' Herald, wen it's out o' hand; don't forget to bespeak the Chronicle; and just bring the 'Tizer, vill you:' and then he'd set vith his eyes fixed on the clock, and rush out, just a quarter of a minit afore the time, to waylay the boy as wos a comin' in with the evenin' paper, wich he'd read with sich intense interest and perseverance as worked the other customers up to the wery confines o' desperation and insanity, 'specially one i-rascible old gen'l'm'n as the vaiter wos always obliged to keep a sharp eye on, at sich times, fear he should be tempted to commit some rash act with the carving knife. Vell, sir, here he'd stop, occupyin' the best place for three hours, and never takin' nothin' arter his dinner, but sleep, and then he'd go away to a coffee-house a few streets off, and have a small pot o' coffee and four crumpets, arter wich he'd walk home to Kensington and go to bed. One night he was took wery ill; sends for a doctor; doctor comes in a green fly, with a kind o' Robinson Crusoe set o' steps, as he could let down wen he got out, and pull up arter him wen he got in, to perwent the necessity o' the coachman's gettin' down, and thereby undeceivin' the public by lettin' 'em see that it wos only a livery coat as he'd got on, and not the trousers to match. 'Wot's the matter?' says the doctor. 'Wery ill,' says the patient. 'Wot have you been a eatin' on?' says the doctor. 'Roast weal,' says the patient. 'Wot's the last thing you dewoured?' says the doctor. 'Crumpets,' says the patient. 'That's it!' says the doctor. 'I'll send you a box of pills directly, and don't you never take no more of 'em,' he says. 'No more o' wot?' says the patient—'Pills?' 'No; crumpets,' says the doctor. 'Wy?' says the patient, starting up in bed: 'I've eat four crumpets, ev'ry night for fifteen year, on principle.' 'Well, then, you'd better leave 'em off, on principle,' says the doctor. 'Crumpets is wholesome, sir,' says the patient. 'Crumpets is *not* wholesome, sir' says the doctor, wery fierce. 'But they're so cheap,' says the patient, comin' down a little, 'and so wery fillin' at the price.' 'They'd be dear to you, at any price; dear if you wos paid to eat 'em,' says the doctor. 'Four crumpets a night,' he says, 'vill do your business in six months!' The patient looks him full in the face, and turns it over in his mind for a long time, and at last he says, 'Are you sure o' that 'ere, sir?' 'I'll stake my professional reputation on it,' says the doctor. 'How many crumpets, at a sittin', do you think 'ud kill me off at once?' says the patient. 'I don't know,' says the doctor, 'Do you think half a crown's worth 'ud do it?' says the patient. 'I think it might,' says the doctor. 'Three shillins' wurth 'ud be sure to do it, I s'pose?' says the patient. 'Certainly,' says the doctor. 'Wery good,' says the patient; 'good night.' Next mornin' he gets up, has a fire lit, orders in three shillins' wurth o' crumpets, toasts 'em all, eats 'em all, and blows his brains out."

"What did he do that for?" inquired Mr. Pickwick abruptly; for he was considerably startled by this tragical termination of the narrative.

"Wot did he do it for, sir?" reiterated Sam. "Wy, in support of his great principle that crumpets wos wholesome, and to show that he wouldn't be put out of his way for nobody!"

W. S. MERWIN: Tergvinder's Stone

One time my friend Tergvinder brought a large round boulder into his living room. He rolled it up the steps with the help of some two-by-fours, and when he got it out into the middle of the room, where some people have coffee tables (though he had never had one there himself) he left it. He said that was where it belonged.

It is really a plain-looking stone. Not as large as Plymouth Rock by a great deal, but then it does not have all the claims of a big shaky promotion campaign to support. That was one of the things Tergvinder said about it. He made no claims at all for it, he said. It was other people who called it Tergvinder's Stone. All he said was that according to him it belonged there.

His dog took to peeing on it, which created a problem (Tergvinder had not moved the carpet before he got the stone to where he said it belonged). Their tomcat took to squirting it, too. His wife fell over it quite often at first and it did not help their already strained marriage. Tergvinder said there was nothing to be done about it. It was in the order of things. That was a phrase he seldom employed, and never when he conceived that there was any room left for doubt.

He confided in me that he often woke in the middle of the night, troubled by the ancient, nameless ills of the planet, and got up quietly not to wake his wife, and walked through the house naked, without turning on any lights. He said that at such times he found himself listening, listening, aware of how some shapes in the darkness emitted low sounds like breathing, as they never did by day. He said he had become aware of a hole in the darkness in the middle of the living room, and out of that hole a breathing, a mournful dissatisfied sound of an absence waiting for what belonged to it, for something it had never seen and could not conceive of, but without which it could not rest. It was a sound, Tergvinder said, that touched him with fellow-feeling, and he had undertaken—oh, without saying anything to anybody—to assuage, if he could, that wordless longing that seemed always on the verge of despair. How to do it was another matter, and for months he had circled the problem, night and day, without apparently coming any closer to a solution. Then one day he had seen the stone. It had been there all the time at the bottom of his drive, he said, and he had never really seen it. Never recognized it for what it was. The nearer to the house he had got it, the more certain he had become. The stone had rolled into its present place like a lost loved one falling into arms that had long ached for it.

Tergvinder says that now on nights when he walks through the dark house he comes and stands in the living room doorway and listens to the peace in the middle of the floor. He knows its size, its weight, the touch of it, something of what is thought of it. He knows that it is peace. As he listens, some hint of that peace touches him too. Often, after a while, he steps down into the living room and goes and kneels beside the stone and they converse for hours in silence—a silence broken only by the sound of his own breathing.

FRANZ KAFKA: Parable of the Law[1]

"Before the Law stands a doorkeeper. To this doorkeeper there comes a man from the country who begs for admittance to the Law. But the doorkeeper says that he cannot admit the man at the moment. The man, on reflection, asks if he will be allowed, then, to enter later. 'It is possible,' answers the doorkeeper, 'but not at this moment.' Since the door leading into the Law stands open as usual and the doorkeeper steps to one side, the man bends down to peer through the entrance. When the doorkeeper sees that, he laughs and says: 'If you are so strongly tempted, try to get in without my permission. But note that I am powerful. And I am only the lowest doorkeeper. From hall to hall, keepers stand at every door, one more powerful than the other. And the sight of the third man is already more than even I can stand.' These are difficulties which the man from the country has not expected to meet, the Law, he thinks, should be accessible to every man and at all times, but when he looks more closely at the doorkeeper in his furred robe, with his huge pointed nose and long thin Tartar beard, he decides that he had better wait until he gets permission to enter. The doorkeeper gives him a stool and lets him sit down at the side of the door. There he sits waiting for days and years. He makes many attempts to be allowed in and wearies the doorkeeper with his importunity. The doorkeeper often engages him in brief conversation, asking him about his home and about other matters, but the questions are put quite impersonally, as great men put questions, and always conclude with the statement that the man cannot be allowed

1. From the chapter, "In the Cathedral," of *The Trial* (1925).

to enter yet. The man, who has equipped himself with many things for his journey, parts with all he has, however valuable, in the hope of bribing the doorkeeper. The doorkeeper accepts it all, saying, however, as he takes each gift: 'I take this only to keep you from feeling that you have left something undone.' During all these long years the man watches the doorkeeper almost incessantly. He forgets about the other doorkeepers, and this one seems to him the only barrier between himself and the Law. In the first years he curses his evil fate aloud; later, as he grows old, he only mutters to himself. He grows childish, and since in his prolonged study of the doorkeeper he has learned to know even the fleas in his fur collar, he begs the very fleas to help him and to persuade the doorkeeper to change his mind. Finally his eyes grow dim and he does not know whether the world is really darkening around him or whether his eyes are only deceiving him. But in the darkness he can now perceive a radiance that streams inextinguishably from the door of the Law. Now his life is drawing to a close. Before he dies, all that he has experienced during the whole time of his sojourn condenses in his mind into one question, which he has never yet put to the doorkeeper. He beckons the doorkeeper, since he can no longer raise his stiffening body. The doorkeeper has to bend far down to hear him, for the difference in size between them has increased very much to the man's disadvantage. 'What do you want to know now?' asks the doorkeeper, 'you are insatiable.' 'Everyone strives to attain the Law,' answers the man, 'how does it come about, then, that in all these years no one has come seeking admittance but me?' The doorkeeper perceives that the man is nearing his end and his hearing is failing, so he bellows in his ear: 'No one but you could gain admittance through this door, since this door was intended for you. I am now going to shut it.'"

"So the doorkeeper deceived the man," said K. immediately, strongly attracted by the story. "Don't be too hasty," said the priest, "don't take over someone else's opinion without testing it. I have told you the story in the very words of the scriptures. There's no mention of deception in it." "But it's clear enough," said K., "and your first interpretation of it was quite right. The doorkeeper gave the message of salvation to the man only when it could no longer help him." "He was not asked the question any earlier," said the priest, "and you must consider, too, that he was only a doorkeeper, and as such fulfilled his duty." "What makes you think he fulfilled his duty?" asked K. "He didn't fulfill it. His duty might have been to keep all strangers away, but this man, for whom the door was intended, should have been let in." "You have not enough respect for the written word and you are altering the story," said the priest. "The story contains two important statements made by the doorkeeper about admission to the Law, one at the beginning, the other at the end. The first statement is: that he cannot admit the man at the moment, and the other is: that this door was intended only for the man. If there were a contradiction between the two, you would be right and the doorkeeper would have deceived the man. But there is no contradiction. The first statement, on the contrary, even implies the second. One could almost say that in suggesting to the man the possibility of future admittance the doorkeeper is exceeding his duty. At that time his apparent duty is only to refuse admittance and indeed many commentators are surprised that the suggestion should be made at all, since the doorkeeper appears to be a precisian with a stern regard for duty. He does not once leave his post during these many years, and he does not shut the door until the very last minute; he is conscious of the importance of his office, for he says: 'I am powerful'; he is respectful to his superiors, for he says: 'I am only the lowest doorkeeper'; he is not garrulous, for during all these years he puts only what are called 'impersonal questions'; he is not to be bribed, for he says in accepting a gift: 'I take this only to keep you from feeling that you have left something undone'; where his duty is concerned he is to be moved neither by pity nor rage, for we are told that the man 'wearied the doorkeeper with his importunity'; and finally even his external appearance hints at a pedantic character, the large, pointed nose and the long, thin, black, Tartar beard. Could one imagine a more faithful doorkeeper? Yet the doorkeeper has other elements in his character which are likely to advantage anyone seeking admittance and which make it comprehensible enough that he should somewhat exceed his duty in suggesting the possibility of future admittance. For it cannot be denied that he is a little simple-minded and consequently a little conceited. Take the statements he makes about his power and the power of the other doorkeepers and their dreadful aspect which even he cannot bear to see—I hold that these statements may be true enough, but that the way in which he brings them out shows that his perceptions are confused by simpleness of mind and conceit. The commentators note in this connection: 'The right perception of any matter and a misunderstanding of the same matter do not wholly exclude each other.' One must at any rate assume that such simpleness and conceit, however sparingly manifest, are likely to weaken his defense of the door; they are breaches in the character of the doorkeeper. To this must be added the fact that the doorkeeper seems to be a friendly creature by nature, he is by no means always on his official dignity. In the very first moments he allows himself the jest of inviting the man to enter in spite of the strictly maintained veto against entry; then he does not, for instance, send the man away, but gives him, as we are told, a stool and lets him sit down beside the door. The patience with which he endures the man's appeals during so many years, the brief conversations, the acceptance of the gifts, the politeness with which he allows the man to curse loudly in his presence the fate for which he himself is responsible—all this lets us deduce certain feelings of pity. Not every doorkeeper would have acted thus. And finally, in answer to a gesture of the man's he bends down to give him the chance of putting a last question. Nothing but mild impatience—the doorkeeper knows that this is the end of it all—is discernible in the words: 'You are insatiable.' Some push this mode of interpretation even further and hold that these words express a kind of friendly admiration, though not without a hint of condescension. At any rate the figure of the doorkeeper can be said to come out very differently from what you fancied." "You have studied the story more exactly and for a longer time than I have," said K. They were both silent for a little while. Then. K. said: "So you think the man was not deceived?" "Don't misunderstand me," said the priest, "I am only showing you the various opinions concerning that point. You must not pay too much attention to them. The scriptures are unalterable and the comments often enough merely express the commentators' despair. In this case there even exists an interpretation which claims that the deluded person is really the doorkeeper." "That's a farfetched interpretation," said K. "On what is it based?" "It is based," answered the priest, "on the simple-mindedness of the doorkeeper. The argument is that he does not know the Law from inside, he knows only the way that leads to it, where he patrols up and down. His ideas of the interior are assumed to be childish, and it is supposed that he himself is afraid of the other guardians whom he holds up as bogies before the man. Indeed, he fears them more than the man does, since the man is determined to enter after hearing about the dreadful guardians of the interior, while the door-keeper has no desire to enter, at least not so far as we are told. Others again say that he must have been in the interior already, since he is after all engaged in the service of the Law and can only have been appointed from inside. This is countered by arguing that he may have been appointed by a voice calling from the interior, and that anyhow he cannot have been far inside, since the aspect of the third doorkeeper is more than he can endure. Moreover, no indication is given that during all these years he ever made any remarks showing a knowledge of the interior, except for the one remark about the doorkeepers. He may have been forbidden to do so, but there is no mention of that either. On these grounds the conclusion is reached that he knows nothing about the aspect and significance of the interior, so that he is in a state of delusion. But he is deceived also about his relation to the man from the country, for he is inferior to the man and does not know it. He treats the man instead as his own subordinate, as can be recognized from many details that must be still fresh in your mind. But, according to this view of the story, it is just as clearly indicated that he is really subordinated to the man. In the first place, a bondman is always subject to a free man. Now the man from the country is really free, he can go where he likes, it is only the Law that is closed to him, and access to the Law is forbidden him only by one individual, the doorkeeper. When he sits down on the stool by the side of the door and stays there for the rest of his life, he does it of his own free will; in the story there is no mention of any compulsion. But the door-keeper is bound to his post by his very office, he does not dare go out into the country, nor apparently may he go into the interior of the Law, even should he wish to. Besides, although he is in the service of the Law, his service is confined to this one entrance; that is to say, he serves only this man for whom alone the entrance is intended. On that ground too he is inferior to the man. One must assume that for many years, for as long as it takes a man to grow up to the prime of life, his service was in a sense an empty for-mality, since he had to wait for a man to come, that is to say some-one in the prime of life, and so he had to wait a long time before the purpose of his service could be fulfilled, and, moreover, had to wait on the man's pleasure, for the man came of his own free will. But the termination of his service also depends on the man's term of life, so that to the very end he is subject to the man. And it is emphasized throughout that the doorkeeper apparently realizes nothing of all this. That is not in itself remarkable, since according to this interpretation the doorkeeper is deceived in a much more important issue, affecting his very office. At the end, for example, he says regarding the entrance to the Law: 'I am now going to shut it,' but at the beginning of the story we are told that the door leading into the Law always stands open, and if it always stands open, that is to say at all times, without reference to life or death of the man, then the doorkeeper cannot close it. There is some difference of opinion about the motive behind the doorkeeper's statement, whether he said he was going to close the door merely for the sake of giving an answer, or to emphasize his devotion to duty, or to bring the man into a state of grief and regret in his last moments. But there is no lack of agreement that the doorkeeper will not be able to shut the door. Many indeed pro-fess to find that he is subordinate to the man even in knowledge, toward the end, at least, for the man sees the radiance that issues from the door of the Law while the doorkeeper in his official posi-tion must stand with his back to the door, nor does he say anything to show that he has perceived the change." "That is well argued," said K., after repeating to himself in a low voice several passages from the priest's exposition. "It is well argued, and I am inclined to agree that the doorkeeper is deceived. But that has not made me abandon my former opinion, since both conclusions are to some extent compatible. Whether the doorkeeper is clear-sighted or deceived does not dispose of the matter. I said the man is deceived. If the doorkeeper is clear-sighted, one might have doubts about that, but if the doorkeeper himself is deceived, then his deception must of necessity be communicated to the man. That makes the door-keeper not, indeed, a deceiver, but a creature so simple-minded that he ought to be dismissed at once from his office. You mustn't forget that the doorkeeper's deceptions do himself no harm but do infinite harm to the man." "There are objections to that," said the priest. "Many aver that the story confers no right on anyone to pass judgment on the doorkeeper. Whatever he may seem to us, he is yet a servant of the Law; that is, he belongs to the Law and as such is beyond human judgment. In that case one must not believe that the doorkeeper is subordinate to the man. Bound as he is by his service, even only at the door of the Law, he is incomparably greater than anyone at large in the world. The man is only seeking the Law, the doorkeeper is already attached to it. It is the Law that has placed him at his post; to doubt his dignity is to doubt the Law itself." "I don't agree with that point of view," said K., shaking his head, "for if one accepts it, one must accept as true everything the doorkeeper says. But you yourself have suffi-ciently proved how impossible it is to do that." "No," said the priest, "it is not necessary to accept everything as true, one must only accept it as necessary." "A melancholy conclusion," said K. "It turns lying into a universal principle."

Zen Parables

Muddy Road

Tanzan and Ekido were once traveling together down a muddy road. A heavy rain was still falling.

Coming around a bend, they met a lovely girl in a silk kimono and sash, unable to cross the intersection.

"Come on, girl," said Tanzan at once. Lifting her in his arms, he carried her over the mud.

Ekido did not speak again until that night when they reached a lodging temple. Then he no longer could restrain himself. "We monks don't go near females," he told Tanzan, "especially not young and lovely ones. It is dangerous. Why did you do that?"

"I left the girl there," said Tanzan. "Are you still carrying her?"

A Parable

Buddha told a parable in a sutra:

A man traveling across a field encountered a tiger. He fled, the tiger after him. Coming to a precipice, he caught hold of the root of a wild vine and swung himself down over the edge. The tiger sniffed at him from above. Trembling, the man looked down to where, far below, another tiger was waiting to eat him. Only the vine sustained him.

Two mice, one white and one black, little by little started to gnaw away the vine. The man saw a luscious strawberry near him. Grasping the vine with one hand, he plucked the strawberry with the other. How sweet it tasted!

Learning to Be Silent

The pupils of the Tendai school used to study meditation before Zen entered Japan. Four of them who were intimate friends promised one another to observe seven days of silence.

On the first day all were silent. Their meditation had begun auspiciously, but when night came and the oil lamps were growing dim one of the pupils could not help exclaiming to a servant: "Fix those lamps."

The second pupil was surprised to hear the first one talk. "We are not supposed to say a word," he remarked.

"You two are stupid. Why did you talk?" asked the third.

"I am the only one who has not talked," concluded the fourth pupil.

OSCAR WILDE: The Doer of Good

It was night-time, and He was alone.

And He saw afar off the walls of a round city, and went towards the city.

And when He came near He heard within the city the tread of the feet of joy, and the laughter of the mouth of gladness, and the loud noise of many lutes. And He knocked at the gate and certain of the gate-keepers opened to Him.

And He beheld a house that was of marble, and had fair pillars of marble before it. The pillars were hung with garlands, and within and without there were torches of cedar. And He entered the house.

And when He had passed through the hall of chalcedony and the hall of jasper, and reached the long hall of feasting, He saw lying on a couch of sea-purple one whose hair was crowned with red roses and whose lips were red with wine.

And He went behind him and touched him on the shoulder, and said to him:

"Why do you live like this?"

And the young man turned round and recognized Him, and made answer, and said: "But I was a leper once, and you healed me. How else should I live?"

And He passed out of the house and went again into the street.

And after a little while He saw one whose face and raiment were painted and whose feet were shod with pearls. And behind her came slowly, as a hunter, a young man who wore a cloak of two colours. Now the face of the woman was as the fair face of an idol, and the eyes of the young man were bright with lust.

And He followed swiftly and touched the hand of the young man, and said to him: "Why do you look at this woman and in such wise?"

And the young man turned round and recognized Him, and said: "But I was blind once, and you gave me sight. At what else should I look?"

And He ran forward and touched the painted raiment of the woman, and said to her: "Is there no other way in which to walk save the way of sin?"

And the woman turned round and recognized Him, and laughed, and said: "But you forgave me my sins, and the way is a pleasant way."

And He passed out of the city.

And when He had passed out of the city, He saw, seated by the roadside, a young man who was weeping.

And he went towards him and touched the long locks of his hair, and said to him: "Why are you weeping?"

And the young man looked up and recognized Him, and made answer: "But I was dead once, and you raised me from the dead. What else should I do but weep?"

MARTIN BUBER: The Query of Queries[1]

Before his death, Rabbi Zusya said "In the coming world, they will not ask me: 'Why were you not Moses?' They will ask me: 'Why were you not Zusya?' "

---

1. From *Tales of the Hasidim*, 1947.

Last Things

J. B. PRIESTLEY

The Ironic Principle

Many years ago, an old friend of my schooldays sent me an inscribed copy of a book he had written on dairy farming, a subject on which he was an authority. I looked at this bulky volume in despair. Clearly I could not give it away or sell it, yet nothing could have been less use to me for I cared nothing about dairy farming. So I pushed it away in some obscure corner of my bookshelves and then forgot about it. But now that I own a dairy herd and am breeding pedigree Guernsey stock, I need that book and I cannot find it. This is Irony at work in private life. It works equally hard in public life. Thus, at this present time, we in Britain are short of petrol and cannot run our cars as often as we should like to run them. This is partly because, in order to break the Russian blockade, we are delivering rations and coal to the people of Berlin by air, the most extravagant delivery service the world has yet known. And this policy is most warmly defended by the very people here who, four years ago, were denouncing the Berliners as subhuman creatures only fit to be exterminated. Again, to take a larger example, it is less than a hundred years ago that the Japanese, still living in a medieval dream, only asked to be left alone by Western Man. But we insisted upon their opening their ports to us, with the result that after a turn or two of the wheel there arrived the disaster of Pearl Harbor and the fall of Singapore. So it goes on. The conquerors enslave the conquered, who in turn begin to shape and color the secret dreams and the culture of their masters. The diabolical prisoners' cage is occupied first by the sadist who designed it. The Duke of Alva ends a career of legendary terror by being breast-fed. English colonels would stamp round India for years, snorting with contempt, and return home to join the Theosophical Society. In large American cities so many people are in a hurry and drive automobiles that traffic in the congested streets goes into slow motion. In England so many people want to live on the edge of the countryside that miles and miles of it disappear into the city. Both whole communities and individuals turn their back on some pitfall and hurry off to land in another, rather deeper. Just when Man thinks he can do everything, he finds himself helpless in the clutch of some unknown force. And in this ironic principle, which appears to govern so much of our lives, I find delight. Even when it comes close and hurts, the delight is still there. "The Old So-and-So!" I mutter admiringly, from that part of me which must be immortal and invulnerable.

ELIZABETH KÜBLER-ROSS

On the Fear of Death

*Let me not pray to be sheltered from
dangers but to be fearless in facing
them.
   Let me not beg for the stilling of
my pain but for the heart to conquer it.
   Let me not look for allies in life's
battlefield but to my own strength.
   Let me not crave in anxious fear to
be saved but hope for the patience to
win my freedom.
   Grant me that I may not be a
coward, feeling your mercy in my
success alone; but let me find the grasp
of your hand in my failure.*

RABINDRANATH TAGORE,
Fruit-Gathering

Epidemics have taken a great toll of lives in past generations. Death in infancy and early childhood was frequent and there were few families who didn't lose a member of the family at an early age. Medicine has changed greatly in the last decades. Widespread vaccinations have practically eradicated many illnesses, at least in western Europe and the United States. The use of chemotherapy, especially the antibiotics, has contributed to an ever decreasing number of fatalities in infectious diseases. Better child care and education has effected a low morbidity and mortality among children. The many diseases that have taken an impressive toll among the young and middle-aged have been conquered. The number of old people is on the rise, and with this fact come the number of people with malignancies and chronic diseases associated more with old age.

Pediatricians have less work with acute and life-threatening situations as they have an ever increasing number of patients with psychosomatic disturbances and adjustment and behavior problems.

Physicians have more people in their waiting rooms with emotional problems than they have ever had before, but they also have more elderly patients who not only try to live with their decreased physical abilities and limitations but who also face loneliness and isolation with all its pains and anguish. The majority of these people are not seen by a psychiatrist. Their needs have to be elicited and gratified by other professional people, for instance, chaplains and social workers. It is for them that I am trying to outline the changes that have taken place in the last few decades, changes that are ultimately responsible for the increased fear of death, the rising number of emotional problems, and the greater need for understanding of and coping with the problems of death and dying.

When we look back in time and study old cultures and people, we are impressed that death has always been distasteful to man and will probably always be. From a psychiatrist's point of view this is very understandable and can perhaps best be explained by our basic knowledge that, in our unconscious, death is never possible in regard to ourselves. It is inconceivable for our unconscious to imagine an actual ending of our own life here on earth, and if this life of ours has to end, the ending is always attributed to a malicious intervention from the outside by someone else. In simple terms, in our unconscious mind we can only be killed; it is inconceivable to die of a natural cause or of old age. Therefore death in itself is associated with a bad act, a frightening happening, something that in itself calls for retribution and punishment.

One is wise to remember these fundamental facts as they are essential in understanding some of the most important, otherwise unintelligible communications of our patients.

The second fact that we have to comprehend is that in our unconscious mind we cannot distinguish between a wish and a deed. We are all aware of some of our illogical dreams in which two completely opposite statements can exist side by side—very acceptable in our dreams but unthinkable and illogical in our wakening state. Just as our unconscious mind cannot differentiate between the wish to kill somebody in anger and the act of having done so, the young child is unable to make this distinction. The child who angrily wishes his mother to drop dead for not having gratified his needs will be traumatized greatly by the actual death of his mother —even if this event is not linked closely in time with his destructive wishes. He will always take part or the whole blame for the loss of his mother. He will always say to himself—rarely to others—"I did it, I am responsible, I was bad, therefore Mommy left me." It is well to remember that the child will react in the same manner if he loses a parent by divorce, separation, or desertion. Death is often seen by a child as an impermanent thing and has therefore little distinction from a divorce in which he may have an opportunity to see a parent again.

Many a parent will remember remarks of their children such as, "I will bury my doggy now and next spring when the flowers come up again, he will get up." Maybe it was the same wish that motivated the ancient Egyptians to supply their dead with food and goods to keep them happy and the old American Indians to bury their relatives with their belongings.

When we grow older and begin to realize that our omnipotence is really not so omnipotent, that our strongest wishes are not powerful enough to make the impossible possible, the fear that we have contributed to the death of a loved one diminishes—and with it the guilt. The fear remains diminished, however, only so long as it is not challenged too strongly. Its vestiges can be seen daily in hospital corridors and in people associated with the bereaved.

A husband and wife may have been fighting for years, but when the partner dies, the survivor will pull his hair, whine and cry louder and beat his chest in regret, fear and anguish, and will hence fear his own death more than before, still believing in the law of talion —an eye for an eye, a tooth for a tooth—"I am responsible for her death, I will have to die a pitiful death in retribution."

Maybe this knowledge will help us understand many of the old customs and rituals which have lasted over the centuries and whose purpose is to diminish the anger of the gods or the people as the case may be, thus decreasing the anticipated punishment. I am thinking of the ashes, the torn clothes, the veil, the *Klage Weiber*[1] of the old days—they are all means to ask you to take pity on them, the mourners, and are expressions of sorrow, grief, and shame. If someone grieves, beats his chest, tears his hair, or refuses to eat, it is an attempt at self-punishment to avoid or reduce the anticipated punishment for the blame that he takes on the death of a loved one.

This grief, shame, and guilt are not very far removed from feelings of anger and rage. The process of grief always includes some qualities of anger. Since none of us likes to admit anger at a deceased person, these emotions are often disguised or repressed and prolong the period of grief or show up in other ways. It is well to remember that it is not up to us to judge such feelings as bad or shameful but to understand their true meaning and origin as something very human. In order to illustrate this I will again use the example of the child—and the child in us. The five-year-old who loses his mother is both blaming himself for her disappearance and being angry at her for having deserted him and for no longer gratifying his needs. The dead person then turns into something the child loves and wants very much but also hates with equal intensity for this severe deprivation.

The ancient Hebrews regarded the body of a dead person as

1. Wailing wives.

something unclean and not to be touched. The early American Indians talked about the evil spirits and shot arrows in the air to drive the spirits away. Many other cultures have rituals to take care of the "bad" dead person, and they all originate in this feeling of anger which still exists in all of us, though we dislike admitting it. The tradition of the tombstone may originate in this wish to keep the bad spirits deep down in the ground, and the pebbles that many mourners put on the grave are left-over symbols of the same wish. Though we call the firing of guns at military funerals a last salute, it is the same symbolic ritual as the Indian used when he shot his spears and arrows into the skies.

I give these examples to emphasize that man has not basically changed. Death is still a fearful, frightening happening, and the fear of death is a universal fear even if we think we have mastered it on many levels.

What has changed is our way of coping and dealing with death and dying and our dying patients.

Having been raised in a country in Europe where science is not so advanced, where modern techniques have just started to find their way into medicine, and where people still live as they did in this country half a century ago, I may have had an opportunity to study a part of the evolution of mankind in a shorter period.

I remember as a child the death of a farmer. He fell from a tree and was not expected to live. He asked simply to die at home, a wish that was granted without questioning. He called his daughters into the bedroom and spoke with each one of them alone for a few moments. He arranged his affairs quietly, though he was in great pain, and distributed his belongings and his land, none of which was to be split until his wife should follow him in death. He also asked each of his children to share in the work, duties, and tasks that he had carried on until the time of the accident. He asked his friends to visit him once more, to bid good-bye to them. Although I was a small child at the time, he did not exclude me or my siblings. We were allowed to share in the preparations of the family just as we were permitted to grieve with them until he died. When he did die, he was left at home, in his own beloved home which he had built, and among his friends and neighbors who went to take a last look at him where he lay in the midst of flowers in the place he had lived in and loved so much. In that country today there is still no make-believe slumber room, no embalming, no false makeup to pretend sleep. Only the signs of very disfiguring illnesses are covered up with bandages and only infectious cases are removed from the home prior to the burial.

Why do I describe such "old-fashioned" customs? I think they are an indication of our acceptance of a fatal outcome, and they help the dying patient as well as his family to accept the loss of a loved one. If a patient is allowed to terminate his life in the familiar and beloved environment, it requires less adjustment for him. His own family knows him well enough to replace a sedative with a glass of his favorite wine; or the smell of a home-cooked soup may give him the appetite to sip a few spoons of fluid which, I think is still more enjoyable than an infusion. I will not minimize the need for sedatives and infusions and realize full well from my own experience as a country doctor that they are sometimes life-saving and often unavoidable. But I also know that patience and familiar people and foods could replace many a bottle of intravenous fluids given for the simple reason that it fulfills the physiological need without involving too many people and/or individual nursing care.

The fact that children are allowed to stay at home where a fatality has stricken and are included in the talk, discussions, and fears gives them the feeling that they are not alone in the grief and gives them the comfort of shared responsibility and shared mourning. It prepares them gradually and helps them view death as part of life, an experience which may help them grow and mature.

This is in great contrast to a society in which death is viewed as taboo, discussion of it is regarded as morbid, and children are excluded with the presumption and pretext that it would be "too much" for them. They are then sent off to relatives, often accompanied with some unconvincing lies of "Mother has gone on a long trip" or other unbelievable stories. The child senses that something is wrong, and his distrust in adults will only multiply if other relatives add new variations of the story, avoid his questions or suspicions, shower him with gifts as a meager substitute for a loss he is not permitted to deal with. Sooner or later the child will become aware of the changed family situation and, depending on the age and personality of the child, will have an unresolved grief and regard this incident as a frightening, mysterious, in any case very traumatic experience with untrustworthy grownups, which he has no way to cope with.

It is equally unwise to tell a little child who lost her brother that God loved little boys so much that he took little Johnny to heaven. When this little girl grew up to be a woman she never solved her anger at God, which resulted in a psychotic depression when she lost her own little son three decades later.

We would think that our great emancipation, our knowledge of science and of man, has given us better ways and means to prepare ourselves and our families for this inevitable happening. Instead the days are gone when a man was allowed to die in peace and dignity in his own home.

The more we are making advancements in science, the more we seem to fear and deny the reality of death. How is this possible?

We use euphemisms, we made the dead look as if they were asleep, we ship the children off to protect them from the anxiety and turmoil around the house if the patient is fortunate enough to die at home, we don't allow children to visit their dying parents in the hospitals, we have long and controversial discussions about whether patients should be told the truth—a question that rarely arises when the dying person is tended by the family physician who has known him from delivery to death and who knows the weaknesses and strengths of each member of the family.

I think there are many reasons for this flight away from facing death calmly. One of the most important facts is that dying nowadays is more gruesome in many ways, namely, more lonely, mechanical, and dehumanized; at times it is even difficult to determine technically when the time of death has occurred.

Dying becomes lonely and impersonal because the patient is often taken out of his familiar environment and rushed to an emergency room. Whoever has been very sick and has required rest and comfort especially may recall his experience of being put on a stretcher and enduring the noise of the ambulance siren and hectic rush until the hospital gates open. Only those who have lived through this may appreciate the discomfort and cold necessity of such transportation which is only the beginning of a long ordeal—hard to endure when you are well, difficult to express in words when noise, light, pumps, and voices are all too much to put up with. It may well be that we might consider more the patient under the sheets and blankets and perhaps stop our well-meant efficiency and rush in order to hold the patient's hand, to smile, or to listen to a question. I include the trip to the hospital as the first episode in dying, as it is for many. I am putting it exaggeratedly in contrast to the sick man who is left at home—not to say that lives should not be saved if they can be saved by a hospitalization but to keep the focus on the patient's experience, his needs and his reactions.

When a patient is severely ill, he is often treated like a person with no right to an opinion. It is often someone else who makes the decision if and when and where a patient should be hospitalized. It would take so little to remember that the sick person too has feelings, has wishes and opinions, and has—most important of all—the right to be heard.

Well, our presumed patient has now reached the emergency room. He will be surrounded by busy nurses, orderlies, interns, residents, a lab technician perhaps who will take some blood, an electrocardiogram technician who takes the cardiogram. He may be moved to X-ray and he will overhear opinions of his condition and discussions and questions to members of the family. He slowly but surely is beginning to be treated like a thing. He is no longer a person. Decisions are made often without his opinion. If he tries to rebel he will be sedated and after hours of waiting and wondering whether he has the strength, he will be wheeled into the operating room or intensive treatment unit and become an object of great concern and great financial investment.

He may cry for rest, peace, and dignity, but he will get infusions, transfusions, a heart machine, or tracheostomy if necessary. He may want one single person to stop for one single minute so that he can ask one single question—but he will get a dozen people around the clock, all busily preoccupied with his heart rate, pulse, electrocardiogram or pulmonary functions, his secretions or excretions but not with him as a human being. He may wish to fight it all but it is going to be a useless fight since all this is done in the fight for his life, and if they can save his life they can consider the person afterwards. Those who consider the person first may lose precious time to save his life! At least this seems to be the rationale or justification behind all this—or is it? Is the reason for this increasingly mechanical, depersonalized approach our own defensiveness? Is this approach our own way to cope with and repress the anxieties that a terminally or critically ill patient evokes in us? Is our concentration on equipment, on blood pressure our desperate attempt to deny the impending death which is so frightening and discomforting to us that we displace all our knowledge onto machines, since they are less close to us than the suffering face of another human being which would remind us once more of our lack of omnipotence, our own limits and failures, and last but not least perhaps our own mortality?

Maybe the question has to be raised: Are we becoming less human or more human? * * * [I]t is clear that whatever the answer may be, the patient is suffering more—not physically, perhaps, but emotionally. And his needs have not changed over the centuries, only our ability to gratify them.

LEWIS THOMAS
The Long Habit

We continue to share with our remotest ancestors the most tangled and evasive attitudes about death, despite the great distance we have come to understanding some of the profound aspects of biology. We have as much distaste for talking about personal death as for thinking about it; it is an indelicacy, like talking in mixed company about venereal disease or abortion in the old days. Death on a grand scale does not bother us in the same special way: we can sit around a dinner table and discuss war, involving 60 million volatilized human deaths, as though we were talking about bad weather;

we can watch abrupt bloody death every day, in color, on films and television, without blinking back a tear. It is when the numbers of dead are very small, and very close, that we begin to think in scurrying circles. At the very center of the problem is the naked cold deadness of one's own self, the only reality in nature of which we can have absolute certainty, and it is unmentionable, unthinkable. We may be even less willing to face the issue at first hand than our predecessors because of a secret new hope that maybe it will go away. We like to think, hiding the thought, that with all the marvelous ways in which we seem now to lead nature around by the nose, perhaps we can avoid the central problem if we just become, next year, say, a bit smarter.

"The long habit of living," said Thomas Browne, "indisposeth us to dying." These days, the habit has become an addiction: we are hooked on living, the tenacity of its grip on us, and ours on it, grows in intensity. We cannot think of giving it up, even when living loses its zest—even when we have lost the zest for zest.

We have come a long way in our technologic capacity to put death off, and it is imaginable that we might learn to stall it for even longer periods, perhaps matching the life-spans of the Abkhasian Russians, who are said to go on, springily, for a century and a half. If we can rid ourselves of some of our chronic, degenerative diseases, and cancer, strokes and coronaries, we might go on and on. It sounds attractive and reasonable, but it is no certainty. If we became free of disease, we would make a much better run of it for the last decade or so, but might still terminate on about the same schedule as now. We may be like the genetically different lines of mice, or like Hayflick's different tissue-culture lines, programmed to die after a predetermined number of days clocked by their genomes. If this is the way it is, some of us will continue to wear out and come unhinged in the sixth decade, and some much later, depending on genetic timetables.

If we ever do achieve freedom from most of today's diseases, or even complete freedom from disease, we will perhaps terminate by drying out and blowing away on a light breeze, but we will still die.

Most of my friends do not like this way of looking at it. They prefer to take it for granted that we only die because we get sick, with one lethal ailment or another, and if we did not have our diseases we might go on indefinitely. Even biologists choose to think this about themselves, despite the evidences of the absolute inevitability of death that surround their professional lives. Everything dies, all around, trees, plankton, lichens, mice, whales, flies, mitochondria. In the simplest creatures it is sometimes difficult to see it as death, since the strands of replicating DNA they leave behind are more conspicuously the living parts of themselves than with us (not that it is fundamentally any different, but it seems so). Flies do not develop a ward round[1] of diseases that carry them off, one by one. They simply age, and die, like flies.

We hanker to go on, even in the face of plain evidence that long, long lives are not necessarily pleasurable in the kind of society we have arranged thus far. We will be lucky if we can postpone the search for new technologies for a while, until we have discovered some satisfactory things to do with the extra time. Something will surely have to be found to take the place of sitting on the porch reexamining one's watch.

Perhaps we would not be so anxious to prolong life if we did not detest so much the sickness of withdrawal. It is astonishing how little information we have about this universal process, with all the other dazzling advances in biology. It is almost as though we wanted not to know about it. Even if we could imagine the act of death in isolation, without any preliminary stage of being struck down by disease, we would be fearful of it.

There are signs that medicine may be taking a new interest in the process, partly from interest, partly from an embarrassed realization that we have not been handling this aspect of disease with as much skill as physicians once displayed, back in the days before they became convinced that disease was their solitary and sometimes defeatable enemy. It used to be the hardest and most important of all the services of a good doctor to be on hand at the time of death, and to provide comfort, usually in the home. Now it is done in hospitals, in secrecy (one of the reasons for the increased fear of death these days may be that so many people are totally unfamiliar with it; they never actually see it happen in real life). Some of our technology permits us to deny its existence, and we maintain flickers of life for long stretches in one community of cells or another, as though we were keeping a flag flying. Death is not a sudden all-at-once affair; cells go down in sequence, one by one. You can, if you like, recover great numbers of them many hours after the lights have gone out, and grow them out in cultures. It takes hours, even days, before the irreversible word finally gets around to all the provinces.

We may be about to rediscover that dying is not such a bad thing to do after all. Sir William Osler took this view; he disapproved of people who spoke of the agony of death, maintaining that there was no such thing.

In a 19th-century memoir about an expedition in Africa, there is a story about an explorer who was caught by a lion, crushed across the chest in the animal's great jaws, and saved in the instant by a lucky shot from a friend. Later, he remembered the episode in clear detail. He was so amazed by the extraordinary sense of peace and calm, and total painlessness, associated with his partial experience

---

1. A doctor's circuit through a hospital ward.

of being killed, that he constructed a theory that all creatures are provided with a protective physiologic mechanism, switched on at the verge of death, carrying them through in a haze of tranquility.

I have seen agony in death only once, in a patient with rabies, who remained acutely aware of every stage in the process of his own disintegration over a 24-hour period, right up to his final moment. It was as though, in the special neuropathology of rabies, the switch had been prevented from turning.

We will be having new opportunities to learn more about the physiology of death at first hand, from the increasing numbers of cardiac patients who have been through the whole process and then back again. Judging from what has been found out thus far, from the first generation of people resuscitated from cardiac standstill (already termed the Lazarus syndrome), Osler seems to have been right. Those who remember parts or all of their episodes do not recall any fear, or anguish. Several people who remained conscious throughout, while appearing to have been quite dead, could only describe a remarkable sensation of detachment. One man underwent coronary occlusion with cessation of the heart and dropped for all practical purposes dead in front of a hospital, and within a few minutes his heart had been restarted by electrodes and he breathed his way back into life. According to his account, the strangest thing was that there were so many people around him, moving so urgently, handling his body with such excitement, while all his awareness was of quietude.

In a recent study of the reaction to dying in patients with obstructive disease of the lungs, it was concluded that the process was considerably more shattering for the professional observers than the observed. Most of the patients appeared to be preparing themselves with equanimity for death, as though intuitively familiar with the business. One elderly woman reported that the only painful and distressing part of the process was in being interrupted; on several occasions she was provided with conventional therapeutic measures to maintain oxygenation or restore fluids and electrolytes, and each time she found the experience of coming back harrowing, she deeply resented the interference with her dying.

I find myself surprised by the thought that dying is an all-right thing to do, but perhaps it should not surprise. It is, after all, the most ancient and fundamental of biologic functions, with its mechanisms worked out with the same attention to detail, the same provision for the advantage of the organism, the same abundance of genetic information for guidance through the stages, that we have long since become accustomed to finding in all the crucial acts of living.

Very well. But even so, if the transformation is a co-ordinated, integrated physiologic process in its initial, local stages, there is still that permanent vanishing of consciousness to be accounted for. Are we to be stuck forever with this problem? Where on earth does it go? Is it simply stopped dead in its tracks, lost in humus, wasted? Considering the tendency of nature to find uses for complex and intricate mechanisms, this seems to me unnatural. I prefer to think of it as somehow separated off at the filaments of its attachment, and then drawn like an easy breath back into the membrane of its origin, a fresh memory for a biospherical nervous system, but I have no data on the matter.

This is for another science, another day. It may turn out, as some scientists suggest, that we are forever precluded from investigating consciousness, by a sort of indeterminacy principle that stipulates that the very act of looking will make it twitch and blur out of sight. It this is true, we will never learn. I envy some of my friends who are convinced about telepathy; oddly enough, it is my European scientist acquaintances who believe it most freely and take it most lightly. All their aunts have received Communications, and there they sit, with proof of the motility of consciousness at their fingertips, and the making of a new science. It is discouraging to have had the wrong aunts, and never the ghost of a message.

LEWIS THOMAS

Death in the Open

Most of the dead animals you see on highways near the cities are dogs, a few cats. Out in the countryside, the forms and coloring of the dead are strange; these are the wild creatures. Seen from a car window, they appear as fragments, evoking memories of wood-chucks, badgers, skunks, voles, snakes, sometimes the mysterious wreckage of a deer.

It is always a queer shock—part a sudden upwelling of grief, part unaccountable amazement. It is simply astounding to see an animal dead on a highway. The outrage is more than just the location; it is the impropriety of such visible death, anywhere. You do not expect to see dead animals in the open. It is the nature of animals to die alone, off somewhere, hidden. It is wrong to see them lying out on the highway; it is wrong to see them anywhere.

Everything in the world dies, but we only know about it as a kind of abstraction. If you stand in a meadow, at the edge of a hill-side and look around carefully, almost everything you can catch sight of is in the process of dying, and most things will be dead long before you are. If it were not for the constant renewal and replacement going on before your eyes, the whole place would turn to stone and sand under your feet.

There are some creatures that do not seem to die at all; they simply vanish totally into their own progeny. Single cells do this. The cell becomes two, then four and so on, and after a while the last trace is gone. It cannot be seen as death; barring mutation, the descendants are simply the first cell, living all over again. The cycles of the slime mold have episodes that seem as conclusive as death, but the withered slug, with its stalk and fruiting body, is plainly the transient tissue of a developing animal; the free-swimming amebo-cytes use this organ collectively to produce more of themselves.

There are said to be a billion billion insects on the earth at any moment, most of them with very short life expectancies by our standards. Someone has estimated that there are 25 million assorted insects hanging in the air over every temperate square mile, in a column extending upward for thousands of feet, drifting through the layers of the atmosphere like plankton. They are dying steadily, some by being eaten, some just dropping in their tracks, tons of them around the earth, disintegrating as they die, invisibly.

Who ever sees dead birds, in anything like the huge numbers stipulated by the certainty of the death of all birds? A dead bird is an incongruity, more startling than an unexpected live bird, sure evidence to the human mind that something has gone wrong. Birds do their dying off somewhere behind things, under things, never on the wing.

Animals seem to have an instinct for performing death alone, hidden. Even the largest, most conspicuous ones find ways to con-ceal themselves in time. If an elephant missteps and dies in an open place, the herd will not leave him there; the others will pick him up and carry the body from place to place, finally putting it down in some inexplicably suitable location. When elephants encounter the skeleton of an elephant out in the open, they methodically take up each of the bones and distribute them, in a ponderous ceremony, over neighboring acres.

It is a natural marvel. All the life of the earth dies, all the time, in the same volume as the new life that dazzles us each morning, each spring. All we see of this is the odd stump, the fly struggling on the porch floor of the summer house in October, the fragment on the highway. I have lived all my life with an embarrassment of squirrels in my backyard; they are all over the place, all year long, and I have never seen, anywhere, a dead squirrel.

I suppose it is just as well. If the earth were otherwise, and all the dying were done in the open, with the dead there to be looked at, we would never have it out of our minds. We can forget about it much of the time, or think of it as an accident to be avoided some-how. But it does make the process of dying seem more exceptional than it really is, and harder to engage in at the times when we must ourselves engage.

In our way, we conform as best we can to the rest of nature. The obituary pages tell us the news that we are dying away, and the birth announcements in finer print, off at the side of the page, inform us of our replacements, but we get no grasp from this of the enormity of scale. There are three billion of us on the earth, and all three billion must be dead, on a schedule, within this lifetime. The vast mortality, involving something over 50 million of us each year, takes place in relative secrecy. We can only really know of the deaths in our households, or among our friends. These, detached in our minds from all the rest, we take to be unnatural events, anomalies, outrages. We speak of our own dead in low voices; struck down, we say, as though visible death can only occur for cause, by disease or violence, avoidably. We send off for flowers, grieve, make ceremonies, scatter bones, unaware of the rest of the three billion on the same schedule. All that immense mass of flesh and bone and consciousness will disappear by absorption into the earth, without recognition by the transient survivors.

Less then half a century from now, our replacements will have more than doubled the numbers. It is hard to see how we can continue to keep the secret, with such multitudes doing the dying. We will have to give up the notion that death is catastrophe, or detestable, or avoidable, or even strange. We will need to learn more about the cycling of life in the rest of the system, and about our connection to the process. Everything that comes alive seems to be in trade for something that dies, cell for cell. There might be some comfort in the recognition of synchrony—in the information that we all go down together, in the best of company.

QUESTIONS

1. Thomas is a physician, a practitioner of what is said to be both science and art. What elements of each do you find in his essays?
2. Thomas says that death now occurs in hospitals, in secrecy, and Elizabeth Kübler-Ross, another physician, also discusses the social phenomenon (p. 1138). Both discussions are essays in professional self-criticism; what do the two writers do, in their essays, to establish their authority for this criticism?
3. Thomas wrote these articles for a medical journal, but they gradually commanded a wider, more general audience. To what would you attribute this general appeal? Can you locate the cause in the actual language of his essays?

JAMES THURBER
The Owl Who Was God

Once upon a starless midnight there was an owl who sat on the branch of an oak tree. Two ground moles tried to slip quietly by, unnoticed. "You!" said the owl. "Who?" they quavered, in fear and astonishment, for they could not believe it was possible for anyone to see them in that thick darkness. "You two!" said the owl. The moles hurried away and told the other creatures of the field and forest that the owl was the greatest and wisest of all animals because he could see in the dark and because he could answer any question. "I'll see about that," said a secretary bird, and he called on the owl one night when it was again very dark. "How many claws am I holding up?" said the secretary bird, "Two," said the owl, and that was right. "Can you give me another expression for 'that is to say' or 'namely'?" asked the secretary bird. "To wit," said the owl. "Why does a lover call on his love?" asked the secretary bird. "To woo," said the owl.

The secretary bird hastened back to the other creatures and reported that the owl was indeed the greatest and wisest animal in the world because he could see in the dark and because he could answer any question. "Can he see in the daytime, too?" asked a red fox. "Yes," echoed a dormouse and a French poodle. "Can he see in the daytime, too?" All the other creatures laughed loudly at this silly question, and they set upon the red fox and his friends and drove them out of the region. Then they sent a messenger to the owl and asked him to be their leader.

When the owl appeared among the animals it was high noon and the sun was shining brightly. He walked very slowly, which gave him an appearance of great dignity, and he peered about him with large, staring eyes, which gave him an air of tremendous importance. "He's God!" screamed a Plymouth Rock hen. And the others took up the cry "He's God!" So they followed him wherever he went and when he began to bump into things they began to bump into things, too. Finally he came to a concrete highway and he started up the middle of it and all the other creatures followed him. Presently a hawk, who was acting as outrider, observed a truck coming toward them at fifty miles an hour, and he reported to the secretary bird and the secretary bird reported to the owl. "There's danger ahead," said the secretary bird. "To wit?" said the owl. The secretary bird told him. "Aren't you afraid?" He asked. "Who?" said the owl calmly, for he could not see the truck. "He's God!" cried all the creatures again, and they were still crying "He's God!" when the truck hit them and ran them down. Some of the animals were merely injured, but most of them, including the owl, were killed.

Moral: You can fool too many of the people too much of the time.

ROBERT GRAVES
Mythology[1]

Mythology is the study of whatever religious or heroic legends are so foreign to a student's experience that he cannot believe them to be true. Hence the English adjective "mythical," meaning "incredible"; and hence the omission from standard European mythologies of all Biblical narratives even when closely paralleled by· myths from Persia, Babylonia, Egypt, and Greece, and of all hagiological legends. * * *

Myth has two main functions. The first is to answer the sort of awkward questions that children ask, such as: "Who made the world? How will it end? Who was the first man? Where do souls go after death?" The answers, necessarily graphic and positive, confer enormous power on the various deities credited with the creation and care of souls—and incidentally on their priesthoods.

The second function of myth is to justify an existing social system and account for traditional rites and customs. The Erechtheid clan of Athens, who used a snake as an amulet, preserved myths of their descent from King Erichthonius, a man-serpent, son of the Smith-god Hephaestus and foster-son of the Goddess Athene. The Ioxids of Caria explained their veneration for rushes and wild asparagus by a story of their ancestress Perigune, whom Theseus the Erechtheid courted in a thicket of these plants; thus incidentally claiming cousinship with the Attic royal house. The real reason may have been that wild asparagus stalks and rushes were woven into sacred baskets, and therefore taboo.

Myths of origin and eventual extinction vary according to the climate. In the cold North, the first human beings were said to have sprung from the licking of frozen stones by a divine cow named Audumla; and the Northern afterworld was a bare, misty, featureless plain where ghosts wandered hungry and shivering. According to a myth from the kinder climate of Greece, a Titan named Prometheus, kneading mud on a flowery riverbank, made human statuettes which Athene—who was once the Libyan Moon-goddess Neith—brought to life, and Greek ghosts went to a sunless, flowerless underground cavern. These afterworlds were destined for serfs or commoners; deserving nobles could count on warm, celestial mead halls in the North, and Elysian Fields in Greece.

Primitive peoples remodel old myths to conform with changes produced by revolutions, or invasions and, as a rule, politely disguise their violence: thus a treacherous usurper will figure as a lost heir to the throne who killed a destructive dragon or other monster and,

---

1. Introduction to the *Larousse Encyclopedia of Mythology*, 1959.

after marrying the king's daughter, duly succeeded him. Even myths of origin get altered or discarded. Prometheus' creation of men from clay superseded the hatching of all nature from a world-egg laid by the ancient Mediterranean Dove-goddess Eurynome—a myth common also in Polynesia, where the Goddess is called Tangaroa.

A typical case-history of how myths develop as culture spreads: Among the Akan of Ghana, the original social system was a number of queendoms, each containing three or more clans and ruled by a Queen-mother with her council of elder women, descent being reckoned in the female line, and each clan having its own animal deity. The Akan believed that the world was born from the all-powerful Moon-goddess Ngame, who gave human beings souls, as soon as born, by shooting lunar rays into them. At some time or other, perhaps in the early Middle Ages, patriarchal nomads from the Sudan forced the Akans to accept a male Creator, a Sky-god named Odomankoma, but failed to destroy Ngame's dispensation. A compromise myth was agreed upon: Odomankoma created the world with hammer and chisel from inert matter, after which Ngame brought it to life. These Sudanese invaders also worshipped the seven planetary powers ruling the week—a system originating in Babylonia. (It had spread to Northern Euope, bypassing Greece and Rome, which is why the names of pagan deities—Tuisto, Woden, Thor, and Frigg—are still attached to Tuesday, Wednesday, Thursday, and Friday.) This extra cult provided the Akan with seven new deities, and the compromise myth made both them and the clan gods bisexual. Towards the end of the fourteenth century A.D., a social revolution deposed Odomankoma in favor of a Universal Sun-god, and altered the myth accordingly. While Odomankoma ruled, a queendom was still a queendom, the king acting merely as a consort and male representative of the sovereign Queen-mother, and being styled "Son of the Moon": a yearly dying, yearly resurrected, fertility godling. But the gradual welding of small queendoms into city-states, and of city-states into a rich and populous nation, encouraged the High King—the king of the dominant city-state—to borrow a foreign custom. He styled himself "Son of the Sun," as well as "Son of the Moon," and claimed limitless authority. The Sun, which, according to the myth, had hitherto been reborn every morning from Ngame, was now worshipped as an eternal god altogether independent of the Moon's life-giving function. New myths appeared when the Akan accepted the patriarchal principle, which Sun-worship brought in; they began tracing succession through the father, and mothers ceased to be the spiritual heads of households.

This case-history throws light on the complex Egyptian corpus of myth. Egypt, it seems, developed from small matriarchal Moon-queendoms to Pharaonic patriarchal Sun-monarchy. Grotesque animal deities of leading clans in the Delta became city-gods, and the cities were federated under the sovereignty of a High King (once a "Son of the Moon"), who claimed to be the Son of Ra the Sun-god. Opposition by independent-minded city-rulers to the Pharaoh's autocratic sway appears in the undated myth of how Ra grew so old and feeble that he could not even control his spittle; the Moon-goddess Isis plotted against him and Ra retaliated by casting his baleful eye on mankind—they perished in their thousands. Ra nevertheless decided to quit the ungrateful land of Egypt, whereupon Hathor, a loyal Cow-goddess, flew him up to the vault of Heaven. The myth doubtless records a compromise that consigned the High King's absolutist pretensions, supported by his wife, to the vague realm of philosophic theory. He kept the throne, but once more became, for all practical purposes, an incarnation of Osiris, consort of the Moon-goddess Isis—a yearly dying, yearly resurrected fertility godling.

Indian myth is highly complex, and swings from gross physical abandon to rigorous asceticism and fantastic visions of the spirit world. Yet it has much in common with European myth, since Aryan invasions in the second millennium B.C. changed the religious system of both continents. The invaders were nomad herdsmen, and the peoples on whom they imposed themselves as a military aristocracy were peasants. Hesiod, an early Greek poet, preserves a myth of pre-Aryan "Silver Age" heroes: "divinely created eaters of bread, utterly subject to their mothers however long they lived, who never sacrificed to the gods, but at least did not make war against one another." Hesiod put the case well: in primitive agricultural communities, recourse to war is rare, and goddess-worship the rule. Herdsmen, on the contrary, tend to make fighting a profession and, perhaps because bulls dominate their herds, as rams do flocks, worship a male Sky-god typified by a bull or a ram. He sends down rain for the pastures, and they take omens from the entrails of the victims sacrificed to him.

When an invading Aryan chieftain, a tribal rainmaker, married the Moon-priestess and Queen of a conquered people, a new myth inevitably celebrated the marriage of the Sky-god and the Moon. But since the Moon-goddess was everywhere worshipped as a triad, in honor of the Moon's three phases—waxing, full, and waning—the god split up into a complementary triad. This accounts for three-bodied Geryon, the first king of Spain; three-headed Cernunnos, the Gallic god; the Irish triad, Brian, Iuchar, and Iucharba, who married the three queenly owners of Ireland; and the invading Greek brothers Zeus, Poseidon, and Hades, who, despite great opposition, married the pre-Greek Moon-goddess in her three aspects, respectively as Queen of Heaven, Queen of the Sea, and Queen of the Underworld.

The Queen-mother's decline in religious power, and the goddesses' continual struggle to preserve their royal prerogatives, appears in the Homeric myth of how Zeus ill-treated and bullied Hera, and how she continually plotted against him. Zeus remained a Thunder-god, because Greek national sentiment forbad his becoming a Sun-god in Oriental style. But his Irish counterpart, a thunder-god named The Dagda, grew senile at last and surrendered the throne to his son Bodb the Red, a war-god—in Ireland, the magic of rainmaking was not so important as in Greece.

One constant rule of mythology is that whatever happens among the gods above reflects events on earth. Thus a father-god named "The Ancient One of the Jade" (Yu-ti) ruled the pre-revolutionary Chinese Heaven: like Prometheus, he had created human beings from clay. His wife was the Queen-mother, and their court an exact replica of the old Imperial Court at Pekin, with precisely the same functionaries: ministers, soldiers, and a numerous family of the gods' sisters, daughters, and nephews. The two annual sacrifices paid by the Emperor to the August One of the Jade—at the winter solstice when the days first lengthen and at the Spring equinox when they become longer than the nights—show him to have once been a solar god. And the theological value to the number 72 suggests that the cult started as a compromise between Moon-goddess worship and Sun-god worship. 72 means three-times-three, the Moon's mystical number, multipled by two-times-two-times-two, the Sun's mystical number, and occurs in solar-lunar divine unions throughout Europe, Asia, and Africa. Chinese conservatism, by the way, kept these gods dressed in ancient court-dress, making no concessions to the new fashions which the invading dynasty from Manchuria had introduced.

In West Africa, whenever the Queen-mother, or King, appointed a new functionary at Court, the same thing happened in Heaven, by royal decree. Presumably this was also the case in China; and if we apply the principle to Greek myth, it seems reasonably certain that the account of Tirynthian Heracles' marriage to Hera's daughter Hebe, and his appointment as Celestial Porter to Zeus, commemorates the appointment of a Tirynthian prince as vizier at the court of the Mycenaean High King, after marriage to a daughter of his Queen, the High Priestess of Argos. Probably the appointment of Ganymede, son of an early Trojan king, as cup-bearer to Zeus, had much the same significance: Zeus, in this context, would be more likely the Hittite king resident at Hattusas.

Myth, then, is a dramatic shorthand record of such matters as invasions, migrations, dynastic changes, admission of foreign cults, and social reforms. When bread was first introduced into Greece—where only beans, poppyseeds, acorns, and asphodel roots had hitherto been known—the myth of Demeter and Triptolemus sanctified its use; the same event in Wales produced a myth of "The Old White One," a Sow-goddess who went around the country with gifts of grain, bees, and her own young; for agriculture, pig breeding and beekeeping were taught to the aborigines by the same wave of neolithic invaders. Other myths sanctified the invention of wine.

A proper study of myth demands a great store of abstruse geographical, historical, and anthropological knowledge, also familiarity with the properties of plants and trees, and the habits of wild birds and beasts. Thus a Central American stone sculpture, a Toad-god sitting beneath a mushroom, means little to mythologists who have not considered the worldwide association of toads with toxic mushrooms or heard of a Mexican Mushroom-god, patron of an oracular cult; for the toxic agent is a drug, similar to that secreted in the sweat glands of frightened toads, which provides magnificent hallucinations of a heavenly kingdom.

Myths are fascinating and easily misread. Readers may smile at the picture of Queen Maya and her prenatal dream of the Buddha descending upon her disguised as a charming white baby elephant—he looks as though he would crush her to pulp—when "at once all nature rejoiced, trees burst into bloom, and musical instruments played of their own accord." In English-speaking countries, "white elephant" denotes something not only useless and unwanted, but expensive to maintain; and the picture could be misread there as indicating the Queen's grave embarrassment at the prospect of bearing a child. In India, however, the elephant symbolizes royalty—the supreme God Indra rides one—and white elephants (which are not albinos, but animals suffering from a vitiliginous skin disease) are sacred to the Sun, as white horses were for the ancient Greeks, and white oxen for the British druids. The elephant, moreover, symbolizes intelligence, and Indian writers traditionally acknowledge the Elephant-god Ganesa as their patron; he is supposed to have dictated the *Mahabharata*.

Again, in English, a scallop shell is associated either with cookery or with medieval pilgrims returning from a visit to the Holy Sepulcher; but Aphrodite the Greek Love-goddess employed a scallop shell for her voyages across the sea, because its two parts were so tightly hinged together as to provide a symbol of passionate sexual love—the hinge of the scallop being a principal ingredient in ancient love-philters. The lotus-flower sacred to Buddha and Osiris has five petals, which symbolize the four limbs and the head; the five senses; the five digits; and, like the pyramid, the four points of the compass and the zenith. Other esoteric meanings abound, for myths are seldom simple, and never irresponsible.

ELDRIDGE CLEAVER
A Religious Conversion, More or Less[1]

Folsom Prison, September 10, 1965

Once I was a Catholic. I was baptized, made my first Communion, my Confirmation, and I wore a Cross with Jesus on it around my neck. I prayed at night, said my Rosary, went to Confession, and said all the Hail Marys and Our Fathers to which I was sentenced by the priest. Hopelessly enamored of sin myself, yet appalled by the sins of others, I longed for Judgment Day and a trial before a jury of my peers—this was my only chance to escape the flames which I could feel already licking at my feet. I was in a California Youth Authority institution at the time, having transgressed the laws of man—God did not indict me that time; if He did, it was a secret indictment, for I was never informed of any charges brought against me. The reason I became a Catholic was that the rule of the institution held that every Sunday each inmate had to attend the church of his choice. I chose the Catholic Church because all the Negroes and Mexicans went there. The whites went to the Protestant chapel. Had I been a fool enough to go to the Protestant chapel, one black face in a sea of white, and with guerrilla warfare going on between us, I might have ended up a Christian martyr—St. Eldridge the Stupe.

It all ended one day when, at a catechism class, the priest asked if anyone present understood the mystery of the Holy Trinity. I had been studying my lessons diligently and knew by heart what I'd been taught. Up shot my hand, my heart throbbing with piety (pride) for this chance to demonstrate my knowledge of the Word. To my great shock and embarrassment, the Father announced, and it sounded like a thunderclap, that I was lying, that no one, not even the Pope, understood the Godhead, and why else did I think they called it the *mystery* of the Holy Trinity? I saw in a flash, stung to the quick by the jeers of my fellow catechumens, that I had been used, that the Father had been lying in wait for the chance to drop that thunderbolt, in order to drive home the point that the Holy Trinity was not to be taken lightly.

I had intended to explain the Trinity with an analogy to 3-in-1 oil, so it was probably just as well.

QUESTIONS

1. Why does Cleaver use the title he does, especially the word "conversion" in combination with a seeming contradiction in the qualification "more or less"?

1. From *Soul on Ice*, 1968.

2. How would Cleaver's account have differed in tone and style if he had been describing a "real" conversion?
3. What attitude does the phrase "sentenced by the priest" reveal? Does Cleaver use the phrase flippantly, objectively, seriously, humorously, or in some other way?
4. Explore the possibilities of Cleaver's analogy of the Trinity to 3-in-1 oil. Could it have been developed appropriately? Why does Cleaver say it was "probably just as well" he didn't use it?
5. From the way Cleaver describes his past attitude—"hopelessly enamored of sin myself, yet appalled by the sins of others"—what do you deduce his present attitude toward sin to be?

RONALD A. KNOX

The Nature of Enthusiasm[1]

I have called this book *Enthusiasm*, not meaning thereby to name (for name it has none) the elusive thing that is its subject. I have only used a cant term, pejorative, and commonly misapplied, as a label for a tendency. And, lest I should be accused of setting out to mystify the reader, I must proceed to map out, as best I may, the course of this inquiry. There is, I would say, a recurrent situation in Church history—using the word "church" in the widest sense—where an excess of charity threatens unity. You have a clique, an *élite*, of Christian men and (more importantly) women, who are trying to live a less worldly life than their neighbors; to be more attentive to the guidance (directly felt, they would tell you) of the Holy Spirit. More and more, by a kind of fatality, you see them draw apart from their co-religionists, a hive ready to swarm. There is provocation on both sides; on the one part, cheap jokes at the expense of over-godliness, acts of stupid repression by unsympathetic authorities; on the other, contempt of the half-Christian, ominous references to old wine and new bottles, to the kernel and the husk. Then, while you hold your breath and turn away your eyes in fear, the break comes; condemnation or secession, what difference does it make? A fresh name has been added to the list of Christianities.

The pattern is always repeating itself, not in outline merely but in detail. Almost always the enthusiastic movement is denounced as an innovation, yet claims to be preserving, or to be restoring, the primitive discipline of the Church. Almost always the opposition is twofold; good Christian people who do not relish an eccentric spirituality find themselves in unwelcome alliance with worldlings who do not relish any spirituality at all. Almost always schism begets

1. From Chapter I of *Enthusiasm*, 1950.

schism; once the instinct of discipline is lost, the movement breeds rival prophets and rival coteries, at the peril of its internal unity. Always the first fervors evaporate; prophecy dies out, and the charismatic is merged in the institutional. "The high that proved too high, the heroic for earth too hard"—it is a fugal melody that runs through the centuries.

If I could have been certain of the reader's goodwill, I would have called my tendency "ultrasupernaturalism." For that is the real character of the enthusiast; he expects more evident results from the grace of God than we others. He sees what effects religion can have, does sometimes have, in transforming a man's whole life and outlook; these exceptional cases (so we are content to think them) are for him the average standard of religious achievement. He will have no "almost-Christians," no weaker brethren who plod and stumble, who (if the truth must be told) would like to have a foot in either world, whose ambition is to qualify, not to excel. He has before his eyes a picture of the early Church, visibly penetrated with supernatural influences; and nothing less will serve him for a model. Extenuate, accommodate, interpret, and he will part company with you.

Quoting a hundred texts—we also use them but with more of embarrassment—he insists that the members of his society, saved members of a perishing world, should live a life of angelic purity, of apostolic simplicity; worldly amusements, the artifices of a polite society, are not for them. Poor human nature! Every lapse that follows is marked by pitiless watchers outside the fold, creates a harvest of scandal within. Worse still, if the devout circle has cultivated a legend of its own impeccability; we shall be told, in that case, that actions which bring damnation to the worldling may be inculpable in the children of light. We must be prepared for strange alternations of rigorism and antinomianism as our history unfolds itself.

Meanwhile, it must not be supposed that the new birth which the enthusiast preaches can be limited to a mere reformation of manners. It involves a new approach to religion; hitherto this has been a matter of outward forms and ordinances, now it is an affair of the heart. Sacraments are not necessarily dispensed with; but the emphasis lies on a direct personal access to the Author of our salvation, with little of intellectual background or of liturgical expression. The appeal of art and music, hitherto conceived as a ladder which carried human thought upwards, is frowned upon as a barrier which interferes with the simplicity of true heart-worship. An inward experience of peace and joy is both the assurance which the soul craves for and its characteristic prayer-attitude. The strength of this personal approach is that it dominates the imagination, and presents a future world in all the colours of reality. Its weakness—but we are not concerned here to criticize—is an anthropocentric bias; not

God's glory but your own salvation preoccupies the mind, with some risk of scruples, and even of despair.

But the implications of enthusiasm go deeper than this; at the root of it lies a different theology of grace. Our traditional doctrine is that grace perfects nature, elevates it to a higher pitch, so that it can bear its part in the music of eternity, but leaves it nature still. The assumption of the enthusiast is bolder and simpler; for him, grace has destroyed nature, and replaced it. The saved man has come out into a new order of being, with a new set of faculties which are proper to his state; David must not wear the panoply of Saul. Especially, he decries the use of human reason as a guide to any sort of religious truth. A direct indication of the Divine will is communicated to him at every turn, if only he will consent to abandon the "arm of flesh"—Man's miserable intellect, fatally obscured by the Fall. If no oracle from heaven is forthcoming, he will take refuge in sortilege; anything, to make sure that he is leaving the decision in God's hands. That God speaks to us through the intellect is a notion which he may accept on paper, but fears, in practice, to apply.

A new set of faculties, and also a new status; man saved becomes, at last, fully man. It follows that "the seed of grace," God's elect people, although they must perforce live cheek by jowl with the sons of perdition, claim another citizenship and own another allegiance. For the sake of peace and charity, they will submit themselves to every ordinance of man, but always under protest; worldly governments, being of purely human institution, have no real mandate to exercise authority, and sinful folk have no real rights, although, out of courtesy, their fancied rights must be respected. Always the enthusiast hankers after a theocracy, in which the anomalies of the present situation will be done away, and the righteous bear rule openly. Disappointed of this hope, a group of sectaries will sometimes go out into the wilderness, and set up a little theocracy of their own, like Cato's senate at Utica. The American continent has more than once been the scene of such an adventure; in these days, it is the last refuge of the enthusiast.

QUESTIONS

1. What devices does Knox use in constructing his definition of enthusiasm?
2. What explanation does Knox imply for the fact that "enthusiasm" is regarded as a pejorative term?
3. What does Knox mean by "ominous references to old wine and new bottles, to the kernel and the husk"?
4. What illustrations might Knox give for his last sentence?

NICHOLAS OF CUSA
The Icon of God[1]

If I strive in human fashion to transport you to things divine, I must needs use a comparison of some kind. Now among men's works I have found no image better suited to our purposes than that of an image which is omnivoyant—its face, by the painter's cunning art, being made to appear as though looking on all around it. There are many excellent pictures of such faces—for example, that of the archeress in the market-place of Nuremberg; that by the eminent painter, Roger, in his priceless picture in the governor's house at Brussels; the Veronica in my chapel at Coblenz, and, in the castle of Brixen, the angel holding the arms of the Church, and many others elsewhere. Yet, lest ye should fail in the exercise, which requireth a figure of this description to be looked upon, I send for your indulgence such a picture as I have been able to procure, setting forth the figure of an omnivoyant, and this I call the icon of God.

This picture, brethren, ye shall set up in some place, let us say, on a north wall, and shall stand round it, a little way off, and look upon it. And each of you shall find that, from whatsoever quarter he regardeth it, it looketh upon him as if it looked on none other. And it shall seem to a brother standing to eastward as if that face looketh toward the east, while one to southward shall think it looketh toward the south, and one to westward, toward the west. First, then, ye will marvel how it can be that the face should look on all and each at the same time. For the imagination of him standing to eastward cannot conceive the gaze of the icon to be turned unto any other quarter, such as west or south. Then let the brother who stood to eastward place himself to westward and he will find its gaze fastened on him in the west just as it was afore in the east. And, as he knoweth the icon to be fixed and unmoved, he will marvel at the motion of its immovable gaze.

If now, while fixing his eye on the icon, he walk from west to east, he will find that its gaze continuously goeth along with him, and if he return from east to west, in like manner it will not leave him. Then will he marvel how, being motionless, it moveth, nor will his imagination be able to conceive that it should also move in like manner with one going in a contrary direction to himself. If he wish to experiment on this, he will cause one of his brethren to cross over from east to west, still looking on the icon, while he himself moveth from west to east; and he will ask the other as they meet if the gaze of the icon turn continuously with him; he will

1. Preface to *The Vision of God*.

hear that it doth move in a contrary direction, even as with himself, and he will believe him. But, had he not believed him, he could not have conceived this to be possible. So by his brother's showing he will come to know that the picture's face keepeth in sight all as they go on their way, though it be in contrary directions; and thus he will prove that that countenance, though motionless, is turned to east in the same way that it is simultaneously to west, and in the same way to north and to south, and alike to one particular place and to all objects at once, whereby it regardeth a single movement even as it regardeth all together. And while he observeth how that gaze never quitteth any, he seeth that it taketh such diligent care of each one who findeth himself observed as though it cared only for him, and for no other, and this to such a degree that one on whom it resteth cannot even conceive that it should take care of any other. He will also see that it taketh the same most diligent care of the least of creatures as of the greatest, and of the whole universe.

JOHN DONNE

Let Me Wither

Let me wither and wear out mine age in a discomfortable, in an unwholesome, in a penurious prison, and so pay my debts with my bones, and recompense the wastefulness of my youth, with the beggary of mine age; Let me wither in a spittle under sharp, and foul, and infamous diseases, and so recompense the wantonness of my youth, with that loathsomeness in mine age; yet if God withdraw not his spiritual blessings, his grace, his patience, If I can call my suffering his doing, my passion his action, All this that is temporal, is but a caterpiller got into one corner of my garden, but a mildew fallen upon one acre of my corn; The body of all, the substance of all is safe, as long as the soul is safe. But when I shall trust to that, which we call a good spirit, and God shall deject, and impoverish, and evacuate that spirit, when I shall rely upon a moral constancy, and God shall shake, and enfeeble, and enervate, destroy and demolish that constancy; when I shall think to refresh my self in the serenity and sweet air of a good conscience, and God shall call up the damps and vapors of hell itself, and spread a cloud of diffidence, and an impenetrable crust of desperation upon my conscience; when health shall fly from me, and I shall lay hold upon riches to succor me, and comfort me in my sickness, and riches shall fly from me, and I shall snatch after favor, and good opinion, to comfort me in my poverty; when even this good opinion shall leave me, and calumnies and misinformations shall prevail against me; when I shall need peace, because there is none but thou, O Lord, that should stand for me, and then shall find, that all the wounds that I have, come from thy hand, all the arrows that stick in me, from thy quiver; when I shall see, that because I have given my self to my corrupt nature, thou hast changed thine; and because I· am all evil toward thee, therefore thou hast given over being good toward me; When it comes to this height, that the fever is not in the humors, but in the spirits,[1] that mine enemy is not an imaginary enemy, fortune, nor a transitory enemy, malice in great persons, but a real, and an irresistible, and an inexorable, and an everlasting enemy, The Lord of Hosts himself, The Almighty God himself, the Almighty God himself only knows the weight of this affliction, and except he put in that *pondus gloriae*, that exceeding weight of an eternal glory, with his own hand, into the other scale, we are weighed down, we are swallowed up, irreparably, irrevocably, irrecoverably, irremediably.

1. Not in one of the four chief fluids of the body or "humors" (blood, yellow bile, phlegm, and black bile), but in the more subtle fluids.

QUESTIONS

Donne is perhaps more famous as a poet than as preacher, yet all that any author writes will in one way or another bear the stamp of his thought and personality. Read the following poem by Donne, and compare it with the sermon. Does the conception of God suggested in the poem resemble that in the sermon? Does the poem accomplish any of the same purposes as the sermon? Is the sermon "poetic" in any way? What differences arise from the fact that in the sermon Donne is speaking to a congregation, in the poem he is addressing God?

Batter my heart, three person'd God; for, you
As yet but knocke, breathe, shine, and seeke to mend.
That I may rise, and stand, o'erthrow mee, and bend
Your force, to breake, blowe, burn and make me new.
I, like an usurpt towne, to another due,
Labour to admit you, but Oh, to no end,
Reason your viceroy in mee, mee should defend,
But is captiv'd, and proves weake or untrue.
Yet dearely I love you, and would be loved faine,
But am bethroth'd unto your enemie;
Divorce mee, untie, or breake that knot againe,
Take mee to you, imprison mee, for I
Except you enthrall mee, never shall be free,
Nor ever chast, except you ravish mee.

—JOHN DONNE

JONATHAN EDWARDS
Sinners in the Hands of an Angry God[1]

Their foot shall slide in due time.[2]
—DEUT. xxxii. 35

In this verse is threatened the vengeance of God on the wicked unbelieving Israelites, who were God's visible people, and who lived under the means of grace; but who, notwithstanding all God's wonderful works towards them, remained (as ver. 28.)[3] void of counsel, having no understanding in them. Under all the cultivations of heaven, they brought forth bitter and poisonous fruit; as in the two verses next preceding the text. The expression I have chosen for my text, *Their foot shall slide in due time*, seems to imply the following things, relating to the punishment and destruction to which these wicked Israelites were exposed.

1. That they were always exposed to *destruction*; as one that stands or walks in slippery places is always exposed to fall. This is implied in the manner of their destruction coming upon them, being represented by their foot sliding. The same is expressed, Psalm lxxiii. 18. "Surely thou didst set them in slippery places; thou castedst them down into destruction."

2. It implies that they were always exposed to sudden unexpected destruction. As he that walks in slippery places is every moment liable to fall, he cannot foresee one moment whether he shall stand or fall the next; and when he does fall, he falls at once without warning: Which is also expressed in Psalm lxxiii. 18, 19. "Surely thou didst set them in slippery places; thou castedst them down into destruction. How are they brought into desolation as in a moment!"

3. Another thing implied is, that they are liable to fall of *themselves*, without being thrown down by the hand of another; as he that stands or walks on slippery ground needs nothing but his own weight to throw him down.

4. That the reason why they are not fallen already, and do not fall now, is only that God's appointed time is not come. For it is said, that when that due time, or appointed time comes, *their foot shall slide*. Then they shall be left to fall, as they are inclined by their own weight. God will not hold them up in these slippery places any longer, but will let them go; and then, at that very instant, they shall fall into destruction; as he that stands on such slippery

1. Only the first part of the sermon is printed here; the "application" is omitted.
2. The complete verse reads: "To me belongeth vengeance, and recompence; their foot shall slide in due time: for the day of their calamity is at hand, and the things that shall come upon them make haste." It occurs in the middle of a long denunciatory "song" spoken by Moses to the Israelites.
3. Verse 28: "For they are a nation void of counsel, neither is there any understanding in them."

declining ground, on the edge of a pit, he cannot stand alone, when he is let go he immediately falls and is lost.

The observation from the words that I would now insist upon is this—"There is nothing that keeps wicked men at any one moment out of hell, but the mere pleasure of God"—By the *mere* pleasure of God, I mean his *sovereign* pleasure, his arbitrary will, restrained by no obligation, hindered by no manner of difficulty, any more than if nothing else but God's mere will had in the least degree, or in any respect whatsoever, any hand in the preservation of wicked men one moment. The truth of this observation may appear by the following considerations.

1. There is no want of *power* in God to cast wicked men into hell at any moment. Men's hands cannot be strong when God rises up. The strongest have no power to resist him, nor can any deliver out of his hands. He is not only able to cast wicked men into hell, but he can most easily do it. Sometimes an earthly prince meets with a great deal of difficulty to subdue a rebel, who has found means to fortify himself, and has made himself strong by the numbers of his followers. But it is not so with God. There is no fortress that is any defense from the power of God. Though hand join in hand, and vast multitudes of God's enemies combine and associate themselves, they are easily broken in pieces. They are as great heaps of light chaff before the whirlwind; or large quantities of dry stubble before devouring flames. We find it easy to tread on and crush a worm that we see crawling on the earth; so it is easy for us to cut or singe a slender thread that any thing hangs by: thus easy is it for God, when he pleases, to cast his enemies down to hell. What are we, that we should think to stand before him, at whose rebuke the earth trembles, and before whom the rocks are thrown down?

2. They *deserve* to be cast into hell; so that divine justice never stands in the way, it makes no objection against God's using his power at any moment to destroy them. Yea, on the contrary, justice calls aloud for an infinite punishment of their sins. Divine justice says of the tree that brings forth such grapes of Sodom, "Cut it down, why cumbereth it the ground?" Luke xiii. 7. The sword of divine justice is every moment brandished over their heads, and it is nothing but the hand of arbitrary mercy, and God's mere will, that holds it back.

3. They are already under a sentence of *condemnation* to hell. They do not only justly deserve to be cast down thither, but the sentence of the law of God, that eternal and immutable rule of righteousness that God has fixed between him and mankind, is gone out against them, and stands against them; so that they are bound over already to hell. John iii. 18. "He that believeth not is condemned already." So that every unconverted man properly belongs to hell; that is his place; from thence he is, John viii. 23. "Ye are from beneath:" And thither he is bound; it is the place that justice,

and God's word, and the sentence of his unchangeable law assign to him.

4. They are now the objects of that very same *anger* and wrath of God, that is expressed in the torments of hell. And the reason why they do not go down to hell at each moment, is not because God, in whose power they are, is not then very angry with them; as he is with many miserable creatures now tormented in hell, who there feel and bear the fierceness of his wrath. Yea, God is a great deal more angry with great numbers that are now on earth; yea, doubtless, with many that are now in this congregation, who it may be are at ease, than he is with many of those who are now in the flames of hell.

So that it is not because God is unmindful of their wickedness, and does not resent it, that he does not let loose his hand and cut them off. God is not altogether such an one as themselves, though they may imagine him to be so. The wrath of God burns against them, their damnation does not slumber; the pit is prepared, the fire is made ready, the furnace is now hot, ready to receive them; the flames do now rage and glow. The glittering sword is whet, and held over them, and the pit hath opened its mouth under them.

5. The *devil* stands ready to fall upon them, and seize them as his own, at what moment God shall permit him. They belong to him; he has their souls in his possession, and under his dominion. The scripture represents them as his goods, Luke xi. 12. The devils watch them; they are ever by them at their right hand; they stand waiting for them, like greedy hungry lions that see their prey, and expect to have it, but are for the present kept back. If God should withdraw his hand, by which they are restrained, they would in one moment fly upon their poor souls. The old serpent is gaping for them; hell opens its mouth wide to receive them; and if God should permit it, they would be hastily swallowed up and lost.

6. There are in the souls of wicked men those hellish *principles* reigning, that would presently kindle and flame out into hell fire, if it were not for God's restraints. There is laid in the very nature of carnal men, a foundation for the torments of hell. There are those corrupt principles, in reigning power in them, and in full possession of them, that are seeds of hell fire. These principles are active and powerful, exceeding violent in their nature, and if it were not for the restraining hand of God upon them, they would soon break out, they would flame out after the same manner as the same corruptions, the same enmity does in the hearts of damned souls, and would beget the same torments as they do in them. The souls of the wicked are in scripture compared to the troubled sea, Isa. lvii. 20. For the present, God restrains their wickedness by his mighty power, as he does the raging waves of the troubled sea, saying, "Hitherto shalt thou come, but no further;" but if God should withdraw that restraining power, it would soon carry all before it.

Sin is the ruin and misery of the soul; it is destructive in its nature; and if God should leave it without restraint, there would need nothing else to make the soul perfectly miserable. The corruption of the heart of man is immoderate and boundless in its fury; and while wicked men live here, it is like fire pent up by God's restraints, whereas if it were let loose, it would set on fire the course of nature; and as the heart is now a sink of sin, so if sin was not restrained, it would immediately turn the soul into a fiery oven, or a furnace of fire and brimstone.

7. It is no security to wicked men for one moment, that there are no visible means of death at hand. It is no security to a natural man, that he is now in health, and that he does not see which way he should now immediately go out of the world by any accident, and that there is no visible danger in any respect in his circumstances. The manifold and continual experience of the world in all ages, shows this is no evidence, that a man is not on the very brink of eternity, and that the next step will not be into another world. The unseen, unthought-of ways and means of persons going suddenly out of the world are innumerable and inconceivable. Unconverted men walk over the pit of hell on a rotten covering, and there are innumerable places in this covering so weak that they will not bear their weight, and these places are not seen. The arrows of death fly unseen at noon-day; the sharpest sight cannot discern them. God has so many different unsearchable ways of taking wicked men out of the world and sending them to hell, that there is nothing to make it appear, that God had need to be at the expense of a miracle, or go out of the ordinary course of his providence, to destroy any wicked man, at any moment. All the means that there are of sinners going out of the world, are so in God's hands, and so universally and absolutely subject to his power and determination, that it does not depend at all the less on the mere will of God, whether sinners shall at any moment go to hell, than if means were never made use of, or at all concerned in the case.

8. Natural men's prudence and care to preserve their own lives, or the care of others to preserve them, do not secure them a moment. To this, divine providence and universal experience do also bear testimony. There is this clear evidence that men's own wisdom is no security to them from death; that if it were otherwise we should see some difference between the wise and politic men of the world, and others, with regard to their liableness to early and unexpected death: but how is it in fact? Eccles. ii. 16. "How dieth the wise man? even as the fool."

9. All wicked men's pains and *contrivance* which they use to escape hell, while they continue to reject Christ, and so remain wicked men, do not secure them from hell one moment. Almost every natural man that hears of hell, flatters himself that he shall escape it; he depends upon himself for his own security; he flatters him-

self in what he has done, in what he is now doing, or what he intends to do. Every one lays out matters in his own mind how he shall avoid damnation, and flatters himself that he contrives well for himself, and that his schemes will not fail. They hear indeed that there are but few saved, and that the greater part of men that have died heretofore are gone to hell; but each one imagines that he lays out matters better for his own escape than others have done. He does not intend to come to that place of torment; he says within himself, that he intends to take effectual care, and to order matters so for himself as not to fail.

But the foolish children of men miserably delude themselves in their own schemes, and in confidence in their own strength and wisdom; they trust to nothing but a shadow. The greater part of those who heretofore have lived under the same means of grace, and are now dead, are undoubtedly gone to hell; and it was not because they were not as wise as those who are now alive: it was not because they did not lay out matters as well for themselves to secure their own escape. If we could speak with them, and inquire of them, one by one, whether they expected, when alive, and when they used to hear about hell, ever to be the subjects of that misery: we doubtless, should hear one and another reply, "No, I never intended to come here: I had laid out matters otherwise in my mind; I thought I should contrive well for myself: I thought my scheme good. I intended to take effectual care; but it came upon me unexpected; I did not look for it at that time, and in that manner; it came as a thief: Death outwitted me: God's wrath was too quick for me. Oh, my cursed foolishness! I was flattering myself, and pleasing myself with vain dreams of what I would do hereafter; and when I was saying, Peace and safety, then suddenly destruction came upon me."

10. God has laid himself under *no* obligation, by any promise to keep any natural man out of hell one moment. God certainly has made no promises either of eternal life, or of any deliverance or preservation from eternal death, but what are contained in the covenant of grace, the promises that are given in Christ, in whom all the promises are yea and amen. But surely they have no interest in the promises of the covenant of grace who are not the children of the covenant, who do not believe in any of the promises, and have no interest in the Mediator of the covenant.

So that, whatever some have imagined and pretended about promises made to natural men's earnest seeking and knocking, it is plain and manifest, that whatever pains a natural man takes in religion, whatever prayers he makes, till he believes in Christ, God is under no manner of obligation to keep him a moment from eternal destruction.

So that, thus it is that natural men are held in the hand of God, over the pit of hell; they have deserved the fiery pit, and are already sentenced to it; and God is dreadfully provoked, his anger is as great towards them as to those that are actually suffering the executions of the fierceness of his wrath in hell, and they have done nothing in the least to appease or abate that anger, neither is God in the least bound by any promise to hold them up one moment; the devil is waiting for them, hell is gaping for them, the flames gather and flash about them, and would fain lay hold on them, and swallow them up; the fire pent up in their own hearts is struggling to break out: and they have no interest in any Mediator, there are no means within reach that can be any security to them. In short, they have no refuge, nothing to take hold of; all that preserves them every moment is in the mere arbitrary will, and uncovenanted, unobliged forbearance of an incensed God.

QUESTIONS

1. Trace the steps by which Edwards gets from his text to his various conclusions about man's state. Are they all logical? What assumptions does he add to those implied by the text in developing his argument? (Before answering these questions you will probably want to check the entire context of the text in Deuteronomy xxxii.)
2. What kinds of evidence does Edwards use in supporting his argument? Are they equally valid?
3. How do the concrete details, the imagery, and the metaphors that Edwards uses contribute to the effectiveness of his argument?
4. One might make the assumption that a society's conception of hell reflects, at least indirectly, some of that society's positive values. What positive values are reflected in Edwards' picture of hell?
5. One of his pupils described Edwards' delivery: "His appearance in the desk was with a good grace, and his delivery easy, natural and very solemn. He had not a strong, loud voice, but appeared with such gravity and solemnity, and spake with such distinctness and precision, his words were so full of ideas, set in such a plain and striking light, that few speakers have been so able to demand the attention of an audience as he. His words often discovered a great degree of inward fervor, without much noise or external emotion, and fell with great weight on the minds of his hearers. He made but little motion of his head or hands in the desk, but spake as to discover the motion of his own heart, which tended in the most natural and effectual manner to move and affect others." Would this manner of delivery be effective for the sermon printed here? Explain.

C. S. LEWIS

Three Screwtape Letters

I

My Dear Wormwood,[1]

I note what you say about guiding your patient's reading and taking care that he sees a good deal of his materialist friend. But are you not being a trifle *naïf*? It sounds as if you supposed that *argument* was the way to keep him out of the Enemy's clutches. That might have been so if he had lived a few centuries earlier. At that time the humans still knew pretty well when a thing was proved and when it was not; and if it was proved they really believed it. They still connected thinking with doing and were prepared to alter their way of life as the result of a chain of reasoning. But what with the weekly press and other such weapons we have largely altered that. Your man has been accustomed, ever since he was a boy, to have a dozen incompatible philosophies dancing about together inside his head. He doesn't think of doctrines as primarily "true" or "false", but as "academic" or "practical", "outworn" or "contemporary", "conventional" or "ruthless". Jargon, not argument, is your best ally in keeping him from the Church. Don't waste time trying to make him think that materialism is *true*! Make him think it is strong, or stark, or courageous—that it is the philosophy of the future. That's the sort of thing he cares about.

The trouble about argument is that it moves the whole struggle onto the Enemy's own ground. He can argue too; whereas in really practical propaganda of the kind I am suggesting He has been shown for centuries to be greatly the inferior of Our Father Below. By the very act of arguing, you awake the patient's reason; and once it is awake, who can foresee the result? Even if a particular train of thought can be twisted so as to end in our favour, you will find that you have been strengthening in your patient the fatal habit of attending to universal issues and withdrawing his attention from the stream of immediate sense experiences. Your business is to fix his attention on the stream. Teach him to call it "real life" and don't let him ask what he means by "real".

Remember, he is not, like you, a pure spirit. Never having been a human (Oh that abominable advantage of the Enemy's!) you don't realise how enslaved they are to the pressure of the ordinary. I once had a patient, a sound atheist, who used to read in the British Museum. One day, as he sat reading, I saw a train of thought in his mind beginning to go the wrong way. The Enemy, of course, was at

---

1. In these letters from Hell, Screwtape, an experienced devil, is counseling his nephew Wormwood, a neophyte tempter, who has ascended to Earth to begin his work.

his elbow in a moment. Before I knew where I was I saw my twenty years' work beginning to totter. If I had lost my head and begun to attempt a defence by argument I should have been undone. But I was not such a fool. I struck instantly at the part of the man which I had best under my control and suggested that it was just about time he had some lunch. The Enemy presumably made the counter-suggestion (you know how one can never *quite* overhear what He says to them?) that this·was more important than lunch. At least I think that must have been His line for when I said "Quite. In fact much *too* important to tackle at the end of a morning", the patient brightened up considerably; and by the time I had added "Much better come back after lunch and go into it with a fresh mind", he was already half way to the door. Once he was in the street the battle was won. I showed him a newsboy shouting the midday paper, and a No. 73 bus going past, and before he reached the bottom of the steps I had got into him an unalterable conviction that, whatever odd ideas might come into a man's head when he was shut up alone with his books, a healthy dose of "real life" (by which he meant the bus and the newsboy) was enough to show him that all "that sort of thing" just couldn't be true. He knew he'd had a narrow escape and in later years was fond of talking about "that inarticulate sense for actuality which is our ultimate safeguard against the aberrations of mere logic". He is now safe in Our Father's house.

You begin to see the point? Thanks to processes which we set at work in them centuries ago, they find it all but impossible to believe in the unfamiliar while the familiar is before their eyes. Keep pressing home on him the *ordinariness* of things. Above all, do not attempt to use science (I mean, the real sciences) as a defence against Christianity. They will positively encourage him to think about realities he can't touch and see. There have been sad cases among the modern physicists. If he must dabble in science, keep him on economics and sociology; don't let him get away from that invaluable "real life". But the best of all is to let him read no science but to give him a grand general idea that he knows it all and that everything he happens to have picked up in casual talk and reading is "the results of modern investigation". Do remember you are there to fuddle him. From the way some of you young fiends talk, anyone would suppose it was our job to *teach*!

> Your affectionate uncle
> SCREWTAPE

II

MY DEAR WORMWOOD,

I note with grave displeasure that your patient has become a Christian. Do not indulge the hope that you will escape the usual penalties: indeed, in your better moments, I trust you would hardly even wish to do so. In the meantime we must make the best of the situation. There is no need to despair; hundreds of these adult converts have been reclaimed after a brief sojourn in the Enemy's camp and are now with us. All the *habits* of the patient, both mental and bodily, are still in our favour.

One of our great allies at present is the Church itself. Do not misunderstand me. I do not mean the Church as we see her spread out through all time and space and rooted in eternity, terrible as an army with banners. That, I confess, is a spectacle which makes our boldest tempters uneasy. But fortunately it is quite invisible to these humans. All your patient sees is the half-finished, sham Gothic erection on the new building estate. When he goes inside, he sees the local grocer with rather an oily expression on his face bustling up to offer him one shiny little book containing a liturgy which neither of them understands, and one shabby little book containing corrupt texts of a number of religious lyrics, mostly bad, and in very small print. When he gets to his pew and looks round him he sees just that selection of his neighbours whom he has hitherto avoided. You want to lean pretty heavily on those neighbours. Make his mind flit to and fro between an expression like "the body of Christ" and the actual faces in the next pew. It matters very little of course, what kind of people that next pew really contains. You may know one of them to be a great warrior on the Enemy's side. No matter. Your patient, thanks to Our Father Below, is a fool. Provided that any of those neighbours sing out of tune, or have boots that squeak, or double chins, or odd clothes, the patient will quite easily believe that their religion must therefore be somehow ridiculous. At his present stage, you see, he has an idea of "Christians" in his mind which he supposes to be spiritual but which, in fact, is largely pictorial. His mind is full of togas and sandals and armour and bare legs and the mere fact that the other people in church wear modern clothes is a real—though of course an unconscious—difficulty to him. Never let it come to the surface; never let him ask what he expected them to look like. Keep everything hazy in his mind now, and you will have all eternity wherein to amuse yourself by producing in him the peculiar kind of clarity which Hell affords.

Work hard, then, on the disappointment or anticlimax which is certainly coming to the patient during his first few weeks as a churchman. The Enemy allows this disappointment to occur on the threshold of every human endeavour. It occurs when the boy who has been enchanted in the nursery by *Stories from the Odyssey* buckles down to really learning Greek. It occurs when lovers have got married and begin the real task of learning to live together. In every department of life it marks the transition from dreaming aspiration to laborious doing. The Enemy takes this risk because He has a curious fantasy of making all these disgusting little human vermin into what He calls His "free" lovers and servants—"sons" is the word He uses, with His inveterate love of degrading the whole spiritual world by unnatural liaisons with the two-legged animals. Desiring their freedom, He therefore refuses to carry them, by their mere affections and habits, to any of the goals which He sets before them: He leaves them to "do it on their own". And there lies our opportunity. But also, remember, there lies our danger. If once they get through this initial dryness successfully, they become much less dependent on emotion and therefore much harder to tempt.

I have been writing hitherto on the assumption that the people in the next pew afford no *rational* ground for disappointment. Of course if they do—if the patient knows that the woman with the absurd hat is a fanatical bridge-player or the man with squeaky boots a miser and an extortioner—then your task is so much the easier. All you then have to do is to keep out of his mind the question "If I, being what I am, can consider that I am in some sense a Christian, why should the different vices of those people in the next pew prove that their religion is mere hypocrisy and convention?" You may ask whether it is possible to keep such an obvious thought from occurring even to a human mind. It is, Wormwood, it is! Handle him properly and it simply won't come into his head. He has not been anything like long enough with the Enemy to have any real humility yet. What he says, even on his knees, about his own sinfulness is all parrot talk. At bottom, he still believes he has run up a very favourable credit-balance in the Enemy's ledger by allowing himself to be converted, and thinks that he is showing great humility and condescension in going to church with those "smug", commonplace neighbours at all. Keep him in that state of mind as long as you can.

Your affectionate uncle
SCREWTAPE

III

MY DEAR WORMWOOD,

I am very pleased by what you tell me about this man's relations with his mother. But you must press your advantage. The Enemy will be working from the centre outwards, gradually bringing more and more of the patient's conduct under the new standard, and may reach his behaviour to the old lady at any moment. You want to get in first. Keep in close touch with our colleague Glubose who is in charge of the mother, and build up between you in that house a good settled habit of mutual annoyance; daily pinpricks. The following methods are useful.

1. Keep his mind on the inner life. He thinks his conversion is something *inside* him and his attention is therefore chiefly turned at present to the states of his own mind—or rather to that very expur-

gated version of them which is all you should allow him to see.
Encourage this. Keep his mind off the most elementary duties by
directing it to the most advanced and spiritual ones. Aggravate that
most useful human characteristic, the horror and neglect of the
obvious. You must bring him to a condition in which he can practise self-examination for an hour without discovering any of those,
facts about himself which are perfectly clear to anyone who has ever
lived in the same house with him or worked in the same office.

2. It is, no doubt, impossible to prevent his praying for his
mother, but we have means of rendering the prayers innocuous.
Make sure that they are always very "spiritual", that he is always
concerned with the state of her soul and never with her rheumatism. Two advantages will follow. In the first place, his attention
will be kept on what he regards as her sins, by which, with a little
guidance from you, he can be induced to mean any of her actions
which are inconvenient or irritating to himself. Thus you can keep
rubbing the wounds of the day a little sorer even while he is on his
knees; the operation is not at all difficult and you will find it very
entertaining. In the second place, since his ideas about her soul will
be very crude and often erroneous, he will, in some degree, be praying for an imaginary person, and it will be your task to make that
imaginary person daily less and less like the real mother—the
sharp-tongued old lady at the breakfast table. In time, you may get
the cleavage so wide that no thought or feeling from his prayers for
the imagined mother will ever flow over into his treatment of the
real one. I have had patients of my own so well in hand that they
could be turned at a moment's notice from impassioned prayer for a
wife's or son's "soul" to beating or insulting the real wife or son
without a qualm.

3. When two humans have lived together for many years it
usually happens that each has tones of voice and expressions of face
which are almost unendurably irritating to the other. Work on that.
Bring fully into the consciousness of your patient that particular lift
of his mother's eyebrows which he learned to dislike in the nursery,
and let him think how much he dislikes it. Let him assume that she
knows how annoying it is and does it to annoy—if you know your
job he will not notice the immense improbability of the assumption. And, of course, never let him suspect that he has tones and
looks which similarly annoy her. As he cannot see or hear himself,
this is easily managed.

4. In civilised life domestic hatred usually expresses itself by
saying things which would appear quite harmless on paper (the
words are not offensive) but in such a voice, or at such a moment,
that they are not far short of a blow in the face. To keep this game
up you and Glubose must see to it that each of these two fools has
a sort of double standard. Your patient must demand that all his
own utterances are to be taken at their face value and judged simply

on the actual words, while at the same time judging all his mother's utterances with the fullest and most over-sensitive interpretation of the tone and the context and the suspected intention. She must be encouraged to do the same to him. Hence from every quarrel they can both go away convinced, or very nearly convinced, that they are quite innocent. You know the kind of thing: "I simply ask her what time dinner will be and she flies into a temper." Once this habit is well established you have the delightful situation of a human saying things with the express purpose of offending and yet having a grievance when offence is taken.

Finally, tell me something about the old lady's religious position. Is she at all jealous of the new factor in her son's life?—at all piqued that he should have learned from others, and so late, what she considers she gave him such good opportunity of learning in childhood? Does she feel he is making a great deal of "fuss" about it—or that he's getting in on very easy terms? Remember the elder brother in the Enemy's story,

Your affectionate uncle
SCREWTAPE

SÖREN KIERKEGAARD
The Knight of Faith

I candidly admit that in my practice I have not found any reliable example of the knight of faith, though I would not therefore deny that every second man may be such an example. I have been trying, however, for several years to get on the track of this, and all in vain. People commonly travel around the world to see rivers and mountains, new stars, birds of rare plumage, queerly deformed fishes, ridiculous breeds of men—they abandon themselves to the bestial stupor which gapes at existence, and they think they have seen something. This does not interest me. But if I knew where there was such a knight of faith, I would make a pilgrimage to him on foot, for this prodigy interests me absolutely. I would not let go of him for an instant, every moment I would watch to see how he managed to make the movements, I would regard myself as secured for life, and would divide my time between looking at him and practicing the exercises myself, and thus would spend all my time admiring him. As was said, I have not found any such person, but I can well think him. Here he is. Acquaintance made, I am introduced to him. The moment I set eyes on him I instantly push him from me, I myself leap backwards, I clasp my hands and say half aloud, "Good Lord, is this the man? Is it really he? Why, he looks like a tax collector!" However, it is the man after all. I draw closer to him, watching his least movements to see whether there might not be visible a little heterogeneous fractional telegraphic message from the infinite, a glance, a look, a gesture, a note of sadness, a smile, which betrayed the infinite in its heterogeneity with the finite. No! I examine his figure from tip to toe to see if there might not be a cranny through which the infinite was peeping. No! He is solid through and through. His tread? It is vigorous, belonging entirely to finiteness; no smartly dressed townsman who walks out to Fresberg on a Sunday afternoon treads the ground more firmly, he belongs entirely to the world, no Philistine more so. One can discover nothing of that aloof and superior nature whereby one recognizes the knight of the infinite. He takes delight in everything, and whenever one sees him taking part in a particular pleasure, he does it with the persistence which is the mark of the earthly man whose soul is absorbed in such things. He tends to his work. So when one looks at him one might suppose that he was a clerk who had lost his soul in an intricate system of bookkeeping, so precise is he. He takes a holiday on Sunday. He goes to church. No heavenly glance or any other token of the incommensurable betrays him; if one did not know him, it would be impossible to distinguish him from the rest of the congregation, for his healthy and vigorous hymn singing proves at the most that he has a good chest. In the afternoon he walks to the forest. He takes delight in everything he sees, in the human swarm, in the new omnibuses, in the water of the Sound; when one meets him on the Beach Road one might suppose he was a shopkeeper taking his fling, that's just the way he disports himself, for he is not a poet, and I have sought in vain to detect in him the poetic incommensurability. Toward evening he walks home, his gait is as indefatigable as that of the postman. On his way he reflects that his wife has surely a special little warm dish prepared for him, e.g. a calf's head roasted, garnished with vegetables. If he were to meet a man like-minded, he could continue as far as East Gate to discourse with him about that dish, with a passion befitting a hotel chef. As it happens, he hasn't four pence to his name, and yet he fully and firmly believes that his wife has that dainty dish for him. If she had it, it would then be an invidious sight for superior people and an inspiring one for the plain man, to see him eat; for his appetite is greater than Esau's. His wife hasn't it—strangely enough, it is quite the same to him. On the way he comes past a building site and runs across another man. They talk together for a moment. In the twinkling of an eye he erects a new building, he has at his disposition all the powers necessary for it. The stranger leaves him with the thought that he certainly was a capitalist, while my admired knight thinks, "Yes, if the money were needed, I dare say I could get it." He lounges at an open window and looks out on the square on which he lives; he is interested in everything that goes on, in a rat which slips under the curb, in the children's play, and this with the nonchalance of a girl of sixteen. And yet he is no genius, for in vain I have sought in him the incommensurability of genius. In the evening he smokes his pipe; to look at him one would swear that it was the grocer over the way vegetating in the twilight. He lives as carefree as a ne'er-do-well, and yet he buys up the acceptable time at the dearest price, for he does not do the least thing except by virtue of the absurd. And yet, and yet— actually I could become dubious over it, for envy if for no other reason—this man has made and every instant is making the movements of infinity. With infinite resignation he has drained the cup of life's profound sadness, he knows the bliss of the infinite, he senses the pain of renouncing everything, the dearest things he possesses in the world, and yet finiteness tastes to him just as good as to one who never knew anything higher, for his continuance in the finite did not bear a trace of the cowed and fearful spirit produced by the process of training; and yet he has the sense of security in enjoying it, as though the finite life were the surest thing of all. And yet, and yet the whole earthly form he exhibits is a new creation by virtue of the absurd. He resigned everything infinitely, and then he grasped everything again by virtue of the absurd. He constantly makes the movements of infinity, but he does this with such correctness and assurance that he constantly gets the finite out of it, and there is not a second when one has a notion of anything else. It is supposed to be the most difficult task for a dancer to leap into a definite posture in such a way that there is not a second when he is grasping after the posture, but by the leap itself he stands fixed in that posture. Perhaps no dancer can do it—that is what this knight does. Most people live dejectedly in wordly sorrow and joy; they are the ones who sit along the wall and do not join in the dance. The knights of infinity are dancers and possess elevation. They make the movements upward, and fall down again; and this too is no mean pastime, nor ungraceful to behold. But whenever they fall down they are not able at once to assume the posture, they vacillate an instant, and this vacillation shows that after all they are strangers in the world. This is more or less strikingly evident in proportion to the art they possess, but even the most artistic knights cannot altogether conceal this vacillation. One need not look at them when they are up in the air, but only the instant they touch or have touched the ground—then one recognizes them. But to be able to fall down in such a way that the same second it looks as if one were standing and walking, to transform the leap of life into a walk, absolutely to express the sublime in the pedestrian—that only the knight of faith can do—and this is the one and only prodigy.

PAUL TILLICH
The Riddle of Inequality

For to him who has will more be given; and from him
who has not, even what he has will be taken away.
—MARK iv. 25

One day a learned colleague called me up and said to me with
angry excitement: "There is a saying in the New Testament which
I consider to be one of the most immoral and unjust statements
ever made!" And then he started quoting our text: "To him who
has will more be given," and his anger increased when he continued:
"and from him who has not, even what he has will be taken away."
We all, I think, feel offended with him. And we cannot easily
ignore the offense by suggesting what *he* suggested—that the
words may be due to a misunderstanding of the disciples. It appears
at least four times in the gospels with great emphasis. And even
more, we can clearly see that the writers of the gospels felt exactly
as we do. For them it was a stumbling block, which they tried to
interpret in different ways. Probably none of these explanations satisfied them fully, for with this saying of Jesus, we are confronted
immediately with the greatest and perhaps most painful riddle of
life, that of the inequality of all beings. We certainly cannot hope to
solve it when neither the Bible nor any other of the great religions
and philosophies was able to do so. But we can do two things: We
can show the breadth and the depth of the riddle of inequality and
we can try to find a way to live with it, even if it is unsolved.

I

If we hear the words, "to him who has will more be given," we
ask ourselves: What *do* we have? And then we may find that much is
given to us in terms of external goods, of friends, of intellectual
gifts and even of a comparatively high moral level of action. So we
can expect that more will be given to us, while we must expect
that those who are lacking in all that will lose the little they already
have. Even further, according to Jesus' parable, the one talent they
have will be given to us who have five or ten talents. We shall be
richer because they will be poorer. We may cry out against such
an injustice. But we cannot deny that life confirms it abundantly.
We cannot deny it, but we can ask the question, do we *really*
have what we believe we have so that it cannot be taken from
us? It is a question full of anxiety, confirmed by a version of our
text rendered by Luke. "From him who has not, even what he
thinks that he has will be taken away." Perhaps our having of those
many things is not the kind of having which is increased. Perhaps
the having of few things by the poor ones is the kind of having
which makes them grow. In the parable of the talents, Jesus con-

firms this. Those talents which are used, even with a risk of losing them, are those which we really have; those which we try to preserve without using them for growth are those which we do not really have and which are being taken away from us. They slowly disappear, and suddenly we feel that we have lost these talents, perhaps forever.

Let us apply this to our own life, whether it is long or short. In the memory of all of us many things appear which we had without having them and which were taken away from us. Some of them became lost because of the tragic limitations of life; we had to sacrifice them in order to make other things grow. We all were given childish innocence; but innocence cannot be used and increased. The growth of our lives is possible only because we have sacrificed the original gift of innocence. Nevertheless, sometimes there arises in us a melancholy longing for a purity which has been taken from us. We all were given youthful enthusiasm for many things and aims. But this also cannot be used and increased. Most of the objects of our early enthusiasm must be sacrificed for a few, and the few must be approached with soberness. No maturity is possible without this sacrifice. Yet often a melancholy longing for the lost possibilities and enthusiasm takes hold of us. Innocence and youthful enthusiasm: we had them and had them not. Life itself demanded that they were taken from us.

But there are other things which we had and which were taken from us, because we let them go through our own guilt. Some of us had a deep sensitivity for the wonder of life as it is revealed in nature. Slowly under the pressure of work and social life and the lure of cheap pleasures, we lose the wonder of our earlier years when we felt intense joy and the presence of the mystery of life through the freshness of the young day or the glory of the dying day, the majesty of the mountains or the infinity of the sea, a flower breaking through the soil or a young animal in the perfection of its movements. Perhaps we try to produce such feelings again, but we are empty and do not succeed. We had it and had it not, and it has been taken from us.

Others had the same experience with music, poetry, the great novels and plays. One wanted to devour all of them, one lived in them and created for oneself a life above the daily life. We *had* all this and did not have it; we did not let it grow; our love towards it was not strong enough and so it was taken from us.

Many, especially in this group, remember a time in which the desire to learn to solve the riddles of the universe, to find truth has been the driving force in their lives. They came to college and university, not in order to buy their entrance ticket into the upper middle classes or in order to provide for the preconditions of social and economic success, but they came, driven by the desire for knowledge. They had something and more could have been given to them. But in reality they did not have it. They did not make it grow and so it was taken from them and they finished their academic work in terms of expendiency and indifference towards truth. Their love for truth has left them and in some moments they are sick in their hearts because they realize that what they have lost they may never get back.

We all know that any deeper relation to a human being needs watchfulness and growth, otherwise it is taken away from us. And we cannot get it back. This is a form of having and not having which is the root of innumerable human tragedies. We all know about them. And there is another, the most fundamental kind of having and not having—our having and losing God. Perhaps we were rich towards God in our childhood and beyond it. We may remember the moments in which we felt his ultimate presence. We may remember prayers with an overflowing heart, the encounter with the holy in word and music and holy places. We had communication with God; but it was taken from us because we had it and had it not. We did not let it grow, and so it slowly disappeared leaving an empty space. We became unconcerned, cynical, indifferent, not because we doubted about our religious traditions—such doubt belongs to being rich towards God—but because we turned away from that which once concerned us infinitely.

Such thoughts are a first step in approaching the riddle of inequality. Those who have, receive more if they really have it, if they use it and make it grow. And those who have not, lose what they have because they never had it really.

II

But the question of inequality is not yet answered. For one now asks: Why do some receive more than others in the very beginning, before there is even the possibility of using or wasting our talents? Why does the one servant receive five talents and the other two and the third one? Why is the one born in the slums and the other in a well-to-do suburban family? It does not help to answer that of those to whom much is given much is demanded and little of those to whom little is given. For it is just this inequality of original gifts, internal and external, which arouses our question. Why is it given to one human being to gain so much more out of his being human than to another one? Why is so much given to the one that much *can* be asked of him, while to the other one little is given and little *can* be asked? If this question is asked, not only about individual men but also about classes, races and nations, the everlasting question of political inequality arises, and with it the many ways appear in which men have tried to abolish inequality. In every revolution and in every war, the will to solve the riddle of inequality is a driving force. But neither war nor revolution can remove it. Even if we imagine that in an indefinite future most social inequalities are conquered, three things remain: the inequality of talents in body and mind, the inequality created by freedom and destiny, and the fact that all generations before the time of such equality would be excluded from its blessings. This would be the greatest possible inequality! No! In face of one of the deepest and most torturing problems of life, it is unpermittably shallow and foolish to escape into a social dreamland. We have to live now; we have to live this our life, and we must face today the riddle of inequality.

Let us not confuse the riddle of inequality with the fact that each of us is a unique incomparable self. Certainly our being individuals belongs to our dignity as men. It is given to us and must be used and intensified and not drowned in the gray waters of conformity which threaten us today. One should defend every individuality and the uniqueness of every human self. But one should not believe that this is a way of solving the riddle of inequality. Unfortunately, there are social and political reactionaries who use this confusion in order to justify social injustice. They are at least as foolish as the dreamers of a future removal of inequality. Whoever has seen hospitals, prisons, sweatshops, battlefields, houses for the insane, starvation, family tragedies, moral aberrations should be cured from any confusion of the gift of individuality with the riddle of inequality. He should be cured from any feelings of easy consolation.

III

And now we must make the third step in our attempt to penetrate the riddle of inequality and ask: Why do some use and increase what was given to them, while others do not, so that it is taken from them? Why does God say to the prophet in our Old Testament lesson that the ears and eyes of a nation are made insensible for the divine message?

Is it enough to answer: Because some use their freedom responsibly and do what they ought to do while others fail through their own guilt? Is this answer, which seems so obvious, sufficient? Now let me first say that it *is* sufficient if we apply it to ourselves. Each of us must consider the increase or the loss of what is given to him as a matter of his own responsibility. Our conscience tells us that we cannot put the blame for our losses on anybody or anything else than ourselves.

But if we look at others, this answer is not sufficient. On the contrary: If we applied the judgment which we *must* apply to anyone else we would be like the Pharisee in Jesus' parable. You cannot tell somebody who comes to you in distress about himself: Use what has been given to you; for he may come to you just because he is unable to do so! And you cannot tell those who are in despair about what they are: Be something else; for this is just what despair means—the inability of getting rid of oneself. You cannot tell those who did not conquer the destructive influences of their surroundings and were driven into crime and misery that they should have been stronger; for it was just of this strength they had been deprived by heritage or environment. Certainly they all are men, and to all of them freedom is given; but they all are also subject to destiny. It is not up to us to condemn them because they were free, as it is not up to us to excuse them because they were under their destiny. We cannot judge them. And when we judge ourselves, we must be conscious that even this is not the last word, but that we like them are under an ultimate judgment. In it the riddle of inequality is eternally answered. But this answer is not ours. It is our predicament that we must ask. And we ask with an uneasy conscience. Why are they in misery, why not we? Thinking of some who are near to us, we can ask: Are we partly responsible? But even if we are, it does not solve the riddle of inequality. The uneasy conscience asks about the farthest as well as about the nearest: Why they, why not we?

Why has my child, or any of millions and millions of children, died before even having a chance to grow out of infancy? Why is my child, or any child, born feeble-minded or crippled? Why has my friend or relative, or anybody's friend or relative, disintegrated in his mind and lost both his freedom and his destiny? Why has my son or daughter, gifted as I believe with many talents, wasted them and been deprived of them? And why does this happen to any parent at all? Why have this boy's or this girl's creative powers been broken by a tyrannical father or by a possessive mother?

In all these questions it is not the question of our own misery which we ask. It is not the question: Why has this happened to *me*?

It is not the question of Job which God answers by humiliating him and then by elevating him into communion with him. It is not the old and urgent question: Where is the divine justice, where is the divine love towards me? But it is almost the opposite question: Why has this *not* happened to me, why has it happened to the other one, to the innumerable other ones to whom not even the power of Job is given to accept the divine answer? Why—and Jesus has asked the same question—are many called and few elected?

He does not answer; he only states that this is the human predicament. Shall we therefore cease to ask and humbly accept the fact of a divine judgment which condemns most human beings away from the community with him into despair and self-destruction? Can we accept the eternal victory of judgment over love? We cannot; and nobody ever could, even if he preached and threatened in these terms. As long as he could not see himself with complete certainty as eternally rejected, his preaching and threatening would be self-deceiving. And who could see himself eternally rejected?

But if this is not the solution of the riddle of inequality at its deepest level, can we trespass the boundaries of the Christian tradition and listen to those who tell us that this life does not decide about our eternal destiny? There will be occasions in other lives, as our present life is determined by previous ones and what we have achieved or wasted in them. It is a serious doctrine and not completely strange to Christianity. But if we don't know and never will know what each of us has been in the previous or future lives, then it is not really *our* destiny which develops from life to life, but in each life it is the destiny of someone else. This answer also does not solve the riddle of inequality.

There is no answer at all if we ask about the temporal and eternal destiny of the single being separated from the destiny of the whole. Only in the unity of all beings in time and eternity can a humanly possible answer to the riddle of inequality be found. *Humanly* possible does not mean an answer which removes the riddle of inequality, but an answer with which we can live.

There is an ultimate unity of all beings, rooted in the divine life from which they come and to which they go. All beings, non-human as well as human, participate in it. And therefore they all participate in each other. We participate in each other's having and we participate in each other's not-having. If we become aware of this unity of all beings, something happens. The fact that others have-not changes in every moment the character of my having: It undercuts its security, it drives me beyond myself, to understand, to give, to share, to help. The fact that others fall into sin, crime and misery changes the character of the grace which is given to me: It makes me realize my own hidden guilt, it shows to me that those who suffer for their sin and crime, suffer also for me; for I am guilty of their guilt—at least in the desire of my heart—and ought to suffer as they do. The awareness that others who *could* have become fully developed human beings and never *have*, changes my state of full humanity. Their early death, their early or late disintegration, makes my life and my health a continuous risk, a dying which is not yet death, a disintegration which is not yet destruction. In every death which we encounter, something of us dies; in every disease which we encounter, something of us tends to disintegrate.

Can we live with this answer? We can to the degree in which we are liberated from the seclusion within ourselves. But nobody can be liberated from himself unless he is grasped by the power of that which is present in everyone and everything—the eternal from which we come and to which we go, which gives us to ourselves and which liberates us *from* ourselves. It is the greatness and the heart of the Christian message that God—as manifest in the Cross of the Christ—participates totally in the dying child, in the condemned criminal, in the disintegrating mind, in the starving one and in him who rejects him. There is no extreme human condition into which the divine presence would not reach. This is what the Cross, the most extreme of all human conditions, tells us. The riddle of inequality cannot be solved on the level of our separation from each other. It is eternally solved in the divine participation in all of us and every being. The certainty of the divine participation gives us the courage to stand the riddle of inequality, though finite minds cannot solve it. Amen.

HENRY SLOANE COFFIN

What Crucified Christ?[1]

Some years ago a well-known British journalist, the late W. T. Stead, after witnessing the Passion Play at Oberammergau, came away saying to himself: "This is the story which has transformed the world." And he seemed to hear an echo from the Bavarian hills about him: "Yes, and will transform it."

Each generation stresses particular aspects of the Gospel; and it must be confessed that in our day, and especially in those circles where Christianity is interpreted in terms of contemporary thought, the cross does not hold the central place in preaching. With many men the Incarnation has taken the place formerly occupied by the Atonement, and the character of Jesus is proclaimed as the supreme revelation of God and the ideal for man. In other circles it has been the religious experience of Jesus which is oftenest preached, and men are bidden follow His way of life with God and man. In still other quarters it is His teaching which is dwelt on and men are enlisted as devotees of the Kingdom of God. But the cross, while it is mentioned as a significant unveiling of Jesus' character, or as the most draining ordeal for which He drew on spiritual resources, or as the climax of His devotion to His cause, is seldom preached as a redemptive act. Indeed few of those who have accepted the current liberal theology devote many sermons to the cross of Christ. They feel themselves incapable of treating the theme.

There are various reasons for this. Our exaggerated individualism renders it difficult for us to think of One bearing the sins of others. Our easy optimism makes us think lightly of sin as an obsession of minds which hold unwholesome views of man and of God. Above all, the luxurious circumstances in which modern American Christians have found themselves have dulled our capacities for appreciating sacrifice. We have surrounded ourselves with conveniences and comforts, and we have tried to banish pain. The tortured form of One spiked on a beam of wood and done to death does not belong in our mental picture. Our ideals and manner of life are incompatible with this tragic and heroic symbol. Preachers have felt an unreality in attempting to explore with their people the meaning of the crucifixion.

---

1. Chapter 1 of *The Meaning of the Cross* (1931).

This neglect of the cross has had something to do with the lack of transforming power in our message. No one can look complacently upon the present condition of our churches. Hundreds of them are barely holding on: they make no gains from the lives about them. In hundreds more, where there is bustle and stir, the activity is about trifles, and lives are not radically altered nor their communities made over. In very few does one find comrades of the conscience of Christ. In most the majority of communicants show no marks of the Lord Jesus in the purposes to which they devote themselves, in their attitudes towards their neighbors, in the opinions which they hold on public questions. Ministers can count on their fingers the number of their people ready to give themselves for an advance of the Kingdom. The wealth in Christian hands in this country is fabulous, but almost all Church Boards are crippled for want of support. More money is taken in at the gates of a single champion prizefight than a million Church members contribute in a whole year to the spread of the Gospel throughout the world. Above all repentance—a fundamental Christian experience— "repentance unto life" as the Westminster divines termed it—is a saving grace seldom seen. That which has most moved other centuries to repentance unto life has been the preaching of Christ crucified. Commenting upon Dwight L. Moody's insistence upon the efficacy of the sacrifice of Christ to do away with sin, Gamaliel Bradford writes:

To some of us, at any rate, whether we can accept this doctrine or not, it seems that the enormous, unparalleled growth and power and majesty of Christianity in the last nineteen hundred years depend upon it.

One would not harshly criticize brethren in the ministry who have shrunk from the word of the cross. We preachers are pitiable men, doomed to be haunted week after week with a sense of the insufficiency of our treatment of subjects obviously too high for us, and on which we are still constrained to speak. We become most abysmally aware of our incompetence when we attempt to set forth the meaning of the suffering and death of the Son of Man. John Milton, who had marvelously celebrated the birth of Jesus in the "Ode on the Morning of Christ's Nativity," attempted a sequel upon the Passion, but after a few exquisite stanzas he ceased in despair, and the fragment is published with the significant note:

This Subject the Author finding to be above the years he had when he wrote it, and nothing satisfied with what was begun, left it unfinished.

And years do not of themselves mature us to deal with this theme. Happily we discover that sermons which seriously try to interpret that supreme event possess a moving power out of proportion to the wisdom of their content.

How are we to preach Christ crucified? We want an interpretation of the cross for our generation which shall move to repentance and faith. In order to remain in close touch with reality, suppose we begin with two questions of history: First, How came it that the Life which subsequent centuries have looked up to as the best ever lived on our earth seemed so intolerable to the dominant groups of His day that they executed Him? Second, Why did Jesus force the issue that made His execution inevitable?

Let us attempt to answer the first question in this initial chapter remembering that we are not attempting a doctrine of the cross for classroom discussion, but for general presentation. How came it that He whom succeeding generations have revered as the best of men was put to death as a criminal? Who were the crucifiers of Christ?

First and foremost the religious leaders whom Church folk respected. It is a tribute to the force conferred by religious conviction that believing men are so often the prime movers in momentous occurrences, both in the blackest crimes and in the brightest triumphs of mankind. Faith, like fire, empowers its possessors whether for woe or for weal. We must not forget that there was ardent faith in God and conscientious loyalty to Him in the Pharisees who contrived the cruel death of our earth's divinest figure. Like one of their own school, they verily thought themselves under compulsion to act as they did.

That is why Church folk should study them carefully. Who were they? The successors of a brave and patriotic company of stalwart believers who had saved the Jewish faith when foreign conquerors attempted to compromise and wreck it by introducing their own customs and worship. They were known for that essential element in vital religion—detachment: they were called Separatists, Pharisees. They were the heirs of a noble army of martyrs. They knew and honored the Bible as the Law of God. They reverenced the scholars who had spent their lives in explaining it and applying it to life. They were the backbone of the synagogues throughout the land. They prayed; they believed in God's present government of His world and in His immediate control of events. They thought His angelic messengers spoke in the consciences of devout folk and watched for good over their steps. They looked forward to the resurrection of the righteous and their life in the Messiah's everlasting kingdom. They were intense lovers of home and country: in their households there was family religion, and boys, like Saul of Tarsus, were brought up to become devotees and leaders of the Church. They supplied the candidates for the ministry—the scribes who studied and interpreted the Torah. They furnished the missionaries who had enthusiasm to compass sea and land for a single proselyte, and had built up around the synagogues of the whole

Mediterranean world companies of the God-fearing who had espoused the faith of Israel.

Men who sincerely try to order their lives by God's will usually work out a system of obligations, to which they hold themselves and seek to hold others. Now some matters can readily be embodied in rules—keeping the Sabbath, observing sacred festivals and fasts, adopting methodical times and habits of prayer, setting aside a tenth of one's gains for religious purposes. And some matters cannot be thus codified—having clean thoughts and generous sympathies, being conciliatory, honoring every human being, however unadmirable, as kin to God, serving him as his heavenly Father understandingly cares for him. And matters which can be incorporated in rules tend to be stressed above those which cannot be precisely defined. And when men have their beliefs and duties clearly stated, and are earnestly living by them, they are not apt to distinguish between more and less important items in their religious code: all of it is precious to them. They do not wish any of it changed. Sincere religion is inherently conservative. It deals with tested values.

Jesus scandalized them by disregarding practices which they considered God's Law. He broke the Sabbath shockingly. When asked to speak in the synagogues, His addresses upset many in the congregation. He associated with disreputable people—with loose women and with unpatriotic profiteering farmers of revenue. He touched the academic pride of their scholars: how should a carpenter correct their explanation of Scriptures which they had spent their lives in studying and for which they had the authority of recognized experts? Many of them had never heard Him for themselves, and at second or tenth hand, when the intervening hands are unfriendly, His sayings and doings appeared even more insufferable. From the outset He was surrounded in their minds with an atmosphere of suspicion. They sent spies to watch Him, and spies have a way of hearing what they fancy they are sent to hear. The Pharisees felt themselves guardians of the faith of Israel. Their fathers had fought and bled for it; their own lives were wrapped up in it; they were holding it in the dark days of Roman dominion for their children and children's children. Could they allow this Innovator, this Charlatan who made preposterous claims for Himself, to go on deceiving simple folk and perhaps wreck the Church? Quite apart from the embittering encounters Jesus had with some of them—encounters which may have been colored in our gospels by the subsequent strife between the Synagogue and the growing Christian Church, there was enough difference between His faith and life and theirs to rouse determined antagonism. In loyalty to God they must put an end to His mischievous career.

A second group were the inheritors of a lucrative commercial privilege—the aristocratic Sadducean priests who controlled the Temple area. They also were churchmen, but in comparison with the Pharisees, their religion was a subordinate and moderate interest. It was an inheritance which they cherished with an antiquarian's regard for its more primitive form. Their thought of Deity was of a remote and unaggressive Being, who left men to work out their own affairs, who certainly did not interfere or help by sending angelic spirits. God wished from Israel a seemly recognition in the maintenance of the time-honored ceremonies. For the rest they were broadminded. Their predecessors had welcomed the culture and customs of the Greeks, and they probably had a much more tolerant attitude in religion than the Pharisees. One might have picked up a Greek poem or drama in their homes; they were interested in the on-goings of the larger world; and after the manner of cultivated liberals they smiled in superior fashion on the narrow preoccupations of scribes with the details of the religious code. They were much more concerned with politics and finance than with religion. So long as Jesus remained in Galilee, they may never have heard of Him; or if some rumor of Him came to their ears, they would pay little attention to it. The alarm of the Pharisees over His teaching would have seemed to them a petty squabble which was no concern of theirs.

But when Jesus invaded the Temple precincts and created a commotion by overturning the tables of the money-changers, these gentlemen were roused. Here was a dangerous social Radical. Doubtless their leasing of space for booths in the outer court of the Temple had been criticized before, and there was popular talk over the prices of doves and lambs, and grumbling at the rate of exchange for the half-shekel. But this was the usual proletarian murmuring. Did they not provide a public convenience in these business arrangements? Were they not assisting worshippers in their religious duties? Did not the ancient Law clearly enjoin that the Temple tax should be paid in a particular coin? And must not someone supply facilities for exchanging the various currencies which pilgrims brought with them from all over the Empire for the proper silver piece? Was not four per cent a moderate broker's fee for such an exchange? The idea of this upcountry Agitator appearing and, without a word to anybody in authority, making this disturbance in the Temple court, and infecting the populace with the absurd notion that there should be no charge for perfectly legitimate ecclesiastical business! Where did He think animals for sacrifice would be procured? What did He consider a reasonable charge for exchange, if He called four per cent robbery? Who was He, anyhow, to take upon Himself to reform the financial methods of men whose forebears had derived their incomes unquestioned from these leases? His attack was a reflection not only upon them, but upon their honored fathers. Annas and Caiaphas had never seen the court of the Temple without booths and stalls; it was to them part of the natural order of things that cattle and doves should be sold there and money exchanged. Further they had been born to the tradition that the sacred area of the Temple belonged to the hereditary priesthood, and that they were to derive their support from its ceremonies. How could they understand the indignant feelings of Jesus? The charge, which the false witnesses brought, that He had threatened to destroy the Temple, may have had some slight basis in fact. Such statements are seldom made out of whole cloth. Jesus may have expressed the feeling that, if this Temple made with hands were destroyed, real religion might not lose much. That would disturb these gentlemen in their family sentiment, in their inherited faith, in their economic interests.

And they were politicians with a keen eye for the political situation. At the moment they were on fair terms with the Roman Empire and were allowed some freedom in the management of local affairs. A demagogue of this sort, as Caiaphas remarked, might stir up a political mess, and embroil them with the Roman authorities. Could they risk allowing Him to go on?[2]

A third figure among the crucifiers is the representative of imperialistic government. He seems to have been impressed by Jesus—more impressed than the scribes or the priests. We pity him as part of a system which our age feels to be inherently faulty. In theory at least we do not believe in one people governing another. It is bad for both peoples. It creates such attitudes as one sees in this scene—the priests fawning upon the governor and Pilate overbearing toward them and insulting the nation by the derisive title he orders nailed above the Victim on the cross. But among imperialistic peoples few have understood their business as well as the Romans. They probably kept Judaea in better order than any native leader could have kept it. They governed brutally, but there are still many who think that inferiors must be made to know their place. Jesus had been struck with their haughty attitude: "Ye know that the rulers of the Gentiles lord it." It may have been partially a patriot's unwillingness to speak against His own countrymen before an overlord which sealed His lips in the judgment hall.

All our narratives agree that the governor was most reluctant to execute this Prisoner. He suggested expedient after expedient to

2. Doctor L. P. Jacks has said of our contemporary churches: "The gravamen of the charge against the Church is not so much that there are definite abuses in its corporate life as that there is a general atmosphere of acquiescence in all that is worldly and conventional. No one knows exactly what ideal of life the Church stands for, unless that it is that of a kindly and good-natured toleration of things as they are, with a mild desire that they may grow better in time, so far as that is compatible with the maintenance of existing vested interests." That is the position of the Sadducee; and Jesus touched it at its most sensitive point when He assailed vested interests [Coffin's note].

obviate it. He tried everything except the direct course of following his conscience and seeking to deal justly towards the Man before him. The system of which he was a part entangled him. Rome asked her procurators to keep the tribute flowing steadily from their provinces and to maintain quiet. No governor wished complaints lodged against him with his superiors. Pilate had to live with these priests, and in the end it seemed easier to let them have their way with this Peasant from Galilee. He was poor and insignificant, and to this day justice is never the same for the unfriended sons of poverty as for the wealthy and influential. Paul, claiming his rights as a Roman citizen, was to have days in court his Master could not command.

To the last Pilate was uncomfortable about the case. He did his best to shift responsibility—on Herod, on the crowd, on the priests. But the priests knew their man and played skillfully upon his loyalties and his fears. The fourth evangelist makes them say: "If thou release this man, thou art not Cæsar's friend." Fidelity to Cæsar was both a Roman's patriotism and his religion. They were appealing to Pilate's principles, and they won their point. Pilate washed his hands, but throughout the centuries his name has been coupled with this event as responsible for it on the lips of thousands who repeat "crucified under Pontius Pilate."

A fourth figure among crucifiers, although he is hardly a decisive factor, is a man of the gay world—Herod Antipas. A scion of an able family, born to wealth and position, brought up in Rome at the imperial court, admitted to the fashionable society of the capital in the golden age of Augustus, a member of the smart set, he knew all about the latest delicacies of the table, had a keen eye for a beautiful dancer, and surrounded by boon companions lived for pleasure. Like many in similar circumstances in contemporary America he had a shabby marital record, having become infatuated with his half-brother's wife, for whom he divorced his own wife and whom he stole from her husband. But divorces even of this sordid variety were not bad form then, any more than they are among ourselves today, and bad form was the only taboo Herod revered. He had a reputation for political shrewdness, and he had burnt his fingers in handling one prophet, John, and was wary of repeating the blunder. Jesus dreaded what He called "the leaven of Herod"—loose morals, lavish outlay, and sharp politics. He had spoken of this tetrarch as "that fox." Now these two were face to face.

Herod displayed a man-of-the-world's versatility in asking Him "many questions"—one wonders what they were. He was clever and was pleased to display his knowledge of religious fine points before his companions and before the priests. It was a chance to impress them. But Herod could make nothing of Jesus. And Jesus could make nothing of Herod. He had borne witness to His Messiahship before Caiaphas and the Sanhedrin; He had admitted His kingship to Pontius Pilate; but He had not a syllable to utter to Antipas. The tetrarch had heard of him as a wonder-worker and craved the chance to see Him do something startling. But Jesus' mighty works are not tricks to entertain and astonish. Herod had a conscience; could not Jesus appeal to that with some piercing story such as Nathan told adulterous David? Did the Saviour ever confront a needier sinner? But He had not a word for him.

Herod was apparently "past feeling," and Jesus gave him up. This clownish roysterer and his cronies could think of nothing to do with their disappointing Prisoner but tog Him out in mock finery and make game of Him. Fancy the mind of Jesus while this went on! It cost Pilate some struggle to condemn Him; but when He was sent away from the tetrarch's palace, Herod had been laughing at Him as a buffoon, and was now smiling at his own shrewdness in outwitting the governor, and handing his awkward case back to him.

A fifth figure among the crucifiers is a disillusioned idealist. We have no reason to think that the man of Kerioth did not enlist in the cause of Jesus from the same high motives as the other disciples. If anything it was harder for him, the only Judaean in the group, than for Galileans. He heard all that they heard and he shared all that they shared, and, like them, he was disappointed. He had looked for a different issue. Jesus outdistanced his ideals; he fancied that Jesus did not measure up to his ideals and he grew critical. With many the attempt "to go beyond themselves and wind themselves too high" is followed by a reaction. What he had hoped for, and hoped for immediately, did not happen, and Judas became bitter. He felt himself duped. The confident attitude of Jesus as He set His face to what seemed to Judas folly and defeat, irritated him. He was no longer the reasonable man he had been. It was that perhaps which led the disciples in retrospect to recall that the devil entered into him. They felt that he was at war with himself. And in such plight men not infrequently turn on those to whom they have been most warmly attached. Their disgust with themselves they are apt to vent on those who make them uncomfortable. Iago says of Cassio: "He hath a daily beauty in his life that makes me ugly." Jesus became hateful to Judas Iscariot. There may be a shred of truth in the theories which make his betrayal of the Master an attempt to force His hand, and compel Him to assume his power.

For what was it that Judas betrayed to the priests? Obviously not merely the spot where their police could arrest Jesus. That was not worth paying for. The police could follow him and find out His haunts. Probably Judas betrayed, as many modern interpreters think, the secret of Jesus' Messiahship, which was talked of in the inner circle but not published abroad. That was not clear to the priests or to the public even after the entry amid hosannas, for the shouts of a crowd are not evidence. Now they had a basis for trial, so Judas was in a sense forcing Jesus to declare Himself. But our narratives imply that Judas did it vindictively, not affectionately.

Disillusioned idealists become sour and cynical. And in cynicism consciences unravel: Judas may easily have grown careless in handling the money in his custody. Avarice cannot have been the main motive in the betrayal, but greed has a place in most ignoble stories. Very trifling sums induce people still to hideous crimes. When a man is embittered, he is capable of anything, and it was a cynic who drove the shabby bargain with the chief priests and went out with thirty pieces of silver jingling in his purse and a betrayed Master on his conscience.

A sixth factor among the crucifiers is a crowd. The individuals who composed it were decent men, kind to their families and neighbors, and personally they would not have been cruel to this Prophet from Galilee. They had a prejudice against Him, and that prejudice was worked up until they were fused into a howling mob. In such a mass a man is lifted out of himself, loses control of his feelings, and his passions surge unchecked and augmented by the passions of the throng around him. He becomes a thousand times himself emotionally. Shakespeare's Bassanio speaks of

> The buzzing pleased multitude
> Whose every something being blent together
> Turns to a wild of nothing save of joy.

And the reverse is true when the crowd is prejudiced and their every something being blended together turns to a wild of nothing save of cruelty.

A crowd, being emotionally intense, is very suggestible. A catchword will set it off. Our propagandists and advertisers have taught us how we can be worked on in masses by names, phrases, pictures. And crowds are much more readily suggestible to the more primitive and coarser sentiments than to the finer. Man is a thinly varnished savage at best, lump him together in throngs and the varnish melts at the touch. When Pilate appeared unwilling to grant the priests' request, the crowd was swayed by nationalism; the priests were their own, and the governor the representative of the hated oppressor. They had a traditional right to claim clemency for a prisoner at the Passover. They will use it, and natural self-assertion impels them not to ask for One whom Pilate would gladly let them have. A suggestion is given them—Barabbas, a popular revolutionary of the crude type—a slogan for the emotions of a crowd.

Jesus can hardly have been popular. How much better "copy" for our own press Barabbas would be than the Teacher of Nazareth!

Besides Barabbas is the nationalistic type Pilate would least like to release. Mobs feel and scarcely think. Could these men as individuals have calmly weighed Jesus and Barabbas, the result might have been different; but they were atingle with their cruder instincts. And a crowd which takes to shouting works itself to a violent pitch, and when thwarted can become fiendishly brutal. The spectators who packed the tiers of the Coliseum, turned down their thumbs at some fallen gladiator and yelled themselves hoarse demanding his death, would not have done anything of the sort by themselves. Each man in the crowd has lost his sense of personal responsibility. It is what men do in a social set, a political party, an economic group, a nation, a religious assembly, that is likely to be least moral and most diabolically savage. Pilate did his weak best not to execute Jesus; Herod found loutish amusement in Him, but showed no desire for His blood; Judas wished Him out of his way, but jail would have satisfied him; the crowd, with their tribal feelings roused—the instincts of the hunting pack—shouted "Crucify Him, crucify Him!"

A seventh factor among the crucifiers was a guard of soldiers. Jesus never spoke harshly of the military profession. One of His rare compliments was paid to an officer who had expressed his faith in terms of soldierly obedience. And probably it was in extenuation of the legionaries charged with the grim details of His execution that He prayed: "Father, forgive them, for they know not what they do." But it was by men prepared for their task by military discipline that He was done to death at Golgotha.

That system is deliberately planned to depersonalize those whom it trains. They are educated not to decide for themselves, but to give machine-like response to a command. Such a system, while it has noble associations with courage, loyalty, honor, and self-effacement, counteracts that which Christianity tries hardest to create—a reasoning conscience. The soldiers who scourged Jesus and spiked His hands and feet to the beams of the cross never thought what they were doing—they were victims of a discipline which had crucified their moral judgments.

Their occupation was held in high honor as the typical and most essential patriotic service. Rome ruled by physical might. She believed in awing inferior peoples and encouraged her soldiers to strike terror into them. The scourging which Pilate ordered—"the terrible preface," as it was called, to capital punishment—was forbidden for Roman citizens, but it was customary for provincials. A small guard was ordered to inflict on Jesus this appalling indignity in public—stripping Him, binding Him to a stake in a stooping position with hands behind Him, and beating Him with thongs at the ends of which were leaden balls or sharp-pointed bones.

And when that prostrating ordeal was over they took Him for further maltreatment to the privacy of the guardroom. Brutal mockery of the condemned was allowed the soldiers in order to maintain their *morale*. All the finer feelings must be overcome in those whose trade is iron and blood. And privacy seems to be an inevitable temptation to men with fellow-beings in their power. Schoolboys, jailors, keepers of the weak in mind or body, generation after generation, have to be watched against outbreaks of savagery to their victims. It was expected of the soldiers—a crude comic interlude of their rough day. But in fairness to these systematically hardened men let us recall that when the Prisoner was uplifted on the cross, slowly bleeding to death in agony, educated and revered religious leaders, professors of divinity, vented their detestation of Him with gibes. Theological animosity renders men as callous as professional hangmen.

Perhaps more so, for these soldiers had to restrain themselves from feeling by gambling at the foot of the cross. They had to sit by while the crucified writhed, and groaned, and cried, in their prolonged misery. It is not surprising that they resorted to the excitement of playing dice as a mental relief. They are typical representatives of callings into which men cannot put themselves—their minds and consciences and hearts. Such callings rob those who engage in them of moral vitality and make them fit agents of tragic occurrences like Calvary.

But there is still an eighth factor without which the crucifixion would not have taken place—the public. Behind the chief actors in the drama at Golgotha we see thousands of obscure figures—the populace of the city. One fancies them getting up in the morning and hearing rumors of a case on before the governor. The city, crowded with Passover pilgrims, would be more excitable and talkative than usual, and news of events at the palace, involving the Sanhedrin, would spread rapidly. Then, as people were in the midst of their morning's work, they would catch sight of that sinister procession tramping through the streets on the way to the place of execution outside the city wall. We can overhear such remarks as "Hello! another hanging today? Who's to be hung? Those two bandits? Who's the third prisoner? That Prophet from Galilee? Oh, they got Him very quickly, didn't they?" And as prisoners and guards filed past, the day's work was resumed.

Behind all earth's tragedies there is a public whose state of mind has much to do with the central event. Even under the least democratic government the authorities dare not go more than a certain distance without the popular will. The thousands of uncaring nobodies, to whom what was done with Jesus was a matter of indifference, gave scribes and priests and governor their chance. These obscure folk felt themselves without responsibility. What had they to do with this Prophet from the north country who had ridden into the city, hailed by a crowd of provincial pilgrims? Possibly it was of them that Jesus was thinking—the public of the capital city—when He said: "O Jerusalem, Jerusalem, that killeth the prophets."

The public is never of one mind; it represents various shades of opinion and feeling—sympathetic, hostile, indifferent; and all shades were there in Jerusalem. But if enough of its inhabitants had really cared about Jesus, He would never have been crucified. The chief handicap of the public is ignorance. The mass of the dwellers in Jerusalem knew next to nothing about the Prophet from Galilee. But Jesus did not weep over them merely because of their lack of information. Religious capitals, like cathedral towns, are proverbially hard to move. Religion was an old story to those who lived in the neighborhood of the venerable Temple and were familiar with the figures of the great doctors of the Law. They were complacent in sacred traditions of the past and not open to fresh incomings of the Most High. Jesus wept over their apathy. To Him it seemed that even unfeeling stones must respond to One who so manifestly represented God. They did not know the things which belonged to peace because they did not wish to know them. Jerusalem slew the Son of God not only because He had won the sharp ill-will of the powerful few, but also because the many did not want to be bothered with Him. And the public of Jerusalem, who thought the fate of this Stranger none of their business, had to bear the doom with their as-yet-unborn children; for judgment brings home social obligations and convinces us that by a myriad unsuspected cords men are tied up in one bundle of life in cities, in nations, in races, and in a world of men. These thousands of citizens of Jerusalem never went through the form of washing their hands, like Pilate. They were unaware of any accountability for this execution. But history with its destruction of the city rendered its verdict upon them.

Such a survey of the factors which crucified Jesus—and a course rather than a single sermon is obviously necessary to treat them with sufficient explicitness—forces men to think. This was the world which executed the Life subsequent generations until this hour revere as the best earth has seen. And plainly it is the world in which we still live. All these forces are present and active in our society—religious intolerance, commercial privilege, political expediency, pleasure-loving irresponsibility, unfaithfulness, the mob spirit, militarism, public apathy. These are perennial evils. They are deep-seated in the very structure of human society. The forms of political and economic and ecclesiastical organization may alter, but these remain under all forms. We should find them in a socialist republic or a communist state, as surely as in an imperial despotism or a capitalist regime. Moreover, they act and react upon each other. The priests help Judas to his treachery and incite the mob; Pilate stimulates the priests to play politics; the political methods of both governor and religious leaders keep the public morally indifferent; their sinister motives interweave into a corporate force for evil. Together they make up what Jesus called "the power of darkness," the satanic kingdom.

It is significant that the national and ecclesiastical capital is the slayer of the prophets. Evil organizes itself with this inherent solidarity and possesses a group—a church, a nation, a race. These forces were present in the villages and towns, but they came to a focus where the organization of the church and the nation had its seat, and where the representative of imperial government exercised his power. Wickedness propagates itself generation after generation. Jesus recognized the unity of the factors with which He was struggling with similar factors, which had always been present in the life of His people, when He spoke of this generation which was crucifying Him having upon it "all the righteous blood shed on earth," from the blood of Abel on the first pages of the Old Testament to the blood of Zachariah recorded on its last pages. Evil spreads itself laterally, building up a corporate force of wickedness, and passes itself on from age to age, linking the generations in a solidarity of sin.

When we examine the factors which slew Jesus, we recognize them at once as contemporaries. We can attach modern names to them. There is nothing abnormal or unusual about these men who rear the cross: they are acting true to type—a type which recurs century after century throughout history. They are average folk. We must not blacken their characters. John Stuart Mill, whose ethical judgments are singularly dispassionate, says of them:

> They were not worse than men commonly are, but rather the contrary, men who possessed in a full, or somewhat more than a full measure the religious, moral, and patriotic feelings of their people; the very kind of men who in all times, our own included, have every chance of passing through life blameless and unspotted.

We can think of no more high-minded young man than the student of Gamaliel, Saul of Tarsus, and we know how cordially he approved the course taken by the leaders of Israel in putting Jesus out of the way.

We can easily multiply from history and literature men far more villainous—a Caesar Borgia or an Iago, for instance. Indeed we can find more depraved figures in almost any community, if we look for them. But the purpose of Jesus and the purposes of even good people clash. The inevitableness of the crucifixion is brought home to us. The issue between the motives of Jesus and those of the mass of mankind is thrown into light. They are irreconcilable. Life is a desperately real struggle between mutually destroying forces. If the motives of Jesus prevail, the factors that slew Him will cease to be. If the motives of Caiaphas and Pilate, of the mob, the soldiers, and the public prevail—there is an execution: "Away with such a fellow from the earth."

There are three crosses on Calvary: on two of them society is trying to rid itself of predatory bandits, on the third it placed One whom it considered also its enemy, perhaps a worse enemy since He was placed on the central cross. We level up with our standards of right, and we also level down. He who is above the conscience of the community is as likely to be slain as he who is below. This is our world; this is the society in which we move; these are the types of people with whom we associate; this is the public to which we belong. The slayers of Jesus are our relatives, kinsmen in thought and feeling. A sense of complicity in what they did comes upon us. We are bound up with them in this bundle of human life. The corporate evil which dominated first-century Palestine and moved these men to kill their Best dominates our world and is compassing similar fell results. Trails of blood lead to our doors. Wretched men that we are, who shall deliver us out of this social body of death?

And these factors are not only about us, they are also within us. As we scan these men who sent Jesus to His death—devout Pharisee and conservative Sadducee, Roman politician and false friend, emotional mob and unthinking soldiers, the host of indifferent or approving faces of the public behind them—their motives and feelings have been and are our own. You may recall in Hawthorne's *Mosses from an Old Manse* the scene where, going through the virtuoso's collection, he nearly falls over a huge bundle, like a peddler's pack, done up in sackcloth and very securely strapped and corded. " 'It is Christian's burden of sin,' said the virtuoso. 'O pray, let me see it,' cried I. 'For many a year I have longed to know its contents.' 'Look into your own conscience and memory,' replied the virtuoso. 'You will there find a list of whatever it contained.' " It is so with the motives of those who planned and carried out the death of Jesus. We do not need to ask: "Lord, is it I?" We are aware of belonging in this same realm of darkness, and of having dealt with His brethren very much as He was dealt with. As we think of ourselves, we shudder—"God, be merciful to me, a sinner."

Men speak of the absence of the sense of sin in our time. It has never been vigorous in any age, save as some judgment of history or the disturbing presence of the ideal has created it. We have witnessed a judgment on a colossal scale in the World War—a judgment upon our entire civilization. Some of us said to ourselves, feeling mankind in the grip of overmastering social forces of passion and greed and brutality: "Now is your hour and the power of darkness." And we know ourselves a long way yet from redemption from the motives which brought it on. Underneath the ease and comfort of our day there is restless discontent. Some of it is crassly materialistic—the common envy of the have-nots for the haves, the craving of the have-littles to have more. But souls are never satisfied with things. Life is in relationships, human and divine, in purposes. And men are dissatisfied with the quality of life. To take them to Calvary and show them the factors which nailed Jesus on the cross is to uncover for them a far more terrible world than they dreamed they were in, and to uncover for them themselves.

This gives us an inkling of Jesus' reason for putting Himself into men's hands and letting them do with Him as they would. His broken and bleeding body on the cross is the exposure of a murderous world. The Crucified becomes one with the unrecognized and misused and cruelly treated in every age. The nail-pierced Figure on Calvary haunts our race as a symbol of what is forever taking place generation after generation, and of what each of us has his part in.

Readers of Ibsen's drama *Emperor and Galilean* will recall how Julian is made to ask—

Where is He now? Has He been at work elsewhere since that happened at Golgotha?

I dreamed of Him lately. I dreamed that I had subdued the whole world. I ordained that the memory of the Galilean should be rooted out on earth; and it was rooted out. Then the spirits came and ministered to me, and bound wings on my shoulders, and I soared aloft into infinite space, till my feet rested on another world.

It was another world than mine. Its curve was vaster, its light more golden, and many moons circled around it. Then I looked down at my own earth—the Emperor's earth that I had made Galileanless—and I thought that all that I had done was very good.

But behold there came a procession by me on the strange earth where I stood. There were soldiers and judges and executioners at the head of it and weeping women followed. And lo, in the midst of the slow-moving array, was the Galilean, alive and bearing a cross on His back. Then I called to Him and said, "Whither away, Galilean?" And He turned His face to me and smiled, nodded slowly and said, "To the place of the skull."

Where is He now? What if that at Golgotha, near Jerusalem, was but a wayside matter, a thing done as it were in passing! What if He goes on and on, and suffers and dies, and conquers, again and again, from world to world!

It is a vivid way of picturing the solidarity of the worlds of every generation, each offering its Golgotha. It is there that men come to themselves and realize their plight and the plight of society. Walter Pater said that "the way to perfection is through a series of disgusts." To let men see the factors which enact the tragedy outside the wall of Jerusalem is to disgust them with their world and with themselves. If some protest that this is not a wholesome state of mind, one may answer in the words of that robust thinker, Walter Bagehot: "So long as men are very imperfect, a sense of great imperfection should cleave to them." It is a necessary part of the process towards genuine healthy-mindedness. When they realize what caused the torture and execution of Jesus, they cry, "O not that! Such a world is intolerable!" And made conscious that they are builders of such worlds, and that their hands are stained, they hunger and thirst after righteousness.

QUESTIONS

1. Indicate each of the principal groups and figures who, by Coffin's account, contributed to the crucifixion of Christ. What leading motive does Coffin ascribe to each? How does Coffin show these motives to be perennial ones, operative now as then? Why does he do so?
2. Examine each of the transitions Coffin makes. How does he proceed from one part to another in his essay? How does he relate part to part? What order of progression is discernible in the essay?
3. Coffin accords the Pharisees considerable praise. Why? What does he imply to be the essential fault of the Pharisees? In what respects does he compare and contrast the Pharisees and Sadducees?
4. Coffin refers (p. 1196) to the "motives of Jesus," but he does not delineate these or discuss them in full. To what extent has he indirectly indicated them in his account of the principal groups and figures contributing to the crucifixion?
5. Consider Coffin's title. Why has he asked precisely that question? Might he just as well have given as title "Who Crucified Christ?" Explain.

GEORGE SANTAYANA

Classic Liberty

When ancient peoples defended what they called their liberty, the word stood for a plain and urgent interest of theirs: that their cities should not be destroyed, their territory pillaged, and they themselves sold into slavery. For the Greeks in particular liberty meant even more than this. Perhaps the deepest assumption of classic philosophy is that nature and the gods on the one hand and man on the other, both have a fixed character; that there is consequently a necessary piety, a true philosophy, a standard happiness, a normal art. The Greeks believed, not without reason, that they had grasped these permanent principles better than other peoples. They had largely dispelled superstition, experimented in government, and turned life into a rational art. Therefore when they defended their liberty what they defended was not merely freedom to live. It was freedom to live well, to live as other nations did not, in the public experimental study of the world and of human nature.

This liberty to discover and pursue a natural happiness, this liberty to grow wise and to live in friendship with the gods and with one another, was the liberty vindicated at Thermopylae by martyrdom and at Salamis by victory.

As Greek cities stood for liberty in the world, so philosophers stood for liberty in the Greek cities. In both cases it was the same kind of liberty, not freedom to wander at hazard or to let things slip, but on the contrary freedom to legislate more precisely, at least for oneself, and to discover and codify the means to true happiness. Many of these pioneers in wisdom were audacious radicals and recoiled from no paradox. Some condemned what was most Greek: mythology, athletics, even multiplicity and physical motion. In the heart of those thriving, loquacious, festive little ant-hills, they preached impassibility and abstraction, the unanswerable scepticism of silence. Others practised a musical and priestly refinement of life, filled with metaphysical mysteries, and formed secret societies, not without a tendency to political domination. The cynics railed at the conventions, making themselves as comfortable as possible in the role of beggars and mocking parasites. The conservatives themselves were radical, so intelligent were they, and Plato wrote the charter[1] of the most extreme militarism and communism, for the sake of preserving the free state. It was the swan-song of liberty, a prescription to a diseased old man to become young again and try a second life of superhuman virtue. The old man preferred simply to die.

Many laughed then, as we may be tempted to do, at all those absolute physicians of the soul, each with his panacea. Yet beneath their quarrels the wranglers had a common faith. They all believed there was a single solid natural wisdom to be found, that reason could find it, and that mankind, sobered by reason, could put it in practice. Mankind has continued to run wild and like barbarians to place freedom in their very wildness, till we can hardly conceive the classic assumption of Greek philosophers and cities, that true liberty is bound up with an institution, a corporate scientific discipline, necessary to set free the perfect man, or the god, within us.

Upon the dissolution of paganism the Christian church adopted the classic conception of liberty. Of course, the field in which the higher politics had to operate was now conceived differently, and there was a new experience of the sort of happiness appropriate and possible to man; but the assumption remained unchallenged that Providence, as well as the human soul, had a fixed discoverable scope, and that the business of education, law, and religion was to bring them to operate in harmony. The aim of life, salvation, was involved in the nature of the soul itself, and the means of salvation had been ascertained by a positive science which the church was

1. The reference is to Plato's *Republic*.

possessed of, partly revealed and partly experimental. Salvation was simply what, on a broad view, we should see to be health, and religion was nothing but a sort of universal hygiene.

The church, therefore, little as it tolerated heretical liberty, the liberty of moral and intellectual dispersion, felt that it had come into the world to set men free, and constantly demanded liberty for itself, that it might fulfil this mission. It was divinely commissioned to teach, guide, and console all nations and all ages by the self-same means, and to promote at all costs what it conceived to be human perfection. There should be saints and as many saints as possible. The church never admitted, any more than did any sect of ancient philosophers, that its teaching might represent only an eccentric view of the world, or that its guidance and consolations might be suitable only at one stage of human development. To waver in the pursuit of the orthodox ideal could only betray frivolity and want of self-knowledge. The truth of things and the happiness of each man could not lie elsewhere than where the church, summing up all human experience and all divine revelation, had placed it once for all and for everybody. The liberty of the church to fulfil its mission was accordingly hostile to any liberty of dispersion, to any radical consecutive independence, in the life of individuals or of nations.

When it came to full fruition this orthodox freedom was far from gay; it was called sanctity. The freedom of pagan philosophers too had turned out to be rather a stiff and severe pose; but in the Christian dispensation this austerity of true happiness was less to be wondered at, since life on earth was reputed to be abnormal from the beginning, and infected with hereditary disease. The full beauty and joy of restored liberty could hardly become evident in this life. Nevertheless a certain beauty and joy did radiate visibly from the saints; and while we may well think their renunciations and penances misguided or excessive, it is certain that, like the Spartans and the philosophers, they got something for their pains. Their bodies and souls were transfigured, as none now found upon earth. If we admire without imitating them we shall perhaps have done their philosophy exact justice. Classic liberty was a sort of forced and artificial liberty, a poor perfection reserved for an ascetic aristocracy in whom heroism and refinement were touched with perversity and slowly starved themselves to death.

Since those days we have discovered how much larger the universe is, and we have lost our way in it. Any day it may come over us again that our modern liberty to drift in the dark is the most terrible negation of freedom. Nothing happens to us as we would. We want peace and make war. We need science and obey the will to believe, we love art and flounder among whimsicalities, we believe in general comfort and equality and we strain every nerve to become millionaires. After all, antiquity must have been right in thinking that reasonable self-direction must rest on having a determinate character and knowing what it is, and that only the truth about God and happiness, if we somehow found it, could make us free. But the truth is not to be found by guessing at it, as religious prophets and men of genius have done, and then damning every one who does not agree. Human nature, for all its substantial fixity, is a living thing with many varieties and variations. All diversity of opinion is therefore not founded on ignorance; it may express a legitimate change of habit or interest. The classic and Christian synthesis from which we have broken loose was certainly premature, even if the only issue of our liberal experiments should be to lead us back to some such equilibrium. Let us hope at least that the new morality, when it comes, may be more broadly based than the old on knowledge of the world, not so absolute, not so meticulous, and not chanted so much in the monotone of an abstracted sage.

GILBERT HIGHET
The Mystery of Zen

The mind need never stop growing. Indeed, one of the few experiences which never pall is the experience of watching one's own mind, and observing how it produces new interests, responds to new stimuli, and develops new thoughts, apparently without effort and almost independently of one's own conscious control. I have seen this happen to myself a hundred times; and every time it happens again, I am equally fascinated and astonished.

Some years ago a publisher sent me a little book for review. I read it, and decided it was too remote from my main interests and too highly specialized. It was a brief account of how a young German philosopher living in Japan had learned how to shoot with a bow and arrow, and how this training had made it possible for him to understand the esoteric doctrines of the Zen sect of Buddhism. Really, what could be more alien to my own life, and to that of everyone I knew, than Zen Buddhism and Japanese archery? So I thought, and put the book away.

Yet I did not forget it. It was well written, and translated into good English. It was delightfully short, and implied much more than it said. Although its theme was extremely odd, it was at least highly individual; I had never read anything like it before or since.

It remained in my mind. Its name was *Zen in the Art of Archery*, its author Eugen Herrigel, its publisher Pantheon of New York. One day I took it off the shelf and read it again; this time it seemed even stranger than before and even more unforgettable. Now it began to cohere with other interests of mine. Something I had read of the Japanese art of flower arrangement seemed to connect with it; and then, when I wrote an essay on the peculiar Japanese poems called *haiku*, other links began to grow. Finally I had to read the book once more with care, and to go through some other works which illuminated the same subject. I am still grappling with the theme; I have not got anywhere near understanding it fully; but I have learned a good deal, and I am grateful to the little book which refused to be forgotten.

The author, a German philosopher, got a job teaching philosophy at the University of Tokyo (apparently between the wars), and he did what Germans in foreign countries do not usually do: he determined to adapt himself and to learn from his hosts. In particular, he had always been interested in mysticism—which, for every earnest philosopher, poses a problem that is all the more inescapable because it is virtually insoluble. Zen Buddhism is not the only mystical doctrine to be found in the East, but it is one of the most highly developed and certainly one of the most difficult to approach. Herrigel knew that there were scarcely any books which did more than skirt the edge of the subject, and that the best of all books on Zen (those by the philosopher D. T. Suzuki) constantly emphasize that Zen can never be learned from books, can never be studied as we can study other disciplines such as logic or mathematics. Therefore he began to look for a Japanese thinker who could teach him directly.

At once he met with embarrassed refusals. His Japanese friends explained that he would gain nothing from trying to discuss Zen as a philosopher, that its theories could not be spread out for analysis by a detached mind, and in fact that the normal relationship of teacher and pupil simply did not exist within the sect, because the Zen masters felt it useless to explain things stage by stage and to argue about the various possible interpretations of their doctrine. Herrigel had read enough to be prepared for this. He replied that he did not want to dissect the teachings of the school, because he knew that would be useless. He wanted to become a Zen mystic himself. (This was highly intelligent of him. No one could really penetrate into Christian mysticism without being a devout Christian; no one could appreciate Hindu mystical doctrine without accepting the Hindu view of the universe.) At this, Herrigel's Japanese friends were more forthcoming. They told him that the best way, indeed the only way, for a European to approach Zen mysticism was to learn one of the arts which exemplified it.

He was a fairly good rifle shot, so he determined to learn archery; and his wife co-operated with him by taking lessons in painting and flower arrangement. How any philosopher could investigate a mystical doctrine by learning to shoot with a bow and arrow and watching his wife arrange flowers, Herrigel did not ask. He had good sense.

A Zen master who was a teacher of archery agreed to take him as a pupil. The lessons lasted six years, during which he practiced every single day. There are many difficult courses of instruction in the world: the Jesuits, violin virtuosi, Talmudic scholars, all have long and hard training, which in one sense never comes to an end; but Herrigel's training in archery equaled them all in intensity. If I were trying to learn archery, I should expect to begin by looking at a target and shooting arrows at it. He was not even allowed to aim at a target for the first four years. He had to begin by learning how to hold the bow and arrow, and then how to release the arrow; this took ages. The Japanese bow is not like our sporting bow, and the stance of the archer in Japan is different from ours. We hold the bow at shoulder level, stretch our left arm out ahead, pull the string and the nocked arrow to a point either below the chin or sometimes past the right ear, and then shoot. The Japanese hold the bow above the head, and then pull the hands apart to left and right until the left hand comes down to eye level and the right hand comes to rest above the right shoulder; then there is a pause, during which the bow is held at full stretch, with the tip of the three-foot arrow projecting only a few inches beyond the bow; after that, the arrow is loosed. When Herrigel tried this, even without aiming, he found it was almost impossible. His hands trembled. His legs stiffened and grew cramped. His breathing became labored. And of course he could not possibly aim. Week after week he practiced this, with the Master watching him carefully and correcting his strained attitude; week after week he made no progress whatever. Finally he gave up and told his teacher that he could not learn: it was absolutely impossible for him to draw the bow and loose the arrow.

To his astonishment, the Master agreed. He said, "Certainly you cannot. It is because you are not breathing correctly. You must learn to breathe in a steady rhythm, keeping your lungs full most of the time, and drawing in one rapid inspiration with each stage of the process, as you grasp the bow, fit the arrow, raise the bow, draw, pause, and loose the shot. If you do, you will both grow stronger and be able to relax." To prove this, he himself drew his massive bow and told his pupil to feel the muscles of his arms: they were perfectly relaxed, as though he were doing no work whatever.

Herrigel now started breathing exercises; after some time he combined the new rhythm of breathing with the actions of drawing and shooting; and, much to his astonishment, he found that the whole thing, after this complicated process, had become much easier. Or rather, not easier, but different. At times it became quite unconscious. He says himself that he felt he was not breathing, but being breathed; and in time he felt that the occasional shot was not being dispatched by him, but shooting itself. The bow and arrow were in charge; he had become merely a part of them.

All this time, of course, Herrigel did not even attempt to discuss Zen docrine with his Master. No doubt he knew that he was approaching it, but he concentrated solely on learning how to shoot. Every stage which he surmounted appeared to lead to another stage even more difficult. It took him months to learn how to loosen the bowstring. The problem was this. If he gripped the string and arrowhead tightly, either he froze, so that his hands were slowly pulled together and the shot was wasted, or else he jerked, so that the arrow flew up into the air or down into the ground; and if he was relaxed, then the bowstring and arrow simply *leaked* out of his grasp before he could reach full stretch, and the arrow went nowhere. He explained this problem to the Master. The Master understood perfectly well. He replied, "You must hold the drawn bowstring like a child holding a grownup's finger. You know how firmly a child grips; and yet when it lets go, there is not the slightest jerk—because the child does not think of itself, it is not self-conscious, it does not say, 'I will now let go and do something else,' it merely acts instinctively. That is what you must learn to do. Practice, practice, and practice, and then the string will loose itself at the right moment. The shot will come as effortlessly as snow slipping from a leaf." Day after day, week after week, month after month, Herrigel practiced this; and then, after one shot, the Master suddenly bowed and broke off the lesson. He said "Just then it shot. Not you, but *it*." And gradually thereafter more and more right shots achieved themselves; the young philosopher forgot himself, forgot that he was learning archery for some other purpose, forgot even that he was practicing archery, and became part of that unconsciously active complex, the bow, the string, the arrow, and the man.

Next came the target. After four years, Herrigel was allowed to shoot at the target. But he was strictly forbidden to aim at it. The Master explained that even he himself did not aim; and indeed, when he shot, he was so absorbed in the act, so selfless and unanxious, that his eyes were almost closed. It was difficult, almost impossible, for Herrigel to believe that such shooting could ever be effective; and he risked insulting the Master by suggesting that he ought to be able to hit the target blindfolded. But the Master accepted the challenge. That night, after a cup of tea and long meditation, he went into the archery hall, put on the lights at one end and left the target perfectly dark, with only a thin taper burning in front of it. Then, with habitual grace and precision, and with that strange, almost sleepwalking, selfless confidence that is the heart of Zen, he shot two arrows into the darkness. Herrigel went out to collect them. He found that the first had gone to the heart of the bull's eye, and that the second had actually hit the first arrow and splintered it. The Master showed no pride. He said, "Perhaps, with unconscious memory of the position of the target, I shot the first arrow; but the second arrow? *It* shot the second arrow, and *it* brought it to the center of the target."

At last Herrigel began to understand. His progress became faster and faster; easier, too. Perfect shots (perfect because perfectly unconscious) occurred at almost every lesson; and finally, after six years of incessant training, in a public display he was awarded the diploma. He needed no further instruction: he had himself become a Master. His wife meanwhile had become expert both in painting and in the arrangement of flowers—two of the finest of Japanese arts. (I wish she could be persuaded to write a companion volume, called *Zen in the Art of Flower Arrangement*; it would have a wider general appeal than her husband's work.) I gather also from a hint or two in his book that she had taken part in the archery lessons. During one of the most difficult periods in Herrigel's training, when his Master had practically refused to continue teaching him—because Herrigel had tried to cheat by *consciously* opening his hand at the moment of loosing the arrow— his wife had advised him against that solution, and sympathized with him when it was rejected. She in her own way had learned more quickly than he, and reached the final point together with him. All their effort had not been in vain: Herrigel and his wife had really acquired a new and valuable kind of wisdom. Only at this point, when he was about to abandon his lessons forever, did his Master treat him almost as an equal and hint at the innermost doctrines of Zen Buddhism. Only hints he gave; and yet, for the young philosopher who had now become a mystic, they were enough. Herrigel understood the doctrine, not with his logical mind, but with his entire being. He at any rate had solved the mystery of Zen.

Without going through a course of training as absorbing and as complete as Herrigel's, we can probably never penetrate the mystery. The doctrine of Zen cannot be analyzed from without: it must be lived.

But although it cannot be analyzed, it can be hinted at. All the hints that the adherents of this creed give us are interesting. Many are fantastic; some are practically incomprehensible, and yet unforgettable. Put together, they take us toward a way of life which is utterly impossible for westerners living in a western world, and nevertheless has a deep fascination and contains some values which we must respect.

The word Zen means "meditation." (It is the Japanese word, corresponding to the Chinese Ch'an and the Hindu Dhyana.) It is the central idea of a special sect of Buddhism which flourished in China during the Sung period (between A.D. 1000 and 1300) and entered Japan in the twelfth century. Without knowing much about it, we might be certain that the Zen sect was a worthy and noble one, because it produced a quantity of highly distinguished art, specifically painting. And if we knew anything about Buddhism itself, we might say that Zen goes closer than other sects to the heart of Buddha's teaching: because Buddha was trying to found, not a religion with temples and rituals, but a way of life based on meditation. However, there is something eccentric about the Zen life which is hard to trace in Buddha's teaching; there is an active energy which he did not admire, there is a rough grasp on reality which he himself eschewed, there is something like a sense of humor, which he rarely displayed. The gravity and serenity of the Indian preacher are transformed, in Zen, to the earthy liveliness of Chinese and Japanese sages. The lotus brooding calmly on the water has turned into a knotted tree covered with spring blossoms.

In this sense, "meditation" does not mean what we usually think of when we say a philosopher meditates: analysis of reality, a long-sustained effort to solve problems of religion and ethics, the logical dissection of the universe. It means something not divisive, but whole; not schematic, but organic; not long-drawn-out, but immediate. It means something more like our words "intuition" and "realization." It means a way of life in which there is no division between thought and action; none of the painful gulf, so well known to all of us, between the unconscious and the conscious mind; and no absolute distinction between the self and the external world, even between the various parts of the external world and the whole.

When the German philosopher took six years of lessons in archery in order to approach the mystical significance of Zen, he was not given direct philosophical instruction. He was merely shown how to breathe, how to hold and loose the bowstring, and finally how to shoot in such a way that the bow and arrow used him as an instrument. There are many such stories about Zen teachers. The strangest I know is one about a fencing master who undertook to train a young man in the art of the sword. The relationship of teacher and pupil is very important, almost sacred, in the Far East; and the pupil hardly ever thinks of leaving a master or objecting to his methods, however extraordinary they may seem. Therefore this young fellow did not at first object when he was made to act as a servant, drawing water, sweeping floors, gathering wood for the fire, and cooking. But after some time he asked for more direct instruction. The master agreed to give it, but produced no swords. The routine went on just as before, except that every now and then the master would strike the young man with a stick. No matter what he was doing, sweeping the floor or weeding in the garden, a blow would descend on him apparently out of nowhere; he had always to be on the alert, and yet he was constantly receiving unexpected cracks on the head or shoulders. After some months of this, he saw his master stooping over a boiling pot full of vegetables; and he thought he would have his revenge. Silently he lifted a stick and brought it down; but without any effort, without even a glance in his direction, his master parried the blow with the lid of the cooking pot. At last, the pupil began to understand the instinctive alertness, the effortless perception and avoidance of danger, in which his master had been training him. As soon as he had achieved it, it was child's play for him to learn the management of the sword: he could parry every cut and turn every slash without anxiety, until his opponent, exhausted, left an opening for his counterattack. (The same principle was used by the elderly samurai for selecting his comrades in the Japanese motion picture *The Magnificent Seven*.)

These stories show that Zen meditation does not mean sitting and thinking. On the contrary, it means acting with as little thought as possible. The fencing master trained his pupil to guard against every attack with the same immediate, instinctive rapidity with which our eyelid closes over our eye when something threatens it. His work was aimed at breaking down the wall between thought and act, at completely fusing body and senses and mind so that they might all work together rapidly and effortlessly. When a Zen artist draws a picture, he does it in a rhythm almost the exact reverse of that which is followed by a Western artist. We begin by blocking out the design and then filling in the details, usually working more and more slowly as we approach the completion of the picture. The Zen artist sits down very calmly; examines his brush carefully; prepares his own ink; smooths out the paper on which he will work; falls into a profound silent ecstasy of contemplation—during which he does not think anxiously of various details, composition, brushwork, shades of tone, but rather attempts to become the vehicle through which the subject can express itself in painting; and then, very quickly and almost unconsciously, with sure effortless strokes, draws a picture containing the fewest and most effective lines. Most of the paper is left blank; only the essential is depicted, and that not completely. One long curving line will be enough to show a mountainside; seven streaks will become a group of bamboos bending in the wind; and yet, though technically incomplete, such pictures are unforgettably clear. They show the heart of reality.

All this we can sympathize with, because we can see the results. The young swordsman learns how to fence. The intuitional painter produces a fine picture. But the hardest thing for us to appreciate is that the Zen masters refuse to teach philosophy or religion directly, and deny logic. In fact, they despise logic as an artificial distortion of reality. Many philosophical teachers are difficult to understand because they analyze profound problems with subtle intricacy: such is Aristotle in his *Metaphysics*. Many mystical writers are difficult to understand because, as they themselves admit, they are attempting to use words to describe experiences which are too abstruse for words, so that they have to fall back on imagery and analogy, which they themselves recognize to be poor media, far coarser than the realities with which they have been in contact. But the Zen teachers seem to deny the power of language and thought altogether. For example, if you ask a Zen master what is the ultimate reality, he will answer, without the slightest hesitation, "The bamboo grove at the foot of the hill" or "A branch of plum blossom." Apparently he means that these things, which we can see instantly without effort, or imagine in the flash of a second, are real with the ultimate reality; that nothing is more real than these; and that we ought to grasp ultimates as we grasp simple immediates. A Chinese master was once asked the central question, "What is the Buddha?" He said nothing whatever, but held out his index finger. What did he mean? It is hard to explain; but apparently he meant "Here. Now. Look and realize with the effortlessness of seeing. Do not try to use words. Do not think. Make no efforts toward withdrawal from the world. Expect no sublime ecstasies. Live. All *that* is the ultimate reality, and it can be understood from the motion of a finger as well as from the execution of any complex ritual, from any subtle argument, or from the circling of the starry universe."

In making that gesture, the master was copying the Buddha himself, who once delivered a sermon which is famous, but was hardly understood by his pupils at the time. Without saying a word, he held up a flower and showed it to the gathering. One man, one alone, knew what he meant. The gesture became renowned as the Flower Sermon.

In the annals of Zen there are many cryptic answers to the final question, "What is the Buddha?"—which in our terms means "What is the meaning of life? What is truly real?" For example, one master, when asked "What is the Buddha?" replied, "Your name is Yecho." Another said, "Even the finest artist cannot paint him." Another said, "No nonsense here." And another answered, "The mouth is the gate of woe." My favorite story is about the monk who said to a Master, "Has a dog Buddha-nature too?" The Master replied, "Wu"—which is what the dog himself would have said.

Now, some critics might attack Zen by saying that this is the creed of a savage or an animal. The adherents of Zen would deny that—or more probably they would ignore the criticism, or make some cryptic remark which meant that it was pointless. Their position—if they could ever be persuaded to put it into words—would be this. An animal is instinctively in touch with reality, and so far is living rightly, but it has never had a mind and so cannot perceive the Whole, only that part with which it is in touch. The philosopher sees both the Whole and the parts, and enjoys them all. As for the savage, he exists only through the group; he feels himself as part of a war party or a ceremonial dance team or a ploughing-and-sowing group or the Snake clan; he is not truly an individual at all, and therefore is less than fully human. Zen has at its heart an inner solitude; its aim is to teach us to live, as in the last resort we do all have to live, alone.

A more dangerous criticism of Zen would be that it is nihilism, that its purpose is to abolish thought altogether. (This criticism is handled, but not fully met, by the great Zen authority Suzuki in his *Introduction to Zen Buddhism*.) It can hardly be completely confuted, for after all the central doctrine of Buddhism is—Nothingness. And many of the sayings of Zen masters are truly nihilistic. The first patriarch of the sect in China was asked by the emperor what was the ultimate and holiest principle of Buddhism. He replied, "Vast emptiness, and nothing holy in it." Another who was asked the searching question "Where is the abiding-place for the mind?" answered, "Not in this dualism of good and evil, being and non-being, thought and matter." In fact, thought is an activity which divides. It analyzes, it makes distinctions, it criticizes, it judges, it breaks reality into groups and classes and individuals. The aim of Zen is to abolish that kind of thinking, and to substitute—not unconsciousness, which would be death, but a consciousness that does not analyze but experiences life directly. Although it has no prescribed prayers, no sacred scriptures, no ceremonial rites, no personal god, and no interest in the soul's future destination, Zen is a religion rather than a philosophy. Jung points out that its aim is to produce a religious conversion, a "transformation": and he adds, "The transformation process is incommensurable with intellect." Thought is always interesting, but often painful; Zen is calm and painless. Thought is incomplete; Zen enlightenment brings a sense of completeness. Thought is a process; Zen illumination is a state. But it is a state which cannot be defined. In the Buddhist scriptures there is a dialogue between a master and a pupil in which the pupil tries to discover the exact meaning of such a state. The master says to him, 'If a fire were blazing in front of you, would you know that it was blazing?'

"Yes, master."

"And would you know the reason for its blazing?"

"Yes, because it had a supply of grass and sticks."

"And would you know if it were to go out?"

"Yes, master."

"And on its going out, would you know where the fire had gone? To the east, to the west, to the north, or to the south?"

"The question does not apply, master. For the fire blazed because it had a supply of grass and sticks. When it had consumed this and had no other fuel, then it went out."

"In the same way," replies the master, "no question will apply to the meaning of Nirvana, and no statement will explain it."

Such, then, neither happy nor unhappy but beyond all divisive description, is the condition which students of Zen strive to attain. Small wonder that they can scarcely explain it to us, the unilluminated.

QUESTIONS

1. What difficulties does Highet face in discussing Zen? How does he manage to give a definition in spite of his statement that Zen "cannot be analyzed"?
2. Why does Highet describe the training in archery in such detail?
3. On page 1210 Highet says that "Zen is a religion rather than a philosophy." How has he led up to this conclusion? What definitions of "religion" and "philosophy" does he imply?
4. By what means does Highet define "meditation"? Would other means have worked as well? Explain.
5. To what extent is Zen "the creed of a savage or an animal"? How does Highet go about refuting this charge?

ALAN W. WATTS
The Answer of Religion[1]

The oldest answers in the world to the problem of happiness are found in religion, for the kind of happiness we are considering belongs to the deepest realms of the human spirit. But this should not lead us to suppose that it is something remote from familiar experience, something to be sought out in supernatural spheres far beyond the world which we know through our five senses. The world of the spirit is so often understood in an almost materialistic way, as a locality infinite in space containing things that are eternal in-

1. From *The Meaning of Happiness*, 1940. (All notes are Watts's.)

terms of time.[2] It is thought to bė a world corresponding in form and substance to our own, save that its forms and substances are constructed of spirit instead of matter, and its operation governed by different laws, for nothing changes—all things are everlasting. To understand the world of the spirit in this way is to make it wholly different from the world in which we live, and when religion is concerned with this kind of spiritualism a great gulf appears between the world of the spirit and the world of everyday experience, contact with the former being possible only in a disembodied condition, as after death, or in a state of consciousness where we acquire a new set of senses, spiritual senses that can perceive things to which material vision is not attuned.

This view of spirituality is so common in religion that many people believe salvation to lie utterly beyond our present life, being something for which earthly existence is only a preparation and which will be inherited when we have passed beyond the grave or when, even though still living, our thoughts have ascended to a higher sphere so that we are in this world but not of it. It is probable, however, that this idea has arisen because so much religious teaching is presented in the form of allegory; spiritual truths are presented in terms of time and space for purposes of simplification. Heaven and hell are removed in time to the life after death and in place to a *different* world-order; eternity is represented as unending time, which is not eternity but everlastingness. This kind of simplification may have its uses, but in many ways it is an unnecessary complication for the conception has greater value if we think of heaven and hell as here and now, and of eternity as the timeless, eternal Now.

Religion as a Denial of Life

However, this is one of the main trends of thought in religion as generally understood, besides which there is yet another believing that spiritual happiness is attainable on earth but in a somewhat utopian and materialistic way. Both of these trends exist in Christianity, some holding that "on this earth we have no continuing home, therefore we seek one to come," and others working for the establishment of the "kingdom of heaven on earth." The Christian holding the former opinion feels that he can never be at home in this world which he regards a kind of anteroom to the life hereafter, a place of trial and temptation where God tests the fitness of His children to enter His kingdom. At the same time he will thank his Lord for all the blessings of this earth, for the pleasures which

2. A remarkable analysis of this confusion is the first chapter of Nicolas Berdyaev's *Freedom and the Spirit* (London, 1935), esp. p. 15. "Spirit," he writes, "is by no means opposed to flesh; rather, flesh is the incarnation and symbol of spirit."

give him joy as well as for the pains which give opportunities to learn wisdom. Yet he is not content with those pleasures, and because they are so fleeting he regards them as mere hints of the glories of paradise which shall endure forever and ever.

But in modern Christianity especially there is another element which existed in olden times, though in a different form. An article of the Apostles' Creed is the belief in the resurrection of the body,[3] the belief that the world to come is not only a spiritual but also a condition of life where the physical world has been recreated by spiritual power. It is said that God will create a new heaven and a new earth, and that "the kingdom of this world shall become the Kingdom of Our Lord and of His Christ." The modern Christian is apt to regard this teaching in rather a different way, for whereas his ancestors viewed it as something which would happen only at the last day when all the dead would rise from their graves, the modern view is rather that the kingdom of heaven on earth is something which man may create by the Grace of God here and now. Hence the increasing interest of the churches in idealistic politics. Morality becomes something to be practiced, not only to insure salvation in the world to come, but to improve the lot of mankind in the world as it is. For Christianity has become linked to the idea of progress, and the churches are the foremost advocates of peace, of social service, and of political and economic justice.

But both among Christians and among followers of other religions there are those who feel that such ideals are rather naive, either because they seem impossible of achievement or else because they do not seem very desirable. Spiritual happiness, as they understand it, has little to do with either material well-being or everlasting glory in a paradise of heavenly music and streets of pure gold. But they share the same suspicion of the world as it is, believing the highest illumination of the spirit unattainable in the flesh or under the particular limitations of the senses which compel us to view life as a transient alternation of pleasure and pain.

For many centureis there has been a tendency of this kind in the religions of the East, of which the most notable example is Hinayana Buddhism—the type of Buddhism with which the West is most familiar. The Hinayana takes the most gloomy view of the world of any religion, and seeks escape from it by the quickest possible means to a stage which is not exactly complete annihilation, but a kind of vague, infinite consciousness from which all personality, all sense of individual identity, and all diversity of form have been removed. In this state there is no pain because there is no pleasure, and no death

3. A refreshingly different interpreta-   Berdyaev, *ibid.*, pp. 40–41.
tion of this doctrine will be found in

because there is no longer anyone to die. The gist of its teaching is that when you realize that your personal self does not exist, then you are free of suffering, for suffering can arise only when there is a person to suffer. The same may be said of pleasure, with the result that the Hinayana ideal is a state of tastelessness which is held to be the highest attainable bliss.

A similar ideal might be found by a casual examination of the teaching of Hindu Vedanta as expressed in the Upanishads. For it seems as if the supreme aspiration of the Hindu yogin is to become merged into the infinite Brahman, the one reality of which all diverse forms are illusory expressions. In common with the Hinayana Buddhist, he finds the world unsatisfying because of the impermanence of its glories. Therefore he fights against all those things in himself which move him to seek happiness in the pleasures of the world, learning to see the changing forms of life as a web of delusion hiding the face of God. To him all things are God; mountains, trees, rivers, men, and beasts only seem to be what they are because of the limitations of his own senses. Once those limitations are overcome, the world of diverse form vanishes and there remains only the vast and void infinitude of Brahman in whom is eternal rest and bliss.

Such ideas are frequent in Eastern thought, although they do not represent its deepest meaning. To most of us they are abstract and incomprehensible. Nevertheless, countless religious people maintain that the end and aim of our life here on earth is an eternal condition whose characteristics may be described in one of the following ways. First, a state beyond death wherein the beauties of life are greatly magnified and all its pains and limitations overcome. Second, a state in this life wherein earthly pains and limitations have been overcome by the exercise of human reason and skill, inspired by the Grace of God. Third, a state attainable either in the body or out of it where human consciousness has been raised above the limits imposed upon it by the personal self and its five senses, wherein all diversity of form, all pairs of opposites, have been merged into the infinite and formless divine essence from which they originally came.

Abolishing the Universe

All these three have certain elements in common. There is a distaste for the world as it is, implying that the wrong is not so much in the external world as in one's own imperfect self, which is either doomed to live in this world on account of those imperfections or else which sees that world falsely, being deluded by imperfect senses. There is also the hope for an eternal state in which good things are made permanent or abolished altogether along with the evil. And, most significant of all, there is the implication that one of these religious states is the ultimate purpose of our earthly existence, from which it must follow that appropriate religious activities are fundamentally the only worth-while pursuits for mankind. All other pursuits must therefore be considered subordinate and ephemeral, and in this view art, literature, music, politics, science, drama, exploration, and sport become vain and empty unless they are regarded simply as means of keeping body and soul together in reasonable comfort, or unless they are used for specifically religious purposes. Apart from these two uses they become simply the trimmings of life, the mere gilt on the pill, mere "relaxations" to assuage in as harmless a manner as possible our carnal nature lest its sufferings become too great for us to bear.

The direction of this kind of religion is even more apparent when we consider the various ways and means prescribed for attaining such ideals. Among civilized peoples there are two principal ways of approach to the religious ideal, both of which have various common elements. Both are founded on the idea that the search for spiritual happiness in worldly pleasures is a snare because those pleasures are impermanent; they do, perhaps, impart a certain happiness, but because that happiness is entirely dependent on external circumstances it disappears as soon as those circumstances change. But there is something in man which makes it exceedingly hard for him to avoid the pursuit of earthly pleasures, and this tendency religion attempts to vanquish by a strongly hostile attitude to them. Hence the general antipathy in religion to all that pertains to the senses, and especially to the most elementary and important of earthly pleasures which are to be found in the sexual functions.

The first of the two ways of approach to the religious ideal is found mainly in Christianity. It is the way of mortification of the flesh in order that the eyes may be turned from the snares of the world to the eternal glories of the world beyond. By prayer, fasting, and acts of charity, by abstinence from fleshly delights, man may make himself fit to receive, feel and rejoice in the Grace of God which senses deluded by earthly things cannot appreciate. If the senses are coarsened by carnal pleasures, man becomes incapable of entering either now or hereafter into that realm of supernatural glory to which the Grace of God belongs. By its light he is not illumined but burned because of his impurities, for only those things which have been refined of all evil can exist within it.

The second way is similar in most respects, save that it is a way of self-development, wherein the individual relies not on God, but on his own power of willing. It is found in Buddhism and Vedanta, and consists of exercises in mortification and meditation whose object is similarly to refine the senses, to turn them away from the snares of the world and finally to root out from the soul the sense of personal identity and self-sufficiency and its desire to find happiness in the forms of life.

Obviously we are discussing some of the more extreme forms of religious theory and practice; generally speaking, their outward forms have been increasingly modified in the course of years. But there has been little change in the underlying philosophy, which amounts virtually to the complete denial of life as we understand it. For according to this kind of teaching the world of the senses has been made for the sole purpose of encompassing the human soul with a variety of snares. Even the "highest" delights of the senses such as are to be found in the arts are "trimmings," and the less refined joys of eating and sex are just tolerated in so far as they are used only for the purpose of maintaining and reproducing life. Today the harsh attitude of religion to these things has been appreciably softened, but this softening is rather a concession to human nature than an attempt to alter the fundamental premises of religious doctrine. And a mere concession to human nature it will remain while so many types of religious philosophy regard the material and spiritual worlds as irreconcilably opposed.

The problem is important because it affects the usefulness of religion to the greater part of mankind. The belief is still generally prevalent that those who wish to "go furthest" in religion must practice extremes of fasting and chastity and other forms of cumbersome discipline to acquire the necessary spiritual sensitivity for making contact with states of consciousness and mystical insight which less refined senses can no more experience than a jaded palate can taste the subtleties of a fine wine. But this refining and exaltation of consciousness by means of asceticism is obviously a vocation for the very few, for even if it were practicable for the majority it would not be altogether desirable to have the world converted into a vast Tibet. It would be wiser to heed the warning of Lucretius, "*Tantum religio potuit suadere malorum,*" or "Too much religion is apt to encourage evil."

But if the highest illumination of the spirit is only attainable by such means, of what use is religion to the ordinary run of mankind? It may encourage them to a greater morality; it may even teach them to love one another, though the course of history does not suggest that there has been much success in this. It may also give them a sense of the reality of a Father God to whom they can pray as "a very present help in time of trouble." But this does not begin to exhaust the possibilities of religion because it comes nowhere near to the real essentials of religion; it scarcely touches what is called "religious experience," without which doctrines, rites, and observances are the emptiest shells. It cannot be assumed that because most religious people are moral, moral people are therefore religious. As Wilde said, "When I am happy I am always good, but when I am good I am seldom happy," and this becomes more true than ever if by happiness we mean the state that arises from religious experience.

The Religious Experience

Religious experience is something like artistic or musical inspiration, though inspiration is a word that through misuse has unfortunate associations; religious experience is not "uplift" or flighty emotionalism. Strictly speaking, a composer is inspired when melody emerges from the depths of his mind, how or why we do not know. To convey that melody to others he writes it down on paper, employing a technical knowledge which enables him to name the notes which he hears in his mind. This fact is important: his technical knowledge does not *create* the tune in his mind; it simply provides him with a complicated alphabet, and is no more the source of music than the literary alphabet and the rules of grammar are the sources of men's ideas. If he is writing a symphony he will want to orchestrate his melody, but to do this he does not look up the books on harmony and orchestration to find out what combinations of notes he is advised by the the rules to put together. He has heard the whole symphony in his mind with every instrument playing its independent part, and his knowledge of orchestration and harmony simply enables him to tell which is which. What music teachers call the "rules" of harmony are just observations on the harmonies most usually used by such people as Bach and Beethoven. Bach and Beethoven did not use them because they were in the rules but because they liked their sound, and if people's tastes change so that they like other sounds then the old harmonic forms are replaced. It is necessary for a composer to study harmony in order that he may be able to identify chords which he hears in his mind, but he does not use his knowledge to *construct* chords unless he is a mere imitator of other people. In the same way, language is used not to create thoughts but to express them, and mastery of prose does not make a great thinker. The spiritual genius works in the same way as the musical genius. He has a wider scope because his technique of expression, his alphabet, is every possible human activity. For some reason there arises in his soul a feeling of the most profound happiness, not because of some special event, but because of the whole of life. This is not necessarily contentment or joy; it is rather that he feels himself completely united to the power that moves the universe, whatever that may be. This feeling he expresses in two ways, firstly by living a certain kind of life, and secondly by translating his feelings into the form of thoughts and words.

People who have not had this feeling make observations on his actions and words, and from them formulate the "rules" of religious morality and theology. But this involves a strange distortion, for as a rule the observer goes about his work in the wrong way. When the mystic says, "I feel united with God," the observer is interested primarily in the statement as a revelation of the existence of God, and goes on to consult the mystic's other sayings to find out what kind of God this is and in what manner He behaves. He is interested only secondarily in the mystic's feelings as a feeling, and it occurs to him only as an afterthought that it might be possible for himself to feel united with God. Whereat he proceeds to achieve this by trying to think in the same way as the mystic; that is to say, he takes the mystic's *ideas* and substitutes them for his own. He also tries to behave in the same way, imitating the mystic's actions. In other words, he tries to perform a kind of sympathetic magic, and in imitating the mystic's external forms deceives himself and others into thinking that he is really like him. But the important thing about the mystic was his feeling, not his ideas and actions, for these were only reflections of the feeling, and a reflection existing without a light is a sham. Therefore just as great technical proficiency will not make a creative genius in music, morality, theology, and discipline will not make a genius in religion, for these things are results of religious experience, not causes, and by themselves can no more produce it than the tail can be made to wag the dog.

The Spiritual Irrelevance of Occultism

This is not the only example of confused thought in searching for religious experience. The other, which we have already mentioned, is the opposition made between the spiritual and the material. Much depends, of course, on the precise meaning given to the word "spirit," but it should certainly not be confused with the word "psychic" and many things described as spiritual are clearly psychic. There is no definite rule as to how these words should be used, so to be explicit we have to make our own rules. And the spiritual, in the sense in which it is used here, is no more opposed to the material than white is opposed to long. The opposite of white is black, and of long, short; white things are no more necessarily short than material things are unspiritual. But we can say that the material and the psychic are opposed, if only in the sense that they are opposite ends of the same stick. Psychic things belong to the world explored by occultism and "psychic science"—telepathy, clairvoyance, mind-reading, and all those phenomena which appear to require sixth or seventh senses whose development seems unquestionably to be assisted by ascetic practices. The so-called spiritual realms inhabited by departed souls, angels, elementals, and demons, and the source of beatific visions, would be most correctly described as psychic if we are to allow that such things have actual, objective existence. And this world is the logical opposite of the material world because it belongs in the same category; it contains forms and substances, even though its substance may be of a wholly different order from what we understand as matter. People who are in touch with this world, however, are not necessarily spiritual people; they may have unusual faculties of perception and be familiar with the beings and ways of a more glorious world than our own, but this is a matter of *faculty* and *knowledge,* not of spirituality. The technique of living employed by such people is more highly evolved than that of ordinary men, just as the technique of the opera is more complicated than that of pure drama. Opera involves not only acting but singing, playing music, and sometimes dancing, but this does not make it a greater art.

Spirituality belongs in the same category as happiness and freedom, and strictly speaking there is no such thing as the spiritual *world.* If psychic people are to be believed, there is a psychic *world,* and because it is a world entry into it is simply an enlargement of experience. But experience as such never made anyone either free or happy, and in so far as freedom and happiness are concerned with experience the important thing is not experience itself but what is learned from it. Some people learn from experience and others do not; some learn much from a little, others learn little from much. "Without going out of my house, " said the Chinese sage Lao Tzu, "I know the whole universe." For the spiritual is in no way divided from the material, nor from the psychic, not from any other aspect of life. To find it, it is not necessary to go from one state of consciousness to another, from one set of senses to another or from one world to another. Such journeying about in the fields of experience takes you neither toward it nor away from it. In the words of the Psalmist:[4]

Whither shall I go from Thy spirit? Or whither shall I flee from Thy presence?

If I ascend up into heaven, Thou art there: if I make my bed in hell, behold, Thou art there.

If I take the wings of the morning, and dwell in the uttermost parts of the sea; even there shall thy hand lead me, and thy right hand shall hold me.

If I say, Surely the darkness shall cover me; even the night shall be light about me.

Yea, the darkness hideth not from Thee; but the night shineth as the day: the darkness and the light are both alike to Thee.

4. Psalm 139:7–12.

In fact the spiritual world, if we must use the term, is this world and all possible worlds, and spiritual experience is what we are experiencing at this moment and at any moment—if we look at it in the right way.

Union with Life

This is the difference between religious or spiritual experience and artistic inspiration; both are analogous, but the latter is particularized. The artist or musician has a special type of creative genius; he creates pictures or music, for his genius is a specialized gift. But the spiritual genius is not a specialist, for he does not just paint or compose creatively: he *lives* creatively, and his tools are not confined to brush, pen or instrument; they are all things touched by his hand. This is not to say that when he takes up a brush he can paint like Leonardo or that when he takes hammer and chisel he can work like a master-mason. Spiritual experience involves neither technical proficiency nor factual knowledge; it is no short-cut to things that must ordinarily be mastered by pains and practice. Nor is spiritual experience necessarily expressed in any *particular* mode of life; its presence in any given individual cannot be judged by measurement in accordance with certain standards. It can only be felt intuitively, for creative living is not always outwardly distinguishable from any other kind of living; in fact, spiritual people are often at pains to appear as normal as possible. At the same time, although spiritual people may do exactly the same things as others, one feels that their actions are in some way different. There is a story of a Buddhist sage who was about to speak to his disciples when he found that he wanted more light. He pointed to a curtain covering one of the windows and instantly two of the disciples went and rolled it up, whereat the sage remarked, "One of them is right, but the other is wrong."[5]

In itself, spirituality is purely an inner experience; it has no necessary effect whatsoever on one's outward behavior judged from the standards of efficiency and worldly-wisdom. This is not to say, however, that it is something absolutely private and personal, finding no expression that others can see. For spirituality is a deep sense of inner freedom based on the realization that one's self is in complete union and harmony with life, with God, with the Self of the universe or whatever that principle may be called. It is the realization that that union has existed from all times, even though one did not know it, and that nothing in all the world nor anything that oneself can do is able to destroy it. It is thus the sense that the whole might of the universe is at work in one's every thought and action,

5. *Mu-mon-kwan,* xxvi.

however trivial and small. In fact this is true of all men and all things, but only the spiritual man really knows it and his realization gives a subtly different quality to his life; all that he does becomes strangely alive, for though its outward appearance is perhaps the same as before it acquires a new meaning. It is this which other people notice, but if he has the gift for teaching they will see it in other ways as well. By his words as well as his deeds and his personal "atmosphere" they will understand that this realization has awakened in him a tremendous love for life in all its aspects.

Prose and the logic of philosophy cannot explain this love; one might as well try to describe a beautiful face by a mathematical account of its measurements and proportions. It is a mixture of the joy of freedom, a childlike sense of wonder, and the inner sensation of absolute harmony with life as in the rhythm of an eternal dance such as the Hindus portray in the interlocked figures of Shiva and his bride.[6] In one sense you feel that your life is not lived by you at all; the power of the universe, fate and destiny, God Himself are directing all your motions and all your responsibilities are blown to the winds. In another sense you feel free to move as you wish; you seem to be moving life with the same vast power with which life moves you, and your littlest acts become filled with gigantic possibilities. Indeed, physicists tell us that the stars are affected when we lift a single finger. The result of these two feelings is that you no longer distinguish between what you do to life and what life does to you; it is as if two dancers moved in such perfect accord that the distinction between lead and response vanished, as if the two became one and the same motion. By the whirling, ever-changing movement of this dance you are carried along without pause, but not like a drunken man in a torrent, for you as much as life are the source of the movement. And this is real freedom; it includes both freedom to move and to be moved; action and passivity are merged, and in spirituality as well as in marriage this is the fulfillment of love.

The Spirituality of Everyday Life

All this, however, does not take place in the ecstasy of trance, in some abstract state of consciousness where all shapes and substances have become merged into a single infinite essence. The spiritual man does not perform his ordinary activities as one in a dream, letting his surface thoughts and deeds run on mechanically. He can become just as much absorbed in the usual affairs of the world as anyone else, but in a certain way he sanctifies them for under his hands sharpening a pencil becomes as much a religious act as prayer or meditation. Indeed, he can afford to become absorbed in

6. See Zimmer, *Kunstform und Yoga* (Berlin, 1926).

everyday affairs almost more than others, and he can do so with a certain zest and abandon for to him ordinary human thoughts and activities are as much included in the dance of the spirit as is anything else. This, indeed, is much of his secret, for he knows that spirituality does not consist in thinking always about the spiritual as such. His world is not divided into "water-tight compartments" and his religion is not a special form of thought and activity, for the spiritual and the material are not separated.

But because a man does not occupy himself with the ordinary pursuits of mankind, this is no indication that he lacks spiritual understanding. He is free to follow whatever occupation he pleases— monk, philosopher, lawyer, clerk, or tradesman, but from the spiritual point of view a priest is not necessarily more holy than a truck-driver. Furthermore, to obtain spiritual experience it is not essential to "vex your mournful minds with pious pains," to spend years in the study of theology, to retire from the world, to become a vegetarian and teetotaler, to practice mental acrobatics and seek out "higher realms" of consciousness, to abstain from sexuality, or to develop such peculiar gifts as "fourth-dimensional vision." Certainly these things are necessary for the professional philosopher or for that particular type of *scientist* whose field of research is the psychic world. If we are going to find out how our present senses may be developed, how we can tap sources of nervous energy as yet unused, how we can understand time in terms of space and see past and future at once, how we can transfer thought or how we can acquire the faculty of immovable concentration, then indeed we have to go in training even more rigorously than the professional athlete. To acquire psychic faculties you must practice just as much as if you wanted to hold the world's record for sprinting or to be able to walk on hot coals without being burned.

The Nonessentials of Religion

Religion as we understand it includes many things which do not strictly belong to it, because in olden times it had to fulfill functions which have now been taken over by scientists, doctors, and lawyers. At one time the major preoccupation of so-called religion was the study and manipulation of the unknown and the unseen; as these things become known and seen they passed out of the hands of priests. But when priests were considered the wisest of all men they were expected to have answers to all the problems which others did not understand. They were expected to know the causes of disease, the behavior and influence of the stars, the origin of such natural phenomena as thunder, storms, and famines, not to mention the more remote questions of what happens after death and whether there are gods and angels.

Many of these problems have now been taken over by science,

though we are still ignorant of the life after death and still have not objective evidence of the existence of "supernatural" beings. Therefore the priests are still the authorities on such matters even though they remain legitimate objects of scientific inquiry and have no essential connection with religion. The day may come when science, physical or psychic, will be able to answer these questions, and some scientists imagine that there will then be no further need for religion, having no clear idea of what religion is. This is not exactly their fault, for religious people seldom understand the true function of religion and still waste thought and energy in a war with science based on wholly false premises.

If it could be proved objectively and scientifically that there was a life after death and that supernatural beings do exist this would have about as much religious significance as the discovery of a new continent, of the existence of life on Mars, or of the uses of electricity. It would be neither more nor less than an addition to human experience and knowledge. It would not necessarily be an addition to human wisdom, and this is the province of religion. For wisdom is not factual knowledge nor mere quantity and range of experience, nor even facility in the uses of knowledge and experience. Wisdom is a quality of the psychological or spiritual relationship between man and his experience. When that relationship is wise and harmonious man's experiences set him free, but when it is unwise and discordant his experiences bind him.

Religion alone can deal with that relationship, and this is its essential function. For what do we find left in religion when its *quasi*-scientific aspect is removed? There is the whole, vast problem of love or spiritual union which is contained in the question, "How can I learn to love life, whose source and essence we call God? How can I learn to be united with it in all its expressions, in living and dying, in love and fear, in the outer world of circumstances and in the inner world of thought and feeling, so that in union with it I may find freedom?" Now science cannot teach any kind of love, not even the love between man and woman, for who ever learned to love his wife out of a psychological textbook on matrimony? Morality, which religion would teach as having supernatural sanctions, is just the expression of love; it follows it as a consequence and does not precede it as a cause. The will of God as expressed in morality is not a ukase which we should merely obey, for the purpose of His will is not that there should be morality, but that there should be love, and morality is just the "outward and visible sign of an inward and spiritual grace."

In so far as religion has diverged from its main purpose into psychism, morality for its own sake, speculative theology, concern for the life after death, and attempts to awaken spirituality by imitating its expressions, it has also put itself out of touch with people who have no desire to be religious specialists. Those who cannot feel that man's principal concern should lie outside this world, who feel that salvation has nothing to do with removal to another realm of experience or with mere obedience to a moral law—such people can find little assistance from religion as usually taught, and to-day they constitute a very large proportion of intelligent men and women. For the nineteenth-century conflict between religion and science was, for those whose eyes were open, a stripping-off of nonessentials from religion, but unfortunately official religion seldom saw it in this way. It clung to supernaturalism, which, rightly or wrongly, rationalist science had discredited, and continued to make it the keystone of spirituality.

But this kind of religion does not encourage the type of love upon which spirituality is founded. We have seen that its technique is imitative and thus unlikely to produce genuine, first-hand religious experience; we have also seen that its contempt of this world and its concentration on the life hereafter has little to do with the essentials of religion. This is not all, for not only has it little to do with such essentials; it is also a decided hindrance to spiritual growth because it encourages a "love" of God on a false basis. God is loved not because He has given us *this* world, but because He is said to have promised a much better world in the life after death. His gift to us of this world is therefore declined without thanks—an effrontery which is softened by describing this world as a place of trial for fitness to enter the world to come, on the principle that if you refuse God's first gift, you will get His second.

The "Higher Sensuality"

But if God created this world only as a temporary place of trial, He seems to have taken a wholly unnecessary amount of trouble in its construction. He gave us senses which as yet we have hardly begun to develop to their full potentialities, and yet religion warns us against those senses as if they were given us simply as a sop to embellish life with such superficial trimmings as art, literature, music, and athletics so that in playing with them we may have a little relaxation from the more important task of fitting ourselves for the hereafter. But there is a way of looking at things whereby these "trimmings" become the main business of life, and religion the means to their fulfillment, on the principle that religion was made for life and not life for religion. For the contempt of the world of the senses is peculiarly like the fable of the sour grapes. Man burned his fingers at the game of pleasure, and instead of learning to play it aright was filled with fear and relegated pleasure to the realms of the Devil and his vanities, crying:

The earthly hope men set their hearts upon
Turns ashes, or it prospers, and anon,
    Like snow upon the Desert's dusky face,
Lighting a little hour or two, is gone.

But the whole point about the beauties of the earth is that they would be intolerable if they did not change and vanish. A woman is not less beautiful and desirable because she grows old and white; if she had eternal youth she would be a monster, as many women are who refuse to accept the different beauties of old age and death. For the beauty of life is not in any one of its stages but in the whole movement from birth to death, and if this movement is in any way resisted or interrupted there come unhappiness, maladjustment and neurotic disease. Those who look pitiful and hideous in their old age are only so because years rankle them, because they have not accepted the rhythm of their life and go forward to old age with regretful glances behind at lost glories.

Certainly all pleasures are transient; otherwise we should cease to appreciate them, but if this be made the excuse for refusing to enjoy them, one must suspect that man's ideas of happiness are horribly confused. The secret of the enjoyment of pleasure is to know when to stop. Man does not learn this secret easily, but to shun pleasure altogether is cowardly avoidance of a difficult task. For we have to learn the art of enjoying things *because* they are impermanent. We do this every time we listen to music. We do not seize hold of a particular chord or phrase and shout at the orchestra to go on playing it for the rest of the evening; on the contrary, however much we may like that particular moment of music, we know that its perpetuation would interrupt and kill the movement of the melody. We understand that the beauty of a symphony is less in these musical moments than in the whole movement from beginning to end. If the symphony tries to go on too long, if at a certain point the composer exhausts his creative ability and tries to carry on for just the sake of filling in the required space of time, then we begin to fidget in our chairs, feeling that he has denied the natural rhythm, has broken the smooth curve from birth to death, and that though a pretense at life is being made it is in fact a living death.

The Problem of Pain

But by itself this philosophy of "higher sensuality" is inadequate, for life is not like a musical masterpiece in certain respects. We may find all of a musical masterpiece beautiful; from the sensual point of view life is only beautiful in parts; it has also ugliness, pain, and horror, and hence the love for a God who will remove these things in the world to come. But this, too, is an avoidance of the problem. For the attitude of ordinary religion to both the pleasures and the pains of this world is negative. Pleasure is suspected, and in the everlasting life pain is not.

But we must now ask whether it is not possible that greater heights of spirituality may be attained by a positive attitude to pleasure and pain in this world. If this is possible, it is clear that religion has no special concern with the life after death and that spirituality has nothing whatever to do with retiring from this world. No one can deny the existence of a life after death, but that it should be a more spiritual life than this one is a wholly unreasonable assumption. If it is true that we are physically reincarnated on this earth or another, the whole picture is changed. But if orthodox Christianity is right in its belief that we have only one material life, then the next life will be psychic because according to our definition there can be no such thing as a spiritual world, spirituality being a quality of life and not a kind of existence in the same category as the material and the psychic.

Spirituality is therefore a way of living in whatever world one happens to be, and is in no way separable from the actual process of living in that world. In other words, there is no difference between religion and ordinary, everyday life; religious ideas and practices (which are no more religion itself than any other activities) exist solely to promote a positive and loving attitude toward ordinary life and what it stands for, namely, God. Unless one happens to be a religious specialist, which is not necessarily the same thing as spiritual person, religious practices are not ends in themselves. They are means to a fuller and greater life *in this world*, involving a positive and constructive attitude to pleasure and pain alike, and thus an increasing ability to learn happiness and freedom from every possible kind of expereience. In this sense, religion is union with life; whether that life is the present life of physical form, of thought and feeling with brain and soul, or whether it is a future life of purely psychic substance is beside the point. These are only different grades of existence; they are not different grades of spirituality, for the same spiritual laws apply in every grade of existence, and when one has learned union with one of them, one has discovered the secret of union with any of them.

We have suggested that the secret of this union lies in a positive attitude toward the world in which we live. To repeat the question which religion has to answer, we want to discover how we can learn to be united with life in all its expressions, in living and dying, in love and fear, in the outer world of circumstance and in the inner world of thought and feeling, so that in union with it we may find freedom and happiness. To be united with life in all its expressions may seem a large demand to make on oneself, for those expressions include disease, pain, death, madness, and all the horrors which man can devise, wittingly or unwittingly, for his fellow-creatures. In fact the "nub" of the whole problem is the acceptance of the dark side of life, for this is the very occasion of our unhappiness. "Acceptance" may seem a weak word for a positive attitude of love, but it is used because the type of love in question is relaxed. It is positive but not aggressive; it grows in its own way and is not forced. Therefore we may say that it is not enough to *tolerate* the dark side of life; acceptance in this sense is much more than a "let it be" with a resigned shrug of the shoulders. Let us call it "creative acceptance," though because this phrase smacks overmuch of philosophical jargon we will write the noun and only remember its qualifying adjective. This is perhaps wise in another way, for a truth oddly comes out of a play on words: to be genuine, acceptance must be unqualified.

ANNIE DILLARD

Sight into Insight[1]

When I was six or seven years old, growing up in Pittsburgh, I used to take a penny of my own and hide it for someone else to find. It was a curious compulsion; sadly, I've never been seized by it since. For some reason I always "hid" the penny along the same stretch of sidewalk up the street. I'd cradle it at the roots of a maple, say, or in a hole left by a chipped-off piece of sidewalk. Then I'd take a piece of chalk and, starting at either end of the block, draw huge arrows leading up to the penny from both directions. After I learned to write I labeled the arrows "SURPRISE AHEAD" or "MONEY THIS WAY." I was greatly excited, during all this arrow-drawing, at the thought of the first lucky passerby who would receive in this way, regardless of merit, a free gift from the universe. But I never lurked about. I'd go straight home and not give the matter another thought, until, some months later, I would be gripped by the impulse to hide another penny.

There are lots of things to see, unwrapped gifts and free surprises. The world is fairly studded and strewn with pennies cast broadside from a generous hand. But—and this is the point—who gets excited by a mere penny? If you follow one arrow, if you crouch motionless on a bank to watch a tremulous ripple thrill on the water, and are rewarded by the sight of a muskrat kit paddling from its den, will you count that sight a chip of copper only, and go your rueful way?

1. Adapted from *Pilgrim at Tinker Creek*, 1974.

1228 · *Annie Dillard*

It is very dire poverty indeed for a man to be so malnourished and fatigued that he won't stoop to pick up a penny. But if you cultivate a healthy poverty and simplicity, so that finding a penny will make your day, then, since the world is in fact planted in pennies, you have with your poverty bought a lifetime of days. What you see is what you get.

Unfortunately, nature is very much a now-you-see-it, now-you-don't affair. A fish flashes, then dissolves in the water before my eyes like so much salt. Deer apparentlyly ascend bodily into heaven; the brightest oriole fades into leaves. These disappearances stun me into stillness and concentration; they say of nature that it conceals with a grand nonchalance, and they say of vision that it is a deliberate gift, the revelation of a dancer who for my eyes only flings away her seven veils.

For nature does reveal as well as conceal: now-you-don't-see-it, now-you-do. For a week this September migrating red-winged blackbirds were feeding heavily down by Tinker Creek at the back of the house. One day I went out to investigate the racket; I walked up to a tree, an Osage orange, and a hundred birds flew away. They simply materialized out of the tree. I saw a tree, then a whisk of color, then a tree again. I walked closer and another hundred blackbirds took flight. Not a branch, not a twig budged: the birds were apparently weightless as well as invisible. Or, it was as if the leaves of the Osage orange had been freed from a spell in the form of red-winged blackbirds; they flew from the tree, caught my eye in the sky, and vanished. When I looked again at the tree, the leaves had reassembled as if nothing had happened. Finally I walked directly to the trunk of the tree and a final hundred, the real diehards, appeared, spread, and vanished. How could so many hide in the tree without my seeing them? The Osage orange, unruffled, looked just as it had looked from the house, when three hundred red-winged blackbirds cried from its crown. I looked upstream where they flew, and they were gone. Searching, I couldn't spot one. I wandered upstream to force them to play their hand, but they'd crossed the creek and scattered. One show to a customer. These appearances catch at my throat; they are the free gifts, the bright coppers at the roots of trees.

It's all a matter of keeping my eyes open. Nature is like one of those line drawings that are puzzles for children: Can you find hidden in the tree a duck, a house, a boy, a bucket, a giraffe, and a boot? Specialists can find the most incredibly hidden things. A book I read when I was young recommended an easy way to find caterpillars: you simply find some fresh caterpillar droppings, look up, and there's your caterpillar. More recently an author advised me to set my mind at ease about those piles of cut stems on the ground in grassy fields. Field mice make them; they cut the grass down by degrees to reach the seeds at the head. It seems that when the grass is tightly packed, as in a field of ripe grain, the blade won't topple at a single cut through the stem; instead, the cut stem simply drops vertically, held in the crush of grain. The mouse severs the bottom again and again, the stem keeps dropping an inch at a time, and finally the head is low enough for the mouse to reach the seeds. Meanwhile the mouse is positively littering the field with its little piles of cut stems into which, presumably, the author is constantly stumbling.

If I can't see these minutiae, I still try to keep my eyes open. I'm always on the lookout for ant lion traps in sandy soil, monarch pupae near milkweed, skipper larvae in locust leaves. These things are utterly common, and I've not seen one. I bang on hollow trees near water, but so far no flying squirrels have appeared. In flat country I watch every sunset in hopes of seeing the green ray. The green ray is a seldom-seen streak of light that rises from the sun like a spurting fountain at the moment of sunset; it throbs into the sky for two seconds and disappears. One more reason to keep my eyes open. A photography professor at the University of Florida just happened to see a bird die in midflight; it jerked, died, dropped, and smashed on the ground.

I squint at the wind because I read Stewart Edward White: "I have always maintained that if you looked closely enough you could *see* the wind—the dim, hardly-made-out, fine débris fleeing high in the air." White was an excellent observer, and devoted an entire chapter of *The Mountains* to the subject of seeing deer: "As soon as you can forget the naturally obvious and construct an artificial obvious, then you too will see deer."

But the artificial obvious is hard to see. My eyes account for less than 1 percent of the weight of my head; I'm bony and dense; I see what I expect. I just don't know what the lover knows; I can't see the artificial obvious that those in the know construct. The herpetologist asks the native, "Are there snakes in that ravine?" "No, sir." And the herpetologist comes home with, yessir, three bags full. Are there butterflies on that mountain? Are the bluets in bloom? Are there arrowheads here, or fossil ferns in the shale?

Peeping through my keyhole I see within the range of only about 30 percent of the light that comes from the sun; the rest is infrared and some little ultraviolet, perfectly apparent to many animals, but invisible to me. A nightmare network of ganglia, charged and firing without my knowledge, cuts and splices what I do see, editing it for my brain. Donald E. Carr points out that the sense impressions of one-celled animals are *not* edited for the brain: "This is philosophically interesting in a rather mournful way, since it means that only the simplest animals perceive the universe as it is."

A fog that won't burn away drifts and flows across my field of vision. When you see fog move against a backdrop of deep pines, you don't see the fog itself, but streaks of clearness floating across the air in dark shreds. So I see only tatters of clearness through a pervading obscurity. I can't distinguish the fog from the overcast sky; I can't be sure if the light is direct or reflected. Everywhere darkness and the presence of the unseen appalls. We estimate now that only one atom dances alone in every cubic meter of intergalactic space. I blink and squint. What planet or power yanks Halley's Comet out of orbit? We haven't seen it yet; it's a question of distance, density, and the pallor of reflected light. We rock, cradled in the swaddling band of darkness. Even the simple darkness of night whispers suggestions to the mind. This summer, in August, I stayed at the creek too late.

Where Tinker Creek flows under the sycamore log bridge to the tear-shaped island, it is slow and shallow, fringed thinly in cattail marsh. At this spot an astonishing bloom of life supports vast breeding populations of insects, fish, reptiles, birds, and mammals. On windless summer evenings I stalk along the creek bank or straddle the sycamore log in absolute stillness, watching for muskrats. The night I stayed too late I was hunched on the log staring spellbound at spreading, reflected stains of lilac on the water. A cloud in the sky suddenly lighted as if turned on by a switch; its reflection just as suddenly materialized on the water upstream, flat and floating, so that I couldn't see the creek bottom, or life in the water under the cloud. Downstream, away from the cloud on the water, water turtles smooth as beans were gliding down with the current in a series of easy, weightless push-offs, as men bound on the moon. I didn't know whether to trace the progress of one turtle I was sure of, risking sticking my face in one of the bridge's spider webs made invisible by the gathering dark, or take a chance on seeing the carp, or scan the mudbank in hope of seeing a muskrat, or follow the last of the swallows who caught at my heart and trailed it after them like streamers as they appeared from directly below, under the log, flying upstream with their tails forked, so fast.

But shadows spread and deepened and stayed. After thousands of years we're still strangers to darkness, fearful aliens in an enemy camp with our arms crossed over our chests. I stirred. A land turtle on the bank, startled, hissed the air from its lungs and withdrew to its shell. An uneasy pink here, an unfathomable blue there, gave great suggestion of lurking beings. Things were going on. I couldn't see whether that rustle I heard was a distant rattle-snake, slit-eyed, or a nearby sparrow kicking in the dry flood debris slung at the foot of a willow. Tremendous action roiled the water everywhere I looked, big action, inexplicable. A tremor welled up beside a gaping muskrat burrow in the bank and I caught my breath, but no muskrat appeared. The ripples continued to fan upstream with a steady, powerful thrust. Night was knitting an eyeless mask over my face, and I still sat transfixed. A distant airplane, a delta wing out of nightmare, made a gliding shadow on the creek's bottom that looked like a stingray cruising upstream. At once a black fin slit the pink cloud on the water, shearing it in two. The two halves merged together and seemed to dissolve before my eyes. Darkness pooled in the cleft of the creek and rose, as water collects in a well. Untamed, dreaming lights flickered over the sky. I saw hints of hulking underwater shadows, two pale splashes out of the water, and round ripples rolling close together from a blackened center.

At last I stared upstream where only the deepest violet remained of the cloud, a cloud so high its underbelly still glowed, its feeble color reflected from a hidden sky lighted in turn by a sun halfway to China. And out of that violet, a sudden enormous black body arced over the water. Head and tail, if there was a head and tail, were both submerged in cloud. I saw only one ebony fling, a headlong dive to darkness; then the waters closed, and the lights went out.

I walked home in a shivering daze, up hill and down. Later I lay openmouthed in bed, my arms flung wide at my sides to steady the whirling darkness. At this latitude I'm spinning 836 miles an hour round the earth's axis; I feel my sweeping fall as a breakneck arc like the dive of dolphins, and the hollow rushing of wind raises the hairs on my neck and the side of my face. In orbit around the sun I'm moving 64,800 miles an hour. The solar system as a whole, like a merry-go-round unhinged, spins, bobs, and blinks at the speed of 43,200 miles an hour along a course set east of Hercules. Someone has piped, and we are dancing a tarantella until the sweat pours. I open my eyes and I see dark, muscled forms curl out of water, with flapping gills and flattened eyes. I close my eyes and I see stars, deep stars giving way to deeper stars, deeper stars bowing to deepest stars at the crown of an infinite cone.

"Still," wrote Van Gogh in a letter, "a great deal of light falls on everything." If we are blinded by darkness, we are also blinded by light. Sometimes here in Virginia at sunset low clouds on the southern or northern horizon are completely invisible in the lighted sky. I only know one is there because I can see its reflection in still water. The first time I discovered this mystery I looked from cloud to nocloud in bewilderment, checking my bearings over and over, thinking maybe the ark of the covenant was just passing by south of Dead Man Mountain. Only much later did I learn the explanation: polarized light from the sky is very much weakened by reflection, but the light in clouds isn't polarized. So invisible clouds pass among visible clouds, till all slide over the mountains; so a greater light extinguishes a lesser as though it didn't exist.

In the great meteor shower of August, the Perseid, I wail all day for the shooting stars I miss. They're out there showering down, committing hara-kiri in a flame of fatal attraction, and hissing perhaps at last into the ocean. But at dawn what looks like a blue dome clamps down over me like a lid on a pot. The stars and planets could smash and I'd never know. Only a piece of ashen moon occasionally climbs up or down the inside of the dome, and our local star without surcease explodes on our heads. We have really only that one light, one source for all power, and yet we must turn away from it by universal decree. Nobody here on the planet seems aware of this strange, powerful taboo, that we all walk about carefully averting our faces, this way and that, lest our eyes be blasted forever.

Darkness appalls and light dazzles; the scrap of visible light that doesn't hurt my eyes hurts my brain. What I see sets me swaying. Size and distance and the sudden swelling of meanings confuse me, bowl me over. I straddle the sycamore log bridge over Tinker Creek in the summer. I look at the lighted creek bottom: snail tracks tunnel the mud in quavering curves. A crayfish jerks, but by the time I absorb what has happened, he's gone in a billowing smoke screen of silt. I look at the water; minnows and shiners. If I'm thinking minnows, a carp will fill my brain till I scream. I look at the water's surface: skaters, bubbles, and leaves sliding down. Suddenly, my own face, reflected, startles me witless. Those snails have been tracking my face! Finally, with a shuddering wrench of the will, I see clouds, cirrus clouds. I'm dizzy, I fall in.

This looking business is risky. Once I stood on a humped rock on nearby Purgatory Mountain, watching through binoculars the great autumn hawk migration below, until I discovered that I was in danger of joining the hawks on a vertical migration of my own. I was used to binoculars, but not, apparently, to balancing on humped rocks while looking through them. I reeled. Everything advanced and receded by turns; the world was full of unexplained foreshortenings and depths. A distant huge object, a hawk the size of an elephant, turned out to be the browned bough of a nearby loblolly pine. I followed a sharp-shinned hawk against a featureless sky, rotating my head unawares as it flew, and when I lowered the glass a glimpse of my own looming shoulder sent me staggering. What prevents the men at Palomar[2] from falling, voiceless and blinded, from their tiny, vaulted chairs?

I reel in confusion; I don't understand what I see. With the naked eye I can see two million light-years to the Andromeda galaxy. Often I slop some creek water in a jar, and when I get home I dump it in a white china bowl. After the silt settles I return and see tracings of minute snails on the bottom, a planarian or two winding round the rim of water, roundworms shimmying, frantically, and finally, when my eyes have adjusted to these dimensions, amoebae. At first the amoebae look like *muscae volitantes*, those

2. An astronomical observatory in California.

curled moving spots you seem to see in your eyes when you stare at
a distant wall. Then I see the amoebae as drops of water congealed,
bluish, translucent, like chips of sky in the bowl. At length I choose
one individual and give myself over to its idea of an evening. I see it
dribble a grainy foot before it on its wet, unfathomable way. Do its
unedited sense impressions include the fierce focus of my eyes?
Shall I take it outside and show it Andromeda, and blow its little
endoplasm? I stir the water with a finger, in case it's running out of
oxygen. Maybe I should get a tropical aquarium with motorized
bubblers and lights, and keep this one for a pet. Yes, it would tell
its fissioned descendants, the universe is two feet by five, and if you
listen closely you can hear the buzzing music of the spheres.

Oh, it's mysterious, lamplit evenings here in the galaxy, one after
the other. It's one of those nights when I wander from window to
window, looking for a sign. But I can't see. Terror and a beauty
insoluble are a riband of blue woven into the fringe of garments of
things both great and small. No culture explains, no bivouac offers
real haven or rest. But it could be that we are not seeing something.
Galileo thought comets were an optical illusion. This is fertile
ground: since we are certain that they're not, we can look at what
our scientists have been saying with fresh hope. What if there are
really gleaming, castellated cities hung up-side-down over the desert
sand? What limpid lakes and cool date palms have our caravans
always passed untried? Until, one by one, by the blindest of leaps,
we light on the road to these places, we must stumble in darkness
and hunger. I turn from the window. I'm blind as a bat, sensing
only from every direction the echo of my own thin cries.

I chanced on a wonderful book called *Space and Sight*, by Marius
Von Senden. When Western surgeons discovered how to perform
safe cataract operations, they ranged across Europe and America
operating on dozens of men and women of all ages who had been
blinded by cataracts since birth. Von Senden collected accounts of
such cases; the histories are fascinating. Many doctors had tested
their patients' sense perceptions and ideas of space both before and
after the operations. The vast majority of patients, of both sexes
and all ages, had, in Von Senden's opinion, no idea of space whatsoever. Form, distance, and size were so many meaningless syllables.
A patient "had no idea of depth, confusing it with roundness."
Before the operation a doctor would give a blind patient a cube and
a sphere; the patient would tongue it or feel it with his hands, and
name it correctly. After the operation the doctor would show the
same objects to the patient without letting him touch them; now
he had no clue whatsoever to what he was seeing. One patient
called lemonade "square" because it pricked on his tongue as a
square shape pricked on the touch of his hands. Of another post-
operative patient the doctor writes, "I have found in her no notion

of size, for example, not even within the narrow limits which she might have encompassed with the aid of touch. Thus when I asked her to show me how big her mother was, she did not stretch out her hands, but set her two index fingers a few inches apart."

For the newly sighted, vision is pure sensation unencumbered by meaning. When a newly sighted girl saw photographs and paintings, she asked, " 'Why do they put those dark marks all over them?' 'Those aren't dark marks,' her mother explained, 'those are shadows. That is one of the ways the eye knows that things have shape. If it were not for shadows, many things would look flat.' 'Well, that how things do look,' Joan answered. 'Everything looks flat with dark patches.' "

In general the newly sighted see the world as a dazzle of "color-patches." They are pleased by the sensation of color, and learn quickly to name the colors, but the rest of seeing is tormentingly difficult. Soon after his operation a patient "generally bumps into one of these colour-patches and observes them to be substantial, since they resist him as tactual objects do. In walking about it also strikes him—or can if he pays attention—that he is continually passing in between the colours he sees, that he can go past a visual object, that a part of it then steadily disappears from view; and that in spite of this, however he twists and turns—whether entering the room from the door, for example, or returning back to it—he always has a visual space in front of him. Thus he gradually comes to realize that there is also a space behind him, which he does not see."

The mental effort involved in these reasonings proves overwhelming for many patients. It oppresses them to realize that they have been visible to people all along, perhaps unattractively so, without their knowledge or consent. A disheartening number of them refuse to use their new vision, continuing to go over objects with their tongues, and lapsing into apathy and despair.

On the other hand, many newly sighted people speak well of the world, and teach us how dull our own vision is. To one patient, a human hand, unrecognized, is "something bright and then holes." Shown a bunch of grapes, a boy calls out, "It is dark, blue and shiny. . . . It isn't smooth, it has bumps and hollows." A little girl visits a garden. "She is greatly astonished, and can scarcely be persuaded to answer, stands speechless in front of the tree, which she only names on taking hold of it, and then as 'the tree with the lights in it.' " Another patient, a twenty-two-year-old girl, was dazzled by the world's brightness and kept her eyes shut for two weeks. When at the end of that time she opened her eyes again, she did not recognize any objects, but "the more she now directed her gaze upon everything about her, the more it could be seen how an expression of gratification and astonishment overspread her features; she repeatedly exclaimed: 'Oh God! How beautiful!' "

I saw color-patches for weeks after I read this wonderful book. It was summer; the peaches were ripe in the valley orchards. When I woke in the morning, color-patches wrapped round my eyes, intricately, leaving not one unfilled spot. All day long I walked among shifting color-patches that parted before me like the Red Sea and closed again in silence, transfigured, wherever I looked back. Some patches swelled and loomed, while others vanished utterly, and dark marks flitted at random over the whole dazzling sweep. But I couldn't sustain the illusion of flatness. I've been around for too long. Form is condemned to an eternal danse macabre with meaning: I couldn't unpeach the peaches. Nor can I remember ever having seen without understanding; the color-patches of infancy are lost. My brain then must have been smooth as any balloon. I'm told I reached for the moon; many babies do. But the color-patches of infancy swelled as meaning filled them; they arrayed themselves in solemn ranks down distance which unrolled and stretched before me like a plain. The moon rocketed away. I live now in a world of shadows that shape and distance color, a world where space makes a kind of terrible sense. What Gnosticism[3] is this, and what physics? The fluttering patch I saw in my nursery window—silver and green and shape-shifting blue—is gone; a row of Lombardy poplars takes its place, mute, across the distant lawn. That humming oblong creature pale as light that stole along the walls of my room at night, stretching exhilaratingly around the corners, is gone, too, gone the night I ate of the bittersweet fruit, put two and two together and puckered forever my brain. Martin Buber tells this tale: "Rabbi Mendel once boasted to his teacher Rabbi Elimelekh that evenings he saw the angel who rolls away the light before the darkness, and mornings the angel who rolls away the darkness before the light. 'Yes,' said Rabbi Elimelekh, 'in my youth I saw that too. Later on you don't see these things anymore.' "

Why didn't someone hand those newly sighted people paints and brushes from the start, when they still didn't know what anything was? Then maybe we all could see color-patches too, the world unraveled from reason, Eden before Adam gave names. The scales would drop from my eyes; I'd see trees like men walking; I'd run down the road against all orders, hallooing and leaping.

Seeing is of course very much a matter of verbalization. Unless I call my attention to what passes before my eyes, I simply won't see it. If Tinker Mountain erupted, I'd be likely to notice. But if I want to notice the lesser cataclysms of valley life, I have to maintain in my head a running description of the present. It's not that I'm observant; it's just that I talk too much. Otherwise, especially

3. Pretension to esoteric spiritual knowledge.

in a strange place, I'll never know what's happening. Like a blind man at the ball game, I need a radio.

When I see this way I analyze and pry. I hurl over logs and roll away stones; I study the bank a square foot at a time, probing and tilting my head. Some days when a mist covers the mountains, when the muskrats won't show and the microscope's mirror shatters, I want to climb up the blank blue dome as a man would storm the inside of a circus tent, wildly, dangling, and with a steel knife claw a rent in the top, peep, and, if I must, fall.

But there is another kind of seeing that involves a letting go. When I see this way I sway transfixed and emptied. The difference between the two ways of seeing is the difference between walking with and without a camera. When I walk with a camera I walk from shot to shot, reading the light on a calibrated meter. When I walk without a camera, my own shutter opens, and the moment's light prints on my own silver gut. When I see this second way I am above all an unscrupulous observer.

It was sunny one evening last summer at Tinker Creek; the sun was low in the sky, upstream. I was sitting on the sycamore log bridge with the sunset at my back, watching the shiners the size of minnows who were feeding over the muddy sand in skittery schools. Again and again, one fish, then another, turned for a split second across the current and flash! the sun shot out from its silver side. I couldn't watch for it. It was always just happening somewhere else, and it drew my vision just as it disappeared: flash! like a sudden dazzle of the thinnest blade, a sparking over a dun and olive ground at chance intervals from every direction. Then I noticed white specks, some sort of pale petals, small, floating from under my feet on the creek's surface, very slow and steady. So I blurred my eyes and gazed toward the brim of my hat and saw a new world. I saw the pale white circles roll up, roll up, like the world's turning, mute and perfect, and I saw the linear flashes, gleaming silver, like stars being born at random down a rolling scroll of time. Something broke and something opened. I filled up like a new wineskin. I breathed an air like light; I saw a light like water. I was the lip of a fountain the creek filled forever; I was ether, the leaf in the zephyr; I was flesh-flake, feather, bone.

When I see this way I see truly. As Thoreau says, I return to my senses. I am the man who watches the baseball game in silence in an empty stadium. I see the game purely; I'm abstracted and dazed. When it's all over and the white-suited players lope off the green field to their shadowed dugouts, I leap to my feet, I cheer and cheer.

But I can't go out and try to see this way. I'll fail, I'll go mad. All I can do is try to gag the commentator, to hush the noise of useless interior babble that keeps me from seeing just as surely as a newspaper dangled before my eyes. The effort is really a discipline requiring a lifetime of dedicated struggle; it marks the literature of saints and monks of every order east and west, under every rule and no rule, discalced and shod. The world's spiritual geniuses seem to discover universally that the mind's muddy river, this ceaseless flow of trivia and trash, cannot be dammed, and that trying to dam it is a waste of effort that might lead to madness. Instead you must allow the muddy river to flow unheeded in the dim channels of consciousness; you raise your sights; you look along it, mildly, acknowledging its presence without interest and gazing beyond it into the realm of the real where subjects and objects act and rest purely, without utterance. "Launch into the deep," says Jacques Ellul, "and you shall see."

The secret of seeing, then, is the pearl of great price. If I thought he could teach me to find it and keep it forever I would stagger barefoot across a hundred deserts after any lunatic at all. But although the pearl may be found, it may not be sought. The literature of illumination reveals this above all: although it comes to those who wait for it, it is always, even to the most practiced and adept, a gift and a total surprise. I return from one walk knowing where the killdeer nests in the field by the creek and the hour the laurel blooms. I return from the same walk a day later scarcely knowing my own name. Litanies hum in my ears; my tongue flaps in my mouth, *Alim non*, alleluia! I cannot cause light; the most I can do is try to put myself in the path of its beam. It is possible, in deep space, to sail on solar wind. Light, be it particle or wave, has force: you rig a giant sail and go. The secret of seeing is to sail on solar wind. Hone and spread your spirit till you yourself are a sail, whetted, translucent, broadside to the merest puff.

When her doctor took her bandages off and led her into the garden, the girl who was no longer blind saw "the tree with the lights in it." It was for this tree I searched through the peach orchards of summer, in the forests of fall and down winter and spring for years. Then one day I was walking along Tinker Creek thinking of nothing at all and I saw the tree with the lights in it. I saw the backyard cedar where the mourning doves roost charged and transfigured, each cell buzzing with flame. I stood on the grass with the lights in it, grass that was wholly fire, utterly focused and utterly dreamed. It was less like seeing than like being for the first time seen, knocked breathless by a powerful glance. The flood of fire abated, but I'm still spending the power. Gradually the lights went out in the cedar, the colors died, the cells unflamed and disappeared. I was still ringing. I had been my whole life a bell, and never knew it until at that moment I was lifted and struck. I have since only very rarely seen the tree with the lights in it. The vision comes and goes, mostly goes, but I live for it, for the moment when the mountains open and a new light roars in spate through the crack, and the mountains slam.

QUESTIONS

1. Is the kind of seeing Dillard talks about at the end of her essay the same as that she talks about at the beginning?
2. What accounts for the intensity of her description of staying at the creek too late (pp. 1230–1231)?
3. How does Dillard establish her authority during the course of her argument?
4. Why is verbalization so important to seeing (p. 1235)?

JEAN-PAUL SARTRE

Existentialism

Man is nothing else but what he makes of himself. Such is the first principle of existentialism. It is also what is called subjectivity, the name we are labeled with when charges are brought against us. But what do we mean by this, if not that man has a greater dignity than a stone or table? For we mean that man first exists, that is, that man first of all is the being who hurls himself toward a future and who is conscious of imagining himself as being in the future. Man is at the start a plan which is aware of itself, rather than a patch of moss, a piece of garbage, or a cauliflower; nothing exists prior to this plan; there is nothing in heaven; man will be what he will have planned to be. Not what he will want to be. Because by the word "will" we generally mean a conscious decision, which is subsequent to what we have already made of ourselves. I may want to belong to a political party, write a book, get married; but all that is only a manifestation of an earlier, more spontaneous choice that is called "will." But if existence really does precede essence, man is responsible for what he is. Thus, existentialism's first move is to make every man aware of what he is and to make the full responsibility of his existence rest on him. And when we say that a man is responsible for himself, we do not only mean that he is responsible for his own individuality, but that he is responsible for all men.

The word "subjectivism" has two meanings, and our opponents play on the two. Subjectivism means, on the one hand, that an individual chooses and makes himself; and, on the other, that it is impossible for man to transcend human subjectivity. The second of these is the essential meaning of existentialism. When we say that man chooses his own self, we mean that every one of us does likewise; but we also mean by that that in making this choice he also chooses all men. In fact, in creating the man that we want to be, there is not a single one of our acts which does not at the same time create an image of man as we think he ought to be. To choose to be this or that is to affirm at the same time the value of what we choose, because we can never choose evil. We always choose the good, and nothing can be good for us without being good for all.

If, on the other hand, existence precedes essence, and if we grant that we exist and fashion our image at one and the same time, the image is valid for everybody and for our whole age. Thus, our responsibility is much greater than we might have supposed, because it involves all mankind. If I am a workingman and choose to join a Christian trade union rather than be a Communist, and if by being a member I want to show that the best thing for man is resignation, that the kingdom of man is not of this world, I am not only involving my own case—I want to be resigned for everyone. As a result, my action has involved all humanity. To take a more individual matter, if I want to marry, to have children, even it this marriage depends solely on my own circumstances or passion or wish, I am involving all humanity in monogamy and not merely myself. Therefore, I am responsible for myself and for everyone else. I am creating a certain image of man of my own choosing. In choosing myself, I choose man.

This helps us understand what the actual content is of such rather grandiloquent words as anguish, forlornness, despair. As you will see, it's all quite simple.

First, what is meant by anguish? The existentialists say at once that man is anguish. What that means is this: the man who involves himself and who realizes that he is not only the person he chooses to be, but also a lawmaker who is, at the same time, choosing all mankind as well as himself, cannot help escape the feeling of his total and deep responsibility. Of course, there are many people who are not anxious; but we claim that they are hiding their anxiety, that they are fleeing from it. Certainly, many people believe that when they do something, they themselves are the only ones involved, and when someone says to them, "What if everyone acted that way?" they shrug their shoulders and answer, "Everyone doesn't act that way." But really, one should always ask himself, "What would happen if everybody looked at things that way?" There is no escaping this disturbing thought except by a kind of double-dealing. A man who lies and makes excuses for himself by saying "not everybody does that," is someone with an uneasy conscience, because the act of lying implies that a universal value is conferred upon the lie.

Anguish is evident even when it conceals itself. This is the anguish that Kierkegaard called the anguish of Abraham. You know the story: an angel has ordered Abraham to sacrifice his son; if it really were an angel who has come and said, "You are Abraham, you shall sacrifice your son," everything would be all right. But everyone might first wonder, "Is it really an angel, and am I really Abraham? What proof do I have?"

There was a madwoman who had hallucinations; someone used to speak to her on the telephone and give her orders. Her doctor asked her, "Who is it who talks to you?" She answered, "He says it's God." What proof did she really have that it was God? If an angel comes to me, what proof is there that it's an angel? And if I hear voices, what proof is there that they come from heaven and not from hell, or from the subconscious, or a pathological condition? What proves that they are addressed to me? What proof is there that I have been appointed to impose my choice and my conception of man on humanity? I'll never find any proof or sign to convince me of that. If a voice addresses me, it is always for me to decide that this is the angel's voice; if I consider that such an act is a good one, it is I who will choose to say that it is good rather than bad.

Now, I'm not being singled out as an Abraham, and yet at every moment I'm obliged to perform exemplary acts. For every man, everything happens as if all mankind had its eyes fixed on him and were guiding itself by what he does. And every man ought to say to himself, "Am I really the kind of man who has the right to act in such a way that humanity might guide itself by my actions?" And if he does not say that to himself, he is masking his anguish.

There is no question here of the kind of anguish which would lead to quietism, to inaction. It is a matter of a simple sort of anguish that anybody who has had responsibilities is familiar with. For example, when a military officer takes the responsibility for an attack and sends a certain number of men to death, he chooses to do so, and in the main he alone makes the choice. Doubtless, orders come from above, but they are too broad; he interprets them, and on this interpretation depend the lives of ten or fourteen or twenty men. In making a decision he cannot help having a certain anguish. All leaders know this anguish. That doesn't keep them from acting; on the contrary, it is the very condition of their action. For it implies that they envisage a number of possibilities, and when they choose one, they realize that it has value only because it is chosen. We shall see that this kind of anguish, which is the kind that existentialism describes, is explained, in addition, by a direct responsibility to the other men whom it involves. It is not a curtain separating us from action, but is part of action itself.

When we speak of forlornness, a term Heidegger was fond of, we mean only that God does not exist and that we have to face all the consequences of this. This existentialist is strongly opposed to a certain kind of secular ethics which would like to abolish God with the least possible expense. About 1880, some French teachers tried to set up a secular ethics which went something like this: God is a useless and costly hypothesis; we are discarding it; but, meanwhile, in order for there to be an ethics, a society, a civilization, it is essential that certain values be taken seriously and that they be considered as having an *a priori* existence. It must be obligatory, a *priori*, to be honest, not to lie, not to beat your wife, to have children, etc., etc. So we're going to try a little device which will make it possible to show that values exist all the same, inscribed in a heaven of ideas, though otherwise God does not exist. In other words—and this, I believe, is the tendency of everything called reformism in France— nothing will be changed if God does not exist. We shall find ourselves with the same norms of honesty, progress, and humanism, and we shall have made of God an outdated hypothesis which will peacefully die off by itself.

The existentialist, on the contrary, thinks it very distressing that God does not exist, because all possibility of finding values in a heaven of ideas disappears along with Him; there can no longer be an *a priori* Good, since there is no infinite and perfect consciousness to think it. Nowhere is it written that the Good exists, that we must be honest, that we must not lie; because the fact is we are on a plane where there are only men. Dostoievsky said, "If God didn't exist, everything would be possible." That is the very starting point of existentialism. Indeed, everything is permissible if God does not exist, and as a result man is forlorn, because neither within him nor without does he find anything to cling to. He can't start making excuses for himself.

If existence really does precede essence, there is no explaining things away by reference to a fixed and given human nature. In other words, there is no determinism, man is free, man is freedom. On the other hand, if God does not exist, we find no values or commands to turn to which legitimize our conduct. So, in the bright realm of values, we have no excuse behind us, nor justification before us. We are alone, with no excuses.

That is the idea I shall try to convey when I say that man is condemned to be free. Condemned, because he did not create himself, yet, in other respects is free; because, once thrown into the world, he is responsible for everything he does. The existentialist does not believe in the power of passion. He will never agree that a sweeping passion is a ravaging torrent which fatally leads a man to certain acts and is therefore an excuse. He thinks that man is responsible for his passion.

The existentialist does not think that man is going to help himself by finding in the world some omen by which to orient himself. Because he thinks that man will interpret the omen to suit himself. Therefore, he thinks that man, with no support and no aid, is condemned every moment to invent man. Ponge, in a very fine article, has said, "Man is the future of man." That's exactly it. But if it is taken to mean that this future is recorded in heaven, that God sees it, then it is false, because it would really no longer be a future. If it is taken to mean that, whatever a man may be, there is a future to be forged, a virgin future before him, then this remark is sound. But then we are forlorn.

To give you an example which will enable you to understand forlornness better, I shall cite the case of one of my students who came to see me under the following circumstances: his father was on bad terms with his mother, and, moreover, was inclined to be a collaborationist; his older brother had been killed in the German offensive of 1940, and the young man, with somewhat immature but generous feelings, wanted to avenge him. His mother lived alone with him, very much upset by the half-treason of her husband and the death of her older son; the boy was her only consolation.

The boy was faced with the choice of leaving for England and joining the Free French forces—that is, leaving his mother behind —or remaining with his mother and helping her to carry on. He was fully aware that the woman lived only for him and that his going off—and perhaps his death—would plunge her into despair. He was also aware that every act that he did for his mother's sake was a sure thing, in the sense that it was helping her to carry on, whereas every effort he made toward going off and fighting was an uncertain move which might run aground and prove completely useless; for example, on his way to England he might, while passing through Spain, be detained indefinitely in a Spanish camp; he might reach England or Algiers and be stuck in an office at a desk job. As a result, he was faced with two very different kinds of action: one, concrete, immediate, but concerning only one individual; the other concerned an incomparably vaster group, a national collectivity, but for that very reason was dubious, and might be interrupted en route. And, at the same time, he was wavering between two kinds of ethics. On the one hand, an ethics of sympathy, of personal devotion; on the other, a broader ethics, but one whose efficacy was more dubious. He had to choose between the two.

Who could help him choose? Christian doctrine? No. Christian doctrine says, "Be charitable, love your neighbor, take the more rugged path, etc., etc." But which is the more rugged path? Whom should he love as a brother? The fighting man or his mother? Which does the greater good, the vague act of fighting in a group, or the concrete one of helping a particular human being to go on living? Who can decide *a priori*? Nobody. No book of ethics can tell him. The Kantian ethics says, "Never treat any person as a means, but as an end." Very well, if I stay with my mother, I'll treat her as an end and not as a means; but by virtue of this very fact, I'm running the risk of treating the people around me who are fighting, as means; and, conversely, if I go to join those who are fighting, I'll be treating them as an end, and, by doing that, I run the risk of treating my mother as a means.

If values are vague, and if they are always too broad for the concrete and specific case that we are considering, the only thing left for us is to trust our instincts. That's what this young man tried to do; and when I saw him, he said, "In the end, feeling is what counts. I ought to choose whichever pushes me in one direction. If I feel that I love my mother enough to sacrifice everything else for her—my desire for vengeance, for action, for adventure—then I'll stay with her. If, on the contrary, I feel that my love for my mother isn't enough, I'll leave."

But how is the value of a feeling determined? What gives his feeling for his mother value? Precisely the fact that he remained with her. I may say that I like so-and-so well enough to sacrifice a certain amount of money for him, but I may say so only if I've done it. I may say "I love my mother well enough to remain with her" if I have remained with her. The only way to determine the value of this affection is, precisely, to perform an act which confirms and defines it. But, since I require this affection to justify my act, I find myself caught in a vicious circle.

On the other hand, Gide has well said that a mock feeling and a true feeling are almost indistinguishable; to decide that I love my mother and will remain with her, or to remain with her by putting on an act, amount somewhat to the same thing. In other words, the feeling is formed by the acts one performs; so, I cannot refer to it in order to act upon it. Which means that I can neither seek within myself the true condition which will impel me to act, nor apply to a system of ethics for concepts which will permit me to act. You will say, "At least, he did go to a teacher for advice." But if you seek advice from a priest, for example, you have chosen this priest; you already knew, more or less, just about what advice he was going to give you. In other words, choosing your adviser is involving yourself. The proof of this is that if you are a Christian, you will say, "Consult a priest." But some priests are collaborating, some are just marking time, some are resisting. Which to choose? If the young man chooses a priest who is resisting or collaborating, he has already decided on the kind of advice he's going to get. Therefore, in coming to see me he knew the answer I was going to give him, and I had only one answer to give: "You're free, choose, that is, invent." No general ethics can show you what is to be done; there are no omens in the world. The Catholics will reply, "But there are." Granted —but, in any case, I myself choose the meaning they have.

When I was a prisoner, I knew a rather remarkable young man who was a Jesuit. He had entered the Jesuit order in the following way: he had had a number of very bad breaks; in childhood, his father died, leaving him in poverty, and he was a scholarship student at a religious institution where he was constantly made to feel that he was being kept out of charity; then, he failed to get any of the honors and distinctions that children like; later on, at about eighteen, he bungled a love affair; finally, at twenty-two, he failed in military training, a childish enough matter, but it was the last straw.

This young fellow might well have felt that he had botched everything. It was a sign of something, but of what? He might have taken refuge in bitterness or despair. But he very wisely looked upon all this as a sign that he was not made for secular triumphs, and that only the triumphs of religion, holiness, and faith were open to him. He saw the hand of God in all this, and so he entered the order. Who can help seeing that he alone decided what the sign meant?

Some other interpretation might have been drawn from this series of setbacks; for example, that he might have done better to turn carpenter or revolutionist. Therefore, he is fully responsible for the interpretation. Forlornness implies that we ourselves choose our being. Forlornness and anguish go together.

As for despair, the term has a very simple meaning. It means that we shall confine ourselves to reckoning only with what depends upon our will, or on the ensemble of probabilities which make our action possible. When we want something, we always have to reckon with probabilities. I may be counting on the arrival of a friend. The friend is coming by rail or streetcar; this supposes that the train will arrive on schedule, or that the streetcar will not jump the track. I am left in the realm of possibility; but possibilities are to be reckoned with only to the point where my action comports with the ensemble of these possibilities, and no further. The moment the possibilities I am considering are not rigorously involved by my action, I ought to disengage myself from them, because no God, no scheme, can adapt the world and its possibilities to my will. When Descartes said, "Conquer yourself rather than the world," he meant essentially the same thing.

The Marxists to whom I have spoken reply, "You can rely on the support of others in your action, which obviously has certain limits because you're not going to live forever. That means: rely on both what others are doing elsewhere to help you, in China, in Russia, and what they will do later on, after your death, to carry on the action and lead it to its fulfillment, which will be the revolution. You even *have* to rely upon that, otherwise you're immoral." I reply at once that I will always rely on fellow-fighters insofar as these comrades are involved with me in a common struggle, in the unity of a party or a group in which I can more or less make my weight felt; that is, one whose ranks I am in as a fighter and whose movements I am aware of at every moment. In such a situation, relying on the unity and will of the party is exactly like counting on the fact that the train will arrive on time or that the car won't jump the track. But, given that man is free and that there is no human nature for me to depend on, I cannot count on men whom I do not know by relying on human goodness or man's concern for the good of society. I don't know what will become of the Russian revolution; I may make an example of it to the extent that at the present time it is apparent that the proletariat plays a part in Russia that it plays in no other nation. But I can't swear that this will inevitably lead to a triumph of the proletariat. I've got to limit myself to what I see.

Given that men are free and that tomorrow they will freely decide what man will be, I cannot be sure that, after my death, fellow-fighters will carry on my work to bring it to its maximum perfection. Tomorrow, after my death, some men may decide to set up Fascism, and the others may be cowardly and muddled enough to let them do it. Fascism will then be the human reality, so much the worse for us.

Actually, things will be as man will have decided they are to be. Does that mean that I should abandon myself to quietism? No. First, I should involve myself; then, act on the old saw, "Nothing ventured, nothing gained." Nor does it mean that I shouldn't belong to a party, but rather that I shall have no illusions and shall do what I can. For example, suppose I ask myself, "Will socialization, as such, ever come about?" I know nothing about it. All I know is that I'm going to do everything in my power to bring it about. Beyond that, I can't count on anything. Quietism is the attitude of people who say, "Let others do what I can't do." The doctrine I am presenting is the very opposite of quietism, since it declares, "There is no reality except in action." Moreover, it goes further, since it adds, "Man is nothing else than his plan; he exists only to the extent that he fulfills himself; he is therefore nothing else than the ensemble of his acts, nothing else than his life."

According to this, we can understand why our doctrine horrifies certain people. Because often the only way they can bear their wretchedness is to think, "Circumstances have been against me. What I've been and done doesn't show my true worth. To be sure, I've had no great love, no great friendship, but that's because I haven't met a man or woman who was worthy. The books I've written haven't been very good because I haven't had the proper leisure. I haven't had children to devote myself to because I didn't find a man with whom I could have spent my life. So there remains within me, unused and quite viable, a host of propensities, inclinations, possibilities, that one wouldn't guess from the mere series of things I've done."

Now, for the existentialist there is really no love other than one which manifests itself in a person's being in love. There is no genius other than one which is expressed in works of art; the genius of Proust is the sum of Proust's works; the genius of Racine is his series of tragedies. Outside of that, there is nothing. Why say that Racine could have written another tragedy, when he didn't write it? A man is involved in life, leaves his impress on it, and outside of that there is nothing. To be sure, this may seem a harsh thought to someone whose life hasn't been a success. But, on the other hand, it prompts people to understand that reality alone is what counts, that dreams, expectations, and hopes warrant no more than to define a man as a disappointed dream, as miscarried hopes, as vain expectations. In other words, to define him negatively and not positively. However, when we say, "You are nothing else than your life," that does not imply that the artist will be judged solely on the basis of his works of art; a thousand other things will contribute toward summing him up. What we mean is that a man is nothing else than a series of undertakings, that he is the sum, the organization, the ensemble of the relationships which make up these undertakings.

When all is said and done, what we are accused of, at bottom, is not our pessimism, but an optimistic toughness. If people throw up to us our works of fiction in which we write about people who are soft, weak, cowardly, and sometimes even downright bad, it's not because these prople are soft, weak, cowardly, or bad; because if we were to say, as Zola did, that they are that way because of heredity, the workings of environment, society, because of biological or psychological determinism, people would be reassured. They would say, "Well, that's what we're like, no one can do anything about it." But when the existentialist writes about a coward, he says that this coward is responsible for his cowardice. He's not like that because he has a cowardly heart or lung or brain; he's not like that on account of his physiological make-up; but he's like that because he has made himself a coward by his acts. There's no such thing as a cowardly constitution; there are nervous constitutions; there is poor blood, as the common people say, or strong constitutions. But the man whose blood is poor is not a coward on that account, for what makes cowardice is the act of renouncing or yielding. A constitution is·not an act; the coward is defined on the basis of the acts he performs. People feel, in a vague sort of way, that this coward we're talking about is guilty of being a coward, and the thought frightens them. What people would like is that a coward or a hero be born that way. . . .

From these few reflections it is evident that nothing is more unjust than the objections that have been raised against us. Existentialism is nothing else than an attempt to draw all the consequences of a coherent atheistic position. It isn't trying to plunge man into despair at all. But if one calls every attitude of unbelief despair, like the Christians, then the word is not being used in its original sense. Existentialism isn't so atheistic that it wears itself out showing that God doesn't exist. Rather, it declares that even if God did exist, that would change nothing. There you've got our point of view. Not that we believe that God exists, but we think that the problem of His existence is not the issue. In this sense existentialism is optimistic, a doctrine of action, and it is plain dishonesty for Christians to make no distinction between their own despair and ours˙and then to call us despairing.

QUESTIONS

1. What are some of the methods or devices Sartre uses to define existentialism? Why does he use more than one method or device? Compare the techniques that Sartre uses with those Knox uses in defining enthusiasm (pp. 1158–1160) or those Highet uses in defining Zen (pp. 1202–1211).
2. What is the significance of the words "if existence really does precede essence"? What does this mean? What is the force of "if"? Why does Sartre repeat the words later in the essay?
3. Why does Sartre use three separate terms—anguish, forlornness, despair? What, if any, are the differences among them?
4. Sartre makes a distinction between treating "any person as a means . . . [and] as an end" (p. 1242). What are the implications of this distinction?
5. Sartre says that the "coward is responsible for his cowardice," since man "is defined on the basis of the acts he performs." Does this notion of responsibility agree with that of Henry Sloane Coffin in "What Crucified Christ?" (pp. 1184–1199)?

RICHARD B. SEWALL

A Sense of the Ending[1]

The last time I appeared on this stage[2] was in a minor part in a Cap and Bells production of *Much Ado About Nothing*. I was Friar Francis. I had nine speeches—six one-liners and two big juicy ones. The two big ones were full of wisdom and sound advice, as befits a friar—or, indeed, a convocation speaker. I read the Friar's part through the other day, to get myself in the spirit of this platform again and perhaps to recall a little bit of the old undergraduate glory. As a matter of fact, for me, it was anything but glorious. My timing was bad on the one-liners, and the big speeches fell curiously flat. Frankly, I don't think I understood them then. But I know more about Shakespeare (and a few other things) now; and, as I read those lines over, they hit me at 67 as they never did at 17. Listen to Friar Francis trying to get his listeners to accept something he feels deeply—in this case, his belief in the innocence of a slandered young lady. One can feel his frustration in every word:

1. Adapted for the *Williams Alumni Review*, Fall 1975. From a convocation address, delivered at Williams College, Williamstown, Mass.
2. As an undergraduate at Williams College.

> Call me a fool;
> Trust not my reading nor my observations,
> Which with experimental seal doth warrant
> The tenour of my book; trust not my age,
> My reverence, calling, nor divinity,
> If this sweet lady lie not guiltless here
> Under some biting error.

Fifty years (between 17 and 67) make a lot of difference, and now at last I know what the Friar felt: the frustration of trying to convey something you feel deeply to an audience that is either skeptical or uninvolved. The Friar put my difficulty plainly, even if it is not quite the same as his. I want to talk to you today about matters which cannot be to you as intensely personal as they are to me; I'm involved as you cannot be, and I cannot bridge the gap by the triumphant march of logic, by statistics, by hard evidence. I want to share with you, simply, a bit of experience I've picked up on the way.

Oh, there are lots of "biting errors" I could expose, were my mood so inclined: educational fallacies rampant in my own beloved New Haven and right here in Williamstown; the sinister drift of our national culture and politics and economy; the global threats to our environment and our peace. I could scare you to death! Or, changing the tune, as appropriate to this day, I could talk about the library as the beating heart of this or any other educational institution. I could talk about Jack Sawyer and all he did for this college. But although all these possibilities are close to my mind and heart, they are not closest, and I decided I must talk about what is closest or I'd better not talk at all. What is closest? Just two things, intimately bound, almost inseparable: love and death.

Shortly after I came to this decision, I ran across a remark by William Butler Yeats. "I am still of the opinion," he wrote, "that only two topics can be of the least interest to a serious and studious mind—sex and death." My first thought was: What a stuffy way to put it! And my second was: Why be so glandular? Why sex and death? I prefer my way of putting it, and Woody Allen's: love and death. I don't intend to be clinical about either, and I am not addressing the "serious and studious mind." I am talking to you as fellow pilgrims—old, middle-aged and young—in this vale of tears and laughter. And I want to share with you a little of what I've learned this past year—I would say the most educational year of my life, the high-water mark of my experience as a human being.

I guess you'll have to know the facts: My wife, Mathilde, died of cancer of the pancreas last November, and my brother John (Williams '28) was killed in a car accident last March. With all the tragedy in the world, you may wonder at my bringing up these two personal losses. It may seem a little impudent of me, even a little embarrassing. "They talk of hallowed things aloud," said Emily Dickinson, trying to explain her aversion to society, "and embarrass my dog." But she was young when she said that. She clammed up, and she was wrong. She was too easily embarrassed.

So here's the first and perhaps simplest thing I've learned this past year: Never be embarrassed to talk about hallowed things, like love and death. We Americans are a little finicky about both. We reduce love to sex and talk about it clinically as in Kinsey and the sex books, or grossly as in *Playboy* and *Penthouse,* or sentimentally as in the popular songs. There's very little talk about the tragic side of love, the comic side of love, love as a discipline, love as a means of education, love as the end and aim of education, the very reason we're here today.

And as for death, we hide from it, pretty it up, pack it away in hospitals, spend millions every year on lavish funerals, or get so glutted with it over the media that we hear or read, with hardly a tremor, about hundreds of thousands dying in Vietnam, or Africa, or Bangladesh. The result is that death is hardly real at all to us. It's a forbidden subject except at funerals and in sermons that aim to take away its sting. I think we'd be better able to cope with it if we talked about it more, if we shared our experience of it more frankly. And so I'm facing you with it—ironically, on this festive occasion, this day of a new beginning when the last thing you want to hear about is the old, old ending.

Which leads me to the second thing I've learned this past year: It's a sense of the ending that makes the beginning, and all that follows therefrom, so much more meaningful. Why deny a reality that, paradoxically, can be so life giving, so enriching?

I heard the other day of a great-great-grandmother who—this was generations ago—amazed her family by announcing one morning: "I want to die in that rocking chair, and I'm going to close my own eyes." She did both. Her name was Experience Bardwell Lyman. The young people called her "Aunt Speedie," and a hundred years later her descendants are still talking and laughing about her and living a little more fully because of her. I wonder if this is what Wallace Stevens had in mind when he wrote, "Death is the mother of beauty."

Her great-grandchildren still point to that rocker. Aunt Speedie knew how to die and how to talk about it. She had a sense of her ending—clear-eyed, frank, unabashed, humorous. My friend Emily Dickinson knew how to talk about it, too—in her poetry:

> By a departing light
> We see acuter, quite,
> Than by a wick that stays.
> There's something in the flight
> That clarifies the sight
> And decks the rays.

"There's something in the flight/That clarifies the sight . . ." or, in the words of the old hymn, takes "The dimness of our souls away." Why do things get so dim and unclear? Going along in the old routine, we get in a kind of acquiescent numbness, we get used to things, we don't see sharply or hear clearly or feel intensely.

I had a teacher of creative writing once who told our class, "You must look at things not only as if you were seeing them for the first time but as if you were seeing them for the last time, as if you were never to see them again and had to take them all in and remember them forever." Keep that in mind the next time you look around at these hills. Never, never get used to them!

We need to be jolted out of our numbness, often not so gently as my teacher did it. "Such men as I," cried Dmitri Karamazov, "need a blow . . ." and he spoke for the whole human race. Sometimes nothing but death will remind us that we are alive. That's a terrible thing to say, but it's true.

Love and death . . . What has tortured me these past ten months since Mathilde died are the things I didn't say, the love I didn't express. Why was I so dim, so finicky, so inhibited, so embarrassed? Or were the look in the eyes enough, the squeeze of the hand, the kiss on the brow? I hope to God they were. Heaven knows she was up to anything. She had nerve for both of us. She and Aunt Speedie would have gotten along fine. A week before she died, I came in her room wearing a new dark-green shirt under an old greenish tweed jacket. "They were made for each other," she said. "You could wear them anywhere—even my funeral." Which I did.

The evening of the night she died, she was hilarious, never wittier, and (as always) a bit of a rascal. She ribbed her doctor about what a lousy skier he was. When a friend asked her why she couldn't eat a bit of the lovely cheese cake she'd brought her, she replied, "Because, my dear, I have a touch of cancer."

It was at the time those three doctors went to examine Nixon in San Clemente to see if he was well enough to testify. In my then state of compassion, I averred as how it was tough on the poor man to have to go through all that examination again. Our cheese-cake friend, a veteran Nixon-hater, said, "Nonsense! Nothing is bad enough for that man," etc., etc. "No," said Mathilde, looking quite saintly on her sickbed, "you're wrong. I'm so full of love I can't wish harm on any one." And with a twinkle she added, "You know, if I should get well, I think I'd be rather nice." ("Death is the mother of beauty.")

Then another friend said, "Tillie, when you get well, I want you to make me one of those saints." (Til was a potter, I should tell you, and did ceramic sculpture. One of her favorite themes was St. Francis and the birds.) "Evaline," she answered, "if I get well, I'll make nothing but saints." Six hours later she was dead. Aunt Speedie was one up on her: Mathilde didn't close her own eyes. Will it shock you—it shouldn't by now—when I tell you that I closed them? It was very simple, very sad and very beautiful.

Love and death . . . It's clear to me that the closer she came to death, the more she learned to love and the more she learned *about* love—and the more she taught us both *to love* and *about love.* The departing light clarified the sight—in all of us. She knew where she was going, and she knew what she was learning, and she talked about it. "These last three months," she told her doctor a few weeks before the end, "have been the best of my life. I wouldn't have missed them for anything."

To understand more fully this remarkable statement, you must hear the last letter she ever wrote. It was to a friend, Holly Tuttle of New Haven, who lost her husband some years ago. The letter says more about love and death than I could in a week of convocation addresses. It's more than just a letter; it's a document. And I read it to you with no embarrassment at all. Remember: "There's something in the flight/That clarifies the sight." All things—individual lives, colleges, libraries, college educations—take on new meaning in the light of their endings—or when they end for you, as they must. *Love them while you can,* and never, never be embarrassed.

And now here's the letter, and I'm done:

DEAR HOLLY—You sent me such a good letter—I do want to answer— The problem of dealing with this fellow Death has been interesting (funny—what would woman's lib. say to my making Death masculine— surely I can't think of myself being swept up by a lady). In the first place—when I saw him come striding up to my house—garbed in all his strange garments that we humans have wished on him—I wasn't in the least spooked. I opened the door and we had a nice little chat, Subsequent chats have been reassuring and I know he's my good friend. I'm sure you too have a nodding acquaintance with him so you have the same feelings.

Then there's LOVE. I feel I'd never have known its endless horizons had I lived out my full span. Somehow in a smooth life we take each other for granted and now even with someone like Richard new little vistas open up—and with casual acquaintances—whole worlds. My plumber—Tommy Citerella—stopped in to see me after he'd attended to my drips and leaks—sat down and looked out at the view I have from my bed—a valley—a mill house—a waterfall—a lake—all hung in the most sensational color—

"Missus" he said—"you have to have faith. You have to pray. God's never failed me. He's saved me three times."

"Tommy," I said, "I don't know where to aim my prayers. God is such a mystery."

"Missus," he said, "don't worry. I'll take over all the praying"—and he took my two hands and leaned down and kissed me on the brow.

So now—what do I have to worry about?

LOVE, TIL

Death is the mother of beauty . . . a sense of the ending. Do you see what I mean?

Notes on Composition

Saying Something That Matters

There is no point in the hard labor of writing unless you expect to *do* something to somebody—perhaps add to his store of information, perhaps cause him to change his mind on some issue that you care about. Determining just what that something is is half the battle; hence the importance of knowing your main point, your central purpose in writing, your **thesis**. It may seem that this step—perhaps in the form of a "thesis sentence" or exact statement of the main point—is inevitably prior to everything else in writing, but in actual practice the case is more complicated. Few good writers attain a final grasp of their thesis until they have tried setting down their first halting ideas at some length; to put it another way, you discover more precisely what it is you have to say in the act of trying to say it. Formulating and refining upon a thesis sentence as you work your way through a piece of writing helps you see what needs to be done at each stage; the finished piece, though, instead of announcing its thesis in any one sentence, may simply imply it by the fact of its unity, the determinate way the parts hang together. There is probably no single sentence in E. B. White's "Once More to the Lake" (p. 84) that will serve satisfactorily to represent the entire essay in miniature, yet clearly such a sentence could be formulated: The pleasure of recapturing the past is heavily qualified by an adult awareness of the inevitability of change. But whether you state the main point or leave it to be inferred, you need to decide what your piece is about, what you want to say about it, why, and to whom.

Sometimes a thesis will rest on a good many **assumptions**, related ideas that the writer may not mention but depends upon his reader to understand and agree to (if he is an honest writer) or to overlook and hence fail to reject (if his real purpose is to mislead). Machiavelli (p. 852) appears to assume that it is more important for a prince to stay in power than to be a "good" man. We may feel the question is highly ambiguous, or we may disagree sharply. But even if we decide, finally, that we can live with Machiavelli's assumption, we shall have acquired a fuller understanding of what he is saying, and of our own relationship to it, for having scrutinized what is being taken for granted. The habit of scrutiny guards us against the careless or cunning writer whose unstated assumptions may be highly questionable. The same habit, turned on our own minds when we become writers, can save us from the unthinking use of assumptions that we would be hard pressed to defend.

Some theses lend themselves to verification by laboratory methods or the like; they deal with **questions of fact**. The exact order of composition of Shakespeare's plays could conceivably be settled finally if new evidence turned up. Whether or not the plays are great literature, on the other hand, is a **question of opinion**; agreement (though not hard to reach in this instance) depends on the weighing of arguments rather than on tests or measurements. Not that all theses can be neatly classified as assertions either of fact or of opinion (consider "Shakespeare's influence has been greater than Newton's"); still the attempt to classify his own effort can help a writer understand what he is doing.

Sometimes a writer addresses himself more specifically to his readers' **understanding**, sometimes he addresses himself chiefly to their **emotions**. Although the process of thinking and of feeling are almost always mixed, still it is obvious that a description of a chemical process and a description of a candidate you hope to see elected to office will differ considerably in tone and emphasis. Accordingly you need to give some thought to the kind of result you hope to produce: perhaps simply an addition of information, perhaps a change of attitude, perhaps a commitment of the will to action.

The Means of Saying It

No worthwhile thesis comes without work, and the work of arriving at a thesis is much like the work of writing itself—developing, elaborating, refining upon an idea that is perhaps at first hazy. For convenience the process may be divided into setting bounds, or defining; marshaling evidence; and drawing conclusions.

DEFINING in a broad sense may be thought of as what you do to answer the question "What do you mean?" It sets bounds by doing two things to an idea: grouping it with others like it and showing how it differs from those others. "An island is a tract of land" (like a lot of prairie or peninsula) "completely surrounded by water and too small to be called a continent" (and therefore different from a lot, etc.). This process of classifying and distinguishing may take many forms, depending on the kind of thing you are dealing with and your reason for doing so. (Artifacts, for example, can hardly be defined without reference to purpose; a lock is a device *for securing* a door; a theodolite is an instrument used to *measure* horizontal or vertical angles). Some of the standard methods are these: by giving **examples**, pointing to an instance as a short way of indicating class and individual characteristics ("*That* is a firebreak"; "A liberal is a man like Jefferson"); by **negating**, explaining what your subject is *not*—i.e., process of elimination ("Love vaunteth not itself, is not puffed up"); by **comparing and contrasting**, noting the resemblances and differences between your subject and something else ("A magazine is sometimes as big as a book but differs in binding and layout"); by **analyzing**, breaking down a whole into its constituent parts ("A play may be seen as exposition, rising action, and denouement"); by seeking a **cause** of the thing in question or an **effect** that it has produced ("Scurvy is the result of a dietary deficiency and often leads to anemia"); or by attributing to a thing an **end** or **means**, seeing it as a way of fulfilling purpose or as the fulfillment of a purpose ("Representation is the end of the electoral system and the means to good government").

When we turn to specimens of writing, we see immediately that the various methods of defining may serve not only for one-sentence "dictionary" definitions but also as methods of organizing paragraphs or even whole essays, where unfolding the subject is in a sense "defining" it, showing where its boundaries lie. Philip Slater (p. 520) draws an extended comparison between two cultures in an attempt to show the necessity of change and the direction it should take. William Golding (p. 127) analyzes thought in general into three distinct "grades" as he recounts his own intellectual development as a schoolboy. The choice of method in the above examples, it will be noted, is not random; each author selects according to his purpose in writing, and what suits one purpose exactly might be exactly wrong for another.

MARSHALING EVIDENCE. Once you have said what you mean, the next question is likely to be "How do you know?" Marshaling evidence may be thought of as what you do to answer that question. Where the matter at hand involves questions of fact, **factual evidence** will be most directly appropriate. (A diary, a letter—perhaps a cryptogram hidden in the text—might prove even to die-hard Baconians that Shakespeare himself did in fact write the plays which have been credited to him). Writers on scientific subjects inevitably draw chiefly on facts, often intricately arrayed, to support their conclusions. But it should not be assumed that factual evidence turns up mainly in scientific writing. Dee Brown's account (p. 911) of the war for the Black Hills is obviously based on facts in the form of historical documents. Anthony Burgess (p. 514), adopting a less direct strategy, adduces many familiar facts that seem to point to the imminent breakdown of American society, but then, through a combination of factual and other kinds of evidence, tries to show that such signs are misleading.

Factual evidence is generally thought to carry more weight than any other kind, though the force of a fact is greatly diminished if it is not easily verifiable or attested to by reliable witnesses. Where factual evidence is hard to come by (consider the problems of proving that Bacon did not write Shakespeare's plays), the opinion of **authorities** is often invoked, on the assumption that the men most knowledgeable in a field are most likely to judge truly in a particular case. The testimony of authorities is relevant, of course, not only in questions of fact but also in questions of opinion. Francis Bacon (p. 279), for example, invokes Solomon and Job to support his ideas about revenge. In general, however, the appeal to authority in matters of opinion has lost the rhetorical effectiveness it once had, perhaps because there is less agreement as to who the reliable authorities are.

As changes in the nature of the question draw in a larger and larger number of "authorities," evidence from authority shades into what might be called "the **common consent** of mankind," those generalizations about human experience that large numbers of readers can be counted upon to accept and that often find expression in proverbs or apothegms: "Risk no more than you can afford to lose" and "The first step toward Hell is halfway there." Such generalizations, whether proverbial or not, are a common ground on which writer and reader meet in agreement. The writer's task is to find and present the ones applicable to his particular thesis and then demonstrate that applicability.

DRAWING CONCLUSIONS. One of the ways of determining the consequences of thought—that is, drawing conclusions—is the process of applying generalizations (**deduction**): "If we should risk no more than we can afford to lose, then we had better not jeopardize the independence of our universities by seeking federal aid." Another way of arriving at conclusions is the process of **induction**, which consists in forming generalizations from a sufficient number of observed instances: "Since universities A, B, and C have been accepting federal aid through research grants for years without loss of independence, it is probably safe for any university to do so." Typically deduction and induction work reciprocally, each helping to supply for the other the materials upon which inference operates. We induce from experience that green apples are sour; we deduce from this generalization that a particular green apple is sour. A third kind of inference, sometimes regarded as only a special kind of deduction or induction, is **analogy**, the process of concluding that two things which resemble each other in one way will resemble each other in another way also: "Federal aid has benefited mental hospitals enormously, and will probaby benefit universities just as much." An analogy proves nothing, although it may help the reader see the reasonableness of an idea and is often extremely valuable for purposes of illustration, since it makes an unknown clearer by relating it to a known.

Turning to our essays, we can see something of the variety of ways in which these three kinds of inference manifest themselves in serious writing: Samuel Johnson (p. 280) deducing from men's customary unwillingness to pay more than a thing is worth the conclusion that the pyramids are a monument to human vanity; Wallace Stegner arguing from a series of particular instances to the general conclusion that a community may be judged by what it throws away (p. 6); Radcliffe Squires suggesting the nature of a blockage in the unconscious creative process by likening it to what happens when "rapid eye-movement" sleep is persistently interrupted (p. 370).

Such a list of examples suggests that in good writing the conclusions the writer draws, the consequences of his thought, are "consequential" in more than one sense: not only do they follow logically from the evidence has has considered, they are also *significant*; they relate directly or indirectly to aspects of our lives that we care about. To the questions suggested earlier as demands for definition and evidence, then, we must add a third. "What do you mean?" calls for precision yet admits answers vast in scope. "How do you know?" trims the vastness down to what can be substantiated but may settle for triviality as the price of certainty. The appropriate question to raise finally, then, is simply "So what?" and the conclusions we as writers draw need to be significant enough to yield answers to that question. We have come full circle back to the idea of saying something that matters.

And the Style

One theory of style in writing sees form and content as distinct: style is the way a thing is said, the thing itself an unchanging substance that can be decked out in various ways. Mr. Smith not only *died*, he *ceased to be*, he *passed away*, he *croaked*, he *was promoted to glory*—all mean "the same thing." According to a second theory, however, they are ways of saying different things: variations in **diction** imply variations in reference. To say that Smith *ceased to be* records a privative and secular event; to say that he *was promoted to glory* (a Salvation Army expression) rejoices in an event of a different order altogether. Content and form in this view are inseparable; a change in one is a change in the other.

In **metaphor** we can see that the two theories, instead of contradicting each other, are more like the two sides of a coin; when one idea is expressed in terms of another, it is the same and yet not the same. To view the passage from life to death as if it were a promotion from one military rank to a higher one is to see a common center of reference and widening circles of association at the same time. This seeing *as if* opens up a whole range of expression, since many meanings reside in the relationship between the two parts of a comparison rather than in either part by itself. Charles Lamb (p. 281), ironically extolling borrowers over lenders, exclaims "What a careless, even deportment hath your borrower!" and then adds "what rosy gills!" His metaphor seems to suggest, approximately, that the borrower's healthy contentment depends on a certain fish-like obliviousness, yet no paraphrase captures the humorous aptness of the metaphor itself.

But style is by no means dependent on diction and metaphor alone. Grammatical relationships yield a host of stylistic devices, most of which can be described in terms of **repetition and variation**. Repetition may exist at every level; as commonly understood, its chief application is to the word (including the pronoun as a word-substitute), but the same principle governs the use of parallelism (repetition of a grammatical structure) within and between sentences, even between paragraphs. Failure to observe that principle—that similarity in idea calls for similarity in form—can be detected wherever a change in form implies that a distinction is being made when actually none is relevant to the context: "Their conversation was interrupted by dinner, but they resumed their discussion afterwards"; "She rolled out the dough, placed it over the pie, and pricked holes in it. She also trimmed off the edge." The corollary of the principle of appropriate repetition is the principle of appropriate variation—that difference in idea calls for difference in form. For every failure to repeat when repetition is called for there is a corresponding failure to vary when variation is called for: "Their discussion was interrupted when class discussion of the day's assignment began"; "It had been raining for many days near the river. It had been rising steadily toward the top of the levee." Failures of this sort, which suggest a similarity in idea or parallelism in thought where none exists, often strike the ear as a lack of euphony or appropriate rhythm: "A boxer must learn to react absolutely instantly"; "The slingshot was made of strips of inner tubes of tires of cars." The principle of appropriate variation applies, too, to sentences as wholes: if a separate sentence is used for each detail, or if every sentence includes many details, the reader may be given a false impression of parallelism or equality of emphasis. Here again variation may be a way to avoid misleading grammatical indications of meaning. In a writer like Samuel Johnson (p. 280), who works deliberately for a high degree of parallelism, correspondence between repetition and sameness of meaning, or variation and difference of meaning, is perhaps most conveniently illustrated.

All stylistic techniques come together to supply an answer to the question "Who is behind these words?" Every writer establishes an impression of himself—a persona—through what he says and the way he says it, and the quality of that impression obviously has much to do with his reader's willingness to be convinced. Honesty and straightforwardness come first— though the honesty of an ignoramus and the straightforwardness of a fool are unlikely to win assent. Some more sophisticated approaches to the adoption of a persona employ irony: the author assumes a character that the reader can see is at odds with his real intention. Whether direct or ironic, the chosen role must be suited to both the subject and the writer himself, who may want to try out several roles to see what each implies. Is he an expert or a humble seeker after truth, a wry humorist or a gadfly deliberately exacerbating hidden guilt? Even writers working in the same general territory—S. J. Perelman (p. 563) and George J. W. Goodman (p. 535), for example, both deal ironically with supposed aspects of the American character—may present sharply different personalities to their readers in their characteristic handling of both thought and expression. A self will be revealed in every phrase the writer sets down—even in details of spelling, grammar, and punctuation, which, if ineptly handled, may suggest to his readers a carelessness that destroys their confidence.

Authors

Frederick Lewis Allen (1890–1954) American social historian and journalist. He is best remembered for penetrating works of social history, including *Only Yesterday*, *The Lords of Creation*, *Since Yesterday*, *The Great Pierpoint Morgan*, and *The Big Change*.

Woody Allen (Heywood Allen) (1935–) American comedian, writer, actor, film director. Author of *Getting Even* (1971) and *Without Feathers* (1975).

Kenneth Allsop (1920–1973) English journalist and broadcaster. Author of *The Angry Decade* (1958), *Scan* (collected journalism) (1965), and *The Bootleggers and Their Era* (1968).

Maya Angelou (1924–) American actress, journalist, television script writer, and civil rights worker; author of *I Know Why the Caged Bird Sings*, *Just Give Me a Cool Drink of Water 'fore I Die*.

Hannah Arendt (1906–1975) German-born American political analyst (New School for Social Research); author of *The Origins of Totalitarianism*, *The Human Condition*, *Eichmann in Jerusalem*, *On Revolution*, *On Violence*, *Men in Dark Times*, *Crises of the Republic*.

Matthew Arnold (1822–1888) English man of letters, poet, and literary critic; author of *Poems*, *Essays in Criticism*, *Culture and Anarchy*, *Literature and Dogma*.

Roger Ascham (1515–1568) English scholar, tutor of Queen Elizabeth I; author of *Toxophilus* and *The Scholemaster*.

Isaac Asimov (1920–) American author, educator; professor of biochemistry at Boston University School of Medicine. Author of 143 books, including *The Stars, Like the Dust*, *Of Time and Space and Other Things*, *An Easy Introduction to the Slide Rule*, *The Left Hand of the Electron*, *Nightfall and Other Stories*, and *ABC's of the Earth*.

W(ystan) H(ugh) Auden (1907–1973) English-born American poet, playwright, critic; author of *In Time of War*, *The Sea and the Mirror*, *Poems*, *The Dyer's Hand*; with Christopher Isherwood, of *Ascent of F-6*, *The Dog Beneath the Skin* (plays); with Louis MacNeice, of *Letters from Iceland*.

Sir Francis Bacon (1561–1626) English politician, statesman, and philosopher; author of *Essays, Advancement of Learning*, *New Organon*, *New Atlantis*.

James Baldwin (1924–) American essayist and novelist; Harlem-bred, one-time expatriate in Paris, political activist for civil rights causes; author of *Go Tell It on the Mountain*, *Another Country*, *Tell Me How Long the Train's Been Gone* (novels), *Notes of a Native Son*, *Nobody Knows My Name*, the *Fire Next Time*, *Going to Meet the Man*, *No Name in the Street* (commentaries).

Jacques Barzun (1907–) American writer and educator. He has written and edited critical and historical studies on a wide variety of subjects, some of which are *Race: A Study in Modern Superstition, Romanticism and the Modern Ego, The Teacher in America,* and *Berlioz and the Romantic Century.*

Saul Bellow (1915–   )
American novelist, story writer (University of Chicago); author of *Herzog, Mr. Sammler's Planet, The Adventures of Augie March, Dangling Man, Mosby's Memoirs and Other Stories.*

Henri Bergson (1859–1941)
French philosopher; author of *The Two Sources of Morality and Religion, Time and Free Will, *On Laughter.*

Bruno Bettelheim (1903–   )
Austrian-born American psychologist (University of Chicago) and psychoanalyst; author of *Love Is Not Enough, *The Informed Heart, The Empty Fortress, Children of the Dream.*

Ambrose Bierce (1842–1914?)
American short-story writer and journalist; author of *Tales of Soldiers and Civilians, The Cynic's Word Book (retitled *The Devil's Dictionary).*

William Blake (1757–1827)
English poet, artist, and engraver, author of *Songs of Innocence, Songs of Experience, *The Marriage of Heaven and Hell, the Book of Thel.*

Wayne C. Booth (1921–   )
American literary critic, dean (University of Chicago); author of *The Rhetoric of Fiction, The Rhetoric of Irony.*

Hal Borland (Harold Glen) (1900–   )
American author, editorial writer. Author of numerous books of verse and novels of outdoor life, including *Heaps of Gold* (1922), *America Is Americans* (1942), *Borland Country* (1971). He says, "I am a fortunate man. I grew up on a frontier, escaped early success, had things to say when I matured. I have been able to make a living at work I wanted to do, to write what I believed and find an audience. My purpose has been to write at least a few paragraphs that will be remembered after I am dead. I have enjoyed life. I still do. What more can a man ask?"

Jimmy Breslin (1930–   )
American newspaperman; syndicated columnist: *New York Herald-Tribune, Paris Tribune,* many others. Author of *Sunny Jim, Can't Anybody Here Play This Game?, Gang That Couldn't Shouldn't Straight,* and *How the Good Guys Finally Won.*

Jacob Bronowski (1908–1974)
British critic and statesman, senior fellow and trustee of Salk Institute for Biological Studies, author of *The Poet's Defence, The Common Sense of Science, Science and Human Values, The Identity of Man, Nature and Knowledge.*

Dee (Alexander) Brown (1908–   )
American historian and writer; author of *Bury My Heart at Wounded Knee, The Galvanized Yankees, Grierson's Raid.*

Norman O. Brown (1913–   )
American scholar and social critic, his works include *Life Against Death, The Psychoanalytical Meaning of History, Love's Body, Hermes The Thief,* and *Closing Time.*

Jerome S. Bruner (1915–   )
American psychologist (Harvard University); author of *The Process of Education, Toward a Theory of Instruction, Processes of Cognitive Growth, The Relevance of Education.*

Martin Buber (1878–1965)
Jewish philosopher and educator. Among his books are *Adult Education, Which Way America?, The New Prometheus, Science and Freedom, *Tales of the Hasidim—The Early Masters,* and *The Next America.*

Art Buchwald (1925–   )
American newspaper columnist, writer, humorist. Author of *Paris After Dark, Is it Safe to Drink the Water?, Counting Sheep, Getting High in Government Circles,* and *I Never Danced at the White House,* among numerous other books.

(John) Anthony Burgess (Wilson) (1917–)
Author of *A Clockwork Orange, Re Joyce, The Novel Now, MF, Tremor of Intent, Enderby, The Long Day Wanes: A Trilogy, The Wanting Seed, Urgent Copy, The Worm and the Ring.*

Samuel Butler (1835–1902)
English sheep farmer, biologist, composer, writer; author of *Erewhon, Erewhon Revisited, Evolution Old and New, Unconscious Memory, *The Notebooks of Samuel Butler, The Way of All Flesh.*

Edward Hallett Carr (1892–)
English historian (Cambridge), journalist, and statesman; author of *The Romantic Exiles; The Bolshevik Revolution, 1917-1923; *What Is History?*

(Arthur) Joyce (Lunel) Cary (1888–1957)
Anglo-Irish novelist, poet, and political philosopher; author of *Aissa Saved, The Horse's Mouth, Mister Johnson, The Captive and the Free* (novels), *A Case for African Freedom, Power in Men, The Process of Real Freedom* (commentaries).

Carlos Castaneda (1931–)
A UCLA graduate student in anthropology who became a sorcerer's apprentice. His book *The Teachings of Don Juan: A Yaqui Way of Knowledge* is a record of the regimen of his apprenticeship.

Lord Chesterfield (1694–1773)
Philip Dormer Stanhope, fourth earl; English statesman and diplomat; well-known letter writer (*Letters to His Son*).

Sir Kenneth Clark (1902–)
English art historian and critic; author of *Landscape into Art, The Nude, Leonardo da Vinci, Looking at Pictures, Civilisation.*

Eldridge Cleaver (1935–)
Black American revolutionary, journalist, social critic; former Minister of Information of the Black Panther Party; author of *Soul on Ice.*

Samuel Langhorne Clemens (Mark Twain) (1835–1910)
American humorist; itinerant journalist; critic and novelist. Author of *Roughing It* (1872), *Tom Sawyer* (1876), *Life on the Mississippi* (1883), *Huckleberry Finn* (1885), *A Connecticut Yankee in King Arthur's Court* (1889), and numerous other works.

Henry Sloane Coffin (1877–1954)
American clergyman and educator; president, Union Theological Seminary; author of *The Meaning of the Cross, Religion Yesterday and Today.*

Robert Coles (1929–)
American psychiatrist (Harvard University); author of *Children of Crisis, Still Hungry in America, The Image Is You, The Wages of Neglect, Uprooted Children, Drugs and Youth, Erik Erikson: The Growth of His Work, *The Middle Americans, The South Goes North.*

Paul Cowan
Staff writer for the *Village Voice.*

Harvey Gallagher Cox (1929–)
American theologian and writer. Author of *The Secular City, God's Revolution and Man's Responsibility, The Feast of Fools, The Seduction of the Spirit, and The Use and Misuse of People's Religion.*

Timothy Crouse
American journalist and author of *The Boys on the Bus* (1973).

Robert Darnton (1939–)
American professor of history at Princeton, formerly on the staff of the *New York Times.* He has written articles on the book trade and on the ideological origins of the French Revolution. Author of *Mesmerism and the End of the Enlightenment in France.*

Clarence Darrow (1857–1938)
American attorney and politician; identified with many prominent cases, including defenses of labor leaders and the Scopes trial; author of *An Eye for an Eye Crime: Its Cause and Treatment; The Story of My Life.*

Stephen Darst (1931–)
Formerly a reporter for the *St. Louis Globe-Democrat,* and presently on

the staff of the *St. Louis Review*, the newspaper of the St. Louis Archdiocese.

Edwin Denby
American writer, critic. Author of *Looking at the Dance.*

Thomas De Quincey (1785–1859)
English essayist and literary journalist; author of *Confessions of an English Opium Eater, *Autobiographic Sketches.*

Charles Dickens (1812–1870)
British novelist, Author of *Pickwick Papers, Great Expectations, A Christmas Carol, Oliver Twist, A Tale of Two Cities, Bleak House*, and others.

Joan Didion (1934–   )
American writer whose works include the novels *Run River* and *Play It As It Lays*, and a collection of magazine pieces, *Slouching Towards Bethlehem.*

Annie Dillard (1945–   )
American writer, editor. Author of *Pilgrim at Tinker Creek* (1974).

John Donne (1573–1631)
English poet and clergyman, Dean of St. Paul's Cathedral, founder and chief exemplar of the Metaphysical School in English poetry: author of *Songs and Sonnets, Devotions upon Emergent Occasions.*

John Roderigo Dos Passos (1896–1970)
American novelist. Novels include *Three Soldiers, Manhattan Transfer*, and *The Big Money*; some of his nonfiction works are *Men Who Made the Nation, Mr. Wilson's War*, and *Easter Island: Island of Enigmas.*

W(illiam) E(dward) B(urghardt) Du Bois (1868–1963)
American author, editor, and teacher; a founder of the National Association for the Advancement of Colored People; relentless exponent of the complete equality of the Negro in America; author of *The Suppression of the African Slave Trade, The Souls of Black Folk, John Brown, Black Reconstruction, Dusk of Dawn, The Black Flame (A Trilogy).*

Jonathan Edwards (1703–1758)
American Puritan preacher and theologian in Massachusetts Bay Colony.

Loren Eiseley (1907–   )
American anthropologist and historian of science (University of Pennsylvania); author of *The Immense Journey, Darwin's Century, The Firmament of Time, The Mind as Nature, Francis Bacon and the Modern Dilemma, The Unexpected Universe, The Invisible Pyramid, *The Night Country, All the Strange Hours.*

George Paul Elliott (1918–   )
American author; professor of English at Syracuse University. Works include *An Hour of Last Things, A Piece of Lettuce, Conversions, Fever and Chills*, and *From the Berkeley Hills.*

Mary Ellmann
American critic, writer. Author of *Thinking About Women* (1968).

Ralph Waldo Emerson (1803–1882)
American essayist, poet, expositor of the intellectual movement known as Transcendentalism; author of *Nature, Representative Men, English Traits.*

Desiderius Erasmus (1465–1536)
Dutch humanist-scholar, satirist; author of *The Praise of Folly, Colloquies, *The Education of a Christian Prince.*

Erik H. Erikson (1902–   )
German-born American psychoanalyst (Harvard University); author of *Young Man Luther, Identity and the Life Cycle, *Insight and Responsibility, Identity: Youth and Crisis, Childhood and Society, Gandhi's Truth* (Pulitzer Prize, 1970).

Shulamith Firestone (1945–   )
Canadian writer, editor, author of *The Dialectic of Sex* (1970).

Janet Flanner (Genêt) (1892–   )
American writer and foreign correspondent for *The New Yorker* magazine. Some of her books include *The Cubical City, American in Paris,*

Men and Monuments, and *Paris Journal.*

E(dward) M(organ) Forster (1879–1970)
English novelist and essayist; author of *The Longest Journey, Howard's End, A Passage to India, Maurice* (novels). *Aspects of the Novel, *Two Cheers for Democracy* (criticism).

Benjamin Franklin (1706–1790)
American statesman, delegate to the Continental Congress and Constitutional Convention, ambassador to France during the American Revolution, inventor, newspaper publisher, and practical philosopher; author of *Poor Richard's Almanack, *Autobiography.*

Erich Fromm (1900–)
German-born American psychoanalyst; author of *Psychoanalysis and Religion, The Sane Society, Sigmund Freud's Mission, The Dogma of Christ and Other Essays on Religion, Psychology and Culture, The Heart of Man.*

Robert Frost (1874–1963)
American poet, lecturer, teacher.

Christopher Fry (1907–)
English playwright and translator; author of the plays *The Boy with a Cart, The Dark Is Light Enough. The Lady's Not for Burning, Venus Observed, A Yard of Sun.*

Northrop Frye (1912–)
Canadian literary critic (University of Toronto); author of *Anatomy of Criticism, Design for Learning, *The Educated Imagination.*

Richard Gambino
American educator who teaches in the Department of Education at Queens College, N.Y.

Peter Gay (1923–)
American educator, author whose works include *The Dilemma of Democratic Socialism, The Poet as Realist, Puritan Historians in Colonial America, The Outsider as Insider,* and *The Science of Freedom.*

Willard Gaylin (1925–)
President of the Institute of Society, Ethics, and the Life Sciences in Hastings, New York, and the author of *In Service of Their Country; War Resisters in Prison.*

William Golding (1911–)
British novelist and poet educated at Oxford. Served as commander of a rocket-launching ship in the Royal Navy; author of *Lord of the Flies* (1954) and *Pincher Martin* (1956).

Emma Goldman (1869–1940)
Russian-born American anarchist, editor, and propagandist; author of *Anarchism and Other Essays, *Living My Life, My Disillusionment in Russia.*

Edna Goldsmith
Formerly a student at Yale University.

George J. W. Goodman ("Adam Smith") (1930–)
American journalist, stock market analyst. Author of several novels but is best known for his books *The Money Game* (1968) and *Supermoney* (1974).

Robert Graves (1895–)
British man of letters; author of *The White Goddess, The Greek Myths, Collected Poems, Love Respelt.*

B. H. Haggin (1900–)
American music critic. Author of *Music for the Man Who Enjoys "Hamlet"* (1944) and *The Toscanini Musicians Knew* (1959).

Elizabeth Hardwick (1916–)
American author and contributing editor of the *Partisan Review, The New Yorker,* and *Harper's* magazines. Author of *The Ghostly Lover, The Simple Truth, A View of My Own,* the *Selected Letters of William James,* and *Seduction and Betrayal.*

Nathaniel Hawthorne (1804–1864)
American novelist, short-story writer, essayist; author of *Twice-told Tales, Mosses from an Old Manse, The Scarlet Letter, The House of the Seven Gables.*

William Hazlitt (1778–1830)
English essayist, critic; author of *Characters of Shakespeare's Plays;*

English Comic Writers; Table Talk, or Original Essays on Men and Manners; *Characteristics.

Ernest Hemingway (1898–1961)
American novelist and story writer. Pulitzer and Nobel Prizes; author of The Sun Also Rises, A Farewell to Arms, *Death in the Afternoon, For Whom the Bell Tolls, The Old Man and the Sea.

Hendrik Hertzberg (1943–   )
Staff writer for The New Yorker magazine. Author of One Million (1973).

Gilbert Highet (1906–   )
Scots-born American classicist and teacher (Columbia) author of The Classical Tradition, The Art of Teaching, The Anatomy of Satire, *Talents and Geniuses.

Edward Hoagland (1932–   )
American novelist, writer. His books include Cat Man (1956) and *The Courage of Turtles (1974).

Eric Hoffer (1902–   )
American longshoreman and social critic; author of The True Believer, The Passionate State of Mind, The Ordeal of Change.

Richard H. Hoggart (1918–   )
British Professor of English at Birmingham University. Author of The Uses of Literacy, W. H. Auden—A Selection, Teaching Literature, The Critical Moment, How and Why Do We Learn, Essays in Literature and Culture, and Speaking to Each Other.

John Caldwell Holt (1923–   )
American educator; author of How Children Fail, How Children Learn, Underachieving School, What Do I Do Monday?

Ada Louise Huxtable
American architectural critic (New York Times); author of Classic New York, Pier Luigi Nervi, *Will They Ever Finish Bruckner Boulevard?

Jane Jacobs (1916–   )
American editor and sociologist; author of *The Death and Life of Great American Cities.

Lenore F. Jacobson
American elementary school principal in San Francisco. Ed. D, University of California at Berkeley, 1966.

William James (1842–1910)
American philosopher and pioneer psychologist (Harvard), pragmatist, brother of Henry James; author of *Principles of Psychology, The Varieties of Religious Experience, Pragmatism.

Elizabeth Hall Janeway (1913–   )
American writer whose works include The Walsh Girls; Daisy Kenyon; The Question of Gregory; The Vikings; Leaving Home; Early Days of the Automobile; The Third Choice; Angry Kate; Man's World, Woman's Place; and *Between Myth and Morning.

Thomas Jefferson (1743–1826)
Third President of the United States, first Secretary of State, founder of the University of Virginia, drafter of the *Declaration of Independence and the statute of Virginia for religious freedom, founder of the Democratic party; also renowned for his talents as an architect and inventor.

Samuel Johnson (1709–1784)
English lexicographer, critic, moralist; journalist (The Idler, *The Rambler); author of A Dictionary of the English Language, Lives of the Poets; subject of Boswell's Life.

Pat Jordan (1941–   )
American sports writer, former minor-league baseball pitcher, author of Black Coach, *A False Spring, and The Suitors of Spring.

Carl Gustav Jung (1875–1961)
Swiss psychiatrist; a founder of analytic psychology; author of Analytical Psychology, The Undiscovered Self, Man and His Symbols, *Modern Man in Search of a Soul, Psychology and Religion, A Theory of Psychoanalysis.

Franz Kafka (1883–1924)
Czech novelist and short-story writer; author of *The Trial, The Castle, Amerika.

X. J. Kennedy (1929–   )
Pseudonym of Joseph C. Kennedy; poet, critic, professor of English (Tufts); author of Nude Descending a Staircase, Introduction to Poetry.

Jean Collins Kerr (1923–)
American author and playwright. Her plays include *Mary, Mary* (1961), *Poor Richard* (1964), and *Finishing Touches* (1973). She is the author of *Please Don't Eat the Daisies*, **Penny Candy*, and *The Snake Has All the Lines*.

Sören Kierkegaard (1813–1855)
Danish theologian and philosopher; author of **Fear and Trembling, Either/Or, Philosophical Fragments*.

Martin Luther King, Jr. (1929–1968)
American Negro clergyman and civil rights leader; president, Southern Christian Leadership Conference; Nobel Peace Prize, 1964; author of *Stride Toward Freedom* and *Why We Can't Wait*.

Ronald Knox (1888–1957)
English Roman Catholic prelate; author of *The Belief of Catholics; The Body in the Silo; Let Dons Delight; *Enthusiasm, a Chapter in the History of Religion*.

Jonathan Kozol (1936–)
American author; recipient of a National Book Award in 1968. Author of *Death at an Early Age* and **Free Schools*.

Mark Kram (1936)
American columnist, senior writer for *Sports Illustrated*, formerly feature writer and columnist for the *Baltimore Sun*.

Joseph Wood Krutch (1893–1970)
American literary and social critic; author of *The Modern Temper, The Measure of Man, Human Nature and the Human Condition*.

Thomas Kuhn (1922–)
American historian of science (Princeton University); author of *The Copernican Revolution, Planetary Astronomy in the Development of Western Thought, *The Structure of Scientific Revolutions*.

Elizabeth Kübler-Ross
Psychologist. Author of **On Death and Dying* (1969).

Charles Lamb (1775–1834)
English essayist, critic; author of **Essays of Elia* and, with his sister, Mary, *Tales from Shakespeare*.

Susanne K. Langer (1895–)
American philosopher and educator (Connecticut College); author of *The Practice of Philosophy, An Introduction to Symbolic Logic, Feeling and Form. *Problems of Art*.

François, duc de la Rochefoucauld (1613–1680)
French moralist; author of *Memoirs, *Reflections or Sentences and Moral Maxims*.

Susan Lee (1944–)
American writer, novelist; from Paterson, New Jersey.

Doris Lessing (1919–)
British novelist. Author of *Children of Violence, Briefing for a Descent into Hell, The Summer Before the Dark*, and a collection of short pieces, **A Small Personal Voice*.

C(live) S(taples) Lewis (1898–1963)
English novelist and essayist whose principal works include *The Pilgrim's Regress* and **The Screwtape Letters*.

Abraham Lincoln (1809–1865)
Sixteenth president of the United States; lawyer, congressman, celebrated for his debates with Stephen Douglas on the question of slavery's extension. His voluminous state papers include the Emancipation Proclamation, the Gettysburg Address, **the Second Inaugural*.

Walter Lippmann (1889–1971)
American politicial philosopher and journalist-statesman; author of *Public Opinion. A Preface to Morals, The New Imperative, The Public Philosophy, The Communist World and Ours*.

Konrad Lorenz (1903–)
Austrian-born German scientist; director of Max Planck Institute for Physiology of Behavior; author of **King Solomon's Ring* and *Man Meets Dog*.

John Livingston Lowes (1867–1945)
American literary critic, scholar, and teacher (Harvard); author of **Geoffrey Chaucer, The Road to Xanadu*.

Niccolò Machiavelli (1469–1527)
Florentine statesman and political

philosopher during the reign of the Medici; author of *The Art of War, History of Florence, Discourses on Livy, *The Prince*.

Sir John Mandeville (1338–1400?)
Fourteenth-century English author of *The Travels of Sir John Mandeville*. Originally written in Norman French, the work became enormously popular and was translated into English, Latin, and most European languages. It purports to recount the author's travels through Jerusalem, Egypt, Turkistan, India, China, and other places.

William March (1893–1954)
Pseudonym of William Edward March Campbell; American businessman, novelist, short-story writer, fabulist; author of *Company K, The Little Wife and Other Stories, Some Like Them Short*, *99 Fables*.

Matthew
One of the twelve Apostles of Christ, author of *The Gospel According to St. Matthew.

W. Somerset Maugham (1874–1965)
English novelist, dramatist, short-story writer; author of *Of Human Bondage* (novel), *The Moon and Sixpence* (novel), *The Circle* (play), *The Summing Up* (autobiography).

Mary McCarthy (1912–   )
American novelist and short-story writer. Novels include *The Company She Keeps* (1942), *The Oasis* (1949), *Cast a Cold Eye* (1950), and *The Groves of Academe* (1952).

David C. K. McClelland (1917–   )
American psychologist, educator. Author of *Personality* (1951), *Talent and Society* (1958), *The Achieving Society* (1961), and *The Roots of Consciousness* (1964).

W. S. Merwin (1927–   )
American poet and translator. His volumes of poetry include *A Mask for Janus, Drunk in the Furnace*, and *Lice*. Merwin is also well known for his translations, among them *The Cid* and *The Life of Lazarillo de Tormes*.

Stanley Milgram (1933–   )
American social psychologist (Yale). Author of *Obedience to Authority.

Elaine Morgan (1920–   )
Welsh writer, teacher. Author of *The Descent of Woman* (1972).

Jan Morris (James Morris) (1926–   )
English writer who underwent a sex-change operation. Author of *Conundrum* (1974).

Toni Morrison (1931–   )
American writer; author of *The Bluest Eye.

John Henry Newman (1801–1890)
English Catholic prelate and cardinal; author of *Tracts for the Times, *The Idea of a University, Apologia pro Vita Sua.

Nicholas of Cusa (c. 1400–1464)
German Catholic prelate (bishop and cardinal) and philosopher, argued in favor of church councils over the pope and for the principle of consent as the basis of government; author of *De concordantia catholica, De docta ignorentia, *De visione Dei* (*The Vision of God*).

Anaïs Nin (1903–   )
American writer. Her fiction, noted for its poetic style and searching portraits of women, includes the novels *Winter of Artifice* and *A Spy in the House of Love*.

George Orwell (1903–1950)
Pseudonym of Eric Blair; English novelist, essayist, and social commentator, satirist of totalitarianism; author of *Down and Out in Paris and London, Homage to Catalonia, *Nineteen Eighty-Four, Animal Farm*.

Walter Pater (1839–1894)
English man of letters, interpreter of Renaissance humanism; author of *Studies in the History of the Renaissance, Marius the Epicurean, Appreciations*.

Robert Pattison (1945–   )
Teacher of English at St. John's University, New York. Ph.D, Columbia. Author of the forthcoming *The Child Figure in English Literature*.

Donald R. Pearce (1917–   )
Canadian professor of English (Santa Barbara); author of *Journal of a War: Northwest Europe, 1944–

1945 and *In the President's and My Opinion.*

Charles Sanders Peirce (1839–1914)
American philosopher, scientist, and logician; author of *Chance, Love, and Logic; Essays in the Philosophy of Science; Values in a Universe of Chance.*

S(idney) J(oseph) Perelman (1904–   )
American humorist. Writer for motion pictures since 1930, named best screen writer of 1956. Author of *One Touch of Venus, *Vinegar Puss,* and *Acres and Pains.*

William G. Perry, Jr. (1913–   )
American educator, director of the Bureau of Study Counsel at Harvard.

Robert Pirsig (1928–   )
American writer and educator. Author of *Zen and the Art of Motorcycle Maintenance* (1974).

Plato (427?–347 B.C.)
Greek philosopher, pupil and friend of Socrates, teacher of Aristotle, founder of the Academy, proponent of an oligarchy of intellectuals based on the assumption that virtue is knowledge; author of *The Republic.*

Norman Podhoretz (1930–   )
American writer, former editor of *Commentary.* Author of *Doings and Undoings, The Fifties and After in American Writing,* and *Making It.*

J. B. Priestley (1894–   )
English novelist, critic, and playwright. Author of *The English Comic Characters, George Meredith, Peacock;* and novels, including *Rain upon Godshill, Let the People Sing, Dangerous Corner, Time and the Conways,* and *Music at Night.*

Adrienne Rich (1929–   )
American poet (Douglass College); author of *A Change of World, The Diamond Cutters, Necessities of Life, Snapshots of a Daughter-in-Law, Leaflets, The Will to Change, Diving into the Wreck, Poems: Selected and New,* and the prose work, *Of Woman Born* (1976).

Theodore Rosengarten
American writer; editor of the autobiography of Nate Shaw, *All God's Dangers* (1974). Nate Shaw (1885–1973) was an American cotton farmer, born in east-central Alabama, the son of former slaves. Active in the sharecroppers' union, a militant organization "for the poor class of people."

Robert Rosenthal (1933–   )
American professor of social psychology at Harvard University. Ph.D., UCLA (1956).

(Victoria Mary) Vita Sackville-West (1892–1962)
English writer whose works include *Selected Poems* (1941), *Pepita* (1937), *The Eagle and the Dove* (1943), *The Devil at Westcase* (1947), and *The Easter Party* (1953).

Margaret Sanger (1883–1966)
American writer and leader of the birth-control movement; organized the first American birth-control conference in New York City, 1921. Among her works are *What Every Girl Should Know, Motherhood in Bondage, My Fight for Birth Control;* editor and publisher of *The Woman Rebel* and *Birth Control Review.*

George Santayana (1863–1952)
American philosopher (Harvard), author of *The Life of Reason, The Realm of Essence, The Realm of Truth,* and *Soliloquies in England.*

May Sarton (1912–   )
American poet and novelist. Among her volumes of poetry are *Encounter in April, In Time Like Air, A Durable Fire,* and *Collected Poems 1930–1973;* her prose works include *Kinds of Love, As We Are Now,* and *Journal of a Solitude.*

Jean-Paul Sartre (1905–   )
French philosopher, playwright, novelist, story writer, social and literary critic, Nobel Prize winner; author of *Existentialism, Existentialism and Humanism, No Exit, The Wall, Imagination; Of Human Freedom, The Problem of Method, The Words, The Transcendence of the Ego.*

Jonathan Schell (1943–)
Writer for *The New Yorker*. His books include *The Village of Ben Suk*, *The Military Half*, and **The Time of Illusion*.

Terri Schultz
Ms. Schultz, a freelance writer, was formerly a reporter for the *Chicago Tribune*. She covered the Wounded Knee episode for the *Chicago Tribune* and *Harper's*.

Chief Seattle (19th century)
American Indian, chief of the Duwampo tribe in Washington Territory.

John Selden (1584–1654)
English politician, jurist, Oriental scholar, and member of Parliament; author of many political tracts and works on law and **Table Talk*.

Richard B. Sewall (1908–)
American professor of English (Yale); recipient of a National Book Award for his biography of Emily Dickinson; author of *The Vision of Tragedy*.

George Bernard Shaw (1856–1950)
Irish playwright and essayist; author of the plays *Saint Joan*, **Man and Superman*, **Major Barbara, Caesar and Cleopatra*.

B(urrhus) F(rederic) Skinner (1904–)
American psychologist (Harvard); inventor of the Skinner box, an artificial environmental system for the control and study of behavior; author of *Science and Human Behavior*, *Walden Two*, *Beyond Freedom*.

Philip E. Slater (1927–)
American sociologist whose books include *Microcosm* (1966), *The Glory of Hera* (1968), and **The Pursuit of Loneliness* (1970).

(James) Radcliffe Squires (1917–)
American poet and editor of the *Michigan Quarterly*.

Jean Stafford (1915–)
American writer whose books include *Boston Adventure*, *The Mountain Lion*, *The Catherine Wheel*, and *Collected Stories*.

Wallace Stegner (1909–)
American essayist, novelist, professor of English (Stanford); author of *Remembering Laughter, The Women on the Wall, Beyond the Hundredth Meridian, A Shocking Star, *Wolf Willow, All the Little Live Things*, and *Gathering of Zion: The Story of the Mormon Trail*.

John Steinbeck (1902–1969)
American novelist, columnist; Nobel Prize winner, 1963; author of *In Dubious Battle, Of Mice and Men, The Grapes of Wrath* (Pulitzer Prize, 1939), *East of Eden, *Journal of a Novel: The East of Eden Letters*.

Laurence Sterne (1713–1768)
English cleric, novelist, and humorist; author of **Tristram Shandy, A Sentimental Journey, Sermons*.

Jonathan Swift (1667–1745)
Irish satirist, poet, and churchman; author of *Gulliver's Travels, A Tale of a Tub, *The Battle of the Books*.

(Louis) Studs Terkel (1912–)
American actor, interviewer, and writer; author of **Hard Times: An Oral History of the Great Depression, Division Street: America, *Working*.

Theophrastus (c. 371–287 B.C.)
Greek philosopher, naturalist, and successor to Aristotle; author of **Characters, Metaphysics, On Plants*.

Dylan Thomas (1914–1953)
Welsh poet, story writer, radio script writer, and broadcaster, author of *Collected Poems (1934–1952), Under Milk Wood* (verse drama), *Adventures in the Skin Trade and Other Stories, Portrait of the Artist as a Young Dog* (autobiographical sketches).

Lewis Thomas (1913–)
American physician, educator and medical administrator. Author of **The Lives of a Cell: Notes of a Biology Watcher*.

Henry David Thoreau (1817–1862)
American philosopher, essayist, naturalist, poet, disciple of Emerson, foremost exponent of self-reliance; author of *Walden*, "Civil Disobedience," **Journals*.

James Thurber (1894–1963)
American humorist, cartoonist, social commentator (*New Yorker*),

playwright; author of *My Life and Hard Times; *Fables for Our Time; *Men, Women, and Dogs; The Beast in Me and Other Animals.*

Paul Tillich (1886–1965)
German-born American theologian, author of *The Interpretation of History, The Shaking of the Foundations, Systematic Theology, The Dynamic of Faith, Christianity and the Encounter of the World Religions.*

Niko Tinbergen (1907–   )
British zoologist presently on the faculty of Oxford University. He was awarded the 1973 Nobel Prize in Medicine and Physiology for his work in reviving and developing the biological science of animal behavior. His best known books are *The Herring Gull's World* and *Curious Naturalists.*

John Updike (1932–   )
American novelist, story writer, poet; author of *Rabbit, Run; The Centaur; Of the Farm; Couples; Bech; Rabbit Redux* (novels); *The Same Door; Pigeon Feathers; The Music School* (stories).

Verta Mae (1938–   )
Black American writer; author of *Vibration Cooking* and *Thursdays and Every Other Sunday Off.*

Ian P(ierre) Watt (1917–   )
English-born American professor of English (Stanford University): author of *The Rise of the Novel.*

Alan W. Watts (1915–1973)
English-born American philosopher and editor; author of *The Legacy of Asia and Western Man, The Supreme Identity, Myth and Ritual in Christianity, *The Meaning of Happiness, Beyond Theology, The Book, Does It Matter?*

Naomi Weisstein (1939–   )
American psychologist (Loyola University, Chicago); author of numerous papers on perception, cognition, information science, memory, and the psychology of differences between men and women.

E. B. White (1899–   )
American essayist, journalist, editor (*New Yorker*); author of *One Man's Meat, *The Wild Flag, *The Second Tree from the Corner.*

Oscar Wilde (1854–1900)
Irish writer, poet, and playwright, whose works include *The Picture of Dorian Gray, An Ideal Husband, The Importance of Being Earnest, Ballad of Reading Gaol,* and the autobiographical *De Profundis.*

Tom Wolfe (1931–   )
American essayist, story writer, social critic; author of *The Kandy-Kolored Tangerine-Flake Streamline Baby, The Pump House Gang, Radical Chic and Mau Mauing the Flak Catcher's.*

Virginia Woolf (1882–1941)
English novelist, essayist, and critic; author of *Mrs. Dalloway, To the Lighthouse* (novels), *The Common Reader, Granite and Rainbow, *The Second Common Reader* (essays).

Alphabetical Index

1271